European Integration

PEARSON Education

We work with leading authors to develop the strongest educational materials in economics, bringing cutting-edge thinking and best learning practice to a global market.

Under a range of well-known imprints, including Financial Times Prentice Hall, we craft high quality print and electronic publications which help readers to understand and apply their content, whether studying or at work.

To find out more about the complete range of our publishing, please visit us on the World Wide Web at: www.pearsoned.co.uk

European Integration

Methods and Economic Analysis

Third Edition

JACQUES PELKMANS

FT Prentice Hall
FINANCIAL TIMES

An imprint of Pearson Education
Harlow, England • London • New York • Boston • San Francisco • Toronto
Sydney • Tokyo • Singapore • Hong Kong • Seoul • Taipei • New Delhi
Cape Town • Madrid • Mexico City • Amsterdam • Munich • Paris • Milan

Pearson Education Limited
Edinburgh Gate
Harlow
Essex CM20 2JE
England

and Associated Companies throughout the world

Visit us on the World Wide Web at:
www.pearsoned.co.uk

First published 1997
Second edition published 2001
Third edition published 2006

ISBN: 978-0-273-69449-6

British Library Cataloguing-in-Publication Data
A catalogue record for this book is available from the British Library

Library of Congress Cataloging-in-Publication Data
A catalog record for this book is available from the Library of Congress

10 9 8 7 6 5 4 3 2
10 09 08 07

Typeset in 9pt Times Roman by 71
Printed and bound by Ashford Colour Press, Gosport, Hants.

The publisher's policy is to use paper manufactured from sustainable forests.

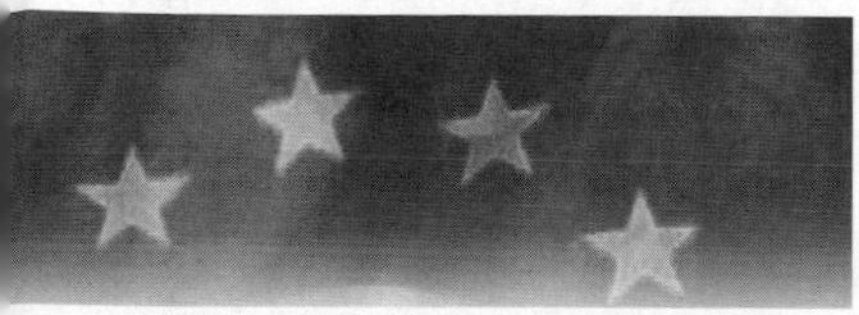

Contents

List of Tables and Figures

List of Case Studies

Preface

This third edition has been drastically revised, indeed so much so that a good deal of the text is new or heavily amended. The revision responds to the rapid developments of the European Union and, to some extent, to expressed preferences of many attentive and supporting readers who have suggested improvements or somewhat different priorities. In some sense it is, therefore, a new book. Yet, at the same time, readers familiar with the structure and the combination of integration methods and economic analysis so characteristic for this textbook will recognise that much of the structure has been retained.

Let me summarise the changes.

First, several chapters are completely new: Chapter 4 on EU regulation and Chapter 19 on the EU budget. In addition, the old Chapter 15 on equity in the Union has been split into two separate ones on social equity (Chapter 15) and on cohesion (Chapter 16), both with significant revisions and additions. The former Chapter 2 on how economic integration emerged after the war and how deepening, widening and enlargement developed over five decades has been deleted in order to make space for other topics – a regrettable but unavoidable choice. Appendix 1.3, though, provides a very brief summary of deepening, widening and enlargement. Secondly, several chapters were almost entirely rewritten and updated where applicable: the subsidiarity chapter (now Chapter 3), the one on EMU (now Chapter 18) and the chapter on Enlargement (now Chapter 20). Thirdly, another group of chapters was significantly revised, constituting around half of the text: Chapter 6 on goods market integration, where the entire second half is new; Chapter 7 on services market integration (now including a systematic treatment of horizontal liberalisation via the so-called Bolkestein directive); and Chapter 11 on the CAP. Fourth, other chapters contain parts that have been substantially revised, such as the chapters on network industries (Chapter 8), on EU trade policy (Chapter 13), the two on factor market integration (Chapters 9 and 10), and the monetary cooperation chapter (now Chapter 17), where the Mundell/Fleming model has been replaced with an open economy model with asset markets.

Fifth, a number of case studies have been deleted or amended and quite a few have been added. With regard to graphs, a few flowcharts have been constructed to substitute for tedious text and some of the more difficult diagrams have been made a little more reader-friendly.

I have decided to refer to the new numbering of the treaties, without mentioning the old numbering any more, except in a few instances. Throughout the text, references are made to the draft constitutional treaty (still to be ratified, with considerable uncertainty after the French and Dutch 'NO' votes in 2005) because this can often be insightful for specific issues.

I am indebted to many colleagues who have helped me to improve this book, including no less than four referees requested by Pearson Education. I specifically wish to thank the following colleagues and friends: Andres Rodriguez Pose, Gerrit Meester, Marko Bos, Bart van Riel, Jean Pierre Casey, Filomena Chirico, Iain Begg, Nicholas Kikidis, Henri Olivier, Dana Greceanu, Niall Bohan and Eric de Souza. Eric is also the co-author of Chapters 17 and 18, for which he wrote specific segments of the new text. Jessie Moerman has skilfully, swiftly and patiently dealt with the entire manuscript, ensuring it would meet the demanding requirements of the publisher in every respect. My wife Annette has once again produced all the new graphs and changes where they were needed. Readers are welcome to suggest improvements or make other comments; e-mail me at jpelkmans@coleurop.be at the College of Europe in Bruges.

Even if it goes without saying, it is worth emphasising that all errors and omissions are the sole responsibility of the author.

Acknowledgements

We are grateful to the following for permission to reproduce copyright material:

Table 6.2 from Sapir, A., 'Regional integration in Europe' Table 2 in *Economic Journal*, Vol. 102, pages 1491–1506, Blackwell Publishing; Figure 6.4 from Kluwer Academic Publishers, *De Economist*, Vol. 130, 4, 1982, 'Customs union and technical efficiency', Pelkmans, J., with kind permission from Kluwer Academic Publishers; Figure 6.10 from 'Product market reforms and productivity: a review of the theoretical and empirical literature on the transmission channels' in *Economic Papers* No. 218, European Commission, (Nicodème, G. and Sauner-Leroy, J. B. December 2004) © European Communities, 2004; Figure 7.3 Reproduced from 'Transport demand, modal choice and the completion of the internal market' in *European Economy, Reports and Studies No 2 – The Impact of the Internal Market on Services*, Publication Office at the European Commission, Brussels © European Communities, (Koopman, G. 1993); Figure 8.1 from F. M. Scherer and David Ross, *Industrial Market Structure and Economic Performance*, Third edition. © 1990 by Houghton Mifflin Company. Adapted with permission; Table 10.1 adapted from 'Sectoral patterns in strategic alliances' in *Panorama of EU Industry 94*, p. 26, Table 5, Publication Office at the European Commission, Brussels © European Communities 1994; Figure 11.7 from 'Effects of the EEC's Variable Import Levies', *Journal of Political Economy*, Vol. 8, 5, p. 1031, University of Chicago, (Sampson, G. and Snape, R. 1980) © 1980 by the University of Chicago; Figure 11.11 Swinnen, 2005. Reproduced by courtesy of Jo Swinnen; Figure 12.3 from Art. 86 'EEC: Economic analysis of the existence of a dominant position' in *European Law Review*, Vol. 4, 4 (December) Sweet and Maxwell, (Baden-Fuller, C. 1979) by permission of Thomson Publishing Services; Figure 13.4 from Shibata, H., 'The theory of economic unions: a comparative analysis of customs union, free trade areas and tax unions' in *Fiscal Harmonisation in Common Markets* Vol. I, by Shoup, C. (ed.) Copyright © 1967 Columbia University Press. Reprinted with permission of the publisher; Figure 13.5 Kluwer Academic Publishers, *Market Integration in the European Community*, 1984, page 233, Pelkmans, J., with kind permission from Kluwer Academic Publishers; Figure 14.1 from Grossman, G., 'Promoting new industrial activities', *OECD Economic Studies*, Vol. 14, Spring 1990 by permission of OECD, Paris; Figure 16.1 and 16.5 from Martin, Ph., 'Are European regional policies delivering?' in *EIB Papers*, Vol. 4, No. 2, 1999 by permission of

Philippe Martin; Figures 16.2 and 16.3 from the *Third Report on Economic and Social Cohesion – COM (2004) 107 of 18 February 2004*, Figs 1.3 and 1.4, p. 11, © European Communities; Figure 16.4 from Puga, D., 'European regional policies in light of recent location theories' in *Journal of Economic Geography*, 2002, October, 2, p. 377, by permission of Oxford University Press, originally taken from a paper by Duro, J. A., 'Regional Income Inequalities in Europe: An Updated Measurement and Some Decomposition Results' with kind permission of Juan Antonio Duro; Figures17.1, 17.2, 17.3, 17.4 and 17.5 Asbjørn Rødseth, *Open Economy Macroeconomics*, (2000), Figures 6.1, 6.2, 6.4, 6.5, Cambridge University Press; Figure 17.7 from *Economics of Monetary Union*, 4th edition, Oxford University Press, Fig 5.10. page 113, constructed on market exchange rates from the European Commission (1993), (De Grauwe, P. 2000) by kind permission of the author; Figure 17.8 adapted from *Economics of Monetary Integration*, Oxford University Press, Fig 6.2, page 136, (De Grauwe, P. 1997) by kind permission of the author; Figure 18.3 Begg, 2005. Reproduced by courtesy of Iain Begg; Figure 18.4 adapted version of figs. 4.2 (p.79) and 4.3 (p. 81) from *Economics of Monetary Union*, 4th ed. by De Grauwe, P. (2000) by permission of Oxford University Press; Figure 18.5 adapted version of fig. 4.4 (p.82) from *Economics of Monetary Union*, 4th ed. by De Grauwe, P. (2000) by permission of Oxford University Press.

In some instances we have been unable to trace the owners of copyright material, and we would appreciate any information that would enable us to do so.

How to Read this Book

This is a textbook about European economic integration. It combines economic analysis of integration with an understanding of the integration methods employed in the European Union. Such a combination is demanding for students and teachers because methods and economic analysis are often dealt with in separate courses.

Economics courses may characterise integration methods as institutional, legal, administrative, political or overly practical. As a result, little attention is given to methods. The present book provides economic integration analysis in a well-defined regulatory or policy context of the Union. This context deserves its own analytical questions as well. One crucial question is how to design proper regulatory and policy frameworks for various intensities of economic integration. Moreover, for policy makers and business, assessing the costs and benefits of alternative integration methods requires an adequate understanding of the methods in the first place.

On the other hand, integration methods as taught by European law or (political) integration courses are far too elaborate and technical for economists. The point for the economics student is to master the economic essence of a regulatory method, of a policy at EU level and of the main concepts of economic integration as practised in Europe. These essentials should be outlined, and details and legal technicalities should be avoided, so that the economic logic and impact can be understood. The present textbook aims to provide exactly that.

In this text, economics students are likely to be confronted with more economic regulation and policies than they are used to. Readers with a 'practical' or legal orientation towards methods are likely to find the book more economic than most other surveys of methods. In combining methods and economic analysis, both types of readers will gain.

Nevertheless, there is a lot of variation possible when reading the book. Many chapters have parts which are facultative readings going into greater detail of methods or of economic analysis. These are indicated by the heading 'Additional reading'. Furthermore, there are many case studies throughout the text, elaborating practical examples or special issues.

Reading the book is facilitated by brief introductions to each of the four parts, as well as by introductory text and summaries within every chapter.

This text aims to enhance understanding and insight, in addition to the inevitable transmission of knowledge. It is not a reference book for data, empirical descriptions, trends, statistics and the like. The student cannot 'learn' these.

List of Abbreviations

ACP	African–Carribean–Pacific (countries with special trade and development cooperation with EU; also called Lomé, and recently, Cotonou group)
AFTA	Asean Free Trade Area
ALS	agro-levy system
ASEAN	Association of South East Asian Nations
ATM	automated teller machines
B2B	business to business
B2C	business to consumer
Benelux	Belgium, Netherlands, Luxembourg (economic union)
CAP	common agricultural policy
CCITT	Committee for Broadcast Standards of the International Telecom Union
CEDEFOP	EU agency for comparison of educational curricula for technical and other schooling, so as to facilitate diploma recognition and entry in labour markets
CEFTA	Central European Free Trade Area
CEN	European (non-electrical) standards body
CENELEC	European electrical standards body
CER	Free trade area of Australia and New Zealand
CERN	particles accelerator in Geneva
CET	common external tariff
CFP	common fisheries policy
CFSP	common foreign and security policy (of the EU)
CM	common market
CRS	computer reservation system (airlines)
COMECON	(former) organisation for trade and economic cooperation of the communist countries (mainly in Europe)
COREPER	Committee of the Ambassadors of the EU Member States, preparing Council decisions
CU	customs union
DIP	deficiency income payments (farmers)
DM	Deutschmark
DPS	deficiency payments scheme (in agriculture)
EBA	everything but arms
EC	European Community
ECB	European Central Bank
ECOFIN	Council of Ministers for Economic Affairs and for Finance
ECSC	European Coal and Steel Community

ECU	European Currency Unit
EDC	European Defence Community (defunct)
EEA	European Economic Area
EEC	European Economic Community
EEIG	European Economic Interest Grouping
EES	European Employment Strategy
EFTA	European Free Trade Area
EIB	European Investment Bank
EMCF	European Monetary Cooperation Fund (of the EMS)
EMI	European Monetary Institute (preceding the ECB)
EMS	European Monetary System
EMU	economic and monetary union (also European Monetary Union)
EOTC	European Organisation for Testing and Certification
EP	European Parliament
EPL	employment protection legislation
EPO	European Patent Office
EPU	European Payments Union (1950–58)
EPC	European Political Cooperation (intergovernmental; EC foreign ministers between 1971 and 1993)
ERC	European Research Council
ERM	exchange rate mechanism (of the EMS)
ESA	European Space Agency
ESCB	European System of Central Banks
ESF	European Social Fund
ESPRIT	EC research programme on information technology
ETSI	European Telecoms Standards Institute
ETUC	European Trade Union Confederation
EU	European Union
EUREKA	European applied research programme (pan-European)
euro	European single currency
FDI	foreign direct investment
FIFG	Financial Instrument for Fisheries Guidance (structural EU Fund for Fisheries)
FSAP	Financial Services Action Plan
FTA	free trade area
GATS	General Agreement on Trade in Services
GATT	General Agreement on Tariffs and Trade
GDP	gross domestic product
GDR	German Democratic Republic (1949–90)
GNI	gross national income (new Eurostat. etc.)
GNP	gross national product
GSM	European standard for digital cellular mobile telephony
GSP	generalised system of preferences
HDTV	high definition television
HICS	Harmonised Index of Consumer Prices
horeca	hotels, restaurants and cafés
HOS	Heckscher–Ohlin–Samuelson (model in trade theory)
HS	Harmonised System (of tariff classification)

IBRD	International Bank for Reconstruction and Development (or World Bank)
ICAO	International Civil Aviation Organisation (UN agency)
IIT	Intra-industry trade
IMF	International Monetary Fund
IPR	intellectual property rights
IT	information technology
ITER	Newest generation nuclear fusion reactor
JET	Joint European Taurus (EU nuclear fusion research)
M&A	Mergers and acquisitions
MCA	monetary compensatory amounts (agriculture)
MEA	Mediterranean Economic Area (proposed in 1995)
MEIP	market economy investor principle
MERCOSUR	Southern Common Market (trading zone in South America)
MFN	most favoured nation (clause in the GATT)
MFA	Multi-Fibre Arrangement
NAFTA	North American Free Trade Area
NAIRU	non-accelerating-inflation rate of unemployment
NATO	North Atlantic Treaty Organisation
NCA	national competition authority
NRA	national regulatory authority
NTSC	US standard for (non-digital) colour TV
OECD	Organisation for Economic Cooperation and Development
OEEC	Organisation for European Economic Cooperation (1948–59)
OMC	open method of coordination
ONP	open network provision (in telecoms)
OPT	outward processing traffic (in textiles and clothing)
OSCE	Organisation for Security and Cooperation in Europe
PAL	European standard for non-digital colour TV
PCT	Patent Cooperation Treaty (worldwide)
PHARE	EU (and Group of 24) technical aid programme for central Europe
PSO	public service obligation
QMV	qualified majority voting
QR	quantitative restriction
R&D	research and development
R&T	research and technology
R&TD	research and technological development
RACE	EU telecoms broadband research programme
RETEX	EU programme for diversification of textile regions
RIA	regulatory impact assessment
SAA	Stability and Association Agreement
SE	Societas Europa (EU company, regulation since 2004)
SECAM	European standard for non-digital colour TV (France/Greece only)
SHEC	safety, health, environmental and consumer protection
SLIM	Simplification of Legislation for the Internal Market (an EC programme since 1996)

STABEX	financial facility by EU (in Lomé treaties) to stabilise export earnings for commodities
SYSMIN	financial facility by EU (in Lomé treaties) to stabilise export earnings for selected minerals
TCE	tonne-coal-equivalent
TEN	trans-European network (infrastructure)
TGV	French rapid train system
TRIPs	Trade-Related Aspects of Intellectual Property Rights (in WTO)
UCITS	mutual funds (officially, undertakings for collective investment schemes in transferable securities)
UMTS	Universal Mobile Telecoms Standard (2nd generation digital interoperability standard, operational by 2002 or 2003)
UNCTAD	UN Conference on Trade and Development
UNIX	standard in information technology (also, group of European IT companies promoting an 'open version' of the standard)
USO	universal service obligation
USSR	Union of Soviet Socialist Republics (defunct since 1991)
VAT	value added tax
VER	voluntary export restraint
VLPS	variable levy with price support (in agriculture)
WTO	World Trade Organisation
WTP	willingness to pay

PART 1 Foundation

European economic integration has become a specialisation in its own right. It has developed its own terminology and concepts. Its current significance is still influenced by its historical background and the forms of development of the European Union since the 1950s. To understand European integration methods, the economic framework implicit in the main treaties should be outlined and inspected more closely. Of course, the given economic framework and integration methods need not be optimal. The normative questions for an economist to ask are, why regulate (or intervene) at the EU or national level of government, and how to regulate.

Together, these concepts, developments, methods and basic questions form the substance of Part 1 on Foundations. Chapter 1 asks, what is economic integration and what is its significance in Europe? In answering these questions it also introduces the necessary terminology and definitions. Chapter 2 provides an economic perspective of the Rome Treaty of 1957, initiating the European Economic Community, and its three revisions: the Single European Act, the Maastricht Treaty and the Amsterdam Treaty. The presentation is kept concise and accessible by means of comparable flowcharts. Chapter 3 addresses the question of what public economic functions the Union should exercise, and how. An economic analysis, based on the subsidiarity principle (a decentralisation principle prevalent in federations), provides a framework for answering these questions in general. Moreover, a subsidiarity test is developed which will be applied throughout the remainder of the book for all kinds of specific economic powers of the Union. Chapter 4 provides an analytical economic framework upon which EU regulation may be properly designed and assessed. Given (cross-border) liberalisation, EU regulation is the core activity of the Union, hence 'good' regulation is essential if economic integration is to bring economic gains.

CHAPTER 1

What is Economic Integration?

Topics covered

Economic integration has attracted increasing attention since the early postwar period. Under the names of 'regional economic integration' or 'economic regionalism', it is distinguished from worldwide integration of national economies.[1] Although the study of economic integration has been inspired, if not dominated, by the European example, less advanced forms of economic integration can now be found in all continents. For analytical purposes, economic integration should be defined independently from the European experience. Section 1.1 defines economic integration and points out its fundamental significance. Section 1.2 briefly discusses the relevance of political integration and various institutional ambitions – especially the 'Community method' – to economic integration in Europe. Conceptual refinements of economic integration are introduced in sections 1.3 (market integration) and 1.4 (the stages of economic integration). The 'stages approach' remains a basic tool for understanding economic integration, although the substance and significance of stages have been amended over time.

Economic regionalism divides the world into preferred and discriminated partners. Therefore, the compatibility of regional integration and the GATT / WTO (section 1.5) is crucial. Finally, there is the increasing similarity between economic integration and economic federalism, the more ambitious economic integration becomes. For the EU this implies that the economics of federalism (a specialisation first developed in public economics) may hold lessons for the economics of integration (section 1.6).

1.1 Definition and significance

Economic integration is defined as the elimination of economic frontiers between two or more economies. In turn, an economic frontier is any demarcation over which actual and potential mobilities of goods, services and production factors, as well as communication flows, are relatively low. On both sides of an economic frontier, the determination of prices and quality of goods, services and factors is influenced only marginally by the flows over the frontier.

[1] 'Regions' in this jargon refers to groupings of countries or continents. However, in the present book, 'regions' will be used to refer to parts of countries, unless stated otherwise. See especially Chapter 15.

There is no *a priori* reason for assuming that economic frontiers coincide with territorial frontiers: countries are demarcated by territorial frontiers, and economies by economic frontiers. Thus, local economies need not always add up to one regional economy if economic frontiers between different local communities persist. Likewise, economic frontiers between regions may inhibit national economic integration. European economic integration is driven by efforts to reduce or eliminate the public role of territorial frontiers with European neighbours as economic frontiers. But, as the definition implies, this is a necessary, not a sufficient, condition for economic integration. Demarcations within and between national economies may remain, perhaps as a result of natural barriers (for example, mountains, sea) the costs of which have not been sufficiently reduced by infrastructural and transport provisions, or perhaps as a result of great disparities in the levels of development, or perhaps as a result of business collusion in a region or country. Even discrepancies in the availability, speed and quality of information might serve as an economic frontier.

The fundamental significance of economic integration is the *increase of actual or potential competition.* This competition is engendered both by market participants originating elsewhere in the country (in case of interregional integration) or group of countries (for example, in the EU), and by their own participants reaching out beyond the traditional confines of the economy.

Competition by market participants is likely to lead to lower prices for similar goods and services, to greater quality variation and wider choice for the integrating area, as well as to a general impetus for change. Product designs, services methods, production and distribution systems and many other aspects become subject to actual or potential challenge. They may induce changes in the direction and intensity of innovation and in working habits. However, as will be shown in Chapter 4, economic integration will also expose regional or national governments to competition, with interesting consequences.

In a fantasy world without national governments or 'nation states', economic integration would boil down to pure market integration – presumably apolitical. In the real world, economic integration is always to some extent political. When modest ambitions prevail, the politics of economic integration will remain largely domestic, apart from coalition formation and negotiation of the classical intergovernmental type. Higher ambitions of economic integration tend to be accommodated by, or to result from, political integration processes.

1.2 Economic and political integration

The relationship between economic and political integration may differ from case to case. Clearly, interregional economic integration within one country assumes a close correspondence between (national) economic and political integration. Nevertheless, the Sun-belt in the USA, after the Civil War (1861–65), remained less than fully integrated in the US economy for perhaps as long as 90 years. Similarly, the Mezzogiorno (Italy, south of Naples) failed to be integrated economically long after political unification of Italy was completed in 1870. The processes of economic and political integration in the EU have been linked from the start. Apart from historical reasons, the perceived threat of communism and the allied cold war played a major role in blending economics and politics. Efforts to forge union in western Europe have been numerous and several attempts preceding the EEC treaty of 1957 were overtly political. Thus, the European Coal and Steel Community (ECSC) was founded in 1951, following a dramatic appeal by French foreign minister Robert Schuman in May 1950 to place the two most important sectors for war-making at the time – coal and steel – under one supranational authority so as to preclude another French–German war. European security was, therefore, the main aim of the ECSC, and sectoral market integration merely the means. In 1952–53, proposals both for a European Political Union and for a European Defence Community were submitted to, for example, the French parliament – and almost accepted. The EEC treaty of 1957 contains traces of the desire for political integration as the preamble avows to strive for 'an ever closer union among the peoples of Europe'.

There is little doubt that the implicit desire to pursue political integration via the economic means specified in the Rome Treaty was a major reason that the UK, Denmark, Norway and some neutral, non-socialist countries did not participate in the final EEC negotiations in 1956.

Although these conclusions are hardly contested, their meaning for the nature and process of economic integration is unclear. Political motives may explain the institutional set-up of the original EEC. But the subsequent development of the Community was driven almost entirely by market integration and selective common economic policies, not by foreign policy cooperation or matters of security or defence, until the late 1980s and early 1990s. Also, key political issues in domestic political processes of the Member States such as employment, inflation, social security, domestic security or societal values were hardly affected by the European Community (EC)[2] for several decades.[3] In practice, therefore, it is exceedingly hard to trace how and to what extent the political aim(s) of the Community have influenced the nature and process of economic integration in the EC. Some landmark decisions in EU history are impossible to explain, however, without recourse to elusive, but persistent, feelings of pursuing common political aims, especially in times of perceived crisis (see Appendix 1.3).

ADDITIONAL READING

Institutional aspects of economic integration

This book will not analyse the institutions and decision making methods of the EU and, more narrowly, the EC. A summary is provided in Appendix 1.1 to this chapter. But in two related aspects the so-called *Community method* implies unique properties which have probably helped the EC to pursue economic integration further than anywhere else in the world and hence ought to be mentioned specifically: supranationality and pooling of sovereignty. Virtually all efforts in the world economy to pursue economic integration in a group of countries, including multilateral reduction of economic frontiers worldwide, are subject to severe constraints imposed by national sovereignty. Countries may, of course, voluntarily limit their exercise of certain sovereign rights in treaties or agreements, for example to liberalise trade in a group or worldwide. But such treaties will always be conditional and all important decisions other than implementation will be taken unanimously. In other words, a country can always exercise its right of veto or opt-out.

Also, judicial review of suspected infringements of the commonly agreed rules will often not exist or not be binding. Lacking judicial review, all that remains are political, quasi-legal or bureaucratic dispute-settlement procedures which carefully avoid touching the sovereignty of the countries involved. The Community method moves distinctly beyond this conditional approach. The ECSC and EEC treaties, and the four revisions of the latter,[4] assign certain competences exclusively to the Community level; both also establish a common Court, the rulings of which override national law or court rulings. This ambitious approach affects national sovereignty, of course, but it does not imply a 'loss' of sovereignty: through 'pooling', *sovereignty is jointly exercised* in the relevant policy areas. The preparedness to go so far removes a major and obstinate political barrier to the pursuit of economic integration. But it is a double-edged sword, as the ambition may, at times, develop from a facilitating factor into a source of profound political discord. This may happen when domestic politics in one or more of the Member States develops extreme sensitivities to the adjustment costs of integration. It is also bound to occur when some countries do not wish to accept the full regulatory or policy consequences of the integration they pledged to pursue. The discord may even go so far as to disrupt economic integration.[5]

Supranationality is closely intertwined with the pooling of sovereignty. The former is associated with the establishment of common institutions, such as the High Authority (in the ECSC), the Commission (in the EEC and Euratom treaties) and the EC Court of Justice, in all of which powers are vested far beyond those normally assigned to international secretariats. For instance, the European Commission has the sole right of initiative in proposing EC legislation. In other words, although the Council of Ministers will dispose (often, together with the European Parliament), it cannot

[2]The EC and EU are not synonymous. In this book the EU will generally be used to indicate the Union in past and present, although formally the Union has existed only since the Maastricht Treaty. EC is used only where legally this is required. Both the EU and the EC refer to treaty articles as well (see Appendix 1.2).

[3]A significant exception was that only democratic European countries with an acceptable human rights record can become EEC members.

[4]The Single European Act, in force since July 1987, the Maastricht Treaty, in force since November 1993, the Amsterdam Treaty, in force since May 1999 and the Nice Treaty, in force today. See Appendix 1.3 and Chapter 2.

[5]An even more general relationship between economic integration and political disintegration is analysed in Alesina *et al.* (2000).

ADDITIONAL READING *continued*

propose draft legislation. In addition, the Commission has tough monitoring powers, as the 'guardian of the treaty', for implementation and as the executive branch at the EC level for selected EC policy areas (for example, competition). The other important aspect of supranationality is the possibility of being outvoted in the Council of Ministers, by simple or qualified majority voting. On the face of it, this is merely a matter of degree since qualified majority voting (QMV) is not entirely unknown in international organisations. There is a significant qualitative difference, however. Its importance in the Union derives from two characteristics. First, the economic importance and range of policy areas subject to (qualified) majority voting has always been much larger than in any other inter-national body, and the four treaty revisions have drastically increased the weight of these policy areas.[6] Second, unlike in other international bodies, the Union has no general opt-out provisions and no recognised right of exit ('secession'), while the Nice Treaty itself does not have an expiry date,[7] all elements which greatly increase the sensitivity to possibilities of being outvoted.

It is not the task of this book to assess or quantify the impact of these institutional properties on economic integration in general. It will be obvious to the reader that when political views differ fundamentally among Member States, even these properties will become less important. However, as will be shown throughout the text, the Union has been able to accommodate a considerable divergence of perspectives and simultaneously achieved far-reaching progress in economic integration. Moreover, the stability of the accomplishments has proved to be robust, despite various upheavals, crises and several enlargements from six to twenty-five Member States. It is hardly conceivable that such impressive results could have been had without the 'Community method', facilitated by a political climate in which ambitious integration was an avowed aim.

At the same time, one should acknowledge that in the actual operation of the Community the notions of pooled sovereignty and supranationality have become blurred. In this respect two relevant characteristics of today's process are 'intergovernmentalism' and 'cooperative federalism'. Both properties are blended with the old ones into a complex and subtle system of decision making that probably increases the legitimacy of the European integration process. Intergovernmentalism refers to classical bargaining and coalition formation among national governments seeking consensus, if not explicit unanimity. As a result of a strong tendency in the Council of Ministers to work intergovernmentally, the scope for (qualified) majority voting in the original Rome Treaty was hardly used. The so-called Luxembourg compromise of 1966[8] led some Union countries to practise a veto policy and thereby undermine this aspect of supranationality. Only after 1985 did majority voting actually become prominent: the old majority-voting articles were regularly applied, once consensus proved impossible, and several important policy areas – including many internal market issues – were newly subjected to majority procedures. Intergovernmentalism also raised its head where powers had been assigned to the European Commission. By what has become known as 'comitology', the Commission sought, or was forced, to consult the Member States on numerous details of implementation decisions. The developments are also related to substance and not merely to procedure. From an economic perspective, the institutional design of the Community is critical for

[6]When the third edition went to press, a fifth revision of the treaty, signed in October 2004, was subject to ratification procedures including many referenda in Member States. This treaty goes under the name 'European Constitution' and has once again increased the number of provisions under QMV. See Appendix 1.2.

[7]The ECSC treaty expired in 2002 and has been absorbed into the EC treaty, as part of the Amsterdam Treaty on European Union. A new Art. 7 EU (note, not EC) enables the Union to suspend certain rights (including voting rights) of a Member State in the event of a 'serious and persistent breach' of basic EU principles. However, the Member State cannot be expelled. In the signed (but not yet ratified) European Constitution, the right of voluntary secession is recognised for the first time.

[8]After an institutional and political crisis about proposed new powers for the Commission and the right of veto in case of a 'vital' interest, Member States 'agreed to disagree' on vetoing in 1966. Of course, the core of the problem was that this right was self-proclaimed and its interpretation would be unilateral by the Member State invoking it.

ADDITIONAL READING *continued*

the efficiency and effectiveness of the public economic functions exercised at EC level. Chapter 3 discusses not only the economic rationale for assigning certain economic functions to the Community level, but also to some extent how these functions ought to be exercised. Least-cost methods of joint regulation and adequate solutions for accountability and legitimacy of public policy will foster efficiency and effectiveness. In this sense, intergovernmentalism, like Janus, has two faces. In some cases it may result in inefficient decision making and excessive Member State control of the Commission, thereby undermining an asset of the Community method. In other cases it may justifiably express concerns of accountability (at least, to Member States' administrations) or legitimacy. If construed in the latter way, it may help the Community to achieve better rules and policies. There is, in other words, an efficiency case for the enmeshing of Member States with Union powers and their exercise. Nevertheless, it is easily abused by the Member States.

Cooperative federalism strengthens the view that Member States' involvement with Union competences need not necessarily imply a breakdown of supranationality. It holds, on the contrary, that once a high degree of market integration has been accomplished, the Union level may find it more effective to share the enforcement and executive functions with the institutions of the Member States. In cooperative federalism, this would work for four reasons: common principles, Commission monitoring, the Commission's 'guardian' function and the EC Court as guarantees for market integration and the desired minimum of communality. At the same time, Union policies and regulation can be based on principles *respecting the remaining autonomy of Member States* as much as possible, while inducing the same Member States to cooperate among themselves and with the Commission to facilitate the achieved market integration (see also Chapter 3).

It may be very misleading to assess institutional aspects of European integration without explicit reference to the achieved degree of economic integration. It is precisely due to the Community method that the *acquis communautaire* – the accomplishments at EC level in Community law and jurisprudence – is robust and not subject to erosion. Intergovernmentalism and far-reaching involvement of the Member States do *not* change that. Rather, given today's *acquis* as well as the 'Community method', intergovernmentalism which adds cooperation to the *acquis*, may even enhance European integration significantly. The EC treaty has been revised four times (and currently the European Constitution ratification might add a fifth one) and this constitutional process itself is, by definition, a matter of intergovernmentalism par excellence, made more difficult still by ratification in all the Member States. Yet, major breakthroughs were adopted (see Chapter 2).

1.3 Market integration and other forms

Economic integration refers both to market integration and (economic) policy integration. Market integration is and remains the essence of economic integration, as is clear from the definition of the latter. Most economic policies directly relate to market conduct, or to structure, performance or distributive outcomes of markets. *Market integration* is a behaviourial notion indicating that activities of market participants in different regions or Member States are geared to supply-and-demand conditions in the entire Union (or other relevant area). Usually, this will also show up in significant cross-frontier movements of goods, services and factors. Even potential, but not actually observed, flows may be important in constraining suppliers' price conduct or in consumer behaviour. In a market of perfectly homogeneous goods or services or one type of financial capital, market integration can be measured by the degree of price convergence.

Compared with market integration, *policy integration* is a less precise concept. It may cover different types of economic policies, using different kinds of instruments. Moreover, the degree of 'binding' and commonality may vary, from consultation and cooperation via coordination and 'approximated' national rules to common policies or fully fledged centralisation. To make matters even more complicated, some elements of policy will be expressed in specific regulation and others in powers leaving a large degree of discretion, the use of which may vary over time and also involve non-regulatory means such as budgetary expenditure. Policy integration cannot, therefore, be measured in any straightforward way. Indeed, whereas there is a strong presumption that market integration (if not distorted) is generally welfare-increasing, more policy integration may or may not be good for aggregate welfare.

Another important distinction is that between positive and negative integration, originated by Tinbergen (1954). *Negative integration* denotes the removal of discrimination in national economic rules and policies under joint surveillance. *Positive integration* refers to the transfer to common institutions, or the joint exercise, of at least some powers.[9] In practice, negative and positive integration will go together. The often heard claim that less ambitious forms of economic integration can solely rely on negative integration is not borne out in actual practice. The EU engages in ambitious forms of economic integration and they require an appropriate combination of positive and negative integration. However, there are no unique solutions or hard and fast rules. This is true even for economic federalism, a level of accomplishment the Union has not achieved: the combinations of negative and positive integration in the Canadian, the US and the EU internal markets – as currently achieved – are all distinct (Pelkmans & Vanheukelen, 1988).

1.4 Stages of economic integration

The complexity of economic integration, and the radically diverging degrees of intensity, have led analysts to distinguish several stages of economic integration. The stages approach dates back to Balassa (1961) and its usage is widespread. Although Balassa's original stages have to be amended in various ways, the approach is indispensable for an understanding of the literature and of key issues in policy making. In addressing the drawbacks one can gain some insight into the learning process which the study of European economic integration has gone through since the early 1960s. Table 1.1 provides the five Balassa stages and describes a few of their characteristics.

Table 1.1 The Balassa stages of economic integration

Stage	Definition	Characteristics/Comments
Free trade area (FTA)	• Tariffs and quotas abolished for imports from area members • Area members retain national tariffs (and quotas) against third countries	Essence of GATT definition; no positive integration
Customs union (CU)	• Suppressing discrimination for CU members in product markets • Equalisation of tariffs (and no, or common, quotas) in trade with non-members	Essence of GATT definition; no positive integration
Common market (CM)	• A CU which also abolishes restrictions on factor movements	Is 'beyond' GATT; definition should also include services; no positive integration
Economic union	• A CM with 'some degree of harmonisation of national economic policies in order to remove discrimination . . . due to disparities in these policies'	Positive integration introduced; extremely vague
Total economic integration	• 'Unification of monetary, fiscal, social and counter cyclical policies' • 'Setting up of a supranational authority where decisions are binding for the Member States'	Centralist; vision of unitary state; supranationality only introduced here

Source: Adapted from Balassa, 1961

[9]The words 'positive' and 'negative' do not have any normative value with respect to 'welfare' or otherwise. They have become mere jargon.

The stages are presented sequentially for analytical reasons. However, there is no compelling reason to follow the sequence rigidly. For instance, the EEC started with a customs union (CU), not a free trade area (FTA). The sequence is helpful for understanding the additionality in each stage when increasing the ambitions in economic integration.

It is important to reflect upon the limitations and problems of this classical view. First, in the world economy today there are a number of preferential trading arrangements whose ambitions do not match even the first stage of Table 1.1. These preferential arrangements may be limited in the scope of products covered, and tariffs (and quotas) for intra-group imports are not fully removed. The General Agreement on Tariffs and Trade (GATT) allows this for developing countries, not for developed ones. A special case is sectoral integration, such as the ECSC for coal and steel or the 1965 US–Canada automotive agreement. For developed countries, such sectoral initiatives require a so-called waiver, that is, a derogation from the GATT.

Second, although the FTA and the CU definitions capture the essence of the GATT definitions and are therefore widely used, the absence of positive integration deprives these notions of practical applicability. This drawback is less severe in the case of an FTA as an FTA does not even have a common external tariff. A simple FTA is the one between the EC and the respective EFTA (European Free Trade Area) countries, established in 1972: positive integration is confined to origin and other customs matters. However, the Stockholm Treaty (1960) establishing EFTA does include modest forms of joint management and, for example, occasional harmonisation in selected cases (Curzon Price, 1974). Recent FTAs among developed countries go further in product scope (for example, including some aspects of services) and in approximation of certain forms of economic regulation. This is true for the CER agreement between Australia and New Zealand[10] and NAFTA.[11] The FTA that goes furthest is the European Economic Area (EEA) concluded between the EC and most EFTA countries in 1992: the EEA is a hybrid of an FTA for industrial goods and for services with far-reaching approximation (that is, making more uniform) of economic regulation, plus a common court (see Chapter 20).

In the case of customs unions, however, the absence of positive integration is simply misleading. It is possible to conceive of a customs union as a tariff union only.[12] Even in that event, however, tariff classifications have to be unified, customs rules harmonised to a large extent and the issue of the distribution of tariff revenues has to be addressed. In practice, many more elements of trade policy will be under pressure to be approximated, made compatible or transferred to common institutions. So, positive integration is already of some importance in a tariff union. This might include anti-dumping, the conclusion of trade treaties and negotiations in the GATT. The EC customs union, and the older Benelux customs union, have gone much further than a mere tariff union. The Community included a common agricultural policy to allow intra-union agricultural trade to become free (see Chapter 11). It also established a common competition policy so that intra-EC trade would not be distorted by adverse business conduct (see Chapter 12). Furthermore, the Community relied upon open-ended provisions for the approximation or uniformity of economic regulation (see Chapters 4 and 5) and some indirect taxation (see section 5.4.3).

Third, the Balassa common market (CM) suffers also from the absence of positive integration. It ignores the cross-border provision of services too. Taking Balassa literally, the CM would imply neither approximation of national economic regulation nor any transfer of regulatory powers to the Union, nor any harmonisation of direct or indirect taxation, let alone any transfer of tax powers or, for instance, Union competences for a common competition policy.[13] The shortcomings of this CM concept are so serious that an adapted definition should be used to prevent misunderstandings: 'a common market attains the free movement of products, services and factors of production accompanied by the necessary positive integration for the common market to function properly'. The stages theory does not answer the question of what that 'necessary positive integration for the common market to function properly' is. This

[10] CER, also called ANZCERTA, is the Australia/New Zealand Closer Economic Relations Trade Agreement, in force since 1983. For a summary view, see GATT (1994b, pp. 30–3).

[11] NAFTA is the North American Free Trade Area, between Canada, the USA and Mexico, concluded in 1992. For an authoriative survey, see Hufbauer & Schott (1992). In fact, both CER and NAFTA contain some elements of a common market in that they deal with intellectual property rights and the right of establishment (without going very far, however).

[12] Assuming quotas to be reconverted into tariff equivalents.

[13] In Balassa (1976) the author revisits his former classification and acknowledges particularly the problem of including the appropriate degree of positive integration for the CM.

question is tackled in Chapter 3, with the principle of subsidiarity – a derivative of the economic theory of federalism. Chapters 7 and 9 deal with the free movement of services and factors respectively, in light of this adapted definition of a CM.

Fourth, there is a conceptual problem about how to distinguish Balassa's common market and economic union. Balassa's economic union comes close to our adapted definition of a CM, combining positive and negative integration. The Balassa definitions in Table 1.1, however, lead to an unhelpful dichotomy between, on the one hand, the CM as confined to free movements without attention to discrimination and distortions, and, on the other hand, the 'higher' stage of economic union, where the liberalisation leading to the free movements is duly accompanied by positive integration with a view to reducing or preventing discrimination and distortions. Unless one is willing to make extreme assumptions about the role of governments in the economy, it is inconceivable that the Balassa CM can exist in its own right.[14] In practice, therefore, his third and fourth stages should be taken together, as is done in our definition of the CM. It prompts the question whether there remains a place for such a thing as an economic union in Union practice. This is not a semantic problem. The EC treaty includes an 'economic union', without defining it, however. Chapter 18 explains the importance of this economic union and provides a conceptual discussion.

Fifth, defining the final stage as 'total economic integration' is unwarranted. The framework of reference would appear to be that of a unitary state, which is unlikely to be appropriate both on economic and political grounds. One could envisage several partial 'unions' beyond the economic union, such as a tax union, a social union, a monetary union and a political union (with the relevant budgetary and economic policy aspects). Whether and why they should be embraced can be analysed with the help of the economic theory of federalism, given alternative political assumptions about the readiness to pool sovereignty. Such an approach rejects the Balassa presumption of 'unification' and seeks to justify the proper degree of (de)centralisation within such 'unions' on economic grounds (see Chapter 3).

Sixth, the introduction of supranationality only in the final stage cannot be justified on either economic or empirical grounds.

1.5 Economic integration and the WTO

Table 1.1 lists three forms of economic integration:

- FTA and CU, recognised in international economic law since centuries (see, for example, Viner, 1950) and codified in the WTO as Article 24 GATT.
- The common market and economic union not specified in international economic law; the terms are widely used, but the definition of economic union in particular varies greatly.
- Total economic integration, a phrase fallen into disuse; however, of the 'partial' unions 'beyond' an economic union mentioned above, the monetary union is often considered as a stage by itself – its essential characteristics are clearly defined, although the desirable budgetary and other policy integration is somewhat controversial; terms such as a 'social union' (applied in the German unification in 1990), a tax union and (the economic elements of) a political union would seem to be more arbitrary.

The present section briefly elaborates on the status of FTA and CU in the GATT. Section 1.6 will relate the higher stages to economic federalism.

The two most important elements of the GATT are the principle of non-discrimination and the drive for multilateral trade liberalisation. The first one is a legal obligation whereas the second is an avowed aim, guided by reciprocity (an agreed balance of concessions among the contracting parties) as a negotiation principle and the 'most favoured nation' (MFN) principle as an assurance of multilateral non-discrimination for any concession made.[15] FTAs and CUs are inconsistent with the principle of non-discrimination, as they are by definition preferential. They may, but need not, be inconsistent with the drive for multilateral liberalisation.

The GATT provides various possibilities for *legal compatibility* of FTA and CU with the non-discrimination and MFN principles. Under Article 25, para. 5, a 'waiver' can be obtained from those obligations: this procedure was used in 1952 to obtain GATT acceptance for the ECSC treaty. A much more common procedure is to refer to Article 24, paras 4 to 9. It is in this article that FTA and CU are defined and minimum conditions for GATT compatibility are prescribed.

[14] Moreover, as Chapter 17 will show, a pure CM *à la* Balassa would be unstable for reasons having to do with financial capital mobility and the autonomy of national monetary and exchange rate policies.

[15] The reader is referred to well-known works on the GATT, e.g. Jackson (1990), or Hoekman & Kostecki (1995); for the Marrakesh (Uruguay Round) package, see GATT (1994a).

ADDITIONAL READING

Article 24, para. 8, is essentially the same as the FTA in Table 1.1 but some interesting specifications are added. First, rather than quotas, the GATT speaks of a much more encompassing category of 'other restrictive regulations of commerce'. In GATT practice, this has covered little more than quotas and import licences for product trade. There is no economic reason why 'other restrictive regulations' could not include a host of economic regulations which somehow restrict exchange in the FTA. As noted, some recently concluded or upgraded FTAs tend to go far beyond the traditional FTAs in these respects. At the same time, many FTAs have kept numerous exceptions in place, given the vagueness of the GATT definition. Second, FTAs can remain economically incomplete, because only 'substantially all the trade' should be covered: it has been commonly accepted that agriculture is excluded (for example in EFTA) or included only selectively (for example, the Union's FTAs with Mediterranean countries); however, many FTAs also employ 'exclusion lists' (for example, the ASEAN Free Trade Area).

Finally, there is reference to products 'originating' from FTA countries. In other words, since products from third countries are subjected to national trade policies in an FTA, and since these will differ, the FTA will need certificates-of-origin. Without such administrative controls, trade would be deflected via low-tariff FTA members, before enjoying zero-tariff access to high-tariff FTA members. The certificates enable customs officers to prevent this trade deflection. These certificates will accompany any intra-FTA import and export of goods. There is an administrative and an economic problem here. The former may become a burden for complex goods with multi-country origin, which is a frequent phenomenon in today's world trade with refined specialisation and global networks of subcontractors. The latter may arise from attempts to reduce the complications of establishing origin, whenever origin from FTA members is not close to 100 per cent. In these cases, usually a simple cut-off rule is applied, say, intra-FTA free trade applies to all goods with at least 50 per cent origin in FTA members. However, such simple origin rules can conceal protectionist attitudes, if the cut-off share is high (for example, 65 per cent for cars in NAFTA), if the methods for establishing the origin share are costly and discretionary, or if there is no cumulative origin for the FTA as a whole but only origin per individual FTA member. Of course, the inclination to employ these technicalities for trade-restrictive purposes will be higher, the wider the absolute and relative discrepancies are among the national trade policies in the FTA.

In addition, the following should be noted. With respect to extra-CU trade – that between the CU and third countries – the notion of a single customs territory is the crucial difference from an FTA. The GATT is not very precise in speaking about 'substantially the same duties and other regulations of commerce' for the group as a whole. However, the EC's customs union simply installed a common external tariff (CET).

About 'other regulations', one may note that even the ambitious EU had major difficulties in unifying its external trade policy. A notorious problem (until 1992) was national quotas for third-country imports, especially in clothing and cars (see section 6.5.3 and Chapter 13). Once quotas are national, traders may profit by trade deflection, even in a CU. Thus, for proper quota enforcement at the national level, the CU will be forced to impose certificates of origin for intra-CU trade. In these products, the CU then functions as if it were an FTA. The GATT does not clearly prohibit this inconsistency.

On the whole, however, the EC has made clear and simple choices: it set out to arrive at a CET, proclaimed a common commercial policy and covered all intra-CU trade (see Chapter 5).

CUs and FTAs differ with respect to the compatibility test the GATT has come to apply over the years. The crux of the matter for other GATT contracting parties is that CUs and FTAs should not raise barriers for trade with third countries, as Article 24, para. 4 prescribes. In para. 5, the FTA test to satisfy this prohibition is simple: no higher level of duties or more restrictive regulation of commerce may be imposed than was previously applied by the FTA countries. Since this refers to an existing set of national trade policies, it is a straightforward rule. But this straightforward test cannot apply to CUs as they will move to a CET, coming from different *ex ante* tariffs, and possibly to other common regulations, with different national ones before. Thus, the GATT says that the duties and other regulations established by the CU must not 'on the whole be higher or more restrictive than the general incidence of the duties and regulations of commerce' previously applied by the CU Member States. This *general-incidence clause* moves the test away from a factual verification of the CET and other measures themselves, and concentrates on the effects of the CU on trade with third countries. This economic test can, in principle, be implemented with the help of the economic analysis of customs unions (see Chapter 6). Without anticipating this analysis, a warning can be formulated about the EC's technique to establish the CET as the arithmetic average of *ex ante* national tariffs (as in the now deleted Article 19 EC). Though seemingly neutral with respect to non-EC countries, this average does not tell the GATT much about the general economic incidence of the CET compared with the general incidence of *ex ante* tariffs. And, even if all CU members had across-the-board tariffs of 10 per cent before the CU, and hence the CET would be 10 per cent too, this does not mean that the general-incidence clause is satisfied. It is this crucial insight that forms the basis for CU theory (see Chapter 6).

The other problem of FTAs and CUs for the GATT is whether regional (product market) integration facilitates or undermines multilateral trade liberalisation. Rather than being building blocks to free trade under the multilateral GATT rules, could a prolification of FTAs and CUs not prove to be stumbling blocks for achieving or even maintaining multilateralism? In so far as the EU is concerned, this question is taken up in Chapter 13.

1.6 Economic integration and economic federalism

The higher or more ambitious the stages of economic integration, the closer is their resemblance to economic federalism. Since all federations in the OECD[16] are not only CUs in the sense of GATT but also common markets as well as economic and monetary unions, some guidance may be had from a comparison with economic federalism.

There is one important caveat, however. Federations are mature political unions with federal government. In such a polity, the 'stage of economic integration' is essentially a product of the degree of *decentralisation,* as determined by a combination of historical tradition, political feasibility and economic costs and benefits. Whatever the chosen degree of decentralisation of public economic functions, the integrity of the federation and its economy are not at issue.[17]

Processes of economic integration among independent countries, even when they increasingly 'pool' their sovereignty, are governed by a radically different political logic. All major steps are subject to unanimity in the group and heavy ratification procedures in each of the Member States. Political sensitivities may, and do, crop up over time, and threats of retrogression are difficult to fend off if the domestic politics in a Member State go against the government or a groundswell of public opinion undermines the legitimacy of integrationist accomplishments. Stability can be greatly strengthened and legal mechanisms and political legitimacy can be fostered by giving electoral political status to common leaders, but the nature and extent of these solutions may themselves be politically controversial. In other words, the integrity of the 'union' economy is itself the issue *par excellence* and the integrity of the federation is not yet accomplished (and may never be).

All federations in the OECD have achieved common markets in the sense that internal factor movements are free and a degree of positive integration helps to make the CM function reasonably well. But this implies neither a counsel of perfection nor one of uniformity between the constituent states, regions, cantons or provinces. In terms of 'completeness' of a CM, one might pose questions about the interstate trade of financial services (banking and insurance, especially) in the CM of the USA, or, about the interprovincial trade of, for example, beer in the CM of Canada. Many federations encounter problems in the free movement of professionals, because the lack of uniformity (for example in diplomas) is not always compensated for by smooth mutual recognition.

It is crucial to appreciate that federalism aims to find *optimal combinations of unity and diversity.* Where positive integration to make a CM function properly

[16]Canada, the USA, Australia, Germany, Switzerland, Austria and Belgium. In some respects one could add Spain and Italy.

[17]With the possible exception of Quebec in Canada. However, despite recurrent threats, secession has never taken place. The splitting up of Czechoslovakia in 1993, while keeping a customs union between the Czech Republic and Slovakia, is a dramatic example of how 'deep' economic interdependence gradually becomes with the highest stages of economic integration and how costly disentanglement can be. See Fidrmuc & Fidrmuc (2000) for the trade effects.

would impose uniformity, the regional preferences for diversity may be suppressed. As a result, any federal CM exhibits numerous trade-offs between the benefits of reducing regulatory discrepancies in the CM and the benefits of satisfying regional preferences. The comparison of the CMs of different federations therefore shows distinct solutions for various aspects. What is achieved by mere liberalisation and strict case law in one federation might be accomplished through almost complete regulatory uniformity (harmonisation or even centralisation) in another one. Great divergencies in regional fiscal autonomy can also be observed, with Switzerland and the USA being rather decentralised, for example, and Germany and Belgium being relatively centralised.

A comparison of federations with respect to economic union would require an authoritative analytical framework, which, as noted, is not available (see, however, Chapter 17). It is worth noting that all federations are also monetary unions[18] with centralised monetary policy functions. The USA has maintained a network of regional central banks in the Federal Reserve System, without, however, compromising the centralisation of monetary (and exchange rate) policy. The eurozone has also maintained the national central banks, without, however, the power to conduct monetary policy (see Chapter 18). The respective monetary unions differ with respect to their budgetary regimes, especially the borrowing autonomy of regions, and the relationship between federal taxation, the (re)distribution of revenues and regional spending. Monetary unions in federations also diverge in their attachment to price stability and the (political) independence and accountability of the central banks. Finally, it should be realised that federal monetary unions invariably function against the backdrop of elected federal governments and federal budgets which amount to an appreciable share of total government spending in the economy. The latter two characteristics are, thus far, absent in the EU. Indeed, in 2005, the euro is the common currency of a monetary union of 12 countries, in an economic union of 25 countries, without a federal government.

1.7 Summary

Economic integration is the elimination of economic frontiers between two or more economies. The fundamental significance of economic integration is the increase of actual or potential competition, and the benefits flowing from this.

Economic integration in Europe should be understood against the backdrop of recent history, political aims and institutional aspects, especially the 'Community method'. The original Community method combined supranationality and the pooling of sovereignty. Later, this was blended with intergovernmentalism and cooperative federalism, magnifying the role of the Member States in decision making as well as implementation and enforcement, respectively.

Besides the distinction between market and (economic) policy integration, negative and positive integration are also useful concepts when understanding economic integration processes.

The Balassa stages of economic integration remain a basic tool of study. Important insights can be gained from several amendments prompted by the absence of positive integration in Balassa's stages of the customs union and the common market. This may also blur the difference between the common market and economic union. Balassa's highest stage is misconceived, inspired as it is by a centralist, rather than a federal, state model.

Economic regionalism is inconsistent with the GATT's non-discrimination principle. The legal compatibility of free trade areas and customs unions with the GATT hinges on certain specific constraints (in Article 24 GATT). In addition, the free trade area test checks whether any more restrictive measure is introduced whereas customs unions are subjected to an economic incidence test.

Understanding the higher stages of economic integration is facilitated by studying the economics of federalism. The two have in common the idea that 'welfare' is best served by the optimal combination of unity and diversity.

[18] In the UK, Scotland has maintained its own banknotes but its issuing authority has no policy discretion. In the case of German unification, the Ostmark disappeared when monetary union was initiated in 1990.

APPENDIX 1.1 European institutions – a brief guide

Nowadays, simple and clear introductions into the institutions and legislative processes of the EU are widely (and often freely) available in many countries of the world. The following description is kept to a minimum and merely serves as a reminder.

Before moving on, a few warnings. The EU system is one of multi-tier government. Thus, despite popular suggestions to the contrary, Member States themselves are just as much a part of the EU as the common bodies at EU level are part of the EU. It is also worthwhile repeating the distinction between EC and EU. EC stands for European Community, legally based on the (main and) first pillar of the European Union (or Amsterdam) Treaty, which also incorporates two (far less comprehensive and less binding) 'pillars': one on foreign policy and security and another one on police and judicial cooperation in criminal matters. The latter 'pillar' used to be called 'justice and home affairs' (mainly, person controls) but, in the Amsterdam Treaty, a considerable part of the issues surrounding person controls was integrated into the EC treaty – that is, the main pillar. Note that, if the European Constitution were to be ratified, the pillar would disappear and a single (EU) treaty would remain. In this book, EU is used to denote the Union in general and, when relevant, the EU treaty itself with those less binding pillars. EC will be used when it is legally necessary in view of the powers in the EC treaty. When referring to the pre-Maastricht period (see Chapter 2), it is sometimes necessary to refer to the Rome Treaty or EEC (European Economic Community). The reader should also not forget that the EU system comprises two other treaties: the ECSC (European Coal and Steel Community) treaty dating back to the Paris Treaty of 1951, included in the EC treaty since 2002, and the Euratom treaty of 1957, which is little used.

Figure App. 1.1 provides a quick guide to the EU-level institutions and what they do. The figure is largely self-explanatory. The European Council[19] consists of the heads of state (only France) and of governments. It provides leadership and meets at least twice a year. Its presidency and that of the Council of Ministers is performed by the same Member State and rotates every six months. The incumbent presidency, and the preceding and following ones form what is sometimes referred to as the 'troika', ensuring continuity in agendas and external representation where needed. The Council of Ministers (usually called the Council) is still the EC's legislator, although the European Parliament (EP) has gradually acquired important powers to co-legislate, to exercise (negative) assent and, in the case of the budget, to take certain final decisions. If the new Constitution (not yet ratified) were to come into force (2009), the EP would become co-legislative in practically all areas. The Commission has the exclusive right to initiate draft laws. In other words, the Commission proposes and the Council (and, increasingly, the EP) disposes. Nonetheless, the Commission wields enormous influence because of the expertise it takes to draft suitable proposals and because of the intense lobbying which surrounds this preparatory work. Moreover, the Commission has several other functions which strengthen its position, the most important one being that of 'guardian of the treaty'. However, the EC policy-making processes are not fully comparable to national ones. The EP controls the Commission (it can even send it home, as it did in 1999) but it cannot directly control the Council, and – by definition – cannot force it to resign. Thus, the fact that the EP is directly chosen by the electorate does not remove the 'democratic deficit', as it is called. After all, the Commission is not chosen by the EP (*de facto,* by the Member States selecting their own Commissioners, although the EP must give 'consent' to the Commission president and interrogates each Commissioner).

The EC Court of Justice has a Court of First Instance which lightens the burden of the (main) Court by focusing on, for example, anti-dumping cases. National courts can (and do) refer to the EC Court to obtain a 'preliminary ruling' on a difficult element of EC law in a national case.

Finally, the past decade or so has witnessed the emergence of a host of specialised agencies at EU level. Usually they perform highly technical functions (for example, the European Medicinal Agency in London, on

[19]Especially outside Europe, the European Council is sometimes confused with the Council of Europe. The latter (dating back to 1949) has Europe-wide membership (thus, also non-EU countries), and focuses on cultural cooperation and human rights, based on the European Convention on Human Rights (1954) and its European Court of Human Rights. It also promotes forms of specific cooperation (e.g. on pharmaceutical practices).

APPENDIX 1.1 *Continued*

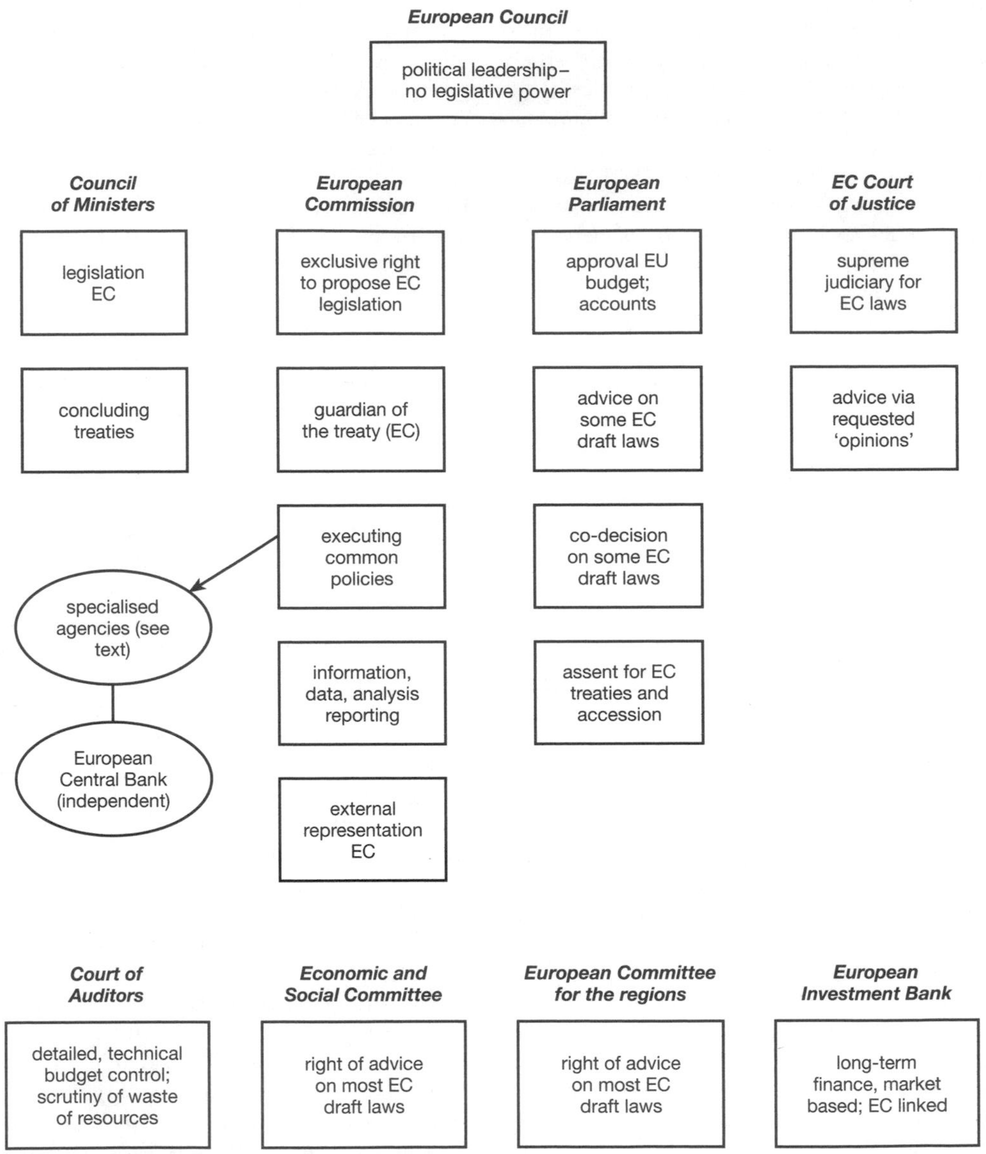

Figure App. 1.1 What the Union institutions do

Note: Member States fulfil important EC functions such as implementation and enforcement of EC laws. Application of EC law by national courts is enmeshed in a single legal system, led by the EC Court.

recognising testing and approval of medicines), analytical functions (for example, the European Environmental Agency in Copenhagen; an agency in Bilbao on health and safety in the workplace) or registration functions (the Office for Harmonisation in Alicante, which deals with trademarks). The European Patent Office in Munich has wider membership than the EU but is nevertheless *de facto* also used as an EC agency.

APPENDIX 1.1 *Continued*

Independent regulatory agencies (as in the USA) do not exist at EU level, with one major exception: the European Central Bank is the first truly independent 'agency' (see Chapter 18).

The legal instruments of the EC are:

- *regulation:* an EC law binding for all legal and natural persons – this is called 'direct effect';[20]
- *directive:* binding with respect to objectives and effect (with varying degrees of detail); the Member States are held to implement directives via incorporation in their national laws in a way suitable to their system;
- *framework directive:* binding with respect to general objectives, and the approach(es) taken, to be followed by a series of specific directives;
- *decision:* binding for a firm or a Member State to which it is addressed;
- *recommendations:* (Council or EP) resolutions, communications, (Commission) White and Green Papers, and 'opinions' may have significant influence, but are not binding.

Decision making is complex in the EU. An understandable reason for that is the plurality and diversity (culturally; big and small countries) of the Union. Also, checks and balances between the institutions may well have greater benefits than costs. More often than not, however, complications arise from stalemate in Council or compromises over treaty revision. The reader is referred to political science literature about the EU institutions and decision making. What should be kept in mind is that the Council may decide by unanimity, by qualified majority voting (QMV) and by simple majority. Two basic factors have pushed the EU towards more QMV and less unanimity: the great EU accomplishments over time (especially with respect to the internal market and common policies – see Chapters 5 to 15), and repeated enlargements up to a group now consisting of 25 Member States (making unanimity more and more costly). QMV means that country votes are weighted by size of the countries but very regressively so. During the intergovernmental conference at Nice, in December 2000, the system of voting for QMV was revised, with a view to giving more weight to the larger Member States. The latter was perceived as counterbalancing the loss of the right of the large Member States to name a second Commissioner, beginning in 2005. At the same time, twelve negotiating candidate countries were also assigned voting weights, anticipating their future entry. Since November 2004, QMV is reached for the EU25 with 232 votes out of a total of 321, and a majority of countries in favour. Large countries now have 29 votes, sliding down via 27 (Spain) and 13 (Netherlands) to 12 (e.g. Greece), 10 (e.g. Austria), 7 (e.g. Denmark) and 4 (Luxembourg) or 3 (Malta). With enlargement, all voting shares have fallen, the big countries tumbling from 11.5 percent to 8.4 percent. Fundamentally, the working of the QMV system has not altered.[21] Coalitions among Member States to push or to block certain draft laws in Council change all the time, although in certain policy areas coalition formation might be more stable.

APPENDIX 1.2 The European Constitution (to be ratified)

On 29 October 2004 in Rome, the 25 Member States signed a new 'treaty establishing a Constitution for Europe'. Although formally still a treaty, it has clear constitutional characteristics, such as an explicit and careful chapter on common values and their enforcement in the EU as well as their pursuit in external relations, a listing of exclusive (to the EU level), shared and complementary powers (competences) between the

[20]Note that, in this book and as is customary in many economic texts, the word 'regulation' is often used in its generic sense as legal interventions in markets. Thus, the EC may develop product regulation (e.g. safety, health) but need not use an EC regulation as the legal instrument to do this (usually, a directive instead). Note also that the new Constitution (not yet ratified) will revamp the set of legal instruments.

[21]The probability of reaching QMV is mathematically reduced with the Nice Treaty. For this and other reasons, the new Constitution (not yet ratified) has simplified QMV. Weighted votes disappear. QMV requires (1) 55 per cent of the Member States (but no less than 15), (2) covering at least 65 per cent of the EU population.

APPENDIX 1.2 *Continued*

EU level and the Member States, a legal personality for the Union (thus far only for the EC as such), and stronger institutional provisions for the three main EU bodies and their interaction. The decade-long battle about a more effective institutional design for the EU (largely failed in the Amsterdam (1997) and Nice (2000) treaties) was finally accomplished in a unifying and comprehensive framework.

No elaboration of this 'Constitution' will be provided here for three reasons. First, the *economic* substance of the former EC treaty was hardly changed. The writing of the Constitution was focused on obtaining a single treaty and on the institutional effectiveness as well as democratic legitimacy ('closer to the people').[22] Second, the ratification process is bound to be difficult, with referenda in 10 Member States. It will take only one country to reject the Constitution and the Union will have to reconsider. Since referenda are less reliable than political coalitions, the risks are considerable. Third, even if ratified in all 25 Member States, it will not come into force until November 2009.

For the main strands and topics of this book, few changes really matter. QMV procedures were changed somewhat (because in Nice they were mishandled), the EP has strengthened its budgetary powers and overall legislative influence (now applicable in many more instances), the European Council replaces a rotational 'presidency' by a president for two and a half years, and matters of justice and home affairs (on asylum, immigration and so forth) will become fully subject to QMV-based methods. Less positively, an exit or secession clause has been introduced. Throughout the book there are occasional references to the Constitution, where relevant.

APPENDIX 1.3 Deepening, widening and enlargement of the EU

The European Community has developed in essentially three ways:[23]

- deepening (of its economic liberalisation, common regulation and policies, and of the commitments and prohibitions of the Member States);
- widening (of the scope of its economic and other powers);
- enlargement (of membership).

As the EEC treaty is ambitious, its faithful implementation is already quite an achievement. However, the EC has actually developed far beyond the original EEC treaty. It has also quadrupled membership. Realising the fragility of the early stages of integration, one should not expect faithful implementation, deepening, widening and enlargement all to go well at the same time – certainly not all the time. There are trade-offs for economic or political reasons between, for example, deepening and widening or deepening and enlargement. This makes for a complex historical development of the EC, one which this book cannot hope to trace in detail.

A careful study of EC history shows that one should be cautious about subscribing to often-heard views that the history of the EC was one of alternating ups and downs. In fact, such views are coloured by a priority of political over economic integration. This idea of successive crises and booms in European integration is also fed by an exclusive focus on the Council and the Commission, hence on legislation, rather than on the Court and judicial review. In addition, many initially insignificant policy actions gradually assumed a prominent place among the activities at EC level.

The EC has *deepened* in several ways. There have been four revisions of the EEC treaty, called the Single European Act (negotiated in December 1985), the Maastricht Treaty (negotiated in 1991, in force since 1

[22]The method of drafting the constitution was undoubtedly more legitimate and transparent than previous amendments of the European treaties. A 'Convention' was called to do it (between February 2002 and July 2003), consisting of national parliamentarians, European parliamentarians, representatives of national governments and two Commissioners. All proceedings, meetings, proposals were public, open and on the internet.

[23]Previous editions of this textbook included a special chapter (Chapter 2) on developing economic integration in the Union. It discussed the policy dilemmas at the outset of the EEC, the aspirations of the founding fathers of the EEC and the lessons which can be learned for (other cases of) economic regionalism.

APPENDIX 1.3 ***Continued***

November 1993), the Amsterdam Treaty (negotiated in June 1997 and in force since May 1999), and the Nice Treaty (2000), currently in force. In addition, a new Constitution was signed by the EU governments' leaders in October 2004, and it finds itself in a ratification procedure in 25 EU countries. They will be dealt with in Chapter 2. But in an incremental fashion, there have been continuous pressures for deepening throughout the history of the EC, especially after its early main task – completing the CU – had been fulfilled. Examples of landmark rulings of the EC Court with respect to economic integration include the *Dassonville* and *Cassis de Dijon* cases (in, respectively, 1974 and 1979) on regulatory barriers hindering imports (see Chapters 4 and 5), the conviction in 1985 of the Council for a 'failure to act' (Article 232 EC) on the establishment of a common transport policy, and the telecoms cases (respectively in 1991 and 1992) justifying Article 86 EC as a basis for a pro-competitive telecoms programme (see Chapter 8). The Court has facilitated deepening in other cases, as will be illustrated throughout this book. Partial changes of the treaty have been few, the most important probably being the 1970 one to endow the EC budget with 'own resources'.

Widening also finds its most prominent examples in the four treaty revisions. Chapter 2 covers this widening in brief. But widening has been a recurrent phenomenon in EC history, especially in economic rules and policies. Ever since the Barre Plan of 1968, the EC has been involved in monetary cooperation and integration. In February 1971 the Council endorsed a resolution on the first stage towards (an ill-defined) economic and monetary union in 1980, a policy which was quietly shelved during the monetary turmoil of the mid-1970s. In 1979 the European Monetary System (EMS) was born (see Chapter 17), but only partially incorporated into the Community (it would be internalised with the Single European Act 1985). Monetary union came back with the Maastricht Treaty, and is now in place for twelve (euro) countries (see Chapter 18).

Widening also occurred as needs arose in flanking economic policies, such as environment and research and technology, regional policies and consumer policy. All of these were initially based on Article 308 EC (often in combination with the preamble or the objectives and instruments of the treaty), a catch-all article enabling the establishment of rules or policies for 'the development and proper functioning of the common market'.

Other instances of widening are easily found, for example the common fisheries policy (two decades after the common agricultural policy), a special (Schengen) convention (adhered to by only thirteen Union countries) for the free movement of persons, and the Social Charter in 1989, a political document about elementary social rights in the EC, from which an impetus on widening social powers was expected (see Chapter 15).

Enlargement has officially taken place five times. When the UK switched from EFTA to the EC (after two failed attempts in 1963 and 1967), it took Denmark with it (because Danish agricultural exports depended heavily on the UK market) as well as Ireland (because it would invalidate the Irish/British FTA and endanger the traditional Irish policy of pegging its punt to the pound sterling). In 1981, Greece changed association for full membership, partly in order to 'lock in' democracy after the colonels' dictatorship. In 1986, Spain and Portugal (the latter coming from EFTA) became EC members. In October 1990 the unification of Germany implied a kind of enlargement through the back door, since a former state (the German Democratic Republic) came into the EC as part of the new Germany.[24] Austria, Finland and Sweden became full EU members on 1 January 1995, whereas Norway did not join after a referendum rejected membership. On 1 May 2004, ten more countries entered the EU: Cyprus and Malta and eight central European countries: Estonia, Latvia, Lithuania, Poland, Czech Republic, Slovakia, Slovenia and Hungary. It is expected that, in 2007, Romania and Bulgaria will join. Croatia and Turkey have entered (long) accession negotiations (see Chapter 20).

[24]It is little known that Greenland – a territory administered by Denmark – chose to leave the EU in 1985.

CHAPTER 2

Economic Constitution of the EU

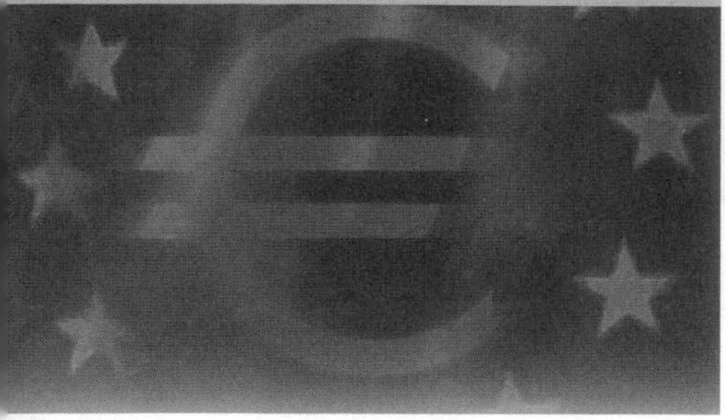

Topics covered

A good understanding of European economic integration requires a basic insight into the nature and economic substance of EU powers. The present chapter provides an economic perspective on four successive EC treaties: the EEC treaty of 1957, the Single European Act of 1985, the Maastricht Treaty of 1991 and the Amsterdam Treaty of 1997.[1]

In considering the treaty as a kind of economic constitution, the chapter can avoid description and concentrate on aims, instruments and principles. The stages of economic integration will also be referred to. The approach facilitates an understanding of the evolution of the economic integration regime of the Community too. Section 2.1 characterises an economic constitution by six key elements and provides some general considerations for their application to economic integration treaties. Section 2.2 uses this framework to outline the economic constitution of the Rome Treaty. Sections 2.3, 2.4 and 2.5 outline the substantive additions incorporated by the Single European Act, the Maastricht Treaty and the Amsterdam Treaty respectively, using the same framework. The four treaties are summarised graphically in four charts with the same structure.

2.1 An economic constitution for integration

When an economic integration treaty includes a considerable degree of positive integration, one may look at the treaty as a kind of economic constitution. In general, a constitution sets out the fundamental rights (and duties) of citizens and firms, besides the powers, and the limits of the powers, of the state. An economic constitution can be seen as a framework of rules and principles for public economic functions, besides the fundamental economic rights (and duties) of private economic agents. Applying this notion to integration would make no sense if only negative integration is agreed; in that case, there would

[1]The Euratom treaty (1957) will not be dealt with, except in passing, as it has largely fallen into disuse. The ECSC treaty is touched upon in Chapter 14. After its expiry in 2002, it has been incorporated in the Amsterdam Treaty. The Treaty of Nice (concluded in 2000) only amended institutional aspects (including a little more QMV) and is of no interest for the subject of the present chapter. Also, the Constitution (not yet ratified) would not prompt any major change in economic substance, although the overall aims of the Union have been formulated in a more coherent fashion.

be no joint public economic functions. All the group members could do would be to voluntarily accept to limit the use of *their own* economic powers (for example, no tariffs for trade within the group in an FTA).

The EEC, and later the EC (and the EU), engaged in extensive positive integration, which has been deepened and widened over time. Looking at the treaties as economic constitutions is a useful way to grasp their economic essence, without going into needless and tedious detail. An added advantage is that the rising integrative ambition in the successive treaties can be easily understood within the same framework. At a general level, there are six basic characteristics of an economic constitution in an integration context:

- the guiding principles;
- the identified stages of economic integration;
- the (economic) aims;
- its public economic functions (scope);
- its economic powers at union level (means);
- its institutions with their various functions.

Guiding principles should determine the nature of the desired economic order. The guiding principles are not always explicit. Especially in the early stages of economic integration, economic relations within the union are likely to be dominated by the economic order of the Member States. Therefore, it might be felt to be a difficult and impractical exercise to define an economic order for the union. With the economic relations and obligations between the Member States not yet being so important, implicit and somewhat vague notions about the economic order will provide much needed flexibility. As integration ambitions deepen or grow more encompassing, guiding principles may have to become explicit.

The *stages of economic integration* need not, of course, comply perfectly with the textbook. However, little can be accomplished if (1) the GATT / WTO status is not explicit (for clearance under Article 24 GATT) and (2) certain basic economic freedoms and common policies are not identified.

The *aims* of an integration treaty can be political and economic (and even cultural). The economic aims should, at least in theory, be expected to be promoted by the means in the treaty (*ceteris paribus*). However, the political aims may well be as important or more important. In other words, one may find that means Y promotes aim Z but that there are more effective ways to promote Z. Thus, the method of (say, partial or sectoral) economic integration in a treaty may be second best or even third best, but the explanation might be found in its political suitability to serve an overriding political aim, for example to prevent wars in the region.

The *public economic functions* are conveniently divided into three: allocative, or those influencing the desired functioning of markets; redistributive (between regions, persons or factors of production); and macroeconomic stabilisation (pursuing low unemployment with the lowest possible inflation, without choking off growth). Specifying the union's public economic functions determines the economic scope of a treaty. Because redistribution and macroeconomic stabilisation exert direct and usually considerable effects upon personal income and wealth, they tend to be sensitive in domestic politics. One would not expect them to become part of an integration treaty without difficulty. Thus, one would not expect an early integration treaty to comprise a monetary constitution (one currency, with the macro policy and institutions needed for this currency to be stable), a fiscal constitution (tax powers for the union, as well as limits on spending and political accountability – with democratic representation – for those who decide), or a social constitution (setting out what redistribution, social insurance and social security system is guaranteed between persons at any moment in time, as well as between generations, between regions and between factors, and how these guarantees are financed).

For allocative measures, matters are more complicated. First, general allocative rules are closely linked to some guiding principles (for example, market versus planning; competition versus intervention; private versus state ownership). Since there is tremendous scope for interpretation, general allocative rules may find little opposition when ending up in an integration treaty. Second, allocative measures can be (and are) fine-tuned enormously in every economy. This will be clear not only from the means (see below) but also from the distinction between negative and positive integration as well as from the enormous differentiation in types of markets (for example, agricultural goods or labour; technology flows or telecoms services; etc.) and the policies related to them. It follows that early integration treaties may pursue market integration with very many degrees of ambition. In part this will be determined by the guiding principles and the identified stage of economic integration; in part, it will be fine-tuned in the treaty; and, finally, it will be fine-tuned during the implementation.

The means specified refer to the *economic powers assigned,* or assigned under conditions, to the union level. These powers can be exhaustively enumerated (as in the US constitution; in Germany the enumerated powers are called a *Kompetenz Katalog*) or they can be enumerated, not exhaustively but subject to discretion.

There are many ways in which this discretion can be used over time. Examples include the subjection of all new assignments to the union level to constitutional revision procedures of a lighter kind[2] (which implies only minimum discretion); the subjection to a special assignment test, based on criteria specified in the constitution; or more open-ended, evolutionary processes, which may become clear over a generation or more. It is important to understand that exhaustive enumeration of union powers is no iron-clad protection for the states against long-term centralisation. Equally problematic, however, is the opposite solution of placing initial economic integration processes in such rigid frameworks that deadlock becomes the 'normal' (but costly) state of the union. In practice, implementation by the various union institutions should eventually lead to a balance of union and state powers which approximates, in some fashion, the preferences of the Member States; exhaustive enumeration is not essential in order for that to happen.

The details of the powers concerned may range over the entire spectrum of possibilities of economic regulation,[3] be it prohibitive[4] or imperative,[5] subsidies, taxation and so on. Common budgets may be established and or one could opt for targeted funds. If so desired, state ownership (for example of companies) can be extended to the union level.

The *institutions of the union* will be divided into the usual legislative, executive and judiciary ones. The greater the autonomy of the union level and the greater the ambition of economic integration, the more important the latter two institutions and the less weight will be attached to unanimity in the legislative.

Another way of looking at the common institutions is to define a little more precisely the functions needed. Thus, one could identify institutions which have the (sole or shared) right to *propose* regulation and taxes/subsidies; which have a role in the decision making (on such issues as whether there is a common parliament and whether there are advisory organs which must be heard); which implement (including the Member States themselves); which monitor implementation, gather data, make technical observations, reports, and so on; which act as a guardian of the union's treaty (if applicable, because this may be sensitive at lower stages of integration; it implies a union prosecutor and first instance judge); and which conduct judicial review (again, in some specified relation with national legal systems). In addition, specific 'agencies' could be singled out under a special legal regime to conduct a specific union assignment (for example, a common central bank for a union currency; a common agency for anti-trust policy).

Given this simplified concept of economic constitution, the successive treaties of the EEC, the Single European Act, Maastricht and Amsterdam can be outlined conveniently. With some degree of specification for the stage of integration and the scope of union powers, the graphical presentation will be based on the four remaining features: economic aims, the means (with some detail so as to specify the methods and scope more precisely), the (guiding) principles and the institutions.

2.2 The economic constitution in the Rome Treaty

Figure 2.1 illustrates the economic constitution of the EEC treaty. Article 2 EEC contains five aims and two very general means. Article 3 EEC specifies in total eleven instruments which together make up these two general means. The instruments are worked out in successive titles and chapters of the substantive part of the treaty. This economic core is complemented by some explicit key principles and limited somewhat by a few exceptions. The economic integration regime should function effectively with innovative and comprehensive institutions.

2.2.1 The economic aims

There are four economic aims and a political one. The upper left box of Figure 2.1 uses original treaty language for the economic aims. As one can see, the wording is ambiguous. Thus, the first two aims would seem to overlap with respect to (continuous) economic growth and its qualities, namely 'balanced' and 'harmonious'. Unbalanced growth was a popular theme in the 1950s, referring usually to a structural or even increasing

[2]In a federation this might require less demanding majorities in the parliament or congress. In an integrating group, it might be that one can avoid ratification of a treaty revision, but the assignment would be subject to unanimity and conditions.

[3]Coming from the union level directly, or via national laws, or via special, assigned agencies.

[4]Prohibiting either economic agents or Member States from acting in specified ways which (could) cause certain unwanted effects.

[5]With different degrees of intrusiveness. Thus, imperative with respect to the objective only, or also the means and perhaps even with all the detailed specifications.

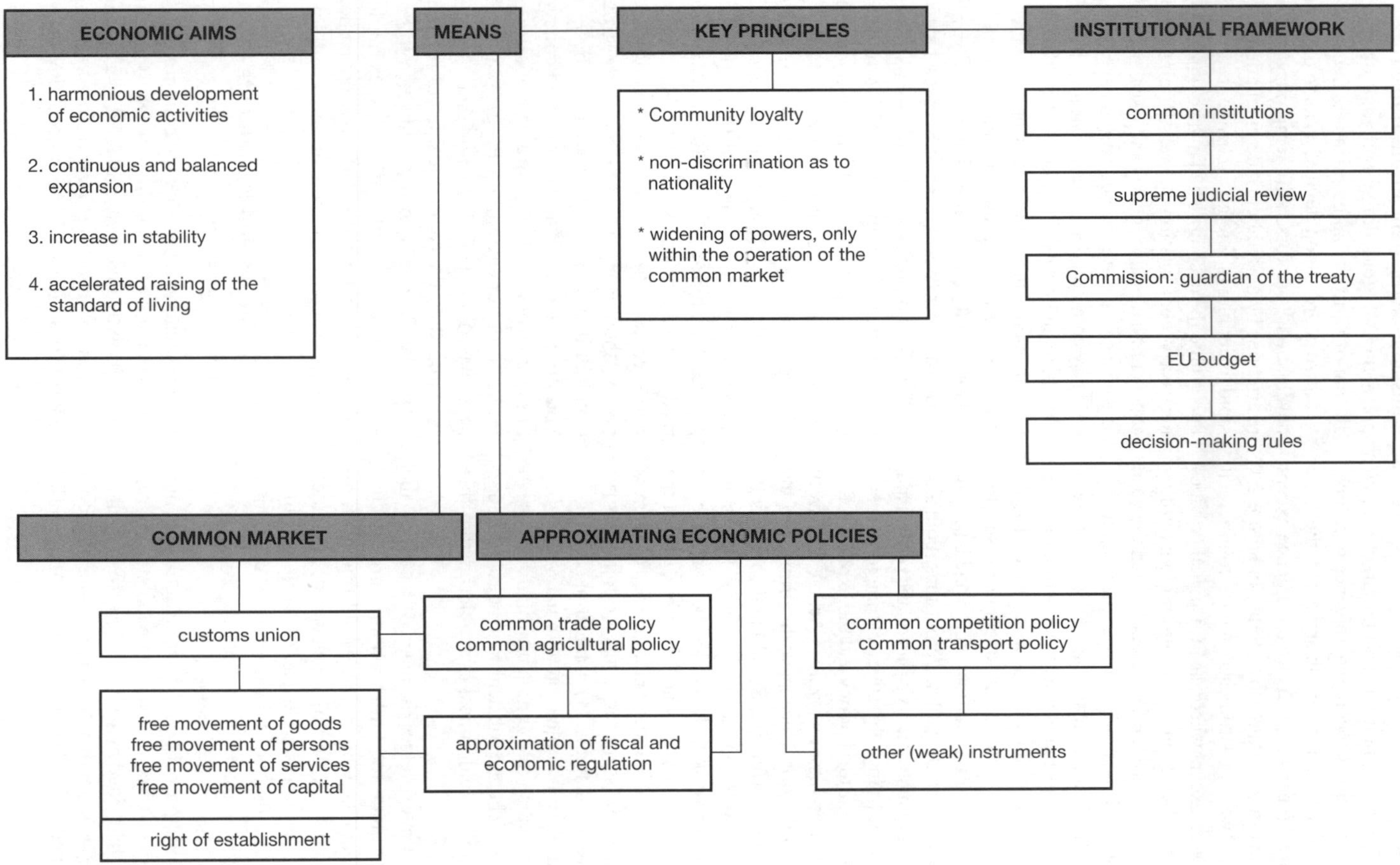

Figure 2.1 Economic structure of the Rome Treaty

income-per-capita divergence between lagging and advanced regions.

The Rome Treaty implicitly relies on market mechanisms to achieve per-capita income convergence over time, if that is what the first aim means. In any event, there are virtually no policy means to promote convergence except the European Investment Bank (to be found in Figure 2.1 in the box 'other (weak) instruments'; it uses commercial principles, however, except where the EC Council provides for subsidies). The beginnings of a joint regional policy were not established until the 1970s. As is often the case with constitutional aims, more than one interpretation is possible. Thus, the first aim may also be read as socially harmonious. In turn, this might refer to industrial relations (the relations between labour and employers) and/or to the avoidance of socially disruptive adjustment processes. Two features support this interpretation: on the one hand, the treaty's social policy and Social Fund provisions (both also in box 'other (weak) instruments') and, on the other hand, the 'fair standard of living' objective (relating to farmers) in the common agricultural policy and the explicit reference to standard of living of workers in Article 3(i). Even if the social interpretation is accepted, the primacy of the first aim remains doubtful. The Social Fund was initially extremely small and its operation restricted. The social policy provisions are weak to the point of being a mere list of desires without EEC instruments. Therefore, neither the regional nor the social interpretation of the first aim is backed up by the necessary regulatory or policy instruments elsewhere in the treaty. By implication, relying on market integration in combination with national policy was assumed to realise this aim. In the Single European Act and the Maastricht and Amsterdam treaties, the notion of 'economic and social cohesion' would change this somewhat.

The second aim expresses the mood of the times: the desire for permanent and high economic growth. For about fifteen years the Community would find itself on a high real growth path, part of which can be attributed to economic integration (see Chapter 6). There was little or no awareness that sustained growth may have increasing environmental costs, hence there is no explicit reference to the environment.

The third aim probably refers to macroeconomic stability. To this end a section on macroeconomic coordination is included, divided into a brief reference to cyclical policy (Article 103) and a 'common concern' about exchange rates and the balance of payments (Articles 107 to 109). The implicit choice was in favour of the adjustable-peg system in the framework of the then prevalent IMF gold–dollar exchange standard. In such a system of rigid exchange rates it is necessary for a CM to utilise coordination devices so as to prevent disruptive devaluations[6] or, worse still, temporary trade and capital restrictions by a Member State in an attempt to prevent a rapid dwindling of foreign exchange reserves. Both would undermine the accomplished market integration. For this necessary coordination to be sufficient, however, the conduct of national monetary and fiscal policies, including sensitive social expenditures, would have to be disciplined either by common decisions or, simply, by external equilibrium requirements. The Rome Treaty does not go so far. Coordination is mainly voluntary and may therefore fail. If it were supreme, it would amount to a major increase in economic and political ambition of the EEC. Therefore, it is part of 'other (weak) provisions' (see Chapter 17).

The fourth aim is again ambiguous. Does 'accelerated' mean a higher growth path? Would the standard of living not automatically go up once aims 1 and 2 are realised? Or is the standard of living a richer concept – as the European consumer movement has long maintained – that is, besides income per capita, does it also relate to the quality of life? This broader perspective formed the basis for the movement's plea to read a 'consumer's doctrine' into this aim. Lacking any reference in the treaty to an overall consumer protection policy, their campaign fell on stony ground as the Council had not adopted this doctrine up to the Maastricht Treaty: it always coupled consumer policy to the internal market. Nowadays quality of life also refers to the environment. Progress in this area was never based on the fourth aim either.

Altogether, the economic aims of the treaty are not very clear. The hard core would seem to be *economic growth under conditionality* (for example, regional convergence, no socially disruptive adjustment, balance of payments constraint, perhaps the quality of life).

2.2.2 Means and instruments

The two general means are the common market and the approximation of economic policies. Both remain undefined. Initially this went unnoticed as a common market appeared to have been well defined since the Spaak report (Spaak *et al.*, 1956). Indeed, the treaty explicitly

[6]IMF rules in those days only allowed a de- (or re)valuation when a 'fundamental disequilibrium' had arisen. This, plus the frequently found political pride of sticking to an overvalued rate, had the effect of enlarging the percentage of a devaluation, once it became inevitable.

mentions in Article 3(c) and Title I the 'four economic freedoms': the free movement of goods, persons, services and capital. A fifth freedom, often compared to the thumb of a hand, is added in Article 106 – the freedom to pay for intra-EC transactions. Moreover, the right of establishment in other Member States was included. Also the definition of approximation of economic policies did not seem to give rise to any problems, as the four boxes attached to this means in Figure 2.1 are all enumerated in Article 3.

This interpretation concealed two phenomenal problems which were to plague economic integration until the Single European Act. The first one is *sequencing*. Building a common market requires more than the imperative of the four freedoms and the right of establishment. Where regulation is economically justified, liberalisation in the form of imposing the four freedoms will require a degree of common economic regulation. Economic justification to regulate can be found in market failures (Chapter 4). Hence, where the common market may 'fail' when functioning freely, appropriate common regulation is economically justified. In a fantasy world of pure functionalism, with the Council and Commission pursuing the ideal Community interest, the nature and degree of approximation of national economic regulation could perhaps be appropriately established in due course. The sequence of harmonisation and liberalisation would matter little as simultaneous moves might characterise the transition. In a political environment, however, where existing national economic or fiscal regulation had generated vested, if not protected, interests, sequencing does matter politically. Usually, there are possibilities and strong incentives for those being regulated to 'capture' the regulators and deeply influence the rules themselves. Capture can be a result of the power of a sector or their hold on technical or other information the regulators need. Such interests will insist on harmonisation *before* liberalisation – but, of course, harmonisation on their terms. Usually it means that they fear competition from competitors in other Member States. With unanimity this is likely to produce vetoes or other stalemates. The upshot would be that the common market would never be completed. The sequencing issue blocked the emergence of the common transport policy until 1985, with the result that no internal market for transport services could emerge. In varying degrees, the problem played a role in numerous goods markets with health and safety regulations, as well as in regulated services markets.

One could have included several partial remedies in the Rome Treaty, such as a shift to qualified majority voting and a common regulatory strategy in the treaty. The former was either absent or politically neutralised; on the latter the treaty is silent. The ideal solution would have been to include in the treaty an unambiguous definition of the common market serving as a 'mother principle' overriding any attempts to misuse sequencing.

The second problem was *conditionality*. The two general means were not independent, as Figure 2.1 shows. Instruments of the common market could only be fully used if certain conditions were satisfied for instruments under the rubric of approximating economic policies.[7] The treaty is rife with conditionality for all four free movements, as will be noticed in later chapters. Suffice to say here that the free movement of goods may suffer from comprehensive derogations for national regulations under Article 36 (now Article 30 EC, for health, safety, environment and consumer protection) which can be 'approximated' under unanimity under Article 100 (now Article 94 EC) but without clear guidelines and deadlines. The free movement of services (for example, financial, transport, telecoms; professional) was conditional in various ways on accomplishments in positive integration on which the treaty was unclear, less than firm, or unhelpful. The free movement of capital was conditional upon adequate macroeconomic coordination. Finally, the free movement of workers was not interpreted as the realisation of a common labour market. An elusive call to harmonise social policies, and some aspects of labour market regulation, is all one may find in the treaty. As a consequence, the free movement of workers acquired a very restrictive meaning (see Chapter 9).

Legally, a common market in the narrow sense of four freedoms plus the right of establishment was, strictly speaking, possible. However, in terms of political economy this makes completely unrealistic assumptions such as a purely functional (that is, apolitical) approach solely interested in accomplishing the treaty's means, backed up by extreme integration loyalty, which would override domestic vested interests or fears of adjustment. In practice, both negative and positive integration can be sensitive and such extreme assumptions are not fulfilled. No wonder that the conditionalities in the treaty are open ended, leaving large discretion to the Member States. Of course, sequencing and conditionality interacted and this made matters worse.

[7]This prompted some leading legal experts to differ on what the common market in the treaty comprised, especially whether (what) common policies 'belong' to the CM. See the example in Pelkmans (1984, p. 186, fn 7).

The economic ambition of the original EEC treaty is therefore not fully reflected in the means and instruments. It is most unlikely that a fully fledged CM can be achieved on the basis of the Rome Treaty. Also the decision rules and consensus habits raised high hurdles against actually achieving a true CM. After 25 years (that is, around 1983), what the Community had achieved covered the following:

- the sections where the treaty was relatively unambiguous (that is, the least regulated parts for the goods markets as well as the common competition policy and common tariffs);
- the areas where sequencing and conditionality were bought off almost irrespective of the costs, that is, the common agricultural policy (CAP).

All other instruments remained weakly developed (for example, social, macroeconomic, Social Fund), incomplete (for example, trade policy), deadlocked (for example, harmonisation of health, safety, etc. regulation) or largely absent (for example, transport policy). The free movements of services, capital and persons were so throttled that they assumed little economic meaning. Fiscal harmonisation had booked one amazing success – the shift to the VAT system in all Member States – and some progress on the VAT base, but there was pure deadlock on any form of approximating the rates or otherwise getting rid of fiscal frontiers.

The common market therefore amounted to a kind of customs union in the goods market supplemented by the CAP and competition policy for goods. Historically, and in comparison with many other attempts of economic regionalism, this was a major accomplishment. The problem, however, is that the treaty aspires to do so much more. This *CU-plus* did not even yield free movement of goods, truncated as it was by the problems specified above.

It was this highly unsatisfactory situation, which was referred to as 'non-Europe' in the Albert and Ball (1983) report. The awareness of 'non-Europe' cleared the ground for what was later to become 'EC-1992' and the Single European Act.

2.2.3 Key principles

In the upper central box in Figure 2.1, three key principles are listed which the Rome Treaty explicitly provided for. Besides these explicit principles, there is one implicit guiding principle which is critical for the understanding of the economic integration regime of the EEC.

The first principle in the box is *Community loyalty* of the Member States (Article 5 EEC, now Article 10 EC). The motive underlying this principle is the far-reaching degree of *decentralisation* of the EEC. This is evident both in legislation and implementation of Community law. Although the Commission has the sole right to propose legislation, it is the Member States in the Council which dispose, often under unanimity *de jure* or *de facto* (before the Single European Act). Community loyalty expressly commits the Member States to legislate in the pursuit of treaty aims. This part of the loyalty principle is little more than a political declaration because in a voluntary peaceful Community there is little one can do if a Member State exhibits outright political unwillingness.[8] If the unwillingness in Council is collective, however, Article 175 (now Article 232 EC) provides a legal basis for the European Parliament (EP) or the Commission to sue the Council before the EC Court for a 'failure to act'. This remarkable and very delicate option was used successfully by the EP in 1984–85 with respect to the failure of getting a common transport policy off the ground.

Community loyalty has more teeth when referring to implementation of Community law by the Member States. This is of critical importance to economic agents in the internal market. The two main vehicles of Community law are the EEC regulation and the EEC directive. The former is normally adopted by Council[9] and is like 'federal' law: it is directly applicable to all economic agents in the EEC. The directive, on the other hand, reflects a more decentralised approach as it provides objectives, broad prohibitions or other principles and criteria, but the exact details of how this is implemented are left to the Member States. The bulk of Community law is formulated in directives. This decentralised approach may be seen as an early attempt to satisfy the subsidiarity principle. But of course it needs a machinery to guarantee that implementation yields the free movements or the approximation of economic laws that was intended. If not, the EEC would lose credibility and market integration would suffer. This book is not the place to discuss implementation in

[8]Note, however, that the EEC has no legal right of secession and its treaty does not expire (unlike the ECSC treaty). Together this should strengthen credibility which, in turn, should facilitate mutual concessions. Note that lack of loyalty has been addressed in Amsterdam (see section 2.5 below). The right of succession is recognised in the constitutional treaty (not yet ratified).

[9]In some cases (e.g. competition policy, trade), the Commission can issue regulations too; in one case the Commission can even issue directives (Art. 90 EEC, now Art. 86 EC).

any detail. Suffice it to note that three elements in the upper central and right-hand boxes form the core of the compliance machinery in the treaty: Community loyalty binding the Member States, the Commission's role as the 'guardian of the treaty' (that is, a watchdog function minimising infringements) and the Court's supreme judicial review. With the rising ambitions of the Community, even this unique machinery turned out to be insufficient.

The second key principle is *non-discrimination as to nationality*. This pervasive principle has tied the hands of the Member States. The ultimate effect of recurrent Commission or other Member States' objections to specific examples of national regulation or administrative implementation has been a thorough cleansing of national laws of numerous instances of subtle or overt discrimination. The greatest impact, no doubt, has been achieved in the free movements of goods and services and the right of establishment. For example, in limiting the derogations of the free movement of goods strictly to non-discriminatory ones, it has been possible significantly to reduce the potential for hidden protectionism.[10] Nowadays, almost all legislation in Member States which has any relation to freedom of movement, actual or potential, is permeated by this principle.

The third key principle is about *widening* (the scope of EEC economic powers) without treaty revision and ratification. Article 235 (now Article 308 EC) provides a legal basis for widening, under unanimity, but only if such a new competence falls 'within' the operation of the common market. Since the common market is not defined in the treaty and since the former is interdependent with elements of positive integration in the treaty – as Figure 2.1 shows – the interpretation of Article 235 has been the subject of legal and political debate. In practice, the Council has shown a considerable degree of political pragmatism in using this option in conjunction with Article 100 (now Article 94 EC) (see the box on approximation of economic policies). In so doing it added a body of environmental, consumer and regional policy laws to the *acquis communautaire*. The old Article 235 could have been used as a substitute for revising the treaty. However, this did not happen.

Finally, a guiding principle which cannot be read from the treaty text but is crucial for an understanding of the Community's economic regime is *rules, not money*. The EEC is a regulatory machinery, not a spending spree. Typical spending ministries such as defence, social transfers, housing, health, education, public transport and infrastructure, have remained national. Where the EEC treaty encourages common policies there is little indication that this would require major budgetary outlays (for example, transport, competition, trade). As noted, the Social Fund remained small and the Regional Development Fund – set up only in 1975 – was kept equally insignificant until the 1980s. New policies under 'widening', such as research and technological development (R&TD), environment and consumer policies were little different. Initial expenditures on R&TD were at best symbolic[11] and spending began to increase only in the 1980s when framework programmes were introduced and European business began to co-finance and co-manage projects (see Chapter 14). Environment and consumer policies were entirely regulatory.

The 'rules, not money' principle has one big exception: agriculture. Price support, structural subsidies and (nowadays) other expenditures are the main instruments for the CAP, not regulatory measures as such. Over time, CAP expenditure rose rapidly for reasons which are explained in Chapter 11. The effect of spending on the CAP but not on other policies was bound to result in the CAP's receiving a totally disproportionate share of the Community budget: for many years this hovered around 65–70 per cent before declining to around 45 per cent currently.

The nature of the Union budget is therefore not comparable to that of a country (see also Chapter 19). Drawing conclusions from that budget about what the EEC does, whether in absolute or relative (for the CAP) terms, is misconceived. In understanding the EEC, one should fully appreciate its regulatory function. The 'rules, not money' principle has governed economic integration in the Community, with only few exceptions, and continues to retain its relevance.

2.3 The value-added of the Single European Act

The Single European Act is a collection of treaty amendments and additions. Its patchy character makes it

[10]See Chapters 4 and 5 below for details about how the Court has imposed additional criteria with respect to Arts 36 and 30 (now, respectively Arts 30 and 28 EC) and, in doing so, has managed to reduce the scope for subtle protectionism to a trickle. See Chapter 7 below for similar case law in services.

[11]The R&TD budget of the late 1970s and early 1980s was still dominated by substantial spending on nuclear research under the Euratom treaty. The text refers to spending on other items.

difficult to grasp the significance for the European integration process. However, within the analytical framework of Figure 2.1, the importance and limitations of the Single Act can be understood more easily. The Single European Act introduces widening and/or deepening in three broad areas: the institutional framework, specific instruments making up the two general means (that is, largely economic) and foreign policy. Many of the provisions reflect the laying down of an explicit legal basis for what had already been in place on the basis of Article 235 (now Article 308 EC) (see section 2.2.3 below). The Single European Act also codified existing instances of cooperation among the Member States, which had remained intergovernmental up to 1985, hence formally outside the realm of Community law. The two main instances of the latter are the European Monetary System (EMS) and the European Political Cooperation (EPC), the voluntary coordination of national foreign policies. In the following the incorporation of EPC will be ignored.

Figure 2.2 illustrates the additions of the Single European Act to the Rome Treaty using the framework of Figure 2.1. Before discussing them it is important to observe that the economic structure of the EEC treaty is only marginally altered. Thus, the economic aims, the common market, the four common policies attached to 'approximating economic policies', the key principles and the basic institutional framework are not touched. Nevertheless, the economic constitution is strengthened considerably.

After the discussion in section 2.2, it is easy to trace the provisions which strengthened the economic constitution. The main reason for rewriting parts of the Rome Treaty was, after all, to have a more solid basis for 'completing the internal market'.[12] All five critical additions to the treaty have a bearing on this effort to 'complete' the internal market. All other additions were either codifications of existing practices or provisions of marginal importance. Those five additions were:

- far more qualified majority voting (QMV) on internal market matters;
- an explicit, unambiguous definition of the internal market;
- mutual recognition as a regulatory principle;
- approximation of health and safety in the workplace;
- economic and social cohesion.

As shown in section 2.2, the first two additions were indispensable. QMV was introduced for the basic approximation article (in a new version, Article 100A, now Article 95 EC) and throughout the treaty for services, free movement of capital and, for example, the extension of the common transport policy (including the free movement of transport services) to air and maritime. Only some aspects of social regulation and all tax matters remained under unanimity. QMV having become routine, behaviour in the Council changed radically. A results-oriented EC-1992 programme for a period as long as seven and a half years suddenly became a realistic aim.[13]

This was greatly helped by the clear definition of the internal market as an 'area without internal frontiers in which the free movement of goods, persons, services and capital is ensured'. In other words, a 'mother principle' as a benchmark for the completed internal market is introduced. In doing so, it greatly reduced the problems of sequencing and conditionality, since the overriding importance of free movement and of the removal of internal frontiers – be they border controls, fiscal or regulatory – could no longer be disputed. And, of course, QMV added the needed political pressure.

Also the methods of approximation or common economic regulation were altered. In the 'old' approach, approximation of national economic regulation usually boiled down to extremely detailed law making at the Community level. Partly, this was caused by unanimity – a recalcitrant Member State could insist on any detail. Partly, it reflected a lack of trust among the Member States. The degree of decentralisation under the Rome Treaty was still so great that approximation only of the objectives (so as to prevent market failure) would have required an enormous compliance machinery to verify implementation by the Member States. Thus, once the EC did regulate, it regulated all the details too, given insufficient monitoring and a very slow and limited compliance machinery. The 'new' approach changed all that. In fact, with the Single European Act, a new regulatory strategy was initiated, which will be explained in Chapter 4. A key element of it was 'mutual recognition'. This addition to the 'approximating economic policies' block, which is also closely connected to the 'common market' block in Figure 2.2, expresses the new strategy.

The specific case of health and safety in the workplace was simply the outcome of a widely held consensus in the Community. A textual improvement in

[12] This is the title of the famous White Paper comprising the initial EC-1992 programme. See COM (85) 314 of 14 June 1985.

[13] For a survey of the accomplishments and significance of EC-1992, see Pelkmans (1994a). For its main elements, see Chapters 5, 7, 8, 9, 12, 13 and 14 below.

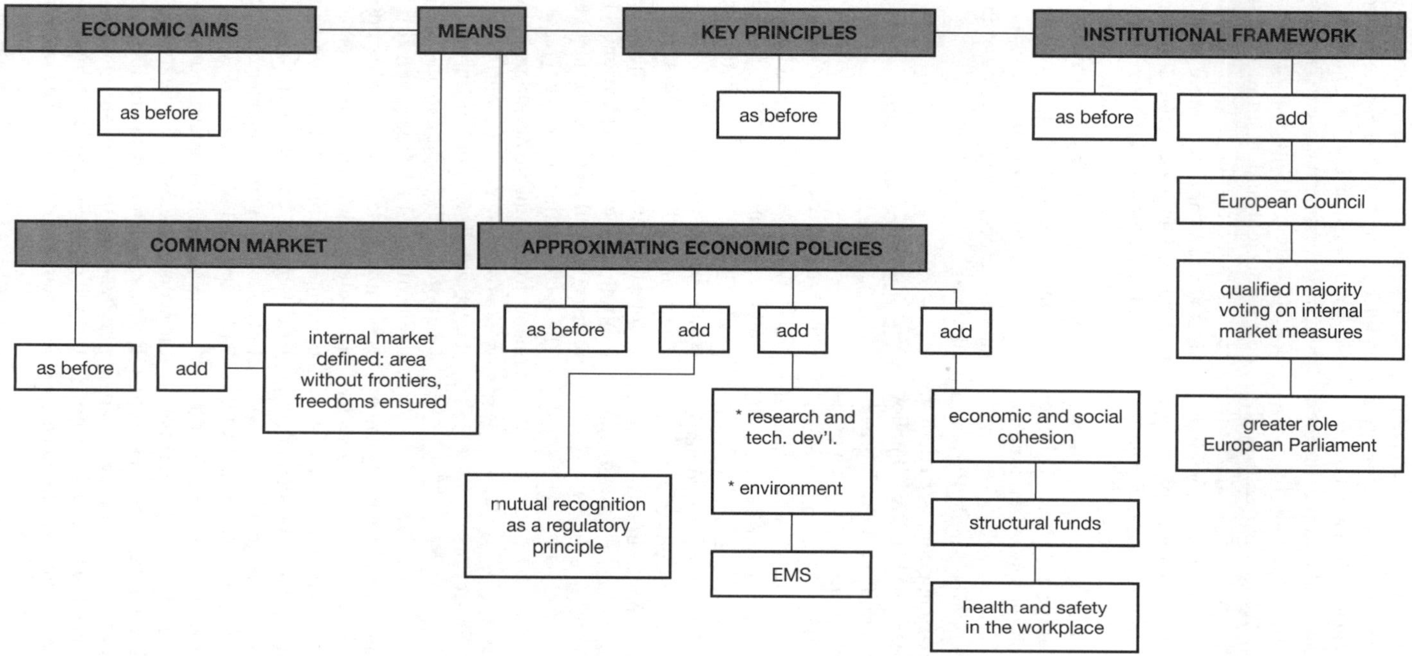

Figure 2.2 Adding the Single European Act to the Rome Treaty

the Rome Treaty and QMV turned out to be sufficient for a successful approximation in this field.

Finally, the insertion of 'economic and social cohesion' has a double significance. No doubt it formed a political condition for what came to be called the four 'cohesion countries' (Greece, Ireland and the new members Spain and Portugal) to agree to the ambitious EC-1992 programme. Yet, it also echoes the debate about the interpretation of the first aim of the treaty (see section 2.2.1 above). In order to ensure that the cohesion concern would not remain empty words, the existing Funds (Social, Agricultural Structure, Regional) were reformed into the Structural Funds and streamlined. In February 1988 their five-year budgets were doubled. The Single European Act also calls for explicit consideration of cohesion in other common policies.

Besides these five additions, the Single European Act codified a number of existing policies, including the European Monetary System (EMS), R&TD policy and environment. It also codified the European Council of heads of state and governments, a top organ operating *de facto* since the mid-1970s. Some genuine additions were also provided, such as the 'social dialogue' between employers and labour unions at EC level (which was little used later on) and a somewhat greater role for the EP, especially for internal market legislation and R&TD. For those concerned and for the specialists, these codifications and additions might be significant, but for the substance of the economic constitution of the Community they were not.

2.4 The Maastricht Treaty

The (first) treaty on European Union, commonly called the Maastricht Treaty, was negotiated only three years after the Single European Act had legally come into force. It was signed in December 1991 in Maastricht (the Netherlands). After a tortuous ratification process – with three national referenda (one of which – the Danish – had to be repeated after a 'reinterpretation' of the implied obligation); constitutional court cases in the UK and Germany, and two exchange rate crises in the EMS, closely related to the treaty's monetary provisions – the Maastricht Treaty went into force on 1 November 1993. An intergovernmental conference about treaty revision was foreseen for 1996; it was expected to aim at improving the institutional framework.[14] Its talks led to the Amsterdam Treaty.

The Maastricht Treaty comprises more widening and deepening than the Single European Act. Whereas the Act pushes the common market closer to its logical conclusion, the Maastricht Treaty signifies a greater departure from the original EEC treaty. This is true for some political and institutional aspects but it also applies to the economic structure. Thus, the economic aims are reformulated and extended, a third general means (economic and monetary union, EMU) is added, a legal basis for a host of new 'instruments' is provided for, and a number of guiding principles is introduced. Though a more systematic revision of the treaty than the Single European Act, it remains possible to utilise the framework of Figure 2.1 to assist in grasping the nature and economic meaning of the amendments and additions.

2.4.1 Economic aims

The 'economic aims' box has been largely rewritten (see Figure 2.3). In the fifth objective the word 'accelerated', which appeared in the old fourth objective, has been deleted. The revisions reflect some of the issues discussed in section 2.2.1 above as well as the emergence of new socio-economic objectives in European society. That 'balanced' growth has become explicit is mere codification. The second aim (a rewrite) as well as the third (new) are related to EMU. The second objective also expresses the EU's commitments to sustainable development within the Union as well as worldwide. The fourth aim explicitly elevates the 'social dimension' of European integration to the level of the EU's fundamental aims. The long debate about quality of life is given full recognition in the fifth aim. Finally, economic and social cohesion is also elevated to the aims (the sixth one). It is combined with solidarity among Member States, which might be interpreted by some as explicitly introducing a permanent redistributive character which the treaty lacked thus far.

The modernisation and more explicit formulation of the economic aims of the treaty can only be applauded. But this does not mean that the (economic) interpretation has become more straightforward. The reason is that the greater clarity of formulation has been blended with new specifications. The latter introduce a series of

[14]For at least two reasons. First, the 'democratic deficit' (see Appendix 1.1 of Chapter 1 above) was only marginally narrowed by Maastricht. Second, the problems of decision making were expected to be exacerbated by enlargement with several EFTA countries. Member States were not prepared to complicate the Maastricht negotiations with enlargement issues.

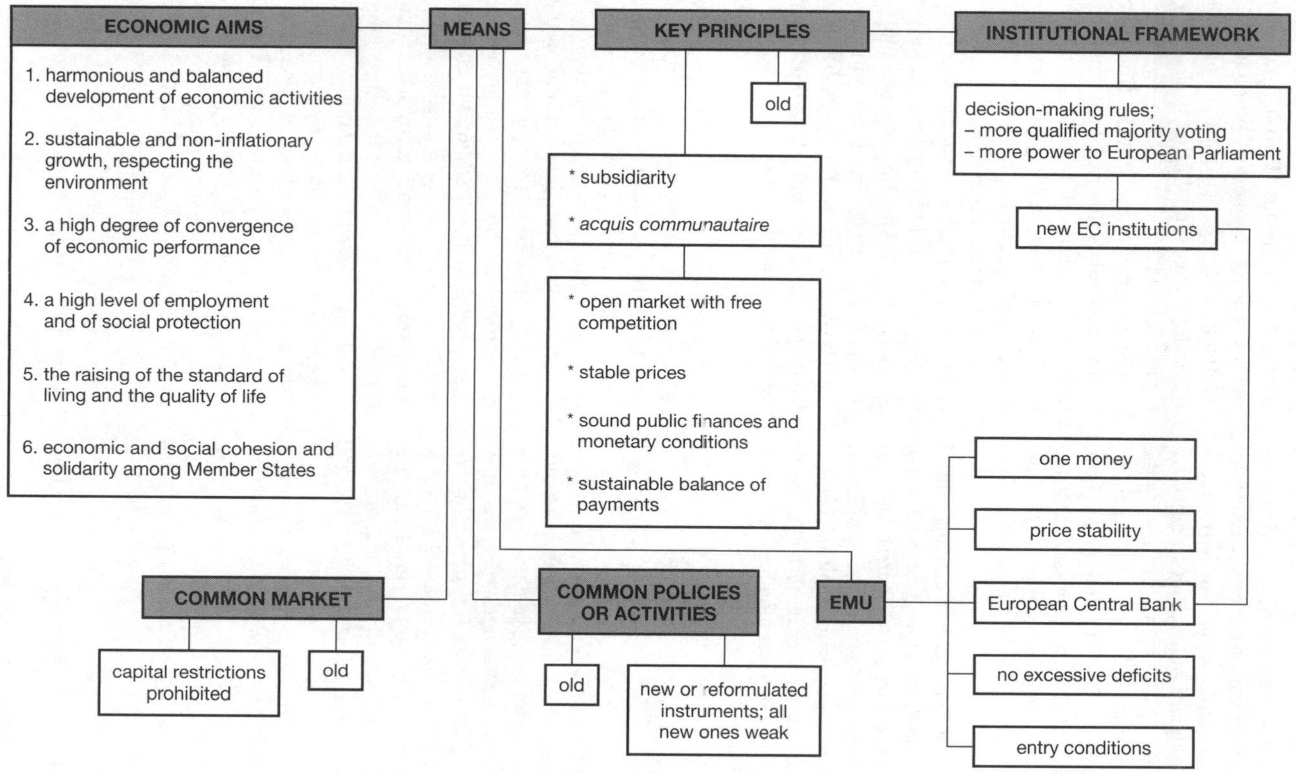

Figure 2.3 Economic structure of the Maastricht Treaty

trade-offs which require political decisions in Council. Sustainable development is a laudable objective but the optimal trade-off may be assessed in radically different ways, dependent on society's preferences, one's access to resources, technology, and so on. Also, a high level of social protection could well be inconsistent with pursuing a high level of employment. Furthermore, as the text suggests, the standard of living is an objective distinct from the quality of life; again, promoting the two will not always be consistent.

And last but not least, if cohesion is interpreted in an 'efficiency' sense (see Chapter 16), that is, equalising the opportunities to exploit the internal market, then the added 'equity' objective of solidarity may reduce the efficacy of the former.

Given the constitutional character of the treaty, general formulations are understandable: a too great precision of the economic aims would perhaps make the treaty obsolescent before too long. At the same time it is hard to escape the conclusion that the aims–means–instruments relations in the Maastricht Treaty are a rather imperfect guide to appreciating fully the economic integration regime.

2.4.2 Means and instruments

The crux of the Maastricht Treaty is found in the general means. A third means (EMU) is added and the label 'approximating economic policies' is replaced by 'common policies or activities', comprising a number of new competences in addition to the relevant *acquis* in Figures 2.1 and 2.2.

The common market, as the first general means, is hardly changed as this had been dealt with so successfully in the Single European Act. Consistent with EMU, restrictions on capital flows in the common market are henceforth prohibited. The 'common policies or activities' block counts no less than thirteen additions. The reader is warned that confining oneself merely to a literal reading of this listing in Article 3 EC is grossly misleading. As one may surmise from the word 'activities', the (economic) meaning of the legal basis for some of these additions is protracted, leading to texts or solutions full of compromises (see Additional Reading below).

ADDITIONAL READING

It is crucial to see that 'instruments' of a very divergent nature are enumerated, some of them virtually without any consequence. Perhaps one can categorise the thirteen added instruments as two strong ones, four with some potential and seven weak ones. The strong ones are cohesion and environmental policy. They represent the *acquis* from the Single European Act, but are now also listed in the instruments, with some added strength.[15]

The four instruments with potential are R&TD policies (also in the Single European Act, but then not in Article 3), infrastructure, consumer protection and the Social Protocol. Consumer protection is new, but whether this will alter actual EC practice remains to be seen. The Social Protocol formally remained outside the treaty, at first in Maastricht, but in Amsterdam it was moved into the treaty. Chapter 15 asks whether this insertion reflects a major shift of social regulation towards the Union. A historically remarkable addition is the introduction of (modest) EC powers for European infrastructure. Thus far, this area had been jealously guarded by the Member States. From an economic point of view this jealousy is clearly suboptimal. An internal market can only be exploited to the full if Europe-wide infrastructure is of high quality and if networks interoperate and interconnect well. It is a classic case of a power that should be coordinated, possibly (partially) centralised. The treaty introduces some EC competence for trans-European networks (TENs) in transport, telecoms and energy (see Chapter 14).

The seven 'weak' additions look like a shopping list.[16] Development cooperation was long overdue

[15]For example, both are also in the aims; a new Cohesion Fund was established (see Chapter 16); QMV is introduced for some environmental measures.

[16]There is little or no substance to instruments such as tourism, civil protection, energy and health. On energy, a declaration, attached to the treaty, promises a separate energy title in the revised post-1996 treaty (but the Amsterdam Treaty did not honour this promise). On education/vocational training and youth, some modest (e.g. exchanges) policies might be built. The Constitution (not yet ratified) has resolved the textual formulations, as well as the (very limited) nature of the EU powers involved, in a much more transparent way. See especially Part III, Chapter V of the Constitution (not yet ratified), on seven areas where the Union may take supporting, coordinating or complementary action.

ADDITIONAL READING *continued*

as the EC had been practising this for a long time. A particular form of industrial policy was introduced, but its nature is pro-market, pro-competitive and anti-protectionist. The sharp debates about this clause, and unanimity, will prevent it from being used in a lighthearted fashion (see Chapter 14). Another interesting feature is a clause on culture. The Union level may develop a cultural policy but only if it 'contribute[s] to the flowering of the cultures of the Member States' (Article 128 now Article 151 EC). Viewing Europe's diversity as a treasure can hardly be expressed more emphatically.

All in all, the 'new' instruments do not imply a great widening of EC powers.

The third new general means is economic and monetary union. Whereas the treaty defines monetary union in detail, economic union remains unspecified. In Chapter 18, three conceptual options for economic union are considered. In Figure 2.3 these options are not included.

Monetary union is both qualitatively and quantitively the greatest addition since the Single European Act. A true monetary constitution is introduced. Extensive procedures on economic (especially budgetary) policy coordination based on explicitly defined and verifiable criteria are followed by detailed provisions on monetary policy and by elaborate institutional provisions. Great care is taken to ensure that EMU would have a sound macroeconomic footing from the start by strict entry conditions and prescriptions for the transitional period. A fully fledged statute of the European Central Bank (ECB) is provided in a protocol.[17] This solid treaty base is no longer comparable with a single-article chapter in the Single European Act about cooperation in economic and monetary policy. The quality jump is so big that it lends support to the criticism of the Balassa stages in Chapter 1. Among modern, open economies, with governments being concerned about allocation, redistribution and macroeconomic stabilisation, a fully fledged common market as a separate stage is either unlikely or unstable. The Rome Treaty and its implementation are consistent with this view, as the common market could not nearly be achieved – and, in fact, was not. The Single European Act and its implementation is also consistent with this proposition as the 'completed' internal market it sets out to realise in less than eight years should be expected to (and, in fact, did) lead to a further shift to the higher stage of EMU. Had Maastricht failed, the internal market would have been combined with inadequate coordination guarantees in an EMS not incorporating all Member States. Lacking credible macroeconomic convergence, this would have led either to misaligned exchange rates (and large subsequent realignments) or outright restrictions in the internal market. In both cases there would be retrogression.

The monetary union is discussed in Chapter 18. Figure 2.3 illustrates five pivotal elements. In Stage 3 of EMU, exchange rates will be irrevocably fixed and, as meanwhile has been decided, one currency (the euro) will replace national currencies. The ECB will issue the single currency and set the volume and growth of the money stock. The ECB's policy must pursue price stability as an overriding goal. National governments are required not to run 'excessive deficits' as doing so could undermine price stability in EMU. Figure 2.3 also notes the strict entry conditions for EMU's third stage. The European Council had to meet in 1996 and find (by QMV) a minimum of seven Member States which met these entry conditions. In that event the monetary union would have started in 1997 (in fact, this proved to be too early). If the group were smaller than seven, any two or more EU Members (fulfilling the conditions in 1998) should start EMU in 1999 in any case. Finally, the Council could set guidelines for the ECB's management of the external value of the single currency.

The two key decisions for credibility of EMU are price stability and the binding commitment to start EMU in any event before 2000.

[17] There is also a protocol on the European Monetary Institute for Stage 2, which started in 1994. Various other protocols also refer to EMU.

2.4.3 Key principles

The Maastricht Treaty adds two groups of guiding principles to those of the Rome Treaty.

The newly inserted Article 3A(3) (now Article 4) of the EC treaty[18] explicitly mentions 'the following guiding principles: stable prices, sound public finances and monetary conditions and a sustainable balance of payments'. Article 3A(1) specifies that 'the activities of the Member States and the Community shall . . . [be] conducted in accordance with the principle of an open market economy with free competition'. This is repeated in Article 3A(2). Both are typically constitutional in nature. Nowhere in the Rome Treaty can these guiding principles be found. They guide both the national and the EC policy makers. The open economy/free-competition principle would seem to represent a definitive shift away from the last remnants of the highly interventionist economic policies of the 1950s (for example, a high degree of state ownership of companies, far-reaching sectoral policies, a tendency to subsidise loss-making firms for purposes of employment, high protection via trade policy or public procurement). The long-term significance of this principle could therefore be considerable.

Two other guiding principles are introduced explicitly. The most important one is *subsidiarity.* First mentioned in the 'common provisions' of the overarching EU treaty (Article B, now Article 2 EU), it is defined in Article 3B EC, now Article 5 EC. The subsidiarity principle is bound to become, and to remain, a critical principle in the development of European integration. From an economic point of view, the explicit reference in the Maastricht Treaty is rather limited as it applies only to cases of shared powers (that is, powers both for Member States and for the EU). The more fundamental economic issue is what assignments to the EU level of government are justified by the economic theory of multilayer government. Put another way, one may assess the Maastricht Treaty with respect to the efficiency of the assignment of (economic) competences to the respective layers of government. An analytical framework to answer such questions is provided in Chapter 3.

The other guiding principle is the maintenance 'in full' of the *acquis communautaire,* a term that is not translated in the English text (Article B, common provision of the EU treaty; see also Article C, now Article 3 EU). In other words, the Maastricht provisions are to be used as additional features, not as a basis for retrogression.

2.5 The incrementalism of the Amsterdam Treaty

The Amsterdam Treaty is of very limited economic significance. It is nonetheless useful to employ the same graphical technique for illustrating the incremental change in main economic areas. A textual exegesis of the lengthy, indeed often declaratory, wording of a range of amendments would be tedious, without adding much to understanding the economic meaning. As Figure 2.4 shows, the main edifice of the Community's economic constitution has not been altered: no additional means, new critical instruments and/or radical institutional innovation are there. The economic aims have been merely recodified and rearranged.

2.5.1 Economic aims

A glance at Figure 2.4 suggests that major change has taken place in the 'economic aims' block. This is, however, largely appearance, with a few exceptions. Though going from six economic aims in Maastricht to eight aims in Amsterdam, a careful comparison shows that the increase from six to seven is due to the textual rearrangement of the aims, whereas only one aim is really new: the equality of men and women. This ethical standard has always been incorporated in the treaty (in Article 141, formerly Article 119 EC), but only for 'equal pay for equal work'. In elevating it to the economic aims without restrictive application, it has become one consensus element in a still diversified notion of the 'European social model'. One result is that Article 141 is extended to 'matters of employment and occupation' and 'full equality in practice between men and women in working life'.

The rearranging is mainly the consequence of functional logic and is unlikely to have substantive implications. Thus 'sustainable' is now an adjective before 'development of economic activities' (no. 1) while reappearing in the growth aim (no. 4), but without the

[18] The EU treaty (a new treaty, overarching the EC and Euratom treaties) lays down a few 'common provisions' followed by the EC treaty. The latter is the new name for the amended EEC treaty (which includes the Single European Act).

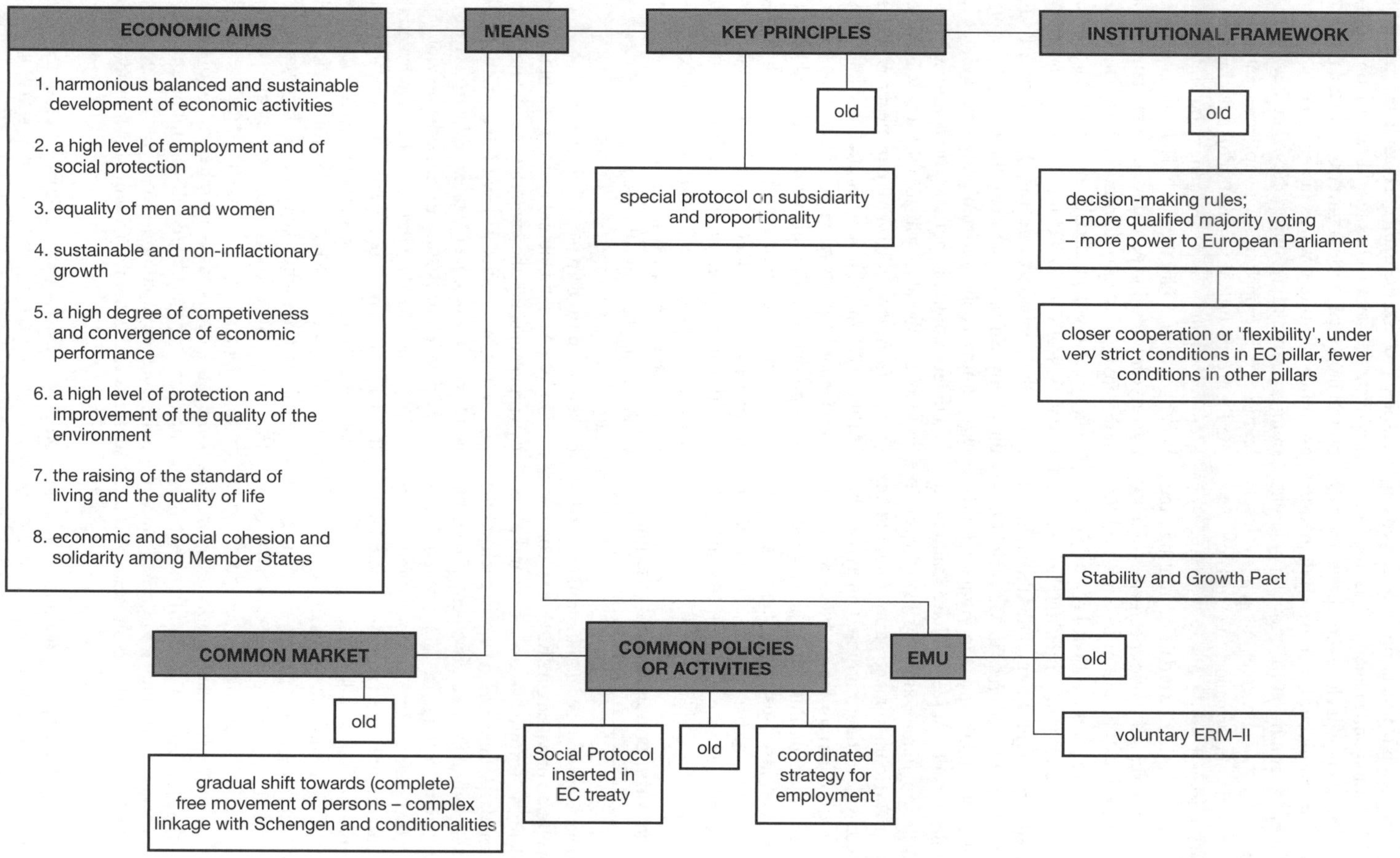

Figure 2.4 Economic structure of the Amsterdam Treaty

superfluous phrase 'respecting the environment'. Thus, the employment and social protection aim moved up from no. 4 to no. 2, without amendment. Thus, the (real) convergence aims (no. 5) now include 'competitiveness'. This insertion of competitiveness can be explained in analogy with the entry condition for monetary union, where inflation rates have to converge, but at a low level. In the case of economic performance, the (real) convergence should be pursued while always striving for 'competitiveness', in other words, emulating the performance benchmarks of good performers. This greater precision could well be meant to condition the (new) employment strategy of Articles 125 to 130 EC (see also 'common policies or activities' in Figure 2.4). Thus, a separate aim (no. 6) now formulates the environmental objectives of the EC, whereas in Maastricht this was attached to the growth aim (no. 2 in Figure 2.3, now no. 4). Here, the drafters do not seem to have maintained discipline. In order to pursue aims by using overall means and more specific instruments, aims ought to be clearly formulated, with distinct wording. Otherwise, the effectiveness of policy can no longer be ascertained. With respect to environment, this clarity and separation between distinct aims is lost: 'sustainable' appears in two aims, even though there is also a separate environmental aim (no. 6) and a reference to the quality of life (in no. 7)

2.5.2 Instruments, principles and 'flexibility'

The three means have not changed and their many instruments have been altered only marginally. Under 'common market', a problematic feature has always been the free movement of persons. Article 3 EC always specified the four freedoms as including the free movement of persons, not 'workers' or 'labour' (see Figure 2.1). But the EC, as such, could never really ensure this freedom of movement because person controls at borders are not carried out for economic reasons alone but also for social and security reasons. With respect to the social aspect, the EC has never had a common immigration policy. With respect to the security (and police) aspects, such powers fall outside the EC treaty and, until Maastricht, even outside the purview of what is now called the European Union. In Maastricht, there was a hesitant recognition that it is inconsistent to pursue a 'completed' internal market without solving the problem of person controls. The period between Maastricht and Amsterdam has induced a learning process, the main conclusion being that the intergovernmental approaches to address person controls have proved unworkable. Both governments and public opinion are slowly shifting towards the acceptance of a common immigration and asylum policy. The key issue here is legitimacy. The upshot is a complicated set of articles in the EC treaty, linked to a protocol, a declaration (by the Member States) and an annex on integrating the Schengen *acquis* into the EU.[19] The crucial Article 61 has a five-year transition period for a programme of measures in the area of asylum, immigration, safeguards for third country nationals in the EU, and so on, and is subject to QMV. Typically when it comes to areas concerning legitimacy, the decision to go for QMV is itself subject to unanimity. Since Amsterdam, the EU is therefore on the way towards a common immigration policy.

Under 'common policies or activities' the Social Protocol has found its way into the treaty as Articles 136 to 145 EC. A new Title on Employment has been inserted (Articles 125 to 130), as a result of an addition to Article 3 on a coordinated strategy for employment. The guidelines produced under this strategy should be part of the 'broad guidelines' which will be formulated annually in the framework of EMU (Article 99 EC). Practically all the formal powers remain at the Member States level. The main underlying issue is, what an effective employment policy should comprise and how interventionist it should or should not be. It would seem that the strategy will not alter much in what the EU and its Member States could do before Amsterdam (see Chapter 15).

Under EMU, the actual start of 'euroland' prompted two provisions. For the countries that did not enter monetary union by 1 January 1999 (UK, Sweden, Denmark and Greece), an exchange rate mechanism (ERM-II) was devised which in essence extends the previous provision (see Chapter 18), though here with reference to the euro. It is voluntary, and should serve as a gateway to euroland. For the eleven Member States (since 2001 also including a twelfth – Greece) who joined euroland, the Stability and Growth Pact was agreed, but merely by a resolution of the European Council. The idea is to respect the medium-term budgetary objective of sticking close to balance or being in surplus, as a member of euroland, by strict commitment to declared self-discipline and unwavering adherence to common sanctions to curb 'excessive deficits'. As Chapter 18 will show, many EU Member

[19]These articles (Arts 61 to 69 EC) are the consequence of the 'area of freedom, security and justice' (see Art. 2 EU). Note that the UK and Ireland, and in a more limited way Denmark, 'enjoy' derogations, with 'opting-in' provisions. The Schengen Treaty goes back to 1985 and is about person controls. Initially only between Germany, Benelux and France, it now governs the lifting of person controls for (practically) all EU25 countries, and is (in 2005) more and more integrated in Union rules and decision making.

States were highly disciplined when the prize to be won was membership of euroland. Once inside euroland, many observers feared that this discipline would wane, and there would be little the EU could do about it. The Stability and Growth Pact is meant to support tough finance ministers when domestic politics create spending pressures, and in doing so, uphold the 'hardness' of the euro.

The 'key principles' did not change. A special protocol on subsidiarity and proportionality merely restates what had become official policy since Maastricht (see Chapter 3). Finally, under 'institutional framework', provisions for 'closer cooperation' or flexibility have been introduced. This applies mainly to foreign and security policy and to police cooperation. Behind these complex new provisions lays frustration caused by the fact that a single Member State can block the wishes of all others, or a 'core group', to deepen or widen integration. For the EC treaty itself, the conditionality (in Article 11 EC) is so strict that it is most unlikely it will ever to be used.[20] In the Nice Treaty of 2000, a range of new provisions has facilitated the use and widened the potential scope of 'enhanced cooperation'. Besides general principles (in Title VII of the EU treaty), which largely reproduce the tough conditionality of Amsterdam and specify that it be 'a last resort', there are provisions for its use under the EC treaty, for foreign and security policy, and for the 'area of freedom, security and justice'. However, its use for policies under the EC treaty is likely to remain exceptional.

2.6 Summary

An economic constitution is a framework of rules and principles for public economic functions, besides the fundamental economic rights (and duties) of economic agents. Applying this notion to integration makes sense once there is a considerable degree of positive integration, that is, joint public economic functions.

In an integration context the six basic characteristics of an economic constitution are: guiding principles, the identified stages of economic integration, economic aims, public economic functions (that is, scope at Union level), economic powers (means at Union level), institutions with their various functions.

Applying this analytical framework to the Rome Treaty shows that, in terms of aims, the EEC pursued economic growth under conditionality. The two general means are the common market and approximation of economic policies. Because of problems of sequencing and conditionalities of instruments, the economic ambition of the EEC treaty is not fully reflected in means and instruments. The common market, even after 25 years, amounted to a kind of 'customs union plus', without genuine free movement. Besides three explicit guiding principles (loyalty, non-discrimination as to nationality, widening of scope under strict limitations), a crucial implicit principle is 'rules, not money'.

The Single European Act added five important elements: more QMV on internal market matters, a clear definition of the internal market, mutual recognition as a regulatory principle, approximation of health and safety in the workplace, and economic and social cohesion. Note that the economic structure of the treaty remains intact.

The Maastricht Treaty is characterised by a revision of the economic aims, the addition of a third means (EMU), new principles, and a host of new 'activities', few of which actually have major new consequences. EMU is firmly grounded in a strict monetary constitution, based on price stability and centralisation of monetary policy. The Maastricht Treaty is explicit about the economic order: principles include 'an open market economy with free competition' and guidance for sound macroeconomic stabilisation policies (for both levels of government). Furthermore, the subsidiarity principle is defined for concurrent powers and the *acquis communautaire* is to be maintained.

The Amsterdam Treaty is, at best, incremental in terms of economic aims, means and instruments – or, for that matter, the institutional framework. The economic constitution was hardly altered. The economic aims were reshuffled and one (on equality of men and women) was added. The Social Protocol was incorporated, an employment strategy was included (with little noticeable value-added), and a complex transition towards a common immigration policy is made possible by bringing 'Schengen' (on person controls) into the main EC treaty. A strict regime for national budgetary policies in a Stability and Growth Pact is meant to strengthen fiscal credibility in euroland.

[20]Article 11 is under QMV. But a Member State, if opposed to QMV 'for important and stated reasons of national policy' may block the application of QMV.

CHAPTER 3

Subsidiarity and Union Economic Functions

Topics covered

3.1 Basic economics of multi-tier government
3.2 A subsidiarity test for the Union
3.3 Application of the subsidiarity test
3.4 Subsidiarity and EU efficiency
3.5 Subsidiarity and EU equity
3.6 Subsidiarity, macroeconomic stabilisation and fiscal powers
3.7 Summary

The positive analysis of the economic constitution of the Community provided in Chapter 2 forms an important basis for any economic study of European integration. The present chapter builds on this by asking the following normative question: Which public economic functions should be assigned to the EU level and which ones should remain at the Member States level? The economic analysis of multi-tier government may help us to identify criteria to justify, on economic grounds, the assignment of public economic functions to the highest (that is, EU) level of government. The functional application of these criteria is constrained, however, by the degree of political willingness to accept fully fledged liberalisation of markets (which reduces domestic autonomy) and to transfer public economic functions to the EU level. As noted in Chapter 1, a minimum commitment in these respects is required before the economic analysis of multi-tier government can be fruitfully applied.

It is therefore not surprising that, once the EC-1992 programme and the Single European Act had been agreed, the Commission asked for a study of the 'systemic' implications for the EC of completing the internal market. The resulting Padoa-Schioppa report (Padoa-Schioppa *et al.*, 1987) gave prominence for policy makers to the economic analysis of multi-tier government via the principle of subsidiarity. Section 3.1 below provides the basic economics of subsidiarity. A subsidiarity test is developed in section 3.2 and applied in a case study about environmental policy. For a more general application of subsidiarity to the EU's public economic functions, the conventional categories of efficiency (market functioning and allocation), equity (redistribution) and macroeconomic stabilisation are employed, hence the subsequent three sections dealing in turn with these public economic functions.

3.1 Basic economics of multi-tier government

3.1.1 Optimal (de)centralisation

The starting point of the economic theory of multi-tier government consists in asking the question whether centralisation of public economic functions is welfare improving. The answer is that all-out centralisation is bound to be suboptimal (see below why). In federal countries this leads to the problem of the optimal degree and forms of *de*centralisation. However, in the process of economic integration between countries which retain the sovereignty to transfer (or not) powers to a common level, it leads (*mutatis mutandis*) to the problem of the optimal degree and forms of centralisation. In purely analytical economic terms, and abstracting from politics, these two questions should functionally come to the same answer. However, the current state of economic integration and Union building in Europe – advanced though it is – is *politically* so radically different from a federation operating as a single country that such a purely theoretical approach adds more to confusion than to insight.

3.1.2 Great caution before applying 'economic federalism'

There are four political differences between European integration and a federal country. First, the political logic of ever more ambitious economic integration is very different indeed from the logic of (economic) decentralisation in a mature federation. Of course, in Europe this is well known.[1] Whereas a considerable degree of centralisation is an established fact in federations, be it with significant variance between federations, the political costs of even minor shifts to more economic or institutional centralisation weigh heavily in European integration. And, until today, every country has veto power on any treaty-based shift, a power which profoundly influences any proposals for centralisation in the first place.

Second, an advanced degree of completion of the internal market must itself be politically acceptable before the economics of subsidiarity can be usefully applied. The completion of the internal market can be justified economically by typical subsidiarity criteria (see section 3.3) but, in theory, that would often be correct at world level too. However, such deepening entails profound and manifold consequences for the domestic capacity to regulate markets, protect workers or consumers and maintain the welfare state, to mention only some aspects. These state activities usually result from intense political debate, based on local preferences. Once there is a minimum willingness to accept a high degree of liberalisation, with sufficiently strong mechanisms to formulate joint regulation where appropriate, the logic of economic integration begins to apply. In the event that the stages of economic integration become ever more ambitious, the subsidiarity question has to be posed ever more insistently.

The EU is still the only instance of regionalism where not simply internal free trade prevails but indeed *free movement,* credibly enforced moreover by a common guardian (the Commission) and a supreme court. This deep commitment to the internal market is ultimately a political prerequisite for the sensible application of subsidiarity. One can envisage a wide spectrum of options for commitments of Member States in economic regionalism, anywhere from very soft and selective to very 'hard'. The 'harder' or deeper the commitment, the costlier it is to continue to allow Members the option of secession (exit). At the far end of the spectrum the commitment can be perceived as federal. Elsewhere on the spectrum it all depends: even the EU, with more and 'harder' commitments than any other instance of economic regionalism, such as NAFTA, Mercosur, AFTA and so forth, the level and scope of commitments are far from federal indeed.

Third, the EU still lacks a number of properties that are taken for granted in a federal country. Since 1999 it has a single currency but there are still three 'outs' in the EU15 and thirteen in the EU25 since May 2004. The EU has no right to tax, no common army or defence, and more an uncommon than a common foreign policy. Even the customs, though operating on exactly the same rules and bound into a common information and management system everywhere, has remained national, despite the courageous abolition of internal frontiers.

Fourth, the EU has no central government.

3.1.3 Making the economic case for centralisation

Given these political constraints, we can now return to the question why all-out centralisation is bound to be suboptimal. Welfare improvement is always a matter of the (better) satisfaction of preferences. If a representative democracy is capable of revealing the preferences of the voters well, the satisfaction of voters' preferences will be the more likely the closer the government is to the voters. There are two reasons for this: on the one hand, proximity to voters will enable policy makers to

[1] Indeed, the 2002/03 Convention on the future of Europe was a unique occasion to verify the explicit choices and preferences of national parliamentarians about national and EU powers, otherwise very hard to measure properly. A routine inspection of the minutes of the Convention plenary and the eleven working groups reveals many examples of inhibitions about (further) transfers of powers to the EU level.

'read' the preferences better than more distant policy makers; and on the other hand, policy makers at the local or regional level will be able to respond to such revealed preferences without having regard to the preferences of other localities or regions, unlike a higher tier of government. In the ideal system, at least for the sake of preference satisfaction, there should be three means of enforcement or discipline: voice, replacement of policy makers and exit. *Voice* refers to the many ways that voters express views between elections as well as in the elections themselves: the probability of re-election drives policy makers. Policy makers who do not respond to revealed preferences can also be *replaced,* and locally this process can be geared to local issues. *Exit* refers to movement (by voters) to other localities or regions in response to a disregard of preferences. If exit is costly in financial or socio-cultural terms, local policy makers enjoy more discretion.

These elementary points underlie the priority that the subsidiarity principle gives to decentralisation. In the theory of multi-tier government the subsidiarity principle is simply an assignment rule for *optimal institutional design:* close correspondence of public policy with voters' preferences will often require the assignment of policy competences to local government. For all-out centralisation to be optimal, one would have to make extreme assumptions like congruent preference sets for all voters in all localities or regions and the full information at the central level about these preferences. Or, alternatively, full information at the central level about the differences in regional preferences and the unrestricted capacity at the central level to differentiate any policy or rule at every level so as to satisfy these preferences at very low costs. It is from the rejection of such pointless abstractions that the subsidiarity principle derives its bias towards decentralisation. It follows that the case for centralisation has to be made.

However, this is not the end but merely the beginning of the story. The implicit assumption in the reasoning so far is that localities or regions are not in any way interdependent. Moreover, there is no mention of cost: certain preferences may require public policies which are too costly to provide locally or even regionally but could be payable if provided by a group of localities or regions or even countries. The *interdependence* between regions in a modern economy is of course very strong. The nature of such interdependence will affect a rational assignment of powers. Cross-border externalities between regions or countries linked together by markets or otherwise can be negative or positive. Positive externalities imply that the local effectiveness of the measure taken in region A is reduced by the positive effects it has on the policy objectives of region B. Decentralisation can then generate a typical prisoner's dilemma in that a refusal of region B to cooperate or pay will make region A reticent to persevere with the measure, with the result that too little is done (hence, satisfaction of local preferences is reduced). At a higher level of government this externality can be internalised. Negative externalities are conflictual as they result from beggar-thy-neighbour policies: the effectiveness of a measure taken in region A is at the expense of welfare in region B. Examples include cross-border pollution or trade protection. Prohibitions or common rules at a higher level of government can internalise these problems.

Where policies are *costly,* especially if the minimum fixed costs are high before any provision is feasible, economies of scale may militate against decentralisation. CERN, the particles accelerator in nuclear physics near Geneva, is supported by many countries for reasons of scale. This example shows that scale, as an argument to move away from pure decentralisation, need not automatically imply centralisation; durable cooperation may do very well. The same goes for a consortium to build a fighter jet.

Therefore, the case for centralisation under subsidiarity hinges on scale and cross-border externalities arguments. Note that this assignment to a *higher* level on functional grounds is just as much 'subsidiarity' as the *a priori* presumption that preferences tend to be better satisfied by *local* government. Subsidiarity is a two-way principle. Its initial bias might be towards decentralisation, yet, once the case is properly made, centralisation can be compelling on the basis of exactly the same (assignment) principle.

Assigning public economic functions to higher tiers of government should only be done whenever, and to the extent that, one or more of the relevant criteria for policy efficiency and effectiveness are fulfilled. The subsidiarity test is about the appropriate application of the criteria for possible assignment of functions to the EU level. The criteria are listed in Table 3.1.

The economic approach to subsidiarity takes for granted a willingness to integrate ('centralise') public economic functions once one or more criteria are fulfilled. The criteria then point to 'welfare' gains from centralisation. It differs from the political approach, where the economic gains of centralisation are weighed against the political costs of centralisation itself. The economic approach provides the analytical basis for a rational application of subsidiarity, but, in practice, an ultimate political judgement remains decisive.

The reasoning behind Table 3.1 amounts to a search of the *benefits* of centralisation and runs as follows. First, establish whether a criterion is relevant (for

Table 3.1 Assignment criteria under subsidiarity

Criterion	Nature	Examples
1. Positive externalities	Reduces regional effectiveness	• An expenditure impulse by a very open economy, unilaterally (given exchange rates)
2. Negative externalities	Beggar-thy-neighbour policies, inimical to adjacent economies	• Water or air pollution • Trade protection
3. Economies of scale	High fixed costs of supply, or 'indivisibilities'	• Defence • Developing a jet fighter plane • Particles accelerator in nuclear physics

example, positive externalities across intra-EU borders). Second, verify what economic policy or regulation gives rise to this observation (see examples). Third, efficiency (the lowest cost for achieving the objective of policy or regulation) and/or effectiveness (actually accomplishing the objective) may then require a degree of cooperation, joint action or fully fledged centralisation. Not included in the table, and subsequent to the application of the criteria, is the consideration of the economic cost of this centralisation: these costs ought to be minimised. This will be discussed later.

By far the most powerful case for centralisation in economic integration is related to the internal market. By and large, it would refer to the criteria of negative externalities: any hindrance of intra-EU movement of goods, services or factors, or any country-specific distortions would in principle qualify. However, the resulting centralisation need not consist of positive integration: negative integration might suffice. The centralisation in case of negative integration would merely consist in the required common regulation prohibiting Member States (and economic agents) to pursue certain actions or measures – in other words, common regulation only for the purpose of intra-EU free movement. Since centralisation may well mean negative integration only, or many mixtures of negative and positive integration, the term 'centralisation' in a subsidiarity test is considered in a purely functional way. The reader is warned that, in the actual political debate in the EU, centralisation often refers to its most extreme variant: the *full transfer* of certain powers to the EU level, if not to the Commission and the EP only. Such a politicised perspective is dysfunctional and may lead to serious misunderstandings – it may cause flawed assignments and hence welfare costs. Other than prohibitions, centralisation also refers to many intermediate variants with different cost/benefit ratios.

The three criteria (negative and positive externalities across intra-EU borders; scale, beyond the national level) are by far the most important ones to consider. However, a number of other criteria may play a role in the EU: they may be subsumed under the three principal criteria (for benefits), or, they are specific criteria for reducing the economic costs of centralisation. Thus, one could favour centralisation on the basis of criteria such as:

- uniformity of Community law, including case law (a special case of scale);
- insurance against macroeconomic shocks which are country specific, by pooling part of unemployment payments among Member States (a special case of scale);
- differentiation of central policies according to national preferences or circumstances (reducing the 'costs' of centralisation, by responsiveness to differences in preferences).

Special mention is due to (common) bargaining power in, say, trade negotiations or negotiations about fishing rights. It amounts to a combination of (a threat of negative) externalities and scale, so it is not an independent criterion. Moreover, the presumption is that the gains in 'welfare' may well be at the expense of others. Finally, one cannot *a priori* exclude the possibility that political homogeneity increases over time in the EU, although one should not push this idea too far. An example is 'solidarity', having been introduced into the aims of the Maastricht Treaty. The Union is still very far removed from the degree of homogeneity similar to that expressed in the idea of 'nationhood'. Thus, there is a big gap between avowed and actual solidarity. The higher actual solidarity, the stronger the argument for transfers via the centre.

The criteria of Table 3.1 suggest ways to rationalise why the assignment of a particular regulatory or policy or tax competence should move beyond the regional/country level. They do not, in and by themselves, suffice to justify centralisation. Since subsidiarity stresses the inherent costs of centralisation, the optimal approach is to maximise the benefits by moving beyond the regional/country level (once a criterion is fulfilled), while seeking degrees and forms of centralisation which minimise its costs. Thus, it may well be possible – as indeed has happened in some of the examples in Table 3.1 – to establish voluntary (ad hoc) cooperation or coordination with a sufficient degree of binding and sufficient additional gains for all to satisfy subsidiarity. Such a solution pre-empts full centralisation. The nuclear particles accelerator CERN in Geneva is a form of ad hoc cooperation beyond the EU. Fighter jets are sometimes produced by ad hoc consortia. Some aspects of pollution may only be fought at world level, inevitably with a moderate degree of binding.

In other words, the criteria in Table 3.1 do not necessarily lead to the conclusions:

1 that a grouping such as the EU is assigned to tackle the problem; the relevant grouping may be smaller (for example, the Rhine Convention) or bigger (for instance, the International Atomic Energy Agency, checking nuclear safety); so, the *level of centralisation* may be variable;
2 that centralisation with strict binding is superior (less costly) than cooperation or coordination or innovative ways to blend centralisation with differentiation; so, the *degree of stringency of centralisation* may also be variable.

3.2 A subsidiarity test for the Union

The analytical framework discussed above can be elaborated and applied to every public economic function in European integration.[2] In the present chapter and in the remainder of this book references to it abound. In principle, it is possible to arrive at a comprehensive assessment of the 'economic constitution' of the Union and its shortcomings or inconsistencies. However, such a normative economic analysis should not be mixed up with the more limited meaning of subsidiarity in the Maastricht Treaty. As noted in section 3.3, an unrestricted application of subsidiarity to the *acquis communautaire* might be inconsistent with the equally prominent stability requirement in the Maastricht Treaty that the *acquis* cannot be affected. No less important, any finding that 'integration deficits' at the EU level would have to be filled with additional competences, would bypass the constitutional process of decision making.[3] As this would undermine the political legitimacy of integration it would be pointless.

For these reasons the Amsterdam Treaty restricts the application of subsidiarity to public economic functions where competences are *concurrent* at (that is, shared between) the Member States and the EU levels. Article 5 EC prescribes:

> In areas which do not fall within its exclusive competence, the Community shall take action, in accordance with the principle of subsidiarity, only if and in so far as the objectives of the proposed actions cannot be sufficiently achieved by the Member States and can therefore, by reason of the scale or effects of the proposed action, be better achieved by the Community. Any action by the Community shall not go beyond what is necessary to achieve the objectives of the Treaty.

Therefore, any action taken by the Community must fulfil two conditions. First, in areas of shared competence, the Community must demonstrate a *need to act in common,* as given by the existence of either economies of scale or cross-border externalities. If either of these conditions hold, non-cooperative policy making would be less efficient, or even detrimental, compared with cooperative policy making. This is broadly in line with the basic economics of subsidiarity. Second, any action must be *proportional* to the desired objective. Again, this is a logical corollary to the primacy of lower-tier government, where possible and efficient: no more than that which is necessary to attain the objective should be done at the 'central' level. Thus, when deciding whether to enact binding or non-binding measures, the EU level must justify the need for non-discrimination and legal certainty (both being indivisible in nature) before considering uniformity in measures. Even then, the EU should demonstrate the costs of differentiation before opting for a high degree of uniformity. The degree of binding could also increase, commensurate with the degree of complexity. If these justifications fail, EU regulations or directives would be disproportionate and only coordination, recommendations or consultation should be pursued. When binding measures (that is, legislation) are needed, framework directives should first be considered as they leave greater discretion to national and regional governments; if they would be inappropriate, directives may still be preferable to EC regulations which are directly binding for all economic agents in the market. Where

[2]See the (anonymous) exercise for applying the criteria to some 75 economic functions – in a slightly different way – in a background study to the MacDougall report (MacDougall *et al.*, 1977), Vol. II. See also CEPR (1993).

[3]It would require an intergovernmental conference, followed by ratification by the Member States (Art. 48 EU).

possible and efficient, Member States should play the primary role in policy implementation.[4]

One important criterion to decide upon the degree of centralisation, once the need-to-act-in-common test is passed, is *credibility*. If all Member States were to cooperate voluntarily on a given policy issue, there would seem to be no need for centralisation. As game theory teaches, simple and repetitive cooperative games lead to 'learning' and may eventually result in efficient bargaining. But non-repetitive cooperation is often difficult to agree upon, for instance when the number of interested parties is large, the range of policy alternatives is wide, the problem is complex, and the relative gains and losses of players are unevenly distributed. What really matters for economic agents in the market, however, is whether cooperation is credible, hence sustainable. Credibility of cooperation is low if information is highly imperfect or asymmetrically distributed, especially in complex policy areas, because this renders it impossible to monitor compliance. Credibility is also low when the incentives to cheat are strong and the ability or willingness to impose collective sanctions is perceived as minimal. If cooperation cannot come about, or it would not be credible, there is a case for centralisation.

The *subsidiarity test* can then derive assignments to the Union level as follows, in five steps:

1 Identify whether a measure falls within the area of shared competences (if exclusive to the EC, the treaty test does not apply).
2 Apply the criteria (scale and externalities, Article 5 EC, and possibly other criteria) – this is the 'need to act in common' test.
3 Verify whether credible cooperation is feasible.
4 If steps 1 and 2 are confirmed, and step 3 denied, then the assignment is to the Union level.
5 Define to what extent (proportionality) implementation, monitoring and enforcement should also be assigned to the EC level, or, indeed, can be assigned to the Member States, perhaps in a common framework.

The test would become fully general – that is, not bound by the treaty's text – if the first step is ignored and all possible criteria are considered in the second step. Note also that step 3 may lead to cooperation at levels lower than the Union level, at continental or world level.

Case Study 3.1 Considers the issue of subsidiarity with respect to environmental policy.

CASE STUDY 3.1 Subsidiarity and environment

The question when applying subsidiarity to the environment is whether the Union level should be assigned powers to pursue environmental policy. To argue for exclusive rather than shared powers (step 1) would surely be inappropriate knowing that EU countries have different national endowments with different environmental absorption capacities, as well as different preferences. Since at least some environmental problems are local, regional or national in nature, these differences can best be taken into account at those levels of governments.[5] But it is also well known that many negative cross-border externalities are to be found in the area of environment. This fulfils one criterion in step 2 of the subsidiarity test.

When setting objectives, three levels of externalities should be distinguished: bi- or trilateral, Community-wide and worldwide. Cooperation (step 3) might be possible in bi/trilateral frameworks but will become ever more difficult as the number of countries increases. Moreover, cooperation might even fail in the bilateral case because the full costs of the 'polluter pays' principle may be resisted. This would satisfy step 4. However, it does not follow that all bilateral problems should be addressed at Union level: cooperation may, and does, succeed (perhaps also because it would otherwise be tackled at EU level). For Community-wide issues, 'internalisation' of the externalities is best done at

[4]This interpretation is close to that actually proposed by the European Commission. See SEC (29) 1990, *The Principle of Subsidiarity*, 27 October 1992. A concise instruction to the various EU institutions, broadly reflecting those considerations, is found in the Protocol on the Application of the Principle of Subsidiarity and Proportionality attached to the Amsterdam Treaty.

[5]The treaty criteria (need to act in common) do not apply. However, some people argue that the Union's citizenship (established by the Maastricht Treaty) could be seen as consisting, *inter alia*, of a set of citizen rights including minimum ambient quality (in turn including minimum public health). If so, the political homogeneity criterion would be satisfied. For the moment the point is a rather speculative one.

CASE STUDY 3.1 ***continued***

EU level. For global issues, a common EU policy stance both reduces the number of countries for worldwide cooperation and might (but need not) provide leadership to arrive at agreement. For the Union countries, unity would also increase negotiating power.

At the level of instruments the problems get much more complicated. To begin with, an objective such as a minimum ambient quality at intra-EU borders may be easier to apply to rivers than to air pollution. This is partly because some sources of air pollution are extremely mobile (cars, sprays containing CFCs, for example). It is probably less difficult to come to a consensus about precise instruments which are easy to monitor than it is to set objectives for Member States, in the presence of mobile, polluting sources. Hence, the EU often uses product standards. Once product standards are chosen for mobile goods, the single market will severely limit the national ability to employ this instrument effectively. Thus, in the single market, either the 'national' product standard will be undermined as imports complying with other standards come in anyway, or steps 3 and/or 4 of the test will apply. Because cooperation is voluntary (hence, every country has a veto), it will not easily succeed since adjustment costs and competitiveness create incentives for avoiding regulation. If step 4 were to imply approximation of technical regulations (Article 95 EC) it would be subject to qualified majority voting, an incentive for more efficient bargaining. Such common mandatory (product) rules will combine the protection of the environment (internalising externalities) and internal free trade. Steps 4 and 5 suggest, however, that Member States are free to impose higher national standards, as long as they do not interfere with free movement. What this means is that the perceived local benefit of additional environmental protection will incur costs which primarily fall on local economic agents.

However, in a more elaborate application of subsidiarity to environmental policy instruments, the nature and efficiency impact of various instruments need to be considered. Thus, ambient quality and diffusion objectives might be achieved more efficiently (that is, with lower welfare costs), with fiscal and economic instruments rather than with regulatory ones (except when risks are intolerably high, such as hazardous waste). Again, such national subsidies, taxes, tradable pollution permits and tax credits may distort competition in the single market and will therefore be limited, conditioned or outlawed in a Community framework. Special 'eco-taxes' impose costs on local sales but cannot prevent users and consumers from switching to untaxed imports from other Member States.[6] This would argue for common minimum eco-taxes, but the difference between steps 3 and 4 is not great, as taxation directives are subject to unanimity.[7] In the special case of a proposed eco-tax on fuels and some other energy products, the externalities affecting competitiveness go beyond the EU, so that step 4 (an EC minimum tax) might well be made dependent on prior cooperation with key OECD countries (step 4, but in a wider context).

Some instruments apply to stationary sources (for example, power plants). Although the free movement of goods is not at issue here, national regulatory discretion may still be circumscribed by effects on competitiveness: differences in national environmental requirements may lead to different prices for energy inputs, which will especially affect the competitiveness of energy-intensive companies (for example, chemicals, aluminium, paper).

Finally, any application of subsidiarity must carefully reflect on step 5. The usual breakdown of public functions here is into problem diagnosis; policy formulation and (if applicable) legislation; implementation, monitoring and control; and enforcement. Diagnosis should be at EU level in all cases where a *prima facie* expectation for spillovers or scale exists; otherwise, the principle of subsidiarity cannot be meaningfully applied. Policy formulation should be at EU level when step 4 of the test is

[6]As long as the destination principle applies. Once the origin principle has been introduced in the EU (see section 5.4.3), it will also negatively affect the export position of producers in the origin country, if the tax is not VAT (VAT is paid back to producers).

[7]There is a difference in credibility, since EC directives cannot easily be undone.

CASE STUDY 3.1 *continued*

reached. However, in the past, the EU has pursued policies which do not pass steps 2 or 3 (for example, the 'cleaning of the Mediterranean sea'). Perhaps the EU should only be a partner in a step-3-type regional cooperation, as currently is the case for the Rhine agreement. Implementation is traditionally assigned to the Member States, except for certain worldwide or continental negotiations. Monitoring and control should be supervised by the EU level (precisely so as to obtain the credibility that cooperation may lack), but can be executed by national agencies. This is also true for enforcement where ultimate resort to (for example) the EC Court should be possible.

3.3 Application of the subsidiarity test

Subsidiarity is often misunderstood and even more frequently referred to in an inappropriate manner. It is crucial for readers to stick to the functional logic of subsidiarity, short of falling back to pure political statements. Thus, a good understanding of the application of the test is indispensable.

The test is a *functional* one and can only be operational if goals and instruments, and indeed the legal basis for the assignment of powers to a higher level, are not themselves controversial. In some areas of today's EU (for example, foreign and security policy) this condition is not fulfilled, and in some other cases the legal issue of whether powers are shared or not cannot always be ascertained.[8] However, these points ought not to be exaggerated, short of going counter to the very essence of subsidiarity itself. As soon as the subsidiarity test *itself* is politicised it becomes worthless and pointless. With political disagreement about goals or too great political sensitivities about central powers, the 'better achievement' of certain policies is logically excluded, hence becomes irrelevant. In such cases, the refusal to consider centralisation is a pure political act – which might be legitimate, of course – but not a 'test'. The test is useful only if it is first accepted that it is a functional one which informs political decision makers about costs and benefits as well as the implications of further (de)centralisation.

The test should also *not* be confused with the ultimate political decision to (de)centralise. Whereas the *test* is functional, the *decision* ought to be political, precisely because of the sensitivity at the level of local/regional preferences, which are often only sufficiently revealed once clarity is provided about the repercussions. Such political decisions have to be made by *elected* agents who are politically *accountable.* Only in such a way can subsidiarity decisions acquire political legitimacy.

The test can be based on Article 5 EC and the Protocol. From an economic point of view the Protocol seems to have little added-value to Article 5 EC. Three guidelines in item 5 of the Protocol are not independent from each other. Indeed, the 'transnational aspects', 'conflicts with the requirements of the treaty' and significant 'damage' to other Member States' interests are all manifestations of cross-border externalities. They will also, more often than not, overlap. In detailed methodologies or subsequent 'manuals', all possibilities must be covered which might render it necessary to verify whether the subtle differences between these three guidelines of item 5 of the Protocol matter in specific instances.[9] The first four steps (subsidiarity) have the purpose of tracing the *benefits* of centralisation and the fifth step (proportionality) should seek for options to minimise the *costs* of such centralisation.

It is perhaps instructive to provide some selective points on the application of the test. First, sometimes it is suggested that the uniformity of Community/Union

[8] The new Constitution (not yet ratified) contains lists of exclusive and shared powers (for the first time) in Arts I-13 and I-14. This helps transparency but does not solve specific issues in all cases.

[9] The same goes for the simplified version of the Protocol attached to the Constitution (not yet ratified). Article 5 of this new protocol combines what are currently items 5 and 9 of the Amsterdam version of the Protocol, in a shorter text. Other than a reference to the implications for Member States in the case of a European framework law (a new legal instrument in the Constitution), the requirements are essentially the same. Moreover, the guidelines in the Amsterdam Protocol remain *acquis* in the event that further precision is needed.

law can serve as a reason to justify centralisation. One can view this uniformity as a public good once the case for it is made in a concrete instance. But it is not always necessary to uphold uniformity; one might needlessly suppress the satisfaction of local preferences when clinging to this notion. Hence, the principles of proportionality and differentiation have to be taken into account. Second, the EU25 is rich in its diversity of preferences. Nevertheless, selective issues might be supported by far-reaching homogeneity because of common elements in European culture or destiny or as a result of a long period of European integration which might prompt intergenerational convergence of preferences. Such degrees of homogeneity are hard to measure and the Euro-barometer is not suitable. Still, recent empirical work on apparent preferences (Calmfors *et al.,* 2003, pp. 85–8; CEPR, 2003, pp. 25–6) shows remarkable similarities between the European peoples on key domains such as internal security and foreign policy[10] which are not reflected in the state of European integration. In the new Constitution (not yet ratified), some new but prudent activities (by subgroups of the EU) in cooperative (not 'common') defence are included, as well as more effective decision-making rules for intra-EU security and common controls of persons at the outer frontiers of the Union. At the level of objectives, such moves are widely supported by voters, as shown in polls. When it comes to details, however, the homogeneity of preferences often breaks down in Europe. Clearly, true homogeneity of preferences would have the effect of strongly reducing the costs of centralisation.

3.4 Subsidiarity and EU efficiency

3.4.1 Assigning powers and policies to the EU level

The efficiency function of the EU refers first of all to the establishment and proper functioning of the internal market. The *establishment* of the internal market, in turn, consists of the fullest possible realisation of free movement and free establishment (called 'liberalisation' of cross-border activities). Where the treaty or, say, unanimity in EU decision making precludes or blocks such liberalisation, the internal market cannot be 'completed'. Since, by definition, cross-border externalities are at stake with (potential) cross-border flows of goods, services or factors of production, we must assume that these inhibitions are based on political refusals or decisions. Given such preferences, all a subsidiarity test can do is to reveal the cost/benefit picture but such a functional approach is not likely to address the motives or perceptions behind deep-seated political preferences. Changing such preferences will take time or perhaps will never take place.

The *proper functioning* of the internal market results from a complicated interplay between three aspects: liberalisation, regulation and competition. As noted in previous chapters, mere negative integration (that pure cross-border liberalisation) will often leave market failures unattended. At the EU level, no less than at Member States level, market failures ought to be overcome in a least-cost but credible manner. For problems of market power or other distortions of competition (for example, state aid), this is done by the common competition policy. For market failures such as externalities or asymmetries of information, this is done by various forms of regulation (see Chapter 4). A special source of (internal) market failure that does not normally have a counterpart in national markets, is the coexistence of disparate national regulation. Such regulatory disparities can have economic effects analogous to border obstacles, frustrating market access or making access more costly than for domestic economic agents, and may thereby distort competition, too. Such disparities will have to be addressed by an effective and least-cost combination of liberalisation (prohibiting or constraining such national regulation, partly or entirely) and common regulation, if necessary. Articles 94 and 95 EC have been designed to address such questions for the 'proper functioning' of the internal market via regulation, in the form of 'approximation' of the national laws. A peculiar class of problems is thrown up in network markets (what used to be public utilities such as postal services, telecoms, gas, electricity, etc.) where national 'exclusive rights' used to be granted to domestic monopolies until the 1990s. In other words, they were carved out of the internal market. For network markets, liberalisation first requires the prohibition of such national exclusive rights. Subsequently, the proper functioning of the internal market of network industries results from appropriate combinations of regulation and competition policy.

Also, fiscal obstacles are likely to hinder the proper functioning of the internal market. For goods and services, indirect taxes (including excise duties) can differ

[10] However, it should be noted that the questions posed were highly general and, of course, the answers were, for every individual, non-committing. This greatly reduces the reliability of such polls.

between Member States as to the tax system, the tax base and the rates. Together, they can lead to crippling disparities which would have to be solved by border-tax adjustments – a time-consuming and costly approach. Such negative externalities clearly show a 'need to act in common'. The next question is whether cooperative arrangements on (say, standardised) border-tax adjustments would be credible and sufficient to remove 'fiscal frontiers'. Given the ambitious concept of the internal market (see Chapter 2), the answer to that question is no. Hence, step 4, an EU system of indirect taxation, is justified. Thus, the EU has legislated a common system (VAT; also excise duties have been harmonised), largely a common tax base (describing which goods and services are taxed) and, for VAT, a minimum rate of 15 per cent for most goods and services. All this has been accomplished despite unanimity. For (free movement of) financial capital and corporate activities (linked to the right of establishment), tax competition can prompt financial capital and legal and fiscal incorporation to shift between Member States. If this were to take extreme forms, one might speak of harmful tax competition, hence, a 'need to act in common'. For purely financial flows, the speed of response to sufficient tax differentials can be so fast and drastic that either a 'race to the bottom' or harmonisation will be the outcome. The EU has, after many years of deadlock, opted for a simple, minimum withholding tax.[11] In corporate taxation, speed of response cannot be very high and the annually mobile tax base cannot be so large because (daughter) companies cannot be shifted so easily across borders. Moreover, there are many determinants of direct investments and the fiscal burden is only one of them. Nevertheless, once corporate tax disparities in the base or the rates (or both) are large enough, this is bound to have an impact over time on new and replacement investment. It could still induce a (slow) 'race to the bottom'. The 'need to act in common' was finally recognised in earnest in the EU in 1997 when a code of conduct against harmful tax competition was adopted (a blend of steps 3 and 4 in the test). The debate on a common tax base and perhaps minimum rates (step 4 of test) is ongoing.

These central questions of the internal market require careful analysis in specialised chapters. Subsidiarity tests are part and parcel of such analyses. Thus, at a rather general level, the economics of EU regulation in the internal market is addressed in Chapter 4. Liberalisation is of course a prerequisite for any EU market integration, but how to do this and how far to go are matters with links to subsidiarity. This is discussed in many chapters of the book but especially in Chapters 5, 7, 9 and 20. Network industries are analysed in Chapter 8. The common competition policy is explained in Chapter 12. Taxation issues are found in Chapters 5, 9 and 10.

The efficiency function of the EU also refers to several other elements including the design of certain common policies such as agriculture and trade, as well as the question whether the EU should provide any 'public goods', a core function of any state. In agriculture (Chapter 11), a subsidiarity test yields different results in terms of (de)centralisation, dependent on the design of the policy, in turn (as will become clear) determined by a powerful political economy. In trade policy (Chapter 13), the imperative of centralisation is too obvious to be controversial. However, a subsidiarity perspective is still interesting with respect to the scope of trade policy, given globalisation and the widening range of activities of the WTO.

Whether the EU should provide 'public goods' is not only, and not primarily, a functional question. Public goods are at the heart of what even the least interventionist countries assign the state to do. Therefore, political legitimacy, sentiments about nationhood and 'belonging' and deep-rooted political perceptions tend to have the upperhand. This does not render the functional subsidiarity test less useful but it would be naive to expect it to play more than a modest role in the background. Public goods such as national (that is, external) and domestic security, and a legal system providing and enforcing basic market rules for every economic agent in the jurisdiction, are typically produced by governments rather than the 'market'. Such 'goods' are characterised by non-appropriability (of adequate revenues) and non-excludability (in consumption) so that they cannot be profitable. In fact, property rights are not well defined and, by the nature of these goods, cannot be enforced *vis-à-vis* individual consumers. As a consequence, in private markets they would either be undersupplied or their supply would break down, or appropriability would be restored by somehow imposing exclusivity, and in so doing sacrificing their public nature. Taxation can overcome non-appropriability, while non-excludability is usually declared a citizen's right as a counterpart. Therefore, it is a paramount political question of legitimacy and authority to supply public goods and be granted the right to levy taxes. Nowadays, the EU hardly provides public goods and, partly as a consequence of this, has no right to tax.

[11]Or a duty to engage in detailed mutual information on the database of taxable foreigners or foreign companies.

ADDITIONAL READING

One could stretch the 'allocation function' much further. One could discuss domains such as justice and home affairs (JHA), common foreign and security policy (CFSP) and defence. These sensitive domains have a much less compelling link with the internal market. JHA emerges (mainly) from the abolition of internal frontiers and testifies how many different meanings are given to the notion of (the free movement of) persons. It also testifies how far one is forced to move in a cooperative, if not centralising, direction for a zone of internal security to be effective. As a (Union) public good, however, a half-baked approach is glaringly inconsistent and will incessantly be exploited by asylum seekers, economic immigrants and criminals. As a consequence, citizens will not find the weak, cooperative solutions credible (remember the wording of step 3 of the test) and this will continue to exert pressures for more efficient and effective solutions. These have to be assessed in detail but inevitably will cause a significant increase in the now trivial JHA Union budget, and prompt, in part, more centralising solutions. A manifestation of this trend is the shift to the Community method for JHA in the Constitution (not yet ratified).

CFSP is typically treated by economists as a Union public good *par excellence.* Analytically, this may be correct but the question is whether this analytical observation brings us any further. The argument for a credible CFSP does not hinge on the discipline of cross-border mobilities in the internal market, one of the two standard criteria for the subsidiarity test. Instead, it is based on convictions that the Union as a Community of 'values' should provide itself with the means to defend and promote these values internally and externally. At this level of abstraction, the argument can be extended to common defence functions of the Union. A related point consists of the discrepancy between the economic might of the Union and its political frailty. Only a properly organised and to some extent centralised CFSP could re-equilibrate this imbalance. This reasoning has only a remote link with the internal market and is primarily concerned with the political willingness to produce and enjoy the public good in common. The cardinal issues here are political preferences and their translation into the public policies and positioning in the CFSP as well as the effective political accountability towards the citizens. At a general level of Euro-barometer (polling) questions, European citizens are indeed massively in favour of a more European approach in foreign and security policy, and, to a lesser extent and with a sharper differentiation between countries, in defence as well. However, preference revelation in specific issues such as the strands of foreign policy or the military and budgetary aspects of a common defence are highly sensitive, even inside the nation states of the Union. So is the permanent process of political accountability in these areas. It is for these important reasons that the simplistic and far too general public goods approach which has been advocated in recent economic papers and reports (for example, Tabellini, 2002; CEPR, 2003) does not add much value. Where the link with the internal market is direct (for example, the scale and externalities arguments are more compelling in joint R&D in military technology, standardisation between NATO and the EU joint Rapid Reaction Force, and joint procurement), a subsidiarity test might be helpful to overcome vested interests.

Applying subsidiarity tests to the efficiency function of the Union has dynamic aspects too. As half a century of European integration has made crystal clear, the EU is a highly dynamic construct. Indeed, in Community law, the legal function of subsidiarity is precisely to govern the *exercise* of shared competences.[12] Thus, even when the treaty, or the new Constitution (not yet ratified), is taken as given, (functionally) testing for subsidiarity remains useful to reveal to policy makers the costs and benefits of further (de)centralisation in cases where blockages or sensitivities are known to exist. Of course, such applications trod on sensitive territory and the logic of subsidiarity may well be resisted. There are two categories of sensitive cases. First, a range of policy issues where subsidiarity is misused or rejected for reasons of political sentiment or influential vested interests, even

[12]Once a competence is conferred to the Union level, Art. I-11 of the new Constitution (not yet ratified) says that the 'use of Union competences is governed by the principles of subsidiarity and proportionality'.

though this is likely to result in lower economic welfare for the Union. Second, some policy domains, which are widely – and correctly – regarded as national competences, might exhibit fuzzy boundaries between what the EU should (not) do and what national governments should (not) do.

3.4.2 Between sensitivities and functional logic

In the first group where subsidiarity is misused to justify the status quo, one finds the prominent example of national labour market regulation and related social policies. The details of this issue are discussed in Chapter15, but a few pointers can readily be understood. The basic socio-political stance of many Member States and most of the labour unions is that social policies and labour market regulation should, on the whole, be nationally dealt with, except for migrant labour under the free movement of workers (Article 39 EC). It is asserted that this is in accordance with subsidiarity since preferences about social regimes differ between Member States and cross-border issues hardly arise because labour migrants crossing intra-EU borders are very few. Note that the issue at stake is not so much whether labour markets and social policies should be (more) 'centralised' – there are good arguments not to do this now and possibly for a very long time still, if ever. Rather, the question is the *improper application* of subsidiarity. Owing to a steadfast refusal to allow labour from other EU countries to influence domestic rules and the welfare state, both the Treaty of Rome and subsequent legislation have been designed such that cross-border labour flows inside the Union can only amount to a trickle. This political preference has long been taken for granted. The 'free movement' of workers under Article 39 EC is severely restricted by what is called the 'host country control principle', which (as Chapter 15 sets out in greater detail) has the interesting effect of formally maintaining free movement while taking away critical economic incentives for migrants. Moreover, unlike for other 'free movements', there has been no interest whatsoever to engage in a programme of approximation to overcome numerous difficult legal, social and fiscal obstacles to cross-border intra-EU migration until a Commission proposal as late as 2001. In order words, cross-border migration in the Union was designed to be 'residual'. Remember that the application of subsidiarity is pointless if there is no acceptance of the mobilities across borders. This is precisely the case here. It is logically flawed to turn the reasoning on its head and conclude from the tiny number of migrants (a residual, caused by restrictions) that subsidiarity suggests that competences remain national.

Other interesting instances can be mentioned where subsidiarity is (improperly) considered to be a 'one-way' principle. It is heralded as a good principle if it supports a case for keeping competences national but rejected if the same test results in a case for greater centralisation. Examples of a one-way approach long included corporate tax issues (but, as noted recently, some beginning of a recognition of the merits of modest centralisation seems to emerge – see Chapter 10), and infrastructure (in so far as it refers to missing links in an EU-wide mobility perspective or plain cross-border questions). Infrastructure is less straightforward. Countries like Canada and the USA promoted common infrastructure as an integrative device during the early years of their countries' modern history. The EU has never done this. The interdependence inside western Europe was so great in the 1950s and 1960s that some degree of cooperation in road and rail infrastructure was accomplished (a kind of step 3, but beyond the EU – mainly in the UN Economic Commission for Europe). However, this cooperation was slow, inefficient and often ineffective in the sense that 'missing links' remained when looking at networks from the pan-European rather than a local perspective. Trans-European Networks (TENs) were introduced in the Maastricht Treaty, and the EC acquired a weak coordination competence for them. Financial means are minimal. For infrastructure one can, therefore, argue that the EU's almost complete decentralisation of infrastructure is suboptimal: step 2 (need to act in common) is accepted only half-heartedly and step 3 (on TENs) is not credible. How much and how to centralise (steps 4 and 5) are difficult questions, not least because they involve major expenditures. One can surmise the reason for these hesitant positions. The need to act in common arises not from negative but from positive externalities. The benefits of considerable expenditures on 'missing links' (given pressures to spend on many other domestic categories, too) would only partly be enjoyed by domestic constituencies and a good deal by users from other Member States. The TEN approach is a kind of step 3 in terms of planning of missing links, but without the certainty of the finance, hence the lack of credibility. A shift to step 4 would require a significant fund in the EU budget for infrastructure, and this goes against the lack of political will to substitute national by EU infrastructural spending as far as missing links are concerned (even if this does not lead to higher taxes, overall). Current solutions include complex compromises on national infrastructural charges for users from other Member States (for example, road haulage in Germany) and loans from the European Investment Bank. After the enlargement towards the east of Europe, the pressures to increase at least marginally the centralisation of TENs have increased as is clear from the Constitution (not yet ratified). Moreover, in poor regions the EU can and does support infrastructure with a view to connect those regions to major European routes or networks.

The second category of sensitive cases concerns policy domains with undisputed national powers. The question is, rather, *where the boundary of that national competence* should be drawn. Subsidiarity tests can serve the purpose of consistently helping to find functional demarcations between what Member States should do and where the Union should or may come in, and possibly how.

Examples of policy domains with undisputed national powers typically include public health and education. Let us illustrate the application with the case of public health. In public health, there are numerous aspects of the internal market that apply in goods markets (for example, medicines and food laws), services (health services offered to patients from outside the provider's normal catchment area) and factor markets (for example, recognition of diplomas). Nevertheless, public health in a narrow sense, that is, the organisation and financing of health care and social protection systems is undoubtedly a national competence. The treaty only allows 'complementary' activities at EU level and this explicitly without harmonisation (Article 152 EC). Free movement and competition policy have never been explicitly restricted, however, with a view to national public health. As a result, the EC Court has initiated case law reducing the 'immunity' of national health systems from the internal market.[13] Moreover, during the 1990s cross-border health threats caused by contagion in instances like SARS, BSE ('mad cow disease') and the fear of humans getting infected, HIV and bird flu required extremely tight EU-wide coordination for which the EU needs to be better equipped ('need to act in common'), recognised by the new Constitution (not yet ratified) in Article III-278). Careful analysis under a subsidiarity test would be capable of generating more clarity about new functional demarcations between the EU and the national public health in the light of these new developments, without giving up the essence of national public health policies.

Finally, what about more *de*centralisation in the EU? It is good to note first that most of the so-called spending ministries are, and have always remained, at the national level: public health, social housing, infrastructure, education, defence, social policy, and justice and policing. These national policies easily cover three-quarters or more of the national budgets. Very few of these expenditures have any counterpart in the (small) EU budget. The overwhelming majority of issues and aspects covered by these domestic activities neither induces cross-border effects nor are they of a scale that the Member States cannot handle alone. Thus, the status quo that many key policies are at the Member State level is justified by subsidiarity considerations.

Beyond that, could a subsidiarity test not clarify that national powers ought to be strengthened or reinstated. In principle, yes. Since the Union has gradually been built up over only a few decades, there are not many candidates for this possibility. One is the CAP, now that agricultural policy at EU level is under quasi-permanent reform (see Chapter 11). Since the instruments of the CAP have recently become far less intrusive and more market based, and since farmers' income is nowadays targeted via direct transfers (so-called direct income payments, under some restrictions), the subsidiarity case for some measure of decentralisation and, indeed, differentiation of payments in accordance with national standards of living is becoming stronger. An added advantage would be that inter-Member-State transfers for the CAP would reduce to a trickle, which would take the sting out of many EU budget disputes (see Chapter 19). Another possible candidate is the class of measures under the Cohesion and Structural Funds. The case for decentralising the funding for relatively poor regions in relatively rich EU countries is no doubt very strong indeed (see Chapter 16). A third example can be found in certain specialised aspects of the common competition policy, namely about Article 81 EC, with respect to inter-firm agreements, where the Union has recently decentralised the policy and enforcement to the national competition authorities. However, in this instance the actual change is minor because the law and policy have remained the same, only the execution is decentralised, with explicit cooperation between those authorities and a residual but crucial role for the Commission.

[13]For those interested, a survey of this case law can be found in Commission Staff Paper SEC (2003) 900 of 28 July 2003, *Report on the Application of Internal Market rules to Health Services (a report addressed to the Member States).*

3.5 Subsidiarity and EU equity

The economics of (fiscal) federalism has generated a body of theory showing that the pursuit of equity, in the presence of high actual or potential mobility of taxable persons or firms between states in a union, has to be largely addressed at the union level. Only at the union level can the negative externalities be internalised (no race to the bottom) (see Oates, 1999).

Social charges and taxation of earnings might differ between Member States and, if one assumes costless mobility of persons and companies, it is possible to envisage a scenario where such disparities in fiscal burdens would lead the richer persons and the profitable firms to move to low-tax/low-social-charges states. In other words, under such extreme assumptions the tax base of a country would itself become mobile and a country could not pursue independent equity objectives. At this level of pure theory, there are two solutions: either one assumes perfect and stable interstate coordination in equity – but the temptation for states to deviate would be very strong – or equity and the way of financing it would have to be centralised, including an agreed formula for distributing the revenue among the states.

Of course, in reality, cross-border mobility is far from costless in pecuniary and human terms, even in the longer run, and therefore this scenario is far-fetched. But a weak version of it, over long periods of time, might have some validity for the more mobile elements of the tax base (not to speak of purely financial capital). As noted, workers in Europe are severely hindered with respect to moving across borders, but it has to be recognised that they are not even very mobile inside countries (at least, given the social protection they enjoy). But companies are more mobile. Multinationals, especially, can be highly flexible at the margin (the extra direct investment) and have to be rational in terms of costs in the long run (relocation, despite sunk costs). In so far as equity is supported by company taxation, Member States are therefore already constrained. However, for personal income taxation, the tax base is in essence immobile and the rules of the welfare states are such – including the links with the labour markets – that it remains carefully protected. Equity in Europe is thus a relatively effective policy at the decentralised level. The Union has no equity assignments and this seems to be correct from a subsidiarity point of view. Nonetheless, there is one major caveat: it does mean that one first accepts the fragmentation of the internal market for labour. Once the fragmentation erodes – that is, the more cross-border labour movement is facilitated and the more that migrants respond to such incentives – some moderate pressures (or disciplines) will eventually arise and prompt the coordination of equity or even the build-up of a two-tier, quasi-federal system.

The question may arise whether it is correct to state that the Union does not have any equity objectives and instruments at all. One is tempted to respond that 'cohesion' represents an equity aim. This is doubtful, however. At the very least it is a mixed efficiency/equity game (see below). Furthermore, the CAP has explicit redistributional goals, protecting farmers' incomes, but this is accomplished via inefficient interventions in the internal market under very strong political pressures. This violates the notion of a 'functional' approach to subsidiarity, adopted here, and the instruments used are 'disproportional' to the objectives (see Chapter 11). Finally, one could situate the permanent debate about a more Social Europe under this heading. Looking through the subsidiarity glass to this excessively vague debate, one cannot but get the impression that a game of (warm) words is played without much of an operational meaning. Social Europe is continuously reaffirmed in dialogues, charters, resolutions, objectives and declarations or, to some extent even in the Lisbon process,[14] without much interest or willingness to add the means to the avowed aims. This is consistent with the state of the art as analysed before. Indeed, how can Social Europe move beyond a general communality of aims if the free movement of workers cannot even be resolved and mutual recognition not even applied?

Economic and social cohesion might perhaps seem to be an exception to the lack of broad EU equity concerns, but a closer look does not affirm that. Social cohesion, an ill-defined term anyway, is usually contrasted with social exclusion, and this is weakly addressed in the 'open method of coordination' (OMC), a soft form of step 3. It does not imply any Union competence. Economic cohesion is routinely defined as the reduction of disparities of real income per capita between regions or countries of the EU over time. It is pursued in three ways: via the convergent impact of the growth effects of the internal market, via the removal of anti-cohesion aspects of EU policies (notably, the CAP) and via budgetary transfers under strict conditionality. Only the latter look like an equity policy, although a weak one because it relies on

[14]The Lisbon process, begun in 2000, aims to make the EU the most competitive knowledge economy in the world by 2010. It is briefly discussed in Chapters 14 and 18.

the weakest federalist instrument, namely, specific-purpose grants.[15] However, the link with 'solidarity' in the ordinary sense of equity motivations is in doubt here. In fact, the aim of cohesion transfers (via the various funds) is 'catch-up growth', which is to say that the solidarity is *temporary*. The real aim is higher *efficiency* combined with infrastructure capacity building, yielding such a high growth rate of less prosperous regions or countries that cohesion policy can eventually be phased out. National equity policies are *for ever*, not temporary, and the handicapped, the old, the sick and the very poor are not expected to disappear.

3.6 Subsidiarity, macroeconomic stabilisation and fiscal powers

Macroeconomic stabilisation assumes a greater importance, the higher is the stage of economic integration and the greater the economic openness towards the integration partners. With the completion of the internal market, the economic significance of stabilisation increased. Disruptive policy has higher costs in a single market, as has been shown in the EMS crisis of 1992–93 (see Chapter 18), which strengthens the need to act in common (step 2). The question, then, is whether cooperation (step 3) is credible and lasting. Given the enormous pressures that can rapidly build up within financial markets, once macro policies or exchange rates cease to be credible, cooperation would have to be so strict and detailed – and accompanied by guarantees, intervention credits, and so on – that it would be far more effective to shift to step 4: centralisation. If properly organised (see Chapter 18), centralisation is likely to be more effective, indeed, but it is *not* indispensable. True, exchange rate stability and predictability are essential prerequisites for the proper functioning of the internal market. However, with deep forward markets in currencies, some degree of exchange rate flexibility need not be a problem for the internal market. And, as we shall see in Chapter 18, flexible (though not gyrating) exchange rates have advantages too. Nevertheless, over a larger timespan and between many Member States, sufficient exchange rate predictability remains a tall order. Recent EU history provides many examples of sudden disruptions. In other words, with free movement of financial services and financial capital, such stability and predictability are hard to accomplish without significantly limiting the macroeconomic policy autonomy of Member States. In macroeconomic stabilisation, therefore, the difference between step 3 and step 4 is more political than economic, at least as long as one strictly adheres to the objectives of stability and predictability.

For a long time, macroeconomic *in*stability at the Member State level was indeed the Achilles heel of the internal market. The EEC treaty was designed with a series of crippling conditionalities, from the conditional liberalisation of financial services, via the even more conditional liberalisation of (financial) capital[16] littered with safeguards, to the infamous Articles 108 and 109 EEC, the safeguards to protect a currency with disruptive means in the event of macroeconomic instability. Very weak instances of step 3, macroeconomic cooperation, were envisaged in the Rome Treaty but, with escape routes and no sanctions, it was grossly insufficient. Nowadays this is history and, interestingly enough, also for the non-eurozone countries. The current division of powers in EMU is monetary centralisation, with one currency, and fiscal decentralisation; plus the complication that 13 of the 25 Member States are not currently members of 'euroland'.[17] Whether this combination can be economically justified, and indeed is a stable solution in the long term, will be discussed in Chapter 18. However, already at this stage, it is appropriate to briefly discuss two crucial aspects in terms of subsidiarity: the autonomy of domestic fiscal policy, and the size and nature of the EU budget.

EMU has centralised monetary policy and decentralised budgetary policy. However, a too literal reading of this statement is probably inconsistent with a subsidiarity perspective and would be dysfunctional. The statement is correct in that EMU, unlike many other monetary unions, has no central budget of any significance (see below). But how decentralised is *national* budgetary policy? The fiscal side is somewhat constrained by prevailing tax harmonisation, mainly of indirect taxes, and the code of conduct on corporate taxation (see Chapter 9). The treaty prohibits excessive deficits and pre-empts any 'bail-out' in case of extreme debt. The Stability and Growth Pact of 1997 further tightens the discipline by prescribing a balanced national budget over the medium run and can apply a staggered financial sanctions regime following a lack of compliance. Future claims on the national budget, in particular pensions, are

[15]See Walsh (1993) for a classification and analysis of federal transfers.

[16]In fact, Art. 67 EEC spoke of 'endeavour'.

[17]In 2005, Denmark, Estonia and Lithuania were in the so-called ERM-II (exchange rates) mechanism, one step before entering the eurozone (see Chapter 18 for details).

nowadays subject to 'open coordination'. The conclusion is that, for the so-called monetary/fiscal policy mix not to become adverse, the EU constraints on decentralised fiscal policy are considerable.

The main reasons for this limitation of national fiscal autonomy are cross-border spillovers and the protection of the euro as a collective good of the participants. The fiscal spillovers may result from free-riding in the eurozone. In a eurozone of many countries, a relatively small excess of the deficit of country A will not amount to an alarming signal for financial markets yet, given the agreed discipline of all others. But this would mean that *all* finance ministers – especially in a recession – might be tempted to allow some overstepping of the deficit rules. In turn, this might eventually induce a higher interest rate in the eurozone for all participants, including the ones that have stuck to a budgetary discipline, in other words, a negative cross-border externality. The other reason is found in the importance of relatively low debt/GNP ratios. High or rapidly rising debt ratios could impair the intra-eurozone trust in a hard euro, which is a collective good. It could also prompt a depreciation of the euro externally. The first consequence is of greater economic importance since more than 85 per cent of the economic intercourse of eurozone countries takes place within the eurozone. In broad terms, therefore, some limitation of national fiscal powers in a monetary union with a hard currency is consistent with subsidiarity.

Despite its absolute size the Union budget is not a macroeconomic policy budget in any serious sense of the word. It is not at all comparable in relative size to the budget of the Member States (2.3 per cent of the aggregate of the national budgets of the EU), its main components are more or less fixed (CAP and cohesion take nearly 85 per cent), it cannot run deficits by law and is not funded by European taxes or by flexible forms of automatic revenue. Moreover, one could argue that, in the long run, the EU budget in its present configuration will 'dry up'. The CAP is gradually moving away from price support to income support, itself subject to a mildly digressive trend until 2013. Indeed, in scenarios up to 2013 inclusive, the share of the CAP in the EU budget is likely to reduce from the current 45 per cent to around 38 per cent. Further reforms might well cut it down even more. In the case of cohesion the story is similar. In 25 years from today it seems reasonable to expect that catch-up growth will have produced convergence, at least among today's Member States, to such a degree that the budgetary outlays for it will begin to shrink. In other words, the long-run perspective of the EU budget is one of further reduction to trivial size, if current policy preferences of Member States are continued.

Even more than today, the upshot would be a monetary union with only trivial central expenditure and this would be unique. For the moment, however, it is imperative to question the Byzantine way in which the Union collects revenue for current expenditures. It is probable that the revenue side artificially suppresses a rational use of joint financing of Union policies, because EU revenues are systematically regarded in terms of net paying positions between Member States. This can only be removed by reducing redistributive policies (CAP and cohesion) on the one hand, and by reforming the instruments of revenue collection on the other. Nonetheless, it would be delusory, even if such reforms were to be successful, to believe that this could soon lead to a central budget with macroeconomic significance. Indeed, a more rational revenue side of the EU budget is unlikely to be acceptable to Member States, unless the expenditure ceilings remain under veto. The Constitution (not yet ratified) has indeed not changed the heavy (in fact, constitutional) procedures for EU 'own resources' decisions. In Chapter 19, a deeper economic analysis of the EU budget as it is and should be, based on a subsidiarity test, will be provided.

3.7 Summary

A crucial element of economic integration analysis is a framework to answer the question, which public economic functions should be assigned to the EU level and which ones should remain at the Member States level? The economics of subsidiarity suggests an optimal approach, maximising the benefits of 'centralisation' – only when certain criteria are fulfilled, however – and minimising the costs by varying the degrees and forms of assignment to the EU level.

Assignment to the EU level will bring benefits if one of three criteria is fulfilled: positive externalities (across intra-EU borders), negative externalities, economies of scale.

Applying subsidiarity to the public economic functions in the EU does not yield results similar to those seen in federations. There are four differences by comparison with federations: the political costs of centralisation weigh heavily in integration processes; the internal

Summary *continued*

market may remain 'incomplete' for constitutional reasons (especially for labour); and the EU lacks both typical federal properties (such as the right to tax) and a federal government. Therefore, a subsidiarity test for the Union is developed, inspired by (but somewhat distinct from) the theory of 'economic federalism'.

The subsidiarity test for the Union goes through five steps: (1) identify whether a measure falls in the area of shared competences; (2) apply the treaty criteria (scale, externalities) – the 'need to act in common' test; (3) verify whether credible cooperation is feasible; (4) if steps 1 and 2 are confirmed and step 3 denied, go for EU assignment; (5) develop ways to minimise the costs of centralisation. The test is illustrated in a case study on environmental regulation.

A wider application of the test helps to understand the (proper) assignment to the EU level of the 'efficiency' or market functioning role of government, by far the most important public economic function of the Union. Given a (high) minimum political commitment to establish the internal market – that is, legally accepting the free mobility of goods, services and factors of production – the proper functioning of the resulting internal market hinges on a complicated interplay of liberalisation, regulation and competition. Although the EU has legally gone quite far in committing to the internal market, there are some political inhibitions, most notably for labour. The interplay of regulation and competition policy requires careful analysis of when and how to regulate in what cases, and, *mutatis mutandis,* for (harmonisation of or competition between) national taxes. Subsidiarity tests are part and parcel of such analyses. This is equally valid for common policies such as agriculture, competition and trade. However, it is crucial to appreciate that 'subsidiarity' is often wrongly (or plainly politically rather than functionally) applied: examples are provided in policy areas such as labour and infrastructure. A subtle application of the subsidiarity test is useful in case national powers are uncontroversial but the 'boundaries' of such powers (*vis-à-vis* what the EU could do better) are fuzzy: an example is found in public health. Lastly, the test can also identify partial or complete reassignments away from the EU level, if the criteria were to bring this out: illustrations might be found in the CAP and, to some extent, in the Structural Funds.

A similar application to the 'equity' function of the Union shows striking differences with federations: unlike the latter, the EU has hardly any equity functions, given (throttled) cross-border migration inside the Union, and given strong resistance against any EU tax power (including social charges), as an expression of firm political preferences. The only minor exception is 'cohesion', and even cohesion turns out to be partly efficiency driven.

Applying the subsidiarity test to macroeconomic stabilisation and fiscal powers, the case for centralisation of monetary policy and decentralised fiscal policies is inspected. A single currency can be underpinned in terms of subsidiarity but such centralisation is not indispensable. Fiscal policies, though decentralised, are not fully autonomous, and that is justified. Finally, the tiny EU budget does not go against subsidiarity, not even in the monetary union. The greater part of the budgets of most of the 'spending ministries' is, justifiably, provided at the Member States level.

CHAPTER 4

The Economics of EU Regulation

For the internal market to get established in the first place there will be numerous instances where Member States expect cross-border liberalisation to be accompanied by some form of regulation. In such cases, the mere *establishment* of the internal market is dependent on agreement in Council about the nature, method and degree of detail of regulation. This may be because Member States already have regulation in place and, for this reason alone, will often tend to expect similar rules at the EU level via 'approximation' under Article 95 EC. One important function of the economic study of European integration is to offer an analytical framework to verify rigorously the justification of such regulation in terms of economic welfare. This chapter provides such an analytical framework. How crucial it is to carefully justify European regulation can be readily understood. Given the imperative of free movement and establishment in the treaty, the 'core business' of the Union is about regulation, not money. As noted in Chapter 3, the EU has only a (relatively) tiny budget and few policy domains are dealt with by means of expenditures, mainly agriculture and cohesion and, to a minor extent, research and technology.

Now that decision making is no longer under unanimity but based on QMV,[1] the establishment of the internal market will only rarely depend on costly compromises to buy off blocking minorities or to pre-empt vetoes. The design of European regulation in the internal market can therefore be governed by a functional approach for which economic analysis has much to offer. The functional approach makes it possible to shift the attention to what matters in the EU context: from the establishment to the *proper functioning* of the internal market because only the latter generates the economic benefits serving the overall goals of the Union.

The economic analysis of EU regulation is always based on three questions: why regulate, at what level of government (EU or Member State or perhaps even a region or *Land*), and how? Together, the answers should result in a maximisation of the benefits and a minimisation of the costs of

[1]With the exceptions of taxation, intellectual property rights and some provisions about social security and related matters. Note that, although unanimity can cause blockages or costly or inconsistent regulation, this is far from always the case. Many internal market regulatory decisions have in fact been adopted under unanimity and many of them have proved to be useful.

EU rules. Section 4.1 asks the 'why' question and sets out the market failures that can justify regulation. A sketch of the EU regulatory *acquis* in the internal market is offered in section 4.2, based upon a classification of market failures. The 'what level' and 'how' questions are addressed in section 4.3, culminating in what can be called the EU regulatory strategy for the internal market.

The methodology of designing 'good European regulation' requires much greater analytical depth than this overall framework. Since regulation under three common policies is dealt with separately (in Chapters 11, 12 and 13), it is broadly correct to focus on 'risk regulation' as the most important and widespread form of EU regulation in the internal market. Section 4.4 gives the basic economics of risk regulation in the EU context, with an illustrative application to EU environmental policy. The final section discusses how to optimise European regulation (at least, in the internal market) given the political economy of over- and under-regulation and the presence of cost-minimising incentives at the Union level.

4.1 Why should the EU regulate?

4.1.1 The public interest approach to regulation

There are economic and non-economic justifications of regulation of market variables or behaviour. Non-economic justifications may include security-of-supply considerations (energy; agriculture) and equity objectives (fair distribution of income).[2] Here, our concern will be with the proper *economic* justification which traditionally consists of overcoming *market failures*. Where no market failures are identified, market processes are superior to regulation as an allocative and cost-minimising device. Even though the benefits consist in overcoming market failures, it is still critical to keep the costs of regulation to a minimum. If the costs of regulation outweigh the benefits, 'regulatory failure' would take the place of market failures and welfare would fall. Clearly, this must be avoided.

Economic theory distinguishes four types of market failure:

- market power;
- externalities;
- internalities;
- public goods.

Such market failures can be tackled with various instruments including, besides regulation, subsidies, public procurement or state ownership. The EU level provides few subsidies (outside agriculture and fisheries), and what is provided is mainly for research and technology far removed from applications in markets. The EU institutions have practically no means for gearing their extremely limited public procurement to problems of market failure, even if they might wish to consider it in the first place. State ownership at EU level does not exist and is almost certainly not considered as an option in the near future. This leaves regulation as the sole option.

The so-called *public interest approach* to regulation is based on the assumption of a benevolent government, solely interested in the best way to pursue economic welfare. In the EU context this would mean that one assumes that the Commission will propose a well-designed draft regulation in the best European public interest and that Member States in Council as well as the parliamentarians in the EP will consider it in the same functional manner before adopting it as law. The public interest approach fits ideally with the economic perspective on regulation, based on the overcoming of market failures. The present chapter reflects the (European) public interest approach. This does not mean, of course, that one can be naive about the day-to-day reality of making regulation in the EU circuit of decision makers and decision shapers. Regulation and proposals are influenced by lobbying of private parties, by specific interests of some Member States, by political preferences (which may diverge in various ways from market failures) and by aspects such as the legal basis in the treaty or the institutional problems of the Union. As an independent academic analyst, one's function is to provide a proper analysis in the European public interest, not least to support the Commission in its crucial role as designer of proposed regulation, as well as to underpin the work of opinion leaders in the European debate. It is up to decision makers to ensure

[2] The efficiency of such regulation remains an economic issue. Thus, as Chapter 11 will show, assuring European farmers a 'fair' income is better accomplished by non-market transfers than by regulating market variables.

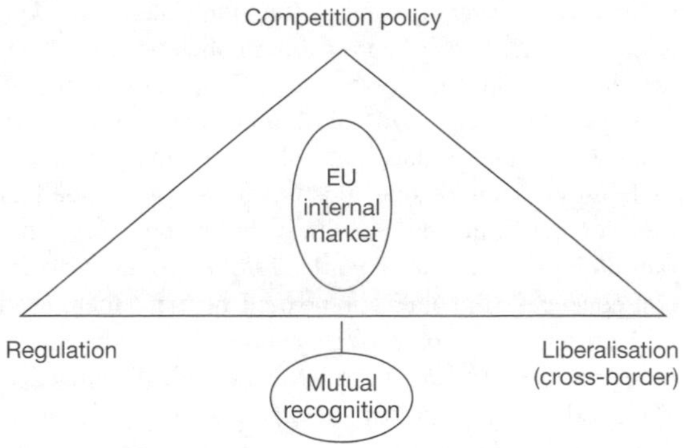

Figure 4.1 Internal market triangle

that the EU approximates as closely as possible the ideal approach.[3]

4.1.2 The internal market triangle

Building the internal market and having it function properly is always a question of seeking the appropriate place in the 'internal market triangle'. The prerequisite for the establishment of the internal market is cross-border *liberalisation* in the Union. The proper functioning, if market failures are identified, hinges on good *regulation* and *competition policy.* Figure 4.1 depicts the internal market triangle.

Liberalisation consists of introducing free movement of goods, of services and of factors of production such as financial or other capital, labour and technology (as intellectual property rights or codified know-how). In addition, it is concerned with the right of establishment for companies or entrepreneurs. The free movement can be automatically derived from the treaty or may require EU regulation in the form of prohibitions for Member States to throw up border or domestic obstacles to cross-border flows. If a Member State cannot invoke the possible derogations in the treaty for goods (for example, Article 30 EC) or services (for example, Article 56 EC) or selected other ones, free movement and establishment simply apply. But if Member States do, with justification, impose obstacles then liberalisation has to be combined with some form of regulation. In factor markets it is a little more complicated. Whereas capital flows enjoy complete free movement (albeit that disparities in the operation of stock exchanges still cause high frontier costs), this is not at all the case for labour migration across intra-EU borders even though the label 'free movement' is employed in Article 39 EC. Also, intellectual property rights were initially only nationally defined which precluded free movement of technology and knowledge in the absence of an adequate provision in the treaty.

It is in all these cases that the regulation angle of Figure 4.1 becomes relevant. The term regulation in the Union context can lead to confusion and the reader ought to be aware of the following. In the internal market (by far the largest area for legislation) EU regulation is more precisely described as 'approximation' of the laws of the Member States in the form of a directive. Thus, in free movement aspects, national regulation is not replaced by an EC 'regulation' (with direct effect upon all EU citizens and companies, and not requiring transposition into national law) as a legal instrument; approximation, usually based on Article 95 EC, is less 'centralist', so to say. In contrast, in common policies the legal instrument of an EC 'regulation' is the routine. For the economic issues at stake (market failures, and securing free movement or market access), the less centralist method is appealing, but in practice the cost/benefit picture turns out to be more complicated owing to the habits of Member States to add other elements to national laws transposing EC directives ('gold plating'). The generic term 'regulation' in this book covers any regulatory influence on markets. Where relevant, the legal EC instrument of a 'regulation' will always be carefully specified so as to avoid any confusion.[4]

[3]The public interest approach to regulation in economics contrasts with the so-called positive theory of regulation. This body of analysis is interested in explaining existing regulation one can actually observe, and not the regulation one prescribes based on a normative economic theory of market failures. The positive theory tries to find consistent theoretical and empirical explanations of why regulation deviates from what the public interest would lead one to expect. The 'government' is decomposed into a set of different actors, all with behavioural functions mixing public or institutional constraints with private objectives (such as more power, a larger operational budget or the probability of being re-elected). Other actors such as regulatory agencies and actual or potential regulators are included too. This is then combined with theories of collective action and lobbying or other insights from 'public choice' in order to arrive at testable propositions about actual regulation and its departure from the public interest, despite the veil of stated public interest motives. This strand of literature is based on Stigler (1971), Peltzman (1976) and many others. In the present book the focus is on the public interest approach – that is, how the EU 'should' regulate – but a fuller appreciation of what it takes to get 'good' regulation does require taking adequate notice of the positive approach as well, in addition to a basic understanding of the political economy of (EU) regulation in general.

[4]In the new Constitution (not yet ratified) the current term 'regulation' as a legal instrument will be renamed as 'European law' and a directive as 'European framework law'. However, the executive and implementation powers of the Commission will be enhanced considerably and this has been done with the help of a new instrument, called 'European regulations' (Art. I-33), which by definition (see Art. I-36) are delegated specifically in laws by Council and the EP.

Whether European regulation in the internal market is justified hinges on an analysis of the relevant market failures, namely, externalities or internalities.

An ingenious intermediate form between liberalisation and regulation in Figure 4.1 is 'mutual recognition'. The idea is charmingly simple: suppose one finds that the regulatory objectives of the Member States are 'equivalent', why would 'approximation' still be necessary? If equivalent, there would seem to be no differences in addressing market failures and hence, free movement should apply without any further act. This simple idea has the potential of being a forceful driver of EU market integration for two reasons. First, once the regulatory objectives are equivalent, the technical details in which national laws on goods or services differ in numerous ways do not matter for free movement any more (a conclusion radically at odds with the traditional notion that national laws must be enforced on each and every specification). But if this corollary is accepted, it must mean that tiresome and difficult 'approximation' on countless details of such national laws is superfluous in every case where objectives are equivalent. Thus, there is liberalisation as well as regulation but explicitly *no European* regulation. Hence, the position for 'mutual recognition' is in the middle of the bottom line of the triangle. Second, as it turns out, there are numerous instances of national regulation, usually concerned with relatively modest risks, where EU Member States do pursue the same objectives but where the specifics in the rules differ for historical or other non-essential reasons. The implication is that mutual recognition should have a significant impact on liberalisation, without delays or other hurdles of designing EU regulation. Mutual recognition is considered in greater depth in section 4.3.3 below.

Even when regulation has correctly addressed market failures such as internalities and externalities, the resulting internal market might fail to function properly because of market power or other distortions of competition. EU competition policy deals with such distortions. The scope of EU competition policy, applicable to goods and services markets in a wide sense, can be explained with the analogy of the hand. Three fingers are about 'anti-trust', fighting the anti-competitive conduct of firms. This includes inter-firm agreements (including cartels), monopoly (or, in EU parlance, abuse of dominant position) and merger control. The fourth finger on the hand refers to a special category of markets populated by 'network industries', often better known as public utilities (see Chapter 8), where competition policy has to work hand-in-glove with regulators in a more direct manner in order to realise the proper functioning of markets. The thumb represents EU control of state aids distorting the competition in the internal market. Unlike in other parts of competition policy where companies are the addressees (here, for the Commission), in state aids the interface is with the Member States. Only very gradually has the EU succeeded in overcoming its leniency in the supervision of state aids for the simple reason that the Member States did not always allow consistent and rational approaches to prevail. More often than not, the consequences of liberalisation would, here and there, lead to the rescue or structural state support of certain sectors or regions or, in the worst case, even individual companies. With today's state aid in the EU drastically declined, market functioning must have improved (*ceteris paribus*).

The present chapter focusing on regulation does not mean that one can ignore the other angles of Figure 4.1. For a good appreciation of market integration the entire picture should be borne in mind.

4.1.3 Market failures in goods and services

In principle, market failures apply equally to goods and services. The four types of market failure will be defined and explained first, followed by a few specific annotations relevant for services. The following merely sketches the highlights of the state of the art in economic regulation theory.[5]

Market power may, but need not, depend on the observation of an apparently high concentration of firms and/or a low elasticity of demand. If there is contestability (a credible threat of potential competition), such market characteristics yield no power. Once barriers to entry keep such potential competition at bay, incumbents may enjoy market power. A barrier to entry into a market is a cost of production for a new entrant that is not incurred by incumbent firms. *Sunk costs* (non-recoverable, market-specific costs) are the only private entry barrier which may justify regulation of some kind. Neither scale nor product differentiation do, in and by themselves. If scale costs can be recuperated upon exit (for example, in second-hand markets), entry is not costly. Once these costs are sunk, entry becomes risky and a barrier exists. Similarly with product differentiation: if incumbents try to prevent entry by what is called 'brand proliferation', this tactic would act as a barrier if, and only if, the establishment of new brands by the entrant implies sunk production and marketing costs. However, sunk costs create risks of exposure as well: excessive entry could be destabilising and entail welfare costs. Long-term contracts are a typical private response to this. The risk-sharing involved may

[5]Authoritative sources in the literature include Spulber (1989) and Laffont & Tirole (1993). A good blend of economics and law is found in Ogus (1994). See also Baldwin & Cave (1999).

permit an increase in irreversible capital. However, there are many problems with such contracts (for example, enforcement in the presence of contingencies; negotiation strategies; market power *vis-à-vis* consumers), such that regulation may be justified. For utilities, with 'natural monopolies' and extremely high sunk costs, regulation may at the same time protect both a firm's right to serve (allowing investment in capital and networks with a long lifespan) and the consumer's right to be served. In cases of less extreme sunk costs, those costs may lead to collusion or monopolistic behaviour which can be mitigated or prevented by competition policy.

Externalities are costs or benefits transmitted between agents, in the absence of any related economic transaction between those agents. By definition, therefore, there is a 'missing market' and the negative or positive benefit remains uncompensated. Examples of negative externalities include pollution, the harm a pedestrian may incur in an accident with a car, or the discomfort of congestion. The concept can be extended to depletable resources such as common fishing grounds and mineral resources. Positive externalities include a bee-keeper benefiting from an adjacent orchard or so-called 'agglomeration effects' (local/regional clusters of complementary and competitive skills and services leading to extremely fine specialisation, with higher value-added or growth or innovation as a positive externality for all, hence tending to attract still more of the most productive factors to the agglomeration). Silicon Valley and the City of London are examples of localities benefiting from agglomeration effects.

It is often said that creating the 'missing market' by defining the property rights completely and exhaustively, 'internalises' the problem and will remove the market failure. However, defining property rights accordingly in the case of the environment is a formidable and costly enterprise, as Spulber (1989) calls it, and might still require regulation. Moreover, 'internalisation' is not a perfect recipe either, as the third type of market failure (see below) will show. Hence, in the case of externalities, regulation is often employed to impose internalisation by equating private and social costs. Doing this properly is very difficult and will invariably introduce some regulatory costs. In the environment, regulation may rely on economic instruments (such as subsidies, penalties, tax credit or tradable pollution permits) or by prohibition and mandatory technical requirements – the 'command and control' approach. Products with health and safety risks may also cause negative externalities (for example, contamination and accidents) for other persons or to society as a whole (for example, in the case of state health insurance).

Internalities refer to costs and benefits of a transaction that the parties to the transaction have not accounted for in the terms of exchange.[6] Unlike the market failures of market power (imperfect competition) or externalities (a missing market), internalities often exist in competitive markets. Harm to a consumer due to product failure, not foreseen or covered in the contract terms, is a negative internality. A breach of contract, with the consequences not reflected in the contract, is another. An example of a positive internality is on-the-job-training of an employee which does not follow from the labour contract. As will become clear in this book, regulation addressing internalities is important to the EU internal market of goods and services.

Internalities are due to special transaction costs or incomplete information. More precisely, sources of internalities are:

- the costs of writing contingent contracts in the presence of risks (the most important case is that of long-term contracts for utilities and so on mentioned above);
- when behaviour is imperfectly observable, the costs of observation and monitoring may be high;
- when parties possess private information, there may be high costs of information gathering and disclosure.

This book deals mainly with EU regulation based on the latter two sources of internalities. Imperfectly observable behaviour gives rise to *moral hazard,* an incentive problem for the design of market contracts. Thus, there may be imperfect incentives for employers to prevent accidents once they have insured their workers, or consumers may use products carelessly once they enjoy warranties from the supplier. Liability reduces but does not eliminate moral hazard. Regulatory alternatives (for example, product standards, workplace safety standards, inspection) may assist in establishing more correct observances, but they entail costs and inefficiencies too.

Private information gives rise to strategic behaviour in markets owing to the asymmetry between the parties in this respect. If parties do not reveal information, the presence of asymmetric information implies that markets may fail even if transactions are made – however, they might also not be made at all. A major problem is *adverse selection.* Insurance markets may fail or even fail to exist if individuals cannot be induced (for example, via *ex post* penalties) to reveal all information for the proper assessment of risk. Clearly, individuals with the greatest health risk have the least incentive to provide

[6]See Spulber (1989, p. 54) for a similar definition.

such information, whereas healthy individuals – though perhaps willing to provide the information – have lower incentives to buy insurance. The market would thus lead the insurance companies to suffer from adverse selection of policy holders, causing unsustainable losses.

In many product markets, adverse selection is a potential problem for which private and regulatory remedies have emerged. The used-car market may turn into a 'market for lemons' ('lemons' being bad cars) because of adverse selection, but guarantees by reputable dealers and reliable private testing and certification (say, based on public safety regulation) can overcome this problem. In the absence of safety regulation, asymmetric information in the labour market may cause workplace safety to be lower than workers expect, whereas, in product markets, buyers may get products which are less safe than they expect. In professional services, buyers generally have no way of assessing the provider's service until after the service is consumed – and frequently not even then. In such cases, minimum entry conditions (for example, diplomas) and publicly acknowledged self-regulation may overcome the market failure. In banking and insurance there is, moreover, the impossibility of knowing for sure whether the institutions holding customers' deposits, securities or premiums are financially sound, which justifies strict and permanent prudential control.

Public goods such as national (that is, external) and domestic security, and a legal system providing and enforcing basic market rules for every economic agent in the jurisdiction are typically produced by governments. They are characterised by non-appropriability (of adequate revenues) and non-excludability (of consumption) – once again, a matter of ill-defined property rights – so that they cannot be profitable. As a consequence, in private markets they would be undersupplied, or their supply would break down, or appropriability would be restored by imposing exclusivity, thereby sacrificing their public nature. Taxation can overcome non-appropriability, while non-excludability is usually declared a citizen's right as a counterpart. Therefore, it is a major political question of legitimacy and authority to supply public goods and be granted the right to levy taxes.

If goods have weak appropriability and weak excludability, collective action in a limited group of producers may internalise the market failure to such an extent that 'free-riding', or avoidance of controls, no longer undermines supply. An example of such an 'impure' public good is a voluntary technical standard which improves the technical efficiency of all suppliers, and thereby the functioning of the market.[7] Another example concerns knowledge, which has strong public good characteristics. Basic research is typically subsidised by government. The more applied, hence specific, the knowledge is, the higher the probability that it can be patented for appropriability and/or that it can be embodied in products which have excludability. However, R&D consortia between firms may, at times, internalise the market failure too.

It is worthwhile digressing on market failures for *services*. The nature of most services differs from that of goods and this has consequences for the manifestation of market failures. Few services are 'search goods' for which the buyer can evaluate quality before consumption. Services are usually 'experience goods' (evaluation of quality is possible only after consumption) or 'credence goods'(quality cannot be evaluated even after consumption). Regulation can be economically justified by three market failures: internalities such as asymmetric information (for example, about quality); market power or imperfect competition; and externalities. All three play an important role in services, although sectoral specificities always need to be taken into account.

The most general market failure in services is *internalities*. This is caused by the fact that services, unlike goods, are non-storable or intangible. This intangible nature makes it even more difficult to assess quality than with products, indeed, it is usually impossible to do so prior to consumption. Services being 'experience goods' rather than 'search goods', services markets should be expected to suffer from asymmetries of information. Usually, this means that the seller knows more *a priori* about service quality than the buyer, although quality may sometimes depend on interaction between buyers and sellers (for example, education, consultancy) and occasionally buyers may cause information problems for sellers (for example, insurance). In the case of moral hazard, suppliers can make higher profits by reducing the quality of the service to below the perceived or expected quality. The problem is acute for non-repeat purchases in the absence of any controlling knowledge (for example, a taxi ride for a tourist). The market solution for moral hazard is to signal commitment to quality

[7] A simple example is the market for beds. By agreeing to limit the number of standard bed sizes to very few, economies of scale can be achieved for the mass market of beds and mattresses, while also enabling the 'unbundling' of the bed–mattress combination, which enhances competition. Since the standard is voluntary, non-standard beds are still produced but at a premium; likewise for the compatible mattress.

by means of investing in reputation, brand names and easy access to complaint procedures. However, since these solutions are not watertight (especially not for high risks such as some insurance or medical services) and, in any case, are based on repeat purchases and comparability,[8] some regulation may be justified.

Adverse selection, caused by asymmetric information, is more evenly a problem of both buyers and sellers. Sometimes sellers may not have (or ask) enough information about buyers to enable them to distinguish them according to risk (hence, pricing, including risk premiums, is problematic). In other cases, buyers may be confronted with a number of service suppliers (say, in a trade directory) but have no way of distinguishing their (divergent) qualities or competence. Market solutions for adverse selection may include self-regulation of (minimum) professional qualities, self-regulation of conduct or standard contracts agreed between, say, consumer bodies and suppliers' associations. Such solutions decrease the uncertainty for buyers because of minimum standards of quality; hence, confidence may be increased. However, self-regulation might only come about when (a credible threat of) regulation exists, otherwise free-riding among suppliers may prevent agreement. The reason is obvious: higher competence and quality services would tend to be driven out of the market as both their prices and frequency of sales would be continuously undermined by charlatans exploiting lack of information on the part of the buyers. Apart from the rationale for 'back-up' regulation, societies have judged the risks to individuals, the impact on individual household expenditure and the smooth functioning of service markets to be so important that all kinds of structures and conduct regulation (including licensing and supervision by special agencies) have been introduced. Sometimes sellers are allowed to refuse buyers if insufficient information is supplied. All this regulation might be wholly or partly justified.

The second market failure is *imperfect competition*. Sellers of many services tend to enjoy some degree of market power. The latter results from a low degree of contestability of the established firms in the market. This may depend on economies of scale or, for multi-services supply, scope, or on product differentiation. But the observation of any of these three is not a sufficient condition. What matters is whether new entrants can enter and exit at such a low cost (and such high speed) that potential competition becomes a credible discipline on the behaviour of established firms or companies. Given such entry and exit conditions, and given that market power is exploited, 'fly-by-night' companies might enter at virtually no cost and erode the profitability of established firms.[9] If the entry costs are determined by the exit costs and are low (that is, if there are well-functioning markets for buildings and equipment so that entry costs can be recouped upon exit), and cost functions of established firms are similar to those of new entrants,[10] contestability is high and market power cannot be exercised.

Among services, contestability varies enormously between sectors. At one extreme of the spectrum, scale and/or scope are absent, whereas at the other extreme, barriers to entry and exit are high. The latter means that costs incurred with entry cannot be recouped upon exit: they are sunk. Thus, one could hardly imagine a well-functioning market to exist for a railway network or a sewage system; however, for aeroplanes, second-hand markets have emerged.[11] So, one has to assess tangible exit barriers from case to case. Intangible entry/exit barriers may be more important in services, however; investment in reputation and consumer loyalty is often specific to the company and, hence, sunk. The costs to acquire reputation and loyalty can be extremely high and may serve as effective barriers to entry (for instance in retail banking or in some network industries).

Of course, internalities and market power may mutually reinforce each other. Thus, consumer loyalty may be due to consumer switching costs, which consumers may perceive to be high between experienced services (from the supplier they are loyal to) and inexperienced ones, the quality of which they cannot judge. It is claimed that this explains consumer loyalty in retail banking. This makes contestability by new entrants difficult (because discounting may be distrusted as low quality) and hence may lead to concerted or parallel pricing behaviour in an oligopoly of the established companies. Another example of interaction between the two market failures is self-regulation which, in addressing the problem of asymmetric information, may actually

[8]Services are extremely differentiated products. Only comparable services can benefit from reputation effects by word of mouth.

[9]Those with an appetite for economic theory are referred to an interesting model by Grossman & Horn (1988). The authors analyse whether protection or (proper) regulation of services trade could best deal with the market failures, here in an infant service, using a two-periods model (which allows protection to be only temporary, that is, only in period 1). See also Sapir & Winter (1994).

[10]Or, better still, if new entrants have lower costs overall.

[11]Especially since specialised leasing companies started operating in the late 1970s.

raise barriers of entry (too much) or stifle innovative conduct. This is often said to be the case for certain professionals, for example, solicitors.

It goes without saying that these features require the application of a sophisticated and active competition policy to services. Unfortunately, asymmetric information (as well as the third market failure, see below) has often prompted regulation, which, in turn, reduces the scope or effectiveness of competition policy. Carefully assessing the complementarity between regulation and competition policy is critical for the understanding of the establishment and proper functioning of the internal market for services.[12]

The third market failure is *externalities*. Where these are negative externalities (for example, for the environment), they may influence the delivery of the services with goods that pollute (for example, trucks, aircrafts, ships). This may give rise to regulation. However, negative spillovers may also be unrelated to the physical means of transport. A significant decline in confidence in a bank or a securities company may prompt a 'run' on the bank, which in turn might undermine confidence in other financial service providers, inducing what is called 'contagion'. This severe negative externality is a 'systemic' risk, which could threaten the financial stability of a country or, if cross-border services exist, of the EU as a whole. Prudential regulation is therefore required. More complicated are the positive externalities in goods and services networks, a subject discussed in detail in Chapter 8.

4.2 The regulatory *acquis* in the internal market

The accomplishments of the Union as accumulated over time are called the *acquis communautaire,* a French term adopted in the treaty in all languages. Apart from the key features of the treaty (as the free movements, the common policies, the euro, and so forth), the *acquis* includes all the regulation in force as well as the achievements of all kinds of EU policies and the case law of the EC Court. Furthermore, it incorporates the institutional developments and political agreements at the European Council level (of heads of government) as, for example, the Charter on Fundamental Rights from 2000, now included in the Constitution as Part II (not yet ratified).

[12]See Chapter 12.

The regulatory *acquis* is perhaps the most frequently discussed part of the overall *acquis*. When the Union enlarges by incorporating new Member States (see Chapter 20), the adoption and transposition of the *acquis* is typically viewed as the greatest challenge. What is meant is (mainly) the regulatory *acquis* of the internal market and the implementing regulation of the common policies in so far as these are necessary at the national level. The regulatory *acquis* of the internal market is large and multifaceted. It is often suggested that it is next to impossible to encompass and appreciate it in its entirety. In some basic sense this is true, just as true as if one were to encompass the entire regulation of a Member State. Once one begins to take some distance for the purpose of an analytical perspective, however, it turns out to be both feasible and helpful to provide an overall view of the regulatory *acquis* of the internal market.

Table 4.1 shows that it is feasible without drowning in a mass of detailed description. More important, it is helpful for the economic study of EU regulation. Table 4.1 combines a common distinction of goods, services and three factor markets with the market failures underlying the public interest approach to regulation. A glance at the twenty entries in this matrix should assist the reader in acquiring some sense of what the internal market regulatory *acquis* is all about and help to classify as well as appreciate the kind of public interest justifications which (should) lie behind the various elements of this *acquis*. For a careful analysis, of course, one would have to 'zoom in' on the domain at issue. It should be realised, too, that such an overview cannot always do full justice to the complicated nature of specific instances of regulation: thus, directives may be justified both by internalities and externalities, or, the distinction between financial services and financial capital is somewhat blurred (hence, more entries might be acceptable). Finally, for a proper understanding of the nature and place of the regulatory *acquis* as summarised in the table, one has to take a close look at the assumptions as listed in the footnotes. One illustration demonstrates how important that is: the focus on regulation proper while assuming (but not specifically mentioning in the entries) free movement/establishment and not specifying the nuts and bolts of competition policy leads to a simple reference in the entry 'internalities/services' to 'all network industries'. This conceals, inevitably, how free movement, competition policy and regulation are intertwined when opening up the network industries,

Table 4.1 Regulatory *acquis* of the internal market

	Type of Market				
Market Failures	Goods	Services	Capital	Labour	Technology
Externalities	Environmental *acquis* Health and safety regulation	Environmental aspects of transport Network security (electricity, air, rail, software)	Anti-money laundering Tax competition (harmful)?	(Selected) professional minimum standards (see services)	
	Industrial • old approach (selected) • new approach (selected)	Systemic case for prudential regulation of financial services; →	Prevention of systemic risk	Health and safety at workplace	
	Agricultural goods • inputs (fertilisers, veterinary medicines) • plants and animal health rules and controls, etc. . . . Food law and mutual recognition Product liability	(selected) professional minimum standards (veterinarians, pharmacists)	Corporate tax (against harmful tax competition)		
Internalities	Health and safety regulation Industrial • old approach • new approach • global approach (testing and cert.) • standardisation • labelling and info. • green labelling and GMOs	Minimum professional qualifications in • transport • financial services • professions Mutual recognition/ origin principle	Disclosure rules Corporate governance; selected other company law	Minimum professional qualifications (see services) Mutual recognition of diplomas (general)	
	Food law and mutual recognition Medicinal law and agency Product liability Consumer protection	All network industries Consumer protection • general • insurance • e-commerce Harmonisation on 'general good'	Accounting standards	Health and safety at workplace	

as Chapter 8 sets out. Indeed, the regulatory *acquis* makes sense only against the backdrop of cross-border liberalisation and in the presence of competition policy.

The purpose of Table 4.1 is not that the student should somehow master and comprehend the regulatory *acquis* of the EU internal market. Rather, it is to help anybody who studies EU internal market regulation (1) to ask the

Table 4.1 continued

	Type of Market				
Market Failures	Goods	Services	Capital	Labour	Technology
Competition • **market power** • **distortion**	(see competition policy) • tax harmonisation/ competition • public procurement rules Uniform customs rules	(see competition policy) • tax harmonisation/ competition • public procurement rules Labour restrictions on modes 3 and 4 (services mode in GATS)	Prohibition exchange controls Clearing and settlement; custody (in stock exchanges) Tax harmonisation/ competition	Portability pensions (Minimum) harmonisation fiscal/health/ social Host country control; (weak) immigration rules	R&D subsidy controls EU common IPRs Harmonised parallel national IPRs Accounting standards (intangibles)
Public goods	Uniformity of EU law (incl. damages for non-implementation) TENs (?)	idem (as in goods) TENs (?)	(Euro?)		Conditionalities EU R&D

Notes: No common policies included; few equity regulatory aspects; no macroeconomic rules included; free movements assumed; free establishment assumed; public goods outside the internal market are excluded (e.g. security and defence).
GATS = General Agreement on Trade in Services; GMO = genetically modified organism; IPR = intellectual property rights; TEN = trans-European network.

relevant economic questions, and (2) to dispose of an easy source of tracing or mapping whatever regulation one encounters in the internal market in terms of the public European interest. A lot of this regulation is technical, expert driven and demanding for almost any reader as indeed a lot of national regulation is too. Nevertheless, the kind of questions prompted by Table 4.1 should always be answered in no uncertain terms, otherwise one wonders, why regulate and how to assess the benefits for the internal market in the first place. A significant advantage of the table is that the general and perhaps somewhat abstract analysis of market failures becomes concrete and applied with the help of the matrix.

This textbook cannot possibly go into all the entries of the matrix. But in all the chapters on the internal market (Chapters 6 to 10 as well as 4 and 5 more generally) and occasionally in the chapters on the common policies (Chapters 11 to 13, possibly 14), on macroeconomic stabilisation (Chapters 17 and 18) and enlargement there are references to regulation. Readers are encouraged to employ Table 4.1 as a tool for understanding.

4.3 At what level and how should the EU regulate?

4.3.1 Subsidiarity and proportionality

The EU should regulate only if the subsidiarity test is passed (see sections 3.3 and 3.4). In most internal market matters, what this means is that one or more of the following applies. For the establishment of the internal market, the blockage of free movement (by definition, an issue of cross-border externalities) has to be removed and if derogations in the treaty are (rightly) invoked, step-3-type cooperative action among the Member States is unlikely to accomplish this (at least, not without some joint regulation or, some agreement to refer to and recognise, say, a European voluntary standard). For sectors more heavily regulated, such as food, network industries or financial services and capital markets, the supervision and/or control systems themselves will have to be regulated both for free movement and for the right of establishment, and the interaction between the two. It is also probable that the greater the acknowledged risks in markets the stronger the incentives to shift to step-4-type common regulation, but, presumably, this would be a smooth process only if the safety or health objectives are regarded as identical in terms of protection of citizens and workers. For the proper functioning of the internal market, and (here) ignoring issues of anti-competitive behaviour or state aids, it may be that mutual recognition causes extra costs which are better resolved via approximation. What has also happened frequently during the process of 'completing' the internal market is that specific areas are tackled via framework directives or partial approaches which subsequently prompt follow-up regulation in order to overcome all kinds of disparities in free movement. Moreover, case law from the EC Court often yields a case-driven improvement in market access without solving wider issues of free movement or establishment, causing new pressures to approximate. However, such case law can also be about the interpretation of non-discrimination (a key principle of EC law, see Chapter 2). Some rulings raised the spectre of such great disparities that the proper functioning of the internal market prompted further approximation.

Of course, the subsidiarity test has to be conducted within the legal limits of Community law. As noted, this first of all implies a reference to shared powers. In the internal market this is rarely a problem, except if (say) case law on free movement has the practical effect of impinging on the effectiveness of what are recognised national powers such as public health or primary and secondary education. In these two policy domains the increased mobility of patients across borders as well as the actual or potential mobility of suppliers or consumers of education (in particular, when privately financed) exploit the free movement opportunities, but a liberal case law in this respect would risk undermining the exercise of what are in essence national powers, clearly supported as such in a subsidiarity test. Another problem is that the limits of Community law can be dysfunctional. One example is the old Meroni doctrine of the EC Court. It holds that, since Member States have conferred powers to the EU institutions, it is constitutionally not possible for the EU institutions to fully delegate these powers in turn to, say, independent regulatory agencies. In network industries but also in food, this leads to the undesirable configuration that, whereas Member States have such independent regulatory agencies in these markets, the internal market for network industries or for food products cannot be effectively supervised and swiftly corrected by similar EU agencies. The double costs of this anomaly are that (1) second-best regulation is adopted instead, the price of which is that the internal market is functioning less well, and (2) so-called autonomous EU agencies are set up which entail high coordination costs and lack powers.[13] The Union, not being a state, can therefore cause some inefficiencies in the internal market, presumably justified by the fear on the part of Member States of the costs of such far-reaching delegation of powers to the 'centre'.

The principle of proportionality plays a major role in the day-to-day practice of EU regulation. There are two overlapping meanings of proportionality for European regulation. First, as noted in Chapter 3, it refers to cost minimisation of central regulation. It will be remembered that this hinges on the answers to questions about binding versus less binding measures; when binding, questions about the (more or less) centralising nature of the instrument so as to leave the Member States some discretion in, for instance, framework directives; and the choice between differentiation (if possible without unduly raising the costs) and uniformity.

Second, it refers to the degree of intrusiveness or restrictiveness of regulation, in other words, the way it attempts to overcome the market failure without restricting more than necessary the freedom of economic agents in markets. In this respect, the two upper entries in the 'goods' column in Table 4.1 are instructive. For health and safety regulation, the initial stages of EU approximation in goods are known as the 'old approach'. What happened was plainly 'disproportional', hence costly. Given the threat of vetoes in those days, and absent the idea of mutual recognition emphasising the equivalence of health and safety objectives and not the nitty-gritty detail of technical specifications in national laws, elaborate technical 'harmonisation' directives were adopted with all the technical specification in text or annexes, including conformity assessment methods. In 1985, a much more proportional 'new approach' was initiated, the essence of which is to agree on the objectives and, where necessary some well-specified effects, while leaving the technical detail to (recognised European) standard bodies writing the relevant standard.[14] The old approach would

[13] Another consequence is that, since the EU has exclusive power in competition policy, a tendency can be observed to overload competition policy in order to compensate for the weakness of regulatory institutions, especially in network industries.

[14] These standards are 'mandated' by the Commission so as to be sure that they properly reflect the objectives and effects of the directive. Once written, they have to be recognised as such. The conformity assessment of whether a company has actually conformed to the standard is left to 'notified bodies', that is, they are recognised by the Commission as guaranteeing a permanent high level of quality giving full confidence to Member States allowing free movement. Given this quality level, there is mutual recognition for all conformity assessment under new-approach directives.

seem to be defensible under proportionality only if risks are very high and restrictive and uniform regulation is the only way to acquire confidence throughout the internal market.

The combination of subsidiarity and proportionality is certainly a useful foundation for EU regulation. However, it is overly general and, moreover, ignores more refined economic assessments of how to regulate. This requires a systematic approach called 'regulatory impact assessment', largely based on cost/benefit analysis, to which we now turn.

4.3.2 Regulatory impact assessment

The methodology of regulatory impact assessment (RIA) should force the preparatory process of drafting Commission proposals to assume a consistent, functional approach to a regulatory issue. This includes the justification of the regulation in the draft, and subsequently information of the decision makers (Council and EP) so as to enable them to take well-informed decisions for which they are accountable. This may sound obvious to economists far removed from political processes, but the systematic use of RIAs would greatly improve the rationality of preparing draft regulation (not only at EU but at national level too). One would consider all relevant alternatives, having regard to societal costs and benefits and justifying explicitly the choice of a particular option in terms of subsidiarity, proportionality (in some detail) as well as costs and benefits in quantitative and qualitative terms. For one thing, it would make it far more difficult for lobbies to 'capture' the Commission or the EU decision makers. The focus in making EU laws in the internal market would justifiably be on the net benefits for the society as a whole and avoid a single-minded emphasis by business only on the costs to them. Such costs ought to be minimised by considering alternative options but, in the final analysis, it is the net benefit which justifies the regulation for the EU. RIAs might also help to preempt a process of overregulation by making explicit the (possibly) negative net benefits of too many specifications or of an unreasonably costly drive to reduce risks. In other words, RIAs are a sensible response to the political economy of (EU) decision shaping and decision making.

The essence of RIAs consists of three elements: consistency in the entire regulatory process in answering a well-defined set of core questions; cost/benefit analysis of the options considered; and explicit justification of a proposal or decision based on the results of the two previous steps.

The consistency refers mainly to analytical discipline in defining carefully the regulatory issues to be resolved; the reasons why the status quo is to be altered; the objectives of a new regulation (or, indeed, perhaps other ways of solving the issue); the various options considered and their instruments; and the explicit analysis of trade-offs in the case of multiple objectives (which European regulation often exhibits). And all of this before a proper cost/benefit analysis can be conducted.

The cost/benefit analysis can take a number of forms.[15] Ideally, a rigorous economic analysis of the costs and benefits for European society of all the options considered is required. In practice, this is extremely demanding in terms of modelling and data. Moreover, certain aspects can be evaluated only in qualitative terms and the weighing of such qualitative effects will ultimately have to be done by politically accountable decision makers. However, the rigour of cost/benefit analysis remains a virtue even when the models and data create serious problems. It should be noted that several alternatives to cost/benefit analysis are sometimes used which are less appropriate. One is 'cost effectiveness' analysis which starts from the assumption or, indeed, political agreement, that the wanted effect (i.e. benefit) can be precisely defined so that one can focus solely on alternative ways to minimise the cost of achieving it, say via various forms of regulation. In highly specific technical regulation this can be a fruitful approach, but for wider regulatory questions or framework regulation the benefits are themselves part of the analysis and hence the approach is flawed. Another approach is called either 'business impact analysis' or (business) 'competitiveness impact analysis', prompted by a fear of high compliance costs for business or even losses of market share or a lower pace of innovation in a context of globalisation. This partial analysis is justified only as far as it goes: it calls attention to aspects or intrusiveness of regulation which may be too easily overlooked or downplayed by politicians or eurocrats but it should not become so prominent as to dismiss or underplay what matters most: the benefits to society of greater safety or health and/or a better environment. It should not be forgotten that excessive 'risk regulation' can

[15] See Pelkmans & Labory (1998), and Pelkmans *et al.* (2000b). See also Pearce & Howarth (2000).

also be very costly to (some) consumers or workers or farmers. Such a wider view would be the outcome of an overall cost/benefit analysis, based on proper risk assessment (see section 4.4.3).

The explicit justification is, and ought to be, a political judgement. An RIA has the virtue of making the justification transparent for everybody. But the weighing of trade-offs, the assessment of qualitative benefits and the tolerance of certain costs can only be decided by those having political legitimacy with voters in representative democracy. The decision makers should be held accountable for the regulation so that voters' preferences are in some sense reflected in regulation.

The actual working of RIAs in the EU context still has to be assessed. The EU started a systematic RIA process of all major draft regulation in 2003 with some 40 instances.[16] The idea is to arrive a what is called 'better EU regulation' for the purpose of a lesser burden for the economy while focusing more sharply on the justified objectives of health and safety.

4.3.3 Mutual recognition, and its costs and benefits

Mutual recognition (MR) starts from the idea that Member States have equivalent regulatory objectives in safety, health, environmental and consumer protection (SHEC) which, in practice in Europe, is very often correct. But if and when objectives are equivalent, and thus the market failure is addressed, approximation should no longer be necessary and free movement could prevail. The notion of *mutual recognition* refers to the implication for national customs or inspectors or regulatory agencies or policy makers that a good entering this Member State from another EU country must be allowed unhindered access, even if the detailed specifications in the relevant domestic regulation differ from those in the country of origin, as long as the regulatory objectives are equivalent. From a narrow regulatory point of view it would thus seem as if the importing country 'recognises' the regulatory regime of the exporting country. Because the principle has general application for the internal market, this recognition is 'mutual'.

Before explaining MR a little more precisely in the EU context, it is crucial to appreciate a few properties. First, mutual recognition must always be understood as an alternative or complement to liberalisation and/or approximation. Therefore, when EU authorities say that MR is a leading principle of the internal market, this should not be interpreted as meaning that it is the sole or overriding principle. Economists ought to analyse the economics of MR in the proper regulatory context. Second, the reliance on MR in the EU is greatly facilitated by the forceful treaty principle of free movement, a principle that does not exist and cannot be expected in international trade law or in economic regionalism elsewhere (whether NAFTA, the ASEAN free trade area, Mercosur, or whatever). Free movement goes much beyond free trade in that the former implies a right to enter national markets. National discretion to intervene exists only when there is an explicit derogation in the treaty. Thus, when the derogation does not apply or when it is narrowly interpreted by the EC Court (which has typically happened in the EU), free movement prevails automatically. And when derogations do apply, the objectives and key aspects can be approximated by common decision making. The originality of 'mutual recognition' is that, before rushing into thousands of approximation exercises, one should first ask the question whether the objectives of national regulation, falling under the derogation, are not equivalent to begin with. If so, MR applies because the purpose (that of overcoming the internal market failure) is then fulfilled and free movement should prevail, irrespective of the details that might differ between those national rules. Third, a supranational EC Court is present neither in the WTO regime nor in other regional trade regimes. It is the combination of these last two aspects (that is, the principle of free movement rather than free trade, and a 'supreme' court) which makes it doubtful whether MR, with all its profound consequences, can be exported to world trade or other trade blocs (see also Pelkmans, 1995). Fourth, MR is not the same as the 'origin principle'. The latter is more radical. What is similar between the two principles is that the regulation of the country of origin being different from the regulation in the country of destination is not a hindrance for cross-border access to the latter country. What is different is that the origin principle does not require 'equivalence' of regulatory goals. This must imply either a presumption that goals are not very different or that regulatory competition is fully accepted. The origin principle is sometimes applied in EU services and is discussed in Chapter 7.

[16]See COM (2002) 276 of 5 June 2002 on impact assessment, and SEC (2004) 1377 of 21 October 2004; see also Radaelli (2003).

ADDITIONAL READING

The remainder of this section endeavours to set out more precisely the MR regime of the EU in its regulatory context. The aim is to have the reader understand that MR can flourish only in a well-defined and hierarchical legal regime (see also Pelkmans, 2005a).

The principle of mutual recognition has been developed by the EC Court in its case law. In its famous *Cassis de Dijon* case, the Court held that, in principle, a Member State must allow a product lawfully produced and marketed in another Member State into its own market, unless a prohibition of this product is justified by mandatory requirements, such as health and safety protection (see below).[17] This means that Member States cannot apply certain specific details of national regulation to intra-EC imports of goods, if the objective or effect of the relevant law in other Member States is equivalent to that of the importing country. The idea behind MR is that all Member States care for their citizens and cannot be assumed to produce, for instance, unsafe or unhealthy products merely because technical specifications differ. Hence, the principle of MR plays a pivotal role in the internal market since it ensures free movement of goods and services without making it necessary to approximate/harmonise national legislation. Since free movement of goods is essential to the internal market, it is not surprising that the burden of proof of 'non-equivalence' of objectives is on the Member State which is unwilling to allow the import of the products concerned.

In emphasising the objective(s), rather than the detailed specifications, in a national product law or decree, both the national regulation and the regulation of Member States where the imported product comes from are forced to concentrate on overcoming the market failure. This will tend to make regulatory failure unattractive. A widespread instance of regulatory failure in Europe was overregulation in the sense that national product laws extended to aspects that had nothing to do with the market failure. At the same time, however, it assumes that the grounds in Article 30 EC (referring mainly to health and safety) represent market failures. If one includes the EC Court's rule of reason interpretation of Article 28 EC, which justifies national regulation involving environmental and consumer protection, and observes that almost all the relevant product regulation related to Article 30 EC is about health and safety protection, this assumption is broadly correct. Those four combine to SHEC which covers practically all relevant market failures for goods.

Where MR fails because of non-equivalence, the EU can decide to take up regulation approximating national legislative provisions in order to ensure the free movement of goods. In an attempt to overcome the drawbacks of the 'old approach' to the abolition of technical barriers to trade followed by the Council since 1969,[18] the Commission launched in 1985 its 'New Approach to Harmonisation and Technical Standards'. The new approach restricts approximation to stipulating essential health and safety requirements, while the specification of these requirements in technical standards is left to the European standardisation bodies (CEN, CENELEC and ETSI). The distinction between the essential SHEC requirements (the regulatory objectives) and technical specifications constitutes the main characteristic of the new approach. This new approach is often denoted as 'minimum harmonisation': what this refers to is not that regulation is somehow (too?) minimalist but that all that is to be approximated are the objectives and their essential links with voluntary, preferably common standards, but no more than that. Once these objectives are approximated, the rest is subject to MR. Common – though voluntary – standards are then desirable instruments to drastically lower information costs and uncertainty for business and technical designers in clarifying what critical specifications are presumed to be in compliance with these (often quite general) SHEC objectives. However,

[17] Case 120/78 *Rewe-Zentrale AG v Bundesmonopolverwaltung für Branntwein* [1979] ECR 649, although this principle was explicitly developed only in Case 113/80 *Commission v Ireland* [1981] ECR 1625.

[18] Adopted on 28 May 1969, (1969) OJ C 76/1. For the drawbacks see Pelkmans (1987).

ADDITIONAL READING *continued*

innovation is not throttled because new solutions may be tested and certified as well, as long as they comply with these objectives. The new approach, with much lower costs and far fewer blockages in the Council, has thus been greatly facilitated by the emergence of MR and is therefore far superior to the old, rigid harmonisation approach the Community applied before 1985.

Mutual recognition is an ingenious European solution to a complex problem of multi-tier regulation, given the obligation of free movement and its (SHEC) derogations. In the following a brief cost/benefit analysis is provided so that the merits and practical problems of this innovation in the internal market can be readily understood. The results are summarised in Table 4.2 (for more details see Pelkmans, 2005a).

The benefits shown in Table 4.2 are many and diverse. Crucial for the legitimacy of the principle is the first benefit: market access of foreign (intra-EU) competitors not precisely conforming to the detailed national rules does not undermine the objectives of national regulation; this is simply because the (SHEC) objectives have to be equivalent to begin with. In practice, EU Member States tend to have many SHEC regulations with very similar objectives and this should provide ample scope for MR.

The main 'case' for MR is both strategic and economic. The strategic benefits are significant and the preponderant ones are probably the first (much more free movement) and the last one (without any regulatory centralisation). The second one is relevant if the local overregulation represents not deeply entrenched preferences but vested interests of a minority. If preferences are the reason of tight regulation, the country would be ready to incur the higher costs since those costs will be outweighed by the benefits one prefers. However, if vested interests suddenly see that protective regulation inflicts costs upon them but not on the new competitors, pressures will emerge to reduce the costs of national regulation. The third benefit, laying the basis for regulatory competition, is addressed in Case Study 4.1. The economic benefits arise from competition across intra-EU borders.

Table 4.2 Mutual recognition: benefits and costs

Benefits	Costs
Regulatory • national regulatory autonomy protected for SHEC objectives • focus on 'objectives', not the technical detail, hence, a bias against regulatory failure	Information costs • mutual recognition 'invisible' for economic agents in many cases • no clarity on 'grey areas', as it is based on EC Court cases, *ex post* • no 'rule book' available
Strategic • in principle, sweeping improvement of free movement • costs of over/misregulation fall now on Member State and its economy, so pressures for less costly rules • lays basis for 'regulatory competition' between EU countries • free movement without more rules at EU level	Transaction costs • costs of monitoring day-to-day MR in markets would be infinite, hence no monitoring • when Member States refuse, little help available • assuring one's rights is costly and slow, unattractive for business
Welfare • pro-competitive	Compliance costs • unknown but probably high costs of market access for *existing* national rules • centralised pre-emption regime drastically reducing costs of *new* national regulation

CASE STUDY 4.1 Regulatory competition

From the perspective of the economics of regulation, it may be argued that an optimal economic strategy would also incorporate regulatory competition between the Member States.

Judicial mutual recognition will expose national regulation to the forces of arbitrage: consumers may choose between (products or services produced under) domestic regulation or that of any other Member State, by importing the relevant products or services.

Regulatory competition is dynamic and takes this process further. It is defined as the alteration of national regulation in response to the actual or potential impact of cross-border mobility of goods, services or factors on national economic activity (Sun & Pelkmans, 1995a). Behind this alteration are complex business–government interactions. Jurisdictions with costly regulations may find business pressing to reduce their regulatory burden when faced with import competition from jurisdictions with 'light' regimes. Alternatively, local business and government may agree on strategic deregulation so as to boost certain activities in the internal market. Since this may also be practised, or responded to, by other Member States, iterative processes of regulatory competition may develop.

As a rule, one would expect a process of regulatory competition to induce a 'market-driven' regulatory convergence in the EC. However, this should not be allowed where 'negative externalities' is the relevant market failure as this would lead to fragmentation of the internal market or underregulation (for example, environment, discriminatory measures); nevertheless it would be suitable if information asymmetries or other 'internalities' are the problem. It could well be economically superior to Council-driven approximation as decision makers cannot be assumed to pursue the general interest unconditionally, as the positive theory of regulation teaches. Unfortunately, regulatory competition may not be as smooth as simple theory might stipulate, because significant distortions can remain. It is nevertheless useful to allow it as an option for Member States. Had the regulatory failure of the 'old approach' remained in place, regulatory competition would be more attractive. After all, the costs of approximation in the new regulatory strategy are incomparably lower than before 1985.

ADDITIONAL READING *continued*

What has long been ignored, unfortunately, is the fact that MR is very demanding in terms of information and proper application. That is the reason why the first strategic benefit, though sweeping, is conditioned by 'in principle'. This benefit is sweeping if and only if the numerous costs are contained in a forceful and credible manner. Apart from the food sector (where so many EC Court cases have been ruled that Member States were eventually forced to revise their many food laws, taking MR into account,[19] this is hardly the case. Many companies do not know about MR, and if they do, they still regard it as an abstract principle which does not tell them whether it applies to their goods in every Member State. More often than not, authorities in all kinds of less heavily regulated sectors, where MR may well apply, are not well informed or are uncertain about 'equivalence' and hence enforce the local rules.[20] Indeed, one cannot 'see' MR in laws unless there are explicit and precise 'equivalence clauses'. This property of invisibility leads to huge knowledge gaps as well as great uncertainty in business circles. Besides these information costs, economic agents are likely to incur considerable transaction costs even if they are confident about the validity of MR. Since independent monitoring of millions of such transactions every day is out of the question, the discretion of

[19]This was combined with a horizontal EU programme of approximation, complementing MR, such as a labelling directive, irradiation regulation, broad sanitary procedures in what is called HACCP rules, etc., so the sector and Member States were well aware of the ins and outs of MR.

[20]For evidence, see COM (1999) 299 of 16 June 1999 and COM (2002) 419 of 23 July 2002 respectively, the first and second reports on the application of the principle of MR. See also Pelkmans (2005a).

ADDITIONAL READING *continued*

national controlling authorities to play it safe in relying on local laws is hardly reduced. Help is hard to come by, although for a few years a SOLVIT service has been providing short-term mediation (which has often led to results, apparently). Few companies believe it is sensible to assure their rights, with an eye on the future business they expect to have in the country of destination. In other words, there is a lack of incentive to reduce transaction costs and the system is not self-policing. Finally, the compliance costs of unexpected additional resources spent on market access can amount to a significant proportion of turnover, especially for SMEs. Repeated complaints have caused European business to turn away from MR and plead for approximation, especially since the 'new approach' with the European standards tends to give business more certainty and allows large production runs for the entire internal market. The gap between the ideal of an ingenious innovation, originated in the EC Court, and the reality of cross-border business demonstrates that the EU can enjoy the considerable benefits of MR only if it invests deeply in cost reduction of its application.

In one respect, the EU has done so, namely, for *new* (goods) regulation by the Member States. A little known procedure under Directive 98/34 verifies all national draft regulation which does not fall under approximation obligations. Some 700 laws and technical decrees pass this committee every year. Potential obstacles to free movement are spotted by the Commission and the (other) Member States; also, equivalence clauses are to be inserted. This strict procedure protects free movement and MR against erosion. Without it, the massive regulatory drive of the Member States might long have undermined the internal market.

4.3.4 EU regulatory strategy

In the 25 years or so since the beginning of the Community, both the decision making about, and the quality of, EU regulation left a lot to be desired. Harmonisation – if it succeeded at all, given vetoes and costly compromises in Council – invariably led to almost full uniformity and excessive detail. In addition, rigidity was such that even revision of details could be problematic. No link with flexible European (performance) standards was pursued at the EU level. The upshot was a double regulatory failure: deadlock due to vetoes, often about trivialities – hence, a fragmented internal market – and costly overregulation on very narrow areas of regulation.[21]

A radically new strategy was badly needed. Such a strategy would have to accomplish no less than four goals:

- improved decision making by allowing qualified majority voting (QMV), instead of crippling vetoes, and better quality of rules by focusing on market failures only;
- a much faster 'completion' of the internal market (especially for goods);
- drastically lower regulatory costs without in any way compromising SHEC objectives;
- as little centralisation as possible.

With the Single European Act (see Chapter 3) and the emergence of MR, this proved feasible.

The strategy consists of a triptych of a political, a judicial and a regulatory panel (see Table 4.3). The

Table 4.3 The EU's new regulatory strategy

Political	Judicial	Regulatory
Qualified majority voting (with a few exceptions)	Judicial MR (given equivalent objectives or if Art. 30 does not apply)	• Free movement • No internal frontiers • Subsidiarity • Minimum approximation/ harmonisation • Regulatory MR
	Proportionality (Member States)	Proportionality (EU level)

[21] An example is the chocolate directive (73/241) of 1973, revised into a much lighter form of regulation only in 2001 after repeated battles in the EP and Council. This 'old approach' directive restricted the name 'chocolate' for free movement to a very precise description of ingredients (thereby limiting food innovation) and, in effect, moving quality standards for upmarket chocolate into the law and, in so doing, restricting choices of informed consumers, without there being an essential health reason for this restriction. The annex with detailed recipe-type descriptions of over 20 types of permitted chocolate varieties leaves practically no discretion to the market.

regulatory panel, in turn, is made up of a quintet. With due account of the political and judicial panels, this *regulatory quintet* is central to the establishment and proper functioning of the single market, the economic hard core of the Union.

The Single European Act removed the veto obstacle. For most internal market matters, QMV was *de jure* and *de facto* introduced. This altered the conduct of Member States' representatives in COREPER and Council. No longer could every detail and every deviation with other Member States be imposed on the Community: compromises were either needed to obtain some concessions from others or were indispensable to form a blocking minority. QMV thereby reduced the costs of 'how' the EU regulated, while significantly lowering the probability of deadlock, so that the internal market could be built much faster.

The judicial panel has its roots in the 1970s, albeit only for goods markets, in the *Dassonville* and *Cassis de Dijon* cases.

Judicial MR proved capable of declaring inapplicable to intra-EU imports a large number of regulatory specifications in food laws, and some in machine safety regulations and construction products. In and by itself, it made superfluous a lot of tedious approximation that was deadlocked on the technical specifications, *not* on the regulatory objectives sought. Just as QMV did after the Single European Act, judicial MR altered the behaviour of Member States. First, it came to be understood that the 'need to act in common' (step 2 of the subsidiarity test) at EU level often did not apply where (national) SHEC objectives were the same. This had the double advantage of *reducing the EU regulatory burden* (that is, less approximation) while exposing national overregulation (with technical specifications) by free movement. The potential total number of goods waiting for EU regulation before free movement became a reality was drastically curtailed. Moreover, existing, often detailed national regulation as well as possible future refinements became unenforceable *vis-à-vis* intra-EU imports.

Second, judicial MR led to a rethink of how approximation could best be tackled whenever there was doubt about the equivalence of regulatory objectives. Approximation was minimised to the 'essential requirements' of health, safety, environmental or consumer protection. Beyond these regulatory objectives, Member States were free to regulate more strictly, but MR (and thus free movement) would apply. This *regulatory mutual recognition* solved the problem of (business) uncertainty about 'equivalence' by defining common minimum requirements in rather general terms, while imposing free movement and MR 'beyond' those requirements. This had the great advantage that agreement in the Council would be far easier to achieve as, in Europe, regulatory objectives hardly diverge in the large majority of cases. It meant that the establishment of the internal market became politically feasible.

The EC Court also introduced another principle, that of 'proportionality'. Because judicial MR may confuse consumers, as they are confronted with goods from different regulatory regimes, it did accept labelling requirements as a 'least restrictive' measure to protect the consumer. Very costly measures such as complete import bans (for example, beer into Germany; pasta not fully made from durum wheat into Italy) had to be removed. Thus asymmetric information can be solved at very little cost and without impeding free movement.

The regulatory panel of Table 4.3 emerged from this evolution. With the Single European Act's removal of internal frontiers and the Maastricht Treaty's adoption of subsidiarity, the quintet was complete. It is hard to overrate the economic significance of the regulatory quintet. The combination of free movement, no internal frontiers and MR as well as proportionality at the Member States level has led to a far greater and more intense competitive exposure of national goods markets than before the Single European Act. Should common regulatory action be necessary, it is nevertheless still bound by the combination of subsidiarity (as in the treaty, Article 5 EC), minimum approximation and EU-level proportionality.

There is one caveat. Establishing the internal market while overcoming market failures and minimising regulatory failures should improve economic welfare, as a rule. But this conclusion cannot be fully generalised. Consider the case of EU countries with very large differences in preferences: in some health, safety or environmental objectives they diverge sharply. An inconsiderate application of free movement would preempt the satisfaction of the strictest local preferences (in, say, environmental regulation). Article 30 EC should prevent this from happening. But approximation may similarly suppress such preferences if QMV overrules the relevant Member State(s). This might mean that common regulation to overcome market failure could *lower* welfare in some Member States. Assuming that the overruled preferences expressed in Council are widely held by the voters in these countries and do not merely reflect overt protectionism, this would be a serious drawback.

There are two possible responses to this problem. First, in Article 95 EC, sub. 4, an escape clause is formulated, under strict conditions, allowing a Member State to maintain stricter legislation *without* MR. This clause has hardly been invoked thus far, showing that it is not a pressing problem in practice. Second, a Member State may maintain or enact stricter legislation, but of course subject to MR. In economic terms, the effect will be that *the regulatory costs will fall on the suppliers in the Member State itself.* If such preferences are truly widespread in the country, the satisfaction of these preferences may well offset the regulatory costs.

4.4 EU risk regulation

Most regulation of the EU, not being part of the common policies, amounts to 'risk regulation'. One can surmise this already from Table 4.1. For the internal market to function properly and the European economy to remain dynamic, it is crucial that European risk regulation is well designed and least cost. This simple statement, which is so easy to agree with, turns out to be a very demanding task. Getting it wrong can be extremely costly. The emphasis here is on the economic approach to EU risk regulation, but it should be clear that subjective factors can and do play a significant role in actual EU practice as well.

4.4.1 The scope of EU risk regulation

EU regulation of risky goods, services, situations at the workplace, industrial processes, transport systems (including traffic rules) and so forth is voluminous. Europeans live in a 'regulatory state', and the regulatory regime has several tiers of government. It is therefore better to simplify in order to grasp the core issues (see Case Study 4.2).

CASE STUDY 4.2 EU risk regulation: what does it cover?

The EU has mainly approximated risk regulation in the following areas: safety of goods and, where relevant, services as well, including some basic aspects of traffic systems ; numerous aspects of public health in goods markets (such as agro-food and fish products, mobile and stationary goods as well as processes, minimum quality of diplomas of medical and paramedical professions); animal health and welfare; nature and biodiversity; consumer protection in a narrow sense (contract requirements, redress, misleading advertising, minimum information and labelling); consumer protection in a wider sense (the financial soundness of banks and insurance providers, for example); investor protection in capital markets (reporting and accounting requirements; prospectuses when issuing shares; financial soundness of investment intermediaries); and finally, health and safety at the workplace for employees. Much of this regulation is linked to voluntary standards with specific links to the objectives of the law. Moreover, various forms of supervision, licensing, inspection or conformity assessment are incorporated in the regulation, mostly at Member States level (based on common criteria) but to some extent at EU level as well.

Besides this myriad of rules, individual companies, consumer organisations, voluntary standard bodies and voluntary conformity assessment institutions provide a market-based set of approaches to reduce risk and thereby acquire consumer or customer trust.

In this book the shorthand employed for most of the risk regulation is SHEC: rules promoting safety, health, environmental and consumer protection. Not only does this abbreviation cover a good deal of internal market regulation, it also accords well with the derogations of free movements under Articles 28 and 30, EC for goods and Article 56 EC for services. When such derogations cause free movement to be blocked and MR does not apply (or is too uncertain), approximation is called for. Given the depth of internal market integration, there has been a steady shift towards more common regulation as well as towards a much closer cooperation of national regulators and supervisors. In some instances, this is complemented by 'autonomous' (but not fully independent) EU regulators or 'agencies' such as the European Food Safety Agency, the European Medicinal Agency (for medicines approval) and common safety agencies for air transport and rail. Euratom has a complementary role in nuclear safety requirements. It is expected (in 2005) that a European Chemical Agency will become operational with the overhaul of the EU's elaborate chemicals regulation.

4.4.2 Economics of risk reduction

The driving forces behind the trend of increasing risk regulation can be traced to the rising prosperity of Europe since the 1950s and the preferences of European society to become more risk averse than in the past. The two are related. It is precisely the rising standard of living which shifts priorities in people's preferences. When living in poverty, individuals are ready to assume considerable risks or might not even take the trouble of informing themselves properly about the risk they might run; poor societies might not offer much of an alternative in the first place. In Europe the demands to be protected against all kinds of risks have been, and continue to be, translated in a steady flow of new and amended legislation as well as market responses based on signalling by companies and (health, safety and 'green') reputations of providers. The radical principles of the internal market such as free movement, free establishment and MR as well as the overhelming evidence that the protection sought was, and is, often highly correlated between Member States, generate very powerful incentives to build up what amounts to a Union regime of risk regulation, with implementation largely at the Member States level. The satisfaction of Europe's risk-averse preferences has made the Union into a much safer, healthier and 'greener' place, no doubt. But risk reduction is no free lunch: regulation is costly and European economic resources will be committed, explicitly or implicitly. In the light of the extremely comprehensive scope of this regime, it becomes ever more important to assume a functional approach so that benefits and costs become explicit as much as possible and no unwanted regulatory burden would gradually suffocate the European economy.

Rules imposing risk reduction carry a cost to society for the benefit of satisfying a preference of greater safety or more of other SHEC objectives. In some way, society must be willing to pay for those benefits, via higher market prices, less choice, rationing or higher taxes. If benefits can be expressed in a money value of 'willingness to pay' and the costs can be calculated, cost/benefit analysis could determine the degree of risk reduction, hence the stringency of regulation, which should not be exceeded. When costs begin to exceed benefits, there is regulatory failure. Optimal regulation would be determined at the point where the net benefits (over costs) is at a maximum.[22] When moving beyond the optimal degree of stringency towards the strictness where costs and benefits are just equal, it is as well to realise that the marginal costs of tougher requirements can go up very fast, for what sometimes might amount to only a trivial extra benefit. For example, dependent on the industry, protecting workers from loud noise is, on average, some 50 per cent more costly when one goes from a protection level of sub-90 decibels to that of sub-80 decibels; in arsenic regulation in the USA, the average cost increase of going from a medium to a tight standard, with one-twelfth of substance per cubic metre for the latter compared to the former, merely doubled but the marginal costs went up sixfold (Viscusi *et al.,* 2000, p. 614). The point is that decision makers must be informed before they can choose and be accountable for their decisions.

More often than not, these marginal costs and benefits are not visible to society without careful empirical risk analysis. Sometimes, however, consumers suddenly realise what ever increasing risk regulation may imply. A well-known example was the withdrawal from the market of the Citroën 2CV ('ugly duckling') car in the early 1990s because increasingly stringent safety regulation in Europe (for new cars) could no longer be met by marginal adjustments and upgrading of this cheap but reliable and popular car dating back to the 1950s. The original idea of a low-cost car which would be cheap to drive (minimal comfort and very low fuel consumption) had been undermined and prices were drifting up to levels at which consumers demanded more comfort and safety. Also, other types of costs of risk regulation may be quite visible: for instance, end-of-pipe solutions in environmental rules usually require extra investments in filters first and R&D in new processes subsequently. Costs could take many other forms, such as more testing and controls, more costly machinery, extra R&D on products and processes, extra insurance, more costly transport or the inclusion of more expensive ingredients or materials which should be anticipated when deciding upon new rules.

The calculation of regulatory costs is not easy, however. A single noise standard may work out very differently in different industries. Second, there are important considerations of time, since resources have an opportunity cost. The discount rate one takes could be adopted from the European market of (long-term) government bonds in euros.[23] Of course, this rate should also apply to the benefits. However, where most of the costs of regulation are incurred up-front, a high discount

[22]For an excellent and non-technical introduction into risk regulation, see Viscusi *et al.* (2000, chapters 19 to 23).

[23]The question one could ask is whether this interest rate properly represents the way society would prefer to allocate social resources over time.

rate would bias the calculation against the benefits because the actual value of those benefits (spread over many years into the future) is bound to shrink rapidly the higher the rate, whereas the costs would not be discounted as they are one-off costs incurred at the outset. Such a seemingly technical issue can play a major role in environmental rules or health regulation where time lags are long (as with asbestos for example). Third, costs depend on risk reduction, but that assumes that risks are precisely known. However, empirical risk assessment is surrounded by much uncertainty. Often, multiple and complex analyses are needed before risks can be properly assessed, and even then margins of uncertainty may remain very large, further complicated by differentiation according to local circumstances (for example, soil, water, air; or, type of persons). Inevitably, this leads to conservatism by basing results on the edge of the high risk boundary around the mean, if not with yet an extra safety margin. It is little realised that, in the presence of large margins and great differentiation, this might push up costs artificially. Ideally, a range of risks ought to be presented and, if practical, alternative regulatory strictness should be scrutinised with respect to costs and benefits. Not risk assessors but accountable politicians should make these choices.

The benefits hinge on 'willingness to pay' (WTP). For most people and in many circumstances, WTP is implicit. It ultimately depends on preferences and these are notoriously difficult to measure properly. Based on WTP, one can calculate 'units' of benefits such as the 'statistical value of life' (SVOL). Note that SVOL has nothing to do with moral or ethical values of life, or with the material losses of death of relatives. It simply measures the society's WTP to reduce fatality risks.[24] If risk is defined as the probability of having a fatal accident or disease caused by a product or site or plant or (say) a certain level of ambient air quality, which can be regulated, and risk reduction – to be accomplished via regulation – is defined as the degree of lowering this probability, then it follows that:

$$\text{SVOL} = \frac{\text{WTP}}{\text{Size of risk reduction}}$$

In other words, SVOL is the value society is willing to pay to prevent one statistical death. Suppose a risk is very small, for example one-millionth, and a person is asked to buy off this tiny risk to die. Typically one would not expect the person (if objectively informed about the risk) to have a high WTP, let us say he opts for €5. The answer would imply a SVOL of €5 million. Economic research in the USA has come up with SVOL ranges of $3 million to $6 million whereas the Commission (for instance, in chemical regulatory impact assessment) has used a conservative SVOL of €1 million. The benefits for an imaginary EU draft regulation would be found as follows. If we assume the risk reduction is translated into an annual reduction of fatalities of 1,000, and this for 20 years, the undiscounted benefits would amount to €20 billion whereas the discounted ones (on a year-by-year basis) would add up to much less, also dependent on the chosen discount rate.

ADDITIONAL READING

Designing EU environmental regulation

In Case Study 3.1, environmental policy was subjected to the subsidiarity test. Here, by way of illustration, EU environmental policy is analysed in terms of the economics of risk regulation. Cross-border externalities of an environmental kind (for example, air and water pollution) and those distorting free movement or free establishment (for example, cost-raising differences in national environmental regulation or taxation; intolerable incentives to shift output to EU countries with lax environmental laws if relevant for intra-EU exchange) are the justifications for the EU level to pursue environmental policy. In addition, some issues (such as global warming or the ozone layer) have to be addressed at world level where the Union performs as a single actor. More controversially, in a few local environmental problems the EU has adopted fairly strict common regulation, apparently based on the notion of homogeneity of

[24] Fatality or death is not the only basis for risk. The World Bank uses DALY, disability adjusted life years, and others use QALY, quality adjusted life years. These variations hinge on interpretations of damage short of having a fatal accident or contracting a lethal disease.

ADDITIONAL READING *continued*

preferences. The most prominent instance is that of drinking water. If preference for the quality of drinking water is influenced by one's level of prosperity (think of the central European Member States), it is improbable that this common regulation is optimal. Quite the contrary, it imposes a considerable cost on the new Member States (because the marginal cost of raising drinking water standards far beyond the minimum WHO requirements is high).[25] Derogations would have been justified for a period of one or two decades after becoming an EU member, by which time catch-up growth would have reduced the income gap appreciably.

Proper design of EU environmental policy should address the 'why' and 'how' questions.[26] In developed economies, the symbiosis between man and nature is broken. The environment is viewed as a 'free' resource since there are no property rights, hence no prices (what is called the 'missing market'). This leads companies and consumers to have regard only to private and not to social costs because the latter are not 'visible' until they are somehow enforced. With private costs lower than social costs, too much of the environmental resources will be used. Consider Figure 4.2.

Figure 4.2(a) shows the market equilibrium P_1Q_1 if only private marginal costs (*MC*p) are taken into account. The leaves the social costs of pollution (spu) unaddressed. If they were addressed, via EU policy, price would move to P_2 and output would reduce to Q_2. Note that pollution is not eliminated as this would entail the disappearance of production. This would be approached if MC_s were very steep, that is, if pollution were socially very costly (thus, heavy metals such as cadmium tend to be outlawed in products or output or their use remains severely restricted). In Figure 4.2(b), two environmental taxes are compared. The simplest form is a fixed tax per unit of output (t_1)

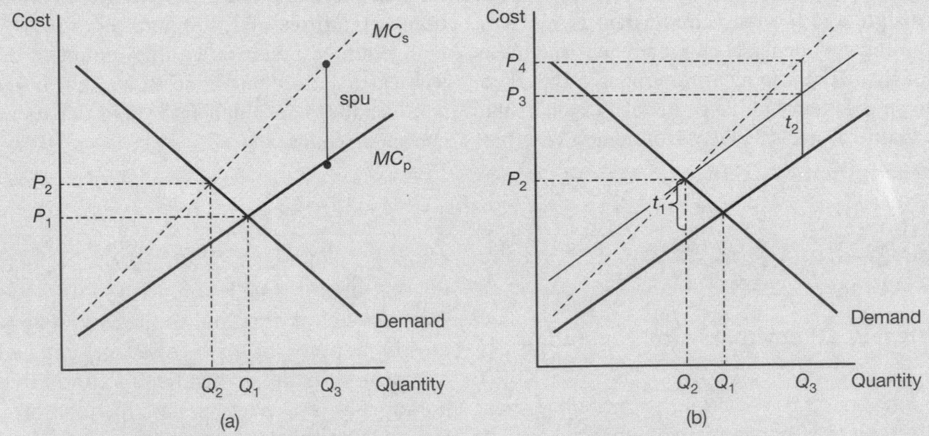

spu social costs of pollution per unit of output
t_1 fixed pollution tax per unit of output
t_2 tax per unit of pollution (e.g. emission)
MC_p private marginal coats
MC_s social marginal coats

Figure 4.2 Policy to internalise pollution externality

[25]For the eight new EU countries that joined in 2004 plus Romania and Bulgaria, rough estimates of these costs of purification installations run into several tens of billions of euros.

[26]For a survey of EU environmental policies, see, e.g., Clinch (2000).

ADDITIONAL READING *continued*

which has relatively low compliance costs for the government. A variable tax, namely, a given tax per unit of pollution (t_2) is more demanding in terms of monitoring the actual pollution per company. The graph is drawn such that at Q_2, the price effect, is the same. However, if demand were to shift over time so that Q_3 output becomes the equilibrium, the variable tax is socially superior as it still fully internalises the externality at P_4, whereas the simple tax does not accomplish that. If the compliance costs of measuring pollution are not too high, t_2 should be preferred.

Of course, the EU itself cannot levy taxes but it can 'harmonise' the calculation of such taxes and the measuring methods. In rare cases it will even go so far as to agree on a tax rate (whether t_1 or t_2) or indicate bands of tolerated taxes. *Mutatis mutandis,* for (fiscal) subsidies to reduce pollution (say, for 'greener' cars). Such harmonisation is typically justified by expected distortions of the internal market. The idea behind Figure 4.2 is also achieved if emission levels are fixed by product or process requirements. In principle, the abatement costs of investing in cleaner processes or products are tantamount to a tax. The more ambitious such emissions requirements, the higher the R&D costs and/or the unit costs of end-of-pipe filters or per-product devices. Indeed, it is conceivable that the EU might in the future set strict requirements with a view to forcing industry or energy providers to devote R&D to new technology and new products. Thus, for cars and heavy goods vehicles the setting of ever stricter EU emissions and fuel requirements has been the policy ever since the mid-1970s, first driven primarily by local air quality objectives and later also by the reduction of greenhouse gases causing global warming.

In the EU, regulation, based on 'command and control', was prominent until the 1990s. Over 300 environmental directives have entered the *acquis.* Many of them set maxima to emissions or to ingredients in products. In practice, however, the costs of enforcing compliance have been high, and too often compliance failed because of high monitoring and inspection costs. Thus, a gradual shift to so-called market-based instruments has been witnessed. Such instruments tend to carry lower compliance costs, including taxes (hence, some harmonisation of them), subsidies (*idem*), voluntary agreements by sectors (under the menace of regulation) and tradable pollution permits.[27] In carbon dioxide emission (the reduction of which is critical against global warming and the EU is a determined leader in the Kyoto process coordinating such policies), the EU has initiated a tradable emission permit system in 2005. The rationale for this approach cannot be deduced from Figure 4.2 since the crux is found in the existence of very different marginal cost curves in sectors. For a given permitted total of carbon dioxide emissions for the EU, subsequently distributed over the EU countries and then by sector, an exchange between firms with high marginal abatement costs (eager to minimise their extra costs) and those with low marginal abatement costs (prepared to fight emission drastically since it costs relatively little to them) will be profitable. At the margin, the high-costs firms are willing to pay for extra permits as long as the permits cost less than the firms' high marginal costs (and that is likely as the permits will come from low-cost firms), and if low-costs firms sell them they will earn a rent. As a result, the target emission total will be accomplished at the lowest cost. Moreover, once the system is in place, its transaction costs are small except for random checks on actual emissions. A problematic aspect of such permit markets is the determination of the initial total and distribution of the allowed pollution. If the EU legislator (EP and Council) does not succeed in fending off lobbying for exemptions and 'credits' for all kinds of reasons, it will end up paying some sort of implicit subsidy to industry by allowing firms to avoid extra costs. The counterpart of that is a low price for carbon dioxide and low effectiveness. Over time, and if the price is high enough, such markets will induce technical progress towards low-emission technology, in particular if stricter limits are announced long before.

Most EU regulation, whether command and control or market based, is founded on the 'polluter pays' principle. In *ex ante* policies, where the

[27]It is not possible to deal with all instruments in an illustrative section like this. One could include environmental liability as well.

ADDITIONAL READING *continued*

polluters are known and targeted beforehand, this presents no problem. *Ex post* or, for instance, in the case of oceanic pollution, the principle is hard to apply. The EU has recently embraced a radically different principle: the precautionary principle. Its application is found in health and environmental areas but only in special instances. If the suspected consequences of substances or emissions are likely to be grave and irreversible, and if scientific knowledge about causes and effects is severely underdeveloped or insufficient, measures should be based on 'precaution'. This idea may or may not be proved correct decades later, but at the moment that regulation is to be decided, traditional RIAs (see section 4.3.2) are bound to be inappropriate since they require science-based risk assessment. Even in such risk assessment, margins of uncertainty are often large but one accepts having to work within them. If the proposed measures under the precautionary principle are far-reaching or very costly (for example, the banning of certain chemicals; short-time reduction paths in carbon dioxide emission for, say, all countries), policies can be extremely controversial, without disposing of a RIA-type discipline to come to a shared assessment of the issue (as, incidentally, the WTO requires before measures impinging upon market access can be applied to WTO partners).[28]

4.5 Is the EU over- or underregulated?

The regulatory *acquis* has enormously increased since the mid-1980s, while at the same time its underlying principles have become more rational. These conflicting signals have caused confusion. It is sometimes claimed that the Union is overregulated. Note first that 'the' Union can, in political discourse, refer to the collection of the Member States. Indeed, in recent economic studies (for example, Nicoletti & Scarpetta, 2003), empirical evidence is provided for overly heavy and costly *national* regulation in labour markets and services. Quite another question is whether, *at the EU level,* the Union is over- or perhaps underregulated. Figure 4.3 sketches a simplified framework to illustrate this crucial issue.

Behind the pressures for *overregulation* at EU level, many factors can be hidden. Figure 4.3 does not pretend that all the ideological or business or NGO motivations are brought into the picture. Almost always, however, is there an initial though diverse 'stock' of regulation at Member States level which somehow has to be accommodated or adjusted. In turn, this stock may entail sunk costs or hidden benefits for some (if national rules were raising rivals' costs, for example) and this may prompt some Member States to favour a replica of their rules at EU level with minimal adaptation. Thus, replacing command-and-control legislation by (EU) market-based policies is bound to be difficult and slow as it may negatively affect vested interests. Also, QMV is a significant improvement compared with unanimity but far from a guarantee of best-practice regulation because it might not always provide enough discipline to a (majority) coalition of regulation-prone countries on a certain issue. Furthermore, a lot of implementation rules (especially with respect to food laws or health and safety in the workplace) are effectively decided in hundreds of committees (of national representatives and the Commission). This so-called comitology is a useful form of delegation of technical regulation except for the lack of a 'guardian' to protect the EU against excessively intrusive rules. Finally, 'overregulation' in the EU need not be attributable to the EU level, or not only to it. One important reason is the incompleteness of the internal market (for example, in labour markets, patent laws, certain services) which leaves in place a myriad of different national laws, without much 'free' movement.

Under unanimity this can lead to excessively costly compromises or a stalemate which may be expensive as well. Another reason is the lack of discipline about 'cumulation' of EU and national regulation (sometimes regional and local, as well) or about the 'gold plating' by Member States of relatively 'light' EU directives, raising the cost of regulation.[29]

[28]For a critique of the precautionary principle, see Majone (2002).

[29]Gold plating occurs when Member States use the occasion of the transposition of a directive into national law for the addition of all kinds of other requirements or procedures, not necessarily for proper implementation. This happens frequently.

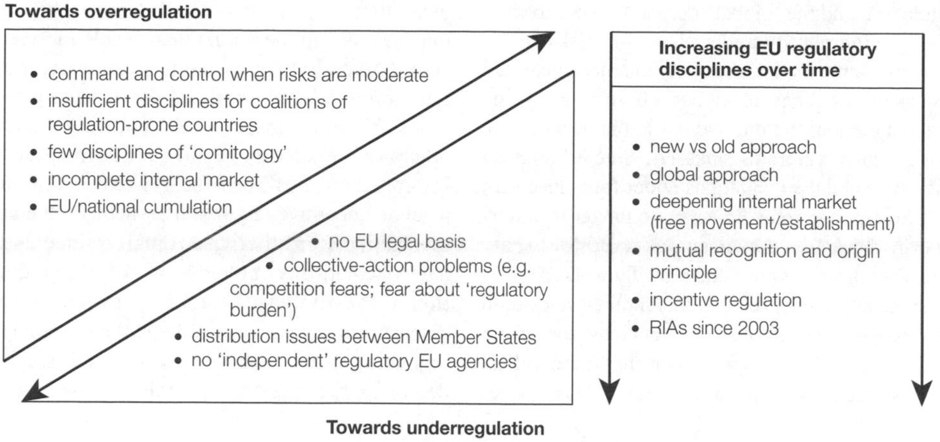

Figure 4.3 Reasons for EU over- and underregulation

A multi-tier system of government that is not a federation also runs the risk of *underregulation.* One obvious reason is the lack of any, or of a sufficient, legal basis in the treaty. If the problem to be regulated is part of the internal market, one can take refuge in the catch-all Article 308 EC, but that is under unanimity. The dreadful saga about the Community patent is one example where the failure of an EU solution has been very costly to the EU economy. A group of no less than 25 Member States is also likely to suffer from 'collective action' problems (as in a prisoners' dilemma) where the uncertainty about the quality of the common solution may eventually lead to the worst solution in terms of welfare. Fears about business' competitiveness in the short run may preclude sensible regulation. This is the more so if regulation is seen to impair EU business prospects in the world markets as well. A similar motive might consist of fears that the EU is, or becomes, 'overregulated', even if the cause of this fear can be traced to the Member State level. An example is the fierce rejection by EU business of a carbon tax as proposed in the early 1990s by the Commission. A carbon tax is a 'regulatory' tax supposed to influence market conduct; it is not meant, in and of itself, to augment tax revenue. Nevertheless, business widely feared that it would do just that: raise the overall tax burden. Note that the EU level does not pocket the tax nor can it decide on the overall level and structure of national taxation. In such a collective action setting, no common action will be possible although the market failure remains. EU measures may also run into opposition from a 'blocking minority' under QMV because enough Member States fear adverse consequences for their business. An example is the takeover bid directive first proposed in 1989 and followed by a litany of amended proposals over a period of fifteen years. In 2004, a directive was adopted because of a stalemate in the EP and against the will of Commissioner Bolkestein.[30] Finally, under the so-called Meroni doctrine of the EC Court, the EU cannot establish independent regulatory agencies except by amendment of the treaty. In network industries, where all Member States find it indispensable to closely guard liberalisation and competition on a day-to-day basis by agencies having *ex ante* and intervening powers, the internal market of network industries must make do with an inferior combination of the competition powers of the Commission, and relatively soft, slow and complicated cooperative mechanisms between national regulators (see Chapter 8).

It is far from easy to draw a general conclusion from these opposing forces about EU regulation. What is possible, however, is to recognise the learning process about EU regulation *over time.* On the right-hand side of Figure 4.3, six important disciplines are listed which have, *ceteris paribus*, led EU regulation to be less heavy-handed or more market based (that is, less costly). The first two (the 'new approach' of minimum approximation mainly as to objectives in

[30]In such a case, the Commission has the option of withdrawing the proposal which makes legislation impossible. However, in a surprising turnaround, the (split) Commission did not support the Commissioner for this withdrawal. The upshot is that the EU may be saddled with a directive that does not solve the problem at hand.

goods regulation, and the 'global approach' of conformity assessment at high quality and scaled as to risk) are an enormous improvement on the detailed and piecemeal 'old approach' in goods. They have also contributed to the faster establishment of the internal market in areas where at first no agreements were feasible. The Single European Act has strengthened the obligations under free movement and establishment (approximation can no longer in and by itself for ever block free movement, as it did for twenty years in transport), and this has undoubtedly worked out as a discipline on subsequent regulation. Another innovation is mutual recognition and, in some services, the origin principle. In section 4.3.3 it was shown that these radical principles are often resisted. Nevertheless, this does not mean that they never work. Whenever they apply, they impose a discipline on national regulation via full exposure to intra-EU competition, without creating any EU regulation. Clearly, without these principles, in some cases free movement would not have arisen, and in others EU regulation would have been agreed. Another improvement has been the gradual acceptance at EU level of 'incentive regulation', whether via market-based mechanisms or otherwise. Finally, since 2003 the EU has systematically applied RIAs for all new draft legislation at the EU level. Ideally, it should be capable of disciplining or exposing at least the tendencies of over-regulation in, for example, the Council. However, RIAs do not apply (as yet) to comitology.

4.6 Summary

Regulation is a core business of the EU. It is forgoing the great benefits of a better functioning internal market if market failure is not corrected; but it is equally important to avoid (EU) regulation when the costs do not outweigh the benefits or when the combination of national regulation with fully applicable free movement is a superior solution. Even if EU regulation is justified by overcoming market failures, the costs can be minimised in a number of ways, dealt with throughout the chapter.

In the overwhelming majority of cases outside agriculture, EU regulation is called for to help establish the internal market and/or to make it function better. This can best be explained with the help of the 'internal market triangle' combining liberalisation, regulation (and mutual recognition) and competition. The four market failures (externalities, internalities, market power, public goods) can directly be connected to the three complements of liberalisation in this triangle. The market failures are first set out for goods and subsequently for services, where especially internalities are a prominent reason to regulate.

The regulatory *acquis* of the internal market is surveyed with the help of a summary matrix, linking the most important topics for regulation based on the four market failures, with the five component markets of the EU internal market (goods, services, capital, labour, technology). This (unique) survey attempts to enhance the reader's understanding of the actual scope and meaning of EU regulation, based on market failures.

The questions of at what level (EU or national) the Union should regulate, and how (and how not), are analysed at length. After testing EU regulation for subsidiarity and proportionality, the merits of regulatory impact assessment, widely practised in the EU since early 2003, are inspected. An important EU innovation aiming to discipline regulatory impulses of Member States, without replacing national rules by EU rules, is 'mutual recognition'. It is shown that the obstacles to enjoying more mutual recognition in the internal market than we do today are attributable not so much to the benefits as to the significant, but so far ignored, costs of the principle. A cost/benefit analysis is provided in regulatory, strategic and economic welfare terms. A wider perspective on the overall EU regulatory strategy concludes this section. The strategy comprises a series of useful disciplines at both levels of government.

Most of EU regulation is risk regulation. The basic economics of risk regulation are set out, including a brief excursion into the 'statistical value of life' approach to measure the benefits of such regulation. An illustration for environmental (EU) regulation is elaborated, with the help of a graphical analysis.

The chapter concludes with an analytical framework to assess whether the EU is over- or underregulated. After emphasising the critical distinction between the 'Europe of Member States' regulating too much or too little versus the EU level as such, the analysis is strictly focused on the latter. It is shown that the answer has three aspects: driving forces over- and underregulating the EU, and a forceful long-run trend at EU level to promote or invent a range of disciplines to contain the reach of EU regulation and/or its costs.

PART 2 Internal Market

The internal market forms the hard core of the Union's economic integration. It is defined as the effective realisation of the relevant freedoms of movement (products, services, factors), with the explicit provision of 'no frontiers', and the freedom of establishment. Part 2 deals with the realisation of the relevant freedoms (negative integration), and the accompanying approximation (positive integration). The other elements of positive integration closely linked to the establishment and proper functioning of the internal market are four common policies (agriculture, competition, trade and industrial), to be addressed in Part 3. Besides the methods of negative and positive market integration, Part 2 provides the basics of theoretical and empirical economic impact analysis. Both normative economic assessment and economic impact analysis are provided.

The structure of Part 2 is simple. Pairs of chapters deal with goods and factors respectively. For services it is slightly different. Chapter 5 goes into the method of EU goods market integration, with the customs union as an intermediate case. Chapter 6 gives the relevant economic analysis, both customs union theory (including instances of imperfect competition) and empirical impact analysis. The economic impact of EC goods market integration (again, for goods only) is dealt with at some length. Chapter 7 deals with both method and economic analysis of market integration of services other than network industries. Brief excursions into the areas of financial services and road transport are made. Chapter 8 is entirely devoted to liberalisation and regulation of network industries in the internal market; telecoms and air transport are studied a little more closely and four case studies illustrate other network industries. Chapter 9 gives a survey of the methods of EU factor market integration, with an economic impact analysis being provided in Chapter 10. Some aspects are intimately linked with the policy chapters later in the book (for example, labour in Chapter 15, technology and intellectual property rights in Chapter 14, financial capital in Chapter 17).

CHAPTER 5

Goods Market Integration: Method

Topics covered

- 5.1 Framework for goods market integration
- 5.2 Building the customs union
- 5.3 From customs union to goods market integration
- 5.4 Removing barriers in the internal market
- 5.5 Summary

The methods for achieving goods market integration are multivariate because goods market integration requires the removal of very different kinds of intra-union barriers. Among modern, regulated economies with interventionist governments, which also impose taxes, the customs union (CU) will not be sufficient to attain a single goods market. The CU will 'merely' remove intra-union tariffs and quotas. Moving beyond the CU to accomplish true goods market integration requires the removal of a host of regulatory barriers, of fiscal barriers and of discrimination in public procurement and public works. Where sectoral interventionism is particularly heavy (for example coal, steel, agriculture in the 1950s), it might even require a considerable degree of joint interventionism before free movement can be realised.

Section 5.1 discusses the Rome Treaty framework for goods market integration as a combination of liberalisation, approximation and common policies for goods. Section 5.2 explains the building of the custom union in some detail, both internal removal and the setting of common tariffs and quotas. The mechanisms for shifting from the CU to true goods market integration is addressed in section 5.3. Section 5.4 provides short surveys of the methods of removing discrimination in public procurement, technical barriers and fiscal ones in the internal market for goods.

5.1 Framework for goods market integration

Goods market integration is governed by a treaty framework going far beyond a mere customs union. As a subset of the structure sketched in Figure 2.1, it contains a mixture of liberalisation, approximated national regulation and common policies. Figure 5.1 depicts these three constituent elements of the Rome Treaty regime and enumerates the most important provisions comprised by each one of them. The picture is completed by a reference to flanking policies and to (temporary and permanent) exceptions to, and derogations from, free goods movement.

5.1.1 Liberalisation and approximation

As noted in section 1.6, the Rome Treaty opted for a CU covering all goods trade. The treaty also takes a comprehensive view of what the GATT, Article 24

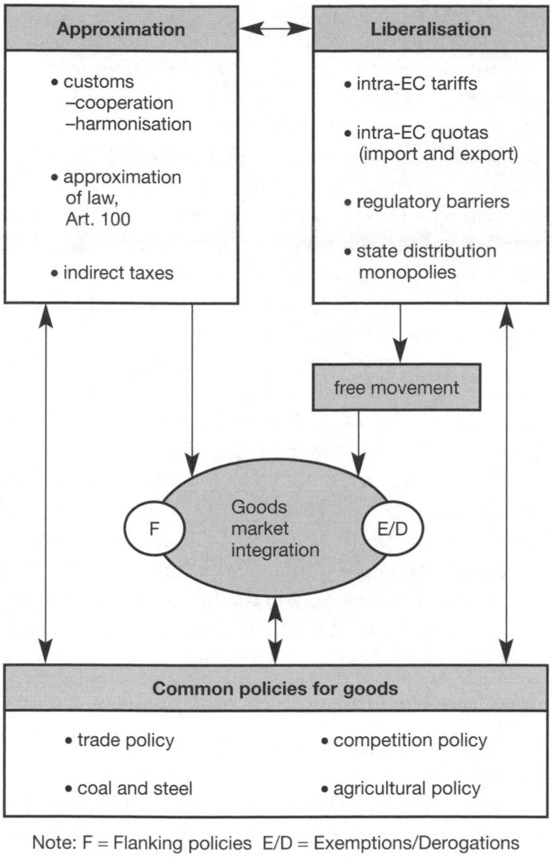

Figure 5.1 Goods market integration in the Rome Treaty

calls 'other restrictive regulations of commerce'. This maximalist ambition should be read in the liberalisation box in Figure 5.1: para-fiscal charges, stamp duties (beyond the cost price of a service provided) and other 'charges with equivalent effects to tariffs'; intra-EC import and export quotas as well as 'measures with an equivalent effect to' quotas; and any discrimination in the purchasing and distribution of goods by the various state trading monopolies still existing in the late 1950s (for example, on tobacco, salt, newsprint paper, matches) were all outlawed. Although more ambitious than any CU thus far, it could still be argued that this CU, essentially the result of the liberalisation box, was within the overall terms defined by the GATT. However, it does have the unique feature of 'free movement', one of the key principles of EC market integration. Since the application of this principle is subject to common judicial review, it has a powerful liberalising effect far beyond a CU as defined by the GATT. The EC framework for goods is moved further beyond a GATT-based CU to a regime for goods market integration by approximation and common policies, on which the GATT is silent.

The aims of the approximation box are unclear because it is open-ended. Its evolutionary character would largely depend on the political will to approximate (or 'harmonise') so as to remove or reduce remaining distortions (indeed, sometimes outright blockages of free goods movement). In a grouping of six, fifteen or twenty-five countries, the perceived need to approximate will rarely be completely uniform. More often than not, distortions hint at vested interests being promoted or protected. Therefore, a critical factor consists in the efficiency of the decision-making system to produce joint regulation, reducing goods market failures of this kind. The most important inefficiency in the early EEC consisted in compromise regulation far beyond the need to deal with the market failure at issue. The latter was generated by an endless search for consensus, under veto threats, resulting in superfluous details so as to 'buy off' the vested interests of one or more Member States. So progress was slow, many failures (that is, vetoes) were encountered and the harmonisation achieved often overcame the market failure in the CU only by imposing a degree of regulatory failure. This flaw would be removed only by a complete overhaul of the regulatory economic strategy of the Union, which emerged from the EC-1992 programme (see section 4.3.4).

The hesitations about scope and economic justification of approximation apply to all three categories specified in the approximation box in Figure 5.1. This is surprising in so far as customs cooperation and approximation are concerned. In the light of the ambitious CU opted for, the liberalisation and approximation boxes were hardly consistent. Thus, whereas the liberalisation box combined with EC competition policy aimed at a competitively functioning internal goods market, the approximation provisions for national customs (Vaulont, 1981) were designed to do no more than the barest minimum, without much regard for the costs of cross-border business. Since the customs also handled the complicated border adjustments for indirect taxes, an EC failure to use the competence for indirect tax approximation exacerbated this inconsistency. The general provision for approximation of laws (Article 94 EC) added to these contradictions: with tariffs and quotas removed, a string of regulatory barriers still effectively prevented goods market integration in the CU. Lacking international precedents in removing regulatory barriers, at first the EC dramatically underestimated both scope and technicality of this kind of approximation. Moreover, one should bear in mind that the postwar period witnessed a significant intensification of economic regulation in the entire developed world. For the EC's goods market integration, this meant that a permanent regulatory drive at national level was not governed by a binding EC framework. All that Article 94 suggested doing was to remove barriers, under unanimity, once they were in place and identified. Unlike tariffs, there was no easy way to identify new regulatory barriers. Apart from a few complaints, numerous new barriers would go unnoticed. Hence, in an almost invisible way, regulatory barriers actually *increased* in the CU. Until 1985, the EC had no regulatory strategy to cope with this profound problem.

5.1.2 Common policies for goods markets

The common policies box is no doubt highly ambitious, at least in a political sense. The economic question is whether the common policies were facilitating goods market integration by addressing actual or potential market failures or removing costly inconsistencies in national policies. Set against this test, the treaty regime is less than satisfactory, or at best open-ended.

The common trade policy appears to match the ambition of the liberalisation box. The establishment of the common external tariff (CET) is largely specified in non-discretionary terms, and a common trade policy, going far beyond the CET requirement in the GATT, is introduced. Both elements are explicitly placed in a liberal context by stressing the goal of contributing to multilateral trade liberalisation. Initially, the Community lived up to such expectations. Although the CET would come into force in 1970, its actual introduction was brought forward by one and a half years. By that time the EC had already negotiated the arithmetically calculated CET in two GATT Rounds, thereby reducing it on average by nearly 30 per cent from the originally foreseen level. Also, at the outset, very few EC-wide quotas were adopted – the thrust was to abolish remaining national quotas as leftovers of the OEEC liberalisation programme of the 1950s.

But in three distinct areas the EC was not living up to the letter or the spirit of the GATT. In agriculture, the GATT had never been allowed to work: European countries (with the partial exception of the UK) had been protectionist and agricultural trade resulted largely from shortages, hardly ever from free trade and specialisation. The USA, though less protectionist on some agricultural goods, obtained a GATT waiver in 1955 for not having to apply GATT rules to agricultural trade. The EEC treaty options of the common agricultural policy (CAP) did not necessitate high external protection, but one could have few illusions about it. Of the six Member States, only the Netherlands practised a mixture of openness and moderate protection of agriculture (see Chapter 11). The second exception were national quotas *vis-à-vis* third countries. A consistent application of the GATT concept of a CU implies either their removal or the replacement of them by CU-wide quotas. *A fortiori,* this would be necessary if the aim is goods market integration rather than a mere CU. In contrast to other rules for the transition to CU, the treaty is not explicit about it. The problem grew worse with the advent of special protection against cotton textiles imports from Asia and some other countries. Led by the USA, the Long Term Arrangement on Cotton Textiles was concluded in 1963, effectively carving this trade out of the purview of the GATT. The Arrangement was first based on national quotas (*vis-à-vis* third countries). As a telling example of inconsistency, while the GATT's Dillon Round and the Arrangement were diplomatically linked, the EC as a whole was involved only in the former while Member States negotiated the latter. The upshot was that hundreds of national quotas were *added* and a common EC trade policy in this sector became illusory (see Chapter 13).

The third exception was preferentialism. The Rome Treaty was negotiated in an era of decolonisation. France, Belgium and the Netherlands insisted on preferentialism with existing or former colonies. Thus, the CET should not apply to them (see Chapter 13).

Competition policy is dealt with in a fairly strict and comprehensive fashion. Both collusion among independent firms and monopoly abuse were prohibited, with explicit criteria for exemption in the case of the former. There was a compromise clause on state-owned enterprise and utilities (Article 86 EC). State aids were also prohibited, with explicit criteria for exemption. These rules were intended to prevent subsidies or restrictive business conduct from replacing the removed tariffs and quotas and to help make the internal goods market function properly (see Chapter 12).

The common agricultural markets and a host of interventionist instruments for them, such as price regulation, production subsidies, 'common machinery for stabilising imports or exports' and, as an option, agricultural guidance and guarantee funds, are already specified in the treaty. The critical Article 33 EC (on objectives and policy constraints) is rife with political and social compromises. These several compromises reflect the political reality that the alternative to the CAP – namely, having *national* protectionist agricultural policies – would have been at least as costly, if not more so. As

Chapter 11 will clarify, the intention was not so much to regulate the market to prevent market failures as to guide a very long-term adjustment process in a socially and politically acceptable fashion.

Two instruments, subsequently chosen in the heavily politicised decision making about the CAP, have caused goods market integration to be realised at extremely high economic costs: the variable levies on imports from third countries and the administrative price level chosen for the linchpin of the most interventionist goods market regime, grain. The variable levies were specified in such a way that they throttled import competition, irrespective of world prices. The intra-EC price level chosen in 1964 was so high that the inefficient German agriculture would hardly be forced to adjust. The implication was that the CU's normal function of stimulating specialisation through trade between areas with different cost levels (caused by comparative advantages and inefficiencies) was largely pre-empted.

Finally, the coal and steel sector fell under the Paris Treaty of 1951. For decades the EEC and ECSC treaties were applied side by side, although the two are quite different for goods markets. First of all, the ECSC treaty has no CET and no common commercial policy. Strictly speaking, it is not a customs union but a free trade area. Second, the ECSC treaty is rather interventionist, especially when a 'manifest crisis' is declared by Council (Article 58 ECSC). Case Study 14.1 on the ECSC and steel crises gives further details.

Gradually, however, the EEC and ECSC regimes began to converge in a pragmatic way. The greatest contribution to this development is, no doubt, the EC Court's doctrine of 'implied powers', pronounced in 1978. It means that the ECSC does imply a common commercial policy if, and in so far as, the pursuit of its objectives and the use of (intra-EC) instruments require such a policy for consistency. In the early 1990s the Union decided to integrate the ECSC into the EC treaty by 2002.

5.1.3 Flanking/supporting policies and exceptions

The triangular regime of liberalisation, approximation and common policies makes for a quite comprehensive system seeking to ensure goods market integration. This was bolstered by flanking policies. Most prominent was the common transport policy as an essential complement of the free movement of goods. Of course, transport is a service, but its free movement was part of a separate treaty chapter on a common transport policy. Two related questions concerned how to make EC transport both least distorted and cheap, and how to regulate at EC level the nationally regulated transport markets while providing the greatest possible freedom for market agents. Again, views differed partly because of a fear of losing market share at home, partly because of national differences in social charges and taxation, partly because the public and economic function of some modes of transport was perceived differently,[1] partly because of fears of free-riding on one another's infrastructure. As a result, the Council was convicted by the EC Court as late as 1985 for a 'failure to act' (Article 232 EC) on a common transport policy. Meanwhile, this policy is in place (see Chapter 7). A third issue was how to obtain an efficient EC transport system serving goods market integration effectively. Great progress has been achieved on this point despite the initial lack of a common policy. The earlier establishment of a common policy could undoubtedly have enhanced the efficiency drive as the response to EC-1992 in transport has shown. In its absence, improvements were obtained through technological progress of the means of transport, and domestic infrastructural investments (weakly coordinated in the UN Economic Commission for Europe and the OECD-linked European Conference of Ministers of Transport, but not by the EC for long), and the resulting shifts in the modal split (especially, the increase in the market share of road haulage).

Exchange rates, or rather balance of payments problems – the form they took in the Bretton Wood system of adjustable pegs, at the time of treaty drafting – constituted another flanking problem. Misaligned rates could cause such tensions in national currency markets and such a drain of foreign exchange reserves that far-reaching national safeguards were provided for in Articles 108 and 109 EEC (now deleted and replaced by EMU articles). No change of regime was introduced once flexible exchange rates had become accepted (after 1970). The upshot was that goods market integration was permanently in danger, and worse, was permanently hampered by retained or varying exchange controls. In 1986, six out of twelve EC Member States still had exchange controls. Measures to restrict intra-EC trade (as distinct from financial) flows had been prohibited by the EC Court in the mid-1970s but the safeguard only disappeared with the EC-1992 programme (see Chapters 9 and 17).

[1]Hence the so-called modal split (the substitution between, and complementarity of, different modes of transport) differed significantly between Member States.

Other flanking policies were of minor importance: an endeavour to come to social policy approximation was very weakly formulated and led to little except for the (explicitly treaty-based) laws regarding equality between men and women; the Social Fund served as an adjustment fund but was trivial; and the European Investment Bank initially remained marginal (see Chapter 15).

Finally, it is interesting to observe that there were exceptions to the regime. The permanent exceptions include some important limitations of the treaty:

- The CU does not apply to military goods; the difficulty is then to delineate double-purpose goods from 'purely' military goods.
- State ownership is entirely a matter of the Member States; the EC never had any influence on privatisation or nationalisation – in practice this weakened the EC competition policy *vis-à-vis* state-owned enterprises up to the 1980s (see Chapter 12).
- Industrial and intellectual property rights are similarly in the purview of national jurisdictions (because they refer to 'ownership' too); this has yielded incentives to exploit the possibilities for price discrimination between Member States; the EC Court curbed this potential by courageous case law but weaker forms of market failure continue to trouble the internal market even today (for example patents, trademarks; see Chapter 9).

The regime of goods market integration is the hard core of the EEC treaty. The goods regime is a condition *sine qua non* for the Union. It is also the regime with the widest scope and the greatest impact.

5.2 Building the customs union

Article 23 EC defines the CU. It is to cover all goods and refers to tariffs and 'all charges having equivalent effect'. Described in this way the CU applies also to agriculture, even though the CAP is treated in a separate title. In a simple economic analysis one could define the CAP as an agricultural CU, with internal and border interventions ensuring a politically agreed minimum price. Article 23 defines the CU purely as a 'tariff union'. Quotas and import and distribution monopolies are dealt with in a separate chapter. Strictly, this is not in keeping with GATT; practically it hardly matters in so far as intra-EC quotas must be removed anyway. For national quotas *vis-à-vis* third countries the distinction does matter and the problem can be resolved only by an appropriate common commercial policy specified elsewhere in the treaty.

ADDITIONAL READING

Internal liberalisation

It is interesting and instructive to study the method of internal (stepwise) liberalisation so as to arrive at the CU. Only some crucial aspects will be highlighted here.[2] Intra-EC tariff removal was expected to take twelve years and would be across the board. The twelve year transition period was broken down into three stages. The timing and percentages sliced off were prescribed for the first two stages. This *automaticity* was combined with modest flexibilities for the first stage, for purposes of varying the speed and reducing the costs of adjustment for sensitive sectors.[3] Though not explicitly mentioned, the idea was to have 60 per cent sliced off after two stages. It did specify the aim for the Member States to slice off at least 25 per cent per tariff line in both stages. Although the third stage is not detailed, the timetable of reductions is subject only to a qualified majority in Council.

Since initial tariffs of some countries were high, tariff disparities were likely to influence the time path and country distribution of adjustment costs. Thus, the first reductions of a prohibitive tariff would have no impact while, at the same time, similar reductions of a medium or lower tariff might cause strong import competition. Later on, a relatively sudden exposure to import competition would follow for the high-tariff country. Not only could this cause social or political resentment, it might have the unfortunate effect that, initially, export opportunities

[2] A little more detail can be found in Chapter 5 of the 2nd edition.

[3] For instance, every tariff line had to be reduced by at least 5 per cent.

ADDITIONAL READING *continued*

would be denied to the adjusting sector in the low-tariff country, whereas such export opportunities would be available for the high-tariff country by the time that sector would be forced to adjust. The treaty could have prescribed an accelerated reduction for peak tariffs or a 'decapping' procedure, cutting off all peaks beyond a given *ad valorem* duty. However, a politically less sensitive obligation was opted for: all tariffs higher than 30 per cent had to be reduced by one-tenth each time in the first stage, allowing no flexibility. The case of dumping was dealt with in the competition rules. Interesting is the 'reverse dumping' clause of Article 91(2) EEC: exploiting tariff disparities via dumping is made risky because dumped goods can be re-imported into the exporting country free of tariffs or quotas. If transaction costs are not too high, 'reverse dumping' sets an effective limit to dumping practices.

The strictness of the internal liberalisation in the transition period was combined with calls upon Member States to accelerate tariff cuts. The latter option was used twice by all the Six together so that the actual transition period was only ten and a half years. Figure 5.2 shows the reduction path.

The success of the internal tariff removal should not mislead the reader into believing that no problems were perceived when negotiating the treaty. Two sets of provisions reflect those: the procedure to move to stage 2 and the 'special regime' for France. A complicated Article 17 EC defines three stages, each of four years' duration. The real problem is feared to consist in the transition from the first to the second stage. Failing unanimity, the first stage can twice be extended for a year;[4] only after six years does the Council shift to qualified majority. Those outvoted could opt for an arbitration procedure described in the same article. Although uniquely strict for diplomatic practices in those days, a measure of uncertainty and political discretion was created. What if no qualified majority could be found for whatever cyclical or other reason? What if arbitration sided with the outvoted Member State? These uncertainties would undoubtedly have been magnified if economic times during transition had been bad. As it turned out, a high-growth/low-unemployment climate facilitated the transition period and the special procedures in Article 17 EC were

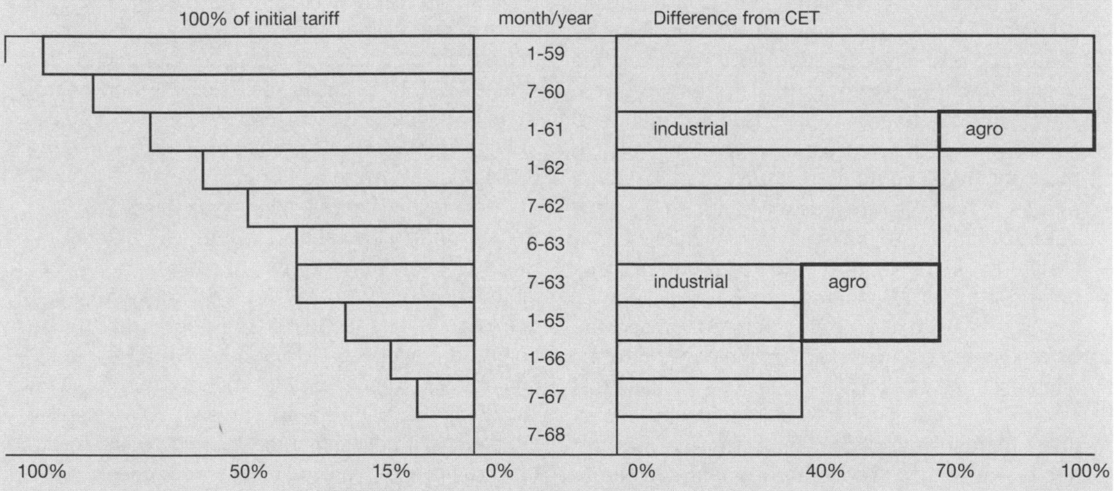

Figure 5.2 Intra-EC tariff reduction and CET building

[4]However, one Member State could not block the decision merely because it had not fulfilled its first-stage obligation in time (Art. 8(3) EEC).

ADDITIONAL READING ***continued***

never used. It should also be noted that greater automaticity was imposed for the other two stages (any Member State could veto a delay) and unambiguous obligations were prescribed for the expiry of the transitional period.

The 'special regime' for France reflected another weakness: a CU with pegged exchange rates is unsustainable if misalignments cannot be prevented or readily resolved. However, imposing far-reaching coordination of macroeconomic policies to prevent realignments and/or common decision making before accepting realignments would have increased the ambition of the CU enormously. Given the lack of macroeconomic ambitions, Articles 107(2), 108 and 109 EEC had to deal with the possibly disruptive consequences of misalignments, a major devaluation or restrictions with a view to upholding the exchange rate at the expense of intra-EC economic intercourse. Worse still, before signing and during the ratification procedure of the Rome Treaty, French attempts to solve the balance of payments problem for the franc area (which included its colonies in West Africa) threatened to undermine intra-EC liberalisation commitments from the outset. In a special protocol, France had been allowed to keep its system of across-the-board export subsidies and special import charges for the protection of the franc until balance of payments equilibrium and sufficient foreign exchange reserves would enable the Council (by qualified majority) to abolish this special regime. This regime amounted to a hidden devaluation. Such a major set of restrictions hardly inspired confidence in the liberalisation process once the EEC treaty came into force (1 January 1958). Other Member States were now dependent on the French political resolve to impose domestic austerity or otherwise face a major devaluation or – worse still – would have to take safeguard measures themselves. After more than a year of hesitation, a new French government decided to opt for a devaluation in late 1958 combined with the abolition of the special regime, just before the first intra-CU tariff reduction would come into force.

The conclusion is therefore that the CU regime combined strictness with some significant weaknesses: automaticity was not fully accepted and the unquestioned preference for pegged exchange rates was tied to inadequate coordination provisions, thereby risking prompting restrictions and safeguards which would undermine the very market integration aimied for.

The internal liberalisation of quotas was tough. First, the quota removal covered agriculture and goods traded by commercial state monopolies. Both were highly sensitive and the unambiguous commitment to liberalise was no mean achievement. Second, a standstill clause and the 'ratchet effect' made rearguard protectionist lobbying practically impossible. The ratchet effect refers to the definitive nature of liberalisation: there being no going back. This was accomplished by a combination of automaticity (based on specific treaty percentages and timetables), the across-the-board coverage rather than discretion per tariff line and the prohibition of unilateral reimposition of quotas. Third, and critical for the preparedness of low-tariff countries to liberalise, the CU imposed tariff and quota removal simultaneously. Fourth, just like in the case of quasi-tariffs, 'measures with an equivalent effect' to quotas would also be forbidden (Article 28 EC), except for certain derogations for health and safety, and so on (Article 30 EC). However, for the latter, 'approximation' was provided for under Article 94 EC. Fifth, not only were quotas under state trading (that is, state import and distribution monopolies) forbidden, but Article 31 EC prescribed that, by the end of the transitional period, all discrimination with respect to imports or domestic procurement and marketing or distribution had to be eliminated.

Technically, liberalisation took place by first transforming bilateral quotas into 'global' quotas, that is, 'open without discrimination to all other Member States' (Article 33(1), now deleted), after one year. Subsequently, these quotas had to be enlarged in value by 20 per cent overall annually, and at least 10 per cent per product. After ten years all quotas had to be equal to at least 20 per cent of the national production of the relevant goods. Unlike tariff removal, no special delays were possible. An acceleration clause was included. At the end of the transitional period, quotas had to be abolished.

Initial intra-EC quota abolition was therefore stricter than tariffs. Discretion was limited and there were no provisions for a staged approach or delays.

5.2.1 Setting common tariffs and quotas

Setting the CET and, where necessary, common quotas, is likely to be more politicised than internal liberalisation. When participating in a CU, all players are expected to accept the GATT rule of zero intra-tariffs and no intra-CU quotas. This is not the case for the CET. One would expect the CET to have a protective function (see also Chapter 6). So, there is bound to be active lobbying for influencing the CET at the level of individual tariff lines, but also with respect to the overall restrictive effect for end products, the structure of tariffs over respective processing stages ('effective protection'), the downward or upward adjustment of tariffs between members with tariff disparities, and the position of outsiders via bilateral pressures and the Article 24 GATT review procedure. All this political economy can be constrained or even pre-empted by automaticity in treaty rules, just as with internal liberalisation. But achieving such rules will be extremely difficult for the CET because setting the CET boils down to a shift from one set of tariffs to another set of tariffs, not to an adjustment from one set of tariffs to zero for all. Moreover, the GATT 'general incidence' clause (see Chapter 1) is vague. Although at the time of drafting the treaty, CU theory (see Chapter 6) was available as a rough guide to interpret the general incidence clause, its practical application leaves ample room for discretion.

Since the negotiators of the EEC treaty wanted simple rules to minimise the political economy and because they did not want to lose the momentum of political will, Article 19(1), now deleted, specifies the CET as the arithmetic average of the *ex ante* national tariffs. This implied that, in most cases, France and Italy had to reduce tariffs and the Benelux countries to increase tariffs. Germany was in an intermediate position. However, as might be expected from the contrast between internal and external tariff adjustment in a CU, all kinds of exceptions and amendments were introduced.[5] In this way a rule-based CET setting was *de facto* transformed in a mixture of basic rules (see Figure 5.2) and negotiated adaptation. Broadly speaking, and excluding agricultural products, the deviations did not have the effect of increasing the protectionist impact, but individual tariffs can be identified where this was the case.

The contrast between tariffs and quotas was even greater on the external side than for internal liberalisation. In the free movement of goods title of the treaty there is no reference to quotas *vis-à-vis* third countries. From an economic perspective this is curious since significant disparities in national (external) quotas are likely to result in different competitive pressures, and hence may create distortions of goods market integration. Whether they will, depends on whether the treaty allows trade deflection to take place. Trade deflection is a response to differentials in external trade policies and hence characterises a free trade area (FTA), not a CU. Thus, an FTA may see imports to high-tariff member B deflected via low-tariff member A if certificates of origin would not prevent this. However, once CU members have very different external quotas (or some have no quotas), national prices will be higher in countries with binding quotas than in those with big or no quotas. Hence, trade deflection will pay. This creates an issue of principle because a CU (like the EEC) would not normally impose certificates of origin for internal trade. In order to control trade deflection, however, it will have to. The silence on this issue in the free movement title is therefore inconsistent with a CU. But Article 133 EC merely speaks about 'uniform principles' such as 'the achievement of uniformity in measures of liberalisation' (here, 'liberalisation' refers to quotas). For almost two and a half decades following the end of the transition period this problem remained unresolved. In a package deal in December 1993, based on the EC-1992 programme, remaining national quotas *vis-à-vis* third countries were finally eliminated (see Chapter 13).

5.3 From customs union to goods market integration

5.3.1 Searching for a mother principle

The *economic* notion behind the EEC CU is not clear. Defined merely as a tariff union (as it is in the treaty, Article 23 EC), it suppresses one type of border intervention for trade without having a clue about the change in quotas, voluntary export restraints (VERs), or fiscal or regulatory barriers. If the latter substitute for the former, the gains from trade may remain small. Even if there is no conscious effort to substitute forgone tariff protection, intra-CU tariff removal is still a far cry from internal free trade in goods. A tariff union would imply neither that all sectors are equally exposed to intra-CU

[5]For details, see the Additional Reading on p. 76 of the 2nd edition.

imports nor that all sectors have equal opportunities to penetrate other countries' markets in the CU.

The *policy concept* behind a CU is problematic, too. The origin of CUs goes back several centuries (Viner, 1950) when levying tolls or customs duties were the only trade interventions (other than import bans). What about other border intervention, today? In fact, the implicit CU concept in the EEC treaty could be said to consist of four elements: a tariff union, an indirect tax union, abolition of internal quotas and 'equivalent effect' measures, and, in principle, uniform external quota liberalisation (the word 'common quotas' is not found anywhere). The latter three, however, entail great problems of interpretation which are hard to resolve without a *mother principle.* A major weakness of the Rome Treaty was the lack of such a basic guideline. As a consequence Member States retained interpretations or vetoed proposals, such that fully fledged goods market integration remained unattainable. In this sense the CU could not be completed.

There are two mother principles which suggest themselves. Applying them would have meant a significant increase in ambition, that is, a 'deepening'. The *economic approach* would use goods market integration as the benchmark: all (artificial) economic frontiers in the goods markets would be removed. This would go far beyond the implicit CU, as described above, as it would also encompass an adequate competition policy, appropriate common sectoral policies where necessary, and such a degree of macroeconomic coordination that safeguards would not be used. All these additional elements have a place in the treaty but they are not sufficient. The ambition of the CU, as defined by the four elements mentioned, would also greatly increase if measured against the benchmark of goods market integration. For example, what are 'measures with an equivalent effect' to quotas (Article 28)?

Initially, the interpretation of Article 28 EC was constrained by the lack of a mother principle; hence Member States took a legalistic view of what the EC could do. The EC Court understood the grave inconsistencies this would give rise to. In the *Dassonville* case[6] it provided an economic definition of such measures: 'all trading rules enacted by Member States which are capable of hindering, directly or indirectly, actually or potentially, intra-Community trade'. In so doing it recognised that regulatory barriers had to be added to the elements of the CU already specified. At the same time the actual application of the *Dassonville* definition was limited by major derogations in the treaty, such as Article 30 EC, which could be resolved only by approximation. Also, there was at best a weak legal basis in the treaty for the application of the CU to (indirect) fiscal frontiers or national external quotas. The conclusion is inescapable: getting goods market integration accepted as a mother principle would require treaty revision.

The *policy approach* would simply carry the notion of a customs union to its logical conclusion: a customs union should apply only union customs rules, and internal frontier controls would therefore have to disappear. From a policy perspective this is attractive for several reasons. First, such a benchmark is straightforward. Its automaticity pre-empts a great deal of political economy, arising from vested interests. Second, it dictates a clear and exhaustive policy agenda and facilitates judicial review. Third, it does not impinge upon national regulatory objectives as long as other domestic instruments are found which do not discriminate imports from other Member States.

Removing internal frontiers was not, however, included in the Rome Treaty, so this approach would also require treaty revision. In the period 1970–85 there were few indications that such a revision was ever going to be undertaken. On the contrary, as late as 1979 the Commission prepared a Multi-annual Programme for the Attainment of the CU[7] comprising all kinds of elementary implementation issues, prompted by the fierce independence of the national customs services. It merely referred to the tariff union and even ignored the customs role for statistics about intra-EC trade.

5.3.2 How the Community pursued goods market integration

The intrinsic difficulties of trying to achieve goods market integration with the three boxes depicted in Figure 5.1 would continue to plague the Community from the end of the transition period (1970) up to 1985. All three boxes suffered from shortcomings and there was no mother principle to remedy them once and for all.

Liberalisation measures were implemented if they did not depend on the other two boxes. The cases of state distribution monopolies led to repeated rulings of the EC Court, with the upshot that most of them became defunct or that discrimination was minimised. However, Article 28 EC, prohibiting 'measures with an equivalent effect to' quotas, only began to bite long after the

[6]Case 8/74 *Procureur du Roi v Dassonville* [1974] ECR 837.
[7]OJ C 84 of 31 March 1979.

Dassonville ruling. Its effective scope was greatly limited by the derogations in Article 30 EC (largely on health and safety), and the derogations developed by the Court under a rule of reason (on consumer protection and the environment) – and therefore by the required 'approximation of SHEC' under Article 94 EC.

However, as noted in section 4.3.4 above, approximation turned out to be a failure in two ways. On the one hand, crippled by the unanimity rule, many proposals were blocked in Council or not even tried out by the European Commission; on the other hand, when approximation did result in EC legislation, a degree of regulatory failure crept in because approximation was invariably interpreted as detailed and rigid 'harmonisation'. Thus, in none of the three items specified in the approximation box of Figure 5.1 did the EC make much progress.

Where common policies were affecting goods market integration, gaps and distortive solutions could be observed, both preventing product market integration from being realised. In trade policy gaps included the failure to remove national quotas *vis-à-vis* third countries for various reasons. In competition policy, the neglect of Article 86 EC (on utilities and state-owned enterprises with 'entrusted tasks') and the weak enforcement of the prohibition of certain state aids were major problems. Also, the sectoral policies for agriculture and coal and steel led, at best, to rather distorted forms of intra-EC trade, and not to the removal of economic frontiers.

All this does not mean that intra-EC trade in goods was not intense. The initial liberalisation in the 1960s had caused rapid growth in intra-EC trade and had pushed up the intra-EC share in every Member State's foreign trade, hovering around 50 per cent after the transition period (see Chapter 6). The CU-plus, accomplished by 1985, exhibited much 'deeper' goods market integration than in regionalism anywhere else on the globe. However, it is still a long away from complying with the mother principles. Based on those benchmarks, achieving genuine goods market integration is a great deal more ambitious than a CU-plus. It required the Single European Act, which incorporates a definition of the internal market (Article 14 EC) embracing free movement and no internal frontiers virtually unconditionally, to encompass the mother principles.

This led to a new regulatory strategy. What is conveniently summarised in Table 4.3 has come about only gradually since the late 1970s. With respect to judicial review of the EC Court, based on *Dassonville,* a case law was built up removing regulatory barriers, or at least minimising their distortive impact. This judicial review had a strongly liberalising effect. Gradually, a doctrine on the free movement of goods emerged consisting of a few basic principles that invariably apply. Ignoring the many subtleties of this judicial review, the more important principles include the following:

- *Non-discrimination:* this is a treaty principle (Article 12 EC); national regulation ought not to discriminate between domestic and other EC goods. In a series of rulings the Court extended this even to extreme disparities between taxing domestic spirits (low) and foreign substitutes (high).
- The *Dassonville* test.
- *Mutual recognition:* if SHEC objectives are 'equivalent' between Member States, goods[8] from other Member States have to be (mutually) accepted, despite differences in the detailed specifications of the relevant national laws (this implies a drastic curtailment of the possibilities to hide behind Article 30 EC to maintain regulatory barriers).
- *Proportionality:* if an objective (falling under Article 30) is pursued in national regulation, the regulatory obligations should be proportional to that objective. In practice, this often means that labelling requirements are sufficient and import prohibitions 'disproportional'.
- *Reversing the burden of proof:* in Article 30 cases, the burden of proof of showing that a SHEC objective justifies a national restriction or is not 'equivalent' to those in another Member State falls on the Member State creating the barrier. Usually, this proof must hinge on objective scientific evidence or measurable differences in, for example, safety preferences.

Since the late 1970s the judicial doctrine on free movement of goods has greatly reduced the number and intensity of regulatory barriers on the internal market. A celebrated example is the German beer purity law (see Case Study 5.1).

From an economic perspective, mutual recognition (MR) would appear to be a useful principle to prevent overregulation and the economic barriers between Member States that might result from it. It also preempts a lot of centralised regulation which might stifle markets, and may even induce regulatory competition (see Case Study 4.1). Table 4.3 also shows the considerable costs of MR (see also Atkins, 1997). As a result, the

[8]Besides goods, the Court has also applied this to (equivalent) testing and prohibited duplication (of identical tests) in other Member States.

Commission has become more vigilant and stepped up infringement procedures on MR while promoting greater awareness (COM (1999) 299 of 16 July 1999 on mutual recognition). These practical problems are important because some 28 per cent of intra-EC goods trade is under mutual recognition (Atkins, 1997, pp. 1–6).

The other approach was regulatory and largely represented by EC-1992.[9] The EC-1992 programme in the 1985 White Paper should be understood against the EC achievements at the time. Figure 5.3 attempts to capture how EC-1992 was designed in one single and simple diagram. The measures at issue are divided into four categories: market access (between Member States), competitive conditions in goods markets, the rules ensuring market functioning by preventing market failures, and a range of initiatives in markets other than goods, but which interacted with activities in goods markets.

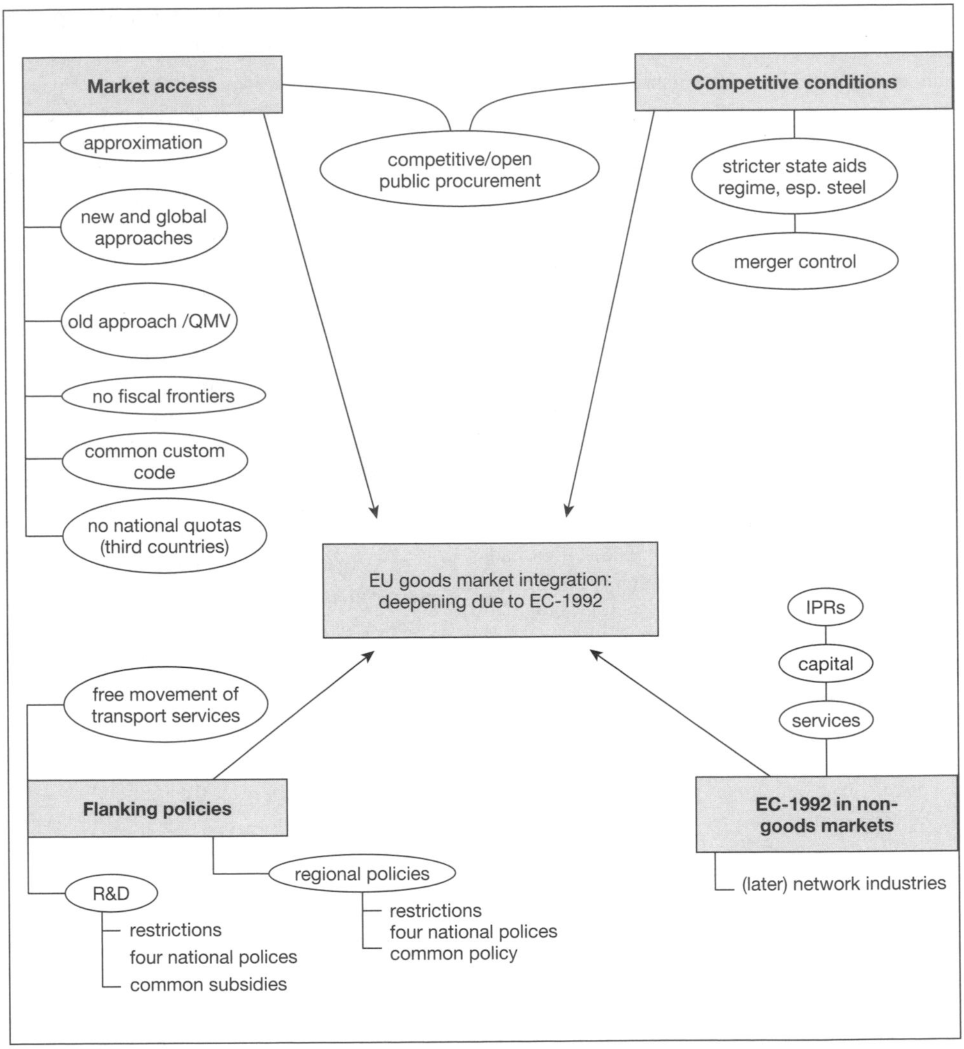

Figure 5.3 How EC-1992 deepened goods market integration

Sources: For details see Pelkmans 1986, 1994a

[9]Not entirely, because two breakthroughs were already accomplished before the 1985 White Paper on EC-1992 was published: a common customs document and the 'new approach' for removing technical barriers. Also, the Court ruling on transport – against the Council – was (one month) before the White Paper.

It shows that the EC-1992 White Paper was ambitious – note that Figure 5.3 mainly refers to the part dealing with goods markets. The customs services and other controls at internal borders were removed, and regulatory and fiscal barriers were tackled with far more resolve. The mother principle had a pervasive effect. However, even this ambition left out the fragmented internal market of energy utilities (gas, electricity), which was added to EC-1992 proposals only in 1988. In the rest of this chapter the methods of removing three main barriers to the accomplishment of goods market integration are briefly elaborated: public procurement, technical barriers and fiscal frontiers.[11]

CASE STUDY 5.1 Beer purity law and judicial mutual recognition

German production and consumption of beer is larger than in any other EU country. Unlike in some other EU countries where dominant brands are often found (in Denmark, 70 per cent of the 1990 home consumption is supplied by Tuborg/Carlsberg; in France, 47 per cent by BSN; in the Netherlands, 50 per cent by Heineken; in Belgium, 60 per cent by Artois–Piedboeuf–Interbrew), concentration in Germany is extremely low. The largest market share of a brewery in Germany (1990) is 6 per cent, with over 1,150 competitors. On the face of it, therefore, Germany is an attractive market for foreign (EU) producers, the penetration of which would not seem to run into a powerful quasi-monopolist.

Yet this inference is incorrect. The German beer market turned out to be very hard to penetrate, for two reasons. First, a technical barrier called the 'beer purity law' (dating back to 1517, when health rules for beer were a major step forward) essentially eliminated the prospects for (foreign or domestic) mass beers, produced with economies of scale, and using chemical catalysts (to speed up the brewing process) and preservatives (for long-distance supplies and storage). A seemingly innocuous regulation thereby protected beers with a short lifespan, produced in small volumes and unsuitable for consistent marketing in distant markets. Second, strong localised preferences for 'own', local brands, and local control of outlets (beer houses) also formed a barrier to entry as the acceptance of 'national' or 'foreign' brands would require very high sunk costs in marketing and distribution.

The internal market regime should have ensured that at least the regulatory barrier was removed or minimised. Judicial MR has accomplished that in the wake of the *Cassis de Dijon* case.[10] Once the health objectives of national regulations on beer are 'equivalent', MR becomes compulsory for Member States. Thus, one would presume that the European Court would apply MR, so that foreign brands, marketed lawfully in any one Member State, could not be prevented from entering the German beer market, even though these brands might contain residues of catalysts or preservatives. Before the EC Court, the German government argued that beer containing additives should be prohibited because of a danger to health. The Court rejected this argument: not only did other drinks (imperfect substitutes for beers) in Germany lawfully contain additives, it also held that other national governments were just as concerned about the health of their citizens; indeed, millions of Germans routinely consumed beers on holidays or travels in the EU without any trace of fear for their health. The burden of proof was reversed (see section 5.3.2) so that Germany had to provide scientific evidence to the contrary. The Court ruling in 1987 confirmed MR on the basis of equivalence, and the 'beer purity law' was held to violate 'proportionality' (note that the Court thereby wisely avoided having to assess the health grounds in detail; it only established equivalence). If consumer protection were to be of overriding concern, proportionality suggests that objective labelling about ingredients should suffice. The ruling implies that German producers therefore face higher costs as the law retains its validity for them (except, of course, for exports).

The Cecchini report (Cecchini *et al.*, 1988), while recognising very fine product differentiation and taste niches, based its estimate of static 'welfare' benefits on scale arguments, given a best guess about (small) import penetration via supermarkets: the range was ECU 90–215 million a year. The actual long-term impact is hard to estimate as contestability of local breweries may slowly increase over time, yet strong preferences for quality beers are unlikely to alter much.

[10]Case 120/78 '*Cassis de Dijon*' [1979] ECR 649.

[11]Customs law is too specialist for the present volume and is ignored. Most other items mentioned are touched upon elsewhere in this book.

5.4 Removing barriers in the internal market

5.4.1 Towards competitive public procurement

The purely formal prohibition of discrimination in national and regional public procurement, established at the end of the transition period, was totally ineffective. Two procedural EC directives (for procured goods and for public works) gave far too much latitude to continue *de facto* discrimination; moreover, they were not enforced or monitored. The Cecchini report's crude estimates indicated that protectionist procurement and monopolistic supplies to state agencies led to welfare losses of perhaps up to ECU 25 billion, quite apart from effects upon innovation.[12] The report also showed that, in failing to tackle public procurement practices, up to ECU 500 billion of demand for goods would be carved out of the internal market. By 1994, and including public procurement of services as well, this had gone up to ECU 721 billion or ECU 2,000 per EU citizen.[13] In a simple CU this might be defended as outside its purview – although even GATT rules have some impact here – but when striving for goods market integration, this huge omission has to be resolved.

However, there are many forms and instances of public procurement and there are tens of thousands of state organs in the EU falling under procurement rules. Detailed requirements can be onerous and costly for such organs. On the other hand, potential suppliers are loath to incur prior costs of tendering if too many bidders are expected or national biases are suspected (despite the EU rules). Yet, lax rules – though less costly – undermine market access for non-locals and many provide too much discretion for state organs. Thus far, several revisions of EU public procurement rules have not yet resolved these dilemmas in a satisfactory manner (see also Case Study 5.2 below).

5.4.2 Removing technical barriers

There are three types of technical barriers to trade; those arising from:

- differences between (national) goods regulations;
- differences between (voluntary) standards;
- differences in, or duplication of, conformity assessment.

Whereas the first one is obvious, the second might be thought to present no problems since market access is not legally blocked. Yet, where local standards are dominant, market share of foreign entrants may not develop before adherence to that standard is observed. The third barrier can be costly if testing and certification have to be performed in many EU countries.

It is hard to generalise on technical barriers, except that, in very different degrees, they arise in many goods markets. In a qualitative sense, the economic effects of removing them include cost savings due to fewer interruptions of scale production and to lower storage requirements; cost savings because retooling is no longer required and conformity assessment is cheaper and faster; and welfare gains following greater contestability of markets as well as greater incentives to compete on the basis of quality.[14]

Since technical barriers are regulatory barriers, the solution to overcome them had to come from the judicial review about the Article 28 EC prohibition of 'measures with an equivalent effect' to quotas, combined with the Article 30 EC derogations and the approximation called for in Article 94 EC. Remember, the 'old' approach to approximation boiled down to a mixing up of regulation and standards, that is, not only health and safety objectives were specified in the directives but exhaustive technical specifications of product aspects and test methods were also included. With such EC laws there were no incentives to write (voluntary) European standards in those fields. In the relatively few cases where EC directives were adopted despite unanimity, all three barriers were removed in one stroke, but at high costs of rigidity and complexity. Moreover, a major economic and regulatory issue for the internal market was that a steady flow of new national regulations was added to the large stock of technical barriers while the speed of removal was extremely slow (see below and Pelkmans, 1987; see also CEPS, 1992a; Nicolas & Repussard, 1995).

The solution was found in a new regulatory strategy. For the removal of technical barriers it took shape as follows. Inspired by the judicial review of the EC Court, a 'new approach' for the regulatory track was developed in 1985. Based on the principle of 'minimum harmonisation', approximation would henceforth consist of harmonising only the 'essential requirements' of SHEC. In other words, the health (etc.) objectives of machine or

[12] The economics of EC-1992, *European Economy,* 1988, no. 35.
[13] *European Economy,* 1996, no. 4, p. 24.
[14] A much richer economic analysis, focused on standards, is found in Blind (2004) and the survey by Swann (2000).

toy legislation would be included in the EC directive but not the technical specifications. This has two economic advantages: first, by referring to European standards, much greater flexibility is achieved for business as CEN and CENELEC[15] will usually prefer performance standards;[16] second, standards are voluntary and leave room for innovators to 'go around' them, if desired.[17]

Besides the new approach to harmonisation, the 'global approach' has removed the barriers in the conformity assessment for regulated goods. The crux here is MR between Member States' mandated bodies, selected on the basis of quality criteria. This implies independence of the country of certification from the country of production or country of sales: so, one can certify in EU country A even though one produces in B. Given minimum quality criteria for test houses, it also leads to competition in testing. The cost reduction from the global approach is therefore likely to be very considerable (for an authoritative survey, see Machado Jorge, 1995).

CASE STUDY 5.2 Economic effects of competitive public procurement

By 1994 the EC had adopted a series of directives imposing strict procedural rules promoting competitive public procurement.[18] The main principles applied include timely and sufficiently detailed publicity (including publication in the EC Official Journal, if the purchase is above a specified threshold), special obligations for tenders restricted to preselected bidders, mandatory reference to European standards and strict monitoring by the European Commission. The latter can intervene if urgent complaints can be substantiated. The scope of the rules goes far beyond goods bought by public buyers in competitive markets: public works, purchases by utilities (whether public or private) and services bought by public authorities are also covered.

The economic effects of this procurement regime are doubtless positive (although the rules are also perceived as costly). But whether intra-EC trade in 'procurement goods' would become comparable (say, in terms of shares) to other goods is not *a priori* clear. Both price and quality of best bidders from other EC countries may be 'matched' by domestic suppliers, thereby realising 'welfare' gains and greater competitiveness at home, without increasing intra-EC trade directly.[19] Also, with respect to major contracts (for example, supplying to utilities), the procurement regime has sparked numerous joint ventures and alliances across intra-EU borders, with much greater possibilities for tendering 'locally'. Again, this form of inter-firm collaboration suggests a strong indirect effect on intra-EC trade. Presumably the greatest economic impact of breaking down procurement barriers is the credible threat of potential competition in many markets where procurement protection had come to be taken for granted. It is this potential competition which removes the very negative effects on technical efficiency and company performance that protectionist national procurement long had.

The 1996/97 Single Market Review found that the initial impact of more competitive public procurement was limited: the direct effect was merely to double the very low share (1.4 per cent) of successful foreign bids to 3 per cent, whereas the indirectly sourced share rose from 4 per cent to 7 per cent. The welfare effects were hard to trace empirically.

[15]CENELEC (the European body for electric/electronic standards) and CEN (the European body for non-electric standards) consist of the national standards bodies in western Europe. For telecoms standards, ETSI was founded in 1988.

[16]Unlike precise and rigid design standards, performance standards focus on what tolerances or other (safety, etc.) performance should be met and, if necessary, how this should be tested. This leaves great discretion for product differentiation and innovation among producers.

[17]Since complying with referred standard is 'presumed' (in the new approach) to be equivalent to compliance with the 'essential requirements', a product solution outside the standard will require independent certification in order to confirm compliance with the directive.

[18]See European Commission (1994), *The Community Internal Market, 1993 Report,* pp. 118–30.

[19]Of course, any domestic suppliers would themselves purchase rationally in the single market or beyond, hence there is likely to be a considerable EU input in their final supplies to the government. For a theoretical 'welfare' analysis see, for example, Tovias (1990).

The new and global approaches in conjunction with the judicial review regarding Articles 28 and 30 EC have created an effective mechanism to tackle thousands of technical barriers. They are complemented by other elements.[20] The most important one of these is the 'information' directive 83/189, revised as 98/34, briefly discussed in section 4.3.3 above. This remarkable directive provides the EU with a power to intervene in national drafting of legislation if the legislation is likely give rise to (new) technical barriers to trade. Prompted by the regulatory drive of the Member States, this unique power is now used routinely. There are 700 (mandatory) notifications a year by Member States, one-third of which give rise to a so-called detailed opinion or indeed a standstill – and sometimes an EC directive instead. This seemingly technocratic instrument has meanwhile become the great protector of market integration against new technical barriers.

It is the seemingly unstoppable regulatory drive of individual Member States that creates a permanent threat of erosion of the internal product market. Although Member States cannot create new regulation for goods under EC directives, and MR has further limited the regulatory discretion of Member States, the number of notifications to the 98/34 Committee has not fallen (as one would expect) but steadily increased. The 98/34 Committee will continue to ensure that such national regulations are not allowed to throw up new barriers and that MR and 'equivalence' provisions are explicitly incorporated. As Pelkmans *et al.* (2000c) show, without this powerful mechanism a steady undermining of goods market integration would be inevitable.[21]

CASE STUDY 5.3 New-approach directives on pressure vessels

Few readers of this book will know what 'pressure vessels' are and yet they are part and parcel of our daily lives. They are intermediary goods inside final products ranging from pressure cookers to huge boilers in ships or power plants or a myriad of machines. Pressures of gas or liquids may cause them to explode or leak in hazardous ways. The infamous explosions of steam boilers on Mississippi passenger ferries in the late nineteenth century prompted the beginning of strict and detailed risk regulation in the USA and Europe. All EU Member States had therefore developed strict and rigid regulations in this area. When the customs union was completed the heterogeneity of national rules, conformity assessment, standards (if the specifications were not incorporated in national laws in the first place) and inspection on pressure vessels threatened to make a mockery of free movement in numerous product markets that, on the face of it, were not subject to a barrier for that final good (but only for the pressure vessels inside them). After difficult negotiations, a framework directive 76/767/EEC was adopted in 1976 but it was optional and allowed for bilateral recognition only. The 'old approach' did not work. The new approach in this difficult and sensitive area has worked, however. Two directives (on simple pressure vessels, 87/404/EEC, and the more general pressure equipment directive 97/23) form the core of the new approach here. The 'essential safety requirements' are specified with considerable room for innovation and flexibility on how to build the products, a body of CEN standards has been built up (mutual recognition of) conformity assessment by 'notified bodies' on the basis of the 'global approach' is organised and, when respecting these standards, there is a 'presumption of conformity', hence, free intra-EU market access anywhere. Further incentives for innovation are provided via so-called European

[20] There are four elements: some 90 approximation proposals for industrial goods and some 75 for agricultural goods and live animals were dealt with following the White Paper – this proved possible because of qualified majority voting; Directive 83/189, now amended as 98/34 (the 'mutual information' directive) dealt with the regulatory drive of the Member States, such that new national regulations could not create new technical barriers (see text); standards not connected to legislation were more often Europeanised; and the EOTC was established in 1990 to promote MR for testing and certification for non-regulated products (on the latter, see Machado Jorge, 1995).

[21] See also the comprehensive Commission report COM (2003) 200 of 23 May 2003, *The Operation of Directive 98/34/EC from 1999 to 2001.*

CASE STUDY 5.3 *continued*

Approvals of Materials, a special clause in 97/23 facilitating 'new, advanced materials' by means of a higher flexible form of standardisation. The first such approval was given in 2004 for new nickel materials used in highly complex chemical installations. For pressure vessels, market size and scale are crucial for competitiveness and also remove a barrier to further innovation (given the fear of not being able to recoup the R&D costs). For many final goods, especially machines (itself a highly diversified set of up to 45,000 differentiated goods) free movement of pressure vessels removes what is probably the greatest impediment to free movement in the single market.

5.4.3 Removing fiscal frontiers

The initial proposals on tax harmonisation were often centralist, rigid and uniformist.[22] These extreme positions kept fiscal frontiers alive in the EC customs union until the early 1990s because Member States neither liked to give up so much tax autonomy nor accepted a looser regime inducing fiscal competition for fears of revenue losses. What are the core economic issues when removing (indirect) tax frontiers, and how did the EU tackle them?

5.4.3.1 The economics of fiscal harmonisation

Tax harmonisation for goods markets refers to indirect taxation, that is, sales taxes (or like taxes) and excise duties. If a CU also wishes to be an indirect tax union, it must remove border tax adjustments under the destination principle. This principle is the customary one for international trade within a CU. The *destination principle* says that goods should be taxed at the place of consumption, at the local tax rate. Since exports are not consumed locally, they ought to be zero rated. In so doing, consumption in the destination country will be trade neutral: if the domestic and import pre-tax prices are equal, the tax-inclusive prices will also be equal. The fiscal frontiers under the destination principle consist of two activities: once the export goods physically pass the frontier, a form will be obtained from customs declaring that they are now eligible for zero rating; upon entering the fiscal jurisdiction of destination, they will become subject to local indirect taxation. Hence, a CU having abolished border instruments of protection for intra-CU trade, such as tariffs and quotas, will still witness double fiscal frontiers. This is the most important reason why the Commission has insisted already for two decades on the eventual switch away from the destination principle. The post-EC-1992 EU indirect tax regime does not really do that, and the compliance costs of this 'transitional' regime seem to amount to a new kind of fiscal frontier, as we shall see shortly.

Today's regime sets intra-CU trade apart from domestic trade for which the *origin principle* is used. According to the origin principle a good is taxed at the place of production irrespective of where it is consumed, locally or abroad. Were this principle to be used for international trade, it would not be trade neutral, but distortive. Only in a purely hypothetical scenario, where all national tax regimes are identical and rates (across many goods) uniform, would the distortion of competition disappear. If that were true, the origin principle would of course be superior since the heavy compliance cost of fiscal frontiers would not arise. Politically, it is unrealistic to expect such a scenario to come true. But defending the origin principle from this perspective is also problematic economically. The most fundamental problems derive from the economic suboptimality of completely uniform tax regimes and rates among countries, even in a CU. Differences in taxation are a function of differences in income levels, and their distribution, and also of different priorities and ambitions in public spending, in turn derived from differences in voters' preferences, revealed in one way or another via the political system. These differences are reflected in disparities in indirect tax structures. Imposing uniformity between the Member States' tax regimes and rates would therefore suppress the satisfaction of preferences in many – if not

[22] An interesting difference with regulatory barriers is, however, that the treaty (Art. 93 EC) speaks of harmonisation in the case of indirect taxation and approximation (Arts. 94 and 95 EC) in the case of regulatory barriers. (However, harmonisation is used in the French text of Arts. 94 and 95.)

all – Member States, in a number of ways. This class of objections forms a strong argument against the early Community pursuit for uniformist tax harmonisation, rather than tax diversity.

In practice, there are three distinct issues behind disparities of indirect taxation between Member States – all three are relevant to the EU experience. First, the *systems* of indirect taxation may differ. During the build-up phase of the CU, all six EC countries except France operated so-called cascade taxes: every sale, at intermediate stages of production and to final consumers, was taxed. This idea leads to arbitrarily different tax rates between (sometimes the same) goods: some goods pass through several stages before reaching the final consumer and others through only one, the latter thus enjoy a lower tax burden. It also led to fiscal incentives for vertical integration: if a three-stage production process could be completed in one company, two intermediate taxes would be avoided. In trade the problems were even greater. Zero rating for exports meant that the pre-paid tax from intermediate sales had to be refunded, but such compensations could only be approximate and case by case. This gave rise to the fear of hidden export subsidies and to numerous complaints by business about too low refunds. Border tax adjustments for imports within the CU tended to be higher the closer the goods were to the final consumer, which again provided discretion for 'protectionist' levies. France, however, operated a value added tax (VAT) where invoices of any sale would always report the tax of the value added (irrespective of the stages it passed through) up to that point. This could be reclaimed by business and tax and additional value added would be shifted to the next user or the final consumer. VAT made both domestic and intra-EC trade fiscally easy, neutral and non-arbitrary, and hence was proposed for all EC6 countries. It was adopted in 1967.

The systems problem was not so great in excise duties where tight tax controls and the absence of complicated processing stages (unlike in car or machinery manufacture) facilitated border tax adjustments.

Second, the *tax bases* may differ. The issue here is which goods are actually taxed and which ones are exempted or treated specially (with higher or lower taxes). Disparities in the tax bases would also cause the origin principle to be distortive. The EU approximated the national VAT bases in 1977 in the 6th VAT directive without making them fully uniform. One might argue for this approximation on the grounds of preparing for the origin principle, because under the destination principle there is no economic reason to approximate.[23] However, such a defence would conceal the real political reason at the time. The EU budget had meanwhile established a system of 'own resources' (revenues), part of which consisted of a tiny share of the national VAT revenues. Since the national tax bases differed greatly, and since the ratio of direct over indirect tax revenues varied significantly among the Member States, the national contributions to the own resources were far from proportional. Approximation reduced these discrepancies. Together, the introduction of VAT and base approximation amounted to a (presumably welfare-increasing) tax reform as it drastically simplified indirect taxation in practically all Member States while simultaneously doing away with all kinds of atavistic taxes. It acted as a welcome tax reform. This was also true for excise duties, the goods basis of which was narrowed to a few major products with special health (alcoholic beverages and tobacco products) and environmental and infrastructural (fuels for transport) problems, causing externalities. It is claimed that, when Greece became a member in 1981, around one hundred different taxes had to be abolished.

Third, the *tax rates* may differ. The case for the origin principle is convincing only if tax rate approximation is not politically restricted. The problem that arises under the origin principle is not only due to tax rate disparities. Even if rates were the same, imbalances in tax revenues may arise between Member States due to trade deficits or surpluses. In reality, rates will always differ somewhat and trade is rarely balanced, so the EU, on shifting to the origin principle, will need a clearing house.

5.4.3.2 Fiscal EC-1992 and beyond

During the 1980s the Community gradually shifted away from the supposed need for uniformist harmonisation of tax rates. A degree of diversity and measured

[23]Under the origin principle and given disparities of national VAT rates, (fiscal) trade deflection could occur (remember, from Chapter 1, trade deflection in an FTA due to tariff disparities) for imports from non-EU countries and knowing the huge intra-EU intra-firm transactions in multinationals, this problem is not trivial. So, given the origin principle, there is an efficiency case for tax rate approximation. Some economists plead for the origin principle precisely because it would induce tax competition and discipline governments. Unfortunately, this is naïve. Member States' treasuries reject the origin principle, mainly for the very same reason: they do not want to sacrifice (VAT) tax autonomy, either via tax competition or via prior VAT rates harmonisation.

fiscal competition among the Member States were accepted towards the end of the EC-1992 process. Thus, low and high VAT goods were defined and fiscal competition among high-VAT goods has been allowed by only establishing a minimum VAT rate of 15 per cent. The Member States acknowledged the imposition by EC-1992 to remove fiscal frontiers but have thus far refused to shift to the origin principle. The view of the EC Commission – that by 2000 the origin principle should govern intra-EC trade – was not supported by the Member States.

The fascinating history of the interaction between Commission and Council will not be dealt with here.[24] The compromise reached is a 'temporary' solution[25] with regular reviews. The comparison boils down to the retention of the destination principle for companies and commercial traders, but without the fiscal frontiers at the borders.[26] As noted above, border controls were used to verify whether zero-rated goods had actually left the exporting country and to ensure that destination VAT was imposed by the importing country. In the post-1992 system these two controls are shifted to the companies themselves.

The problem is that this shift has proved to be very costly. Careful empirical work by Verwaal & Cnossen (2002) shows that the compliance costs amount, on average, to no less than 5 per cent of the value of their intra-EU transactions, with large variations around this average, in particular for one-third of the firms, which have relatively few intra-EU (taxable) transactions (for them, 12 per cent or more was reached). Clearly, if this research is correct, the EC-1992 removal of fiscal frontiers has been a regulatory failure, or, at best, has not reduced compliance costs, only the form. One reason is that Eurostat still imposes intra-EU trade statistics linked to VAT; another cost-raising factor is the 'listing' system (reporting to both import and export countries), which implies a lack of cooperation between Member States. The Benelux system prior to EC-1992 did not have this, for example.

ADDITIONAL READING

The benefits of removing customs controls for tax purposes have to be weighed against the actual administrative burden at the company level plus the costs of close administrative cooperation between the tax authorities of Member States to prevent or detect fraud. The enforcement problem can be resolved by tax audits and administrative supervision at national levels and intensive administrative information and cooperation between national tax authorities. If the enforcement problem is effectively resolved at low cost, this transitional system of cooperation is in accordance with the subsidiarity test of Chapter 4.

The compliance costs and estimates of residual fraud[27] are among the reasons for proposals to shift, in future, to the origin system. The origin

[24]See, e.g., CEPS (1989) and Smith (1993).

[25]Commissioner Monti presented proposals for a common VAT, based on the origin principle, to be realised by 2000. See COM (96) 328 of 22 July 1996. Given the resistance of practically all Member States (mainly out of fear of problems with the clearing house, see Additional Reading below), all the Commission could do was to propose a practical refinement of the current 'transitional' system, based on the destination principle for goods, yet without the (formal) fiscal frontiers. See COM (2000) 348 of 7 June 2000 for the proposals. A technical interim report of a range of cost-reducing measures to simplify and modernise VAT in the Union is found in COM (2003) 614 of 30 October 2003, *Review and Update of VAT Strategy Priorities.*

[26]Note that this destination principle applies for companies, but no longer for individual consumers who do cross-border shopping. Since they have no VAT number, the origin principle applies (except for large values and special items such as cars). In other words, Member States have tolerated the (minor) fiscal competition arriving from cross-border shopping. Except sometimes in case of disparate excise duties and (rarely) disparities in VAT rates, cross-border shopping leaves national tax autonomy largely in place.

[27]The self-reinforcing nature of VAT drastically reduces the incentive for fraudulent business behaviour. Suppose it is feared that a zero-rated export good is to be diverted back into the domestic economy, facilitated by the lack of customs control. First, the tax authorities would not refund the accumulated VAT without proof of paid invoices or delivery forms. Even if that failed somehow, the user or distributor would have to collaborate (as they cannot reclaim VAT either) and final consumers (including businesses reclaiming VAT) should be expected not to report. This would seem unsustainable on a large scale. An ingenious loophole (carousel fraud) has recently been exploited by blending (zero-rated) exports and (taxable) domestic goods. More intense tax cooperation and stricter rules are expected to close this loophole.

ADDITIONAL READING *continued*

system would do away with zero rating for intra-EC exports, but it would protect the Member States from revenue shocks by the setting up of a clearing house. The importing company would claim the VAT paid in the origin country from the destination country's tax authorities (against the company's own VAT liability). This would maintain neutrality for trade and competition. The policy problem would be found in the changes in revenues of the Member States. However, in this form, the administrative costs would be considerable as every national tax authority would have to handle millions of invoices from all Member States. The revenue problem is not trivial either because the system would positively affect revenues of Member States with above-average VAT rates (origin rates) as well as those with bilateral trade surpluses within the Union, and engender revenue losses for deficit and relatively low tax countries.[28] The Union clearing house would bring together the accumulated net bilateral claims and make transfers accordingly. Apart from the need to do this by statistical approximation (as the transactions-based approach would be too cumbersome), there is a problem of enforcement asymmetry (Smith, 1993). Whereas 'output' VAT (in the destination country) will be controlled as usual, the origin country may feel few incentives to control 'input' VAT (on its exported products) because the destination country is held to pay the 'input' to the origin country unless fraud is suspected. Why would the origin country's administration audit VAT claims which are not submitted to its own administration?

To overcome the Member States' fears about incorrect clearing of tax revenues through the EC clearing house, and in order to reduce incentives to commit fraud, Keen & Smith (1996) have proposed an ingenious, yet simple solution. They propose to introduce a special, uniform VAT rate for business-to-business (B2B) transactions, while keeping fiscal sovereignty about the business-to-consumers (B2C) VAT rates (except that they cannot, of course, be lower than 15 per cent for most goods). In addition, exports would no longer be zero rated, but taxed at the (EU) B2B rate, as long as the buyer can report a VAT number (if not, he is a final consumer and the origin system *de facto* applies, as it does today in cross-border shopping). Under this regime, VAT fraud between low and high VAT countries is no longer interesting between businesses. As to national revenues, they are not affected by the intermediate, common rate but by the final (nationally distinct) rates. Clearing will now be far easier. Moreover, since the B2B rate will be commonly set, Member States can reduce the net payments flows to 'restore' the revenues that the destination principle would have given them, by lowering the B2B rate. A final advantage of this simple solution is that VAT rate approximation is less pressing than under a pure origin system, which might induce trade deflection prompted by VAT rate disparities. After all, B2C VAT rates would be irrelevant for business, and the B2B rate would be uniform.[29]

5.5 Summary

The Community has gone through different aims in pursuit of product market integration. The Rome Treaty implicitly comprises a tariff union, complemented by open-ended approximation (under unanimity) and four common policies: trade policy (though incomplete), competition policy, agricultural policy and – based on the Paris Treaty – coal and steel.

Although complicated by various protocols and stages of liberalisation, the internal tariff removal turned out to be easy, owing to a high degree of automaticity in the treaty and the favourable economic climate. The internal removal of quotas was almost entirely automatic. The problems of the customs union were minor with respect to the CET – again, due to far-reaching automaticity – but

[28]For some indicative short- and long-run calculations, see CEPS (1989). These calculations combine the 1987 proposals on rate harmonisation with the clearing house.

[29]Other interesting proposals to overcome fears about the origin principle include McLure (2000) and Bird & Gendron (2000).

enormous and stubborn with respect to quotas *vis-à-vis* third countries. The latter turned the CU into an FTA for certain products, above all textiles and clothing.

Moving beyond the CU to true product market integration really required a 'mother' principle. Two overlapping 'mother' principles are suggested: the ideal one of explicitly defining product market integration (an area without economic frontiers in the product market) as the benchmark, or the less far-reaching one of removing of all internal frontier controls. Article 8A (now Article 14 EC) of the Single European Act comprises the second one and goes far along the path and in the direction of the first. The famous EC-1992 programme brings this out (Figure 5.3 provides a summary of the EC-1992 proposals in goods markets).

Apart from the physical removal of the customs services and other controls at the internal borders of the Union, three kinds of barriers were removed by a combination of negative and positive integration:

- *Discrimination in public procurement:* this led to more competitive purchasing with potentially large 'welfare' gains; actually realising (and measuring) such gains is far from easy.
- *Technical barriers* (technical regulations which differ between Member States; similarly for standards and conformity assessment): a huge area of regulatory barriers held another promise of great welfare gains, although only after a long lead time to write European standards for reference. Two case studies illustrate important aspects of how to remove technical barriers. Although MR is important too (28 per cent of intra-EC goods trade falls under it), there are problems of practical enforcement.
- *Indirect tax frontiers:* the key issues there are whether a degree of fiscal competition is accepted by Member States (in VAT this was accomplished) and whether the origin principle is introduced for the EU (this was delayed); the origin principle turns out to have a complex cost/benefit picture; Member States mostly fear the revenue risks of the proposed clearing house; a uniform business-to-business VAT rate might be the basis for a solution.

CHAPTER 6

Goods Market Integration:
Economic Impact Analysis

Topics covered

Goods market integration has been the subject of an extensive literature both in economic theory and empirical analysis. This chapter addresses simple trade and (static) welfare effects, several 'pro-competitive' effects, macroeconomic effects and the remaining economic potential for deepening the single market still further. As noted in Chapter 5, goods market integration includes, but goes far beyond, the mere establishment of a CU. Removing quotas for third countries, while dismantling regulatory and fiscal barriers among members and, at the same time, preventing private anti-competitive behaviour, is an ambitious balancing act. If successful, it should lead to strong tendencies towards price convergence in the union. The present chapter is limited to the main themes and reduces technicalities to a (graphical) minimum. The first three sections deal with the basic economics of a CU. The scope and assumptions of basic theory are restrictive. The typical impact of a CU in this analysis includes trade and (static) welfare effects. Trade creation and diversion, and some other (static) effects of a CU, are analysed, including the CU's impact in the presence of scale economies and (initial) technical inefficiency. Section 6.4 discusses the empirical literature studying the emerging European CU in the 1960s, using the basic (static) CU theory as the frame of reference.

Only when the restrictive assumptions of the basic theory are further relaxed can the pro-competitive effects of a CU be better understood. Section 6.5 discusses four such effects: intra-industry trade, deepening goods market integration under imperfect competition (making price discrimination no longer possible), an extension to oligopolistic goods markets in the Union, and, in an Additional Reading, removing national quotas *vis-à-vis* third countries. The macroeconomic effects of the removal of 'trade costs' and the subsequent pro-competitive pressures are divided into productivity impact and growth effects, against the backdrop of the Cecchini and Monti reports on EC-1992. The discussion of the further economic potential of deepening deals with the new 'trade costs' literature, the trade impact of the euro and price convergence.

6.1 Basic theory of customs union

Any economic theory of (regionally) discriminatory trade has to address the question whether the preferential arrangement would be superior to worldwide liberalisation. If not economically superior, why do it, and how could (net) costs be minimised? Given a decision to go for regionalism, a further choice is to be made between the various methods of regional trade liberalisation. Different options can be defined dependent on whether one wishes to leave some national trade policy autonomy or not, and how one copes with different national protection *vis-à-vis* third countries. If one wishes merely to liberalise intra-group trade, and refuses to constrain national trade policies, massive transit trade would arise. Economic agents would exploit differences in protection among partners by leading imports from third countries through the partner country with the lowest protection. This is called 'trade deflection'.

Following section 1.5, a *customs union* (CU) can be defined as a group of countries eliminating tariffs for intra-group trade and unifying their national tariffs into a common external tariff for trade with third countries. A customs union differs from a free trade area in the way it prevents trade deflection: in the free trade area, the national tariff disparities remain but their exploitation is outlawed with enforcement based on certificates of area origin, whereas in the customs union, tariff disparities are simply eliminated by erecting a common external tariff. As noted in Chapter 2, the European Community has explicitly opted for a customs union rather than a free trade area.

The question addressed in basic CU theory is what the trade and 'welfare' effects are of a change from national (tariff) protection to a CU. In fact, this is a more general and precise formulation of what was called the 'general incidence' in section 1.5. Our exposition of the basic theory of CU will be built upon a set of standard assumptions, taken from the standard theory of tariffs.[1]

6.1.1 Trade creation and diversion

The central tenets of basic customs union theory can be explained in a graph as simple as Figure 6.1. The world price P_C is constant (in other words, the partner countries A and B are 'small'), initial tariffs are t_A and t_B and the CET (common external tariff) is a simple average of the two (as the EU did).

Now, consider Figure 6.1, where A's market for X has been portrayed.

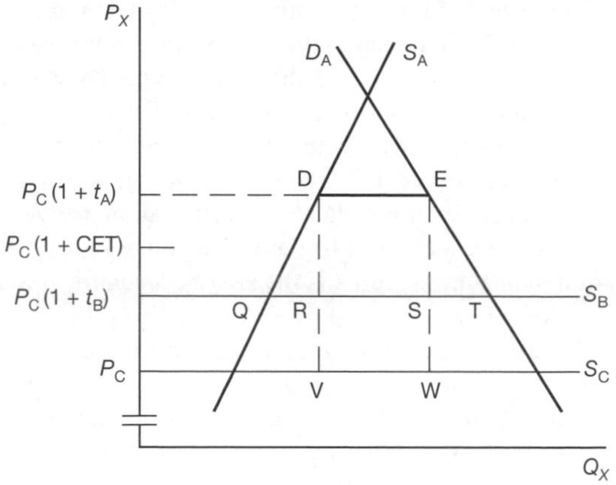

Figure 6.1 Customs union: trade creation and diversion

In the figure, A's supply schedule S_A shows increasing costs; B and C (the rest of the world) supply at constant costs, C being the lowest-cost supplier. The situation before the CU in the A-market is that A imports DE from C at $P_C(1 + t_A)$, yielding a tariff revenue DEWV. After the CU is established, B will supply A the volume of QT of X behind the CET at the price $P_C(1 + t_B)$. Although t_B has moved up to CET, perfect competition prevents B suppliers from pricing up to $P_C(1 + \text{CET})$. Basic CU theory, developed from Viner's (1950) pioneering study, defines the following effects:

- *trade creation* is the welfare change due to the replacement of (higher-cost) domestic production of import goods by (lower-cost) imports;
- *trade diversion* is the welfare change due to the replacement of imports from a low cost source by imports from a high cost source.[2]

In terms of the world allocation of resources or the world division of labour, it is clear that trade creation is beneficial to 'welfare', whereas trade diversion worsens allocation. Applied to Figure 6.1, trade creation is the welfare gain from the replacement of QR production, previously supplied by A itself, by imports from B: this is DRQ. Trade diversion is the resource costs of

[1]See any good textbook on international economics for standard tariff theory. Thus, the following is based on static reasoning, perfect competition if not stated otherwise, no internal or external (dis)economies, the same technology everywhere, etc. Extending this to CUs requires at least three countries (two partners making the CU, plus the rest of the world), assumptions on costs and demand elasticities, various scenarios on tariffs levels and changes (including the common tariffs) and, in more sophisticated theory, more than one good. The present chapter will stick to one-good analysis, for simplicity; this good can be homogeneous (sections 6.1 to 6.3, for example) or differentiated. For the purposes of this book, relatively simple economic impact analysis can show all the main results.

[2]The reader is warned that trade creation and diversion are frequently referred to in trade flow, rather than in welfare, terms. Trade flow changes are not a precise indicator of welfare changes; sometimes they are even misleading. (See, e.g., Tovias, 1982; Pelkmans & Gremmen, 1983.)

replacing DE of imports from C by intra-CU imports (free of tariffs, and behind the CET which, in this case, keeps C out) from B: this is the tariff revenue, now lost for A, minus the gain to A-consumers (DESR), being RSWV. Besides trade creation and diversion, there is a *consumption effect* EST, the 'welfare' gain of the increase in consumption due to the price fall of *X* in A.

These effects can also be derived as follows: the total gain in consumer surplus is the area between the price axis, the line P_C $(1 + t_A)$ up to E and S_B up to T; A-producers see their producer surplus decrease by the area between the price axis and D and Q whereas the government loses DESR as part of the lost revenue. Hence, DRQ and EST remain as net gains; RSWV is the uncompensated part of revenue loss and represents a net loss. As drawn, 'welfare' remains roughly the same once trade creation, the consumption effect and trade diversion are added up. It is expressed in static 'welfare' terms, under restrictive assumptions.

Several conclusions follow from this analysis. First, to call a CU 'trade diverting' or 'trade creating' is often inappropriate: in a product analysis as simple as Figure 6.1, the CU gives rise to both effects at the same time.

Second, the naive idea that CUs are necessarily a step towards free trade – an idea that underlies the GATT exemption for CUs (and free trade areas) – is incorrect. In Figure 6.1 it all depends on a series of variables. Viner's contribution consists in dealing a fatal blow to this naivety by a simple device: once trade creation and diversion are defined, it follows that the net effect on the world efficiency of production can be either positive or negative. Adding the consumption effect does not alter this fundamental conclusion. Later, Viner's insight has been generalised in the theory of second-best: the shift from one suboptimal situation to another does not permit generalisations on the direction of the change in 'welfare'. The conclusion extends to trade flows as well. The GATT condition on the 'general incidence' may well be violated; in Figure 6.1, C is pushed out of the CU.

Third, the likelihood of welfare gains increases if *ex ante* tariffs are high, *ex ante* imports from the rest of the world are low, *ex post* CU prices are close to the world level and if the number of Member States were large relative to that in the rest of the world.[3]

Fourth, static 'welfare' effects (for a given world terms of trade) are small. Empirical studies usually find effects for the EC6 in the 1960s ranging from 0.15 per cent (Balassa, 1975) to no more than 0.5 per cent of GDP. Intuitively, this is not hard to understand once it is realised that trade creation for the bigger EC countries will reduce the domestic supply to domestic consumption by only a few percentage points. Also, the triangles' vertical lines (Figure 6.1) only measure the tariff decrease to the level of the CET (say, for Italy in 1958, on average, perhaps from 25 to 15 per cent) and this, in turn, is only 10/115 of the relevant price (multiplied by half, so as to get the area of the triangle). Only under extreme differences in costs and/or tariffs and very large replacements would these effects become more significant; this is only to be expected in a few sectors, if indeed the political economy were to allow such shifts to take place rapidly.

Consider, next, Figure 6.2. The purpose of Figure 6.2 is to explain the basic economics of the 'general incidence' clause of the GATT, Article 24 (see section 1.5 above). In Figure 6.1, the 'incidence' of the CU for the rest of the world, C, was pretty drastic: in the *X*-market, C lost all exports which previously went to country A. However, the assumption of both B and C having constant costs (in *X*) is rather extreme and should be replaced by a more realistic scenario. Figure 6.2 is based on rising costs for the union partners A and B. C is assumed to be so large that constant costs is a reasonable assumption. To concentrate on what matters economically, the query posed in Chapter 1 is taken up here: if all A and B tariffs are equal across the board and equal to each other, hence the CET will also be at this level, should not the 'general incidence' clause be satisfied? Figure 6.2 shows that this is not normally the case; as depicted, the clause is violated. The reasons for this include different cost structures and demand elasticities. Figure 6.2 depicts both countries A and B in the same graph. Prior to the CU, (inefficient) country A imported BE from C at the price P_C $(1 + t_A)$ $(t_A = t_B = \text{CET})$, hence, at P_{CU}. Country B was satisfied at self-sufficiency F; its potential exports to A at *P*CU, namely CE, cannot compete with C's exports as they have lower costs. Once the CU is formed, B meets no tariff barrier any more in A (whereas C does). Adding the export supply schedule of B horizontally to S_A,[4] one sees immediately that, in the CU, B will supply BD to A, tariff-free, and replace C exports. For C, only DE of exports remain. In trade flow terms, BD is trade diversion because the costs of these

[3]Think of the following example. If two (small) high-tariff countries form a CU, the CET is likely to be high as well, yet world imports may nonetheless remain sizable (small countries typically cannot produce all goods efficiently). The presumption, following from the text, is that this CU would be bad for 'welfare' as it magnifies trade diversion, combined with relatively minor trade creation.

[4]The export supply schedule can be found by measuring the quantity of exports (here, of B), hence, horizontally, for every price level. At F, exports of B are zero, below F they are negative and for prices higher than at F, they become positive. At P_{CU} they are CE (= BD).

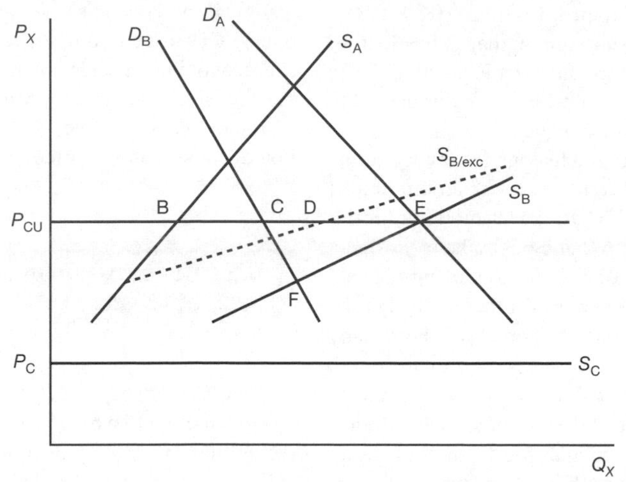

Figure 6.2 General incidence of customs union, all tariffs identical

exports are higher than if they had been produced in C. The conclusion is clear: despite the full equality of all tariffs and the CET, which might mislead one into believing that no adverse effect to C could possibly occur, the 'general incidence' (as far as good X is concerned) is negative. The graph can easily be manipulated for a demonstration of less or more adverse impact on C. If (for given elasticities of S and D curves) F were lower (that is, B would be still more efficient), CE would widen and could perhaps squeeze out all prior C-exports to A. This could also be the case if S_B were much more elastic, for example. Therefore, the general incidence clause will require solid empirical economic analysis rather than naive suppositions before one can be reasonably sure it is satisfied in GATT consultations.

Of course, Figure 6.2 is peculiar. In a CU, as indeed in the EU as well (see Chapter 5), a key issue is the precise level at which the CET will be fixed. Figure 6.3 is more general in this respect. Now, the CET is some kind of average between two disparate *ex ante* tariffs t_A and t_B. Also, both partners are *ex ante* importers from C.

In country A, the previous imports DE (from C) rise to QT, with QR supplied by partner B and RT by C. This gives a trade creation of DRQ and a consumption effect of EST. Whether there will be trade diversion depends on the reactions in B's X-market. What one might fail to see in a one-country diagram, focusing on country A, is immediately obvious in a union diagram: the chosen CET changes country B from an importer (D'E' from C) to an exporter (QR) to A. Figure 6.3. has been drawn in such a way that D'E' = ST. Thus, the *ex ante* imports of the two CU partners from C are equal to RT. Since RT = HK (by definition), it follows that – as drawn – C's exports to the customs union have remained constant. The QR part of the extra imports of A represents trade creation as it comes from a cheaper source (B) than domestic producers (though not from the cheapest source, C). However, as soon as B's exports to A become larger than QR, B would encroach upon the *ex ante* A-imports from C (DE = RS) and this would amount to trade diversion. This would occur when S_B became more elastic than drawn, or when the CET became a little higher than indicated in Figure 6.3.

The 'welfare' effects are quite complex. Trade creation is DRQ in A, but in B trade creation is *negative* (D'LF) as relatively inefficient B-production replaces C-imports.

Trade diversion may or may not occur dependent on whether B's exports to A are bigger or smaller than QR.

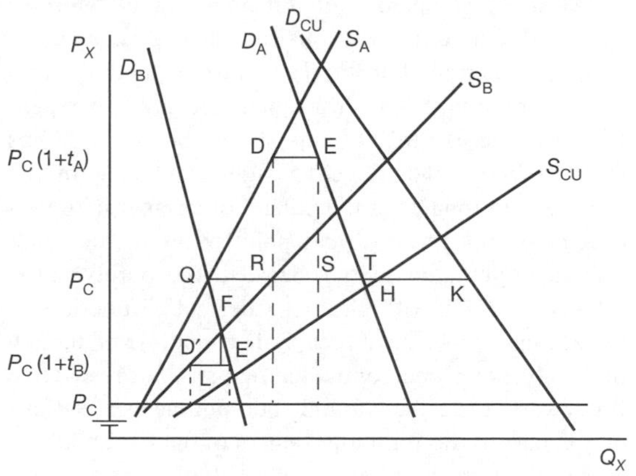

Figure 6.3 Customs union, both partners rising costs

It also matters how the CU tariff revenue (HK × CET), collected by A, will be shared now that B has lost all tariff revenue. The consumption effect is positive (EST) in A but *negative* in B (FLE'), while net gains accrue to B from becoming an exporter (FQR).

Two other interesting conclusions follow from this analysis. The first one is concerned with an implicit, if not explicit, purpose of all CUs: the promotion of intra-group trade. Figures 6.1, 6.2 and 6.3 make clear that a CU can promote trade among its member countries only if the CET is distinctly protective for the relatively efficient producer in the union (here, B). For many agricultural products, the EU raises high to very high border levies, that have enabled explosive growth in intra-EC agricultural trade at the cost of substantial trade diversion, with France, Ireland, the Netherlands and Denmark being relatively efficient exporters of well-protected non-Mediterranean products. Spain, and to a lesser extent Greece and Italy, have boosted citrus and olive exports to EU partners based on high protection too. In textiles and clothing, EU tariff and volume protection has long enabled Italy, and later Portugal, to expand greatly their intra-EU exports, while in automobiles British volume protection *vis-à-vis* Japan since 1977 has led to a substitution of British production by more efficient EU imports during the 1980s.

The second conclusion is concerned with C's market access. It is usually incorrect – though often stated – that regionalism would lead to a closure of the (CU's) market, a kind of a 'fortress'. In the case of the EU, only in agriculture was the CU explicitly used for this purpose (see Chapter 11). Figures 6.2 and 6.3 are relevant for industrial goods. In Figure 6.3, C's exports to the union remain exactly the same. An increase in the CET could let HK shrink to zero and a lower CET would induce even larger exports from C to the union than before.

All in all, some additional insights can be obtained by introducing complications such as increasing costs and the averaging of tariffs. The fundamental drawbacks of a CU remain, however. From a theoretical perspective, a range of other effects should be addressed as these effects have played a significant role in the European rationale for the pursuit of an internal goods market. From an empirical point of view, the other effects might also matter because the purely static effects of a CU of otherwise perfectly functioning markets are, as we have seen, rather small. Even though the analysis will be conducted in a similar, restrictive framework, the effects found underpin the expectations on the part of the founding fathers of the EU about the economic impact of goods market integration. Two among these effects are singled out: the removal of technical inefficiencies (a major problem in the 1950s) due to CU-driven competitive imports from partners, and economies of scale when exploiting the much lager market size (the most prominent argument for the 'common market' in the 1956 Spaak report, the foundation document of the Rome Treaty).

6.2 Customs union and technical efficiency

Technical efficiency is defined as input minimisation at any given output level, given the employment of the best techniques available. To suggest that firms are technically inefficient (often called X-inefficient) must imply that, somehow, competition is not perfect, permitting departures from cost minimisation without going bankrupt. For enterprises, competing in markets from day to day, this is not a particularly surprising insight. For entrepreneurs and managers, competitive firm behaviour is a complex variable not insensitive to the overall state of competition in the goods and factor markets, or indeed in the relevant economy as a whole. From there it is a small step to suggest that various forms of private or public shelter from (perfect) competition will eventually lead to higher costs per unit of marketable output than necessary.

In actual practice, therefore, firms will not exhibit equal performance in cost minimisation: every sector will have best-practice firms and higher cost ones. However, in basic CU theory, this crucial notion is assumed away by postulating perfect competition. For policy makers and business, on the other hand, it is important to understand whether a CU intensifies competition, and thereby induces (technical) efficiency gains.

In the western Europe of the 1950s many observers were of the opinion that a number of industries were technically inefficient due to numerous public interventions, public regulations, border protection and, occasionally, highly traditional patterns of organisation of industry (see, for example, Scitovsky, 1958). It was believed that European industrial market integration could have a 'cold shower' effect on the competitive behaviour of industrial firms. To put it in more analytical terms, decreases in the degree of technical inefficiency of European industry could be induced by decreases in the degree of border protection – giving rise to import competition and export opportunities in the EC customs union – complemented with a tougher surveillance of restrictive business practices via a common competition regime.

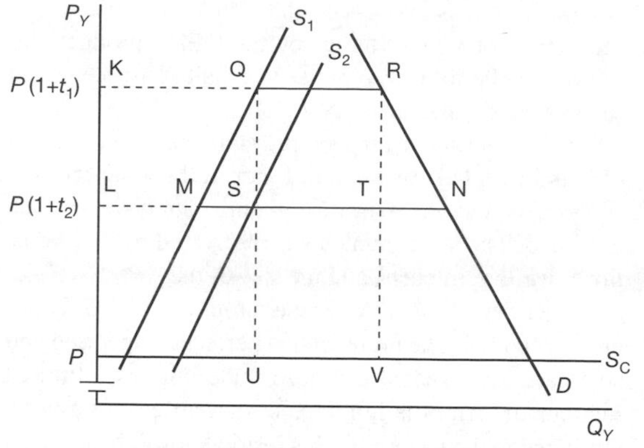

Figure 6.4 Technical efficiency and lower protection

Source: Pelkmans (1982b)

It can be shown that the 'welfare' consequences of an improvement of technical efficiency after the reduction of protection are likely to be many times larger than the usually rather trivial net gains from trade creation over trade diversion.

The essential argument is that a gain in technical efficiency, leading to a cost reduction per unit of production, would remove 'waste' and therefore constitute a gain to society. No netting of producer vs. consumer surpluses would be required, let alone losses of tariff revenues. It is also important to see that the gains relate to the entire output, which, for import competing sectors, is usually much larger than the relevant trade volumes.

Consider Figure 6.4 (Pelkmans, 1982b) where the home country has rising costs as output of *Y* increases and an initial tariff t_1. Supplies from the rest of the world S_C are at constant costs. Now, assume a tariff decrease to t_2. Because of the cold shower of sharply increased foreign competition on the domestic market (the foreigner's *Y*-market share would rise from QR/KR to MN/LN), assume that technical efficiency of home *Y*-producers improves and that this results in a downward shift of S_1 to S_2. For simplicity, the resulting cost difference (QS) is supposed to be equal to the absolute tariff difference per unit of the *ex ante* output. In this case, the triangle gains *only* would be QSM + RTN, whereas the technical efficiency gains comprise KQSL – the 'cost reduction' of the entire *ex ante* production – a multiple of the triangles. It should be emphasised that, *ceteris paribus,* for a given tariff reduction and a given efficiency improvement per unit of output (in Figure 6.4, both QS), the ratio of technical efficiency gains over triangle gains increases the smaller the initial market share of foreigners is and the more inelastic demand and supply are. The extent of technical efficiency improvement per unit of output, in turn, may also be related to the *ex ante* market share of foreigners. It seems plausible to expect that the possible leap from a small market share to what rival home producers might think of as a 'large' market share, would induce a relative big technical efficiency improvement compared with the cost reduction induced by enlargement of an already sizable market share. It follows that truly sheltered economies can reap large X-efficiency gains (and, of course, the triangle consumer gains as well) by engaging in trade liberalisation.

The analysis can be extended to a customs union. In Figure 6.5, country A's market for *X* is depicted. The initial tariff is t_A, the common external tariff (CET) is either CET or CET', depending on the arithmetical average of all EC tariffs (the former Article 19.1 EEC), S_{CU} is the union supply of *X* in A (the horizontal addition of S_A and the export supply schedule of partner B) and S_C is perfectly elastic world supply. It is assumed that the 'cold shower' shifts A's supply schedule from $S_A{}^1$ to $S_A{}^2$, that is, from Q to S.

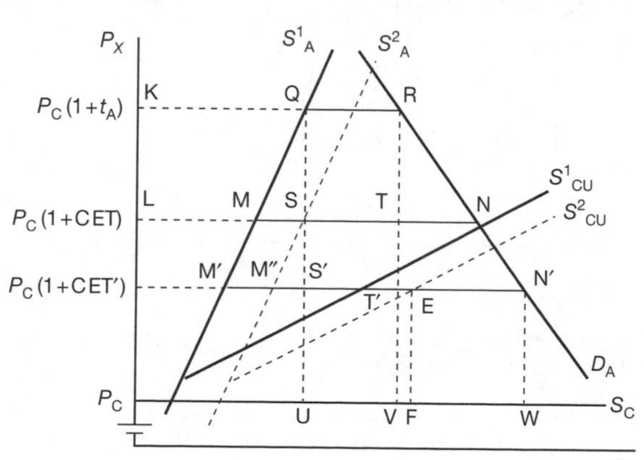

Figure 6.5 Technical efficiency and customs union

For the higher CET, trade diversion (S' TVU) would clearly outweigh trade creation (MSS' + RTN), had technical efficiency not been improved. The cold shower alters the picture since the 'cost reduction' effect is KQSB which is (drawn such as to be) approximately equal to the trade diversion, minus the consumption gain of RTN. However, the case of the relatively higher CET would be atypical since C-exporters lose all access to the customs union. (MN exported from country B to country A).

For CET', C's exports would still be EN, yielding a union tariff revenue of EN' WF. The overall effects of the customs union would then be the 'cost reduction' effect (KQSB) plus trade creation (on the production side: SM' S"; on the consumption side: RT' N'), plus the *ex post* tariff revenue (EN' WF), minus a tiny trade diversion (S" EFU). It is obvious that the formation of such a customs union would be highly advantageous in 'welfare' terms.[5] Although hard to prove, there are many indications that the customs union has engendered a more competitive climate in the EU.[6] To the extent that this inference is correct, non-trivial (static) gains can be attributed to goods market integration, especially in the 1960s.

6.3 Customs union and decreasing costs

The EU's founding fathers, including Spaak (1956, report), and Jean Monnet, were convinced that market size was crucial for Europe's industry to regain competitiveness *vis-à-vis* the USA, by means of economies of scale. Studies by the OEEC productivity centres (in the follow-up of the Marshall Plan) seemed to support these convictions.

In this section, a very simple static analysis of scale effects in a CU is presented. Later in this chapter, in a richer framework, a more dynamic analysis will be provided. The static analysis is motivated by two additional welfare impacts, and the size of them.

Other than scale, the basic assumptions of CU theory are maintained. The problem that perfect competition and scale are inconsistent (because scale implies a limited number of firms) is ignored, so that all effects can be attributed to the CU itself. This restriction will be dropped later in the chapter. The reader will remember that scale curves are average cost curves, not fully comparable to the marginal-cost-based supply schedules in previous figures.

Consider Figure 6.6. If A and B have equal access to well-known process technology, it is a reasonable simplification to assume that $S_A = S_B$. This scale curve may be above the world price for *X*, even at its lowest point, because of different factor prices. Initially, let $D_A = D_B$. As drawn, both countries produce *X* before the union and their (different) tariffs are necessarily prohibitive. A produces at E' and B at K', sales prices being determined by the tariff-inclusive world price in the two economies (we assume that monopoly pricing in A and in B would lead to still higher prices – not drawn – but this is prevented by competing imports at tariff-inclusive prices).

If the CU is established, one of the two countries will capture the entire market. Given the assumptions of

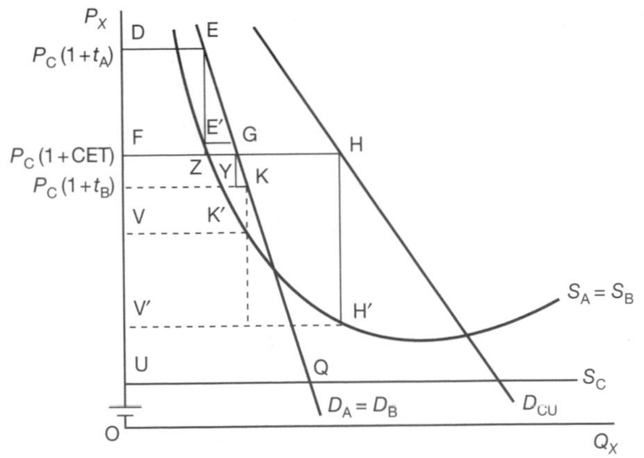

Figure 6.6 Closed customs union with decreasing costs

[5]There are a number of qualifications of this analysis. See Pelkmans (1982b).

[6]A special instance of the 'cold shower' debate was the expected 'cold war' for the UK industry once the UK entered (it did in 1973). There were indications of X-inefficiency in Britain. A recent study with a much more sophisticated model (Gasiorek *et al.*, 2002) arrives at far higher efficiency ('welfare') benefits than traditional studies but this is also attributable to changes in competitive behaviour (not included in Figure 6.4), and not merely to cost efficiency.

equal access to technology and complete information, both countries' X-industries could invest in large-scale technology as soon as the CU treaty is signed. In this case, we do not know which country's industry will be wiped out. One might replace complete information by short-sightedness of the most protected industry, in which case B will capture the market since it enjoys an initial cost and price advantage. At any rate, if B supplies the entire union, and the average CET is adopted, the 'welfare' effects of producing at H' will be as follows. Consumers in A would enjoy a considerable gain as the market price falls to P_C (1 + CET), that is, EZG + DEZF; consumers in B would suffer a tiny 'welfare' loss (GYK + FG × GY). Trade creation is harder to determine: since A will henceforth import from B, the trade flow effect is DE; since trade creation is a production (supply) effect, it is the cost differential (not the price differential) which counts; hence, trade creation is the rectangle DE × (D V – EE'). Note that, under scale, a given trade-flow-based trade creation (here, DE) reflects a rectangle of 'welfare' gains, rather than a triangle, and would therefore seem to be double the size of a given trade-flow-based trade creation under rising costs. But in fact it is far more since it relates to the entire *ex ante* production (here, of A). Another difference comes with a new effect, introduced by Corden (1972): the *cost-reduction effect.* The entire *ex ante* production of B (VK') is made cheaper, because of scale, from OV per unit to OV' per unit: the cost reduction effect is VK'VV'. This is an improvement of technical efficiency. Unlike in section 6.2, where slack is the reason for initial technical inefficiency, here initial inefficiency is caused by a lack of demand in B. The CU means market enlargement and, in case of scale, technical efficiency gains can therefore be large, especially if small countries first protect scale sectors. This is precisely the kind of benefits the Spaak report had in mind.

In the real world with political economy, the CU as shown in Figure 6.6 is unlikely to be established in this form. It is easy to see that, while A's X-industry dies, that of B enjoys huge rents in the CU. The sole reason is that the CET is not adapted to the new cost structures. If this CU subsequently offered considerable reductions in a GATT Round, reaching a CET-inclusive price of OV', the CU will still be autarkic, yet reverse the distribution effect to the benefit of consumers (including a reversal of B's negative consumption effect).

It should be noted that the welfare gains from the scale effects of a CU are often – but not necessarily[7] – a multiple of those under increasing costs. For example, in Figure 6.6 country A experiences substantial trade creation and a positive consumption effect without any negative effects (assuming an average CET), while B's negative consumption effect is amply overcompensated by the cost reduction effect (assuming both to produce initially).

Moreover, trade creation and the cost reduction effect due to scale (being rectangles) are not just double their analogue under increasing costs (being a triangle). Trade creation with increasing costs relates only to that part of domestic *ex ante* production which is replaced by cheaper imports, while both trade creation and the cost reduction effect, due to scale, relate to the *entire ex ante* domestic production. Thus, strictly on the production side, and dependent on *ex ante* import/production ratios for the increasing costs case and the extent of cost decreases in the case of scale, it is easy to conceive of 'welfare' gains of scale of a dozen or more times the size of trade creation under increasing costs.[8]

The thus derived (stronger) economic case for the CU is, of course, based on restrictive assumptions. Figure 6.6 assumes an *ex post union monopoly* in the homogeneous good X. This is a useful procedure to isolate the 'welfare' gains from exploiting economies of scale but it raises important policy questions. The redistributive effects of excessive market power are especially unlikely to be acceptable and there are likely to be welfare losses from exploiting monopoly power (not drawn). Moreover, if there were no serious competition in the union X-market, one might question the persistence of technical efficiency of the monopolist. A practical consideration of utmost importance is, therefore, that the size of the CU market should be such that the *exploitation of economies of scale can be combined with effective competition* among firms. In the Union this combination is practically always possible. For purposes of economic analysis, one has to find ways to allow more firms, under economies of scale. As we shall see in sections 6.5 and 6.6, the analysis can give insights both for a given number of firms and for a variable number of firms, because the latter may illustrate how firms restructure when confronted with goods market integration.

[7]Figure 6.6 is kept extremely stylised and simple. It does not cover situations where trade diversion would occur (namely, when one of the countries is an *ex ante* importer). In that event, trade creation cannot occur at the same time, so the net benefits can be positive only if the cost reduction effect is large enough.

[8]The major exception seems to consist in cases where both A and B are *ex ante* importers but wish to establish their own production above the world price level. The CU is then considered to be a means to generate sufficient demand strictly for union products. Such a move results in both trade diversion and negative trade creation and is costly.

6.4 Empirical studies of the early EU

The impact of goods market integration can, in principle, be studied for many variables, not only trade flows, 'welfare', market structure, but also macroeconomic variables such as the price level, employment or growth. This section focuses on trade flows and related 'welfare' changes. In the 1960s, empirical studies were all based on the partial and simple analysis, as in Figures 6.1, 6.2 and 6.3, and could not analyse any macro effects.

Empirical studies of EC goods market integration come in many kinds but these various techniques need not concern us here.[9] Most studies are interested in the trade effects only. This might mean that welfare effects are assumed to be proportional to, say, the induction of intra-CU trade – which is not necessarily the case as footnote 1 above emphasised. Alternatively, it might mean that business and policy makers are primarily interested in (intra-CU) trade opportunities perhaps because of the mercantilistic notion that export expansion is the key to a CU. For the economy as a whole, this is mistaken because it ignores the benefits of import competition and fails to distinguish trade creation from trade diversion. The studies have gradually increased in sophistication although the majority model only the demand side of importing countries, or merely extrapolate a few general trends from the past. Both partial and general equilibrium approaches have been published. All the studies up to the mid-1970s concentrate on the formative years of the Community's CU (the 1960s). Some additional effects arise because where partner countries (for example, Benelux) had to raise tariffs to the CET, negative trade creation is induced as Figure 6.3 shows (called 'trade erosion' in some studies); external trade creation emerges when the CET is lowered as was the case in the Dillon and Kennedy Rounds of the GATT. Table 6.1 lists some well-known *ex post* studies of EC trade flows in manufactured goods.

Table 6.1 Trade creation and diversion in EC trade flows of manufactured goods (values in US$ billions)

Author(s)[a]	Year	Trade creation[b]	Trade diversion[c]
Aitken (1973) (projection)	1964	5.7	0.2[d]
	1965	6.9	0.0[d]
	1966	8.6	-0.2[d]
	1967	9.2	-0.6[d]
Truman (1969) (1958 base)	1964	4.5	-1.6
Williamson & Bottrill (1973)	1969	9.6	0.0
Truman (1975) (projection)	1968	5.7	-3.7[e]
Balassa (1975)	1970	11.4	-0.1
Resnick & Truman (1975)	1968	1.8	-3.0
Verdoorn & Schwartz (1972)	1968	10.1	-1.1
Kreinin (1972) (US normalised; adjusted)	1969/70	7.3	-2.6
Prewo (1974)	1970	18.0	-3.1

[a] *Ex post* studies only.
[b] Trade creation is defined as a decrease in domestic production by Truman (1969), Truman (1975) and Resnick & Truman (1975); for the others it is either the increase of intra-EC trade (*vis-à-vis* the anti-monde) or the latter minus what is considered as trade diversion.
[c] Trade diversion is defined as the decrease in the outsiders' supply to the EC (*vis-à-vis* the anti-monde).
[d] Only trade diversion *vis-à-vis* EFTA.
[e] 'Trade diverted plus trade eroded'.

Since trade creation and trade diversion both augment intra-EC trade, Table 6.1 suggests that a share of 1970 intra-EC trade in manufactures in the range of, approximately, one-quarter to one-half could be attributed to EC market integration. This is of no mean importance: with hindsight one can reasonably claim that the EC as such has brought about a 50–100 per cent increase in the 1959 intra-EC trade in manufactures. Of course, this is merely an estimate of the 'static' effect; it does not take account of the direct and indirect impact of market integration on economic growth, which, in turn, will induce further increases in (all) imports. Also note that the actual (real) increase of intra-EC trade was much higher still. Of the estimated increase in intra-EC trade, trade diversion in manufactured goods was low in most studies though not in all. Since Table 6.1 excludes agriculture the picture is too positive, because in the static

[9] For surveys, see Mayes (1978), Winters (1987) and Ohly (1993). Thus, one finds *ex ante* and *ex post* studies (the latter using data about the actual CU experience), those with 'residual imputation' (the difference between the postulated determinants of trade, and an 'anti-monde' of the same relations without the CU – hence, it is *ex post*), *ex ante* studies with an 'anti-monde'; studies with varying techniques and degrees of generality.

effects of the CAP trade diversion must have been significant,[10] given the protectionist nature of the CAP.

The welfare effects of the increase in intra-EC trade are small, however. Balassa (1975) estimates them to be about 0.15 per cent of GNP. The reader can do a 'back of the envelope' check of this figure as follows.[11] Take the average EC manufactures tariffs in 1959 to be 12 per cent and a rounded trade creation figure from Table 6.1 to be $10 billion in 1970. This gives a trade creation welfare triangles effect of $0.12 \times 10 \times 0.5 = \$0.6$ billion, a trivial sum compared with the then GNP of the EC6. The contrast between the considerable trade impact and the minimal 'welfare' impact is striking. As noted in sections 6.2 and 6.3, the neglect of X-inefficiency (undoubtedly prominent in the pre-EC days) and of scale effects (of which major examples have been studied) may lead one to miss out the (much) greater part of the welfare improvements. In *ex post* studies, X-efficiency improvements and scale influence the trade effects in complicated ways, but these influences are not modelled. So, calculating the welfare effects as pure reallocation effects in the form of trade creation and diversion is then inappropriate. Other reasons for a too low estimate of welfare effects induced by the observed increase in intra-EC trade may include the removal of quotas and some other non-tariff barriers, both of which have had the effect of adding (unknown) tariff equivalents to *ex ante* tariffs.

It is also important to pay attention to what is called the 'regionalisation' of overall EC trade, measured as the share of intra-EC trade in total EC trade. CUs typically aim to boost intra-CU trade, but this inevitably adds trade creation and diversion. As shown, the effects may well be more complicated still, dependent on what cost assumption and technical efficiency improvements play a role. Table 6.2 indicates regionalisation over a period of 32 years, with three enlargements. Note that the shares refer to a trade volume probably more than six times as large by 1990 than at the outset. Note also that the fluctuations

Table 6.2 Regionalisation of EC trade, 1958–90 (intra-EC as a percentage of all EC trade)

		EC12	EFTA	Eastern Europe	Mediterranean countries	ACP	Other developing countries	Industrial countries
Exports	1958	37.2	12.2	2.7	7.8	6.6	15.3	18.2
	1965	49.6	13.0	2.9	4.8	4.4	9.4	15.9
	1970	53.4	11.7	3.4	4.8	3.6	7.1	16.0
	1975	52.4	10.6	4.9	6.7	3.6	9.6	12.2
	1980	56.1	11.2	3.5	5.9	3.5	9.2	10.6
	1985	55.2	10.0	2.8	5.2	2.3	8.7	15.8
	1990	61.2	10.4	2.3	4.2	1.6	7.3	13.0
Imports	1958	35.2	9.3	2.9	4.5	6.8	19.2	22.1
	1965	44.9	9.0	3.4	4.7	5.2	12.7	20.1
	1970	50.3	8.7	3.2	4.7	4.4	10.3	18.4
	1975	49.5	7.9	3.5	3.8	3.8	16.3	15.2
	1980	49.3	8.6	3.7	4.2	3.8	15.6	14.8
	1985	53.4	9.4	3.9	5.1	3.5	9.8	14.9
	1990	59.0	9.6	2.7	3.8	1.8	8.2	14.9

Source: Sapir, 1992, Table 2

[10]See Chapter 11 below and Thorbecke & Pagoulatos (1975) who discuss the literature of the 1960s and arrive at a fairly careful estimate of US$740 million in 1969; a more simple indicator of trade diversion in agriculture is found in Table 5 of Sapir (1992).

[11]As suggested by Hine (1994, pp. 256–7).

on the import side can be explained mainly by oil price volatility. The EC12 has shown a strong degree of further regionalisation, starting from an already medium/high share (37 per cent in 1958). The EC12 and EFTA reached nearly 72 per cent in 1990. What is to be explained from Table 6.2 is the combination of the considerable increase in EC regionalisation with the gradual, but all-in-all far-reaching, external liberalisation of trade. Other than in agriculture, trade protection has either strongly decreased or been eliminated. Regionalisation should not only be explained by integration effects: what may seem integration effects may in turn be partly explained by shortening of economic distance (infrastructure, transport, and communication technology).

We now turn to more 'realistic' analyses of product market integration. The main difference is that the perfect competition assumptions are dropped. It enables the analysis of a customs union, given different degrees of competitive exposure in national markets. The impact of a customs union is then likely to be 'pro-competitive', something completely excluded in classical customs union theory. In the EU, the pro-competitive effects of the CU have been, and still are, important. Moreover, such approaches facilitate the study of all kinds of non-tariff barriers to fully fledged product market integration, as described in Chapter 5. In section 6.5 we discuss important theoretical aspects, whereas in section 6.6 both the *ex ante* and *ex post* empirical studies of EC-1992 will be highlighted, based – in large part – on the 'pro-competitive' impact.

6.5 Pro-competitive effects of a single goods market

In basic CU theory, perfect competition is assumed. Product differentiation and product innovation are ignored. Of course, this amounts to a drastic simplification. The analytical problem is how to overcome it. A number of approaches have been developed, often in distinct analytical frameworks. These approaches have in common that they regard degrees of goods market integration as degrees of exposure to competition, in turn leading to changes in conduct and/or market structure (for example, the number of firms). Trade is often important in these analyses, but it need not be. Indeed, we shall discuss an influential model where a decline of intra-EU trade is the direct result of welfare-improving market integration. In other words, it is the actual or potential competition which is critical to the analysis. In section 6.2 it was shown that an improvement of X-efficiency may be a relatively strong, welfare-improving result of a CU. However, the downward shift of the supply schedule was merely postulated: it might be induced by actual new import competition in the CU or by the mere threat of it. A similar behaviour might take place in the case of economies of scale. The Italian 'white goods' industry was the first to apply scale technology, imported from the USA, in this sector – precisely when the intra-EU tariff reductions began. The result was what economic theory would lead one to expect – the myopic competitors elsewhere in the EEC6 were largely wiped out and the entire industry of washing machines and refrigerators went through a process of drastic restructuring ending up in much higher concentration in the early 1970s. The sectoral welfare benefits (Mueller, 1981) were a multiple of the static ones found in section 6.4. It is for this kind of reason that economists have long suspected the main benefits of (goods) market integration to result from greater exposure to competition. Scale and X-efficiency are undoubtedly major instances of this approach. Their explanation in sections 6.2 and 6.3 is not satisfactory, however, as scale is combined with perfect competition (for reasons of convenience) and neither X-inefficiency nor its improvement is explained by the model itself.

In this section we consider the pro-competitive effects of deepening, beyond the mere customs union. For simplicity, we call it a single goods market. As Chapter 5 explains, the degree of deepening depends on overcoming regulatory, technical, fiscal and procurement barriers and, perhaps, restrictive business practices as well. Therefore, there is an entire spectrum of ever further deepening towards a (perfectly) single goods market. The analysis will treat four aspects. First, allowing differentiation of goods, market integration will yield greater variety, hence, more consumer choice while still keeping the kind of cost reduction, made possible by the much larger size of the market. Second, price discrimination (between national markets in the single market) and its collapse with further deepening will be studied. It is inspected both for homogeneous and differentiated goods.[12] Third, the pro-competitive

[12]For the special case of a monopolist in one member country, unwilling to export to the rest of the single market, see Pelkmans (1984, pp. 72–5). One can show that such exports would have an ambiguous effect on profit (combining a lower price and higher sales). However, with deepening, the monopolist would, sooner or later, have to respond to import competition or arbitrage, prompting local prices to fall.

effects of greater deepening are derived for oligopolistic markets, with the number of companies being variable. Fourth, in an Additional Reading, the anti-competitive impact of national quotas *vis-à-vis* third countries is analysed, hence, the benefits of removing those.

6.5.1 Intra-industry trade

In the early years of the EC it was observed that inter-industry specialisation was not the general market response to the CU. Also, the expectation that high-tariff countries would experience a shrinkage in production of protected goods often did not come true. What was observed was two-way trade in similar, sometimes identical, products (in terms of factor inputs and consumption): so-called intra-industry trade.

Intra-industry trade (IIT) will occur in the presence of product differentiation and fixed costs to variety (hence, scale).[13] The extent of scale economies in a given national market will limit the number of producers. Suppose entry barriers are low so that monopolistic competition will emerge. A CU is supposed to affect all varieties similarly – per country – as all of them will tend to fall under one tariff heading. Figure 6.7 shows the impact of the CU on one of the established firms in a member country. Of course, firms may differ marginally in the fixed costs of their variety and some varieties are likely to be more popular than other ones. These degrees of realism are ignored in Figure 6.7 which, for convenience, assumes the established company to be representative of all such firms in all Member States.

The initial equilibrium (P_1, q_1; marginal cost MC = MR, marginal revenue) at B shows a fairly inelastic (residual) demand schedule for the firm (D_1). With the CU, two effects will occur simultaneously: some demand for this firm's variety will develop in other CU countries so that D shifts to the right; at the same time the number of competing varieties will increase, which will cause the demand schedule, which every established firm will face, to become more elastic.

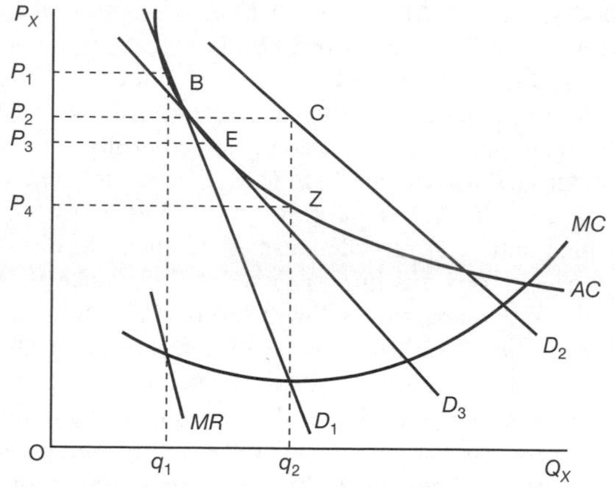

Figure 6.7 A customs union under monopolistic competition

The extra demand from other CU countries will still allow monopolistic pricing. Figure 6.7 is drawn such that D_1 also represents the (new) MR-line (belonging to D_2); at sales q_2. the new $MR = MC$, hence price P_2 at C. The profits are high now, with a price/cost margin of CZ/P_4. This will attract entry, shifting back the residual demand schedule to D_3. with sales at E. The cost reduction effect is Oq_1 ($P_1 - P_3$) and variety has increased. The intra-industry trade the CU induces is pro-competitive and beneficial in terms of 'welfare'.

The empirical issues for intra-EC IIT are essentially three:

1. To what extent has intra-EU trade become intra-industry trade?
2. Is market integration, in and by itself, a stimulus to IIT?
3. Has IIT helped to lower the costs of adjustment to greater competition and specialisation in the single market?

As to the first question, the short answer is that the bulk of intra-EU trade has become IIT.[14] For the EC6 (Balassa, 1975), the IIT index rose from a range of

[13]This statement should not be read such that intra-industry trade could not be explained by other supply or demand factors. Authoritative work has been provided by Helpman & Krugman (1985), Krugman & Venables (1990), introducing a 'home market effect' based on a wide concept of 'trade costs', and Markusen & Venables (1996), connecting this with multinationals in a general equilibrium setting. For the considerable empirical literature on the determinants of IIT the reader is referred to Greenaway & Milner (1986), Kol (1988) and the survey by Greenaway & Tortensson (1997). For the IIT indices, see any standard textbook on international economics.

[14]This book cannot go into the long debate about proper empirical measurement of IIT. See, e.g., Kol (1988) and Somma (1994). The text refers to measurement at fairly high level of aggregation such as three-digit level, except when stated otherwise. See Somma (1994) for a case study on intra-EC IIT in computers at eight-digit level.

0.42 (Italy) to 0.61 (France) in 1958 to a range of 0.59 (Italy) to 0.73 (France) in 1970. For the EC8 (Sapir, 1992, Table 4), defined as the EC12 minus the four cohesion countries (Spain, Greece, Portugal, Ireland), the range (in a slightly different measurement) in 1970 was from 0.41 (Denmark) to 0.76 (France), moving to a range of 0.57 (Denmark, Italy) to 0.83 (France), of which only Italy recorded a small decline. The cohesion countries are in a special category since it is well-established that a lower level of development (*ceteris paribus*) exerts a negative influence on the degree of IIT. This is readily explained by the positive correlation between the level of development and the scope for product differentiation. Thus, the Cohesion-4 have IIT indices in 1970 (when they were non-members) ranging from 0.22 (Greece) to 0.36 (Ireland), moving up to a range of 0.31 (Greece) to 0.64 (Spain) in 1987.

The second issue is problematic because, in the EU case, market proximity largely overlaps with EU membership, not just in terms of physical distance but also in terms of cultural affinity and market structure similarities. Greenaway's (1989) survey identifies three channels exerting a positive influence on IIT which are themselves a positive function of market integration: overlapping demand, exploiting scale economies and factor mobility. Therefore, EU membership adds an extra stimulus to the degree of intra-EU IIT.

With regard to the costs of adjustment, it is widely suspected that IIT growth entails lower costs of adjustment than growth of inter-industry trade. A unique study by Adler (1970) shows this empirically to be so even for what would seem, on the face of it, to be a homogeneous goods sector such as steel. In the EC, specialisation in different steel products was deepened to such an extent in the 1950s and 1960s that the sharp distinction between winners and losers, expected under pure inter-industry scenarios in steel, hardly arose. More generally, smooth adjustment made possible by IIT specialisation may well have supported a higher EC growth rate, in so far as it lessened the pressures to slow down adjustment by trade protection or subsidies (Greenaway & Hine, 1991). The EC-1992 process has fostered yet more IIT. As to IIT, the EC-1992 programme has coincided with (perhaps even caused) a steady increase in IIT of a 'vertical' kind (that is, in differentiated products), while 'horizontal' IIT (that is, in similar products) remained about the same (in terms of shares of all intra-EC trade). Strikingly, inter-industry trade (indicating country specialisation, often based on different factor endowments and less on product differentiation) saw its share decline steadily between 1985 and 1994 (CEPII, 1998). Since this new work is done at the eight-digit level of product disaggregation, the IIT ratios are not comparable with those mentioned above. With this refined measure, a much better correspondence between the level of development and the share of (both horizontal and vertical) IIT can be found (with the exception of Denmark due to extreme sectoral specialisation). Thus, by 1994, IIT shares for Ireland, Portugal and Greece ranged between 43 and 14 per cent, while Spain and Italy hovered around 55 per cent. The other EC countries have shares between 60 and 70 per cent, with about two-thirds of it in differentiated products. The latter shares invariably increased from those in 1987.

A fully fledged internal market, including no internal frontiers, may prompt companies to exploit 'corporate integration' over the entire EU (see Chapter 10) to the full. It could well imply even greater specialisation among plants within one company located in different EC countries. Hufbauer & Chilas (1974) showed that intra-US IIT was lower than intra-EC IIT and it is possible that EC-1992 may move EU trade marginally towards the US pattern. If so, IIT may not increase, but might even decline somewhat.

6.5.2 Price discrimination and the single market

Price discrimination between national markets in the single goods market must imply that some kind of barriers keep up degrees of segmentation which companies can exploit. First, there is the case of homogeneous goods. Consider Figure 6.8; showing a firm with market power, facing different demand elasticities for its goods in the two EU countries A and B. When segmentation is made possible by non-tariff barriers, pricing uniformly at P_{CU} throughout the CU would not maximise profits. P_{CU} is found by adding horizontally the two marginal revenue schedules; this joint *MR* line cuts the marginal cost curve (*MC*) at *S* (hence, *R* and P_{CU}). The analysis runs as follows. At the uniform price P_{CU}, the firm would sell Oq_2 (at F) in country A. Marginal revenue is negative (extend the line fQ_2 down until it cuts MR_A). In B it would sell OQ_1 with positive marginal revenue (at E). Thus, by reducing sales in A, loss making at the margin is reduced, indeed it is eventually eliminated, while selling this part in B adds considerable marginal revenue. This sales adjustment would pay up to the point where marginal revenues are equal, and equal to the marginal cost of supplying both countries (that is,

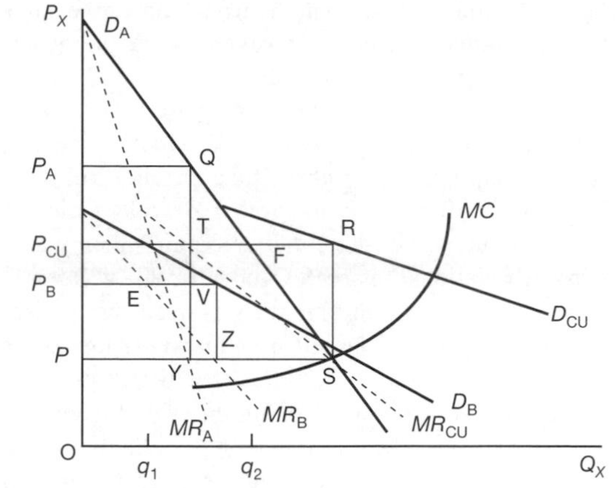

Figure 6.8 Removing price discrimination in a single goods market

in S). It yields MR_A (at Y) = MR_B (at Z) = MR_{CU} (at S) = MC = OP. Such price discrimination will lead to A-consumption at Q and B-consumption at V, hence considerable price differentials, made possible by market power, sustained by barriers of one kind or another.

When the barriers between A and B are removed, the threat of arbitrage will force uniform pricing. Besides the redistribution of the profit reduction to consumers, there is the pro-competitive effect of reducing the dead-weight loss of market power in the single goods market.[15]

Let us now consider the case that both national markets A and B have a firm with market power, f_1 and f_2 respectively. These two firms produce similar but differentiated goods. In the single goods market, this will lead to reciprocal 'fringe competition'[16] Initially, prices will be higher than under competitive equilibrium, though between A and B national prices are likely to differ. National market power is bolstered by non-tariff barriers and goods differentiation geared to local preferences (styling, brand names and so forth.) These access and entry barriers will make f_1 a fringe competitor in B and f_2 one in A. To make a dent in the market share of f_1 in A, f_2 will sharply lower prices for intra-EU exports, while retaining high mark-ups at home; f_1 will act similarly in response. This constellation is not far-fetched. Car markets may have had these properties in the first decades of the EU. Hocking (1980) shows how such fringe competition worked in the car markets of Italy, France, Germany and the UK. This reciprocal 'fringe competition' has the curious effect of increasing intra-EU trade artificially in these products (at least, if trade prices are pushed below those that would have prevailed under intra-EU barrier-free trade).[17] The economic impact of removing non-tariff barriers fully (say, because of EC-1992) may then go through two stages. Regulatory and other non-tariff barriers (for example, controls) increase trade costs. Removing barriers will first eliminate these unnecessary extra costs of intra-EU trade which should be welfare increasing; at the margin, it should sharpen fringe competition, too. Except for peculiar quota (or VER) cases (see next section), the Cecchini report (European Commission, 1988) has shown that the extra costs caused by barriers in product markets are moderate.[18] Hence, it is unlikely that national market power is undermined by removing them. It takes a change in conduct for that to happen, triggered perhaps by the adoption of EU-wide strategies of some incumbents (including takeovers in various national markets). Stage two would then prompt unrestricted EU-wide competition, putting an end to price discrimination. This would add a significant further increase in 'welfare', even though intra-EU trade might fall as trade prices rise and domestic prices decrease. In this scenario the single market would have a strong pro-competitive effect.

[15]This is not written into Figure 6.8 so as not to overload the graph. It can be seen by comparing the reduction of the welfare loss in A (the triangle with QT) and the extra welfare loss in B (a triangle, not drawn, from V straight up to the P_{CU}R line and left until the point where D_B cuts P_{CU}R.

[16]For a seminal article in international trade theory, see Krugman (1979).

[17]Following Krugman (1979) and, for example, Harris (1984), Smith & Venables (1988) and Venables (1990) have formalised these effects, which hinge on scale and product differentiation.This goes beyond the present book. The informal reasoning in the text attempts to capture the essence of this approach.

[18]This formulation should be read carefully. In services rather than goods markets, this may not be valid (see, e.g., Chapter 7). Also, in some goods markets, non-tariff barriers are not the problem, e.g. in medicines where price levels are determined largely by national reimbursement schemes of (social and private) insurance (see Case Study 6.1 below).

6.5.3 Restructuring and efficiency gains of single market deepening

In many industrial goods markets, especially for intermediate but to some extent also for final goods, competition has gradually become oligopolistic. This development is driven by (the fixed costs of) economies of scale and scope, as well as the fixed costs of offering a variety of slightly differentiated goods by a single firm. If oligopolistic competition takes place in national markets in the EU and barriers retain some importance in segmenting the national markets (that is, deepening of the single market still has to be pursued), there is a high probability that national market will be 'too small' for all efficiency gains to be reaped. Why? National markets are likely to have only few firms and they will therefore have relatively high mark-ups, as you would expect in oligopoly.[19] In such a setting, the few firms have no incentive to push output as far down over the scale curves as possible because this would lower their profits, hence a degree of inefficiency remains. Now assume that deepening of the single market occurs in a credible way (as EC-1992 did). This increases the exposure to EU-wide competition and makes the residual demand of every firm more elastic. Mark-ups will fall for two reasons: import competition in the home market and an increase in intra-EU exports to other national markets now also exhibiting lower margins. Thus, output per firm will increase, which should lower average costs. Since the 'welfare' effects of scale always relate to total output (see section 6.2), such pro-competitive effects are likely to be much larger than the trivial allocative gains of (net) trade creation. However, these gains are augmented significantly once the firms start changing their pricing rules altogether and relate them henceforth to the entire single goods market. In practice, this will not happen overnight. Once pricing rules of oligopolists will become 'integrated' over the Union, it is their Union market share that determines their mark-up in each 'national' market. Over time, this will imply a sharp cut in the 'home' mark-ups because no firm will (normally) have a large *Union* market share. As we have seen (in section 6.5.1), domestic prices may fall so sharply that intra-EU trade might even decrease in the first instance. The cut in mark-ups is likely to lead the less efficient firms to make losses and they will exit the market or be acquired in takeovers or mergers. Such a merger wave would thus be a process manifesting the pro-competitive and welfare-improving restructuring of the EU's supply side. If intra-EU competition is effective, it would be wrong to measure the concentration in individual goods markets on a national basis: of course, a national measure would result in seemingly high concentration as if oligopoly had been tightened. If competition is effective across intra-EU borders, EU-wide oligopolies (if they emerge in the first place) would have many more viable players, presumably in effective rivalry. So, over the entire Union, the number of players must have decreased but the remaining ones all compete with each other. Therefore, it is precisely upheavals such as restructuring that will ultimately bring much larger welfare gains from a deepening of the single goods market.[20]

[19]For the reader interested in the underlying microeconomics, consider the following. Suppose there is Cournot-type competition, that is, the few players know that they are interdependent and each sets the quantity of sales and output, based on an expected quantity of output of the rivals. This leads to best-response functions (reaction curves) and a Cournot–Nash equilibrium. A standard result in such analysis is: the greater the number of competitors, the smaller each firm's market share and the less its market power, expressed by the mark-up. With fixed costs, firms need to capture a minimum market share and a sufficient mark-up over marginal costs to cover their fixed costs; this will put a limit on the maximum number of viable firms in the national market (for a formal analysis, see any good textbook on industrial economics, e.g. Church & Ware, 2000, chapter 8). If barriers to entry raise the costs of entry and/or if insufficient deepening of the single market smothers intra-EU import competition, even fewer firms might be a stable outcome, all with high mark-ups.

[20]A good deal of the underlying microeconomics in the 1988 Cecchini report (see fn 25) is based on a partial equilibrium approach attempting to model this reasoning in a two-stage approach, that is, first a moderate increase in cross-border competitive exposure due to the reduction of, what is for simplicity called, 'trade costs' (the barriers removed by EC-1992) and, subsequently, a simulation based on EU-wide pricing rules of the oligopolists. See Smith & Venables (1988) and Gasiorek *et al.* (1992). For a more general approach, see Baldwin & Venables (1995, pp. 1605–14). Whereas the Cecchini report was *ex ante,* the Monti report was written after EC-1992 (see fn 31). It used the same ideas but with more technical sophistication, including econometric and computable general equilibrium approaches. See Allen *et al.* (1998) and the comments by Flam (1998) and Sorensen (1998).

ADDITIONAL READING

Gains of removing national quotas

In textiles and clothing, cars and footwear, *national* quotas or voluntary export restraints (VERs) *vis-à-vis* third countries were reintroduced in the 1970s and early 1980s, making the EU look more like an FTA than a CU.[21] The trade policy aspects are discussed in section 13.4.

Removing (binding) national quotas is pro-competitive if they are not replaced by EU quotas (as this removal would cause quota profits to disappear and cause lower prices, especially sharply down in the least efficient Member States). If they are replaced by EU quotas or if existing EC quotas are no longer apportioned nationally, the critical question is whether there is 'room' in the previous quotas of 'liberal' EU countries. Thus, one could argue that, by the late 1980s, the clothing quotas of the UK, Germany, Benelux and Denmark were no longer binding for their local demand. Giving up the national apportioning by January 1993 must have implied that previously restricted importers in other EU countries obtained (EU) import licences which used to be earmarked for Benelux, the UK, and so on. This will make the overall EU quota 'binding' but in most cases still have a pro-competitive effect. However, it cannot be generalised, because one could, for instance, envisage a common EU quota emerging from the removal of only two or three national quotas. Adjustment fears in footwear were such that this (temporary) solution was opted for: many non-quota Member States were brought under an EU VER *vis-à-vis* South Korea and Japan (up to 1993 only) which had to be restrictive enough to continue to protect the ones with existing quotas.[22] Clearly, in such a case, there is a high probability that this 'integrity' of the single market is bought at the price of increasing protectionism.

Clothing markets are characterised by a multitude of suppliers and competitive pricing. In the case of car the numbers of firms were quite low and competition left much to be desired. The British VER *vis-à-vis* Japanese car imports, dating from 1977, was one important reason why Japanese cars remained consistently much higher priced than the same cars in nearby Benelux.[23] What happened was that the VER permitted collusion, which did not have to be explicit ('tacit'). A more pertinent case is the dominance of Fiat in the Italian car market (54 per cent market share in the late 1980s) in the presence of intra-EC fringe competition and a very small quota for Japanese cars. The pro-competitive effects of removing (national) quotas in the presence of market power may be significant. Figure 6.9 illustrates why.

To focus on the anti-competitive effect of (national) quotas, let us simplify a case similar to the Italian car market as follows. Ignoring for a moment EC imports and domestic fringe competition, the monopolist would be disciplined under free trade by Japanese imports at P_w. Now assume that the quota for Japanese cars (q_2q_3) is just equal to free trade

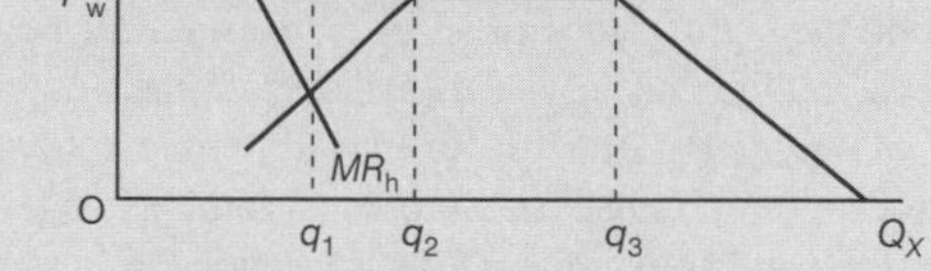

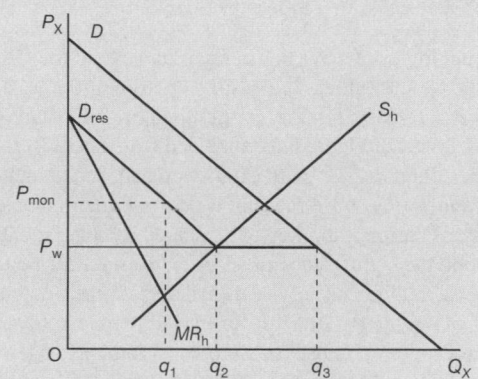

Figure 6.9 Quota removal undermining market power

Source: Flam, 1992

[21]Indeed, as section 13.7.2 (on the economics of FTAs) shows, such truncated 'free' movement can cause persistent price disparities (not due to price discrimination). Carl Hamilton (1991) wrote an influential article showing that intra-EC trade would fully eliminate the price differentials (in clothing) in the EC due to national quotas. However, in the first edition of this book (p. 97, Figure 6.8) a graphical proof is provided that this is not correct in a two-country model with increasing costs: price disparities remain.

[22]Something similar happened in a few products such as silk and selected clothing items *vis-à-vis* China in 1994.

[23]That this is (also) an issue of competition policy is clear from the way arbitrage was prevented: Japanese car dealers are not allowed to ship cars from the Benelux to the UK and this restrictive business practice was condoned under an exemption from Art. 81(3) EC (see Chapter 12 below). In 1993, the EC Court ruled (against the EC Commission) that this condoning of the VER was illegal.

ADDITIONAL READING *continued*

imports at P_w (as drawn). As a consequence, the residual demand schedule the incumbent faces is D_{res}. Note that even a quota equal to imports under free trade will not lead to P_w but to P_{mon} as the prevailing price in 'Italy'. Since the Japanese exporters are constrained they cannot capture sales from the monopolist, so the latter feels free to pursue monopolistic pricing (equating MR_h with S_h, assuming S_h to represent marginal costs). In this static graph the gradual enlargement of the quota (for Japanese cars, until 1999, when car quotas have been eliminated) will discipline the monopolist by shifting residual demand D_{res} to the left, with a net 'welfare' gain of $(q_1q_2)\times\frac{1}{2}(P_{mon}-P_w)$. In all likelihood, there will be dynamic repercussions as well in terms of improved cost minimisation and quality.[24] Therefore, the removal of national quotas not only 'completes' the internal market but also contributes critically to competitive exposure. In this sense, the internal market will promote greater competitiveness, helped by beneficial Japanese competition.

Would intra-EU competition from German or French car makers reduce British or Italian mark-ups when the quota for Japanese cars still existed? The answer is hardly or not at all. In cars there is oligopolistic rather than perfect competition. EC competitors would follow the local price leader(s), and indeed the Japanese suppliers will too (as they gain no market share by pricing low). Therefore, the entire EC/EFTA car sector has shared in the rents induced by national quotas, even though these national quotas (or VERs) existed only in the UK, Spain, Italy and France. No wonder that the revitalisation of the European car industry was only beginning in earnest when EC-1992 was perceived to be credible, spelling the end of these quotas.

6.6 Macroeconomic impact of market integration

Deepening goods market integration beyond the CU is likely to strengthen the pro-competitive effects. The impressive supply-side programme of EC-1992 (as summarised in Figure 5.3) combined wide-ranging cross-border liberalisation with (new-approach, hence lighter) harmonisation, both facilitating cross-border contestability of national markets, via actual or potential entry. Beyond the significance of specific measures for sectors or horizontally, this very wide and deep further 'completion' of the internal market was bound to have noticeable macroeconomic impact as well. We discuss the once-for-all income and employment effects (section 6.6.1) as well as productivity and growth effects (section 6.6.2).

6.6.1 EC-1992: how good for income and jobs?

In terms of economic analysis, the impact of EC-1992 blends estimates of reducing 'trade costs' (such as the removal of border controls, of the extra costs of double testing, and so on – all direct cost reductions for market participants) with estimates of the (net) benefits of the changes in conduct and structure, induced by the greater competitive exposure made possible by this liberalisation and approximation. The discussion here sketches the main results and insights from the Cecchini report of 1988 (an *ex ante* analysis), with our emphasis being on goods markets (for services, see Chapter 7), followed by some interesting features and the main results of the 1996/97 *Single Market Review* – an *ex post* analysis).

The Cecchini report[25] attempted to simulate the economic effect of an exhaustive implementation of the White Paper on the completion of the internal market (see Chapter 5). It sparked a lively and ongoing debate among economists about the merits and shortcomings of the analyses.[26] In at least three ways the Cecchini report moved the analysis of market integration forward: it undertook a major (often, first) effort to measure empirically the economic impact of numerous regulatory barriers (including border controls), it tried to come to grips with the so-called dynamic effects of market integration (based on imperfect competition and scale) and it attempted empirical measurement of selected services liberalisation. The Cecchini report also took an aggregate

[24]There is ample empirical evidence about the European car industry being behind in the 1980s in these two aspects *vis-à-vis* the Japanese. See European Commission (1994c).

[25]See European Commission (1988) and twenty volumes of background reports in the Documents series of the EC Publications Office (Luxembourg) under the title *Research on the Costs of 'Non-Europe'* (1988). For an informal account, see Cecchini *et al.* (1988).

[26]See, *inter alia,* Pelkmans & Winters (1988), Italianer (1990, 1994), Siebert (1990), Winters & Venables (1991), Flam (1992), Pelkmans (1992a), Winters (1992), Hoeller & Louppe (1994), and various issues of *European Economy* in the period 1989–92.

view by simulating macroeconomic (growth, employment and price level) effects, resulting from 'shocks' prompted by EC-1992.[27] The simulated outcome included a 6.5 per cent addition to EC GNP, 1.8 million extra jobs (after an initial fall) and a modest drop in the price level. Of course, this overall macro effect includes far more than goods markets only.

The crucial element in the Cecchini report was the modelling of the pro-competitive effects.[28] A two-stage approach was worked out. First, the removal of physical and regulatory barriers (see Figure 6.3) is simplified into a reduction of 'trade costs', set at 2.5 per cent of the intra-EC trade value (in fact, not so far from what the Cecchini report found overall). In a setting of oligopolistic interaction, with price–cost margins endogenously determined (as in section 6.5.3), the subsequent increase in intra-EC trade will imply lower margins on average (less 'national' market power) and some shifting of sales to markets with lower margins. This will induce companies to increase overall output, which, given scale, should reduce average costs. Since the 'welfare' effects of scale always apply to total output (see section 6.2), such pro-competitive effects could be substantial. Based on average costs declining up to 2 per cent, the welfare effects of EC-1992 could easily reach 1 per cent or more of output. However, a serious drawback to these calculations is that the empirical estimates of sectoral scale effects are dated and might have become inapplicable.[29]

Second, while the first stage only reduces the segmentation in the internal market, the second stage does away with segmentation altogether. This integrated market approach could well reduce intra-EC trade in cases where national market power was initially very strong (see section 6.5.2); in any event, it further magnifies 'welfare' effects – up to 5 per cent of output in highly concentrated industries. It is this work that has been taken as the basis for the 'market integration effects' of the Cecchini report, possibly adding up to 2 per cent (of GDP) to the simulated outcomes. In aggregate studies, following the Cecchini report, the impact estimates are lower, ranging from 0.4 per cent of GDP to 1.18 per cent of GDP (but this merely concerns manufacturing, only one element of EC-1992).[30]

A few years after EC-1992 had ended, the European Commission redid the type of work undertaken by the Cecchini report under the series heading 'Single Market Review,'[31] this time, of course, as an *ex post* study, with even wider scope. From this extremely rich set of empirical studies, we only focus on the pro-competitive effects of further goods market integration. The pro-competitive effects have been addressed in a similar two-stage approach to the *ex ante* studies about EC-1992.[32] The direct demand effect follows from the reduction of 'trade costs' and the pro-competitive effect is obtained by allowing price–cost margins to change in response to changing market shares, induced in the first stage. Since, typically, 'domestic' market shares are relatively large, prices go down more in domestic markets, resulting in an increase of domestic market shares, in order to counteract some of the loss experienced elsewhere in the internal market. This feature is more pronounced if the remaining market segmentation is lifted altogether. Once companies' pricing rules are 'integrated', it is their market share across the whole EU that determines the price–cost margins in each 'national' market. This removes the 'home bias' from companies' behaviour, resulting in the 'home' margins being cut sharply; hence 'domestic' market shares increase and (on this account at least) intra-EC imports fall. Moving to a long-term perspective, the analysis can allow the number of firms to be variable. Thus, some companies which lose market share initially, especially at home, might not be able to cut margins enough and are forced to exit the market or are acquired in a restructuring wave. This wave might well lead to somewhat higher concentration, measured nationally, but – if market integration works – disciplined by EC-wide competition.

[27]This was done by aggregating all the microeffects into four categories and treating them as 'shocks' (e.g. price reductions) in two different macroeconometric models for the European economy.

[28]See Smith & Venables (1988) (a partial equilibrium setting) and the elaboration in Gasiorek *et al.* (1992). For an explanation of the kind of models involved, see Baldwin & Venables (1995, pp. 1605–14).

[29]The scale estimates are taken from Pratten (1988) and discussed, e.g., by Geroski (1989b).

[30]See the brief survey in Baldwin & Venables (1995, pp. 1661–3).

[31]The main economic report is *Economic Evaluation of the Internal Market,* a special issue of *European Economy,* Reports and Studies, 1996, no. 4 (December). A popular version is M. Monti (1996). The 38 background reports were published in 1997 and 1998 jointly by the Office for Official Publications of the EC (Luxembourg) and Kogan Page (London), under the overall series title Single Market Review.

[32]The differences (from, e.g., Smith and Venables (1988) etc.) consist not only in that the new study is *ex post,* that is, it could use actual data (but in fact hardly beyond 1991/92, even though restructuring may come later), but also in its far greater technical sophistication. See Allen *et al.,* (1998). Both econometric and computable general equilibrium approaches are used and (uniquely) the one is used as input for the latter. But this sophistication does not necessarily improve the quality and reliability of the results, especially the ones in the long run. See Flam (1998) and Sorensen (1998).

'Welfare' effects are far larger than in previous studies, perhaps because of the 'limit case' of a fully integrated internal market. Such welfare effects are also relatively large for smaller economies, but this implies they undergo far greater restructuring. Since a merger wave (see Chapter 10) and other strong indicators confirm a forceful increase in restructuring in the EU since about 1987, the general approach is not implausible. The overall income effect of the Single Market Review is lower than in Cecchini, probably due to implementation lags of EC-1992 and the incomplete restructuring in the years for which full data were available (at the latest 1992).

6.6.2 Productivity and growth effects

Another macroeconomic impact of EC-1992 is that on economic growth. After showing how deepening of (EU) market integration impacts, via three channels of efficiency improvement, on (factor) productivity, the elementary Solow model is used to illustrate what Baldwin (1989) has called a 'medium-term growth bonus'.

Figure 6.10 illustrates the transmission of the better functioning of the internal (goods) market, via pro-competitive effects, hence higher efficiency, to higher productivity. Pro-competitive effects work directly on allocative and technical efficiency, as has been discussed before. The pressure on mark-ups and intra-firm reallocation of factors of production result directly from fiercer price competition. Reallocation of factors between firms may result from exit or shrinkage of some firms, outcompeted by others.

The greater competitive pressure will also reduce X-inefficiency (slack, for a given scale and and product structure of output per firm). In addition, it might prompt restructuring, that is, a larger scale (via mergers and acquisitions, or, additional investment in scale) or, via a reduction in – perhaps excessive – product differentiation, hence, the product structure of output. Indeed, EC-1992 was an important factor (besides globalisation of markets, to some degree) for companies to focus on their 'core business' and sell less profitable product lines or outsource certain inputs, initially produced internally.

A new element, not discussed thus far, is the effect on innovation. It is well known that companies in non-homogeneous goods markets attempt to escape from fiercer competitive pressures by resorting to product innovation. More generally, there is a large literature on the question whether sharp competition or monopoly is best for innovation. Over the spectrum from perfect competition all the way to fully fledged monopoly, the recent consensus in industrial economics points to an inverted U-curve. In other words, under very sharp competition, no firm can afford to divert significant resources away from production since mark-ups are minimal or zero. But with monopoly, while the resources for R&D are available, the incentives for innovation may be weak for two reasons: the goods currently in the markets serve as cash cows for the monopolists and hence change is rationally resisted, and, second, the 'quiet life' and lack of rivalry may well fail to bring a sense of urgency to management and workers about the need for timely

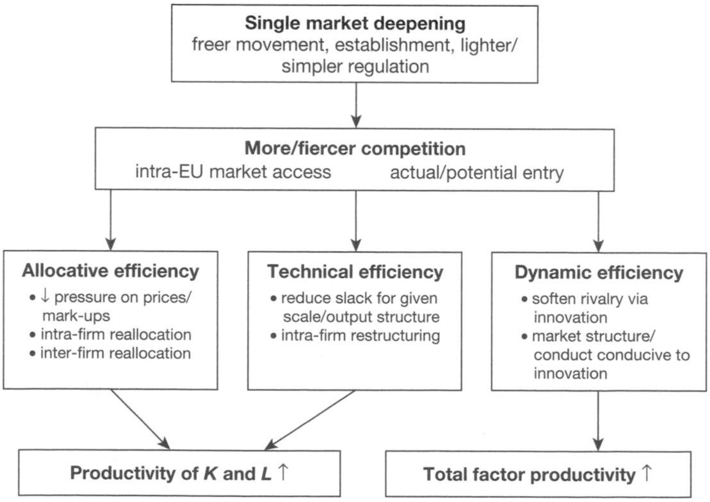

Figure 6.10 How deepening boosts EU productivity

Source: Adapted from Nicodème & Sauner-Leroy, 2004, p. 19. *Economic Papers* No. 218, © European Communities, 2004

innovation. Thus, with an inverted U-curve over this spectrum, if EC-1992 has augmented competitive pressures on thus-far shielded domestic oligopolists, the effect could well be a move higher up the inverted U-curve, hence, more innovation. This would be observed macroeconomically as higher total factor productivity (i.e. not explained by more capital or more labour but 'technical progress').

ADDITIONAL READING

Let us now turn to economic growth. The link between Figure 6.10 and the following is straightforward: once (marginal) factor productivity goes up, it becomes more attractive to expand factor input. Below, this is derived for capital as it is simple to grasp in the context of the Solow model.

Consider Figure 6.11. The higher curve $f(k)$ is the production function (expressed per worker) where $k = K/L$. For any specific capital/labour ratio on the horizontal axis, one can trace a $y = Y/L$, output or income per capita, on the vertical axis. After a steep beginning, the curve bends more and more to the right; this flattening reflects the gradually diminishing marginal productivity of capital (which must be equal to the marginal return on investment) in generating additional income. The lower curve is the (gross) investment function. Given Solow's assumption of a fixed saving rate (s), the function is sy or $sf(k)$ and hence it also bends ever more to the right. However, net investment (the addition to the capital stock, or, accumulation) must take account of depreciation, being δK. If we assume that labour input is constant, the accumulation is $sy - \delta k$. In Figure 6.11 the given depreciation rate is the line δk. Where the gross investment function $sf(k)$ is above this line there will be net investment (such as i_n). This implies that k rises and the economy moves towards the right to E at k_1 where the net investment is zero. Beyond k_1, net investment would be negative and the economy would move towards the left until E is reached. E is therefore an equilibrium. The corresponding per-capita income is y_1, reached at F. If EC-1992 or a further deepening of market integration generates the productivity improvements as depicted in Figure 6.10, it means that the same factor input can produce more output, in other words, $f(k)$ shifts upwards to $f(k)_2$ and since this applies just as much to new capital, $sf(k)$ also shifts upwards to $sf(k)_2$. For any given k (say, k_1) on the horizontal axis, the allocation

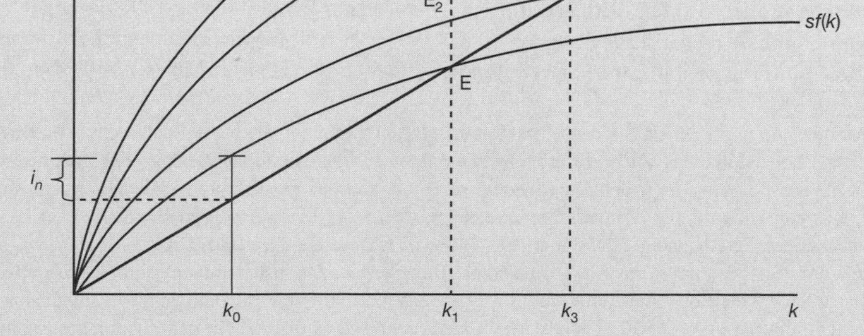

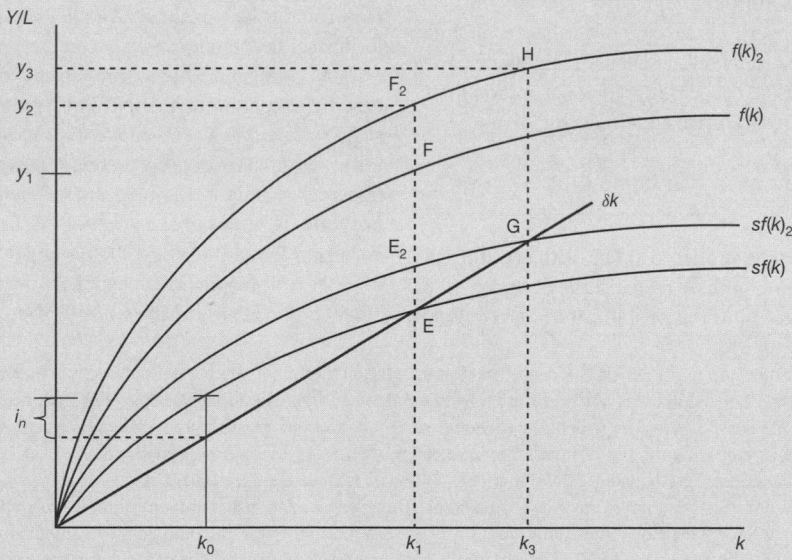

Figure 6.11 Growth bonus of deeper market integration

ADDITIONAL READING *continued*

effect can now be expressed in a rise in income from y_1 to y_2. But k_1 is no longer the equilibrium capital/labour ratio because at k_1 the gross investment curve is above the depreciation line. The new equilibrium is at G, and for output at H, which implies a 'medium-term growth bonus' of y_3 - y_2. The productivity boost stimulates investment and this generates further income gains for the Union. The bonus does not go beyond the medium run since, after a few years, a new equilibrium would be reached at G and (at that higher income per capita) the growth rate is bound to go back to its normal: no extra investment is made any more.[33]

6.7 Economic potential for further deepening

The internal market for goods is practically fully liberalised, unlike those for services or labour, for instance. But that is the legal outlook. Although those legal prerequisites are crucial, they should and cannot be confused with market integration itself. As we have see in Chapters 4 and 5, free movement, in and by itself, does not guarantee that goods move freely across intra-EU borders. Harmonisation, mutual recognition and inter-Member States cooperation are indispensable in preventing or removing market segmentation in the Union.

Yet, this intricate combination of negative and positive integration might still not lead to a market as 'single' as national markets. In an economic sense, further deepening is still possible and indeed worthwhile from a 'welfare' point of view. Three ways of further 'economic' deepening will be briefly discussed: reducing 'trade costs' in the internal market, deepening market integration in the eurozone, and increased price convergence.

6.7.1 Trade costs and home bias

It is well known that 'trade costs' in ordinary international trade are quite high. A recent survey (Anderson & van Wincoop, 2004) put the overall multi-sectoral and multi-country average at 170 per cent of the price at the factory gate. This includes transportation costs (including insurance and time), tariff and non-tariff border measures, information costs, contract enforcement costs, costs associated with the use of different currencies, regulations and legal systems, as well as wholesale and retail distribution costs. For 'deeper' market integration in the EU, transport and distribution probably matter less than 'border costs'.[34] Since tariffs do not exist in the EU and regulatory barriers in the goods market have become relatively low, we should expect EU consumers from any Member State not to make much difference between domestically produced goods and goods originating from the rest of the EU.[35] However, this expectation is not borne out at all: there is a powerful 'home bias' in national purchases in the Union. Head & Mayer (2000) found that, after controlling for distance, Europeans purchase fourteen times more from domestic producers than from equally distant foreign EU suppliers. How can this be explained? And does it suggest an agenda for further deepening?

The 'home bias' literature is strictly empirical and not based on economic theory. The trade costs literature suggests five types of 'border costs': language differences, information barriers, contracting costs and insecurity, lingering regulatory barriers, and different currencies. The last one is the subject of section 6.7.2. Worldwide, Anderson & van Wincoop (2004) suggest a tariff equivalent of 7 per cent for the inconvenience of speaking different languages.[36] Head & Mayer (2000) find that if the Union

[33]An alternative question to ask is whether deeper market integration might not make it more attractive to invest in the EU, quite apart from productivity boosts. In other words, the propensity to invest (s) would no longer be fixed but itself be a function of better market functioning. If so, the gross investment curve would move up, and this must imply a growth bonus, a shift *along* the $f(k)$ curve to the right. Remember that the extra investment induced by deepening the internal (goods) market can be domestic as well as foreign direct investment, and the latter can be intra-EU and/or from third countries (see Chapter 10).

[34]After four decades of goods market integration and some fifteen years of 'transport liberalisation', it is unlikely that transport (see also Chapter 7) and local distribution would differ much between foreign (in the EU) and domestic goods, for a given distance.

[35]Except for a very limited group of final goods which are recognised as distinct (in quality) for geographical reasons: e.g. cheese, wine, Delft Blue tiles, Venetian glass, etc.

[36]Note, however, that the language 'barrier' (and the other 'border costs') can only be measured for a given substitution elasticity between foreign and domestic goods. Anderson & van Wincoop show (pp. 716–7) that differences in this elasticity matter a lot for the height of the 'barrier'.

were to speak one language, home bias would drastically fall. Thus, the great cultural diversity of the EU25 is an asset with large, intangible benefit, but apparently it does carry the costs of putting a brake on deeper market integration. The research on information barriers suggests some borders costs as well but results are hard to generalise (perhaps some 6 per cent). As to contracting costs and insecurity, the literature typically compares trade costs inside multinationals or inside networks with trade outside those two and finds significant differences (perhaps some 3 per cent).[37] As to regulatory barriers, Head & Mayer show that these 'border barriers' have gradually fallen between 1976 and 1995. In their empirical estimates, the regulatory barriers of today remain insignificant.

Since there is no underlying theory for much of this work, and since the home bias reduces but does not disappear when taking the 'border costs' into account, Head & Mayer suggest taste differences as the principal explanation behind the home bias in EU countries. If true (but the authors do not offer empirical evidence), the remaining 'cost' differentials would be rational, and no cause for explicit 'deepening' measures.

6.7.2 Does the euro boost intra-EU trade?

Rose & van Wincoop (2001) find a 14 per cent tariff equivalent of conducting bilateral trade between countries with different currencies.[38] If correct for the eurozone as well, one should expect the 12 countries in euroland to receive a boost in intra-trade starting in 1999. Some positive effects of the euro on intra-EU trade are widely expected but the question is, how much? Since the DM-zone exhibited exchange rate stability for many years before the euro and prospective eurozone countries stabilised their DM exchange rate shortly after the EMS crisis of 1992/93 (see Chapter 17), the impact of the euro might be of minor significance. Moreover, the EU15 had long developed intra-trade of goods and services, with a further rise of the intra-EU share during the 1990s. Therefore, few economists anticipated a major trade bonus from the euro.

In a seminal paper, Rose (2000) came to a different conclusion. Although not directly dealing with the eurozone, he found an empirical regularity in many currency unions over five decades: a common currency tended to augment intra-trade up to 200 per cent (a factor of 3). This sensational result was found improbable and a large literature developed to discuss the impact. After all, why would a common currency make so much difference? For business, hedging is not very costly. Furthermore, there is likely to be a causality problem since currency unions are typically formed by countries already trading intensely with one another – this is certainly true for the EU. A recent survey by Rose & Stanley (2004) attempts to correct for a range of possible biases and other problems and still finds that a currency union increases intra-trade somewhere between 30 per cent and 90 per cent. Of course, in a few years from today, direct tests on the eurozone should be possible, taking account of the 2001–03 recession in the EU and other factors that might disturb the impact found. All that can be said thus far is that no conspicuous kink in the trend of intra-EU trade has been experienced since 1999. An early study by Micco *et al.* (2003) found an increase, starting 1999, of 8–16 per cent.

6.7.3 Price convergence

Goods market integration should ideally lead to price convergence for identical goods over the entire internal market, ignoring indirect taxes and unavoidable transport cost differences. As the present chapter has shown, up to EC-1992 there were several reasons why price convergence could not be expected, such as insufficient competitive exposure, national quotas and remaining regulatory barriers. The Cecchini report (Cecchini *et al.*, 1988) has used a data set with carefully 'homogenised' goods at a high level of disaggregation, taken from Eurostat, to investigate the issue. It was found that, in 1985, price dispersion was considerable, with the greatest deviations in consumer goods.[39] This leads to two questions.

First, even when acknowledging some price dispersion as inevitable, can one detect increasing market integration over time, shown by a gradual move towards greater price convergence? The empirical evidence would seem to suggest a conditional yes in answer to this question. Langhammer (1987), using a data set on cost of living indices for capital cities, finds both a modest move towards price convergence between 1970 and 1985, and a significant difference between intra-EC (and also EC/EFTA) and countries such as the USA and Japan. Note, however, that inflation and tax differentials as well as exchange rate swings have to be properly accounted for. The Cecchini report suggests a distinction between sectors suffering disproportionally

[37] The 3 per cent might not seem so significant but this is partly the consequence of fairly high substitution elasticities (reducing the tariff equivalence for importing buyers).

[38] With a substitution elasticity of 8.

[39] This was measured with the coefficient of variation, that is, the standard deviation as a percentage of the average EC price. For details see Cecchini *et al.* (1988) and *European Economy,* 1988, no. 35 (March).

from intra-EC barriers and other sectors which did not (over 1975–85): the former show greater price dispersion over time, whereas the latter enjoy a tendency towards price convergence. This is a strong empirical confirmation of the expected pressure for reduced price dispersion which market integration should bring about.[40]

Second, would deepening of goods market integration bring 'complete' price convergence and, if not, why not? One should expect EC-1992 to lead to a higher degree of price convergence, but no more. First of all, there are a few very special cases such as pharmaceuticals (see Case Study 6.1).[41] When ignoring those, convergence pressures would arise from direct reductions of the costs of border-crossing and of indirect tax-rate differentials as well as from greater actual and potential competition. Yet, there are two principal reasons why 'complete' convergence should not be expected. To begin with, prices also differ within countries, within cities and even between shops. Competition keeps the dispersion in check. However, only under zero search costs for consumers and perceived perfect identity of both goods and shops (or suppliers) would complete convergence arise. This leads to a closer inspection of actual market structure and business conduct. The expectation of full price convergence would ignore the four determinants (cf. Diller & Bukhari, 1994) of price dispersion in the actual EU marketplace:

1. *The prevailing price structures*: the business problem is that a single EU price may lead a product in EU country A to move out of the market segment in which it is strategically positioned (for example, the watch market in Italy has a high premium on luxury watches).
2. *Oligopolies*: (national) oligopolies, in so far as EC-1992 does not undermine them, practise rigid pricing (see section 12.4.1) for fear of ruinous price wars; also, different phases of the product life cycle in different countries may impose differential pricing.
3. *Distribution structure*: market integration exerts pressures to internationalise distribution, but this process is disparate between Member States, leading to disparate convergence pressures.
4. *Consumer behaviour*: this refers to different elasticities combined with subtle forms of actual or perceived product differentiation; some scope for differentiation is virtually always possible.

CASE STUDY 6.1 Disparities in intra-EC medicines prices

A very special case of price disparities in the internal market is found for medicines, or pharmaceutical products. Among several reasons why very large disparities have persisted for decades one may mention national licensing procedures (allowing a medicine on the market), patents, the hindrances for 'parallel' intra-EC imports (that is, by independent importers), trademarks and brand names for generics (no-longer-patented medicines) and differences in labelling and packaging among Member States. Yet, these together are not as important as the national reimbursement schemes for health insurance, prompting severe price controls in some countries and not in others. The enormity of the disparities is clear from Figure CS 6.1.

EC-1992 has removed some regulatory discrepancies in marketing, transparency of price-setting by Member States and licensing. After EC-1992 a European Medicinal Agency was established (begun in 1995) to perform certification at EU level for medicines based on bio-technology and some others; moreover, it will serve as an arbitration point in case of licensing conflicts. Via judicial review and otherwise, parallel trade has slowly been facilitated. Parallel trade by independent traders is attractive given the price disparities, but proof of identity of the medicine is not always easy for non-manufacturers. The rising share of generics and the Europeanisation of wholesalers are also beginning to exercise a dampening effect on the price disparities.

However, EC-1992 could not tackle the root of the problem – reimbursements – as this is possible only with a far-reaching degree of approximation of the reimbursement systems. As they are part of the social dimension, this is not to be expected soon. Moreover, with disparities in the level of development there are limits to price convergence, even if approximation of reimbursements were ever to be attempted.

[40] See also Diller & Bukhari (1994) for a detailed comparison in four consumer products.

[41] Another one is the car market, but for completely different reasons than for medicines. In the EU car market a restrictive dealer-system was long exempted from the working of Art. 81 (against collusion; see Chapter 12) and this is suspected to have facilitated far-reaching price discrimination, with large and lingering price differentials. See Case Study 12.1. However, the exemption has been tightened considerably since 1995. Goldberg & Verboven (2005) show that the deepening of market integration forces a slow but steady decline of the price differentials over time and that the structural factors causing such differentials are fading in importance.

CASE STUDY 6.1 *continued*

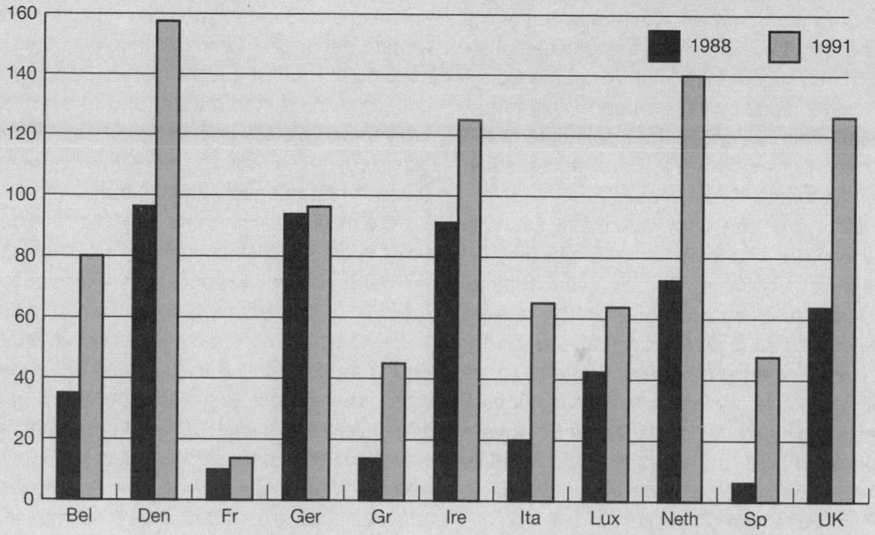

Figure CS 6.1 Medicines' price disparities in the EU depicted as the percentage difference between EU Member State and Portugal

Source: Data from European Commission

The general expectation of further price convergence induced by EC-1992 is confirmed by the Single Market Review,[42] and also applies to Spain and Portugal, having joined in 1986. As expected, highly traded goods sectors exhibit a stronger tendency of price convergence. Further econometric work has attempted to identify the many factors which (could) cause price disparities. Apart from obvious factors such as languages, 'home bias' in purchases, taxation (for example, in alcoholic beverages and cars) and business strategies clearly play a role. Thus, in homogeneous goods markets, price convergence can be observed after 1985. However, in vertically differentiated product sectors (for example, televisions, electronic equipment, optical instruments) which are both research and advertisement intensive, sunk costs on R&D and marketing often create high entry barriers and intra-EU trade is often intra-firm trade (hence, does not increase local competitive pressure) – here, price disparities are quite high and stable. Finally, and perhaps not surprisingly, a high degree of concentration in national markets tends to favour price disparity. Slow but continued price convergence can be detected during the 1990s, as well (Engel & Rogers, 2004).

6.8 Summary

Goods market integration includes, but goes far beyond, the mere establishment of a CU. Also, quotas *vis-à-vis* third countries, regulatory barriers, and possibly fiscal barriers should all be removed and anti-competitive behaviour along national lines ought to be prevented.

The basic theory of CU was set out in section 6.1. Trade creation and diversion are central to this theory; conditions for maximising the net static 'welfare' benefits of CU were derived. If a CU aims to promote intra-CU trade (and this is to be expected), the CET has to be distinctly protective for the relatively efficient producer in the union.

Once CUs are thought to exert a 'cold shower' effect on X-inefficient industries, because of heightened competitive exposure, the gains may well be a multiple of (net) trade creation. The reason is that 'cost

[42]See *European Economy,* Reports and Studies, 1996, no. 4 (December), section 5.4 and annex 4 to chapter 5.

Summary *continued*

reduction' refers to the entire *ex ante* production of the importing country. In the case of scale economies, too, the benefits can easily be a large multiple of the typical trade creation under rising costs. Also here, cost reduction refers to the entire *ex ante* output, this time of the surviving industry. Only in very protectionist cases can scale actually lead to (significant) losses.

Empirical studies of the early CU of the EC have shown that 1958 intra-EC trade had increased by 50–100 per cent purely on account of the CU itself (that is, ignoring growth and so forth) by around 1970. However, the welfare benefits of trade creation and diversion were small though clearly positive (for manufactures). These studies do not incorporate improvements of X-inefficiency and scale effects. It should be noted that the EC12 have strongly 'regionalised' their trade over time, for example in exports, moving from 37 per cent of all trade being intra-EC trade to no less than 61 per cent in 1990.

Goods market integration can best be conceived of in terms of degrees of exposure to competition. Thus, intra-industry trade increases can be interpreted as pro-competitive moves in monopolistic competition. Intra-industry trade has greatly increased over time in the EU.

Removing price discrimination is analysed for two cases. Given homogeneous goods, for companies with some market power and supplying two or more national markets in the EU it is profit maximising to exploit different elasticities of demand by charging distinct prices. With further deepening, the barriers separating these national markets will disappear and arbitrage will eventually force uniform pricing. The results will consist in some redistribution of profits to consumers as well as a welfare gain for society as a whole given the lower deadweight loss of market power. For differentiated goods, sufficient competitive pressure from what initially are fringe competitors in one another's domestic markets will eventually compel oligopolists to cut their relatively high margins at home, resulting in considerable welfare gains. One further step in the analysis – and indeed the actual practice in deepening the internal market – is to consider the number of oligopolists as variable. Once oligopolists are forced to set the mark-ups with a view to the entire single market, concentration will be much lower than at home and the cuts may well be significant. As a result, some companies will become loss making and will exit the market or be acquired in a merger wave. Such a restructuring will increase the scale-driven output per remaining firm, hence, lower costs, in a more competitive environment. Simulations show considerable additional welfare gains after restructuring. The case of removing specific national quotas for price-competitive third country suppliers can be shown to exercise a greater pro-competitive effect than the mere additional imports expected; it also removes market power for residual local demand (after deducting the quota).

The macroeconomic impact of the single market deepening is first discussed on the basis of the simulations in the 1988 Cecchini report (which includes much more than goods markets only) and came with a full implementation effect of more than 6 per cent addition to EU GNP and some 1.8 million extra jobs, after an initial adjustment. The *ex post* Single Market Review of 1996/97 is analytically more sophisticated and even more comprehensive in scope: its income effect is up to 1.5 per cent, among other things perhaps due to reliance on data no later than 1991 or 1992 when the impact of EC-1992 was far from complete. Another approach to macro effects is to study the three main channels of productivity increase, based on the previous static and pro-competitive effects, and subsequently attempt to understand the 'growth bonus' implied by the higher marginal productivity of capital. This medium-run effect may well add up to one-half a per cent or so to the EU growth rate for a number of years, although this is a very rough calculation.

After the turn of the century the deepening of the single market has not fizzled out, particularly in markets other than goods. However, even for goods, three aspects of deepening are worth inspecting. Economists have observed a strong 'home bias' in Europe, in that Europeans buy a large multiple from domestic producers rather than from equi-distant other EU producers. The recent literature on trade costs can be used in trying to explain what further 'border costs' could be tackled in the EU so as to reduce the home bias, a clear sign that markets are not fully integrated. Second, the euro might eventually prompt a significant boost to intra-EU goods trade, if a statistically significant pattern found in many currency unions were also applicable in the eurozone. There are early signs that some such effect might occur. Finally, the degree of price convergence – an economically meaningful indicator of market integration – may well be increased. From empirical research over decades, a secular trend of slow price convergence can be observed, up until today, but there are odd cases with major disparities. Moreover, at the micro level, there are rational limits to price convergence.

CHAPTER 7

Services Market Integration: Method and Economic Analysis

Topics covered

Services market integration differs in many ways from goods market integration. The analogy between Chapters 5 and 6 on the one hand and Chapter 7 on the other is therefore limited. Cross-border services are rarely tangible and are not subject to tariffs, hence there is no such thing as a services CU. The EC treaty, especially the Rome Treaty version, contains a stark contrast between detailed liberalisation obligations for goods and a virtual absence of details on services liberalisation, which is also conditional in important cases. In addition, the history of the EC differs sharply between the two: whereas the CU was achieved by mid-1968 and regulatory barriers were at least addressed subsequently, almost nothing was accomplished in services until the mid-1980s.

From an economic point of view this was a curious form of neglect. The 1990 market services share of GDP was up 10 percentage points from 1970, to reach 48.2 per cent, while job creation between 1980 and 1990 amounted to 10.4 million for market services (compared with a loss of manufacturing jobs of 3.6 million).[1] Even without non-market services, the economic importance of services exceeds that of agriculture and industry together. In the years after EC-1992 a neglect of services market integration would be a serious omission. This is above all true for producer services, led by the narrower category of business services[2] in view of the close relationship between those services and the 'europeanisation' of production and sales. In the EU12, intra-EU trade in goods grew annually by 4.6 per cent from 1984 to 1993, in services overall by 6.4 per cent but in business services by 14 per cent (Rubalcaba-Bermejo, 1999, p. 297). In 2001, business-related services (business services, financial, distribution and networked services) employed 55 million persons in the EU15, or 55 per cent of total employment of non-government jobs. Job growth in business-related services (1990–2001) is, by far, the main source of job creation in the EU15 and exceeded the US job growth in this sector in at least nine Member States (European Commission, 2003, pp. 11–13). Productivity per person employed grew by 1.7 per cent per year between 1995 and 2001; however, this was lower than manufacturing (except in telecoms and finance). This discrepancy in productivity growth between manufacturing and services is usually referred to as Baumol's law.

[1] All data from Buigues & Sapir (1993).

[2] Business services (NACE 72–74) include computer activities, R&D services, legal and accounting, market research, management consulting, architecture and engineering, testing and analysing, advertising, industrial cleaning, and so on.

Bearing this in mind, services market integration is dealt with in the present chapter, combining methods of integration and economic analysis. Given the limited familiarity with the entire family of services, and the distinct characteristics of various categories of them, which have to be dealt with differently in liberalisation and regulation, a survey of the family of services and the relevant classification is first provided. The methods of achieving services market integration are dealt with in section 7.2. After a glance at how services are dealt with in the treaty, the EC Court case law and the 'origin principle' will be discussed, followed by the fundamental issue of how to tackle effectively the question of horizontal services liberalisation. Though reminiscent, at times, of the method for goods markets, services market integration is in fact rather different. A great problem of services liberalisation is its sector-specific nature. Many service sectors have distinct characteristics, terminology and regulation. However, there is the special category of network industries, which are all services in their retail or distribution aspects but may be either goods (for example, gas, electricity, water and sewage) or services (for example, airlines, broadcasting, postal, telecoms and rail) in production and, where relevant, transmission over networks. Network industries have peculiar economic properties and are demanding in terms of both liberalisation and regulation; therefore, Chapter 8 is devoted to them. Following horizontal liberalisation, some attention is paid to sectoral liberalisation other than network industries, for two big sectors: financial services (section 7.3) and road haulage (section 7.4). A case study on accountancy services (Case Study 7.1) illustrates the special problems of services provided by professionals.[3]

7.1 A primer on internal market services

Defining what services are and how to classify them in meaningful categories for the purpose of building the internal market is not so easy. The reader may wish to take a pause and attempt to define services and their categories, before reading the following. One reason for the difficulty of categorising services is the extremely diversified nature of services, a result of the old, threefold division of the economy into agriculture (and fisheries), industry and (the remainder being) services. Another reason is the intangible character of services, making them incomparable to goods. Most goods are 'search goods' (see Chapter 4) whereas services often are 'experience' goods or even 'credence' goods. The simple fact of not being able to see, let alone 'inspect', a service greatly reduces the familiarity of people with services in numerous specific instances. It is interesting that even official statistical offices have been struggling for decades with services statistics. When the EU announced what was called a strategy for completing the internal market in services, as part of the Lisbon agenda of 2000, one element was a multi-annual programme of revising and improving the Union's services statistics.

In Figure 7.1, a classification of services is utilised which should assist the reader in grasping the nature and requirements of an internal market of services. For this purpose, it is essential to know whether services are 'tradable' across intra-EU borders, whether there is a possibility of choosing the mode of 'establishment' in another Member State to serve clients (even when the service itself is not tradable), and whether the service is regulated, since unregulated services should not present any problem in finding clients throughout the internal market. If regulated, the EU will often impose a distinction between B2B and B2C, based on the idea that individual consumers suffer far more from asymmetries of information than business; the upshot is that B2C tends to be more strictly regulated in view of consumer protection. Moreover, Figure 7.1 incorporates categories which relate to the various provisions in the treaty for them, such as networked services (former public utilities), transport, financial services, pure government services, and education and public health in so far as the latter two are not commercial (which is overwhelmingly the case in Europe).

Of the roughly 70 per cent of GNP which services generate in the EU15 (and some 60 per cent and rising in central Europe), not all activity will become part of the EU internal market. The non-tradable category is quite big, ranging from 20 per cent to more than 30 per cent, depending on the Member State. Ignoring pure government services (local, regional or national), a significant share of service activity is purely local. The celebrated example is a haircut but, more generally, practically all retail shops and the bulk of wholesale is local or regional in nature. This is also applicable to the 'horeca' (hotels, restaurants, cafés) sector and some consumer and business services which are tradable but, in terms of turnover, will nevertheless largely be supplied locally or regionally.

[3] The reader interested in other business services is referred to Rubalcaba-Fermejo (1999). For the study of advertising in the Single Market Review, see Bocconi (1997).

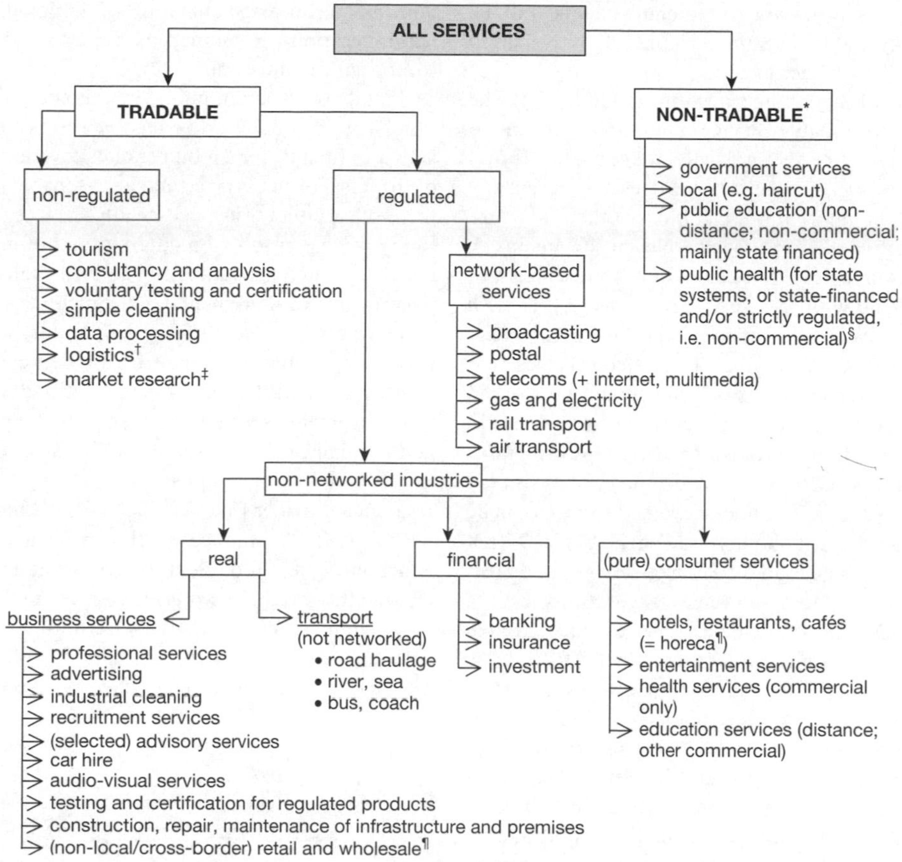

Figure 7.1 Services in the internal market

Notes:

1. The examples mentioned are for illustration only; these lists are not exhaustive.

2. Trade or 'establishment' services may be B2B or B2C.

*Non-tradable, commercial services might still exploit the right to establishment across intra-EU borders.

†Unregulated, other than transport itself (which is regulated).

‡Unregulated, other than laws on privacy (partly EU).

§Patients can, of course, move across EU borders, and case law exists about who pays for what hospital and non-hospital care.

¶Retail, wholesale and horeca are almost entirely domestic, although there might be limited 'establishment' in other EU countries.

Similarly, it is bound to be the case for a very large part of education and health. The strong local/regional bias in services provision is immediately explained by two related characteristics of many services. First, many simple services are usually produced and consumed at the same moment, unlike goods. Second, the relationship between the provider and the client is often based on familiarity and trust. The remaining 40 per cent or more of value-added in services is potentially tradable but this does not mean that, even when the internal market functions properly, the actual cross-border share will come anywhere near to this figure. Still, there is another mode of supplying services across borders, namely, establishment in another Member State, and, potentially, this mode might well be more important economically. Indeed, if trust between provider and client is crucial, it is only through this mode that regular service provision to 'foreign' clients will be commercially viable. Therefore, Figure 7.1 always has to be read with both modes in mind.

A few words about the categories in Figure 7.1. The *non-regulated* tradable services enjoy free movement. The biggest service sector of all – tourism – is, for all practical purposes, unregulated and does not present any problem in the internal market. Most of the other subsectors mentioned are primarily relevant for business, and free movement would seem to work well. The issues are to be found with *regulated* services as well as with the sensitive distinction between public and commercial education and health services. Regulated services first have to be divided into networked and non-networked services. The former are subject to Article 86 EC in addition to the treaty provisions of free movement of services and those for free establishment. They are the subject of Chapter 8. The non-networked services can be usefully broken down into four categories: transport (not networked), financial, pure consumer services and business services. Most non-networked transport, a considerable part of financial services and variable shares of the different business services are B2B. Only few of these subsectors are pure business services, however. Some will be B2C and this has often implications for free movement: in B2C the requirements of consumer protection may be such that detailed harmonisation must accompany liberalisation for tradable services. In such instances, the mode of 'establishment', usually via direct investment or acquisition, might enhance competition somewhat but a genuine internal market will not emerge. In B2B regulated (non-networked) services, there may be special sections in the treaty such as for financial services and transport or there is a direct link with (EU) regulated goods under the new and old approaches (see Chapter 5) such as with testing or certification. The EC-1992 programme has greatly contributed to progress in these areas, with a combination of minimum harmonisation and mutual recognition. In other business services, in construction and construction-related professions (for example plumbers, electricians) and some consumer services (for example entertainment), it is less obvious why free movement might be throttled or blocked. Even if local laws apply, there would seem to be no reason why the service job could not be competed for by providers from other Member States, unless it might turn out that the Member State of origin fails in, say, adequate diploma levels or administrative controls on dubious companies. However, as will become clear in the following, matters are not at all simple, and as late as 2002 the Commission published a painful survey of the widespread protectionism, red tape and arbitrary behaviour of national and local administrations in numerous services of this kind (European Commission, 2002).

Finally, what about public health and public education? The internal market legally refers to economic activities (that is, for a remuneration covering most or all of the costs of the service and a reasonable profit) and, therefore, publicly financed health services (which may imply price controls of medicines and of medical acts under regulated insurance, and so forth) fall outside the purview of free movement. On the margin, there may be cases where the client (here, the patient) seeks health treatment in other EU countries. In that event, the EC Court has ruled that patients are entitled, in enjoying free movement as a right, to unconditional payment for non-hospital care (up to the cost of the same treatment at home) and that hospital care has to be agreed with the insurance provider first. Analogously, publicly financed education (thus, practically all primary and secondary education and a good deal of tertiary education) falls outside the internal market. However, distance education, adult education, MBAs, retraining, on-the-job training and all kinds of seminars do fall under free movement and can thus be provided cross-border.

7.2 Method of achieving services market integration

The establishment and proper functioning of the internal market for services has been problematic from the start. The legal details go much too far for the present textbook. However, the enormous economic importance of intra-EU services trade, actually or potentially, and of 'establishment' in services across borders, compels us to gain a basic understanding of the method of accomplishing the services internal market. First, the basic provisions in the treaty (which have remained unchanged in substance) are set out briefly. Second, a few crucial rulings of the EC Court are summarised since these have laid the foundation for the liberalisation of those services not treated sectorally in the treaty. Third, the horizontal approach of the proposed services directive is explained and its possible reach and derogations.

7.2.1 Services in the treaty

The treaty section on services contains virtually no detail on how and what should be liberalised. Large sectors such as transport and financial services are either under a special regime or conditional. No clear stages are defined[4] and no timetable is foreseen.[5] The related section on the right of establishment is clearer but, typically, this applies equally to goods and services suppliers.

The reasons for this asymmetry are not hard to find. They include the (in the mid-1950s) very limited share of tradable services in total services output, the inherent difficulties in providing many services – requiring trust and close contact between supplier and consumer – in other jurisdictions with different languages and customs, and the then low stock of EC direct investment in the EC (providing few incentives for producer services to 'follow' their customers). Accomplishing approximation was probably seen as a daunting task, given idiosyncratic regulatory and supervisory regimes[6] in the Member States. Initially, therefore, little more than tourist services (for which there is little to liberalise) and transport services (as a necessary corollary of goods market integration) could be identified as being of any economic significance for cross-border transactions in the Community.

There are four ways of providing cross-border services.[7] Recasting them in EC treaty language, one may distinguish temporarily or permanently provided services in another Member State.[8] The *temporary* services are defined as 'services' within the meaning of the treaty (Articles 59 to 66 now Articles 49 to 55 EC). The three temporary services consist of pure cross-border services (between immobile consumers and immobile providers), or, alternatively, services for the consumption (or provision) of which the consumer (or supplier) crosses borders. The permanent provision of services in another Member State falls under the regime for the right of establishment (Articles 52 to 58 now Articles 43 to 48 EC).

Both services and establishment in the treaty framework suffer from considerable limitations, be it for different reasons. The services chapter would seem to be generally applicable but it is not. Transport services are dealt with in a separate 'transport' title of the treaty, pursuing what is called a 'common transport policy'. In the 1950s, the various modes of transport tended to be subject to restrictive national regulation, including (major) subsidies, administered prices, discriminatory taxation and managed intermodal competition. Reasons included forms of 'capture', protectionism, limitations of infrastructure, 'public service' obligations and even national security (for maritime shipping). This explains the ambiguous wording of the transport title, suggesting a balance between 'harmonisation' of socio-economic interventions and liberalisation. As a result, progress on transport services remained largely deadlocked until the European Parliament won an EC Court case against the Council, in 1985, accusing it of a 'failure to act' (Article 175, now Article 232 EC). Ever since, the emphasis has heavily been on liberalisation, limiting approximation merely to 'essential requirements' (safety, professional competence and so on). Rapid progress was the result.

Financial services liberalisation was conditional upon 'the progressive liberalisation of movement of capital' (Article 61.2 EC, now Article 51.2 EC; see also Chapters 9 and 17 below). But as late as early 1986, six out of twelve Member States still practised exchange controls and one had a dual currency market; little liberalisation had actually taken place except in the right of establishment for banks and insurance companies.

Network industries or their (retail) distribution did not fall under Article 59 (now Article 49 EC) – at least not at the outset. For all practical purposes, they had been carved out of the services chapter. Article 86 EC was widely interpreted as accepting (national) 'exclusive rights' for network industries and a national universal service obligation. As a result, Article 49 on the free movement of services was simply not applied to services of networks industries for a long time. Liberalisation, under conditionality, only began in the late 1980s.

But what economic meaning did the treaty's services chapter have without such important services sectors?

Indeed, such economic significance was initially very limited. The most important overall category outside big and free-market tourism comprises cross-border services by professionals such as lawyers, accountants, architects, physicians and pharmacists. However, in these cases other obstacles arose, such as

[4]Article 63 (now Art. 52) EC speaks of a 'general programme' to be drawn up, or, in its absence, of a stage in the liberalisation of a specific service, without elaboration.

[5]After the first stage (four years, that is beginning 1963). However, directives would be voted on by qualified majority.

[6]Including self-regulation of professional services with *de facto* entry barriers for non-nationals.

[7]Note that, nowadays, the WTO's General Agreement on Trade in Services also distinguishes these four models, inspired by the Rome Treaty.

[8]As subsidiarity would suggest, intra-Member State services do not fall under EC competences.

a lack of mutual recognition of diplomas. The diploma issue is somewhat special here as national laws and practices (for example for lawyers and notaries) or health traditions and insurance conditions (for example for doctors, pharmacists and dentists) may justify local traineeships or some measure of local education. Nonetheless, there are strong indications that 'capture' plays a role here as well, in other words, that diploma recognition is made more cumbersome than is justified in order to protect vested interests by extra barriers to entry. At the same time, it is as well to realise that even with recognition, the economic incentive for temporary cross-border services of most professionals is weak; non-incidental services will require close and regular contact with the customer, so that services will eventually prompt local establishment. One interesting exception is consultancy, where little regulation applies and cross-border services are more often an alternative to establishment. The reader is also referred to Case Study 9.3 where diploma recognition is discussed (the idea being that establishment of professionals is a cross-border factor movement) and Case Study 7.1 (below) on accountancy, showing that a single market for accountancy services is impeded by a host of obstacles, not just diploma recognition.

The establishment regime has different limitations. In analogy with goods, obligations to abolish restrictions are imperative and Article 44 in particular details a number of specific duties for Commission and Council. Indeed, this framework has formed a good basis for direct investment (see Chapter 9) and some specialised service sectors with a low degree of (self-)regulation (for example, consultancy, voluntary certification). Where regulation is prominent, however, achieving freedom of establishment proved difficult. For financial services, establishment directives were adopted only after the transition period – a decade too late. In telecoms, television, postal, air and rail transport, legal or factual monopolies in public ownership at first made establishment in another Member State taboo. Furthermore, Article 46 allows significant derogations of the kind that Article 30 allows for goods, which requires well-developed case law to prevent misuse. As noted, a major services area where establishment could have an impact is in professional services. The stumbling block was similar to the removal of technical barriers under Article 94: an extremely strong attachment to the very details of education, training and examination of professionals, backed up by unanimity – all the drawbacks of the old approach in goods.

CASE STUDY 7.1 The uncommon market for accountancy services

Once one steps outside the big four regulated service sectors (transport, financial services, network industries and health) and unregulated tourism, one encounters the many complex cases of professional services. As with other professional services, a single market for accountancy is in (slow) process for almost four decades. The reasons are complex. First, the initial approach to recognition of professional diplomas was wrong, based as it was on total harmonisation in the 'old' approach. It also suffered from the sequencing problem (see section 3.2.2) in putting harmonisation before liberalisation. Second, there is a strong interdependence between the free movement of these services and the right of establishment, at any moment in time as well as over time. Third, accountants work both as individuals, with or without specific authorisation to supply specific services, and as firms, with or without such authorisations. This means that both freedoms (services and establishment throughout the Union) should apply to both types of suppliers, and currently they do not. Fourth, accountants supply many services (statutory audit, accounting for firms, merger audit, public sector audit, insolvency practice, expert witness, tax advice, client representation, consulting and so on) and only statutory audit is subject to EC regulation. This leaves many subtle regulatory barriers for other accounting services untouched, if restrictively regulated by one or more Member States and (presumably) left unchallenged as being justified in the general interest.

What has been achieved thus far? The fourth and seventh company law directives define the obligation for all firms in the EC, above a certain turnover threshold, to have a statutory audit of accounts, for individual company accounts and for consolidated accounts. Apart from some basic principles, the method of the audit and the criteria for authorising (that is, how and who) remained to be decided by the

CASE STUDY 7.1 *continued*

Member States. The eighth company law directive, adopted in 1984 and partly, on professional qualification, an 'old' approach – was concerned only with the approximation of conditions for authorising statutory auditors. Implementation is far from identical in Member States because there is leeway with respect to independence, liability and the level (not the topics) of the required knowledge in examinations. Nevertheless, in some Member States it has had a major impact: for example, in the Netherlands, a large group of second-tier accountants entered the market for statutory audits and altered market structure in a pro-competitive way (Maijoor, 1995).

The new approach switched to broad notions of mutual recognition of diplomas in three directives (see also Case Study 9.3). The idea – applicable to accountants – is that the authorisation, rather than the details of education and professional organisation, in Member State A should be the main reason to mutually recognise in B. Of course, when in B, the accountant is subject to all professional and ethical rules valid in B, but the authorisation itself should not be a problem. In accounting, all Member States still impose an aptitude test, but this has primarily to do with the local law and to ensure locally relevant good practice. A better way to facilitate cross-border services and movement, the new approach is itself under a process of gradual development. Moreover, it applies to persons, not to accounting firms.

Some pressure emerged from the EC Court. The *Ramrath* case[9] facilitated the free movement of accounting services on the basis of judicial recognition. The Court applied (besides the obvious non-discrimination test) the three tests: justification, mutual recognition or home country control, and proportionality. The ruling confirms precisely the freedom to provide services in the form advocated above, both for individuals and firms. It was only after 2000 that significant progress could be observed, helped by broader incentives of diploma recognition as well as by harmonisation of accounting standards and the general move to improve the horizontal liberalisation of services. A new directive on the recognition of professional qualifications, consolidating and simplifying no less than twelve specialised directives on professions as well as the application of the three general diploma directives to the professions, was adopted by the Council and EP in June 2005 (see Case Study 9.3). It establishes a lighter regime for cross-border services than for establishment, for example. In this sense it is a corollary of the proposed horizontal services directive (see section 7.2.3.). The substantive work of accounting and auditing in the internal market has at long last been (quite radically) harmonised, first, by Regulation 1606/2002, imposing the use of International Accounting Standards by 2005 for all listed companies in the Union and, subsequently, by a major amendment of the eighth company law directive, in that all EU statutory audits will have to be carried out in accordance with the new Directive on international standards of auditing, based on COM (2004) 177 (adopted October 2005, not yet published). Undoubtedly, these measures will improve the functioning of the internal market for accountancy services while, at the same time, remove costly obstacles in globalised equity markets.

Establishing an internal market for services hinges on free movement.[10] The provisions are also silent on whether there should be an external policy for services, and whether the EC has exclusive power (as with trade in goods). In the transport title Article 84 (now Article 80) caused great uncertainty because it seemed to make free movement in sea and air transport service optional, at the discretion of the Council.

The method of accomplishing the right of establishment is broadly similar to that in services. There are three

[9]Case C-106/91 *Ramrath v Ministre de la Justice* [1992] ECR I-3351.

[10]It combines (1) an obligation (in Art. 49) to abolish restrictions on the free movement of services, (2) a standstill clause, (3) a programme approach (in Art. 52), and (4) a non-discrimination clause for remaining restrictions extended to all residents. The scope does not extend to nationals of a third country, except when the Council so decides.

differences, and all three are important. First, rather than having a non-discrimination clause, companies receive 'national treatment'.[11] National treatment, a principle in EC and GATT law, refers to treatment of non-domestic establishments being no different from that of domestic companies. Second, as noted there are wide derogations in Article 46, similar to Article 30 for goods.[12] Via a cross-reference in services (Article 55), these derogations are applicable to services too. This raises the question of how widely or narrowly the EC Court would interpret these rules. Again, these ambiguities have not helped to make progress in these areas. Third, regulatory mutual recognition was introduced for diplomas of professionals but at first in an 'old' approach, hence based not on minimum, but on extensive, harmonisation. As noted, this has proved no less cumbersome than old-approach approximation under Article 94 for goods.

7.2.2 Case law and the origin principle

The case law on the free movement of services has gradually become similar to that for goods, with a delay of a decade or so. Of course, this applies to the principles, not to the specific details.[13] This interpretation has helped the integration of the services market to move forward.

As with goods, there is first the distinction between discriminatory and non-discriminatory barriers. Discrimination on account of the provider's nationality[14] or the provider's Member State of establishment is prohibited, but broad derogations under Article 46 are possible. For non-discriminatory restrictions, it would seem that the case law on goods (that is, Article 28) has inspired the jurisprudence on services, too. In the *Säger* case[15] and later, there is an analogy with *Dassonville:* restrictions 'liable to prohibit or otherwise impede' cross-border services of the 'temporary' type are not allowed (see section 5.3.1 above). This economic approach covers those measures affecting the ability to provide, those increasing the cost of the relevant service (a very wide-ranging prohibition, as in *Dassonville*), and those discouraging its provision. Interestingly, it also explicitly protects consumers who are prevented from receiving the services of their choice.

It is then a small step to introduce the analogy with *Cassis de Dijon* (see Case Study 5.1). A Member State cannot normally prohibit the provision, in its own territory, of a service lawfully provided in another Member State, even if the conditions in which it is provided are different in the country where the service provider is established. If there are no justified derogations (see further) this looks like mutual recognition (MR). But is it? The case law for regulated goods makes this dependent on the *equivalence* of the objectives under derogations (like SHEC) in the origin and destination countries. If equivalent in objectives, the differences in specific details in the laws of the Member State(s) of origin, and of destination are irrelevant for free movement. However, if 'equivalence' is not specifically mentioned, and therefore does not matter, one often denotes the *Cassis de Dijon* quote (above) as the origin principle. *Whether the two principles converge or not, hinges therefore on the way the derogations are disciplined (that is, limited):* equivalence of objectives, or a weaker or no discipline. If and in so far as the discipline is weaker or absent, the origin principle in combination with these 'undisciplined' derogations leaves more discretion to Member States. However, exactly for that reason, 'equivalence' (hence, MR) would give more certainty to firms and Member States and help free movement more. The case law on services is not entirely clear on the distinction. It is crucial to understand why.

The main reason is the imbalance in services between the legislator (EP and Council, on proposals of the Commission) and the judiciary. Why? The EC Court has been faced with many cases, because, especially in service sectors, possible market failures not clearly specified in the treaty (thus, other than transport, finance and the professions), the EU legislator has long failed to engage in (minimum) harmonisation. Without guidance from what Council and EP wanted to regulate, the EC Court was forced to stress a fairly radical free movement approach, but also prudently *permit very wide and many derogations in fairly general wording.* Rather than a consistent and straightforward application of the origin principle, which might have undermined much regulation in destination countries, the EC Court could do no more than 'wait' until the EU legislator determined what the proper limits of the derogations

[11]Except for 'post-box' establishments; their registered office, central administration or principal place of business (Art. 48) is needed. Note that national treatment is similar to non-discrimination but may facilitate market access.

[12]Article 46 specifies, in very broad terms, 'public policy, public security and public health'.

[13]An extremely detailed survey of EU case law on services is published by the Commission (DG Internal Market) as *Guide to Case Law, Freedom to Provide Services* (2001). The text above highlights only a few basic principles.

[14]Services provisions cannot be reserved for nationals only, except when the derogations in Art. 46 make this restriction indispensable (but the Court assesses this carefully, see further).

[15]Case C-76/90 [1991] ECR I-4221; ruling 1991.

should be. The EU legislator took up this challenge in a few remarkable directives where the origin principle is explicitly the basis of free movement (for example, the TV without frontiers directive (see Chapter 8) and the e-commerce directive 2000/31), but refrained from doing so more generally for services. It is only after the discovery of many obstacles to service trade and establishment in 2002, that the Commission was finally in the position to propose horizontal services legislation (see section 7.2.3).

In analogy to Article 30 the wide derogations of Article 46 and a host of related other objectives[16] legally need not be incompatible with free movement of services. To verify whether this is so, national regulations have to pass three tests. The first one is the justification test, that is, overriding reasons related to the public interest. But this is restrictively interpreted (indeed, like Article 30). Thus, economic aims or administrative convenience do not qualify. Second, there is a kind of home country control test. Statutory conditions (if equivalent), already satisfied in the home country, cannot be duplicated by the host country, and the supervisory authority of the host country must take into account supervision and verifications in the home country.[17] Finally, there is the proportionality test: the restrictions should be indispensable and least restrictive (that is, no less restrictive means should be available).

7.2.3 Horizontal liberalisation of services: merits and traps

The combination of a highly conditional 'free' movement of services, a lack of treaty specifications on how to actually accomplish the process of horizontal liberalisation (that is, outside sectoral liberalisation), and extensive EC case law compelled to employ broadly formulated derogations (in the form of principles, much more than 'rules') given the failure of the EU legislator to engage in clear harmonisation, did not augur well for the completion of the internal services market. It was only once a 'services strategy' had been agreed in 2000, in the framework of the Lisbon goals to make the EU perform economically far better (see Chapter 18), that decisive improvements of the functioning of the single market of services could become a serious priority for the EU legislator. Given the tremendous specificity of services and the complicated EC case law, the regulatory design of the legislation matters a lot. In particular, what combination of liberalisation, prohibitions of types of national measures, harmonisation for aspects which the EC Court placed under 'derogations' (and the limits of them) as well as cooperation between the Member States for purposes of home-country measures and in avoiding red tape hindering free establishment, is desirable? How could that combination be optimal in balancing the great need finally to liberalise and the justified minimum regulatory protection in the public interest?

Figure 7.2 provides the basis for an optimal regulatory design for horizontal and sectoral services liberalisation. One can read the schema as a clarification of the so-called services draft directive[18] which has been widely misunderstood. However, as will be shown, no matter how this horizontal draft directive eventually looks like in terms of detail, it will be hard to escape the logic of Figure 7.2. Where certain elements of the regulatory design, as depicted in Figure 7.2, would be modified, it is easy to trace the ramifications of such a choice for other elements in the flowchart.

As noted before, but too often forgotten, services liberalisation in the EU is always about free movement and free establishment. Moreover, it applies solely to economic services, hence not to non-economic services of a social or cultural nature, or, indeed, to publicly financed and/or (non-commercially) regulated services such as (most) public health and public education. Figure 7.2 is relatively clear about free establishment (the right-hand side). While a number of overly restrictive or unreasonable measures or requirements of Member States, or regional authorities, should be unambiguously forbidden (the third arrow), positive measures include conscious administrative simplification such as 'one-stop shopping' for licences or other red tape (where Member States should act in the common EU interest, which they evidently have not, thus far) and cooperation between authorities in different jurisdictions for quickly retrieving the proper information, and some degree of harmonisation of criteria for licensing and procedures. Given the existing uncertainty for a myriad of services, a screening process of national laws in EU working groups should provide all necessary information about

[16]The Court has referred to all the essential requirements specified in the old Art. 36 as, in principle, applicable to services too, as well as to some other ones (which it calls 'mandatory'), e.g. 'coherence in the tax system' (C-204/90, *Bachmann;* ruling 1992). See the Commission survey of 2001 (in fn 13).

[17]In goods there is an anology with the Court's principle that identical testing should not be duplicated.

[18]COM (2004) 2 of 13 January 2004, *Proposal for a Directive on Services in the Internal Market* (informally known as the Bolkestein directive).

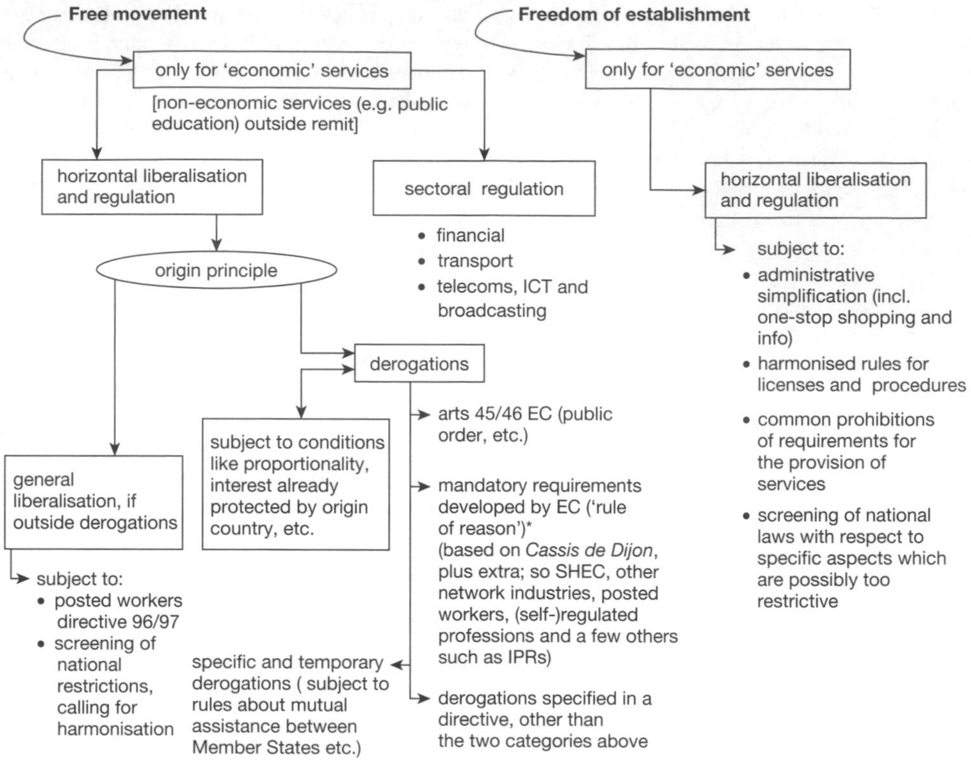

Figure 7.2 Regulating services liberalisation

*Note that, if structural assistance between Member States and some further harmonisation are dealt with, the EC Court is likely to reduce significantly the number and scope of derogations regarded as mandatory requirements.

further simplification or abolition of red tape, or, in exceptional cases perhaps harmonisation.

The problem of free movement is a good deal more complicated and the sensitivities are not to be underestimated. If one ignores sectoral liberalisation, dealt with under special regimes in the EU, the starting point of horizontal liberalisation is to ask what core principle ought to be applied over the range of services sectors: mutual recognition or the origin principle. What they have in common is the idea that, except for derogations, a Member State cannot normally prohibit the provision, in its own territory, of a service lawfully provided in another Member State, even if the conditions in which it is provided are different from those in the country of destination. Where the two principles differ is that the origin principle stops right there, whereas MR (at least, if inspired by the tradition in goods markets) adds a qualification for the derogations: if the objectives behind the derogation(s) are 'equivalent' (for example, for typical SHEC-motivated rules, see Chapters 4 and 5), free movement still applies. There are two ways to determine whether objectives are 'equivalent': the EU case law and (minimum) harmonisation, focused on goals only. The upshot is that the origin principle may override some of the worst, protectionist rules for services that cannot be justified, but otherwise will merely invite a litany of derogations, the limits of which are hard to foresee and for which only generally worded disciplines, such as necessity and proportionality, will be available. This is indeed what happened with the draft services directive of 2004. In Article 16 the origin principle is stated as: 'Member States shall ensure that providers are subject only to the national provisions of their Member State of origin which fall under the coordinated field'. Wisely, this is first followed by a list of what in any event is prohibited for Member States. But, as Figure 7.2 shows, the economic meaning of the origin principle is hard to determine in the light of many derogations. The discipline of the derogations is mentioned in the box left/below the derogations and comprises, *inter alia*, the criterion whether or not the 'interest is already protected by the rules of the State where the service provider is established'.[19] The difference between the origin principle and mutual recognition vanishes if this quote of the case law is interpreted to mean that the objectives of the relevant laws of the two countries are 'equivalent' (what the EC Court calls 'interests . . . already protected').

Once free movement, based on the origin principle, is not reduced or blocked by the derogations, general liberalisation applies (lower left). However, since service provision is labour intensive and, in some sectors such as construction and construction related professions (painters, plumbers, electricians) and simple 'horeca' labour services, heavily dependent on labour costs, the posted workers directive (Directive 96/97) governs any contracts under this general liberalisation. As will be discussed in Chapter 15, this directive largely prevents the provider applying the labour costs of the country of origin for a temporary service in the destination country.[20]

CASE STUDY 7.2 Economic impact of services liberalisation

Cross-border services liberalisation has not received nearly the same attention from economists as freeing cross-border trade in goods. Two studies have attempted to simulate the economic impact of horizontal services liberalisation as proposed in the EU in 2004. As Figure 7.2 clarifies, the scope and economic meaning of the proposals are difficult to determine due to the many derogations and the complicated regulatory design of the draft legislation. But it is also true that no authoritative economic methodology exists to analyse the problem. In Kox *et al.* (2004), the previous empirical OECD work on regulation (for example, Nicoletti & Scarpetta, 2003, and referred literature therein) is used to calculate bilateral heterogeneity-of-regulation indices between Member States. It can be shown that the differences in regulation as well as in their restrictiveness between Member States is a major reason for low levels of services exchanges and establishment across intra-EU borders. The magnitude and economic significance of these indices is estimated. The next step is to what extent it is expected that these heterogeneity indices will decrease as a result of horizontal services liberalisation. With these lower indices, the impact on trade, direct investment flows (establishment) and (net) job growth is simulated. For both commercial services trade and the stock of direct investments in the EU, the authors find an increase in the range of 15 to 35 per cent.

Copenhagen Economics (2005) bases its calculations on 'tariff equivalents' of a range of barriers to intra-EU services trade, derived by converting qualitative into quantitative obstacles in a 'restrictiveness index in services' for the internal market. 'Cost-creating' tariff equivalents (causing higher costs for capital and labour) are distinguished from 'rent-creating' tariff equivalents (throttling competition). The tariff equivalents fall in various ways owing to liberalisation. Model simulations at the micro level, giving the effects of the lower tariff equivalents, are imputed into a macro model. The authors expect a welfare gain for the Union of 37 billion (0.3 per cent of EU GDP) and 600,000 extra jobs after adjustment.

[19]Quoted from the *Guiot* case, C-272/94, [1996] ECR-I 1905 para. 13; see Commission survey, 2001, as in fn 13, p. 116. Similar, in the *Säger* case, C-76/90 [1991] ECR I-4221 para. 15, Commission survey, op. cit. p. 119 ff.

[20]One reason the draft services directive is so sensitive in the EU of 2005 is related to the uncertainty on the part of labour unions in the EU15, whether the draft was closing all possible loopholes to get around the posted workers directive. This goes far beyond what a textbook should deal with, short of observing that only very special instances can be imagined. The real reason behind the fear of EU labour unions was probably that enforcement of the posted workers directive by the Member States is sloppy, and that a complicated services directive would only enhance the incentives to practise illegal services provision, especially where central European workers would be involved given the enormous wage discrepancies with the EU15. Furthermore, as with free establishment, a screening period can be used to discover any additional need to harmonise and more intense cooperation between the Member States should help to support the actual exploitation of free movement.

7.3 Financial services: the EU regulatory framework

Traditionally, one distinguishes three financial services: banking, insurance and investment services.[21] In Europe, unlike in the USA, banks provide the bulk of investment services because of the continental tradition of 'universal' banks. Nowadays, banks and insurance companies can link up or merge in the EU. Thus although the services are distinct, separately regulated, and governed by different supervisory arrangements, the providers are often financial conglomerates or at least carry a mix of services. Nowadays, some national supervisors are also conglomerate in the sense that they control all three financial services, based on their distinct regulation. Another conceptual issue is the often less than clear cut distinction between financial services and capital (the latter being a factor of production, and is hence dealt with in Chapters 9 and 10). In any event, there are complex linkages, and cross-references are indispensable for a good understanding. In turn, the two are crucial for the operation of monetary policy (see Chapter 18). In the EU financial services sector, the distinction between services and capital as a factor of production – crucial for the lubrication and growth functions of finance for the European economy as a whole – is hardly used. The distinction that matters in markets and for purposes of regulation is wholesale versus retail. In the present chapter the focus is on retail, after a brief exposition of the method of pursuing a simple market for all financial services. Thus, in section 7.4, banking and insurance will be singled out, whereas investment services are dealt with in Chapter 9. A further difficulty with the traditional threefold distinction of financial services consists in the importance of 'risk management' for business. Traditional insurance is about physical events, not about financial events such as hedging cash flows. Thus, one may view 'derivatives trade' as an insurance policy against financial events risk. However, this is too specialised and the reader is referred to appropriate texts (for example, Steinherr, 2000).

The quality of the overall framework for a properly functioning single market for financial services depends on the appropriate nature and degree of liberalisation, approximation and indeed centralisation in other sensitive financial fields. These functional linkages entail major policy implications for national economic, fiscal and monetary policies in the eurozone. If there is insufficient willingness to adjust or centralise these policies, where appropriate, the functioning of the internal market for financial services will remain suboptimal. Thus, such a broad notion of a European financial area would consist of four elements:

- the internal market for financial services;
- the internal market for financial capital and money;
- a single currency;
- fiscal and accounting approximation.

The Rome Treaty explicitly recognised the linkage between the first and the second element, but in such a way that the failure to accomplish the second led to a blockage of the first one. As to the third, in the pre-EMU stages of the Maastricht Treaty, the existence of different currencies (which were not irrevocably fixed) led to risk-based price differentials between transactions denominated in different currencies. Failing to address the fourth element may severely undermine the economic incentives for cross-border consumption of some financial services and distort the internal capital market, even though – formally – free movement of services is not impaired.

EC-1992 and the Maastricht Treaty have caused a sea-change in the pursuit of a European financial area. Establishing the internal market for financial services was seriously pursued for the first time, following the abolition of exchange and capital controls. The abolition of the latter is complete and without reciprocity for third countries.[22] However, one should not jump to the conclusion that cross-border capital mobility is now close to perfect and comparable to domestic capital mobility, as Chapter 9 will show. Critical is the distinction between the money markets (assets with a maturity less than one year), which have become fully integrated in the eurozone, with a converged interest rate, and equity and bond markets with (much) longer maturity, and serious obstacles despite the legal free movement. The introduction of the euro in January 1999 in a zone of twelve EU countries had a major impact, providing a new impetus to improve the first, the second and the fourth elements of the European financial area.

For a proper understanding of the regulatory framework permitting liberalisation in the internal market, without market failures, one has to be able to answer a range of questions: Is the provision of financial services temporary and/or permanent (that is, establishment)? Is the provision between immobile suppliers and immobile

[21] A fourth one is 'asset management'. However, this is about financial capital as a factor of production and is treated, therefore, in Chapters 9 and 10.

[22] See Directive 88/361, in OJ L 178 of 8 June 1988. See further Chapters 9 and 17 below.

consumers in different Member States? Is the consumer moving across the border or is it the supplier, or, indeed, does provision take place via e-commerce? What are the market failures involved in the three types of services and what is the necessary regulation ('proportionality' and minimum approximation) to overcome them? Can one merely focus on the institutions (prudential control) and/or do the services themselves require regulation and/or supervision? Should wholesale markets (that is, among financial companies directly), corporate clients and retail consumers be regulated differently, given different internalities? How do services link up with capital aspects and the introduction of the euro?

There is no need for the reader to become expert in financial services markets, but the nature of these questions and the economic (that is, market failure) reasons why they are posed should be appreciated. The EU has gone through four stages in establishing and deepening its financial market integration, here mainly retail. The methods employed are interesting and partly novel in regulatory terms. They are summarised in Table 7.1.

Financial services market integration began in the late 1970s (many years after the transition period) with the 'right of establishment' (permanent provision). It required little adjustment, other than a licensing system in all Member States. Insurance and securities markets were still so segregated that the supervisors were not coordinating. A

CASE STUDY 7.3 Why regulate financial services?

Building on the analysis of market failures made in Chapter 4, the complexities in financial regulation can be readily understood, even if the details are left to the specialists (for an excellent survey, see Llewellyn, 1999, on which the following is based). Financial regulation pursues three objectives: (1) to sustain systemic stability; (2) to maintain the safety and soundness of financial service providers; (3) to protect the consumer. The market failures at issue consist of externalities (relating directly to the first objective) and internalities, especially asymmetric information. But regulating too strictly to overcome these two market failures might, in turn, prevent competitive challenges (say, by new entrants) from ever bringing down any incumbents, thus risking too high a concentration or the permanence of lax competition. The pursuit of objective no. 2 is done by means of 'prudential regulation'. Consumers cannot judge the soundness of financial service providers and, in any event, can never know what subsequent behaviour providers will display after signing the contract. Regulation and permanent supervision need to ensure this. The third objective is mainly, though not exclusively, approached via 'conduct of business' regulation. It comprises mandatory information disclosure, the honesty and integrity of firms and their employees, the level of competence, fair business practices and minimum standards in marketing.

Systemic stability is critical because of the pivotal role of banks in clearing and payments systems, the dangers of bank runs and the adverse selection and moral hazard induced by guarantees such as the lender of last resort (the central bank providing liquidity to solvent banks, in case of crisis) and deposit insurance (this desirable protection of the deposit holder might push the provider into excessively risky conduct, without having to bear the consequences if it goes wrong). The problem of consumer protection is that the case in general is easily made but popular pressures, often after a scandal, may cause it to become excessive, with (in the EU) restrictive positioning as a result, causing the internal market to suffer. The mantra of the 'general good' (see Case Study 7.4) has permitted too much protection, but finding the appropriate level of harmonisation in the presence of diverse preferences might also fail. Solid providers have every interest (indeed, with the consumers) to require minimum standards, yet if these standards are set too high they will act as entry barriers, throttling competition. A particular problem with banks is herd behaviour, causing extreme pressures to exploit short-run gains from risk taking even if one is conscious about it. The reason is usually that banks fear (or, observe) that competitors will do this anyway, and they have no choice other than to follow. Setting common conduct standards is then next to impossible and a regulator can break the gridlock.

banking supervisors committee was formed because large intra-EU payments (over the SWIFT system) and the interbank and currency markets implied systemic risks (see Case Study 7.3 for market failures underlying financial regulation). The second stage, that is EC-1992, turned to cross-border service liberalisation. This could potentially be far more significant, especially if suppliers can solicit business in other Member States without necessarily establishing there.

At this stage, the EU made two fundamental, regulatory choices: (1) approximation would relate primarily to the soundness of institutions, via prudential regulation and supervision, and would *not* be about the details of the *services* provided – thus avoiding the nightmare scenario of endless, detailed approximation, like the 'old' approach in goods (Chapter 5); (2) even for the institutions, prudential regulation would be minimal, with supervisors mutually recognising each other's licences under a radical new principle: *home country control.* In other words, consumers and businesses in Spain could be supplied with financial services by company H from Denmark, and their confidence in H would be based on a licence ('single passport') to offer financial services. This single passport would result from 'home (prudential) control' by the Danish supervisor, and would be (indeed, must be) recognised by the Spanish supervisor. Home country control with minimum approximation has great advantages: it obviates endless arguments about licences for non-national operators, often raised to block foreign entry; it facilitates EU-wide strategies where feasible in these services and thereby introduces potential competitive pressure into often overly protected national markets; and it enables mutual recognition and perhaps even regulatory competition in the services themselves, as long as there is equivalence in objectives (for example, consumer protection).[23] This possibility is important for services innovation and consumer choice since, until the mid-1980s, many EU countries maintained rigid regulation on financial services. As Table 7.1 shows, home country control and the single licence (or passport) were introduced in all three types of financial services, albeit half-heartedly at first in investment services (which was overcome in 2004).

As a services integration method, home country control received acclaim both inside and outside Europe. But did it work? If it did at all, its impact in retail remained far below expectations (see section 7.4). The Member States, whether because of initial protectionism, consumer pressures or incipient loss of power of regulators, did not allow free movement of financial retail services to work. First, the 'general good' clause, left undefined by the EC court, was open to a large degree of discretion by national supervisors or regulators to prohibit or condition cross-border services, even though the provider formally enjoyed the 'single passport'. Lacking approximation, except some minor instances of retail regulation (see the third stage in Table 7.1), the Commission was forced to narrow the application of the 'general good' clause in two interpretative documents in 1997 and 2000. Case Study 7.4 explains the issue: B2B services may escape the 'general good' clause but little, if any, progress was made on true retail. Second, key subsectors such as (supplementary) pensions were excluded from the insurance and securities liberalisation and approximation, or – like mutual funds – were narrowly defined and otherwise restricted.[24] Third, the lack of other framework conditions frustrated actual (free) movement – such conditions include, for example, appropriate tax harmonisation and accounting standards. Thus, the cross-border provision of mortgage credit, already problematic owing to currency risks until the euro, was killed by an amazing ruling of the EC Court,[25] holding that the interest payments are not tax deductible in the country where income tax is paid if the mortgage is obtained from a provider from another EU country.[26] The Court invented the dubious public interest justification of the 'coherence of the tax system' (of the country where the interest would be deducted)[27] for this purpose.

[23]As noted in section 7.1, the EC Court has developed case law about this last point, in anology with *Cassis de Dijon.* However, this will work only if the 'general good' clause is narrowed down considerably (see Case Study 7.4).

[24]For example, marketing and management of funds remained under host country control, and tax distortions throttled cross-border provision from all EU countries except (zero-tax) Luxembourg. These restrictions were later tackled under the Financial Services Action Plan (see further).

[25]C-204/90 *Bachmann* [1992] ECR 249.

[26]Besides the huge disincentive on the demand side, there is also a major disincentive for cross-border suppliers. The latter pay a withholding tax on interest paid over mortgages (and consumer credit). A domestic lender can 'net' this against corporate tax whereas this withholding tax is non-refundable for the foreign (EU) supplier.

[27]Consistency in using this justification would render it straightforward to convict (zero-tax) Luxembourg for its refusal to agree to a withholding tax on interest income earned on capital or savings or to supply detailed and full information, because this distortion has caused a clearly unwanted loophole in tax systems of other Member States (if only because of equity reasons) while lowering their (*ceteris paribus*) tax revenues. See also Case Study 9.1. Such a conviction never happened but the underlying tax issues for interest earned on savings or capital was resolved in 2003 (via a directive) and with foreign tax havens in 2005.

Table 7.1 EU financial services: four stages of deepening the internal market

Stages	Banking	Investment services	Insurance
↓	←	Host country control	→
(Mere) establishment (1970s)	No approximation	Minor approximation (listing)	No approximation (life and non-life)
↓	Banking Supervisors Committee	No committee	No committee
(1st generation)	Home c.c.	(Mixed) home/host c.c.	Home c.c.[a]
(EC-1992) Cross-border service liberalisation	←	MR of home c.c.	→
	←	Single 'passport'	→
↓	Approx. prudential rules[b]	Approx. prudential rules[c]	Approx. prudential rules[d]
			Insurance Supervisors Committee
Retail/consumer protection	Minor/selected approx. (credit cards/cross border payments) + deposit guarantee	Minor approx. (e.g. investor compensatory schemes)	No approx.
↓	Mostly still different, hence, 'general good' inhibits (retail) cross-border services (see Case Study 7.4)	Mostly still different, hence, 'general good' inhibits retail cross-border services and transaction costs of cross-border securities purchase excessive	'General good' inhibits retail cross-border services
(2nd generation) Deepening (via FSAP)	←	Minor further approximation of prudential rules	→
(except wholesale capital markets, see Chapter 9)	Some approx. of services offered, of retail level[e]	Securities Supervising Committee	Approx. of insurance brokers

Notes: Apart from a few illustrations, the table is about 'methods' only. The reader is advised to read section 9.1 as well (wholesale/capital). FSAP = Financial Services Action Plan (2000–05).

[a] On car insurance (compulsory in EU) and liability of car drivers, there is a mix of host country control and MR (e.g. one green liability card for Europe).

[b] Directives on 'own funds' of banks, solvency, no large exposures, consolidated supervision.

[c] Capital adequacy of investment service providers (merchant banks, etc.).

[d] Directives on solvency, on the investment of technical reserves, maxima for assets according to risk, diversification and currency matching.

[e] For instance, on information to be provided to consumers (distance selling of financial products) as well as on mortgage credit (excluding tax breaks) and e-money.

Table 7.1 also illustrates the reluctance of regulators and supervisors in stage 3 to cooperate in bringing the internal retail market forward. Supervisors tend to be followers and it is probable that they would defend their turf. And they tend to view greater competition as a potential threat to the stability of the financial system for which they are responsible. Indeed, whereas competition in many other markets may result in failing firms, a failing bank is often regarded as a failure by the regulator. So, regulators tend to err on the side of (excessive) prudence, which *de facto* reduces competition. The banking supervisory committee had existed since 1977 but was, at first, low key. With home country control the committee was strengthened, yet the debacle with the BCCI bank[28] prompted more stringent coordination. Yet, the question arises whether basic directives plus a web of bilateral commitments among supervisors is an appropriate application of subsidiarity. In terms of the subsidiarity test laid out in Chapter 3, the cooperative approach amounts to step 3 and should be credible to market participants relying on home country control. In insurance, a committee was installed only in the mid-1990s; and in securities the advisory committee, which emerged in the 1990s, was reformed only under the Financial Services Action Plan (FSAP) in 2002.

The unsatisfactory framework of the first three stages would probably have lingered, perhaps with a gradual improvement due to outside pressures of globalisation in the finance industry. However, two radical changes have prompted a renewed acceleration of liberalisation and approximation: e-commerce (and e-money), and the introduction of the euro. The fourth stage of Table 7.1 comprises several older proposals which have become politically acceptable as well as new ones, explicitly to address electronic financial services.[29] The euro has also removed currency risks (at least in the eurozone) and this has helped pension funds to appear on the agenda. In addition, the euro has re-ignited the debate about further centralisation of prudential supervision, especially for securities, because most of these are not traded on the basis of physical presence on the trading floors of exchanges. Systemic risks are thus more prone to EU-wide contagion than before and the euro reinforces this. Linked to this is the issue of the lender of last resort in the Union. In case of a financial crisis (for example, a bank run or contagion), central banks would temporarily provide enough liquidity to trusted financial institutions to prevent sound providers from suffering from a liquidity squeeze and to bolster up consumers confidence. However, such temporary liquidity expansion can nowadays only be decided, and instructed, by the European Central Bank (ECB). In 2003, a Memorandum of Understanding between the ECB and national supervisors was signed to address these issues (step 3 of the subsidiarity test).

All in all, the deepening of financial services market integration has moved to the top of the EU's agenda, be it more for wholesale than for retail. The biggest unknown is probably the actual use of cross-border e-commerce in financial services, which vitally depends on legal certainty and sufficient contractual information to consumers. It brings to the fore a range of consumer protection issues for retail. In turn, this pushes Community law into domestic civil law (namely, contract law), because legal redress for e-consumers from other countries would become very difficult, and indeed for each Member State. The current EU rule that e-consumers should always be able to rely on their domestic contract law, might facilitate matters for consumers but may well throttle the emergence of financial e-commerce from the supply side as too complicated and costly.

So far in this book, one specific cross-border service has not been addressed at all: cross-border payments. Of course, with exchange controls removed, such controls no longer seemed to pose a problem for credits or financial capital transactions, whereas for goods they had always been unrestricted. However, the excessive costs of cross-border money transfers emerged as an issue in the early 1990s, discrediting the single financial services market in the eyes of the ordinary consumer. Studies in the early 1990s showed that average transfer costs of ECU 100 in the EU amounted to no less than ECU 24, and the number of days exceeded those of domestic payments. Clearly,

CASE STUDY 7.4 General-good clause: protectionism or consumer protection?

Both in banking and insurance, the 'single-passport' to provide retail cross-border services under mutual recognition and home country control, remained of limited economic significance due to the restrictive application of the 'general good' clause in many Member States. The root of the problem is found in the regulatory strategy applied for the establishment of the internal market for financial services, namely, an emphasis on the soundness of banks and insurance companies (that

[28] A bank active only in the UK, whose clients were almost entirely Arab, Indian and Pakistani, and with its formal headquarters in Luxembourg, turned out to have been supervised neither by the UK nor by Luxembourg.

[29] The debate on regulatory reform as a way to provide an extra impetus to EU economic growth, which had been relatively low during the mid-1990s, also helped in this respect. See Chapter 10 on the potential growth impetus of the FSAP.

CASE STUDY 7.4 *continued*

is, the institutions). In contrast, there has been no approximation of, for example, consumer protection regulation with respect to the services themselves, except for some aspects of consumer credit and distance marketing of financial services. The EC Court has long recognised the 'general good' as a justification for restrictions of the free movement of services (since 1979). But it has never been willing to define the concept, and saw itself eventually forced to admit an incredible laundry list of (national) objectives as 'imperative reasons' in the general good. Such recognised objectives include: protection of workers, social protection, consumer protection, preservation of the good reputation of the national financial sector, prevention of fraud, social order, cohesion of the tax system, protection of creditors, and a host of others.[30]

No wonder fragmentation of the internal market has not been overcome. What is striking is the apparent violation of the notion that a Member State should respect equivalence of objectives in other Member States, for example the home country, even when the details of a service regulation differ. Some Member States have even gone so far as to apply the 'general good' clause in the very few areas where some approximation of services has been accomplished (for example, consumer credit). Clearly, solutions involving less restriction must be possible here. The Court has attempted to introduce a test to check whether protectionism is masquerading as consumer protection but giving no benefit to the consumer. In the *Mars* case[31] it introduced the 'circumspect consumer', able to judge for himself only if properly informed. This would no doubt be valid for B2B services across borders (as recognised in insurance). The Commission believes that the general good clause cannot normally be invoked in such B2B services. Member States have also tried to hide behind the defence that provisions in contracts (for example, banking) fall under contractual rules, and thus civil law and only weak intergovernmental conventions apply, not Community law. Suppose country B requires loan contracts to have a fixed interest rate. This might prevent the sale of a variable interest loan in Member State B from a financial service provider in country A, and – according to the Commission – this clearly is overridden by (supreme) Community law on trade between Member States; the service of the provider in A should not need to be modified in cross-border provision. The *Caixa* case,[32] ruled by the EC Court on 5 October 2004, is relevant here, although it is about the right of establishment. The Court ruled that the French prohibition on the remuneration of 'sight' accounts in euros amounted to an unjustified restriction for foreign entrants (such as the Spanish Caixa bank), which do not dispose of extensive branch networks, and hence can hardly compete otherwise than by rendering their services more attractive.

Given the pervasive and somewhat arbitrary application of the general good clause, three options present themselves. First, a blank form of mutual recognition could be envisaged, but this might confront the consumer (who is not always fully informed) with all kinds of services originating from (perhaps up to 24) Member States with different details on consumer protection. Second, at the other extreme would exist an approximation of services in so far as consumer protection requires this. Since views differ between EU countries, this process would be slow, although it might be accelerated by the pressure arising from (financial) e-commerce. There is a serious risk of too high protection (as consumer associations demand 'maximum harmonisation' (sic); one ought to submit this to regulatory impact assessments, as Chapter 4 notes). Third, an interim solution could consist of far higher standards of information disclosure and EU-wide codes of conduct by associations of financial service providers. This could serve as the basis for what is sometimes called a (parallel) 26th regime for retail finance in the single market.

[30]See OJ C 209 of 10 July 1997, p. 15 and OJ C 43 of 16 February 2000, pp. 17–18.
[31]Case C-470/93 *Mars* [1995] ECR I-1923.
[32]Case C-442/02 *Caixa* [2004] ECR I-8961.

such charges and delays are inconsistent with a single financial services market. There was a host of reasons for these costs, including the (costly) recourse to correspondent banks, lack of adequate interbank infrastructures, and lack of standards and procedures internal to banks. In the euro area, these excessive costs are even less tolerable. Decisive progress for 'small transfers' and ATM withdrawals was made in the eurozone, after some foot dragging by the banks in Europe. In Case Study 18.2 the issue is dealt with in a eurozone context.

7.4 Financial services: the economic impact

Measuring or even discussing in qualitative terms the impact of removing intra-EU barriers to financial services market integration is difficult for several reasons. First, the removal has been done in stages, as Table 7.1 shows, including the FSAP.[33] Second, because (minimum) approximation of retail services regulation has hardly taken place, the 'general good' clause and consumer difficulties in assessing the legal consequences of cross-border services have acted as strong breaks to mutual interpenetration. It is not clear whether a blend of new approximation and 'regulatory competition' may eventually reduce such actual and perceived obstacles, but this is bound to be a slow process. Third, the three subsectors in financial services show signs of convergence and this complicates the impact analysis. Of course, the convergence process is, in part, a consequence of the 'universal bank' model of the EU, which has now explicitly been allowed to encompass the insurance business as well. Fourth, all three subsectors have been subjected to other shocks in the same period (say, since 1988) which creates a problem of causality. Shocks were probably greatest in the securities business, closely followed by banking. Thus, it might be difficult or inappropriate to attribute observed changes in economic variables such as efficiency, market structure or, indeed, degree of competitive pressure to single market initiatives. Fifth, it is somewhat artificial to ignore the abolition of exchange (or capital) controls in the EU in 1988, which was made irreversible by the (Maastricht) Treaty from 1994 onwards. Indeed, this book employs a distinction between goods (Chapters 5 and 6), services (Chapters 7 and 8) and factors of production (Chapters 9 and 10), but financial capital is so difficult to define that the separation remains to some extent arbitrary. It is not possible effectively to liberalise cross-border services and establishment – certainly not for wholesale markets and corporate clients – without abolition of exchange controls (see also Chapter 9).

In the following, the discussion distinguishes between the banking, insurance and securities subsectors, though a degree of fluidity is emerging among these three via finance conglomerates or *bancassurance* (or *Allfinanz*). The present chapter, being more focused on retail, discusses only banking and insurance. In Chapter 9 the securities markets and the significance of the FSAP are dealt with.

7.4.1 Banking

The attribution problem in banking is considerable because, in the 1990s, European banking was subject to a range of shocks or trend changes, whilst another one (the euro) was looming. The single market initiatives were only one of those shocks.[34]

First, EC-1992 and its follow-up were one (major) element of much wider regulatory reform. This trend included, besides the EU liberalisation, national regulatory reform (especially in EU countries with restrictive banking rules), a wave of privatisations, and the increasing application of national and EC competition rules to banks. One upshot of the EU prudential directives was that the practice of employing restrictive conduct of business rules (in, for example, Italy and Spain) for prudential purposes disappeared via national regulatory reform. Although this did not remove the 'general good' type restrictions, it introduced new or more intense international competition almost overnight. In addition banks were, far more than in the past, subject to shareholder pressures, inducing a greater focus on return on equity and return on assets.[35]

Second, new technology has had a profound impact on banking. It has enabled a higher quality of service and lower costs in cash transactions (using ATMs and so on), and further reduced the use of cheques (which are used in only about half the EU countries, electronic transfer between accounts being routine in the other half). New

[33] See COM (1999) 232 of 11 May 1999. The FSAP was virtually completed early 2005. See http://europa.eu.int /comm./internal_market/en/finances/actionplan/stocktaking_en/htm. See also Chapter 9.

[34] See Inzerillo *et al.*, (2000), Gros & Lannoo (2000) and Walter & Smith (2000) for careful surveys with somewhat different emphases.

[35] Inzerillo *et al.* (2000, p. 297), show that, as recently as 1997, return on equity of private banks in Europe was two to three times that of state-owned banks, dependent on the type of bank.

technology also facilitated small and personal loan provision by relying on large data sets, and so reducing adverse selection (of bad borrowers) and moral hazard on the side of the banks. Possibly, some cost reductions were obtained by (IT) capital/labour substitution.

Third, there is a trend of increasing diversification of financial assets. This tends to exert a negative influence on the traditional banking business as savings may now go to mutual funds, various ('life') insurance products, supplementary pensions, or indeed personal equity portfolios. But since Europe has universal banks, this 'new' business (new, at least, for traditional banks) was largely internalised by the incorporation of investment funds and insurance companies.

Later in the 1990s, the introduction of the euro was certain and had begun to influence the strategies of all financial service providers in the EU (and to some extent, beyond). The euro has eroded traditional bank business even further as it eliminates the bulk of the revenue from intra-EU currency trading.[36] The major impact, however, is felt in the securities trade; but in Europe this is also dominated by the banks (see Chapter 9).

It is in this light that the impact of EC-1992 on banking services has to be assessed. Economic Research Europe (ERE, 1997) reporting for the Single Market Review, reached the following key conclusions:

1 It has intensified banking competition, with price reductions identified in selected activities and countries.
2 However, price differentials between EU countries have hardly reduced, except for credit cards and mortgages.[37]
3 Cross-border financial services have registered strong growth, but not in retail, and foreign (EU) branches and subsidiaries have increased rapidly (but from a low base).
4 There is only weak evidence of scale effects (to be exploited through increased market size) – this accords with (many) other estimates;[38] there is also some evidence that intra-EU liberalisation has led to better exploitation of economies of scope (that is, a differentiation of many services, with a major element of joint costs, hence cheaper than stand-alone provision). Many studies show, nevertheless, that any scale and scope effects in banking are swamped by the differences in operating costs. Hence, greater competition is the key to higher efficiency, not so much market size.
5 A dominant strategic response has consisted in domestic mergers of a defensive kind, often to reduce 'overbranching' or to widen the bank's activities to insurance and/or specialised investment services. This has led to increased concentration – indeed, worryingly so in some of the smaller EU countries.[39] This trend has been reinforced after the EC-1992 period itself was over. Between 1991 and 2003, domestic bank mergers dominated cross-border ones in number (often tenfold) and value (often fifteenfold) (see Walkner & Raes, 2005, p. 23).

By 2005, a single banking market at the retail level was still far off. A review solicited by the Commission made this very clear.[40] Apart from the severe problems in diverse consumer protection (hence, the virtual impossibility to design EU-wide retail banking products), and (tax and other) difficulties in creating true pan-European banks, it is also interesting to reflect on some drawbacks of the EU regulatory strategy, as set out in Table 7.1. There are two clear drawbacks. First, the single licence, a courageous step at the time, does not appear to be effective in promoting cross-border banking services. Precisely because so many other barriers (in retail) have remained, its merit is doubtful. Second, and closely related, home country control – a novel idea at the time – is not accompanied by the right incentive structure. It applies only to branches of foreign (EU) banks, not to subsidiaries. The latter are subject to host country control, in other words, a pan-European bank has to deal with several dozens of supervisors. Where branches are used, the home country supervisor bears the cost while the host country supervisor receives the benefits of reliability and soundness.[41] A special new feature is the banking sector in central Europe.

[36]Dermine (1998) also points to the need to diversify the loan portfolio beyond the national market in order to counter the negative impact of a possible asymmetric shock (see also Chapter 18); the permanently low inflation in the eurozone has already reduced the interest margins on deposits. Other possible repercussions are discussed in White (1998, pp. 8–9).

[37]Kleimeyer & Sander (2000) find some convergence of retail lending rates, based on co-integration techniques, for the period 1985–96.

[38]See Inzerillo *et al.* (2000, annex) and the survey by Dermine (1999).

[39]The 'relevant market' can still be considered national. In retail that was and is no doubt the case but 'contestability' might now increase because of internet banking. The problem is precisely whether internet banking can really work across intra-EU borders.

[40]Review of FSAP, reports of four independent expert groups, 7 July 2004.

[41]However, this might be less lopsided than it seems at first sight. Remember that cross-border market penetration may go both ways, hence the problems may cancel out.

Banking is rapidly improving in the new Member States[42] even if the level of financial intermediation is still relatively low (ECB, 2005). Conspicuous is the very strong foreign presence: 72 per cent of bank assets in 2003 were foreign-owned, mainly by banks from the EU15. Thus, a transmission of shocks from the EU15 may have a much greater impact in a new Member State than the other way around. Moreover, a foreign branch in central Europe might have 'systemic' importance in the host country (while being very small for the bank overall), and hence the home country supervisor might not observe a problem while the host country supervisor might fear to struggle with a threat to stability.

7.4.2 Insurance

Insurance has not been swept by national deregulation trends ahead of EC-1992 and the liberalisation of capital flows has probably not had a major impact on intra-EC insurance business. Impact analysis is thus focused on EC-1992. However, it took three generations of insurance directives before the internal market was established and the implementation calendar is such that the impact only became observable by the late 1990s. The following is therefore largely an analysis of the expected impact.[43]

As to the nature of competition, confidence and close contact with the customers (often via brokers) are critical in this service market, with potentially serious asymmetries of information in the case of individuals and small firms. The degrees of product differentiation and scale economies are moderate. In non-life insurance, products are relatively standardised, and in life insurance and pensions, the greater scope for product innovation is often reduced by regulation. Even if product regulation is liberal, new products tend to be imitated swiftly since there are no patent laws in insurance. Fairly strict regulation and supervision and high switching costs for consumers have led to attitudes of building reputation by solidity and service in case of claims, at the cost of price competition and innovation. Only since the mid-1980s have competitive pressures been on the rise, due to the encroachment of banks, the influence of information technology, and the entry of foreign insurers into local markets.[44] Scale economies derive from the need to have an adequate information base to price risks accurately and to make use of modern IT systems. Scale on the demand side is helpful in the perception of consumers: it gives them confidence that the insurance company can and will honour its payment commitments at any time. It should be realised, however, that firm size and the law of large numbers are not correlated: risk absorption can be done by relatively small companies as they can rely on well-developed reinsurance markets.[45] For all these reasons, both national and European concentration is low,[46] although domestic concentration would seem to be on the rise everywhere.

The first response to EC-1992 was generated by the major insurance companies serving corporate clients. With those clients spreading production, transport, distribution and sales all over EU and EFTA in response to EC-1992, if not before, insurers began to invest in European networks to be able to supply wholesale service. This motive became mixed with the desire to share in the greater growth opportunities of the Mediterranean EU countries which tended to be relatively underinsured. This drive is now spreading to the new Member States. Such cross-border establishment has been more pronounced in non-life than in life insurance, both because corporate clients concentrate on the former and because turnovers in life insurance are (still) growing everywhere so the incentive to seek turnover elsewhere is small. After a time lag, medium-sized companies have reacted to this networking by defensive, domestic mergers and cross-border strategic alliances.[47] This has led to greater competitive pressures in non-life markets. Globalisation has added strength to the process, as follows. Multinationals have increasingly centralised corporate treasury and financial management functions, including insurance. Often this led them to rely on self-insurance for small losses and set up 'captive' insurance companies for the remainder. Such companies can take away a segment of the corporate non-life market because they have resort to reinsurance directly. Even if they

[42]Non-performing loans and doubtful loans were (in 2003) still fairly high, though.

[43]It is based on Dickinson (1993) and Cegos (1998).

[44]Following the co-insurance and establishment directives adopted in the late 1970s.

[45]Reinsurance is the specialised wholesale market for insurance companies: it is only lightly regulated and is highly international. A reinsurance supervision directive was adopted in 2004.

[46]In 1990 some 2,500 independent groups controlling around 4,000 insurance companies existed in the EU and EFTA.

[47]Cegos (1998) reports a trend of upstream and downstream (cross-border) partnership agreements, affecting – in contrast – the life more than the non-life sector. They also discern the first examples of Euro-products, i.e. identical insurance products for different EU countries.

choose to go through other insurers, their bargaining position causes margins to fall.

A second indirect effect of EC-1992 is potential. As EC-1992 is itself a product of a pro-market undercurrent in Europe, it interacts with national tendencies to allow greater private initiatives in social security related instances of insurance, such as pensions, health care, worker disability insurance and the like. For tax and other reasons these markets are still very much national, and local presence is needed to benefit from the opportunities. As Table 7.1 shows, the supplementary pensions market should gradually become a single market, especially in the eurozone, if tax problems can be solved.

The impact of home country control and a single passport to supply insurance directly across intra-EU borders is likely to be minimal because the contract law is that of the insurer (which makes consumers very wary). The 1992 *Bachmann* case[48] has made it virtually impossible, however, to sell life insurance across borders, given strong tax disincentives.

With respect to the pro-competitive effect of EC-1992 insurance, two important aspects of the regulatory reform should be noted. First, in countries (notably, Germany and Italy) where very detailed service regulation (on premiums, contract conditions, types of service innovations allowed after scrutiny) was held to prevent insolvency more effectively, a pro-competitive effect (lower prices, more variety) can be observed, since this detailed overregulation has been removed. How far such reform should go in the liberal direction so that costs and cartel-type rents can be reduced without introducing instability is less easy to answer, and is also unclear from empirical research.[49] Second, while promoting competition by liberalisation and some approximation, the EU has also allowed a major exemption of competition law (Article 81.3 EC) so that companies can cooperate. The idea is that insurers need to pool information on the claims records so as to arrive at highly accurate loss probability tables. Although this pooling might be defended as a 'public good', it is not *a priori* clear why a regulator could not do this for the companies. Worse, the EU has allowed insurers to go beyond information collection and set common risk premium tariffs, even to set common standard policy conditions. Unless the Commission succeeds in extremely tight monitoring, this risks (as Rees & Kessner (1999, pp. 376–7) argue) the substitution of public detailed regulation (now largely removed in Germany and Italy) with private, cartel-like regulation of the market. By 2005 this state of affairs had changed little, except for the emergence of some pan-European insurance groups. Since branching across borders hardly happens in insurance, home country control is hardly applied. The barriers are so numerous that the FSAP review group for insurance[50] proposes the study of a 26th regulatory regime (parallel to 25 national ones) and business-generated standardised pan-European insurance products.

7.5 Road haulage

There are six modes of transport (road haulage, air, rail, maritime, river and buses) and one close substitute for some bulk services (pipelines). After the 1985 Court ruling convicting the Council of a 'failure to act' upon its duty to set up a common transport policy, an internal market has been established for all modes of transport services. Given its space limitations, this text deals only with road haulage, by far the most important mode economically. Air and rail transport, being network industries, are discussed in Chapter 8.

7.5.1 Establishing an internal market for road haulage

The internal market for road haulage was prevented from actually being established by national quotas and access restrictions. Fairly centralist proposals for a common transport policy, including common minimum and maximum prices, never made it through the Council in the 1960s. Renewed attempts based on harmonisation without centralisation, dating back to the second half of the 1970s, foundered on the rocks of unwilling Member States insisting on maximum, not minimum, fiscal and social harmonisation. It was only in November 1985 that the Council agreed to liberalise, while reducing harmonisation ambitions. Minimum harmonisation in road haulage focused on entry conditions such as technical regulations, like weight and length of vehicles, and (minimum) professional qualities, as well as on social aspects (maximum number of driving hours and the size

[48]Case C-204/90 *Bachmann* [1992] ECR 249.

[49]Rees & Kessner (1999) attempt to demonstrate empirically that German insurers are less efficient than British insurers (operating in a loosely regulated market).

[50]Review of FSAP, 2004, op.cit., fn 40 above.

of cabins). Liberalisation was accomplished by the gradual enlargement of bilateral quotas, the abolition of bilateral quotas and intra-EC-wide permits by January 1993. The really serious problems arose in two areas: taxation and user charges; and cabotage – the right for non-domestic carriers to supply domestic services. Indirectly, the issue of European transport infrastructure had also begun to play a role in the 1980s and more explicitly with the promotion of trans-European networks (TENs) provided for in the Maastricht Treaty.

The burden of taxation and user charges for road transport differs considerably between the Member States. Some countries, by virtue of their peripheral location, will tend to be net users of roads in other Member States; in some Member States, roads will tend to be used relatively heavily by non-domestic carriers. If there are no user charges (tolls), such as in Germany, Denmark and Benelux, domestic users may find they suffer from higher congestion and higher taxes. Germany's location and convenient transit-roads prompted this country during the EC-1992 process to insist on the *territoriality principle*. This principle says that the road user should be taxed by the country whose infrastructure is being used. Levying tolls is one way of doing so. In the north-western EU countries, the *residence principle* used to be applied, implying taxation by the home country of the carrier. Germany, Benelux and Denmark prefer not to introduce tolls, even though they may serve as ideal user charges. Germany's problem was exacerbated by domestic distortions in inter-modal competition between rail and road haulage, leading to cross-subsidisation from the latter to the former.[51] This had to be abolished in the internal market, but was fiercely resisted. A cumbersome solution was found, as a proxy to the territoriality principle, in the 'Euro-vignette' for trucks in Denmark, Germany and Benelux.[52] The revenues from the charges due before obtaining the vignette flow into a common fund of the five countries, from which Germany receives 73 per cent. This negotiated allocation was sufficient for Germany to lift its veto on outstanding EC decisions. Observe that this issue of user charges for infrastructure may also impact on competitiveness, since the Euro-vignette has reduced discrepancies among truck taxes between carriers from different Member States.

Cabotage is defined as (road) transport services between two points within a Member State, by a foreign (EU) service provider. It implies that the segmentation between domestic and cross-border transport services is reduced. Once mobile communications and Europe-wide logistics permit a home office to trace trucks and loads at all times, it becomes possible for international hauliers to compete with domestic ones. If timing and routing match the return trip, this could even be offered at barely more than marginal costs. This sharpened competition at the margin was feared by the less competitive trucking companies, but has finally been agreed to. It was also feared that relatively low-wage countries in the EU (Greece, Spain, Portugal) would quickly enlarge market share in high-wage countries via cabotage, a kind of 'social dumping' as it was called.

Finally, the removal of internal frontier controls in the EU in January 1993, though a horizontal measure, was expected to impact positively upon road transport.

7.5.2 Economic impact of road haulage market integration

As with banking and insurance, the impact of EC-1992 on road haulage is hard to isolate, as it is blended with some underlying economic trends affecting transport demand and supply in the EU.[53]

Initially, let us proceed at fairly aggregate level, while ignoring intermodal competition. Three effects of EC-1992 should be expected. First, as intra-EU road haulage since 1970 has grown almost twice as fast as industrial production, the expected growth impulse of EC-1992 should translate into a much larger demand impulse for road haulage services. Second, to the extent that plant economies of scale could be more fully exploited due to EC-1992, centralisation of production in fewer plants would augment transport costs (as average distances would increase significantly). If the latter costs are lower than the benefits of centralisation of plant output, the consequent centralisation should be expected to increase the demand for transport services. In Figure 7.3 the relation between estimates of scale economies and transport costs (both as shares of total costs) is depicted. It indicates that basic metals, cars, electromechanical products, machines, paper and wood, and instruments should be expected to show tendencies of plant centralisation. This should benefit road haulage, especially where high value per weight is relevant. The impact could be strong if one

[51]Initially via quota restrictions, and more generally via high truck taxes, the competitiveness of freight rail services was prompted artificially.

[52]Officially called 'Euro-regional disc' (for lorries above 12 tonnes). This has been in force since January 1995 (and revised several times since).

[53]The following is based on Sleuwaegen *et al.* (1993), Koopman (1993) and NEA (1997– for the Single Market Review).

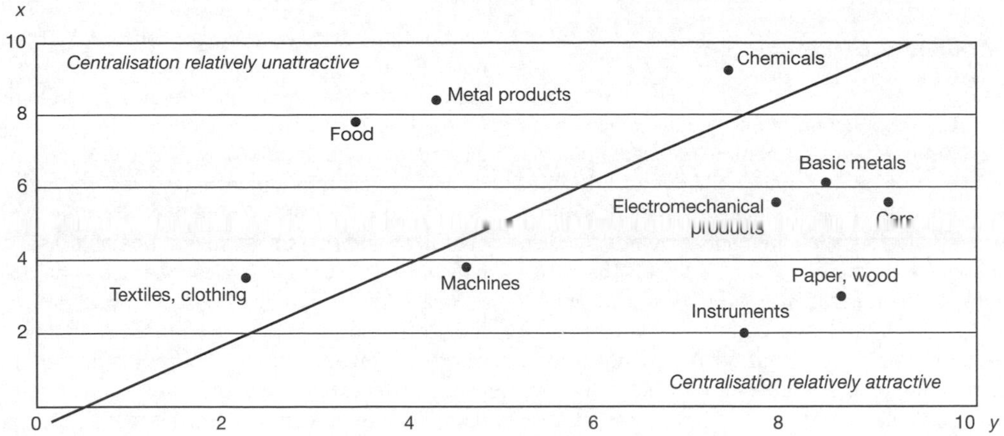

Figure 7.3 Plant scale economies and transport costs

Source: Reproduced from the original figure taken from *European Economy, Reports and Studies No. 2 – The Impact of the Internal Market on Services,* published by the Publication Office, Brussels 1993, © European Communities.

considers that a doubling of the transport costs share (observe, in Figure 7.3, say for instruments, from 2 to 4 per cent) would still leave a net benefit to be reaped. But a doubling of this share means a greater than double expansion of transport in terms of tonne-kilometres, given the high fixed cost share in road haulage. Therefore, the scale effects will boost transport services.

Third, EC-1992, by removing various barriers – especially internal customs and tax frontiers – rendered centralisation of stockholdings more attractive to industry. There are some scale economies in distribution, and, above a critical mass, it becomes profitable to employ modern, capital-intensive stock techniques.[54] Again, this trend increases average distances to users and consumers and thereby exercises a positive effect on demand for haulier services.

Some other effects of EC-1992 include greater efficiency, the emergence of transport brokers, and strategic alliances and pan-European networks. Efficiency has improved due to a reduction of own-account (that is, in-company) trucking, which tends to underutilise truck capacities, and to the permission for cabotage. Cabotage is likely to happen at just above marginal costs, but is possible on a routine basis only if demand and supply can be matched almost instantaneously (here emphasising the importance of telemetrics). At this point, brokers come in, a new phenomenon in road haulage in Europe. Brokers may also service companies which do not need sophisticated logistical systems and hence wish to shop around for competitive prices. The more efficiently brokers can serve them, the less these companies will rely on own-account trucking. Cabotage turned out to be relatively little used (0.2 per cent of national road transport between 1996 and 1998 – see European Commission, 2000) and was initially not used by hauliers from relatively low wage EU countries. The Dutch, Belgian and French hauliers make the best use of the cabotage rights. When cabotage became fully unconstrained (in July 1998), there was hardly any further increase. Apparently, only sophisticated logistics and large, diversified fleets make systematic use of cabotage possible. Its pro-competitive effect will therefore remain limited.

There is also a rapid 'Europeanisation' of road haulage. The major firms engage in domestic and cross-border acquisitions in attempts to build up European networks under their full control. This is combined by service differentiation and specialisation according to types of freight or sectors. Smaller companies respond by cooperative ventures in strategic alliances. They attempt to realise scale, scope and network economies without losing ownership. Such alliances might not obtain long-term logistical contracts as easily as the major companies do, but may build up a customer base of regular exporters.

However, the upheaval in road transport generates social costs as well. Before jumping to conclusions about the benefits of EC-1992, it should not be forgotten

[54]Combining IT and robotics. Note that the average variance in calls on stocks in a centralised warehouse is lower than in a decentralised system, so that the average stock level is lower (hence, the capital tied up is lower too). This reduces costs as well.

ADDITIONAL READING

An explicit introduction of intermodal choice points to a continued strengthening of road haulage. However, this is only marginally due to EC-1992. The (non-local) road haulage market has three segments: logistical chain management, dedicated transport and simple road haulage. The latter segment is contestable as entry is easy, competition is price-based and sunk costs are minimal (hence, exit is at low cost) in the presence of a well-functioning second-hand truck market. Numerous small companies with only a few trucks characterise the supply in this segment. Dedicated transport refers to refrigerated products, chemicals and, for example, live animals. Niche specialisation and close relations with shippers make this a special segment, with some barriers to entry but still considerable competition.

Logistical chain management exhibits scale, network effects and much stronger concentration; competition is service-oriented and transport contracts with major shippers (often, multinationals with many loads per day) tend to be long term. Scale, network effects and high quality services (especially by forward integration into logistics including forwarding, warehousing and European distribution centres) create high barriers to entry and exit. Simple road haulage is often complementary to rail and river transport for short hauls, but has to compete in the margin for long hauls with low-priced rail and river shipments. Logistical chain management shows much higher growth and can benefit much more from internal market effects. The desire of EU companies (shippers) is to minimise total logistics costs (some 10–15 per cent of total costs on average, consisting of transport, handling and inventory) while retaining full control because of specialisation and just-in-time production systems. What counts for the major clients of road hauliers is the combination of quality and costs of the logistics system. Quality is measured in terms of reliability, frequency and speed, in addition to the fullest possible association with the client's logistical needs and an ability to locate freight (that is, the trucks or any freight in a distribution centre) at any time, irrespective of where it moves. Simple road haulage transport cannot effectively respond to these demands. The occasional exception is air freight (but at a variable costs of five times per tonne-kilometre). As noted, this trend – facilitated but not 'caused' by EC-1992 – is more pronounced for high value-per-weight goods. Moreover, there is an autonomous trend favouring a rise of value per weight due to dematerialisation, miniaturisation and lighter materials, which should benefit this kind of road haulage. As a case study by Ponti & Cappiello (2000) shows, the continued interventionism in Italian road haulage (domestic quotas, various state aid, price regulation) until the late 1990s has shielded (small) domestic hauliers from clear market signals, preventing new strategies and restructuring. Hauliers have massively stayed in regional transport, with the result that no less than 65 per cent of international freight in Italy is carried by foreign (EU) hauliers. Via cabotage, foreign hauliers further exercise competitive pressure and Italian hauliers are not competitive enough (precisely in logistics) to compensate this in the rest of the single market. As with financial services, the liberalisation at EU level necessitates domestic regulatory reform, if only to boost competitiveness *vis-à-vis* EU-wide competitors.

that infrastructural issues, congestion, environmental objections and remaining problems of taxation necessitate an overall EC transport policy of a much wider scope. The secular growth of road haulage has long been higher than that of GNP in the EU, and this trend is expected to continue at least another decade, if not beyond 2020. Both carbon dioxide emissions (related to climate change) and rapidly increasing congestion have prompted a much greater awareness of what is called 'sustainable mobility' in the Union.[55] Road vehicles (trucks and cars) are responsible for some 28 per cent of all EU emissions of carbon dioxide. This has lead to EU regulation about (far) better fuel standards, and alternative fuels and strong pressures to link fuel taxation to (unpaid) external costs. Higher fuel taxes should increase incentives to come up with

[55]See Pelkmans & White (2000) and the Commission's White Paper (2001).

low-carbon cars, and perhaps eventually with hydrogen cars (zero carbon dioxide). Congestion is also rapidly increasing in the EU. Daily traffic jams on the EU motorways reach some 7,500 km and are a clear sign that the use of bottlenecks is underpriced and/or that infrastructural investments have fallen intolerably behind demand.

Congestions charging will become more prominent in the Union as a rational method to internalise these costs, even if the sensitivity about 'road pricing' is very high.[56]

7.6 Summary

Services market integration is different in nature from goods market integration. For a proper understanding, Figure 7.1 offers a classification of services to help to appreciate how the internal services market may be liberalised and regulated. Thus, services are first divided into economic and 'non-economic', into tradable and 'non-tradable', and into regulated and 'non-regulated'. The regulated ones are subdivided into networked and 'non-networked' ones, and the latter into transport (in so far as non-networked), financial, pure consumer services and business services.

The original treaty section on services contrasts starkly indeed with the treaty sections on goods market integration. Moreover, the economically important services (financial, telecoms, postal, all transport modes) are under separate treaty sections, with initially very little progress in intra-EC market access. Of the big services sectors, only the unregulated tourism services escaped special treatment, but in this case there is next to nothing to liberalise. Among the other services without special sections in the treaty, the overall category of cross-border services provided by professionals is the most important one. Severe difficulties in the mutual recognition of diplomas for professionals have long throttled the provision of these cross-border services.

Both the right of establishment (for services and for goods suppliers) and the free movement of services suffer from considerable derogations. In the 1980s and early 1990s, EC case law on services gradually developed principles similar to those protecting the free movement of goods, for example, formulations similar to the *Dassonville* and *Cassis de Dijon* cases (see Chapters 4 and 5) and proportionality tests.

The crux of the matter is therefore how to accomplish 'horizontal service liberalisation', that is, outside all the sector-specific cases in the treaty. As Figure 7.2 shows, the core problem about free movement is how to discipline the many derogations that have been granted to Member States by the EC Court, and given the lack of relevant harmonisation.

A single market for financial services can only function properly in the context of a Union-wide financial area, including also free movement of financial capital and money, a single currency as well as fiscal and accounting approximation. The regulatory principles for establishing the internal market for financial services include, besides free movement of course, minimum harmonisation (focused on financial institutions, not so much on financial service products), mutual recognition based on home country control of financial institutions operating across intra-EU borders and limited host country control. Progress has been made but obstacles such as fiscal barriers and different accounting standards remain. The barriers in retail financial services are still formidable, however. The 'general good' clause is a culprit, although it has now been overcome for B2B services. The impact of EC-1992 in financial services has been considerable, in some EU countries little short of drastic. The first empirical indications for banking show attempts to avoid sharper price competition (not unusual in oligopolies), a strong increase in mergers and acquisitions, and higher productivity combined with cost cutting. In insurance, competitive pressures in the non-life markets have gone up. Other effects are not yet observable because the insurance directives were implemented later than those for banking and the impact of the single 'passport' to supply insurance directly to consumers are minimal.

The single market for transport services has become possible only after the 1985 Court ruling that the Transport Council of Minsters had failed to act on its main treaty obligation. Harmonisation since that date has been mostly technical (and 'minimal'), while

[56]See also ECMT (2003) for detailed analysis and simulations.

Summary *continued*

liberalisation has practically been completed in all the modes. In road haulage, the conflict about the proper allocation of infrastructural costs centred around the territoriality principle (the user pays charges where and when they use the infrastructure) versus the residence principle (taxation in the home country). Cabotage (the right of foreign firms to supply intra-national services) has been implemented in road transport but is little used. In road haulage there are direct and indirect determinants of an increase in demand for road transport, all prompted by EC-1992. The benefits will mostly be captured by the sophisticated segment of logistical chain management offering a full range of logistics services, over ever more integrated Europe-wide company networks. EC-1992 has also led to the emergence of road haulage brokers, not least because of cabotage. Regional transport and simple road haulage are subject to perfect competition; and the scale of exit/entry being permanently tiny make it impossible to compete with value-added, EU-wide services.

CHAPTER 8

The Internal Market for Network Industries

Topics covered

8.1 Network industries and the EC treaty

8.2 The economics of network industries

8.3 Air transport

8.4 Telecoms

8.5 Summary

Since the mid-1980s the EU has gradually introduced internal market principles and competition in the network industries. Network industries are special. Because of their characteristics and initial position (complete monopoly, usually), introducing economic integration had to be done in ways which, to some extent, could not be compared with 'ordinary' goods and services markets. The purpose of the present chapter is to set out and assess the methods of economic integration in this category of industries, and to analyse the actual or expected economic impact.

Network industries, referred to in this chapter, include airlines and rail; gas and electricity; telecoms and postal; and multimedia, internet and broadcasting.[1] They represent over 6 per cent of GDP in the EU. However, the economic[2] significance of network industries is greater because practically all other economic activities use the output of these industries as input. Also, the quality of life of households (a treaty objective) is heavily dependent on being connected to such networks and on the quality and price of the goods and services delivered over them.

Section 8.1 explains the key articles of the EC treaty and the current interpretation of them, an interpretation which is radically different from that accepted in the period before the mid-1980s. Section 8.2 sets out the economics of network industries: natural monopoly and what has remained of it; how to combine universal service with competition; and network externalities. Section 8.3 discusses the economic impact of over a decade of air transport liberalisation, and section 8.4 that of telecoms liberalisation. Short case studies on rail, postal, gas and electricity, and broadcasting services are provided for illustrative purposes.

8.1 Network industries and the EC treaty

Network industries, formerly called 'public utilities', were almost invariably state owned in Europe before, say, 1980 (with some exceptions in, for example, water and radio broadcasting). The relevant treaty article, Article 86 (formerly Article 90) EC, indeed, begins by mentioning public 'undertakings and under-

[1]This list is not exhaustive. We could include (cross-border) bus services liberalised under EC-1992; water and sewerage (not interesting for EU level because there is no cross-border trade – although there are cross-border mergers and acquisitions (M&A); district heating (idem); local and regional public transport (idem).

[2]The sectors also have an important social and political meaning (see text).

takings to which Member States grant special or exclusive rights' as if they logically constitute a single category of firms. However, it was drafted in early 1957.

The EC treaty is neutral with respect to ownership (Article 295, formerly Article 222). But the existence of state-owned companies does not imply a right to distort the competition on the internal market. In fact, the treaty does not make a distinction between state-owned and private enterprises as such. Both are subject to the same rules, including competition policy. A Member State cannot 'use' a state-owned enterprise (in a way that distorts competition) to achieve policy objectives. Article 86(1) allows Member States to grant certain enterprises (not necessarily state owned) exclusive or special rights for what the EC Court calls 'legitimate national objectives'. When doing so, the Member State shall neither enact nor maintain in force any measure contrary to the rules of the treaty, in particular Article 12 (formerly Article 6, prohibiting discrimination as to nationality) and Articles 81 to 89 (formerly Articles 85 to 94, on practices distorting or eliminating competition in the internal market). Strict application of this provision raises the question of why a Member State would wish to have or maintain state-owned enterprises. A network industry may be given exclusive rights if the objective is 'legitimate' but this does not hinge on its being state owned. If a company is state owned, but has no special rights for 'legitimate' reasons, why keep it in state ownership? Among the few reasons left are the protection of national ownership itself – for example, a takeover can never be 'hostile', whether domestic or foreign – and if it involves a strictly local product or service which does not affect cross-border intra-EC trade in any way. In other cases, insisting on state ownership of companies would seem to be pointless in the EU.

For decades, however, the implementation of Article 86 was taboo in the Community. In other words, state-owned enterprises enjoyed *de facto* greater discretion as long as Article 86 and control over state aids to state-owned companies (Article 87) were not properly enforced. In different degrees, Member States maintained widespread state ownership as an alternative or complementary means to market processes, or indeed to regulation, for the allocation of resources and the control of market outcomes. Historically this was due to remnants of 'indicative planning' (in France), the notion of the developmental state (in Italy), or residuals of early moves towards nationalisation (for example, in the UK, Spain and Portugal). In any event, for a long while there was little attention to whether rules, policies or state aids were supporting the competitive position of state-owned enterprises in one way or another, in violation of Article 86(1). During the 1980s and 1990s this changed radically. First, on their own initiative, Member States have privatised many state-owned companies, often after first 'incorporating' them (that is, changing them from a unit within the public administration to a genuine company, though still in state ownership). These moves are likely to have reduced the actual distortions of the internal market made possible by the lack of enforcement of Article 86(1), although some privatisations have been executed in a form implying hidden, one-off state aids. Second, after 1980, the EC Commission began to enforce the equality of state-owned and private enterprise much more rigorously, beginning with hidden state aids to state-owned enterprises.[3]

But Article 86 is basically about utilities or network markets and this brings in much more difficult economic and political issues. At stake is whether and when exclusive rights at national level can be justified legally and economically by the Community. Article 86(1) allows Member States to grant special or exclusive rights but subject to conditions, for example, there must be a 'legitimate national objective' and other treaty rules cannot be violated. The corollary is Article 86(2) which comprises a derogation for companies that enjoy special or exclusive rights, especially firms 'entrusted with the operation of services of general economic interest'. The latter is Euro-speak for public services of an economic nature. Decisions to impose public service obligations on specific firms are a Member State matter – such public services may require exclusive rights but this needs to be justified under EC law. An important, specific example of such a 'legitimate objective' in public services is 'universal service', as in telecoms and postal services (see below).[4] Since universal service in telecoms and postal services, as well as other public service obligations, used to be defined at Member State level, the exclusive rights are nationally (or regionally)

[3]By means of the so-called transparency directive 80/723 (as amended in 1985) and several times amended since. Note that this is a Commission (not a Council) directive, based on Art. 86(3), upheld by the EC Court in 1982. This way of getting round Council's resistance has played a major role in the debate on Art. 86.

[4]Article 86(2) also mentions firms 'having the character of a revenue-producing monopoly' (e.g. for spirits or tobacco); since Art. 37, now Art. 31 (on goods, not services) applies to them, this provision is largely redundant.

defined too. This violates free movement in the internal market. The derogation implies that the EC competition and internal market rules apply only in so far as their application does not obstruct the performance of the particular tasks assigned to such utilities and in so far the development of trade is affected to an extent contrary to the interests of the Community. The test is, therefore, to balance the public service obligations of the Member State and the interest of the Community, especially competition and services trade in the internal market. Since exclusive rights lead to monopoly, the interaction between the EC regulatory activity in the internal market and judicial review under competition policy is based on Article 86 in combination with Article 82 (formerly Article 86) and Article 49 (formerly Article 59).[5]

8.2 The economics of network industries

In this section we briefly analyse three economic characteristics of network industries: natural monopoly, the (proper) combination of USOs with competition, and network externalities. In addition, two central economic policy issues are addressed: the advantages of having a regulator rather than 'mere' competition policy, and the regulatory requirements to overcome asymmetries of information between the regulator and the established firms (or dominant players).

All network industries link upstream supply of goods or services with downstream customers via networks. The fixed costs of building a network in the first place are

ADDITIONAL READING

The gradual application of the derogation can be summarised as follows:

- Since the *British Telecom* case[6] of 1985, the burden of proof of whether the 'universal service' obligation imposed upon the monopolist actually requires exclusive rights rests upon the monopolist; this principle is also used for Article 30, (goods) and Article 46, (services), both derogations to free movement.
- Whereas the grounds for derogations of goods trade (Article 30) and services trade (Article 46) are non-economic (for example, social, public education and non-commercial public health), Article 86 blends economic and non-economic elements; network industries typically perform an *economic* activity but 'universal service' is based on non-economic objectives of a social and regional nature. Since the 2004 White Paper,[7] the EU distinguishes 'services of general interest', which are clearly 'non-economic' (such as social services, public education and non-commercial public health) from services specified in Article 86(2). The former services are considered to fall outside the internal market.
- Universal service refers to a defined set of services, made available to all customers (throughout the country or jurisdiction) at an affordable tariff, sometimes even at the same price throughout the country; in other words, a (domestic) letter mailed from whatever location would cost the same and similarly for local telephone calls in, say, all towns (that is, this must imply cross-subsidisation between cheaper and higher-cost parts of the network).
- This brings in the proportionality principle (just like Articles 30 and 46); if the granting of an exclusive right is justified by universal service obligations (USOs), what exact rights are and are not necessary, and is there a less restrictive alternative available?
- Once the proportionality test is passed, the EC has come to favour EC regulation, clearly specifying that these well-defined services are 'reserved services'; other ones should be liberalised, that is, become subject to competition in the internal market. This kind of regulation was applied to telecoms before 1998 and is still applied to postal services.

When exclusive rights were challenged in Court on competition grounds, judicial review moved

[5]The following is based on Gyselen (1994) and Olsen & Pelkmans (1996), among others.
[6]Case 41/83 *Italy v Commission* (generally known as '*British Telecom*') [1985] ECR 873, [1985] 2 CMLR 368.
[7]COM (2004) 374 of 12 May 2004, *White Paper on Services of General Interest.*

ADDITIONAL READING *continued*

towards the same position (especially since the *Corbeau* ruling[8] of 1993).

The EC Court, in *Corbeau,* verified whether Mr Corbeau's local postal service (in Liège) had 'value-added' features and concluded it did (for example, collection at business premises). The Court held that, for such service, exclusive rights were not necessary (proportionality test) and should be subject to competition, but with one proviso: the Belgian Post, entrusted with universal service obligations, should not see its financial viability undermined. However, once the exclusive rights are not justified, enjoying this right can be an abuse of a dominant position in breach of Article 82. The crux of interpreting Article 86(2) on utilities boils down to an economic analysis of 'natural monopoly' and/or the need for a distribution monopoly to live up to the universal service obligation. Since the mid-1980s affirmative answers to these two questions have no longer been taken for granted in the microeconomic analysis of utilities. Where justification fails, competition and the free movement of products and services should prevail in the internal market, be it often in combination with selective regulation.

very high. Usually, they are sunk too, so that a 'natural monopoly' might exist. Pushing for competition in the case of a natural monopoly is not in the (European) public interest. It should be realised that even today, after decades of liberalisation, natural monopoly is thought to apply to interregional rail infrastructure, transmission and distribution of electricity over high voltage networks and (often) high-pressure gas networks (as well as water and sewerage). In other parts of these network industries and in the other network industries, there is little or no economic evidence supporting natural monopoly.

Consider Figure 8.1, where long-run average costs (*LRAC*) continue to fall in the relevant range of demand. If several small suppliers coexisted, the supply schedule would be *S*, with each one producing the equivalent of Oq_1. Consumers would pay P_3 (in A). An X-efficient monopolist would produce at q_3 (where marginal costs (*LRMC*) and marginal revenue (heavy dashed line) intersect). This outcome would serve the consumer well because he would sell at $P_2 < P_3$. The producer efficiency gains are even more impressive as $P_1 << P_3$; in fact, supply by several competitors would result in a loss of P_3ABP_1 to society. Hence, competition would be bad and monopoly good. If this could be shown to be the case, the exclusive right might be justified under Article 86(2). A serious problem in Figure 8.1 is the assumption of X-efficiency – entrenched monopolies tend to develop large X-inefficiencies over time, which would push 'up' *LRAC*, possibly wiping out the advantages of monopoly provision. Therefore, one could argue that a true natural monopoly should not receive 'exclusive rights' – if X-inefficiencies become too large, less inefficient entry (or by-pass) will eventually occur, disciplining the monopolist somewhat. This argument hinges on the possibility of limited entry.

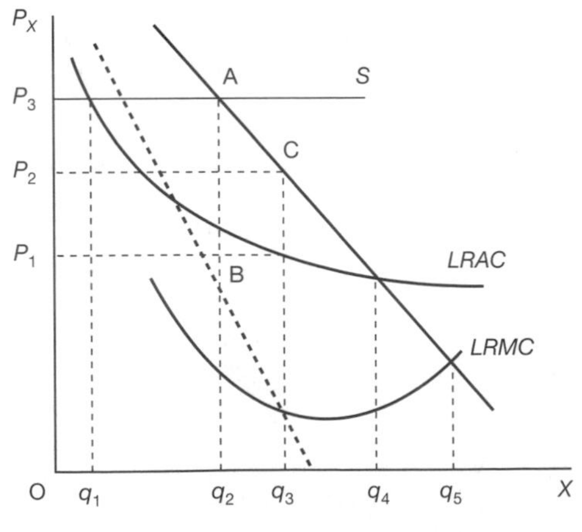

Figure 8.1 A network industry with natural monopoly

Source: from F.M. Scherer and David Ross, *Industrial Market Structure and Economic Performance,* Third edition. © 1990 by Houghton Mifflin Company. Adapted with permission.

Universal service obligations – the second economic characteristic of networks – could also be brought into this analysis. Critical are 'affordable rates' (for example, for a letter) for consumers, sometimes even the same rates irrespective of location. This could be achieved by regulating the network industries, compelling it to supply at q_4 at much lower prices. If prices were forced down to long-run marginal cost (the price for sales at q_5), this would mean that losses would have to be covered by subsidies (the vertical difference between *LRAC* and *LRMC,* at q_5, times output volume).

If there is not a single price, cross-subsidisation may pre-empt loss making. Even with a single price,

[8]Case C-320/91 *Corbeau* [1993] ECR I-1477, [1995] 4 CMLR 621

cross-subsidisation may suffice, but then the price must average between high cost and low cost parts of the network, for example between urban areas and the periphery (not indicated in Figure 8.1). In fixed-lines telecoms, low local rates and low (and uniform) line rental charges used to be subsidised by revenues from long-distance and cross-border calls (with a much lower share of non-business demand). In postal services, loss-making services in remote areas are compensated for by profitable services in densely populated areas. Such forms of large-scale cross-subsidisation have to be protected by exclusive rights. Were entry made possible, while the established postal firm kept its universal service obligation at a single price, new entrants would target only the dense markets. They would set prices lower than the utility's average price but still make profits since costs in the dense parts of the market are very low. This selective competition is called 'cream skimming'. With effective cream skimming, the established postal firm would eventually become a loss maker. But cross-subsidisation, hence exclusive rights, are not the only and often not the best way to guarantee USOs. Thus, introducing competition – while maintaining this 'universal service' – can work with explicit subsidies for serving the costly periphery. A key question is whether – with cream skimming in the cities (postal) or over trunk lines between cities (telecoms) allowed – subsidies to remote areas would have to be larger as scale or network effects would be smaller. This brings in the financial viability issue of the EC Court in the *Corbeau* case. Were explicit subsidies combined with competition to take the place of exclusive rights, the empirical problem is whether the expected efficiency benefits of competition outweigh the subsidies. Recent experiences in postal services and telecoms in Europe suggest that the reductions in X-inefficiency (the benefits) are large when competition is introduced and that the actual (net) costs of universal service is low or practically zero in postal and telecoms.

The justification for exclusive rights due to natural monopoly is subject to several strong qualifications. The greatest problem is no doubt that the long-run position of the scale curve is likely to be much higher than necessary due to X-inefficiencies induced by the lack of competition. If this is a matter of unit costs, franchising might be an alternative option in some cases. Thus, every five or ten years, there would be competition *for* the market (namely, the franchise), yet no competition *in* the market. If it is a matter of service quality (for example, a telephone connection in only a few days) or innovation (since lack of competition reduces the responsiveness to new demands of consumers for example, added-value services), fringe competition may be an effective means to contain X-inefficiency. This is now recognised to be the case for courier express services. In the EC judicial review this fringe competition is allowed unless it would demonstrably undermine the financial equilibrium of the utility.[9] Value-added services in telecoms (for example, data transfer) were liberalised by the EU in 1992 for the same reason.

The other important qualification relates to new technologies, which play a major role in telecoms. The fixed-line telecoms sector has been challenged by mobile telephony, especially digital cellular mobile phones (GSM in Europe, now succeeded by 3G). Moreover, telecoms services traffic has increased so much, new network equipment (for example, optical fibres) has fallen in price (per unit of capacity) so much – and the convergence of information technology, broadcasting and media services and telecoms has proceeded so far – that competition between networks (especially long distance) has become possible without losing the cost advantages of scale.

The upshot has been that the most entrenched barriers in the internal market – exclusive rights – can be, and are challenged to a considerable degree by EC judicial review and regulation in all seven network markets. In the process, related (and long unquestioned) import prohibitions to protect the energy monopolies have also been dismantled.

A third economic characteristic of networks is found in network externalities. Externalities create a wedge between the private and social costs or the private and social benefits of individual decisions, reflecting a suboptimal performance of a market. In networks, externalities are bound to be strong because all subscribers are linked to major parts of, if not to the entire, network. Thus, a potential subscriber will tend to join one network rather than another one dependent on a mixture of quality and price. Particularly in the case of new entrants or, more drastically still, completely new markets (for example, GSM mobile phone services, digital pay-TV), the potential subscriber will base his or her decision on perceived quality (including performance and innovation) and expected prices. This generates a peculiar set of dynamics because, often, the actual quality of the (new) network is a function of the expected quality, via a size effect (more subscribers enable the company to deliver the quality via investment and human resources). The size effect is, in turn, a function of prior investment (in technology and infrastructure) or the mere credibility of announcing it, as well as the entry price, much more than the actual service tariffs.

[9]Note that in recent Commission decisions on the Dutch and Spanish Post Offices, undermining was found not to be the case.

This has several implications for (European) public policy. First, for network competition to be successful, reputation effects and credibility as well as 'penetration pricing'(for example, selling a mobile phone at a giveaway price, but tying it to a subscription with fixed costs and possibly high or intransparent service fees) are essential. If an established firm offers too little and is slow, ample scope is provided for network competition; if relatively agile, however, it might cleverly increase switching costs for subscribers and, possibly, abuse its dominant position. For competition policy this will not be easy to prove. Thus, one could ask whether frequent flyer loyalty schemes are anti-competitive or not; certainly, they raise switching costs and the scheme's attractiveness is a positive function of the size of an airline's network. On the other hand, are they critical for some airlines to enable them to take on other established firms, and thus pro-competitive?

Second, for competition *on* networks, network externalities work like the positive or negative interdependencies of the members of a club. They are positive in the classic case of (old) telephone networks: the decision of a third subscriber C has a positive welfare effect on existing subscribers A and B as they can now call more people. This positive network externality can rationalise USOs, simply by ensuring all-to-all connectivity, be it on a single monopoly network or via smooth interconnection. Note that it does not follow that all-to-all interconnectivity should necessarily be 'affordable', let alone be uniformly priced; this might be commercially attractive and, if not, it is a matter of equity and 'cohesion'. However, negative network externalities exist as well, such as network failure (for example, power), quality or integrity of the network (for example, distribution, interference, internet viruses) and congestion (rail, airports, internet, Christmas mail, etc.). It is a difficult issue whether, and to what extent, a monopolist or a few oligopolists should be regulated with respect to quality and capacity investments, so as to minimise negative network externalities. And if regulation is accepted, whether this be done at EU level, national level or both.

However, once the various network industries which – potentially or actually – can develop cross-border trade and hence fall under EC jurisdiction have begun to be liberalised, a complex two-level mixture of regulation and competition will be required before the internal market for network goods and services can be expected to function properly. In other words, the EU-level is compelled to adopt fairly detailed minimum rules about (national) regulation and supervision. It is easy to understand why. With established firms so powerful and their networks present everywhere, entry into the market requires very close supervision indeed. Such rules and supervision have three objectives: they should enable competition between networks (new and old); they should ensure effective and undistorted access for new goods or service providers to networks in the Member States, hence competition on networks, as well as cross-border exchange or transit – that is, free movement; and they should ensure that even where monopoly is (justifiably) retained, private ownership or franchising should be open to all EU companies.[10]

Two key economic issues in all this regulation are the initially overwhelming power of the established firms, deterring entry, and asymmetry of information between the regulator and the establishment. Entry into the market is bound to be considered as a daunting adventure by potential competitors unless an independent regulator can supervise and correct on a very short-term basis. Perhaps it is necessary to introduce, on a temporary basis, so-called asymmetric regulation, preventing the established firms from responding to new entry in certain ways, or giving new entrants a minor competitive edge in order to allow them to get established. When competition between networks cannot be expected, because of too high sunk costs, entry will take the form of competition on, or 'by-pass' of a selected part of, the network (where feasible). In both cases, interconnection with the network or the terms of access to the network are vital for the entrant to survive. Competition policy would be an inferior alternative to the combination of regulation and supervision. The guarantee of regulation and hands-on (independent) supervision is likely to be a prerequisite for entrants to enter in the first place – the long and demanding procedures of competition policy are not suitable for providing certainty and the protection of emerging competition in these peculiar circumstances.[11]

Asymmetry of information is a profound problem between regulated monopolies and the regulator. Once competition is allowed, two main issues need to be solved. First, if the established firm keeps 'reserved' (that is, monopolised) activities such as the very high

[10]Franchising in this context refers to a tender contest for running an existing monopoly network, and possibly its services as well. In principle this is possible in water, sewerage and rail, for example.

[11]Sometimes, competition policy has been adapted in such a way that it can respond like a regulator would do. An example is the 1991 Commission Guidelines for predatory price and non-price behaviour in air transport, with the power of interim rulings in a matter of weeks. Such guidelines are quasi-regulatory and the response is that of a regulator. Without such tools, a small new entrant could die or withdraw before a (normal) ruling has been made.

voltage electricity transmission network but has to compete in generation (for example, of electricity) and final supply, it is essential that the incumbent cannot cross-subsidise competitive activities from revenues in the monopoly segment. Preventing this requires the fullest possible separation (legally separate companies; but, at the very least, separate financial accounts audited by external accountants for the regulator). Second, because interconnection between networks is so crucial, as well as access to networks, it is essential to regulate basic principles of access/interconnection (for example, an obligation for the established firm to accept it, on a non-discriminatory basis). Beyond that, there is a problem of price – what is the cost price, plus a reasonable margin, for network access/interconnection? The technical issues here are beyond the scope of this book, but it does mean that the regulator must have full information about the cost accounting of the established company. Indeed, even the method of calculating the cost price may be prescribed by the regulator so as to prevent abuse of dominant position. This might be so because most networks have a high share of joint/common costs for the delivery of a good or service, and what part of that should be billed for interconnection is, to a degree, arbitrary. The key issue here is that the established firm should not manipulate the interconnection tariff so as to throttle competition.

ADDITIONAL READING

Establishing the internal market for network industries

We shall simplify the method of establishing the internal market for network industries by outlining six steps (see Pelkmans, 2001, for a more detailed exposition). Since the focus is on a horizontal approach, it emphasises the similarities between these industries for the building of the internal market. The reader should be aware that, in so doing, the sectoral differences remain hidden.

Consider Table 8.1, which summarises the six steps. The left-hand column provides a short-hand version of the policy issue, the middle column indicates the kinds of measures the EU ought to decide upon, and the right-hand column specifies the assignments to the two levels of government.

Step 1 is about the nature of competition. If there is a 'natural monopoly', the only option is competition *for* the market and the internal market regime is largely irrelevant except for (non-discriminatory) transit. If competition is possible *on* the networks, and perhaps also between networks, the internal market and competition should be properly introduced. Step 2 begins by incorporating 'undertakings entrusted with the operation of services of general economic interest' (Article 86(2)) as ordinary companies (state-owned or not). In the late 1980s this was important not only for transparency of costs, but foremost because *de facto* regulatory functions about the network and equipment were transferred to a regulator; those functions were also made explicit and subject to judicial review.[12] The best solution is to make the regulator fully independent, both from the incumbent and from the government (especially if the established firm is state owned). In some sectors (for example, gas and electricity), EC directives allow Member States' governments to act as the regulator (subject to EC rules and national appeal procedures), which can be explained by lobbying and a fear of the impact of liberalisation. Where a sector has a natural monopoly on only a part of the network, the established firm has to be split into separate companies (or at least business units) for the competitive business and the 'reserved' activities. This should prevent cross-subsidisation and facilitates independent auditing as an *ex post* verification.

Steps 3 and 4 are about the desired level of universal or public service. To appreciate fully the importance of these steps in the European context, it ought to be realised that public utilities used to be highly ambiguous about public service. On the one hand, USOs and PSOs[13] were viewed as critical objectives for the public at large as well as for all business customers. For a long time it was believed

[12] The main idea behind this is, of course, the avoidance of conflicts of interest when allowing other service providers on the network or when preparing interconnection between new and established networks. But regulatory functions also refer to technical standards, compatibilities, certification of technical equipment, etc.

[13] A USO (universal service obligation) refers to a service provided to everyone irrespective of location at an affordable rate; sometimes even at the same price. A PSO (public service obligation) refers to service obligations of network industries reflecting socio-political objectives without the requirement (or the possibility) of universality and sometimes with specific pricing constraints.

ADDITIONAL READING *continued*

Table 8.1 Establishing the internal market for network industries

Policy issues		Policy measures/regulation	EC level and/or Member State
1	Nature of competition	• In the market (between or on networks) • *For* the market	EC and national National (except transit)
2	Introducing competition (unbundling of accounts, or legal, or even ownership)	• Independent regulator • Separate 'reserved' and competitive business	EC basic regulation EC basic regulation plus EC competition policy
3	Protecting public service levels	• Universal service (USO) • Public service (if not USO) (Both include quality)	EC minimum rules, plus national
4	Non-distortive financing of USO/PSO	• Targeted subsidies, from taxes • USO fund, based on turnover levies • Access charges	EC basic rules, plus national options
5	Non-distortive access to network(s)	• Non-price access/interconnection rules • Access price rules	EC principles EC rules plus national rules supervision
6	Non-distortive cross-border trade	• Non-price rules (e.g. technical; capacity) • Removal old 'frontier' prices	EC free movement and transit rules

(or asserted) that competition was incompatible with the maintenance of USOs and PSO as traditionally conceived in the national political debates. On the other hand, the actual practice did not accord well with those laudable objectives. As it turned out, few EU Member States had carefully spelled out what exactly USOs or PSOs implied (although this differed from sector to sector), hence, it was hard to verify the performance of utilities. Moreover, the costs of such USOs/PSOs at first remained a subject of great controversy because poor internal costing procedures in public utilities rendered it impossible to verify service-based cost prices. Early examples of liberalisation (for example, in the USA, the UK and Sweden) confirmed the widespread suspicion in Europe that (1) the costs of USOs/PSOs could be cut dramatically, and (2) clear definitions and agreed costing methods could greatly help in introducing competition without lowering public service levels. Thus, the 'benchmarking' about USOs/PSOs in Europe has been a healthy and revealing exercise in itself, apart from laying the foundation for EC minimum approximation. Step 3 is necessary for two reasons: (1) to ensure that a national USO/PSO cannot be misused as a pretext to throttle entry in an arbitrary way; and (2) as the basis for step 4. In so far as USOs/PSOs entail costs, the financing of those excess costs should be non-distortive. The best solution would be to provide targeted subsidies (say, to serve a peripheral region, or to serve the disabled, by giving them vouchers) paid from general taxation (sometimes practised in public transport). A 'sectoral' solution is a USO/PSO fund, paying, say, the established firm which is obliged to provide such commercially non-viable services; the fund would receive revenues from a sharing mechanism between all market players (for example, turnover levies). Least recommendable are access charges because this forces the regulator to establish the 'normal' cost price of interconnection so as to prevent the network holder from charging too much (and thus reducing competition).

Step 5 is to ensure easy and properly priced access to networks, for service providers, and easy and properly priced interconnection between networks. Of all the steps this is the critical one – often, it is a life or death issue for new entrants. Non-price access rules (on, for example, non-discrimination, capacity constraints, technical

ADDITIONAL READING *continued*

interoperability) will require a set of EU-level principles, including reference to EU technical standards (if available) and certification procedures. The details need to be closely supervised by national regulators in order to prevent abuse of dominant position. Access price rules (for example, interconnection tariffs for telecoms, interlining tariffs in air transport, and so on) create still greater problems because general EC rules on cost price methods are necessary but insufficient to discipline a powerful established firm. Such methods leave too much discretion for charging a high tariff, unless the national regulator is able – and willing – to impose strict costing rules.[14] The dilemma of the national regulator is that the investment strategies of new entrants are a function of the permitted tariffs, whether regulated or negotiated, between market participants. If access/interconnection tariffs are low, new entrants may not build new networks (the profit incentive may be too low); if tariffs are high, entrants may build, but in the meantime competition is weak and the established firm may entrench its position while learning how better to compete. If 'competition between networks' is not really possible (for example, freight by rail, which is bound to remain 'service competition' with access), cost-price methods become decisive for any anti-trust ruling on 'abusive' tariffs.

Step 6, finally, amounts to the liberalisation of cross-border trade. In the old world of national state-owned utilities, international 'cooperation' employed rather peculiar 'frontier prices', such as (very high) 'accounting rates' for telecoms[15] and 'terminal dues' in postal services. In railways it is still true that cross-frontier passenger services are priced higher than a similar distance within a Member State (see Case Study 8.1). In this respect a fully fledged internal market will be achieved more rapidly in competitive network industries than in those where the scope for network competition is severely limited.

CASE STUDY 8.1 Liberalising the railways in the EU

The rail share of the EU internal market for freight was 7.8 per cent in 2001 (against 21 per cent in 1970) and the market share for passengers was barely 6 per cent (down from 10 per cent). This dramatic economic performance is partly due to structural change (for example, shift to services; just-in-time in industry, which favours road haulage) but no doubt also to a total lack of (intramodal) competition and automatic, annual state aids. But the 'internal market', here, is just an addition of national turnovers, not a functioning economic reality. Until the 1990s in Europe, there was nowhere 'free movement' or free establishment, and practically nowhere any competition. The national railway companies had traditionally 'cooperated' for cross-border services (both passenger and freight) but the inefficiencies in pricing, working practices, allocation of slots on the networks, terminals procedures, technical incompatibilities, service quality and frontier problems confirmed people's worst beliefs about monopoly practices. This resulted in an average speed of rail freight of 16 km per hour (hopelessly uncompetitive even for bulk) and a 1.5 year wait for a quoted price to use Deutsche Bahn's network for specified freight services by a private provider.

The problem is how to introduce free movement, free establishment and competition, especially for cross-border rail services, on existing networks (which have hardly been expanded except for the TGV, the very rapid trains) and given the entrenched anti-competitive habits of the established firms and the powerful trade unions. The implications are distinct for passenger rail (with public service obligations) and freight by rail, where the public interest may comprise offering a less polluting alternative to road haulage. The

[14] In telecoms, the European Commission cleverly went around this delicate issue by recommending 'benchmark' interconnection tariffs (near the lowest ones found in the EU) without imposing details. During 1998 and 1999 this stimulated a rapid downward convergence of such tariffs.

[15] For GSM mobile, transposed into very high 'roaming' fees.

CASE STUDY 8.1 *continued*

deep resistance to liberalisation can be traced back to the very high degree of unionisation in a sector with considerable overmanning in the low-skilled categories.

At the same time it should be realised that liberalisation of rail is a complicated process in densely populated western Europe, where new infrastructural works are both expensive and resisted by the population. As a result, capacity problems can quickly throttle the potential for commercial entry. With Directive 91/440/EEC, the railway market was formally opened, but all it did was a slow shift to accounting separation of the track ('natural monopoly') and the services. Two directives in 1995 dealt with licensing, the allocation of railway infrastructure and the charging of infrastructure fees. All these proved no more than initial steps, with loopholes and derogations to get them adopted. The so-called First Railway Package of 2001 tightened the two 1995 directives and added Directive 2001/14 on allocation of pathways and infrastructure charges (equal for incumbent services and entrants). In terms of Table 8.1, the competition is thus on the networks. The new proposals are firm on full accounting separation between tracks and services, besides account separation between freight and passenger services (critical to pre-empt cross-subsidisation, since passenger PSOs are heavily subsidised: see step 4 of Table 8.1). The independent regulator for rail is mainly of importance for allotting capacity in a fair and non-discriminatory fashion, based on scarcity and other criteria. The idea of the First Package was to liberalise freight rail on specific EU rail corridors. In the Second Package (2004) this was to be extended to the entire EU network by 2006. Access pricing in rail takes the form of infrastructural fees; the proposal suggests marginal costs plus a margin for external costs and a scarcity premium. This would eventually remove 'frontier prices' in rail as well. Safety and interoperability directives have been adopted as well, and a European Agency for it started operating in 2005. A Third Package on passenger rail liberalisation by 2010 was proposed in 2004. For an economic appraisal, see di Pietrantonio & Pelkmans (2004).

8.3 Air transport

8.3.1 Method

Air transport as an industry is not easy to classify. Although a network industry in some respects (see below), it was not viewed as a typical 'public utility' – yet, airlines in Europe used invariably to be state owned and were burdened with PSOs (domestic, ex-colonies). For some decades, air transport was also kept outside the realm of the 'common transport policy' because Article 84 (now Article 80) EC made inclusion conditional on unanimity in Council.

However, the EC Court ruled in 1974 that the general rules of the treaty (for example, free movement of services and competition rules) also applied to sea and air transport. A first attempt to formulate a common air transport policy, proposed in 1975, failed hopelessly. It was the Single European Act,[16] with the 'area without frontiers' formula (see section 2.3), and a few successive Court cases, that led to a sequence of 'packages' finally resulting in the accomplishment of an internal market of air transport services.

To understand the basic regulatory economic issues, it is essential to distinguish three subsectors: charter, cargo and scheduled passenger traffic. The European charter market refers to low-cost, highly competitive service activities bringing package tours and a residual of seat-only trips to (usually Mediterranean) tourist destinations. Intermodal competition is intense (especially from cars) and there are no network effects, only point-to-point services. This subsector was virtually unregulated in Europe, except for the careful separation between this subsector and scheduled traffic.[17]

[16]Not the 1985 White Paper on the completion of the internal market, which, curiously, proposes only weak liberalisation measures in air transport.

[17]The charter market in Europe is larger than the scheduled market in terms of passenger-kilometres (± 55 per cent market share), though not in revenues. The reader should note that, for this reason, alone, the EU passenger air transport is different from that in the USA, where the charter market is tiny. Numerous cheap flights in the USA in the scheduled market have their counterpart in the huge European charter market (with fierce competition), if holidays or leisure are involved.

Cargo also enjoys a light regulatory regime and is competitive. The EU regulatory and liberalisation problems were found in the scheduled passenger market.

Scheduled passenger air transport is not comparable with road transport. Whereas the key issue in the latter is free movement, it is effective competition and competition policy in the former. Moreover, intra-EU competition is hindered by world regulation of air transport in bilateral agreements. This has an economic reason. EU major carriers earn most of their revenue intercontinentally. Their being big in the EU internal market does not depend in the first place on the effectiveness of exploiting intra-EU opportunities. Thus, for new entrants to compete (given strong network effects) requires equally good access to intercontinental routes. Based on restrictive interpretations of the Chicago Convention of 1944, most bilateral agreements in the world do not allow free access but insist on fine-tuning reciprocity in landing rights, frequency and even capacity.[18] While restricting established companies, bilaterals virtually bar new entrants in the intercontinental market. Only recently is there a global tendency to allow less restrictive interpretations, but this is a far cry from equal opportunities between established firms and new entrants. This is one reason why intra-European concentration remains high. Indeed, the large majority of city-pair routes are still duopolies of established companies.

As safety regulations are strict worldwide (via de ICAO, a UN agency), harmonisation was not too difficult in the run-up to full intra-EU liberalisation. Liberalisation was achieved by the freedom of establishment – doing away with exclusive rights of state-owned flag carriers – and by gradually improved free movement of services. Cabotage was introduced in 1997.

Given a history of state support and regulatory protection, the efficiency of European flag carriers was long lower than the leading US carriers, though the discrepancy has now become small. A liberal external policy might therefore be the best form of competition policy. However, deeply engrained attitudes of reciprocity worldwide make this very difficult to achieve.[19] Only since 2004 has the EU entered negotiations with the largest air market in the world (the USA) to shift to EU-wide bilaterals.

ADDITIONAL READING

In terms of Table 8.1, the competition takes place 'in' the market, especially between (airline) networks. Since air transport networks cannot be separated from the service provider, there is no competition 'on' the network, but 'interlining' (connecting a passenger from one network to the other) is commercially negotiated between airlines.[20] PSOs are of minor importance in air transport.[21] Interlining tariffs create problems for no-frills entrants wishing to offer their passengers further connections. Since networks are expensive to build up and maintain, interlining is too expensive for no-frills airlines, so that (thus far) they provide merely point-to-point services. Cross-border trade is no longer an issue in European air transport but some cross-border traffic is artificial because the external bilaterals prevent the start of intercontinental flights of incumbent carriers from any other country than the home country. Thus Air-France–KLM cannot fly Rome–New York, only Amsterdam–New York or Paris–New York, hence KLM might try to attract passengers to fly via Amsterdam, 'within' the KLM network, using competitive rates. Without the bilaterals, some of this 'feeder traffic' to the hub would disappear in Europe.

[18]Bilateral agreements are needed because landing rights have to be legally granted. Since the 1947 Bermuda-I bilateral between the USA and the UK, highly mercantilistic practices have become routine in worldwide civil aviation. A liberal interpretation of the Convention is possible but a liberal revision with access obligations would be far superior.

[19]Moreover, air transport ('hard') rights have been excluded from the Uruguay Round. In a landmark ruling of the EC Court in November 2002, the Court sided with the Commission in that national bilaterals with third countries fragment the internal market (just like national goods quotas *vis-à-vis* third countries, see section 6.5.3), hence, the EU as such can pursue a joint external policy. The Commission now strives after EU-wide bilaterals, beginning with the USA.

[20]For feeder (usually regional) airlines flying to a 'hub', this is so vital that they often end up as a daughter or alliance partner of a major carrier at the hub.

[21]An example is the steady services supplied to the many Greek islands, all year round, from the Greek mainland.

8.3.2 Economic impact analysis

Impact analysis for civil aviation should distinguish autonomous, worldwide trends of gradual liberalisation as well as the influence of rapid globalisation of this service industry from the consequences of liberalisation of the internal market itself. Furthermore, such liberalisation is only relevant for the scheduled passenger submarket and hardly or not at all for the (big) charter market or the one for cargo, as both are relatively free and fiercely competitive. In the long run, a single market for air transport might blur the distinction between charter and scheduled, but seasonality, the popularity of package tours and specificity of charter destinations strongly suggest that a significant, specialised charter market will remain in Europe. The critical economic difference between the charter and the scheduled market is the absence of network externalities in the former.[22] This is a crucial point in assessing the potential for greater competition in a single market for civil aviation, because – apart from possible non-EU entrants – charter companies were expected to be the only credible candidates for entry once the scheduled market became contestable. The challenge that charter companies face is whether they can risk huge sunk costs upon entry, before network externalities are built up. In some larger domestic markets in the EU, charter companies have entered in a modest fashion. Instead, low costs, no-frills new entrants (also, point-to-point) emerged in the 1990s and began to challenge the incumbents and, indirectly, the charters as well (see further below).

Up to the mid-1980s, scheduled air transport in Europe was characterised by little price competition, heavy collusion (mostly authorised or allowed by captured regulators), severe regulatory constraints (far more restrictive than in road transport) and residual forms of non-price competition. To understand whether airline liberalisation, in and by itself, would induce effective competition requires an economic analysis of how this market would operate without restrictive regulation, other than bilaterals with third countries. As is explained below, the impact of the liberalisation of the internal market has come out very gradually. Establishing a single market for civil aviation is necessary but far from sufficient. In this peculiar oligopolistic market, one cannot take for granted that competition, other than fringe competition, will emerge by itself. The core issue is therefore the proper functioning of the single market by *improving its contestability* and/or by active EC competition policy.

After briefly recalling some underlying worldwide trends in civil aviation, the problem of improving the *contestability* of scheduled air transport – and more specifically the one in Europe – will be analysed. Only by understanding this fundamental issue will it be possible to design a combination of (pro-competitive) regulation, competition policy, external services trade policy and market developments, bringing about a properly functioning single market in all forms of civil aviation.[23]

CASE STUDY 8.2 Towards a single market in gas and electricity

In regulatory debates the gas and electricity industries are often viewed together. Indeed, they are both network industries in energy and they have a somewhat similar structure. However, gas can be stored (at a cost, of course) and electricity cannot. Electricity systems have to be balanced every second, hence electricity wholesale trading (for example, generators and final supply) is always done beforehand; a true forward market. Gas, like oil, requires exploration and extraction, unlike electricity. Yet, electricity can be produced at any scale: by power generators, ranging from tiny ones (including windmills) and hydro to huge plants using coal, oil, gas or nuclear. With new production technologies such as CCGTs (combined cycle gas turbines) and CHP (combined heat and power), environmental emission standards and efficiency are enhanced considerably. Gas production depends

[22]The most important entry barrier in the charter market is the ability to tap mass tourist demand. Only tour operators and networks of travel agents can do this effectively (i.e. routinely achieve load factors of 100 per cent). It also explains why charter companies of destination countries are at a disadvantage compared with those from origin countries. (Note, the load factor of an aeroplane is the share of sold seats in the total number of available seats.)

[23]The following is based on Pelkmans (1992b), McGowan (2000), CAA (1998), AEA (2005) and *The Economist* (2004).

CASE STUDY 8.2 *continued*

on relatively few source countries (say, the Netherlands, the UK, Norway in the extended internal market, called the EEA; Russia, Algeria and the Arab peninsula outside it) and hence suffers from a formidable security of supply problem in the long term (70 per cent imports in 2020).

In 1996, the electricity directive (Directive 96/92) liberalised the market for generation as well as final supply to large (that is, business) customers. In 1998, the gas directive (Directive 98/30) did more or less the same. Both directives were incomplete (only business liberalisation) and weak. They have been overridden by firmer ones in 2003 (Directives 2003/54 and 2003/55) with a path to full liberalisation in 2007, and regulation on access and (cross-border) interconnectors (including pricing principles, for example Regulation 1228/2003). In terms of Table 8.1, the competition is *in* the market for generation and sales to large customers, but significant natural monopolies remain. In electricity, the high voltage transmission grid is undoubtedly a natural monopoly and a transmission system's operator must be established; thereby, the ownership and the actual use of the grid are effectively separated. As to generation, self-generation (for example, in companies some minimum capacity may be kept for emergency purposes) is free and all other production is subject to licensing or tendering, based on prescribed principles. The medium voltage distribution is also a natural monopoly, and distribution systems operators must be established as well. In gas, partial duplication (that is, dedicated pipeline) of the network can be cost effective for large customers (for example, a bulk chemical plant).

In 2003, step 2 (Table 8.1) has been improved to legal unbundling and independent national regulators. Uniform tariff USOs (step 3) are explicitly allowed (relevant for electricity only). In step 4, regulated distribution tariffs for USO purposes are allowed – their financing in such cases is therefore not explicit. The access rules (step 5) are based on (regulatory) third-party access to the transmission/distribution. Cross-border trade (step 6) is liberalised (that is, exclusive import or export rights are abolished) and transit trade is almost free (at €1 per megawatt-hour) subject to capacity constraints. However, these constraints are severe and to overcome them requires major investment. The internal market may thus remain rather fragmented for some time. One immediate benefit is clear: the costs of business energy inputs have already begun to decrease. However, electricity prices still differ a lot in the EU and arbitrage is insufficient, given capacity constraints over interconnectors. In gas, price differences can be observed, too. Gas prices fluctuate to some extent with oil prices and this may swamp liberalisation effects.

ADDITIONAL READING

For decades, the growth of passenger air transport has been far above GDP growth. The trend can be explained by sustained technological progress, permitting rapid improvement of aircraft productivity. This has gradually pushed costs and yields[24] down. In the 1960s, this made the emergence of the European holidays charter market possible. By the 1980s the scheduled market also saw yields decline via a gradual increase of the share of discount tickets. Where load factors permitted, or the charter market caused some indirect competition, the practice of 'deep discounts' developed – essentially sales just above (low) marginal costs.[25] Prosperity in OECD countries, and more recently in other parts of the world, caused the non-business travel demand to rise very rapidly. Eventually this led to the following market structure in Europe. The flag carriers responded to the emergence of a huge charter market in Europe[26] by discounting and

[24]Yields are defined as the amount of revenue per passenger-kilometre.

[25]Above the break-even load factor, selling seats at very low prices still adds to profits.

[26]Some 55 per cent of all passenger-kilometres flown in Europe is covered by the charters.

ADDITIONAL READING *continued*

deep discounting in a highly prudent fashion, via service differentiation and restrictions on discount tickets. In addition, they ensured, via captured regulators, that the scheduled and the charter markets remained largely separated, while engaging in partial ownership of some charter carriers. By the use of such strategies, the high-priced business travel segment remained protected from effective price erosion until the deep civil aviation crisis of 1992–93. At the same time, the flag carriers focused heavily on worldwide connections with the arrival of wide-body planes. Owing to restrictions in bilateral air transport agreements and greater scope for low pricing for non-business travel in wide-body aircrafts, European charters were pre-empted in penetrating the world tourist market. Today, non-European air transport services make up close to 70 per cent of capacity and over 50 per cent of revenue of scheduled services by European flag carriers. Hence, economically, the single market (plus EFTA and other Europe) is hardly the mainstay for European scheduled air transport, the more so as the world segment is growing faster. The strong internationalisation has had a pro-competitive impact on the European carriers, despite the restrictive bilateral agreements on which world air transport is built. However, this is still a far cry from the European market being contestable.

The contestability of scheduled air transport in Europe has markedly increased only since full (intra-EU) liberalisation, that is, since the mid-1990s. How far the contestability goes is unclear. Assuming a second-hand or lease-market for aircraft, some economists first maintained that entry and exit would be at very low cost (that is, making it contestable). So suppliers, but equally new entrants, in using airplanes, would only incur 'marginal costs on wings'. Economies of scale in hardware are modest.[27] These arguments for high contestability are overridden, however, by other features. The economies of scale in branding and marketing are large, helped by computer reservation systems (CRSs). CRSs address an important asymmetry of information in air travel, namely the search costs of finding out all competing offers for a desired trip. Even when CRS are not biased in favour of dominant airlines (at first, the owners of a CRS), access to CRSs is privileged for airlines and travel agents, which have little incentive to promote sales of low-margin tickets of new entrants. Building up one's own CRS is extremely costly, not only for reasons of development but also because there is an installed base with thousands of travel agents worldwide which somehow has to be penetrated. These barriers to entry and exit used to be formidable indeed. However, internet ticketing has caused these barriers to melt away. Economies of scope and other network externalities for airlines have proved to be equally formidable barriers, at least for typical 'network passengers'. Smooth connections to continental and intercontinental networks, as well as to regional 'feeders', are so crucial for business and some non-business passengers that economies of network size may not be exhausted before a carrier effectively operates worldwide, be it alone or in alliances spanning the continents. Scope is also enhanced by hub-and-spoke systems[28] which allow less used routes to be flown profitably (as spokes) but which require major sunk-cost commitments. Entry on just a few routes or expanding from a regional to a limited main-cities carrier will at most serve as fringe competition. If prices of such an entrant are low, established airlines can respond by matching those prices by deep discounting for a few seats only or even by predatory practices (such as a sudden increase in frequency to weaken the entrant on the relevant route).

In Europe, contestability is further weakened because bilaterals control third country competition and because of the (public) ownership of most

[27]So-called economies of route length and of density can be measured but they do not make a compelling case for overall size carriers (i.e. for a multitude of routes).

[28]A hub is a major airport used by an airline as a home base or as a central point on another continent. Spokes are connections to the hub. The key advantages of a hub-and-spoke system are superior connections and clustering of passengers for less-used (i.e. thin) routes, which (without hubbing) would not be viable or would have far lower frequencies.

ADDITIONAL READING *continued*

carriers. And a history of protection and state aids reduce the prospect of successful rivalry among the flag carriers.

Initially, this structural lack of challenge and price competition, led to a legacy of high-cost European airlines. Although costs were high compared with those of US airlines, there are also great differences among the European scheduled carriers (see CAA, 1993, appendix 2). Since the inefficiencies are typically of the X-inefficiency type, the economic gains of fiercer competition in a single market should be large.[29] Almost certainly it would necessitate mergers or alliances and a different fleet composition to cut costs for less profitable routes – all features of the adjustment of EU airlines during the 1990s.

The initial market impact of intra-European liberalisation has been modest but real. Low contestability has been confirmed by the (harsh) test of the market: between early 1993 and early 1999, no less than 131 airlines (with schedules services) entered, of which 56 per cent have exited in the same period. Of the 124 established airlines (many of which are in the fringe) in early 1993, 55 have ceased to operate (AEA, 1999). However, all major carriers remained in business, though six of them received significant state aids in the mid-1990s.

Competitive pressure did increase somewhat (see CAA, 1998). The major carriers' dominance declined: their aggregate share of output on all scheduled routes within the EU fell from over 80 per cent in late 1992 to well under 70 per cent by late 1997; in their domestic markets, the decline was even sharper – from 75 per cent to a little over 60 per cent, due to new entry. Note, however, that many feeder airlines have code-sharing or franchising agreements with the majors, so formal market share declines may be the result not of competitive entry but of complementary networks. At the level of individual intra-EU cross-border routes, the share of those with more than two airlines increased only from 4 to 7 per cent. Focusing on only the densest routes – the ones where competitive entry is viable – the increase is significant, from 12 to 26 per cent. For domestic routes the analogous increase was from 10 to 20 per cent. Alliances and hub-based exploitation of network effects have increased, and cabotage rights are hardly used, both signs that the EU market has become more and more dichotomised between network-based (major) airlines and feeders on the one hand, and point-to-point no-frills scheduled and charter airlines on the other.

Later in the 1990s, and up to 2005, the upheaval in EU civil aviation has become greater. The first 'deeper' contest would consist of rivalry on the home-ground of main carriers, because the removal of exclusive rights and profitable routes (with load market power) looked like a standing invitation to penetrate. In 2002, the average cost advantage of no-frills, compared with network carriers was some 57 per cent, almost two-thirds of which was due to high-density seating, station-handling costs and airport charges, followed by discontinuance of in-flight catering and avoidance of travel agent commission. Some of these items cannot but apply to short-haul; some other items (such as electronic ticketing and internet booking) can be imitated by network airlines. So can the refined yield management, raising prices as planes fill up. Under low contestability one would expect a price response only with actual entry rather than potential entry. But the costs of 'earning' credibility upon entry are extremely high. A deterrent example is that of Deutsche Britisch Airways (DBA) trying to challenge Lufthansa on the busy Frankfurt–Munich route. As Figure 8.2 illustrates, Lufthansa launched a price war to protect its dominance on this domestic route, but only once DBA announced entry, and more forcefully still once DBA initiated the services. All further price decreases by DBA were matched by Lufthansa for all three fare levels. Note that DBA is a daughter of what was then Europe's biggest and most profitable airline, yet the losses

[29]Since overstaffing is one serious reason for X-inefficiency, these gains will lead to significant shedding of labour. These adjustment costs have to be deducted.

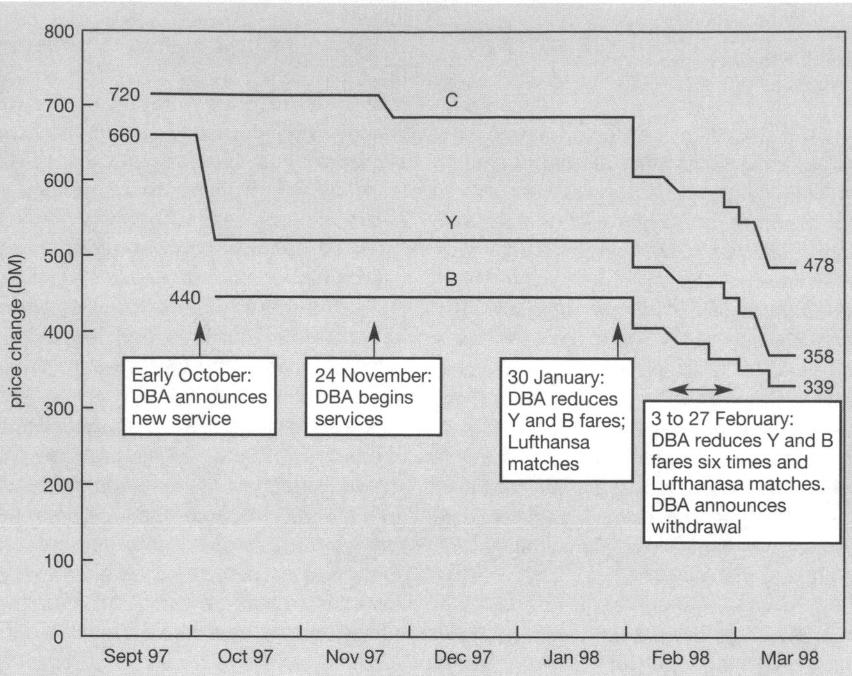

Figure 8.2 Competitive entry and price-war deterrence in EU air transport: change in Lufthansa return fare on Frankfurt–Munich route following DBA's entry

Source: CAA, 1998, p. 295

ADDITIONAL READING *continued*

became unbearable and DBA pulled out. Smaller and financially vulnerable entrants will avoid such major challenges or enter with fringe products (for example, turbo prop services).[30] Second, since the late 1990s, the low-cost no-frills airlines have enjoyed phenomenal growth rates. Clearly, this has benefited the price-sensitive leisure traveller and can be judged positively. But thus far, practically all this air traffic is additional to the existing scheduled services, with many passengers who would simply not have opted to fly otherwise. Many flights take off and land on little-used airports (to cut costs) and services are typically point-to-point with no interlining. In 2000, their total seats offered were approximately 8 per cent of intra-European seats offered by the major scheduled airlines, up to more than 16 per cent by 2004.[31] These airlines have reached the point when further growth will imply head-on competition on major routes with the former flag carriers. One powerful effect of the no-frills is the drastic cost-cutting in network industries. So, even when it seems that the first high-growth period of the no-frills is over, their impact on the other airlines is significant. However, with major routes, costs are higher, while the old carriers have become lean. And going interconnected is harder still.

[30]Another example of building a major presence (here, in France) is the merger of TAT and Air Liberté, partly owned by BA.

[31]They include Ryanair, Virgin Express, easyJet, Buibaby, Basiq Air, Volare Web and (e.g.) Sky Europe (all in 2004; there is a lot of entry/exit in this market).

CASE STUDY 8.3 Postal liberalisation: rowing against the tide

Postal services traditionally consist largely of letter mail (including the lucrative direct-mail submarket), periodicals and relatively small parcels. It is a network industry with essentially four business functions: collection, sorting, transport and delivery. The sector is under significant competitive pressure because e-mail substitutes for ordinary letters (local, national and European), broadcasting and internet can be seen as substitutes for direct mail, while private carriers have grown into major rivals for express courier services. Privatisation of the established postal companies used to be rare – even in the UK (and the USA) the postal monopolies are state owned. The Dutch Post (now TPG) privatised fully in the mid-1990s and subsequently developed (via acquisitions) as a postal and logistic multinational. Deutsche Post followed a few years later. Liberalisation at the Member State level is uneven in the EU: in five EU countries (including Sweden and Finland), there is no postal monopoly any more, and in 2005 the UK and several other countries were considering ending the postal monopoly. Some other EU25 countries have shrunk the 'reserved' activities for the monopolist further than the second postal directive (2002/39).

In 1994, the Council agreed, by resolution, to engage in a process of 'gradual and controlled' liberalisation of the sector. This decision alone was the outcome of a tough political battle. Most postal jobs are low skilled. In 2003, of the 1.7 million persons employed in the sector, 1.1 million are employed by USO-based postal operators. In December 1997, the postal directive (Directive 97/67) was finally adopted, but the scope for competition is very limited.

In terms of Table 8.1, step 1 is simple, in that natural monopoly does not apply, yet also complicated, because some B2C activities and C2C mail are under sensitive political constraints. The postal network of collection, transport and delivery is logistical, not physical. The sunk costs would not suggest the necessity of monopoly provision. As to delivery – a labour-intensive activity absorbing 60 per cent of all costs – a company might specialise in it and accept mail from several providers in a single delivery round per day. Because of technological progress, sorting has become highly automated, raising fixed costs for lightweight letters; with more and more centralised sorting, scale might perhaps require 'access' rules.

Step 2 foresees an independent regulator, but this can be a ministry. The key provision in the postal directive is the split between 'reserved' and competitive business. Whereas Directive 97/67 maintains that 'reserved business' are letters under 350 grams (unless the customer is willing to pay five times the regulated tariff, for value-added, for example courier services which are under competition), Directive 2002/39 narrows the 'reserved business' for the monopolist to letters under 100 grams until the end of 2005, and under 50 grams (or two and a half times the tariff) as of 2006. The move from 100 grams to 50 grams adds some 7 per cent of the letter business. Altogether, no more than 16 per cent of the letter business will be free in 2006. Note that direct mail and (incoming) cross-border mail are also part of the monopoly business. USOs/PSOs (step 3) are defined in the 1997 directive and are wider than the 'reserved' activities. That means that new (licensed) operators have to comply with USO rules, yet in a competitive environment.

Universal service obligations are ambitious: letters, books, catalogues, newspapers and magazines up to a weight of 2 kg, as well as registered and insured items, and freight up to 10 kg and possibly 20 kg. Financing the USO (step 4) can be done via cross-subsidisation or a USO ('compensation') fund. Entry into the market can be made subject to general and/or individual licences, with requirements about USOs or their (co)financing. Access to the network (step 5) is a special heading in the directive but no provision specifies access conditions (or rights) . The *Bronner* case[32] tested the nature of access to postal and related distribution networks. A small Austrian newspaper demanded access to the home-distribution network of a major producer of newspapers. The small newspaper claimed that the distribution network was an 'essential facility', indispensable for the fringe competitor to compete effectively. The relevance to postal distribution is obvious. The EC Court rejected the demand, noting that only when it is economically impossible to duplicate the facility,

[32]Case C-7/97, [1998] ECR I-7791.

CASE STUDY 8.3 *continued*

is it 'essential' and could 'access' be required. As to step 6, cross-border trade, the Reims II agreement[33] has done away with the highly distorted 'terminal dues'. The dues for processing and delivering incoming cross-border mail (from EU countries) are 'cost-related' and tied to quality levels. By 2004 this had led to a dramatic quality increase in cross-border mail services in the EU.

8.4 Telecoms

8.4.1 Method

Telecoms have generally been regarded in Europe as a utility or public service. Until the early 1980s, telecoms services were under national exclusive (that is, monopoly) rights, provided by the same organisation as the one owning the single, fixed wired network and selling exclusively telephone sets and telexes. In most Member States this was also combined with the postal monopoly. Article 86 EC was ignored or interpreted as a recognition of the exceptional status of utilities.

Since 1983, a complicated process has unfolded, ending in the full liberalisation of telecoms services and infrastructures in the EU by early 1998. Nowadays, in terms of Table 8.1, competition is in the market, and both on and between networks. This section focuses solely on the essential regulatory framework for telecoms services of the internal market. Thus, it disregards non-service elements in the liberalisation of telecoms in the EU.[34]

In 1990, the liberalisation in telecoms services began prudently with the following steps:

- The *separation of regulatory functions from network operations* (step 2, in Table 8.1).
- A split between *'reserved' services,* that is, those remaining under monopoly rights,[35] and *competitive services,* mainly value-added services such as data transmission, interbank transfers, and so on (step 2, in Table 8.1). Since having or building a network was still monopolised initially, guarantees of access to the network had to be provided in order for competitive services to be supplied at all.
- A framework for *open network provision* (ONP) (step 5, in Table 8.1). The right of access to the network is given to users and providers of value-added services but at conditions which should ensure undistorted competition (especially between the competitive services of the incumbent and those of new entrants).[36] The main point of ONP is to discipline the monopolist and create equal opportunities for competitive services.

These first steps were useful exercises in liberalisation, especially against the backdrop of a wave of privatisation at Member States level and rising pressures of business

[33] See the definitive commission approval in OJ L 56/76 of 24 February 2004.

[34] Such as the liberalisation of the terminal equipment market in 1988, 1991 (see Pelkmans & Young, 1998, chapter 6), and in 1999; the introduction of competitive procurement of network equipment (cables and switching) (see section 5.4.1) and supporting measures such as common R&D in the RACE programme and issues of standardisation and interoperability. Telecoms standards have been developed and adopted (voluntarily) in ETSI (European Telecoms Standards Institute) since 1988. For the critical common standard, namely the GSM standard for digital cellular mobile communication, see Case Study 14.2 on high-tech standards; see also Pelkmans (1999).

[35] As far as EC legislation is concerned, Member States were free to liberalise nationally, as the UK, Finland and Sweden progressively did.

[36] Thus, cross-subsidisation from the earnings of reserved services of the incumbent to its competitive services is prohibited. In 1994, Deutsche Telekom was convicted for cross-subsidising its (competitive) data services activities to the tune of several hundreds of million Deutschmarks. More generally, the ONP framework directive specifies access conditions, imposed on incumbents, such as transparency, non-discrimination and least-restrictiveness of measures related to (data) security and network integrity.

user groups (much wanted clients for any service provider) to allow more liberalisation. Nevertheless, the opening up for competitive services left some 85 per cent of the incumbents' revenues untouched, those arising from voice telephony, fax and telex, as reserved services; also, the rapidly growing mobile sector was 'reserved'.

The pressures to liberalise became rapidly stronger. One traditional defense of exclusive rights – natural monopoly – had crumbled for terminal equipment and competitive services. With the needed investments in cellular mobile being relatively low, sunk costs reduced and competition became possible.[37] The UK and other early liberalisers showed that the other traditional defence of exclusive rights – universal service – could be achieved in a competitive environment without large cross-subsidies from (business-dominated) trunk calls to local ones, and from cities and trunk lines to the periphery.

In 1993, the Council agreed to go for full liberalisation of telecoms services. In 1994 it also adopted a proposal to liberalise network infrastructures and set a timetable up to 1998 for services liberalisation. Focusing on the main issues among many, five can be identified as critical: the proper costing principles, the approximation of universal service obligations, the achievement of an 'information society', competition policy and subsidiarity (see Additional Reading below for elaboration).

ADDITIONAL READING

Costing principles are a major issue for reasons of cross-subsidisation, the (true) costs of universal service and the proper pricing of interconnection. The current view is that the costs of universal service need not throttle competition at all. Studies have shown that the additional costs of USOs are between zero and 2 per cent of revenues. Only in cohesion countries, where networks were not fully completed, could the costs (temporarily) be higher. Second, the most extreme costs used to be incurred in peripheral and mountainous regions, whereas, today, modern radio communications or digital cellular mobile have become superior and far cheaper alternatives. By 1998, when the internal market was fully liberalised, thirteen out of fifteen Member States did not even opt for a sharing mechanism to cofinance USOs and only France and Italy actually imposed it – for just two years.

Costing principles are also important to verify whether interconnection tariffs (of dominant established companies) are abusive. A consensus is emerging that the best pricing rule is that of forward-looking long-run average incremental costs plus a mark-up (see Figure 8.1).[38] After some initial disputes in 1998, the Commission began to promote 'benchmark' interconnection tariffs simply by recommending the average of the lowest interconnection tariffs in the EU, on a regular basis. Given the highly competitive environment, and pressures from business, a process of downward convergence could be observed during 1998 and 1999.

As to USOs, the EU incorporated minimum specifications in the 1997 ONP voice telephony directive (for details see Pelkmans & Young, 1998, chapter 8), with half-yearly reporting requirements on national USOs and their realisation. What had long been a sensitive political obstacle for liberalisation, with reservations on the part of some Member States to assign the EU level with the task of approximation, in the end became a fairly well defined set of quality requirements for EU consumers. Moreover, since 1998, both competition on and between networks as well as careful comparative reporting have proved to be conducive to the realising of fairly ambitious USOs, an achievement not comparable with the situation of two decades earlier.

The advent of the single market in telecoms services has been greatly boosted by the arrival of the 'information society', merging telecoms, information technology and multimedia in business services and at home (see Case Study 8.4).

Competition policy in telecoms is often almost indistinguishable from (liberal) regulation. The key problem with competition policy is that, with the initial dominance of incumbents, it is far too slow

[37] Note, however, that mobile service providers still need access to a fixed network as well.

[38] For an authoritative discussion of various pricing rules and their application, see *European Economy,* 1999, no. 4, Reports and Studies, Part B, pp. 132–67 (by Laffont *et al.*). See also Cave & Valletti (2000). A careful technical elaboration is in ERG (2005). Forward-looking means based on current costs (which in telecoms, usually means, downward). Incremental costs are like marginal costs except that marginal costs strictly refer to the *last* extra unit added, not just one extra unit. In practice, the two are equivalent.

ADDITIONAL READING *continued*

and uncertain with regard to details. Another crucial issue is the existence of extreme asymmetries of information between incumbents and general competition authorities. A specialised regulator with permanent access to detailed information and with safeguards against 'capture' is likely to be greatly superior. However, regulators in EU telecoms are nowadays at the national level whereas competition policy exists at both levels of government (see Chapter 12). The principle of subsidiarity prompts reflection about the pros and cons of an EU regulator (see Sun & Pelkmans, 1995b; Pelkmans, 1998). In 1998, with full interoperability, free competition and no 'frontier effect' (the costs of cross-border calls would be priced according to distance, irrespective of the border – see step 6 of Table 8.1), liberalisation would initially have been well served with a centralised regulator. In those early days, many decisions should have been taken speedily for the whole of the single market, in particular for licensing and interconnection.

First movers, in particular, attempting to set up pan-European telecoms networks – a reflection of single market opportunities – suffered delays and severe losses which should have been prevented by a centralised regulator. A much improved and more simple EU telecoms regime was adopted in 2002. It is based on the idea that lighter regulation is justified by prevailing competition. The text of the directives is inspired by competition policy. Indeed, national regulators are assigned to conduct detailed economic market analysis of eighteen (potentially 'relevant') wholesale and retail services markets, and if, and only if, these are found not to be competitive, can they intervene. Even so, interventions remedies are scaled, with competition policy remedies first, and if insufficient, regulatory ones. This way, abuse of dominant position is preempted (*ex ante*) by remedies. It has led to price regulation, for example of (initially high) fixed-to-mobile interconnection tariffs, and of urban leased lines, needed for fringe competitors.

CASE STUDY 8.4 Information and media services on convergent networks

Barely having concluded the long and tortuous road to full liberalisation of telecoms equipment, services and network markets, rapid technological progress already foreshadowed yet another revolution in markets and EU (networks) regulation. Under the label of 'convergence', hitherto separated activities such as broadcasting, pay-TV, value-added and internet services, telecoms, film and video distribution and publishing all expected their traditional ways of creating value to be deeply affected, if not transformed. The underlying technological drive is digitisation: in principle, it became possible for all these goods and services to be produced and distributed in digital form, and possible to adapt network technologies in such a way as to transmit the 'bits' over any electronic network. Thus, TV cable companies could offer not only telephony and internet but also interactive pay-TV; traditional telecoms companies saw 'telephony' becoming a commodity and wished to penetrate the higher value-added internet and 'content' industries; film producers, already magnifying their revenues via video and TV rights, saw (interactive) pay-TV as another outlet, especially with broadcasting and TV sets becoming digitised as well; internet services widened to include (cheaper) telephony, still and (subsequently) moving pictures, with web-TV emerging as an infant-industry; a major upheaval might be caused by (almost free) VoIP (Voice over Internet Protocol worldwide); publishing (for example, newspapers, encyclopaedias, academic journals) has also gone electronic quite rapidly.

This upheaval generates a range of regulatory issues for network industries. First, broadcasting – a public utility in Europe until the early 1980s – has been subjected to an internal market regime in 1989 (in the 'TV without frontiers' directive). Only 'public

CASE STUDY 8.4 *continued*

TV' (state-owned or not) has PSOs and can receive state aids to finance it. It should be noted that the dual (private/public) TV system is typical for Europe; indeed, a special protocol on public broadcasting was attached to the Amsterdam Treaty. The question is how this regime will survive the emergence of web-TV (thus far, of much lower quality), digital pay-TV and 3G mobile technology with still pictures, mobile pictures and mini-TV. Difficult issues about how dominance of digital pay-TV providers can be combined with open network access in what (because of language and culture) are still national markets have caused several vertical mergers to be prohibited (see Case Study 12.3). Second, the phenomenal rise of the internet precisely in the period that EU's telecoms liberalisation took place radically shifted the preferences of consumers, business and policy makers alike. The new 2002 telecoms regime takes convergence fully into account – neutrality with respect to the underlying technology whether cable, satellite, fixed-wire, various forms of wireless – and greatly simplifies the regime, with compliance costs expected to be lower. Also, the local-loop (connccting homes and businesses to networks) had to be unbundled by the established telecoms companies so as to facilitate consumer choice for all digitised network services. So, broadcasting falls under this regime as far as electronic transport is concerned, but not with respect to content. The future is likely to be for single-provider packages of different electronic communications, with content included: a cable TV operator may offer internet and fixed voice as well, and the consumer might opt for pay-TV as an extra.

8.4.2 Economic impact analysis

In telecoms, probably more than any other network industry, changes in economic variables observed after liberalisation may have been caused by drivers, other than EU liberalisation itself. The most powerful driving force of liberalisation consisted in rapid and pervasive technological change in equipment, network hardware, services (for example, mobile and internet), and capacity, besides the shift to digitisation. Even in 2005, the pace of change shows no sign of slowing in the immediate future; if anything, convergence (see Case Study 8.4) may well act as a strong incentive for even more intense innovation. Other driving forces included incessant pressures from business eager to economise on high telecoms bills while insisting on higher quality, and globalisation, which prompted business to find ways to avoid the most inefficient and costly monopolies. Therefore, one finds cost reductions as early as the mid-1980s. Bossard *et al.* (1997) find large cost reductions for interregional and international calls and some new entry, all since the early 1990s when EU-wide liberalisation began. In the following we focus first on short-term liberalisation effects in 1998/99, and subsequently provide evidence of the very considerable medium-term success of EU telecoms liberalisaton.[39]

First, there has been massive entry in public fixed voice telephony and substantial entry in mobile telecoms. By August 1999 there were 343 local and 545 national fixed-wire telephony providers in the EU15 (these two groups partly overlap) and many more licensed, without having begun services. The established operators tend to lose market share the quickest in long-distance and international operations. In mobile, competition is even more effective. Thus, the market share of the mobile subsidiarity of the established fixed operator, adding analogue (where the monopolists did not have to compete as a rule until the mid-1990s) and GSM, declined to between 37 and 68 per cent, dependent on the Member States. Equally, where the established operator's subsidiaries act as an internet service provider, they are up against fierce competition, with market shares generally between 20 and 50 per cent.[40]

Second, how forcefully competition has increased can also be read from the supergrowth in interconnection agreements[41] (from 442 in August 1998 to 820 in August

[39]Early data from the Commission's fifth implementation report, especially annex 4, COM (1999) 537 of 10 November 1999.
[40]Outliers were France (60 per cent) and Portugal (65 per cent), as well as Spain (8 per cent).
[41]For call termination on fixed networks, that is, fixed-to-fixed and mobile-to-fixed.

1999). Data show a rapid convergence of interconnection tariffs to the EU best-practice levels, which means that interconnection itself has become a competitive business.[42]

Third, price levels have come down rapidly. Given the history of cross-subsidisation for USO purposes one should expect entrants to target international and interregional call markets, since it is easy to undercut those artificially high tariffs. These differences might perhaps even have induced inefficient entry.[43] To withstand this massive entry, the established operator must 'rebalance' its tariff structure rapidly, without losing revenue if possible. This requires either an increase in local call charges (and initial access charges as well as rentals) or sharp improvements of cost levels. However, it is politically (and commercially) hard to justify a rise in bills to consumers and small businesses at a time when telecoms liberalisation is, it is claimed, cutting prices dramatically. Therefore, tariff rebalancing can best be spread over a number of years, during which incumbents improve efficiency and gradually cut trunk and international call charges. Not only were expenditures on a given basket of calls for residential users highest in late liberalisers such as Austria, Belgium, Spain and Portugal (and this pattern is even more pronounced for business users), local call charges had to be increased (between 1997 and 1999) sharply by Greece, Spain, Austria and Portugal, with Belgium alone sharply raising the price of regional calls. The EU average price fall for long-distance calls over 1997 to 1999 amounted to 30 per cent, and 42 per cent for international calls. Also, trends in leased-line tariffs are sharply down, even though prices remain much higher than in the USA, for example. Meanwhile, even though the fixed voice segment was still growing by nearly 5 per cent a year, mobile remained in the 15–20 per cent growth bracket, and internet subscribers almost doubled year on year up to 2000. It would be misleading to ascribe these growth figures to the single market in telecoms alone, or even primarily (technology and service innovation are primary influences), although there is more justification in the case of mobile (given GSM and roaming) than internet.

The medium-run effects as well as the spreading of the liberalisation to the ten new Member States show more of the same positive effects.[44] Starting in 1998 (thus, ignoring price falls before 1998), the average decrease in the cost of international calls up to mid-2003 was more than 40 per cent both for residential users and for business. Such price reductions in the EU15 are beginning to flatten but declines in central Europe were still steep in the year of joining the EU (2004). In terms of overall monthly spending on telecoms (the bills, calculated for a fixed basket of services), the EU25 declines are more gradual (owing to tariff rebalancing) but the impact continues through 2004. In EU15 fixed voice, incumbent market shares keep on falling: down to 60 per cent for international calls but even for local calls (the 'local loop' is typically owned only by incumbents) to 75 per cent in December 2003. One reason is carrier (pre-)select (alternative service providers), reaching 31 per cent in July 2004. In mobile (EU15), by 2000 the market shares of competitors became larger than that of the incumbent's daughters, amounting to 56.8 per cent by 2004, against 43.2 per cent. Also, leased line tariffs keep on declining in the EU25.

In the near future, the application of the new telecoms regime is likely to induce drastic reduction of roaming charges (GSM calls in other countries, essentially) and a hand-offs policy about VoIP, which will put further pressure on cross-border (fixed) calls worldwide.

8.5 Summary

Network industries, formerly called 'public utilities', were almost invariably state owned in western Europe before 1980. The EC treaty is neutral with respect to ownership. But the existence of state-owned companies does not imply a right to distort the competition in the internal market. A network industry may be given exclusive rights if the objective is legitimate (for example, universal service), but under proportionality; if not legitimate or if disproportional, the services come under free movement and competition, with less restrictive means to fulfil public service obligations.

The three important characteristics of network industries are: natural monopoly or, if not, considerable sunk costs; the (proper) combination of USOs with

[42]However, the tariffs from fixed-to-mobile proved to be far out of line. The Commission DG for competition initiated proceedings which led to sharp cuts in 2000. Further cuts have been imposed by national regulators later. Nonetheless, by 2004 fixed-to-mobile interconnection rates were roughly eight times the (regulated) rates for fixed-to-fixed.

[43]Inefficient entry means that the *costs* of the entrant on the relevant (here, dense) routes are higher than those of the established operator, but the latter's price is higher initially (see text).

[44]All data from the 10th Commission report on telecoms. See COM (2004) 759 of 2 December 2004, *European Electronic Communications Regulation and Markets 2004,* and annex.

Summary *continued*

competition; and network externalities. Under natural monopoly, competition is bad and monopoly is good, as long as X-efficiency can be maintained. Universal service obligations may well (have to) imply large-scale cross-subsidisation; if so, exclusive rights are one way to protect against 'cream skimming'. However, USOs can be combined with competition (if natural monopoly is absent) if targeted subsidies are used. This combination of targeted subsidies with competition may be superior in squeezing out the often large X-inefficiencies that exist. Network externalities have major implications for competition between networks (for example, new mobile networks, airline networks) as well as for competition on networks. This is one reason why network compatibility standards can be strongly pro-competitive.

The internal market for network industries requires a complex two-level mixture of regulation and competition. Rules of supervision should ensure effective, undistorted access for new providers to networks (competition on networks), competition between networks and free movement. Especially for initial entry and some aspects of access or interconnection, regulation is likely to be superior to sole reliance on competition policy, also at EU level.

Establishing the internal market for network industries can be outlined as a six-step procedure, applicable (broadly speaking) to all the relevant network industries horizontally. This is to be complemented with the sectoral specificities, which can be many. Step 1 is about competition 'in' the market or (under natural monopoly) 'for' the market. Step 2 is how to introduce competition: establish an independent regulator and separate (unbundle) 'reserved' from competitive business. Steps 3 and 4 are about public or universal service, defining the levels and regulating their non-distortive funding. Step 5 is all about (non-distortive) access and interconnection, and the supervision of it. Step 6 is how to realise non-distortive cross-border trade.

The chapter illustrates four network industry liberalisations in case studies. In rail, progress came with two packages in 2001 and 2004, after a long period of mostly (formal) liberalisation since 1991. The major gains are expected in rail freight, subject to capacity problems. In gas and electricity, liberalisation will be complete at EU level in 2007 but has often been realised earlier at Member State level. However, significant (transmission) natural monopolies remain, and a true single market has not yet been achieved owing to capacity constraints of cross-border 'interconnectors'. In postal services resistance has been fierce, mainly because it is feared that low-skilled labour will be laid off. A sector with less extreme sunk costs and mainly logistical functions, it will eventually have to open up entirely. Also, some postal services risk becoming obsolete owing to electronic substitution. As to internet and media services (on converged networks), there is much less regulatory emphasis (except public TV; access, for example, with respect to cable TV) because convergence and competition cause an incredible transformation with 'easy' entry and innovation.

Two network industries are elaborated in terms of method and economic analysis. In air transport, the issues are in the scheduled passenger market (cargo and the huge charter market being highly competitive). Given the oligopolistic market structure, EC competition policy is crucial. Liberalisation inside the single market (and the EEA, Switzerland and some countries in eastern Europe) is complete, be it that slot allocation at congested airports is conservative. However, for intercontinental traffic, restrictive bilaterals concluded with Member States (not the EU) throttle entry, aggravated by network effects and the weight of intercontinental turnover for European trunk carriers. The core economic issue in scheduled air transport is contestability. This has improved greatly, at first in modest degrees, hence the initial liberalisation gains are positive but not large. With the entry of the no-frills low-cost airlines, which have tapped new, additional demand, contestability has increased. Their future growth depends on whether they can take on the majors. Entry by majors into one another's 'domestic' trunk routes is a lethal business, leading to price wars.

Telecoms services have been liberalised since 1998. Liberalisation followed all the six steps summarised in Table 8.1. Universal service obligations are provided competitively by established operators. Access, interconnection and cost-price calculation in the presence of high joint/common costs of networks are the three key regulatory issues in this sector. The economic impact is extremely beneficial, but this mixes liberalisation effects with those of technology. Telecoms is now competitive in fixed telephony (except for the local loop and call termination), in mobile and in internet provision, and growth rates are high in the latter two. A new, competition-policy-based regulatory regime for telecoms and (transport of) media/internet came into force in mid-2003.

CHAPTER 9

Factor Market Integration: Method

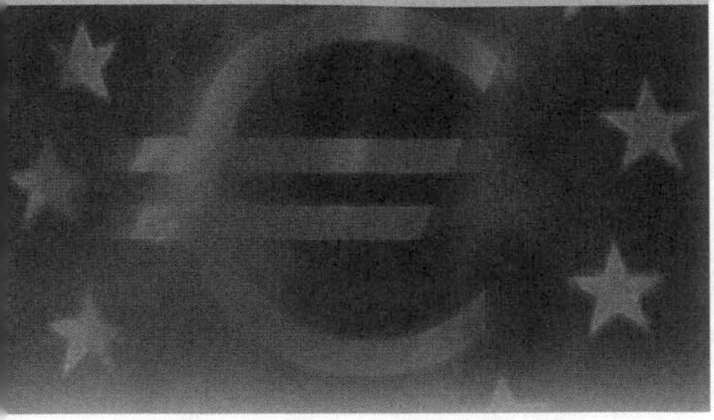

Topics covered

- 9.1 Financial market integration: deepening and widening
- 9.2 Labour
- 9.3 Technology and commercial ideas
- 9.4 Corporate control and mobility of tangible assets
- 9.5 Summary

The conceptual innovation of a 'common market', launched by the Spaak report, found its way into the treaty. Although in the Treaty of Rome the common market was not explicitly defined (see Chapter 2), it was clear that the freedoms of movement for persons (to some extent, workers) and capital were a *conditio sine qua non.* How much of positive integration was to be pursued, and what the nature of such provisions would be, remained far less clear. The present chapter introduces the methods of integrating the markets for factors of production.

The economic logic of a common market suggests that all potentially mobile factors of production should enjoy free movement. This idea underlies the present chapter and its sequel, Chapter 10, on economic analysis of factor market integration. But the treaties are unclear on the scope (all factors, or not?) and the degree of market integration. Indeed, for four and a half decades the Community has struggled to put substance and coherence into the notion of a common market.

Section 9.1 explains the pre- and post-Single European Act regimes for financial capital and makes intelligible the further deepening and widening via the Financial Services Action Plan (see also Chapter 7). There is a case study on EU tax coordination on interest income. Section 9.2 attempts to take a similar approach to the free movement of labour and the professions. There are numerous inconsistencies, and illustrations using two case studies are provided to help reach a better understanding. Section 9.2.2 sets out what it would take before an EU internal market for labour can come into being. Section 9.3 is about the emerging common market in knowledge and ideas, above all, technology and intellectual, industrial and commercial property rights. The chapter closes with a discussion about what is sometimes called 'corporate integration' in Europe: the free movement of tangible assets under corporate control. This includes intra-EU production across borders, the direct investment necessary for it, cross-border relocation and strategic business alliances across intra-EU borders. Recent progress on corporate governance and the facilitation of cross-border mergers (including rules for takeover bids) is relevant, here. There are case studies on EU company law and regulatory competition, and on the novel legal possibility of a 'European Company', the SE.

9.1 Financial market integration: deepening and widening

It is useful to distinguish money and financial capital from direct investments and other control-related factor flows such as management. This distinction does not imply that no overlap between the two exists, but rather it implies that the economic and legal justification for treating them differently is borne out by the actual behaviour of market participants. The EC method of capital market integration is also based on this distinction. This section deals with money and financial capital; section 9.4 deals with direct investments, relocation and corporate control. Another prior distinction is that between the macro- and microeconomic relevance of the free movement of capital. The EU has, above all because of initial treaty inconsistencies, paid attention first to the macro aspects (section 9.1.1) and only later to the microeconomic improvements of how capital market integration should best be pursued for allocation, risk taking and growth (section 9.1.2).

9.1.1 Liberalising financial capital movement

The Rome Treaty is so conditional with respect to financial capital market integration that it is difficult to see how the latter could have been achieved on a permanent basis under that regime. This is not the case for payments in so far as they are connected with liberalised flows in the common market (Article 106 EEC, now deleted).

ADDITIONAL READING

Traditionally the free movements of goods, services, capital and persons were seen as the four fingers of a hand, and the old Article 106 EEC as the 'thumb'. This 'hand' symbolised the treaty notion of the common market. The logic seems compelling: what is the point of accomplishing free flows if they cannot be paid for? But in the old treaty text this logic was far from fully pursued. Article 106 EEC is in the balance of payments chapter of the Rome Treaty, and this chapter is precisely concerned with the overriding priority of protecting the value of national currencies. The sequence of liberalisation will therefore be determined by macroeconomic priorities. To the extent that a free movement would be achieved, Article 106 would guarantee the free flow of payments for any transaction of that kind. But where macroeconomic conditionalities were built into the liberalisation (such as exchange controls) or pre-empted liberalisation from becoming permanent, new safeguards restricting payments could never be excluded. In Chapter 7 we noted the conditionality with respect to financial services liberalisation. Since capital flows are usually operated via the activities of financial services institutions, the two are intimately linked (as indeed Article 61(2), now Article 51(2)), on the liberalisation of banking and insurance services explicitly does). Hence, the conditionalities in the treaty could be overcome only if financial capital could enjoy full liberalisation.

But capital market liberalisation is prescribed in Article 67(1) EEC (now deleted), to 'the extent necessary to ensure the proper functioning of the common market'. This leads to a circular reasoning: how can the establishment itself of the common market be conditional upon its proper functioning? The chapter on capital (Articles 67 to 73, now all deleted) is littered with safeguards and conditions. The reason for this serious inconsistency was the priority of national macroeconomic policy autonomy, as expressed in the balance of payments chapter (Articles 104 to 109, now deleted or revised). The definitive accomplishment of capital market integration would thus require two, probably simultaneous, revisions of the treaty: on the one hand doing away with the conditionalities so that the free movement of financial capital emerges as an imperative principle for the establishment of the common market; on the other hand reducing the national autonomy of macroeconomic policies to such an extent that resorting to safeguards, disrupting the free movement, can be

ADDITIONAL READING *continued*

excluded (see section 17.1.) The history of financial capital market integration during the first three decades (that is, up to the late 1980s) reflects these treaty inconsistencies. Capital and exchange controls persisted in different degrees among the Member States and even liberal countries employed ingenious methods to maintain a degree of protection for 'their' national capital markets.[1] Exchange controls varied greatly in methods and in intensity, also over time.[2] The EC Court confirmed in 1982 that there was no legal basis to impose (unconditional) free movement of capital.[3] This boils down to saying that establishing the common market was at the discretion of the Member States – the concept was too weakly codified. However, in 1974 the Court did prohibit exchange controls affecting the free movement of goods.[4]

The first step to overcome the inconsistency was made in the Single European Act. Its Article 8A (now Article 14 EC) defining the internal market as an 'area without frontiers' also applied to (financial) capital. The Member States accepted the consequences and adopted a directive in 1988 to fully remove exchange controls. But this bold move is not consistent with the maintenance of autonomous macroeconomic policies. More precisely, *free movement, pegged exchange rates and national autonomy in macroeconomic (especially monetary) policies cannot go together*. Once the Single European Act made free movement imperative, either flexible rates would have to be fully accepted or credible coordination underpinning a system of pegged rates would have to be established, implying greatly reduced autonomy. By the time the Act was ratified the European Monetary System (EMS) had existed for seven years. The EMS aims to achieve and maintain monetary stability, in any event exchange rate stability. It was incorporated in the Single European Act. However, as shown in section 17.4, the EMS was insufficiently stringent to guarantee the needed degree of macroeconomic coordination. Moreover, its membership was incomplete.[5] Thus, having rejected flexible exchange rates, Member States were faced with the choice of sticking with the modest EMS but no longer having resort to exchange controls (hence, restricting the autonomy of national monetary policy) or creating a permanent and more credible arrangement to lock the exchange rates (that is, giving up autonomy in a different way).

The Maastricht Treaty constituted the second step in overcoming the Rome Treaty's inconsistency. It codified a detailed route to EMU, thereby fully removing the remaining inconsistency between free movement of financial capital (and of financial services and any flow of payments) and macroeconomic policy making. This regime will be explained in Chapter 18, whereas the capital movements component is set out below. Before looking at that, however, it should be realised that the Maastricht solution is not watertight. The problem is that some EU Members might not (ultimately or for a long time) become EMU members. For non-EMU EU members (the 'outs'), some kind of a new adjustable (but 'joint') peg *vis-à-vis* the euro has been devised, called ERM-II (see Chapter 18).

The Maastricht Treaty's regime for capital movements distinguishes two stages before EMU has been finalised. Up to 1994, the Rome Treaty chapter was maintained, but this should be understood against the backdrop of the 1988 directive already having led to removal of all exchange controls. Since January 1994 the second stage of EMU has been in force. The new Article 73a–g[6] incorporates the essence of the 1988 directive, thereby assuming a constitutional character. The core of the present regime is a strict prohibition of capital and exchange controls between the Member

[1]Thus, countries not employing exchange controls could often still place public bonds in a privileged way with national institutional investors, for example.

[2]See, for example, Bakker (1996).

[3]In the *Casati* case; see Petersen (1982).

[4]When Italy imposed interest-free deposit requirements for importers to prevent a fall of the lira.

[5]All EU Members were EMS members, but that was a formality. The crux is the exchange rate mechanism for which a degree of credibility of macroeconomic policy convergence to support exchange rate stability *vis-à-vis* other participating currencies is required. Not all EMS 'members' participated in the exchange rate mechanism.

[6]The Amsterdam Treaty deleted Arts 73a and 73e; the other ones are now Arts 56 to 60 EC.

States (Article 56). The safeguard in Article 59 EC is totally different in nature from that in the Rome Treaty: it does not refer to (national) balances of payments or currencies, but to 'serious difficulties for the operation of EMU' and relates only to extra-EC capital movements.[7] The only problem remaining is a fiscal one (Article 58). The national taxation of interest from savings and capital income in an environment of high capital mobility gives rise to sharp fiscal competition, except if and to the extent that a minimum threshold is agreed or full information is shared between the national tax authorities. Case Study 9.1 explains the ingenious solution to this tricky problem, requiring strong intra-EU as well as external cooperation.

The freedom for financial capital in the EU also applies *vis-à-vis* third countries. During a currency crisis in 1992 Spain (using a derogation then still valid) attempted temporary exchange controls, but they were quickly eroded.[8] This lesson is important for Article 57 which requires unanimity for any retrogression of the EU openness *vis-à-vis* the world capital market.

CASE STUDY 9.1 Taxing interest income: EU coordination against evasion

Free movement of financial capital is, of course, no reason to allow tax evasion. However, in the EU in 1989 taxation of the interest from savings was made very difficult because Luxembourg had a zero rate and bank secrecy. There were also opportunities to move financial capital to tax havens such as the Channel Islands or the Dutch Antilles or to countries with bank secrecy such as Switzerland (and to some extent Austria, in the EU). When Germany nevertheless imposed a withholding tax, some DM 80 billion moved to Luxembourg in a matter of days and the measure had to be withdrawn. Luxembourg was in a difficult position. No doubt, its specialisation in banking on this basis had brought it prosperity which it defined as a vital interest. Yet, the negative externalities were severe as free movement was causing a fiscal racc to the bottom. Member States see their tax revenues undermined and will, for any desirable amount of revenue, have to raise other taxes. In addition, the failure to agree on a minimum tax rate leads to tax evasion having regressive effects (as savers going to Luxembourg are typically found in high income groups – indeed, it is often referred to as the 'Belgian dentist' problem). In terms of the subsidiarity test, there is a need to act in common (step 2), but step 3 was at first refused (cooperation on information about non-resident savers) as well as step 4 (a directive on a minimum (withholding) tax rate).

The eventual compromise solution was engineered over a period of sixteen years until, in April 2005, the negotiations with a group of tax havens were concluded successfully. Among the many difficulties were the UK fear that the (tax-free) eurobond market might be hit; the Austrian problem of a change in the constitution (for its bank secrecy); the Belgians wishing to keep their withholding tax; the pivotal role of the Swiss in accommodating the EU desire to block this escape route and, once accepting this, enabling the Union to put pressure on other tax havens as well. Directive 2003/48 of 3 June 2003 entered into force on 1 July 2005. This directive, once tax havens have cooperated, imposes a regime on the Member States either to routinely report to other Member States the relevant data about savings of non-resident citizens, or to impose a withholding tax for a transition period. The latter would be 15 per cent for the first three years, go to 20 per cent for another three years and then reach 35 per cent until the transition period is terminated. The revenues from the withholding tax are transferred to the other Member States with savers in the taxing country (with 25 per cent of revenue for the taxing country). Belgium, Luxembourg and Austria have opted for a temporary withholding tax, the other EU countries for automatic mutual information. This solution avoids tax harmonisation, yet is likely to be effective.

[7]It is only in Art. 60 that a Member State may take unilateral measures against a third country, but it refers to a situation of war (see also Art. 297).

[8]See Garber & Taylor (1995) for details.

The third step involves approximation and mutual recognition. For a while it was thought that negative integration (that is, the removal of exchange controls) would be sufficient for the free movement of financial capital, except for some fiscal problems, as discussed. The close linkage of financial flows with financial services necessitates a minimum degree of approximation of prudential rules, and home country control, leading to the 'single passport' – also applying to securities firms or banks dealing with securities (see Chapter 7). As section 9.1.2 shows, the required deepening and widening for a proper functioning of the internal financial capital market was seriously misjudged and only began to be tackled with the arrival of the euro.

The growth and 'Europeanisation' of the financial capital market also prompt a new look at prudential supervision and the lender of last resort. There is a tendency to separate this (micro) supervisory function from the assignment of central banks, so as to avoid conflicts of interest. At the same time, there is a subsidiarity issue: should this supervision not be centralised more (say, in a tightly coordinated two-tier national/euro-based system) and should the ECB not be permanently informed? Should not, at the same time, the ECB Statute be amended, so that the assignment of the lender of last resort function to the ECB is unambiguous, and that guidelines[9] are agreed on how to act in case of emergency? Failing to address these questions can, one day, severely impair the confidence in the proper functioning of the internal market for financial capital and money. Meanwhile, these issues are recognised and permanent consultation between supervisors and the ECB has been organised on the basis of a Memorandum of Understanding. Whether this step 3 of the subsidiarity test is sufficient remains to be seen.

9.1.2 A proper functioning EU financial market?

Following Table 7.1, the EU financial markets after EC-1992 had begun to be more Europeanised. However, in the mid-1990s, it began to dawn on market players and Member States, not least those in euroland, that the intermediation, lubrication and growth functions of capital markets in Europe were far below US standards. Sometimes this was a matter of size (liquidity, efforts to find counterparts), but, more often, it was a question of costs, lack of speed, service quality and, indeed, competition and regulation. In 1999, the Financial Services Action Plan (FSAP) was born, prompting a further deepening and widening of financial market integration, against the backdrop of the arrival of the euro. The FSAP is complex, large and technical. A detailed treatment will be avoided here. Figure 9.1 provides a bird's eye view so as to be able to appreciate the main idea.

The two critical elements of the deepening consisted of two key areas where vested interests had thus far throttled effective (conditions for) 'deep' market integration: wholesale (securities and asset management) and supervision.

The wholesale markets in the EU had not been effectively integrated with the 1992 investment services directive (partly based on host country control). It turned out that a series of barriers kept market fragmentation in place (Giovannini, 2002; Levin, 2003). A number of them have been tackled in FSAP as the upper left box in Figure 9.1 shows.

9.2 Labour

9.2.1 Ineffective free movement

The problems in achieving a European labour market are far greater than those in financial capital. This is not immediately obvious when reading the Rome Treaty (again, in contrast to the case of capital). Article 48.1 EEC (now Article 39 EC) would seem to be unconditional: 'Freedom of movement for workers shall be secured within the Community by the end of the transitional period at the latest'. And so it happened. By 1968, Article 48 had been implemented. Before inspecting more closely what this 'free' movement does and does not mean, let us first spell out what the chapter on workers stipulates.

What is pursued combines the abolition of any discrimination based on nationality between workers of the Member States with 'national treatment'. Therefore, a Belgian working in Spain is to be treated like a Spanish worker in Spain. Workers are entitled to accept job offers throughout the internal market, to move freely to take up

[9]For instance, liquidity provision should only be foreseen if macroeconomic instability may occur; if individual banks could expect liquidity, for any reason other than a macro risk, this invites 'moral hazard'. There are also adverse selection and other issues. See Gros & Lannoo (2000, chapter 4).

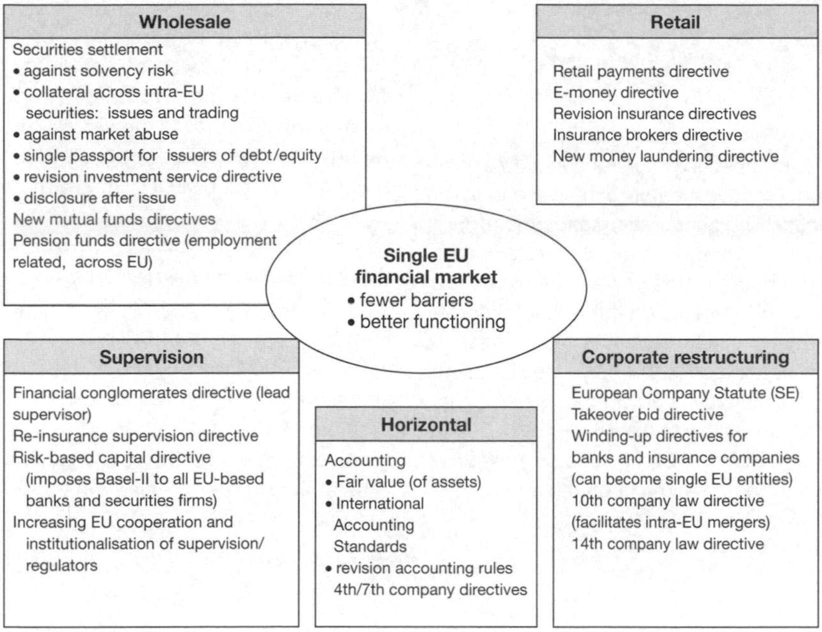

Figure 9.1 Deepening financial market integration after EC-1992 and the euro

ADDITIONAL READING

At the time of writing (spring 2005), no proposal had been tackled on what is called 'clearing and settlement' in securities trade, an excessively costly post-trade item for equity trade across borders in the EU. Since domestic equity trading has become competitive in the EU, owing to liberalisation, internet trade, alliances between stock markets and better information, the (high) cost differential is due to (largely unnecessary) legal and technical standard issues. With clearing and settlement approaching domestic cost levels, equity markets in Europe will compete much more intensely still, and it is probable that only a few truly European ones remain.

With the FSAP, finally, the investment regulation of pension funds has become EU-wide, rather than (often) national, as well as more rationally based on risk analysis (with better return expected). The revised investment services directive[10] has two objectives: investor protection and more effective integration of equity markets in the Union. It shifts more firmly to home country control (compare with stage 3 in Table 7.1). As recital 71 of the directive puts it, an integrated EU financial market 'requires the establishment of common regulatory requirements relating to investment firms wherever they are authorised in the Community and governing the functioning of regulated markets and other trading systems so as to prevent opacity or disruption on one market from undermining the efficient operation of the European financial system as a whole'. It should also be noted that asset management, sometimes seen as a distinct financial service business, is well served with the upper left box of Figure 9.1, due to the new mutual funds directive and the pension funds directive. Although serious tax problems remain for EU-wide management, a horizontal asset management directive is not necessary (Lannoo & Levin, 2003).

The other key area which was insufficiently addressed in EC-1992 was supervision. The lower left box shows that gaps have been filled up, and that EU-wide cooperation between supervisors has

[10] Directive 2004/39 on markets in financial instruments, of 21 April 2004, OJ L 145 of 30 April 2004.

ADDITIONAL READING *continued*

greatly intensified. In accomplishing this, risk elements and information costs are bound to decline and this should reduce capital costs in the long run (*ceteris paribus*). The cooperation takes the form of step 3 of the subsidiarity test for all three groups of supervisors: in banking, insurance and investment services. The notion of a 'single' regulator for all three, as now practised by several Member States, is not yet addressed at EU level. It might well be useful to include asset management, given its special characteristics and requirements (Lannoo & Levin, 2003). A common EU regulator is sometimes suggested as well but (as in Chapter 8) this requires a change in the treaty, besides being sensitive politically.

The FSAP has marginally improved retail (upper right box), without genuinely overcoming the fragmentation of the internal market. Accounting standards (lower middle box) have been internationalised, especially with a view to globalisation and OECD-wide harmony in disclosure rules.

The lower right box shows that considerable political and legislative effort was spent to overcome deep-rooted barriers. The European Company Statute is explained in Case Study 9.3 in section 9.4. The 2004 takeover-bid directive has been through many versions since 1989. It is discussed in section 9.4 as well. Finally, for banks and insurance companies, the winding-up directives should bring about better organisation of internal market business.

the offer, and to stay after the job is finished. The self-employed (for example, in retail) also enjoy this free movement. Jobs in the public service of Member States do not have to be open to workers from other Member States, but the EC Court has interpreted this narrowly (for example, state-owned enterprises or the fire brigade are open to all EU nationals).[11] The other provisions elaborate on the freedom of workers' movement (for example, on 'aggregation' of social security entitlements among the Member States) or are of trivial importance. The chapter on the free movement of workers has not been changed either in the Single European Act or in the Maastricht Treaty.[12] The treaty's approach to free movement is *not* concerned at all with the actual possibilities and economic incentives to move across intra-EU borders, only with the legal right to do so. Surely, the legal text does *not* provide the basis for exploiting an internal market for labour for the overall economic benefit of the EU, as was the case with goods, services or capital. For labour, the obstacles and disincentives are the crux of the matter. There is little point in getting national treatment if the movement itself is strongly discouraged by restrictive regulations and by financial and other problems thrown up by the Member States.

The most fundamental reason why the movement of workers in the EU is 'unfree' has to do with social protectionism. 'Free movement' is under 'host country control' which means, among other things, that wages and secondary benefits are hardly negotiable for the migrant, if at all. Whereas in goods, many services and capital, free movement implies price competition – indeed, that is a major incentive as well as a source of welfare gains – for intra-EU labour mobility, incoming workers cannot compete by offering or accepting lower wages. Of course this prevents low-skilled workers from relatively low-wage EU countries from exploiting what would be their critical advantage. This pre-emption, in turn, protects the local workers against such competition, and *significantly reduces the demand for non-local EU labour* (*ceteris paribus*). Since, at least for low-skilled labour, local workers will easily outcompete the incoming workers with respect to language, work habits, networks, and so on, the inability to compete on wages and secondary benefits tends to lead to a collapse of

[11]The main criterion is that a nationality requirement is only allowed when a function in the public service is part of exercising public 'authority' (e.g. the police). (See Art. 55 EC (now Art. 45) for a similar restriction in services.)

[12]Since the Single European Act, however, there is qualified majority voting on most implementation directives (but not social security; Art. 42 EC). The EP's influence has increased too. Thus, since Amsterdam, the EP has co-decision on Art. 42 EC, yet the Council still acts by unanimity – hence, a stalemate is conceivable between the two bodies.

cross-border mobility.[13] Host country control is a highly effective protectionist principle and confirms the 'fortress' character of national labour markets.[14]

Apart from this fundamental economic reason for 'unfree' labour movement, a battery of regulatory, social security, tax, health insurance, housing and other reasons (for example, diploma recognition) must be addressed as well. In a book like this it is neither possible nor desirable to describe this labyrinth of obstacles and difficulties. In the Additional Reading a regulatory framework for (an as yet non-existent) EU labour market is sketched. The gap between that framework and today's 'free' movement of workers is telling. Another telling illustration is the unwillingness of Member States to deal properly with the problems of frontier workers. Frontier workers live in Member State A but work 'over the border' in Member State B. Although their social security rights are subject to EC directives, the resolution of their tax problems is dependent on poorly functioning bilateral cooperation among the Member States. Numerous conflicts about health and other insurance, restrictions resulting from car taxes (dependent on the licence plate) and a host of other questions, including extreme hurdles which must be overcome to obtain redress, show the justification for mandatory EU action.[15] As if this battery *and* host country control are not enough, with the enlargement from the EU15 to EU25 (1 May 2004) many EU15 Member States opted for temporary quantitative restrictions for inward migration from central European new Member States. Such restrictions are reviewed after two years and can be kept up to a maximum of seven years (2011). It is a clear case of coordination failures at EU level: once some countries (with Germany as the prime 'target country' due to networks of former immigrants) had decided to raise new barriers, other Member States feared a deviation of migration, resulting in a 'race to the (restrictive) top'.

All that can be said about this free movement is that it is a necessary but grossly insufficient condition to achieve an internal labour market. The contrast with financial capital is striking. Whereas capital controls were explicitly allowed under treaty derogations (until recently), no such restrictions or safeguards are mentioned in the case of labour. The removal of capital controls was often unilateral and their final prohibition in 1988 required relatively little in the form of 'approximation' or centralisation of measures concerned with capital markets. Also, the market response was overwhelming, indeed so much so that excessive fiscal competition emerged (see Case Study 9.1). On the other hand, the removal of discrimination with respect to foreign (but EU) workers was a slow and difficult process, under unanimity until 1987, and little if any unilateral anticipation took place. Indeed, not a single Member State took an *a priori* liberal view on these measures. The market response to the formal right of free movement of workers was negligible, except where income differentials were very high. It is not an exaggeration to say that, both in an economic and a regulatory sense, a high degree of capital market integration now (see section 10.1) compares with a very low degree of labour market integration in the Community. In fact, there is no such thing as an EU labour market.

Of course, in a multilingual Union with a significant degree of cultural diversity and subtle, but sensitive divergences in social customs, industrial relations, hierarchies and family ties, one should not expect capital and labour market integration to be fully comparable. Thus, actual and potential cross-border labour mobility will never be very high in the EU. This fact of European life not only reduces the responsiveness of workers to inter-country disparities in earnings, but also allows vested interests to push the regulatory behaviour of the Member States into a much more restrictive direction. Given such national restrictiveness, the need for positive integration increases considerably before free movement acquires any economic meaning. It is one thing to argue that cultural diversity in Europe will always show up (*ceteris paribus*) in a much lower income elasticity for labour mobility than in, for example, the USA. It is quite another to assert that this is the only reason why free movement of workers has a trivial impact in the EU. The latter is also caused by the failure to establish an EU labour market.

[13]Surprisingly, the literature on the determinants of intra-EU migration (see Chapter 10) pays virtually no attention to this crucial disincentive.

[14]Or, the import of workers occurs illegally, which even happened during the construction of the new EU Council building in Brussels.

[15]The Veil report (Veil *et al.*, 1997) has dealt with this issue only *à la* carte, without proposing adequate EU rules which protect workers rather than relying on inadequate cooperation between the Member States.

CASE STUDY 9.2 Host country control for posted workers

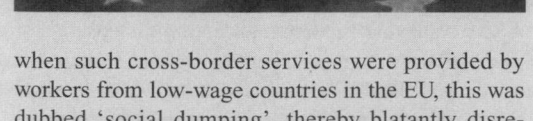

Cross-border labour migration in the EU can take a number of forms including the regular acceptance of a job in another country, the establishment of a person as an 'independent' (for example, an entrepreneur opening a restaurant in another Member State) and the temporary provision of labour in the framework of a temporary cross-border provision of a service. All three are subject to host country control, an expression of the fortress character of national labour markets. The suggestion that more liberal principles such as mutual recognition or the origin principle should apply, typically prompts loud protests about alleged 'social dumping'. The protectionist effect of host country control in the presence of large differences in national real wages in the EU has been discussed in section 9.2.1. For independents, there should be the normal entrepreneurial risks. The problem here is that, in some sensitive instances such as the building industry, the difference between an immigrating 'independent' and a migrating worker has remained unclear and this has fuelled fears of a clever by-pass of labour protection. This leaves the special case of 'posted workers' in the framework of a temporary cross-border service provision.

In so far as cross-border movement of temporary services is competitive owing to significant differences of wages and non-wage labour costs between the country of origin and the country where the service is provided – and this is typically the case in short-term services in the building industry for construction and major repairs as well as in the hotel/restaurant/café business and, sometimes, for industrial cleaning, where specialised skills or local, tacit knowledge play a minor role – such services provision is quickly regarded as undermining the jobs and competitiveness of the local suppliers of such services as they are held to apply local labour standards and/or collective agreements. For the EU trade unions it was crucial to 'raise rivals' costs' by imposing a kind of host country control for the labour component of such services. Rather defensively, when such cross-border services were provided by workers from low-wage countries in the EU, this was dubbed 'social dumping', thereby blatantly disregarding the anti-social character of not giving precisely the workers from such relatively poor EU countries a possibility to use their competitive advantage to the full (for short periods).

The posted workers directive (Directive 96/71) imposes a far-reaching but incomplete form of host country control on the treatment of workers from country A providing a service in country B. It applies to personel with normal labour contracts of a firm from A, taking the workers into B; to secondment within multinationals (which, unlike typical service jobs, can be for a much longer time) and to posted workers by private employment agencies from A in country B (for a short period). Host country control is applied to a core cluster of social provisions such as minimum wages, holidays, working hours and rest periods, occupational health and safety, and some other aspects. Local collective agreements can (but need not) be imposed, except for the obligation to do this in the building industry. The only important origin-based aspect that remains is social security premiums. Interesting (though little known) is that most of these aspects are already covered by minimum social harmonisation, except for minimum wages. There can be no doubt that the posted workers directive hardens the deep fragmentation of European labour markets by throttling almost any arbitrage even for short-term work, especially in the lower- and modest-skill segments of the labour markets. Indeed, it seems that Member States go to great lengths to protect national labour market regulation, even for highly skilled workers. In an interesting preliminary ruling by the EC Court on 28 January 1999, the Dutch provisions causing a temporary (highly skilled) worker in the UK to pay more tax in the Netherlands because of the secondment were considered to violate EC law, as an obstacle to free movement.

ADDITIONAL READING

How to establish an EU labour market

What would be required to arrive at an EU labour market? The necessary condition is, of course, free movement. This has been formally achieved, including full aggregation of social security between countries (for migrants), as well as national treatment. Not unlike goods and services, however, a number of other measures are to be adopted before the regulatory framework is sufficient for labour market integration. Here, we consider five: approximation of national labour market regulation, mutual recognition of diplomas, EU-wide access to social security, supporting measures, and a common immigration policy.

Approximation of national labour market regulation

In goods and services markets, it has come to be accepted that national regulation often has to be approximated (otherwise, derogations allow these regulations to block free movement or make it more costly). There is, however, little approximation in labour markets. The lack of approximation is a serious problem in an economic perspective of free movement precisely because labour markets are heavily regulated in Europe. Laws on minimum wages, collective contracting, hiring and firing, duration of the working week, flexible labour contracts, qualifications, and a host of entitlements differ among the Member States. The diversity and complexity of these laws have a very discouraging effect on cross-border labour migration: few workers will have access to information of a quality reassuring them about their risks and opportunities, hence uncertainties abound. In subtle ways, many national provisions also make market entry for non-nationals more risky, costly or impractical. For goods, the *Dassonville* test would apply in such cases (see section 5.3.1.). Services have moved in the same direction (see section 7.2). All there is in the case of labour is non-discrimination for those non-national workers already having a job (offer). This ignores the crucial issue of free entry.

Free entry would mean that the worker from B could freely compete with workers in A, irrespective of the regulation in A (origin principle or, combined with 'equivalence' in mutual recognition), or, as with many goods and services markets, compete on any terms at or above the minimum regulatory standards to be set at EU level. Remembering the regulatory strategy for goods and services (see section 4.3.4.), national regulation could remain in place in A but, as potential and active competition from workers from EU countries B, C, D and so on would emerge, it would be subject to regulatory competition above common EU regulatory standards. Since labour mobility will never be very high in Europe, the scope for national regulatory autonomy would still remain considerable.[16]

By and large such approximation for the establishment and proper functioning of the internal market for labour (that is, for efficiency purposes) has been avoided. As noted, migrant workers enter national labour markets entirely within regulatory terms set by host country control. Since the Single European Act and the Maastricht Treaty, a modest degree of approximation has been pursued without doing much about the economic (dis)incentives for EU workers.

There are two clear exceptions to the lack of (economically relevant) approximation. The first one, based on a market failure argument, is about health and safety in the workplace. Article 118 EC[17] sets as the objective 'the harmonisation of conditions in this area' in a context of 'encouraging improvements', subject to qualified majority voting (QMV).[18] The upshot has been a series of directives, setting (high) minimum conditions of health and safety for the workplace. It is widely agreed that no competitive advantages should be obtained by making the paint shop in a car plant less healthy in one Member State or by allowing excessively heavy physical burdens on workers in another. The

[16]Mutual recognition in EU labour markets has been analysed in detail in Kostoris Padoa-Schioppa, 2003.

[17]Introduced by the Single European Act, and revised twice.

[18]Note also that Art. 95, sub. 3, prescribes a 'high level of protection' concerning, *inter alia,* health and safety.

ADDITIONAL READING *continued*

potential externalities are serious here and such distortions have no justification.[19] The second one, based on equity considerations, is about equal pay for equal work between men and women (Article 119, now Article 141, as revised). The article arose from French fears (in the mid-1950s) that its own non-discrimination provision might result in competitive disadvantages for its firms. It was therefore included not for purposes of a European labour market but for preventing a distortion in goods markets. Its implementation has not been without consequences, as Chapter 15 sets out. Yet, while removing a potential distortion for cross-border labour flows, it does little to reduce the segmentation between national labour markets.

Mutual recognition of qualifications of workers and professionals

In the area of mutual recognition (MR) too, there are serious difficulties. After a very long gestation period, a special EU agency (called CEDEFOP) began a systematic and detailed identification of requirements as the basis for MR. A case-by-case approach, equally meticulous, was practiced by the professionals (see Case Study 9.3).

This old approach to arrive at 'mutual recognition' of diplomas has very little to do with the notions of MR (spelled out in Chapter 4), accepted after the mid-1980s. The latter notion sharply distinguishes objectives (of regulatory protection) and means (the detailed specifications). If the objectives are 'equivalent' or harmonised at EU level, the specifications matter less and, hence, different regulatory specifics are to be mutually accepted. Where appropriate, minimum requirements (expressing the agreed objective) can be set at EU level, beyond which variations in national regimes cannot be enforced on imports.

EC-1992 has also had a positive impact here. Three broad (so, not detailed) directives on MR of higher education diplomas have meant a breakthrough, although aptitude tests can still imply high entry barriers.[20] Vocational training is explicitly promoted at EU level in order to facilitate cross-border mobility.

The difficulties have far from disappeared, however. No certification or accreditation systems for schools, academies and universities exist at EU level, as is often the case in the USA. High informal barriers persist due to severe biases towards national education and to languages. Since the Bologna process began in 1999, there is a long-run prospect of easier mutual access based on higher-diploma recognition and equivalence.[21]

Union-wide access to social security

This has remained a total taboo in the Community. Federal countries grant internal migrants access to social security, irrespective of place and status (worker or unemployed), as part of their citizenship. This requires a federal commitment to equity, usually complemented by (differentiated) state-level social security. The beneficial upshot is, however, far greater efficiency in the functioning of the labour market.

The EU does not pursue this removal of an important barrier to cross-border mobility. In the Amsterdam Treaty, the new Article 137(3) places draft directives on social security and social protection under unanimity, a strict provision, but already progress has been made compared with the purely consultative and facilitating work to promote close cooperation between the Member States (now in Article 140). This should not be confused with the directives for the adding up (aggregation) of social

[19]There is, however, criticism that harmonisation of health and safety in the workplace is too detailed and hence unnecessarily costly. This might be the result of not using the 'new approach' (see section 5.4.2) which would reduce regulatory costs greatly. See, e.g., Baldwin & Daintith (1992).

[20]Directives 89/48, 92/51 and 1999/42.

[21]The Bologna process, spearheaded by the EU15 but a pan-European initiative, seeks to reform university and some other tertiary education on a voluntary, national basis, yet based on a single bachelors/masters structure with roughly similar minimum requirements. This should facilitate cross-border exchange of students, promote the transparency about 'equivalence' in job markets and render European degrees more transparent for the rest of the world.

ADDITIONAL READING *continued*

security rights between jobs in different Member States for migrant workers (Article 42 EC). This security does little or nothing about the discrepancies between Member States in rights and the great uncertainty about them, without any 'federal' minimum. Therefore, a serious asymmetry in information about jobs and the implied rights, as well as about access to jobs, remains between nationals and non-nationals in the EU: cross-border job searches are difficult for those already with a job, while, in addition, they entail a financial risk for the unemployed which is perceived as being potentially very high. Thus, the absence of EU-wide minimum social security provides considerable implicit protection of national labour markets. Combine this implicit protection with the actual and perceived costs of entry from another Member State due to a lack of approximation, and one begins to appreciate what prevents an EU labour market from coming into being.

Supporting or flanking measures

Some supporting measures are essential for migrant workers, such as access to (mostly low-cost) housing and health insurance as well as portability of pensions over intra-EU borders. High income earners may be inhibited by costly interruptions of their supplementary pension build-up, in the absence of portability. Before EMU, portability was hard to accomplish in a commercially attractive way; the exchange risks were unknown for such long periods. In the eurozone, portability of (euro) pensions will undoubtedly be tackled.[22] Low-cost housing in Europe is often accomplished under rent control, which discourages supply. This results in rationing which forms a barrier to free labour mobility because long waiting periods amount to a high barrier for migrant workers. Health insurance beyond national borders may cause prohibitive barriers if insurance companies (or state insurance) in different Member States do not adopt a mutual acceptance commitment. In the absence of such commitments, cross-border labour movements would be biased towards young and healthy workers. Flanking and support measures have been tackled only selectively, thus retaining yet another discouraging influence for potential cross-border job searchers.

A (more) common immigration policy

Since the Schengen treaty of 1985 has moved 'into' the EC treaty,[23] the questions of non-economic (for example, asylum, visa, crime fighting and gun control) and economic persons controls have increasingly moved in parallel. Thus, Article 63(3) provides a legal basis for EU action with respect to legal and illegal economic immigration. The constitutional treaty (not yet ratified) in Article III-267 is unambiguous that 'The Union shall develop a common immigration policy aimed at . . . the efficient management of migration flows'.[24] Even if the EU cannot set the actual access of non-EU workers to national labour markets in terms of numbers or timing, the subsidiarity case for a (more) common immigration policy is powerful. Unilateral policies of EU countries create not only cross-border externalities for individuals that need to be addressed at the EU level, such as the right to travel in the Schengen area (nowadays most of the EU25 plus Switzerland even) and to move to other Member States once long-term residence status has been obtained, but also policy spillovers such as the recent 'race to the top' in restrictiveness of admission procedures between Member States, the selective rivalry between Member States to attract

[22] For a careful survey, with recommendation, see Mortensen (2003).

[23] The Schengen group has gradually grown to comprise all of the EU25 minus the UK and Ireland. Its purpose is to avoid (passport) controls of persons at frontiers, just as with goods. In the Amsterdam Treaty, complicated procedures have been introduced to gradually bring the Schengen *acquis* into the regular EC treaty. The UK and Ireland have meanwhile selectively joined some arrangements. The European Constitution (not yet ratified) has fully integrated this area on a QMV basis (for most issues).

[24] In a subtle application of subsidiarity, given the political constraint that labour markets are 'national' despite the internal market, the article continues: 'This Article shall not affect the right of Member States to determine volumes of admission of third-country nationals . . . to their territory . . .'. So, a true internal market for labour is, once again, resisted.

ADDITIONAL READING *continued*

scarce high-skilled talents from other continents and potential 'free-riding' in the enforcement of border controls for both legal and illegal immigration. Moreover, with the increasing average age of the EU population a well-designed immigration policy is bound to alleviate to some degree the worst shortages or gaps that are likely to arise and it is sensible to do this on the basis on some common principles and procedures.[25] However, progress here is slow, caused by a sense of stagnation in the EU15 (not in the new Member States), the existing sensitivity about intra-EU migration from central Europe and the fears about the risks for a permanent surge in welfare payments. These inhibitions will eventually subside with the impact of ageing and the gradual convergence of real wages over the EU25. For the next decade or so, however, immigration from the rest of the world will thus not exercise much, if any, influence on the further integration of the national labour markets.

Therefore there is no such thing as an EU labour market despite the Euro-speak of an 'internal market' for labour.

CASE STUDY 9.3 Diploma recognition for professionals

Professionals such as dentists, physicians, accountants, lawyers, notaries and pharmacists, could in principle benefit from the (QMV) directives on the mutual recognition of diplomas, to be enacted under Article 47 EC. Article 47(3) EC calls for coordination of the relevant provisions for the medical, paramedical (for example, nurses, midwives) and pharmaceutical professions. However, lawyers specialise predominantly in national law, and enforcement via national courts so the mere fact of being a competent lawyer in Member State A is an insufficient condition to be recognised in B. For notaries, Article 45 EC can be invoked, which specifies a derogation of the right of establishment in case of the exercise of 'public authority'.

The key issue from an economic point of view is how to combine justified regulation with the greatest possible scope for free movement and establishment. Ideally, this could be achieved by a careful assessment of the respective national regulatory regimes for professionals (asking the question: What regulation is justified on public interest grounds, and what not?). Subsequently, the EC method of integration should seek the least-regulatory-cost approach to accomplish free movement (and free establishment). Initially, neither of those two rules of thumb was applied. Unconditional free movement and establishment assessment rules are not easy to justify on subsidiarity grounds since deeply held values, sensitivities and practices may be at stake which differ between Member States. Imposing uniformity in the presence of disparate preferences violates the subsidiarity test, too, except if the net benefits could be shown to be significant – yet, for professionals the net benefits would be elusive and doubtful. This could justify the current host country control. But there are good reasons to be sceptical that domestic rules serve only the 'public interest'. Why? Asymmetries of information are so great between professionals and 'society at large' that there is ample scope for regulatory capture. In other words, it is plausible that the disparities in national preferences result, in part, from anti-competitive regulation, engineered by vested interests among professionals (for practical and economic evidence supporting this suggestion, see COM (2004) 83 of 9 February 2004 on competition in professional services).

Also, the initial method of diploma recognition was a clear instance of regulatory failure. The 'old approach' of harmonisation was used, on a case-by-case basis, defining extremely detailed requirements on which agreement proved difficult even after

[25] See COM (2004) 811 of 11 January 2005 on an EU approach to managing economic migration, for a spectrum of immigration policy options.

CASE STUDY 9.3 *continued*

decades of negotiation. Rather than defining general, commonly agreed objectives, with mutual recognition of different specifications flowing from that, in fact every detail was subjected to excessive harmonisation. There is a strong presumption that the process was captured by the national associations. Capture is relatively easy because professionals tend to enjoy a high degree of public and self-regulation and are tightly organised on a national basis.

The 'new approach' is a considerable improvement. Directives 89/48/EEC and 92/51/EEC on recognition of higher education diplomas are based on mutual trust among the Member States. The idea is that no Member State has an interest in low-quality professionals; hence, the different end products of national education systems should, in principle, be compatible. All that may be required are corrective measures to compensate for crucial differences. Such compensation mechanisms may consist either of an aptitude test or an adaptation (stage) period.

However, the first directive, while having a positive impact on the free movement of teachers (according to a Commission report on the period 1991–94), still leaves major barriers in place for the regulated professions. While the EU has meanwhile simplified the rules by codifying 35 earlier directives into a single one (Directive 1999/42 in OJ L 201 of 31 July 1999), and simplifying it via Directive 2001/19, a further simplification (and facilitation of free movement and establishment of professionals) was adopted only in June 2005, with the consolidation of the twelve professional directives then still in place.

9.3 Technology and commercial ideas

Markets for knowledge are highly imperfect and tend not to function properly if left on their own. This is due to the public good characteristics of knowledge severely discouraging supply of knowledge and investment in original research. The problem of non-appropriability (though perhaps less that of non-excludability in consumption) extends to the ideas shaping or differentiating goods and services, whether they be copyright, design or even image tied to reputable names.

There are three broad responses to improve the functioning of markets for knowledge and ideas. First, supply can be subsidised by government. This tends to be done if, and to the extent that, the public goods characteristics are preponderant (for example, basic research). Second, companies will attempt to internalise the market (with its externalities) by controlling internal R&D and the subsequent commercialisation. Third, new knowledge and ideas are codified in property rights which enjoy regulatory protection for certain periods. The protection boils down to a temporary monopoly to use the ideas and so on in commerce and to obtain the implied monopoly rents in order to recuperate the costs of R&D and retain a profit. All three methods entail some imperfections but these are too complex to examine here (see, however, Chapter 14).

The EU internal market for knowledge and ideas has only slowly come about, and not all problems have been fully resolved. With respect to *subsidisation,* the problems relate to non-distortiveness. The EU regime for state aids (see section 12.6) also applies to R&D subsidies. Ceilings have been set for subsidies to R&D beyond the stage of basic research; the latter typically takes place in universities and lacks marketability. What the EU calls 'pre-competitive' research would include basic research by companies which is still far away from commercialisation. Once research comes closer to the market, especially with product and process development, the subsidy surveillance becomes stricter. More direct assurance of non-distortiveness should in principle result from EU rather than national subsidies. Since the Single European Act, the EU spends considerable sums on R&TD subsidies, though probably still no more than some 6 per cent of what the Member States together do (but the latter includes all basic research). In the recent R&TD framework programmes of the Union there is more attention on what is critical to the proper functioning of the internal market for technology and ideas: knowledge diffusion throughout the Union.

With respect to *internalisation by companies,* the relevant aspects are the degree of Europeanisation of the company and its participation in inter-firm R&D collaboration. For companies with a spread of production and possibly even R&D over the EU, knowledge travels easily across intra-EU borders but it is captive within the company. This may well result in a skewed distribution of company R&D over the Union, with higher shares in the relatively developed economies, boosting resources accentuating their comparative advantages. Inter-firm R&D collaboration falls under regular EU competition policy: under certain conditions, it is exempted from the prohibition of collusion (see section 12.3.2). The EU R&TD subsidies typically promote cross-border inter-firm collaboration so as to induce a spread of knowledge-related activities throughout the internal market (see section 14.4). It is coupled to an obligation to facilitate diffusion under conditions.

Where *property rights* come in, however, the internal market has progressed very slowly. Legally, the reasons are not hard to find. Article 222 (now Article 295 EC) says that this 'Treaty shall in no way prejudice the rules in Member States governing the system of property ownership'. The problem with this categorical statement is that there are no exceptions or even avowed endeavours to overcome resulting barriers. It is one thing to leave state ownership of companies untouched,[26] but quite another to grant unrestrained autonomy to national patents, trademarks and so on. Sticking to national patents will keep in place two barriers: one in the internal goods market and one in the market for knowledge and ideas.

ADDITIONAL READING

The barrier in the goods market is explicitly exempted under Article 30.[27] Articles 295 and 30 together may cause national goods markets, governed by national 'rights', to become fully separated. Indeed, as Wyatt & Dashwood (1980, p. 342) clarify, 'the holder of a patent or trade mark right protected under the law of Member State A may be entitled to oppose a parallel patent or bearing a parallel mark protected under the law of Member State B. And this may be so even if the holder of the patent or mark in Member State B is none other than the company in A itself or a subsidiary or licensee'. A faithful implementation of the freedom to trade goods is obviously undermined if firms may compartmentalise the Union market by relying on rights with respect to intangible assets.

This major flaw in the Rome Treaty has been tackled only gradually in three different ways. The subsidiarity test, step 2, clearly identifies a 'need to act in common'. The first method to at least reduce the inimical effects of the flaw was due to EC Court rulings within the existing Community legal framework. Given the economic definition of 'measures with an equivalent effect' (now Article 28), as in *Dassonville* (see section 5.3.1), the Court distinguishes the *existence* of the property right, being unassailable, from the *exercise* of this right in the internal market. This exercise could be improper if it were of 'such a nature as to maintain or effect artificial partitions within the common market'.[28] In increasingly refined case law the Court has greatly limited the potential for price discrimination between national markets segmented by property rights.[29] The second method is an example of voluntary but credible cooperation (step 3 of the subsidiarity test) to further reduce the costs of the flaw, without going as far as approximation or unification. The European Patent Treaty of 1973 centralises the application and registration procedures for many European countries in the European Patent Office (EPO), but retains the (different) national patent laws. It represents a clear instance of the scale criterion for cooperation: in going for this 'European' patent via a single procedure: the costs of patenting in many countries are

[26]Though not their conduct; see Art. 86 EC, and Chapter 8 above.

[27]Remember that Art. 30 exempts certain categories from the prohibition in Art. 28, of 'measures with an equivalent effect' to quantitative restrictions. Article 30 expressly speaks about restrictions 'justified on grounds of . . . the protection of industrial and commercial property'.

[28]In case 119/75 *Terrapin v Terranova* [1976] ECR 1061–1062.

[29]One example is the principle of the 'exhaustion of rights': one cannot rely on legal protection (namely Art. 30) in case the good, the import of which is sought to be excluded, has been lawfully marketed in another Member State by the holder of the right or with the holder's consent. So, parallel (re-)imports via independent traders are then legal (see, e.g., Case Study 6.1 on medicines prices).

ADDITIONAL READING *continued*

drastically reduced for the applicant. Also, by pooling highly specialised engineers and other experts, quality and scope of patent research are boosted for all countries but especially for the smaller economies. It may not pay if the patent is for only one or two countries (for this case, the national patent would suffice), but the savings are significant if patenting is sought for the whole Union. What is not approximated or unified are the underlying national patent laws and their methods of enforcement.

The third method attempts exactly that: approximation and unification. In patents, the intergovernmental Community Patent Convention was concluded in 1975, with a related Agreement in 1989, but they have never been ratified by all the Member States. Towards the end of the 1990s the EU finally began to discuss the high costs of patenting in the EU (compared with in the USA), and in 2000 the Commission proposed a genuine Community patent.[30] By November 2003 the Community Patent Regulation was practically agreed. The Community Patent will exist parallel to national patents, has a duration of twenty years (from the date of filing) and is to be published in English, French or German, with the claims translated into Italian and Spanish. This (for the EU) very modest language requirement is the outcome of a true language battle, and should keep the costs low; indeed, the translation is even paid for by the EPO. A Community Intellectual Property Court will guarantee unity of law and consistent case law (hence, a form of centralisation justified by subsidiarity). However, after nearly 42 years (a first EC patent was proposed in 1962), the Council failed to reach unanimity once again: on the legal validity of translations of the 'claims' (a return to all EU languages) and deadlines. In trademarks, both approximation of national trademark law and a parallel EU-wide trademark (with the curiously named European Office for Harmonisation, in Alicante) were adopted as a result of EC-1992. The EU has also adopted copyright regulation (via adherence to the Berne and Paris Conventions, by Member States) and several specialised items of property rights.[31]

Sticking to national patents and so forth also creates a barrier in the internal market for knowledge and ideas. National property rights reduce the incentive to invest in R&D, process technology, design and copyright over the entire EU, relative to national incentives. Even more important may be the speed and geographical spread of diffusion of inventions, innovations and new designs. Appropriate incentives for diffusion may well be as important for the competitiveness of industry, agriculture and services in the EU as innovation subsidies or centres of research excellence. Segmentation of national markets by property rights or inhibitions about the transfer of knowledge across intra-EU borders (when property protection is not the same) add to the incentives of European companies to internalise their intangible asset diffusion. For the numerous companies for which this is beyond their capabilities, even this diffusion mechanism will not work. Ultimately, this will lead to a lower growth rate and a slower adjustment to (new) comparative advantages by the EU in the world economy.

9.4 Corporate control and mobility of tangible assets

In this section we deal with the regulatory framework for cross-border enterprise in the EU. In some publications this is called EU-wide 'corporate integration'. A fully fledged internal market would have no economic frontiers for cross-border entrepreneurial activities; in fact, managers would think and act Union-wide without finding any reason to call this 'cross-border'. Apart from trading goods and services, or granting licences for production elsewhere, what we refer to is intra-EU production across borders, the direct investment required for this (whether as acquisition, merger, greenfield investment), cross-border relocation and strategic

[30]See COM (2000) 412 of August 2000 (as a regulation, not a directive).

[31]For example, for chips topography, software, etc. as well as protection of geographical origin (appellation, etc.).

business alliances across intra-EU borders. It goes without saying that one critical element of this is the approximation or mutual recognition of company law.

Direct investments were liberalised in the early 1960s. Formally, this liberalisation is *erga omnes,* that is, third country investors are basically free to invest anywhere in the EU, subject to normal regulatory constraints (for example, environment, land zoning, and so on). The Union has no policy on direct investment, either for European companies or for companies of non-EU origin. Once the latter invest and incorporate legally in any Member State, they are Community firms (Article 58 EEC, now Article 48 EC) and enjoy national (hence EC) treatment.[32] The policy issues surrounding direct investment therefore have different reasons. Two such issues stand out: local contents requirements and industrial policy. Neither of them inhibits the free movement of direct investment.

It has often been asserted that direct investments in the EU were conditioned by local content requirements. This is incorrect, but it is useful to understand why. National or regional authorities cannot impose local contents requirements as this would violate Article 28 EC: it is a prohibited 'measure with an equivalent effect' to quantitative restrictions. Informal 'understandings' to this effect, in order to obtain regional subsidies are unenforceable. Nevertheless, a company may live up to such an understanding given its desire to be what is called a good 'corporate citizen', that is, integrate well into the regional economy via subcontracting, local supplies and sourcing for local skills. Also at EU level, no local content requirements exist. The only problematic issue concerns trade policy. Where anti-dumping duties or, in the past, quotas hit product *X* from a third country *Y*, production in the EU may be set up purely with the intent to circumvent the trade policy measure. For instance, it may be a pure assembly operation with very low value-added (possible when the components are not hit by the trade policy). Clearly, this is not a problem for intra-EU direct investment, only for third countries.[33]

Another assertion is that national industrial policies lead EU countries to pursue direct investment policies. When countries do that, the instruments will be rather constrained. National, regional and local subsidies give some margin for manoeuvre, but under scrutiny of the European Commission. However, when regional subsidies take the form of (corporate) tax breaks, the leeway has thus far been considerable (see section 12.6). In fact, what can be observed is sharp competition between EU countries and regions to attract direct investors, often cancelling out the differential attractiveness of subsidies (hence, a waste of public money). What remains are mainly locational advantages, be they natural or artificial (see Chapter 10). Accentuating locational advantages, promoting centres of excellence for research and tax breaks touch upon some of the many determinants of direct investment, but more often than not locational decisions tend to be business driven, not policy driven. In the late 1990s, the tax breaks offered by many Member States to internationally operating companies were said to draw the Member States into ever more 'harmful' corporate tax competition. In fact one may distinguish two somewhat different interpretations of 'harmful' tax competition in the EU. One type is clearly highly distortive, as it consists of offering tax rates and privileges to offshore companies and financial holdings, very different from the tax treatment of other companies in the same country. The 1997 EU Code on Harmful Tax Competition agreed first a standstill and subsequently the Primarola list of 66 'harmful' instances (with the Netherlands and Ireland as major sinners) which had to be removed by 2003. The other type of 'harmful' tax competition is non-discriminatory and refers to disparities in tax base and rates. The economics of this corporate tax competition (not yet formally addressed by the EU) is provided in Case Study 10.1.

But liberalisation of direct investments alone will not suffice. Approximation is needed to facilitate intra-EU mobility of tangible assets under corporate control. Thus, direct investments need not be greenfield investments or expansions of plants or distribution networks. They may take the form of acquisitions or mergers. For a long time, cross-border mergers were next to impossible in the Union for legal and fiscal reasons. EC-1992 has removed some obstacles by approximating elements of company law (for example, bankruptcy provisions for such cross-border mergers) and by a few fiscal directives.

A rather different approach than approximation of national company law is the notion of a *Community*

[32]The Court has stated that pure 'postbox' companies do not qualify; there should be some economic activity.

[33]In anti-dumping the solution is to have a clear GATT rule about circumvention of anti-dumping; this failed in the Uruguay Round. For quotas, the matter acquired (in the late 1980s) some political significance for Japanese cars built in the UK: Would they enjoy free movement even though there were national quotas *vis-à-vis* Japanese cars in some Member States? Such quotas have meanwhile disappeared.

CASE STUDY 9.4 EU company law and regulatory competition?

The harmonisation of company law has been a slow and selective affair. A series of basic requirements (including on audits etc.) of national company law has been approximated but the diversity in the EU is still great. There are questions whether such a diversity is not generating more costs than benefits in ever deeper market integration. Since the late 1990s, new developments might generate information on the desired degree of convergence of national company laws. EC Court rulings seem to provide some scope for regulatory competition, which might reflect what markets want. In the *Centros* case[34] the Danish refusal to register a branch of a company incorporated in another Member State (here, in the UK, because the Danish owners wanted to circumvent the Danish capital requirements to set up a company) was found to be contrary to the right of establishment. Once companies attempt more frequently to get around restrictive clauses in national company law by setting up in other Member States, regulatory competition might prompt regulatory changes reducing the disparities between national provisions. As long as more liberal provisions do not allow market failures, such regulatory competition could be welfare improving. The *Überseering* case[35] forced a decision in a similar case with conflicting national laws, but this time the issue was about what is probably the most divisive of all company law provisions in the EU: the real-seat doctrine versus the incorporation approach. The real-seat doctrine ignores the state of registration and focuses on the location of the head office; if the latter is in state B even if the former is in state A, the law of state B applies. In contrast, the incorporation approach is interested only in the place of formal registration of the company – it is the law of that country which applies. It is obvious that this longstanding issue in EU company law cannot be resolved as the two approaches exclude one another (at least, where the real seat is outside the country of incorporation). The *Überseering* case prompted the Federal Court of Germany to ask the EC Court whether a Member State is held to apply the incorporation principle to determine legal personality, in view of the fact that, presumably, otherwise the freedom of establishment would be violated.[36] The EC Court held that the freedom of establishment requires that proper recognition is given to companies validly incorporated under the law of another Member State. Other EC Court cases have amplified the scope for at least some degree of regulatory competition in this area.

company, the 'Societas Europa' (SE). Community law would create EU-wide jurisdiction to incorporate firms as SE, existing parallel to nationally incorporated firms. At first (early 1970s), the SE idea proved too cumbersome in the presence of large differences of national company law. To prevent substitution effects, the SE was not allowed to be legally more attractive than nationally incorporated firms. This led to deadlock until 2001, when the SE Regulation was finally adopted (see Case Study 9.5). One original offshoot of the SE debate has been legislated under a special EC regulation[37] as a cross-border non-profit joint venture, called the European Economic Interest Grouping (EEIG). Until its recent incorporation, Airbus has been a EEIG among four national participants in the UK, Germany, France and Spain.

[34]Case C-212/97; ruling of 9 March 1999.

[35]Case 208/00; ruling of 5 November 2002.

[36]Note that Germany applies the real-seat doctrine, and the legally Dutch company, with German owners and all its business in Germany, was not recognised to exist by a lower German court, as it was not registered in Germany.

[37]Regulation 2137/85 (OJ L 199 of 31 July 1985).

CASE STUDY 9.5 On SE, European Company

After 35 years of debate, Regulation 2157/2001 of 8 October 2001[38] established the legal basis for a European Company, under the abbreviation of SE (Societas Europa). It went into force on 8 October 2004. The SE is a response to the difficulties encountered for cross-border mergers in the EU, even if such problems have decreased over time with selective harmonisation of company law and a few corporate tax directives. The recitals refer explicitly to giving companies 'the option of combining their potential by means of mergers . . . [because companies] . . . should be able to plan and carry out the reorganisation of their business on a Community scale.' More generally, it is stated that the 'completion of the internal market' means that 'the structures of production must be adapted to the Community dimension'. The SE is a European public limited liability company, with shares, basically like national ones. SEs may arise in four ways: via a merger (of two companies in at least two different Member States), a holding SE (in the case of public and private limited liability companies, at least two of which have had a subsidiary in another Member State for two years), a subsidiary SE (with similar conditions) and via a transformation of a public limited liability company with subsidiaries in two or more Member States. An SE may also set up subsidiaries as an SE. Normally, the registered office of the SE will be in the same Member State as the head office. Regulation 2157/2001 is not very detailed on corporate governance (for example, a one-tier or two-tier system as it is called are both possible, see Article 38), partly because national law also continues to play a role. That is also the case for taxation, intellectual property rights or insolvency, knowing that some degree of approximation has taken place in these areas. The most problematic sticking point before the SE regulation could be adopted was the influence of workers, given the fear that (at least, in a number of Member States) the SE might be misused as a vehicle to undermine or escape from co-determination or cooperative arrangements with worker representatives. Directive 2001/86 of the same date is designed to ensure that employees have a right of involvement in issues and decisions affecting the development of the SE. The directive forms an 'indissociable complement to' the regulation. Indeed, a SE may not be registered unless an agreement on employee involvement based on this directive has been concluded (Article 12(2)). Altogether, it remains to be seen to what extent the SE option will be taken up by business in the Union.

ADDITIONAL READING

It is often suggested that EU industry adjusts too slowly, in other words, are there too many obstacles or disincentives to restructuring, rationalisation and change in the internal market?

For acquisitions the disparities in the EU were, and to some extent still are, striking. There is no single market for corporate control. It is relatively easy to pursue a takeover in the UK and much harder in Germany, with other countries assuming an intermediate position. Hostile takeovers are practically excluded in Germany because on both the capital and the labour side management is severely constrained, and because takeover bids can be pre-empted by legal constructions (for example, multiple voting or preferential shares). Protective legal constructions have been somewhat reduced by modest EC company law directives but several countries (for example, the Netherlands) still have many firms using them. Given such protection, the market for corporate control does not work properly and this may impinge on the long-term efficiency of companies. A protected

[38] In OJ L 294.

ADDITIONAL READING *continued*

management need not fear that its weak performance, resulting in falling share prices, will attract takeover bids seeking to exploit the assets of the firm better. Against this view, there are two counter-arguments. First, in Germany[39] banks have traditionally served as a partial substitute for the market discipline exercised by the threat of takeover bids. By taking a shareholding stake and assuming the role of a well-informed 'house bank', firms could assume a long-term, strategic view for R&D, alliances, new product lines or new markets. The bank would be more willing to finance risky long-run ventures than would the arm's-length capital market, and hence this construction would be economically superior in the long term. The capital market would either hold back (given asymmetries of information and lack of control) or generate takeover bids during the periods of low shares/low profits suppressed by long-term projects. If these features were structural, one would expect German firms not to emphasise profits to the extent that UK firms would, which is borne out by the data.[40] However it is still true that hostile takeover bids by other German or EU companies remain virtually impossible, given the powerful financial protection of the large banks.[41] The European debate between (UK-type) 'short-termism' and the (German-type) trade-off between long-term risk orientation on the one hand, and excessive legal protection on the other, is far from over. An entire literature has sprung up about what is called corporate governance. It has turned out to be exceedingly difficult to demonstrate what an 'optimal' system is, in part because national preferences and a myriad of variables play a role. Approximation should therefore not be pursued unless the case can be made. Securitisation and the demands of powerful institutional investors about better disclosure and so on might create enough market pressures to effect change.[42]

Second, there is the influence of labour, the strongest form being the German model of co-determination.[43] Takeover bids may be welcomed when a firm is on the verge of bankruptcy but, generally, labour tends to take protective positions in view of job losses when inefficient firms have to rationalise or be broken up. The good aspect of takeovers is that they provide exactly the shock and impetus that can turn around inefficient performers. At EU level, this issue has led to heated debates about rather modest substance. It is generally agreed that the restructuring of industry and services, prompted by EC-1992 and fiercer global competition, will have to alter the structure of many companies, their product range, their 'Europeanisation', their rates of innovation, their skill structures and so on. Pressures both in goods and services markets and in the market for corporate control are indispensable to overcome profound resistance. Two proposals of the European Commission seek to build in some degree of countervailing (labour) power for such restructuring processes. The first one goes back to the early 1980s[44] and aims for compulsory consultation with workers in case of relocation or major direct investments in other Member States. From a social policy point of view and in a philosophy of consensus models, this is appropriate. For purposes of restructuring, in contrast, it raises yet another obstacle in a field already littered with

[39]And in Japan, in the company networks called 'keiretsu' which includes a 'house bank'.

[40]See de Jong (1995).

[41]Romano Prodi, former president of IRI, once said that to take over a German company one would first have to buy 'Deutsche Bank'. On the other hand, data shows that German companies have often been the target of acquisition or mergers, perhaps all 'friendly' ones.

[42]See for authoritative surveys on 'corporate governance' in an EU context, Berglöf (1997), Lannoo (1999) and Renneboog (1999).

[43]It implies that one-third of the board is chosen by the workers of the company (renewable). Behind co-determination there is a philosophy that a firm is not merely a collection of capital and marketable assets, but that all factors of production are crucial ('stakeholders'), as are harmonious relations between them.

[44]Known as the Vredeling draft directive, named after the social affairs commissioner at the time.

ADDITIONAL READING *continued*

vested interests. In 1994, the EU finally adopted a directive on 'works councils' for large companies with production in several Member States. These works councils would operate at EU level and have a consultative function. The second proposal, going back to the 1970s, eventually came to accompanying the SE regulation (Case Study 9.5). The heated debate on the countervailing power of labour is symbolic for the sensitivity of restructuring, and above all, relocation of plants across the EU or beyond, in a period of high unemployment.

Opportunities for securities trading are at a premium once mergers and acquisitions (M&A) are likely or are explicitly announced.[45] In principle, there are good economic reasons for that. The main motive for M&A is the value creation resulting from operating or informational synergies (scale, scope and so forth). This means that the allocation of factors of production improves. In the USA and the UK, and to a weaker extent in continental Europe, (hostile) takeovers can also act as a disciplining force to remove poorly performing management. Again, this improves factor allocation, hence, should improve economic welfare. Whereas the former motive is widely supported, the latter is more controversial, in that long-term risk taking (for example, in R&D) might be unduly suppressed so as to keep dividends high. Thus, making it too easy for hostile takeovers is likely to induce short-termism, which, in turn, could undermine long-run growth of target firms. The difficulty in practice, however, is that legal and other defences may be motivated by vested interests, be they of managers or of overly prudent (or protected?) workers, or even of fearful suppliers.

Since 1989 the EU has been struggling with variants of a takeover bid directive which would reduce but not fully eliminate the (often) multiple defences against takeovers. Such a 'European market for corporate control' should stimulate industrial and services restructuring in the Union, and help boost economic growth. Consider the following stylised facts: shareholding concentration is much higher in continental Europe than in the UK and the USA; complex (for example, holding) ownership structures exist in continental Europe to retain control, even when firms are listed; the continental European corporate sector owns a large stake in itself; and, especially in the UK, institutional investors and directors are the main shareholders, the latter ownership being so prominent that managerial entrenchment is often suspected.

In Europe, the average premium for targeted firms (over the pre-announcement price) upon a takeover is 21.3 per cent; for the bidders, returns are positive but close to zero. A takeover bid directive therefore has the potential merit of improving the functioning of European securities markets, presumably with knock-on effects on economic growth. With 'board neutrality' (no sudden defences, after announcement – however, this restraint has become optional only), a mandatory bid rule (to protect minority shareholders, key in Europe given the high concentration of major shareholders) and some other requirements, managers of listed firms would be forced to perform well. Directive 2004/25 was adopted after a tough battle, but whether it suffices to induce active corporate restructuring in the Union remains to be seen.[46]

[45]The following is based on McCahery *et al.* (2003).

[46]In Directive 2004/25 of 21 April 2005 (OJ L 142 of 30 April 2004) it is also optional, rather than compulsory, to adhere to a 'breakthough rule' (that is, during the bid, multiple voting rights and appointment rights are 'frozen' temporarily), thereby allowing practices in some Member States to continue which render takeovers very difficult. Furthermore, very large majority shareholders (over 90 per cent) have a right of 'squeeze out' (buy up the minority) and a minority can demand a 'sell out'.

The disincentives to set up multi-country production in Europe ('corporate integration') and cross-border business alliances have reduced over time. Some fiscal distortions have been removed as a result of EC-1992.[47] Approximation of company law (and accounting rules) has helped too. Business alliances, cross-border or not, are subject to scrutiny of EC competition policy (see section 12.3.2).

Finally, it is worthwhile reflecting briefly on a secular trend since the early 1980s towards privatisation. In the light of Article 295, the EC remains fully neutral with respect to state ownership versus private ownership. But the strong shift towards greater market orientation and the strict EC surveillance of the conduct of state-owned companies (including state aids; see section 12.6), has led to a gradual but continual decline of state ownership in EU Member States. Once state-owned companies become market oriented and their conduct cannot be manipulated (except under exclusive rights), why have state-owned enterprises? Almost by definition, the privatisation wave amounts to a major improvement of the EU market for corporate control since these companies become subject to stock market discipline, and may even be potential targets for takeovers or minority holdings.[48] Indeed, the converse is also relevant: retention of state ownership may be a perceived disadvantage to pursue cross-border mergers or other forms of restructuring. In 1993 the move from mutual minority holdings between Renault (state-owned) and Volvo to a fully fledged merger failed at the last minute because of a lack of trust in Renault's long-term independence from the French government.

9.5 Summary

For four decades the Community has struggled to put substance and coherence into the notion of a common market, with respect to factors of production. The accomplishments have been mixed thus far although the post-1992 period has shown selective progress.

For financial capital, EC-1992 and the increasing robustness of the EMS meant a watershed. Before the Single European Act, financial capital liberalisation was conditional and unlikely ever to become permanent. Since 1988, exchange controls have been abolished. The Maastricht Treaty has prohibited their reintroduction since 1994, also as a rule *vis-à-vis* third countries. The Financial Services Action Plan is explained with a simple flowchart, illustrating also the difference in progress between (fast) wholesale and (slow) retail. Case Study 9.1 shows how, at long last, tax coordination (without harmonisation) about interest income from almost perfectly mobile financial capital has been accomplished. Altogether, this second move of financial integration has meant a significant deepening.

The accomplishments in labour markets contrast starkly with those in capital markets. In a mostly formal sense, the free movement of workers was accomplished decades ago. National treatment for migrants (especially for social security and such like) now works well. However, the disincentives to move across borders are very large in the Community. There is no such thing as an internal market for labour. Establishing a properly functioning one would require a great deal more approximation of labour market regulation (preferably with mutual recognition), mutual recognition of diplomas, Union-wide access to social security (not to be expected for a long time) and some supporting measures. Cases on posted workers (a restrictive regime for the social treatment of workers, moving over the border for a service) and diploma

[47] For instance, a common taxation for parent companies and their subsidiaries (so that profit transfers to the parent remain untaxed), elimination of specific cases of double taxation, and a common system of taxation for cross-borders mergers, split-ups and exchanges of shares (all in OJ L 225 of 20 April 1990). But EU countries having many head offices of European companies in their fiscal jurisdiction still block, for instance, a draft directive on consolidation of company losses (in Member State A) and profits (in B and C), as this would amount to pure revenue losses for their governments. In the tax 'package', there is a proposal to deal with the taxation of cross-border interest and royalty payments.

[48] If 'golden shares' for the government or other constructions do not prevent that. But the Commission, helped by EC court rulings, has insisted in many cases on reducing or deleting golden-shares clauses.

Summary *continued*

recognition among professionals (which moves ahead slowly) illustrate some of the numerous obstacles to be overcome before free movement of labour can become genuinely free.

The EU internal market for knowledge and ideas has only slowly come about, and not all problems have been fully resolved. In particular, patents and other industrial, commercial or intellectual property rights have caused fragmentation. After 'integrative' judicial review about the limits of the exercise of patent rights, and establishing the European Patent Office (reducing the costs of multi-state filing of patents), a Community patent was proposed only in 2000 but political agreement is stuck on the symbolic (but costly) issue of translations. Thus far, the role of European Patent Office has been useful, but a true Community patent is badly needed. An EC trademark and harmonisation of national trademarks have been accomplished. As incentives for appropriation, hence for R&D of European business, these accomplishments are crucial.

With respect to tangible assets and corporate integration, direct investments were liberalised early on. Company law, however, has proved to be difficult to approximate (although Case Study 9.4 on regulatory competition in this field shows some moves). For acquisitions, for example, the EU has no single market for corporate control, but a 2004 takeover bid directive improves matters somewhat. Resistance has come both from companies and from labour. The ideal of the 'Societas Europa' (SE) – an EU-wide company under EU law directly – has finally been accomplished.

CHAPTER 10

Factor Market Integration:

Economic Analysis

Topics covered

- 10.1 Factor mobility in simple two-country models
- 10.2 Economic significance of factor market integration
- 10.3 The EU financial capital market
- 10.4 An emerging Euro-labour market?
- 10.5 An EU market for technology?
- 10.6 Europeanisation of business
- 10.7 Locational competition for mobile assets
- 10.8 Summary

As a sequel to Chapter 9, on the integration methods for realising an internal market for factors, the present chapter assesses factor market integration in the EU. The reader is warned that such a task is difficult for several reasons. First, economic theory and empirical analysis of factor mobility in general is underdeveloped. In the EU context, it implies that there is no identifiable body of economic analysis called factor market integration theory. Second, not unlike services, it is inappropriate to generalise about factors: any assessment has to do sufficient justice to the particular properties of the various factors. Inevitably, this gives the chapter a somewhat disparate character. Third, empirical data about factor flows and research about their determinants leave much to be desired. The consequence is that the economic assessment uses conjectures as well as limited data.

Section 10.1 provides the basic partial and general equilibrium analysis of free factor movement in an internal market of two countries. It is followed by a section with caveats and extensions, including that of convergence versus divergence of incomes between core regions and the periphery of the Union. Section 10.3 discusses the Community's financial capital market, its significant potential to increase economic welfare, and some indications of the rapid deepening of cross-border financial exchange in the EU. Section 10.4 explains the residual character of intra-EU labour mobility by a detailed analysis of the determinants of intra-EU migration as well as empirically, and adds some notes on the emerging common immigration policy. Section 10.5 tries to come to grips with the economic importance of the EU internal market for technology. Attention is paid to the success and limits of European patenting. Perhaps even more difficult is the answer to the much posed question of whether business is 'Europeanising' (section 10.6). Although all the available indicators of such 'corporate integration' point to a recent boost in Europeanisation, the interpretation remains difficult. A note on locational competition, with Case Study 10.1 on the impact of corporate tax competition on the location of business, closes the chapter.

10.1 Factor mobility in simple two-country models

In simple models mobile factors of production are indistinguishable from goods. Of course, factors are very different from goods in practice, and different types of factors have distinct characteristics. But, as Figure 10.1 shows, some basic

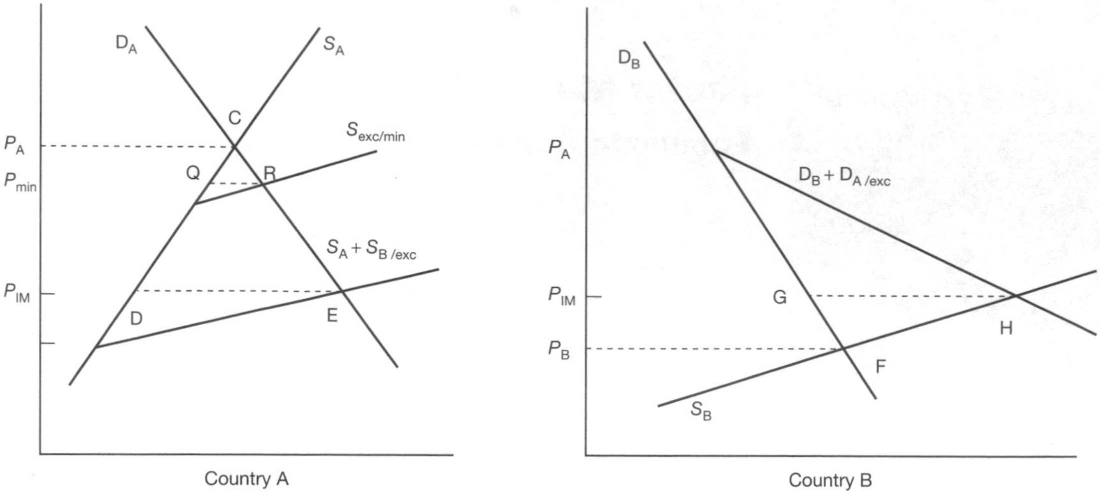

Figure 10.1 Wage convergence in a common labour market

effects of cross-border flows are similar to those in trade. It provides the basic rationale for (the gains from) an internal factor market.

Figure 10.1 assumes that the common factor market is closed for third countries. Let us suppose the graphs depict the labour market, so that prices represent wage rates. The *ex ante* wage rates (P_A and P_B) differ considerably and can persist due to barriers to migration across borders. Since the labour markets are assumed to clear, given flexible wages, there is no unemployment. Once free movement of labour is introduced, the excess demand of country A employers at wages below P_A will be exercised in country B, while B workers (if well informed or attracted by active A employers) will offer to work in A at higher wages than P_B. If migration is costless,[1] the total demand for B workers is expressed by the ($D_B + D_{A/exc}$) schedule; total supply of workers in A by the $S_A + S_{B/exc}$ schedule.

In equilibrium, GH = DE workers migrate from B to A and the converged internal market wage rate is P_{IM}. Overall, the welfare effects are showing a net gain for the internal market: CDE + GHF. But this conceals the winners and losers. A workers lose because their wages fall – they have to compete with migrant labour willing to work for lower wages. B employers lose as they have to pay higher wages. B workers, home or migrant, gain and A employers gain as well.

Although Figure 10.1 is a simple graph with full employment, some general facts about redistribution strategies concerning factor market integration can be readily explained. Trade unions of high wage countries find reasons to resist the shift from a customs union to a common market, whereas trade unions of low wage countries (with a tight labour market) will favour labour migration, even if not a single migrant is unionised. Employers in high wage countries with tight labour markets (for example, France, Benelux, Germany in the 1960s) would favour a common market and they may even be willing to absorb the migration costs. Figure 10.1 also provides a good illustration of the protectionist effect of the 'host country control' principle applied to intra-EU 'free' movement of workers. If the wage differential (*PA* – *PB*) is large, the minimum wage in A (P_{min}) will throttle almost entirely A's demand for B workers. The potential inflow of GH shrinks to a trickle, the actual inflow QR. Country A has become a fortress.

A simple general equilibrium approach is found in the MacDougall diagram (Figure 10.2).[2] Again, this graph can, in principle, be used for capital or labour interchangeably. We shall assume Figure 10.2 to represent interest-rate equalisation induced by capital market integration. Note that 'capital' in this neo-classical approach makes no distinction between, say, portfolio capital or direct investment; also, there is perfect competition,

[1]If B workers could absorb the cost of migrating to A, equal to *m*, the excess supply added to S_A would not start at P_B but at $P_B + m$. Similarly, if A employers absorb those costs, excess demand added to D_B would not start at P_A but at $P_A - m$. Compared with Figure 10.1, the flow of migrants would be smaller and, if workers pay, wage convergence will be incomplete by *m*.

[2]Introduced in MacDougall (1958, in Bhagwati, 1969).

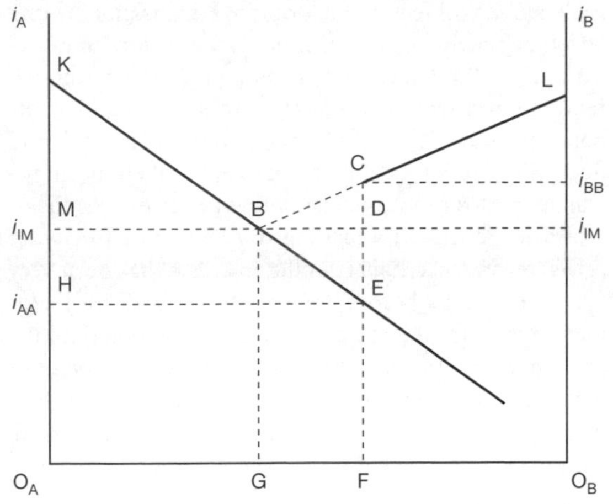

Figure 10.2 Interest equalisation in a common capital market

hence the marginal productivity of capital, so defined, is equal to the interest rate. It is assumed, too, that the labour market clears and that labour, complementing capital, will adjust to whatever the size of the utilised capital stock. These admittedly extreme assumptions may be interpreted as being very long run.

In Figure 10.2 the capital stock of EU countries A (left) and B (right) is added up to get the horizontal axis O_AO_B. The downward-sloping schedules KE and LC indicate that the marginal product of capital falls the greater the utilised capital stock. Before the removal of capital controls, country A employs O_AF of capital at interest rate i_{AA} while B employs O_BF at i_{BB}. The interest rate differential is thus considerable. As capital is relatively abundant in A, its relative income ($i_{AA} \times O_AF$) is modest (labour income is KHE); in B, capital income is relatively large ($O_BF \times i_{BB}$) compared with that of labour (the triangle with CL as diagonal).

When the internal market is established, interest rates converge at i_{IM}, with FG of capital having migrated to B. As drawn, it would imply a major cutback in A's production (GBEF), but its national income would rise because the initial capital income GBEF is augmented with BDE by shifting the capital to B. B's gross income goes up by GBCF; after payment of capital earnings to A, the net increase is BCD. This general equilibrium diagram brings out something that Figure 10.1 cannot: A's labour will lose from the establishment of the internal market (MBEH) and might oppose this direct investment outflow. This fall in labour income may well take the form of job losses if rigid wages prevent the labour market from clearing. Incoming direct investment tends to be welcomed for the opposite reason in B.

10.2 Economic significance of factor market integration

Simple models, as seen in section 10.1, help us to understand the basic economic effects of factor market integration: factor pay convergence and net allocative gains. But the economic significance of factor market integration is far more complicated than suggested above and should also be placed in a wider framework.

The purpose of this section is to indicate five aspects which illustrate the economic significance of factor mobility in the EU. The remainder of the chapter provides some empirical evidence for the four forms of factor market integration distinguished in Chapter 9. The five aspects to be discussed in the present section are: a critical look at the restrictive assumptions of the simple models, the substitutability between capital and labour flows, the substitutability of trade and factor flows, the problem of spatial concentration, and the debate between the income convergence and divergence schools.

The assumptions underlying Figures 10.1 and 10.2 are highly restrictive. The analysis is static, with technology given and accessible for all. The flexible adjustment of both factors suggests that these models should be seen as explaining driving forces (towards convergence) only in the long run. These two characteristics – long run and static – sit uneasily together because sustained factor flows will not just induce an allocative improvement for the internal market countries together, but will also exert a differential impact on growth rates which could become substantial over time. This is particularly true if capital flows are interpreted as direct investments (see sections 10.5 and 10.6) or as 'corporate integration' over the internal market because such movements often entail technological change. Even in a short- to medium-run perspective the models fail to bring out the crucial distinction between portfolio capital and direct investments (that is, a tailor-made package of tangible and intangible assets, under corporate control). With respect to labour, the refinement of different labour skills is also necessary, especially because only unskilled labour does not encounter problems of mutual recognition.[3] Furthermore, the suitability of the analysis

[3]It is also important for the political economy of (not) allowing free immigration. Razin & Sadka (1995) show that, in a model with wage rigidity, the inflow of unskilled labour may reduce the total share of local labour in GDP. Also, it may increase the burden on the welfare state. See Sinn & Ockel (2003) for an elaboration of the latter problem for the case of Germany just before the eastern enlargement.

of common markets also depends on the simultaneity of trade in goods (or services) with factor flows, a question which is touched upon below. Probably the most important objection to the models is the extreme simplicity of the determinants of not only, for example, labour mobility, but also non-portfolio capital or arm's-length technology (in, for example, licences and know-how agreement). This is important because, whereas in trade or, indeed, portfolio capital the removal of intra-EC barriers would give rise to noticeable increases in intra-EU flows, low mobility in skilled labour or direct investments or arm's-length technology need not be caused by controls or prohibitions. Just one example: in Benelux, Flanders and the Netherlands speak the same language (Dutch) and have enjoyed free movement of labour in the Benelux economic union for four decades, yet very little cross-border mobility has been observed. It may not be possible to compare the nature of the controls with that of controls in trade, again because the determinants are very different. Take the influx of US direct investment into the EC (in the 1960s) or of Japanese direct investment into the EC (1985–91) – these moves have complex explanations, but issues of controls played virtually no role as direct investments encounter few formal barriers. The point about the assumptions is thus to take these simple models for what they are. They cannot be used for anything more than basic arguments, and, when doing so, mainly for portfolio capital and unskilled labour.

One reason for the complexities in factor movements is the possibility of various substitutabilities and complementarities. First, capital and labour flows may be viewed as substitutes in the following sense. In a multicultural Community with stark income differentials,[4] it might be a better policy to induce direct investments or relocation to low income regions than to have massive migration flows in a search of jobs in the high income regions. The nature of EU social policy accentuates this view by pre-empting, as much as possible, regulatory competition between, or mutual recognition of, national social regimes, and thereby direct wage competition between workers from different countries (see Case Study 9.2 and Chapter 16). Thus, Slovakian workers in Belgium earn Belgian wages, not by consent but by law. Although this host country principle is protectionist, at least – for comparative disadvantage goods for Belgium – it increases the incentive to invest in low income regions.

Second, trade and factor flows can be substitutes. In a simple Heckscher–Ohlin–Samuelson (HOS) model, trade alone will lead to factor price equalisation, taking away the incentive (in this model) for factors to move. Mundell (1957) has shown that, in a similar model, factor movements can equalise relative endowments between countries, hence taking away the incentive to trade. The HOS model is restrictive, but there is empirical support for the conclusion that trade reduces factor scarcities, eventually leading to a tendency for factor price convergence. Since, in the EU, there has been very active trade long before the legal framework for factor market integration was anywhere near completion, the economic significance of factor market integration must have reduced considerably. With increased services trade, presumably a similar effect should be expected, though the effect would be weaker as services are traded less intensely.

Third, both factors between them, and factor flows and trade can be complements. With direct investments or 'corporate integration' this is most clear. Here, the term 'capital' flow is often a misnomer – the tailor-made packaging of complementary factors such as technology, management, design and access to distribution networks may be coupled to financial capital, which may or may not come from the 'sending' country and might even be borrowed. Direct investment may substitute and be complementary to trade. In the product life cycle, direct investment is usually seen as replacing existing exports, but what often happens is that exports of final products are substituted by exports of crucial components as inputs for foreign production. Inside the EU internal market this complementarity of production and trade within multinationals reflects a combination of the logistically optimal geographical spread of plants and specific location determinants for the distinct production units making various components (in so far as these are not subcontracted). Given the importance of such corporate integration, a lot of intra-EU trade is actually intra-industry trade in networks of suppliers and assemblers as well as intra-firm trade, yet it is the ultimate result of complicated packages of factor flows. Clearly, such a setting is not reflected in Figures 10.1 and 10.2.

A major concern about factor mobility has traditionally been *spatial concentration* of economic activity. In principle, trade alone could cause that. The addition of factor flows may cause what Myrdal (1956) has dubbed 'cumulative causation'. The origin of these fears can be traced back to the long periods of stagnation or decline in southern Italy, Bavaria and the sunbelt of the USA, following national economic integration of, respectively,

[4]The income ratio between the lowest and highest income region in the EC25 is about 1 to 6. At country level, several new Member States were near only 40 per cent of the EU15 income level when they entered the EU in 2004. See Chapters 16 and 20.

Italy, Germany and the USA.[5] With capital not flowing to the weaker regions and labour flowing to the high productivity ones, weaker regions lose their best labour, will have low savings and little local investment, cannot support new infrastructure and will typically be short of all forms of higher education and skills training. These consequences are far worse than if there were no factor mobility. In a dynamic setting these effects can be aggravated by agglomeration effects for specialised skills, a spatial concentration of product innovation and generation of new technology, and the concentrated availability of specialised information and services. These would tend to widen the gap between high and lower performing regions even further. As long as diseconomies of agglomeration (such as congestion) do not become very serious, the result is 'unbalanced growth'. It was this fear which prompted Italy to push for 'balanced' expansion in (the second aim of) the Rome Treaty (see Figure 3.1). Ultimately, this has led to a literature about the economics of agglomeration, relevant to (real) economic convergence or divergence under economic integration. It will be discussed in Chapter 16 on cohesion.

10.3 The EU financial capital market

Since the late 1980s, the EU has progressively moved ahead in deepening financial capital market integration. In this section we deal with three economic aspects (for the regulatory aspects, see Chapter 9): a briefing on the removal of exchange controls as a necessary first step to allow free movement of financial capital; the long-run potential of financial integration in terms of economic 'welfare'; and a few empirical indicators about the impact thus far.

As to the first aspect, it should be realised how much Europe has changed given domestic and EU-wide liberalisation. One critical result is that financial capital is more and more fungible, hence continuous, and at times very swift substitution takes place between currency flows, bank loans and very liquid securities, or between various types of securities. In addition there was an important external factor. The so-called eurocurrency and eurobond markets exploded in the 1970s and 1980s and swamped most attempts to impose effective capital and exchange controls. The euromarkets emerged in London in the 1960s as offshore markets, that is, falling outside the British or any other regulatory system with respect to exchange controls or, for example, interest rate ceilings[6] and restrictive rules for trading. Hence, the euromarkets are in effect world markets and the currencies used for money or bond transactions now include the euro, the dollar and the yen. The euromarkets, the rapid globalisation of capital markets and financial innovation they prompted (also boosted by instantaneous information via telematics) caused ever greater problems for the effectiveness of capital and exchange controls. While such controls may have been moderately effective in the 1960s and early 1970s,[7] it has become virtually impossible today to achieve comparable effects, short of using extreme administrative controls. This raises two questions. The first is about the actual effectiveness of exchange controls practised by some EU countries before the controls were abolished in the late 1980s. There is considerable doubt about their effectiveness (Gros & Thygesen, 1998, pp. 128–37). When the UK (1979) and Denmark (1983) abolished them, no change in flows could be observed. Yet, some observers attribute the gradually accomplished exchange rate stability in the EMS of the 1980s (see section 17.4.3) for France and Italy to their exchange controls, pre-empting the worst of speculative attempts. It is important to realise that Italy and France were prepared to go very far in tightening exchange controls in response to speculation.[8]

The other question is whether a very special type of 'new' exchange control could serve a useful purpose in today's EU, with the euro and complete liberalisation of capital flows. More precisely, could extreme volatility of the euro – if caused by herd behaviour of speculators and

[5]Note that the examples are also often cited as evidence of the risk of monetary union. In so far as productivity differentials are significant, and perhaps growing, the loss of competitiveness of less performing regions would require separate currencies, and hence depreciation. This is ignored here; see Chapter 17.

[6]One reason this market emerged was regulation Q in the USA (an interest rate ceiling for deposits). Note that the euromarkets are not without supervision: solvency and some rules of conduct are scrutinised. The worldwide Basle accords on capital requirements (in force since the early 1990s) apply to euromarket participants too. Eurobonds are tax free, however. Meanwhile, both corporate and government bonds denominated in euro have become an important market, but they have nothing to do with the 'old' so-called euro (tax-free) bonds (Gros & Lannoo, 2000).

[7]Although the classic work by Cairncross (1973) already showed that this required widespread and heavy-handed systems with high costs.

[8]In 1974 Italy even required high deposits (interest free) before importing goods – this was forbidden by the EC Court.

institutional investors – be discouraged without hindering non-speculative capital flows? This idea gained currency after the 1993 EMS crisis (see Case Study 17.1) where, for example, the speculation against the French franc was clearly not based on economic fundamentals (inflation differentials with Germany, public deficit and so forth). It is argued by some (Eichengreen *et al.*, 1995) that a tiny tax on such transactions – known as the Tobin tax – or interest-free deposits in some cases could throw 'sand in the wheels' of speculators, thereby preventing unjustified exchange rate volatility. As Garber & Taylor (1995) convincingly show, this form of exchange control can almost certainly be circumvented fully and at virtually no cost. They also show how temporary controls of a much more restrictive nature, introduced by the Spanish authorities during the peseta crisis of September/October 1992, were also swiftly circumvented. Only draconian controls can be effective but at very high costs to international finance and business at large.[9]

The second aspect is about the ultimate case for financial integration in terms of higher economic welfare for the Union. Although there are a number of solid economic justifications for regulatory intervention in financial markets (see section 7.3), it is just as important to appreciate the great scope for too detailed or too wide restrictions in order to protect inefficient business practices, including the persistence of local non-competing oligopolies. The experience since the late 1980s has much more clearly revealed the anti-competitive effects of restrictive regulation at the national level, especially at the retail level but at first also at the wholesale level. Exactly where to draw the line and to what extent this ought to be differentiated according to national preferences is exceedingly hard to determine (especially since banks and other incumbents may support restrictive consumer protection, but for protectionist motives, and this might then be conceived as the preferences to be catered for). Nevertheless, so much pro-competitive free movement and cross-border entry can be held compatible with a range of financial regulatory devices (as the diversity in the Union convincingly shows) that it would seem entirely defensible to demonstrate the potential in terms of welfare of pro-market reforms to some predetermined 'proven' standard. There are broadly two strands in economic impact analysis here. A macro approach focuses on how deeper financial integration leads to lower prices for financial services at retail and wholesale levels and, via lower interest rates, to higher investment (*ceteris paribus*), in turn imputed into macroeconomic models. First attempted in the Cecchini report[10] and recently by London Economics (2002), for example, it shows considerable gains in the long run, possibly as high as almost 1 per cent of GNP. A microeconomic approach faces the difficulty of avoiding a too partial approach while also having to employ a benchmark for comparison. Giannetti *et al.* (2002) studied EU Member States in terms of their financial level of development as compared with the USA as 'standard'. Whereas EU countries with sophisticated and innovative financial sectors (such as the UK and the Netherlands) benefit little from deepening, many other Member States do benefit to different degrees, with an overall simulated growth effect for the EU15 of 1 per cent. Three key variables are used in the Giannetti *et al.* study: the degree of creditor's protection, the stringency of accounting standards and the rule of law. Interestingly, better accounting standards contribute the most. It was also found that, more than large companies, it is particularly SMEs which benefit greatly from better and cheaper (or more innovative or varied) access to financial markets; SMEs suffer the most from a lack of reform and too little rivalry among fiancial institutions.

The last point deserves attention. The banking sector, especially, should consolidate (but it has done that mostly on a domestic basis) and accept outright much more competition. Many studies (for example, Gual, 2003; Walkner & Raes, 2005) show that the sector fails, in a pan-European perspective, on both accounts, even if in 2005, for example, several major attempts of cross-border mergers were observed (for example, Uno-Credito and Hypo-Vereinsbank creating the ninth largest bank in the EU25; ABN-Amro bidding for Anton-Veneto in Italy). Competition in retail in Member States is so weak that the European Commission has announced a special investigation. The potential economic gains of deepening in financial integration can, of course, only be realised if the market opportunities created by removing restrictive but unjustified regulation or supervision are not taken up due to a lack of competition.

As Chapter 9 showed in some detail, financial market integration has made great strides since the late 1990s in the EU. As before when discussing integration impact, it is far from easy to solve the attribution problem. Is what we notice in European financial markets all due to EU liberalisation? Undoubtedly not. Drivers such as globalisation, ICT and other technology, a search for efficiency gains from scope (and a little from scale, dependent on what market one operates) and conglomeration all matter. Moreover, microeconomic financial market integration has also been facilitated by the arrival of the euro.

[9]Interestingly, there were pressures in the EP in 2000 to amend the treaty and provide a legal basis for a Tobin tax, in case of a future need.

[10]The economics of EC-1992, *European Economy,* 1988, no. 35 (April).

Nevertheless, there are powerful indicators which point to quite a radical shift to EU financial integration in all but the retail sector. A selection of such pointers can illustrate this:[11]

- The (unsecured) money market is fully integrated; the three-month interest rate converged fully the very first day of the euro (2 January 1999). Interestingly, close to convergence also took place for the 'outs' (non-euro), showing the centripetal function of euroland.
- The level of dispersion in national bank lending rates has gone down between 1996 and 2002.
- Bond yields have been converging ever since the early 1990s, in part helped by increasing cross-border trading volumes.
- Equity returns have become increasingly sensitive to European shocks, rather than to pure local shocks.
- On equity markets, the proportion of shares held by non-residents exceeds 20 per cent in most national markets, ranging up to 35 per cent in some.
- Financial institutions have rebalanced their asset and liability management into a much more European perspective (for example, eurozone counterparties; more European investment horizons) and this includes pan-European risk management (for example, derivatives).
- On competition, the indicators are mixed: there is both increased rivalry (for example, bond underwriting fees have fallen steadily over 1995 to 2001) and high concentration rates (national market share of the five largest banks and the five largest insurance companies, averaged for the EU, is over 60 per cent).
- Everywhere, one observes the rise of financial conglomerates with a European outlook but unclear impact on competitive markets.

Meanwhile only few stock exchanges have remained in Europe (from more than thirty a decade ago) and alliances and even consolidation takeover attempts are engineered, leading eventually to one or only very few financial centres for equity and perhaps for a range of wholesale activities. This will only amplify the retail/wholesale dichotomy which marks EU financial market deepening.

10.4 An emerging Euro-labour market?

In Chapter 9 we concluded that there is no such thing as a Community labour market. This section can therefore limit itself to the residual (intra-EU) labour mobility that does (or did) occur and the possible effects of third-country immigration on intra-EU factor market integration. Before doing so, a few misunderstandings about the European labour market should be cleared up.

In the EU institutions and sometimes elsewhere, the phrase 'European (or Union) labour market' is liberally used in the policy debate and in publications. Although rarely defined precisely, the phrase usually refers to the collection of *national* labour markets in the Union. All of them suffer from a number of common problems and the EU (Commission, Council, EP, and the Economic and Social Committee) is extremely active in promoting joint analysis and consultation. The cooperative strategy is a typical example of step 2 of the subsidiarity test – identify a 'need to act' but without any degree of binding and purely in a parallel fashion among the Member States. The approach has been intensified by what is called a 'coordinated strategy for employment' (the new Article 125 EC), by regarding 'promoting employment as a common concern' (Article 126 EC), and much consultation about guidelines and best practices. How jealously national social regulation is guarded (hence, the fragmentation of the EU labour market) is immediately clear from Article 129 where (incentive) measures 'shall not include harmonisation of the laws and regulations of the Member States'.

10.4.1 The determinants of cross-border labour mobility

Cross-border intra-EU labour mobility is *residual* in character. This is neither the case in financial capital nor in direct investment (nor, for that matter, in goods). Relative scarcities of low-skilled labour in national markets tend to induce several responses other than intra-EU labour flows: capital–labour substitution in different degrees, outward direct investment or relocation for relatively labour-intensive goods production, adjustment towards activities with higher labour productivity (so that the low-skilled labour-intensive production is subcontracted from elsewhere, as in outward-processing traffic in clothing) and regulatory or protectionist activities in the political market. If legal access were as easy and economic incentives to enter national labour markets were as powerful as for goods or capital, none of these responses would be needed to the same extent or be sustainable.

The determinants of intra-EU labour mobility are set out in Figure 10.3. Although wage incentives do play a role, both in a long-run general equilibrium context (as

[11] The following is based on COM Staff Working Document SEC (2004) 559, *Financial Integration Monitor 2004* and ECB (2004).

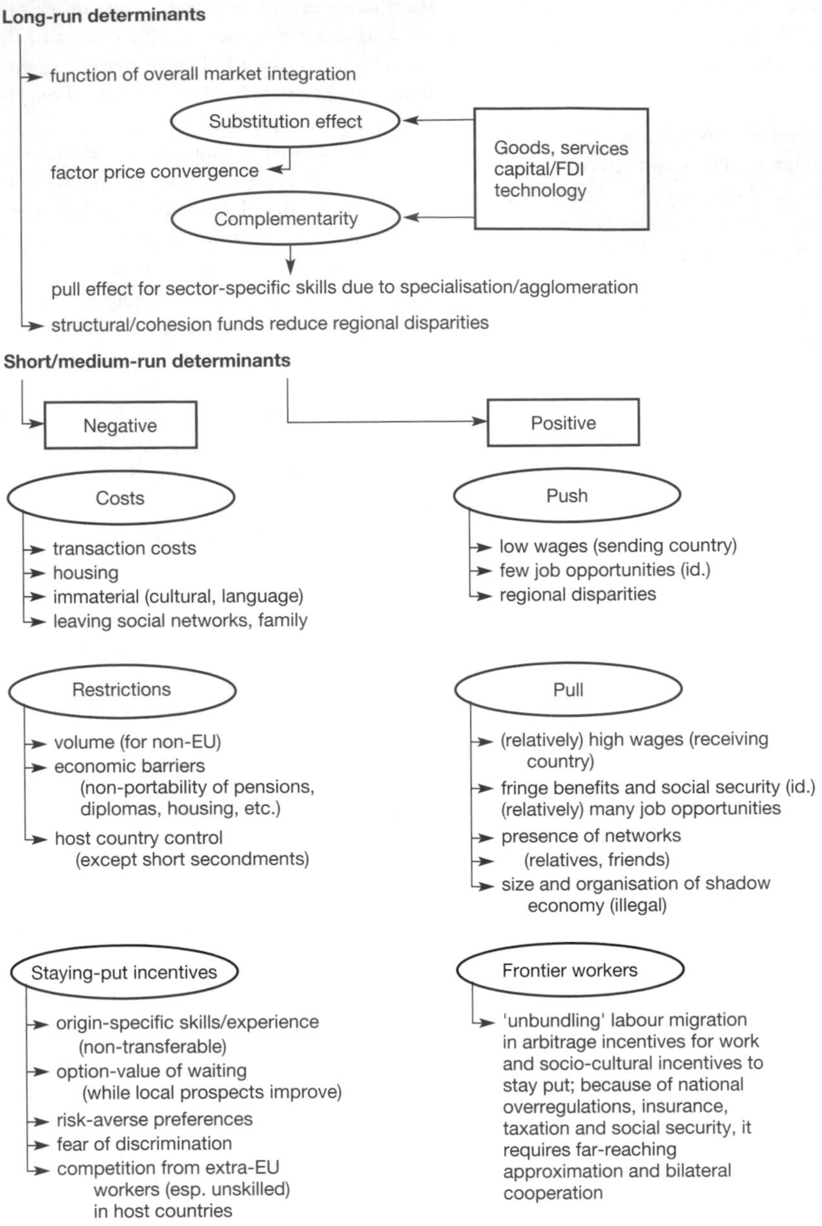

Figure 10.3 Determinants of intra-EU labour mobility

Note: As the main text reiterates, cross-border intra-EU labour migration is residual; heavily regulated national markets make labour market integration impossible. Note, also, that the *domestic* labour mobility has weaker push and pull: housing acts as an incentive to stay and there is no restrictive regulation; however, social security does not vary with interregional immobility. Some economists hold that the absolute level of income (or purchasing power) can pass a threshold beyond which the propensity to migrate falls significantly.

Sources: Molle & van Mourik, 1988; Bauer & Zimmermann, 1999; Boeri & Brueker, 2000; Hönekopp & Werner, 2000

in Figure 10.1 and section 10.2) and in the individual decisions of workers, many other determinants matter as well. As to the long-run context, the substitution effect between labour mobility and overall market integration (in goods, services, capital) has traditionally outweighed any complementarities. Rising incomes in relatively poor regions (gradual EU factor price convergence) tend to reduce actual as well as incipient cross-border labour mobility. Since EU membership implies deep market integration in goods, services, capital (including FDI) and technology, labour mobility from (lower income) Member States such as Greece, Spain, Portugal and Ireland has weakened, if not reversed, over time. This will eventually happen with Europe too. Within sending countries, large regional disparities may also be reduced by EU policy, especially the Structural Funds and the Cohesion Fund, sometimes helped by agro-payments as well (see Chapter 16). This matters too, because once migrants from poor regions are uprooted, their decision to move across borders becomes less difficult. Cohesion policies might thus eventually reduce intra-national and cross-border intra-EU labour mobility, at least of low-skilled workers.

In the short/medium-run context, still in Figure 10.3, workers decide on mobility by weighing costs, restrictions and 'stay-put incentives', on the one hand, and push and pull factors on the other. A special category of frontier workers is in the position to move for work and yet stay put, in the socio-cultural sense; as noted in Chapter 9, however, this 'arbitrage' requires far-reaching protection from the Union, as Member States tend not to invest in sufficient bilateral cooperation to facilitate such 'free' movement. The traditional European view is that it is particularly the non-material costs (languages, culture), and the leaving behind of family and social networks, that are the crucial reasons why cross-border labour mobility in the EU is low. These elements play much less of a role in the USA, which would explain the far higher US interstate labour mobility. Figure 10.3 clarifies, however, that this view is only one part of a far more complex set of determinants. Another critical set of determinants includes a range of legal and economic barriers in the EU, for which there is no equivalent in the USA. In particular, 'host country control' is a protectionist principle, removing the trump card of the low-skilled migrant (namely, the willingness to work for a wage that is between those of the home and the host countries). The upshot is that the competition with local workers will be on non-wage characteristics where locals tend to enjoy advantages of language, work cultures, networks and so on.[12]

On the pull and push side, wages and job opportunities are dominant determinants, but usually only in combination with the presence of networks in host countries (at least, for the low skilled). Typically, forecasts or simulations of migration flows are based on the combination of these three variables.

10.4.2 The impact of free movement and immigration policies

It is exceedingly hard to conduct genuine, respectable economic impact analysis. Figure 10.3 shows the great complications if ever one would wish to model it. Also, there are shifts and indeed reversals of flows over time. And, as to third-country workers, the cautious move towards a more common immigration policy is still under way, while EU countries retain the power to set quotas for third-country nationals immigration. Therefore, the following helps to understand such flows, but it cannot pretend to amount to a fully fledged impact analysis.

The totals of EU migrant workers are low. In 1997 the total was about 2.9 million, including frontier workers. This amounts to some 1.7 per cent of the EU15 active labour force, and this share has remained roughly constant ever since Spain and Portugal joined (in 1986).[13] Approximately half of these workers originate from the four 'cohesion' countries: Greece, Spain, Portugal and Ireland.[14] Interestingly, their numbers have gradually declined. The first three countries were

[12]Host country control is side-stepped in the 'grey' economy but such illegality increases risks (no insurance; expulsion)

[13]For 1995, Luxembourg (36 per cent of domestic labour force) and Belgium (5 per cent), with the EC institutions (and the international 'circuit' around it), register by far the highest domestic shares. Next comes Germany, with a share of 2.9 per cent of its domestic labour force, but this represents some 38 per cent of all intra-EU cross-border migrants. On the other hand, countries such as Italy and Spain are *de facto* 'closed'. Note that 'workers' and 'persons' are not always distinguished in migration statistics. For the latter the totals are almost double (5.1 million in 1995). See Eurostat's *Labour Force Survey: Results 1997,* and Kiehl & Werner (1998) for all data.

[14]In fact, of the 210 bilateral host/origin combinations in the EU15, a mere 5 combinations add up to almost half the total for 1995: Austrians in Germany (126,000), Greeks in Germany (232,000), Italians in Germany (365,000), Portuguese in France (373,000) and Irish in the UK (245,000). The large majority of combinations shows trivial or no numbers: a clear confirmation of the residual nature of migration in the EU.

restricted in the freedom of movement for workers during seven-year transition periods, and by the time these restrictions were lifted, unemployment in the high-income countries greatly reduced the 'pull'. It is probable that, for these countries, the partial income catch-up in that period also reduced the push factor. At first, migrants had great economic significance for these countries.[15] Once these three countries returned to democracy (in 1974/75) and modernised rapidly, the push factor is likely to have been weakened. Another restraining factor might have been the competition from non-EU labour, especially from Mediterranean countries, for similar jobs in, for example, Germany and France.

A similar tale can be told for Italian migrants of the 1950s and early 1960s. Italy experienced rapid catch-up and the domestic labour market tightened, causing a net return migration in the early 1970s. One can conclude, therefore, that the legal 'free movement' is not the trigger for intra-EU cross-border labour mobility. Domestic and destination economic push and pull factors are. In the EU25 of today, matters are hardly different though the perception is that of large (incipient?) flows. In 2001 (before the EU enlarged further), the EU citizens in other Member States (but already counting the EU as EU25) amounted to 6 million (of a total of 455 million). Since about half of them or less actually work, the share in the labour force might well have decreased compared with 1995. If there is 'a problem' at all, it relates to (low) skill levels since the employment rates of high- and medium-skilled EU nationals are extremely high (in 2002, 81.6 per cent and 89 per cent, respectively). The restrictions on migration from the new Member States to most of the EU15 have, of course, kept the inflows low in 2004, but it is anything but clear whether these flows would have been much higher without curbs. Economic growth in the new Member States is healthy (4–6 per cent real annual) and steady, and intra-country mobility is often low (just like in western Europe). Of course, there are illegal flows, but the greater risks, better enforcement of host country controls and improving prospects at home would seem to render them selective.[16]

Non-EU migrants outnumber EU migrants. The sending countries (at first Turkey, Tunisia, Algeria, Morocco and the former Yugoslavia) have far lower wages still. The influx of Mediterranean labour is likely to have exercised a dampening effect on wage increases in unskilled jobs (industry, services, domestic assistance), to the detriment of migrants from cohesion countries. It would seem that relatively little local labour competed with non-EU labour, except in temporary jobs. But non-EU migration is more restricted, and return programmes have reduced the flow to a trickle – many workers have remained and have begun to assimilate. It is typical for the segmented European labour market that (long-term resident) non-EU labour was granted free movement only in 2003. Non-EU immigration received a sudden boost in the 1990s with the opening up of central and eastern Europe and the war in former Yugoslavia. This has prompted a sharp increase in the restrictiveness of immigration and asylum procedures in EU countries and prudent moves towards a common immigration policy. The notion of a common immigration policy, except if highly restrictive, sits uneasily with the maintenance of highly inflexible, over-regulated (national) labour markets, backed up by generous (national) welfare states, and has therefore long been resisted. The trend nowadays is to begin to accept a common policy, but with many traits which keep it restrictive. One extra reason is that third-country workers tend to have higher unemployment (often low-skilled related) and some nationalities have disproportionate shares in social security and welfare programmes. Although this can be related to the risk profile of their jobs, it nonetheless confirms the fears of many, and has fuelled calls for tighter restrictions, except for high-skilled workers.

10.5 An EU market for technology?

It is extremely difficult to get to grips with the notion of an EU market for technology. We use the word 'technology' here to mean all the intangible inputs for production and R&D, which derive from generation and diffusion of knowledge.[17] A lot of the generation and diffusion is, however, not at arm's length. In essence, there are three organisational forms under which technology is generated and can travel: markets, hierarchy (within firms) and networks (OECD, 1992, pp. 77–80).

[15]Molle (1994, p. 201) quotes data for 1973: 19 per cent of the Portuguese labour force, 9 per cent of the Greek and 4 per cent of the Spanish were employed in the EC9. Transfers from these workers as a share of imports ranged from 0 per cent (Spain) to 37 per cent (Portugal).

[16]COM (2004) 508 of 16 July 2004.

[17]Tangible inputs – technology embodied in machines – may be a partial substitute. Note also that intangible inputs in marketing and sales, such as fashion designs, copyright and trademarks, are excluded as they bear little relation to technology.

Markets are based on property rights and fairly detailed contracts, including prices and delivery. Networks are based on complementary assets – usually firm-specific, proprietary knowledge – of the participants, on reciprocity and trust, and on a preparedness to pool resources for the purpose of the network.

Since all three forms have greatly intensified cross-border intra-EU activities, two methodological questions arise. First, should cross-border intra-EU movements under all three organisational forms be considered to be elements of the EU internal market for technology? The answer is affirmative. Free movement of technology should not be limited to a legalistic notion of contracted sales under EU property rights. A legalistic notion of free movement is an inappropriate all-or-nothing concept, rather unhelpful in grasping the economic significance of mobile technology. Thus, the lack of free movement (for example, because of a lack of EU-wide property rights or other barriers) may be a costly inconvenience for business, but it does not mean that technology is not mobile within the EU. Stronger, the gradual achievement of EU property rights need not imply that technology will henceforth only be sold and bought in the open EU market. In this sense, technology (as defined here) is different from goods. As noted before, the choice of the organisational form is determined by appropriability considerations as well as by crucial aspects for competitiveness in some sectors such as speed of innovation, learning processes (which cannot be marketed, by definition) and the need for specialised R&D input which is simply not for sale.

ADDITIONAL READING

The second methodological question is, in describing the EU market, can cross-border activities of all forms actually be observed, and if not, how selective and misleading is the picture? Unfortunately, observations are fragmentary and few. Any precision in conclusions from such evidence would itself be misleading. We present some data which may be suggestive of the nature of technology market integration. They include several indicators about European patenting beyond national markets, and intercompany technology networks.[18]

Figure 10.4 shows the three most important activities of the European Patent Office (EPO). Given the cost reductions for multi-country filing as well as the EPO's quality and the large database for searching,[19] the European patent has become an attractive option. Annual output of European patents granted rose quickly to 37,000 in 1993. Following a slow decline to 2000, a steep rise occurred, reaching 59,000 European patents granted in 2004.[20] Total filings exhibit a strong and steady upward trend. An important reason for this are the Euro-PCT filings. PCT refers to the Patent Cooperation Treaty (72 countries adhering in 1994); when international applications are filed under the PCT, European patents may be granted in a second, 'European' phase.[21] This cooperative response to globalisation may serve as a substitute for direct European patent filings in case patenting is sought in many countries outside Europe as well. That the European patent means

[18]One could include data about the private/public cooperation in the many (cross-border, multi-company) research programmes sponsored by the EU in the R&TD framework programmes (see Chapter 14). Except for EUREKA (which is not only EU), they are prior to commerciable activities in this field. Although by definition cross-border, they focus on input R&D and it is unclear to what extent they may serve as a proxy of technology flows in the internal market. A second category of data could consist of paid-for technology flows expressed in royalties, licence fees and so on. The paucity of relevant data on paid-for technology flows is such that not even proxies of intra-EU flows can be made. Interviews confirm that, apparently, the bulk of the payments for royalties, licence fees and so on are not at arms' length but intra-firm or intra-network. It should also be noted that technology is diffused in many other ways such as imitation 'around' patents, co-makerships and industry-wide standardisation.

[19]The enormous patent and database has made EPO into a worldwide leader (with Japan and the USA) in European and international 'searches'. Some 89,000 searches in total were conducted in 1993 and 116,000 in 1999, rising to 166,000 in 2004, of which 66,000 were for non-Europeans.

[20]Always remember that a 'European patent' strictly refers to EPO's examination being favourable; the legal patents are then national. The Community patent proposal is stuck in Council, mainly on the issue of translations (see Chapter 9).

[21]Although also a unified procedure (like that for the European patent), the simplified form of PCT necessitates either a national or European second round.

ADDITIONAL READING *continued*

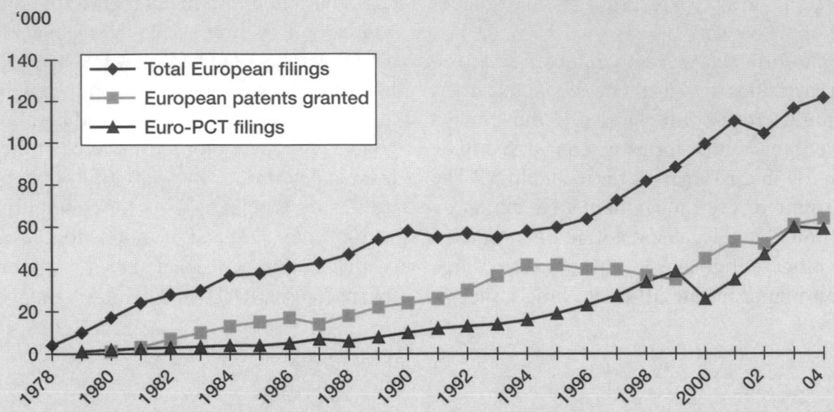

Figure 10.4 European patents: applications filed and patents granted, 1978–2004

Sources: European Patent Office, *Annual Report over 1999* (2000); idem, *Facts and Figures* (2005)

great progress for the internal market for technology is also clear from the absolute and stark relative decline of national applications in the thirty EPO states[22] compared with European patent applications for those countries. The absolute decline of national patents is diminished by the upsurge in PCT applications for national patents.

The significance for the internal market (both that of goods and of technology) is proxied by the average rate of almost eight designated EPO countries per application.[23] As one would expect, by 2004 the five biggest EU countries are designated far more than others: for above 90 per cent of the granted patents (Germany, UK and France), or as high as 76 per cent (for Italy), followed by 59 per cent (for the Netherlands and Spain).

Another measuring rod might be intercompany technology networks. Important work by Hagedoorn (1996) and Narula & Hagedoorn (1999) has shed some light on these links. For information technology in the broad sense of the word,[24] the network density strongly increased in the course of the 1980s, including a strong boost in both private and EC-sponsored EC-based networks. Technological complementarity and reduction of the innovation period are of particular importance in partnerships for new technologies. With increasing experience in technological partnerships by practically all multinationals, some substitution of joint ventures (often highly unstable, with a failure rate of around 50 per cent) to contractual arrangements can be observed. Hagedoorn (1996) provides evidence that multinationals prefer intercontinental partnerships to intra-European ones: from 25 per cent of all partnering in the 1970s to 9 per cent in the 1990s. This might indicate attempts to strengthen intra-EU positions while keeping potential US or Japanese entrants at bay and yet operate world-class technology. Alternatively it might be considered as the consequence of EU weakness in new technologies, many firms wanting to partner with leading US or Japanese companies. It is mainly in networks subsidised under EU technology (framework) programmes that intra-EU alliances can be found (see Hagedoorn & Schakenraad, 1993).[25]

[22]EU25, except Malta and Latvia, plus Switzerland, Liechtenstein, Monaco, Ireland, Cyprus, Romania, Bulgaria and Turkey. Latvia and Malta are applicants and more countries line up.

[23]Some 94,000 inventions were designated for all EPO countries (stock figure in 1993).

[24]Computers, microelectronics, software, telecoms, industrial automation, other information technology.

[25]For a survey of trends in cross-border technology trends, see Koopman & Muennich (1999). This rich survey clarifies that empirical work does not and often cannot distinguish EU and non-EU in such a sharp way.

10.6 Europeanisation of business

An increasingly important manifestation of factor market integration is the change from national to European enterprises.[26] Dunning & Robson (1987) call this 'corporate integration', the vertical and horizontal integration of separate economic activities located in different countries in order to capture a set of transactional benefits derived from placing these activities under common ownership. Such transactional benefits could not arise if all markets functioned properly, including effective competition and absence of market failures. Corporate integration, and its most important vehicle – direct investment across borders – is a response to improperly functioning markets.

Indeed, under corporate integration, both the nature of the firm and the nature of the economic environment are radically different from traditional trade theory. The corporate environment is fraught with imperfections and uncertainties. Not all markets may function efficiently owing to market failures and government intervention; technologies are continuously changing and not freely accessible; there is product differentiation and product innovation; goods and factor markets may have few sellers; factors may be firm or industry specific. In such a world there are numerous tangible or intangible assets that enable positive quasi-rents. Hence, firms will attempt to find such forms of economic organisation as will generate and reproduce continuously assets for extracting profits or quasi-rents in every market they operate.

Following Dunning (1979) the economics of foreign direct investment (FDI) have been based on the so-called OLI framework. A FDI decision may be expected if:

1 there are firm-specific advantages (O for ownership advantage);
2 it is beneficial to internalise rather than externalise those advantages through licensing (or other contractual resource transfers) (I for internalisation);
3 assuming 1 and 2 to be satisfied, it is expected to be beneficial to exploit these advantages abroad in conjunction with some other input, presumably country-specific to the host country (L for location-specific advantage).

If 1 and 2 apply but not 3, the firm would prefer to supply the foreign market by exports; if only 1 applies, the firm would opt for international licensing. The nature of firm-specific advantage 1 is essentially that of a set of barriers to entry.

These general insights have driven a lot of new theory formation, for two reasons.[27] First, the OLI framework needs to be elaborated in more rigorous modelling to understand better its links with trade, especially the explanation of complementarity between the two. Second, the OLI framework is too generic for rigorous empirical analysis; for example, it does not explain the sharply upward trends in FDI, both in the EU and worldwide in the 1990s. Economic theory has succeeded in developing (restrictive) models in which multinationals emerge endogenously. In world markets, 'vertical' FDI will be of some importance, driven by differences in relative factor endowments. In Europe this is often denoted as 'delocalisation': the transfer of, for example, labour-intensive parts of manufacturing to labour-abundant countries. In the internal market, however, 'horizontal' FDI should be expected to be predominant except in countries such as Portugal and those of central Europe. In the EU15, factor endowments tend to be rather similar and FDI will be driven by 'market seeking'. Ownership advantages such as intangible assets are likely to be enjoyed at the firm level, whereas scale advantages are exploited at the plant level. The more important the intangible assets are relative to the fixed costs of setting up more plants, and the higher transport costs, the more likely FDI will be. This will be horizontal FDI and it can be two-way; indeed, it might well displace some existing intra-industry trade. In such theories, the analysis is focused on ownership and location advantages, while taking internalisation as given.[28]

[26]In the 'economic' sense. Since 2004 it has been possible to incorporate as a 'European company' (SE; see Case Study 9.5) as well, but how much this will be done is hard to predict. What matters economically, however, is corporate control and production in several 'national' markets or throughout the internal market.

[27]The following cannot possibly do justice to the results of a burgeoning literature. For recent surveys, see Markusen (1995) and Segre (2000). See also di Mauro (2000).

[28]An exception is Ethier (1986) who explicitly models internalisation too. One important reason why the new models on multinationals are restrictive is the assumption of free entry and exit of firms. An original approach avoiding this is found in Neary (2002). He explores three motives for FDI in (or out of) the EU: tariff-jumping (more FDI, the higher the CET and the lower the fixed cost of a new plant), export platform motive (only a single plant for the Union, rather than exporting) and sharp competition from local EU firms (say, due to EC-1992 or further deepening) forces some multinationals to leave. The tariff jumping is closely linked to older literature on FDI when the CU was under formation, and the CET was still relatively high. The empirical literature, dating back to the 1960s and early 1970s is based on the Scaperlanda model. For a survey, see Pelkmans (1984, pp. 123–5). See also Yannopoulos (1990) for a classification of how the CU impacts on FDI (also in 2nd edition, p. 194).

In the empirical analysis of FDI and its relationship to EU market integration, the issues are timing and the identification problem. Timing refers to the sequential pattern over time of the stages of integration as they have a bearing on FDI. In the EU there was first the customs union (and internal quota removal), then a judicial and, since EC-1992, also regulatory removal of numerous regulatory and fiscal barriers, and finally progress with the facilitation of cross-border corporate control.[29] So, initially, intra-EU FDI was small and often a result of remaining barriers in public procurement and regulation.[30] When market integration deepened over time, intra-EU FDI intensified too, especially during the EU-1992 programme. However, it is difficult to interpret it because the increase is the outcome of two opposing effects of 'deepening' the EC framework for intra-EU FDI. On the one hand, as fewer barriers lower the costs of intra-EU trade, it reduces the need for barrier-hopping FDI (especially because such plants are typically at suboptimal scale). This 'rationalisation' of fragmented multi-plant production could be observed following EC-1992, for example.[31] On the other hand, 'deepening' facilitated the managerial efforts and enhanced the potential benefits of having integrated production, logistics and supplies throughout the common market. Thus, freer intra-EU trade and services as well as more suitable conditions in the factor markets made it easier to exploit the advantages of corporate integration across the internal market. An indirect indication is also that the upward trend in intra-EU FDI in the 1990s was accompanied by a substantial increase in both levels and shares of intra-industry, as well as intra-firm, intra-EU trade.

Empirical analysis of FDI is also hindered by an *identification problem* arises. The overwhelming impression is that EC-1992 has prompted a boost in intra-EU FDI. Is EC-1992 the only explanation, not a general trend towards globalisation?[32] Whereas in the empirical analysis of CU effects on trade one can model an 'anti-monde' – modelling what would have happened without the CU (see Chapter 6) – this is unlikely to be possible for FDI. Moreover, unlike trade, there is a stock-flow problem. Thus, it is known that, in the early 1990s the intra-EU FDI first levelled off and subsequently shrunk before strongly increasing again. After taking recessionary circumstances into account, would a shrinkage indicate a corporate *disintegration* in the EU? Almost certainly not. What ultimately matters for corporate integration are the stocks of FDI and the degree of corporate control, both across intra-EU borders. Paying attention merely to a flow measure which is positive but just lower than that in peak years says little about the stocks[33] and does not affect existing forms of control.

Brenton (1996) has employed a gravity model to verify the single market impact on intra-EU FDI and on FDI from Sweden (before membership), the USA and Japan. He finds that GDP has a strong effect on FDI flows;[34] indeed stronger than export. In the period 1982–93 the EU-effect is significant for EU investing countries – France, the UK and Germany – and it is much more pronounced in the (EC-1992) period 1988–93. More precisely, FDI outflows to other EU countries are much higher than can be explained on the basis of GDP, population and distance (and this is controlled for the enlargement with Spain and Portugal). Explaining this disproportional response by EC-1992 accords well with business surveys. It once again underlines that EC-1992 represented a unique episode.[35] Egger & Pfaffermayr (2004) confirm the EC-1992 effect. The authors find that, for EC-1992, the enlargement of 1995 (with Finland, Austria and Sweden) and the European

[29]Examples of facilitation include some harmonisation of company law including the SE, EU-level merger control, free movement of financial capital, genuine liberalisation of services and a mixture of approximation and some unification of property rights at EU level.

[30]For data on the early period, see Pelkmans (1984, pp. 140–2). See also Dunning (1997).

[31]Neary (2002) gives a rigorous proof, in theory, of this rationalisation effect.

[32]Also, worldwide FDI increased rapidly in that period, up to four times as fast as world trade growth.

[33]Although there is a presumption that the stocks should increase if the flow overcompensates depreciation or helps to finance the generation of firm-specific assets locally.

[34]As noted before, the reliance of FDI flows statistics is problematic. Not surprising, Brenton's results are subject to very high standard errors for the estimated equations. For an attempt to recast this type of analysis into a stock-flow adjustment framework, see Menil (1999), especially the annex.

[35]With ever increasing globalisation, driven by the FDI, it is becoming harder to isolate such 'special' causes. An example may illustrate that. In 1999 the FDI inflows into EU countries from other EU countries increased by no less than 80 per cent, after a similar hike in 1998. However, between 1993 (where EC-1992 ends) and 1997, intra-EU FDI grew only moderately. The advent of the euro has probably next to no role here (see *European Economy,* Supplement A, no. 12, December 2001). It is also true that, in those years, some huge single cases of M&A greatly influenced the overall 'flows'.

Agreements all boosted FDI but only for a few years.

Corporate integration can also be read from trends, levels and forms of extending control of entrepreneurial activity across borders. We briefly discuss mergers and acquisitions (M&A).

Trends in M&A are not easy to read because there are no official statistics and longer period series are often based on different definitions (for example, what deals are registered; number versus 'value'; only majority owners, hence no joint ventures). Some trends are sufficient, however, to indicate that the significance of the internal market has increased since the 1980s.[36]

- M&A deals tripled in number in the EU between 1987 and 1998 in one source. Starting from the early 1990s, however, the EU (and the world at large) show a clear cyclical pattern with a peak around 1999–2001 and a return to early 1990s' levels by 2003. This suggests that EC-1992 and other deepening has caused a once-and-for-all amplification of M&A activities inside the EU and with EU companies up to the early 1990s, and that later trends essentially move with globalisation trends.
- 'Pure' intra-EU M&A (that is, an EU company bidding for another EU company but across intra-EU borders) as a percentage of all M&A with an EU company (that is, also domestic and with non-EU) moved up a little from around 10 per cent before 1990 to 15 per cent by 1997, and then starts hovering around 17 per cent before returning to 15 per cent by 2003. This can be interpreted as a facilitation of EU corporate integration but only modestly so; the bulk of M&A takes place inside Member States and might well be seen as 'defensive' in the first instance; if not anti-competitive, it could still serve efficiency in the longer run.
- Sectorally, services attract about two-thirds of M&A activity, in other words, a higher share than tradable services make up of EU GNP. Since exports are far less easy or economically sensible in services (see Chapter 7) companies tend to revert to M&A more easily.
- Globalisation plays an ever increasing role in explaining intra-EU M&A.[37] EU companies invest far more than before in central Europe and Asia and probably the same goes for non-EU companies (in particular, those dependent on relatively low-skills-intensive products, or, for India, certain services). For instance, of all M&A conducted by EU15 companies worldwide, the share of intra-EU15 fell between the early 1990s and 2000–03 from 61 per cent to 48 per cent whereas the share of 'rest of Europe' (mainly the accession countries) jumped from 12 per cent to 19 per cent: at the same time an internal market and a globalisation effect. The relative attractiveness of Asia and central Europe forebodes an ever deeper trend of globalisation in the future and is, in and by itself, not worrying but a natural consequence of open markets both for factors and for trade.

ADDITIONAL READING

In these respects a more business-oriented approach to OLI – ownership, location and internalisation – may well be more useful. Table 10.1 identifies ten motives which can be interpreted as manifestations of OLI. However, this matrix was developed in a study of EU strategic alliances, where corporate control is partial or cooperative. Minority holdings or joint ventures are often used if companies, wishing to enter markets, have to get around legal or fiscal problems connected with mergers or full acquisitions. Therefore, the form may differ somewhat from FDI but the underlying advantages sought do not. Table 10.1 is developed to understand (FDI and) inter-firm collaboration ventures as responses to EC-1992 and other competitive challenges.

Except for motives no. 4 (R&D cost sharing) and no. 10 (orderly withdrawal), the alliance advantages may equally well apply to single-firm FDI. The matrix brings home the point that FDI can only be fully understood at the firm-strategic level.

[36]We employ three not entirely consistent Commission sources as the basis of these inferences: *European Economy,* Supplement A, no. 2, February 1999; *European Economy,* Supplement A, no. 12, December 2001; European Commission, *Mergers and Acquisitions: Note,* October 2004.

[37]M&A are not identical with FDI flows because greenfield investments, reinvested earnings and intra-company loans are included in FDI flows as well. Moreover, M&A statistics are based on 5 per cent ownership and FDI on 10 per cent ownership.

Table 10.1 Motives for EU alliances by sector

	Identifying and obtaining new technologies	Achieving or retaining cost leadership	Search for innovation even if possible alone	R&D cost sharing	Survival through special-isation on core com petences	Exploiting new product op-portunities	Exploiting opportunities in new geographical market	Re-establish critical mass	Scale economies	Orderly withdrawal
Air transport							X	0	0	X
Aerospace equipment	X			X				0	X	X
Computer	0					0	X			
Food and drinks			X			X			X	
Chemicals excl. pharma	0	X		X	0					X
Pharmaceuticals	0			0		0				
Biotechnology	X			X		X				
Telecoms equipment	X		X	0	X	X	0	X		0
Semi-conductors	X	X		X		X		X		
Auto components										
Vehicle assembly		X						0	X	X

0 = very important factor; X = important factor
Source: Adapted from the original table taken from the *Panorama of EU Industry'94*, © European Communities 1994

10.7 Locational competition for mobile assets

The greater the mobility of tangible assets of companies, the greater the importance of locational factors of regions and countries. Greater factor market integration induces fierce competition among regions in the EU to attract mobile, tangible assets such as production plants, distribution centres, services providers, research laboratories or indeed head offices of multinationals. This *locational competition* is driven not only by natural advantages, agglomeration effects (for example, centres of excellence, specialised skills) and specific forms of sourcing (for example, labour, sea harbours) but also by 'policy competition' and tax competition (see Case Study 10.1). Of course, locational competition is not a purely intra-EU affair: EU regions are keen to attract non-EU FDI as well.

Research on locational competition and regional policy (see Chapter 16) shows that there is not one single overriding location determinant or even one successful strategic 'package' of determinants. The interesting question in the context of this chapter is whether the nature, size and direction of asset mobility in the internal market are influenced by locational competition. There is important qualitative evidence (European Commission, 1991) that locational competition does play a role in all three aspects of this question. In appreciating business location decisions likely to involve the mobility of various factors, one has to realise the interconnection of the internal market for goods, services and factors alike, often in a context of globalisation as well. The nature of asset mobility has changed with deepening market integration. Many more non-EU multinationals have sought or now seek to establish themselves in the EU, with distribution on an EU-wide scale and/or with manufacturing or assembly. European and non-European established companies have frequently responded to EC-1992 with rationalisation and/or more EU-wide strategies. This has prompted intensified competition among regions for location or, indeed, relocation. Non-cost factors such as quality and availability of labour, and quality of infrastructure as well as the general business climate in the country (which is usually not region-bound) then become decisive elements. What this implies is that:

- the nature of asset mobility is not affected by locational competition, but changes in the former have greatly intensified the latter;
- the direction of asset mobility, however, is influenced. In the commission survey (1991), 75 per cent of the companies first chose an EU country, then the region, but 25 per cent chose between competing regions in different EU countries;
- the overall size of asset flows affected by locational competition cannot be measured, but there are indications that agglomeration effects are potentially strong. Reasons for mobile assets to cluster include (intermediate) supplier relationships, specialised skills, specialised services, access to information of high value, and proximity to business customers. As a result, regional clustering may to some extent imply sectoral clustering as well. However, agglomeration also involves trade aspects and is critical for regional and structural policies. That is why we return to the problem in Chapter 16.

CASE STUDY 10.1 Corporate tax competition in the internal market

The sensitivity of Member States' governments in the EU25 about corporate tax competition has greatly increased since the 1990s. Countries such as the new central European Member States and Ireland typically use statutory corporate tax rates far lower than customary in most of the other EU countries in order to attract FDI from multinationals, possibly to compensate for peripheral location or other disadvantages. More generally, corporate tax rates seem to have declined over a long period in Europe and, even in 2005, Germany announced further rate cuts. As noted in section 9.4, the EU had already agreed to tackle discriminatory corporate tax rates aimed solely at inducing profit shifting (via transfer pricing and otherwise) without a direct connection to the location of real economic activity in the country of taxation, via a wide-ranging code of conduct. This is bound to hit new EU countries (for example, Cyprus) as well in the future.

Is corporate tax competition influencing the location of economic activity and does it erode revenues (race to the bottom)? First, some generalised facts

CASE STUDY 10.1 *continued*

and subsequently an economic assessment (see Devereaux *et al.*, 2002). The generalised facts are: (1) statutory tax rates did fall over the 1980s and 1990s; (2) but the tax base (especially by reducing the scope of allowances for depreciation) was broadened almost everywhere which, of course, counters the first generalised fact; (3) the effective marginal tax rate has remained more or less stable (consistent with the combination of (1) and (2)); (4) effective average tax rates declined, however, notably for projects earning higher profits and more so for more profitable ones; (5) corporate tax revenues did not decline as a percentage of GDP but did as a percentage of overall tax revenue.

Simple models of tax competition are often said to explain corporate tax competition but they do not explain these trends in the internal market. These theories reason as follows. If capital is mobile in the internal market (a legal must and an observable fact), the post-tax rate of return earned on capital should be equated among EU countries. Thus, relatively high taxes in country A will raise the required pre-tax rate of return of capital and thereby prompt (some) capital to move to other EU countries: a negative spillover effect. Therefore, the optimal tax rate is lower than in the absence of capital mobility and, to the extent that only this revenue pays for public goods, it might lead to an underprovision of public goods. A serious weakness of this approach is that no distinction is made between the statutory rate and the tax base, essential in the generalised facts. Apart from distortive tax competition purely for profit shifting (see section 9.4), what can explain the slow decline in tax revenue as a percentage of overall revenue is the targeting of highly profitable multinationals. The latter tend to be more profitable than domestic firms (everywhere in the world) and, if not too footloose, can be expected to yield significant economic benefits to the local economy via firm-specific advantages, upgrading local suppliers, setting quality standards, learning effects, spreading knowledge about other markets, and so on. Thus, other tax revenue is likely to increase as a result of successfully attracting FDI. All in all, it is plausible that the location of economic activity in the internal market is influenced somewhat by corporate tax competition but this seems far removed from a 'race to the bottom'. If and to the extent that such corporate tax competition is perceived as an erosion of the economic activity in 'old' Member States, and strategic interaction between Member States intensifies this, some modest harmonisation of the tax base could be a good solution as the distortions arising from endlessly playing around with the tax base amplify the already high transaction costs of firms operating throughout the internal market. Tax rates should either not be harmonised, however, or be free above a low minimum rate so as to maintain some exposure to tax competition, which is a healthy check on (Leviathan-type) governments.

Relocation of tangible assets often implies delocation for other regions or countries. Although costly because of severance packages for workers, EC-1992 has not on the whole experienced significant resistance against relocation, as part of restructuring and rationalisation. But there is one exception, to be discussed in Case Study 15.1 on social dumping: if asset mobility is induced by (downward) competition in social policies between Member States, sensitivity in Europe is great. Locational competition is now practised by virtually all regions in the EU. In Chapter 16 we shall have occasion to study more closely the likelihood of agglomeration, locational competition and regional disparities and the role of EU structural policies in this respect.

10.8 Summary

Factor market integration in the EU is multifaceted and its economic analysis is hindered by caveats about economic theory and available data.

In a simple partial-equilibrium two-countries model, the net welfare gain of labour mobility is unambiguous, although there are losers too. In a simple general equilibrium graph of a common capital market, one may explain why trade unions of the capital outflow country may resist free movement of capital.

Among a series of caveats and possible extensions, one may emphasise the various substitutabilities and

Summary ***continued***

complementarities between different types of factor flows as well as between factor flows and trade (both in goods and services). A sensitive issue is also the question of whether free factor flows would not cause an increasingly wide income gap between core and peripheral regions in the EU (more on this in Chapter 16).

Financial capital market integration has been greatly strengthened by EC-1992 and, subsequently, by the arrival of the euro and technology for remote access to securities trade. However, there is doubt whether exchange controls had been effective, before their abolition, or had merely altered the structure of capital movements in the medium term by finding substitutive transaction patterns not caught by controls. Deeper financial integration is good for economic welfare and growth, but, in EU practice, the dichtomy between (integrating) wholesale activities and (fragmented) retail is so sharp still, that reaping all of the potential economic gains is not going to happen soon.

Cross-border intra-EU labour flows are residual in character. Various market mechanisms other than intra-EU labour flows tend to respond to relative scarcities of labour (with different skills). Third-country labour may have reduced incentives for intra-EU low-skilled labour to migrate in the EU, even though the former could not move across intra-EU borders for work until 2003. It is possible to identify the long-term and short/medium-term determinants of intra-EU migration – with cost items, restrictions and staying-put incentives being negative ones, and push and pull factors being positive ones. A common immigration policy is slowly coming into being, hard pressed by a peak of political and economic refugees and migrants in the 1990s, up to 2003.

The functioning of the internal market for technology is difficult to verify since a lot of technology flows remain within (EU-wide) firms or within networks. The success of the European Patent Office in reducing transactions costs of filing is impressive. There is some empirical evidence that business alliances and networks (not necessarily only within the EU) have greatly increased in importance for the generation and diffusion of technology and know-how.

Also, the Europeanisation of business has received a strong boost since the mid-1980s. Gravity models have demonstrated strong intra-EU FDI effects from EC-1992. Other data, such as those relating to mergers and acquisitions, point in the same direction. However, globalisation also begins to determine choices of 'vertical' FDI, including alternative locations for part of the value chain (such as central Europe and Asia).

Locational competition, especially among regions, for mobile, tangible assets has greatly increased with factor market integration, along with goods and services market integration. There are indications that such competition does affect the direction, and possibly the size, of factor mobility in Europe. Corporate tax competition in Europe does have an impact on FDI flows and a measured case for harmonisation (of the tax base, not the rate or only at a low minimum) can be made.

PART 3

Common Policies

From the outset of the EEC, the novel idea of a common market was inextricably related to common policies. No other postwar attempt of economic regionalism anywhere in the world has assumed such demanding ambitions. The three 'heavy-weight' common policies – agriculture, competition and trade – are a direct consequence of the kind of common market wanted. In agriculture, sacrificing heavy interventionism for the sake of free movement in agricultural goods was politically unthinkable. Whereas EFTA chose to leave agriculture out, incorporating it in the EEC was bound to be conditioned by common interventionism before allowing intra-EC market integration. A common competition policy resulted from the importance of letting the common market function properly, once established. This can be expected neither from national competition policies – and surely not from those in the mid-1950s – nor from their coordination. A common trade policy is a logical part of the comprehensive form of product market integration. Building on the CU with a CET (and common quotas), the intra-EC removal of regulatory and fiscal barriers for free movement of goods requires a much more ambitious common trade policy.

Of the other common policies, the common transport policy has finally come to mean little more than regulatory approximation and (some) fiscal harmonisation so as to permit free movement of these services (see Chapter 7). The rising status of environmental regulatory approximation amounts, thus far, mostly to a prerequisite to prevent regulatory barriers or distortions of competition in the internal market. It is in principle no different from national environmental policies, but the necessity of constraints or minimum requirements in the internal market may justify EU rules or policies (see Case Study 4.1). Therefore, there is no separate chapter in this book. The only major exception is that the EU acts and speaks as 'one' in world climate policies. A choice is made to deal with the EU's industrial policy, including sector, technology and horizontal policies. Altogether, not only is this complex set of policies important for the proper functioning of the internal market and future wealth creation, but it has also been a controversial issue for decades which justifies a discussion of crucial analytical issues about good and bad economic policy.

Part 3 incorporates both methods and economic analysis in every chapter. Chapter 11 surveys the common agricultural policy and reform issues. Chapter 12 is about the common competition policy, including anti-collusion; anti-monopoly (together 'anti-trust'), merger control and the regime on state aids. Chapter 13 addresses the common trade policy, including tariffs and volume protection, anti-dumping (which overlaps with competition policy), EU's preferentialism and the Union's general stance on multilateralism. Chapter 14 inspects industrial policy, its economic justification and today's and past manifestations at EU level.

CHAPTER 11

Common Agricultural Policy

Topics covered

The customs union or the free movement of goods in the common market does not automatically extend to agricultural trade. Article 32 EC stipulates that the 'common market for agricultural products must be accompanied by the establishment of a common agricultural policy among the Member States'. There should be no illusion about the interventionist nature of such a common agricultural policy (CAP), even if several reform waves since the early 1990s have altered the 'old' CAP considerably. In Europe, modern agronomic intervention goes back more than a century. In the 1950s, the six founding countries all applied border protection, combined with a variety of domestic interventions with different intensities. Agricultural quotas had been notoriously difficult to remove in the OEEC liberalisation attempts while a Green Pool of freer trade had failed. The upshot was that intra-European agricultural trade had a residual character and was heavily distorted. The GATT had effectively taken agriculture out of its tariff rounds.

Since the CAP is a sectoral policy, the chapter begins with an attempt to formulate a case for the CAP on economic and social adjustment grounds. Section 11.2 discusses the objectives, principles and instruments of the CAP. Since income support for European farmers is prominent among the objectives, four types of income policy used in the CAP are analysed in section 11.3 with respect to welfare effects and, in a limited way, political economy. They include agro-levies as such and agro-levies with intra-EU price support, deficiency payments, direct income payments and supply quotas. Section 11.4 provides an economic assessment of the actual performance of the CAP, before the reform waves set in, with respect to market integration, the five treaty objectives (in Article 33), the costs to consumers, the EU budget and the costs to third countries, as well as the much neglected macroeconomic costs. Section 11.5 addresses CAP reform, beginning with a brief explanation of the initial 'reform resistance' of the CAP in terms of political economy. It also provides a discussion of the four main drivers of CAP reform. Subsequently, the transformation from the 'old' CAP to the 'new' CAP is set out in section 11.5.2. The economic and regulatory principles which should underlie further CAP reforms are brought together in section 11.5.3.

11.1 A case for the CAP?

Income support has social and political reasons. An economic case for the CAP's income support is difficult to make in a market economy where economic agents in other sectors also face the risk of gradual or sudden income decline.[1] This is not to say that agriculture does not suffer from special income effects. These relate to the structural level of income and its short-term instability. They help to explain certain features of agricultural policies, but they do not justify the CAP as it emerged.

The structural level of agricultural income can only increase under special conditions. Most agricultural produce is a part of the food budget of citizens, and income elasticities are therefore low (Engel's law). In consequence, demand expansion of the agricultural sector must largely arise from the increase in the population rather than from the rise in income levels. On the supply side, a steady technological progress has easily kept pace with the secular population increases. Hence, supply has tended to outgrow demand at the ruling prices: a structural excess supply of agricultural workers was created. This would be no special problem if there were a continuous increase in the demand for labour in the industrial and services sectors. Assuming a given cost of physical capital input, farmers' income need not fall if, for a given product demand, labour exit matches the increase in labour productivity. Should the price fall, however, it will cause only a marginal increase in demand because of saturation of food consumption in high-income countries (low price elasticity of demand). Neither will the price fall cause a contraction of the volume of supply, as farmers typically do not leave the land once settled, and capital investment will have to be recouped in order to service debts (that is, low price elasticity of supply). The upshot is a structural downward pressure on absolute agricultural incomes – dependent on agricultural technical progress and agricultural labour exit – as well as on relative agricultural income (*vis-à-vis* industry). If enough agricultural workers and farmers leave the sector, absolute incomes may grow but relative agricultural income might still fall.

The short-term stability of agricultural income is threatened by price instability. The source of instability is usually on the supply side and may consist of bad weather or exogenous changes in the costs of inputs. This will lead to sharp price variations. If upwards, it may induce short-run investments, giving rise to magnified supply increases in later seasons, causing a price fall again: the well-known 'cobweb analysis' (sometimes called the pig cycle). A cobweb converges to an equilibrium price if the (absolute) price elasticity of demand is greater than that of supply; if not, it is explosive. In developed countries, demand elasticities tend to decrease with a secular rise in income (people can afford the same volume at a higher price, at least over the short run), while supply elasticities do not change much. Therefore, high-income countries have, *ceteris paribus,* a higher degree of uncertainty about future agricultural incomes, derived from free markets, than in the past.

In general terms, however, one can formulate a case for the main objectives of the CAP when considering Europe's transformational processes over a generation or so. The case is not purely economic and is temporary. This case for the CAP objectives should also not be confused with the reasons advanced by the European farmer organisations, although they partly overlap. The present case is formulated as a conscious choice for a second-best policy, knowing that the collection of national policies is unlikely to be better. The weakness of the case is that it is focused solely on the objectives, seemingly justifying whatever instruments are needed to pursue the former.

The EC6 had nearly 23 per cent of the workforce in agriculture in 1958, down from over 30 per cent in the late 1940s. For another generation or longer, a high rate of labour exit from agriculture was expected to be part of a transformation to an industrial, and later a service, society with much stronger urbanisation and a rationalised agro-industrial complex (for the actual labour exit, see Figure 11.1[2]). A failure to absorb this labour into other sectors would cause relative, and possibly even absolute, agricultural income to fall steadily. This would destabilise society and in any event be unacceptable in a period when the European welfare states were being constructed. Rationalisation of Europe's agriculture would occur via market integration – the CU part of the CAP – and technical progress. At the same time, the CAP would protect farmers' income without the latter being on the social

[1]Unless one assumes, with Corden (1975), that individual 'welfare' functions are interdependent. For instance, there may be grounds to believe (or the farm lobby succeeds in having people perceive) that major or secular decreases in farmers' income inflict marginally upon one's own utility. If so, (rational) income protection *à la* Corden would imply a utility increase for non-farmers equal to the latter's utility decrease due to the farmer's income decline in the absence of such protection.

[2]For comparison, the new Member States (Poland, Hungary) have been included in Figure 11.1. Both countries have also experienced a considerable fall in this share of agricultural workers but the harmonised Eurostat data do not go back far enough to show this trend for them as well.

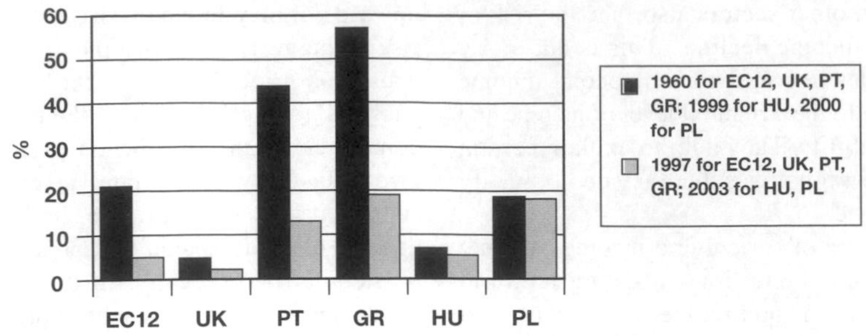

Figure 11.1 Share of agricultural in total working population

payroll (which farmers refused even to consider). The Community's strong growth orientation in the Rome Treaty could ensure a steady rise in the demand for labour.

Basing the case for a CAP on the transformation of Europe's economy and society would seem to have been implicitly accepted for several decades. It accorded well with another political driver to create a CAP, namely, the wish of EEC6 countries to be or remain largely self-sufficient (be it in a small group of associated countries) after the war experience of 'hunger winters' and food shortages. The social and the self-sufficiency rationals have probably facilitated the electorate's tolerance of the negative effects and costs of the CAP as implemented. For it is the instruments and their application which present the real economic policy problem. Even when the case is granted as a good argument during a generation or so, the question remains: if income protection is desirable, how is this best done? How did the actual CAP pursue this key goal and how was this combined with product market integration? How should the results be assessed? These questions will concern us in the remainder of the chapter.[3]

11.2 Objectives, principles and instruments

The Rome Treaty defines the objectives of the CAP; a conference was held in Stresa in 1958 to work out the details. Since Stresa, three principles would seem to be carved in stone: a single product market, so-called Community preference (that is, high trade barriers around this single market), and financial solidarity among the Member States (sharing levies and other revenues as well as the overall intervention costs). The first two together could be interpreted as a CU with a sufficiently high CET. Because of income protection, however, the CET at the product level was made into a variable one. The variable levies governed trade with third countries until 1995, when they were converted into (high) fixed tariffs. This is supplemented by intra-EU price support for which the third principle prescribes joint financing. Stresa and the early 1960s witnessed the emergence of four ways to intervene in markets for purposes of income protection and subsidiary goals: the variable levy/price support systems for core agricultural product markets with low elasticities of supply (for example, grain, sugar, dairy, beef and pork, table wine and certain fish products, and selected fruits and vegetables); variable levies only; deficiency payments; and direct income payments under specific conditions.

For a good understanding of the CAP, its evolution, its several reforms in the 1990s, the triangular relationship between objectives, principles and instruments should be kept in mind. Figure 11.2 summarises its formal structure.

It should be observed that there are several serious problems with the list of five CAP objectives. Objective 2 in Article 33 EC is preceded by the words 'thus to ensure' (a fair standard of living), implying that objective 1 (efficiency) is considered instrumental to the objective of agricultural incomes. As has been set out above, productivity increases in agriculture should be matched by a decrease in factor inputs, especially labour, before efficiency translates into (fair)

[3]In practice, a dramatic politicisation of the CAP has taken place. This book cannot go deeply into the political economy of the CAP. However, for a full understanding of the CAP it is neither fruitful nor realistic to ignore the politics of this common interventionism. See the essays in Pelkmans (1985a) for public choice, political economy and historical explanations of the actual implementations of the CAP. See also Munk (1994).

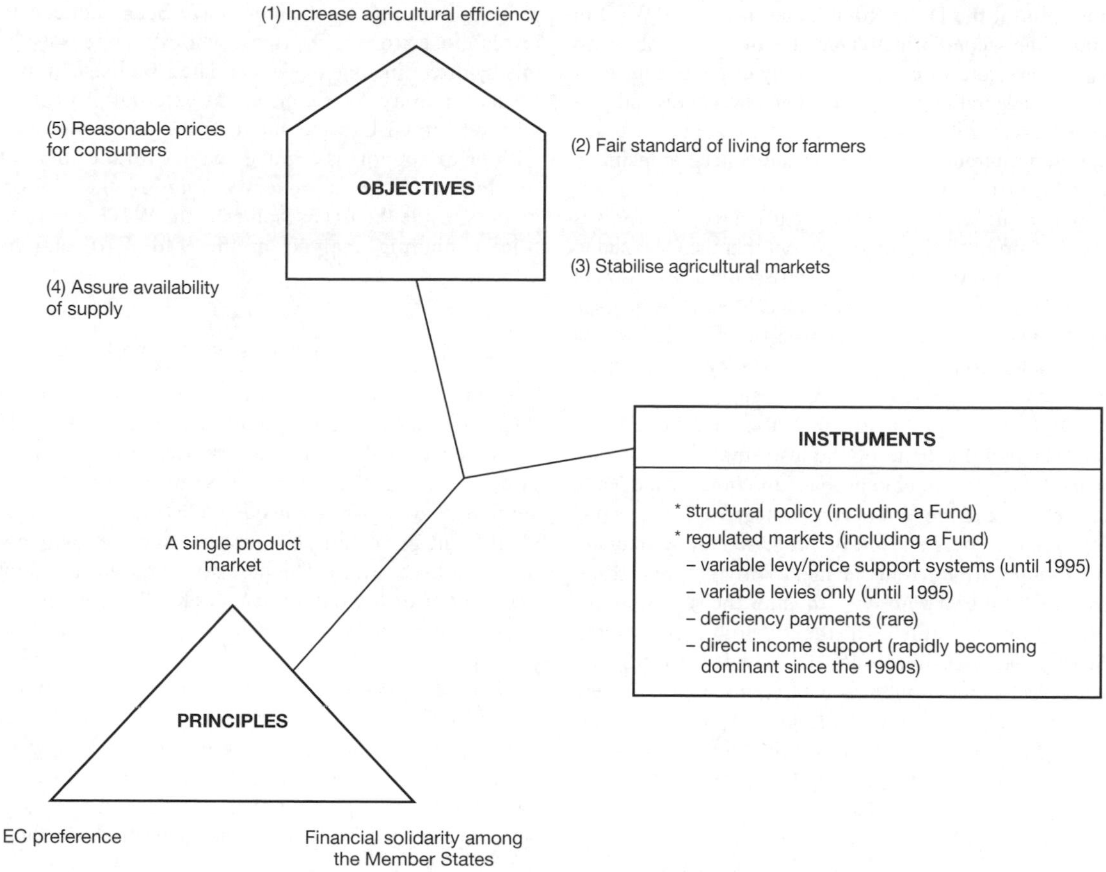

Figure 11.2 The CAP's triangle

incomes. Perhaps the link between the first and the second objective should be related specifically to the 'optimum utilisation of all factors of production', a phrase that could mean the appropriate rate of decrease of labour input. However, if this were correct, one would expect a view on how the desirable labour mobility can be made to match technological progress. Since the treaty is silent on this important issue, one has to presume that the growth climate of the 1950s, with close to full employment, was considered sufficiently conducive to generate labour mobility without noticeable absorption problems.[4]

The actual practice of the CAP has clearly shown that the (level and stability of) income objectives are paramount among the five CAP objectives. However, the instruments used cause negative side-effects *vis-à-vis* other CAP objectives and the overall objective of integration itself. Indeed, as the first CAP principle says, the five objectives must be pursued under free trade within the CU (called the 'common market' in Article 32). This obviously relates to the optimum utilisation of factors (objective 1), implying regional specialisation in the CU. The principle was not adhered to during periods of exchange rate volatility. Faced with the choice between the avoidance of income adjustment to currency appreciation and the single market, the latter was sacrificed time and again. Another constraint has undoubtedly been neglected. Article 18 (now deleted), on the common external tariff of the CU, explicitly mentions the Member States' 'readiness to contribute to the development of international trade and the lowering of barriers to trade'.[5] In the CAP the declared readiness was simply

[4]Article 36 provides for exceptions, based on structural or natural conditions or within the framework of economic development programmes.

[5]Similarly positive intentions can be found in the Preamble, in Arts 27 and 131.

absent until the Doha Round, ongoing in the WTO in 2005. The second principle and the overriding objective of income protection ensure a totally different climate. It is not exaggerating to say that there always was and, to a lesser extent, still is a readiness to frustrate international agricultural trade (by export subsidies) and to maintain very high barriers.

Once one realises the full significance of objectives and constraints, it becomes evident that the CAP had to be constructed in some compromise form. The constraint of (external) trade liberalisation has literally been given up. However, that by itself conflicts with objective 5 on reasonable consumer prices, and may occasionally conflict with objective 4 on supply security.

Objectives could also conflict among themselves, but that would depend on the instruments chosen (see below). One formidable problem of choice is hidden in the second and most important objective. The question is, *which* farmers should be promised a fair standard of living: all current farmers only, or also their existing children who wish to enter the sector, or any other new entrants? In the twenty-first century, farming as a professional activity is still a sector where (EU) employment is contracting. Given modern agricultural techniques and optimal farm sizes, the ratio of agricultural to total working population can be very low without generating a shortage of domestic supply.

11.3 Income protection, alternative CAP methods

The four CAP methods of income protection indicated in Figure 11.2 will be dealt with.[6] Three out of four methods have led to severe budgetary problems which, in some cases, are contained by supply quotas. A brief look at such quotas is therefore included as well.

11.3.1 The agro-levy system

The agro-levy system (ALS) was, until 1995, the core of the CAP. It no longer is today for two reasons: the Uruguay Round has turned the variable levies into fixed levies, usually very high ones, and intra-EU price guarantees for farmers have been reduced to levels closer to world prices, while 'compensating' this by direct income payments. The ALS exists in two forms: the pure ALS consists of external protection without intra-EU price support; the ALS combined with price support is a much heavier form of market regulation. A good understanding of the reform process inside the EU as well as in the WTO requires a brief economic analysis of the 'old' CAP and its effects.

11.3.1.1 Trade policy as income protection

The pure ALS uses trade policy as the means to protect intra-EU prices, which, in turn, are expected to yield desirable income levels for farmers. Hence, no minimum prices are upheld via the purchase of incipient excess supplies. Good harvests inside the EU may thus cause significant price falls but non-EU supplies will not undercut high prices. The pure ALS is used for about one-quarter of EU output, namely for flowers, quality wine, rice, certain fruits and vegetables, eggs and poultry.

The levy system shields domestic agricultural prices from those in the world market by import levies if the world market prices are lower, and by export levies if world prices are higher. In theory, the ALS can be used for pure short-term stabilisation purposes. The two (tough) conditions are that domestic agricultural

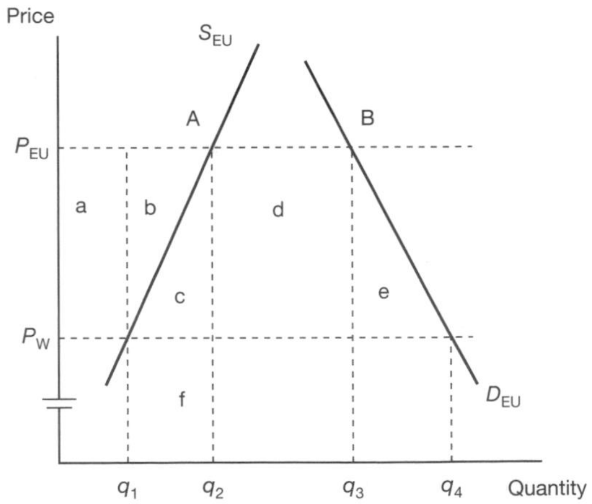

Figure 11.3 Agro-levies: EU imports

[6]The literature on the methods is large and need not to be quoted here. The author has benefited in particular from various manuscripts of Gerrit Meester.

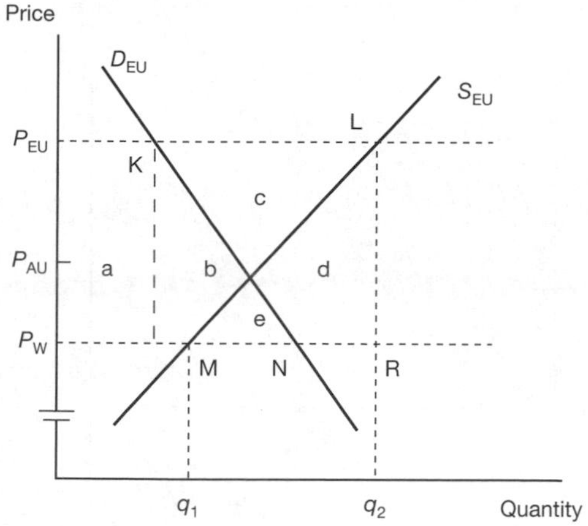

Figure 11.4 Agro-levies: EU exports

prices follow world prices, except for sudden price jumps or dives, and that intervention should automatically fade out in the short run, over, say, one or two seasons.

However, it is the longer-term deviation from world prices, irrespective of their level or direction of change, which makes the ALS a true income policy. The approach is totally protectionist: before 1995, no link between domestic prices and world prices was permitted.

In Figures 11.3 and 11.4, the static 'welfare' and redistributive effects have been illustrated. If the EC's autarky price lies above P_W (the world price), the levy $P_{EU} - P_W$ restricts imports from the world to AB (Figure 11.3). This high price policy serves as an income policy since it increases domestic agricultural income with a + b. The consumers pay these higher incomes through higher prices. However, they pay much more, because, in addition to a + b, they pay d as levy revenue to the Agricultural Fund and c and e as 'welfare losses', due to excess production costs over those of imports (c) and due to a net deterioration of consumption possibilities for those not willing to pay P_{EU} (e). The levy revenue d is used for export subsidies in other agricultural products, or for export subsidies in the same product at some later date (in case self-sufficiency is reached).

Figure 11.4 portrays the case of excess supply KL, carrying an export subsidy per unit of $P_{EU} - P_W$ to enable EU producers to find an outlet on the world market. At *P*w the EU would import MN. Production at L increases agricultural income with $P_{EU}L(P_{EU} - Pw)$ of which the Agricultural Fund pays $(P_{EU} - P_W)$KL to the farmers exporting to the world. The Fund is paid by taxpayers and, for import-competing goods, by consumers. The high welfare costs to the EU of export subsidies (so, quite apart from the damage they inflict on third countries) can be read from the shrinkage of consumption (to K, causing b + e as consumption losses of which e remains uncompensated by producer gains), the increase of inefficient production (to L, with e and d as excess production costs over those of the world competitors), and the budgetary 'loss' of the EU (KL × LR). The costs are so high because export subsidies must imply artificial surpluses, prompted by high protection, which are subsequently dumped: in fact, three times welfare costs are incurred.

Assessing pure ALS can be done with the help of three criteria: least social costs, the benefits for small versus large farmers, and other costs of government failure. Using least social costs, ALS is not a matter of pure transfers to farmers: the net 'welfare' costs to the domestic economy (c + e) are an extra burden. The world economy does not suffer given the assumption of a given world price (as the EU is big, this assumption will be dropped later).

In a multi-product analysis costs are higher. Feedstock grains protected by levies are substitutable by goods that are duty free (as, in the EU, is the case for soya beans, corn gluten and tapioca). Dependent on the degree of substitutability (which tends to increase price elasticities of supply), welfare costs may be larger for this product but negative for others. However, it requires a multi-product framework, with alternative input structures and data on the coverage of the ALS, before detailed conclusions can be drawn. Nonetheless, there is a presumption that prices will rise for many more agricultural goods than those falling under the ALS as cost rises in inputs cannot be fully prevented via substitution, and will be shifted to consumers.

The second criterion, the income redistribution between large and small farmers, cannot be applied without additional knowledge about cost functions for both types. For a large number of agricultural products, there tends to be a negative relation between average costs and the quantity of inputs such as (roughly homogeneous) land, technology or physical capital (including cattle). It follows that, for income policies to be effective for the marginal, often small and backward farmer, prices have to be set substantially beyond the costs for efficient large farmers. In so doing, the large farmers benefit disproportionately from the CAP, although the 'standard of living' problem resides with the marginal farmers. Consider Figure 11.5 where the left graph shows the marginal

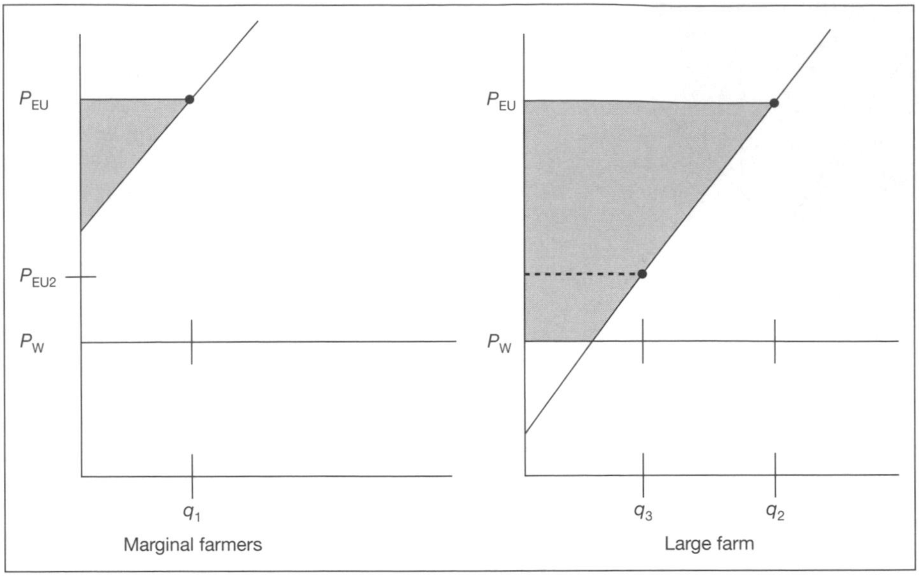

Figure 11.5 Inequitable CAP

farmers with steep marginal cost (supply) schedules, beginning at a cost price much higher than P_W. The right-hand graph depicts larger farmers who could even compete in the world market for a limited output. Figure 11.5 assumes that $q_2 = 3\ q_1$, that is, the output of large farms is three times that of marginal farms. The marginal farmers could not survive without a high P_{EU} guarantee. For them, a 'fair standard of living' is an existential issue. As drawn, the larger farmers obtain roughly five times the revenue (shaded areas) of the marginal farmers, and, of course, this discrepancy is amplified if counted per single farm (because there are far fewer large farms).

This causes a number of secondary effects that static graphs do not reflect. One such effect is that large advanced farmers can (and do) purchase even more technology, physical capital and, possibly, land. In turn, this leads to a rise in the price of land which, if anything, works against income improvement for the marginal farmer. It also creates great obstacles for new, well-trained entrants into farming.

Even if transfers to farmers are politically accepted, there may be other costs. Politicians prefer the 'invisible' transfers from consumers to farmers via higher prices (just as they prefer tariffs) to 'visible', income subsidies, despite the lower social costs of direct subsidies. The most important reason for avoiding tariffs – the threat of retaliation – used to be practically irrelevant in agriculture since it was left out of GATT negotiations up until the Uruguay Round. Administratively, levies are easy to implement. So, administrators are likely to favour the comfort and certainty of the ALS over systems with direct subsidies, tax preferences or hybrids of tax and subsidy with all their administrative cumbersomeness and a significantly lower degree of control. There is also an administrative convenience in the ALS to market integration since it applies a common tariff for the CU as a whole.

But additional costs do arise in the case of export subsidies. They are administratively cumbersome and verification is tedious. The EC Court of Auditors, and more and more often the Commission, uncover numerous cases of sloppy application and even outright fraud. A special EU anti-fraud taskforce has been in operation since 1991.

11.3.1.2 Agro-levies with intra-EU price support

For the core of non-Mediterranean agricultural products such as grain, beef, pork, milk and sugar, but also for table wine and fish products, levies are in fact a supplement of intra-EU price support. This system of market regulation (here, denoted as ALPS – agro-levy price support) is analysed under three simplifying assumptions: given intra-EU exchange rates, a given world price for the relevant product, and no substitution effect in the use of acreage, in feedstock or otherwise. The restrictiveness of these assumptions will be discussed later.

Five prices enter the analysis. Three prices are *ex ante* prices (that is, before crop growing), based on forecasts of demand and supply and decided upon in highly politicised marathon meetings of the EU Council of Ministers. The *target price* is that price with which EU farmers are supposed to maintain to appropriately increase their standard of living. It follows that the target price is a political price. It also serves as the linchpin of the support system. The target price can be higher than, equal to or lower than the autarky price. The *threshold price* is a price for customs officers: it is the world price plus the relevant levy – since the world price varies over time, the threshold price for every agro-product also varies over time.[7] Since the early 1990s, reforms have tackled the target price but not the threshold price – the latter is only reduced in the WTO context. For grains, the 1992 reforms left the threshold price untouched at a very high level, while the target price was reduced by one-third. The Uruguay Round subsequently reduced threshold prices by cutting the levies by 36 per cent. In the Doha Round, the EU has offered levy cuts of up to 65 per cent.

The *intervention price,* or floor price, is the minimum wholesale price for farmers that is guaranteed by political decision and upheld by offices authorised to make intervention purchases. Intervention offices act whenever there is excess supply.

Two prices are *ex post* prices determined by private and public demand and supply. One is the *world price.* Since many countries in the world practise protectionist agricultural policies, the world market is a residual market and prices sometimes fluctuate wildly. In other words, protection can be seen as the export of instability. In addition, the EU frequently unloads excess production on the world market with the aid of 'export subsidies' (in Community language, 'restitutions'), further adding to instability and artificially depressing prices for foreign suppliers in the world market. As we shall see, the EU export subsidies have drastically declined, but only very recently. Our assumption to take the world price as given, therefore, assumes away some serious problems (see section 11.3.1.3).

The fifth price is the *actual market price* in the EU which must be equal to or above the intervention price.

Consider Figure 11.6, with a higher threshold (border) price P_{thr1}, a lower one P_{thr2}, and the intervention price P_{int} (considerably above the world price P_W). There is one EU demand schedule D_{EU} and two supply schedules, S_{1EU} and S_{2EU}, the latter of which is more elastic owing to structural productivity increases and/or the weather. Assume, first, that at the end of the season S_{1EU} prevails, as forecast. For simplicity, we can think of market clearance at F as precisely what the agricultural ministers had in mind when setting the target price. Observe that this self-sufficiency is protected from world supplies by the higher threshold price P_{thr1}. There will be no external trade, no tariff revenue, but also no export subsidies. The EU consumers are stuck with high prices and the farmers (presumably) earn a 'fair standard of living'. Now, the threshold price falls to P_{thr2}, say, because of the Uruguay Round. What

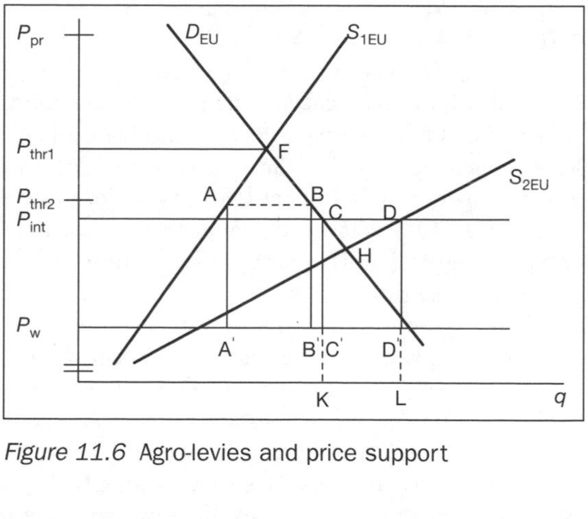

Figure 11.6 Agro-levies and price support

[7]Of course, this is no different from the intra-EU price of any imported good subjected to the CET (see section 6.1). However, this is new for EU agriculture. Up to 1995, the threshold price was calculated differently, namely, it would be derived from the target price, for example by deducting the transport costs from major harbours to a central place of consumption. This meant that, usually, the threshold price was high (to protect the EU farmers) and fixed in ECU (because the target price was fixed in ECU). To keep the threshold prices fixed, the influence of fluctuating world prices had to be eliminated. This was done by making the levy variable: no matter how low the world price fell, it would (still) not improve the levy-inclusive price – the levy would simply be increased on a weekly basis – the EU agro-market for all goods remained insulated. The Uruguay Round has outlawed variable levies. So, today, levies are fixed, hence the levy-inclusive prices of imports vary with world prices.

happens is that world imports have market access (AB) and the tariff revenue for the EU is ABB′A′. Figure 11.6 is drawn such that the cuts in levies agreed in the Uruguay Round lead immediately to actual access. In fact, agro-levies were often so high that even a 36 per cent cut did not result in imports such as AB; the initial levies were prohibitive (like P_{pr}). The present Doha Round might change that, if cuts of 50–65 per cent are indeed agreed.

Note that, for S_{1EU} as given, the intervention price P_{int} is of no consequence. It is obvious that P_{thr2} will never be below P_{int}, because it would force EU intervention for outside suppliers. However, P_{int} becomes important once the supply rotates to the right. For S_{2EU} and given demand, there is excess supply CD at P_{int}, but, since this would tend to force the market clearing price down to H, EU offices would intervene. The EU buys up the surplus CD at a cost of CD × P_{int}, so that at least this (gross) income for the farmers remains guaranteed. If these goods are not perishable (soon), for example grains or milk powder, the EU has traditionally sought outlets on the world market for these surpluses. Ignoring for the moment that the EU is a big player in world agro-markets, and the more so since global agro-trade is 'residual' due to protectionism all around, we assume that P_W is not influenced by this dumping. In that case, the EU will recuperate C′D′LK as sales revenue. If farmers themselves seek outlets on the world market, they receive 'export subsidies' CDD′C′ and C′D′LK as sales revenue.

The first serious reform of the CAP in 1992 (the MacSharry reforms) reduced grain prices by one-third. How can this move be incorporated into Figure 11.6? What happened was that the intervention price was pushed down to ECU 100 per tonne, then close to the world price. If P_{int} is lowered, it might come close to or or end up lower than H, and thus the surpluses would dry up. Yet, the threshold price was kept at ECU 155, which, in Figure 11.6, could be said to be reflected by P_{thr1}, if not higher. Still, the economic impact was not entirely domestic for the Union. If CD shrinks (due to a reduced P_{int}), export subsidies are likely to shrink as well, hence the reduction or removal of a very disturbing distortion of world markets. This effect is amplified by a likely shift of D_{EU} to the right, because, with grain prices close to world prices, it becomes attractive for EU farmers to substitute imported feedstock by EU-origin grains. As a result, we should expect the grain surplus to disappear and export subsidies of, for example, flour from grains, to dry up. Market access for competitive grain suppliers such as the USA, Australia, Canada and Argentina remains impossible, be it that the Uruguay Round reduced P_{thr} by 36 per cent.

The second CAP reform, called Agenda 2000, finally agreed in Berlin in 1999, was less convincing. In grains, the price reduction was 15 per cent. Although weaker, the analysis is similar to the one above.

11.3.1.3 Export subsidies and perverse trade

Given widespread agricultural protection practically all over the world, given low elasticities, and given the sheer magnitude of EU residual demand and supply (the EU being the largest trade bloc in the world), the assumption of the EU facing an infinitely elastic world supply at constant prices seems unduly restrictive. Dropping this assumption leads to three principal effects. First, the EU will acquire a terms-of-trade gain under the ALS, when it is an importer. Second, it will incur a terms-of-trade loss once it becomes an exporter, dumping surpluses on the world market. Third, it will, by implication, export instability. Although most GATT / WTO members are protectionist in agriculture, the ALS did not permit any transmission of price fluctuations from the world market (until 1995) and this tended to amplify price fluctuations in the world market.

The first two effects are illustrated in Figure 11.7, where excess supply and demand schedules are depicted for the EU (right-hand quadrant) and the rest of the world (W) (left-hand quadrant, defined positively). The world's excess supply S_W turns into excess demand D_W in the right-hand quadrant. At the equilibrium free trade price P_{FT} the EU imports OB = OA from the rest of the world. The target CAP price is

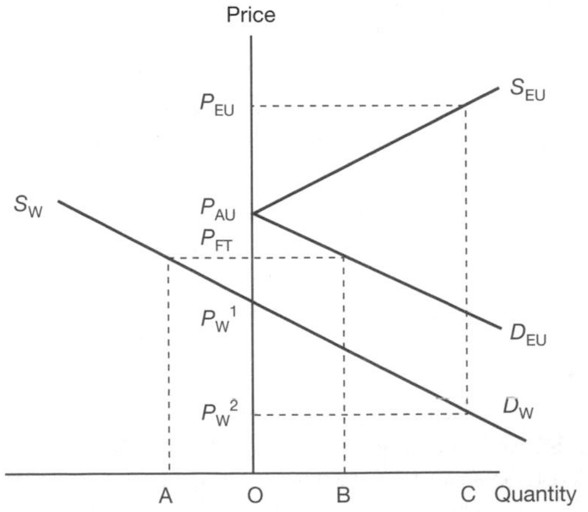

Figure 11.7 CAP export subsidies and terms of trade

Source: Adapted from Sampson & Snape, 1980, p. 1031, © 1980 by the University of Chicago

P_{EU}, yielding a surplus of OC. If the EU merely keeps its market closed, any EU price P_{AU} (autarky price) or higher would force the world market price down to $P_W{}^1$. This must mean that, as long as the EU is still importing, it will obtain a terms-of-trade gain. However, if it provides (variable) export subsidies, the price fall in the world market must be much larger. This prompts a perverse trade pattern.

In order to find sufficient demand in the world market to sell its surplus OC, the necessary export subsidy per unit is $P_{EU}-P_W{}^2$. Hence the mere disposal of OC at such huge subsidies turns the rest of the world from an exporter into an importer. This trade inversion is bound to deny many marginal non-EU producers the possibility either to export or to receive prices sufficient for their standard of living. Figure 11.6 also makes clear that reforms for grains should, in reducing or eliminating export subsidies, raise the world grain price perhaps up to $P_W{}^1$, *ceteris paribus.* Would EU grain be used for feedstock again, because of the price fall (a lower P_{EU}), the autarky price P_{AU} will increase. However, since there will be a big wedge between the threshold price (say, the old P_{EU}) and the world price without EU exports ($P_W{}^1$), the world price cannot further improve on account of world exports to the EU. The EU, on the other hand, will recoup its *ex ante* terms of trade loss. We conclude that CAP reforms, which lower the internal intervention price, are even more beneficial under variable world prices. The reduction or elimination of export subsidies leads to a restoration of world prices, coming closer to reflecting comparative advantages. The EU itself will incur a smaller (or no) terms-of-trade loss.

11.3.2 Deficiency payments

Deficiency payments schemes (DPSs) are also based on an *ex ante* guaranteed price for all EU farmers for a given product. Deficiency payments to farmers cover the 'deficiency' between the market price, which is dependent on the world price *through free imports,* and the price guaranteed to the farmers.

In Figure 11.8, a DPS is compared with a levy system. Deficiency payments relate to levies just as subsidies relate to tariffs. More accurately, deficiency payments reflect a subsidy per unit of *x* produced. It is well known that production subsidies (*ceteris paribus*) create fewer distortions than comparable tariffs. In Figure 11.8, the net 'welfare' costs of the DPS are c, compared with c + e under the ALS. Also, the 'invisible' income redistribution from consumers to producers a + b + c and to the EU d, available for agricultural income policy via the Agricultural Fund (e being an uncompensated loss for consumers) is replaced by a 'visiblc' one in the sense that the total government subsidy a + b + c appears on the budget. Although the DPS is naturally fitted for importing countries, it could be applied to exports. The results are quite odd, however. Going back to Figure 11.4, it would not mean an export subsidy of $P_{EU}-P_W$ on KL but the same subsidy on the entire production up to L.[8] The case of exports with a DPS is therefore identical as regards price effects to that of ALS, although the income redistribution in the DPS goes entirely via the budget. But the trade and welfare effects are different. Note that export subsidies in a DPS will assume a different meaning: since there is free trade, consumers will import all consumption (P_WN in Figure 11.4) at P_W. Clearly, this will not be sustainable, unless other barriers keep out those imports. Given the trade effects, then neither are the 'welfare' identical to those under an ALS.

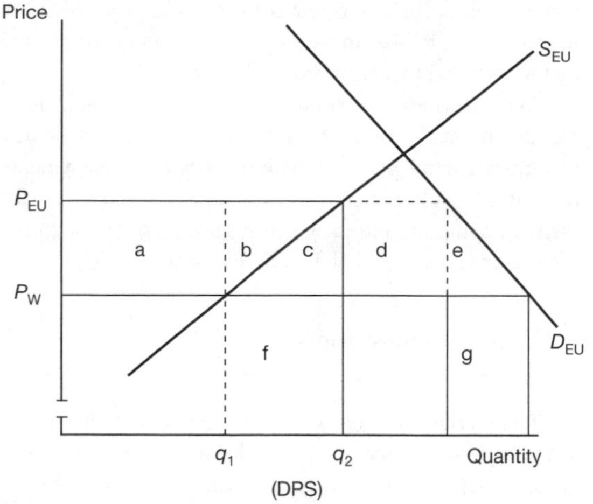

Figure 11.8 Deficiency payments versus agro-levies

11.3.3 Direct income payments

It seems a rather straightforward idea to pursue income policies with instruments that directly touch upon the incomes themselves, rather via the prices of products sold. Direct income payments to farmers (if set high enough, of course) would immediately solve the policy

[8]The policy relevance of DPS for exports became clear in the Uruguay Round when the USA had to accept that its DPS in fact implied export subsidies too.

issue. This is the textbook solution to any problem of income redistribution since it does not create price distortions and therefore no static 'welfare' costs.

Four alternative forms come readily to mind: deficiency income payments per unit of land, deficiency income payments per animal, deficiency income payments per family head in farming, and a negative income tax for farmers. Only the latter two forms are comparable to the lump-sum transfer so beloved in microeconomics.

11.3.4 Supply quotas

If direct income payments prove to be unacceptable owing to too high budgetary costs or perhaps too high implementation costs, one may return to the costly price-based income policies but limit their secondary effects on production growth. High CAP prices strengthened the trend towards EU self-sufficiency, in turn reducing the benefits of the intra-EU (agricultural) division of labour. In addition, under the ALS, achieving higher self-sufficiency implies increasing budgetary outlays for government stockpiling or export subsidy. Hence, supply quotas, discouraging undesirable production expansion, seem an appealing instrument to CAP decision makers. In some products, notably dairy products as well as sugar, the long-term effect of high prices on supply elasticities has been so large that production had to be discouraged. One method of doing this is by limiting the price guarantee (and therefore domestic intervention and export subsidies) to production quotas for the EU, if desirable divided per region or country, or per farm.[9]

ADDITIONAL READING

In Figure 11.9 a levy or export subsidy $P_{EU} - P_W$ maintains the price P_{EU}. Suppose the supply quota, for which the price guarantee is upheld via export subsidies (or government stockpiling), is decided to be equal to production at world prices, that is q_4. Beyond q_4 EU suppliers would find their marginal costs (assumed to be expressed by the supply schedule) to exceed the revenue P_W per unit. Hence, the relevant supply schedule will become QNT. Compared with Figure 11.3 there is a gain in avoiding the 'welfare' costs c and a decrease in income distribution to farmers (via export subsidies) of b + c. The evaluation of the ALPS quota crucially depends on the size of the quota and the prevailing levy. Furthermore, the purpose of the quota ought to be kept in mind. In Figure 11.9 quotas serve to reduce the government's budgetary burden (by b + c), without reducing the price per unit for farmers and without touching upon domestic demand. Given the price P_{EU}, world interests are either served (when P_W was variable, unrestrained subsidised EU exports would have tended to depress the world price further) or left unaffected. Intra-EU quotas for EU budget purposes can therefore be helpful to the GATT / WTO as well.

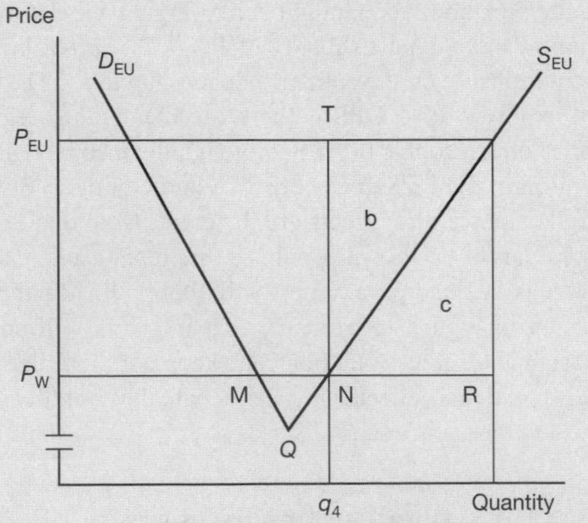

Figure 11.9 Supply quotas and price guarantees

[9]Thus, in the Berlin European Council of May 1999 it was decided that the milk quota system would be maintained until 2005, and milk reforms abolishing quotas would be gradually introduced in the period from 2005 to 2008. However, in the third CAP reform of 2003, yet another postponement to 2014 was agreed, in view of the eastern enlargement. In sugar, the quota system (including a purchased quota from the ACP (Cotonou) group) had escaped two reforms, but was finally tackled in 2005 as a result of the 2003 reforms.

11.4 Assessing the CAP before the reforms

This brief evaluation of the CAP asks the following questions:

- Has the CAP resulted in agricultural market integration?
- Has it realised the five treaty objectives (Article 39EC, now Article 33EC)?
- What have been the costs to consumers, taxpayers and the EU budget?
- What have been the costs to outsiders and in terms of trade conflicts?
- Are there macroeconomic costs to the EU economy?

The assessment refers mainly to the first three decades of the CAP, that is, *before* the three CAP reforms began. Indeed, when going through the evaluation, question by question, several 'drivers' for CAP reform will be identified.

11.4.1 CAP and agro-market integration

The CAP has made intra-EU free trade in agricultural goods possible. Remembering the situation of the mid-1950s, this is no small achievement. During the 1970s and 1980s, however, two important barriers to a single agro-market remained. One consisted of a set of veterinary and phytosanitary controls at the national level; they were at long last removed in the EC-1992 programme by means of (minimum) harmonisation of the required domestic controls and mutual recognition of inspections and certificates. The other barrier was irregular and caused by exchange rate volatility.[10] The introduction of the euro has removed this problem, and non-euro countries are now tied to stricter conditions.

The victory of realising a single agricultural goods market carried 'welfare' costs (as, no doubt, continued national protection would have done as well). There are strong indications that trade diversion swamped trade creation if defined in trade flows terms. In contrast to a minor growth disparity between intra-EU and extra-EU trade in all products, the disparity between the two in agricultural trade is large and striking.[11] It ought to be noted that the net diversion effect has been reduced sharply by the fact that feedstocks such as soya beans, tapioca and corn gluten have remained levy free, having caused strong substitution effects and a rapid extra-EU increase of such imports. It should furthermore be noted that the CAP gradually exerted dynamic influences, for example, shifts of the supply schedules to the right and increasing elasticities. Hence, a proper use of the static trade creation/diversion analysis is impossible when the period of observation is very long. Of course, on intuitive grounds, the high, often prohibitive protection of temperate zone agro-goods is almost certainly still leading to significant trade diversion today.

11.4.2 CAP and treaty objectives

Has the CAP realised the five objectives of Article 33EC (see Figure 11.2)? The first objective of the CAP may be simplified to mean productivity increase and regional specialisation. Agricultural labour productivity in the EC6 between 1963 and 1977, and in the EC9 between 1972 and 1977, has sharply increased, and more so than in the (national and Community) economy at large.[12] In Thomson (1994) these trends are confirmed for 1973–90. Excluding (the strong increase in) intermediate inputs, primary factor productivity rose over this period at an

[10] Monetary compensatory amounts (MCAs), being the intra-EU border taxes/subsidies when green rates (exchange rates, defined for farmers when paid 'restitutions' or surpluses) differed from actual exchange rates. Particularly 'positive' MCAs (for appreciating currencies such as the Deutschmark and the guilder) proved to be highly resistant to removal, as this would imply income reduction in local currency. In certain periods with larger de- or revaluations, MCAs were large, making a mockery of the single agricultural goods market.

[11] In a survey by Thorbecke & Pagoulatos (1975, especially pp. 297–300), a large number of *ex ante* and *ex post* studies are shown to find trade diversion effects on the CAP, exceeding trade creation (in trade flow terms) in virtually all agricultural product groups. The only rigorous attempt, however, is that of Thorbecke & Pagoulatos themselves, using 14 product-wise import demand functions and Balassa's definitions of trade creation and diversion. On top of the caveats to this method, set out in Chapter 6, it should be appreciated that the CAP creates great difficulties for this type of empirical work. The authors have also taken world price as given and encountered problems with the price elasticities. Their estimate of trade diversion was US$740 million (for 1969). However, Kreinin (1972) arrives at the same overall conclusion.

[12] See Meester (1980, pp. 95–100). The measure of labour productivity is the average annual percentage increase in gross value added per unit of labour, at market prices.

annual average rate of 3.6 per cent for agriculture, considerably higher than average real GDP growth of the EU12. The question is whether this was promoted by the CAP as implemented. Indications are that technological progress and capital investment were fostered by the CAP, but regional specialisation in the internal market far less. The underlying economic reason is that market integration, in so far as it results from the actual supply and price behaviour of market participants, was long constrained by the imposed high CAP price level. After all, only Germany had to decrease its price-level – and only a little – when common prices were first determined (in 1964), while the other five, and three adherents (in 1973) all had to raise theirs. In the absence of minimum prices, it would have been (more) worthwhile for efficient producers to export aggressively to low-efficiency regions throughout the EU and so induce more regional specialisation and still higher productivity.

The second objective is the 'fair' income of farmers. The measurement of 'real farming income' used by the European Commission is rather crude: net value added in agriculture per worker, in real terms. This measure increased by 1.4 per cent annually between 1973 and 1990 for the EU12, but with considerable volatility (Thomson, 1994, pp. 51–2). Since GNP per person rose faster, this measure of farmer's income implies a relative decline *vis-à-vis* the rest of the EU economy and hence an apparent failure of the CAP to realise this political priority in spite of heavy-handed interventionism. While this conclusion is correct as formulated here, it does not mean that the *actual* income position of farmers deteriorated. There are two reasons for this surprising point. First, of the 8 million persons in the sector in 1993 EU12, only 2.2 million are classified as being full-time. Thus, the measure used above does not properly reflect the actual income position of part-time farming. This poses the question (see section 11.2), which farmers ought to receive income support: part-timers as well as full-timers? Second, even full-time farmers have, on average, one-third non-farm income, including pensions. In Larsen *et al.* (1994, p. 5), it is shown that, at the level of agricultural households, average disposable income (net of tax) in the late 1980s was higher than that of all households in all EU countries except Portugal. This strongly suggests that the much-discussed income gap between agricultural and non-agricultural personal incomes has disappeared for the sector as a whole. The real problem is the divide between small, marginal farmers, mostly in need of income support, and large farmers. Roughly 80 per cent of income-related support ends up with the 20 per cent of the farmers with above-average farm size. This stable ratio discredits the social case for income support.

The third objective is market stabilisation. If interpreted as short-run price stabilisation, the results are satisfactory (Meester, 1980, pp. 130–2). Given the type of instruments the CAP employs, however, producer-price stability is hardly surprising. There are also indications that annual price increases over longer periods do not compare unfavourably with developments in non-EU countries. However, if market stabilisation is to be interpreted as long-term equilibrium of supply and demand, several indicators point to a failure. Not only have EU self-sufficiency ratios increased for many agricultural products over a long period, but more and more do they surpass a ratio of 100 per cent.[13] Unless one is prepared to argue that these trends consistently reflect improved comparative advantages, the conclusion of structural excess supply at ruling CAP prices is inescapable.

Another indicator consists in Community budgetary outlays for stockpiling purchases and export subsidies. Although the increases in absolute outlays for milk and dairy products were very large, the relative ones for olive oil and tobacco were much larger.[14] Thomson (1994, p. 60) shows that real EU expenditure for storage (of surpluses) increased with an annual average of 6.3 per cent over 1973 to 1992. Clearly, this is unsustainable and can scarcely be called stabilisation. The budgetary and political costs of the export subsidies also rose sharply in that period. The explanation of these trends is that the EU was gradually turning into a net exporter and this is very expensive: 'import-levies' revenue dries up and export subsidies get ever more expansive (see also Figure 11.7). In milk in 1984, a 'super-levy' (on milk output) was introduced in order to stem the growth of the 'milk lakes', in fact, a precursor of CAP reform.

Objective 4 – security of supply – is hard to interpret analytically. What is an appropriate self-sufficiency ratio for supply security? A low ratio with reliable non-EU suppliers, feeling bound to honour long-term supply contracts, might be better than a higher one with unreliable suppliers. A wide geographical spread of outside suppliers may also increase security. At any rate, even when focusing only on self-sufficiency ratios it seems impossible to defend above 100 per cent ratios for a

[13]In Thomson (1994, pp. 57–8) selected data for trends between 1956–60 and 1989–90 and detailed data comparing 1979–91 show that the EU has become more than self-sufficient (and increases its surpluses) in many products.

[14]As a percentage of gross output, olive oil and tobacco reached 23 per cent and 62 per cent respectively, while milk and dairy products reached 'only' 13.5 per cent (1975–77). All data from Meester (1980, p. 138).

large and increasing number of agricultural products on account of security. After the end of the cold war, ratios below 100 per cent should present no problem if sourcing is diversified.

The fifth objective is about reasonable consumer prices. The problem here is one of comparison. It is widely known that EU agricultural prices tend to be higher than world prices (except in 1973–74 and, partly, in 1995). But, as noted, world market prices would probably be higher if the Community did not repeatedly dump heavily subsidised surpluses on the world market and became instead a net importer (hence, exerting more demand for world imports). Figure 11.7 supports this point. However, it is important to realise that real agricultural producer prices have structurally declined (3.7 per cent annually over 1979 to 1991; see Larsen *et al.,* 1994, p. 17). World market prices fell more sharply still, at a real rate of 6.7 per cent annually between 1979 and 1991. As a result, the nominal rate of EU protection (as levies were then still variable) *increased* – in other words, the consumer benefited from a real price decline but far less than would have happened under fixed tariffs.[15] The very nature of the CAP instruments therefore further divorced EU market conditions from the world market until 1995. Real consumer prices, though falling, became even less 'reasonable'. Ironically, it is, in part, the EU itself that induced sharper declines in world prices via export subsidies.

11.4.3 CAP and costs to consumers, taxpayers and the EU budget

The costs of the CAP to consumers and tax payers in the EU are provided in Table 11.1. They are huge, ranging from €110 billion (82 plus 82) in 1986–88 to €123 billion for the EU25 in 2004, falling from some 55 per cent of value-added at the farm gate to some 45 per cent.[16] For a family of four persons, the transfer hovers around 1,000 annually, a relatively high sum with a regressive effect given the prevailing income distribution. The transfers per full-time farmer hide the very unequal distribution: large farmers (roughly 20 per cent) obtain about 80 per cent of the CAP support, even though their relative income levels do not justify an income policy. The reason for this skewed transfer was that price support used to be tied to output, though contained by supply quotas and, recently, some reforms: hence, the importance of 'decoupling' support and output in future reforms (see section 11.5). It is, however, important to realise that the price paid by consumers and taxpayers does not all end up with the farmers. Some of it (although less and less) may benefit Egyptian consumers of grain flour, some may benefit large landowners and some may go to import supplies (for example, fertilisers).

Table 11.1 Agricultural transfers of consumers and taxpayers to farmers (€billion)

	EU 15		EU 25	
	1986–88	2003	2004 (p)	2004 (p)
Producers support estimate, of which:	92	104	100	108
market price support	80	57	54	57
% PSE of output	41	36	34	33
transfers from economies	82	58	55	58
transfers from taxpayers	28	61	59	65

p = provisional
Source: Data as in OECD, 2005, p. 85

The EU budget pressures induced by the CAP are hard to sustain in a Community that basically relies on liberalisation and regulation (that is, not on the budget) to achieve its goals. The real EU agricultural budget costs rose at an annual rate of 5.1 per cent between 1973 and 1991, far beyond the real EU growth rate. Including ECU 3 billion for structural measures, the total outlays amounted to ECU 33 billion in 1990, close to 60 per cent of the EU budget. Adding national spending of the Member States as well (for example, on agricultural R&D) the total is close to ECU 50 billion. For economic, financial and political reasons this development would seem to be unsustainable.

[15]Apart from poultry and eggs, annual growth rates of the nominal rate of protection (1979–91) hover between 2.1 per cent and 9.5 per cent; for poultry –1.2 per cent; for eggs –5.1 per cent. Average 2.8 per cent for all products.

[16]The reader is warned of the technical difficulties in such calculations, hence the problems in comparing results about 'transfers'. See Munk & Thomson (1994) for details.

11.4.4 CAP, costs to outsiders and trade conflicts

The costs to outsiders are manifold and varied. It is useful to realise that it is arbitrary to single out the CAP when considering the distortions of world agro-markets. All countries which do not heavily rely on agricultural exports engage in agricultural protectionism. What made the EU a target of special criticism is, first, that tariffs were variable up to 1995 and hence insulated the EU from the world market, and second, that export subsidies are automatic, massive and without (almost) any budget constraint. Though beneficial to (especially poor) food importers such as Egypt, these CAP instruments are inimical to comparative advantage exporters of temperate zone products.[17] Problems for citrus fruits, some other fruits and olives are somewhat less severe because some imports are possible (often off-season) and export subsidies do not exist. As the Uruguay Round imposed the fixation of variable tariffs (at high maximums, though – see section 13.4) and some cuts in export subsidies, as well as (low) minimum import shares, the costs to outsiders have reduced somewhat, and world prices have improved a little. A major improvement will only be accomplished, however, if further CAP reform is pursued. As noted, there are plenty of reasons to do so, both economic and political. The careful empirical analysis in Tokarick (2005) illustrates some of the points. First, the costs to outsiders notwithstanding, up to 90 per cent of the welfare gains of full liberalisation in agriculture is reaped by the countries removing the distortions. So, the EU has every interest to pursue vigorously further CAP reform. Second, net exporting third countries enjoy a double gain, that is, agro-liberalisation would lead them to reap a terms-of-trade gain (as their export prices go up) and an efficiency gain. But even net importing third countries, though suffering from a terms-of-trade loss, would enjoy the efficiency gain and, in a number of cases, the latter would exceed the former. However, liberalisation of grains (wheat and maize) would badly hurt countries such as Egypt, Mexico, Marocco and the Philippines, given their dependence on flour imports. If the EU and other OECD countries were to liberalise fully, countries such as Argentina, Brazil, India and many in sub-Saharan Africa would enjoy net gains, even if – once again – over 90 per cent of world welfare improvement would end up in OECD countries themselves. Liberalisation of milk and dairy as well as beef would prompt quite spectacular changes, including large price falls in formerly protected countries (alas, these major adjustments are also an indicator of the expected resistance to reform by EU farmers). Third, there is a discrepancy between the impact of tariff liberalisation and the removal of subsidies (be they for output or exports). Whereas the net effect of the latter is modest (the gain for taxpayers cancels out the loss for farmers, so only indirect gains matter), tariff liberalisation induces gains up to almost ten times higher. Thus, for CAP reforms, the follow-up in the WTO is even more essential for insiders than for outsiders.

One additional reason is that the CAP has repeatedly led the EU into trade conflicts: examples include the chicken war with the USA (1963), the sudden closure for beef imports from Hungary in 1974, the refusal to adhere to two negative GATT panel verdicts on oilseeds in the late 1980s and early 1990s, the 1982 conflict with ASEAN over a 'voluntary' export restraint on Thai tapioca exports, a subsidy war on flour exports to Egypt with the USA (mid-1980s), frictions on citrus fruit and olives with Mediterranean countries after the Iberian enlargement, and so on. Again, this should not be interpreted as a unique feature of European agriculture since agro-trade is sensitive almost everywhere. Now that the EU has turned into an exporter in many products, it has far greater political and economic interests to reduce the costs of the problems in the world market which are partly of its own making. Further CAP reform – and its being bound by the new GATT / WTO rules – will significantly reduce the potential for trade conflict, while inducing other GATT / WTO partners to open up as well.

11.4.5 CAP as a drag on economic growth

As if all these drawbacks are not enough, it is little realised that the CAP also causes a 'drag' on the growth potential of the EU economy. Long-term adjustment out of agriculture, having little comparative advantage, would yield a considerable improvement in the overall allocation of productive resources in the Union. This would raise productivity, hence overall income. This point is of particular significance for the new Member States. Indeed, the eastward 'export' of the CAP to new Member States, is, of course, greatly welcomed by their farmers (not least, since income support is in euro, based on EU averages, so very advantageous to them), but is bound to slow down badly needed adjustment via inter-sectoral factor flows between less and more productive activities. The risk of lower

[17] For example, Argentina, USA, Australia and Hungary for beef; USA, Argentina for grain; USA, Brazil for corn; New Zealand for dairy; many countries for sugar, as cane sugar may substitute for beet sugar; and so on.

CASE STUDY 11.1 Common fisheries policy: why and how?

Agriculture and fisheries are often viewed as a natural pair. But the common fisheries policy (CFP) of the EU is very different from the CAP, old or new. First, the objectives of the CFP are justified by the public interest and also call, inevitably, for a firm approach at the EU level (or, indeed, wider if at all possible). The seas and oceans, fishing stocks and their regeneration capability are a 'common resource', a kind of collective good. Given the large capacity of the EU's fishing fleet, overfishing has become a pressing problem. It presents a classic dilemma: if countries credibly cooperate (and indeed accept lower catches, hence, a reduction of *their* capacity), their national fishermen keep a viable prospect for their standard of living; if countries shy away from a joint regime, or, do not enforce, or, subsidise new capacity while scrapping old, all others will be inclined to do the same and a lack of mutual trust will undermine the CFP's effectiveness, to the detriment of all. Second, the instruments of the CFP consist of national quotas for types of (endangered) fish, besides free access to each other's territorial waters and a single market for fish. The quota approach is only partly successful because (1) it is annual rather than medium run, (2) it is weakly enforced and too politicised in Council.

The hostility of fishermen against the CFP cannot be explained by its basic rationale. Sooner or later, fishermen do understand and accept the necessity of keeping 'their' resources alive on a medium-term basis. The real problem is overcapacity, caused by a very low rate of labour exit (in turn, caused by the lack of alternative employment in fishing regions) and the enormous jumps in capacity when modernising fishing boats and techniques. Given this predicament of EU fishermen, they all attempt to 'free ride' and wait with adjustment, in the hope that colleagues exit first. Moreover, they hunt more and more aggressively for catches in other seas of the world, sometimes helped by the EU purchase of 'fishing rights' from poor countries, for example in West Africa. The long-run solution of the CFP consists of more (subsidised) capacity cuts, greater 'ownership' of the medium-run policy by the fishermen themselves and somewhat greater centralisation of enforcement in order to restore mutual trust.

growth than otherwise obtainable follows directly from the incentives of very-low-productivity farmers *not* to leave their land, thereby hindering shifts to better factor use.[18]

11.5 Reforming the CAP

Only four years after 1964 when the CAP's linchpin – the then ALPS for grains – had become operational, Commissioner Mansholt presented the first, quite radical reform plans. In those days the transfers to producers were only 5 per cent of value added at the farm. The reform proposals were not accepted. Ever since, numerous reform proposals, official or academic, have been presented. The need for reform by 1990 was far greater than in the 1960s but the EU was forced to become accustomed to powerful lobbying by farmers and severe politicisation in the Agro-Council.

This section first summarises the drivers of CAP reform, subsequently discusses three recent reforms and ends with general principles (including subsidiarity) for further reform.

11.5.1 Drivers of CAP reform

The analysis in section 11.4 is quite critical, in particular as to static and dynamic (overall) economic welfare and as to economic growth potential. Such economic assessments of the CAP have a long tradition in academia and among

[18] In the second edition, a graphical (macro)analysis of the point was provided and the interested reader is referred to Figure 11.9 and related text in that edition. A rough idea of the order of magnitudes is given by an estimate of up to 3 per cent (of GNP) EU15 output forgone.

think-tanks, but it is as well to realise that they have failed to impress farmer lobbies and agricultural decision makers in Council and the EP. Indeed, the political economy of CAP decision making strongly suggests – up until the 1990s – a high degree of insulation from 'public interest' arguments such as efficiency, the pursuit of equity with direct payments, low external protection and acceptance of GATT disciplines. While this textbook cannot go into the political economy of the CAP in any depth (see, for example, the contributions in Pelkmans, 1985), the reader should realise a few 'deep' reasons for this insulation.

First, up to the early 1990s, the implicit foundation of the 'old' CAP was a French/German political understanding (1) that agriculture had to be part and parcel of the internal goods market, (2) that this would be pursued behind very high protection, 'good' for farmers in both countries (continuing the *exante* protection they enjoyed nationally), and (3) that internal free agro-trade would be based on prices, above floor prices, close to the inefficient German level so as to minimise adjustment for (West) German family farms. This deal could be sold to the fearful German farmers, but it was also highly advantageous for French (and, incidentally, Dutch and, later, Danish) farmers, as they enjoyed a major price increase. Since Germany was a net agro-importer inside the EU, the by-product of protecting its inefficient farmers was a major net transfer to other EU suppliers (including France), which were at least relatively efficient.[19] For decades the politically powerful farm lobbies felt assured by this 'deal' and could afford not to 'listen' to sound economic or policy analysis.

Second, the well organised farm lobbies had no natural or effective counterparts in Brussels. For consumers, somewhat higher prices for a small part of people's household budget were no reason to demonstrate (as the farmers massively did, time and again) or organise political pressure. European business increasingly raised its voice, in particular when agro-goods became too expensive as inputs. Typically, such complaints were bought off by special measures, further raising the costs of the CAP. Later, business became preoccupied about the negative effects for the GATT Rounds or in bilateral trade wars, but lobbying against the CAP never became a priority, hence decision makers ignored it when tough choices had to be made.

Third, the CAP's status in European integration also shielded it from criticism for a while. It is true, for a sector starting from a collection of extremely interventionist national policies, the construction of a common (interventionist) policy, complete with minimum price setting and joint financing, is a baffling success story. A swift glance at how other examples of regionalism in the world deal with agriculture shows how extraordinary the emergence of the CAP must be. In the transition period up to 1970, the EEC6 managed to have the CAP in place and working before the (much easier) CU and before regulatory harmonisation began in earnest. As the process of deep integration is a fragile one, especially in the early years, the CAP and the annual marathon meetings about price setting in the Agro Council retained an 'achiever' status for many years.[20] Deeply reforming what politically was an incredible accomplishment, was initially taboo. For these and other reasons, initial reform 'debates' remained 'dialogues of the deaf'.

Since the early 1990s, the insulation has been over. Figure 11.10 provides an overview of the numerous drivers of CAP reform. A good number of those have been identified in section 11.4. Together, they explain the incessant pressures to mitigate the adverse consequences of the CAP, and in the end, to start questioning its very foundations.

There are four permanent drivers of CAP reform: budget pressures, every six or seven years when the multi-annual 'financial perspectives' have to be negotiated; mounting pressure from world trade partners, in particular since the Uruguay Round; a series of intrinsic policy failures of the CAP, causing ever greater dissatisfaction with the instruments, even when supporting the objectives; and, finally, the quest for rural development which requires a policy vision in which other determinants than CAP-related factors are preponderant. The first two are in bold in Figure 11.10 because they are most prominent politically.

The *EU budget quarrels* are, by definition, political. It is a political judgement whether the current overall EU payments for the CAP (including a small but increasing part for rural) of €45 billion is too much or

[19] Thus, Germany's role as 'paymaster' of Europe was to some extent self-inflicted.

[20] Trade partners, especially the USA, have long interpreted this 'status' in a much more intrusive way, which is not what the text above implies. They perceived that the CAP was the centrepiece of European integration, and that its methods reflected European performances for protectionism and market intervention. Thus, when EC-1992 began, it was immediately dubbed 'Fortress Europe' in the Washington debate about the US Trade Act of 1988. The (false) perception was that any major initiative of European integration would be inspired by the CAP. In fact, the CAP has always been the exception to a market-oriented process of European integration, where commonly set prices, budget transfers driven by output, or extreme protection played no role.

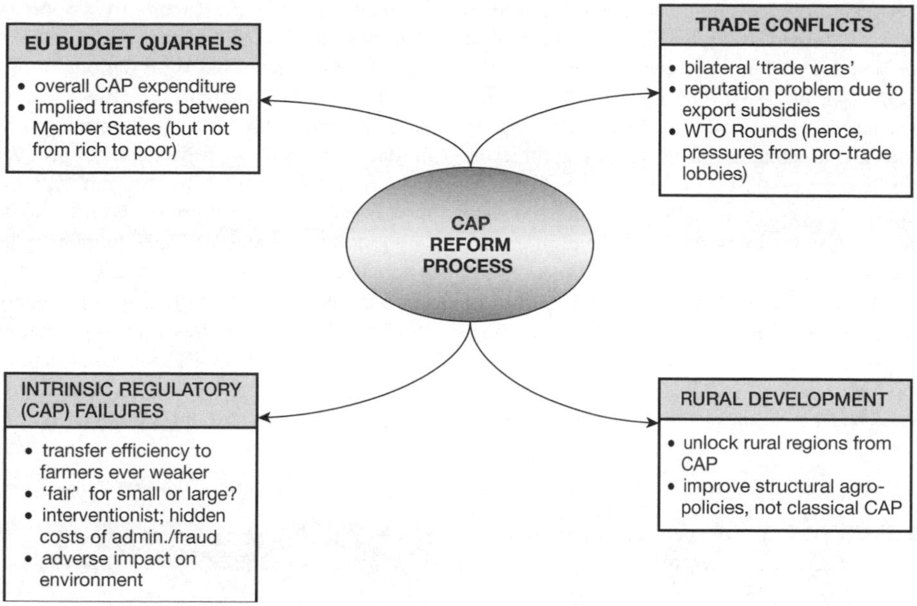

Figure 11.10 Drivers of CAP reform

not. Some reasons suggest it is not much of a 'burden': as a percentage of EU GNP it barely reaches 0.4 per cent (and, by 2013, even less), some of which would undoubtedly have to be handed out to marginal farmers if they were instead on the social payroll of Member States. Also, the composition of the expenditure matters: once the money is no longer spent on surpluses and export subsidies, as is mostly the case in 2005, the political protests dwindle rapidly.

Nonetheless, there are powerful arguments for cutting the total spending drastically. They include the privileged status of farmer subsidies (why subsidise agriculture when other sectors are not?); the paralysing impossibility of a major shift in EU spending to R&D and other determinants of future European growth (an issue addressed in Chapter 19), given that Member States are not prepared to increase the EU budget overall; and the 'one-farm-fits-all' approach of EU direct payments in euros to farmers, irrespective of the country's standard of living. The latter results in huge differences between the Member States in the local socio-economic impact of equivalent payments. This issue is discussed in section 11.5.3. In the final analysis, even these impressive arguments might not be the most incisive ones politically. The common financing principle of the CAP causes transfers between the Member States which are not based on a poor/rich country distinction (a distinction quite acceptable in the EU). The transfer issue has politically become very costly indeed and is used (by opponents) as leverage to obtain support for the other reasons to cut CAP spending.

The second driver, *pressures from trade partners* has already been discussed. The EU has become much more receptive to pressures from developing countries in a multilateral context (in the Doha Round) as well as bilaterally (for example, opening up to Mercosur countries)[21] and even unilaterally (fully open access for the 48 least developed countries in the 'everything but arms' liberalisation by the EU in 2003). See also Case Study 11.2 on sugar reform.

A third driver is a combination of many defects of the 'old' CAP, even when its principles, the primacy of farmers' income protection and productivity increases are taken as a given. So, these issues are not a normative criticism but refer to 'intrinsic regulatory failures'. In fact, one might call them *design failures.* Some of these are beyond the scope of this book,[22] such as administrative complications and fraud, the adverse impact on the environment (given the strong incentives for larger quantities of output, automatically paid for at at least P_{int}) and the disregard of animal welfare in 'industrial' farming. The distributional

[21] The emerging common market between Argentina, Brazil, Paraguay, Uruguay and, as associated countries, Bolivia and Chile.

[22] The 2nd edition, Table 11.2 (p. 219) provides a detailed explanation of no less than seven such failures of the 'old' CAP, called 'positive' (as against 'normative') regulatory failures.

inequity between large and small farmers' subsidies has been dealt with, helped by Figure 11.5. The decreased 'transfer efficiency' refers to the net benefit for the farmers from CAP interventionism. The decline of this efficiency is the consequence of many secondary effects of the CAP such as the capitalisation in higher support levels on to higher land prices, the ever rising debt levels of new entrants and second-generation farmers, rising price elasticities and steadily declining world agricultural prices, partly due to the EU itself.

The fourth driver is the prospect for *rural development* throughout the Union. The CAP has had the effect of 'locking' rural regions into agricultural activities. Where this had powerful effects on long-run productivity increases (for example, in East Germany after 1990 and in Ireland), it tends to support rising living standards and agro-business competitiveness. More often than not, however, rural regions were, or still are, populated by marginal farmers. In such cases, the lock-in has hampered the level and long-run growth of overall productivity. Why? Upward trends of productivity ought to be fostered by a shift to high-performance agribusiness (hence, structural policy, not the CAP) and, more importantly, a structural change to industry and services, whereas the CAP subsidies and guarantees kept low-productivity farmers on the land for generations. Thus, rural development implies a much greater emphasis on the structural policies for European agriculture (long the stepchild of the CAP) as well as general structural and 'cohesion' policies (see also Chapter 16).

CASE STUDY 11.2 Europe's artificial sugar markets and proposed reform

A major test case of the 'new' CAP is the sugar reform and liberalisation. Sugar long escaped reforms even though it is a classic instance of the many drawbacks of the 'old' CAP. The old regime was initiated in 1968 and kept until 2005. It consists of five features: an intervention price for sugar beet growers and two intervention prices for sugar refineries (one for raw sugar and one for white), production quotas (as in Figure 11.9, except that there are A-quota prices for the first 82 per cent and lower B-quota prices for the remaining 18 per cent), high tariffs, and specific import quotas and export subsidies. This complex system is geared to keep the intra-EU price of sugar at three times the world price. The world price is to some extent a residual price as many other countries protect their sugar farmers too. Still, the EU exacerbates the problem by dumping up to 5 million tonnes excess output on the world market at prices below its own production costs. This massive dumping causes havoc among many small sugar growers in poor countries eager to export cane sugar. At the same time, the EU has honoured privileges for its former colonies in the African–Caribbean–Pacific (ACP)/Cotonou group and India by granting tariff-free import quotas up to roughly 1.5 million tonnes, which are bought by the EU at the very high EU intervention prices, a boon for those countries. However, since the EU's high prices already cause surpluses, the Union is forced to dump these imports back on the world markets. Thus, in addition to discriminating one set of developing countries against another, the former are also to suffer from subsequent dumping. The budgetary costs of the sugar regime are not trivial (€1.4 billion in 2004, down from €2.1 billion in 2000) but surely not as high as one might have expected; the trick is found in the quotas which serve to contain the costs to the budget without improving the allocation of productive resources at all.

The dumping question is interesting for other reasons as well. Dumping of sugar can take place under the A-quotas and the B-quotas, at the prices that they give; however, it also applies to the imports from ACP and India which get A-quota intervention prices. Brazil, Thailand and Australia filed a WTO case, however, accusing the EU of cross-subsidising so-called C-sugar, which is outside quotas, hence formally unsubsidised. Both the panel (October 2004) and the Appelate Body[23] sided with these countries, holding that the intervention prices for sugar are so high that cross-subsidisation is a major factor behind some 3 million tonnes of sugar exports of the EU. Moreover, in so doing the EU also overstepped its volume limits of export subsidies as fixed in the Uruguay Round.

[23]WTO, Appelate Body report AB-2005-2 of 28 April 2005.

CASE STUDY 11.2 *continued*

The Commission started a reform debate in 2003, saw its first reform proposals stranded in Council in July 2004 and tabled more radical reforms in June 2005.[24] Since the sector is not competitive by any standard, creeping steps would never do. The proposed price cut is 39 per cent in two steps. Direct (compensation) payments of 60 per cent of the income loss will be incorporated in the single farm payments of the relevant farms (most farms grow sugar besides other crops). Note that the current production levy will disappear and this will further raise the compensation level. A single quota will be installed. Subsidies for biofuel and for restructuring and exit will be available. The intervention price for refineries will be removed.

The impact for developing countries is complicated and not necessarily positive, curiously enough. The ACP countries and India will obtain a lower price for their exports to the EU (still quite attractive though). Modest 'special preferences' will be eroded (up to 150,000 tonnes) by the 'everything but arms' initiative which gradually opens up for sugar until 2009 (when access will be free). EU sugar exports will be drastically reduced as the WTO has ruled and this is likely to lift the world price somewhat; the Doha Round may end all remaining export subsidies anyway which would be still better. Since the ordinary tariffs for sugar are very high and a special safeguard clause augments this tariff considerably, it is critical for market access to know what tariff reductions will apply to sugar after the Doha Round. With a possible cut of 50 per cent, market access might become possible for the most competitive performers such as Brazil. Unfortunately, even if the EU were to open up completely, the winners would probably not include the poorest sugar producers: Haiti, Dominican Republic and Angola. Precisely the countries that filed the WTO case are likely to swamp the market with low-priced sugar.

The final 'food for thought' for the reader is the following. How is it possible that a very small subsector with only 135 refineries in the EU15 and another 90 in central Europe can exercise such an extraordinary power and obtain such privileges for so long? Processed sugar is oligopolistic or even monopolistic in all Member States and restrictive practices in the UK have been fined by the Commission in the past. The 'sugar barons' were of course very useful in keeping the administrative nuisance of the quota system and intervention prices to an absolute minimum. Profits and rents both of farmers and processors were high despite (or, rather, because of) the absurdity of the arrangements. What could be the political economy logic of immunity for the sugar sector for decades?

11.5.2 From 'old' to 'new' CAP

The drivers for CAP reform being many, and some of them very powerful, sooner or later the 'immunity' of the CAP to reform and liberalisation had to be given up. Since the early 1990s, it has become increasingly clear that the EU is gradually discarding its 'old' CAP and building a 'new', quite different one. And the process is far from petering out. Already in 2005, several political decisions by the European Council stretch to 2013 and 2014. The details of CAP reform are often very technical and go beyond the scope of this book. What we try to show here are the central measures of reform and liberalisation, leaving out numerous technicalities or measures for minor crops or activities. Even when focusing only on the major moves, there is still a risk of being overwhelmed by the sheer number of smaller steps, if looked at one by one (the 'trees') in a series of reforms, rather than discern the overall direction towards a 'new' CAP (the 'forest').

Table 11.2 provides a comprehensive overview, yet has a surprisingly simple structure. It brings together the two sides of transferring the CAP: intra-EU reforms (the top panel of three waves) and external agro-trade liberalisation (the lower panel of three distinct waves in opening up).

The top panel of Table 11.2 uses the same structure for the three waves, emphasising cuts of intervention prices and the shift towards direct payments to farmers. The key to render this shift effective is decoupling the direct payments from output. Initially this was done only hesitantly, especially because it would have meant a huge fall in the subsidies going to large farms. In the third wave (the 2003 Mid-term Review), however, the single farm payment implies a further decoupling and a

[24]See COM (2005) 263 of 22 June 2005.

Table 11.2 From 'old' to 'new' CAP: reforms and liberalisation

First reform wave (MacSharry)	Second reform wave (Agenda 2000)	Third reform wave (Mid-term Review)
1. *price cuts* (intervention) • 33% for grains • some cuts for substitutes (oil seeds; protein crops) • cuts for downstream products (beef)	1. *price cuts* (intervention) • 15% for grains • milk and dairy 15% • beaf/veal 20%	1. *price cuts* (intervention) • minor for grains • big for rice • milk and dairy sharp (17%; 35%)
2. *direct payments* • partially decoupled • (seen as) compensation for price cuts • 'set aside'	2. *direct payments* - as before, but - degression over time was deleted	2. *direct payments-* • further decoupling • single farm payment • broken up in 'rights'; tradable • larger farms get less (up to 19%)
3. first *environmental* disciplines	3. *budgetary ceiling* • Until 2006, market costs of €38 billion (1999 prices) • first rural budget	3. *cross-compliance* • payments linked to 'good agro-policies', and envir./animal health
		4. *budget ceiling* • real reduction of CAP spending up to 2013 with 1% a year; milk quotas until 2014
Note: milk and sugar escape	*Note:* sugar escapes	*Note:* reforms announced for sugar, olive oil
External liberalisation via Uruguay Round	**CAP tariff protection more porous via bilateral FTAs**	**External liberalisation via Doha Round (EU offer, Oct. 2005)**
• variable levies terminated	• agro in FTAs with MED countries	• EU: unilateral opening 2003 in 'everything but arms' for 48 least developed countries (even sugar, in 2009) (in force)
• most quotas 'tariffied'	• agro in Europe Agreements of candidate countries	
• (very high) tariffs cut by 36%	• some agro concessions in FTAs with Mexico/S. Africa	• deep tariff cuts offered: if tariff >90%, cuts 60% or 50%; max. agro-tariff at 100%
• domestic support cut by 20%	• more agro access for Cotonou countries	• drastic cuts in domestic support; 70% in trade-distorting aid; some cuts in partially distorting aid
• cuts of export subsidies 20%		• offer in 2004: end of all export subsidies
• some min. imports compulsory (5% of home consumption)		• larger volumes under tariff quotas

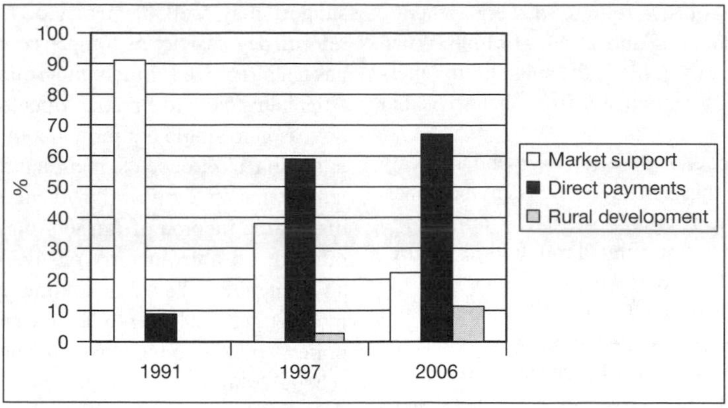

Figure 11.11 Shift to direct income payments

Source: Swinnen, 2005. Reproduced by courtesy of Jo Swinnen

beginning is made with cuts for large farms. Figure 11.11 shows the dramatic shift towards direct payments and away from price support in just one and a half decades. One can also observe other disciplines emerging which reduce the design failures of the CAP, such as environmental rules, regulation on animal health and on food safety (based on standards for good agricultural practices). Complying with these disciplines is a prerequisite for receiving the single farm payment. Finally, budget disciplines have been imposed in view of the fact that the early reforms of the CAP (though in the right direction) did nothing to halt the secular, absolute increase of the EU agricultural spending. In October 2003, the European Council agreed that the nominal agro-budget up to 2013 could not increase by more than 1 per cent a year; given the 2 per cent inflation in the EU15 (and the rapidly falling inflation in central Europe), this implies an annual real reduction of 1 per cent, reducing the expected share of agricultural spending in 2013 to 37 per cent (down from today's 45 per cent).

The lower panel of Table 11.2 is just as important for an appreciation of the 'new' CAP. After decades of undisciplined protection and distortion of world markets (with export subsidies), a longer-run perspective on agricultural trade liberalisation since the early 1990s reveals a manifest trend of opening up the EU. One can credibly argue that the Uruguay Round did little more than bring the EU's CAP under GATT disciplines, while entertaining an expectation for better market access in future Rounds. As the Doha Round is not yet finalised (2005), one has to be prudent in assessing today's positioning. Nevertheless, the offers in the lower right panel of Table 11.2 are nothing short of drastic and are incompatible with the 'old' CAP given its insistence on Community preference. If these offers are going to be agreed, there will still be considerable agro-protection in the EU, but a range of goods will be confronted with import competition and potential import competition will discipline intra-EU prices. Moreover, export subsidies (already reduced radically to only 10 per cent of the level in the early 1990s) will disappear, improving world prices and making investment decisions of farmers in third countries more predictable. Also, the external disciplines of intra-EU subsidies (if not fully decoupled) are sharpened appreciably. For very sensitive goods (often seasonal), tariff quotas will allow import volumes eligible for low tariffs to increase.[25] The transformation to the 'new' CAP is so intrusive that no sector will easily escape reforms and some liberalisation. The stubborn resistance in sectors such as sugar and milk has caused delays but reforms have now also affected these goods (see Case Study 11.2). The repeated delays in milk and dairy output quota removal, now to 2014, can be explained by the fear of huge compensation payments from the EU budget.

11.5.3 Further reforms without treaty revision

There is little doubt about an ongoing transformation of the CAP for many years to come. This reform and liberalisation process should best be guided by the four 'Ds'

[25] A tariff quota works as follows. For a specified volume of initial imports, the tariff is low or zero; beyond this volume, a much higher tariff will be applied.

and subsidiarity. The four Ds refer to: direct payments, their degressivity, decoupling and decentralisation. When these four Ds are properly applied, the subsidiarity question will come to a different answer from that arrived at under the 'old' CAP.

There is perhaps not enough reason to amend the treaty objectives, difficult as this is in any event. As to the principles, in particular the financial solidarity among the Member States could be interpreted much more restrictively. A 'new' CAP will greatly facilitate this.

Of the five objectives (see Figure 11.2), the first and the second need to be disentangled: promoting efficiency and income objectives with one instrument – price – is costly and, in the end, ineffective. So, a greater market orientation of the CAP refers to the clearance of markets by the normal price mechanism, with intervention and price stabilisation being only for the short run and for temporary use. Any such intervention price would have to be close to world market prices (say, a three-year average). Over a longer period this would also mean far lower protection and the disappearance of export subsidies (already long forbidden in the GATT rules for industrial trade). Such a market orientation supports objectives 1 (in short, efficiency) and 5 (reasonable consumer prices), while guaranteeing market integration in the EU. Objective 4 (security of good supply) is scarcely the problem today, to put it mildly, but any long-run concern is best addressed by providing export prospects for a multitude of external suppliers, so that there is diversification.[26] Objective 3 (price stability) is better achieved on world markets when they do not serve as 'residual markets'. For farmers' income, price stability matters less nowadays because there is a separate income policy instrument.

Direct income payments have now become the main instrument for minimum income protection. Once prices are no longer a policy instrument for farm incomes, and come down, the price of land is bound to fall eventually. This would help to reduce the cost of entry into farming. The short-term adjustments (given capital depreciation, debt service and inter-sectoral labour movement) may, however, be difficult, hence temporary, degressive income support may well be justified. However, in the 1999 reform, degressivity of compensatory payments over time has been removed, which undermines market incentives. After adjustment to a market-oriented CAP there would be no reason to single out farm incomes as special. As noted in section 11.4, once the marginal farmers have gradually left the market, empirical evidence suggests that personal disposable income of farmers may well be higher than other disposable income on average. Therefore, after adjustment and based on adding up farm and non-farm income, there is likely to be no case for a special income policy. An adapted extension of national social security schemes should suffice, just as for any other economic activity. Since social issues are dealt with at national level (see Chapter 15), given large income discrepancies and preference differences, the principle of subsidiarity suggests that this income policy should no longer be pursued at EU level. In leaving this to the Member States, and considering the lower prices over a wide range of products as well as the removal of export subsidies, the budgetary squabbles between the Member States would greatly reduce as well. What financial solidarity (the third principle) would remain would refer to common structural measures, occasional interventions, short-run compensation measures, joint R&D, the promotion of forestry, and so on. The long-term reform scenario is primarily characterised by *decoupling* (income payments from output) and *decentralisation* (income payments mostly at Member States level). This would be combined with prices around the level of world prices and low protection.

A central condition to make this reform scenario work is full confidence of the Member States (and the farmers) that EU competition policy – especially with respect to keeping state aids non-distortive or otherwise banning them – is effective when decentralisation of income policy takes place. In farming, subsidies are part of a deep-seated culture, and pressures at national level can be very strong. Perhaps the state aids regime in agriculture demands a special set-up to underpin this confidence (for example, subsidies conditioned on independent EU approval before disbursement).

11.6 Summary

The CAP is probably the most severely criticised EU policy. Precisely for this reason it is appropriate to understand the (initial) case for having the CAP. The central argument is that a possible failure to absorb

[26]One historical reason for the oilseeds conflict with the USA was the USA's sudden export ban on soya beans in 1973, depriving EU farmers of cheap inputs for one season. The USA was virtually a monopoly supplier.

Summary *continued*

a high rate of labour exit from agriculture would cause a relative and perhaps absolute decline in agricultural income for a (then) substantial part of the population, which would destabilise society and in any event not be socially acceptable. The problem with this case is that it justifies important goals behind the CAP but not its actual instruments. Since the early 1990s, several CAP reform waves have tackled exactly the instruments, thus gradually generating a 'new' CAP.

The three principles underlying the CAP are a single product market, EC preference (that is, protection) and financial solidarity among the Member States. The five objectives are the increase in agricultural efficiency, a fair standard of living for the farmers, agricultural market stabilisation, supply security, and reasonable prices for consumers. The instruments include structural ones (via an Agricultural Fund) and those for regulation of agro-product markets, such as (variable) levies – with or without intra-EU price support – deficiency payments, direct income support under various conditions and supply quotas.

Variable levies became fixed tariffs in 1995 because of the Uruguay Round. Such (fixed) agro-levies are so high that they keep practically all imports at bay in the core CAP products. Besides inducing an income transfer to farmers, they cause 'deadweight' losses to the EU economy. Agro-levies with intra-EU price support used to worsen this picture considerably, since their long-run effects included a secular increase in self-sufficiency causing surpluses which – owing to price guarantees – required huge subsidies before they could find buyers in the world market. Also, large farmers benefit disproportionately because high prices apply to all output, no matter how big, and because their marginal costs are lower.

The 1992 CAP reform is successful, having brought down the grain intervention price by one-third (and lower price reductions for, for example, beef), but it has remained partial. A second reform in 1999 (with consequences, for example, for milk quota removal) up to 2008, is also insufficient and selective. The 2003 reform has pushed 'decoupling' from output and from the means of production much further.

Deficiency payments are in effect subsidies per unit of output. As long as the EU is an importer, such payments are preferable to agro-levies. Direct income support is the socially least-cost form of (agricultural) income policy. However, there should be no link with farm size or output (that is, there should be decoupling). A possibly effective way to limit social and budgetary costs of price-based CAP income support is to impose supply quotas, limiting the price guarantee to maximum volumes. The implementation costs are high, however, and there are serious risks that rigidities ossify agricultural output structures.

When assessing the CAP in terms of policy costs and effectiveness before the reform wave, it does not get high marks. The agricultural CU has long remained without truly free movement. In terms of the five objectives of the treaty (Article 33), efficiency in the sector has gone up, but because of technical progress and heavy investment in powerful inputs, rather than because of trade-induced regional specialisation. The 'fair' income of farmers in terms of 'real farming income' has declined relatively, despite the costly and sustained interventionism. Surprisingly, actual overall (disposable) income of farmers was higher on average than that of other households (in the late 1980s). The market stabilisation objective is achieved in the EU, though at increasing costs. The security of supply objective was exceeded with many product self-sufficiency ratios above 100 per cent. This has proved to be so expensive that the EU became interested in reforms. Consumer prices were much higher than they need have been. The overall costs to taxpayers and consumers is high, €123 billion in 2004 (EU25). The cost of the CAP in terms of trade policy conflicts was very high over its history.

Given a range of design failures as well as welfare costs, but especially trade conflicts and EU budgetary pressures, the reform wave became inevitable. Even products that used to escape (above all, sugar) were included and a better 'decoupling' of direct income payments from output was accomplished. Further CAP reform should be guided by the four Ds: direct payments, degressivity, decoupling and decentralisation; and in the WTO it should be accomplished by opening up the internal market to competitors.

CHAPTER 12

EC Competition Policy

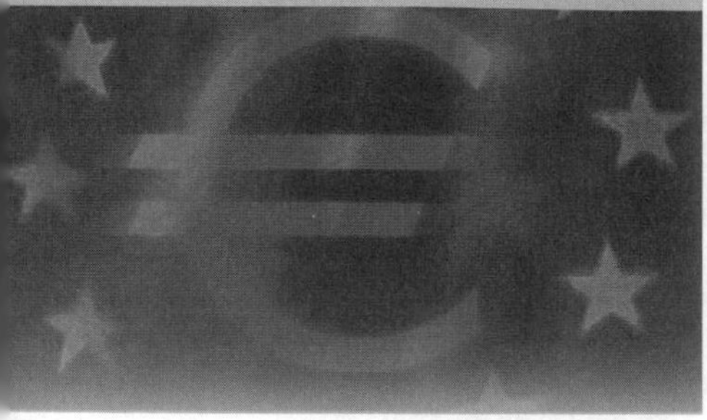

Topics covered

Competition policy is crucial in the economic constitution of the Community for two main reasons. First, there is the underlying idea that competition and competitive markets are the principal way to serve the economic aims of the treaty. Already important in the Rome Treaty, the idea has been elevated to an explicit guiding principle in the Maastricht Treaty (see Figure 2.3). Second, the establishment of the internal market may fail or yield unsatisfactory results if restrictive business practices at the national level could form effective barriers against competition from other Member States. Such private barriers might emerge or be perfected as a response to the required removal of public barriers. Competition policy should ensure that the substitution of public by private barriers cannot arise, and hence cannot endanger what the EC Court calls 'the unity of the internal market'.

After first dealing with the underlying justification for competition policy, the subsidiarity test is applied to explain why the EU level should be assigned with the power to ensure competition in the internal market. Whereas the basic subsidiarity test is easy to do, the subtleties arise in where the exact line should be drawn, for example in merger control and in anti-collusion issues. Section 12.2 gives an overview of the Community's regime for competition. The sections on anti-collusion (section 12.3) and anti-monopoly (section 12.4) are divided into an analytical economic subsection and a policy subsection. There are case studies (12.1 and 12.2) on the block exemption for car distribution and Tetra Pak's abuse of dominant position respectively. Merger control at EU level is treated, analytically and in policy terms, in section 12.5, with Case Study 12.3 on refusals of mergers. Why and how state aids are controlled in the Union is dealt with in section 12.6.

It cannot be emphasised enough, for business and economics students, that it is crucial to develop a minimal understanding of EC competition policy if they wish to comprehend the economic core of today's European Union.

12.1 Why EC competition policy?

Market integration implies more than the removal of national barriers. After all, the internal market, like national markets, might fail to function optimally. The proper functioning of the internal market requires the prevention of market failures.[1] Competition policy is geared towards the prevention of market power and other distortions of competition, and thereby helps to make the market function properly. For the Community it means that both the establishment and the proper functioning of the internal market are essential for the pursuit of the aims of the treaty. In this section two questions will be raised: first, why a competition policy for the internal market, and second, why a *common* one?

12.1.1 Why a policy for competition?

Behind the term 'proper functioning' different schools of thought may be hidden, with different views on the desirability and technical approaches of competition policy. It is important to understand the basic tenets of these different philosophies. Most economists would agree that the proper functioning of a market refers to its effect on the allocation of resources leading to the highest level of economic welfare (ignoring, here, the distribution of income). Markets can do that when they are characterised by competition.[2] Thus, 'the prime purpose of competition policy is . . . to promote and maintain a process of effective competition so as to achieve a more efficient allocation of resources' (Vickers & Hay, 1987, p. 2). This view is supported by static microeconomics, although in comparative statics in the presence of scale economies, trade-offs can be identified between market dominance and efficiency (see section 12.4.1). A fundamental objection against this view arises, however, when one considers the incentives behind competition. Ultimately, competition is driven by the market rewards of being better, cheaper or more original than one's competitors, thereby enlarging one's market share and profits. Sustained success in this respect might lead to market dominance. This has led to the fear that a policy going against market power might inadvertently end up as 'winner-bashing', because the dominant firm's competitive strategies may too easily be considered as abusive. Penalising efficient 'winners' undermines the ulterior motive of big firms to compete and, in so doing, precisely the process of competition the policy is supposed to maintain. Unfortunately, economic theory is not a clear guide to the long-run dynamics of competition processes.[3]

A strand of more laissez-faire oriented literature goes further still. The claim is that the dynamics of technology, product innovation, new entry as well as the erosion of efficiency of incumbents when not subjected to effective competition, ultimately renders monopolies and cartels unsustainable. Such forms of market power generate high profits or a 'quiet life' (a lower pace of work and innovation, and relatively high remuneration of the factors of production) which, except in some extreme cases, are precisely the incentives needed for others to challenge these positions. In the laissez-faire view, these market-led incentives to overcome market power should be expected to generate outcomes superior to policies executed by bureaucrats and based on laws formulated by politicians. The upshot would be that competition policy against market power (in the USA, called 'anti-trust') is undesirable, except in some extreme cases.[4] Such a conclusion is not widely supported because the empirical evidence is ambiguous and, more importantly, the time-paths of the competition dynamics are unpredictable, leaving markets functioning suboptimally for possibly very long periods. In a subtle application of competition policy, checking the abuses of market power need not throttle the competitive dynamics over the long run. The evolution of competition tends to be driven not by selectively restricting market power but by other determinants such as new technologies, product innovation or new combinations.

The following example is instructive. In 1984 the European Commission instructed IBM to be more forthcoming to competitors about its interface standards and changes of them in the mainframe computer market. Detailed provisions and annual monitoring had to ensure that competitors could guarantee IBM compatibility for complementary equipment. Up to that time, IBM complementary equipment repeatedly gained and regained first-mover advantages *vis-à-vis* competitors owing to delays in the provision of information or to recurrent

[1]As noted before, besides in the provision of public goods, markets may fail because of externalities, internalities and market power or other distortions of competition.

[2]With some notable exceptions, see Chapter 8.

[3]One can go a few steps further and ask the empirical, instead of theoretical, question whether (EU) competition policy has, systematically and over decades, engendered verifiable consumer benefits. There are no studies tackling this question, perhaps because the detailed data are not made available. This is also true for the USA, although Crandall and Winston (2003) have collected selective evidence. The authors caution that competition policy should make a stronger, empirical case before tackling the less clear-cut cases.

[4]In cases where competition is actually inefficient ('natural monopoly', see Chapter 8), competition policy may be inferior to optimal economic regulation as a means to obtain the highest economic welfare.

standard switching, thereby underpinning IBM's hold on the entire market (mainframes plus complementary machines such as printers). In 1994, however, IBM was absolved from these obligations due to the dramatic increase of the market share of personal computers, the partial substitution of mainframes by ever more sophisticated PCs and the much greater competitive challenge that IBM faced due to a user-led drive for open standards. The employment of competition policy initially promoted competition but in no way prevented the competitive dynamics in the computer market from developing, with the final result of making the intervention irrelevant.

Political philosophies, often mixed with economic arguments, also guide competition policy. In the EU, some non-economic objectives do play a role. Since competition policy is to some extent discretionary, the influence of divergent perspectives reduces its coherence and complicates the understanding of EU policy. The origins of EC competition policy date back to the 1950s when few Member States had developed competition policies. Market interventions (if not 'indicative planning', as in France) were condoned much more widely than in the 1990s. From an *interventionist* perspective, the costs of misallocation are usually weighed against the perceived political or social benefits of intervention. A prime example consists in the suggested use of deliberate exemptions from competition policy to promote 'European champions', big and fit enough to compete worldwide. A second one is crisis cartels: facilitating adjustment and restructuring to lower sector-wide capacity by allowing coordinated scrapping of capacity among competitors. Competition policy then risks becoming an interventionist industrial policy. The economic justification for these approaches is often spurious (see also Chapter 14). More likely, the arguments are of a social nature in crisis cartels, and of a nationalist character in the case of Euro-giants (safeguarding a national firm among the few). With the much greater intensity of market integration nowadays, the influence of interventionist thoughts has waned but not died.

From a *liberal/democratic* perspective economic arguments about the virtues of a market economy are blended with political values such as freedom in society and democracy. The non-economic function of competition is openness and freedom of choice and initiative in society. Economic concentrations may be considered anti-democratic if the great influence wielded by them is used in subtle political ways to obtain special privileges or protectionism. This might discredit property-owning democracy.[5] The goal derived from these considerations is diffusion of economic power. That is, in some situations, an explicit protection of (small) competitors may override the protection of a totally free competitive process. Examples of this goal include the provisions against the abuse of dependence of suppliers in German and French competition law (Fishwick, 1993, pp. 25–6) and the EU position that (indirect) support for small and medium-sized enterprises contributes to the maintenance of the competitive process (Fishwick, 1993, p. 93). Recently, however, EU competition has shifted to a more singular emphasis on the consumer only, without undue regard to competitors.[6]

12.1.2 Competition policy and subsidiarity

Once it is agreed that competition policy needs to promote a proper functioning of the internal market, does it follow that a *common* competition policy is necessary? Could not the Member States' policies be coordinated yielding the same result? There are two reasons for not assuming the latter approach. First, EC competition policy finds part of its justification in the potential conflicts between national jurisdictions, i.e. a case of negative cross-border externalities. When the Rome Treaty was negotiated, only Germany (among the EC6) had developed a strict competition law; Italy, for instance, had none at all and the Dutch one was lax. A belated introduction or adaptation of national policies would have been a slow and uncertain process. Once in place, the discretionary nature and fine-tuning which competition policy inevitably requires, would have implied a very demanding and detailed, permanent coordination. Its complexity, uncertainty and long delays would almost certainly have been far more costly than a common policy.[7] Second, national competition policies would tend not to take into account the repercussions of

[5]See, e.g., Jacquemin & de Jong (1977, pp. 198–9) and Cairncross *et al.* (1974).

[6]The debate on 'protecting competition or competitors' suggests a far too sharp dichotomy for EU competition policy. But it is true that competitors in Europe could, by filing a case against a leading company, force the Commission into actions it might not always have initiated itself. See Commissioner Kroes (2005a) for a new emphasis on consumers.

[7]Interestingly, today all EU Member States have well developed competition policies which have gradually been attuned closely to the main rules of the EU-wide regime. So it would seem that the common policy, in conjunction with deepened market integration, has induced approximation of the (residual) national regimes. One wonders whether this outcome would have been accomplished merely via coordination.

national measures (or inaction) for other Member States. Step 3 of the subsidiarity test (cooperative common action) would not be effective and swift. Only a common policy can take repercussions into account. So, even if national competition policies had been based on some commonly agreed principles and procedures, externalities induced by focusing on national markets and interests would still make this set-up suboptimal. Together, the two grounds yield a strong justification for the EC treaty competition regime for the internal market or any substantial part of it. National competition policies (can) remain, but only in so far as the distortions of competition affect the domestic market without having an appreciable impact on actual or potential intra-EU trade.

The actual division of labour between the two levels of government has long remained uncontroversial for anti-collusion (Article 81 EC) and anti-monopoly (Article 82 EC) policies. It has always been a difficult issue in merger control, even after its overdue introduction in 1989. Today's EU competences in merger control have remained too limited and this unwillingness of Member States to centralise more generates costs of uncertainty, delays and compliance (for example, when obtaining approvals in two, three or more Member States) (see section 12.5).

However, in 1999 the Commission proposed a decentralisation of the enforcement of Articles 81 and 82 EC,[8] a complete break with nearly forty years of exhaustive notification obligations to the EU level for, especially, intercompany agreements. It came into force in 2004. The idea is that national competition authorities and national courts should (largely) enforce, the Commission intervening only when uniformity of Community law would be undermined or when more than three Member States are involved. The Commission would then focus on major European cartel or monopoly cases. The key rationale is the great workload with regard to numerous innocent agreements while resources for truly anti-competitive cartels or abuses remain too limited. Of course, workload has nothing to do with subsidiarity. If the EU level is properly assigned with a task, then the human resources must be given to the Commission to prevent loss of credibility. However, the elaborate notification system has been abolished too, and exemptions from the collusion prohibition will be 'directly applicable' (see Appendix, Chapter 1), that is, enforceable before national courts. This solution will accord well with subsidiarity only if local courts are qualified and uniformity of exemption policies throughout the internal market can be maintained at low cost. All this shows that step 5 of the subsidiarity test can lead to complex debates in EU practice which can help to reduce regulatory costs.

The proper functioning of the internal market depends not only on anti-trust. Two other distortions of competition suggest a policy assignment at EU level. First, state aids to businesses distort competition by providing artificial advantages not available to competitors. The EU has developed a complex effect-based regime in an effort to separate subsidies which do not distort the internal market (or which even help to improve its functioning) from those which do. The latter are prohibited (see section 12.6). Second, EC competition policy has a set of provisions on companies (state-owned or not) with special or exclusive rights operating in typical network markets, such as utilities. Such provisions are needed because specific economic regulation and state ownership were long used in Europe as alternative or complementary means to the process of competition for the allocation resources and the control of economic outcomes. Because they are national means for the national economy, they are likely to throttle, distort or eliminate competition in the internal market. This is a fundamental problem of the economic order for the Community. After all, a rigorous application of EU competition policy (and free movement and/or establishment) might undermine the very reasons for national state ownership and is inconsistent with exclusive rights. Chapter 8 deals with the revolutionary changes in the EU regime applied to network markets since the mid-1980s. The chapter shows how liberalisation (free movement and establishment) is combined with competition policy and specific regulation.

12.2 The Community's competition regime

The competition regime of the EU can be both widely and narrowly defined. In the wider conception it would refer to all provisions dealing with private and public distortions of competition in the internal market. Besides the issues mentioned in the previous section it would also include remaining regulatory barriers, intra-EU border interventions or fiscal disparities having an effect on intra-EU economic intercourse. In

[8]See COM (1999) 101 of 28 April 1999, *White Paper on Modernisation of the Rules Implementing Articles 85 and 86 of the EC Treaty.*

other words, to the extent that the establishment of the internal market leaves distortions in place, its proper functioning is also negatively affected. In a narrow conception, however, the removal of barriers via liberalisation and joint regulation is ignored and competition policy refers merely to the total set of provisions governing public and private behaviour affecting the competitive process in the internal market. This more limited conception is summarised in Table 12.1.

Table 12.1 Competition regime in the internal market

Nature	Substance	Provision[a]	Scope
General rules	• objectives and general means	Art. 2	All markets
	• Specific means: 'system ensuring that competition . . . is not distorted'	Art. 3g	Internal market generally
	• No discrimination as to nationality	Art. 12	Internal market generally
Behaviour private firms ('anti-trust')	• cartels, concerted practices (or, 'anti-collusion')	Art. 81	Goods and services
	• abuse of dominant position (or 'anti-monopoly')	Art. 82	Goods and services
	• merger control	Reg. 139/2004	Goods and services
Behaviour public agents	• Firms with special or exclusive rights	Art. 86	Network markets
	• State/regional aids	Arts 87 and 88	Goods and services
	• State distribution monopolies	Art. 31	Goods
Special regimes	• Transport	Arts 73 and 80	Air–sea transport
	• Agriculture	Art. 36	Agro-goods under market organisations

[a] All articles refer to the EC pillar of the Amsterdam Treaty.

The core provisions are contained in Articles 81 to 89 of the treaty plus the 2004 merger regulation; special provisions exist for transport and agriculture. The boundaries between the competition regime, on the one hand, and liberalisation and regulation on the other are sometimes unclear. This is the case where regulation deals with actual behaviour: neutralising the effect of state distribution monopolies on competition may be defined either as the establishment of the common market (also in view of its place in the treaty) or as ensuring its proper functioning (in view of two decades of litigation about anti-competitive behaviour).[9] A similar border case is Article 86, with respect to 'exclusive rights': given the limitations of EU-wide regulatory provisions on these network markets, successful litigation under competition rules was used in the early 1990s in order to initiate a process of liberalisation and regulation in, for example, telecoms (see Chapter 8).

It is crucial to understand the place of this competition regime in a wider context of other EU provisions and policies. Thus, the actual and potential competition in the internal market is influenced not only by competition policy but also by the internal market regime (free movements, mutual recognition, approximation) and by the impact of various EU policies (such as trade, transport, agriculture). The various policies may complement or (partially) substitute for each other. Thus, open EU trade policy can be regarded as a highly effective form of competition policy as it exposes (EU) business to actual or potential competitive pressures, even in cases where intra-EU competition would otherwise not be aggressive. Jacquemin & Sapir (1988) provide econometric evidence showing that external exposure tended to exercise greater competitive discipline on EU firms than intra-EU competition (before EC-1992) did.

Thus, once the liberalisation of national transport markets enables the establishment of the internal transport market, an adequate application of competition policy may greatly reduce the regulatory requirements of the common transport policy. Indeed, the latter may largely confine itself to minimum harmonisation of some essential requirements (safety, compatibility and so forth) and the critical aspects of transport infrastructure. Thus, the more 'complete' the removal of barriers

[9]The main reasons for the initial resistance against the rigorous application of Art. 31 are (1) the revenue function for the state's finances (e.g. salt in Italy); (2) a universal service functioning for 'essential' commodities (e.g. petrol stations in Portugal); (3) a public service function of preventing undesirable private concentation of power for overriding public policy reasons (e.g. the paper for newspapers in France). Whatever the reasons, Art. 31 does not permit 'exclusive rights' in goods, certainly not for import/export and wholesale. These issues now seem to be settled.

in the internal market, the lower the probability (*ceteris paribus*) that competition policy will have to intervene to promote or restore competition.[10] The more pro-market EU policies are, the greater the scope and intensity of actual and potential competition in the internal market and the more critical is the role of EC competition policy to prevent this competition from being eroded.

Since the late 1990s, the detailed implementation and to some extent the substance of EC competition policy has been subject to a sustained process of reform and modernisation. Figure 12.1 provides the highlights of the modernisation process in stylised form. The technicalities and details of the many revisions need not concern us here

However, some drivers of this ongoing reform process can be spelled out. First, there is a marked shift from a two-tier complementary set-up, with the Commission dealing with EC law, and the national competition authorities (NCAs) with national competition law, to a more joint enforcement of European competition policy via decentralisation and intensive networking among NCAs and the Commission. This has become a regular mode of 'competition governance', so to say, for a range of network markets[11] and under the new enforcement rules for Articles 81 and 82 EC.[12] Second, another major shift is the sharper focus on (economic) effects of possibly restrictive practices, rather than the legalistic 'object' of such clauses. Third, reforms are driven by rationalisation of procedures, both with regard to the transaction costs of certain aspects of competition policy (for example, state aids, notifications under Article 81) and greater efficiency, effectiveness, openness and proper 'hearing' of companies by DG Competition of the Commission. Finally, there is a possibility (although as yet no proposals) that the Commission might propose a framework to facilitate private competition cases in courts, a routine way to go in the USA. If the EU could avoid the drawbacks of the US incentive system (including certain types of class actions and inflated damages), private

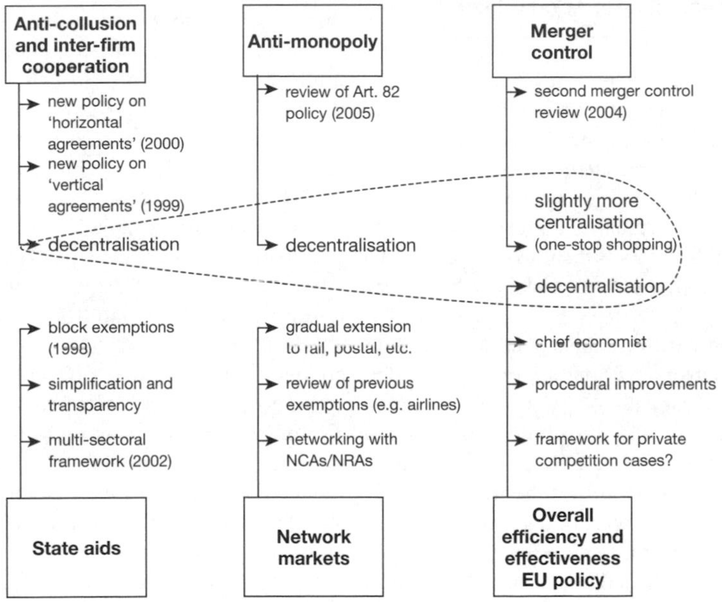

Figure 12.1 Modernisation of EU competition law

[10]This is working well in road transport, the most important one of the six transport modes. In airlines and rail transport, harmonisation is more extensive. In airlines, competition policy has now become critical to a much better functioning internal market for airline services. In rail, it is far more complicated (see Case Study 8.1).

[11]In network markets, it is a little more complex, as noted in Chapter 8, because the competitive framework is the result both of regulation and competition law together. Thus, Member States may have assigned powers to NCAs, to NRAs (national regulatory authorities for network markets) or to both, so that the networking with the Commission is on a sectoral basis.

[12]Regulation 1/2003 in OJ L 1 of 4 January 2003.

action in the EU could contribute to better enforcement of competition rules in the internal market. Figure 12.1 calls attention to the wide range of reforms but also to the rethink of more decentralisation in collusion and monopoly cases and slightly more centralisation (given the benefits of one-stop shopping; see section 12. 5) in merger control.

12.3 Anti-collusion policy

This section deals with cartels, concerted practices, other forms of business collusion and with the clearing of inter-company agreements which are not anti-competitive. After a brief excursion into the underlying economics, the essence of the treaty provisions and Commission policy are set out, complemented by Case Study 12.1 for purposes of illustration.

12.3.1 The economics of anti-collusion

Anti-collusion policy is the prevention of collusion among otherwise independent firms, which restricts, distorts or eliminates competition. In setting out the economics of anti-collusion, attention is focused on economic welfare effects (for example, changes in consumer and producer surplus). If collusion is perfect and encompasses all suppliers,[13] then, in simple micro-economics, this is no different from monopoly. Consider Figure 12.2.

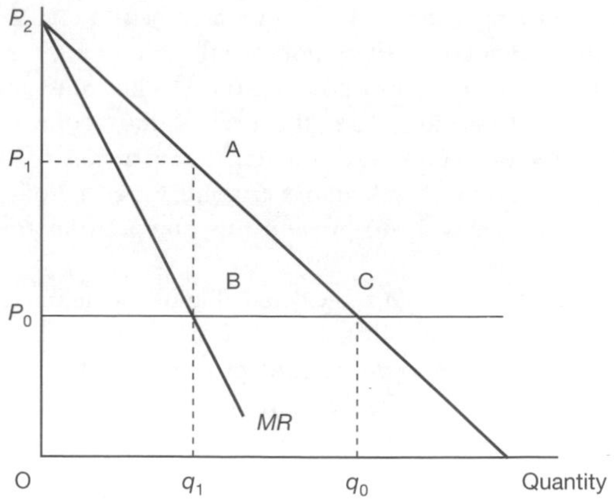

Figure 12.2 Perfect collusion or monopoly

In atomistic competition (numerous sellers) P_0 equals marginal and average costs (assuming no scale effects). The market clears at C (P_0, q_0). If collusion is perfect and costless a *de facto* monopolist would emerge. All individual firms face a given price, in other words perfectly elastic demand. But the industry as a whole – here, the cartel – faces a downward-sloping demand curve. Were one firm to raise the price beyond P_0, it would lose all customers. For the cartel to accomplish a price rise, it must cut the quantity supplied. If the demand schedule is known precisely, hence also the marginal revenue (*MR*) schedule, supply will be shrunk to Oq_1, where marginal costs equal marginal revenue; the resulting price is P_1. This reduces consumer surplus by P_1ACP_0, of which P_1ABP_0 is captured by the cartel.

The uncompensated loss to society is ABC: it represents the loss of welfare for those consumers willing to buy above P_0 and lower than P_1, but being frustrated in this search. Note that the consumers buying at P_1 are satisfied, given the scarcity. Note, also that P_1ABP_0 might be objected to politically as the reflection of undesirable (market) power, though in the simple economics of this figure it is merely a transfer from consumers to producers, without a net effect on welfare.

There are many real-world complications concealed by this graph. To begin with, collusion is not costless, hardly ever perfect and rarely encompasses all suppliers. If entry is free, the cartel would be disciplined at P_0 and become pointless. If new entrants (or established firms in the cartel) were to compete with product differentiation, prices would come down less but 'cartel' profits would disappear. Therefore, cartels in markets with many sellers and/or low entry barriers, are unlikely or are highly unstable. Indeed, cartels are often unstable because members have an incentive to cheat: for each single member, the marginal revenue of producing more than its quota of the joint-profit-maximising cartel quantity is higher than the marginal costs (see, for example, Martin, 1993, pp. 162–3). Instability is also a result of significant differences in the marginal costs of cartel members: since joint-profit maximisation requires marginal costs to be the same, the high-cost firms must accept a lower quota (and much lower profits)

[13]Buyers can also collude. However, oligopsonies and monopsonies are ignored in this text. Though rare, they do seem to occur in Europe (e.g. purchasing syndicates of supermarkets).

than the low-cost members.[14] The costs of coordination and monitoring are much lower in oligopolies, especially when scale is combined with virtually no possibility for product differentiation (for example, cement, bulk chemicals, simple steel, flat glass). If entry barriers also serve as exit barriers – in other words, the investment and other expenditures to enter the market are sunk and cannot be recouped upon exit – the market is characterised by low 'contestability'. Without outside contenders, oligopolistic behaviour is usually dictated by the interdependence between firms in strategy and performance. It can be shown that this leads to excessive price stability in oligopolistic markets, without there necessarily being a cartel.

Another way of making the same point is that if overall excess capacity in the industry exists (say, because it is sensitive to the business cycle as, for example, bulk chemicals typically are), prices would still remain sticky out of fear that any individual firm's price cut would immediately be matched by all others.[15] After the upswing, with all firms producing at full capacity, such fears disappear as competitors have no excess capacity to supply the extra quantity that would be demanded if they were to keep their prices constant. In all probability, all prices would go up and would tend to persist in the subsequent downswing. A celebrated example is the *Woodpulp* case,[16] where price rises over the upswing were followed by a ratchet effect (that is, resistance to going back to the *ex ante* situation) during excess capacity. Although the Commission was of the view that this was the result of an oligopolistic cartel, aiming at price concertation, the mere observation of pricing behaviour may just as well be explained by independent conduct of individual firms as shown above.

In oligopolies producing typical consumer products (for example, simple cosmetics, detergents, toothpaste, toilet paper, cigarettes), *non-price* competition attempts to get around the inevitable oligopolistic détente on price. Image or brand name competition is largely conducted with heavy advertising aiming to enlarge or stabilise market share. If matched by all oligopolists, such strategies may actually be wasteful for the economy. This could also be the case if firms proliferate their brands for different market niches (entry deterrence or pre-empting further growth of a competitor's share). Product innovation which is duplicated in a wave of 'me-too' products implies wasteful research expenditure and perhaps a loss of economies of scale. The conclusion is that collusion is not always easy to prove. Even when oligopolists do not collude, the functioning of markets may be far from satisfactory, with a possible economic waste of resources.

Second, Figure 12.2 is static, excludes the presumably high costs of X-inefficiency induced by the lack of competition and ignores other virtues of competition. Stable oligopolies, let alone cartels, may suffer from X-inefficiencies as long as new entry is not actually taking place or a downswing would not cause structural overcapacity (assuming that structural, as distinct from cyclical, overcapacity would force a restructuring for survival). The long-run impact of oligopolistic competition on innovation is ambiguous. As a form of non-price competition, an innovation strategy may be attractive for oligopolists facing pricing constraints because of a fear of price wars. However, inside every company, new products or processes are seen as successful only once they upset the prevailing market structure. In the actual practice of competition policy, it is almost impossible to employ long-run conjectures about the benefits of oligopolistic firms' innovative conduct in concrete cases at a given moment in time.

12.3.2 The EC's policy on anti-collusion

Article 81 EC prohibits, and explicitly declares automatically void, 'as incompatible with the common market: all agreements between undertakings, decisions by associations of undertakings and concerted practices which may affect trade between Member States and which have as their object or effect the prevention, restriction or distortion of competition within the common market'. Examples are given in the article, such as price fixing, quantitative restrictions on production, investment or R&D, market sharing and tying of supplementary conditions to sales. The above can 'be declared inapplicable' (so-called exemptions) if four conditions are fulfilled simultaneously:

1 contributing to improving production, distribution or promote technical or 'economic' progress;
2 allowing consumers a fair share of the benefits;

[14]The graphical illustration is equivalent to that of the large versus the marginal farmers in Figure 11.5. In the CAP, the price is politically set, whereas in a (market) cartel, the price follows from equating marginal revenue and costs for the entire cartel. Once the price is known, however, the inequalities are the same.

[15]Analytically, this can be shown with the help of the 'kinked demand' schedule. See, for instance, Martin (1993, pp. 404–7).

[16]See OJ L 85 (1984) for the Commission decision and Cases 125–129/85 before the EC Court.

3 avoiding restrictions that are not indispensable to the attainment of conditions (1) and (2) (that is, the notion of proportionality, so often applied in Community law);
4 not affording the undertakings the possibility of eliminating competition in respect of a substantial part of the products in question.

Under the reform of Article 81 EC,[17] wide-ranging (so-called) block exemptions are provided, with notification only in specified cases (for example, for verticals, above 30 per cent market share) and a blacklist of 'hard-core' restrictions which are always forbidden. Guidelines explain, in particular, the 'economic effect' test and analysis. Restrictive agreements can be horizontal, such as price cartels or market-sharing ones, and vertical, such as selective or exclusive distribution, exclusive purchasing (for example, petrol stations and alehouses) and resale price maintenance. Horizontal agreements operate at the same stage of production or distribution. Not all horizontal agreements are cartels, and cartels are not always engaged in price fixing and market sharing. For instance, a seemingly innocuous agreement to exchange sales information may facilitate collusion, especially in oligopolies. A cartel might also agree on, for example, a short lifetime for the product (tyres, light bulbs) which may pre-empt innovation on longer lifetimes or the use of new technology as it would reduce current or future earnings for the group. Their form does not detract from the basic conclusion of Figure 12.2: unless one can demonstrate offsetting benefits, horizontal agreements have a negative effect on economic welfare. This supports the clear prohibition in the EC treaty. Still, since the reforms, the first step is often crucial for companies: does the interfirm agreement have a restrictive economic 'effect' in the first place, that is, is it caught by Article 81(1) at all? It is there that the modernisation is most sensible. Many innocuous agreements now simply do not fall under Article 81(1) EC. However, when they do, exemptions would be justified only when benefits of business cooperation exceed the social costs – a condition often called the 'efficiency test'.

As noted above, Article 81(1) permits exemptions. The offsetting benefits should, in the EU, contribute 'to improving the production or distribution of goods or to promoting technical or economic progress'. This vaguely worded sentence, without clear criteria grounded in economic analysis about such an 'efficiency' test (see, for example, George & Jacquemin, 1990, p. 211), has gradually gained credibility over time. The simultaneity of the four conditions helps to ensure that the competitive process and consumer benefits are not throttled.[18]

The only major issue is that of 'crisis cartels' allowing a concerted reduction of capacity for the purpose of restructuring an industry in decline. In atomistic markets such as clothing and shoes, there have been periods in EU history when such restructuring was complemented by conditional state aids (and EU trade protection) as an incentive to forgo non-cooperative behaviour. Although this combination was aimed at reducing adjustment costs, it is likely to have been a slow and costly method; permitting it under competition policy is questionable. One EC crisis cartel emerged in an oligopolistic market, that of synthetic fibres, and was initially rejected, though allowed under strict conditions later.

The main instruments of implementation of Article 81 (3) are general and specific block exemptions. Under strict conditions, which vary according to the kind of block exemption, forms of intercompany cooperation are permitted. Such permissions have been issued for horizontal R&D collaboration, know-how agreements and certain specialisation agreements.[19] A general block exemption deals with vertical agreements and specific ones exist, for example for agreements between car makers and car dealers (see Case Study 12.1). In so doing, block exemptions are used as an instrument to help smaller companies to compete more effectively without losing their independence and to provide more legal certainty.

Vertical agreements have two effects on economic welfare which may either strengthen or offset one another: the impact on *inter-brand* competition and that on *intra-brand* competition. Restrictive vertical agreements such as exclusive distribution arrangements or resale price maintenance will, in the language of Article 81, prevent, restrict or distort intra-brand competition.

[17]See, for vertical agreements, Reg. 2790/1999 (in OJ L 336 of 29 December 1999) and the subsequent Guidelines (OJ C 291 of 13 October 2000). For horizontal agreements, Reg. 2658/2000 and Reg. 2659/2000 (both in OJ L 304 of 5 December 2000) and the subsequent Guidelines (in OJ C 3 of 6 January 2001).

[18]The new Guidelines for the application of Art. 81(3) EC explain the 'objective economic benefits' which should outweigh any negative effects of the interfirm agreement. See OJ C 291 of 13 October 2000, as quoted above, section 1.4.2. and the entire section 2.

[19]Some exemptions are truly restored, take the ones for insurance and for interlining among airlines (the 'tariff' conference of IATA).

However, if there are quality reasons behind such agreements, the arrangements could actually be pro-competitive between different brands. Suppose, a brand from EU country Q wants to penetrate EU country R, the market of which is dominated by a few major, well-known brands. The strategy of the new competitor might be to select a single distributor in R who, in turn, may select a limited number of retailers and provide them with territorial protection (a monopoly for that brand in a sales area and a prohibition for other, non-selected retailers to sell in that area). In return, these agents would create and maintain a high-quality image, guarantees and favourable after-sales service. The investment in standards, certification and presentation as well as the costs of an after-sales and repair apparatus will not easily be made by shop owners knowing the existing consumer acceptance of major brands. If they still agree to invest, they wish to be assured that the return of these investments will not be eroded by 'free-riding' sellers exploiting the reputation without actually offering the quality and services themselves (but precisely for that reason being able to offer lower prices). This example shows that restricted intra-brand competition can be a strategy to increase inter-brand competition. In so doing, it may also help to strengthen intra-EU market integration, unless the territorial restrictions (and the market power of upstream producers) are such that it facilitates a fragmentation between sales areas or EU countries, with price discrimination as a result (see Figure 6.8 and Case Study 12.1 below).

ADDITIONAL READING

The intra-brand/inter-brand combination requires a careful analysis. Intra-brand restrictions may be part of cartel-like arrangements to reduce inter-brand competition. This is obvious if the intra-brand restrictions are collective for a group of brands – collective resale price maintenance is not allowed by the Commission. The same goes for reciprocal exclusive dealing as this would severely limit market entry possibilities (unless intra-brand competition is very strong). Neither will arrangements for collective rebates be tolerated.

Nowadays there is a consensus that, on the whole, vertical restraints are less harmful for competition than horizontal ones. The reason is that 'verticals' concern complementary, not substitute, goods. The exercise of market power by one producer of substitute goods always benefits the other producers of substitute products. If the goods at stake are complementary, however, the demand for the complement will reduce if the price of the good produced by the company with market power goes up. In other words, due to this conflict of interest, 'verticals' tend to be 'self-policing' except when this policing mechanism does not work. As will be outlined below, this has led to a more precise and focused policy about verticals by the European Commission. The consensus is summarised by Neven *et al.* (1998) as follows. (1) Are the goods concerned (indeed) complements? In that event, vertical agreements should be presumed to be compatible with EC competition rules. (2) Yet, it ought to be verified whether inter-brand competition is weak or not. If weak, ask whether (if the parties were vertically integrated) they would enjoy substantial market power. If yes, then (3) the SANE test should be employed: is there evidence of a Substantial Adverse Net External effect on third parties such as consumers, existing competitors or potential entrants? If no, the 'vertical' is legal. Since collective verticals undermine or pre-empt inter-brand competition, and almost certainly damage third parties, they tend to be forbidden. For individual verticals, however, this 'new' perspective has profound implications. It means that the very foundation of the Commission's policy on Article 81 was far too restrictive. Remember that Article 81 speaks of the 'object or effect' of intercompany agreements. The new perspective on verticals is clearly 'effect-based' and suggests a liberal policy of non-notification, given the answers to questions (1) and (2), even if the object of the agreement is restrictive. Yet, the practice in the EC during the 1960s was exactly the opposite. The Commission assumed a bureaucratic approach by requiring notification for almost any vertical (given its restrictive object), and subsequently was inundated by so many notifications that it came up with block exemptions, clearing various categories of agreement under specific conditions.[20]

[20]This approach was bolstered by the *Technique Miniere* case (1966) where the Court sided with the Commission in ruling that a focus on 'object' was sufficient to fall under Art. 85 (now Art. 81(1).

ADDITIONAL READING *continued*

The Commission has now switched[21] from a form-based to an effect-based approach, with one wide-ranging block-exemption, and a 'blacklist' of verticals which are not exempt. This should drastically lower enforcement costs for business for many innocent agreements. A fourfold classification is proposed where the effects could well be anti-competitive, other agreements being cleared *a priori*. Three of these classes concern competition directly: exclusive distribution,[22] single branding,[23] resale price maintenance.[24] The fourth one is typical for the EU: partitioning of the internal market and the facilitation of price discrimination between different 'national' markets. Crucial for this fourth class is that 'parallel' imports between the Member States should never be restricted in intercompany agreements as this would undermine market integration and might sustain intra-brand price discrimination between Member States.[25]

After decades of a fairly strict EC anti-collusion policy (with high fines), business behaviour has undoubtedly become more pro-competitive. This does not mean that cartels no longer exist or that major incidences are not discovered. In the late 1980s and the 1990s the Commission discovered classical cases of market sharing or cartels, such as that between Solvay and ICI on soda-ash (total fine ECU 47 million in 1990) or a cartel among welded steel mesh producers (total fine ECU 9.5 million in 1989). In a far more complex case (because of Dutch legal provisions, seemingly condoning these business practices), a cartel-like arrangement among 28 construction associations in the Netherlands on bidding and price regulations in the process of awarding contracts was condemned in 1992 (fine of ECU 22.5 million). A textbook case; as Commissioner van Miert called it, was the cartel of seventeen EC12 and Scandinavian steel beam producers: price fixing, market sharing and systematic exchange of confidential information (fines imposed in 1994 amounting to ECU 104 million).

A (then) record fine of ECU 280 million was set in 1994 by yet another classical case, the European Cement Association. The basic rule in the industry was to avoid penetration of each other's home markets. A range of practices were discovered such as permanent exchange of price information, discussion about 'fair competition' among the competitors, identical pricing methods, a no-dumping principle of surpluses, bilateral market-sharing agreements between producers in pairs of countries and instances of regulating the cement trade. Recent examples include a sugar cartel in the UK and a Union-wide cartel among the producers of district-heating pipes, led by ABB, with a fine for ABB alone of no less than ECU 70 million. In the period 2001–03 the Commission strengthened anti-collusion policy, among other things, with the help of a new leniency policy,[26] which led to many new discoveries. Total fines in these three years moved up to €3.2 billion.[27]

Article 81 EC has also left its mark on services. This is perhaps obvious in oligopolistic industries such as air transport, but it has become routine in other services too.

[21]See Peeperkorn (1998), and the Guidelines on vertical restraints in OJ C 291 of 13 October 2000, which explain aspects such as the 'economic approach', effect-based, checking market power and inter-brand competition first.

[22]Also exclusive supply (e.g. to alehouses, pubs, etc.), quantity forcing via incentive schemes, and selective distribution. The idea is that they may lead to foreclosure of certain buyers, the reduction of intra-brand competition, and/or to less in-store inter-brand competition.

[23]Non-compete clauses and quantity forcing may have similar effects in exclusive distribution.

[24]Besides no intra-brand competition, the price transparency facilitates collusion because monitoring is easy.

[25]This intertwining between competition policy and market integration goes back to the landmark *Grundig/Consten* case of 1965. Parallel imports are a major issue in the exemption, under Art. 81(3), for exclusive dealerships in the car sector (see Case Study 12.1) and in pharmaceuticals (see Case Study 6.1).

[26]A leniency policy creates incentives for 'whistle-blowers' to report collusion and for firms to request low (or no) fines if they provide hard evidence of the restrictive practices they are (were) involved in.

[27]European Commission (2004) *23rd Report on Competition Policy*, pp. 23–4.

CASE STUDY 12.1 Exclusive distribution and EU car price disparities

It has long been suspected that the car dealer system in the EU is exploited by the car manufacturers to practise price discrimination between national car markets. In the early 1980s, very considerable price disparities for identical models had survived the CU and subsequent approximation (see Pelkmans, 1984, pp. 214–16, for data). However, it was argued, with good reason, that barriers such as a lack of harmonised safety regulations, national inspection, certification and registration effectively segmented national markets, quite irrespective of the dealer system. This argument was gradually undermined by EC-1992. Can today's price disparities be attributed to price discrimination?

Regulation 123/85 exempted car manufacturers from Article 81 prohibitions, in having an exclusive distribution system. Dealers could only sell one make of car, in return for an exclusive geographical area (territorial protection). The conditions under Article 81(3) were considered to be met on safety grounds (for example, strict repair obligations), consumer protection grounds (such as far-reaching guarantees, and the quality of specialised after-sales service for that brand) and competition grounds (identification with a brand would fuel inter-brand competition in every dealer's territory). In a major investigation by the Commission, following a formal complaint from the European consumers' association BEUC, enormous price disparities were established for the years 1989 to 1991. Thus, for a Ford Fiesta, price disparities ranged from 28 per cent (1990) to 47 per cent (1991); for a VW Audi 80 between 15 per cent (1989) and 41 per cent (1990); for a Honda Accord between 30 per cent (1989) and 44 per cent (1990). Nonetheless, the Commission did not trigger the clause that, once price disparities would go beyond 18 per cent, arbitrage would be allowed again, because, allegedly, rigorous proof of causation (the dealer system 'causing' the price discrepancies) was said to be difficult.

A new regulation (1475/95) extended the exemption on somewhat stricter terms, and only until 2002. Meanwhile, the euro had eliminated exchange rate changes (in the eurozone) and the quotas *vis-á-vis* Japanese cars (see Chapter 13) had been removed. This leaves tax disparities as the only other possible cause.

Car makers have repeatedly attempted to frustrate the weak arbitrage allowed under the old exemptions. Examples include the conviction of Ford by the EC Court (1982) for a refusal to deliver right-hand drive cars to Flemish dealers (for UK clients), the Court ruling (1994) that parallel imports of Peugeot cars into France by Eco System was legal, the complaint in 1994 by another parallel importer (SGA) that Peugeot harasses its dealers in Italy or Spain not to deliver cars to SGA, and the Court ruling of February 1996 that the exemption refers only to authorised dealers, not to independent dealers which, somehow, legally obtain cars from the car makers and can trade freely. In 1998, VW (in Italy) and, in 2000, Opel (in the Netherlands) were fined heavily for harassment of dealers selling cars to non-domestic EU clients (that is, frustrating arbitrage). The newest exemption in Regulation 1400/2002 amounts to a partial 'liberalisation' in that trade in parts is freer and several different car marques can be sold by one firm (but in distinct showrooms). In 2005, the so-called location clauses were removed from these 'verticals'. This should step up intra-brand competition as dealers can now open sales outlets (under strict quality conditions) anywhere in the EU. Since 2002, car prices have slowly converged in the EU. In 2005, the convergence was strongest in the new Member States. The stricter exemptions and the euro (facilitating price comparison) are the likely causes.

An example is the Eurocheque system, run by Europay. In 1992, the Commission fined Europay ECU 1 million and the French contractor GB (Groupement des Cartes Bancaires, of the French banks) ECU 5 million for a secret (Helsinki) agreement, imposing an obligation on the French banks to charge commission on top of the regular interbank commission (allowed by an exemption of Europay throughout Europe, under the old Article 85(3)). The Commission felt that the agreement amounted to price fixing. In cross-border ferry services the Commission discovered cartel practices in 1992 for five Cross-Channel ferries and in 1998 for seven companies operating services between Italy and Greece. In 2002, eight Austrian banks were fined €124 million for a wide-ranging price cartel.

However, in many product markets, and increasingly in services markets, the competitive context is accepted as a fact of European business life and the policy focuses largely on exemptions for beneficial agreements.

12.4 Anti-monopoly policy

12.4.1 The economics of a dominant position

In a simple graph such as Figure 12.2, a dominant firm will extract monopoly profits and, in doing so, causes a suboptimal allocation of resources. However, this prompts the question why other firms do not enter this market and share some of these profits. In other words, in economic theory, dominance can exist only if there are barriers to entry. It can persist only if the nature of these barriers is preventing or deterring entry for a long period of time. The barriers may be a result of market structure or of business conduct, or both. In practice it is not always easy to fully disentangle the two. Entry barriers should also be judged with respect to the possibilities for recouping the entry-investment upon exit. Clearly, if a new challenger considers entry while facing a dominant company, this is a high-risk strategy, especially if the established company might wage a price war or use other entry-deterring tactics (and competition policy does not discover them or cannot prove that they are illegal – see below). A market is called *contestable* if entry investments are not 'sunk' but can be recouped upon exit. Of course, contestability hinges upon the speed of reaction of the established firm: if the latter is capable of responding swiftly with price cuts or other tactics, the recoupment condition would imply that a 'hit-and-run' challenge will still not lead to sunk costs. This condition is somewhat academic,[28] but as a theoretical benchmark it is useful. The implication is that persistent dominance can only occur in markets which are not contestable. If contestable, the relevant market would include potential competition which disciplines the established company so effectively that the latter must behave as if there are numerous sellers.

The barriers to entry traditionally mentioned are economies of scale, possibly combined with product differentiation, as well as intellectual property rights including the patent protection of product and process knowledge. Since the latter is legal and temporary, we concentrate on the former. The reader is first reminded of the crucial point that these traditional barriers to entry ultimately still depend on the 'sunk cost' argument (see Chapter 3). Thus, a new entrant may find it risky actually to enter the market with a newly differentiated product because the sunk costs of gaining an attractive market share in competition with established companies may be very high. Upon failure, these costs cannot be recouped. Consider Figure 12.3.

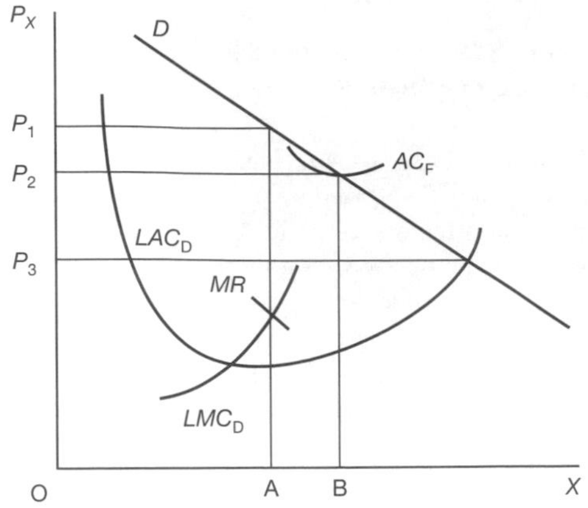

Figure 12.3 Dominant firm with fringe competitor

Source: Baden-Fuller, 1979

The dominant firm D behaves in a similar fashion as in Figure 12.2 since it equates marginal revenue with marginal costs (long-run marginal costs curve LMC_D), at output volume OA. This yields the relatively high price P_1. However, it could price down as low as P_3, say, if it were forced by potential competition. As one may observe, this case of dominance allows a fringe competitor F to exist who prices at P_2 (and produces AB). The latter's scale curve is not the lowest one possible. Presumably, producing on a lower-cost scale curve would require major investments in process technology and equipment, and require a credible prospect of sufficient turnover so as to get a positive return on those investments.

As drawn, this is not the case. If F were to attempt to challenge D, D would cut prices to P_3 at which F could not survive either with its current scale curve or with one comparable to LAC_D, unless one assumes that F's strategy of producing at much larger scale would ensure

[28] One could speculate that, in some cases, entrants operating via the internet could assume a 'fly-by-night' character and significantly increase contestability.

massive switching by consumers to F's products (and D is incapable of responding). Figure 12.3 suggests that a market supplied by a few firms, one of which is as large as or larger than all others, is not really an oligopoly but a monopoly with fringe competition. The question for EC competition policy is: is this state of the market mere dominance, or indeed 'abuse' of dominance (in this case, excessive prices)? The problem is a fundamental one because if D were to eliminate excessive prices, it would thereby eliminate the moderate competition that does exist.

Industrial economics has moved beyond this analysis in many ways. Rather than matching prices upon a threat of entry, dominant firms may employ a range of entry deterrence tactics such as brand proliferation (making it more difficult to occupy initial market niches from which to build up further market penetration), tie-in contracts, rebate systems (making it costly to switch between suppliers), exclusive dealer agreements, proprietary standards, incompatibilities for add-on equipment, and heavy image advertising. Moreover, excess capacity may be kept as a strategic device to enable highly targeted predatory pricing in the margin (for instance, in air transport on routes where entry might be attractive). Yet another possibility is vertical integration, for example ownership of distribution channels or concluding contracts with distributors imposing an automatic right to match new features or lower prices of new entrants.

All these complications do not detract from a basic issue alluded to in section 12.1. Can dominant firms legitimately defend their interests without this being interpreted as an attempt to maintain their dominance (let alone increase market share)? If dominant firms could not always do this, it would mean that large size is penalised (even if efficiency is the origin of it) and that conduct permissible for relatively small companies may not be permissible for market leaders.

12.4.2 EC anti-monopoly policy

Article 82 EC says that 'any abuse by one or more undertakings of a dominant position within the common market or in a substantial part of it shall be prohibited as incompatible with the common market insofar as it may affect trade between Member States . . .'. Four examples are mentioned.[29] What Article 82 strongly suggests is that it is not market structure but the firm's conduct that is relevant in assessing whether competition is touched upon. This formulation goes to the heart of industrial economics, with respect to the structure–conduct–performance paradigm. In simple, static partial equilibrium models it is the (large) market share that can cause market outcomes to be less efficient than they would be with many sellers. The jump from a test of market share to a test of a firm's conduct and performance is then straightforward. But these models are based on such simple assumptions that their validity for legal cases is doubtful: *inter alia,* they suppose a knowledge of the supply of competitive firms and they are static. Moreover, it is not clear what makes a firm a price leader and what would erode its position. As noted above, once various non-price strategies (scale, investment, product differentiation, product or process innovation, entry deterrence tactics) and uncertainty are introduced, a more operational notion of dominance in a context of greater or lesser contestability can be developed. But entry deterrence and other corporate strategies are clearly behaviourial. In other words, in this richer view of dominance it becomes much harder to separate it from 'abuse'.

The EC Court's definition of dominant position can be found in the *United Brands* case (ruling 1978):

> The dominant position referred to in this Article relates to a position of economic strength enjoyed by an undertaking which enables it to prevent effective competition being maintained on the relevant market by giving it the power to behave to an appreciable extent independently of its competitors, customers and ultimately of its consumers.[30]

This definition combines structural and behaviourial aspects and its employment requires a thorough economic analysis of market position, strategies and potential competition.

Note that Article 82 EC does not incorporate an exemption clause, for example, for an 'efficiency defence' so that the conflict between competition and (scale-based) efficiency is apparently assumed not to arise.[31]

[29]They are, in short, unfair prices (e.g. too low, too high or predatory), unfair trading conditions, discrimination among customers or suppliers, and various other limitations of supplies or contracts.

[30]*United Brands Continental BV v Commission* [1978] ECR 207.

[31]In the review of Art. 82 enforcement (see Figure 12.1), consideration of an efficiency test for dominant firm behaviour has been explicitly raised. In Kroes (2005b), Commissioner Neelie Kroes clarifies that she thinks of a test similar to that in Art. 81(3), if only because there are forms of restrictive conduct that occur under both Art. 81 and Art. 82 (consistency argument). Often, this test will simply not apply in anti-monopoly cases, and, if relevant, it is likely to be a tough case to make.

As Figure 12.3 shows, there can be a trade-off between competition and efficiency, in other words, if one wants efficiency one must accept dominance as inevitable. However, for tradable goods and services it might suffice to have open market access, if this would lead to a more credible threat of potential or actual competition from outside. Also, now that EC-1992 has removed borders as well as many regulatory barriers within the internal market, the trade-off may only rarely occur. For sectors where market integration is accomplished, EU demand is almost always a multiple of the minimum efficient scale of output, hence allowing at least oligopolistic competition. The further opening up of the EU market since EC-1992 and the Uruguay Round (see Chapter 13) should increase the degree of contestability (*ceteris paribus*).

ADDITIONAL READING

One could interpret the 'abuse of dominant position' clause as a relatively tolerant attitude towards big firms. It is sometimes suggested that the founding fathers may have felt that anti-monopoly policy should not stand in the way of building large European firms, but act only when these companies 'abused' these positions. The bigness syndrome intensified ten years later (in 1967) when Servan-Schreiber published his book *The American Challenge*. Even today, the problem of interpretation has not entirely disappeared. In EC competition policy (strictly speaking), however, this complete separation of dominance and abuse is not accepted.

There are several policy problems with Article 82. First, in Commission and Court practice[32] dominance and abuse are almost indistinguishable. This inevitably leads to the position that a certain conduct, permissible for smaller firms, may be held to be abusive for a dominant firm. From an economic perspective, stressing that competition policy should not frustrate the inbuilt incentives and rewards of market processes, this is hard to support.

Indeed, only behaviour made possible by the freedom to act independently from competitors (that is, dominance) should be singled out as abusive. Second, beyond defensive responses of a dominant firm, any offensive action to strengthen its position may be illegal in the EU, as being intrinsically anti-competitive. Such a view focuses merely on the structure of the market and seems to ignore the insights about behaviour and contestability. The reform (Figure 12.1) should end this reasoning, as it is not 'economic effect' based. Third, there are cases under Article 82 where consumers in the final market are not affected and the 'abuse' relates merely to competitors in an upstream market. If the final goods market is highly competitive, this implies that aggregate welfare is not affected, even though a redistribution of profits between suppliers in the upstream market may have been forced by the abuse. Should Article 82 be interpreted as a protection of competition for the purpose of welfare in society or, rather, as a protection of (small or dependent) competitors, thereby serving the objective of diffusion of power? Commissioner Kroes (2005b) is clear about it: '. . . it is competition and not competitors . . . to be protected. . . . I like aggressive competition – including by dominant companies – and I don't care if it may hurt competitors – as long as it ultimately benefits consumers.'[33] If one focuses strictly on (ultimate) benefits, what matters is the assessment of competitive harm, not whether there is 'dominance' or 'abuse'. Dominance would merely be a warning signal.

[32]See Fishwick (1993, pp. 104–7) for references to rulings in the *Continental Can* (1973) and *Michelin Nederland* (1983) cases.

[33]Commissioner Kroes is careful to add that the short-run price effects might be beneficial but the medium- and long-term effects (of excluding or hurting competitors) might be harmful for consumers. These so-called foreclosure effects therefore need a proper assessment.

CASE STUDY 12.2 On Article 82 – Tetra Pak and AstraZeneca

Commission and Court cases on Article 82 are relatively few. The proof of the specific infringement is often difficult. The first case on predatory pricing (AKZO, in the homogeneous benzoyl peroxide market, a flour additive) was ruled only in 1991, but the infringements dated back to 1980–82.

The *Tetra Pak* case,[34] ruled in 1994, is remarkable in that the usual difficulties did not play a major role. The nature and scale of infringements make it a textbook case for what abuses of a dominant position may mean in business practice.

Tetra Pak has a very strong position in the market for packaging liquid food and beverages, including milk. The market for carton packs is divided into an aseptic sector (includes sterilisation, which is technically difficult with cartons) and a non-aseptic sector. Both sector markets comprise the cartons and the packaging machines. The aseptic market is monopolistic, with Tetra Pak holding more than 90 per cent share; the non-aseptic market is oligopolistic with market shares of 50–55 per cent Tetra Pak, 27 per cent Elopak, 11 per cent PKL, 12 per cent others.

Tetra Pak's strategy is to exploit as fully as possible its competitive advantage, including innovation, in the market. It does not grant manufacturing licences for its products, does not use independent distributors (no intra-brand competition), has an elaborate patents policy, very strict conditions for both sale and leasing of equipment, and uses an aggressive pricing policy especially in the non-aseptic market. The establishment of dominance is straightforward once one accepts the relevant market as defined above. Of course, the accused company will always try to widen the relevant market so as to appear less dominant (that is, in this case, including the competition from glass bottles and plastic containers). The Commission and the EC Court also deemed the two sector markets to be closely related. Because only Tetra Pak was strong in both, the company could cross-subsidise to support abusive trading policies in the non-aseptic market, attempting to drive out competitors (as indeed Elopak in Italy complained).

Tetra Pak was fined the very high total of ECU 75 million because no less than six types of abuses (with different instances for each type) were established. These abuses include, *inter alia,* restriction of supply and compartmentalising the internal market, very strong tie-in contracts (throttling competitive entry), discriminatory and predatory pricing both for cartons and for the machines, and non-price predation (for example, an Italian dairy magazine was made to agree not to accept advertisements of Tetra Pak's competitors).

In June 2005, AstraZeneca was fined €60 million for illegally attempting to block parallel imports of generics competing with its successful anti-ulcer medicine Losec.[35] AstraZeneca did this, first, by obtaining five years' extra patent protection (however, misleading the authorities about the conditions) and, second, by altering the packaging of Losec (from a capsule to a tablet) and (mis)using this as a reason to deregister the medicine temporarily. In those days, generics did require a 'reference authorisation'. By temporarily withdrawing it, AstraZeneca could delay or frustrate new generics competition.

12.5 Merger control

One conspicuous gap in the original EC treaty provisions (whether in Article 82 or elsewhere) is the lack of merger control. There are different explanations for this omission. They range from an implicit political bias in favour of strengthening European companies, to a fear in Member States at the time that this would imply, in practice, EU control over *national* mergers (because cross-border mergers on the continent were then rare and legally very difficult). The omission also reflected the fact that no founding Member State had national merger control yet. And despite all of the following, one should never forget that the economic premise in case

[34] *Tetra Pak v Commission* [1994] ECR II-755.

[35] Europa Press Release IP/05/737 of 15 June 2005. Case not yet reported.

of mergers is very different from that of collusion or monopoly: mergers are a natural market phenomenon, as a vehicle for restructuring or consolidation or market penetration or innovation. In other words, mergers are 'not a sin, except if'. It is the 'except if' (mergers are anti-competitive) which is the topic of this section, but it is as well to note that an overwhelming majority of mergers are simply vetted.

Since mergers may, in certain market situations, establish or strengthen a high degree of concentration, the process of competition might be endangered by a lack of merger control. When spotting this omission firms might be tempted to look for acquisitions or merger partners as an alternative to the prohibited and carefully watched options of collusion or anti-competitive conduct of dominant firms. This would undermine the credibility of EC competition policy and, if widely used, entail significant welfare costs for the Community. After a struggle of two decades[36] the adopted EC merger control regulation applies only to mergers with a 'Community dimension', leaving other mergers to the discretion of the Member States (which, by now, all have merger control). Ideally, the proper economic way to determine a Community dimension should be based on a combination of (*ex post*) dominance (say, in terms of expected market share) and an assessment of the contestability of the 'relevant market'. The relevant market should reflect sufficient cross-border activities for the companies involved, for it to be dealt with at EU level. Since this economic evaluation is cumbersome and slow, firms would not know when to notify, let alone whether the merger would have a high probability of not being blocked. Therefore, EU decision makers have opted for a much more simple, fast-track procedure. A rule of thumb for compulsory notification was laid down in 1989: a worldwide turnover threshold of ECU 5 billion for the firms concerned, besides a Community-wide turnover of each of at least two companies concerned of ECU 250 million. The latter criterion is subject to the proviso that the EU turnover (of each one of the firms concerned) should not be concentrated in a single Member State – this concentration threshold is two-thirds of EU turnover.

This triple rule of thumb for notification is meant to express, respectively, a size criterion, an impact criterion supposedly capturing potentially significant effects on the internal market, and a competence criterion (that is, whether the assignment of the merger control is at EU level or at national level). All three criteria can be criticised on economic grounds, although they do have the virtue of transparency and greater certainty. The *size criterion,* that is, the turnover threshold, is inappropriate because what is economically relevant is dominance in the relevant (product or service) market. Thus, a threshold as high as ECU 5 billion will undoubtedly leave unchecked mergers (and acquisitions) between smaller firms producing a narrow line of products but with a leading position in the relevant market. Producers of specialised machinery[37] or specific medicines could well be examples. Whether national merger control would vet them (properly) is not *a priori* clear, and, in any event, not with a view to the impact in all national sub-markets in the EU.

The *impact criterion* is arbitrary. However, the proper alternative is costly and slow because it would have to be based on future market share and strategic positioning. To do this adequately would substitute analysis for mere notification, and the criteria are precisely meant to provide clarity about when to notify. The *competence criterion* is a consequence of the desire of European business to have 'one-stop shopping' for companies faced with merger control. With a simple dividing line between what the European Commission does, and what Member States (may) do, there are no qualms about how to apply subsidiarity. Of course, in a purely economic approach to subsidiarity, the two-thirds ratio is arbitrary since such 'national' mergers may have cross-border spillover effects via the actual or potential impact on intra-EU trade and competition. In the extreme one may argue that a 'national' merger could be 100 per cent

[36]Already in the late 1960s the Commission had voiced its concern about the lack of a merger control. The EC Court acknowledged (in *Continental Can* [1973] ECR 215) that Art. 82, could be used to prohibit mergers *ex post.* In the *Philip Morris* case (730/79, [1980] ECR), the Court concurred with the Commission that Art. 81 could be used to block 'friendly' mergers when they took the form of agreed share transactions between the partners. The first draft merger regulation dates back to 1973. The resistance of the Member States weakened gradually for a number of reasons, including the two Court cases, a few conspicuous interventions by the Commission (e.g. when British Airways acquired British Caledonian), the EC-1992 process, and the rapid increase of cross-border mergers as a response to EC-1992. Business (once many Member States had also introduced controls) facilitated the Council decision too, by pressing what was called 'one-stop shopping': the preference to have only one, single EC merger test. The adopted EC regulation is 4064/89 in OJ L 257 (1990, corrected from L 395 in 1989).

[37]Note that, on the single market, an estimated 45,000 different types of machines are sold, many of which are so specialised that very few suppliers survive.

domestic (in terms of turnover) but, by making entry in the national market more difficult, would still have to be blocked at EU level. Fortunately, most Member States have themselves introduced merger control and this should normally help to resolve the problem. For the case where national merger control is more strict than at EU level, the 'German clause' (Article 9) allows referral to national authorities upon request. This has been used only once in the first three years of EC merger control.

Although the triple rule of thumb may provide one-stop shopping for very large firms involved in M&A, it leaves important mergers and acquisitions below the thresholds in a multi-control jam of several – perhaps many – Member States (if sales are spread wide enough). A simple way to obtain one-stop shopping for companies confronted with two, three, four or five national merger controls, is to agree EU-wide strict cooperation procedures (with deadlines) or to transfer the case to the Commission, taking explicit account of the view of national authorities. This would follow directly from the subsidiarity test (Chapter 4). The 2004 merger regulation goes some way into this direction by tightening the 'referred' system (from the relevant Member States to the Commission) in case of effects on cross-border trade.[38] At first, EU merger control was focused entirely on the creation or strengthening of a dominant position, as a result of which effective competition would be significantly impeded in the internal market. And if it would impede competition, no efficiency defence was incorporated. In the new Merger Regulation 139/2004, the focus is squarely on whether a merger impedes competition. Thus, a merger that does, is forbidden, but one that 'would not significantly impede effective competition in the common market . . . in particular as a result of the creation or strengthening of a dominant position, shall be declared compatible with the common market' (Article 2.2). Also, when there is no dominance, yet it is expected to be anti-competitive, the merger will be refused.[39] Finally, an explicit provision for an efficiency defence is included in Article 2.1(b), with the wording: 'the development of technical and economic progress [will be taken into account] provided it is to consumers' advantage and does not form an obstacle to competition'. This introduction of an efficiency test for mergers is interesting because it forces the authorities to make a clear choice for a 'welfare' standard based solely on the consumer interest or on a broader consumer-plus-producers (aggregate) welfare test. Figure 12.4 helps us to analyse the issue.

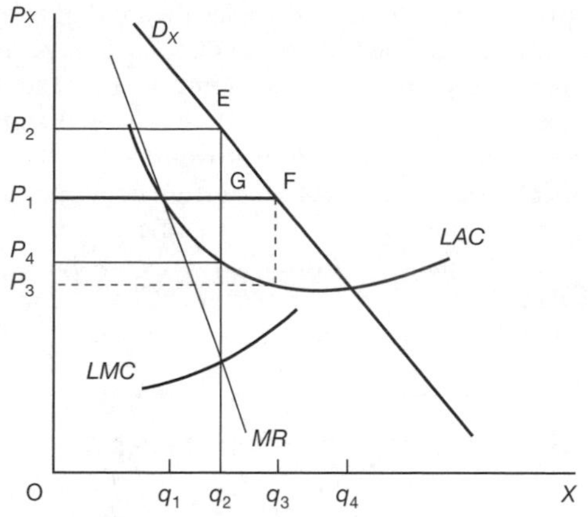

Figure 12.4 A merger raising efficiency

Source: Based on Williamson, 1968

Before the merger the market is made up of two equal-sized duopolists in vigorous competition. Each of them produces on an identical scale curve *LAC* (long-term average costs) a volume of Oq_1 yielding P_1, as if there were atomistic competition ($P_1F \times Oq_3 = 2 \times Oq_1$). The merger will join the two productions and, after adjustment, a volume Oq_3 could be produced at P_3. If the market were contestable this is what would happen. In case the merger creates a dominant position which will not easily be contested, the new monopolist will produce only Oq_2 at P_2, although its costs per unit would fall to P_4. Under the merger regulation the merger would be blocked for the (expected) price effect of the new monopoly. However, the net welfare effect on the EU is not necessarily negative because there is a trade-off between the cost efficiency improvement of the *ex ante* output (which remains) $(P_1 - P_4) \times Oq_2$ and the loss of consumer surplus (EGF). The trade-off represents the efficiency defence if EGF $< [(P_1 - P_4) \times Oq_2]$.

[38]Regulation 139/2004 of 20 January 2004, OJ L 24 of 29 January 2004 (the second revision of the EC Merger Regulation). There are four simultaneous thresholds: (1) the combined turnover of all companies must be larger than €2.5 billion (so, half the size of the Community dimension, see above); (2) in each one of three Member States the combined turnover be €100 million; (3) individual turnover of two companies in at least three Member States be larger than €25 million; (4) EU-wide turnover of at least two of the companies be larger than €100 million.

[39]Note that this sharper focus on impeding effective competition brings EU merger control closer to the US core criterion of 'lessening competition'.

It is easy to see that, as long as the minimum-efficient scale is not reached, the net effect will be positive except for very small cost improvements. There are two caveats here. First, this model, based on Williamson (1968), is far too simple for real-world cases. Second, empirical research about the efficiency effects of mergers has failed to uncover actual efficiency improvements in the majority of M&As, probably due to the non-technical problems of mergers.[40] This important empirical point therefore supports the absence of an efficiency defence for EU mergers. It suggests that, at the time of the merger, companies overestimate the gains and underrate the problems.[41]

Behind the efficiency defence lies the controversy between a pure consumer-welfare standard for competition policy and a traditional aggregate economic welfare standard. In the latter, redistribution effects (in Figure 12.4 the rectangle P_2EGP_1) are netted out and the efficiency test remains. In the former, the extra P_2EGP_1, is viewed as harming the consumer – for an

CASE STUDY 12.3 Refusals of mergers

After fifteen years of EC merger control, only 19 mergers had been refused out of a total of nearly 2,700. The low refusal rate is explained by amendments of merger plans after informal contacts with the Merger Task Force, or formal negotiations in stage two of the procedure. A well-known example of renegotiation in stage two is the Nestlé acquisition of Perrier, a leading French brand of mineral water (also controlling several other brands in the French market). Nestlé is a worldwide food company, owning two mineral water brands in the French market. Having established that the relevant market is that of bottled water from mineral and other wells (and not that of, for example, all soft drinks as well) in France (and not other countries, as it was difficult to penetrate the French market for business and reputation reasons), the merger was only allowed on conditions. These include that a third competitor would take over several brands together, the buyer would have to be approved (that is, be strong enough) and Nestlé was banned from buying back any brand for ten years. In other words, the Commission wished to 'create' competition for the merger to be allowed. This stretches the merger regulation: what if no appropriate buyer is found? Would the merger be called off a year later?

The first refusal (in 1991) was the takeover of De Haviland by ATR, a joint venture of Aerospatiale and Alenia, producing commuter aircrafts.[42] The relevant market was found to be the world market (except central/eastern Europe and China); in product terms that of regional turbo propeller aeroplanes with 20–70 seats. The new firm would have 50 per cent of the world market and 65 per cent of the internal market. Over the total range of commuter aircrafts, only the subsegment of 20–39 seats would remain competitive. Thus, the Commission decided that the new combination would be able to act to an appreciable extent independently from competitors and customers (see section 12.4.2, citation from the famous *United Brands* case) and refused the merger.

The second refusal is uncontroversial. In November 1994, a (so-called) concentrative joint venture – MSG Media Service – by Bertelsmann (the world's second largest media group), Deutsche Telekom (then a monopolist in Germany for telephone and cable TV networks) and Taurus (a German supplier of films) was blocked.[43] MSG would provide services to pay-TV channels. The joint venture would be likely to lead to a fairly long-term monopoly for installing decoders and conditional access systems (set-top box); preclude future competition in the German software market for pay-TV precisely between potential competitors; and result in the likely pre-emption of alternative cable networks after 1998 when the broadband monopoly of Deutsche Telekom would (by EC law) be ended.

[40]Such as different corporate cultures, long-term adjustment problems in management and the workforce, disparities in market orientation and disagreement about corporate strategy.

[41]The suggestion that private motives – such as temporarily boosting the value of stock options of managers – play a role, can only be accepted if capital markets would not 'understand' this. For a survey of empirical evidence on failed mergers and on explanations of why many mergers are 'strategic' (rather than wealth creating), see Schenk (1999).

[42](Case No. IV/M.053 – Aerospatiale–Alenia/De Haviland), Council Regulation (EEC) No. 4064/89. Decision of 2 October 1991 declaring the incompatibility with the common market of a concentration.

[43]Commission Decision of 9 November 1994 relating to a proceeding pursuant to Council Regulation (EEC) No. 4064/89 (IV/M.469 – MSG Media Service) (94/922/EC).

CASE STUDY 12.3 *continued*

In 1998 this was followed by a very similar merger between Bertelsmann and Kirch's (the owner of Taurus) pay-TV interests. Deutsche Telekom was indirectly (but crucially) involved because it had chosen the d-box set-top technology for its cable network (the only one in Germany covering the entire country); this technology was owned by Kirch. A reshuffling would make Premiere the *de facto* sole provider of pay-TV services, as the assets of DF1 (the only competitor with a separate technical platform) would be transferred to Premiere. Kirch still controlled pay-TV rights for Hollywood films and for major sports events (via a channel called DSF). This emerging supermonopolist in German-speaking Europe with integration of the network, access technology and content would have made access of new entrants close to impossible for a long time (this is called 'market foreclosure'). The merger was forbidden.[44] The case was followed by a controlling joint venture between Deutsche Telekom and Kirch's subsidiary Betaresearch, the legal owner of the d-box. For reasons of vertical integration causing foreclosure, it too was forbidden.

The nineteen refusals of mergers are not always final. Appeal to the Court of First Instance or the EC Court itself is possible. In three well-publicised cases (*Tetra-Laval/Sidel,* final EC Court ruling in 2005; *Schneider/Legrand,* Court of First Instance rulings in 2004; and *Air Tours*), refusals were overruled. Reasons included the need for higher standards of economic analysis and improper procedural aspects.

efficiency-raising merger (as in Figure 12.4) to be approved, cost reductions would at least to some extent have to be passed on to consumers.

Roberts & Salop (1996) have proposed a framework to analyse mergers in a dynamic rather than a static way. In a dynamic perspective, cost reduction via innovations will diffuse with a delay and thereby stimulate competition, with significant spillover benefits for consumers. One can simulate the critical (variable) cost reductions, under a pure consumer welfare standard, for given demand elasticities and a given number of competitors in the market. In view of the great uncertainty, the authors adopt a very high discount rate (25 per cent). Low demand elasticities and a lower number of firms cause the required variable cost reductions for consumers to benefit – hence, for the merger to pass – to increase sharply. It is therefore possible to introduce a (case-by-case) efficiency test for mergers in the EU without harming the Union's consumer.[45] Finally, Figure 12.4 can be drawn in such a way that even dominance after a merger will result in a win–win situation: a cost gain for producers and lower prices for consumers. For this to be obtained, the reader should 'stretch' the scale curve, such that it continues to fall for any relevant section of demand (as is the case in Figure 8.1), and rotate the demand schedule anti-clockwise, around F, making it more elastic. Once this is done, a merger may well *increase* output beyond q_3 at a lower price for consumers.

The actual EC procedures are in two stages. When the thresholds are exceeded, notification has to take place (within a week) and the Commission has 25 working days to inspect the merger. This sharp deadline is used to single out the suspect cases for stage two, an in-depth investigation of another four months. Such rapidity can be explained by an implicit bias in the Council to allow mergers in the process of restructuring to the greater competition resulting from EC-1992 as well as from globalisation. But it is political too, since especially Germany and the UK only reluctantly transferred (some) merger control powers to the EC Commission. In practice, the Commission has stood the test: in the fifteen years since 21 September 1990 (until

[44]Commission Decision of 27 May 1998, relating to a proceeding pursuant to Council Regulation (EEC) No. 4064/89, (Case No. IV/M.993 – Bertelsmann/Kirch/Premiere).

[45]For proposals and elaborate economic analysis, see Ilzkovitz & Meiklejohn (eds) (2006).

30 September 2005), it has had to process 2,633 cases in stage one (cleared or for other reasons not going to stage two) and this has worked well: swift and surprisingly unbureaucratic. Of the 147 cases investigated in stage two, 74 were resolved by successful negotiation about remedies so as to avoid refusal, and 19 led to a refusal.

The facilitating attitude of the Merger Task Force can be defended as long as it is not pushed too far. Mergers and acquisitions are important market responses to the need for restructuring. Restructuring is a permanent activity and reflects all kinds of adjustment needs of companies, whether for reasons of technological change, structural alteration of demand, responses to new entrants or globalisation. Hence, facilitation, speed and maximum certainty (within the confines of the law) are proper ways to reduce regulatory costs.

CASE STUDY 12.4 The relevant market

In cases about the abuse of dominant position and in merger control, the question of what constitutes the relevant market is often crucial. In collusion, the nature of the case or the agreement itself is sometimes sufficient to pinpoint the relevant market. There is a relevant product (services or goods) and a relevant geographical market. The purpose of such a market definition need not be the same as identifying a 'market' for purely commercial reasons – the point of the relevant market is to be able to identify the competitors which are or might be capable of disciplining the investigated firms or preventing the latter from behaving independently from users or consumers. For this relevant market, market shares can be calculated which will form a preliminary indicator of market power. Firms are subject to three main sources of competitive constraints:

- demand substitutability (of goods/services, as regards use and price; with cross-elasticities of price or substitution elasticities or other tests (see any textbook on industrial economics);
- supply substitutability (if sufficiently rapid and effective);
- potential competition (hinges on barriers to entry).

It should be remembered that (high) market shares indicate market power only if the (relevant) market is not – or hardly – contestable because of sunk costs or other barriers to entry. If at all possible, a SSNIP test is conducted in anti-monopoly cases: a 'small but significant, non-transitory increase in price' of 5 per cent should indicate to which other suppliers the customers turn and which potential competitors start supplying close substitutes within a year. These suppliers belong to the 'relevant market', as they might discipline the monopolist.

Since the establishment of the relevant market is so crucial for a case, the Commission is at times sharply criticised (indeed, in a few cases by the Court; more often, of course, by the accused companies which always argue for a wider product and/or geographical market than the Commission, so that their market shares look much lower). In fairness, one should realise that suitable, independent data (or elasticities) are rarely available at the required level of disaggregation so that more arbitrary methods tend to prevail.

12.6 Controlling state aids

Both the ECSC and the Rome treaties, in principle, prohibit subsidies if they distort competition in the internal market, that is, between enterprises in different Member States. Articles 87 and 88 EC contain this principle and the derogations allowed, either directly by the treaty or after the Commission declares the subsidy 'compatible' with the common market. There are basic political and economic reasons to justify this EU competence. The political rationale is that the establishment and proper functioning of the internal market would not be guaranteed merely by the liberalisation of market access and the appropriate approximation of economic regulation. As has been argued in section 12.1, behaviour of private firms might prevent or make more costly the entry of potential competitors into a highly concentrated national market or a market dominated by a cartel. But similarly, national or regional governments may subsidise local firms or sectors, thereby making possible a change in relative prices between Member States analogous to tariffs or quotas. When negotiating the treaty, Member States were not willing to expose their national markets to EU-wide competition, if companies in other Member States would enjoy artificial competitive advantages by means of subsidies. Since the alternative means of counter-subsidies would further add to the distortions in the internal market and may well result in a subsidy race, with the upshot that the European economy at large would lose – even though some (producers) might gain – common rules and supervision are the superior option.

The economic rationale consists in the thrust, underlying the EC treaty, that undistorted competition would be the best incentive for technical efficiency and innovation by companies and the most effective route to realise an EU-wide division of labour and specialisation. Aid might also help the less efficient to survive at the expense of the more efficient. Thus, strict controls would generate the economic gains desired.

However, these seemingly plausible arguments do not carry us very far. They beg several questions such as: when is a state aid really a distortion of competition, and when does it induce significant cross-border externalities (justifying centralised EU control)? Consider the following food for thought, inspired by Besley & Seabright (1999). In terms of the first question, at least two points are of critical importance, yet often overlooked. For a state aid to be distortive, the goods or services market at stake must be imperfectly competitive; under perfect competition the benefiting company may enjoy positive profits but all other companies continue to face the same competitive disciplines as before. Thus, equity (between firms) or the taxpayers' concern about 'waste' or favouritism might be issues, but not efficiency as such. Perhaps even more important, if the aid is paid to overcome a market failure, it is not distortive – indeed, it is to restore efficiency. If market failures are similar in kind in different Member States but require disparate amounts of aid, these are also not distortive.

As to the second question, if applied to mobile resources (see Case Study 10.1 on corporate tax competition), one may distinguish greenfield FDI from relocation of existing resources. Whereas aids to induce the latter bring with them a clear negative cross-border externality and ought to be outlawed by the EU, is this also true for government (tax) competition for greenfield FDI? The probable waste of resources will constitute a burden for local taxpayers of the aid-giving country, but is there significant damage (for example, 'harmful tax competition') for other EU countries? Case Study 10.1 suggests that, in some situations, this is the case.

In the mid-1980s, and compared with Japan and the USA, EU countries were typical subsidisers (Ford & Suyker, 1990). This is no longer the case. Overall state aid has fallen significantly over two decades. Starting from 1992 to 2003 inclusive, state aids in the EU15 have halved.[46] In 2003, 55 per cent of the total EU15 state aids went to manufacturing, 6 per cent to services, 26 per cent to agriculture (note, national aid not CAP), 1 per cent to fisheries, 10 per cent to coal and 2 per cent to transport other than rail. However, unlike one or two decades ago, there is a steady shift towards 'horizontal' and away from sectoral or (individual company) rescue aid. No less than 79 per cent of EU15 aid was horizontal in 2003, but in ten of the fifteen Member States, the share had moved beyond 90 per cent. The idea is that horizontal aid is less (or not) distortive and can be better geared towards market failures.[47] A corollary is that a more general EU framework for sectoral aid is emerging which incorporates (at first, separate) aid to the car sector, synthetic fibres and so on, while phasing out any lingering operational sectoral aid, as in shipbuilding.

Shipbuilding is the oldest EU problem. In Article 87(3)(c) it is already mentioned specifically, never changed since the Rome Treaty. During the 1970s and most of the 1980s, shipbuilding was a shrinking activity in the EU, due to sharp competition from Korea and Japan as well as to occasional world surplus capacity. A subsidy race between Member States made a mockery of undistorted intra-EU competition. It is only since the mid-1980s that the Council could finally agree on a steady, though slow, reduction of subsidy ceilings. A sharp fall in shipbuilding aid occurred between 1988/90 and 1990/92 – in terms of value-added, from 33.8 per cent to 14.6 per cent. By 2003, all aid amounted to €685

[46]Total aid, less agriculture, fisheries and transport as a percentage of GDP fell from 0.84 to 0.40 per cent; total aid less railways as a percentage of GDP fell from 1.09 to 0.5 per cent (COM (2005) 147 of 20 April 2005; *State Aid Scoreboard – Spring 2005 Update,* table 2).

[47]Typical horizontal objectives or areas include R&D, environment, energy saving, SMEs, employment creation (general), (re)training, regional development.

million and by 2005 all operational aid in this amount (about half) became illegal. Repeated crises in the steel industry have also prompted heavy subsidisation over long periods of restructuring. A combination of factors[49] caused a major crisis and heavy subsidisation between 1977 and 1985, which only subsided slowly after a special Aid Code was concluded in 1981. Although much of this aid was social in nature, reducing the high, often regionally concentrated adjustment costs, it was nevertheless severely anti-competitive because it frustrated the market rewards of the efficient, non-subsidised mills for years. Steel aid (€95 million in 2003, all environmental) has come down to a trickle (see Case Study 14.1).

ADDITIONAL READING

Subsidies tend to be justified economically by the presence of 'market failures'. Social justifications consist in intolerable adjustment burdens for highly specific groups or 'universal service' considerations (for example, for railways and postal services), implying a compensation for (non-commercial) discount consumers or for the high-cost connections.[48]

For agriculture and shipbuilding, long-run adjustment processes undoubtedly play a role, but the CAP should take care of agriculture at the EU level. The national aid complements this with R&D, environmental and landscape services, food image campaigns, and so on. In shipbuilding, neither a common policy nor a pre-emption of a subsidy war appeared politically feasible for a long time and only now has aid declined so much that the problem has become a minor case.

With respect to market failures, one should make a distinction between whether the EU itself subsidises (which is *not* part of its competition policy) and whether this can be justified, on the one hand, and how to deal with national state aids, which may distort the internal market even when they are justified nationally, on the other hand. The former will be dealt with in chapters on common policies such as industrial policy. The latter may occur in the case of cross-border externalities.[49] The practice of the EC surveillance of state aids is complex. The legal basis for transport aid (for example, Article 77, now Article 73 EC), steel (the Aid Codex of 1981, in fact amending the ECSC treaty) and agriculture (Article 42, now Article 36 EC) are special (though major) cases. Also, the enormous state aids to coal (in 1996–98 amounting to €44,173 per employee for the five EU coal countries remaining – but in Germany this was 50 per cent higher still) are a flagrant violation of Article 4 ECSC, which pronounces a total ban on such aids. Instead, they have been based on the catch-all Article 95 ECSC and in essence amount to operating aids over very long periods, prompted by considerations of regional employment and social policy. There are no economic arguments to support coal as world coal prices are low, supplies (import) diversified and world stocks very large. It should be said that output is steadily decreasing and so is the absolute amount of aid.

Article 87 EC is complicated in its own right. Paragraphs 2 and 3 of the article give the derogations. Apart from special or uncontroversial cases,[50] they include regional problems, important projects of Community interest (the initial Airbus aid is one of the rare applications of this clause) and aid to 'facilitate the development of certain economic activities', all

[48]A special issue is (covert) state aids for state-owned enterprises and, in particular, whether an increase in (state) capital for the company can be justified. The latter is evaluated by asking the question whether a private investor would have done the same ('market economy investor principle' or MEIP). Matters can get even more difficult if restructuring and privatisation occurs. See Harbord & Yarrow (1999) for a careful analysis.

[49]In Meiklejohn (1999) nine main types of market failure are briefly analysed with a view to possible subsidisation. They include public goods, merit goods, increasing returns to scale, externalities, imperfect or asymmetric information, institutional rigidities, imperfect factor mobility (e.g. between regions), frictional adjustment problems and subsidies given to foreign competitors elsewhere. These nine types do not enjoy equally strong justifications for subsidies, and do not necessarily imply that cross-border externalities arise.

[50]For example, certain social aids to consumers, aid connected to natural disasters and a serious disturbance of a Member State's economy.

ADDITIONAL READING *continued*

subject to Commission policy and surveillance.[51] Moreover, there are horizontal and sectoral aids as well as 'general measures'. Competitive advantages arising from the latter have to do with differences in general economic, fiscal or social policy and fall under the little used Articles 96 and 97 EC. They are not state aids since Article 87(1) prescribes that those must benefit *certain* undertakings or the production of certain goods. But until the early 1990s, national general investment aid schemes had been allowed for decades. The critical difference with 'general measures' is that the schemes are discretionary; general (for example) fiscal policy is not. Clearly, there is a grey zone here exemplified by the case of general employment and training aid.[52] In fact, by reviewing all those old broad schemes and disallowing continuation, a large number of them have disappeared since.

In the new Member States of 2004, the pre-accession process has gradually reduced the level and sectoral nature of state aids. It should be realised that the new Member States came out of the 'transition' process towards full market economies (see Chapter 20); during this turbulent process, aid to coal, steel and the banking sector was sometimes indispensable for viability or was a corollary of privatisation. Ignoring such emergency aids before entry into the EU, state aids amount to 0.67 per cent of GDP (average 2000–03), a little higher than the EU15.

A detailed survey is of course beyond the purpose of this book. What is important to understand are the following two basic conclusions:

1 Controlling state aids is to serve a proper functioning internal market in which the competition is not distorted. Unlike the anti-trust part of competition policy, however, major exceptions were allowed for many years in state aids which heavily distorted competition. The drastic decline in the totals and the decisive shift towards horizontal aid can only mean that (on this account) the internal market functions much better today.

2 State aids tend to be politicised in several ways and this reduces the effectiveness of the surveillance in the EU regime. A gradual shift towards a pro-market attitude in Europe as well as EC-1992 and budget constraints (in the framework of EMU) have made it politically possible to tighten state aids surveillance considerably. Nevertheless, the politicisation has long remained a fundamental weakness, as shown by the great problems in checking a new wave of steel aid in 1993–94 and the high and contested aid (in the form of capital participation) to no less than six airlines, including Air France and Iberia in 1994–95. Overall, state aids to industry are now better controlled and a larger part of them are justifiable economically. However, the remaining 'special' sectors and occasional rescue operations continue to be politically influenced.

12.7 Summary

The prime purpose of competition policy is to promote and maintain a process of effective competition so as to achieve a more efficient allocation of resources. However, it should avoid penalising efficient 'winners' in the market. Different emphases in competition policy may be attributed to at least three currents in the literature: laissez-faire oriented, interventionism, and liberal/democratic. The EU level of competition policy is justified by (1) potential conflicts between national jurisdictions, and (2) the neglect of externalities across borders of national approaches to competition cases.

[51]The shipbuilding aids are decided (by QMV) by the Council under Art. 87(3)(d) and this may partly explain their quasi-permanence.

[52]Some €2,300 million annually in 1996–98 for the EU15, but the bulk is constituted by €846 million of employment subsidies in Italy and €585 million of training aid in the UK. See *8th Survey on State Aids in the EU,* COM (2000) 205 of 11 April 2000.

Summary *continued*

The EU competition regime consists of general rules, anti-trust provisions (anti-collusion, anti-monopoly and merger control), rules about the conduct of public agents (including firms enjoying exclusive rights), and special regimes for transport and agriculture. However, competition in the internal market also depends on the internal market regime and the (pro-competitive) nature of other EU policies (for example, trade policy).

The economics of anti-collusion can be traced back to the analogy with the costs of monopoly (namely, perfect collusion). In practice, cartels are stable only in oligopolistic markets, usually those with low contestability; indeed, even excessive price stability may occur, but the complication is that this need not point to cartel behaviour but may reflect intense oligopolistic interdependence. Active cartels in relatively homogeneous goods are still being discovered today (for example, steel beams, cement). However, the key aspect of Article 81 is the (block) exemption on the basis of an efficiency test, prescribed in Article 81(3). It is used with relatively little controversy for, for example, R&D cooperative inter-firm agreements. Exemptions for vertical agreements are more complex to analyse; it is critical that, *inter alia,* inter-brand competition (not so much intra-brand) remains effective and that price discrimination is prevented. The bureaucratic and all-encompassing approach to 'verticals' that the Commission employed for decades has now been replaced by an 'effect-based' approach, except for a short list of outlawed types of verticals. This is economically sound and implementation is less costly. The block exemption for car dealers, long problematic, has gradually become less restrictive and car prices are now less varied across the EU.

The economics of a dominant position is complicated by the potential of fringe competition and a range of entry deterrence tactics. The standard definition of dominance used by the EC Court since the *United Brands* case blends structural and conduct aspects. Any offensive action by a dominant firm to strengthen its position may be illegal under Article 82 EC (as the *Tetra Pak* case illustrates) but this is so only if contestability is low. A current review of Article 82 pratices may well shift the EU towards a stronger emphasis on 'competitive harm' caused by a firm's behaviour (effects based).

Merger control at EU level is justified by subsidiarity, but the thresholds (the size, impact and competence criteria) for the so-called Community dimension can only be defended on grounds of legal certainty; the economic justification is lacking. Economic theory points to a possible efficiency defence of mergers, but empirical research barely supports it. The 2004 merger regulation allows an efficiency defence and has also become more effect (on competition) based. Merger control has worked well, thus far, pursuing a flexible, fast-track approach with minimal costs for business. Apart from routine negotiations to modify notified mergers in a pro-competitive way, only 19 mergers had been blocked up to September 2005 out of 2,700 notifications.

Controlling state aids in the EU has gradually led to a sophisticated, effects-based regime. Undoubtedly the Commission has, step by step, reduced or eliminated a number of open-ended state aid practices while it has rationally conditioned other ones. In three non-manufacturing sectors, national state aid is still high: railways, coal, and agriculture and fisheries (note, not counting EU subsidies for agriculture and fisheries). The key problem is both social and political. Since the Commission confronts Member States, being accountable for the aids given, politicisation is sometimes weakening the EU control (for example, airlines in 1994–95).

Overall, state aids are slowly declining and the policy is beginning to be based more on economic criteria.

CHAPTER 13 Common Trade Policy

Topics covered

From the outset, the EU's trade policy has been one of its more important instruments. Under GATT rules, as a CU it must have a CET and some other common provisions. However, even in the Rome Treaty, the Community opted for a more comprehensive approach. One of the main problems in developing the common trade policy has been to agree how comprehensive its scope would be. This question was (and to some extent still is) exacerbated by the great deepening and widening of EU economic integration. Should the scope of the policy include all goods (for example, including coal, despite the ECSC's lack of a common trade policy), allow a special place for agricultural and fishery goods, and cover (all?) services? Yet, it may also be connected to the 'external' aspects of various other EU policies (for example, immigration or international cooperation in competition policies) and to a veritable host of possible instruments. Finally, it is influenced by multilateral progress (the scope of GATT / WTO) and by plurilateral agreements (such as commodity agreements). And now that the EU contains a eurozone of twelve countries, questions arise about monetary union that are manifestly not questions of trade policy.

The present chapter focuses on trade policy for goods (except for a few notes on services). As will be clear from Table 13.2 – on the links between trade policy and other EU policies – however, a further delimitation is desirable to keep this chapter coherent. This is achieved by reference to other chapters in the book.[1]

After inspecting the possible justification of (a common) trade policy (in section 13.1) with Case Study 13.1 (on its scope), and a survey of its instruments (in section 13.2) and seven types of trade policy (section 13.3), sections 13.4 and 13.5 will, respectively, deal with EU tariff and volume protection, including Case Study 13.2 on the latter. Anti-dumping is analysed in section 13.6 (illustrated by Case Study 13.3), followed by a brief excursion on the EU's preferentialism (section 13.7). Section 13.8 discusses how the EU has combined multilateralism in GATT/WTO with regionalism and whether, as the largest trader in the world,

[1]Thus, the establishment of the CET is dealt with in section 5.2.1; the removal of national quotas *vis-à-vis* third countries is addressed in sections 5.2.2 and 6.5.3; external economic impact analysis (of the CU) in section 6.4 and (of EC-1992) in section 6.6; agricultural trade policy is found in Chapter 11; and a range of trade liberalisation questions in the context of pan-European integration are discussed in Chapter 20. Furthermore, trade policy has a great actual and potential impact on competition, quite apart from the issue whether anti-dumping policy belongs to trade or competition policy. Another close link is that with industrial policy (see, e.g., Table 14.1 on industrial policy instruments).

it has been a follower or a leader in world trade liberalisation. It includes Case Study 13.4 on the Union's 'market access strategy'.

13.1 Why a common trade policy?

As with other EU policies, the heading of this section in fact comprises two questions: why trade policy, and why a common EU one?

13.1.1 Why have trade policies?

Asking why countries, or regional groupings, have trade policies leads to a multitude of answers, such as fiscal (customs) revenue, mercantilism (resisting imports and boosting exports), specific vested interests, foreign policy, import substitution. The question we are interested in here is whether having a trade policy can be justified economically.

The conventional answer in trade theory is that, at least for small countries, free trade is first best. Thus, traditional trade protection finds no economic justification. Other than emergency rationing during and shortly after wars or disasters, the customs should merely be employed for reasons other than protection of domestic business and workers, such as border tax adjustments, specific enforcement (for example, hazardous waste rules) and trade documentation. This conventional recipe has come under attack from two types of alternative approaches: the optimum tariff argument (for large countries) in traditional models, and a breed of new models with scale and imperfect competition.[2] The fundamental weakness of the optimum tariff argument is that it requires other countries not to pursue optimum tariffs as well. Once retaliation is allowed for, one needs complex game-theoretic approaches going beyond the present book. The policy conclusion is ambiguous. On the one hand, one may argue that one ought to make use of trade policy in order to be a credible retaliator in case major trading partners pursue optimum tariffs. On the other hand, this argument is weak for small countries as they are price takers.[3] Nor is it a reliable guide for big countries as they are bound to get into a trade war of iterative tariff reactions resulting in sharply reduced trade and uncertain outcomes.

The new models have qualified the conventional economic case for free trade. Further qualifications can be accomplished when introducing, for example, targeted R&D subsidies on exportables. The main point is that comparative advantage is no longer the sole explanation for the gains from trade (as in conventional models).[4]

There are two important reasons why the free trade recipe is nevertheless still broadly adhered to. First, the conventional (general equilibrium) argument for free trade has always consisted of two elements: allocative gains and technical efficiency gains. Fascination with analytical rigour has caused economists to focus disproportionately on the allocative gains, assuming technical efficiency. But allocative gains have consistently been shown to be very small, except for some extreme cases.[5] It is the exposure to actual and potential external competition which usually yields far larger gains (improvement in technical efficiency). One contribution of the new models is that they have strengthened the analytical underpinning for precisely this argument. It can be extended in a dynamic perspective of innovation and change.

Second, few policies tend to be more influenced by vested interests than trade policy. Political economy tries to explain why trade policies have, more often than not, been geared to producers' rather than consumers' or overall economic interests. If this explanation is accepted, the free trade benchmark becomes a rule of thumb, with the burden of proof for exceptions shifted to those who seek it.[6] The advantages of competitive exposure should weigh heavily in any assessment of derogations. In a GATT/WTO framework these rules of thumb can be multilateralised, including the case for exceptions.

The conclusion is that the economic justification for having trade policies is weak at best. Trade policies are no

[2]It is assumed that the student knows the optimum tariff argument. See, for example, Krugman & Obstfeld (1991, pp. 217–18 and pp. 237–9). The new models are touched upon in, e.g., section 6.5.2. There is now a burgeoning literature. See, e.g., Krugman & Obstfeld (2003, ch. 6).

[3]The extreme is represented by city states such as Hong Kong and Singapore which practise free trade policies (in goods).

[4]Thus, first-mover advantages ('who was first' in the presence of large-scale effects and steep learning curves) and reciprocal dumping may provide an economic rationale for trade without relying on conventional comparative advantage. In other models, import protection can serve as export promotion, with a positive effect on national welfare. See also section 6.5.2.

[5]An example of an extreme case is when access to technology is free and the product can only be produced with labour-intensive methods, a rapid increase in inter-industry north–south trade can force adjustment with large gains (assuming full employment). With unemployment, however, adjustment costs may be considerable.

[6]Krugman (1987), a main contributor to the new models, relies strongly on political economy arguments to recommend free trade.

good for national market failures, since these require solutions directly addressing the failure without deadweight welfare losses which protection inevitably brings about. Trade policies are a possible, but unreliable, instrument to bring other countries to the negotiating table. Given the possible damage of trade wars to trade and investment, it is preferable to do this in a GATT / WTO context. The best use of trade policy is for the purposes of gradual liberalisation, pursuing technical and allocative efficiency gains, also over time. The preferred solution to 'anchor' such a long-run strategy is to accept legal, multilateral commitments, both as a proof of credibility to trading partners and as a robust disarmament of powerful domestic producer (and labour) lobbies seeking protection.

13.1.2 Why a common trade policy?

Why the EU needs a common trade policy is straightforward. As noted, the GATT (Article 24) requires a CU to have a CET and some other common provisions, although these remain ill-defined. For the EU, having moved far beyond the GATT notion of a CU from the outset, the case for a common trade policy is based on the application of subsidiarity. Of the criteria mentioned in Table 3.1, negative externalities, generated by disparate national trade policies in a Union with free movement, is the key one. One may also mention bargaining power and legal uniformity throughout the Union (which lowers uncertainty and transaction costs).

National trade policies form a beggar-thy-neighbour approach, inimical to economic agents in other Member States. Given the accepted objective (now in Article 14 EC) of a completed internal market, with undistorted competition, a comprehensive common policy becomes a logical complement. Maintaining national trade policy instruments, applicable only to third countries, can also not be justified economically in this approach. Two examples may suffice. The retention of national quotas for clothing imports from specific third countries'

CASE STUDY 13.1 The scope of EU trade policy

The Uruguay Round (1986–93) greatly widened the scope of multilateral trade rules. When it came to ratification by the EU, the question arose as to who should ratify? The Court was asked for an opinion. Behind this seemingly formal issue, looms the problem of what falls under the (exclusive) EC competence, what under concurrent competences, and what under Member States' competence? As noted in Chapter 5, a failure to establish common market access rules leads almost certainly to distortions of competition on the internal market. Now that national quotas *vis-à-vis* third countries have finally disappeared for goods (see sections 5.2.2 and 13.4), the problem resurfaces for the external aspects of services liberalisation and other 'new' trade policy issues. In air transport, for example, the Member States were long jealous about their powers to negotiate bilateral agreements with third countries (still the mercantilistic basis of almost all cross-border civil aviation outside the Union – see section 8.4.1) and it took a Court ruling in 2002 to overcome this. More liberal access in air transport is a bilateral issue, however, because it has carefully been kept out of the remit of the GATT rules until today. The EC Court Opinion (1/94) of November 1994 is therefore crucial for economic and policy reasons. The highest judges said that the common trade policy in goods also includes agriculture and coal and steel, if they are a part of multilateral (or plurilateral) agreements. This is equally true for cross-border supplies of services. The three other modes of services trade (see section 7.1) do not fall within the scope of the common trade policy. On transport specifically, the treaty chapter on transport has to be used – for air transport, this means Article 80 EC. With respect to intellectual property rights, counterfeit goods fall under exclusive EC competence but other TRIPs (trade-related aspects of intellectual property rights) are under shared (concurrent) competence. Realising that such a complex treaty regime on common trade policy was therefore potentially inefficient, the Court stressed the obligation of the two levels of government to cooperate closely during negotiations and when about to sign. It also imposed a 'requirement of unity' in the international representation of the Union. These additional conditions imposed by the Court caused attempts to renegotiate the basic policy article, now Article 133. Although an extra clause was inserted in the Amsterdam Treaty, no breakthrough was achieved on the centralisation of trade powers in services and TRIPs.

exporters does distort the internal market, as shown in section 6.5.3. The insistence on keeping national export credit (and credit insurance) powers for exports to third markets equally induces distortions of competition on the internal market.[7]

The argument of legal uniformity and certainty is based on the problems caused by differential customs treatment between any two or more ports of entry into the Union. This grows less and less tolerable the more ambitious the internal market arrangements become. Thus, while the Maastricht Treaty has kept in place the vague Article 27 on approximation of customs law,[8] in practice, the EU felt compelled to develop a common body of law (the common custom code) which was completed in 1992. Hence, the old Article 27 was deleted in the Amsterdam Treaty. Nevertheless, the EU does not have a Union customs, nor is this required on the basis of subsidiarity.

As noted in section 3.1.3, the criterion of bargaining power in fact amounts to a combination of the negative externality (or a threat thereof) argument with scale. Therefore it is not an independent criterion. From the point of view of EU countries and institutions, bargaining power obviously strengthens the case for a common trade policy. However, the EU gains in welfare may well be at the expense of others. For instance, the EU as a whole will have a higher optimum tariff than individual Member States.

13.2 Principle, objectives and instruments

It is not easy to deduce a clear framework for trade policy from the treaty. Far more than the CAP (see Figure 11.2) and competition policy (Table 12.1), trade policy is based on unclear, and at times implicit, objectives. There is a wide range of instruments which are nowhere fully specified. Transparency is a problem: although trade policy is highly complicated, there is no annual report, unlike with several other common policies.[9] It took the mid-term review of the Uruguay Round in the GATT to fill this gap with the biannual, detailed and authoritative Trade Policy Review.[10] Moreover, EC history is not a particularly useful guide because, precisely where protectionist sentiments were greatest, the development of the common policy was often blocked by a refusal to forgo remaining national protection. The situation in 2005 is completely different. With EC-1992, the common policy has definitively been established. The following outlines the framework.

The *principle* governing EU trade policy since the Maastricht Treaty is that of 'an open market economy with free competition' (Article 4 EC). How operational this reference to an 'open' economy is, is not clear. It certainly does not mean, in practice, that the EU will now do away with all remaining protection, merely as a consequence of this provision. What it might mean is, for instance, a prohibition of a movement towards more protection. If such a ratchet effect could be sustained by the EC Court, it would be an important constitutional principle. In any event, to give the principle any meaning, the very least one could demand is public accountability about the grounds for any move which reduces market access to the EU.

The *objectives* of the common trade policy used to read like a list of good intentions. This is evident from the two articles on the CET, which are largely historical.[11] For trade policy more generally – that is, besides the CET, including quotas, regulatory and other barriers as well as safeguards and export policy – the aims mentioned in Article 131 EC are 'the harmonious development of world trade, the progressive abolition of restrictions on international trade and the lowering of customs barriers'. One may read a pro-trade bias here since the 'common commercial policy shall take into account the favourable effect which the abolition of customs duties between

[7]For a detailed study, see Abraham *et al.* (1991).

[8]Article 27 reads: 'Before the end of the first stage, Member States shall, in so far as may be necessary, take steps to approximate their provisions laid down by law, regulation or administrative action in respect of customs matters . . .'.

[9]This, for example, is the case for the CAP, competition policy, the Structural Funds. Since the early 1980s, however, annual reports on anti-dumping have been produced, at the request of the EP.

[10]The TPRs of the EC were published by GATT in 1991 and 1993; and by WTO since 1995. For the latest one, see WTO (2004). See also Pelkmans & Carzaniga (1996).

[11]Article 18 EC (now deleted) and Art. 29 EC (now Art. 27). Article 18 was a declaration of intent ('readiness') to negotiate a lower CET in the GATT than the EC had decided to do (see Figure 5.2). This has been pursued during the transition period of the EEC, in both the Dillon and the Kennedy Rounds. Article 27 specifies four guidelines, including 'the need to promote trade between Member States and third countries' and 'developments in conditions of competition within the Community in so far as they lead to an improvement in the competitive capacity of undertakings'. Does this mean that a lack of competitiveness of enterprises is a reason to be restrictive in trade policy? This would be the wrong sequence; rather, openness should stimulate competitiveness through exposure.

Member States may have on the increase in the competitive strength of undertakings in those States'. The overall impression is one of conditional readiness to lower external Community protection and liberalise world trade at large. But exceptions to this attitude have long existed in agriculture, textiles and clothing, cars, coal and steel, shipbuilding and, more generally, services. When an EC Court case on the International Agreement on Natural Rubber came up, the Court ruled that the aims mentioned above are not binding: '. . . although it may be thought that at the time when the Treaty was drafted liberalisation of trade was the dominant idea, the Treaty nevertheless does not form a barrier to the possibility of the Community's developing a commercial policy aiming at a regulation of the world market for certain products . . .'.[12]

The *instruments* of EC trade policy are not exhaustively specified in the treaty. Exhaustive specification is difficult because modern protectionism has been inventive in finding new tools. Another problem is that the scope of trade policy is steadily widening; increasingly it comprises regulatory barriers which have a domestic origin and are not necessarily enforced at borders. Furthermore, international services trade and issues of intellectual property rights (such as counterfeiting) have stretched the range of external measures far beyond the traditional boundaries of trade policy. The main instruments used in goods markets are specified in Table 13.1, with some explanatory notes.

Table 13.1 EU trade policy instruments in goods markets

Instruments	National/EU	To be noted
Tariffs	EU	GATT-bound, and autonomous
Preferential tariffs (or tariff quotas)	EU	MFN-duty beyond low-tariff quota
Quotas	EU	Few left (only agriculture and fisheries)
Voluntary export restraints	Both	Removed in WTO before 1999 (cars: 1999)
Anti-dumping duties	EU	Max. 5 years (review possible)
Price undertakings	EU	Floor price instead of anti-dumping duties
Regulatory barriers	EU (most); national	Mostly technical
Export subsidies	EU	Agriculture only
Domestic subsidies	Both	Both EU and WTO rules apply
Licences (automatic)	National	For the whole internal market; strict EU rules

MFN = most favoured nation

13.3 Types of EU trade policy

The Union utilises trade policy as a tool for seven different types of common policy, summarised in Table 13.2. As indicated in the introduction to this chapter, the separate chapters on agriculture, pan-European integration, competition and industrial policy address these linkages. Commercial diplomacy and developmental trade policy are dealt with in the present chapter. This book does not deal with trade aspects of foreign policy.

13.4 Tariff protection

For non-agricultural products (excluding petroleum), the simple average tariff of the CET schedule was 6.9 per cent in 1995 and 4.1 per cent in 2000. Because of extra commitments in the framework of the (WTO) Information Technology Agreement, this reduces to 4 per cent. For agricultural tariffs, the WTO (2005, p. 41) estimates a simple average of 16.5 per cent, although the better access *within* tariff quotas is not included here. The weighted tariff averages are significantly lower. As discussed in section 13.7, a 'pyramid of EU preferences' including a generalised system of preferences (GSP) for developing countries, the Cotonou Treaty, and a series of free trade areas and customs unions the EU has concluded, leads to the remarkable result that very few countries actually face these tariffs. Most favoured nation (MFN) tariffs are relevant only for the USA, Canada, Japan, Australia, New Zealand, South Korea, Singapore, Hong Kong and non-WTO countries (such as Russia and Ukraine). Tariff protection should be distinguished from price

[12]Quoted from Steenbergen (1980, p. 240; Case 1/78, ruling of 11 October 1979).

protection which, besides the former, used to include variable levies, anti-dumping duties, price undertakings and voluntary export restraints (VERs) with floor prices. Of these, only anti-dumping duties and 'price undertakings' are now allowed in GATT / WTO. A still wider concept of price protection would also comprise various forms of price subsidies (for example, deficiency payments if applied to exports, see Chapter 11; subsidies to induce local purchases of coal far above world prices). If price protection were to substitute for tariff protection, liberalisation would be compromised at the extra cost of less transparency.

Since the Uruguay Round required 'tariffication' of quotas and variable levies, it is now easier to calculate simple averages including agricultural tariffs. Across all goods, this average is 9.6 per cent (WTO, 1995, p. 52). However, the tariffication of the variable levies has been carried out in a way that reduces transparency: in many cases, a high specific duty is levied, plus a relatively low ad valorem tariff, sometimes with seasonal differences too.[13] Both elements of agro-protectionism have been reduced, on average, by 36 per cent by the year 2000.

Basic features of today's CET are:

- Strong reliance on ad valorem duties for non-agricultural goods, but widespread use of specific duties in agricultural goods, together with ad valorem duties (so-called compound tariffs).
- All EU tariffs are now (GATT) bound; binding of agricultural tariffs is, generally, at high levels, with a few remarkable exceptions at or close to zero, encouraging huge imports (for example, tapioca from Thailand; corn gluten, oilseeds, soya beans from the USA and Brazil).
- Tariff peaks in non-agro-food products are few and moderate. The highest one for EU's 2004 applied tariffs is for trucks (22 per cent). The peak in footwear (17 per cent) is the next highest. Still, they remain exceptions. The highest textiles and clothing tariffs are 12 per cent. Many tariff lines (24 per cent) have zero tariffs. Agro-food tariffs[14] can be extremely high: applied 2004 tariffs peaks include dairy (up to 209 per cent, the record), cereals (up to 101 per cent), food items made from vegetables or fruits (up to 150 per cent),

Table 13.2 EU trade policy employed for other policies

Policy	Main instruments	Purposes
1. Commercial diplomacy	Tariffs, and, formerly, quotas, VERs	Market access; freer trade; slowing down adjustment
2. Agricultural policy	Variable levies (now illegal); specific levies; export subsidies; seasonal tariffs	Price/income goals EU farmers; supply security
3. Economic integration with non-members	Free trade areas or customs unions (for some in 'association')	Preferentialism, or future EU membership
4. Development policy	Preferential tariffs; tariff quotas; duty/quota-free (unilateral GSP; negotiated special preferences)	Export promotion for beneficiaries (trade as aid)
5. Competition policy	Anti-dumping and countervailing duties; competitive exposure for concentrated goods markets	Against predatory pricing; against state aids; discipline by potential competition
6. Industrial policy	VERs, now illegal; anti-dumping duties in absence of predation; excessive subsidies; some public procurement (only non-discriminatory under reciprocity)	Competitiveness of sectors/firms ('Eurochampions'); product development; subsidies; etc.
7. Foreign policy	Embargoes; boycotts; control of dual-purpose goods; special procurement	Human rights; war; UN resolutions

[13]Ad valorem duties are calculated as a percentage of the customs value. Customs value is determined with procedures specified in the customs valuation code of the GATT (preventing all kinds of dubious customs practices). Specific duties specify euros per kilo or litre or bale (etc.); their percentage equivalent varies inversely with the value of the consignment taxed.

[14]Note that the data are from WTO (2004, pp. 40–6). The WTO has calculated the *ad-valorem tariff equivalent* because, in agriculture, specific duties or other 'non ad valorem' duties are rather frequent (often as 'compound' tariffs).

mushrooms (134 per cent), garlic (150 per cent), wild rice (101 per cent) and meat (up to 192 per cent). However, in all these two-digit categories with peak tariffs there are (higher-digit) tariff lines with zero tariffs as well. As noted, some zero-tariff lines attract enormous imports (for example, corn gluten, soya, tapioca). Some tropical agro-food products come in without barriers but others (sugar, up to 114 per cent, ad valorem only; cacao, up to 76 per cent) are highly protected. Finally, one should note that specific tariffs and – for some fruits and vegetables – 'entry price systems' complicate the picture one gets if one merely focuses on ad valorem tariffs.[15]

- There is still tariff escalation in selected products such as fish, tobacco, leather, rubber and textiles (for details, see WTO, 1995, chart IV.3).

Figure 13.1 provides the product structure of EU tariff protection in agricultural and manufactured goods panels. For the agricultural (ad valorem or equivalent) tariffs, the lower rates for the year 2000 have not been indicated (on average some 36 per cent reduced). The determinants of the product structure of tariffs are found in political economy, combined with historical factors, the availability of raw materials, energy dependence and so on. Standard trade theory would lead us to expect that, to the extent that the product structure of trade can be explained by relative factor endowments in the trading countries, nominal tariffs would protect the remuneration of the relatively scarce factor(s) used to produce import-competing products.

Before applying this insight empirically, one has to take account of the fact that non-price elements play a role in trade of goods using intensively skilled labour and R&D. Since this reduces price sensitivity, it tends to reduce (*ceteris paribus*) the demand for protection in such products. The hypothesis would therefore be that EU tariffs tend to be relatively high, and relatively resistant to GATT Rounds liberalisation, for unskilled labour-intensive products. Unfortunately, empirical work on this question is somewhat dated.

Constantopoulos (1974) has tested a simple two-factor model comprising unskilled labour and capital in order to explain the tariff structures of five Member States before their signing of the EEC treaty in 1957. Interestingly, although nominal tariffs were disparate, national tariff structures were not significantly different. This implies that the original, averaged CET hardly altered the relative protection between different products. It turns out that goods using a relatively high share of unskilled labour and those with a relatively high R&D input received high tariff protection in the early days of the Community.

Riedel (1977) addressed the political economy of EU tariff reduction in the Kennedy Round. The hypothesis is that inter-industry variation in percentage tariff reduction reflected a trade policy minimising unskilled labour adjustment costs. Contrary to Cheh (1974) for the USA, Riedel finds a positive correlation between *ex ante* tariff peaks and the measure of tariff reduction. This curious result[16] can be explained by pointing to the EU's insistence that the USA remove tariff peaks in the Round – so it had to set the example to some extent – and by the preference of sectors using low-skilled labour intensively to opt for volume protection and other barriers instead. Note that the tariff peak issue has never gone away. In the Doha Round, a formula has been negotiated to have tariff peaks go down more than lower tariffs.

13.5 Volume protection

Low tariff protection is meaningless if volume protection is 'binding', that is, if incipient import demand at the world price is larger than permitted imports. Binding quotas or VERs cause prices to rise in the import country. Rents are reaped by exporters under a VER if allocation of export rights takes place in the export country; it acts as a market-sharing cartel. A regular quota also yields rents, but they will be captured by traditional importers who can purchase early on at competitive world prices because they are assured of getting the bulk of the quota permits.

The EU's history shows that it has heavily leaned on volume protection. Today, this is no longer the case.[17]

[15] In WTO (2000, pp. 44–45 and chart III.1) the complicated 'entry price' regime for lemons is explained and depicted. The purpose is to protect EU lemon producers, especially during their harvest season. A year is divided in six periods, each one having a price band. The curious property is that the tariff consists of an ad valorum and a specific part, the latter being set differently for different entry prices. Thus, when entry prices are low, they tend to get an ad valorem tariff equivalent of some 77 per cent, but for higher prices the specific part is lower or absent; however, at what (higher) prices this moderation takes place depends on the season. *De facto,* such imports are contracted (consignment basis), hence import prices are *de facto* derived from selling prices in the EU – clearly, this magnifies the potential for (seasonal) protection.

[16] As it would appear to go against received trade theory and the literature on political economy of protection, as inspired by the Stolper–Samuelson theorem. See any handbook of international economics.

[17] In the second edition, section 13.5.1 provides a brief history of EU volume protection. The interested reader is referred to this text. It also contains an economic perspective on the car quotas and VERs, practised by some EU countries *vis-à-vis* Japanese cars in the period 1977–94 (the UK) and up to 1999 (when Italy terminated its quota).

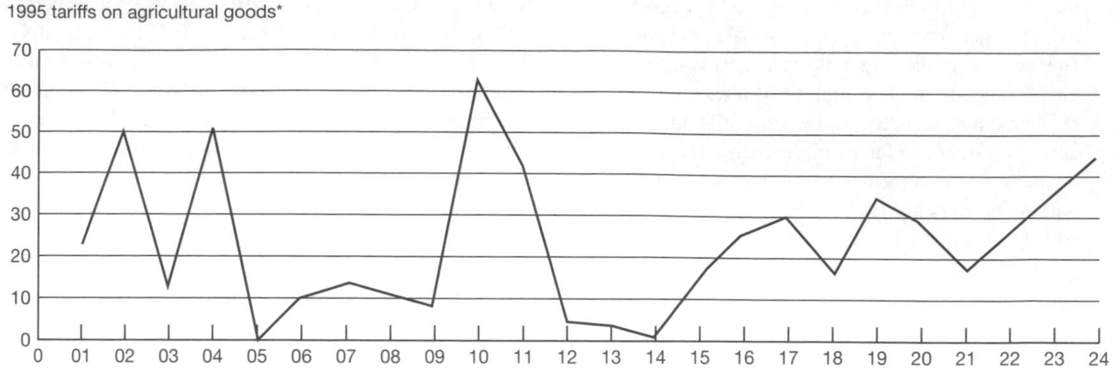

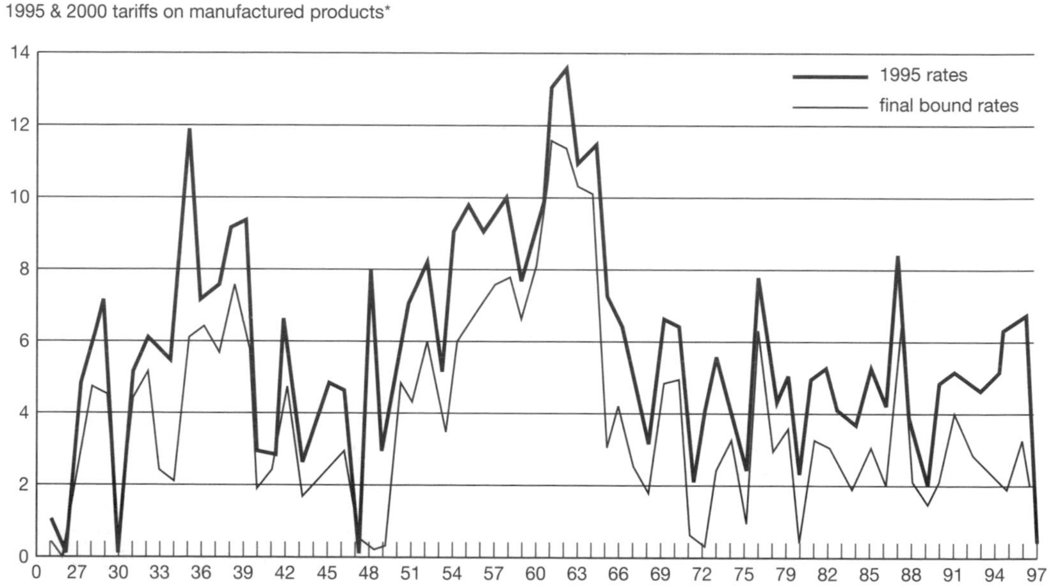

Figure 13.1 Product structure of EU tariff protection

Notes: The Harmonised System (HS) is the harmonised customs tariff classification system achieved in 1988. Numbers along the horizontal axes refer to a two-digit HS chapter. Agricultural goods' peaks (upper graph) refer to: 02 = meat and edible meat offals; 04 = dairy produce, birds' eggs, honey; 10 = cereals; 11 = products of the milling industry; wheat gluten; 24 = tobacco. Manufactured goods' peaks (lower graph) refer to: 35 = albuminoidal substances, starches; glue; 37 = photographic goods; 57 = carpets; 58 = special woven fabrics; 61 = apparel/clothing accessories (knitted); 62 = idem, not knitted; 64 = footwear; 76 = aluminium; 87 = cars and other road vehicles.

* Average tariff rates by HS chapter, in per cent

Source: WTO, 1995

EU volume protection in 2005 is therefore incomparably more liberal than ever before in Community history. The EU nowadays comes close to the WTO principle of not relying on quotas at all. National quotas and all national and EU-wide VERs have been removed. The EU was a long-standing participant in the Multi-Fibre Arrangement (MFA), with numerous restrictive quotas against developing countries' textiles and clothing exports. It was agreed in the Uruguay Round that the MFA would be 'integrated' into the GATT by 2005 in four steps. The final step (late 2004) was by far the most sensitive one: a good deal of the 'cold shower' for the EU textiles and clothing industry would not come until 2005. As it turned out, several EU countries could not stand the cold shower – in particular, from China – and prompted the EU to revert to selective quotas, once again (see Case Study 13.2).

Quotas that remain are either of trivial importance or apply between the EU and non-WTO members.[18] The only case of some importance is a set of iron and steel quotas with Russia, Ukraine and Kazakstan – all under bilateral agreements with these non-WTO countries. Finally, the WTO Safeguards Agreement has terminated

CASE STUDY 13.2 New clothing quotas against China

Barely three months after the expiry of the Multi-Fibre Arrangement, the USA and the EU reverted to selected volume protection against China. They could legally do this owing to the Textiles-Specific Safeguard Clause written into China's Protocol of Accession to the WTO in 2001. On 6 April 2005, the EU published 'guidelines' so that the nature, restrictiveness and determining factors of possible safeguard action against China would be 'predictable'. Only one month later, safeguard action was triggered by EU import growth in the relevant clothing items exceeding the guideline thresholds. Those thresholds (in percentage growth over 2004) were high (100 per cent or 50 per cent) for clothing items where China held a low market share, and low (30 per cent or 10 per cent) for goods where China had already acquired large EU import shares (respectively 20–35 per cent, and beyond 35 per cent). The EU safeguards were agreed with the Chinese, which renders them WTO-compatible for three years (unilateral safeguards, only for one year). In ten product categories, the actual percentage increases of EU imports from China ranged from 51 per cent to 534 per cent (January to March, comparing 2005 with 2004). In part, these import jumps can be explained by the strict binding nature of the last MFA quotas in 2004. To some extent, however, they do not represent a net increase in EU imports since many developing countries saw their exports to the EU in these items fall drastically. Indeed, under a quota-free system with (for the EU) moderate tariffs (of at most 12 per cent), the poorest developing countries were losing their comparative advantage *vis-à-vis* China. Why? The fragmentation of the textiles and clothing value chain over the world economy was artificially encouraged by constraining the highly competitive countries combining low wages with an ability to organise most or all of the value chain. With MFA quotas out of the way, pure assembly clothing exporters incur (double) transport and quality supervision costs, in addition to time loss, a key factor in fashion clothing markets (see, for example, Pelkmans, 1994b; OECD, 2004). Thus, for the large retail chains in Europe, dominating clothing markets, the post-MFA competitiveness lies in well-organised sourcing from China and a few other low-wage countries capable of organising much larger parts of the value-chain. Hence, the pure clothing-assemblies (often least-developed countries) lose out.

The China–EU Safeguards Agreement runs to the end of 2007. It does allow import growth of between 8 per cent and 12 per cent annually in these items. The idea is to provide the clothing industry in countries such as Portugal, Italy, France and Greece (yet another period of) 'breathing space'. Also, the new Member States will be able to adjust, after having enjoyed strong export growth to the EU15 for over a decade. However, once Romania and Bulgaria join the Union (in 2007), adjustment problems might be considerable as these countries attracted many hundreds of footloose assemblies in clothing after 1995. Their only option is to move upmarket and capture larger parts of the value chain and, in so doing, exploit the time-to-market advantage that their proximity to the EU15 gives them.

All safeguard action against China will become WTO-illegal after 2008. The adjustment burden in the EU25 is often concentrated in relatively poor regions and disproportionately with (low-skilled) women.

[18] There are only a few quotas under bilateral agreements with, for example, Belarus, China; OPT quotas (for outward processing traffic in texiles and clothing) with Belarus and Ukraine; and a few quotas left under the 'state trading regime', a regime which is becoming obsolete because of the demise of communism, except for North Korea.

the very old coal quotas by Germany, yet allowed some price – or volume – based safeguards.[19]

This virtual demise of EU volume protection is historically remarkable. Since it is certain to accelerate adjustment in sensitive sectors, it is important to understand the factors behind this shift to exposure to world competition. This would also help to answer the question whether this liberalisation might easily be reversed in times of stagnation. The question is pressing since it is often held that the EU would be particularly prone to (reverting to) protectionism, given the compromise character of its decision making (see, for example, Winters, 1994).

There are five reasons explaining the U-turn in volume protection. First and foremost is the EC-1992 programme. As noted in Chapter 5, EC-1992 centred around two ideas: no internal frontiers (whether physical borders or regulatory barriers) and greater acceptance of market forces so as to regain competitiveness and dynamism on the supply side of goods and services. National volume protection was manifestly in conflict with the first idea.[20] The lack of exposure to world competition and market forces, and the worldwide accusation that the EU was a 'Fortress Europe', militated against the second idea. The comprehensive nature of EC-1992 made it possible to liberalise markets with deeply entrenched interests in, for example, services and public procurement, thereby creating a political climate in which vested interests in volume protection for sensitive product markets also had to give way. Second, volume protection was often ineffective: import growth continued and domestic EC market shares were falling. Because volume protection was porous and volatile, adjustment did take place. This facilitated the removal later. Third, the period 1986–91 was a boom period for Europe and this weakened the socio-political case for the protectionists. Fourth, the Uruguay Round, finally concluded late 1993, contained several broad-based measures against volume protection such as tariffication of certain quotas (especially in agriculture), an obligation to remove grey-area protection such as VERs within four years (and a 'roll-back' even during the negotiations), and the removal of the MFA by 2005. Fifth, and harder to trace in detail, the rise of globalisation, outsourcing and worldwide direct investment have demonstrated the irrelevance of protection for many involved in global business, while creating explicit free trade lobbies objecting to and working against protectionism.

Could volume protection come back? The clothing quotas against China in 2005 show that policy reversals remain possible. However, it would be totally misleading to regard this as more than the exception confirming the rule. Short of apocalyptic scenarios for European integration, national quotas will not return as they are firmly prohibited under Community law. EU-wide quotas could come back only if the WTO dispute procedures did not work and the socio-economic climate in Europe worsened considerably. Even then it is unlikely to assume significance as this would invite retaliation which is not only costly to the EU but will also cause internal division.[21] VERs are forbidden under Article 11 of the WTO Safeguard Agreement and this prohibition is under multilateral surveillance. The EU will not lightly violate this explicit rule. A more realistic possibility is that protectionist demands will seek satisfaction by trying well-accepted tools such as anti-dumping duties and price undertakings, to which we now turn.

13.6 Anti-dumping: trade policy instead of competition policy

Dumping is a form of price discrimination, in the sense of charging different prices in economically separated geographical markets at a given moment in time. Price discrimination is sustainable (and is profitable) if (1) the two markets exhibit disparate price elasticities (in other words, some market power in at least one market), and (2) arbitrage is costly or impossible because the markets

[19]So-called snap-back tariffs have been applied when import prices fall below 'trigger' prices or import volumes exceed 'trigger' volumes. Price triggers applied typically to poultry and turkey meat; volume triggers for certain fruits and vegetables including lemons (see fn 15), which were thereby protected even more.

[20]A CU, in contrast to an FTA, does not (need) to check the origin of goods at intra-CU borders. National quotas violate this condition. For such quotas to be effective, trade deflection via other Member States has to be controlled and this requires intra-EU border checks on (third-country) origin. The EEC treaty contained Art. 115 (now Art. 134) as an escape clause, used by the EU as a legal basis for such intra-Union border checks. After the transition period, reliance on this article was popular with the Member States and the Commission was forced to employ a very convenient interpretation of 'economic difficulties' so as to approve scores of such controls (often with annual renewal, for one and a half decades). Once reliance on the old Art. 115 EEC had reduced rapidly under EC-1992, national quotas had become less interesting because of ineffectiveness. Note that (national) VERs cannot, by their nature, be enforced at intra-EU borders. Restrictions were apparently policed via distribution systems; however, this worked, for example, with cars but not with shoes.

[21]Third countries, presumably large ones, can be expected to retaliate in goods or services other than the ones at stake, thereby forcing the EU to decide on trade-offs between groups of goods and between Member States with different export specialisations.

are segmented by distribution or trade policy barriers. Sustainable price discrimination in a single market is a competition issue as market power is exploited (see section 6.5.2 and section 12.2).[22] In international trade, however, no world competition rules exist, and indeed barriers of all kinds may impede arbitrage. So, there is likely to be price discrimination in world trade. This may be a second-best reason to employ trade policy, under special GATT / WTO rules, since first best is not feasible.

Dumping in GATT / WTO, and hence in EC law *vis-à-vis* third country imports is *not* defined as above, hence it overlaps only partially with an approach based on market failure. In GATT / WTO it refers to 'export prices being lower than prices in the domestic market of the exporter'. This rule is unfortunate since it implies that firm behaviour, allowed inside the internal market, may be prohibited for exports to the EU, if causing (or threatening to cause) 'injury'. Thus, the mere fact that a company Fq (from non-EU country Q) – charging a domestic price of 100 and a price in the EU of 90 – may gain a larger EU market share, is sufficient for it to have anti-dumping charges slapped on its exports to the EU. If company Fq were inside the EU, this might only happen if it were to employ predatory pricing (abuse of dominant position), not because it took market shares from other firms. To make matters worse, there is latitude on setting anti-dumping duties and there is no WTO surveillance. Of course, the GATT / WTO definition is far too wide: profit-taking may be less because of a lack of reputation abroad, temporary losses may be accepted to build up market share, or, because of taste differences or competing brands it is simply not a product that yields a premium everywhere. Recognising this, dumping is actionable under WTO rules only when there is (material) injury. The EU normally imposes duties no higher than the 'injury margin', that is, that part of the dumping margin which is thought to cause injury (how problematic this is, is clear from the simple consideration that non-price factors may cause market shares to shift; if prices also happen to differ, the shift may be attributed to 'dumping').

For EU anti-dumping measures to be taken, imports must be dumped, this must have caused material injury, and the Council must find it in the 'Community interest'. Measures consist in anti-dumping duties (usually less than the dumping margin, but sufficient to remove the injury) or in price undertakings (higher minimum prices, subject to monitoring) by the exporters concerned. These measures are not comparable to tariffs. The greatest difference is, of course, that the former suddenly emerge as a new – possibly high – barrier, long after investments, production and market penetration have begun; tariffs are known *ex ante* and, in the EU case, are always bound in the GATT. Anti-dumping duties are short-term remedies when they are provisional, while definite duties expire after five years, unlike tariffs; moreover, they apply only to specific companies' exports of well-specified products from one or a few countries. It is therefore likely that, if the dumping were sustainable in the absence of anti-dumping duties, the duties would cause trade diversion both inside the EU and between other non-EU suppliers, not hit by anti-dumping duties, and those hit by the duties imposed.[23] Other responses are also possible, such as direct investment, particularly if the shift of production to the EU would have been expected in the product life cycle anyway. Sometimes, there is 'absorption' of the duties by the exporter so that the landed price is not raised (the EU may punish this by extra duties, since the dumping, as defined, is not stopped).

The EU used to be a heavy utiliser of anti-dumping, competing in this respect with the USA for first place worldwide. It seems that, since the turn of the century, EU's anti-dumping has become less aggressive. Whereas in the period 1991–95 the annual average number of initiated anti-dumping proceedings was 31, and 44 in the period 1995–99, it was only 20 in 2002, and 7 in 2003.[24] Anti-dumping duties range from 0 per cent (if companies do not cause injury) to 75 per cent, with an average of 25 per cent (WTO, 2004, p. 57). East Asian countries (led by China) were hit mostly in the period 1991–2003. Homogeneous, scale-driven goods were hit mostly from a sectoral point of view, for example base metal and chemicals together took 50 per cent.[25]

[22]It would hardly ever lead to actual complaints by business since 'reverse dumping' is possible, that is, companies which fear injury from dumping (in the GATT sense, see text above) can return the goods to the sender's market and undercut local prices. See also Art. 91 EEC (now deleted) which facilitated reverse dumping in the CU in the transition period.

[23]A study by Lasgni (2000) found the median of import values from countries hit by EU anti-dumping duties (or price undertakings) to fall by 60 per cent after three years, yet, at the same time observing a rise of 40 per cent of imports from third countries not hit. In other words, the protective effect for EU industry is likely to be small.

[24]The stock (rather than flow) measure gives a less benign picture: in 1995 the stock of anti-dumping measures in force was 147, in 1999 156 and in 2003 once again 147. So, there is a lag of several years before the anti-dumping stock falls.

[25]This sectoral bias can be explained theoretically (see Veugelers & Vandenbussche, 1999) and by policy consideration (see, e.g., Holmes, 1997). The 50 per cent is for 1991–2003 (see WTO, 2004).

CASE STUDY 13.3 Biased anti-dumping in photocopiers

In 1985, four European photocopier producers and Rank Xerox (Europe) filed a complaint about Japanese dumping. In February 1987 definitive anti-dumping duties of, on average, 18.1 per cent were imposed on photocopier imports from Japan. Although dumping cases are minefields of legal technicality (both in the EC and elsewhere), the photocopier case is often viewed as concrete evidence of the excessively wide discretion the Commission has under GATT rules – this discretion can be abused for protectionism, but only if the political pressures are strong enough.

Consider the following curious elements of this anti-dumping case. First, the European subsidiaries of Canon were not recognised as European producers, whereas the Rank Xerox subsidiary was (note also that Canon (Europe)'s production was as big as that of the four European producers). Second, Japanese sales in the EU grew much faster than 'European' sales, which was used as the basis for concluding injury (caused by dumping). However, the four hardly produced small personal copiers; they sold them, under their own name, after buying them from exactly the Japanese suppliers now accused of dumping. Excluding personal copiers, Japanese sales' growth was about the same as sales from EU firms. Was this infant industry protection so that Europeans could build up scale and enjoy learning effects in personal copiers? Third, the price undercutting was acknowledged not to be substantial, yet an artificial price adjustment (for example, for more features) served as the basis for concluding that prices 'should' have been higher for Japanese sales.

The anti-dumping duties did not actually 'protect' the European producers. Not only did imports from Hong Kong, South Korea and Taiwan start to come in (5 per cent EC market share by 1989), Japanese producers circumvented the anti-dumping duties by importing parts and components into the EU. Whereas in 1985 the Japanese share in overall EU imports was about 70 per cent, it had fallen to about 25 per cent by 1989, while at the same time the volume of parts (as a percentage of the volume of copiers) in EU imports from Japan rose from less than 25 per cent (1985) to about 110 per cent (1989). Also, EU-made European sales did not increase market share. Messerlin & Nogushi (1991) estimate the static welfare loss at about ECU 209 million annually. In 1988, the Commission had imposed anti-circumvention anti-dumping duties (that is, on imported parts), which caused further price increases and welfare losses. Note, finally, that a GATT panel, shortly thereafter, concluded that – although circumvention could be sanctionable (the USA has such measures, too) – the EC anti-circumvention anti-dumping directive was incompatible with GATT rules.

It is cases like photocopiers which lead many to suspect that anti-dumping is not a mere application of rules, but a policy – indeed, a policy with a protectionist bias when politically convenient.

The economic assessment of anti-dumping is complicated because of the data requirements, the necessary study of the nature and development of the product market in question, the intricate issues of measurement and procedure,[26] and the great variety of cases. There is also a growing political economy analysis.[27] Some empirical findings (and see Case Study 13.3) may shed some light on it:

- Price undertakings reduced from about three-fifths of all measures in the period 1981–85 to about two-fifths in 1986–91; one reason is that 'state trading dumping' was often resolved with price undertakings. At the end of 1999, of the 100 anti-dumping measures, on a product basis (so, one or more countries may be hit), 16 were price undertakings.[28]
- Undertakings tend to have a more restrictive effect on trade than duties.
- According to Messerlin (1989), relative to intra-EU prices, prices of dumped imports subject to measures rose by 17 per cent over the three years following the initiation of the investigation.

[26]There is extensive criticism about the technical details of EU anti-dumping. The reader is referred to, for example, Bellis (1990) and Nicolaides & van Wijngaarden (1993). Note that the second edition of the present textbook contained a more elaborate discussion of the economics of anti-dumping in section 13.6.

[27]See, e.g., Tharakan & Waelbroeck (1994) and the literature quoted there.

[28]COM (2000) 440 of 11 July 2000, *18th Anti-dumping Report,* annex O.

Anti-dumping policy remains a protectionist danger in a Community which (other than for agricultural products) has become a very open economy. The prominence of China in the past ten years or so of the EU's anti-dumping policy seems to confirm that. Nevertheless, the politics of anti-dumping in the Union point the other way. According to Evenett & Vermulst (2005), one probable reason that the EU has reduced dumping cases is that, in the EU15, a stalemate of two blocks of Member States, systematically voting for and against anti-dumping duties for 85 per cent of all cases, had emerged in the late 1990s. This 'new' anti-anti-dumping block of Member States is likely to be strengthened by the new Member States since eight of the ten rarely used anti-dumping before EU membership.

13.7 Preferential trade policy

The Union is a strong supporter of GATT / WTO but, for a long time, not always in a manner appreciated by (some) other GATT partners, above all the USA and Japan. The EU has consistently attached great value to two elements of the GATT in particular: multilateral trade liberalisation and respect for world trade law (see below, section 13.8). One may observe some ambivalence with respect to a third key element, indeed the cornerstone of the original GATT: non-discrimination. Where most favoured nation (MFN) treatment is crucial to tariff negotiations in Rounds or for other liberalisation purposes, the Union has consistently been a strong supporter of the principle. But at the same time, it has, in practice, been by far the most heavy user of Article 24 GATT for what has come to be called its 'pyramid of preferences'. The Union's preferentialism has, if anything, become more pronounced in the 1990s up to today, but nowadays practically all WTO partners, too, engage in a combination of preferentialism and multilateralism. The EU's 'pyramid of preferences', and how it has changed dramatically since 1991, is first explained. Subsequently, in an Additional Reading, an economic analysis of FTAs is presented. Since most EU preferential agreements are FTAs, this analysis should help understand an impact analysis. Finally, where EU preferences are unilateral (GSP) or 'one-way' (the old Lomé Treaty, now Cotonou, until 2009), the idea is to provide 'trade and aid'. This idea is analysed in Figure 13.4, theoretically.[29]

13.7.1 A pyramid of preferences

The problems that other GATT / WTO partners have with EU's preferentialism are twofold: (1) discrimination of non-Europe OECD enjoying most favoured nation treatment but actually getting *least* favoured access; (2) discrimination among those who are favoured so that a hierarchy, or indeed a pyramid, emerges. It is precisely this division of one's trading partners into friends, lesser friends and foes, that Article 1 of the GATT on non-discrimination aims to prevent. Such trade policies are seen as a reflection of mercantilism or of otherwise undesirable politicisation of world trade, which goes against the very rationale of having exposure to world competition (that is, not only to some but to any). Not least, when mixed with foreign policy, discrimination can heighten tensions in the world, as the 1930s and other episodes have shown. The latter argument used not to be relevant to the EU because, until Maastricht, it had no foreign and defence policy whatsoever: Shonfield (1973) called it a 'civil Community'.

This book will not go through the tortuous history of EU preferentialism. It is a series of ad hoc decisions, often as opportunistic responses to political pressures or to the embarrassment that old 'bonds' might be affected. No grand design is behind it.[30] However, recent changes in the 'pyramid' have been so dramatic that the status quo in 2004 has become completely different.

Consider Figure 13.2, showing the pyramid in mid-1991. From the top down, only the sixth layer of (non-European) OECD and South Africa enjoyed ordinary MFN treatment. The state-trading countries were subject to an inferior regime as their GATT status (and their pricing, 'tariff' and trade monopolisation practices) could not be handled with reciprocal MFN treatment. Due to the opening up of central and eastern Europe (CEE) in 1989–90, in 1991 the EU was in the process of negotiating regular trade agreements with the former USSR countries and the Baltic states (shifting them to the OECD layer) as well as what later would become 'association agreements' with the CEE6 (shifting them up three layers). The first, second and fourth layers had long been rather stable, but important changes have meanwhile taken place in the context of 'pan-European integration' (see Figure 13.3 and Chapter 20).

This leaves two layers: ACP and GSP. The African–Caribbean–Pacific (ACP) or Lomé group resulted from a long post-colonial history of preferentialism, above all by France, Britain, Belgium and the Netherlands: it is

[29] See, e.g., World Bank (2000).

[30] See, e.g., Pomfret (1988) and Grilli (1993).

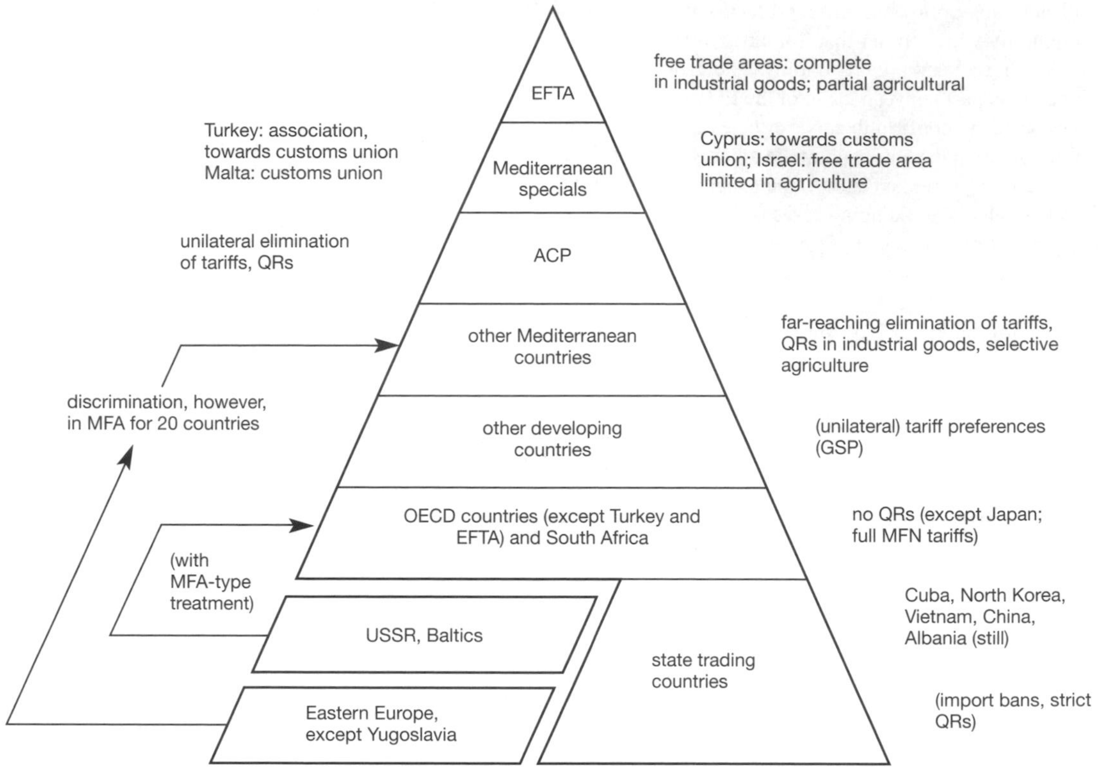

Figure 13.2 EC's pyramid of preferences in 1991

briefly discussed in section 13.7.3. GSP refers to the generalised system of preferences for developing countries (here, to the EU variant of this): the basics are set out in section 13.7.2.

Now consider Figure 13.3, showing a very different pyramid of preferences, as it stood at the end of 2004. Note first that state-trading has practically disappeared owing to the massive transition of communist countries to market economies. So, the bottom of the pyramid now consists of the non-European OECD countries (except Mexico) with regular MFN-based access to the EU. A higher layer are the many countries enjoying unilateral preferences, other than ACP (that is, GSP and EBA – everything but arms), but many EBA countries are also in ACP. It should be realised that EBA evolves up to 2009 when its economic significance for these very poor countries would justify placing it in a higher layer.

The following two layers comprise FTAs, either under negotiation or accomplished or recently deepened (hence, the arrow pointing upwards). Dependent upon political stabilisation in the western Balkans, these countries will likely enjoy a new variety of Europe Agreements, perhaps eventually leading to EU membership (see Chapter 20).[31] The MED (southern and eastern Mediterranean countries other than Israel) countries can already be found in Figure 13.2. Ever since the second half of the 1990s, the EU has renegotiated the former quasi-unilateral preferential access agreements with the MEDs into (fairly deep) FTAs, with the MEDs following a slow path of opening up. The problem with the MED FTAs is that these countries typically have maintained relatively high protection, which, in an FTA, creates a serious risk of trade diversion, as described in the Additional Reading below. It is therefore critical that the EU and the MEDs be capable of engineering a gradual reduction of the external protection of the MEDs, so that exposure to world competition can go together with the fruits of free access to the EU25.

Higher up the pyramid one finds 'deeper' FTAs with Israel, Mexico, South Africa and Chile. The special layer for Switzerland is explained by the Swiss refusal (in a referendum in 1991) to join the European Economic Area

[31]Note that Croatia is already a candidate country, in pre-accession. Several Balkan countries have declared their interest in future EU membership.

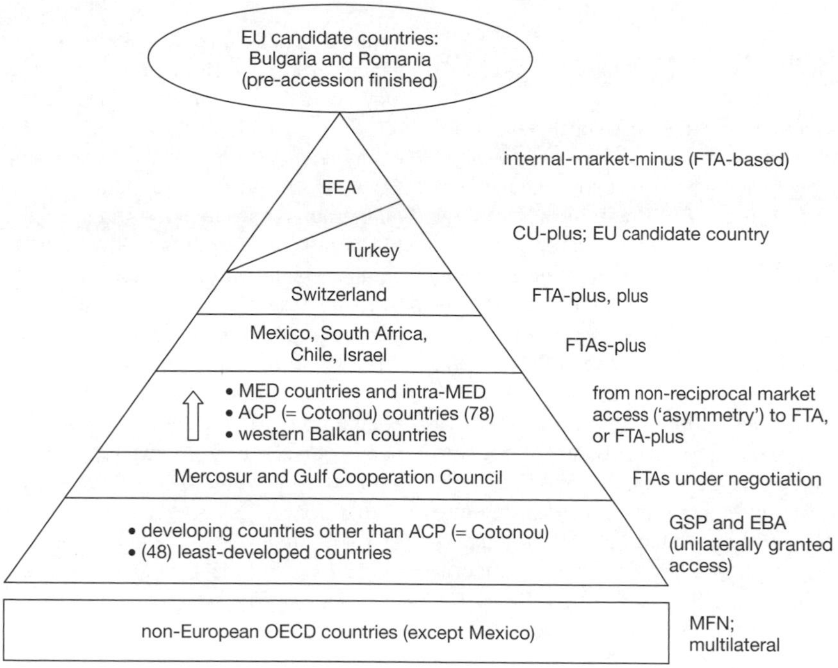

Figure 13.3 EU's pyramid of preferences in 2004

Notes: State-trading (see Figure 13.2) has virtually disappeared; the Multi-Fibre Arrangement (MFA) has expired, end 2004; western Balkans comprise former Yugoslavia countries (except Slovenia, now EU member) plus Albania.

(EEA), which is located at the top of the pyramid. The EEA was concluded shortly after 1991 with Norway, Iceland and Liechtenstein. Its purpose is in essence to participate in the EU's internal market without being a EU member. In Figure 13.3 it is called an 'internal-market-minus'. What Norway did was to negotiate a number of critical exceptions to the internal market *acquis* (such as a common trade policy, agriculture and fisheries, and free movement of workers), yet accept the ambitious regulatory and judicial framework of the internal market for all who would be 'in' the EEA, including the unique common EEA Court for competition, regulation and (remaining) free movements.[32] This internal-market-minus was too ambitious for Switzerland. Its strategy became to negotiate a large series of specific and sectoral agreements (especially on services) and thereby more or less approximate similar degrees of mutual opening with the EU as the EEA would have given it. Finally, one finds Turkey in the top of the pyramid, a candidate country, now engaged in formal accession negotiations. Turkey differs from all others in the pyramid in that it has formed a CU with the EU since 1996. Beyond the top of the pyramid, Romania and Bulgaria are depicted. They have concluded the accession negotiations and are expected to become EU members by 2007 (or 2008 if conditions to be fulfilled should take more time).

The changes in the pyramid notwithstanding, it still has six layers. The principal reason for having the higher layers is that the EU goes so much further in 'deepening' than any other region when practising economic regionalism. The 'depth' of the bilateral agreements the EU has with European and other countries in its 'orbit' is without precedent.

13.7.2 Economic analysis of a free trade area

The regionalism the EU engages in with many third countries takes the form of free trade areas. The welfare analysis of FTAs is analogous to that of CUs, although a new effect (indirect trade deflection) has to be incorporated. What is distinct is the likelihood of price disparities, even when disregarding transport costs.

[32]See Emerson *et al.* (2002) and Vahl (2003) for detailed analysis.

ADDITIONAL READING

The many bilateral FTAs the EU has concluded call for an economic analysis of their effects.[33] One might also use the analysis below for an appreciation of the old EFTA, before most EFTA members switched over to the EU.[34] Although an FTA does not have a common external tariff, the economic analysis displays several analogies with that of a CU. The differences can matter, however, depending on the economic characteristics of the countries and their export competitiveness in the FTA.

Suppose that countries A and B form an FTA while C is the discriminated third country, the rest of the world, supplying at a constant price P_c (see Figure 13.4). A and B supply at rising costs. Before the FTA is formed the high-tariff country A imports AB from C and the low-tariff country B also imports from C (S_b is horizontally added to S_a). Since B's demand is not explicitly given, one cannot deduce exactly how much B will import *ex ante*. The reader may wonder why the excess supply schedule of B is not introduced into A's market (as we did in, for example, Figure 6.5, or, for the Union, in Figure 11.7). However, this procedure would make little economic sense because the crucial point of the FTA is that the excess supply of B would be irrelevant. Consider what B-suppliers would do if there were no transport costs and the FTA began. B-suppliers would observe the *ex ante* price P_a in A. They would massively sell in A because for every unit of good X they expect to obtain a much higher price than P_b. If possible, they would sell their total supply, not just their excess supply. Hence, it is relevant to construct $S_{(a+b)}$ representing total FTA supply in A. $S_{(a+b)}$ is relevant neither below P_b nor above P_a: below P_b because the alternative of B's own supply is tariff-inclusive imports from C, and not above P_a as A will then import from C as well.

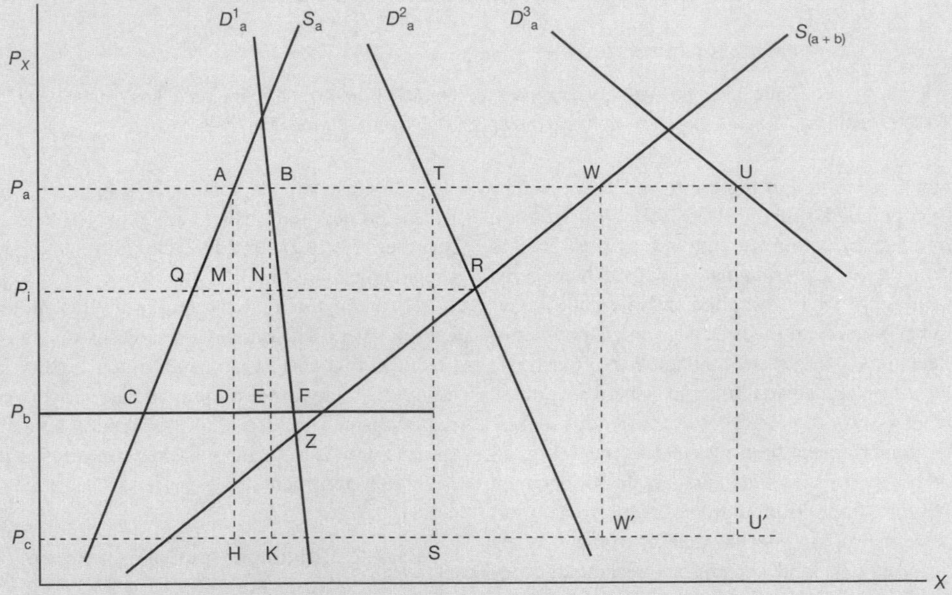

Figure 13.4 Price divergence in a free trade area

Source: From Shibata, H., in *Fiscal Harmonisation in Common Markets*, Shoup, C. (ed.). Copyright © 1967 Columbia University Press. Reprinted with permission of the publisher

[33] For a somewhat different analysis, see de Melo *et al.* (1993). However, their focus is solely on welfare effects, ignoring the questions of price disparities and 'indirect trade deflection' in the FTA.

[34] The second edition, section 18.2.1 comprised an economic assessment of EFTA (the European Free Trade Association), based on the Stockholm Treaty of 1959. Readers interested in this classical, modest but successful FTA are referred to this section. Its assessment can be instructive for new attempts to start FTAs in other parts of the world.

ADDITIONAL READING *continued*

In Figure 13.4 three demand-schedules for A are drawn to represent three cases. Take first the case of D_1^a, that is, limited and inelastic A demand. At P_b B's supply exceeds A's excess demand (CF) so the intra-FTA price will become P_b. Trade creation (in trade flow terms) is CD plus EF and trade diversion is DE. But trade creation CD + EF is different from that of a CU: once B supplies A with these quantities, the country will simultaneously import the very same volume from C to satisfy local B demand. What is trade diversion with respect to A (AB = DE) is not necessarily lost to C, depending on what B imported before the FTA. If B had very limited imports or was just self-sufficient at P_b before the FTA, C would 'regain' AB in country B and, in addition, supply CD + EF there. As drawn, tariff revenue losses are likely to be small, so that this FTA is likely to enjoy major net welfare gains. Needless to say, it is a roundabout way of achieving those gains, at least for A, as it might also reduce its tariffs to the B level (and keep some tariff revenue as well). Thus, the question arises why A would opt for this FTA. If not for plain political reasons, one possible answer could be that transport and transaction costs render such a massive 'sell-out' of B supplies to A impossible. Another possible answer could be that D_1^a represents a special case for one product, but the FTA will cover many products (as the GATT requires) and other products may exhibit another demand/supply structure.

An important conclusion from this first case is that *indirect trade deflection* occurs: transit trade from C via B to A is outlawed, but a similar effect is induced by the replacement of B's local supplies by imports from C, all at P_b. In the present case, B supplies to A are so large relative to A's limited demand that the *ex ante* observation of P_a is a misleading incentive for B suppliers: the *ex post* FTA price will immediately fall to P_b and there is full price convergence.

With D_2^a there is *ex post* price divergence. The *ex post* price in A will be P_i and that in B remains P_b. Trade creation is QM + NR and trade diversion MN = AT. C's exports are squeezed out in A but how much C can switch to B (indirect trade deflection) depends on B's supply capacity at P_b, which is CZ, as drawn. B enjoys export gains in the FTA as well as extra tariff revenue on imports from C, but the FTA as a whole is far less likely to enjoy net welfare gains (for example, because A loses huge tariff revenue) due to trade diversion. Were A demand represented by D_3^a, B's supplies will not fully replace A's imports from C at P_a. Price divergence is now at its maximum, there is considerable trade diversion and no trade creation. A will incur major tariff revenue losses. Thus, if A's demand is strong and the tariff disparity in the FTA is large enough, the FTA is highly inefficient and likely to lead to net welfare losses.

In policy terms, the conclusions are that:

- FTAs are not fully effective in preventing trade deflection, even with certificates of area origin, because of indirect trade deflection;
- an FTA induces pressures to reduce tariff disparities due to welfare costs and uneven distribution of gains and losses among FTA members; in other words, tariff autonomy of FTA members is *de facto* undermined by concessions, or exception lists will be negotiated.[35]

13.7.3 Trade as aid: the GSP

Based on a 1968 GATT decision, the Community introduced a GSP for developing countries in 1971. GSP is unilateral and small changes have been introduced every year since. With longer intervals, reforms were introduced by the EU but only the 1995 reform would seem to bring a really new system.

The original economic motives in the GATT and UNCTAD debates to introduce GSP were interesting. In the final analysis, the idea was to use trade as the 'handmaiden' to growth and development. This sound strategy ran up against two practices: import-substitution strategies in developing countries and a tariff structure of OECD countries biased against processed and manufactured goods in which developing countries tended to

[35]Other possibilities are that intra-FTA value-added is so low that area origin (here, for B) would not be (fully) recognised, or, that FTAs become politically feasible only once tariff disparities have shrunk due to GATT Rounds. This might explain their recent popularity in the world.

have or to generate comparative advantage. The reasoning was that developing countries suffered from underinvestment in potential comparative advantage goods because of infant industries[36] and lack of scale, since their market demand was too limited. There were two ways to enjoy export-led growth, namely rapid overall tariff reduction and preferential access for developing countries. As long as GATT tariff reduction in OECD countries was too slow and indeed minimal for precisely the typical comparative advantage goods of developing countries, it would be more effective to enjoy preferential access for one or two decades until, hopefully, multilateral reduction would have 'caught up'.

A survey by Langhammer & Sapir (1987) has shown that the actual 'benefits' of the EC's GSP were low though perhaps not trivial. Recent analysis (Panagariya, 2002; Özden & Reinhardt, 2003) confirm that the old motive of stimulating a more competitive export performance is accomplished only to a minor extent. With the continued multilateral tariff reductions of the Tokyo and Uruguay Rounds, however, GSP has become a side issue. As noted before, EU volume protection has been far more important as an access issue, and its recent removal is of greater actual and potential economic significance to developing countries.

Some of the reasons why the EU GSP had little economic impact include:

- the EU already had preferences for some developing countries such as the Lomé group and Mediterranean countries;
- protectionist pressures, having pushed the EU to more and refined volume protection in the 1970s and later, were also successful in limiting GSP margins (or duty-free volumes, via tariff quotas) in 'sensitive' products; the application of GSP in the Community became more and more discretionary;[37]
- a host of technical and administrative problems (for example, origin rules) made the system less transparent and created uncertainty, thereby exactly going against the ulterior motive for GSP – to stimulate long-run investment incentives in export industries in developing countries;
- political window-dressing by putting oil derivatives (etc.) under GSP, leading to much higher 'eligible' GSP imports, even though these imports had zero – or very low – MFN duties.

The practical effects of the EU's GSP would ideally benefit those developing countries that are early in their industrialisation process. For them, demand limitation and infant industry arguments are likely to be most important. Developmental success should ideally lead countries to 'graduate' to ordinary GATT MFN status. However, in practice, this has happened with only a few countries (such as Singapore and South Korea). Graduation turned out to be highly sensitive politically and the major beneficiaries of the EU GSP have consistently been successful exporters such as the East Asian countries, Brazil and, early on, Yugoslavia (Langhammer & Sapir, 1987). The latter effect happened despite the numerous tariff quotas in the top export products of these countries.

The EC GSP reform of 1995 would seem to be based on a recognition of most of these criticisms.[38] Moreover, 'graduation' has become less sensitive because, in joining the WTO, developing countries have assumed many regular GATT obligations, though with specific derogations. Furthermore, EU volume protection has virtually disappeared. This provides opportunities to tailor-make GSP for developing countries in the early stages of development and radically to simplify GSP, thereby increasing certainty and lowering transaction costs. Besides this change in the right direction, the new GSP is entirely based on tariffs – this is in line with the GATT / WTO emphasis on 'tariffication'. So, rather than bringing in discretionary volume protection, GSP margins are differentiated for 'sensitive goods' irrespective of country origin, indeed a major simplification.[39] Another differentiation of GSP margins will slowly be pursued for purposes of 'graduation', in order to achieve a concentration of GSP benefits with the least-developed countries. Graduation is said to be driven by economic criteria,[40] not

[36]The infant industry argument is based on external economics (that is, between industries, via knowledge or 'experience' embodied in inter-sectoral factor flows or otherwise) and the reader is recommended to consult a textbook on international (development) economics. Aid or intervention is thus justified by social returns being higher than initial private returns to investment.

[37]A few recent data sheds some light on this discretion. In COM (94) 212 of 1 June 1994 it is noted that reintroductions of MFN duties, after import ceilings had been exceeded, increased from 76 in 1986 to 172 in 1992. Tariff quotas, which have a similar impact, though automatically, were 'reviewed' year by year – the result was an increase from 91 in 1981 via 116 in 1986 to 189 in 1993.

[38]See COM (94) 212 of 1 June 1994 on the role of GSP in the period 1995–2004.

[39]Sensitive GSP goods comprise the bulk of agricultural goods and such industrial goods as textiles, clothing, carpets and footwear.

[40]By a combination of a 'development index' (including per-capita GNP and an overall trade indicator) and a 'specialisation index' (a variant of Balassa's revealed comparative advantage index). Although arguably 'objective', the 1995 Trade Policy Review of the EC by the WTO shows that the new GSP is biased against big countries, even when they are poor. Product examples are given for both India and China. See WTO (1995, pp. 33–5).

ADDITIONAL READING

The graphical analysis of tariff preferences brings out the 'aid' element in the improvement of access, but highlights some of the costs of this discriminatory approach as well. In Figure 13.5, the home country A has a steeply rising cost schedule, the excess supply of trading partner B is horizontally added (which yields S_b1) and the rest of the world supplies at constant costs P_c (along S_c). A represents the EC as a whole, whereas B represents the group of GSP recipients.

The initial situation is without a GSP. This means that B's and C's exports are subject to the same MFN (common) EC tariff, leading to $P_c\ (1 + t)$. At this EU price the poor countries supply AB and the rest of the world BD, with a total tariff revenue of ADTO. Establishing a modest, preferential tariff for partner B, the supply schedule would become S_{b3}. In trade flow terms this leads to a trade diversion of BC; in 'welfare' terms, it is BC × LL′ because the costs of additional B supplies are pushed LL′ above the world price level. It is this kind of impact that dominated the trade preferences debate initially. Note that the EU itself would enjoy lower revenue (namely, BC × LL′), but experience no price reduction for consumers, or any shrinkage of its domestic supply. The trade diversion was thus viewed as a pure transfer of 'aid' to B's exports. Since the rest of the world suffers from this discrimination, and since it is not a CU or an FTA, a special GATT decision was required to enable this one-way preferentialism under specific conditions.

However, the extent of the tariff concessions matter. S_{b4} represents the case of far-reaching tariff preferences. As drawn, C would be squeezed out of the A market. Trade diversion now becomes BD × GG′, as the costs of B supply have moved further

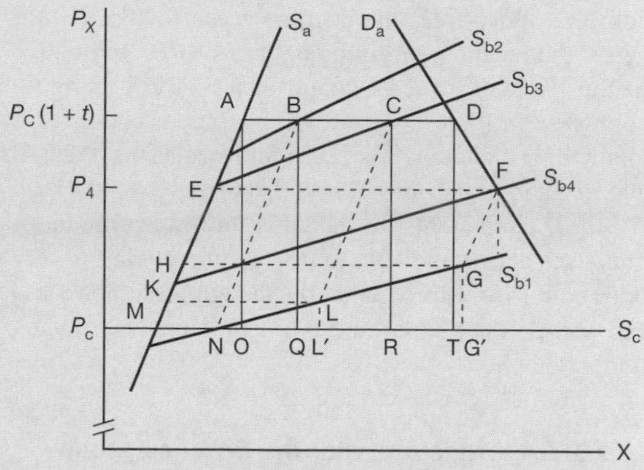

Figure 13.5 Static effects of tariff preferences

Source: Pelkmans, 1984, p. 233

beyond the world price line. New tariff revenue will be EFGH, replacing ADTO; this is, but need not be, smaller. At the same time there are modest trade creation and consumption effects as the EU price falls to P_4. In practice, however, the EU (not unlike the US GSP) limits the concessions for 'sensitive' products in order to prevent the shrinkage of its domestic production in such products. Thus, if B is not permitted to export EF at the low GSP tariff, but has to pay the MFN tariff after some GSP tariff quota is filled, the price reduction will not or will not fully materialise. From the developing countries' point of view, aiming to enhance exports rapidly, the trade creation, consumption and diversion effects (in trade flow terms) would be added together as all would enhance export-led growth. However, the GSP reduces the incentive to raise the competitiveness of the exporter. Squeezing out non-preferential exporters but more competitive exporters may indeed lull the preferred exporter. It also creates vested interests in keeping the preference margin high (and hence future overall tariff reduction of the EU minimal).

commercial (read protectionist) ones. On the other hand, discretion is enhanced by all kinds of new and special considerations, which make GSP an EC negotiation tool to influence policies in developing countries. Extra GSP margins can be given in respect of international social or environmental minimum standards and of TRIPs in the GATT / WTO while cumulation of origin (for regional blocs) will not be undermined by graduation.[41]

The conclusion is that GSP is no longer of great importance as GSP margins have become insignificant for most products. GSP reform has rendered the EU variant simpler than before, but still far from simple.[42]

[41]For details of its current application, see WTO (2004, pp. 34–5).

[42]For the complications of GSP and EBA, see Brenton (2003). The simplicity and eligibility problems lead to unsatisfactory effects on how often GSP countries actually do pay duties. Thus, in 2003, EU imports from China paid full MFN duties over 45 per cent of import value, EBA (non-ACP) countries 40 per cent (due to the early stage of EBA), GSP countries 17 per cent and countries with bilateral FTAs with the EU only 9 per cent (European Commission, 2005).

Because least-developed countries already have virtually complete duty-free, quota-free access to the EU for years, the recent 'everything but arms' (EBA) initiative of the EU will not be a major step forward for these countries. In EBA, access for 48 very poor countries is totally duty and quota free, even for bananas (as of 2006) and rice and sugar (as of 2009). However, given the high EU tariff equivalents for the latter three agro-products, duty-free access is likely to be a genuine help for very poor countries. More generally, though, GSP new style can only produce export incentives for them via 'graduation' of others.

13.7.4 Trade and aid: the Cotonou group

The fourth and last Lomé Convention (1990–2000) was negotiated between the EC12 and 68 ACP countries. It combined trade preferences with development aid in a unique, common institutional framework based on partnership and equality. For a host of reasons, however, the discrepancy between commendable principles and objectives, on the one hand, and the (in)effectiveness of Lomé for the development of ACP countries, on the other, has only increased over time. For most provisions, the Lomé Agreement will be continued in the 'Cotonou' ACP–EU Partnership Agreement until 2007 (see below).

The history of Lomé goes back to the Rome Treaty when an FTA between the EC6 and 22 (colonial or ex-colonial) countries and territories was arranged. As of 1963, two successive Yaoundé agreements turned this into (18) separate FTAs and the EC6. Following British EU membership, EU preferences became unilateral in the first Lomé Convention of 1975, to be followed by three more up to the year 2000.

The unilateral preferences ended a post-colonial era during which the EU wished to maintain good relations with ex-colonies, as 'associates'. This was, at least at the rhetorical level, substituted by partnership and equality in a common institutional framework headed by an ACP Council. The trade concessions to the ACP countries go far. Exports of tropical products and manufactures enter the EC duty free. The partial preferences for agro-products competing with CAP products were significant under Lomé I, in the sense that some 70 per cent of those ACP exports enjoyed *de facto* duty free entry into the EU. Altogether, 94.1 per cent of tariff lines are duty free for ACP exports to the EU. The simple average of agro-tariffs is about half that of MFN (WTO, 2000, p. 47). Nevertheless, the economic significance of the preferences remains limited, even today, since up to 60 per cent of ACP exports to the EU consist of raw materials and fuels that do not carry duties anyway. Free access for industrial products is of obvious potential importance but it should be realised that the ACP group comprises many industrially undeveloped economies.[43]

Brenton & Ikezuki (2005) estimate the value of ACP-African countries of no more than 4 per cent of 2002 exports to the EU, with only five countries enjoying values greater than 10 per cent.

However, the Lomé Agreement and the new Cotonou Agreement of 2000 have a greater economic significance than those from trade preferences only. ACP countries benefit from three major commodity arrangements as well as additional development aid. STABEX ensures the stability of export revenues of a bundle of commodities by financing shortfalls due to price instability. However, unlike the facility of the IMF, compensatory finance under STABEX takes place for single commodities, irrespective of the revenue fluctuations on other commodities. How important STABEX could be under price volatility is evident from the fact that, in 1977, no less than 33 of the then 46 ACP countries had one export product which accounted for more than 50 per cent of the total exports to the EC (Grilli, 1993, p. 30).[44] It can be seen as a new, and objective, way to distribute EC aid to the Lomé countries according to needs. SYSMIN is an insurance system against reductions of mine output for five mineral products (and iron), and may be seen as a security of supply device for EC users too.

The Sugar Protocol is a curious instance of favourable treatment by the EU, a follow-up of a similar arrangement in the British Commonwealth. In the presence of EU self-sufficiency at a very high CAP price, ACP countries are guaranteed a fixed volume of cane sugar exports to the EU, at the CAP price and without duty, for an unlimited period. As Case Study 11.2 shows, this highly preferential, indeed subsidised, access is not GATT compatible and the EU will have to seek other ways or reduce ACP sugar benefits.

ACP countries have been unable to reap 'development' gains from preferential access. The ACP share of EU imports fell from 6.7 per cent in 1997 to 3.1 per cent in 2002. It is telling that other developing countries, with (a less favourable access through) GSP, increased their

[43] A number of them are essentially mono-cultures, with (for some) extra earnings from tourism.

[44] STABEX has other positive features: there is no payback obligation for the least-developed economies; the finance carries no interest rate; and partial conversion into grants is possible for 'more' developed countries.

share in EU imports. Supply factors include mistaken development policies (for example, overvalued exchange rates, tax burdens on exports, lack of competition, the persistence of typical 'high-cost' underdevelopment), very weak infrastructures pushing up local logistical costs and an export bias towards goods facing inelastic EU demand such as beverages (making it difficult to benefit from the few cases with high preference margins). A lack of political stability in many ACP countries has also exerted a negative impact. The new Cotonou Agreement will transform the unilateral preferences into FTAs, as the GATT rules require. The FTAs will aim to promote 'sustainable development', combine a 'deep' FTA (with regulatory disciplines) with development domestic reforms. Cotonou will also promote intra-ACP regionalisation in various ways. The EU–ACP FTAs will be 'asymmetric', in the sense that market-building will precede market opening for ACP.

13.8 Multilateral trade policy

At the basis of EU trade policy lies multilateralism. This can be deduced from various treaty articles (see section 13.2) and the major role it has played in the GATT from the outset in the late 1950s. Nevertheless, in the past the EU has often been accused of having an ambivalent attitude towards the GATT. As noted in section 13.6, of the three fundamental elements of GATT, the EU has been an active supporter of (1) trade liberalisation via Rounds and (2) the notion that GATT is building up a body of world trade law, much less of (3) the scrupulous adherence to the non-discrimination principle of Article 1 GATT.

The present book is not the place to provide an overview of the EU's past activities and positioning over time in GATT (see, for example, Hine, 1985; Murphy, 1990; Pelkmans & Carzaniga, 1996.) We will merely discuss, first, the reasons for the EU's active support of the first two fundamental GATT elements and end with a discussion on how the EU views the compatibility of multilateralism and regionalism.

Of the eight completed GATT Rounds, the four since the EU emerged have led to far-reaching trade liberalisation. This consisted of substantial industrial tariff reduction, practically complete quota liberalisation, and greater market access due to a host of regulatory frameworks or minimum rules with respect to regulatory barriers and administrative and customs handling. Although the 'anti-monde' without the EU remains a counterfactual speculation, a case can be made that without the EU the Dillon and Kennedy Rounds would have been less successful. Indeed, the Kennedy Round might not have been launched at all.[45] It should not be forgotten that the treaty-based CET, in force by mid-1968, had already been cut by the Dillon Round by over 15 per cent, years before it was actually applied. And in 1968 a five-year cumulative reduction, due to the Kennedy Round, began; as a result, at the end of the foreseen transition period the CET was close to 30 per cent lower on average than the treaty said it would be. Also in the other two GATT Rounds the process has largely been led by the USA and the EC together.[46]

Is it true that the EU was, by virtue of its being a bloc with a common trade policy, a difficult negotiating partner? There is little doubt that the intra-EU decision-making mechanism is slow and clumsy, and tends to generate such painfully negotiated compromises that the Commission mandates are rarely flexible enough for initiative and leadership in GATT. This was always the case for the CAP and issues revolving around safeguard clauses which the EU wished to have selective. However, in the Uruguay Round the experience from, and confidence brought about by, EU-1992 enabled the EU to initiate and exercise leadership in several fields. The Community's major problem is really the CAP and the grass-root resistance to radical reforms, let alone genuine market opening in temperate zone products.[47]

The Community has always attached great value to an emerging body of world trade law. The internal aspect of this appreciation resides in the existence of supreme

[45]President Kennedy's call for a new more ambitious GATT Round contained an offer to grant more radical concessions in sectors where 'principal suppliers' (a GATT expression for the main trading nations) would cover 80 per cent of world trade flows. In those days this meant the USA plus the EC6 plus the UK, hence an attempt to promote both European integration and the GATT.

[46]For the Uruguay Round, see Pelkmans and Murphy (1992) and Pelkmans (1995).

[47]However, one should realise that most GATT / WTO partners are protectionist in agriculture – this is true even for several Cairns group countries, the presumed frontrunners in promoting freer world agricultural trade. Note also that the USA had obtained a major GATT waiver on agriculture in 1955. Moreover, despite the selective, (almost) prohibitive agro-tariffs, agricultural market access to the EU is not at all trivial or residual. Many tropical goods come in, often at low or zero duties. A few zero-duty lines of temperate-zone products (e.g. corn gluten, soya) lead to multi-billion euro imports as feedstock. Bilateral FTAs, GSP, EBA and minor concessions in the Uruguay Round have altogether induced substantial agro-imports. The upshot is that the EU is by far the largest agro-importer and, moreover, absorbs no less than 70 per cent of world agro-exports of the least-developed countries (the USA only 17 per cent).

Community law, a key point often overlooked by economists and political scientists. After every GATT Round, the new GATT rules become EC *acquis* via amendments of and additions to Community law. The actual, restraining effect of this GATT-based internal *acquis* upon EU policy makers increased considerably with the 'deepening' of the internal market *acquis,* since all national options and some dubious (former) EU practices are no longer feasible. Given the fact that EU law is deeply entrenched in national law as well, and given its fairly strict enforcement (despite some lingering problems), the EU has in fact come to serve as the guardian of the GATT in the Community. It is unlikely that, in an 'anti-monde' without EC law, GATT rules (before 1995, when the WTO changed GATT into a formal treaty) would have been implemented and enforced so well in all EU countries. Moreover, this refers to a period when the GATT's dispute settlement mechanism was notoriously weak. Precisely because the European integration is legally and economically so advanced, did the European Commission serve as the guardian of the GATT in the EU, simply because the Commission is the guardian of EU law (see Chapter 1, Appendix 1.1).

But there is also an external side to the preference of a body of world trade law. The Community has long preferred a treaty status for the GATT since this would 'bind' all partners into permanent rules, as the EU does internally. Given US leadership in GATT, the very weak legal status of GATT in the USA (until WTO) was long the Union's greatest concern. The EU knows that the federal power structure in the USA creates what in Europe are seen as excessive fears about loss of sovereignty. Since the USA also made use of strong, unilateral trade remedies,[48] and used these procedures in many bilateral issues (though rarely until the final retaliation), the EU understandably wondered about the US adherence to the notion of a world body of trade law, multilateral surveillance and binding dispute settlement. It has long attempted to lure the USA into modes of adherence to this body of law that would come closer to (supreme) treaty position of the GATT in the USA, thereby yielding greater certainty for world business and for trade negotiations. With the conclusion of the WTO, ratified by 148 countries (including the USA) uncertainty has reduced significantly.

Unfortunately, the EC has not been consistent in these pursuits. Quite the contrary. It has joined most other OECD countries in practising grey-area measures (such as VERs) in the 1970s and 1980s, under the pressure of lobbies and in the knowledge that GATT rules were weakly enforced by the GATT itself. Again, this inconsistency would seem to have greatly reduced with the Uruguay Round as well as with EC-1992. Altogether, it would seem that the pro-market, pro-structural adjustment view of the European economy, that was at the base of EC-1992, has also favourably affected EC attitudes during the long Uruguay Round. This also applies to its own trade remedy provision (see Case Study 13.4).

CASE STUDY 13.4 Promoting EU access to third markets

With the steady liberalisation of EU trade policy on the import side, and having taken due notice of the 'vigilant' US approach to prise open foreign markets since the 1978 Trade Act, the EU has gradually strengthened its 'market access strategy'. The basic idea is that the openness of the EU economy is in its own interest (now codified in the treaty, Article 4 EC). However, market access elsewhere remains important for exploiting comparative advantages and scale and should not be pursued only in GATT Rounds via reciprocal concessions. Where possible, active (GATT-compatible) bilateral negotiations should be pursued to reduce barriers to EU exports. Also, dubious implementation of WTO obligations, hindering EU exports, should be acted upon routinely and effectively, as a core activity of the Union's trade diplomats. Since 1996 this strategy (see COM (1996) 53) has been elaborated, supported by a large Market Access Database and active reporting of dubious practices of third countries by EU business. With non-WTO countries, the bilateral negotiation approach is the only tool. With WTO

[48]The 301 and Super 301 measures, named after an article in US trade law.

CASE STUDY 13.4 ***continued***

members, the Trade Barriers Regulation[49] provides a highly structured approach (with deadlines for the Commission, etc.) to EU business to act when its exports are frustrated by illegal barriers. As the Commission puts it: it 'gives industry the right effectively to oblige the Commission to initiate an investigation procedure which could lead to recourse to the dispute settlement procedures of the WTO'.[50] However, it will first attempt bilateral consultation (as indeed is expected by the WTO). Between 1996 and early 2005, 23 procedures were initiated, five of which led to WTO dispute settlement procedures. Examples include: (1) Brazilian exports subsidies (via favourable interest rates) on commuter planes, (2) an allegedly improper use of the trademark 'Parma ham' by the Canadian producers, (3) Korean discrimination in pharmaceutical pricing and reimbursement rules, (4) Argentinean excessive customs requirements for textiles and clothing products, and (5) certain old provisions of the US Anti-Dumping Act of 1916 were GATT-incompatible (but applied to EU steel exports to the USA).[51]

Where the EU has always assumed a special position is on the problem of how properly to combine economic regionalism with multilateralism. It is not easy to formulate the EU position accurately because it has gradually emerged from four decades of history, with highs and lows for trade liberalisation. Moreover, the nature and scope of its integration transformed with deepening, widening and enlargement. Finally, there is an understandable confusion whether or not to attribute specific actions or episodes of the EU protectionism (or refusals to liberalise in a GATT Round) to EU's regionalism as such, or rather to a kind of political economy driven by vested interests and fear of adjustment which rears its head everywhere in the world.

There have been currents in the literature and in commercial diplomacy claiming that 'trade blocs' endanger, if not undermine, the GATT and make GATT Rounds more difficult. Since the EU is the only 'trade bloc' that has a common trade policy, it is a small step to attribute the weaknesses of GATT to the EU or to its example for 'regionalism'. Moreover, the EU is the largest trader in the world economy so that all other GATT / WTO partners have a great interest in market access and its leadership, or the lack of it, in the GATT. Especially in recessionary periods, fears about (the EU's) regionalism being a stumbling block for multilateralism tend to flare up. In appreciating these criticisms it is crucial first to distinguish a great number of weaknesses of the GATT – all addressed to some extent in the Uruguay Round – which cannot be attributed to the EU or at least not solely to it.[52] The second point to consider is that the drawback of the non-discrimination principle of the GATT has been recognised more openly in Europe. Non-discrimination is compatible with any level of protection. Thus, while respecting the great importance of the principle of 'non-discrimination', in and by itself it does nothing to promote trade liberalisation. Especially in the first decades after World War II, when tariffs were high and quotas routine, European countries desperately needed market access for economic growth. Hence, for relatively small, open economies such as the constituent countries of the Community, reducing the level of protection in the GATT was, and often still is, more important than merely upholding non-discrimination in a tariff- and quota-ridden world economy. For the USA of the 1950s and 1960s, when it was a relatively closed economy with a strong export position, this was less

[49]Regulation 3286/94 in OJ L 349 of 22 December 1994.

[50]COM (2000) 440 of 11 July 2000, p. 122.

[51]See http://europa.eu.int/comm/trade/issues/respectrules/tbr/index_en.htm.

[52]When the Uruguay Round began (1986), there were five main weaknesses of the GATT: large derogations (e.g. agriculture); grey-area measures (including MFA); unilateralism (e.g. the US 301 weapon); matters 'beyond' GATT (e.g. TRIPs, services); and institutional and legal weaknesses (e.g. dispute settlements mechanism and the weak legal status of the GATT).

compelling. As a result, the route of a faster and more regional trade liberalisation was opted for in Europe, broadly compatible with Article 24 GATT.

The multilaterial policy problem can therefore be formulated as follows: can regionalism be practised in such a way that (1) it is not at the expense of GATT / WTO partners, and (2) if possible, it is conducive to multilateral liberalisation?[53]

For the first part, the WTO should have an economically sound and legally binding review procedure of any regional trade scheme, notified under Article 24 GATT. The Uruguay Round has produced two steps in the right direction, the biannual Trade Policy Reviews of WTO and an amendment of Article 24. What has irritated other GATT partners in different degrees about the EU, however, is the very emergence and persistence of the pyramid of preferences itself. As noted in section 13.7.1, a hierarchy of friends, lesser friends and foes is surely not in keeping with the spirit of Article 24. The new version of Article 24 cannot undo that. However, the pyramid of 2004 (see Figure 13.3) is more concerned with regulatory 'deepening', even if some discriminatory effects remain undeniable. Since the early 1990s, however, economic regionalism has become popular all over the world, and the 'special' position of the Union no longer exists.

For the second part of this policy issue, the history of the EU's own regionalism is instructive (see, for example, Lawrence, 1991). With trial and error, its pyramid of preferences has eventually induced many countries to liberalise more than one might have expected, *ceteris paribus*. And the EU's own deepening and widening has, step by step, prompted enlargement and better market access for third countries. This is obvious for the entire European continent and the EU's 'orbit' beyond it (see Chapter 20). The other bilateral FTAs with the EU tend to be more 'building blocks' than 'stumbling' blocks' for deeper and wider multilateral liberalisation (Pelkmans & Brenton, 1999).

This is not to say that EU (or other) regionalism could not be a danger to multilateralism, if handled improperly. It also does not mean that the present economic size of the Union does not give it special responsibilities to assume leadership in WTO. The Union's ability to assume leadership will mainly be a function of its internal ability to pursue sound economic policies, so that adjustment is seen not as a threat but as a series of opportunities for change and growth, and its determination to formulate better decision making about trade policy.

In an era in which economic regionalism has become a worldwide phenomenon, with almost frantic bilateral regionalism in East Asia (see, for example, Pangestu, 2003), one might have some fears about further progress in multilateral trade liberalisation. One might surmise that the EU, with its continental economic integration plus its many bilateral FTAs with countries in other parts of the world, would only pay lip service to the importance of the 9th GATT (Doha) Round. This is not the case but, it must be realised, the Union does have a major problem of credibility. The Doha Round is regarded by all WTO partners as a 'development Round'. This implies that the EU's natural interest in deepening and widening the WTO in regulatory issues (for example, services, competition, investment, environment) cannot be expected to accord well with the WTO priorities of developing countries. They emphasise the elimination of agro-export subsidies, substantial and meaningful agro-market access and secure market access for textiles and clothing and their other typical comparative-advantage goods. After failures in Seattle (1999) and Cancún (2003), the Doha Round became serious only in 2004/05 when the EU made major concessions in agriculture and showed flexibility in industrial market access issues. In October 2005, the EU even offered to eliminate agro-export subsidies (if the USA and others would do the same), to bind its decoupling of subsidies to farmers (as decided in the 2003 reform; see Chapter 11) in GATT / WTO and to cut its agro-tariffs by an average of 46 per cent, with peak tariffs cut by as much as 70 per cent, and a maximum tariff of 100 per cent. Inside the EU, this offer was regarded as too far-reaching (for example by France), demonstrating once again the limits of what might be accomplished in the Doha Round. Nevertheless, this offer cannot, in earnest, be typified as minor or as a sign of disinterest in multilateralism. In many temperate-zone goods, tariffs would no doubt still allow 'Community preference', but rarely would they be prohibitive any more. It remains to be seen whether this offer is going to be decisive in bringing about a successful conclusion to the Doha Round, but it might well restore sufficient credibility for the EU to accomplish just that.

[53]This book cannot deal with the broader issue of 'regionalism' in a world trade and development context. For an excellent and highly accessible survey, see World Bank (2000) and Schiff & Winters (2003).

13.9 Summary

The economic justification for having a trade policy is weak at best. Trade policies are no good for overcoming market failures since there are deadweight welfare losses in not tackling such failures directly. That the EU needs a common trade policy is first of all required by GATT / WTO (Article 24). Given the fact that Member States initially had national trade policies – justified or not – a common trade policy is justified by the subsidiarity test (negative externalities generated by disparate national trade policies in an internal market with free movement; also, requirement of legal uniformity). The scope of the common trade policy (Case Study 13.1) is comprehensive for goods, but its (EC) exclusivity is circumscribed for services.

The character of EU trade policy is multifaceted, given vague treaty objectives, the non-exhaustive specifications of instruments in the treaty and up to seven types of trade policy, including interaction with agricultural, development, competition and industrial policies.

Tariff protection has become relatively unimportant in the EU, except for agriculture, food and a few industrial goods. Today's CET exhibits a strong reliance on ad valorem duties for non-agricultural goods and widespread use of (high) specific duties in agricultural goods. All EU tariffs are bound in the GATT. Tariff peaks in non-agricultural goods are few and low (except food and tobacco).

The EU, and its Member States, used to lean heavily on volume protection, until recently. This is no longer the case. The product scope of volume protection included textiles and clothing, leather goods, footwear, steel, colour TVs, certain electronic goods, cars and motorcycles. The intensity increased in the 1970s and the first half of the 1980s, at both national and EU levels. After the mid-1980s, EC volume protection declined drastically: first, because EC-1992 did away with all national instances of such protection; and second, because quotas and VERs were abolished (or expired) during and at the end of the Uruguay Round. The Multi-Fibre Arrangement in textiles and clothing expired late 2004 (ending all quotas), but China's powerful export drive forced the EU into temporary safeguards (Case Study 13.2).

As a form of discriminatory pricing over different and presumably separated markets, dumping is a matter of market power and competition. Inside the EU this is so (since the transition period), but in world trade there is no free movement and access to the market of the 'dumper' may be costly or impossible. In world trade, anti-dumping is a matter of trade policy, as a second-best solution. There are a number of problems with anti-dumping. First, the EC rules are based on GATT rules (dumping refers to export prices being below domestic market prices, which does not always have an economic justification). Second, rules allow considerable discretion, although this is reduced given the disappearance of state-trading and some tightening of GATT rules. Third, there is no WTO surveillance of anti-dumping, especially the delicate issue of the 'right' dumping margin and injury. There is scope to misuse anti-dumping for anti-competitive or industrial policy purposes (Case Study 13.3). Recently, the Union's anti-dumping activity has declined.

The Community has long shown some ambivalence about the non-discrimination principle enshrined in the GATT (Article 1). Its 'pyramid of preferences' seemed to rank its trading partners into friends, lesser friends and foes, which caused widespread political irritation, as well as distortions. As recently as 1991, only the sixth layer (non-European OECD and South Africa) enjoyed ordinary MFN treatment. Others included associates from central Europe, the European Economic Area (not then ratified), Mediterranean preferential partners, the Lomé (ACP) group and GSP (for all developing countries). By 2004, however, the 'pyramid' had altered drastically. The EU has concluded a range of bilaterial FTAs and an economic analysis of FTAs shows that 'indirect trade deflection' can exert a quasi-liberalising, pro-competitive effect. GSP is a unilateral granting of preferences – allowed by the GATT for developing countries – hopefully stimulating export-led growth (hence, 'trade and aid'). In the 1980s, the EC's GSP had a limited, though not trivial, stimulating impact, concentrated on relatively few countries. The 1995 GSP reform introduces 'objective' graduation, simplification and multi-annual duration. The impact of GSP has become small because MFN tariffs are generally low. For the Lomé or Cotonou group the EU has practised 'trade and aid'. The ad hoc aid components (including STABEX) are helpful, but the economic significance of the preferences is modest. Apart from the ever lower preferential margins, the Cotonou group's competitive position is too weak to exploit these advantages.

The Union's stance on multilateralism can be assessed by focusing on the three fundamental

Summary *continued*

elements of the GATT. First, the EU has been essential to the last four GATT Rounds (Dillon, Kennedy, Tokyo, Uruguay); indeed it has – more often than not – exercised joint leadership with the USA. Its main problem in this respect was, and remains, the CAP. Even in the Doha Round, and despite the CAP reforms, this is the case. Second, the Community attaches great value to an emerging body of world trade law. Because GATT law is incorporated into EC law, compliance is in principle ensured. Unfortunately, owing to grey-area measures in the 1970s and 1980s, the EC was anything but stringent when it was politically convenient. Third, the EU has traditionally assumed a somewhat special position on how properly to combine economic regionalism with multilateralism. Regionalism should not be at the expense of WTO partners (and here, the 'pyramid' may be damaging) and, if possible, it should be conducive to multilateral liberalisation (here, the EU score is better).

CHAPTER 14

EU Industrial Policy

Topics covered

- 14.1 How to justify industrial policy
- 14.2 Why a common industrial policy?
- 14.3 Sector policies
- 14.4 Policies stimulating the EU knowledge economy
- 14.5 Horizontal policies
- 14.6 Summary

Industrial policy is a controversial topic, whether in Europe or the rest of the world. It is therefore important to be explicit about how it is defined and what falls outside its scope. Furthermore, one should be clear about whether or not to include services. In any event, in business services the borderline between industrial and service activity is often fuzzy (for example, software development).

In our definition, industrial policy is about incentives for the supply side. More precisely, it comprises all government interventions affecting the incentives to produce industrial goods or incentives to enter/exit specific industrial goods markets. We will refrain from giving a survey of many other definitions of industrial policy and their implications.[1] Industrial policy is a fairly wide-ranging concept. That is why a focus on government-driven incentives is a better guide than a catalogue of policy areas falling under it.

The chapter begins with the economic justification of industrial policy. In the decades preceding the Maastricht Treaty many false 'economic' arguments were brought to the fore, both at national and EU levels, to plead for industrial policy interventions, which were, in fact, driven by protectionism and a fear of too rapid adjustment. Section 14.2 discusses EU and national industrial policy assignments in the light of subsidiarity. The following three sections look at EU industrial policy from three angles: sector (or vertical) policy in section 14.3 (with Case Study 14.1 on steel), technology policy in section 14.4 (which mixes vertical and horizontal elements) (with Case Study 14.2 on high-tech standards), and horizontal measures in section 14.5.

14.1 How to justify industrial policy

Any careful attempt to find economic justifications for industrial policy should first identify what industrial policy is not. Industry lobbying and positioning

[1]The gains of studying many definitions of industrial policy are doubtful, and the marginal returns of the efforts fall rapidly. The interested reader may wish to consult the following works so as to get an idea of the great confusion and discrepancies in conceptualisation of industrial policy: Pelkmans (1984, pp. 252–5); Geroski (1989a); European Commission (1970); Jacquemin & De Jong (1977); Diebold (1980); Bangemann (1992); Nicolaides (1993). A classic and powerful refutation of the whole idea of industrial policy is found in Schultze (1983). The horizontal approach (see text, below) is addressed in Lawton (1999). See, for a very wide-ranging collection of approaches and aspects, Bianchi & Labory (2006).

will be about the 'overall set of policies somehow affecting industry'. It goes without saying that industrial policy is just a narrow subset of this range of policies. Also wider than industrial policy but narrower than the overall set affecting industry are 'policies for industry'.[2]

There is no authoritative way rigorously to separate industrial policy from policies for industry.[3] Restrictions or obligations of the industrial sector may simply protect established companies from new entrants or from foreign competitors without any intent to influence industrial change. But, of course, one may argue that the imposition of rigidities or the favouring of established firms amounts to a refusal of industrial change, hence falls under industrial policy. This wholesale approach to industrial policy has made the term a suspect one among economists. Whether on ideological anti-market grounds, for redistributive reasons, for the sake of industrial employment, for the purpose of maintaining 'strategic' sectors, or plainly for the cushioning of vested capital or labour interests, almost any conceivable measure has been proposed somewhere in Europe. Until the early 1990s, such justifications were readily accepted in EU countries. Since then, interventionist inclinations have become much weaker, yet when there is recession or a higher pace of structural change, these motives tend to reappear. This is why it is critical to substantiate analytical economic grounds before using industrial policy.

14.1.1 Economic arguments

Economic justifications all relate to market failures, real or perceived, thereby missing out on economic growth, or competitiveness[4] or incurring excessive adjustment costs for immobile factors of production. There are essentially four types of economic arguments that may have some analytical validity (Grossman, 1990): firm size arguments, externalities between companies, capital market imperfections, and quality reputation. In addition, there is the second-best argument that rigidities in the labour market may unduly increase adjustment costs for one group in society caused by industrial change.

Firm size arguments have a long history in Europe. As early as the Spaak report (1956), scale and firm size were seen as critical for the needed productivity increases of the EC6, although a customs union and a common market were proposed as the remedy and not industrial policy. Servan-Schreiber's *The American Challenge* (1967) mixed size arguments with those suggesting a better exploitation of the opportunities of the common market, still very incomplete in those days. His book had a major impact on the debate and led to the Colonna–di Paliano memorandum (European Commission 1970), the first explicit plea by the Commission to have an EU industrial policy. Later, recurrent waves of advocating 'European champions' could be observed. The economic question here is not the one analysed in Chapter 6, namely, what the welfare economics are of a customs union in the presence of economies of scale. The concern in that era was whether Europe could close the 'technology gap' purely by market-led catching up or whether an artificial promotion of firm size would strengthen Europe's presence in advanced product markets. There is little evidence that firm size is systematically related to better performance in this respect.[5] However, there remains the problem whether entry or learning-by-doing should be subsidised or otherwise artificially promoted.

Suppose firm F knows that if it could enter the market for a new product *X*, it would have a monopoly, but the fixed costs are estimated to be too high, even at the volume where marginal revenue equals marginal costs. Figure 14.1 shows that a subsidy of DCBE would make entry possible as it would cover expected operating losses.

Consumers appreciate this entry despite monopolistic prices, as they gain BEF. Even if the monopoly were worldwide, the Community-part of BEF could be big enough to justify the subsidy. But there are several caveats. First, the nature of the subsidy matters. As drawn, the operating losses are caused by the need to

[2]Policies for industry have a potentially much wider scope than industrial policies as the former might, in addition, comprise state ownership (for non-economic reasons), price controls, regional industrial planning, buy-national campaigns, tied development aid, as well as general subsidies to standards bodies, to infrastructure, to technical schools or to overall export promotion bodies. Some of these interventions have reduced in importance in Europe or have disappeared altogether. The entire set of policies somehow affecting industry is wider still, the important additions being social policy and fiscal and macroeconomic stabilisation measures as well as policies affecting agricultural, energy or services inputs for industry. See Pelkmans (2006, figure 2.1).

[3]In Pelkmans (2006), a categorisation is provided, however, which should be helpful in most instances. Some modest degree of overlap can nevertheless not be avoided.

[4]At the firm or sector level presumably, because macroeconomically international competitiveness is determined by the exchange rate, influenced in turn by the monetary/fiscal policy mix, and overall wage developments. See section 14.5.

[5]For critical surveys see Geroski (1989b) and Kay (1993).

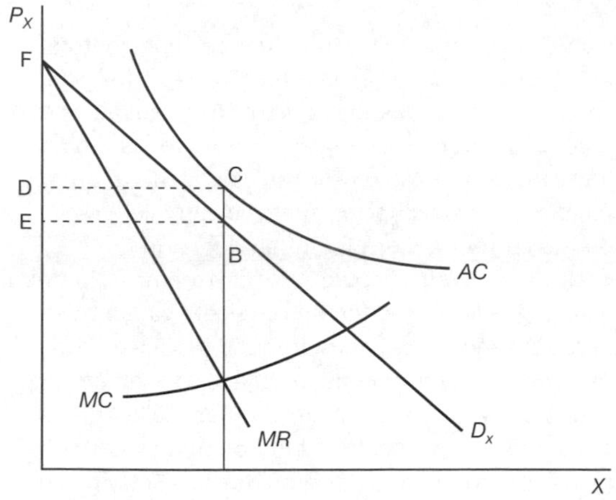

Figure 14.1 Subsidised entry with large fixed costs

Source: Based on Grossman, 1990, p. 97

recoup the fixed costs. But how long would this take? The firm would enter only if it could obtain either a reduction of its annual depreciation costs over many years or a major lump sum initially with the same economic result; however, covering operating losses for one or two years would not do. Given the many uncertainties in the parameters (for example, how much demand? Can the scale curve be forecast so exactly?), such a major production subsidy would be hard to justify in political practice. Second, complications arise with a second potential entrant. If the second entrant is an EU firm, it would be hard to refuse it entry too. Assuming the two firms did not collude, the new price would be lower than in Figure 14.1. This would add to consumer surplus but, at the same time, reduce profits for the first entrant (lower prices, probably far lower sales) while average costs must be higher. So, the welfare calculus becomes more conditional. If the first firm were to be subsidised just enough to enter, a decision to have two entrants must increase the subsidy to the first one. There is also the problem that the EU market is open and the second entrant could be a firm from a third country. In this case everything depends on the shape of the scale curve: the question is whether two or more firms are viable in the world economy. If only one firm is viable without a subsidy, and that firm is a foreign one about to enter, this leaves the EU only one option for industrial policy: strategic entry promotion (Dixit & Kyle, 1985). It would have to be so manifest in its policy to support the EU entrant that the foreign one would opt out. The credibility of industrial policy is critical here. If credibility is insufficient, the foreign firm might hold up, and EU subsidies would have to overcome the subsequent cost rises and operating losses. Also, foreign governments might enter the game because strategic entry promotion is a pure beggar-thy-neighbour policy. This would lead to excessive entry and losses all around.[6]

The overall conclusions are that it is (1) very difficult to know beforehand what new product to support, (2) likely that the social benefit of any support stems from R&D and not from output *per se,* except where 'learning' is very strong and entry artificially restricted. Apart from this last case, strategic entry promotion is a hazardous game, easily leading to excessive entry. *Externalities* could justify industrial policy intervention if this would increase the overall benefit to society which a private firm would not take into account. We focus on R&D and investment in human capital.

ADDITIONAL READING

Real-world cases are rarely as simple as the static example of Figure 14.1. A scale curve is usually not 'given', certainly not for a new, highly complex product. As there will be very few firms, all extremely specialised in a new field, there will be no independent suppliers of process technology. In such new products, with large-scale effects, there will be learning-by-doing effects, internal to the firm (aircraft, computer chips and so on). Learning-by-doing results from experience over time, so learning effects are a function of cumulative turnover over time. If learning effects are strong, although perhaps not entirely predictable, the subsidy argument becomes less vulnerable. In the extreme, it might suffice to provide the entrant in Figure 14.1 with a kind of regulatory or trade protection so as to enable it to recoup fixed costs by rapidly increasing

[6]It is sometimes suggested this is the case for medium-sized commuter planes where demand volatility and subsidisation (e.g. in Canada, Brazil, Indonesia) have probably caused excessive entry, with (political) exit barriers. The demise of Fokker in early 1996 and its long history of problems despite its excellent product range should be seen in this light. The political sensitivity of the Commission's disapproval of the takeover of De Haviland (see Case Study 12.3) is also related to these features.

ADDITIONAL READING *continued*

profits due to rapidly falling costs (both scale and learning). After having ensured considerable sales, it might lower prices in order further to increase sales, thereby further lowering its costs. Once this is achieved, it amounts to a strategic entry deterrence because both entry and exit costs for others (starting at high average costs and with little prospect to realise the same sales volume) will be prohibitively high.

This scenario is sometimes outlined to explain some successes of Japanese consumer electronics companies. A combination of input suppliers and final producers, united in groupings (called 'keiretsu'), with a strong grip on the distribution system in Japan, made it possible to build up volume and anticipate 'learning'. This was achieved – so much so that firms felt secure enough to price low, early on, causing demand to increase so rapidly that their costs became unachievable for competitors. In the USA and the EU, such anti-competitive structures would be forbidden under competition rules. However, the non-application of competition rules in Japan caused European competitors to argue for industrial policy, ultimately due to this strategic entry deterrence. The European companies' lobby also added another dynamic component, namely reinvestment of profits into R&D for the next generation of electronic products, something that had become increasingly difficult for the European competitors. In other words, whereas (in Figure 14.1) the Japanese could risk investing in fixed costs, and recoup through 'learning', the Europeans would have to be subsidised for the next generation of products too, while facing strategic entry deterrence on the current generation of products. In the end, what the EU felt it could do was to employ anti-dumping policy since the anti-competitive structure in Japan (and Korea) permitted the Japanese firms to 'dump' the final products in export markets at prices below those in Japan. The beneficial effects of entry into new scale industries and those with learning effects do exist empirically.[7] Entry often only takes place when one or two initiatives have demonstrated (to potential entrants) that the new industry is viable and that product innovation pays. It is precisely in this early phase that the social returns to the fixed costs of innovation exceed (often by a large multiple) the private returns, so that subsidies would be justified. On strategic entry deterrence, there is a well-known simulation study on the Boeing Airbus case of large jets (Baldwin & Krugman, 1987). The conclusion is that entry promotion seems to have come at considerable welfare cost to the USA, with little if any net gain for Europe, but (since monopoly pricing was broken) clear gains for the rest of the world. The Baldwin–Krugman study is likely to underestimate the subsidy race considerably.[8] Similar work in computer chips has shown excessive entry and welfare losses in both the USA and Japan.

Spillovers in the production of knowledge are such that R&D will be underprovided in free markets. For basic research this is widely recognised and subsidisation occurs in many countries worldwide. Selected applied research and product development are more difficult because spillovers reduce and are harder to gauge anyway. Other than tax credits or accelerated write-offs (not an option for the EU, only for the Member States since the EU does not have the right to tax), it is exceedingly hard to derive precise policy conclusions. Intra- and inter-industry spillovers of R&D are considerable[9] but it is also likely that direct project subsidies have a lower social return than company-financed projects. Allowing (via competition policy) or promoting (via marginal subsidies and a favourable framework) joint research may lead companies to internalise the externalities to a much greater degree.[10] In the EU this has purposefully been promoted in numerous

[7]Grossman (1990, pp. 101 f.f) surveys a number of studies.

[8]On the US side, the indirect subsidies via defence contracts are thought to be very high; on the European side, the German exchange rate guarantees (for the dollar), later outlawed by the GATT, were considerable. Neither is included in the study. In 2004/05, a WTO dispute between the EU and the USA was building up over renewed subsidies, presumably as a result of Airbus having surpassed Boeing in world sales.

[9]See Grossman, (1990, pp. 101 ff.).

[10]See, for example, d'Aspremont and Jacquemin (1988) for a rigorous analysis.

multi-annual programmes, on the condition of cross-border participation, so as to increase the likelihood of exploiting the internal market as a whole later. The use of trade protection to foster R&D will not be effective in overcoming the market failure, as this is a matter of appropriability. By raising the price of final goods, trade protection will attract free-riders using the R&D results of other firms, and this will make existing firms reticent to increase R&D.

Vocational training, retraining and upgrading of the skills of workers may be undersupplied by firms if there are no restrictions on inter-firm mobility. Such mobility will enable workers to capture the rents in other companies too.[11] The right industrial policy is to encourage companies using similar skill profiles to form cooperative ventures for skill-formation, thereby ensuring a much higher degree of appropriability.[12] The classic example is the German apprentice system (see, for example, Audretsch, 1993). Despite the appreciation for it in other EU countries, it has turned out to be very difficult to get firms to commit themselves on an industry-wide basis, in ways as effective as in Germany. The argument can be extended to the entire internal market and is the reason why the EU has attempted to subsidise cross-border apprenticeship exchanges in various programmes, compensating for the lack of EU-wide arrangements at industry level (inhibited by language and social barriers).

Capital market imperfections may also give rise to pleas for industrial policy. Where subsidies or instruments are unavailable or insufficient, companies will often be forced to consider external debt or equity finance. From society's point of view, an efficient capital market should price borrowed funds at social costs plus a reasonable premium for the company's risk. If there is a general short-sightedness on the part of banks or other lenders, this should not be countered by subsidies to credit or credit insurance. There is no reason why governments would be able to assess the riskiness better than capital markets. Rather, as is suggested in the literature on German and Japanese banks and corporate finance, short-sightedness may be the result of the impossibility of monitoring and correcting a company's conduct and strategy. The latter requires the greater involvement of banks in industry, especially inside information at board level. In other words, financing risky and long-term strategies requires a type of bank (special industrial banks or universal banks) whose interests in such finance is matched by mechanisms which are no longer at arm's length.[13] The EU has, in liberalising the internal market for banking, explicitly allowed for universal banking.

Chapter 7 mentioned *reputation for quality* in the context of services and asymmetries of information. For goods, it is necessary to have measures that provide a differential incentive for firms to produce goods of high rather than low quality. The market may provide solutions such as brand names, trademarks, warranties and certificates based on (voluntary) quality standards. The EU's industrial policy could, by creating the appropriate legal instruments at EU-wide level and by fostering EU-wide (voluntary) structures, greatly improve the reliance on these market-led devices. EC-1992 has done this in many respects (see Chapter 5 and below in this chapter). In some cases, minimum quality could be prescribed by EU directives as mandatory, but this would be appropriate only if the asymmetry could lead to hazards (with externalities or social costs going beyond the price of the goods) such as dangers to health, safety or the environment. Otherwise, an obligation of adequate labelling should do.

Finally, declining industries are too often cushioned with a view to reducing *adjustment costs*. The problem here is what one is willing to accept as the benchmark of economic analysis.[14] In the presence of structural unemployment, adjustment costs can run high and they may temporarily eliminate the net gains from extra imports. But adjustment costs are often inflated by a number of rigidities such as the unwillingness to accept lower wages upon inter-sectoral mobility (as the skills and sector-specific experience in sector A may not be valued

[11]Strictly speaking, perfect capital markets would render the underprovision argument irrelevant, as workers could finance their extra training themselves. This point is surely valid for upgrading or learning different skills; it may not apply to vocational training as the collaboration of the firms is indispensable for such investment in human capital.

[12]Curiously, this solution is not mentioned by Grossman (1990).

[13]The reader may be interested in the closely related problem of 'adverse selection' in the case of very risky projects. See Grossman (1990).

[14]The problem for (EU) policy makers is not so much the overall recognition that worldwide competitive pressures and the nature of economic growth require adaptability and change of industrial structures. See COM (1999) 465 of 5 October 1999, *Structural Change and Adjustment in European Manufacturing,* and COM (2005) 474 of 5 October 2005, *Implementing (etc.) a Policy Framework to Strengthen EU Manufacturing,* p. 5, for clear confirmations for this strategic economic perspective. Rather, when it comes down to specific aspects or, for instance, fear of 'de-industrialisation' and 'relocation' of manufacturing, pressure groups and national policy makers might push for special measures.

in sector B), the unwillingness to relocate interregionally,[15] the unwillingness to be retrained, or the provision of high unemployment allowances (leaving little differential with the relevant wages). When skills are less industry specific, general wage rigidities caused by collective contracting may prevent shed labour from offering competitive wages in order to obtain new jobs. Apart from retraining programmes which the EU used to finance (for example for clothing workers under the RETEX programme), it is hard to justify other intervention, let alone trade protection, in order to compensate for badly functioning labour markets. Tackling the labour markets problems directly, however, has proved to be extremely difficult in Europe for socio-political reasons.

14.1.2 Institutional arguments

Besides justification by market failures, industrial policy may be justified by institutional failures. But the arguments may cut both ways, that is, they may also weaken the case for (EU) industrial policy. 'Institutional' is a general label encompassing political processes, policy implementing institutions and what is called (national) 'innovation systems'. The latter focus on the market institutions and how they foster innovation. Pavitt & Sharp (1993) distinguish, for example, myopic and dynamic innovation systems, the former having a set of institutions, skills and methods that systematically undervalue intangible, firm-specific learning.

It is crucial to grasp the basic underlying idea that *market institutions matter*. Neither markets in general, nor (say) scale and learning curves are entirely exogenous. As Pavitt & Sharp (1993, p. 70) put it: 'Learning curve advantages are essentially people – and institution-embodied'. In principle, therefore, industrial policy can occupy itself with shaping the optimal institutional market environment. This should also apply to the optimal (that is, dynamic) as distinct from merely proper (that is, least-distortive in a static sense) functioning of the EU's internal market. In a turnaround against blanket interventionism in two important European Commission papers on industrial policy (European Commission 1990, 1994a), a clear awareness of the importance of market institutions for the dynamic performance of European industry forms the foundation for market-based policy proposals.

Apart from these institution-shaping policies, however, the institutional arguments generally go *against* the pursuit of industrial policy, especially if it is specific and selective. Political processes do not necessarily serve the overall economic welfare of the country or the Union, as is well known from the theory of government failures. And administrative and regulatory failures also exist, explained by 'capture' (for example, of the regulators or the policy makers, by the firms being regulated) or biases prompted by self-interest. This book is not the right place to elaborate on the extensive theoretical and empirical literature.[16] It is crucial to keep in mind that the economic justifications found in section 14.1.1 do not suffice as conclusive arguments for industrial policy. Various institutional–political failures may easily cause adverse selection among those clamouring for policy intervention or lead certain sectors to argue for trade protection and/or subsidies where adjustment was too long resisted or is still being resisted.

What is more, the efficiency-based reasoning in section 14.1.1 has purposely excluded the impact of protection, subsidies or special regulation on cost-minimising behaviour of companies benefiting from it. In fact, it is more realistic to expect X-inefficiencies to emerge upon special treatment or, worse still, X-inefficiencies to continue precisely because special lobbying has ensured some form of cushioning under the label of industrial policy.[17] In turn, this tends to perpetuate the calls for regulatory, trade or subsidy protection as undistorted competition would likely expose such companies or sectors to sharp adjustment pressures. As profits fell, new R&D may come under threat and, as workers would be dismissed, social arguments for a 'breathing' period would be hard to resist. For the Union as a whole, allowing such national derogations or privileges to continue would first of all distort the internal market. Taking a long-term perspective, it may well saddle the EU with an excessive degree of specialisation in declining sectors clamouring for continued shelter (for example, those having lost comparative advantages or which failed to restructure)

[15]This may be due to collapsing regional housing markets for owners if declining sectors are regionally concentrated (e.g. coal, steel, clothing), causing severe capital losses for individuals. It may also be due to social or linguistic barriers.

[16]See, for example, Gatsios and Seabright (1989) and the literature cited therein; Galli & Pelkmans (2000); Labory & Malgarini (2000) and Pelkmans *et al.* (2000b).

[17]Examples that come to mind are the car industry in several EU countries in the period that Japanese competition arose, or consumer electronics in the 1980s.

and with lame-duck national champions shielded against takeovers by, say, more successful world competitors.[18]

14.2 Why a common industrial policy?

The economic arguments for sector-specific industrial policy are weak and uncertain, while the risk of government failure is high. Therefore, most pleas of such a kind are likely to be based on the cost of adjustment. However, the arguments for a measured technology policy and for horizontal measures are stronger, under certain conditions. This leads to the question whether such justified industrial policies should be pursued at national or EU level (or both). Since industrial policy often employs instruments from other policies (such as trade and competition policies), we first try to disentangle the actual assignments since the Maastricht Treaty. Subsequently, subsidiarity criteria are be applied, similar to the chapters on other common policies.

14.2.1 EU industrial policy powers

The phrase 'industrial policy' appeared neither in the Rome Treaty nor in the Single European Act.[19] The ECSC treaty did not employ the term but contained a number of provisions allowing specific sectoral interventions (but in 2002 the ECSC treaty expired). The Maastricht Treaty contains a new article, Article 157 under the title 'industry' which focuses on 'conditions necessary for the competitiveness of the Community's industry'. It reflects the debate following the Bangemann memorandum on industrial policy (European Commission, 1990). Little if any basis for *dirigisme* or 'picking winners' can be derived from the article. It explicitly excludes Community measures 'which could lead to a distortion of competition', emphasises consultation and coordination between the Member States, allows specific EU measures only 'in support of action taken in the Member States' and such measures are to be adopted with unanimity. The aims mentioned for coordination and possible measures are commendable: the adjustment of EU industry to structural change, promotion of initiative (especially small and medium-sized enterprises), creating an environment favourable to intercompany cooperation and fostering better results from innovation policies in the market. In a second industrial policy memorandum (European Commission, 1994a), Commissioner Bangemann has attempted to continue the previous emphasis on horizontal measures, this time with a more explicit reference to the promotion of competitiveness as expressed in Article 157.[20]

Based on our definition of industrial policy, it is, however, more insightful not to focus narrowly on Article 157 even if technology policy is also taken into account. A more complete view is provided by Table 14.1. Two distinctions are made: that between EU and national industrial policies (and how they complement and constrain each other) and that between specific and horizontal instruments.

Table 14.1 has similarities with Table 13.2. What measures are aiming to influence industrial change by affecting the incentives for industrial companies to produce, innovate, enter or exit particular goods or

Table 14.1 Industrial policy instruments since Maastricht

	EU	National
Specific	Trade policy subsidies	Public procurement; state ownership; subsidies, tied development aid
Horizontal	Competition policy • company conduct • state aids Factor market policies; subsidies; standards/quality	Factor market policies; subsidies; standards/quality

[18]See, e.g., Geroski and Jacquemin (1985) for the argument that X-inefficiency rather than (firm) size was the critical obstacle for Europe's industrial competitiveness in the early 1980s.

[19]The Single European Act contains provisions about R&D policies with a view to competitiveness of EU industry. With only slight alteration, they are now found in Arts 163 to 173 EC.

[20]Competitiveness of EU industry was a major theme of the December 1993 White Paper (European Commission, 1993) and this also influenced the second Bangemann memorandum. Note, furthermore, that in terms of broad guidelines and market-driven directives, this horizontal EU industrial policy is supported widely. See Council resolution of November 1994, OJ C 343 of 6 December 1994 and Smith (1999). See also the annual competitiveness reports of DG Enterprise, since 1997. For the difficulties in rendering a 'competitiveness' based EU policy operational, transparent and consistent over time, see Galli & Pelkmans (2000), and Pelkmans (2006).

service markets? They could be part of four policy areas: internal market provisions, competition policy, trade policy or policy initiatives directed to technology and other spheres (for example, small and medium-sized enterprises) not relying on the first three policy areas but instead on subsidies, information, exchange of specialists and so on. In EU practice, evaluating EU industrial policy will necessitate a wholesale inspection of how the EU employs its surveillance competences in competition policy, and actively uses trade policy and internal market rules for industrial policy goals, including sectoral ones if any. In addition, Member States' policies will have to be studied not only because certain powers are exclusive to Member States (public procurement; state ownership of firms; tied development aid) but also in view of the complementarity between EU and national measures where powers are shared (factor market policies such as vocational training; standardisation and voluntary conformity assessment for quality). In subsidies, Article 157 provides a basis (given unanimity) to coordinate national subsidies so as to achieve greater effectiveness, quite apart from the check under Article 87 with respect to their non-distortive character.

14.2.2 Subsidiarity and industrial policy

Assessing whether the policy assignments between the EU and national levels in Table 14.1. are appropriate is far from easy. First, we should identify what industrial policy measures at Member States level distort competition in the internal market (criterion no. 2 of the subsidiarity test of Chapter 3). For those measures the EU should justifiably be given powers to prohibit or to constrain them, or, perhaps, to substitute national measures by EU measures. Once national measures are substituted at EU level, step 5 of the subsidiarity test asks how this should be done, in view of proportionality. Since industrial policy 'borrows' instruments from other EU policies, the EU-level question is often resolved already and the 'how' question is the critical one. Second, questions should be asked about appropriate complementarity between national and EU measures in case of shared powers.

There is no doubt that, over the past decade or so, the Community has greatly improved its score on the subsidiarity test when applied to industrial policy. EC-1992 has eliminated the residual national trade policies (such as national quotas) which caused the competitive exposure of certain national product markets to world competition to differ sharply, thereby distorting the internal market. It has reduced significantly the distortionary impact of national public procurement practices and reduced or eliminated distortionary differences in national product regulation, which sometimes prevented competition or adjustment. Harmonisation and common regulation in intellectual property rights, as well as capital market integration, have greatly reduced distortive effects of national factor markets policies aimed at influencing industrial change. The boost to European standardisation and, in its wake, European conformity assessment via the EOTC[21] procedures and principles is currently in the process of removing numerous actual or perceived artificial national advantages for national industry, which tended to hinder access or facilitated tacit collusion.

Previously existing policies at EU level have been sharpened since EC-1992. This has particularly been the case with the state aids surveillance (see section 12.6).

With respect to industrial cooperation between firms there is the surveillance via the more economic approach to 'horizontals' under EU competition policy since 2001 based on Article 81(3) EC. The encouragement of an environment conducive to inter-firm collaboration, as specified in the new Article 157 is highly general, and restricted to non-distortive provisions. National discrimination or non-trivial preferential treatment of foreign investors (for example, by regions) are forbidden in the internal market, let alone national requirements of export targets or local content.

At EU level, specific industrial policy is weakly manifested in trade policy for declining sectors, as tariff concessions for these sectors have remained below average, and exceptions to GSP still exist. However, all national quotas *vis-à-vis* third (WTO) countries have long been deleted. New trade policy measures other than anti-dumping are rare in the EU. The TV directive[22] is a unique example of requiring a majority of European production for cultural, film and documentary broadcasts. In 1994, the Commission proposed an explicit industrial policy for the European broadcast industry while maintaining this trade policy measure. However,

[21]The European Organisation for Testing and Certification, founded in 1990, deals with voluntary testing and certification, and strives for one-stop conformity assessment (that is, also including mandatory testing and certification under the 'global approach'). See section 5.4.2.

[22]Television without frontiers, Directive 89/552 in OJ L 278 of 17 October 1989 amended as Directive 97/36 in OJ L 202 of 30 July 1997.

this 'quota' system was contested and subsidies were argued to be more appropriate.[23]

This brief survey goes to show that, broadly, the assignment of competences to the EU level would seem to be justified. The major problem is really subsidies, an item appearing in all four categories in Table 14.1. Apart from the political and social sensitivity of curbing state aids to restructuring sectors, several other problems present themselves. First, Article 87 allows distortive subsidies if the subsidised activity is declared to be in the Community interest. This could be a basis for 'picking winners'. The only important case has been Airbus. The justification and public scrutiny of this one very large derogation for two decades has been scant. At least one potential entrant for the smaller end of the family of airplanes (Fokker) may well have suffered from heavy initial subsidisation of Airbus and discriminatory procurement policies by the related national airlines.

Second, the coordination of national subsidies (for example, in R&D) is rational if wasteful duplication can be prevented. However, very little would seem to have been accomplished here, and even this is likely to be suboptimal. EU subsidies tend to go to special cross-border programmes, and directly to firms; these measures have not been used to coordinate national policies. How important coordination might be is highlighted by one figure: EU high-tech programmes account for a budget of roughly 5 per cent of the total of national high-tech budgets, often in similar products, materials or processes. In other words, coordination at the EU level of national R&D programmes could improve 95 per cent of the overall funds in the EU.

14.3 Sector policies

The Union has moved away from selective industrial policies since the 1990 Bangemann memorandum. The trend is clear but gradual. Thus, in the mid-1990s the aircraft sector still received special treatment while several others continued to be seen as requiring a range of stimuli and/or adjustment assistance. In the early 1990s, EU sector policies were adopted or adapted for textiles and clothing, electronics, shipbuilding, machines and footwear (and, in services, for airlines). Influenced by the pro-market philosophy since 1990, all these and other EU sector policies tend to avoid direct intervention and try to improve factor inputs (such as skills and technology), information, standardisation and the performance of small suppliers, while often encouraging the Commission to pursue better market access elsewhere. Adjustment assistance increasingly takes the form of retraining and cross-border exchange programmes.

Other than specific technology promotion (see below), the three main instruments of EU sector policies are: surveillance of state aids and crisis cartels, adjustment assistance from the Structural Funds (when declining sectors are geographically concentrated), and trade policy.

As shown in section 12.6, EU state aids surveillance has gradually become stricter. In the period before the 1990s, serious adjustment problems, often regionally concentrated, made it socially and politically very difficult to prevent distortive sectoral aids by Member States. Shipbuilding subsidies have been given as long as the EU has existed and only in the 2000s have these subsidies become rather marginal. Steel went through two waves of heavy subsidisation (see Case Study 14.1). Special prohibitions on state aids for capacity expansion were laid down for cars, synthetic fibres, and textiles and clothing, which did reduce the subsidy race considerably. Yet another special case is airlines, in the mid-1990s, where heightened competition due to EC-1992 and overcapacity on Atlantic routes, as well as a deep recession, caused tremendous losses covered by rescue aid. Some very large 'final' subsidies were permitted to Sabena, Air France and Iberia, for instance. In 2005, such state aids have been removed, the bankruptcy of Sabena (and the example of the low-cost carriers – see Chapter 8) served as a wake-up call, and EU airlines complain now about indirect state aids (for example, insurance, loans) in the USA. A sharp contrast with the past, indeed. Finally, there is the perennial coal problem where a few countries (above all, Germany; also Spain and, to a lesser extent, France and the UK) have obtained derogations for gradual decreases of extremely high subsidies. While it is true that some Member States have at long

[23]This book cannot go into this fascinating but complex case. In essence there are two very different questions at issue. First, is the quota system protecting a European 'lame duck' against effective US competition? (The answer is yes as far as films are concerned, but see also Case Study 8.4). Second, should free trade and free markets be allowed to undermine the preservation of the many national cultures in Europe (which would also be against the spirit of Art. 151 EC)? In the GATT, the EU and USA have failed to agree here. See also Motta & Polo (1997), COM (2003) 784 *On the Future of European Regulatory Audiovisiual Policy,* and Katsirea (2003).

last given up subsidisation (Belgium, Portugal) in this sector, slowly declining subsidies hinder a properly functioning internal market. Imports of coal from third countries (at much lower world prices) remained at 150 million tonnes in the face of a steadily declining EU demand (1992–99).[24]

CASE STUDY 14.1 EU steel policy: from crisis-prone to healthy industry

The Union began, in 1951, with sectoral coal and steel integration in the ECSC. Unfortunately, the actual performance of coal and steel has been a major problem for decades. The decline in Europe of both sectors led the Union to pursue the kind of industrial policies which have very high static and dynamic costs.

Steel was in permanent crisis between 1974 and 1986. Reasons included: (1) a structural decline in demand (lower infrastructural expenditures; substitution of steel by aluminium, new ceramics, hard plastics or extremely strong fibres; saturation level of steel-using final products (cars, refrigerators); (2) new entrants in world trade such as Japan, South Korea and Brazil (see Figure CS14.1); (3) a long period of very low growth after the first oil shock. Owing to very high fixed costs, price wars were fought on low marginal costs, and losses were unavoidable all around. However, structural adjustment was not rapidly accepted. New capacity was still built in peripheral regions and regional concentration of old capacity caused strong resistance against job losses. First, a subsidy race started, even though Article 4 ECSC contains an outright prohibition of state aids (that is, not an effects-based regime as under the EC treaty; see section 12.6). By late 1977, the USA (Solomon Plan) and the EU (Davignon Plan) cooperated in using external volume protection based on minimum prices (short of anti-dumping action). A crisis cartel was organised by the Commission with voluntary production cuts and talks about capacity reduction. Heavy state aids, cheating (that is, hoping others would close capacity first),

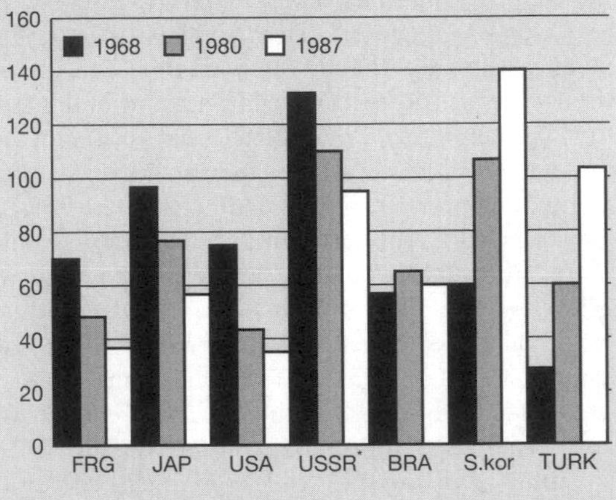

Figure CS 14.1 Steel intensity, 1968–87 (selected years)

Note: Steel intensity is the ratio of steel consumption to GDP.

* USSR + eastern Europe

Source: Data from ESB, 28 October 1992

new capacity and new 'mini mills' destabilised the crisis cartel so that in 1981 a special steel Aid Codex and the Manifest Crisis (Article 58 ECSC) were imposed. Strong centralist powers were used to impose restrictive rules on intra-EU steel trade, capacity cuts, state aids and EU social aids. Up to 1986 the industry lost over 300,000 jobs and capacity was reduced by about 40 million tonnes.

A second crisis occurred after the 1992–93 recession. Especially in Italy and Spain, further capacity cuts had been postponed, while in former East Germany the steel industry had collapsed but

[24]In fact, one may wonder whether an internal market for all coal has ever existed. As early as 1958 (the year that the EEC began), Germany invoked a GATT Art. 19 safeguard, only revoked in 1997. The German cost price of coal in 1992 was ± ECU 145 per tonne-coal-equivalent (TCE), facing a world price of ± ECU 40 per TCE. In 1999, the German cost price had come down to ± €115 facing a world price of €30. Aid, output and employment are currently declining according to a plan up to 2005. Direct (non-social) state aid of Germany for 1999, approved by the ECSC, was €4,600 million, more than €75,000 per miner. This does not include indirect aid to pension funds. The EU coal sector has shrunk to a fraction of its size when the ECSC began in 1951. All data in COM (2000) 380 of 23 June 2000, *Report on State Aid to the Coal Industry in 1998 and 1999.*

CASE STUDY 14.1 *continued*

the leftover of EKO-Stahl nevertheless still meant additional capacity with badly needed state aids. Small but low-priced imports from central Europe broke the oligopolistic price stability, while exports to the USA were closed off by a US voluntary export restraint imposed on the EU. This time no Manifest Crisis was imposed. A restructuring plan sponsored by the Commission foundered on mistrust from the private steel firms about the credibility of the capacity cuts of the state-owned firms (September 1994). Immediately thereafter, the Commission reinvigorated its actions against the state aids. It also acted against steel cartel practices (see section 12.3.2) in a major way. Early in 1996 the industry had little more than 250,000 workers (less than half of those in 1986) and most inefficient plants had been mothballed or scrapped. More mills were privatised. External quota protection is now gone, except quotas *vis-à-vis* Russia, Ukraine and Kazakhstan; steel tariffs are now low or zero. The Community proved to be a slow and costly adjuster. But the results are commendable. State aids for restructuring (which is the bulk) fell by no less than 80 per cent from €1,530 million (annually) in 1994–96 to €260 million (annually) in 1996–98 and are now practically phased out. In October 1999, the Commission reported (COM (1999) 453) that, at long last, the EU steel industry was among the most modern and competitive in the world and the conditions for facing future challenges are good.

Crisis cartels are allowed only under very strict conditions, and this policy has broadly stuck (at least under the EU treaty; for steel, see Case Study 14.1). Crisis cartels may be an alternative to state aids. Such cartels pursue an orderly reduction of capacity in industries suffering from overcapacity. The purpose is to prevent destructive competition causing excessive adjustment costs and possibly adverse selection in bankruptcies. Adverse selection of survivors of such destructive competition means that the survivors might be those with the deepest financial pockets (say, as part of large conglomerates, or because of state ownership) rather than the most efficient companies. If this were to happen, recent modernisation investment and good management might be punished by bankruptcy, which is bad for overall economic welfare while also undermining the basic incentive of markets rewarding best-practice performance. Japan and Germany have provisions for crisis cartels.

Trade policy as a sectoral form of industrial policy has been used by practically all trading countries in the world economy. It used to take the form of variations in tariff (and quota) levels and of preferential treatment. It used to include voluntary export restraints (VERs); nowadays, it might still include discretionary use of anti-dumping and perhaps even specification of origin rules for the application of anti-dumping duties.

Since EC-1992 has removed the remnants of national trade policy in the EC, and since the Uruguay Round has severely circumscribed grey-area measures such as VERs, the possibilities for EU common trade policy to serve as an instrument of industrial policy have become rather limited. As shown in Chapter 13, there is some degree of discretion in anti-dumping policy, but, with the technical improvements of the Uruguay Round and the virtual disappearance of state-trading countries, this discretion has shrunk. Still, there is little doubt that the EU has employed anti-dumping as a defensive industrial policy in electronics.

The product structure of the CET has not changed much over time. Owing to GATT bindings, tariff manipulation for industrial policy purposes is most exceptional.[25] In a unique case in 1983, the EU temporarily raised the

[25]The 1994 Commission memorandum on industrial policy (European Commission, 1994a, p. 34) lists as one of the action points: 'continue to improve the structure of the common customs tariff in a manner which reflects the industrial interests of producers and users'. The scope for doing this is, however, extremely limited, unless this phrase refers to unilateral tariff reduction for inputs. Neutral 'tariff reshuffling' is bound to be contested in GATT / WTO. The EU did reshuffle tariffs for consumer electronic products on 1 January 1986, again a unique instance. But, of course, some tariffs may remain constant in a GATT Round (e.g. cars, at 10 per cent in the Uruguay Round) when many others are cut.

tariff for compact disc players from 9.5 to 19 per cent, with compensation offered in the GATT to Japan (then the only competitor).[26]

Apart from the TV directive (see section 14.2.2), quotas are no longer an accepted instrument in industrial EU trade: with the demise of the MFA in 2005, EU quotas have become rare (see section 13.5). In 2005, the Commission proposed to abolish TV (minimum) quotas for European programmes, even if European production continues to be promoted.

ADDITIONAL READING

A crisis cartel is in fact a common scrapping programme with a degree of binding and common floor prices or an agreement not to reduce prices (backed by the authorities). Without the latter two, 'free-rider' problems are bound to arise (Pelkmans, 1984).

The crux of the crisis cartel is that the free-rider in a scrapping programme (probably the same firm that would be most aggressive in price competition) is offered a higher market share or such prices that it would realise positive profits, even in the recession. The financially strong firm might agree: first, because it will be incapable of estimating what losses ruinous price competition will impart on itself, and, second, because the weaker firms might be able to obtain state aid, which would reduce or eliminate its competitive advantage. The stronger firm would be attracted if the capacity reduction assigned to it were proportionally less, with an increase in market share. However, agreement would be hard to achieve, if the weaker firms are vulnerable precisely because it is the recently added products that have caused overcapacity and high indebtedness: it would lead to scrapping some of the modern and most productive units of overall capacity. It would be even harder when capacity is still coming on stream due to lead times of half a decade.[27] Finally, there is the problem that the dividing line between capacity-enlarging investments (which are prohibited in a crisis cartel) and capital deepening is sometimes arbitrary, which may lead to frictions destabilising the cartel.

Besides the problem of stability there is a host of other problems with crisis cartels, not least discretion and lack of transparency. Crisis cartels also lead to vested interests in organising the market. In effect, this would mean not merely that consumers and user industries have to bear higher prices, but also that rationalisation is likely to take longer in a crisis cartel.

In 1978, the synthetic fibre industry in the EU achieved an informal agreement with the Commission's DG for Industrial Policy, that was subsequently shot down by the entire Commission itself, yet agreed in another form later on (see Shaw & Shaw, 1983). Two years later, a crisis cartel in steel was adopted by the EU on the basis of the special provisions in the ECSC treaty. In September 1982 the six major EU zinc producers notified a crisis cartel for concerted shutdown of capacity, but in the autumn of 1983 the crisis cartel was terminated before it was ever formally approved. In 1994, the Commission approved a crisis cartel of sixteen Dutch brick producers scrapping eight obsolete plants in a time of overcapacity.

Adjustment assistance from the structural funds is, in principle, least distortive. It usually emphasises retraining of workers, marginal support for restructuring indirect stimuli to help attract alternative regional employment, and other measures of an indirect nature. An important difference from some forms of rescue state aids consists in the much lower levels of support per worker and the common agreement in Council. It is unlikely, therefore, that the Structural Funds have a considerable effect on industrial structure; rather they facilitate positive industrial adjustment.

[26]After this measure expired, anti-dumping cases were filed by EU industry. Interestingly, anti-dumping cases against Taiwan, Malaysia and Singapore exports of compact disc players, initiated in 1992, were withdrawn in 1993 because the two leading EU producers had relocated production to East Asia.

[27]During the steel crisis of 1993–94, even the dramatically reduced former East German capacity (concentrated in EKO-Stahl) caused great problems as its restructuring implied a modernisation with added capacity (which also received German state aid given the extreme transition problems).

Interestingly, EU sector subsidies other than via technology programmes or the Structural Funds[28] do not exist. The kind of subsidies that Member States often give, the EU has never provided thus far. This restraint is crucial. If European champions are supported otherwise, it is done by Member States subject to state aid surveillance of the Commission. Airbus remains the only major exception where a perceived 'Community interest' had led the Council to dispense with such a surveillance. But Airbus receives only national, and no EU, subsidies except via (modest) EU R&D programmes for aerospace.

The problem with the emphasis on horizontal measures is that the measures are not tailored to the needs and peculiarities of sectors. Yet, an interventionist sectoral approach will not return. The most recent EU industrial policy initiative attempts to fine-tune for sectors without falling back to interventionism.[29] The approach combines seven horizontal initiatives (like actions against counterfeiting, the competitiveness aspects of energy and environment, a new initiative on market access to third countries and managing structural change) which have more significance for some sectors than for others, with seven sectoral initiatives (on, for example, pharmaceuticals, chemicals, ICT, and mechanical engineering), which however remain non-interventionist. A border case is skill shortages which is presented as a horizontal issue but specified for six selected sectors. Unfortunately, the impact assessment does not provide much guidance on the expected effects of this approach.

14.4 Policies stimulating the EU knowledge economy

Structurally higher economic growth in an open EU economy, participating in a globalised world economy, requires a relentless pursuit of the exploitation of ideas, knowledge and skills. Well-informed and properly functioning markets can do a lot to propel such a pursuit. But market failures, coordination failures between levels of government, national budget outlays and the incentives they bring about, as well as attitudinal issues in Europe such as risk aversion, rigidities and resistance to change, amount to as many reasons to define ambitious strategies at the policy level too. The aim of the Lisbon process, defined by the European Council in 2000, is undoubtedly correct in spirit and strategic direction: the EU should become 'the most competitive knowledge economy in the world' (by 2010). In the present chapter, the Lisbon process and its coordination mechanisms will not be studied (see Chapters 15 and 18 respectively). The reason is that this process is deeper and wider than even a broad concept of industrial policy might be. More precisely, the emphasis in the Lisbon process is not only, and perhaps not even primarily, on the specifics of knowledge-related policies, but on social and economic reforms, better market functioning and deepening of the internal market. Moreover, Lisbon is a product and process of the Member States; the EU level merely facilitates and complements.

In the following, we zoom in on the knowledge-related polices of the EU. After subsidiarity arguments and some problematic conceptual issues (Is all of this 'industrial policy'?), we briefly touch upon the following themes: research and education, EU technology policy and EU innovation policy.

14.4.1 Economic significance of knowledge-related policies

The economic rationale of knowledge-related policies has to do with the expected impact on total factor productivity (see Figure 6.10) in relation with the long-run comparative (dis)advantages of the EU as a highly developed economy in the world division of labour. Increasing the value-added in the EU will have to come more and more from goods and services, if not ideas and technology as well, with a high degree of originality or complexity or with unique attributes of differentiation which are hard to imitate. This is challenging. One needs to innovate at the technology frontier, to compete at (and with) high levels of skills, to be supported by wide and deep research and development capabilities (which are kept excellent by competitive mechanisms and peer review) and to be embedded in a stimulative environment of market rewards and a positive attitude to change. The EU is conscious of this strategic need, both in business and politics, but, so far, it has proved difficult to match genuine and effective policy action with the ambitious wording of goals. Subsidiarity arguments are convincing. Scale, if interpreted as cross-border

[28] In a strict sense, the Regional and Social Funds do not even provide sectoral subsidies, but adjustment assistance is sometimes *de facto* related to sectoral decline in, for example, textiles and clothing, and shipbuilding. The social subsidies in steel are funded by the steel sector itself.

[29] COM (2005) 474 of 5 October 2005, *A Policy Framework to Strengthen EU Manufacturing – Towards a More Integrated Approach for Industrial Policy;* see also SEC (2005) 1215, as an annex, and SEC (2005) 1217, impact assessment.

R&D networks or as the sheer magnitude of some research centres or equipment or as international quality control, is becoming an ever greater necessity for progress at the frontier. The scale argument also applies to risk sharing in very-long-run experiments (such as CERN or nuclear fusion or space research and development). More simply, but of great significance, there is a critical advantage in EU policies in overcoming the parochial attitudes of Member States and their vested interests in local research communities and locally protected and cherished institutes. Here, the question is a *fear* for European scale and even more so, the loss of reputation if tested EU-wide, or the loss of autonomy and low pace. This parochialism is hidden behind the neutral phrase of 'better coordination of national R&D policies and spending'. Such coordination is so critical because the national budgets are a large multiple of the EU budget. Thus far, the cautious approach has typically been one of 'management by speech', and this without any genuine EU 'say' over national spending. Clearly, for the 'coordination' to be effective in overcoming entrenched parochialism, one needs to invent new mechanisms with true leverage.

Cross-border externalities are also relevant in at least two ways. First, a genuine single market is a great stimulus to R&D because of better prospects (*ceteris paribus*) of return on knowledge investment and as a result of facilitating factors such as common standards and a common set of intellectual property rights. Second, there is the more general economic argument of cross-border knowledge spillovers. The more open an economy is, the greater the benefits that economy will enjoy from R&D efforts made by foreign companies (see, for example, Soete & ter Weel, 1999). But these spillovers tend to be sizable only among countries with strong economic interdependence (for an empirical study see, for example, Jacobs *et al.,* 2001). Altogether, the case for an EU role in knowledge-related policies is therefore well established.

It is, however, not immediately clear what shape and ambition such an EU role should assume. For present purposes, the question is whether and to what extent knowledge-related policies can be considered to be 'industrial policy'? Thus, is higher education to be regarded as industrial policy? This would go too far, probably. But it goes without saying that European business should be able to count on societal efforts to have ambitious higher education and to rest assured that a wide range of medium and high skills routinely flows from schools and universities in Europe. Since there are significant gaps and shortcomings here, there is a close link between industrial policy and the more general educational policies in the Union. Another query can be posed about innovation. While innovation is often associated with technology (and rightly so), there is much more to innovation, and these other aspects have a much wider and deep-seated relation with the attitudes and incentives in European society at large (think of attitudes to risk taking, the appreciation of novelty and the willingness to change). Such considerations go far beyond industrial policy, too. Therefore, what follows is inherently limited to what can reasonably be said to be industrial policy.

14.4.2 Research and education

Research can be viewed together with (higher) education. Typically, this would refer to more fundamental research, far removed from the market. Such research has strong 'public goods' properties and tends to be underproduced without subsidies. Some such research may take the form of spin-offs from technical universities or 'science parks' and might be closer to commercial exploitation. When one would go one step further and research directly serves the development of products or processes, hence is marketable, the case for subsidies or tax relief is weak or absent, and the only stimulus that might be considered is an exemption of horizontal cooperation between companies under competition law. This type of R&D is discussed in section 14.4.3, although, admittedly, the line between the two is not sharp.

Research and higher education are closely linked as the quality of advanced teaching and the research at the frontier are strongly interdependent. The quantity and quality of European research ultimately hangs together with the overall climate for higher education and the incentive structure in it. Leading researchers and the best talents in universities are mobile internationally and, given the public good character of what they produce, it is easy, indeed, rewarding, for them to be attracted to a more stimulating research and learning environment. Europe generates numerous fine talents but the overall environment is not so rewarding for them. There has been massive migration to the US research communities, both business and non-profit, so much so that in 2004 an estimated 400,000 European researchers and university teachers were thought to be working in the USA. The counterflow is quite small. The shortcomings in the EU have much to do with the combination of (1) a lack of investment in research and in higher education, with (2) a lack of competition and challenge in research, and (3) a crippling fragmentation and waste in sticking to (many) national traditions in determining policies, structures and incentives, with the European dimension as a marginal afterthought. On all three accounts, researchers are disillusioned, the more so as the EU continues to employ the rhetoric of the 'knowledge society' without living up to it. The past two decades have witnessed a slow but steady rise in the Europeanisation of academic research and publications, which helps in overcoming (2). The cultural diversity in Europe was often misused by academics to 'hide' their published articles in national languages, thereby offering protection to all but the finest minds, who would seek world class journals anyway.

Nowadays, prominence of scholars is determined mainly by European (if not worldwide) recognition and by operation in European associations. The Lisbon process (since 2000) has finally set a more ambitious target for overcoming the lack of investment in R&D: by 2010, EU countries should spend 3 per cent of GDP on R&D, one-third of which in public-funded research and two-thirds in business (which is even more behind the standards set by leading OECD countries). The problem is that these decisions are taken at the national level and/or in business: for public research the required annual growth rate in order to attain the goal would be 6 per cent for a period of eight years consecutively, and for business even 9 per cent. Such growth rates in spending can only be expected if strict priorities are set at the national level.

Even more problematic than the lack of investment is the fragmentation and waste in research in Europe (item (3)). Career perspectives are rigid and strictly national, funding is tied to national procedures and (not infrequently distributive) practices, often excluding European partnerships, foundations tend to be national and tie their projects to nationals, support for many specialisations (no matter how tiny and marginal) is not combined in an EU-wide perspective, funding is routinely related to primary flows for teaching which may splinter research efforts and creates language barriers for non-national scholars, and so on. The problem is deep-seated for reasons of protectionism, no doubt, but also because education has always been regarded as a Member State power *par excellence.* The latter is valid for primary and secondary education and is closely intertwined with culture and customs as well. The case is a good deal weaker, however, for higher levels of education and is almost certainly turning into a case for Europeanisation for the highest levels of academic teaching, let alone research. The High Level Expert Group (2005) has formulated the case for Europeanisation of research in a convincing way.[30] The question now is how to manage change in numerous universities and research centres which have vested interests in slowing down the process and in resisting mending their ways.

One result of the Lisbon process is the idea of a European Research Area.[31] Apart from a better use of the five-year framework programmes for EU research, the idea is to remove at least barriers in national funding for EU-wide work, to redirect national policies into a European direction for questions such as career/appointments, and to stimulate private research by a range of measures in the realm of the internal market (such as IPRs, standards, competition rules, fiscal aspects). In addition, the establishment of a European Research Council (ERC) has been advocated widely (for example, by Sapir *et al.*, 2003). The High Level Expert Group has made the case for an ERC in some detail since it would be a rigorous overhaul of the Union's fragmentation and insufficient competitive spirit in research.[32]

A parallel route consists in the waking of European education ministers to the importance of a European dimension. The EU now seeks to develop what is called a 'Europe of education and training' by 2010.[33] This parallel route focuses on greater mobility of students, professors and teachers in new, more ambitious programmes as well as via national grants and mutual recognition of modules, an emphasis of European qualifications or certificates besides the traditional (but ill-functioning) mutual recognition of diplomas and the support of the so-called

[30]Their arguments include, e.g., reinforcing excellence, linking science to innovation, competing for scarce talent, encouraging investment. The EU value-added, as they call it, consists of: encouraging and supporting the finest European talents (and therefore making it attractive to stay in the EU), the combination of selectivity, agility and focus, dynamic effects in the European research system, etc.

[31]See COM (2003) 226 of 30 April 2003, *Investing in Research: An Action Plan for Europe.*

[32]The reader should nevertheless realise that the mere fact that the fragmentation is discussed precisely by national ministers hinders a full appreciation of several European success stories. EIROforum brings together seven world class, intergovernmental research bodies in nuclear research (CERN), fusion (EFDA), molecular biology (EMBL), space (ESA), astronomy (ESO), radiation (ESRF) and neutron beams (ILL), all European. These top institutes fall outside the regular EU-driven research coordination, intergovernmental as they are. Now that the ERA seems to become a reality, their leadership could hardly be missed. See EIROforum (2005) *Towards a Europe of Knowledge and Innovation,* http://www.eiroforum.org/efarchives/efsciencepolicy05.pdf.

[33]See, e.g., COM (2003) 685 of 12 February 2004, *Joint Interim Report on Education and Training 2010,* and SEC (2004) 73 of 21 January 2004 on indicators and benchmarks (a COM staff paper, based on the Lisbon process).

Bologna process in which many European countries (also non-EU ones) have agreed to adopt a US-type bachelors/masters structure so as to facilitate European recognition and transparency of national degrees in a splintered Europe. This fresh approach and the combination with the European Research Area has finally activated the European universities as well. The Glasgow Declaration[34] is squarely placed in the European knowledge society and is far more proactive on European issues of mobility and quality than ever before. This is bolstered by the support from national education ministers (a U-turn compared with the past) to have the EU level deal directly and proactively with the universities.[35]

14.4.3 EU technology policy

Discussions about EU R&D, or technology, policies are usually focused on the *input* side. This will be the focus here as well. Before pursuing this approach, however, the importance of a market-led framework with the right incentives to obtain an optimal *output* of R&D needs to be stressed. It is important to realise that the establishment and proper functioning of the single market is by far the most important incentive for private innovation. In the final analysis the guarantee of EU-wide market access at least costs and without discrimination provides an enormous impetus for process innovation to be exploited via large sales and higher transient profits. In principle, world free trade has similar effects and this can be pursued simultaneously. The case for a suitable EU framework on the 'output' side of R&D is far stronger than for feasible options at world level, however. The EU has full control over its own single market and its proper functioning. Apart from access to the entire Community market, appropriate and least-cost property rights at EU level such as patents, and software and industrial design protection, are major incentives and are (generally) superior to a collection of national property rights. Competition policy can – and does – allow for inter-firm collaboration, especially 'pre-competitive' research (that is, before firms take the firm-specific innovation track), thereby internalising the problems associated with appropriability and free-riding. Finally, standards setting can be a crucial incentive to proceed from inventions to (costly) innovations and this is far more difficult to accomplish at world level. In other words, the 'horizontal' focus of industrial policy is vital for companies in the EU to exploit the output of their innovative efforts.

In a rare example of simulation of (EU) options in R&D policy to stimulate economic growth, Eaton *et al.* (1998) draw some remarkable inferences. First, EU measures (national or EU level) to increase research output are effective in raising EU productivity (hence, growth), but would also positively affect productivity throughout the OECD. Such measures would include R&D subsidies, stronger patent protection or enhanced research productivity.[36] Second, the simulations show the enormous potential for free-riding if research policy is conducted at the national level. Pre-empting such free-riding – as a huge disincentive – is a formidable argument supporting any of the following policy options: further 'completing' the internal market, as the authors show that (large) increases in intra-EU market outlets stimulate R&D output; a true Community patent, valid for the entire single market; reducing duplicative 'waste' in national research by strict coordination on this score, which effectively raises R&D subsidies.

The appropriability issue for (business) innovation in the EU is a serious one. The costs of patenting for the entire single market are extremely high – despite the single application via the European Patent Office (see Chapter 10) – due to many translations and up to 25 annual renewal fees, quite apart from the multiple costs of possible patent law cases all around. And these costs weigh heavily on medium-sized and large business, by far the most research oriented. Improving the incentive to exploit patent protection at much lower initial and annual costs, and without a high hazard rate of imitation in some national markets (where patents were not sought for cost reasons), seems bound to raise research output in the EU considerably. A Community patent[37] would improve this incentive appreciably, thereby enhancing the proper functioning of the single market, with significantly higher growth rates according to Eaton *et al.* (1998).

[34]European University Association (2005).

[35]COM (2003) 58 of 5 February 2003, *The Role of the Universities in the Europe of Knowledge;* COM (2005) 152 of 20 April 2005, *Mobilising the Brainpower of Europe.*

[36]Another simulation was carried out in the *Impact Assessment for the First Proposal of the 7th Research and Technology Framework Programme;* see SEC (2005) 430 of 6 April 2005. A doubling of the EU-level research would eventually yield an extra GDP (over a business-as-usual scenario) of between 0.45 per cent and 0.96 per cent. In a richer simulation, where research output impacts positively on the quality of goods and services, the extra GDP might reach 1.66 percent as a maximum.

[37]As proposed by the Commission in COM (2000) 412 of 1 August 2000. See Martinez (2000) for a microeconomic assessment. See also section 10.5. By late 2005 the EU patent had still not been adopted, owing to practical language issues.

Community technology policy reflects a mixture of selective and more horizontal approaches. Both aspects are fuzzy. Selectivity rarely goes so far as 'picking winners', but broad choices are clearly made. The horizontal approaches are less general than, say, a guarantee of intra-EU market access or the establishment of an EU-wide patent. The two key issues to be addressed are: (1) whether there is an economic case for technology policy, and (2) what elements should be pursued at EU rather than at Member States level.

Full consideration of the first issue goes beyond the scope of this book, but a few critical points are indispensable for a proper assessment of the case for technology policy. Paraphrasing Pavitt & Sharp (1993), technology can be defined as the combination of skills, equipment and organisation necessary to produce marketable products, processes and services. Unlike in basic CU theory (see section 6.1), technology is not exogenous and not costless; it is often firm specific and tacit, that is, not fully codifiable. Among the important implications of this view of technology are that:

- technological development is cumulative (because of learning-by-doing) and search for variations of technological trajectories (or new ones) is severely constrained by existing skills in the region of location. The fact that science is a (worldwide) public good does not mean that, for that reason alone, technological capacity will be equalised worldwide;
- technology transfer and imitation are costly; at the same time, catching-up attempts by second-movers can be successful when based on effective exploitation of existing clusters of skills. Without the latter, second-movers will face very high catch-up costs.

As the arguments in section 14.1 demonstrate, identifying market failures is not a sufficient case for technology policy. Choices of instruments, of what is to be stimulated and in what institutional setting matter too. The presence of imperfect competition greatly limits the analytical power of the microeconomics of technology. For (EU or national) policy makers there is also the problem that numerous companies have become so internationalised that the micro and macro gains expected from policy may not easily be harvested in the same (EU or national) economy. This is an important reason to focus on skills and embodied learning as these are internationally less mobile. In conclusion, the economic case for technology policy is circumscribed, and its effectiveness may be problematic for a host of reasons.

What elements should be pursued at EU rather than national level? Subsidiarity suggests the criteria of scale and externalities (both positive and negative) beyond the national level. In some specific aspects the case for a common approach is strong and resistance from vested national interests prevent it from being effectively pursued. Examples include common (or, coordinated) rather than fragmented public procurement in, for example, defence equipment, and incentive-driven regulation for newly emerging markets. The former has at least formally been realised in the constitutional treaty (not yet ratified).[38] The latter is exemplified in the Disability Act in the USA, which has greatly stimulated new technology for the disabled. Furthermore, technology policy should contribute to the establishment of the internal market (for example, research for European standards, which in turn limits research options) and main EU policy objectives such as cohesion[39] and selected elements of common policies, for example, transport safety.

CASE STUDY 14.2 High-tech standards and industrial policy

When black and white TV was upgraded to colour TV, three different standards emerged: the US NTSC standard, PAL (most of Europe, most of Asia, Africa) and SECAM (France, Greece, part of Africa). The NTSC standard is an example of 'too early adoption': in 1954 commercial pressure forced a decision whereas the Europeans (behind in income and hence still beginning with mass TV) could wait and wished to improve colour TV further. PAL and SECAM are variants of a better quality TV system, introduced in 1963 in Europe. France used SECAM as industrial policy but PAL was taken up by most European countries. The incompatibility between the two split the EU

[38]Article III-212 establishes a European agency for armaments, research and military capability under the Council.

[39]This may imply inefficiencies in project funding by letting research centres in cohesion countries participate. For policies stimulating diffusion it can be highly rewarding, however.

CASE STUDY 14.2 *continued*

market and led to extra costs of production and inconveniences for consumers. Japan, in 1960, adopted NTSC under US pressure.

Japanese dissatisfaction with low NTSC quality prompted them to start developing a new colour TV system with much higher resolution (that is, sharper image). A Japanese proposal in the CCITT (a broadcast committee of the International Telecom munications Union) in 1985 was blocked in 1986 by the Europeans. They felt this MUSE transmission proposal was disproportionately costly to most of the world (PAL and SECAM) as it was totally incompatible (also US frequencies per second were used, different from Europe). The installed base of TV sets, broadcasting equipment and cameras in Europe would have to be replaced and this would give the Japanese a huge competitive advantage (as they had already developed 'high definition' TV sets). The EU sponsored a EUREKA project to develop a backward-compatible HDTV system with D^2-MAC as the broadcast standard. The next step would be HD-MAC. The problem is known in economics as cooperative standardisation with network externalities. Such standards can be adopted too early or too late and the adoption is primarily determined by a conviction among consumers that the said standard will indeed be widely adopted (see also section 8.2). Buying a colour TV is a major expenditure and marginal improvements such as D^2-MAC will not induce consumer conviction. In 1989, the die was cast by the commercial satellite TV producers who decided to go for PAL. This broke cooperative standardisation and created doubts about the EUREKA project.

Meanwhile, in the USA, rather than industrial policy, a competitive tender for HDTV was used. This gave a chance to an even newer technology – digital TV – and ultimately the key players developing analogue HDTV in EUREKA now also developed digital TV in the USA. In the early 1990s, it became clear that digital TV is viable and that the high demands on broadcasting via satellite and cable can be resolved by new techniques. Both Japanese and European industrial policies had failed. The world is now moving to digital TV.

However, cooperative standardisation with network externalities, and some public intervention, need not always go wrong. The digital cellular mobile telephone GSM, developed on the basis of an open EU standard set in 1987 and elaborated in great detail up to 1990, has overcome the fragmentation of the EU mobile market with a new technology. It became a worldwide success. The 'openness' of the standard may well have contributed to this – access for non-European firms was free and indeed was used by Motorola and others. Curiously, another helpful factor is likely to have been the unfailing commitment by fifteen (mostly state-owned) monopolistic telecoms operators (Pelkmans, 2001a). With the third generation of mobile telecoms (3G), leadership shifted to the equipment producers and this in a fiercely competitive market. This made standards cooperation for UMTS far more difficult, although a compromise was hammered out in early 1999. It has also turned out that 3G applications and extra gadgets (such as cameras) prove decisive for competitive advantage, which helped the Japanese consumer electronics companies to capture higher market share.

ADDITIONAL READING

Large *scale* projects at European level include the JET (Joint European Taurus) on nuclear fusion, now succeeded by ITER, a higher-generation prototype fusion reactor (with the USA, Japan and Russia), and JESSI (on advanced chips) in the EUREKA programme. R&D for space is, however, organised at the ESA (European Space Agency) and for particle circuits at CERN, both organisations going beyond the EU. This goes to show that the specific cost effectiveness and other benefits of common EU technology programmes should be carefully compared with looser coordination alternatives.

ADDITIONAL READING *continued*

In fact, EUREKA (for R&D which is closer to the market than 'pre-competitive' research) provides a flexible formula for project cooperation with variable country membership. Hence, scale is an argument for going beyond the national level but does not automatically justify assignment to the EU level.

The same goes for *externalities,* especially positive externalities. However, because of free-riding it may be crucial for the EU to assume leadership, after which non-EU countries may be more willing to associate themselves. The telecoms broadband network research in RACE and the EUREKA project on HDTV were well-known examples; the GEANT super-network for universities and the Galileo satellite GPS system are recent examples.

The greatest gains from EU assignment are likely to arise from coordination between the Member States' national efforts, with a view to preventing wasteful duplications. A certain degree of duplication or even competition among nationally sponsored R&D efforts is desirable. It is exceedingly hard to identify what the optimal rate of duplication is, though wasteful duplication is widely suspected to involve large resources in Europe. Since non-military R&D spending per capita in Europe is considerably lower than in Japan or the USA, greater effectiveness of resources (for example, via increased specialisation and complementarity) would almost certainly add value for the Union as a whole.

In practice, EU technology policy is operated within five-year framework programmes. The institutional provisions for these programmes are highly inefficient,[40] due to Member States' unwillingness to transfer competences in an effective way and the complex role of the European Parliament in this case. The emphasis on (nuclear) energy research, inherited from a now largely defunct Euratom has disappeared (from 50 per cent in the mid-1980s, through 14 per cent in the early 1990s to 8.4 per cent in the fifth framework programme (1998–2002)). Some 40 per cent used to be spent on ICT (in the fourth programme, up to 1998), down to 35 per cent up to 2006. The main economic argument remains the upgrading of European skills and learning. Indeed, the new objective is called 'a user-friendly information society', for instance in eEurope (2001–05) and i2010, the newest project. It is also hoped that IT, as a generic industry, will support competitiveness in other industries. Certainly, the competitiveness of both software and hardware sectors of the EU ICT industry is already subject to programmes since 1981 (ESPRIT), and yet little, if any, improvement of its competitiveness has been accomplished (Dang Nguyen & Genton, 2005). Could it be that the availability of subsidies prompts adverse selection, that is, too many projects with learning and inventions are ultimately loss making (short of subsidies) because innovation follows only too rarely? Or is Europe's weakness in converting inventions into innovations due to other factors, and, if so, is it the task of EU technology policy to address these problems? It is likely that both questions can be answered with a partial yes. Adverse selection may be possible because of 'capture', for which there are indications.[41]

CASE STUDY 14.3 Technology platforms – a new formula for success?

A promising new method to bring together research communities and industry while promoting public–private partnerships consists in European technology platforms. The platforms set long-term research agendas in a very concrete way, strongly driven by business perspectives about the prospects to arrive at marketable goods and services. This is supposed to overcome innovation gaps (see section

[40]After the Maastricht Treaty it took up to three years to decide one. Time overlaps between successive programmes were accepted to minimise the costs of these inefficiencies. The Amsterdam Treaty has simplified the procedure somewhat.

[41]*The Economist,* 9 January 1993, pp. 21–3, speaks about a 'closed circle . . . unreceptive to outside influences', for example.

CASE STUDY 14.3 *continued*

14.4.4.) precisely in areas and technologies where regulators or public policies are also prominent. In 2004,[42] there were 25 such platforms, and they are seen as exercising strong leadership. There are indirect (but no automatic) linkages with the framework programmes for research subsidies but it is characteristic of the platforms that they also seek their own financing. Their coordination and mutual stimulus in a jointly agreed, bottom-up voluntary process would seem to be the key to their success. Platforms go through three steps. First, they agree on a strategic vision document which specifies the strategic importance, specifies objectives of the future work and sets basic principles. Second, a research agenda is agreed, with priorities, networks and clustering of R&D capacities on a voluntary basis – this agenda is made up by stakeholders but is actively monitored by a 'mirror group' of specialists from the Member States. Third, a deployment strategy is laid out, including demonstration activities and the search for finance (which may include the framework finance but normal procedures will have to be followed). Where collaborative research is essential for the spreading of (long-term and/or very high) risks and are considered important for European business competitiveness, the platforms can be succeeded by Joint Technology Initiatives. These JTIs are dedicated legal structures which are eligible for a multitude of financial sources and subject to conditional exemptions of competition policy. Advantages are the assurance of industry's long-term commitment in the presence of considerable risks, the accomplishment of 'critical mass' and the expected greater leverage of EU subsidies. Examples of JTIs include areas such as hydrogen and fuel cells, aeronautics, nanotechnologies and embedded computer systems. Such JTIs might take the form of so-called joint undertakings under EC law (Article 171 EC), as was already the case with Galileo (the European satellite-based GPS system) and JET (fusion).

14.4.4 Innovation and skills

A persistent complaint about Europe's industry is its weakness in innovation. The Commission White Paper (1993) gives five reasons for the difficulties of converting inventions and ideas into innovations, that is, viable goods or services in the market: inadequate links between universities and business, lack of risk capital, R&D not being a leading factor in many corporate strategies, obstacles for researchers when starting a business and weak market research.[43] The problem for an EU-level role is less a matter of EU versus Member States (although this does play a role as well) and more a matter of how the EU can prompt European *business* to become more innovative. Innovation is very much an entrepreneurial activity, and the relevant question is therefore what the weaknesses in the incentive structures in the EU are which ought to be overcome. Some of the five items mentioned have been tackled since the mid-1990s. In 1999 the EU launched a Risk Capital programme, the reduction in the costs and delays of start-ups have been addressed and monitored with a good deal of publicity and the earlier fears of link-ups between business and universities have faded somewhat. The lack of prominence of R&D in corporate strategy would seem to be a specific problem of the more traditional SMEs. This is, for example, one reason why Italy's score on R&D is so conspicuously low. Italy's industrial strength is largely due to successful medium-sized companies with strong world export performance but often in traditional goods; these SMEs have practically no R&D activities and their innovation is mainly design and quality based. Although such a niche can work, it remains vulnerable to new rivals in other continents. Despite a greater awareness of the innovation gap, the Commission still spoke about inadequate innovation performance in 2003.[44] The EU level meanwhile employs a battery of instruments such as an annual Innovation Scoreboard, a Trend Chart on Innovation in Europe (based on the Lisbon process) and a range of minor tools to insert innovation into other EU

[42]SEC (2005) 800 of 10 June 2005, *Report on Technology Platforms (etc.)*.

[43]See also the UNICE (2000) report on innovation in Europe.

[44]COM (2003) 112 of 11 March 2003, *Innovation Policy.*

policy areas such as regional development, technology (including a special Environmental Technologies programme). It is unclear what the effectiveness of such tools is.[45]

Innovation and technology together hinge on the presence of the right quality of skills. Skills in business are fundamental to an enterprise's capacity to acquire and absorb knowledge as well as the significance of new ideas, *a fortiori,* for their exploitation in innovative ways.

The Union suffers from skill shortages in ICT and shortages might multiply in other fields with ageing in the near future. A deeper internal labour market could offset national and regional shortages to some degree. There is of course a business interest in developing skills inside companies but there is nonetheless an industrial policy concern about the proper matching of college graduates and the needs in the labour markets. An increasing awareness has emerged, for example, that European education does not generate nearly as many graduates, at the various levels, in technical fields and exact sciences as do (proportionately) the Japanese, Chinese and US education systems. Innovation is a function of the skills present, and from that perspective it is essential that skill shortages are prevented in the Union. Since education is a national competence, only the Lisbon process can be used to press this need, but even that is entirely voluntary.

14.5 Horizontal policies

Horizontal policies consist of (1) those setting the regulatory and competitive framework conducive to competitiveness or industrial performance, and (2) more specific activities going across many industries and services.

The overall EU framework conducive to industrial performance has been the mainstay of EU industrial policy since 1990. It consists of five broad elements: the establishment of the internal market; the quality and proper justification of its regulation; competition policy; an open trade policy; and an EU-wide, if not pan-European, promotion of infrastructural networks facilitating specialisation and competition in the single market – these are the building blocks of this framework. The framework should reflect the principle of 'an open market economy with free competition' (Article 4 EC) and the coordination article (Article 157 EC) as discussed in section 14.2. The second Bangemann memorandum (European Commission, 1994a) is essentially a refinement of this policy orientation. For all the many details of sectoral and technology policies or other specific measures, the pro-market foundation remains the key to Europe's industrial competitiveness.

The most important recent manifestation is the attention to regulatory reform at EU and national level so as to limit regulation to cases and forms which are justified by cost/benefit analysis.[46] This should improve business performance because undue regulatory burdens will be removed without sacrificing justified regulation.

As Table 14.1 shows, specific yet horizontal activities should be considered as well. Apart from competition policy (see Chapter 12 and section 14.3), this concerns three types of measures: factor market policies, subsidies and the standards/certification/quality nexus.

Factor market policies concern mainly the promotion of venture capital markets and of intangible investment in human resources, including cross-border mobility, exchange and vocational training. The latter are 'top objectives' according to the second Bangemann memorandum and, subject to subsidiarity, can be justified economically.

Subsidies of a horizontal nature refer especially to positive externalities and public goods such as detailed market analysis, economic information and economic research grants. Also, much greater emphasis is laid on SMEs, and special subsidies are supposed to overcome their problems in certification, quality assurance, joint venture feasibility studies, access to information, modern management and so on. All these subsidies are rather marginal and their effectiveness is hard to measure.

The most important component is the standards/certification/quality nexus in the internal market. The EU's primary role is to ensure the proper regulatory strategy for products with health, safety, environmental

[45]In 2005 the Commission proposed to integrate its Entrepreneurship and Innovation programme, with the ICT policy support and the Intelligent Energy – Europe programme into a (hopefully more coherent) Competitiveness and Innovation framework programme for 2007–2013. See COM (2005) 121 of 6 April and the impact assessment SEC (2005) 430 of 6 April 2005.

[46]See Galli & Pelkmans (2000), Vol. I on horizontal issues, Vol. II on three goods sectors, three services and three network industries. On simplification (in the SLIM programme) see COM (2000) 104 of 28 February 2000, *Review of SLIM.* More broadly, we refer to Chapter 4, especially the role of RIAs. A clear case where 'industrial policy' took the form of reducing the initially proposed regulatory burden on (the chemical) industry, is REACH. See Pelkmans (2005b).

or consumer information problems, so as to prevent market failure (see section 5.4.2). Beyond that, the question arises as to what the EU role should be, if any, for standards not prompted by regulation as well as for voluntary conformity assessment and quality issues. These are essentially market issues. What the EU has done, in the framework of EC-1992, is to bring about a European institutional framework for voluntary conformity assessment (especially with respect to mutual recognition based on quality criteria for conformity bodies) while stimulating majority-voting and flexibility in European standards bodies. This is justified by the overall economic interest the EU has in fostering market-driven European standardisation and competitive, least-cost, EU-wide conformity assessment.[47]

The same interest is less clear for quality promotion and the sponsoring of quality management. When there are no health or consumer problems, competition will determine a range of quality levels attuned to consumer price/quality preferences. All the same, Member States do pursue quality promotion, with a view to industrial competitiveness. The underlying idea is that, in an era of globalisation, the high unit cost of European products necessitates a strong presence in the high value-added segments of industrial product markets. Since these policies do not distort the internal market in any meaningful way, subsidiarity[48] cannot be invoked to justify an EU competence. All the EU should do, therefore, is to increase the awareness of business in the EU via its general subsidies for information and studies (Aichinger, 2001).

A special subset of voluntary standards may justify EU involvement. This is the case where the achievement of coordination to write common standards cannot come about without special EU subsidies or regulation. An old example of the latter is the attempt by twelve European IT companies to achieve an open IT standard, based on UNIX, for which an exemption under Article 81 EC was obtained.[49] An example of the former (subsidies) is the endeavour in EU technology policy to agree on *ex ante* standards. The idea is to limit the large number of trajectories for R&D at a very early stage of basic research, so that costly research is prevented from going in an incompatible direction. The problem here is not the general argument but its specific application. Uncertainty, asymmetries of information and 'capture' may all cause biases as well as a refusal to adjust if the choice turns out to be wrong. When there are network externalities and an installed base (for example, as with television), standards may be set too early, causing costly lock-in effects for subscribers. But a refusal to move to a new standard may block the costly R&D altogether.

14.6 Summary

Industrial policy is defined, in this book, as government incentives for the supply side. There are many false economic justifications of (EU) industrial policy. Only four justifications may have some analytical validity, given certain caveats: some special (but not general) firm size arguments (for example, subsidised entry or learning-by-doing, with severe practical problems, however), externalities between companies (for example, spillovers in the production of knowledge; investment in human capital), capital market imperfections, and quality reputation. Reduction of adjustment costs for declining industries, possibly a valid argument, may degenerate into a third-best policy if labour markets are very rigid. In a dynamic view of the economy, 'innovation systems' might also justify measured intervention – since learning curves are embodied in people and institutions. More often than not, however, institutional aspects have contributed to failures of industrial policy.

Applying subsidiarity to EU industrial policy begins with identifying which industrial policy measures of the Member States distort competition in the internal market. If and when such measures are substituted at EU level ('need to act', to be affirmed), the 'how' question (step 5 of the subsidiarity test) is the critical one. A long history of government failures (at both EU and Member States levels) sounds a pertinent warning. Next, questions would be asked about the appropriate

[47] See, for these various issues, SEC (98) 291, *Efficiency and Accountability in EU Standardisation* (a Commission communication); OECD (1997), Vol. I, chapter 6 on standards; Blind (2004); WTO (2005, Part II); COM (2004) 130 of 25 October 2004, *Integration of Environmental Aspects into European Standardisation.*

[48] As noted before, subsidiarity cannot be used to correct unjustified policies of Member States, as long as externalities (or scale) are not at issue. Note also that Art. 157 requires unanimity.

[49] In the end the attempt failed for other reasons.

Summary *continued*

complementarity between national and EU measures (a highly complex matter, see Table 14.1).

Recent EU industrial policy has become market oriented; for a few years it has even been called 'enterprise policy'. The shift is clear from the much more critical look at sector policies, although the difficulties in coming to grips with national sector subsidies are only slowly fading. Now, airlines and steel (both long dependent on aid) are subsidy free, while shipbuilding and coal have finally succumbed to (much) lower subsidies. In crisis cartels, the Commission's approach has been relatively strict under the EU rules; in steel (ECSC rules), the 1981 Manifest Crisis and severe politicisation have compounded adjustment (for example, capacity cuts) considerably and a competitive steel industry only re-emerged in the late 1990s (Case Study 14.1). Where trade policy was used as industrial sector policy, the disappearance of volume protection (see Section 13.5) has drastically reduced the possibilities under this option. Two Commission memoranda on EU industrial policy in the 1990s are based on horizontal and pro-market approaches. The recent emphasis is strongly on competitiveness.

Stimulated by the Lisbon process, the recent emphasis in the EU is on the knowledge economy. The economic rationale behind the knowledge economy is the expected positive impact on total factor productivity, the only road to higher growth the EU can take. The EU level can be given assignments here, based on scale and externalities arguments, but this does not provide clarity about the desired type of broad industrial policy. We distinguish three elements for purposes of EU industrial policy: research and education, technology policy, and innovation and skills. The key issues in research and education are the drastic reduction of national parochialism and fragmentation in research, its Europeanisation in a European Research Area and a tougher competitive spirit, driven by the new European Research Council.

What is labelled as Community technology policy reflects a mixture of selective and horizontal approaches. Both aspects are fuzzy. The economic case for (EU) technology policy is circumscribed (especially because of globalisation) and might best be focused on the less mobile aspects of skills and embodied learning. Although, in general, large-scale research projects and the better functioning of the internal market are proper arguments for EU technology policy, the 'how' question is even more difficult here than in other policies, since technological trajectories are hard to anticipate. The examples of HDTV (Case Study 14.2) and 25 years of ICT programmes, from ESPRIT (1981) to the newest i2010, are instructive. A seemingly successful combination of market-driven, bottom-up technology trajectory, with firm business commitment, has now been developed in 'European technology platforms', in no less than 25 areas. Also, the problem of converting inventions adequately and rapidly into innovations – so critical for industrial competitiveness in the EU – is addressed at both EU and national level.

How effective all this policy attention is, is hard to say. Perhaps, incentive structures in Europe stimulate European entrepreneurs insufficiently. Horizontal EU policies attempt to build an overall EU framework conducive to industrial performance. It is the mainstay of current EU industrial policy, including pro-market factor market policies (for example, vocational training), horizontal subsidies of a modest nature, and the promotion of the standards/certification/quality nexus in the internal market.

PART 4

Equity and Stabilisation

Parts 2 and 3 deal with the establishment and proper functioning of the internal market, and therefore also with the regulation and common polices required for this purpose. The orientation is microeconomic and the public economic function at stake is 'allocation' (of factors of production, by market forces and/or by EC and national rules and policies). Until the end of the 1980s, there was no doubt that the hard core of EU economic integration consisted merely of this allocative function. Beginning with the Social Charter in 1989, the reformulation of the EC objectives in the Maastricht Treaty and the introduction of monetary union, the economic study of European integration has to ask the question whether equity and macroeconomic stabilisation functions are also exercised by the Union, whether these are justified by subsidiarity and what main elements of this *acquis* can be usefully identified.

Part 4 deals with equity (via redistribution, perhaps also via the EU budget, and minimum requirements) and macroeconomic stabilisation (via monetary, fiscal and exchange rate policies, and possibly the EU budget). The economics of subsidiarity (Chapter 3) would lead us to expect that, once the internal market is truly integrated (including labour), strong pressures would emerge to shift (some of the) equity function to the EU level as well as the macroeconomic stabilisation function. If indeed the single market were so 'complete', these pressures could be resisted only at a cost. Such costs may consist in keeping the internal market partly fragmented or in choosing cooperative solutions (step 3 of the subsidiarity test) which are not credible over longer periods, and hence are unstable and disruptive. The present state of European market integration is characterised by far-reaching deepening of the internal market, except for labour. The exception reflects the resistance 'at a cost', or, at the very least, it coincides with a very prudent attitude of Member States about the emergence of a 'social *acquis*'. In a more complicated fashion, it might well be related to the shift of the macroeconomic stabilisation function to the EU level: in Maastricht the EU opted for a mixed solution, that is, centralisation of monetary policy, while keeping fiscal policy and equity-based expenditures almost entirely decentralised.

Chapter 15 analyses whether and to what extent a social *acquis* should be pursued at the Union level and how it is being pursued at the present stage of European integration. It addresses the notion of a European labour market (building on Chapters 9 and 10), social policies, spending and regulation as well as the EU Social Fund. Chapter 16 discusses economic cohesion, the market and policy approaches for the reduction of income per capita disparities between regions and even countries in the EU. Chapter 17 analyses what the case was, and to some extent still is, for EU macroeconomic cooperation, for economies so open to each other. In particular, the credibility of national macroeconomic policies (including independent exchange rate policies) is emphasised and the method and practice of the European Monetary System is studied. Chapter 18 is about the economic and monetary union. The emphasis is first on the costs and benefits of monetary union, both theoretically and in the case of the EU. The methods of what is presumably meant by the 'Economic Union' (undefined in the treaty), the passage to the euro, the objectives and instruments of monetary union and possible further deepening and enlargement (to 24 members of the eurozone, or more) are set out. The chapter also provides a basic analysis of the monetary policy of the ECB. Chapter 19 considers what public economic functions are justified for the EU budget. Based on this subsidiarity framework, the nature and (desirable) structure of the EU budget is analysed.

CHAPTER 15

Social Equity for the Union?

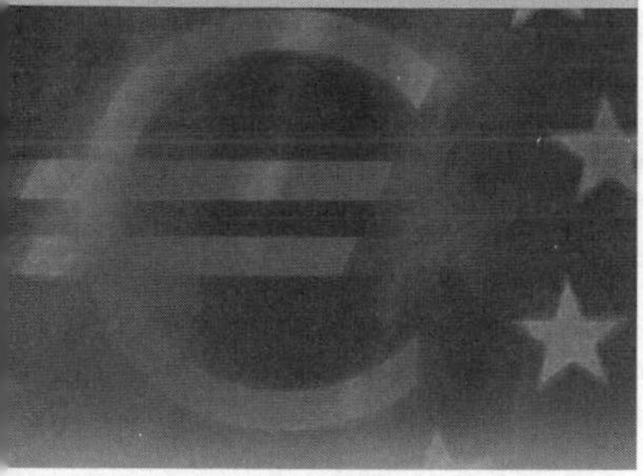

Topics covered

With the deepening and widening of the internal market, following EC-1992, it could be expected that questions about the equity and macroeconomic stabilisation functions of the Union would arise sooner or later. The Padoa-Schioppa report (Padoa-Schioppa *et al.,* 1987) squarely addressed this fundamental assignment problem: in a deep internal market, should equity and macroeconomic stabilisation functions also begin to be exercised by the EU level, wholly or partly?[1] The present chapter focuses on the social *acquis* as a major aspect of equity; Chapter 16 will address economic cohesion as the other major equity topic at EU level.

With the politically agreed Social Charter of 1989 and the fourth objective of the Maastricht Treaty ('a high level of employment and of social protection'), the suggestion that the Union would henceforth pursue equity could not easily be dismissed. In the Amsterdam Treaty, the 'equality of men and women' was added to the EC objectives. Moreover, a 'European employment strategy' was inserted in Article 125 EC (and others), while some crucial aspects of the Social Charter were placed in the treaty once the UK government had given up its objections. The Commission pronounced a medium-term Social Agenda in 2000 and once again in 2005.[2] Since 2003, the European Council has annual Social Summits with the social partners, organised at EU level. The Lisbon process, aiming to make the EU the most competitive knowledge economy by 2010, comprises a considerable social agenda and employs a range of social and employment indicators. Last but not least, there is an intense debate about what is called the 'European social model', a term suggestive of an EU equity function.

The reader is warned that there is a huge gap between European rhetoric and what the EU level is exactly doing in social issues. The deepest reason for that is the ambiguity of the term 'European': does 'European' refer to the *EU as such*[3] or does it refer to the *collection of European countries* assembled in the Union? In the public debate the two are often not clearly distinguished, resulting in undue expectations about, and misplaced demands from, the EU level. This makes it so important, therefore, that a careful normative and descriptive analysis of the social *acquis* is provided.

[1]For early contributions, see Vol. II of the MacDougall report (MacDougall *et al.,* 1977) and Pelkmans (1982a).

[2]See COM (2000) 379 of 28 June 2000 and COM (2005) 33 of 9 February 2005.

[3]The practice of mixing up the EU with 'Europe' is a little unfortunate since, even when the EU has 27 countries in 2007, there will be another 15 European countries which are not EU Member States.

For present purposes, social policies refer to social interference by the state (here, also the EU) across most or all citizens. Different countries in Europe would include most or all of the following elements: social security, social insurance, social welfare, social protection, occupational health and safety, legal and mutually agreed restrictions in the labour market (alternatively, viewed as 'entitlements'), workers' consultation, and various aspects of employment policy such as active mediation and support, retraining, adjustment assistance and vocational training.

Section 15.1 addresses the subsidiarity question, for labour market issues, social expenditures and industrial relations. Section 15.2 describes the social *acquis* at the EU level as it stands in 2005, again with respect to these three aspects. Section 15.3 goes a little deeper into social dilemmas for EU countries, in particular, the ambiguities in the European employment strategy and the reform capability of the respective 'social models' in the Member States. Several case studies illustrate the variety of the issues in the social area.

15.1 Subsidiarity and the social *acquis*

For simplicity we shall distinguish three components of social policy in a wide sense, which could, in principle, make up the social *acquis:*

1. *Social expenditures,* either directly by the state (such as old-age basic pensions, transfers for the disabled, social welfare, social housing subsidies, health subsidies for lower incomes) or payments which could fall under 'insurance' arrangements but are, to some degree, topped up or guaranteed by the state (such as unemployment benefits, sickness funds, disability insurance); in addition, one could include here the spending on 'active' labour market policies such as wage subsidies for structurally unemployed, retraining, upskilling.
2. *Labour market regulation,* including 'employment protection legislation' (EPL), working hours, vacation days and allowances, occupational pension rights, minimum wages, occupational health and safety rules, equal treatment of men and women, rules protecting workers with temporary jobs as well as young employees.
3. *Industrial relations,* that is, the relationships between workers and employers, including wage bargaining traditions, the (automatic?) extension of collective agreements to a sector, consultations at the company, sectoral and/or national level, and (in Germany) co-determination (the inclusion of representatives in the company board, elected by the workers).

The subsidiarity test will be applied to these three categories one by one. The criteria for the test are taken from Chapter 3, hence, scale and cross-border externalities. However, in the social area, it is essential to have special regard for the actual or perceived diversity between Member States given their own histories of social strife and idiosyncratic national compromises. In terms of the subsidiarity analysis of Chapter 3, this amounts to heterogeneous preferences. The greater this heterogeneity is, the weaker the case to shift powers to the EU level. Or, putting it differently, in the event that a spontaneous convergence of preferences is observed over time (given the intense cooperation between EU countries and the great exposure of national solutions to alternatives elsewhere in the EU), the cost of finding common solutions at the EU level is bound to decline.

15.1.1 Social expenditures

Social expenditures are equity driven and not (usually) motivated by market failures. There is little reason to believe that nationals of one country in the Union have a preference to express 'solidarity' with the nationals of other EU countries, as reflected in social charges and (progressive) taxes, on the one hand, and social expenditures, on the other. The starting point of a subsidiarity test is therefore a deeply embedded feeling of the nation state as a 'social union', as against none of this for the Union at large. The clearest revelation of this contrast consisted in the unification of Germany in 1990, where its economic and monetary union proposed in late 1989 (in the run-up to unification in October 1990) was immediately combined with a 'social union' between East and West Germany. Sentiments of solidarity (East Germans could not become second-class citizens with much lower social protection and substantially lower wages) were overriding the economic rationale of associating real wage levels with local productivity levels or the compatibility of 'western' social allowances with local incentives to work. Even weak echoes of such sentiments are never heard about inter-country solidarity in the EU, except in a minor way via economic cohesion (see Chapter 16). For this reason alone, the structure of preferences in the Union clearly dictates that no, or only minimal, social expenditures would be allocated to the EU level.

Against this backdrop, could arguments of scale or cross-border externalities or perhaps a gradual convergence of preferences between countries provide a case of selected EU social expenditures?

As to scale, one might surmise two reasons for an assignment at the EU level. One could be a scale advantage in implementing social security. When testing this for efficiency differences between large and small EU countries, Dekker *et al.* (2003), found that big countries were no better (if not worse) in fighting social inequality than were small countries. The other reason consists in more effective unemployment insurance at the EU rather than the national level. This idea has repeatedly been proposed by economists in Europe (first in the Marjolin report on EMU (Marjolin *et al.,* 1975) and illustrated with simulations by Italianer & Vanheukelen (1993)) because its logic seems persuasive. In so far as macroeconomic shocks are asymmetric for EU countries, such countries could receive unemployment payments from a fund fed by other EU countries not hit by such a shock or finding themselves in an upswing. Owing to the insurance principle, only a very moderate regular payment would be needed for the fund to have added value for the receiving countries. It would result in smoothing the national unemployment allowances, which is clearly advantageous and cannot be accomplished by the country alone.[4]

As to cross-border externalities, matters are a little more complicated. We shall discuss three arguments: the fear of 'welfare tourism' and other migrants causing extra burdens; the scope of the rights of EU citizenship; and a cluster of issues related to social policy competition between Member States. When Greece joined the EU in 1981, some feared a jump in what was called 'welfare tourism': the take-up of a job in relatively rich EU countries, with the intention of quitting subsequently and enjoying welfare benefits. These 'tourists' never showed up, however. Not only was Greece subject to a seven-year period without free movement of workers, but even subsequently the combination of unemployment allowances being related to the duration of one's work and the incentives to 'stay put' (see Table 10.5) simply pre-empted any sizable flow. Recently, similar fears were uttered with respect to migrants from central Europe. Apart from the fact that these workers are also subject to migration restrictions up to (possibly) 2011, the UK (which did not have restrictions) did not experience such tourism after the eastern enlargement. The fear has not waned, however, because in a number of Member States immigrants turn out to be disproportionately represented in the groups enjoying welfare and unemployment allowances. However, these immigrants are typically not the migrants from Member States that joined in the 1980s nor (as yet) those from central Europe but Mediterranean workers who arrived in Europe in the 1970s (and the second generation of them) or new immigrants with asylum. This might point to a deep societal integration problem or to a legacy of 'hard jobs' with higher risks, rather than welfare tourism. The real issue is therefore one of domestic societal integration, by definition a local problem.

An extension of this problem does, however, have profound consequences at the Union level. To the extent that the reduced costs of worldwide mobility turns Europe into a magnet of prosperity for third countries' immigrants, a cascade of national restrictions over time would certainly amount to a negative cross-border externality. In the end, the purpose of new national restrictions would merely be to prevent migrants refused in Member State A to burden Member State B. Such a negative spiral can only be stopped by a common immigration policy at EU level, at least for asylum seekers. This is exactly the direction of EU policy making in the area of justice and home affairs. However, even national immigration policies motivated by economic considerations might be affected. Recently, EU countries have realised that selective immigration for (highly skilled) 'knowledge workers' is attractive for their comparative advantage in a globalised world. The risk is, however, an undue rivalry of national 'special' immigration regimes for such specialists which is likely to be counterproductive. For example, it would be in the common interest to offer such workers fully free mobility in the internal market, similar to the rights of EU workers, as this is more attractive for them.

All nationals of EU countries are also 'EU citizens'. However, the rights associated with this citizenship are only political (for example, one can vote in local elections), not social. In federations, citizenship typically confers a right to the individual to federal social security. Federations tend to have a two-tiered social security system, with variations only as to the state (or provincial) level. The guarantee of federal social security facilitates the functioning of the internal labour market as workers can assume greater risks when searching for jobs elsewhere. In the EU, social security is national only, and is usually tied to work. Rather than facilitating the functioning of the EU internal labour market (which is already fragmented, as noted in Chapter 10), this set-up discourages further cross-border searches for jobs. In fairness, one has to realise

[4]There might be a moral hazard problem in that countries might be less active in preventing unemployment since others share in the payment of unemployment allowances. In everyday political economy, with great sensitivity for higher unemployment, such a free-riding attitude is highly uncertain, however.

that an unconditional access to (say, a minimum of) social security for EU citizens in every Member State would have drastic consequences: it would almost certainly prompt a major demand for harmonisation, first, and probably require a clearing fund in order to even out unequal burdens between Member States, if not some basic common social expenditures. For all these reasons, this externality argument is likely to be dismissed without further ado.

Social policy competition refers to a complex set of issues and is not necessarily good or bad. One way to look at it is as competition between different social systems or models. The idea would then be that better performance would consist of a good combination of social and economic indicators, such that social policies remain sustainable in the long run. For social expenditures it could mean that high spending (for example, on social services) would have to go together with low unemployment and high participation in order to be sustainable. This is typical for the so-called Nordic social model which is often regarded as a good performer. If competition between systems works, it must mean that other systems see compelling reasons for drifting towards the best performing model. Such reasons could be found in people 'voting with their feet' or in the unsustainability of their system. However, it is far from obvious that these two reasons might play more than a very marginal role in Europe. All the diverse social models in Europe have adjusted, and continue to do so, precisely with a view to remaining sustainable, perhaps with some accommodation of elements of other models. Indeed, it is often overlooked that the Nordics themselves have been cutting their overall public expenditures enormously since the early 1990s, whereas Italy, an example from the so-called Mediterranean model, has steadily increased its social expenditure over the past decades, thereby giving up one of its earlier characteristics. Systems competition in general does not seem to generate cross-border externalities which could justify an EU role in social policies. In section 15.3.2 we shall discuss one exception, asking the question whether the distinct reform capabilities of different social models in Europe are not a hindrance to the restoration of dynamism in the EU economy.

Another way of looking at social policy competition is far more focused. It is about the (unwanted) implications of comparative advantages or locational attractiveness of other countries for one's own social strategy. Emotional misnomers such as 'social dumping' are routinely used in such debates (see Case Study 15.1).

The issue is about the fear of a race-to-the-bottom, either because one is convinced that social charges and

CASE STUDY 15.1 A case for fighting 'social dumping'?

The misnomer 'social dumping' is often used in social debates in Europe to refer to 'unfair' competition driven by, or competitive advantages derived from, lower social standards. Only a 'level playing field' would be 'undistortive'. The point is false for a number of reasons. First, the label 'dumping' is wrong. As Chapter 13 clarifies, dumping is a form of price discrimination – in the WTO the export price must be lower than the domestic price for there to be dumping. Social dumping is not dumping because these conditions do not apply. Second, different social standards are not necessarily distortive; indeed, they are a function of genuine differences existing between open economies, whether within Europe or worldwide. Preferences for social security, leisure, regulatory social minima and so on, differ between EU countries. To some degree they vary as a function of levels of income and development. If, and in so far as, national regulations differ because they reflect these diverse preferences, there is no artificial distortion. Quite the contrary, a 'level playing field' would be distortive and the comparative advantages of (say) the new Member States – low wages, combined with considerable skill levels – would be undermined, hence, a major driver of their catch-up growth. However, if comparative advantages of relatively low wage EU Member States were weakened by the extra costs of higher (EU) social standards, real wages would have to adjust.

The problem is often the other way around: raising 'social standards' unilaterally may affect competitiveness, and this may prompt a Member State to argue for EU-wide regulation. The oldest EU example is Article 141 (equal pay for men and women, see Case Study 15.2). Abraham (1992) defines a level effect and a strategic effect of 'social

CASE STUDY 15.1 *continued*

dumping'. The former is the labour cost advantage of the cohesion countries in the EU; this considerable advantage almost disappears when corrected for labour productivity differentials. In other words, it is part of comparative advantage and is desirable for their catch-up. The strategic effect is the deliberate unilateral lowering of labour costs to expand output and employment – it is a beggar-thy-neighbour policy, with negative externalities on other Member States. Abraham's simulations show the overall externalities to be small, except in competitive markets. Note that these externalities need not be countered by common regulation: it suffices ('proportionality') not to lower one's 'social standards' without EU agreement.

In early 1993, Hoover announced its decision to close a vacuum cleaner plant in Dijon, France (700 workers), and move the production to an underutilised plant in Scotland. This led to an outcry in France and from labour unions more generally that British 'social dumping' had beggar-thy-neighbour effects in the common market. Indeed, Mr Foust, president of Hoover Europe, stated that non-wage labour costs were about 10–15 per cent on top of wages whereas they amounted to 40–45 per cent in France; the wages themselves differed little. However, the low non-wage costs are forced upon new workers (in Scotland) by limited contract work, no pension rights for the first two years, highly flexible work times and so on. To make matters worse, the pound had left the ERM (see Chapter 17) and had depreciated some 20 per cent by early 1993.

However, even in the Hoover case, 'social dumping' is not likely to be the determining factor. In general, 'social dumping' can be counterproductive: it is much easier and cheaper to close plants in the UK. When Thompson closed its television plant in Gosport (UK) in 1992, the average redundancy payment per worker was one-seventh of that in Spain. There may also be a skill-lowering effect of 'social dumping'. Returning to Hoover, the company made losses and had to restructure so as to exploit scale better. A far more problematic case is the closure of the Renault plant in Vilvoorde, Belgium (3,100 workers) in March 1997. Vilvoorde was profitable and modern. Renault was said to have chosen Vilvoorde because it was easier and cheaper to lay off workers in Belgium than in France. It also violated an EC directive, but the small fine was no deterrent for Renault.

taxes (for that purpose) raise overall labour costs and hence damage competitiveness, or, that other governments employ social charges strategically so as to boost competitiveness as well as to attract foreign investors (which might even relocate from other Member States for this purpose). For the second option there are anecdotes (see Case Study 15.1) which go both ways, but little if any systematic evidence in the EU15. There are good reasons to back another hypothesis which has empirical support: as a result of the democratic process and due to ageing in Europe, social charges (rather than being lowered for competitiveness) are gradually raised over time in order to pay for higher pensions and health care. This would well explain the trend growth of social spending in Italy, for example. As far as the new Member States are concerned, the real issue is low wages, and this is their comparative advantage. The first option is also not clear because companies are often capable of shifting the social burden on to the workers (see, for example, Nickell & van Ours, 2000). If this is true, all that higher social charges do is to alter the overall composition of total labour costs. All these considerations lead one to a simple conclusion: there seems to be no compelling reason in cross-border externalities to assign the EU with harmonisation or far-reaching coordination of social expenditures.

A third criterion used for the subsidiarity test is homogeneity of preferences. When it comes to social expenditures, all one could observe recently is that EU countries seem to be slowly converging. Not only is this clear from the changes in Italy and the Nordics over time, as noted, but this can be shown to be a general trend.[5]

Finally, one can also approach social expenditures the other way around. It is easy to see that a large part

[5]Dekker *et al.* (2003): figures for beta convergence (an inverse relationship between the initial level and the growth rate) and sigma convergence (the spread between EU countries of social expenditures, as indicated by the coefficient of variation (= standard deviation divided by the mean)) reduce over time. Both point to greater convergence.

of them are truly local or domestic, suggesting no EU role whatsoever. This would apply to welfare spending, social housing, basic state pensions for the elderly, basic health care and care for the disabled. When social expenditures are linked to work and can, in principle, be insured, the sensitivity to cross-border externalities may apply: think of unemployment benefits, sickness leave payments, occupational pensions and disability derived from work. Even so, as shown above, this sensitivity does not necessarily prompt a 'need to act in common', step 2 of the test. And where it might, modest cooperative solutions or (perhaps) minimum requirements in selective harmonisation may suffice.

15.1.2 Labour market regulation

Regulation of labour markets is driven by the desire to overcome market failures. Before applying the subsidiarity test, it is useful first to study the market failures and understand the justification (or not) of regulation. We briefly touch upon asymmetric and/or imperfect information, negative and positive externalities and problems of market power.

Asymmetric and/or imperfect information and negative externalities constitute proper arguments for minimum health and safety regulations for the workplace, and these reasons apply equally well in the EU as a whole. Beyond those minimums, company level contracts could set higher standards, helped by professional advice[6] and encouraged by insurance policies. The EC regulation is thus economically justifiable in terms of objectives, but its reliance on a traditional approach, with excessive detail and rigidity, is perhaps questionable.

A more difficult case of positive externalities is the involvement of workers, as a factor of production, in strategic decision making for the company. It is argued that such involvement would reduce the incentives for inter-firm job switching, and hence would increase the probability for companies to appropriate the return from investment in human capital. With regulation, the incentives of competitors to buy out workers having benefited from private investment in their human capital (and appropriating the rent, leaving the company with a sunk cost) would reduce, and this would have positive externalities for the economy as a whole. This argument is sometimes employed to provide an economic rationale for German co-determination. The point is hardly convincing, however, since there are less costly alternatives. Regulation of influence, let alone co-determination, would appear to be a disproportionate instrument to achieve this goal. Companies, in an era of globalisation, need active human resource policies as a matter of self-interest. Contracts with workers could specify payback obligations or voluntary obligations to serve a minimum term.

Other forms of imperfect or asymmetric information could be overcome by regulation or by an adequate information and (legal) support policy of the government. As with basic insurance policies, standard contracts could be certified by labour offices and most variations could be verified at low marginal cost. Thus, there could be a case for basic social regulation and protection, expressing certain general rights and objectives. Beyond that, the case for detailed (and often rigid, hence costly) social regulation is much harder to make.[7] The heavy regulatory bias in Europe's labour markets also has roots in another market failure: *market power.* It is likely to explain much better the far-reaching restrictions of labour markets than are economic arguments. In Europe, labour unions take pride in having accomplished labour standards as 'entitlements' after more than a century of social strife – traced back to the fear of the market and contractual power of employers *vis-à-vis* workers, beyond asymmetry of information. Labour has organised itself as a countervailing power based on the rights of association and the right to strike. They are seen as (social) human rights, in the framework of democracy. However, exercising these rights and imposing restrictions on the functioning of the labour market have costs. Without in any way questioning the existence of the rights, economies at large, and labour markets in particular, need mechanisms to identify and minimise those costs.

Labour markets in Europe no longer function well because the regulatory rigidities prevent price and non-price flexibilities which would help clear the market. Long periods of unemployment averages of 8–9 per cent are a clear sign of badly working labour markets. The

[6]Based on arguments of 'scale' and positive externalities, an Agency on Health and Safety was set up by the EC in Bilbao in 1995. There is also a consultancy market.

[7]At European level, diversity would occur under a contract-based system of labour standards (other than health and safety), assuming basic social regulation to be in place. In the presence of adequate information and considerable freedom to express one's own preferences, such diversity would merely reflect diverse preferences and trade-offs, hence, not be distortive. A contract approach would also reduce the regulatory fragmentation of the EC labour market, without going for uniformity. Well-developed, even subsidised information and legal advice may promote both contractual labour standards and an internal market for labour.

persistent differences between good and bad performers (countries in the EU) show that wage formation can be organised in such a way that it is not inconsistent with keeping many social entitlements, without excessive rigidities and without giving up 'the European social model'. Constraining the costs of these distortions is – imperfectly – taking place via two outside mechanisms: the competition in goods and services markets (EU-wide and globally),[8] and political decision making. If labour standards reduce the competitive position of a firm or industry, often labour-saving responses emerge to cut costs. More generally, demand for labour will tend to fall, and unskilled labour will tend to be substituted by technology, labour on immediate demand only, or moonlighting. This causes severe negative externalities since, first, the 'welfare state' has to take over (for example, Saint-Paul, 1994) and, subsequently, regulatory barriers to entry restrict the possibilities for the unemployed ('outsiders') to offer labour on other terms. Political decision making also has drawbacks, which are exacerbated precisely by the corporatist influence claimed by the social partners. Depending on party links and political positioning, outright 'capture' of government policy may occur.

The traditional recipe against market power is competition policy. But there is no tradition of applying competition policy in the labour market, either in Europe or in the USA. Labour unions are viewed as forms of 'countervailing power' to the power of, hence dependency from, the owners or managers of a company. Since switching jobs, especially in times of unemployment, may imply high transaction costs plus uncertainty for workers, there is great scope for opportunistic behaviour by employers. Proper monitoring and enforcement of millions of contracts is likely to be difficult and costly, and may generate great problems for employees in the meantime. Countervailing power, collective contracting and extensive labour law respond to these issues. Competition policy works well only if the number of cases is limited and their urgency not great. Minimally regulated labour markets do not fulfil those conditions and hence a regulator is needed instead. However, in the European environment the regulator is bound to be captured at least to some degree by one or both social partners. More fundamentally, how could competition policy or a regulator break the 'countervailing power' without undermining the 'right' of association and the 'right' to strike?

The subsidiarity test will again use the criteria of scale, cross-border externalities and heterogeneity. It is hard to find scale arguments for a 'need to act in common', other than good statistics and quality studies.[9] This is in sharp contrast with cross-border externalities in labour markets. In Chapters 9 and 10, it was concluded that there is no such thing as an EU-wide labour market. In and of itself, this amounts to a formidable 'need to act in common'. For a very long period, severe and many negative cross-border externalities were accepted by the Union in labour markets, although similar obstacles and distortions would never be tolerated in goods, services or capital markets. Only since 2001 has the EU been following a programmme of removal of barriers to the 'free movement of workers'. The pursuit of removal is made exceedingly difficult by the implications that such removals might have for the nature or costs of the respective social models of the Member States or for domestic labour market regulation. A simple example about occupational pensions can illustrate the kinds of problems encountered. In 2005, the Commission announced proposals to harmonise occupational pensions schemes so as to render them portable over intra-EU frontiers, thereby overcoming one of the major obstacles to (economically) free movement. However, this will require significant adjustment of pension funds and insurance companies and these costs may prompt resistance. But the real culprit is taxation: portability without costs for the worker requires similar fiscal treatment of pension premiums between Member States and mutual (fiscal) recognition of the built-up claims. Another issue concerns the link between the formal free movement of workers and non-discrimination. Host country control can be defended on the basis of non-discrimination among all workers in the country of destination. In the presence of sharp wage differentials, however, the upshot will be (see Figure 10.1) a drastic curtailment of the demand for migrant labour. Host country control serves as a major hindrance to the emergence and proper functioning of an EU-wide labour market. Greater or selective flexibility in applying host country control, if not mutual recognition above certain minimum social requirements or within maximum deviations of the local wage, are needed to bring about an economically meaningful intra-EU labour migration. Without it, labour will flow illegally or be blocked.

[8]For a rigorous analysis of the connection between goods and services markets and labour markets, see Boeri *et al.* (2000). The authors show, also empirically, that restrictive regulation of the labour market may prompt restrictive regulation of goods and services markets, thereby weakening indirect, competitive pressures. See also *OECD Economic Outlook,* no. 72, 2002, chapter VI.

[9]The annual report *Employment in Europe* published by DG Employment and Social Affairs is a rich source of statistics and trend studies, for example.

Distinct social models also impact in diverse ways upon the better functioning of a European labour market. A crucial issue in this respect is the trade-off between more or less restrictive employment protection legislation (EPL) protecting ('insider') jobs, and the scope and quality of the social safety net. In the Nordic model and (in slightly different ways) the Anglo-Saxon model, the labour market is more flexible and EPL is rather soft, which is compensated by a wide safety net for those who lose their jobs, whereas in the Mediterranean model (and, to some extent, in the Continental model), insiders in the labour market do not easily lose their jobs as firing is forbidden or very costly severance payments have to be paid, which, in turn, shields the state from having to keep up extensive safety nets. In this stylised description, access of migrants to flexible markets will be easier than in the Mediterranean model where a meaningful form of access would probably require a softening of EPL and other changes. Socio-political reality demonstrates that softening of EPL is fiercely resisted, thus far at least. In this situation, harmonisation is unlikely and cross-border externalities will not be internalised in the internal labour market.

The heterogeneity criterion can be captured by the four stylised social models practised in Europe (see section 15.3.2). The differences between these models are, of course, stylised and evolve in practice. Above, we noted the empirical evidence that, at least in terms of social expenditures, the models seem to be on a converging path. In terms of labour market regulation, the discrepancies may well be less extreme. At a high level of generality, the Social Charter of 1989 formed a political expression of a European consensus about social rights and minimum social requirements. In the constitutional treaty (not yet ratified), Chapter II specifies a number of what are called 'social rights' in Articles II-87 to II-96, such as workers' rights to information and consultation within companies, the right to conclude collective agreements and to strike, right of access to placement services, fair and just working conditions, social security and assistance, the prohibition of child labour and the right to paid maternity leave, besides the even more fundamental one of the right to freedom of association (Article II-72). Moreover, in the EC treaty there is a section on social provisions (Article 136 to 145) including harmonisation, minimum requirements and 'coordination' where the line between measures justified by cross-border externalities and those justified by a common perception of homogeneity is often hard to draw. Most of the specifications are on labour market regulation but aspects of social security and industrial relations are also explicitly mentioned. In principle, this can be justified in social policy in view of the strong interdependence between the nature and impact of labour market regulation and the role and ambition of social expenditures. In so far as heterogeneity prevails, and given the current (and apparently wanted) fragmentation of the EU labour market, the 'need to act in common' has to be identified case by case. Where the political imperative of host country control has to be accepted for the time being, the cross-border externalities will be minimised and the 'need to act in common' might best be pursued by cooperative means (step 3, with various degrees of commitment).

15.1.3 Industrial relations

Industrial relations – the formal and informal modes of conduct between employers and workers or their associations – are characterised by a considerable dose of idiosyncracy grown out of each country's history of social strife and accommodation. Thus, the heterogeneity is strong. Nevertheless, the 'Europeanisation', if not globalisation, of business has exposed the ever more severe limits of inward-looking models of industrial relations. This tension used to be relativy strong in multinational business but, with the deepening of the internal market, the exposure has spread to practically all companies producing goods and more and more companies providing services or technology. As fewer firms are 'sheltered' against cross-border competition, this must have implications for industrial relations.

A pure scale argument for 'European' industrial relations can be identified where and when the law makers at the EU level wish to harmonise or coordinate and consult the social partners. The EU social partners ETUC (labour unions) and UNICE (European industry and some services)[10] play an increasing role in decision shaping in Brussels and beyond and this seems broadly justified by the underlying market integration. In the eurozone, a possible extra argument would consist in proper and timely mutual information about wage formation in the eurozone so that the ECB could take this into account (or, the other way around, social partners might reconsider once the ECB has informed them of its assessment).

[10]The EU has a tradition of including the CEEP, an association of state-owned enterprises, often emerging from a tradition of public utilities. However, membership of the CEEP has shrunk dramatically due to privatisation, and its representativeness among the 25 EU countries is very uneven.

Note, however, that this argument assumes eurozone-wide collective wage bargaining orchestrated by ETUC and UNICE, and this is still very far off.

Cross-border externalities might also play a role. Deeper integration and the transnational character of numerous enterprises render purely national industrial relations less and less sensible for workers in such companies. There is a host of sectoral or more general social provisions where social partners have not only a common interest but also superior information on how to pre-empt undue differences in working conditions or how to act properly in cases of restructuring (more often than not, at a European scale) or how to stimulate retraining and upskilling of employees. It is far from clear that it is necessary or desirable to proceed with such issues in the framework of EU law making, in particular when social partners agree on their common, EU-wide social interests. In transnational companies operating in several EU countries, there might be a case to institutionalise mutual information and consultation at the (EU-wide) company level, besides regular industrial relations at the subsidiary level. In particular, workers can be regarded as stakeholders, and the productivity of companies (other than assembly) depends on their skills and tacit knowledge. It is thus sensible to discuss competitive advantages, exposure and strategy with employees and, to some extent, jointly anticipate restructuring and consolidations.

15.2 The modest social *acquis* of the Union

The striking fact when observing the Union's social *acquis* in 2005 is that by far the larger part of powers and actual policy making is in the realm of the Member States. By implication, the EU social *acquis* is modest, and this is likely to remain so in the near future.[11] This state of affairs is not entirely in line with the subsidiarity test, in particular where the fragmentation of the EU labour market is concerned. The problem is that, once the EU labour market is genuinely liberalised and made to 'function properly', it is bound to have knock-on effects for common regulation and, possibly, industrial relations too. For social expenditures, the *acquis* is negligible, except for the harmonisation of entitlements for migrants in the EU and some minor 'coordination' aspects. Since such expenditures are equity-driven, the EU cannot be expected to have more than a marginal role. Note that social expenditures in Member States hover between 20 and 30 per cent of GDP and none of that is at EU level, except for a miniscule Social Fund (of barely 0.1 per cent of GDP). Altogether, the permanent debates in the Union about a 'Social Europe' and the numerous declarations about the 'social dimension of European integration' should therefore not be misunderstood. If these 'warm words' create expectations with citizens, they might sooner or later backfire because the EU cannot be expected to create jobs via its social policies or its employment strategy as such (it does create jobs via the proper and dynamic functioning of the internal market, however). Indeed, the assignments to the EU level are such that Member States do not allow that in the first place. What the main players in the EU social debate refer to, although often in ambiguous language, is the Union as the collection of Member States. The combination of deep economic interdependence and far-reaching social autonomy sows confusion and, sometimes, frustration in that 'Europe's' socio-economic performance leaves much to be desired.

In the following, a brief account is provided of labour market regulation and of industrial relations at EU level. As to regulation, Article 137 EC provides a legal basis for harmonisation in the form of minimum requirements with respect to:

1 health and safety of workers (QMV);
2 working conditions (for example, maximum number of hours per day and in total) (QMV);
3 information and consultation of employees (QMV);
4 equal treatment of men and women (QMV);
5 social security and social protection of employees (unanimity);
6 EPL (unanimity);
7 influence of workers on management, including codetermination (unanimity);
8 conditions of employment of legally residing third country residents (unanimity);

while explicitly excluding from this harmonisation the remuneration for work and the rights of association and to strike.

The three categories (QMV, unanimity and excluded aspects) show the degrees of sensitivity connected with

[11]See COM (2005) 33 of 9 February 2005 on the Social Agenda until 2009. Note, also, that during the Convention writing the draft of the constitutional treaty, Working Group 11 (on social policies) explicitly decided not to touch the 'status quo' in this area. This decision has been upheld and the constitutional treaty (not yet ratified) essentially reproduces the current EC treaty, except for the explicit formulation of the 'social rights' in Chapter II (which broadly reflect a consensus in Europe, anyway).

different social models and the desire of autonomy of national social partners. Broadly spoken, the QMV articles closely hang together with the approximation under the internal market (Article 95 EC). The best example of that is occupational health and safety which is better regarded as a consequence of the competition on *goods and services* markets than of the labour market as such. Since the Single European Act introduced QMV in this area, social partners and Member States have been united about the idea that competitiveness in goods and services markets cannot be acquired 'over the back' of the workers' health and safety. The *acquis* in this area, based on Framework Directive 89/391, is powerful and justified by subsidiarity. Whether it is always proportional, given an old-approach type of detail, is harder to judge. Beyond minimum requirements, it is probably better to let social partners decide on their preferred combination of (informed) risk and security as the marginal costs of the latter may go up quickly (see section 4.4 and Chapter 5). The equal treatment of men and women is directly regulated in the treaty and its consequences have been impressive (see Case Study 15.2). Besides these two areas the regulatory *acquis* is tiny, with the very few directives usually having a minimum requirements character. These minima reflect a consensus in the EU and hardly alter domestic requirements.

The few 'social' directives that exist include directives on working time, atypical workers (such as those on nightshifts), part-time workers (harmonising a threshold of working hours per week above which (national) social security and pension rights would become compulsory in order to prevent distortions of competition), and work councils for large companies with establishments in several EU countries. The 1989 Charter

CASE STUDY 15.2 Gender equality in the EU

The Community has gradually developed a forceful gender equality policy. This is amazing because many other social concerns are not dealt with so firmly at EU level. The policy could evolve from an unconditional article (Article 119 EEC) amidst otherwise weak social policy provisions. This article was introduced in the Rome Treaty by France. It prescribes equal pay for equal work between men and women. France had legislated an equal-pay clause before the Rome Treaty and feared a negative impact on industrial competitiveness. In forcing a package deal during the treaty negotiations, it insisted on Article 119 EEC (now Article 141 EC). Whatever the ethical merits of the case, economically this negotiation tactic is clearly an instance of 'raising rivals' costs'.

However, by the mid-1970s it turned out that the principle was not adhered to as widely as one might have expected for a straightforward treaty article. In 1976, the EC Court ruled that Article 119 EEC had 'direct effect' – in other words, it could be invoked in national courts irrespective of national regulation. In the same period the Council adopted two approximation directives. In the crucial *Barber* case (ruling 17 May 1990), the EC Court ruled that work-related pension arrangements fall under Article 119 EEC. Since women were, or had been, treated unequally in many cases in many Member States for decades – sometimes married women were excluded altogether – draconian retroactive claims loomed on the horizon. Hence, the EC Court blocked retroactive action except for those already having initiated legal action. Protocol no. 2, attached to the Maastricht Treaty, further limits potential retroactive claims. Nonetheless, in a series of connected EC Court rulings (*Vroege, Fischer, Shell,* among others) of 28 September 1994, this protocol was undermined with respect to women who have been refused access to pensions. Restoration – on request – is obligatory, although both employer and employee should pay their premiums for all those years. In some cases, men can benefit from these rulings, too. In 1995 the Commission proposed approximation legislation incorporating the *Barber* case and the 1994 rulings.

The Amsterdam Treaty deepened and widened gender-related EU policies. Article 2 EC now comprises a general objective to promote 'equality between men and women', hence equality is no longer limited to wage equality. This is reiterated in Article 3 EC (about the instruments and activities of the EC). A new Article 13 EC provides a legal basis to combat discrimination based on (*inter alia*) sex or sexual orientation. Directive 2004/113/EC of 13 December 2004 (OJ L 373 of 21 December 2004) on equal treatment in the access to and supply of goods and services, is based on Article 13 EC. The new Article 137 (taken from the Social Protocol, meanwhile

CASE STUDY 15.2 *continued*

inserted into the treaty) allows the Council (under QMV; co-decision EP) to adopt measures relating to equality between men and women with regard to labour opportunities and treatment at work. Finally, Article 141 EC has been revised: not only is 'equal work' complemented by 'work of equal value' but a legal basis is also created for equal opportunity measures in matters of employment and occupation. In the constitutional treaty (not yet ratified), Article II-83 simply speaks about the equality between men and women 'in all areas'.

A recent Commission report (COM (2005) 44 of 14 February 2005) on equality between men and women found the gender gaps in many respects still to be considerable. Thus, in higher education, women outnumber men in the EU25, and 41 per cent of PhD graduates in 2003 were women. The EU25 gender gap in employment was 15.8 per cent, but female employment rates are rising. The gender pay gap is about 16 per cent and is stable. One factor is the huge difference between 30 per cent of women taking part-time work compared with only 6.6 per cent of men. Gender policies become more pronounced e.g. in gender 'mainstreaming' (gender tests in all EU policies where relevant) and the Commission plan to establish a European Gender Institute.

is now referred to in the new Article 136 (revised from the former Article 117 EC). In other words, the objective is to prevent competitive 'deregulation' in social laws in attempts to gain a competitive edge in the completed and open internal market.[12]

As far as industrial relations are concerned, they have remained overwhelmingly national, with two exceptions (the Social Dialogue and the Work Councils) and one optional issue (EU-wide wage or non-wage coordination inside companies or across sectors). Under the Social Dialogue, a regular setting of consultation and negotiation between the European social partners, agreements on certain non-wage issues can lead to draft legislation taken over by the Commission[13] and legislated under routine EU procedures. The Social Dialogue is an active form of cooperation, yet without centralisation: by early 2004, some 40 cross-industry joint texts and some 300 sectoral texts had been agreed between the European social partners on a host of social issues directly relevant to the stakeholders. So far, six agreements have become directives.[14] Given the different social models, assigning diverse weights and influence to social partners, the Social Dialogue seems to develop into a consensual form of selective 'Europeanisation', based on subsidiarity.[15]

European Work Councils (under Directive 94/45) are compulsory for the largest enterprises in the EU. In 2004, around 650 such Councils had been set up and about an equal number are still expected to be instituted. They aim at intense consultation and information at the European enterprise level, thereby going beyond such processes at the subsidiary level in Member States. In fact, the Councils have increasingly resorted to European in-company agreements, too. The Social Dialogue and the practices of Work Councils have stimulated the further exploration of EU-wide or more limited cross-border

[12]The (perceived) costs of EU social regulation were feared to be high by the UK, and at times by European industry. However, there are only three instances where a marginal increase in the 'regulatory burden' can be discerned: maternity leave (14 weeks mean a few weeks more than before in a few Member States), part-time workers (but here the threshold is always arbitary) and Work Councils.

[13]Article 138 EC provides leadership on the part of the Commission; Art. 139 EC gives the initiative to the social partners, a unique provision.

[14]Three general ones (on parental leave, part-time work and fixed-time work) and three specific ones for three modes of transport (seafarers, civil aviation, railway workers for cross-border interoperable services). See COM (2005) 557 of 12 August 2005 on the Social Dialogue.

[15]Social partners in Europe stress a slightly distinct concept of subsidiarity, besides the classical one between tiers of government. Their emphasis is on whether or not the state is justified (better reflecting preferences and more effective too) in solving an issue when social partners (or, in other cases, the civil society, for example) can come to a consensus, likely to be superior in satisfying preferences of the stakeholders themselves and, for that reason alone, effective. The Social Dialogue reflects this idea of autonomous responsibility, under constraints of the public interest.

collective bargaining, which could be seen as a bottom-up approach to industrial relations at the Union level. The Commission is examining how a framework could be formulated for such cross-border bargaining in the EU, even if this framework is merely supportive and in any event completely voluntary.

It is a natural extension to reflect on the possibility of EU-wide wage coordination or even collective bargaining. For the present book, it goes too far to assess the (de)merits of this option. Some elementary aspects will be readily understood by the reader. Such bargaining is meant to restore the countervailing power of the unions, eroded by deep market integration and globalisation. Dependent on the dialogue with the ECB, the ETUC may or may not incorporate the inflation risks in its demands for higher wages. A greater danger is an increased wage rigidity over several countries, in the presence of distinct labour productivity levels. In countries such as Italy, Spain and Germany (after 1990), centralised wage bargaining occurred despite large productivity differentials between lagging regions and the agglomerations. The upshot has been a sharp increase in, as well as persistence of, regional unemployment. Similar undesirable developments might result from cross-border agreements, if they set wage levels or (for many years) the annual increments determined by productivity improvements. This would add further rigidities to what are still quite inflexible labour markets in a number of EU countries. In any event, such bargaining cannot include the new Member States as their labour productivity level will simply be too far below the levels of the EU15 for a number of years to come.

What is the likelihood of such collective bargaining emerging in the Union ? Apart from a soft declaration of intent in Doorn in 2000, there are few, if any, signs of such deep coordination between national labour unions. The trends are to stick to local sectoral agreements or even at the individual firm level, as much as possible. Moreover, unionisation in Europe has declined in both the public and the private sectors, which renders credible coordination very difficult.

15.3 Social dilemmas for the Union

The Union's ambivalence in social affairs results from deep hesitations to empower the EU level, without, however, at the same time earning credibility for effective reform measures at the national level. We discuss two such dilemmas in brief: the EU employment strategy and the question of credible social reform by Member States trapped in social models ill-adapted to today's challenges.

15.3.1 Does a European employment strategy make sense?

A politically important 'widening' of the social *acquis* is the insertion of Union-level employment strategies in the Amsterdam Treaty. In the EU treaty itself, Article 2 has been amended by inserting 'a high level of employment' among its objectives. Note that this objective had been incorporated in the EC treaty since Maastricht. In Amsterdam, Article 2 EC was reshuffled so that eight, rather than six, objectives emerged (compare Figures 2.3 and 2.4), but the objective of a high level of employment (and social protection) did not change – it simply moved up two places in the priorities of the article.

The main idea behind the insertion of an entirely new Title VIII on Employment in the EC treaty is to balance the (agreed) importance of price stability in EMU with an explicit priority for a high level of employment in the EU. The issues here have, of course, little or nothing to do with a newly discovered desire to pursue full employment – all EU countries have considered this a leading objective for decades. There are two real economic policy issues. First, the subsidiarity question can be posed as follows: What can the Union level do that the employment policies of the Member States cannot, or not do as effectively? Second, even if there is a case for EU-level employment strategies, what form should it take, what (EC) powers would be required, and what constraints would Member States be willing to accept as a corollary?

Neither question has been seriously addressed by the Amsterdam European Council. One gets the strong impression that the textual as well as the coordination and consultation provisions in Articles 125 to 130 are largely cosmetic. They first of all serve the political message to EU citizens that the Union also gives priority to a 'high level' of employment and not just to monetary stability. Both are now a 'common concern'. But, whereas for monetary stability policy has become fully centralised (in the euro area) and otherwise subject to fairly ambitious macroeconomic coordination (see Chapter 18), for employment the policies have remained almost entirely in the hands of the Member States. Also, the new Employment Committee (Article 130 EC) cannot exercise anywhere near the same policy influence as its counterpart, the Economic and Financial Committee (Article 114 EC).

As to the second question, Member States are divided.

Some of them preach (weak) remnants of Keynesian expenditure policies but the new articles provide no new funds to pursue this at the EU level.[16] Most economists would now agree that, short of dramatic declines in aggregate demand,[17] employment levels should be enhanced via the better functioning of labour markets – that is a microeconomic approach. This is expressed as pursuing greater flexibilities in European labour markets. At the rhetorical level this has been widely agreed in the EU for at least a decade. However, there is widespread and deep resistance against the idea that such flexibility be accomplished by questioning (any) entitlements. As a result, the initial 'Luxembourg process' trying to implement the European Employment Strategy (EES) from 1997 onwards was solely formulated in terms of 'positive' approaches such as enhancing 'employability' of workers, stimulating start-ups (entrepreneurship) for unemployed and promoting 'active labour market policies', in particular for the structurally unemployed. Nobody is against such approaches in Europe, it is more a matter of resources and priorities and the depth of reforms helping such policies. Greater labour market flexibility was a taboo term as it was regarded as negative (undermining entitlements) and the soft reference used was 'adaptability' of workers (which clearly leaves entitlements untouched). Therefore, the insider/outsider problem of strict EPL or other design failures of European labour markets could not be addressed. This evasion of what is probably the biggest of EU's labour market problems might well be due to the initial capturing of the Luxembourg process by the social partners.

Since 2003, a new approach has been initiated which is part and parcel of the overall Lisbon process. Both the Lisbon process and its social precursor (the EES) are based on the so-called open method of coordination (OMC), an attempt to keep the national autonomy in these policies while making the most of 'coordination' given the 'common concern' about high unemployment, if not in combination with lacklustre growth in the EU15. OMC tries to go beyond the OECD approach of comparing and 'policy learning' by organising a framework (which the OECD cannot do) of common objectives, 'shaming and faming' good and bad implementation of what was first agreed, benchmarking and peer review (at ministerial level) and employing relatively precise 'indicators' as targets for success. OMC is, in principle, a matter among the Member States but, in practice, the Commission plays an increasingly active role as reporter (for example, of implementation) and analyst.

Neither the Lisbon process more generally (see Chapter 18) nor the EES is a resounding success. In the margin the EES has greatly increased awareness of shortcomings or inefficiency of specific labour market or social policies, but the actual reforms have been modest, particularly in countries with weak employment performance and in the issues where reforms are urgent such as EPL. This is due to a mixture of social resistence and the lack of domestic commitment to the EES (which is construed in EU circles, without much of a secure domestic political base).[18] One extra problem is that the required social and labour market reforms are coinciding with controversial pension reforms. Although reasons for pension reform include fiscal sustainability (given ageing in Europe) and the avoidance of undue burdens in future on the shoulders of the young generation – and therefore are very different from those underlying the labour reforms – for many citizens the quadruple effect of labour reforms, the disciplining of the welfare state, the reduction of pension rights (or the greater private contribution to it) *and* a low-growth climate is tantamount to a decline of the social values of the continent. A fifth element, the free inflow of workers from the new Member States putting wage levels and entitlements under pressure, too, especially in a few vulnerable sectors (for example, building; hotels, restaurants and cafés; and road transport), further augments feelings of social insecurity. In this climate, social reform can go only very slow and requires firm majority governments. Otherwise, the EU becomes a culprit of all bad social messages beamed at the workers, with the serious risk that the internal market, the euro (which blocks any inflationary way out and disciplines the fiscal relief sought by some) and the EES are all thereby discredited, which would be a highly perverse result of OMC.

Nowadays, the EES is embedded in a wider European strategy of economic growth and what is called sustainable public finance.[19] The Kok *et al.* report (2003) recommended a greater focus on four priority areas of action: increasing adaptability of workers, attracting more workers to the labour market, investing in human capital and far

[16]Article 129 EC says that the Council may adopt 'incentive measures', but mainly for analysis and 'best practice' comparison. A special Declaration of the Member States further limits this modest provision.

[17]As Chapter 18 explains, the Stability and Growth Pact (also concluded in Amsterdam, in the framework of EMU) allows some degree of temporary budget deficits, as a consequence of automatic stabilisers, in the event of such downfalls.

[18]This book cannot go into the debates about the (in)effectiveness of the EES. See, for the early years, COM (2002) 416 of 17 July 2002 and Kok *et al.* (2003); see also WRR (2003, chapter 4), Esping-Andersen *et al.* (2001) and Best & Bossaert (2002). (For a concise recent survey see European Commission, *Employment in Europe 2005,* chapter 2.)

[19]See, e.g., the overview and many details in the second report on the implementation of the 2003–2005 broad economic policy guidelines (*European Economy,* 2005, no. 1).

better implementation of the EES. The report was inspired by best practices of some of the Member States (and thereby implicitly criticise the rigidities in some other countries) but otherwise was 'more of the same' of the early EES. Other than the coherence among the EES and the support by the European Social Fund (see Case Study 15.3) and peer review and benchmarking, it is hard to identify concrete benefits from 'coordination'. Almost all the significant reforms in the labour market, and even more so in social polices, Member States can do for themselves and out of self-interest.

Conversely, when the socio-political climate in a Member State disfavours reform, the EES cannot contribute anything. Nevertheless, in a more general sense, one can underpin the 'common concern' with a genuine EU common interest. First and foremost, the internal market is severely curtailed if labour migration is 'unfree' in an economic sense (which is what matters for its

CASE STUDY 15.3 Understanding the European Social Fund

The European Social Fund (ESF) is one of the four Structural Funds (see Chapter 16). Over the period 2000 to 2006 it can disburse €80 billion. It would seem that there has been relatively little analytical attention paid to this Fund. All EU countries receive allotments (per year) for this period and can organise application and management themselves, of course within the EU framework. Although the degrees of co-financing by the Member States are higher for non-cohesion countries and also differ among the three types of regions under the Structural Funds in general (see Chapter 16), it is nevertheless a flow of funding that does reach richer EU countries as well. This might be thought of as weakening the equity character of the Fund. Among (project) stakeholders, however, that is typically not the prevailing view. Also, the ESF has undergone profound changes since its inception in 1958, when it was designed as a pure (and tiny) adjustment fund for workers 'losing out' from market integration. Nowadays, the ESF operates in the framework of the European Employment Strategy and focuses on 'employability' of people in the widest sense of this term. It promotes employment, training (again, in a number of forms) and all kinds of ways of countering social exclusion, in particular for vulnerable persons. It is worthwhile raising a few analytical questions about the ESF because its place and effectiveness are not obvious.

Its justification under a subsidiarity test is probably the greatest puzzle. After all, neither scale nor cross-border externalities apply. The ESF is explicitly charged to complement (that is, co-finance) initiatives at the Member States level and it is hard to come up with arguments why 'scale' at EU level would facilitate feasibility or lower the cost. Since there is no such thing as the internal market for labour, cross-border externalities do not apply either, or marginally at most (common adjustment of sectors in decline and forced to restructure might be helped by EU support; for the role of the ESF and other EU approaches, see COM (2005) 120 of 31 March 2005 on restructuring and employment). Indeed, the five 'policy fields' of the Fund (see below) do not target the existing and serious cross-border externalities discussed in Chapter 10 and the present chapter. Yet, there is emphasis on 'the' labour market but this is the national or even local labour market. So, if the ESF were to have an 'allocation function', there would be no need to act in common in step 2 of the test.

Hence, the only way one might justify the ESF of today would be to consider that the Fund has an equity function about which Member States agree. The treaty speaks about 'social cohesion' and some of the social issues in the treaty might well be part of this agreed 'equity' function. In a wider perspective, this equity function is tiny (only 0.1 per cent of EU GDP). The equity function is nevertheless not easy to define because all countries are eligible. For social cohesion, this would be right because it might affect all EU countries. The ultimate motives behind the ESF are probably more abstract: they include better functioning (national) labour markets – but that is viewed as in the common interest of the EU too, given the Lisbon aims – and the targeted focus on structurally unemployed and/or 'socially excluded' who might best be 'included' via access to jobs, in turn facilitated by retraining, adaptability

CASE STUDY 15.3 *continued*

and so on. The huge problem with such motives is that they may have political and social appeal but they are difficult to operationalise or measure, leave a lot of discretion to both the Commission and Member States, and – perhaps most serious of all – accept the given social situation which might well be the outcome of wrong incentives or bad policies. In the present chapter the example has been given of the misguided idea of central wage bargaining in EU countries with large discrepancies in regional labour productivity. Rather than targeting numerous piecemeal projects funded by the ESF, the better solution would be to shift to decentralised wage bargaining. More generally, even if one accepts the political imperative of this equity motive, should one not ask the question whether the ESF can promote, for example, 'active labour market policies' better than the Member States themselves can?

The five policy fields of the ESF are: (1) active labour market policies (tailor-made to individuals), (2) promoting equal opportunities in order to fight social exclusion (of the disabled, ethnic minorities and so on), (3) training/lifelong learning as a means of greater employability and mobility, (4) adaptability of workers (which is even linked to entrepreneurship and start-ups), and (5) measures to improve women's access to the labour market. It is analytically unclear why most of the issues under these five headings could not be done at least as well by the Member States themselves. Given the harsh criticism of the ESF's significant bureaucratic burden (see, for example, House of Commons, 2003) a purely national or local approach is likely to be superior, except for recognition of certification and the only cross-border progamme (namely, EQUAL).

The overly general equity motive also renders it exceedingly difficult to conduct a rigorous impact analysis. It remains true, of course, that the EU has been crystal-clear about the willingness to give the ESF this role. A benign interpretation could be that the European Employment Strategy needs a 'hard' tool in order to avoid remaining a mere talkshop. With the ESF, initiatives everywhere in the Union have to be disciplined, structured according to the guidelines and, in the margin, stimulated to be 'additive' (that is, have added value that otherwise would not have come about).

dynamic potential) and even more if labour linked to the provision of services (see section 7.2) is throttled, failing thereby to exert its pro-competitive effects. Domestic labour reforms make it easier to accept a better working internal market and, in so doing, interacts positively with the Union's growth strategy. Second, for the eurozone, the sacrifice of national exchange rates (even if Chapter 17 will show that the 'sacrifice' was not so great in fact) requires considerable flexibilities in EU economies so as to minimise adjustment costs in cases of asymmetric shocks. This is elaborated in section 18.1. The common concern here is very concrete: the higher the net gains of monetary union, the greater a country's adjustment capacity.

15.3.2 National social reform in the EU interest

The obverse of the EES is 'autonomous' national social reform. Given idiosyncrasies and the question of democratic legitimacy, it is really national social reform which matters. Of course, it matters most for the country concerned, yet, in the final analysis, it matters for the economic performance of the EU as well. The 'common concern' derives from the deep economic interdependence among the Member States and the endogenous (that is, self-inflicted) lack of dynamism in the internal market and its further deepening. But the need and capabilities of such reforms differ considerably between the 25 EU countries. The social dilemma here is the mirror image of that in section 15.3.1: the problem is (here) not so much how EU countries' policies and reforms can be stimulated to fit common objectives more closely, to match numerous detailed social indicators, and thus also how the countries might be blamed and shamed for poor implementation, but rather how domestic reforms can tackle inefficiencies and design failures of its own 'social model' for its own immediate interest of a better economic performance, which, in turn, is bound to have positive externalities for the Union at large as a natural side effect. The fact that the EES very much remained an exercise of a European policy elite, without deep socio-political roots in the domestic politics of each Member State and, hence, without commitment and domestic political accountability, is almost certainly due to the inevitability of national reform being a highly sensitive process which critically depends on the programme and status of each and every elected cabinet of ministers and their parliamentary backing, and with at least some tacit support from the social partners. Such processes are not, and cannot be expected to be, driven directly by EU-set indicators and overall implementation reports, when the recognition of full social autonomy of the same Member States is so explicit.

An insightful, if stylised, way of thinking about this national approach to social reform is to analyse the four social models which are employed by the Member States in the EU. The reader is warned that the fit of specific countries with 'social models' is always imperfect, but this should not hinder the reasoning too much. Table 15.1 provides a simplified view of the four social models in terms of three key features and a crude assessment of performance with respect to the reduction of income

Table 15.1 EU15 social models and reforms

Models	Key features	Performance assessed		
		Reduction of income inequality/poverty	Social insurance	Participation
Nordic (DK, FI, SW, partly NL)	• High social spending • Active labour market policies • Compressed wage structures	Redistribution strong; low poverty rate	EPL soft, but generous unempl. benefits	Overall employment very high; also for older; youth unemployment low
Anglo-Saxon (UK, IRE)	• Large safety net (last resort) • Active labour market policies and tough conditioning of benefits • Relatively pronounced inequality of incomes and many 'working poor'	Redistribution moderate; poverty rate (relatively) high	EPL very soft, generous unempl. benefits	Overall employment very high; also for older; youth unemployment lowest
Continental (A, B, F, D, Lux, partly NL)	• Insurance-based unempl. benefits; and pensions • Collective agreements cover all workers in many sectors (incl. EPL) • Considerable social spending	Redistribution moderate; low poverty rate	EPL strict, generous unempl. benefits	Overall employment fairly high; for older persons low; youth unemployment quite high
Mediterranean (GR, I, P, SP)	• Social spending focused on pensions • EPL plus early retirement very prominent • Compressed wage structures	Redistribution relatively low; poverty rate (relatively) high	EPL very strict, but relatively low unempl. benefits	Overall employment quite high; for older persons fairly low; youth unempl. high

Notes: (1) redistribution via social charges and taxes range between 42 per cent (strong) and 35 per cent (relatively low); (2) employment rates hover between 73 per cent (very high) and 62 per cent (fairly high); (3) youth unemployment ranges from lowest (10 per cent) to high (22 per cent).
Sources: Boeri, 2002; Sapir, 2005

inequalities (including poverty), the protection against uninsurable labour market risks ('social insurance') and labour market participation.

A close inspection of the table shows that some models perform distinctly better than others, and further analysis (cf. Sapir, 2005) brings out a strong connection between instruments and performance. Thus, it does show that EPL, when strict, is detrimental to employment whereas protecting workers with unemployment insurance (and, one should add, active labour market policies that can be linked to it) is potentially useful for employment. One can also show that poverty is (in the EU15, where redistribution differs but is never below 35 per cent per cent) best fought by investing in the human capital of workers because the relatively minor differences in redistribution explain relatively few of the discrepancies. The real problem here is the Mediterranean model where typical indicators of human capital score far lower than in the other three groups of countries. If incentives are seen as a sign of 'efficiency' and a low risk of poverty as 'equitable', then the Nordic model does not seem to suffer from a trade-off between equity and efficiency: it performs well on both scores. And neither does the Mediterranean model suffer, but this time because it performs badly on both scores!. The Continental model is not so efficient but is equitable whereas the Anglo-Saxon model is efficient but not equitable. Given ageing and globalised competition, according to Sapir (2005), there is also a problem of sustainability: when regarding public debt, the two inefficient models (Continental and Mediterranean) have relatively high debt ratios (both considerably above the 60 per cent, the norm in the eurozone) and their spending and incentive structures suggest further increases without deep reform. It is, above all, their inefficiency that poses a threat to sustainability.

This stylised analysis shows that the reform issues at national level are profound for some EU countries and that citizens and social partners will have to accept that 'more of the same' is not feasible. The resistance against reforms which will alter their habitual social model is impinging on the growth rate of the EU at large. Model simulations show that the potential growth rates of the EU15 have gradually come down. Some countries (for example, Germany, Spain and, in other ways, Austria) have at long last initiated a serious reform path, but Italy, Greece and, to a lesser extent, Belgium (with low participation of older persons, for example) still face strong domestic resistance. France is an intermediate case. Benchmarking at EU level might be helpful but it is more likely that the public debate is more selective: if major but thus far hesitant reformers such as Germany and Italy were to make profound reforms (for example, on EPL and on pensions, or on a later pension age), the impact would likely to be drastic all over the Union. Their failure to do so may well discourage other countries of the less performing social models and this could drag the EU into a too slow process of social change. The social *acquis* will largely be irrelevant to this process.

15.4 Summary

There is a huge gap between European rhetoric and what the EU level is exactly doing in social issues. The deepest reason for that is the ambiguity of the term 'European': in social affairs, 'European' refers to the 'collection of European countries' most of the time, and only rarely to the EU level.

A subsidiarity test for social assignments to the EU level shows that the case for a social *acquis* is at best modest and selective. For social expenditures there is a case only if one were radically to open up the internal market for labour or if a European unemployment fund (based on insurance principles) were to be set up. Both seem far off. Arguing for an EU role due to social policy competition (or even 'social dumping') is not convincing. In labour market regulation, the case of common occupational health and safety regulation is powerful (not least because it concerns competitive goods and services markets as well). It is really market power and the ensuing social entitlements at national level (in turn, linked to the welfare state) that impair the good functioning of labour markets, and the emergence of an internal market for labour. Adjustments and national reforms will have to be very deep, however, before free movement really works. Therefore, while the cross-border (negative) externalities arguments in labour regulation suggest a strong functional case for EU freedoms, less reliance on host country control, and minimum EU regulation, one should realise that the socio-political feasibility of this happening is low nowadays. In industrial relations, the scale criterion is weakly fulfilled with the EU-wide consultations of

Summary *continued*

the social partners. Inside multinationals operating in the internal market, the cross-border spillovers may be such that intra-firm social consultation can be organised across the EU.

The existing social *acquis* of the Union is modest, though not altogether trivial. In social expenditures, there is none, with the tiny exception of the Social Fund. Small as it is, it is not straightforward to justify the Social Fund on the basis of subsidiarity. In labour market regulation, there is a prudent legal basis but in a layered form: some provision under QMV (where the EU case is strong or the treaty imposes a strict requirement such as equal treatment of men and women), some under unanimity, and some areas are explicitly excluded from harmonisation. Given host country control, the internal market pressures for more than cosmetic approximation have remained weak. The shining exception is sexual equality where the treaty, the EC Court and the Commission are strict and the impact has been impressive. As far as industrial relations are concerned, they have remained overwhelmingly national. The Social Dialogue at EU level has proved to be useful and operational, especially at sectoral level where hundreds of joint texts have been negotiated. A few have been converted into EC directives. Work Councils at EU level, within large European companies, are slowly gaining acceptance. European wage bargaining, however, not only remains far off, but could never work in the presence of the great disparities in labour productivity.

The EU's ambivalence in social affairs can be well illustrated with the European Employment Strategy – an initiative incorporated in the treaty but essentially a voluntary process among the Member States – and with the differential capacity of the four stylised 'social models' implemented by the Member States.

The EES is a strengthened OECD-type of benchmarking, but in a more ambitious EU framework of common objectives and more precise indicators. There is likely to be some 'policy learning' but this would lead to reforms only when national governments and parliaments are seen (and held) to deeply commit to EES targets. So far, it is not clear whether the EES can prompt (more) reforms than Member States themselves can (or do) pursue. The four social models which stylise how Member States combine labour markets and the welfare state (Nordic, Anglo-Saxon, Continental and Mediterranean) exhibit distinct reform capabilities. In particular, the Nordic model would seem to avoid a painful choice between equity and efficiency whereas the Mediterranean one scores badly on both. A striking feature of the Mediterranean model is the low score on human capital, a threat for future competitiveness and a good predictor of (relative) poverty. The social predicament of 'Europe' is determined by the capacity to learn from this competition between models, but the EU social *acquis* in the strict sense is irrelevant to these models.

CHAPTER 16

The Economics of Cohesion

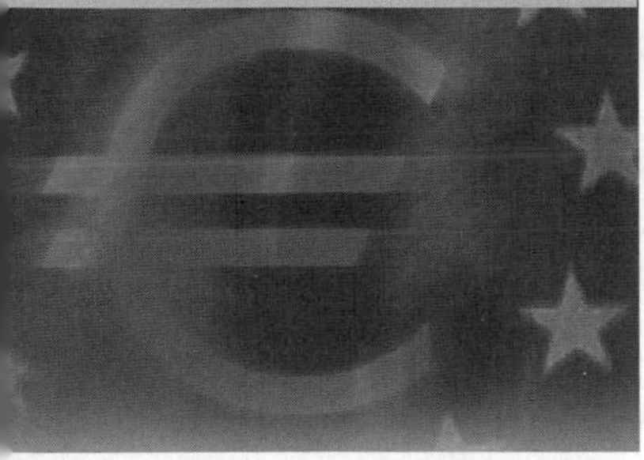

Topics covered

- 16.1 The economic cohesion pursued by the EU
- 16.2 Convergence and divergence in economic theory
- 16.3 How the internal market promotes cohesion
- 16.4 Are the EU Funds effective?
- 16.5 Designing effective cohesion policies
- 16.6 Summary

Economic cohesion can be viewed as the other equity issue at EU level, besides questions of social policy. The present chapter considers economic cohesion mainly from an economic standpoint. Other perspectives are neglected but that is not to be interpreted as irrelevance. Indeed, the political economy of cohesion is likely to explain the gradual rise to prominence of the cohesion issue, starting from the UK's entry into the EU in 1973 (the UK insisted on a Regional Development Fund that was established in 1975), the emphasis Greece laid on cohesion immediately after its entry in the early 1980s, the entry of Spain and Portugal in 1986 (exactly when the EU ambition to deepen the internal market would intensify the exposure of these weaker regions to competition almost right from the beginning), and 'eastern' enlargement in 2004 and its second wave in 2007. There is also merit in analysing the institutional and administrative aspects of cohesion because the design of policy methods can imply great differences in transaction costs. We do not deal with the administrative technicalities of cohesion. Even the description of the Structural and Cohesion Funds will be kept to a minimum in a case study. The focus is on the hard economic questions in theory, empirical analysis and EU policy making.

After an introductory section on the treaty concepts and their meaning, the ambiguities in economic theories about cohesion are set out in a simplified fashion. An elaboration of recent theories falls outside the realm of a textbook like this. The core issue has, for decades, been whether market integration, if left on its own, would generate convergence or divergence between countries and between regions. Section 16.3 addresses the four channels in the internal market which could help – but does not guarantee – to generate convergence. Section 16.4 asks the question whether the ample funding via the four Funds of the Union has actually been effective. The empirical literature is not unanimous on this but there are strong indications that effectiveness can at the very least be significantly improved; hence, the relevance of a better design of cohesion policies (section 16.5).

16.1 The economic cohesion pursued by the EU

If the idea of a 'Community', let alone a 'Union', means anything at all, it is bound to imply some kind of solidarity. The preamble of the Rome Treaty and the reference to a 'harmonious development' among its economic objectives (see Figure 2.1) pointed early on to a shared concern for 'balanced growth'. But all the treaty did was to establish the European Investment Bank (EIB), with the task of facilitating the economic expansion of lagging regions in the Community.[1] The EIB is market based, and borrowing regions will gain only a marginal interest advantage owing to the triple-A status of the Bank in the world capital market. Interest subsidies are possible only if first introduced in the EU budget itself and then transferred to the EIB. One is led to conclude that the founding fathers believed in 'real convergence' (of per-capita incomes) through market forces. In other words, it was the proper functioning of the internal market that contained the incentives for lagging regions to 'catch up' in per-capita income. Implicitly, the assignment for regional policy remained fully with the Member States.

Over time, however, explicit EU assignments for what is now called 'cohesion' were developed. In 1968, the Structural Agricultural Fund[2] was established to promote the modernisation of agriculture (hence, indirectly helping lagging regions as they typically tend to have many people working in low productivity agriculture). This Fund would later be explicitly assigned to promote the economic viability of rural areas. In 1975, the Regional Development Fund was set up, giving infrastructural and investment subsidies to underdeveloped regions.[3] Also, the Social Fund became geared towards vocational training in problem regions.

The major changes are of more recent date. The Single European Act introduced 'economic and social cohesion' (Articles 158 to 162). The cohesion articles depart from the underlying presumption that real convergence should merely come about from market integration. Transfers via a real doubling of the Structural Funds (between 1988 and 1993) have become a main instrument to achieve 'cohesion', in fact, real convergence. A further boost to transfers as a means to promote cohesion followed from the Maastricht Treaty, especially in view of EMU. A Cohesion Fund was established, with eligibility for (four) countries, not regions, and conditional upon their abiding with the EMU's (nominal) convergence criteria (see Chapter 18).

There is no doubt that the transfers via the respective funds have gradually assumed a redistributive character (via the demand side), even though the targeting of the subsidies would seem to be efficiency based (to the supply side).

Over the years 2000 to 2007, and in 1999 prices, the three cohesion countries not yet having caught up sufficiently (namely, Spain, Greece and Portugal) received an annual total together of around €15 billion (Ireland, the fourth cohesion country, moved to the EU average income per capita by the end of the 1990s). This annual sum is a little less than in the 1990s because Spain and Portugal were subjected to modest forms of 'phasing out' given the prosperity of core regions. Moreover, relatively poor regions in countries such as Italy, Germany, the UK and France also received the non-negligable sum of more than €13 billion annually (together). In addition, the idea was that some moderate shifts of funding should be foreseen for the eastern enlargement, before the overall renegotiation of the medium-term EU budget ceilings by 2006. During the 'pre-accession' of these countries, some cohesion money flew to them but under enlargement lines in the EU budget. For the first three years of EU membership (2004–06), however, the eight EU countries in central Europe, together, received around €7 billion annually. To put this annual flow in perspective, one should realise that per-capita incomes in central Europe are much lower than the EU average and, in most cases, also lower than those in Greece, Spain and Portugal.

The increasing emphasis on transfers via the Structural and Cohesion Funds since, say, 1988, has become so dominant in EU politics that, more often than not, 'cohesion' is considered equivalent to 'funding'. This is both unfortunate and wrong. The EU approach to 'cohesion' is based on three complementary routes: (1) deepening and widening of the internal market so that relatively poor regions and EU countries can exploit all the opportunities to get the most out of their (dynamic) comparative advantage inside the EU; (2) the removal of all biases against cohesion in EU policies (for example, the CAP, the steel subsidies by rich countries in the 1980s; possibly, EU regulation imposing undue burdens on relatively poor countries); (3) specific-purpose grants (transfers) via the Structural Funds with a view to facilitate and propel catch-up growth. If the first two routes were to work, there would be no need for the third one. If the third one is not effective in prompting convergence on its own, it does not automatically mean that the other two routes are to be forgotten – they may still be useful. Even though the EU Funds are likely to go on dominating the Union's cohesion debate, the reader is advised to engage in the following thought experiment. When the poor and underdeveloped city of Singapore was

[1]Article 256 EC. Significantly, it has to do this with a view to contributing to the balanced and steady development of the common market. The Rome Treaty also established the Social Fund but this was, initially, not focused on lagging regions.

[2]Officially, the Guidance section of the European Agricultural Fund.

[3]Again, this occurred in the framework of the common market, based on the catch-all Art. 235 EEC (now Art. 308 EC).

expelled from the Malaysian Federation in 1965, and found itself in what was then considered a far-flung corner in the world economy, surely, it had no hope whatsoever of receiving funding of any kind. Nevertheless, Singapore has been able to move on a steep path of catch-up growth for decades. It was not part of any deep internal market and world trade was more tariff-ridden than today. What this example shows is that funding cannot possibly be the only way to view cohesion, and an obsession with funding may pre-empt a search for the right questions to ask.

The economic cohesion the EU pursues is clearly the reduction of disparities of income per capita, and presumably also the reduction of other disparities which are structural (for example, those in regional unemployment). But it does that with transfers which are only a very small fraction of what federations do in various ways. This raises the questions whether the rhetoric of 'real convergence' is truly reflected in the design of cohesion policies, and whether funding is the inevitable route EU decision makers are forced to take when relatively poor EU countries demand clear and straightforward manifestations of EU 'solidarity' or 'equity'. It is the first question that will occupy us for the remainder of the chapter.

16.2 Convergence and divergence in economic theory

Since the mid-1950s, if not earlier (Ottaviano & Thisse, 2005), economists have been ambivalent about the long-run tendencies of market integration to lead to (real) convergence or divergence. Nowadays, one could summarise the state of the art by saying: it all depends what theory or theories one relies on. One empirical reason why the interest in explaining divergence has increased recently is that decades of monitoring European economic integration has yielded a mixed picture, with both convergence and divergence occurring, and this not just over time but simultaneously. In other words, some countries have converged and other countries (for example, Greece as EU member before the mid-1990s; Ireland as an EU member before the late 1980s) only in some periods and not in others. A more general observation has also been that, whereas relatively poor EU countries sooner or later found themselves on a convergence path, their weaker regions tended to suffer from divergence, that is, a slower pace of growth, inevitably resulting in (relative) falling behind.

The neo-classical theories of growth and of trade generate real convergence. Both theories are to be interpreted as long-run. Growth theory employs constant or diminishing returns (see Figure 6.11) which explains catching up, and the Heckscher–Ohlin–Samuelson (HOS) theory even yields factor price equalisation (full convergence as it were). Divergence can be explained by endogenous growth theory (based on increasing returns of human capital and innovation), by the 'new economic geography' (based on the economics of agglomeration, involving externalities and transport and trading costs), and by a range of more institutionally oriented economic theories (including 'social capital').

ADDITIONAL READING

The contrast will be outlined analytically but in a simplified approach.[4] The starting point will be three mechanisms which determine convergence and, each time, consider deviations or limitations. A graphical analysis is added. The three mechanisms are: decreasing returns, technological diffusion and structural change (in the sense of long-run reallocation of factors; de la Fuente, 2000). The standard neo-classical growth model incorporates a few factors of production and capital typically is subject to decreasing returns – a necessary condition for convergence. Decreasing returns mean that output grows less than proportionally with the stock of capital. Thus, the marginal productivity of capital will fall with accumulation (as with Baldwin's growth bonus, see Figure 6.11), in turn reducing the incentive to save (as interest rates are equal to the marginal productivity of capital) as well as the contribution to growth of a given addition to the capital stock (investment flow). As a result, growth will slow down over time. If rich countries/regions have a large capital stock – as they do – and poor ones do not, the latter will tend to grow much faster and gradually converge. The speed of convergence depends on the initial discrepancy.

[4] The literature has swollen enormously in recent years. A selection of theoretical contributions the reader is referred to includes Krugman & Venables (1995), de la Fuente (2000), Thisse (2000), Alonso-Villar (2005) and Ottaviano & Thisse (2005). A critical review is Neary (2001).

ADDITIONAL READING *continued*

If one were to assume increasing returns, the model would produce divergence – in the extreme this could even be explosive. Is it realistic to assume increasing returns? Here, we face a drawback of simple models: what is capital? In the 'endogenous' growth models, the notion of capital is widened to include human capital and knowledge or even 'innovation capacity' – and if this is the case it is conceivable that returns to 'capital' are not decreasing, hence, that inequalities might be permanent.

Early growth models have taken technological progress as given. However, if countries or regions differ in their generation or adoption of new technologies, we have another source of convergence or divergence. The question then becomes whether the stock of (productive) knowledge is subject to decreasing returns. Because (productive) knowledge is also an elusive concept, some economists argue that the cost of innovation may well fall with experience (especially where there is a large pool of human capital and skills). On the other hand, technological catch-up by absorbing technology and other relevant knowledge should be far easier than generating innovation at the technology frontier, particularly if human capital is beginning to be sizable and incentives exist to absorb rapidly and adapt where appropriate. If technological catch-up works, one should expect convergence on this account.

A third basic mechanism is structural change. Its simplest form is the structural transformation from low-productivity agriculture to relatively high productivity industry in developing countries. Cohesion countries all came into the EU with relatively large agricultural sectors and structural change is likely to have contributed to a reduction in productivity differentials over time. Clearly, for cohesion purposes it is important that this transformation can take place smoothly and is not frustrated by inappropriate policies.

If one places this discussion in a context of trade and FDI, the basic insights need not change. But it is possible that the process is accelerated. Thus, in a simple Heckscher–Ohlin–Samuelson model (see any textbook on international economics for an explanation of the HOS model), two countries with different initial factor endowments could experience factor price equalisation due to trade alone. Mundell (1957), in a similar model but without trade, has shown that such equalisation can be accomplished with one factor being mobile, let us say, capital. Stronger (free) trade will also prompt the reallocation of factors over time. It is only in the connection between trade and technological progress where standard trade theory has been less helpful.

All this fairly straightforward theory does not square with important observations in Europe. The most striking one was long considered to be the Mezzogiorno, which – along with some other stagnant or declining regions – caused Myrdal (1956) to formulate his theory of 'circular cumulative causation'. Though not analytically rigorous, his views were highly influential at the time of drafting the Rome Treaty and for a long time after. The core of his reasoning is based on two aspects not present in standard neo-classical analysis: agglomeration and complementary factor flows. Agglomerations enjoy (positive) externalities, which might be technological, informational or pecuniary (that is, via the price mechanism). They may also be dynamic, that is, intensify over time. In turn, they will induce complementary factors (for example, labour and capital) to flow in. Agglomerations would suck in the better labour from the regions and thus render it unattractive for capital to move out. Regions would typically not enjoy the level and diversity of services enjoyed in agglomerations; they would, as a result, tend to stagnate and subsequently decline. Decline would set in because basic infrastructure (for transport, communication and education) would tend to lag behind, reducing the remaining factors' productivity. Eventually, the reduction of demand would reduce the local tax base for public services and the supply of attractive shopping or leisure activities. In short, Myrdal and others were interested in regional deprivation *as a result* of agglomeration. In recent (new economic geography) theories, similarly, agglomeration tends to increase when income equalities increase. This is so since firms will relocate in markets with higher purchasing power or where intermediate supplies can be networked at low costs.

Attention is paid to the causes of such agglomerations in the first place. The two variables that play a crucial role are transport costs (probably in the wider

ADDITIONAL READING *continued*

meaning of all trading costs as in section 6.7.1 and Anderson & van Wincoop, 2004) and labour mobility. As long as workers are mobile between regions, transport costs (and especially transport costs between intermediate and final goods) keep firms more easily in one region, which subsequently attracts labour, in turn initiating a cumulative process ending in divergence. We shall not discuss the intricacies of this theory. However, it is intuitively clear that agglomeration is efficiency driven: some degree of further agglomeration, even though it would increase interregional disparities, is good for the economic growth of, say, a member country. In other words, there is a *trade-off* between efficiency (in the sense of what generates a higher growth rate of country A in the EU) and equity (in the sense of cohesion as defined between regions, both in A and between the poor regions of A and the EU income average).

A simple graphical illustration is provided in Figure 16.1. There are three curves:

- The *AA* curve expresses that the degree of agglomeration[5] (*A*) is a positive function of interregional income disparities (*R*). With trade free (in the internal market) and transaction costs lowered (say because of 'deepening' of integration), economic integration renders it more attractive to locate in the agglomeration. This shift of activity continues until profits in the core and peripheral regions are equal. *AA* is thus an equilibrium relationship.
- The *RR* curve shows a negative relationship between agglomeration and inequality, based on a competitive market for innovation. It works as follows. Agglomeration yields pecuniary externalities (lower-cost inputs, for instance) and local technological or informational spillovers (as in Silicon Valley or the City (London), to take extreme cases) between firms. All this reduces the cost of innovation, hence increasing the rate of innovation. In competitive markets, this brings about new entry, competing with established firms. Entry lowers profits of firms used to having some market power and which are heavily concentrated in the rich region. This has the effect of reducing the income disparities between regions, hence the slope of *RR*.
- The *SS* curve in the lower quadrant (positively defined) shows that agglomeration tends to have a positive effect on the rate of innovation – this rate is 'endogenous' in this model – and hence on the rate of growth. Note that this is the rate of growth of the overall (presumably, the national) economy, not just that of the agglomeration. Thus, *SS* expresses a trade-off between efficiency and equity: going against agglomeration by promoting equity (cohesion) tends to cause a loss in efficiency (lower growth rate).

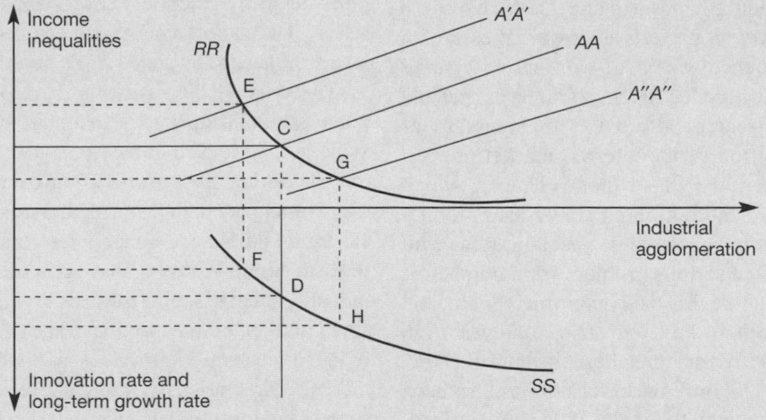

Figure 16.1 Agglomeration and interregional divergence

Source: Adapted from Martin, 1999

[5]For example, A is the ratio of the number of firms in the rich region to the total number of firms. R is an index of inequality, for example, the ratio of income in the rich region to income in the poor region.

ADDITIONAL READING *continued*

The equilibrium levels of agglomeration, inequality, and innovation and growth rates are given by intersections C and D.

There are empirical indications that convergence and divergence trends occur simultaneously in the EU. The explanation is found in the difference between interregional trends inside and between EU countries. Two reasons suggest themselves to explain this simultaneity of convergence and divergence. First, the Myrdal-type phenomena of agglomerations (that is, positive spillovers between firms) and complementary factor migration (which makes agglomerations swell, while depriving the periphery) are clearly regional, or at least intra-national, in nature. Spillovers tend to be far more powerful when based upon social interaction, hence when local or regional. Labour migration – although not high in Europe – is still much larger inside EU countries than between them. The same applies for numerous investments by intermediate input suppliers and service providers. Second, the reduction of transaction costs, although clearly also an EU phenomenon, is likely to be more powerful inside countries than between countries – the most forceful expression is the 'home country bias' discussed in Chapter 6.

Thus (slow?) convergence may well be possible in Europe based on neo-classical mechanisms, in particular if FDI can be attracted as well. At the same time, however, intra-national divergence may increase or stubbornly refuse to diminish.

16.3 How the internal market promotes cohesion

The internal market enables four mechanisms to exert positive effects on cohesion: product and process specialisation in products and services markets; foreign direct investment; competitive exposure; and the reduction of distortions.[6]

Standard trade theory teaches that the exploitation of comparative advantage leads to higher welfare for all participants. Intra-industry specialisation in the single market will have similarly positive effects. Whatever the nature of *specialisation*, it exerts an upward pressure on the productivity, hence wages, of workers with skills demanded for export production. In so far as capital and technology were scarce before EU membership or before the completion of the internal market, market integration will tend to make them cheaper, which should help adjustment to higher value-added production. It is important to choose those specialisations with a long-run view. One serious problem for a number of lagging regions in the EU (for example, Spain and Portugal) is that their key industries enjoyed high national protection before membership, and that EC trade protection is not only far lower but has also been declining secularly since the mid-1980s (for example, textiles and clothing, steel, shipbuilding via subsidies). So adjustment takes place through a steady exit of firms and workers. Rationalisation will have to be combined with product innovation and better market responsiveness to make the remainder of the industry competitive. The much wanted catch-up process of these regions is conditional on radical diversification leading to absorption of the human resources left idle (presumably helped by retraining). The EC has, fortunately, not yielded to the short-run pressures of keeping, for example, the clothing protection high, even though some regions in cohesion countries suffer disproportionately from adjustment pressures prompted by liberalisation. In targeting these regions, the EU's RETEX programme refrains from any direct support to the textiles and clothing industry and focuses instead on retraining, diversified local education and other measures which facilitate new establishment in different sectors. The choice of promising new activities is at least no longer influenced by price signals distorted by protection.

The crux of the matter is therefore consciously to pursue the appropriate adjustment strategies, so as to avoid getting locked into comparative advantages inside the EU which are, or will soon become, comparative disadvantages in the world division of labour. Such strategies should encourage intersectoral resource shifts towards higher-value-added activities as well as intra-industry specialisation towards higher segments in the final market of the product. The single market with reduced protection provides a huge and diversified market characterised by more appropriate relative price signals and incentives than in the past. Other things being equal, exploiting the single market via regional specialisation is therefore promoting convergence, or cohesion.

Capital market integration allows creditworthy investors in the less favoured regions to tap the financial

[6]This section draws on Pelkmans (1991).

resources of the agglomerations. Everything else being equal, this should facilitate investment-led growth dynamics in the less favoured regions. Thus, extensive capital inflows have financed the post-accession investment surge in Spain, which would otherwise have been choked off by the low level of domestic savings (OECD, 1990).

Foreign direct investment (FDI) constitutes an important channel for the transfer of resources and know-how which may initially be underprovided in the less favoured regions. It will allow the mediation of a package of marketing and organisational expertise, product/process innovations, and other firm-specific advantages. The initial FDI can catalyse the reorganisation improvement in the less-favoured regions.

Introducing FDI widens the scope of economic opportunities for poor regions and may go against the negative consequences of agglomeration for them. If factor endowments, hence relative costs, differ between poor and rich regions in the EU, 'vertical' FDI will tend to exploit differences through concentrated output in the poor regions and exports to the entire EU (see also section 10.6). It should be pro-convergence, other things being equal. The 'new economic geography' tends to ignore this. Some of the initial FDI flows to Ireland in the 1980s and much of the FDI to Spain and Portugal the first decade after their accession was of the vertical kind, and a considerable part did not go to the national agglomerations. 'Horizontal' FDI is based on scale economies at the company level, which implies that headquarters tend to establish in agglomerations and several (low-scale) plants are scattered through Europe, in order to be close to customers. Large, rich and growing markets are then the most attractive. However, national redistribution mechanisms in EU countries are strong enough to limit the interregional discrepancies considerably, so that the scattering of 'horizontal' plants is still very wide. With the accession of the central European countries to the EU, one should expect vertical strategies to be dominant for quite a while because the disparity with the EU15 is much larger.

Competitive exposure is the only genuine test for competitiveness of products, services, factors and companies. The single market increases competitive exposure and this may entail drastic consequences for weak regions with sectoral concentration. In the long run, however, only competitive exposure will generate viable firms, sustaining the economic fabric of regions. Therefore, competitive exposure should be welcomed. The single market initiative has more often than not broken through restrictive domestic institutions and so promoted competition even at the national level. The policy problem then becomes how to reduce intolerable adjustment cost, in what timeframe and under what conditions.

The establishment and proper functioning of the internal market implies the prohibition of numerous national and regional measures making access difficult or distorting competition otherwise. In *reducing distortions* the internal market is not necessarily beneficial to less favoured regions; in principle, it all depends. In EU practice, the overall impression from the wide-ranging EC-1992 experience is that liberalisation and the limitation of regulation to 'essential requirements' has removed numerous distortions which had crippling effects on peripheral regions. Faini *et al.* (1992) found that credit market distortions in Italy played a substantial role in accounting for the poor performance of the Mezzogiorno. In Greece and possibly other cohesion countries, a heavy involvement of public enterprises in weak regions, often in a lax competitive environment, has enabled regions to keep unemployment artificially low, but with little prospect for self-sustained development or private entrepreneurship.

Yet, the internal market also helps to improve the access for specialisations that the less favoured regions produce. For instance, the Commission has repeatedly stressed that the actual capability of giving state aids in the highly developed EU countries has proved to be far greater than the actual state aid handed out in cohesion countries. One implication, for a long time, was that Spanish intra-EU steel exports were artificially depressed by subsidies given by other EU countries to their own industries, worsening the adjustment problems unjustifiably.

These four factors show the positive impact of the internal market on the less favoured regions. In and of themselves, they might or might not suffice to yield and sustain real convergence. This depends on whether and to what degree agglomeration effects are actually at the expense of the regions, whether good national and EU infrastructure would actually tend to widen or narrow the gap, and whether and how other national policies (especially collective labour bargaining and fiscal stabilisers) influence real convergence. But it does remind the reader, and hopefully policy makers, that 'deep' economic integration implies powerful mechanisms of convergence, even without any regional policy.

16.4 Are the EU Funds effective?

If the EU Structural and Cohesion Funds are considered to be purely political bribes or gestures of political 'solidarity', their effectiveness does not matter. However, if the Funds have catch-up growth as their aim, their effectiveness is crucial. But even this catch-up growth, or real convergence, can be looked at in several ways. Suppose that the cohesion countries of the EU show faster economic growth (per capita) for a sustained period. Does this mean that the Funds have worked? It could well be that internal market-driven, and presumably neo-classical, processes were at work and that the Funds have not added much or indeed any marginal growth. Conversely, suppose cohesion countries were observed to exhibit neither convergence nor divergence – their growth over a few business cycles is roughly the same as for the EU at large. Does this mean the Funds have been ineffective? Perhaps this is not the case, because if divergence theories hold, the Funds might have compensated the lack of underlying growth.

We first provide a basic description of disparities in the EU27, followed by some key conclusions of the empirical literature.

16.4.1 Disparities

For our purposes, there are three critical disparities for economic cohesion. First, there is the disparity in real incomes per capita among the EU27 countries. Figure 16.2 gives a snapshot for 2002 on a purchasing power basis. The first thing to note is that the EU average itself has been reduced from the EU15 average by some 12 per cent. Beginning with Slovenia (SI) and the Czech Republic (CZ), all the countries in the right-hand part of the bar chart are far below the (already reduced) EU25 average or very far below. Romania and Bulgaria were at roughly 30 per cent of the EU average in 2002.

Spain is above 90 per cent and Greece and Portugal are both around 80 per cent. The new Member States as well as Bulgaria and Romania are growing quite fast (at some 5 per cent annually since the turn of the century) which means that they are catching up steadily. The convergence path is long, however, and has to be thought of as decades. In the EU15, Ireland moved out of cohesion status by 2000 after a phenomenal decade of around 8 per cent growth per year. Spain is no longer a cohesion country if the current 90 per cent criterion is applied (this is the criterion of the Cohesion Fund). This leaves Greece and Portugal, besides the new and arriving Member States. The Spanish problem consists more in the internal disparities. Whereas the country should no longer be subject to subsidies from the Cohesion Fund (which targets only countries), some of its regions are clearly lagging and ought to remain eligible for funding from the Structural Funds such as the Regional and the Fisheries Funds. That the disparities inside EU countries can be very large (though not for all countries) is clear from Figure 16.3.

Second, the EU suffers from a simultaneity of convergence between countries and divergent trends between regions. Figure 16.4 shows this dichotomy for a period of thirteen years. As we analysed before, this dichotomy might well be explained by newer theories on cohesion. This trend creates potential problems of effectiveness for the Funds. Theory leads us to expect that a priority for reducing interregional disparities might hinder the convergence of EU countries. This point is elaborated in section 16.5.

Third, apart from real convergence, there are other structural disparities, and by far the most important one is that in employment and unemployment. Whereas the EU27 average unemployment rate in 2002 was 9.1 per cent, unemployment rates in poor regions ranged up to 25 per cent (Calabria). Whereas about half the EU27 countries had no region with unemployment rates above 10.5 per cent, and Denmark, the Netherlands and Austria not even above 5 per cent, Spain, Italy, Greece and Germany had one or more regions with unemployment above 13.45 per cent and Poland, Lithuania, (practically all of) Slovakia and Bulgaria had no region with less than 13.45 per cent of unemployment. In some

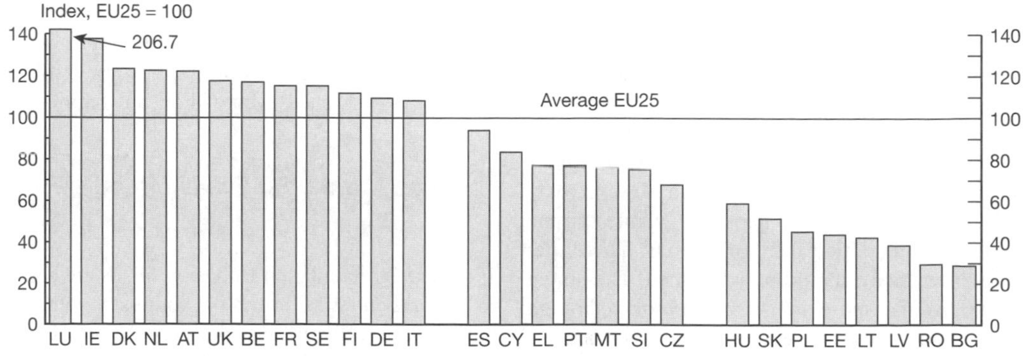

Figure 16.2 GDP per capita (PPS), 2002

Source: European Commission, February 2004. Reproduced from the original figures taken from the *Third Report on Economic and Social Cohesion – COM (2004) 107 of 18 February 2004*, © European Communities

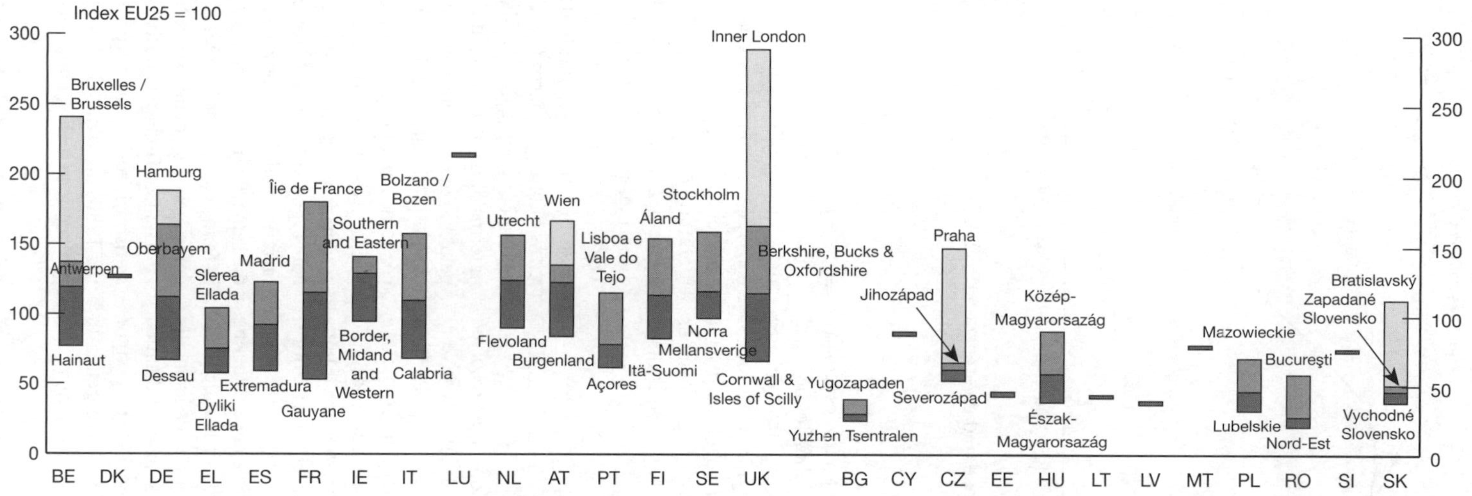

Figure 16.3 GDP per capita by country and regional extremes, 2001

Source: European Commission, February 2004. Reproduced from the original figures taken from the *Third Report on Economic and Social Cohesion – COM (2004) 107 of 18 February 2004*, © European Communities

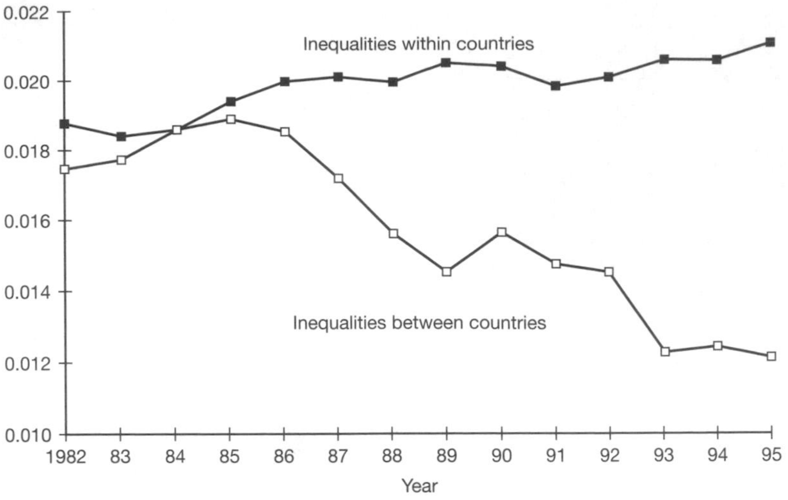

Figure 16.4 Simultaneous convergence and divergence, 1982–95

Note: Based on a Theil index.

Source: Puga, 2002

of the problem regions the employment rates (especially of women) are relatively low too. According to the Third Cohesion Report (European Commission, 2004, chapter 1), the unemployment rates in poor regions have fallen, but this is mainly true for Ireland and Spain, hardly for Greece and Portugal and even less for the new Member States where structural unemployment is high as a legacy of transition (see Chapter 20).

16.4.2 Impact of EU transfers

There are at least two empirical questions to be resolved if one wants to know whether the Funds are effective in lowering disparities. The first question is whether plain trend statistics of the kind used in section 16.4.1 are sufficiently informative regarding convergence and divergence trends. The second is whether the Funds succeed in shifting trends in the direction of (more) convergence, that is, less divergence.

With respect to the first question, there are conflicting results in the literature. In other words, it is much less clear than might at first appear whether one can actually observe convergence. On the basis of a range of detailed indicators Boldrin & Canova (2001) conclude that on the whole there is neither convergence nor divergence in terms of 'real convergence'. What has converged, according to these authors, is the rate of growth itself which is of course inconsistent with catch-up growth, since this would require a much higher growth rate in poor regions than in rich ones. Incidentally, these findings also reject, by implication, most of the agglomeration literature. Also, Puga (2002) finds that the evidence on convergence is at best mixed and that, in any event, disparities between rich and poor regions have widened. There are weak signs that production structures in EU countries are beginning to develop in distinct ways. In terms of unemployment rates, he even speaks about polarization between regions as the disparities are larger than in terms of per capita income. Ederveen *et al.* (2002) use beta and sigma convergence (for definitions see fn. 5, Chapter 15) and find that, as far as countries are concerned, both beta and sigma parameters show convergence over the two decades from 1977. As to regions, evidence is weaker but, again, both beta and sigma convergence is found.[7] However, if controlled for some factors (conditional convergence), the conclusions remain the same but are not universally correct: beta convergence is found except for Sweden, Italy and France, and sigma convergence is found except for the UK.

The fact-finding is further complicated by the delay of statistical work. The above conclusions rely on data from the 1980s up to mid-1990s. Since strong cyclical effects play a role in regional imbalances over specific periods and

[7]In 'The EU economy: 2004 review' (in *European Economy*, 2004, no. 6, pp. 95–102), the Commission also tests for beta and sigma conversions over a period similar to that of Ederveen *et al.* The results confirm gradual and steady country conversions and faster (not slower) regional conversion.

since the Third Cohesion Report is more optimistic about overcoming intra-national disparities, it is exceedingly hard to be firm about the actual trends in economic cohesion in the Union. If even the facts can be disputed, the problem of attribution (what is and is not due to the Funds) becomes almost impossible to resolve with authority.

The second question, that of whether the funds succeed in shifting trends towards convergence, has been answered in the literature in conflicting ways. A mistake one ought to avoid is to confuse demand-led effects with the impact on the capacity to grow faster, a supply-side effect. The direct demand effect on regions in cohesion countries, and possibly on regions in relatively rich EU countries as well, can be sizable. Indeed, in countries such as Greece and Portugal the immediate impact on short-run demand may well be up to 3 per cent of GDP nowadays.[8] In the new Member States, this could become even higher if they prove to be capable of 'absorbing' so much annual aid in valuable projects and programmes. To the extent that the new Member States in central Europe run into a savings gap (given their high public investment needs) and otherwise import private capital on a considerable scale, the EU Funds may well reduce or eliminate this gap. One well-known tool to study the demand-led impact is found in macro-econometric models, such as that of Christodoulakis & Kalyvitis (2000) for the effects of the Funds on Greece and the Commission's simulation exercise with the QUEST model which (for the period 2000–06) gives slowly rising effects for Portugal and Greece above 2 per cent of GDP and less than 1 per cent for Spain.[9] De la Fuente (2002) explicitly models the supply side and finds (for the period 1994–99 for Spanish Objective 1 regions, that is, those below 75 per cent of the EU15 average income per capita at the time) that the transfers have added one percentage point per year to output growth and 0.4 points per year to employment growth (or 27,000 new jobs). In the medium run, the accumulated impact on employment exceeds 300,000 new jobs and the contribution to growth in output in the less favoured regions is more than 6 percentage points (that is, 20 per cent of the initial income gap per capita between those regions and the rest of Spain). However, a survey of the earlier literature by Ederveen *et al.* (2002, pp. 37–49) brings out inconsistent and widely different results from negative to positive and sometimes large effects. Although this clusters together both actual impact studies and simulations of the potential impact, the picture remains confusing. The authors' own empirical work yields at best a moderately positive picture. Cohesion transfers foster economic growth of lagging regions if they are relatively open. Since the authors employ 'conditional convergence', that is, in controlling for country-specific factors each cohesion country grows towards *its own* 'steady state' (see Figure 6.11) and not an EU-wide steady state, they find a strong impact of the Funds. This positive impact largely melts away if one assumes a European convergence. Moreover, the authors make a (unique) empirical attempt to estimate 'crowding out' of national regional support by EU funding and find an average of 17 per cent per euro of cohesion funding.

Even more critical is the analysis in Rodriguez-Pose & Fratesi (2005) who motivate their search for impact by the observed lack of upward mobility of lagging regions ('out of' cohesion support, as it were) and the absence of regional convergence. They first show that regional convergence that does show up in statistics is due to national growth rates and that Objective 1 regions, as a subset, exhibit only a slow convergence. This might be explained by adverse specialisation patterns (high-value-added activities go to agglomerations and lagging regions are stuck with low-value-added manufacturing, non-market services and agriculture). Interestingly, the authors empirically test the effectiveness of the various types of spending of the Structural Funds and find expenditure on human capital to be effective on all counts, whereas that on infrastructure and environment is invariably ineffective. The spending on rural and agriculture works only in the short run and withers away almost immediately thereafter. The authors hold the view that this empirical study demonstrates that the Funds should directly tackle (1) the development problems of each and every region, above all addressing their shortage of skills or the mismatch between supply and demand of labour for higher-value-added activities, and (2) the overall underutilisation (low employment rates) of the regional labour force. The low returns on infrastructural investments might be explained by the fact that the agglomerations can also benefit from lowering trading costs with lagging regions (see section 16.5) as well as by the fact that such investments will raise the quality of life of citizens in the region (therefore, a political demand for such spending will easily develop)

[8]*European Economy*, 2000, no. 71, pp. 199–200.

[9]The Commission uses two very different models, namely, HERMIN and QUEST. For their distinct assumptions, see the box on p. 203 in *European Economy*, 2000, no. 71. The HERMIN model does include some supply-side effects and tends to yield a much higher impact, for example, no less than 6 per cent during the programming period for Greece and Portugal and still some 2 per cent after 2006 (assuming the inflow of EU transfers stops). For East Germany, simulation with HERMIN yields about 4 per cent real GDP impact (idem, p. 202). One reason for the QUEST results being lower is 'crowding out' of private investment, via an appreciation of the real exchange rate.

but, in and of itself, might not induce a higher growth rate. Nevertheless, it is not easy to reconcile these findings with those of de la Fuente (2002) who finds a positive impact arising from infrastructural investments.

The conclusions cannot be very firm. Nonetheless, there seems to be a consensus that funding is likely to be more effective if it is geared to the specific developmental problems of Objective 1 regions and towards the distortions or imbalances which characterise the internal economic integration of cohesion countries (and countries such as Germany and Italy). Given the strong initial demand effects and the popularity of infrastructural spending (if only for the quality of life), there are reasons to believe that the (political) equity motives are at least as important as efficiency considerations about 'catch-up growth'. If these conclusions were incontestable – but, given the controversies in the literature, that is far from being accepted – the implication could well be that general-purpose grants (without detailed conditions and with mainly national discretion how to invest the funding) would outdo the current specific-purpose grants of the EU Funds. Why? With general-purpose grants for Objective 1 regions, it is possible to better respect the specificities of the regions and the crowding-out issue need not arise. Moreover, the considerable bureaucracy of the cohesion policy would largely be eliminated. However, such a policy would introduce other risks such as a lack of quality of local projects (especially in less experienced central Europe) and local forms of corruption.

16.5 Designing effective cohesion policies

In addressing the quest for greater effectiveness of cohesion policies, we shall go through three steps: first, a brief excursion into subsidiarity (inspired in this case by federalism), some analytical considerations about current policies, including an extension of the analysis of Figure 16.1, and, finally, a few thoughts on design issues of the EU cohesion strategy. Case Study 16.1 provides basic information about the Structural and Cohesion Funds.

16.5.1 Cohesion and subsidiarity

In the economic theory of federalism there are two main reasons for the assignment of transfers to the highest tier of government: a minimum Union equity standard, and guaranteeing the effectiveness and sustainability of redistribution at state level.

Given low cross-border mobility of workers, interpersonal redistribution via income taxes and social security need not, and should not, be an EU assignment. In contrast, the lion's share of redistribution in existing federations is achieved via the vehicles of interpersonal redistribution.

In the literature a comparison is made between mobility in the EU, being low both nationally and EU-wide, and that in the USA. Not only is actual mobility far higher on average in the USA, but potential mobility is particularly so. In states where the jobless rate goes up sharply, most of the subsequent fall can be ascribed to emigration. To what extent this reflects preferences of migrants is unclear: the typical lifespan of unemployment benefits in the USA is much shorter than in Europe. Consequently the EU worker has neither the necessity to move nor much of an opportunity in other Member States. Moreover, migrating US workers will also find that the much greater regional wage flexibility in the USA enhances their probabilities of finding a job. The point is that mobility is not exogenously determined: to a significant degree the Union has the low degree of mobility it should expect given the restrictions it allows. Low intra-EU mobility is explained not only by linguistic and cultural differences but also by important regulatory barriers.

This leaves the other option: a *minimum union equity standard*, somehow decided politically on the basis of Union consensus (the 'homogeneity' criterion discussed in section 3.1.1). The political determinants of EU solidarity need not concern us here. In any event, there is no economic criterion to establish how 'high' equity-based transfers should be. In existing federations, federal taxes and transfers together may narrow the interregional income gap by as much as 30 per cent or more (see Chapter 18). As it turns out, the interregional redistribution is greater the greater the fiscal and borrowing restraints are for the sub-federal governments. One should expect redistributive transfers on account of cohesion alone, in an EU not disposing of EU social charges or having the right to tax, to be rather small at best.

This leaves interregional transfers as the remaining option, whether they are general purpose or specific purpose (usually, matching) grants. *General-purpose grants* are purely equity oriented and hence carry no conditions: they aim at a desired degree of equalising fiscal capacity. The EU does not do that. Going by federal experiences, it will take a far greater degree of solidarity before the EU finds it politically desirable to provide general-purpose grants.

Specific-purpose grants have both efficiency and equity goals. In existing federations the redistribution element in these interregional transfers reduces the interregional income gap by about 6 per cent (with transfers of about 2.5 per cent of GDP). This can be compared with the EU Structural Funds plus the Cohesion Funds – both provide specific-purpose grants – with about 0.4 per cent of EU GDP in 2005. What makes grants specific purpose is their allocative conditionality.[10] Acting on the supply side, the growth potential of peripheral regions is to be raised by raising the productivity of the existing endowment of factors and/or by factor inflows (for example, capital, technology). It is this weakest of all forms of solidarity discussed so far that is relevant in the EU. In the final analysis, the equity motive is hoped to be temporary. The conditionality should have the effect of inducing a 'catch-up' process, eventually eliminating the issue. Critical to the justification of the EU assignment for such transfers is that they be 'additional'. No additionality due to full substitution of EU funding by, say, national budget cuts, would mean that the recipient country treats the transfer as pure equity (in this case, for lower taxes). Additionality has been an official condition of the Structural Funds since the 1988 reform. Although understandable from a political point of view of the net contributing EU countries, it might actually magnify the impact of policy design mistakes.

In all of the above, the focus in using the subsidiarity test has been on justifiable assignments to the EU level. However, in one respect, the assignment *to Member States and the regions themselves* should also be addressed. This is when regions initiate or intensify competition between them to attract mobile resources such as FDI, capital and skilled labour. This competition can be benign – not at the expense of other regions – and bring about better policy making and governance in regions as a favourable factor in locational competition (see section 10.7). However, policy competition between regions can be counterproductive, if not harmful, when subsidy wars, fiscal competition or a race-to-the-bottom in social standards would occur (Abraham, 1999). A wider policy perspective than 'cohesion policies' is required to prevent such policy competition. State aid control in competition policy (see section 12.6), the prevention of harmful tax competition (see Case Study 10.1), and basic minimum requirements in social policy should suffice to do this without too much rigidity. A firm EU hand against national and regional beggar-thy-neighbour policies is entirely justified by subsidiarity.

16.5.2 Targeting cohesion transfers, an analysis

The effectiveness of cohesion policies can also be enhanced by a clever choice of the options for the targeting of transfers. The clever choice is rendered more difficult, however, by trade-offs between objectives.

ADDITIONAL READING

First, let us study a transfer to the poor region, the most common instrument used. Note that the analysis here refers to an unconditional transfer, whereas Structural and Cohesion Funds provide conditional transfers (see below). Consider Figure 16.5.

An unconditional transfer will, other things being equal, have a redistributive effect: for any given spatial distribution of firms, income inequality will be lower. In Figure 16.5 this leads to a leftward shift of *RR* to *R′R′* because the improved prosperity in the poor region will stimulate some relocation to it. In going from C to K, the agglomeration index falls. However, there is a cost, as the lower quadrant shows. The corresponding move from D to L means a lower rate of innovation and a lower overall growth rate.

Second, and closer to EU policy, is to condition the transfer. Conditionality is supply oriented. About one-third of the Structural Funds is aimed at the financing of infrastructure, both in regions and the links with agglomerations. The idea – no doubt politically appealing – behind this aim is that 'opportunities' in the single market are equalised if infrastructural barriers are eliminated. Indeed, the disparities in infrastructural terms are perhaps even larger than those in terms of incomes. But in Figure 16.1 this simply means a lowering of transport

[10]One could make an argument that general-purpose grants or even fiscal stabilisers serve allocative purposes too when they help less favoured regions to uphold certain (public) services or more generally sustain a critical demand for the viability of crucial economic activities.

ADDITIONAL READING *continued*

and other transaction costs. In a single market with all free movements respected, it matters whether the transaction costs are lower within the poor region or between the poor and the rich region. If, within the region, such a cost reduction is tantamount to an autonomous increase of demand, then new firms will be attracted into the region. In Figure 16.1, the curve *AA* shifts to the left to *A′A′* (for a given level of income inequality, agglomeration declines). But, in going from C to E income inequality increases, despite the good intentions behind the Structural Funds. Why? The diversion of firms to the poor region(s) will cause a lower rate of innovation, in turn lowering entry in the agglomeration, prompting higher profits there. Again, a trade-off emerges: locational inequality falls while income inequality goes up.

If transaction costs are lower between the poor region(s) and the agglomerations (something the EU bodies may well find the most appropriate as it would improve links between all parts of the single market), then *AA* shifts to the right to *A′′A′′*. In going from C to G, income inequality falls but agglomeration increases. This mirrors the effect of the *A′A′* case: at H the innovation rate is higher, inducing entry, which lowers profits, hence income inequality (at G) will be lower (than at C). Again, a singular focus on income inequality may lead one to approve of this policy; in terms of (reducing) agglomeration (often connected to job opportunities in the cohesion debates), the policy is a failure.

A third set of instruments does not suffer from this trade-off, however. Here, instruments target innovation by, say, reducing the (regulatory or institutional) barriers to innovation or by reducing the costs of innovation directly. The interesting point is that the instruments which may achieve this are not typically 'regional': R&D subsidies, education infrastructure (for example, technical schools, apprentice systems, retraining facilities), venture capital markets to finance start-ups, and even the facilitation of entry in goods and services markets by reducing barriers to entry. When the costs of innovation are lowered by policy, the outcome will be, in business parlance, a win–win situation. Consider Figure 16.5. An autonomous reduction of the cost of innovation shifts *SS* down to *S′S′*, as the growth rate will increase for a given level of agglomeration (from D to D′). But, of course, the rate of innovation will increase at the same time, with costs being lower; this will induce entry, hence lower profits, in turn reducing income inequality. This improved prosperity in the poor region(s) will

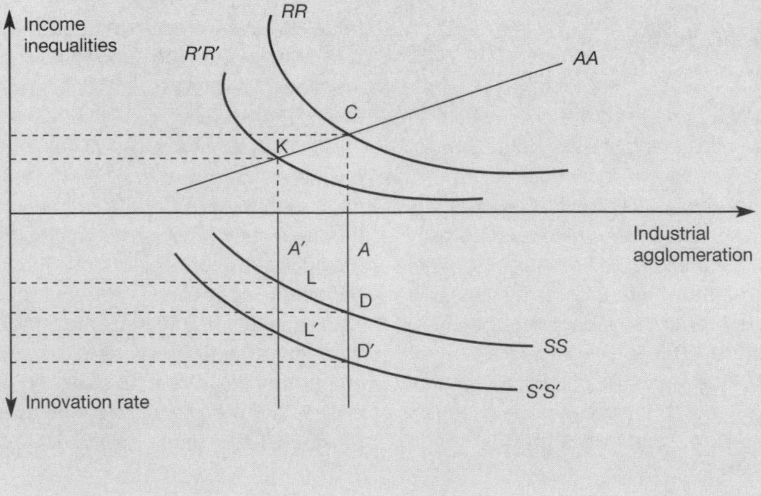

Figure 16.5 The differential impact of cohesion policies

Source: Adapted from Martin, 1999

ADDITIONAL READING *continued*

prompt a shift in the *RR* curve to *R′R′*, because some firms will now relocate to those regions. The new equilibrium is at K and L′, implying both a reduction in income inequality and in agglomeration (so, no trade-offs). Better still, L′ implies a higher overall growth rate for the economy. A similar effect could be achieved if the capacity of poor regions to absorb new technologies or to innovate themselves could be enhanced. One instrument with such an impact is the financing of high-quality information and telecoms networks, an infrastructural support that would tend to reduce agglomeration effects (unlike transport infrastructure).

16.5.3 The EU's cohesion strategy: design issues

The administrative and technical aspects of EU's cohesion policies are a specialised topic, going beyond this book. Rather, we invite the reader to give some thought to the design issues of the EU cohesion strategy in the EU27. First, the narrow focus is on the association of cohesion with budgetary transfers. As Case Study 16.1 indicates, these transfers are conditional upon a number of principles, yet they cause dilemmas of good design. Second, we remind the reader of the non-financial aspects of cohesion which too often tend to be ignored. Convergence can be fostered if these aspects are carefully exploited in the Union. Third, a brief discussion of two new features of cohesion since 2000 is provided: monetary union and enlargement.

If and to the extent that a system of conditional transfers is going to be continued, and at the time of writing (2005) this is practically certain, the design of the strategy will be strongly influenced by the solution of several trade-offs.[14]

CASE STUDY 16.1 A briefing on the Structural and Cohesion Funds

Since the reform concluded at the Edinburgh European Council of December 1992, there have been four Structural Funds (for regions) and a Cohesion Fund (for the four cohesion countries). Besides the Regional, Social and Agricultural Funds, a fisheries fund (Financial Instrument for Fisheries Guidance, FIFG) was established; however, the 2000 expenditure (€46 million) was tiny.[11] Table CS 16.1 provides a convenient summary of the main characteristics of the Funds' operations and transfers. It is self-explanatory. One element not spelled out in the table are the Community-wide programmes of the Structural Funds. There may be reasons such as externalities (cross-border regional problems) or scale (a sectoral decline or various adaptations to industrial change which occur throughout the EU) which justify a Community approach. To assess such a justification would require going into details which are beyond the present book.[12] However, for 2000–06, the budget for EU-wide programmes has been almost halved.

There is little doubt that the Structural Funds have improved since the early 1980s when various constraints and pitfalls undermined the credibility and effectiveness of the efforts.[13] The evolution of the Funds is not just a matter of increasing transfers ('more of the same'); qualitative reforms in 1988 and in 1992 have been in the right direction, broadly speaking. Nevertheless, study of the EC

[11]Note, however, that, up to 2006, another €130 million per year is available for fisheries from Objective 1 funding (i.e. the Regional Fund).

[12]Examples of EU-wide structural programmes include Interreg (cross-border interregional cooperation); Horizon (access to jobs for the handicapped), RETEX (diversification for textile regions) and Now (equal opportunities for women on the labour market). Between 1989 and 1993, ten more such EC programmes existed. Several of them will disappear in or after 2000.

[13]To mention a few: strong *juste retour* attitudes of Member States (i.e. all countries wanted money 'back', hence, no concentration; less transfer), ambiguous objectives, no additionality requirement, major administrative inefficiencies, a refusal of (some) Member States to allow the regions to work directly with the Funds, a project approach.

CASE STUDY 16.1 *continued*

Table CS 16.1 Characteristics of Structural and Cohesion Funds, 2000–06

Characteristic	Specification	Elaboration
Structural Fund, five principles	• concentration • partnership • programming • additionality • efficiency	70 per cent of all SFs on Objective 1 'regions' with regional bodies and social partners i.e. not a project approach EC transfers not to replace national funds
Structural Fund, objectives	Obj.1: less developed regions Obj.2: structural decline regions Obj.3: education and employment	task: development and structural adjustment task: conversion task: improve employability
Structural Fund, transfers	• Member States' structural programmes get 94%; EC-wide ones 6% • 2006 commitment appropriations €27,193 million	in euro of 2000
Cohesion Fund, three principles	• to countries, not regions • GNP per capita below 90% of EU average • only two narrow objectives	eligible countries are Greece, Spain, Portugal, Ireland environment and trans-European networks (note: projects)
Cohesion Fund transfers	• 2006 commitment appropriation €2,553 million	in euro of 2000

Sources: European Commission, *General Budget of the EU for the financial year 2000: the figures*, January 2000; Berlin European Council, Conclusions of the Presidency, 25 March 1999.

Court of Auditors' reports on the implementation of the Funds shows how difficult it is in practice to convert a political promise of EC specific-purpose grants into an actual contribution to real convergence at the regional and country levels. Thus, the Berlin European Council of March 1999 aimed at further improvements by concentrating the previously six objectives into three (see Table CS 16.1), tightening financial management, and simplifying the administration of the Funds. The Cohesion Fund was initiated in 1993 in response to EMU. Now that all four cohesion countries are in the eurozone, its link with EMU has fallen away.

The first trade-off is that of *equity versus 'juste retour'*. Cohesion policy is an expression of an EU equity aim. However, in the current set-up, many regions that are relatively poor in the richer Member States are also eligible. The total of funding flowing to these regions is about 40 per cent. It is not sensible to let rich (nowadays, usually net-paying) Member States first pay to the EU budget, then get cohesion conditionalities attached subject to programming proposals, and subsequently witness some of this money flowing back to their weaker regions. It is creating extra bureaucracy, may not be tailored to the needs of their regions as much as national policy might be, and is ultimately paid – to a large extent – by these rich countries themselves. This roundabout funding is a direct result of the *juste retour* mentality in budget discussions and even in cohesion negotiations. *Juste retour* refers to the idea that Member States should more or less get out of the EU budget what they put in, a notion that generates inefficiencies and political constraints for many forms of expenditures in the Union. Politically, *juste retour* is critical to the domestic debates of the net-paying countries. But it negatively affects 'equity' in the sense

[14]This subsection is inspired by Ederveen *et al.* (2002), even if our text is organised somewhat differently.

that poor regions of the relatively poor countries, with a distinctly smaller capacity to pay for their own weak regions, obtain less funding. Future cohesion transfers ought to eliminate this absurd 'pumping round' of money from rich countries' capitals via Brussels to their weak regions: this would serve equity motives at EU level and be consistent with subsidiarity (a better knowledge of local problems and how to address them).

The second trade-off is that of *national versus regional* redistribution. From a detached, analytical point of view it is hard to grasp why the EU level would be more capable of dealing with the specific needs of regions than would the Member States themselves. Apart from the equity argument above, there is a question of fairness between Member States. Not only do Member States which have never allowed great disparities between their regions get less EU support than those with great disparities, but the richer ones among them also find themselves paying more merely because other rich Member States can claim money for their weak regions. We have also seen before that national efforts for regions pre-empts 'crowding out' which gives an extra boost to cohesion. The problem with all these functional arguments is not that they are wrong but that they tend to be superseded by political considerations. Regions often do not trust their own capitals or politicisation emerges which negatively affects the continuity of subsidy flows: a kind of government failure perhaps. The EU regime is determined for seven years and, for all its problems, is more objectively organised and guaranteed. This argument is amplified in central Europe where the institutional experience is still modest and the risk of corruption is higher. The EU level with its strict procedures and tight controls is regarded as a protection of regions against the capitals, and in regions, as a protection against the lures of misusing money flows.

The third trade-off is that of *additionality versus absorption*. Given that the EU refuses to provide general-purpose grants and sticks to specific-purpose (that is, conditional) grants, additionality is the principle that should pre-empt crowding out. In other words, when EU funding flows to a region in country A, the national regional aid of A to its region should not be lowered. It should be realised that all structural and cohesion funding is subject to national co-financing which, in and of itself, forces country A to maintain an appreciable stake in regional aid. Nevertheless, Ederveen *et al.* (2002) found that some 17 per cent of national regional aid is crowded out. At the same time, the conditionality causes severe problems of absorption. Programming is tested quite rigorously (if only because of critical reports by the European Court of Auditors in the past) and it requires a well-established and skilled machinery at local and regional level to come up with ideas which genuinely tackle local development needs, and also fit the targeted activities in the EU policies. One reason for the Irish success, starting from the late 1980s, is their proficiency in coming up with solid, well-elaborated projects. This proficiency has spread to Spain and Portugal, and later still, to Greece: a good example of benchmarking. One can observe that their absorption rates have gradually moved up. In central Europe initial absorption rates are expected to be very low due to co-financing (these countries invariably have budget deficits already, and are quite poor) and a lack of experience. Thus, what is a trade-off (given the logic of conditionality) in relatively rich countries, becomes less and less a trade-off when it comes to the poorest of the EU Member States: their national aid would almost certainly be very modest indeed compared with what can be expected from the EU. This suggests a different design from the current one: be strict on additionality for Spain, Portugal and Greece (or, more radical still, shift to general-purpose grants as a means to avoid crowding out altogether) and use lower co-financing rates for countries according to their convergence gap. In addition, for central Europe, the environmental *acquis* (set by the rich EU15 before, hence less appropriate for the preferences of central Europe) and infrastructural needs will be disproportionally high for at least a decade or so. It is therefore less difficult to formulate a series of urgent and sizable projects for the initial period (say, up to 2013) which could significantly increase their absorption rates. Some of these projects might also benefit from trans-European network funding. Other efforts to raise the absorption rates can then be directed in particular at funding for human capital, as theory (section 16.5.2) and empirical analysis (Rodriguez-Pose & Fratesi, 2005) strongly suggest.

With respect to the non-financial aspects of cohesion, it is crucial to exploit the proper functioning of the internal market as much as possible. In a simulation, Lejour *et al.* (2001) find that the combination of free intra-EU trade, moderate FDI inflows and associated technology transfers may well raise the growth rate of new Member States by 0.7 per cent a year for the next two decades. We shall elaborate on EU-induced catch-up growth in Chapter 20. Of course, there is a risk that this additional growth might not be to the benefit of the weaker regions in central Europe, not least because some of them have profound deficiencies (for example, in human capital) in development terms. Ederveen *et al.* (2003) suggest that cohesion can add another 0.7 per cent structurally to the growth rates of the new Member States. Even if one should be cautious about the outcomes of such simulations, they underline forcefully that the sole focus on transfers is mistaken. Another plank of the non-financial aspects of cohesion is the avoidance of anti-cohesion biases in other EU policies. Until recently, the CAP was a culprit here, due to the alleged 'northern agro-goods' bias in price support. For two reasons this is less of a problem. First, central Europe produces northern goods in large quantities. Second, the CAP reforms (see Chapter 11) have shifted support away from price support to direct income payments in a radical fashion. These direct income payments have a historical link with former price setting in the EU15 (given the income objective of the CAP) and, for that reason alone, are relatively high for farmers in low-income economies. These direct payments will increase (as a share of what the EU15 farmers get) annually by 5 percentage points, reaching 100 per cent in 2013. There is no doubt that this construction acts as an additional transfer to agriculture in central Europe. The main beneficiaries will be the larger farmers but it also means mean that deprived and low-productivity rural areas in central Europe will receive a strong relative demand boost. The key question is how these transfers can be used for structural improvements of productivity and how they can be complemented by effective rural policies inducing marginal farmers to shift to higher-productivity jobs in other sectors.

Finally, EU cohesion strategy has to take into account two important changes in European economic integration: monetary union and enlargement. Future cohesion policy in the EU27 is essentially about central Europe, even it should be acknowledged that specific regions, including islands, in Greece, Spain and Portugal continue to require attention. Given the current climate in the Union, enlargement will lead to some reshuffling in a constant (or perhaps even shrinking) cohesion budget, away from the three EU15 cohesion countries towards the new Member States. As noted before, this could be facilitated by the termination of cohesion support to the weaker regions in rich EU countries. The reshuffling in a constant budget towards a large group of new Member States will reduce the funding per capita compared with the past. However, the effect of this should not be exaggerated since a euro in central Europe still buys far more than a euro in the EU15. Moreover, the internal market and the attraction of FDI (central Europe being successful by any standard, see Chapter 20) are just as much cohesion tools as money flows. The deeper development problems of the poorest regions in central Europe will require intrusive and ambitious efforts in upgrading human capital and in building effective institutions both for properly functioning markets and for good policies. After an initial emphasis on environmental projects (for example, living up to the EU water directives and fighting air pollution) and some urgent infrastructure, lifting the poorest regions out of their predicament is possible only when tackling their true development capabilities.

The arrival of monetary union was used as an argument in the Maastricht Treaty to establish the Cohesion Fund. Although perhaps politically understandable, the economic rationale for this linkage is at best dubious, except for short-run adjustments. But short-run adjustments are not structural, and are thus inconsistent with the remit of all cohesion efforts of the Union. In so far as the EU15 cohesion countries are concerned, one can argue that the longer-run benefits of the eurozone include a low nominal interest rate, which lowers the debt burden in the national budget and should, other things equal, stimulate investment (unless real interest rates were temporarily high). Of course, this is true for all countries in euroland but the three Mediterranean cohesion countries were all suffering from relatively high inflation (in different degrees), so this could well imply an impetus to their growth. The notion that monetary union is more costly to relatively poor than to rich EU Member States has little, if any, economic underpinning. Indeed, the first five years of EMU since 1999 exhibited a striking contrast between the four cohesion countries (all in the eurozone) and some of the key countries of the eurozone, such as Germany, France and Italy. All the cohesion countries outperformed the three big ones and a country like Spain proved capable of introducing long-postponed reforms in its labour markets and welfare state, with spectacular improvements as a result. A good working of EMU requires more flexible labour markets (see Chapter 18) and cohesion countries, just like other ones, will be affected negatively if reforms are resisted. It is sometimes held that fiscal stringency at the national level, as required by EMU, might impinge on the cohesion countries' ability to co-finance EU funding. If the debt level of a cohesion country is low, the strict rules of the Stability and Growth Pact (essentially, a medium-term budget-neutral stance, with annual fluctuations as 'automatic stabilisers' up to a maximum of 3 per cent of GDP) are a constraint. This does not apply in the three remaining EU15 cohesion countries. But it might be a point once central European countries, with generally low debt ratios, enter the eurozone. The first ones are expected to enter in 2007 and others in early 2008. In the case of central Europe, there is the more general issue of allowing a slightly higher rate of inflation at the time of entry into the currency union than that allowed by the formal rules of entry in the treaty. This has to do with the so-called Balassa–Samuelson effect (see Chapter 18) which generates a higher inflation rate which is the result not of money creation or asset bubbles but is a development effect. Suppressing this inflation, only for the temporary purpose of entering the eurozone, is irrational and could (for a few years) damage catch-up growth. And it is beyond any doubt that, even with unbalanced growth in the new Member States, a country's overall catch-up growth is crucial for the weaker regions too.

16.6 Summary

Cohesion is the Union concern to narrow interregional disparities of wealth and economic performance via negative and positive integration. Cohesion blends equity and efficiency motives. The Rome Treaty is based on the notion of real economic convergence via market integration. However, in economic theory as well as in policy analysis, processes leading to real economic divergence have also been identified. Well known is Myrdal's 'circular cumulative causation', holding that peripheral regions are deprived, relatively or absolutely, as a result of agglomeration effects. Recent economic analysis shows that there is a trade-off between efficiency (what generates a higher growth rate of country A in the EU) and equity (in the sense of cohesion as defined between regions, both in A and between the poor regions of A, and the EU income average). This is due to agglomeration effects. The Structural Funds respond to the latter fear and help regions to exploit market integration better. Nevertheless, it matters how one goes about this: targeting the regions will serve equity but might well be less 'productive' than investing in agglomerations (efficiency) as the latter might lift a country's overall growth rate more. At the same time, however, research has shown that major distortions at the national level, which heighten interregional disparities, have to be removed; a prominent example is central wage bargaining in the presence of strong interregional disparities in labour productivity.

The internal market exerts positive effects on cohesion in four ways: via specialisation based on comparative advantage, foreign direct investment, competitive exposure (forcing higher productivity, though with adjustment costs) and by reducing a number of national distortions. In designing cohesion policies, besides the internal market, it is crucial to get around the trade-off (see above). One way to do this is to target (or reduce the costs of) innovation, as well as telecoms infrastructure. Targeting transport infrastructural links with agglomerations might be counterproductive as firms might be tempted to serve regional markets from the agglomerations.

Transfers at the Union level are specific-purpose grants. More ambitions types of redistribution, known from economic federalism, do not apply in the EU. The key principles of the Structural Funds are: concentration (on target regions/groups under three objectives), partnership (for example, with regions), programming (rather than projects), additionality and efficiency. The Cohesion Fund is based on three principles: to countries (not regions), with a GNP per capita of below 90 per cent of EU average; only two narrow objectives (infrastructure/environment).

On two core issues, the economic literature gives confusing signals. The first is whether one can actually observe economic convergence or divergence in the EU. Between countries, real convergence is undisputable but there are strong indications that weaker regions have not kept up, or have even fallen further behind. Still other authors claim that there is neither real convergence nor divergence but a convergence of growth rates (which excludes any 'catch-up'). Unemployment disparities (long even more extreme) have recently narrowed somewhat, but not yet in central Europe. The second core issue is the effectiveness of the Structural and Cohesion Funds. Of course, the immediate demand effects are considerable, up to 3 per cent of GDP for counties such as Greece and Portugal (and probably for central Europe too). What matters for catch-up growth is the supply side, the enhanced capacity to generate a higher growth path for decades. Empirical economic literature is divided on this question, although there seems to be consensus that investment in overcoming skill shortages and human capital support can be very effective.

Designing effective cohesion policies should be consistent with subsidiarity. Problems of too much uniformity, too little information at the central (EU) level and insufficient possibilities for adequate differentiations for all the lagging regions, suggest a relatively modest, complementary role for the EU itself. In designing cohesion strategies well, one should have regard for three trade-offs: equity versus *juste retour* (and equity should prevail), national versus regional redistribution, and additionality versus absorption. Moreover, the non-budgetary aspects of cohesion (for example, the internal market and the removal of anti-cohesion bias in other EU policies) are too often underplayed. Finally, the eastern enlargement is drastically changing cohesion strategy, far more than a mere reshuffling of funds.

CHAPTER 17

European Macroeconomic Cooperation

Topics covered

- 17.1 Macroeconomic cooperation under the Rome Treaty
- 17.2 Autonomy versus cooperation in an open economy asset markets model
- 17.3 Credibility and macroeconomic cooperation
- 17.4 The European Monetary System
- 17.5 Why beyond the EMS?
- 17.6 Summary

Chapters 17 and 18 present the methods and economic analysis of the macroeconomic stabilisation function at union level.[1] Chapter 17 discusses relatively modest cooperative ambitions for this EC function, notably the European Monetary System. Chapter 18 deals with the much higher ambition of monetary union.

The difference between a customs union (CU) and a fully fledged common market (CM) is of fundamental significance for the national ability to achieve macroeconomic stability. The reason is capital mobility. When moving from the pure CU to the kind of CU-plus, as identified in section 2.2.2, some elements of a CM are added. Thus, the addition of non-financial services and of technology and (the modest intra-EU) labour flows will strengthen economic interdependence, and thereby increase somewhat the importance of intra-EU exchange rates for domestic macroeconomic variables. However, a fully fledged CM is accomplished only when realising free movement of financial capital and the free movement of financial services. In other words, once the Single European Act is assumed to be fully implemented, this may entail far-reaching consequences for macroeconomic policies.

This chapter discusses the problems of autonomous versus cooperative macroeconomic policies among Member States, given fixed or flexible exchange rates and the restriction of (say, in a CU), or complete freedom (say, in a CM), for capital mobility. As always in this book, the analysis will be graphical. It is assumed that the student knows the basics of open macroeconomics.[2] The chapter begins with a review of the macroeconomic section of the Rome Treaty, in the light of subsidiarity and the relevant stage of economic integration. This is followed, in section 17.2, by an open economy asset markets model of the IS-LM-BB type, with restrictive and free capital mobility. The results of this analysis are reappraised in the light of the credibility issues of disinflation policies. A brief discussion of a simplified Barro–Gordon model is included.

Section 17.4 discusses the emergence, development and performance of the European Monetary System (EMS), after the demise of the Bretton Woods system

[1] The revision of both chapters has been co-authored by Eric de Souza of the College of Europe, Bruges. I am much endebted to Eric for his contribution.

[2] See, e.g., Krugman & Obstfeld (2003, chapters 12–19) or similar textbooks. Given the space constraints for this book, it is impossible to provide a comprehensive account of all the analytical issues. The reader will be referred to the relevant literature. Note also that, for students not acquainted with open macroeconomics, the larger part of the analytical sections is presented as 'additional reading', and the remainder is kept as accessible as possible.

and the volatile 1970s. Some attention will be paid to the role of exchange controls in the early EMS. Case Study 17.1 is provided on the major EMS crisis in 1992–93, when fully free financial capital mobility in the EU had been accomplished. The chapter closes with the analytical and empirical arguments for moves going beyond the EMS, that is, beyond macroeconomic cooperation with only a modest degree of binding. Case Study 17.2 studies the impact of the large depreciations of non-core EMS currencies on the functioning of the single market.

17.1 Macroeconomic cooperation under the Rome Treaty

As is clear from Chapters 2, 5, 7 and 9, the Rome Treaty did not provide the substantive basis for a genuine common market. The most appropriate characterisation is an implicit 'customs union plus' (see section 2.2.2). As a reminder of some crucial weaknesses, note that the treaty provided neither for the removal of customs frontiers in the EU nor for an adequate regulatory regime to remove regulatory barriers; nor did it serve as a sufficient basis to accomplish, in substance, the free movement of non-financial services and non-financial factors. The most striking weakness, however, is that concerning the relationship between financial (services and capital) flows and macroeconomic provisions. The latter relations are characterised by (1) heavy conditionality of the liberalisation, (2) a lack of binding commitments for macro policy makers, and (3) open-ended escape and safeguard clauses. Even if the fully fledged CM could have been established on this feeble basis, it could surely not have functioned properly.

Two key ingredients have changed since the 1960s. First, after the demise of Bretton Woods in 1971, flexible exchange rates became much more popular and the EU faced the issue of opting for a 'joint float' (with internal pegs). Second, economic analysis and policy experiences have thoroughly altered the conduct of macroeconomic policies in EU countries. To understand these ingredients better, sections 17.2 and 17.3 present the economic analysis of these questions. Section 17.4 then discusses the EMS in this perspective.

ADDITIONAL READING

Article 61(2) EEC (now Article 51 EC) says that the liberalisation of banking and insurance services 'connected with the movements of capital shall be effected in step with the progressive liberalisation of movement of capital'. But the latter is conditional upon 'the extent necessary to ensure the proper functioning of the common market' (Article 67(1) EEC).[3] Since the common market is not defined in the Rome Treaty (see section 2.1), this creates a *trap* into which the Community was bound to fall. And indeed it did.[4] Either the CM is defined as in Chapter 1 above: in that case, the condition ('to the extent necessary . . .') is superfluous because the free movement of capital is a *sine qua non* for the establishment of a CM. But the treaty chapter on capital movements is inconsistent with this interpretation as it is littered with safeguards and conditions which prevent progress or induce easy retrogression.[5] Or, the definition problem is left unresolved: in that case, a 'mother principle' is lacking and neither the free movement of services nor that of financial capital will be accomplished. Even if accomplished, say, on account of a strong political will to 'complete' the CM on the basis of the Rome Treaty, it would be sustainable only if the macroeconomic reasons for reintroducing capital controls (see Articles 70 and 73 EEC as well as Articles 108 and 109 EEC)[6] would not arise. But for the credibility of the latter achievement it is indispensable that macroeconomic coordination is strong and binding, so that no exchange rate (or balance of payments) crisis will provoke new exchange controls. In terms of the subsidiarity test (see section 3.2), there would be a

[3]Articles 67 to 73 all became obsolete by 1 January 1994, as stipulated in the Maastricht Treaty, Art. 73a. They have been deleted following Amsterdam.

[4]Only the essentials will be set out here. For a full exposition see Pelkmans (1985b, pp. 384–90).

[5]A few telling examples should suffice. Article 68(3) EEC explicitly recognises the segregation between national capital markets (as it imposes prior bilateral agreement in case Member State A wants to obtain capital in B); Art. 70(2) EEC, in case of disagreement on exchange control removal (which is easy enough, due to unanimity); the very weak standstill clause in Art. 71 EEC; the double safeguard clauses (re)introducing capital controls, in Art. 73 EEC.

[6]Articles 108 and 109 EEC (now Arts 119 and 120 EC) will continue to exist formally as long as not all EU countries have joined euroland. See Art. 122 EC.

ADDITIONAL READING *continued*

compelling 'need to act in common' (step 2), and coordination (step 3) would have to be so robust that national policy autonomy would largely vanish. However, the Rome Treaty does not provide for more than weak cooperation, incapable of achieving such credibility.

The macroeconomic section of the Rome Treaty consists of a brief provision on conjunctural[7] policies ('. . . a matter of common concern', Article 103 EEC) and several articles on exchange rate and balance of payments issues in a context of macroeconomic stabilisation.[8] The underlying assumption is the prevalence of pegged, but adjustable exchange rates under the Bretton Woods system. The policy autonomy of the Member States is hardly impaired by EC rules. Even though exchange rates are 'a matter of common concern' (Article 107(1) EEC, now revised as Article 124 EC), a Member State itself decides upon realignment of its exchange rate, subject only to constraints about ('serious') distortions of competition. The exchange rate rigidity which prevailed for most of the 1960s cannot be attributed to this provision – it is a derivative of the pegs to the US dollar, and possibly to some extent to the attachment in the EU to the CAP prices which were expressed in a common unit of account. As soon as balance of payments pressures arose, the reintroduction of (some degree of) exchange controls under the provisions for capital mobility would find its macroeconomic counterpart in Article 108 EEC. The only difference is that the Commission may propose 'mutual assistance' to or among Member States, including credits. This option of avoiding 'jeopardising the functioning of the common market' (Article 108(1)) was not very helpful in practice because there was a tendency in the Bretton Woods system to avoid realignments for as long as possible.[9] It easily led to crises, in turn prompting (stricter) exchange controls under Article 108, or unilaterally and immediately under the safeguard clause of Article 109 EEC.[10] This happened in the case of France in 1968 after the 'May revolt' – even so, France still had to devalue a year later.

Macroeconomic cooperation, as a framework for facilitating the definitive removal of capital controls, was thus simply not provided by the EEC treaty. Consistent with the implicit notion of a CU-plus, the EC Court ruled in 1974 that exchange controls should not affect intra-EC *trade* (in goods) directly. It confirmed in the famous *Casati* case, as late as 1982, the 'trap' that the CM need not be completed with respect to *capital* movements, due to balance of payments risks.[11]

17.2 Autonomy versus cooperation in an open economy asset markets model

The analysis first deals with fixed and flexible exchange rates under different assumptions about capital mobility, in the asset market approach to open economy macroeconomics.[12] This approach is an extension of the Mundell–Fleming model.[13] The analysis is 'additional reading'. However, the summary conclusions are not optional – they have been kept non-technical.

The conclusions of the 'additional reading' below can be summarised as follows. Three factors influence the

[7]To be read as cyclical, or short-run macroeconomic; in the Maastricht Treaty the wording became 'economic' policies but the new elaborate article (now Art. 99 EC) is completely different from the old Art. 103 EEC.

[8]Macroeconomic stabilisation is defined in Art. 104 EEC as a high level of employment and a stable level of prices, while maintaining confidence in the currency. Article 104 EEC has disappeared and Art. 98 refers to the objectives of the Community, and these include the same objectives as in Art. 104 EEC.

[9]This was caused by a mixture of political pride, pressures from traders, and the IMF requirement that balance of payments disequilibria had to be 'fundamental' before a re/devaluation was permitted.

[10]Combined with Art. 73(2) EEC.

[11]For a full discussion, see Petersen (1982). The reader is encouraged to scrutinise the ruling for its circular reasoning on the establishment and proper functioning of the CM.

[12]Readers of the first and second editions might have expected the Mundell–Fleming model here. However, the omission of an explicit asset market is problematic. Hence, the choice to opt for a more appropriate variant of the open economy model.

[13]The approach used here is based on Rødseth (2000) who refers to it as the Mundell–Fleming–Tobin model.

effectiveness of fiscal and monetary policies: (1) the exchange rate regime (fixed or floating), (2) the monetary policy regime (interest rate policy, monetary targeting policy, no sterilisation), and (3) the degree of capital mobility.

Fiscal policy is effective under both fixed and flexible exchange rates. It is most effective when the central bank targets the interest rate. High capital mobility increases its effectiveness under fixed exchange rates, but reduces it under flexible exchange rates. Thus, in a liberalised financial environment (say, after 1988, when the EU liberalised capital flows fully), without exchange controls in the EU and with massive liquid securities which permit funds to be potentially very mobile, fiscal policy under flexible rates has very little impact. The effectiveness of monetary policy depends on the degree of capital mobility. As capital mobility increases, the effectiveness of monetary policy falls under fixed exchange rates and rises under flexible ones. When capital mobility is perfect, monetary policy is ineffective under fixed exchange rates.

The autonomy versus cooperation issues can be brought into sharper relief in two-countries models. Foreign output (that of the 'second' country) and the equilibrium EU (or, if the EU is 'open', world) interest rate are then no longer given, but (endogenously) determined by mutual interaction. This analysis goes beyond the present book. However, a flavour of the policy problems may be had by noting the following. Although, in the case of fixed exchange rates, the effectiveness of fiscal expansion would tend to spill over to the 'second' country (a positive externality, if the second country suffers from unemployment), this need not always be so. If the rise of the world interest rate exerted a strong negative effect on EU (or world) spending, it is possible that a 'beggar-thy-neighbour' effect would arise for the 'second' country. Under flexible exchange rates the latter negative transmission, to the 'second' country, following fiscal expansion in the first, cannot occur: both countries go to higher output, though at a higher level of interest. We shall see that this negative spillover under 'pegged' exchange rates did occur in the EU during the first few years of the 1990s.

ADDITIONAL READING

Fixed exchange rates and macroeconomic policy

We have two countries, the home country and the foreign country which can be considered as the rest of the world. Each country produces only one good which is distinct from that produced by the other country. The good produced by each country can be considered as an aggregate of domestic production. The amount produced of each good is determined by demand. In other words, the supply of a good is infinitely elastic to its price. This supposes that there is some slack in the two economies which allows supply to increase without any pressure on prices. We also suppose that the country is small. Home-produced goods cost the same in both countries, as do foreign-produced goods, once the exchange rate conversion is taken into account.

The real side of the economy is represented by the IS schedule which is the the locus of combinations of i (interest rate) and Y (real national income) at which the goods market[14] is in equilibrium. The financial side of the economy is represented by three markets: the domestic market for domestic money, the market for bonds denominated in domestic currency (domestic bonds), and the market for bonds denominated in foreign currency (foreign bonds). The financial wealth of the private domestic sector is allocated between these three assets. The quantity allocated to each asset depends on the level of financial wealth, the level of domestic output, the domestic interest rate, i, and the risk premium, r, which is the difference between the domestic interest rate, i, and the foreign interest rate, i_*, adjusted for an expected depreciation of the domestic currency, e_e.[15] A higher level of financial wealth leads to a higher demand for all domestic and foreign bonds but does not directly affect the demand for money. A higher level of output increases the demand for money which results in a lower demand for domestic and foreign bonds. A higher domestic interest rate increases the opportunity cost of holding money and, therefore, lowers its demand.[16] And, finally, an increase in the risk

[14]Consumption, investment, government consumption and net exports (trade balance) may all contain services as well.
[15]In other words, $r = i - (i_* + e_e)$.
[16]The demand for domestic and foreign bonds is also affected through the resulting change in the risk premium.

ADDITIONAL READING *continued*

premium lowers the demand for foreign bonds and increases the demand for domestic bonds. The *LM* schedule is the locus of combinations of *i* and *Y* at which the money market clears: a higher interest rates reduces the demand for money and, therefore, requires a higher level of output to maintain money market equilbrium. The *BB* schedule is the locus of combinations of *i* and *Y* for which the domestic bond market is in equilibrium: a higher level of output increases the demand for money and reduces the demand for domestic (and foreign) bonds, which in turn requires a higher interest rate to maintain the demand for domestic bonds. In virtue of Walras' law, we do not explicitly model the equilibrium of the foreign bond market. On account of the slack in the goods market, there is no trade-off between unemployment and inflation (no Phillips curve). Policy makers are typically interested in pursuing 'a high level of employment' (Article 104 EEC, and nowadays also in Article 2 EC) without – in this model – having to worry about inflation. General macroeconomic equilibrium is represented in Figure 17.1.

The question now is whether fiscal and monetary policy are effective under restricted and under free capital mobility. Introducing unhindered capital mobility is supposed to represent the move to a single market. The effects of fiscal and monetary policy will depend on the monetary policy regime in place, and consequently which financial market equilibrium condition is constraining, that is, which equilibrium condition is not affected and, therefore,

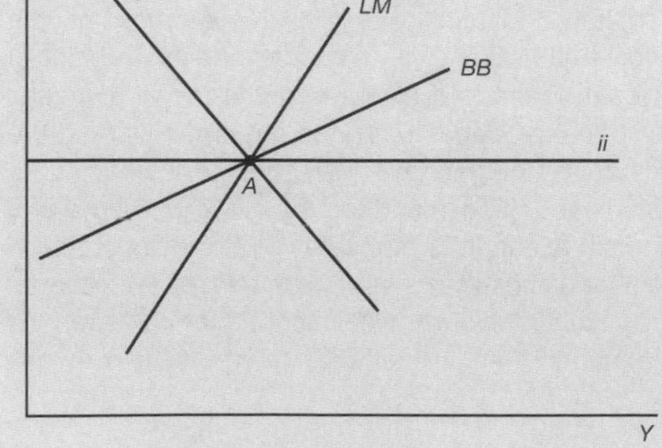

Figure 17.1 General macroeconomic equilibrium

Source: Based on Rødseth (2000), p.172, Fig. 6.1

whose corresponding schedule does not move. If the money supply is targeted, the *LM* schedule is constraining and the supply of domestic bonds must adapt: we can ignore the *BB* schedule. In this case, the effects of a policy or shock on the money supply is fully sterilised or neutralised. If there is no sterilisation, the *BB* schedule is constraining and the money supply becomes endogenous: we can disregard the *LM* schedule. A third monetary policy regime, and the most common one in practice, is an interest rate policy where the central bank sets the interest rate. In this case, both the *LM* and *BB* schedules are endogenous and financial market equilibrium can be represented by a horizontal line at the level of the interest rate set by the central bank. We call this the *ii* schedule.

Consider first an expansionary fiscal policy which is bond financed. This is represented in Figure 17.2. The *IS* schedule is drawn for a given fiscal stance; a rise in public spending would cause the *IS* schedule to shift to the right. An increase in government expenditures results in an increase in output, *Y*, for any given interest rate, *i*. The *IS* curve moves to the right. The increase in *Y* is given by the Keynesian multiplier. What happens next will depend on the monetary regime in force.

- *Interest rate policy.* The increase in *Y* leads to an increase in the transactions demand for money: domestic bonds are sold by the private sector in exchange for money. This would normally cause a fall in the price of those bonds and a concomitant rise in the interest rate. In order to avoid this, the central bank undertakes an open-market purchase of domestic bonds. Foreign exchange reserves remain unchanged. In Figure 17.2, the economy moves from its initial equilibrium at point A to point B: the fiscal expansion has its maximum effect on output.
- *Full sterilisation.* The rise in output following the fiscal expansion increases the transactions demand for money and cause the interest rate to rise. This attracts investors to domestic bonds at the expense of foreign bonds, and leads to an appreciation of the domestic currency. In order to avoid this, the central bank intervenes in the foreign exchange market, increasing its foreign exchange reserves. If the central bank is targeting the money supply, it must then sterilise the effects of its intervention by selling domestic bonds. This causes a further

ADDITIONAL READING *continued*

drop in the price of domestic bonds and rise in the domestic interest rate. The economy moves from its initial equilibrium at point A to point C.

- *No sterilisation.* If the central bank is not targeting the money supply, it does not sterilise its interventions in the foreign exchange market. The money supply increases by the amount of the purchase of foreign exchange by the central bank. The economy moves from its initial equilibrium at point A to its new equilibrium at point D.

In the case of full or no sterilisation, the rise in the domestic interest rate dampens the multiplier effect of the expansionary fiscal policy on output. This dampening effect is known as the crowding-out effect.

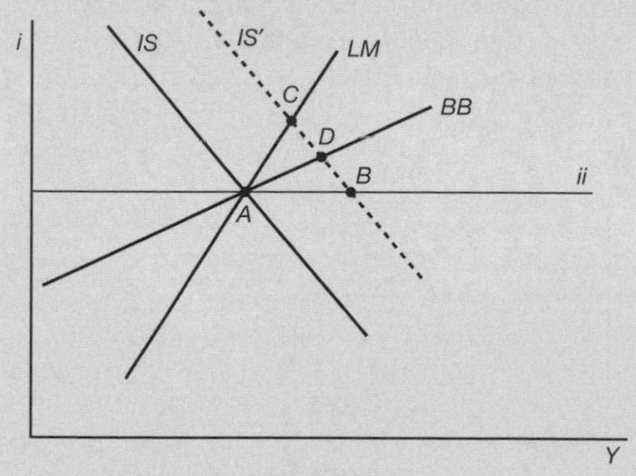

Figure 17.2 Fiscal policy (fixed exchange rates)

Source: Rødseth (2000), p.172, Fig. 6.1

The effectiveness of fiscal policy also depends on the degree of capital mobility: the extent to which domestic and foreign bonds are substitutes for each other. Perfect capital mobility means that domestic and foreign bonds are perfect substitutes for each other. In this extreme case, the risk premium is equal to zero, and the domestic interest rate is determined by the uncovered interest rate parity condition: $i = i_* + e_e$.[17] It is equal to the foreign interest rate when there is no expectation of a realignment. As the degree of capital mobility increases, the *BB* schedule gets flatter. When capital mobility is perfect, it is horizontal; and fiscal policy has its maximum impact on output: there is no crowding out.

Consider now an expansionary monetary policy in the form of an open market operation of the central bank in which the central bank purchases domestic bonds in exchange for money. The initial equilibrium is at point A in Figure 17.3. The *LM* and *BB* curves move to the right. The *IS* curve does not move. The effects of the open-market operation will depend on the monetary regime. Clearly, the interest rate must change to allow for adjustment in the money and domestic bonds markets. Consequently, a fixed interest rate policy is not compatible with an open-market operation. Indeed, central banks use open-market operations mainly to steer the interest rate.

- *No sterilisation.* The contraction in the supply of domestic-currency denominated bonds results in a rise in its price and a fall in the domestic interest rate. This has two effects. In the goods market, the drop in the interest rate will stimulate consumption and investment and lead to a rise in output. In the foreign exchange market, it will lead to an outflow of capital (a sale of domestic bonds for foreign bonds). The central bank will intervene to avoid a depreciation of the currency, thereby reducing its foreign currency reserves as well as money supply. The interest rate too rises slightly, compared with the initial drop to C. The final increase in the money supply is, therefore, smaller than the initial rise following the open-market operation. In Figure 17.3, the economy settles down at point B on the new *BB* curve, indicated by *BB'*.

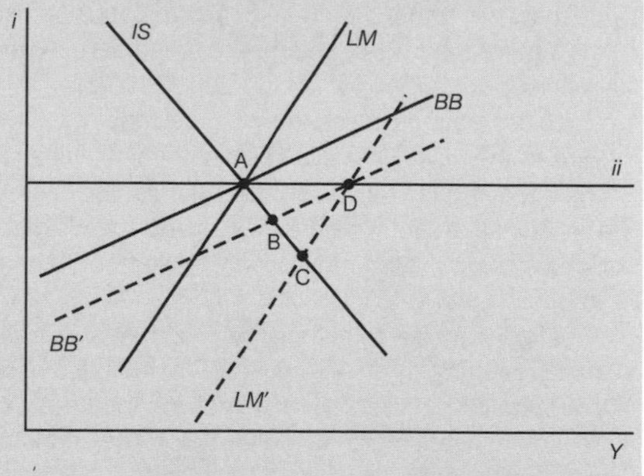

Figure 17.3 Monetary policy (fixed exchange rates)

Source: Rødseth (2000), p.174, Fig. 6.2

[17]For example, see Krugman and Obstfeld (2003, chapter 13).

ADDITIONAL READING *continued*

- *Full sterilisation.* The central bank can always sterilise the effects of its intervention in the foreign exchange market by purchasing domestic bonds. The interest rate drop and the reduction in foreign reserves is larger, as is the increase in output, Y. The new equilibrium is now on the *LM′* curve in Figure 17.3, at point C. Note that, with full sterilisation, the total purchase of foreign bonds is larger than with no sterilisation.

Flexible exchange rates and macroeconomic policy

The analysis for flexible exchange rates is not radically different, though the results are. The exchange rate is now determined in the foreign exchange market, the market for foreign currency. It depends on the interest rate differential, $i - i_*$, and the degree of intervention (via purchases and sales) of central banks in the foreign exchange market. When there is no central bank intervention, we speak of a clean float; otherwise, of a managed or dirty float. We consider the case of a clean float below. The *IS* schedule is drawn so as to take into account the endogeneity of the exchange rate: the exchange rate is replaced by its determinants.

A fiscal expansion increases output and, consequently, the demand for money. This provokes a rise in the interest rate and an appreciation of the domestic currency.

Under an interest rate policy, the central bank will expand the money supply to eliminate the increase in the interest rate. This also avoids the appreciation of the exchange rate, which remains unchanged. There is no crowding out. The economy moves from A to B in Figure 17.4.

Under a money target regime, the interest rate will rise, resulting in an appreciation of the domestic currency. Both these effects will reduce the impact of the initial fiscal expansion on output. The economy moves from A to C in Figure 17.4.

An increase in the money supply will cause a drop in the interest rate, *i*, and an exchange rate depreciation. Both of these will cause output to expand. The increase in Y is larger than in the fixed

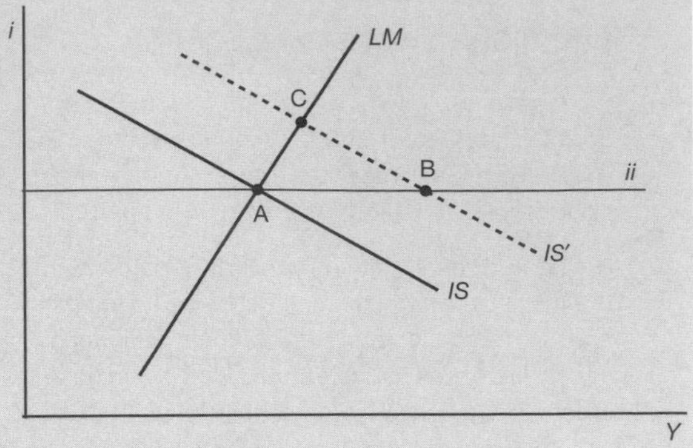

Figure 17.4 Fiscal policy (flexible exchange rates)

Source: Rødseth (2000), p.181, Fig. 6.4

exchange rate case. The *LM* curve moves to the right. A drop in *i* will be accompanied by an exchange rate depreciation, both of which will lead to an expansion of Y. The *ii* curve moves down. An interest rate policy or a money target policy produces the same effects. See Figure 17.5.

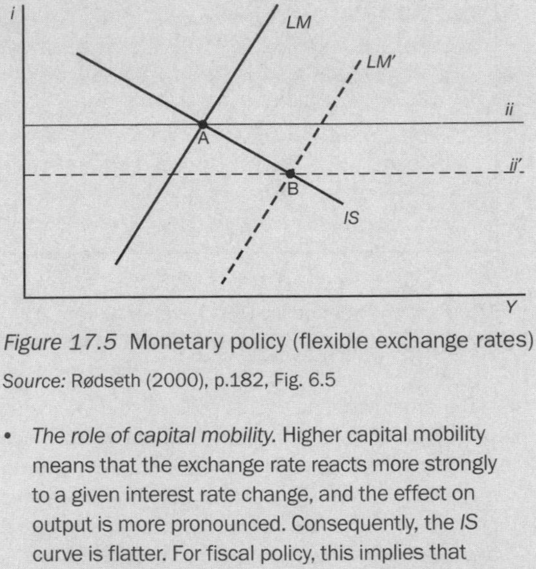

Figure 17.5 Monetary policy (flexible exchange rates)

Source: Rødseth (2000), p.182, Fig. 6.5

- *The role of capital mobility.* Higher capital mobility means that the exchange rate reacts more strongly to a given interest rate change, and the effect on output is more pronounced. Consequently, the *IS* curve is flatter. For fiscal policy, this implies that capital mobility reduces its impact: the point C approaches the point A in Figure 17.4. It can be shown that as long as exchange rate expectations are regressive, the *IS* curve will remain negatively sloped even with perfect capital mobility. For monetary policy, the higher the degree of capital mobility, the stronger the impact of a given increase in the interest rate because of the larger change in the exchange rate.

17.3 Credibility and macroeconomic cooperation

The asset market approach to open economy macroeconomics developed above assumes fixed wages and prices. During the 1970s and 1980s, however, Europe experienced inflation, rising wages and increasing unemployment. This phenomenon was referred to as 'stagflation'. While these developments can be incorporated into the theoretical framework developed above, we shall not do so here.[18] Most European countries attempted to fight the rising unemployment by running appreciable budget deficits and accomodative (lax) monetary policies. But fiscal policy may affect cyclical unemployment, not structural employment which has steadily increased for microeconomic reasons. It should therefore be reduced by microeconomic reforms in the labour market as well as by a reduction in the taxation of labour. The policies followed set public sector debt on an unsustainable path, moderately high levels of inflation and an increasing level of unemployment. Devaluations of the domestic currency sometimes brought temporary relief in the form of increased competitiveness, but, in the end, only resulted in higher inflation because of wage indexation mechanisms. Clearly something had to be done. But people had lost much faith in the ability of governments to seriously attack these problems. There was a credibility issue.

The credibility issue has arisen from two sources: actual experience and political economy. Judging experiences, the long-run impact of macroeconomic policy was disappointing: cyclical unemployment can be reduced but only at the costs of more inflation (fixed exchange rates) and long-term rising debt; monetary policy may have temporary effects at best, and the same goes for devaluations. But at higher inflation, it becomes harder and harder to 'surprise' and so 'buy' extra jobs. In the end, only higher inflation would result.[19] Yet, at least three drawbacks of inflation would remain: for wealth holders (including private pensions), for the proper functioning of markets, and for the stability of exchange rates in the internal market. Reducing inflation would thus entail positive welfare effects.

Monetary (and exchange rate) policy, then, should control inflation and active fiscal policy should be abandoned (the passive fiscal stabilisers would already dampen cyclical effects). From a political economy point of view, however, this prescription is not convincing. It presupposes that central banks and governments pursue the public interest in some idealised way. But if short-run macroeconomic policy pays off politically to the government and to the central bank, or the latter is not independent from politics, the idealised prescription would not be followed. Furthermore, since expectations are taken into account, the authorities have incentives to act differently from what they say, that is, to engineer a surprise inflation (to create jobs before an election) or to devalue despite promises to the contrary. These incentives are weaker the greater the society's preference for low inflation (as the electorate would reduce its support) and the more independent the central bank (so that it is assessed purely on its task of maintaining the purchasing power of the currency).

However, if such a political-economic perspective of macroeconomic policy making is accepted, differences in credibility of policy announcements will exist among EU countries' authorities. This will deeply influence expectations in money and currency markets as well as those of trade unions, possibly even voters. In turn, that means that mere announcements of low inflation targets and a pegged exchange rate for some countries will not be credible to markets. Worse still, given high inflation resulting from successive accommodating policies following the first and the second oil shocks (1973–74 and 1979) and the recession of 1981–82, even costly policies of disinflation will not be credible without evidence of the socio-political willingness to incur those costs. Otherwise, the options of depreciation or of still allowing automatic price compensation remain politically too attractive.

It is worthwhile illustrating these issues graphically.[20] In Figure 17.6 the Member States A (a low inflation country) and B (one that compromises on inflation for purposes of short-run employment gains) are juxtaposed. The closer to the origin, the lower inflation and unemployment. For simplicity the

[18] See Blanchard (2005).

[19] When inflation does not come as a surprise but is expected, the Phillips curve shifts upwards as lower unemployment would now require expected as well as surprise inflation. The Phillips curve shows the trade-off between inflation and unemployment. When workers learn to anticipate inflation, or price compensation becomes automatic, the effects of upward-shifting curves is eventually such that there is no impact on unemployment from a rise of inflation. This long-run Phillips curve is vertical at the natural rate of unemployment (often called NAIRU), determined by the taxation of labour and microeconomic aspects in the labour market.

[20] The following is based on de Grauwe (2000, pp. 46–52).

Phillips curves (convex, as seen from the origin) are supposed to be equal in the two countries (note that p is the rate of inflation and u is unemployment).[21] The vertical lines are the natural rates of unemployment (which may well differ). The indifference curves of the (preferences of the) authorities in the two countries are drawn as concave, seen from the origin, because, as the inflation rate declines, the authorities tend to attach more weight to unemployment. Country B typically has 'steep' indifference curves as it is willing to accept much extra inflation for a reduction in unemployment; country A has 'flat' ones. For both governments, moves towards the origin are viewed as beneficial.

The basic idea of this Barro–Gordon model is that the government plays a game with the private sector under rational expectations. Private economic agents follow optimal strategies in response to government strategies. As it turns out, the private sector responses greatly influence the effectiveness of macroeconomic policy.

Supppose the government of B announces a zero inflation monetary policy and the private sector believes this (hence, the inflation expectations are zero). So country B will find itself at Q. But the government has an incentive to cheat on its announcement, since an unexpected increase of inflation would move the economy to R on the same Phillips curve, but now on I_0 (rather than I_2), much closer to the origin. If the government took a long-run view of the economy, there would be no incentive to cheat because, in period 2, the Phillips curve would shift upwards (given revised expectations about inflation), with unemployment increasing again (say, to S). Furthermore, in period 3, this would lead to a further shift (since, in going from R to S, inflation has further increased, hence shifting expectations again), until, after several periods, the natural rate of unemployment is reached at a high level of inflation (at T). The upshot is that T is on an indifference curve (I_n) further removed from the origin than the one Q is on (I_2), hence, the final result is a significant deterioration. However, the point is that governments tend to take a short-run view, and if they do that, their announcements become what is called 'time inconsistent': as governments solve the policy problem each period, every announcement is incompatible with the incentives for the government in that period.

In country A, a similar announcement sets the economy off at E. If the government cheats, and the multi-period adjustment is over, A has passed via D to C, a relatively low rate of inflation. If A and B are two EU countries, Figure 17.6 shows that B would have to devalue continuously. Country B's problem is therefore one of credibility: the incentive structure should be changed such that a low inflation policy is believed. Once that is the case, B would reap significant welfare gains. It is here that intra-EU monetary cooperation comes in. Suppose B announces fixed exchange rates between A and B. If credible, B would eventually find

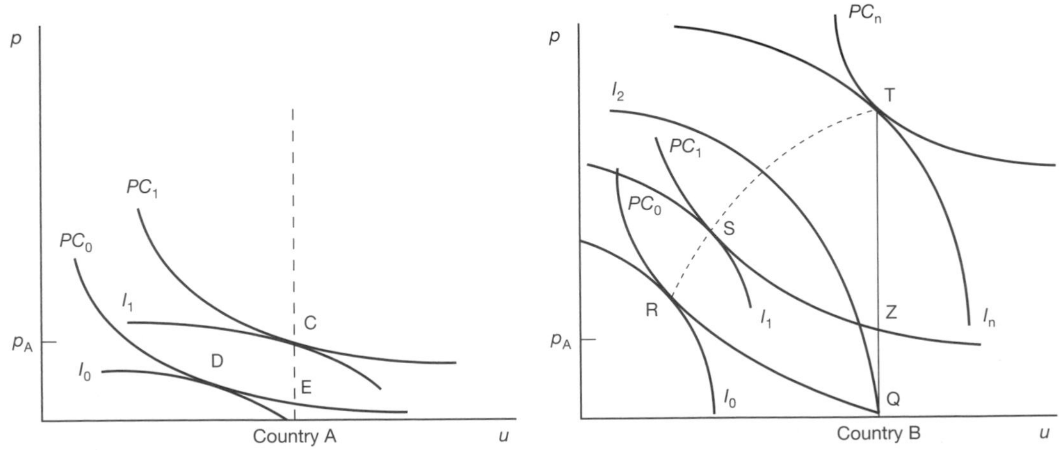

Figure 17.6 Inflation differential and the costs of autonomy

Source: Based on de Grauwe (2000)

[21] The attentive reader will have noticed that these Phillips curves are not related to changes in wages but to those in prices. For given productivity changes, the difference between the two approaches vanishes, however.

itself at Z, with A and B having p_A as inflation rate. Unfortunately, this announcement is not credible either, because the government's incentive is to move to S. It could do that by engineering a surprise devaluation, leading to a surprise inflation. Later, however, the economy will again end up at T.

The conclusion is that a devaluation may help once, but lingering expectations that it may be used again in the future make macroeconomic policy more difficult – policies will not easily be believed any longer. Indeed, devaluations cannot be used at will. Using them changes private expectations at once, and revising those new expectations towards low inflation is a long and painful process.

There are two ways out of this dilemma. Both are forms of macroeconomic cooperation. One is not merely to announce a peg (before the 1990s, typically to the Deutschmark as the currency with the most credible policy of low inflation) but to 'tie one's hands' in the framework of an EU-based system of obligations about exchange-rate stability. This external tying of hands is then presented domestically as vital for the country's 'reputation' in Europe (and beyond), thereby hoping to spread the costs of disinflation over some years of adjustment. As we shall see later on, after some initial failures due to insufficient binding, high-inflation EU countries have successfully pursued this strategy since about 1983. But this requires full acceptance of adjustment at home; if not, the peg may not reduce inflation enough and real appreciation will follow, causing a loss of macroeconomic competitiveness.[22] Ultimately, this insufficient disinflation is unsustainable and the peg has to go.

The other way is explicit coordination among (EU) countries, in the framework of a joint peg. The difference from a self-chosen path of disinflation is probably very small, because the onus is still on the high-inflation country. Only if coordination assumes a more centralist character (in the subsidiarity test, a shift from step 3 to step 4), would it be possible to influence the policy mix in Germany too. But in that case the difference, with monetary union, becomes extremely small. Indeed, coordination is costly and can be slow – so it generates its own credibility problems – and a shift to monetary union may then become a better option (section 17.5).

17.4 The European Monetary System

17.4.1 A preference for exchange rate stability?

There is a long-standing controversy going back to the mid-1950s about the desirability of fixed versus flexible exchange rates in economic regionalism. This has culminated in the theory of optimum currency areas, to be dealt with in Chapter 18. This theory focuses on the question of whether the costs of adjustment in the absence of the exchange rate instrument are low enough to enjoy the (net) benefits of one currency.

But even after the Bretton Woods period (1971), the EC9 clearly expressed a strong preference for exchange rate stability. This can probably be explained by three reasons. First, most European countries saw the demise of Bretton Woods as a dollar problem. Although the dollar exchange rate was, after 1971, no longer an important policy variable for the US authorities in a relatively closed economy, this did not apply to the open European economies. This argument led to empirical literature on whether (nominal) exchange rate volatility had a negative effect on trade due to uncertainty and hedging costs. The thrust of that literature is that the impact is probably rather small because practically all fluctuations relevant to trade transactions can be covered at small costs in the forward market.[23] Nevertheless, in business circles and among European monetary authorities, sudden wide swings in currencies, above all the dollar, were considered to be unduly costly.

Second, not only were the EC9 open, they also traded heavily with one another. Similarly, EFTA countries traded intensively with the EC9, and this could only further augment with the industrial FTA between the EC9 and EFTA, beginning in 1973. The countries (and business) felt strongly that tariffs and regulatory barriers had been broken down, only to see them reappear as costs of uncertainty and hedging. Even if these costs were not so high for trade, they complicated costing for assembly and intermediate products, created far greater uncertainty for (cross-border)

[22] That is, the relatively high inflation would require a depreciation of the currency, which is impossible with 'tied hands'. See section 17.4.4.

[23] See, e.g., IMF (1984) and Sekkat (1998) for surveys. A new variant of this literature (de Grauwe & Skudelny, 2000) employs a (sohisticated) gravity model applied to intra-EU trade; the short-run impact for the period 1972–95 is found to be nearly 1 per cent (annually). The long-run effect is higher but the authors (for technical reasons) cannot calculate these – they suggest, however, that it could be up to six times larger.

mergers and plant rationalisation, and discouraged intra-EU direct investments.

Third, the common prices in the CAP were expressed in a common unit of account (after 1979, in the ECU). Since the devaluation of the French franc and the revaluation of the Deutschmark in 1969, 'green exchange rates'[24] applied to CAP interventions in the case of surpluses or exports to the world market. Though complicated, EU countries swiftly learned to live with this special CAP regime. The weight of this argument for exchange rate stability has never been very great. One reason for this lack of weight is that the economic importance of agriculture in Europe is modest, in contrast to the political sensitivity of the CAP.

The three arguments together led to a strongly held view that the EU (plus perhaps EFTA) needed a 'joint float', if not a single currency. The economic and monetary union (EMU) approach was started with the The Hague summit of 1969, leading to the Werner report of 1970 and a non-binding political Council resolution in early 1971 to enter a 'first stage' towards EMU in 1980 (see, for example, Bakker, 1996). As Chapter 18 will show, this approach was not credible: neither the E nor the M of EMU were properly addressed and the degree of binding was very low.[25] The first EMU approach failed hopelessly.[26]

After this disillusion the emphasis in the EU shifted to exchange rate stability. There were two differences compared with complete exchange rate fixity: a band around the peg (or central rate) and the option of realignment of the exchange rates. Such a form of exchange rate stability looked like a replica of Bretton Woods, European style. Yet, the differences relative to Bretton Woods were important, too. They included the absence of the key currency as the anchor of the system (with the dollar's price in gold as the basis), the worldwide shift to greater exchange rate flexibility, the increasing importance of financial capital mobility (especially from offshore centres in the eurocurrency and eurobond markets) and the absence of a neutral monetary authority like the IMF had been during Bretton Woods.

The EC9 pursued its replica approach in 1972 narrowing the exchange rate band to 2.25 per cent (2 × 1.125 per cent) in the broader band of 4.5 per cent (2 × 2.25 per cent) agreed worldwide. This was called the 'snake in the tunnel': over time the joint float could move like a 'snake' in the wide band. The experiment failed. As noted in section 17.3, EU countries with a greater emphasis on short-run employment gains (than on low inflation) would have both strong incentives and easy options to pursue this course. Over time they accumulated higher inflation which was inconsistent with a joint peg. Short of drastic disinflation obligations, the peg would be tested by the markets and probably prove unsustainable, even with joint interventions based on swaps by the central banks of the snake. And so it happened, indeed, as early as in 1972: the UK and Italy were forced to withdraw within months (free floating). France wavered by adopting an-opting-in-opting-out approach in the mid-1970s in the aftermath of the first oil shock. The upshot was a Deutschmark-zone with Benelux and Denmark, and fairly large swings of exchange rates in the common market which the EU had precisely wished to avoid. Sometimes, the swings were amplified by differential responses of capital in- and outflows to dollar fluctuations, differences which expressed different degrees of confidence (in 'reputation') of European currencies. Italy, France and the UK (as well as Denmark; and Belgium with a dual currency market) tried to stem resulting fluctuations by variations in their capital and exchange controls, thereby moving away from the notion of a true common market.[27]

The European Monetary System (EMS) was based on the lessons from this failure.

17.4.2 The EMS framework

In March 1979 the EMS started functioning. Right from the start the system was characterised by an ambiguity. It was a remarkable agreement at the time but, in substance, the EMS began as a weak form of cooperation. It was remarkable because Germany agreed to automatic intervention obligations and an elaborate system of credit facilities despite its fears (or rather those of the Bundesbank) that it might thereby have to import inflation in times of exchange rate crises. Also the French preparedness to subject realignments to common decision making was noteworthy. 'Symmetry'

[24]Officially 'monetary compensatory amounts' (MCAs), a system of borders taxes and subsidies implicit in the difference between a country's green rate and its nominal exchange rate.

[25]The Marjolin Committee declared EMU 'dead' by 1975.

[26]For a detailed exposition, see Tsoukalis (1977).

[27]Sometimes the DM (and the Swiss franc) were seen as 'safe havens' by hot money flows, forcing these countries to employ temporary measures to stem the inflows by interest-free deposit obligations, as sterilisation became impossible.

was crucial for France: the intervention obligations on two extremes of the EMS band (hence, for both the strong and the weak currency at any such moment) and the 'divergence indicator' (see below) were indispensable for the agreement. Italy used the EMS as leverage for the government to try to break the endless inflation–devaluation spiral with full automatic price compensation (yielding no extra jobs in the end): its entry was less binding with a band of (2 ×) 6 per cent instead of 2.25 per cent. The UK (and Greece as of 1981) did not join the core of the EMS, the exchange rate mechanism. The UK joined the pooling of reserves (for 20 per cent, for each participant) because legally the pooling was hardly binding.[28] Table 17.1 sums up the main properties of the initial EMS and the exchange rate mechanism.

Table 17.1 Characterising the European Monetary System in 1979

Elements	Specification
Goal	'zone of monetary stability'
Exchange rate mechanism (ERM)	• between the central banks (not the governments) • formally outside Community law • central rates in ECU • intervention obligations (symmetric) • realignment subject to common agreement
Credit facilities	• automatic, unlimited swap facilities (up to 45 days) between the central banks (called 'very short term') • short-term facilities up to 9 months between central banks, unconditional (they already existed before) • medium-term credits, conditional upon an applicant's measures to promote 'economic convergence', and subject to an EC Council decision
Reserve pooling	• 20 per cent of national gold and foreign exchange reserves to be deposited for three months, with automatic renewal, into the EMCF • EMCF could issue ECUs against these deposits (under a Council regulation), but only for use among central banks
European Currency Unit (ECU) (for ERM countries only)	• introduced by an EC regulation • ECU is – unit of account – means of payment, only among central banks, but the receiver was obliged only to accept a maximum of ECUs – legal tender for the system
Divergence (for ERM only)	• attempt to introduce 'symmetry' and indicator coordination • fixed at 75 per cent of the margin • the indicator serves as a flashlight; the country with the deviating currency being subject to a 'presumption to act' or otherwise explain in consultations why it did not act

[28]The telling construction was chosen to pool for three months only, with automatic renewal in the absence of a notice to the contrary. The gold and foreign exchange reserves were shifted to the European Monetary Cooperation Fund, but it was a mere bookkeeping operation.

There are many studies of the EMS.[29] For our purposes we focus only, in the present section, on (1) the improvement over the macro section of the Rome Treaty (see section 17.1), and (2) its main weaknesses. Sections 17.4.3 and 17.4.4 provide a short summary of the EMS's performance over fifteen years and an economic assessment, respectively.

The five improvements of the EMS over the Rome Treaty include the common decision to de- or revalue (rather than the exchange rate being of 'common concern'), the elaborate credit facilities (the treaty provides for 'mutual assistance, including credits', so the EMS is best seen as a form of deepening), the strict obligations on both the weakest and the strongest currency to intervene (no such specifications can be found in the treaty), the greater encouragement to coordinate national policies with a view to 'economic convergence' and a few symbolic elements the actual significance of which is unclear (for example, the ECU, pooling of reserves, the European Monetary Cooperation Fund (EMCF)).

But these improvements have to be set against a few serious weaknesses which are evidence of the low degree of binding in the cooperation agreed to. First, the coordination mechanism is not credible, and hence 'convergence' is not *a priori* to be expected. The 'presumption to act' (see Table 17.1) may fail as the divergence flashlight is merely consultative. Only if medium-term loans are provided (for example, to Italy and Greece in the 1980s) can conditionality be fairly strict. Second, although realignment is made more difficult, the very existence of the option reduces credibility of coordination not only in the EMS but also at home (under disinflation) and in currency markets. Low credibility drives adverse expectations and the defence of the peg may require high to very high short-term interest rates and massive interventions. Third, the EMS allows opting in and opting out. The option of leaving the exchange rate mechanism may fatally undermine disinflation policies at home if competitiveness is gradually eroded because disinflation is not radical enough (as with Italy in 1992). The option of entry 'at will' creates problems of credibility, too. Countries may enter with a built-in misalignment and there is no formal decision making that can prevent this (for instance, the UK in 1990). Opting in and opting out together have led to the curious situation that, since the EMS began and until EMU took over in 1999, the EU internal market was never governed by the EMS alone: Greece never entered the exchange rate mechanism, the UK, Spain and Portugal joined late, Italy and the UK left again in 1992, and Italy returned in 1997.

The crux of the matter can already be surmised when observing that 'a zone of monetary stability' remains undefined. Surely, this refers to exchange rate stability but does it also imply the stable purchasing power of the currencies participating?

17.4.3 Performance of the EMS

The development of the EMS has gone through four periods, leading to a gradual transformation of the original system as described in Table 17.1. In Table 17.2 the EMS is characterised for each of the four periods, in terms of four criteria: realignments (that is, 'external stability'), inflation, methods to defend exchange rates, and reform ambitions of participants.[30]

If the EMS performance is assessed in this way, the first period does not score very well. Having inherited fairly high inflation rates after the first oil shock of 1974–75, a second oil shock in the very year that the EMS started (1979) pushed inflation into double figures. Nominal divergence at high levels of inflation was bound to lead to repeated realignments, often with some turbulence in currency markets. The *raison d'être* of holding the EMS together could be little more than preventing a harmful process of competitive depreciations, which had been perceived to be a menace around 1975–76.[31] One is left wondering whether the no-realignment criterion is an appropriate one in a period in which the EMS was tested so severely right after its birth. In this period, rather frequent realignments may be considered as a proper policy response – the point was to decide jointly while building a consensus for a long-run stability strategy. The latter was found in 1982.

The second period is one of discipline and disinflation, even though the US dollar declined sharply after early 1985. This 'success' had its costs, however, as we shall see later. The third period gave the impression for as long as five and a half years that the EMS had become a quasi-monetary union. Convergence was strong at low levels of inflation and with declining interest rates, while exchange rates became frozen. The lira went into the narrow band, and the pound, peseta and escudo all entered the ERM. Prospective EU Members shadowed the ERM fully (Austrian schilling, Finnish mark, Swedish krona). Capital market integration appeared, if anything, to be stabilising,

[29] See, e.g., Giavazzi *et al.* (1989) and Gros & Thygesen (1988, 1998).

[30] Table 17.2 is based on the authoritative account by Gros & Thygesen (1998, chapter 3).

[31] The Duisenberg plan of target zones (1976) was prompted by fears of competitive depreciation among EU Members.

Table 17.2 The changing character of the EMS, 1979–95

Period	Characteristics
March '79 – March '83	• realignment frequent • nominal convergence limited • no reforms • methods (symmetric interventions, credit facilities) barely held EMS together
April '83 – early '87	• realignment less frequent • nominal convergence improved steadily • no EMS reforms, but Single European Act introduced capital market liberalisation • more intra-marginal interventions
early '87 – Sept. '92	• no realignment (until Sept.'92 crisis) • incomplete convergence (in inflation and interest rates) • reforms (Basle–Nyborg and 1st stage EMU) • more currencies in ERM (UK, Spain, Portugal) • exchange controls abolished
Sept. '92 – mid-'96	• several realignments • lira and pound out of ERM • widening of band to (2 ×) 15 per cent • exchange rate stability/convergence restored in '94

Source: Based on Gros & Thygesen, 1998, chapter 3

rather than being incompatible with exchange rate stability, as had long been feared in France, Spain and Italy. The EMS came to be bound up with EMU, having been endorsed and detailed in the Maastricht Treaty. Although the first possible date to decide on monetary union was foreseen for 1996, the entry requirements (for EMU) of no-realignment for at least two years (see Chapter 18) were interpreted by authorities as a credibility test: forgoing realignment was helpful in domestic political economy while, externally, it was hoped to 'earn' the disappearance of the interest rate premium *vis-à-vis* the Deutschmark. In other words, a realignment *after* the EMU negotiations were already under way would destroy credibility, leading to high costs of divergence, both domestically and in capital markets. The currency would risk being relegated to the latecomers in monetary union. As a result, exchange rates actually became locked in, even though nominal convergence remained incomplete and cumulative losses of competitiveness were becoming unsustainable. However, the EMS as a quasi-monetary union proved to be an illusion.

The fourth period is characterised, initially, by crises and soul-searching, and later by a core ERM group playing by somewhat different rules (see Case Study 17.1 on the 1992–93 crisis). A critical weakness of the system (fairly narrow bands, providing one-way-bet options to speculators), was removed by widening the bands to (2 ×) 15 per cent.[32] But this begs the question of whether the EMS still existed: what do exchange rate stability and realignments mean if there is a target zone of 30 per cent allowing very wide fluctuations? However, the goal of the EMS is 'monetary stability' and this is still feasible,

[32]Because the treaty contains a two-year no-devaluation rule, and since 1996 was nearing, a very wide band would keep the options open for all ERM countries.

CASE STUDY 17.1 The 1992–93 EMS crisis

As noted in Table 17.2, the period from early 1987 to mid-1992 was characterised by immovable central rates in the ERM (except a small lira devaluation when Italy entered the narrow band in 1990; however, this devaluation remained in the former, broader band, see Figure 17.7 in section 17.4.4 below) and convergence of inflation at fairly low levels. However, convergence was insufficient. Countries not having been in the core of ERM, or not for a long time (for example, UK, Italy, Spain, Portugal), experienced a higher inflation on average than the core ERM countries (plus Austria which maintained a tight peg to the Deutschmark). Diverging trends in relative costs led to ever widening gaps in cost competitiveness (measured by real effective exchange rates). Whereas the core group had no or minimal current account deficits, the (re-)entrants Spain, UK, Italy had deficits of, respectively, 2.5, 3.8 and 1.3 per cent of GDP. Also, the public sector deficit in Italy (10 per cent of GDP) and high private debt in the UK played a role. Finally, the weakening of the US dollar traditionally puts extra pressure on the weaker European currencies and this also happened in 1992.

The strains in the EMS were, however, accepted by financial markets. After all, inflation convergence had been impressive and countries seemed to prepare for EMU, anticipating the ratification of the Maastricht Treaty. Once the Danes voted 'no' in the early June 1992 referendum, the unanimity required for Maastricht, hence for EMU, seemed forgone. Doubts about the success of the French referendum added to nervousness in currency markets. Suddenly, the market tested the weaker currencies and in September 1992 the lira and the pound left the ERM. The peseta and escudo devalued several times, the Swedish krona gave up its peg to the ECU and the Irish punt devalued 10 per cent early 1993 due to the close links between the Irish and UK economies. The lira, the pound and the krona depreciated very rapidly (around 15–20 per cent). All of this did not calm markets. In the summer of 1993 there were speculative attacks on the Danish krone, and the French and Belgian francs. These attacks were hard to justify by the economic fundamentals as inflation was low (although the Belgian fiscal situation was worrisome) and current accounts looked healthy. In August 1993 the ERM band around the central rate was widened to (2 $\times$) 15 per cent. This led to rapid depreciation of all three currencies against the Deutschmark, but only for a few months. By January 1994 they had all returned to their pre-August 1993 position. The worst EMS crisis ever was over.

indeed, it was exactly what was accomplished as early as 1994. By that time, the French franc, the Belgian franc, the Spanish peseta and the Irish punt had all returned to the 'old' narrow band where the Deutschmark and the Dutch guilder had remained. So convergence and exchange rate stability were still pursued – but without much of a risk of disruptive, one-way speculation. Meanwhile, it should be remembered, the second stage of EMU under the Maastricht Treaty had started and this greatly bolstered the incentives to pursue convergence. In a way, stability in a wide band is a victory because the discipline needed for convergence and exchange rate stability was apparently accepted even without the rigour of formally aligned rates. Almost certainly, such great discipline is sustainable only if the costs of a devaluation are pushed up significantly. The run-up to EMU has had exactly this effect.[33]

If one accepts this interpretation, the 'new' EMS makes more economic sense than the old one. But the crises entailed other features, causing some observers to speak of the collapse of the EMS. Two big EU countries – Italy and the UK – dropped out of the ERM and only Italy returned in 1997, with a view to EMU membership. In 1993–95 their currencies probably undershot temporarily with large depreciations, causing anxiety in business circles throughout the internal market (see Case Study 17.2 on exchange rate movements and the internal market). Also, for a few weeks, exchange controls were reinstalled by Portugal and Spain, exactly the kind of retrogression discussed in section 17.1 and Chapter 9.[34] Nevertheless, the new EMS overcame these severe strains by 1994: once the overvaluations, evident in 1992, of the lira, pound and peseta were corrected, and the Maastricht Treaty was in

[33]See, e.g., de Grauwe (2000, pp. 100–101 and 127) for a graphical illustration of this effect.

[34]See Pelkmans (1982a) and Padoa-Schioppa *et al.* (1987) for the instability of a pure CM without advanced monetary cooperation, if not integration.

force, a deep recession was over and the German unification was no longer throttling German growth, the regained stability appeared firm.

17.4.4 An economic assessment of the EMS

Following the survey by Gros & Thygesen (1998, chapters 4 and 5) an economic assessment of the EMS can be based on six analytical questions. Table 17.3 provides a summary of this assessment.

The overall goal of the EMS, the first query in Table 17.3, has been accomplished, but it is doubtful whether and to what extent the 'internal' stability (lower inflation) can be attributed to the EMS itself (see also the third question). Up to 1983, a soft currency block centred around the French franc.

Exchange (and capital) controls appear not to have been essential for the realisation of exchange rate stability in the EMS (second query in Table 17.3). Exchange controls have not been effective in insulating or reducing domestic interest rates in the long run. But in one other respect they were important, perhaps essential. This aspect refers not to the goal of the EMS but to its survival capacity. Pegged but adjustable exchange rate systems are plagued by the one-way-bet problem which has been greatly magnified by the enormous depth of world capital markets. The one-way bet refers to very low cost of moving out of liquid positions in a weak currency, and the potentially very high return when returning to that currency after devaluation. Unlike uncoordinated, random speculation which tends to be stabilising in the presence of many buyers and sellers, weak 'fundamentals' of the economy or lack of credibility can make currency speculation one-way and self-fulfilling. In the old EMS, once an

Table 17.3 Economic assessment of the EMS

Key word	Research question	Assessment
Stability	Successful as a 'zone of monetary stability'?	Exchange rate variability sharply reduced up to 1992; inflation strongly reduced, but not clearly due to EMS
Exchange controls	Exchange rate stability due to capital controls?	Helpful short-run device before realignments (when bigger than band, i.e. 4.5%) Empirical evidence on insulation very weak up to 1992
Disinflation	EMS reduced the costs of disinflation?	No, because: • empirical evidence for non-EMS not very different • Germany can only lose in this thesis • exchange controls lower credibility
External shocks	EMS, a shock-absorber mechanism?	Yes, because: • intra-EU shocks were symmetric • outside shocks no longer prompted divergent responses
Symmetry	Was the actual functioning of the EMS symmetric?	No, because: • Germany anchor ($n - 1$) • Germany not totally insulated
Growth	Has the EMS caused fiscal policy to be deflationary?	Probably not, because: • theoretically unlikely • empirical evidence at best ambiguous, if not weak

Source: Based on Gros & Thygesen, 1998

exchange rate lost credibility, capital markets would start testing the resolve of the authorities to defend the rate. Without capital controls, there are limits to this defence because the potential of speculative capital flows is so huge that it may easily swamp any offsetting intervention. The limits are less clear with interest rates[35] but a prolonged interest rate defence of a weak currency may be costly in terms of growth and jobs. Capital controls may, at least temporarily, throttle huge speculative attacks.

Why would capital markets react so massively? The reason is a combination of two expectations: the expected percentage change of the rate and a self-fulfilling imitation process of expecting the one-way bet to succeed once markets have signalled serious problems and other market players consider the signals and join (at very low costs). In the EMS, realignments could either stay within the 4.5 per cent band (or the 12 per cent band for Italy, later Spain and Portugal too) or go beyond it. If speculators knew that realignments would always be small (that is, new central rates would remain in the previous band), capital controls would not be necessary because the actual market rate need not change at all after realignment. This is illustrated in the top panel of Figure 17.7 for the DM/lira exchange rate: the change of central rates is never bigger than the (in this case, wide) band and the actual declines of the exchange rate following a realignment are modest.

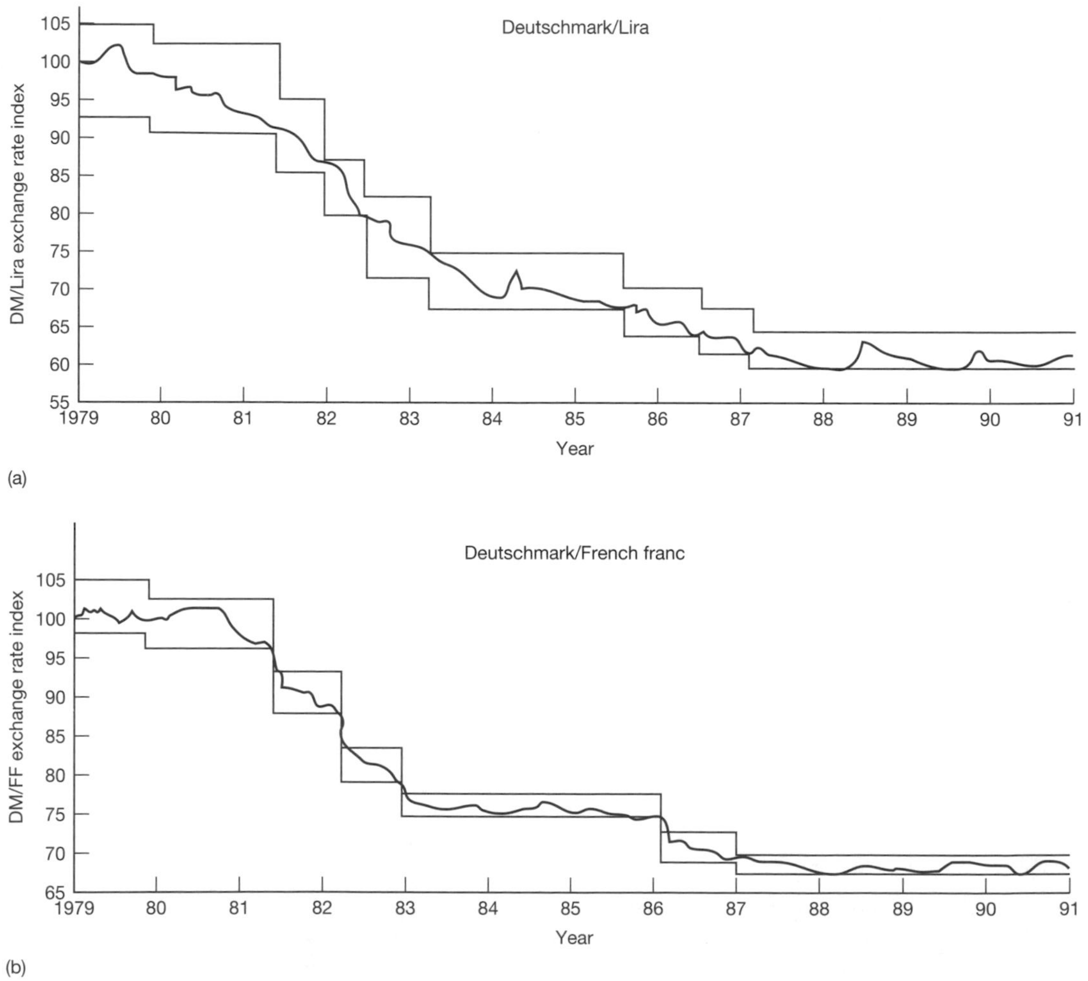

Figure 17.7 Realignment inside and outside the bands

Source: de Grauwe, 2000, p. 113

[35]Sweden, a close 'shadow'-follower of EMS exchange rates up to mid-1992, once allowed the overnight lending rate to go up to 500 per cent.

It has the effect of reducing the profit incentive for speculators. The bottom panel shows the DM/French franc rate, with realignments always delayed until the percentage-jump had exceeded the (here, narrow) band. Gros & Thygesen (1998, p. 129) note that a 4.4 per cent change in the actual rate after realignment implies an annual interest rate of 16 times the invested sum,[36] whereas the costs of the larger transactions are trivial. This extreme imbalance, once expectations are strong, illustrates that the delays practised by France would surely not have been possible without strict controls (say, up to 1984).

But there is another solution to the one-way-bet problem. Since exchange controls were abolished due to EC-1992, this other solution was imperative for the survival of the EMS. It consisted of widening the bands for all ERM currencies – in fact, as wide as 2 × 15 per cent – to heighten the uncertainty for the speculators. This remedy could work only if the other features of the EMS – especially convergence and an attachment to exchange rate stability – remained firmly in place.

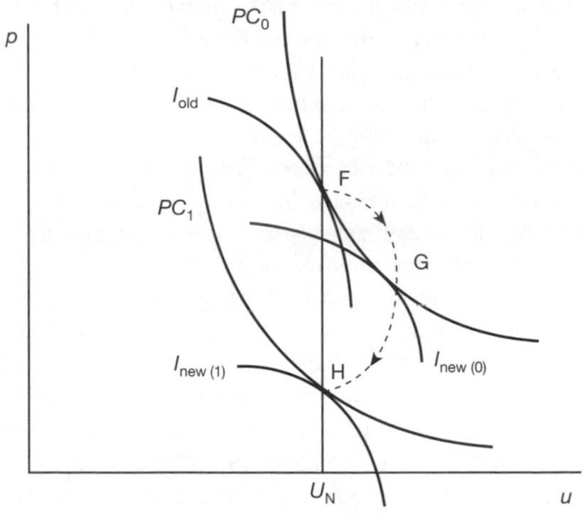

Figure 17.8 Costs and benefits of tying-the-hands disinflation

Source: Adapted from de Grauwe, 2000, p. 51

The third query in Table 17.3 is whether the EMS reduced the costs of disinflation. With inflation running high before the EMS, and even higher during the first few years of its existence, an important question is whether the inevitable (and socially and politically painful) disinflation is less costly within or without the EMS. In section 17.3 we discussed the credibility problem lurking behind this question. The costs of disinflation cannot be lowered before the expectations of markets about the incentives for authorities to engineer a (new) surprise inflation are decisively lowered, too. This requires a change in 'reputation' and that hinges precisely on the proven willingness to accept the unemployment costs. This circular reasoning can be broken in the EMS, by 'tying the hands' of the authorities. Pegging the exchange rate to the Deutschmark would alter expectations if done in the EMS framework which commonly decides about realignments and promotes convergence at low inflation rates. After doing so, markets would begin to accept that the weaker EMS countries were committed to reducing inflation. However, the empirical evidence for EMS, non-EMS EU and non-EU (European) countries does not suggest support for this hypothesis. Others apparently did not need the EMS to do as well, if not better, though that conclusion is sensitive to the period and the base year. One explanation might be that, for countries such as France, and certainly Italy, the EMS had two softening features which the Barro–Gordon model does not contain: a band (for Italy, even a wide band) and exchange controls. In the model's reasoning such soft features undermine 'credibility' and make it difficult to build a 'reputation' in markets. Indeed, one might argue that only when Italy had entered the narrow band (January 1990) and abolished exchange controls, could the hypothesis begin to be tested fully. But, in contrast to France, Italy did not pursue disinflation all the way to eliminate the differential with Germany, and thus cumulated a competitiveness gap which became unsustainable in September 1992.[37]

Figure 17.8 may help to understand the Italian policy dilemma. Short of drastic monetary reform, the tying-the-hands strategy will imply gradual disinflation in Italy, based on flatter indifference curves of the authorities than before. At F the equilibrium is still based on very steep indifference curves (like I_{old}). The announcement that the authorities tie their hand in the EMS is not credible because realignment and exit are both possible and have been used by Italy in the past. Consequently, economic agents in markets want to be convinced, and it will therefore not be possible to 'leave' the higher Phillips curve before the unemployment costs of disinflation are actually incurred, say, at G. This revelation of the authorities' preferences will be the basis for a shift in expectations (flatter indifference curves I_{new}), so that ultimately H can be reached. The problem now is twofold: the costs of this

[36]This 1,600 per cent assumes that moving out of the currency and buying it back later takes one business day. Because of the (possibly self-fulfilling) imitation effect, currency crises have tended to shorten their duration but not as short as one day.

[37]Note that the tying-one's-hands hypothesis also creates a problem for Germany. Although other EMS countries might gain, Germany may only lose, in the sense that the incentives for German authorities to engineer a surprise inflation would increase.

slow process are high, and the result may still not be that the German level of inflation is fully achieved after several years (that is, H in Figure 17.8 is above Z in Figure 17.6). The upshot is that the credibility, slowly earned at high cost, will be under threat by the ever widening gap in competitiveness between core EMS countries and Italy, given fixed exchange rates. Yet, a devaluation would ruin the tying-one's-hands strategy. The only way out before the markets could start their one-way-bet attacks is to forgo the exit and devaluation options, giving up monetary autonomy in all but the name. Failing to do this would ultimately lead to a defeat of the strategy.

The fourth question goes back to the origin of the EMS in the mid-1970s when the 'benign neglect' of the US authorities for the exchange rate allowed wild fluctuations of the US dollar. These external shocks prompted divergent policy responses among EU countries. Since national monetary policies cause externalities, a coordinated approach in Europe would lead to a better shock-absorption. The EMS can be seen as a cooperative solution (step 3 of the subsidiarity test), with relatively little centralisation and soft features, yet with one great advantage facilitating agreement: pegging exchange rates is easy to monitor and pre-empts cheating. It is held that detailed policy coordination (rather than mere exchange rate stability) would be too complex to monitor, or, alternatively, too centralising. In any event the EMS has clearly made the policy responses to outside shocks similar among the Member States, in sharp contrast to the 1970s.

Whether or not the EMS actually functioned symmetrically is the fifth issue. This query should not be confused with the problem of whether the shocks to the EU economy are symmetric (see above). The symmetry of the EMS itself refers to similar rights and obligations for all country participants. Hence, the costs of adjustment would not only fall on weaker currencies. In section 17.4.2 we noted how the 1979 EMS deal attempted to introduce symmetry by the obligation of automatic, reciprocal intervention by the weakest and strongest currency countries when one of them (or both) reached the limits of the band. Also, the divergence indicator expressed the symmetry preference: a flashlight would amount to a 'presumption to act' and this was equally applicable to Germany.

But symmetry is inconsistent with the low degree of centralisation of the EMS. Were monetary policy to be decided jointly, or perhaps if some common rules were to be agreed, symmetry may well be possible in practice. In the EMS, realignments have to be jointly agreed, but the basic agreement contains no rules or guidelines for it. Thus, centralisation goes no further than modest cooperation to keep a pegged but adjustable exchange rate system together. However, in a system of pegged rates, there is a redundancy problem (in the absence of centralisation): with n participating currencies, there are only $n - 1$ independent exchange rates. If the 'anchor' for monetary policy is not jointly decided, the nth country – the 'leader' or hegemon – will determine its own monetary policy and thereby anchor the system. Otherwise, the system would be indeterminate. The anchor typically should be a relatively sizable country with a monetary policy that the others find attractive to hook up to. Germany naturally came to assume this role, given its economic size and strong preference for price stability, both with the authorities and the people.[38]

However, this implies that, for the EMS to enjoy exchange rate stability, it had to be asymmetric. Gros & Thygesen (1998) find that the actual asymmetry was strong (that is, long-run German monetary policy was independent from EMS partners) but insulation was nevertheless incomplete. After German unification (as of 1990), with its soaring fiscal burden and initial inflationary threat, monetary policy was tightened and the costs of this policy mix fell partly on EMS partners having to keep interest rates high despite the post-Gulf War recession. (The reader will remember that this reflects the negative spillover, discussed earlier.) This episode revived the attention for the costs, rather than the benefits, of asymmetry in the EMS.

Finally, has the EMS caused national fiscal policies to be deflationary? The affirmative answer, popular in the mid-1980s, derived from conspicuously low growth in the EMS, together with an old argument about fixed exchange rate systems. In the EMS no single country has an incentive to expand because of positive externalities ('leakages' of the stimulus to trade partners). With such positive externalities the expanding country (such as France in 1982) ends up paying the costs (external deficits, hence realignments) and the benefits are largely given away to trading partners.[39] Without coordination, all would therefore be locked into unnecessarily strict fiscal policies so as to prevent these 'giveaways'. Only coordination of fiscal policies would make it possible to 'internalise' the externalities to a large extent.

In two-country models, with capital mobility, fiscal policy can actually exert beggar-thy-neighbour effects.[40] This is exactly what happened with German unification: a

[38]See de Grauwe (2000, pp. 108–10) for an elegant derivation why self-interested EMS countries would choose Germany as the EMS leader (in the Barro–Gordon framework).

[39]Assuming unemployment in those partner countries too, so that the demand stimulus is welcome.

[40]Going back to Mundell (1968). See, for example, van der Ploeg (1991).

very expansionary fiscal policy, only partly financed by higher taxes, and not accommodated by the Bundesbank, pushed up the German interest rates. Because of the incipient capital outflows, EMS partners had to raise their interest rates, which depressed their demand.

On the empirical side, EMS countries' growth rates recovered quickly after the mid-1980s and the deflationary bias was forgotten. In addition, there is the issue of accumulation of public debt. Once high (and increasing) debt and interest burdens cause a currency to be weak due to low credibility, fiscal consolidation may well have a positive impact on expectations. The cases of Denmark and Ireland in the 1980s tend to support this point (Gros & Thygesen, 1998).

CASE STUDY 17.2 Currency swings and the single market

The relationship between the EMS and the single market (or the EEA, Section see 20.1.3) was important in two ways for member countries: they are open in terms of trade in goods and services (so relative price changes of tradables have important short-run effects on the whole economy, hence, a preference to avoid currency swings) and they trade mostly with EU partners (62 per cent of total goods exports for the EU15 in 1994, ranging from a low of 53 per cent (UK) to a high of 80 per cent (Portugal)). The role of the US dollar had less to do with the EU trade with the USA (7.5 per cent of EU total trade) and more to do with its asset function. Whenever the dollar is considered weak, capital moved out of dollars into the Deutschmark and other strong currencies, thereby forcing other ERM currencies to increase their interest rates so as to avoid exchange rate volatility.

The EMS helped to promote exchange rate stability between, say, 1983 and 1992. The turbulence in 1992–93 (see Case Study 17.1 on the EMS crisis) abruptly ended this. The sharp depreciation of the lira, punt and peseta in a completed single market created irritation in business circles of core ERM countries and, by 1995, to some of their governments. In fact, all three currencies went on depreciating bilaterally against the Deutschmark in 1994 and up to mid-1995: the bilateral depreciation between the third quarter of 1992 (when the EMS crisis started) until mid-1995 amounted to 26 per cent (peseta), 25 per cent (lira), and 20 per cent (pound). (The Swedish krona 30 per cent; the Portuguese escudo 18 per cent.) The 'second round' of depreciation was partly caused by a weakening of the dollar in the spring of 1995 and was largely reversed later in 1995.

Can we speak of competitive depreciation, as a kind of beggar-thy-neighbour policy to boost (national) employment at the costs of core ERM countries? Was business justified in complaining that a single market with such currency swings is a fragmented market, full of (currency) risk for trade, long-run contracts and investment? First, one should not forget that, as shown in the Case Study 17.1 on the EMS crisis, the depreciations were primarily a correction of existing misalignments. Second, using depreciation for employment gains (beyond a correction of misalignments) works, if at all, only for the short-run – see sections 17.2 and 17.3.

Nevertheless, there might have been 'undershooting'. That is, an excessive response in stock-adjustment of assets between weak and strong currencies, not justified by the economic fundamentals. A Commission analysis (*European Economy*, Reports and Studies, 1995, no. 4) find the following:

- The currency turmoil has reduced overall EU growth by one-quarter to one-half of a percentage point (note that Bini-Smaghi & Tristani (1995) find 0.25 per cent to 0.4 per cent for France and Belgium, the same order of magnitude).
- Overall (for example, in terms of the trade balance), depreciations explain only little of changes in trade performance, or do so only for 1993; other factors, such as domestic demand (recession), cost competitiveness, denominations of (for example, Italian) exports in key (rather than own) currencies and incomplete 'pass-through' of swings (by varying profits margins, rather than final price) have all played a role.
- If anything, the swings have impacted on imports more than on exports; thus, it may have become more difficult to penetrate Italian and Spanish markets.
- The car sector clearly suffered from the currency swings between core ERM and hesitant EMS countries, to the (export) advantage of the latter group; for other sectors, the effects are minor or absent.

The reader may now begin to appreciate how theoretical analysis and actual performance of the EMS interact. Both are needed to comprehend the economics of European macroeconomic cooperation. It also lays the groundwork for the debate surrounding the Delors report (next section) and the entire question of monetary integration, as laid out in the Maastricht Treaty (Chapter 18).

17.5 Why beyond the EMS?

When the Single European Act was negotiated (between October and December 1985), there was little interest in increasing the ambitions of macroeconomic cooperation. The urgency felt focused entirely on the internal market. Admittedly, the EMS showed signs of greater convergence and exchange rate stability but only since mid-1983 and with exchange controls still practised by France and Italy. Last but not least, several EU countries (the UK, Greece) did not participate in the ERM, the new members Spain and Portugal were about to double this group, and the lira moved in a wider band. There was an intellectual debate about the strong link between a completed internal market and the nature of the EMS but this had little impact on the negotiators. Padoa-Schioppa (1984)[41] stressed that the combination of free trade, free movement of capital, fixed exchange rates and national monetary autonomy is impossible: at least one of the four has to give way. The significance of the Padoa-Schioppa thesis was not perceived by many. After all, capital controls were still possible, and would remain possible (for exchange rate reasons) under the Single European Act, while the EMS explicitly allowed both realignments and opting out. Germany took the precaution of inserting into the Act a clause stating that a monetary union could not come into being as the 'inevitable' result of a completed internal market, combined with an eventual commitment of EMS members to forgo realignments. As a result, the Single European Act specifies that a monetary union requires a new treaty.[42]

Barely two years later the climate changed radically. After what Table 17.2 calls the second EMS period, the demands for reforms of the EMS grew quickly. Following some minor reforms in the Basle–Nyborg accord among the central banks,[43] agreement was reached to abolish all exchange controls. Because realignments had become less frequent before 1987, and none occurred after January 1987, the Padoa-Schioppa thesis suddenly became relevant. In the course of 1987 the Padoa-Schioppa group produced a far-sighted report, on request of Commission president Delors, on the implications of the completion of the internal market for the three public economic functions of the EU: efficiency, equity and stabilisation (Padoa-Schioppa *et al.,* 1987). The changing economic nature of the EMS also prompted several national memoranda in early 1988 on further moves beyond the EMS, if not to EMU. The Hannover European Council meeting (June 1988) appointed the Delors Committee, including all central bank governors of EU countries and some independent experts. When the Delors report (Delors *et al.,* 1989) was published, the move 'beyond the (old) EMS' had reached the very top of the agenda.

Can we utilise the analysis in section 17.4.3 to understand the fundamentals behind this higher ambition of macroeconomic cooperation? To a considerable extent we can. There was wide agreement[44] that exchange stability was desirable, certainly with a single market, and this required strong policy commitments. Given this premise of exchange rate stability, some of the issues in Table 17.3 help us to comprehend the pressures for moving beyond the old EMS.

The most prominent reason was, no doubt, the question of symmetry.[45] It was noted that symmetry is inconsistent with the very low degrees of binding and centralisation of the old EMS. A desire for symmetry must imply a far more centralising mechanism to 'anchor' monetary policy. Both Italy and France insisted on a search for such a new EMS, if not outright monetary union following their sacrifice of exchange controls.

There were subsidiary reasons to enhance coordination in the EMS, such as the coordinated response to external shocks and the lingering fear that a lack of coordination of national fiscal policies might unduly throttle growth in a Europe with such a high jobless rate.

[41]Up to 1984, he was head of DG Economic and Financial Affairs, European Commission.

[42]Hence, an Intergovernmental Conference under Art. 236 EEC, now transferred to the EU treaty as Art. 48 EU. Germany insisted on the clause for constitutional reasons.

[43]Including systematic intra-marginal interventions. For details, see Gros & Thygesen (1998).

[44]Except some UK-based economists, few seemed to consider a completed internal market with flexible (but stable) exchange rates.

[45]See Gros & Thygesen (1998) for the run-up to the Delors report.

For Italy, 'tying the hands' of the authorities was crucial. A more ambitious EMS, with preferably no realignments and without exchange controls, would finally enable Italy further to reduce the costs of disinflation. If successful it could then move into the narrow band (which it did early in 1990) to strengthen credibility further. Spain also found this argument attractive.

By 1988 the first two issues of Table 17.3 had been fairly well resolved. With convergence so firmly under way (inflation differentials were only a few per cent, ignoring Greece), the fear about giving up exchange controls reduced swiftly. It was observed that neither the UK (in 1979) nor Denmark (in 1983) had suffered from any noticeable disturbance after the removal of exchange controls.

All this would imply that, from Padoa-Schioppa's quartet, the one element to give way would be national monetary autonomy. The upshot was a two-track development in the EU: on the one hand, the strengthening and enlargement of the EMS, with *de facto* exchange rate rigidity; on the other hand, the preparation, negotiations and ratification of EMU, as comprised in the Maastricht Treaty. Initially parallel tracks, in the early 1990s they became directly linked. The EMU route chosen indeed amounted to a gradually more stringent EMS, over three stages, until it was transformed into a fully fledged EMU.

17.6 Summary

Once the internal market *acquis* excludes exchange and capital controls, national macroeconomic policy autonomy is drastically curtailed. Given the preference for exchange rate stability among the very open economies of the EU Member States, trading predominantly with each other (both in goods and services), the question arises whether more binding cooperation in, or even centralisation of, macroeconomic policies would not be preferable.

Macroeconomic policy cooperation in the Rome Treaty was weak and not credible. The corollary was a very weak and conditional commitment to accomplish free movement in financial services and financial capital. Safeguard clauses permitted any Member State to reintroduce exchange controls for balance of payments reasons. New approaches to open macroeconomics and costly experiences with adjustable pegs and flexible exchange rates eventually laid the basis for a more cooperative approach in the EMS, and its gradually greater emphasis on convergence.

In an open economy asset markets model of macroeconomic policy in the presence of capital mobility, the analysis suggests that national fiscal policy is effective under both fixed and flexible exchange rates. It is most effective when the central bank targets the interest rate. High capital mobility increases its effectiveness under fixed exchange rates, but reduces it under flexible exchange rates. However, in two country models, a non-cooperative approach may cause beggar-thy-neighbour effects.

In the 1970s and early 1980s, stagflation occurred. Stuck with relatively high inflation, high unemployment and high debt levels, the key issue became: how to return to low inflation and low debt, under stable exchange rates, and with adjustment costs (unemployment) as small as possible? It can be shown that the capacity to pursue effective macro policies in this respect is a function of the credibility of the authorisation in that country. For erstwhile 'autonomous' countries, the costs of disinflation may be very high. In the Barro–Gordon model it is shown how a credible and lasting sacrifice of autonomy may well be the least-cost solution in terms of adjustment cost, but this may be politically difficult. Doing it jointly might help. The combination of binding cooperation (in an EU system) and a 'tying-one's-hands' strategy *vis-à-vis* a credible and stable monetary hegemony is the best option.

The EMS has been a partial answer to this problem. The original system introduced symmetry with respect to exchange rate (and intervention) obligations among the participants of the ERM (exchange rate mechanism). Also, realignments were decided jointly. However, the degree of binding was low because devaluations and exit remained policy options. The character of the EMS altered over time. By the mid-1990s, the acceptance of nominal convergence was much greater and a core group of permanent ERM participants had greatly increased credibility. Inflation in this group has converged to low levels. Improved convergence was, of course, also due to the requirements (of the Maastricht Treaty) for entry into EMU. Only a few years earlier, however, a major EMS crisis occurred (in 1992–93, see Case Study 17.1). Interestingly, it has hardly affected the core ERM group although the bands around the

Summary *continued*

central rates had to be widened to (2 ×) 15 per cent. After the crisis, the core-ERM currencies remained in or quickly returned to the 'old' band.

An extensive economic assessment of the EMS is provided, based on six questions. The conclusions are: (1) the EMS was indeed successful for exchange rate stabilisation, for the core; (2) capital controls were helpful for the survival capacity of the early EMS (against the one-way bet); (3) the EMS did not noticeably reduce the costs of disinflation; (4) the EMS (and the completion of the single market) made intra-EU shocks more symmetric and responses to outside shocks less divergent; (5) symmetry in obligations did not work – asymmetry was actually essential to the working of the EMS ($n - 1$ problem); (6) evidence that the EMS has caused fiscal policy to be deflationary is ambiguous, if not weak. Case Study 17.1 about the impact of the 1992–93 crisis on the functioning of the single market shows that the short-run effects were negative, though minor overall; however, some sectors (for example, cars) have been affected disproportionately. Many other determinants of trade performance (for example, recession, cost-competitiveness, margins, denomination of contracts in other currencies) dampened or fully compensated the effects after a short while.

CHAPTER 18

Economic and Monetary Union

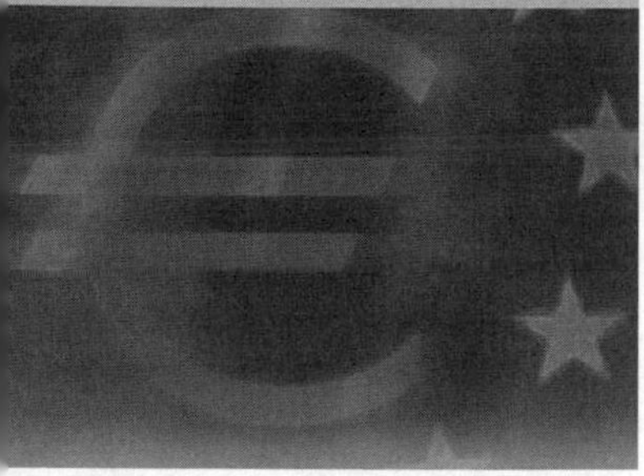

Topics covered

18.1 Economic union

18.2 Costs and benefits of monetary union

18.3 Towards monetary union

18.4 What kind of monetary union?

18.5 Monetary and fiscal policies in the eurozone

18.6 External aspects of the euro

18.7 Summary

In the aftermath of the Delors report (1989) it was decided to start the first stage of EMU in July 1990. As defined, the first stage did not require treaty amendment and, therefore, could precede the negotiations for the Maastricht Treaty. On the face of it, the first stage seemed to add little to the (new) EMS, especially if seen in combination with EC-1992, the cohesion decisions of early 1988 (doubling the Structural Funds) and the widely shared conviction that fiscal consolidation was anyway overdue for several EU Member States. What was different, however, was the intention to avoid a multi-speed EU: all EU currencies were to enter the narrow-band ERM and the use of the ECU would be extended.

The Maastricht Treaty, concluded in December 1991, establishes a firm route to EMU and provides a solid monetary constitution for the third and irreversible stage of EMU. It is likely that political reasons to go for EMU have been decisive. A consensus emerged that the best response to German unification and the opening up of central Europe was to tie Germany even more firmly into the Community. The present chapter discusses only the economic aspects of EMU, however.

Section 18.1 deals with the E of EMU, the economic union. Two concepts are set out, one with and one without monetary union. The system of (soft) economic policy coordination, as it has emerged in the economic union since, say, 1997 is spelled out. A lengthy section 18.2 analyses the benefits and costs of monetary union. The costs are to be minimised and the theory of optimum currency areas should help in the design and membership of a monetary union in order to accomplish that. The benefits are split into (various) lower transaction costs and strategic benefits; in the EU especially the latter are appreciable.

The road to monetary union *à la* Maastricht is discussed in section 18.3. A clear distinction should be made between the characteristics of EMU itself, once the third stage had begun, and the transition towards that stage. Most attention has been focused on the latter, due to criticism of the nominal convergence criteria as entry requirements, and the suspected costs and instability of the transition period. In the final analysis, the quality of the ultimate EMU remains the overriding issue.

Section 18.4 discusses the main characteristics of EU's monetary union: centralisation of monetary policy, and of exchange rate policy (if any), independence of the ECB and, most important, price stability above all. Section 18.5 goes into the method of monetary and fiscal policies in euroland, followed by a short evaluation of ECB policy and the (now revised) Stability and Growth Pact. The chapter ends with the external aspects of the euro, especially its international roles and the option of an exchange rate policy. Case studies on the neglect of economic union in the first EMU attempt (1971), on payment systems in euroland and the EU, and on how the euro was introduced, are included.

18.1 Economic union

Ever since Community leaders decided, in The Hague in 1969, to pursue an economic and monetary union, the notion of 'economic union' has been around officially in the EU. In very general terms, the connection between the two terms 'economic union' and 'monetary union' is obvious: a monetary union implies the prior existence of a fairly advanced degree of economic integration in the relevant group of countries. In the Balassa stages of Table 1.1, economic union might not be so clearly defined but in any event it does refer to considerable depth in economic integration. In this general sense, the term 'EMU' was meant to express that monetary integration was not a purely monetary affair for policy makers: in order to make economic sense, countries should already have developed extensive economic intercourse and, preferably, in a framework with sufficient binding so that predictability and commitment could underpin a monetary union. Few, if any, economists would disagree with these general statements. Nevertheless, there is something curious about the 'economic union'. Neither economic theory nor the actual practice of the EU have accomplished much clarification of the concept.[1] What this means is that, nowadays, the EC treaty contains articles on 'economic union' although it is far from clear what exactly is referred to. EU countries are in the 'economic union' but the value-added of that reference is unclear. And, not least, the monetary union depends or relies or is built on 'economic union' but what the relation between the two is, or should be, remains an open question. This section addresses the relation between the E and the M of EMU and attempts to demonstrate that, even if one cannot establish a precise connection between the two concepts, it is flawed and costly to disconnect the two altogether. We shall also clarify that the two concepts lead to two distinct forms of economic coordination in 'EMU'. Among economists, (very) different definitions can be found in the literature going back to 1949 (see Pelkmans, 1991, annex 2). In the following it is submitted that it is useful to reduce the conceptual problem to only two distinct forms.

18.1.1 What is economic union?

In Figures 18.1 and 18.2 two operational concepts of economic union are illustrated. The two figures take as their starting point that economic union as a concept requires deep integration first. Labelling something an 'economic union' risks becoming a semantic exercise if it is applied to integration stages as low as the CU, or the pre-EC-1992 situation which we denoted as a CU-plus. Yet, this was precisely the ill-considered way of defining stage 1 of EMU in the Council resolution of 1971 (see Case Study 18.1 on the first EMU plans of the 1970s). The following is based on a single market idea for both concepts. The first concept is a 'stand-alone' one; the second is explicitly serving the good functioning of monetary union.

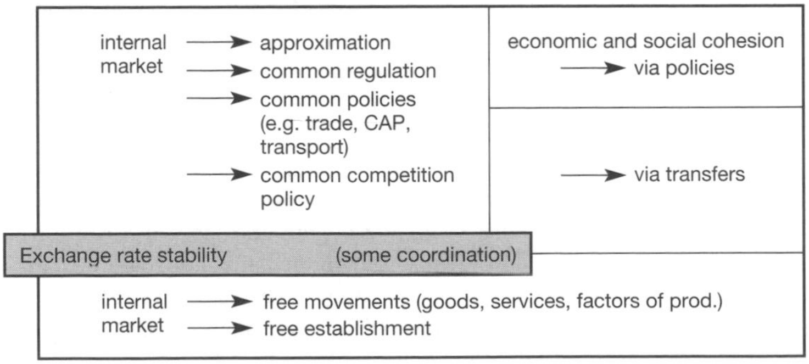

Figure 18.1 The basic concept of economic union

[1]Unlike Canada, for example, where the 'Canadian economic union' was extensively studied and discussed in the 1980s when Quebec considered political independence while remaining in the 'economic union'. For details, see, e.g., Courchene (1986, chapter 9) and Pelkmans & Vanheukelen (1988).

monetary union	→ irrevocable exchange rates / euro → price stability → European Central Bank → entry conditions → policy obligations/Growth and Stability Pact
EMU	→ fiscal conditionalities
economic union	as figure 18.1, with appropriate adjustment capacity, → Member States level (structural change/mobilities) → social partners/flexibilities → (possible) stabilisers (MS/EU levels) → regulatory reform at EU and MS levels

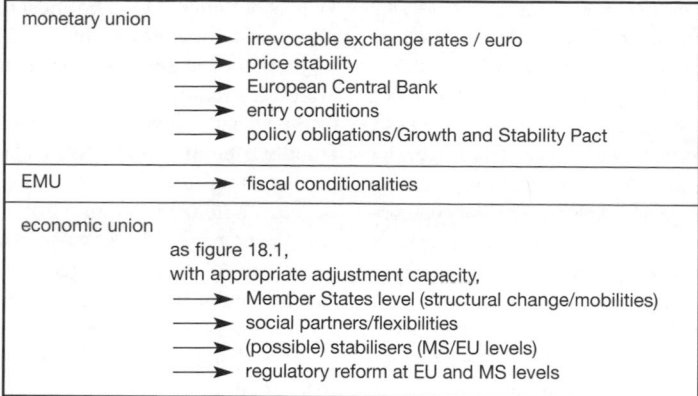

Figure 18.2 Economic union serving monetary union

The first concept defines economic union as a completed internal market, including all positive integration needed to make this internal market function properly (see also section 1.5). The present book shows that this is an ambitious concept. Such an economic union does not require a monetary union; what it needs to function properly is *exchange rate stability*. The practical problem in the EMS, aimed precisely to provide such stability, proved to be that the removal of capital controls (an internal market requirement) presented an actual or potential threat to exchange rate stability. This ultimately leads to an all-or-nothing choice: if the internal market is sacrosanct (so controls cannot be reintroduced), one returns either to flexible exchange rates or to a form of monetary union. If flexible rates are not accompanied by coordination of macroeconomic policies, very wide swings may occur, which – once again – may add to the pressure to fall back to safeguard restrictions in the internal market.[2] But ambitious and credible coordination is equally required if, under pegged exchange rates, one wished to avoid major realignments or currency crises. So, this concept in Figure 18.1 does not require monetary union but there is no denying that fairly ambitious forms of macroeconomic coordination will be required to guarantee exchange rate stability.

Figure 18.1 includes negative integration (free movements and free establishment), the four elements of positive integration of the single market (approximation, joint regulation, common policies and competition policy) and cohesion. As noted in Chapter 16, the single market itself has proved to be a permanent (though slow) source of cohesion: besides, transfers and policies can strengthen the process. Including cohesion in the notion of economic union can be justified in two ways. One is political. Economic union is supposed to serve the aims of the treaty, and 'economic cohesion' is one of the aims. The other is economic. It is hoped that poor regions, in moving resources out of low-productivity agriculture and/or traditional industrial sectors, not only raise their growth rates but also diversify into a range of industries and services. If they do, this would structurally lower adjustment costs in the Union.

The second concept concentrates on the macroeconomic stabilisation rather than the efficiency function of the EU level of government. Again, it assumes market integration to be in place to an appreciable extent. The problem then is what *economic,* as distinct from strictly monetary, integration it takes for the monetary union to function properly. An economic union *needed for monetary union to function properly* would have to live up to two requirements:

1 an appropriate adjustment capacity of the union's economy;
2 fiscal policy coordination with such a degree of binding that the price stability of the monetary union cannot be endangered.

The first requirement is the subject of optimum currency area theory, dealt with in section 18.2. The second requirement is controversial because it substitutes policy coordination for the discipline of capital markets. A high degree of binding is seen as desirable by those who believe that capital markets are (too) imperfect in disciplining deficit-prone governments, which

[2]Eichengreen (1993, p. 1331) concludes that in 'this sense and this sense alone, monetary unification is a logical economic corollary of . . . market integration'. See Pelkmans (1982a) for an early exposition of this point.

can no longer rely on monetary financing. Figure 18.2 has drawn the fiscal conditionalities in an intermediate EMU layer because they can be regarded as 'economic' (as the treaty officially does in Article 104 EC) or as a crucial part of monetary union. In some basic sense, fiscal policy is not monetary because it is largely or wholly tax based or supplemented by borrowing in capital markets. The decisions are not made by monetary authorities. However, the only purpose of the fiscal constraints of Member States is the *proper functioning of the monetary union*, as will be set out later. The bottom part of Figure 18.2 is a more demanding economic union in terms of adjustment and flexibilities. In fact, what is specified are policy responses to the great need to keep the costs of monetary union as low as possible. It includes flexibilities in the labour market and appropriate stabilisers. However, for the proper functioning of monetary union it is important to promote jointly the strategies at Member States level to enhance the working of markets (for example, facilitating structural change, regulatory reform).

In well-established states, which the EU is not (and might never become), the idea of economic union can be pushed further than in Figure 18.2, as for instance in Canada. Thus, all three public economic functions are (also) exercised at the Canadian union level: efficiency, equity and macroeconomic stabilisation. This would surely not fit the EU of today as the present book has shown with the help of subsidiarity tests in a number of chapters.[3] Nevertheless, the Union's reticence to bring politics squarely into EMU is a mixed blessing. The reason is the independence of the European Central Bank (ECB). Germany, in particular, holds the view that a society's acceptance of ECB independence (and given a strict constitutional obligation to pursue price stability) hinges on a minimum Union capacity to define the broad guidelines of the economic order as well as to pursue equity goals and facilitate social adjustment. This view is not only held in political circles but also explicitly argued, for example, by former president Tietmeyer of the Bundesbank. 'For, even if it were possible to establish a monetary union in Europe in the second half of this decade, it would remain fragile without a more ambitious political framework' (Tietmeyer, 1994, p. 457 [author's translation]). It would have to express an irrevocable 'solidarity community' and should, where competent, be able to act swiftly and with legitimacy.

Figure 18.2 does not live up to that. The 'proper functioning of the monetary union', supposedly served by the economic union as depicted in Figure 18.2, assumes that the socio-political issues of smooth adjustment are dealt with at the national level.

18.1.2 Policy coordination in the economic union

Returning to Figure 18.2, it is as well to realise that 'euroland' – the twelve countries with the euro – fully applies this concept of economic union. Note that the Member States which have not entered euroland (in 2005, the new Member States and the UK, Sweden and Denmark) are not 'in' Figure 18.1, but in an incomplete version of Figure 18.2: without fiscal conditionalities,[4] but otherwise with everything of the economic union which serves the euro. Since Maastricht, the treaty is written for an EU-wide monetary union: the 'outs' have a 'derogation'; *all* EU countries have an obligation to pursue price stability, sound public finance and monetary conditions (see Figure 2.3, principles); and *all* Member States participate in treaty-based economic coordination. There is ample coordination in EMU. A good deal of this activity could be classified as being part of the economic union (*à la* Figure 18.2) for the EU25. However, the treaty itself is mainly procedural about it. Article 99(1) EC says that 'Member

[3]Sometimes, more ambitious blends of politics and economics are connected to 'economic union' in Europe. The reader is warned that the debate has been, and often still is, hopelessly undisciplined. All kind of labels may enter the debate. A few examples may illustrate the nature of the issues. German unification in 1990, by definition a political union of an ambitious kind, was widely perceived as the combination of an EMU with a social union and a tax union. The immediate introduction of a social union was a political decision to pre-empt migration and to compensate for the harsh and sudden adjustment expected to result from exposure to West German competition, at a high exchange rate for the old Ostmark. Of course, German unification is a unique case. In the European debate, loose references to social and fiscal elements of 'political union' are frequently made. In the negotiations of the Maastricht Treaty there was, at first, a two-track approach: one for EMU and one for 'political union'. A plethora of proposals reached the negotiators dealing with 'political union', which, in effect, amounted to elements of a richer economic union. The economic union negotiated in the 'monetary' track was strictly limited to Figure 18.2. Besides the fiscal conditionalities, little was specified about the lower panel, other than coordination procedures. The substance was to be filled in over time. When the two-track approach was finally abandoned, the 'political union' idea disappeared – it is not to be found in the Maastricht Treaty and has not been discussed in Amsterdam. An isolated feature of it did enter the treaty in Amsterdam: the employment strategy (see Chapter 16).

[4]Even this is not fully correct. Denmark (and Greece until its entry into euroland) has a convergence report (every two years), which includes fiscal conditions.

CASE STUDY 18.1 Economic union in 1971: a neglected stepchild?

The first attempt to move towards economic and monetary union in the EU was based on the Werner report (Werner *et al.* 1970) and a Council resolution in March 1971. There would be three stages (seemingly, as in the Maastricht Treaty), but little else of the long road was decided upfront. The final date (1980) was set without any clarity about the institutional requirements, the exact definition of the monetary union and/or the 'economic union' underlying it. Already, the Werner report, which was much clearer about what it would take to have a monetary union, showed deep political rifts if one reads the sharp differences between the interim and the final report. Whereas the monetary union decision in the 1990s was kept as apolitical as possible (but, remember, section 18.1.1 above speaks about that being a 'mixed blessing'), and what elements inevitably were a top political decision were unanimously shared by the EU12, the resolution of March 1971 was entirely politicised (see Tsoukalis, 1977) between Gaullists and other conservatists refusing to specify the end goal and its far-reaching institutional requirements (such as centralisation of monetary policy) and 'integrationists' who insisted on clarity right from the first step. Another division popped up between 'monetarists' (not those building on the 'quantity theory of money', but experts believing that monetary union would force the pace of economic integration, because obviously both would be needed) and 'economists' insisting that monetary union be built on economic union, and 'crown' it, as it were. What is clear from hindsight is that, had the first monetary union not been pre-empted by a total lack of political will and of proper understanding (Marjolin *et al.* 1975), and been built faithfully on the March 1971 resolution, it might well have turned into a disaster. Why? Because the resolution does not lay a serious and consistent basis for 'economic union', even if that is exactly what was attempted, in trying to avoid the bickering about the final stage. The emphasis was on new 'coordination' mechanisms for convergence (but with weak powers and a surprising confidence in quantitative recommendations), a range of EU policies which are flanking issues for EMU (such as energy policy, industrial policy), indirect tax harmonisation (showing how shallow even goods market integration was in those days) and eventual liberalisation of financial capital (but this in an era when exchange controls were heavily used to protect currencies; see Chapter 9). Thus, the implicit economic union, as far as the resolution can be called that, did not explicitly mention services market integration at all, was excessively vague on factor market integration and did not impose strict and detailed obligations to achieve a fully fledged internal market. Finally, nowhere was there any mention of QMV, without which the accomplishment of an internal market is impossible, and certainly in a timespan of less than ten years.

States shall regard their economic policies as a matter of common concern and shall coordinate them'. In the treaty itself, phrases such as 'multilateral surveillance', 'closer coordination', 'sustained convergence of economic performance of the Member States' and 'broad guidelines' (all in Article 99 EC) are used without much clarity about substance and complementarity. In this case, the open formulation may well have been a wise decision for two reasons. First, the Member States, sensitive to the loss of ever more instruments of economic policy, opted for a formulation recognising the importance of coordination without a transfer of competences. Coordination may thus mean exchange of information, peer pressure (between ministers) about 'best practice', or recommendations. Do these procedures have teeth? Here, one sees the advantage of Figure 18.2: it depends where, in Figure 18.2, the 'coordination' is located. Fiscal coordination in euroland does have teeth and has been separately organised in the Stability and Growth Pact. It is discussed in section 18.5.2. Coordination failures in the economic union, as depicted in the bottom half of Figure 18.2, are not expected to undermine, directly, the stability of prices or of the euro, so that the degree of binding has remained low. It is discussed in the present section. Article 99(4) goes furthest in making (presumably confidential) recommendations to a Member State public if national economic policies are not consistent with the 'broad guidelines' or if 'they risk jeopardising the proper functioning of economic and monetary union'.[5]

[5]In case of enduring conflict jeopardising EMU, the Member State will also violate Art. 98 EC ('Member States shall conduct their economic policies . . . in the context of the broad guidelines') and this might mean they are convicted by the EC Court, given Art. 98's strong language.

Second, in Maastricht there was great uncertainty about economic policy coordination–in sharp contrast to the meticulous preparation of the monetary union. As noted, the literature about economic union was not particularly helpful to negotiators. The upshot of the open formulation and too little theoretical guidance has been a serious confusion up to today. After a quick proliferation of all kinds of processes and an ever heavier 'coordination' agenda,[6] the regime was consolidated in 2005 with the re-launch of the so-called Lisbon process. Figure 18.3 brings all economic coordination, also the fiscal one, into a single overview.

As Figure 18.3 indicates, there are three consolidated agendas for economic coordination: a strict one for fiscal policy of countries in euroland (the Stability and Growth Pact, see section 18.5.2), and two loose ones for all EU Member States on employment policy and on structural reforms. In addition, there is a macroeconomic dialogue of a triangular kind among the Council, the social partners at EU level and the ECB. To the extent that social partners work at EU level, and not nationally (the overwhelming part), one might see a rationale for this macro dialogue. However, it is nonetheless hard to discern value-added for the players because wage setting is not done at EU level and it is precisely wage setters and monetary policy makers who must be mutually well informed (in order to pre-empt mistakes on either side). The Lisbon process has inherited and widely applied an allegedly new method of coordination: the 'open method of coordination'. In fact, it is little more than an OECD-plus approach in a range of areas of (especially, 'active') labour market policies, social policies in the framework of the welfare state (for example, to reduce 'social exclusion'), pensions and their reform, aspects of education and health polices, and so forth. The 'plus' consists of stronger incentives to learn and adopt 'better' models, via benchmarking, peer review, setting targets and common objectives (which the OECD would not easily do) and harsh implementation reports which do not shy away from 'naming and shaming' those not getting closer to the indicators/objectives, while 'faming' those who do. The Achilles heel of this process is its place in the domestic politics of every

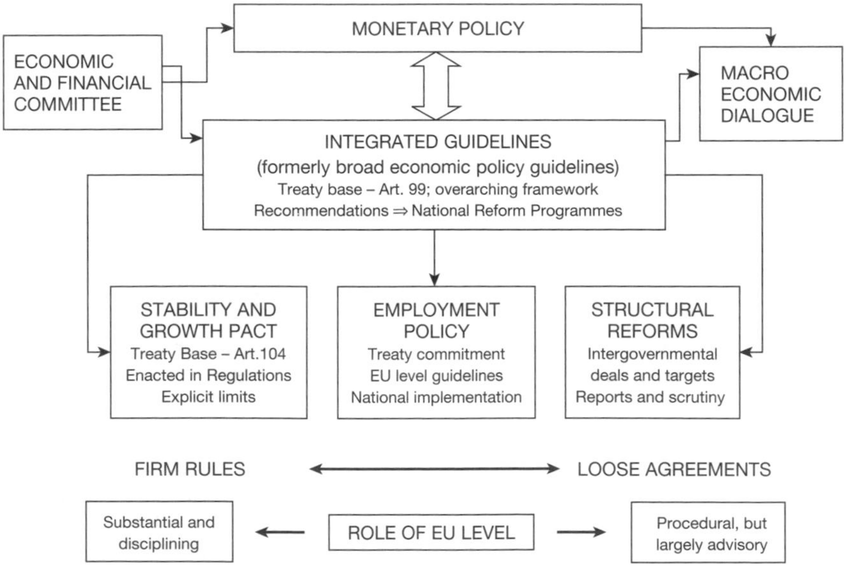

Figure 18.3 Economic coordination in the wider EMU

Source: Begg, 2005. Reproduced by courtesy of Iain Begg

[6]The second edition, pp. 354–5, describes the Cologne, Cardiff and Luxembourg processes, meanwhile joined by the Lisbon process and its 'relaunch' in the spring of 2005. The present book will not deal with history, nor with the details of the Lisbon process. See, e.g., Sapir *et al.* (2003), Pelkmans & Casey (2004) and the Kok *et al.* (2004) report on Lisbon for critical assessments. There is a sizable economic and political economy literature on EU (soft) coordination. See, e.g., Begg (2005), Ederveen *et al.* (2005), Hishow (2005) and *CESifo Forum*, Vol. 6, 2, Summer 2005. Most economists are very critical.

Member State. Because Lisbon is about national, not EU, competences, there is no way one can 'infuse' domestic politics with exactly the same indicators and objectives, tied to political consequences. Put differently, every Member State – once having learned 'better' policies from other EU countries – is entirely capable of achieving the reforms on its own. If Lisbon were truly rooted in domestic politics, there might be some delays but no fundamental doubts about the process. If Lisbon is merely a policy makers' 'carrousel', however, national political leaders and their cabinets will just see ideas as one of many and assume their own socio-political course. This is largely what happened. The 'integrated guidelines' (in Article 99 EC called the 'broad guidelines on the economic policies of the Member States') first became a labyrinth of detailed recommendations without any effect in domestic politics. In 2005 they became far more sober and streamlined, but the ones not directed to individual Member States, but to the EU at large, look more like a manifesto (one nobody is against, presumably) than operational policy guidelines. It reflects the real coordination problem of the economic union: in many EU countries, the resistence against reforms is considerable and pushing them through is electorally hazardous – no Lisbon can change that. These blockages slow down the otherwise effective mechanism of 'policy competition' between the Member States and lead to a worrisome result: too little reform not only with Lisbon but also without. Pisani-Ferry (2005) has argued that the top linkage in Figure 18.3 might help. The ECB could lubricate the system once convincing evidence of deep labour market, and possibly services markets, reforms becomes apparent. Pisani-Ferry holds that one key reason for the reform reticence in the Union is the fear of adjustment or adverse prospects. The ECB, at the same time, insists on reforms as an essential improvement of the adjustment in the eurozone (remember the text explaining Figure 18.2). If each waits for the other to move decisively, a reform paralysis might plague Europe, a true coordination failure. Despite all the criticism, the EU cannot do without a growth-oriented coordination *à la* Lisbon. Mutual economic interdependence and indeed the good functioning of the economic union amount to a strong common interest in rendering the Union economically more dynamic. In addition, it will also help the better functioning of the monetary union, as we shall see shortly.

18.2 The costs and benefits of monetary union

When the EU began to consider the idea of a monetary union, decades ago, the obvious query was why and how one would do this. It goes without saying that the 'why' question must first be addressed. The 'how' question is dealt with in sections 18.3 and 18.4. In economics, the 'why monetary union' question boils down to the costs and benefits of a single currency.

18.2.1 The theory of optimum currency areas

What is the economically optimal size of a currency area? Is it that of a small EU country, a large one, a subset of the EU, or the EU as a whole? The basic answer is: that area for which the cost of giving up flexible exchange rates or the realignment option is lower than the benefits of a single currency. In the theory of optimum currency areas the focus has traditionally been on the costs, as the benefits of having a joint currency – even for the whole world – were taken for granted. Some attention is given here to both the theoretical and the empirical benefits.

Currency unification forces us to reflect on the economic justification of having exchange rates in the first place. This is an old issue in economics.[7] The main argument remains the ease, hence the low costs, of adjustment to a shock. Just as it is far easier to adjust to a centrally decided summertime for daylight saving, with all the benefits this implies, the adjustment to a shock to a (national) economy is easy to achieve through a change in the nominal exchange rate. Or is it really?

Analysing the issue for a group of integrating countries like in the EU requires us to address four questions:

1 What are the nature and the sources of such shocks?
2 If national exchange rate autonomy is sacrificed, what alternative adjustments need to take place in the market?
3 If market adjustment is sluggish, what national or EU policies might bring about adjustment?
4 Also, in the light of the answer to question 3, is the irrevocable fixing of exchange rates really a sacrifice for short-run macroeconomic stabilisation, in particular in Europe?

[7]The classic source is Friedman (1953).

The following goes step by step through these questions in order to develop a case for or against monetary integration in the Union. If the costs of giving up a national exchange rate turn out to be low, the case for a currency union is supposed to have been made.

The seminal contribution on optimal currency areas by Mundell (1961) introduced an exogenous downward shift in the demand schedule for the goods exported in one of two regions together making up a currency area. This sudden change is called an asymmmetric shock, in that it applies solely to the first region, not to the second one in the currency area. In order to establish external equilibrium (external to the first region), a real depreciation is required. Mundell suggests that the region would be best off if it were to have its own currency and devalue. The author arrives at this finding because he suspects other adjustment mechanisms do not work, that is, the first region will not lower its wages in response to unemployment, and workers will not migrate to the second region. However, in the latter region, (wage) inflation will then be inevitable as its goods are more in demand. If inflation is not wanted, only a real appreciation via separate currencies would solve the problem. This has led to a vast literature about the nature and sources of such shocks. To begin with, the shock ought to be specific to the (EU) country at stake. If the shock were symmetric to all EU countries, of course, intra-EU realignments would not be called for.

Why would shocks be nationally differentiated? The instructive example by Mundell is so extreme as to be irrelevant in a context of highly developed trade with numerous very different products.[8] Furthermore, the bulk of goods trade (in Europe) is intra-industry trade, hence two-way. There is little reason to suppose that numerous microeconomic demand shifts (with given exchange rates, and *ceteris paribus*) would not roughly cancel out. However, this conclusion need not follow if, in the long run, permanently fixed exchange rates would cause spatial concentration of certain industries to increase.

Yet the main policy issue is undoubtedly a shock of domestic origin, such as a national wage explosion. The question here is whether the workers, pushing for wage increases far above productivity growth, do not realise the consequences once exchange rates are fixed. If the fixity is permanent, the reduction in competitiveness is bound to lead to unemployment, supposedly forcing a (slow?) reduction in real wages later. It is in these cases that the difference between the initial EMS and EMU is most striking. The old EMS kept the realignment option wide open and, in turn, this may have led trade unions to push for short-run wage claims in the hope that the adjustment would be softened by devaluation. In any event, since Mundell (1961), the literature about the pros and cons of monetary union is dominated by the search for the nature and probability of asymmetric shocks.

The second question is about market-led adjustment. There are three market mechanisms for adjustment: labour mobility, capital mobility and wage/price flexibility. Doubts about the speed and effectiveness of all three are precisely the ground for the traditional preference for exchange rate autonomy. Labour migration from a region or country with a rising unemployment rate would obviously help adjustment. Mundell's proposition was that a single currency is demanding in terms of (interregional) factor mobility. A lack of such mobility would make the single currency area suboptimal; separate currencies and realignments would be less costly. Capital inflows could finance the external deficit; indeed, they will be automatic in a single market. Unlike in a fixed but adjustable peg system, foreign exchange reserves do not act as a constraint under a single currency. But borrowing in the low-demand region is bound to decrease, which is likely to reduce expenditure in due course. Capital inflows are therefore of little help in addressing the demand shortfall itself.

Wage and price flexibility is, in a macroeconomic sense, the counterpart of nominal exchange rate flexibility. The asymmetric shock requires a real depreciation and, for a given nominal exchange rate, this can be achieved through real wage reductions. If there were real-wage rigidity (for example, in the case of automatic wage indexation), the exchange rate cannot serve a useful purpose: the gain in competitiveness is immediately 'undone' through a concomitant rise in wages. McKinnon (1963) has pointed to the degree of openness of the economy as a key variable to be taken into account. In open economies, the competitiveness gain acquired by a devaluation is likely to be small since imported inputs and final goods will rise in price immediately. If, in addition, real wages are sticky downwards, discrete realignments would destabilise the price level even more. This point is obviously of critical importance for the European national economies, most of which are small and have very high trade/GDP ratios.[9]

[8]The exceptions that come to mind are oil and gas (for goods) and tourism (for services), where Europe exhibits sharply different endowments among Member States.

[9]The countries of euroland are, of course, a blend of bigger countries with ratios of intra-euroland goods trade over GDP of just over 20 per cent and smaller countries with ratios from 30 per cent up to 70 per cent or more. When the euro started, in 1999, the euroland average ratio was 29 per cent (EMU after five years, *European Economy,* Special report, 2004, no. 1, p. 146). The new Member States' ratios in 2002 hovered between 50 and 75 per cent (idem, p. 217).

Realising that market adjustment is either sluggish or ineffective, the third question is, what policies might bring about adjustment? There are two rather different points here that should be distinguished. On the one hand, successful devaluations tend to be accompanied by a policy mix which ensures that the real depreciation is not undone. In such cases the devaluation is usually quite large and partly justified by the psychological shock, which provides the government with the discretion to impose strict spending constraints. Such successful realignments (as with the Belgian franc in 1982) cannot be repeated easily, precisely because markets (and voters) will resist that. Nevertheless, if successful realignments are not excluded, the loss of the exchange rate instrument may imply a cost.

A very different issue is whether expansionary fiscal policy could be used domestically to compensate a loss of competitiveness (hence, demand), if real wages and prices are sticky. A single country cannot do this because of positive externalities which are unsustainable without coordination with its main trading partners. If alone, some of the additional spending will 'leak' across borders via extra imports; if many countries boost spending, externalities will go both ways, overcoming the external constraint (for pegged exchange rates). In 1982–83, France attempted to stimulate its economy, but this policy rapidly enlarged its external deficits and recurrent realignments followed. France switched to domestic austerity once its call for EU-wide coordination, that is, fiscal stimuli in all Member States, fell on deaf ears.

But in the theory of optimum currency areas one has to take the reasoning one step further. Once in a single currency area, the current account imbalances an expansionary fiscal policy would give rise to would remain 'invisible' (except in the stock of public debt, so the policy is a temporary one). Hence, fiscal policy may compensate losses of competitiveness due to wage/price stickiness. But this is of doubtful merit. Whereas the EMS might have had a deflationary bias (see section 17.4), unconstrained fiscal policies in a monetary union may then generate an inflationary bias. Altogether, the policy constraints of bringing about adjustment are considerable.

With severe (though not total) inhibitions on the use of exchange rate changes, and considerable constraints for adjustment via policy, the fourth question becomes relevant. The fourth question focuses on whether irrevocable fixation of exchange rates is really a sacrifice for the purpose of short-run macroeconomic stabilisation. As we have seen in Chapter 17, keeping the realignment option is costly. Markets lower their inflationary expectations only very slowly, even after a long period of disinflationary policies. A notorious example is the French franc in the early 1990s, carrying a costly risk premium despite more than half a decade of disinflationary policy. Thus, the realignment option is likely to raise actual inflation and add a premium to nominal interest rates. One might raise credibility if authorities 'tie their hands' – in the EMS, Italy did that by forgoing realignments after January 1987, by abolishing exchange controls and by entering the narrow band in January 1990. However, as it turned out in 1992, this was insufficient, since market adjustments led to a real appreciation which became, in the end, unsustainable. What should convince markets in earning credibility is a *change of regime*: making exchange rates irrevocably fixed. But if credibility cannot be earned otherwise, it must mean that there is no cost to giving up the exchange rate. Indeed, when frustrated about being stuck with an unwanted reputation for giving priority to employment rather than price stability, irrevocable locking of exchange rates will provide an immediate benefit: both inflationary expectations and actual inflation will fall.

18.2.2 The benefits of monetary union

Until recently, relatively little attention was paid to the benefits of monetary union. Another contrast with the debate on the costs is that the latter is mainly focused on macroeconomic (policy) effectiveness, whereas the analysis of benefits tends to be microeconomic. Monetary union, for present purposes, is simply defined as irrevocably fixed exchange rates. If this is 'upgraded' to a single currency, some additional benefits accrue (see section 18.2.5).

There are four microeconomic benefits of irrevocably fixed exchange rates: avoiding the costs of exchange rate volatility, avoiding transaction costs, various avoided costs of exchange rate uncertainty, and the weakening of 'home bias'. The costs of exchange rate volatility in terms of trade forgone are not high, perhaps up to 1 per cent annually (see Chapter 17), although the costs of misalignments are far higher. The impact on FDI is not known. Avoiding the transaction costs of having many currencies in a single market appeals, of course, to everyone crossing a border or making cross-border payments. But in fact, besides the (costly) trade of cash, there are three other transaction costs which will be avoided in a monetary union: interbank transactions, transactions between banks and others (except cash), and company internal costs (IFO, 1998).

Third, there are possible gains from removing uncertainty about exchange rates. It should be said that these gains are controversial and we report only one of them here:[10] increasing the quality of information (price transparency) provided by the price mechanism. This is probably most relevant in the goods and the capital market. In the goods market, multiple currencies reduce price transparency and this might lead to or bolster price discrimination in the single market between (national) currency areas. This argument is unlikely to carry much weight as sections 6.5, 6.6 and 12.3 illustrate.

When purchases have a high price (such as cars, TV sets), European consumers and certainly intermediate traders will not be misled by the quotation in different currencies. The obstacles lie elsewhere, be they taxes, procedures or (as in cars) the drawbacks of current exemptions for dealers. When purchases are not large, the problem is similar to that of cross-border shopping and VAT (see section 5.4.3). Since this is applicable mainly to consumers close to a border, the transparency problem is unlikely to be relevant. In a careful analysis, Gasiorek *et al.* (2004) distinguish search costs for consumers (which may be marginally reduced), facilitation of arbitrage (in turn, increasing the elasticity of demand) and facilitation of collusion among producers of different countries. The first two will reduce price-cost margins, the third one would increase them. Their simulation over 15 countries and 50 sectors (all in manufacturing) shows increased output due to increased price transparency in most sectors and lower mark-ups in all but one sectors. Thus, if consumers gain more price transparency than producers, from the introduction of the euro, pro-competitive effects will result and output will increase. Empirically, the attribution will be difficult, however.

The same attribution question might play a role with the 'home bias' in trade of goods and services. As noted in section 6.7, the home bias in Europe (and the USA and Canada) is strong, even though frontier controls have disappeared. However, there is no clear understanding of what exactly the determinants of 'home bias' are, besides language, personal networks and cultural affinity. Currencies play a role, no doubt, but is that still correct once one controls for transaction costs and exchange rate volatility?

18.2.3 A graphical synthesis

It is also possible to stylise the costs and benefits of monetary union in a graphical analysis. For the reader it may be helpful to collapse a complex debate in such a way.

ADDITIONAL READING

This section sums up the economic crux of the monetary union debate with the help of two simple but insightful graphs. Figure 18.4 relates the costs and benefits of monetary union to the degree of economic openness, thereby stylising the monetarist and the Keynesian views (as in Mundell, 1961).

The benefits of monetary union are mainly two: avoiding the costs of exchange rate volatility and avoiding transaction costs. Both of these benefits increase with the degree of openness, because in more open economies (in goods and services) more economic activity will benefit from avoiding these costs of multiple currencies. Hence, the benefits line B has a positive shape. The costs line C is sloping downwards but this derivation is more complex. The first step depends on whether 'deep' market integration leads to more concentrated economic activity, which would increase the probability of asymmetric shocks, or to less divergence in this sense. The empirical evidence in recent, very detailed work is that:

- at the regional level, the period 1980–95 shows an increasingly similar specialisation pattern. To some extent, this is a result of the structural change from manufacturing to services (see Hallet, 2000);
- at the country level, for the same period, there is a very slow increase in dissimilarity (see Midelfart-Knarvik *et al.*, 2000). However, this applies only to industry, not to services (traded or not); with services included, and their share of GDP growing steadily (see Chapter 7), this weak and slow trend may or may not be valid.

Given this evidence and knowing that intra-industry trade shares are high in the EU (so that

[10] We do not deal with the welfare gains of removing uncertainty in prices, influenced by exchange rates since they are ambiguous (de Grauwe, 2000, pp. 61–4), and the temporary increase of the growth rate via a decline in the real interest rate, in turn caused by the reduction of systemic risk under permanent fixity of exchange rates. The latter goes back to the Baldwin argument in section 6.6.

ADDITIONAL READING *continued*

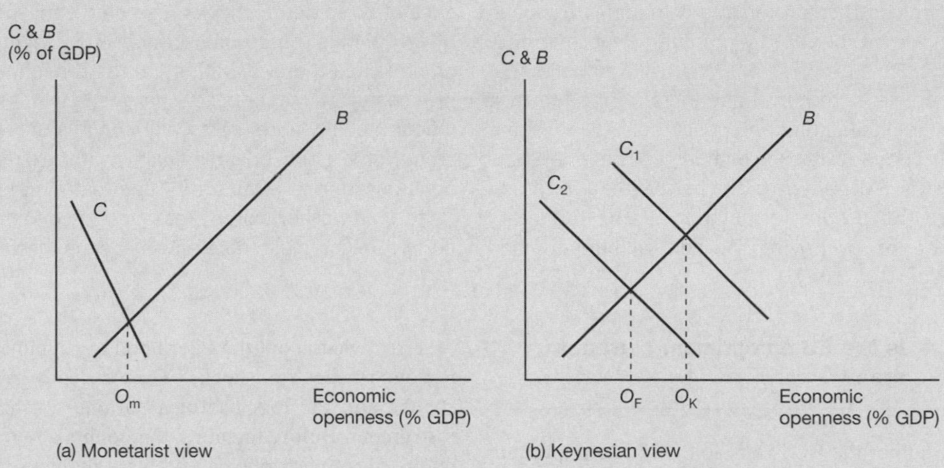

Figure 18.4 Costs and benfits of monetary union

Source: de Grauwe, 2000. Adapted version of figs. 4.2 (p.79) and 4.3 (p.81) from *Economics of Monetary Union*, 4th ed. by de Grauwe, P. (2000) by permission of Oxford University Press

final demand is similarly affected), one could support the view that asymmetric shocks will be less likely the 'deeper' market integration is. It would take far-reaching concentration of activity around single sectors before one should expect integration to enhance the probability of asymmetric shocks. If this would ever occur, it might take decades.

The second step is that more open economies will incur higher costs with exchange rate variability (than less open economies), simply because the supply and demand effects of de/revaluations will apply to larger shares of economic activity (McKinnon, 1963). Hence, a monetary union becomes less and less costly the more open the economy. Taking the two steps together, market integration (or economic openness towards union partners) reduces the costs of a monetary union.

Figure 18.4 implies two central conclusions of the monetary union debate. First, as EU countries display different degrees of economic openness, the cost–benefit analysis about joining monetary union may differ. The EU15 consists of three clusters if it comes to economic openness: Ireland and the Benelux countries (with very high openness), a middle group of relatively small countries (Portugal, Sweden, Finland, Denmark, Greece and Austria)[11] and the five larger economies (Germany, France, Italy, the UK and Spain).[12] Of course, openness is not the only factor. Thus, if credibility can only be earned with a 'tying-one's-hands' strategy, even less open economies may find joining advantageous. Second, Figure 18.4, left-hand panel, shows that the monetary view sees few costs in sacrificing the national currency as it is regarded as an ineffective instrument for macroeconomic stabilisation. The Keynesian view (right-hand panel), as expressed in the classical optimum currency area theory, regards the exchange rate as a tool to lower adjustment costs in the presence of rigidities (here, wage stickiness and no labour mobility to the booming region). Hence, the costs of sacrificing the exchange rate are high. Simplifying a little, one could see the amazing move to EMU by no less

[11]For Greece, Austria and Portugal, tourism (as a service) considerably adds to their openness in goods.

[12]Adding exports and imports of goods as a percentage of GDP the 'Big Five' have ratios between 21 and 26 per cent; again, adding the service sector raises openness considerably.

ADDITIONAL READING *continued*

than twelve EU countries in a demanding treaty as being the result of the gradual shift of policy makers in Europe from the right-hand panel perspective to the left-hand panel perspective. If there are no significant policy costs and some benefits, and if there are important political arguments for EMU anyway, it is better to go for it and ensure the proper formulation of the monetary constitution by having the central bankers and finance ministers draft it. This is in essence what happened in the run-up to Maastricht.

We have also seen that adjustment costs, in the case of asymmetric shocks, can be greatly lowered by flexibilities. This is illustrated in the right-hand graph (since there, rigidities are the reason for the high costs). Market or policy changes to foster higher labour mobility (inter-sectorally within countries, or cross-border) and/or wage flexibility (for example, a bonus system or temporary wage restraints) shifts C_1 to C_2. In other words, less open economies, if flexible, might find it more advantageous to join.

18.2.4 Is the EU an optimum currency area?

Asking whether the EU15 or the EU27 is an optimum currency area has become a widely accepted step in any analysis of EMU. And the answer is usually very similar for the EU15: it is unlikely to be optimal, but some criteria are fulfilled and countries or economic actors may well adjust to some extent to the requirements of EMU, hence get closer to optimality.[13] In the following, we go into some detail, even if we already know the overall assessment. Why still do this? The reason is that, once the monetary union is in place, the non-fulfilment of certain criteria is bound to lead to frictions between countries who will find the central monetary policy badly timed (for them), the real interest rate too high or too low or the ECB not responsive enough to what that country perceives as urgent. The smaller the divergences between countries, and the more synchronised the business cycles, the better the ECB can respond to what is needed in most or all eurozone countries.

What exactly is optimal in practice is also not easy to establish. To get around this, many authors have utilised the USA as a benchmark. Should the EU have adjustment properties as good as those of the USA, the monetary union should at least be workable.[14] In the following we apply the first three questions of section 18.2.1 to the EU, with occasional reference to the USA.

First, what about the likelihood of asymmetric (that is, country-specific) shocks? The less likely asymmetric shocks are, the less useful a national exchange rate instrument. Before the euro, the doubts about the optimality of the eurozone caused fears about a serious risk of asymmetric shocks, especially a lack of synchronisation of business cycles in euroland. However, as Eijffinger & de Haan (2000, pp. 22–6) show in an overview, already during the EMS an increased synchronisation of the business cycle could be identified. The USA as a benchmark seems only helpful as a contrast. Thus, Bini-Smaghi & Vori (1993) find that:

- on average, the differences between regional production structures are much larger within the USA than within the EU, that is, EU national economies are much more alike than US regions;
- differences in economic performance in the EU are due not to differences in the structure of production but to different policy responses; moreover, whereas such responses in the EU tend to offset the effects of sector-specific factors, the opposite is true in the USA.

These conclusions suggest that at least EU6 countries are less likely to suffer from asymmetric shocks than US regions and, hence, that the (national) exchange rate is a less useful instrument of adjustment in the EU than it would be in the USA.[15] The empirical evidence in the first years of EMU is mixed, though leaning towards

[13] Two expert views as an example; de Grauwe (2003, p. 103) and Baldwin & Wyplosz (2003, p. 350).

[14] Note that the USA is not an optimal currency area, only a 'workable' one. Based on a simple model, capturing the essence of optimum currency area theory, Ghosh & Wolf (1994) find that optimal combinations of US states can be found which can reduce the stabilisation costs. The problem with their approach is that their benchmark is (zero costs for) a currency for every state. Five contiguous intra-US monetary unions would reduce the costs from 2.63 per cent of US GDP to 2.08 per cent; five non-contiguous monetary unions would do better still: 1.68 per cent of US GDP.

[15] Note that Kenen (1969) already stressed that a high degree of diversification in the economy reduces the need for a separate exchange rate.

the notion of greater convergence. The Commission study 'EMU after five years' finds that the dispersion of 'output gaps' first increases between 1999 and 2001 and subsequently decreases, all at historically low levels.[16] An alternative measure, the correlation of Member States' business cycles (that is, do they move in tandem?), scores even better since the degree of cyclical co-movement is slightly better than during the 1980s and far better than in the first half of the 1990s. There may be some 'endogeneity', in that the very existence of EMU, as a regime change, has strengthened the 'stability culture' in all EU countries (the lack of which was one source of divergence) and, in intensifying trade and financial market integration, has helped converging tendencies to some degree.

Would asymmetry itself alter once a monetary union were in place? Would not EMU prompt greater geographical specialisation in the long run, as the USA has meanwhile achieved (see also Chapters 10 and 16)? For asymmetric shocks to matter, this would presume rather extreme agglomeration effects for which there is little or no empirical basis, as discussed above.

Second, let us look at two main market adjustment mechanisms to maintain (or quickly restore) a high level of employment. Real wage rigidity is typically feared to be robust in the EU, which is confirmed by empirical analysis; it is also greater than in the USA.[17] Again, this underscores that the exchange rate is a less useful instrument for adjustment in the EU than it would be in the USA.

Labour mobility is notoriously low in the EU. The contrast between (low) cross-border labour migration in the EU and the prominent role of outmigration from depressed US states in reducing unemployment is widely known.[18] This has led to fears that EMU would lead to unemployment for which labour migration would, in practice, not be a remedy. Those fears are only partly justified, however. First, what counts for the effectiveness of exchange rates in a diversified economy (that is, unlike Mundell's simple example) is labour mobility within countries but between sectors. If there is price rigidity, hence also relative price rigidity, sectors not hit by a specific shock will benefit more from the general demand increase that a devaluation would lead to. This should lead to inter-sectoral labour flows away from the negatively affected sectors to other ones. If this were not observed, the conclusion would be that the exchange rate is ineffective in making adjustment easier. Several authors[19] have found evidence that labour mobility within EU countries is indeed low; for Italy, Spain and the UK even lower than among other EU countries.

This leads to a second qualification. Unemployment is costly, but so is labour mobility in both social and economic terms. In Europe, the costs of labour mobility are perceived as high. Not only is cross-border labour mobility viewed as socially disruptive given assimilation and other problems in culturally diverse Europe, but also capital losses on property sold in depressed regions, ill-functioning housing markets, lower wages given competitive disadvantages of involuntary migrant workers and other adjustment costs raise serious questions about labour mobility as a short-run stability device. Of course, all this is a matter of degree. Within today's national currency areas, both social and economic adjustment costs of labour mobility are smaller and yet major discrepancies in regional unemployment rates persist. There is likely to be a strong link with welfare state benefits: in the EU they are strictly national – seeking jobs across borders is not facilitated by 'federal' social security of any kind; in the USA, benefits are generally lower and of shorter duration, but eligibility is USA-wide,[20] which facilitates inter-state labour mobility. The conclusion is that low labour mobility in EMU is scarcely a greater problem than it is within EU countries (with their own currencies), whereas the perceived costs of cross-border labour mobility in Europe are high.

Third, we address adjustment helped by fiscal policy, as an alternative to realignments. The point here is not so much the option of a coordinated fiscal stimulus, which would only be relevant in a true depression. What can be usefully compared with the USA is the extent country-specific shocks (in the USA, region-specific) are compensated by fiscal policy, in its role as 'stabiliser'.[21] The key issue here is the extreme decentralisation of

[16]EMU after five years, *European Economy*, Special report, 2004, no. 1, pp. 48–55.

[17]See McMorrow (1996), who finds that real wages in the USA and Japan are more flexible than in the EU, and that, in the long run, Japanese wages are most flexible.

[18]For a fascinating juxtaposition of Belgium and Michigan in this respect, see de Grauwe (2000, pp. 85–90).

[19]For example, de Grauwe & Vanhaverbeke (1991) and Bini-Smaghi & Vori (1993). Note, however, that the evidence is indirect; what they measure are the (trends in) domestic interregional dispersion of unemployment rates. This should, at least to some extent, be a proxy of inter-sectoral adjustment. See also Gros (1996b), Mauro *et al.* (1999) and Braunerhjelm *et al.* (2000).

[20]The state component of the payment differs among the states; the federal component is the same everywhere.

[21]Note that fiscal policy may also have redistribution and allocation purposes, and that part of the stabilisation function may also be pursued via an 'insurance' pool among Member States.

fiscal stabilisers in the EU versus a federal mechanism in the USA. The MacDougall report (MacDougall *et al.* 1977) advocated a more sizable EU budget precisely to generate some scope for centralised fiscal stabilisation. This is widely rejected by the Member States and not even on the EU agenda. In fact, there has never been much support for more EU budget centralisation (see Chapter 19). However, now that the eurozone is a reality, the question arises whether some degree of budget centralisation can be justified for the purpose of fiscal stabilisation. In the USA, when a state's income falls, disposable income falls less because (1) taxes and social charges to the federal treasury will reduce and (2) (personal) transfers from the federation as grants in aid will increase. The actual reduction of the income decline, which is absorbed by the federal government, has been the subject of some controversy: estimates range from 10 to over 30 per cent.[22] This role as 'stabiliser' is separate from the redistributive function of federal fiscal policy (or the EU budget, if any) which is not related to short-run falls in income but to structural discrepancies in income levels between regions or states (this effect is estimated as 22 per cent for the USA by Bayoumi & Masson (1995)).

For the EU to be an optimal currency area, in the restricted sense of doing as well as the US benchmark, the question is whether its decentralised fiscal policy can accomplish similar results. Although most federations in the OECD utilise federal fiscal stabilisation, one hardly does: Switzerland. So, it is not *a priori* clear whether the federal fiscal solution is necessary, or, for that matter, superior in case of monetary union. The Union budget is extremely small, being around 1 per cent of EU GDP in 2005. The Structural and Cohesion Funds have a small redistributive effect for the cohesion countries only (ranging at most between 1.5 and 4 per cent; see section 16.4). But the EU budget clearly has no stabilisation role whatsoever. Bayoumi & Masson (1995) find that national taxes and personal (social) transfers in EU countries reduce income fluctuations by around 31 per cent, which amounts to the highest estimates for the USA.[23]

The conclusion is that the 'federal' fiscal stabilisers are not the only option: even though the EU has no centralised fiscal stabilisation policy, decentralisation will do. As noted in section 3.1.1, extreme forms of decentralised stabilisation can be a stable solution only in the absence of labour (and voter) mobility across borders. Thus, the strong EU preference to retain national fiscal stabilisers interacts favourably with the strong preference to seek jobs in the national economy, in turn also permitting some degree of divergence between social policies and regulation. It is this combination of deep-rooted national socio-political preferences, and the willingness to pay (taxes and social charges) for them, which renders it most unlikely that significant roles of stabilising income fluctuations or of redistribution (beyond 'cohesion') will be shifted to the EU budget.

In conclusion, it would seem that such an EMU, without redistribution and stabilisation at central level, is possible and may well be stable. There are costs in terms of unemployment but similar costs have already been incurred at the national level. Although cross-border labour migration is very low, the social and economic costs of higher intra-EU labour mobility mitigate the potential of this adjustment channel. In any event, a national exchange rate is not a useful instrument if one regards the low probability of asymmetric shocks, their limited impact on employment and the persistence of real wage rigidity.

Simplifying somewhat, it is possible to illustrate the debate graphically. Figure 18.5 brings real divergence (in the sense of a greater probability of asymmetric shocks) and flexibility (in the sense of relatively

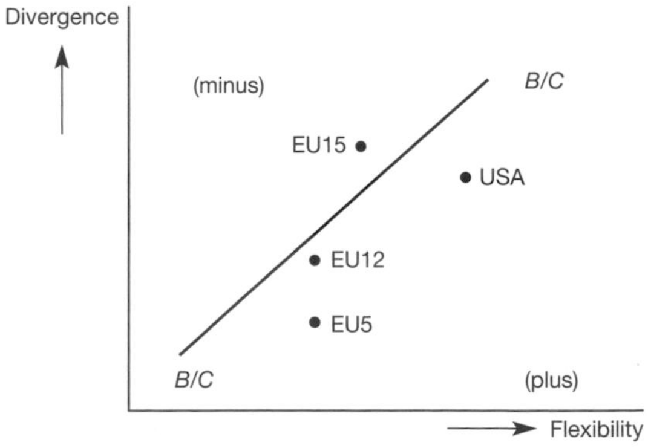

Figure 18.5 Real divergence and flexibility in a monetary union

Source: Adapted version of fig 4.4 (p.82) from *Economics of Monetary Union*, 4th ed. by de Grauwe, P. (2000) by permission of Oxford University Press

[22]See Sala-i-Martin & Sachs (1992) and Bayoumi & Masson (1995) and the literature quoted in the latter paper for the higher estimates. See Gros (1996a, annex 4) for estimates around 10 per cent.

[23]The authors also show that Canada, which has both greater fiscal autonomy for the provinces and a constitutional obligation to provide 'equalisation' transfers to poorer provinces, reaches a stabilisation of only 17 per cent, with redistribution of as much as 39 per cent.

smoothly working adjustment mechanisms) together. In this way the central message of the optimum currency area theory can be visualised.

The *B/C* line is the locus of all combinations of real divergence and flexibility, for which the costs and benefits are cancelled out. The greater is real divergence, the higher are the costs of giving up the exchange rate (as it would be needed to reduce short-run adjustment costs in case of asymmetric shocks). The greater is flexibility, primarily in the labour market (real wage responsiveness and/or labour mobility between sectors, regions or cross-border), the lower are the costs of giving up the exchange rate instrument. Above the *B/C* line the costs of (great) divergence dominate the lower cost of flexibility, for a given level of benefits (as discussed in section 18.2.2). Below the *B/C* line, the lower cost of (higher) flexibility dominates for a given level of benefits of monetary union.

The empirical literature can be (roughly) summarised as follows. The EU15 is not an optimum currency area (above the *B/C* line) as divergence dominates. In fact, this boils down to the UK, because now that the eurozone has twelve countries (and the Danish krone is tightly pegged to the euro), the only other country 'out' is Sweden (a small economy). In fact, the empirical question here is whether the UK's slightly greater flexibility (more to the right than EU12 or EU5), moving it closer to the *B/C* line, is insufficiently compensated by the gradual reduction over time of the (greater) probability of asymmetric shocks. The latter might be explained by a somewhat larger trade in goods and services with non-EU countries and by lower oil and gas production: thus, the EU15 might move 'below' the *B/C* line over time. However, if one adheres more strongly to a 'monetarist' view (see Figure 18.4), the EU15 might already be below the line, as exchange rate changes cannot deal with real variables such as output and employment, even less when they are caused by structural changes between sectors.

The literature is firm about the 'core' of the eurozone being the EU5 (France, Germany, Benelux),[24] in that real divergence is low. Real divergence is no doubt larger in the EU12. And larger still in the EU25, let alone, the EU27. Given the rapid structural changes in and swiftly deepening of integration with central Europe, it is hardly possible to do more at the moment than take a snapshot as far as the new Member States are concerned, which we will do in section 18.3.2.

Finally, it is important to note that, perhaps because of the prospect of monetary union, extreme rigidities in the labour market in Europe are being reduced. However, labour market reforms are slow, uneven and often still timid.[25] Nonetheless, greater flexibility in countries such as Ireland, the Netherlands, Spain and finally Germany, as well as the absence of policy reversals in the UK after 1997 (with a Labour government) do point to the possibility that the EU may move to the right in Figure 18.5. The Commission study 'EMU after five years' also sees glimmers of hope, but otherwise finds the labour market reform picture disappointing.

18.2.5 Tracing the benefits of the euro

Can we identify, and perhaps quantify, the benefits of monetary union in the EU? This section provides the empirical evidence in three steps, summarised in Table 18.1.

The overall conclusion of Table 18.1 is that the benefits of monetary union are larger and more numerous than was realised at first. This is true even if one takes the (unduly) narrow perspective of ignoring items 2 and 3. The trade gains under item 1.1 (see de Grauwe & Skudelny, 2000) and the relief from transaction costs (IFO, 1998) are both somewhat larger than estimated in the well-known Commission report 'One market, one money' (Emerson *et al.*, 1990).[26] Of course, these benefits are still not impressive – if the costs of divergence and/or inflexibilities are not low, such benefits will not justify joining the euro. Once one goes beyond the mere irrevocable fixing of exchange rates, to a single currency, some one-off savings can be had from the pooling of foreign exchange reserves. The seignorage gains[27] are permanent–they are less than 0.5 per cent of GDP, even when the euro assumes an international role (see section 18.7).

Less frequently discussed in the economic literature – in contrast to policy circles – are the strategic gains of the euro. In strict analytical terms, one could argue that there is no necessary causal relationship between 3.1 and 3.2 in Table 18.1 on the one hand, and the euro, on the other. After all, in principle, it is possible to pursue deepening

[24]In fact one might add Austria and even Denmark (despite the referendum on the euro in 2000, when the Danes narrowly rejected entry into the eurozone) and possibly Italy.

[25]See Boeri *et al.* (2000, p. 372).

[26]It is as well to realise that the transaction costs in case of irrevocable fixing will not fall to zero. The bid–ask spreads will only lower somewhat. It takes a single currency as legal tender to squeeze them out altogether.

[27]The net revenue to the authorities of issuing money (at low costs).

Table 18.1 Identifying the benefits of the euro

Type of benefit	Magnitude
1. Benefits of irrevocable exchange rates	
1.1 no exchange rate volatility	
• trade gains	Up to 1% of intra-EU trade (annually)
• FDI	Slight[a]
1.2 no transaction costs (see 18.2.2.) (IFO, 1998)	1% of EU GDP
1.3 no exchange rate uncertainty	(doubtful)
1.4 less 'home bias'	(unclear, if controlled for 1.1 and 1.2)
2. Benefits of the euro as a single currency	
2.1 savings due to lower reserves	small
2.2 seignorage gains	
• in eurozone	small
• with international role	small extra
3. Strategic gains	
3.1 positive feedback for market integration	
• financial services	powerful, but
• capital markets	unquantifiable
3.2 credibility gains	irreversible (pro-growth)
• solid monetary constitution	
• strong incentive for sound policies	

[a]There is little evidence except for Morsink & Molle (1991) and Eichengreen (1993, p. 1228) for FDI.

of financial services and capital market integration without the euro. Indeed, the UK and Sweden are strong supporters of the Financial Services Action Plan (see section 7.3). Similarly, the credibility gains can also be obtained by national decisions to write a strict 'monetary constitution' as well as strict (indeed, partly constitutional) rules about deficits and debts (as some US states have done). However, such a purist position sits uneasily with the very reasons why the link between credibility and monetary union is so strong. The ultimate reasons are found in political economy. Governments may not be credible because they have political incentives to cheat (for example, lower unemployment raising the probability of re-election for the government in office). Once one assumes a political economy perspective, one can ask the more relevant question: would the euro have been agreed without a strict EU monetary constitution? If the answer is no, then the causal link is established and the gains of 3.2 in Table 18.1 should be included. In section 18.3 we shall see that the answer is indeed no. Despite considerable swings in the US dollar, a stock market plunge in 2001 and a recession in 2002–03, the seven years of the eurozone until the end of 2005 were characterised by predictability, an absence of exchange rate crises (so frequent in the EU of the 1970s, 1980s and well into the 1990s) and consistent price stability, not to speak of the achieved (and reasonably maintained, compared with the last few decades) fiscal consolidation. Of course, these strategic benefits are part and parcel of the kind of monetary union the EU has opted for (see sections 18.3 and 18.4) and are not the consequence of just any currency union. These macroeconomic benefits are appreciable and permanent.

The positive feedback for market integration is already powerful. In financial market integration, the euro has engendered further deepening and intensification. In trade in goods, estimates vary,[28] but relatively short-term effects between 7 and 20 per cent, or even 30 per cent have been published whereas long-term growth of intra-eurozone trade might even reach 50 per cent. This seems to confirm the work by Rose & Stanley (2004) and section 6.7.2 that monetary unions generate a lot of extra intra-group trade. There are indicators that FDI is also biased in favour of EMU: the Commission study shows (p. 147) that the share of inward FDI of the EU15 going to non-eurozone countries declines quite dramatically (from 37 per cent in 1998 and 31 per cent in 1999 to 11 per cent in 2002); this is so dramatic because the three 'outs' are otherwise performing rather well in economic terms in the period.

18.3 Towards monetary union

This section discusses the road towards monetary union in two parts: the three stages of EMU, and the entry conditions.

18.3.1 The stages before monetary union

The EC treaty amounts to a compromise between two schools, often termed the 'economist' and the 'monetarist'[29] schools, terms adopted from the debate on

[28]See the Commission study 'EMU after five years', op. cit., fn 16 above, pp. 145–6.

[29]This term should not be confused with the monetary theory based on the quantity theory of money. For a survey of the debate of the 1970s, see Tsoukalis (1977).

EMU of the 1970s. Where both schools nowadays agree is that 'economic union' is a prerequisite for monetary union (unlike in 1971, see Case Study 18.1) and this should in any event include a 'deep' internal market. The former sees monetary union as the 'crowning' of a process of convergence towards price stability, in an economic union as defined in Figure 18.2. In the treaty this approach finds its expression in the strong emphasis on the nominal convergence criteria, as conditions for entry into monetary union. The 'crowning' view is in fact widely shared in Europe. Where the 'monetarist' view makes a difference, is the assertion that early (or easy) irrevocable pegging will greatly facilitate the adjustment of expectations and hence the adjustment and convergence process, while lowering the interest bill of indebted governments. This would, in turn, greatly help in taking tough domestic adjustment measures in a short timespan without too much political risk. The latter conviction found expression in the idea of a timetable over three stages, and the provision that monetary union would begin *in any event* in 1999, possibly with a smaller group (unless the criteria were met by only one or two). The two concrete provisions avoid the trap that conditionality would never actually lead to monetary union, as the lack of commitment by others would fatally undermine the domestic political resolve to converge firmly and sufficiently.

CASE STUDY 18.2 Payment systems and monetary union

Payments constitute a key element where internal market issues and the proper functioning of monetary union combine to accomplish genuine Europeanisation. We are concerned here with large-value payments (wholesale) and cross-border retail. Member States differed greatly in the organisation, supervision and pricing of payment services.

Large-value cross-border payments have increased enormously since the late 1980s and this may have resulted in an increase of systemic risk. In financial circles in the EU, it was felt that EU-wide 'real-time gross settlement' in large-value payments (mainly between banks) would be the simplest way to reduce settlement risk and systemic risk. Of course, for cover of net positions either a system of statutory reserves or the constitution of collateral (with marketable assets) would be needed. This would entail extra costs for banks – the former solution more than the latter – on top of reserve requirements for monetary policy purposes.

The TARGET system was developed in anticipation of the centralisation of monetary policy and the introduction of the euro in the wholesale markets. In effect, TARGET had to be created as the infrastructural condition for an efficient interbank market in the eurozone. There are many participants in TARGET and therefore net positions can be minimised fairly easily. The system has been recognised as safe and flexible. It should be realised that TARGET represents an enormous improvement over a system relying on corresponding banks, in place until 4 January 1999. By September 1999 the number of payments was 165,000 a day, with a total value of €880 billion. Apart from being efficient (that is, instantaneous and 'deep') and safe, TARGET also greatly facilitates the conduct of the ECB's monetary policy. Moreover, it renders arbitrage in the euro money markets more efficient.[30]

Cross-border retail payments have long suffered from very high 'frontier prices' just like, for example, telecoms services or cross-border air transport in the past. A 1993 Commission report found that a cross-border payment of ECU 100 cost an average ECU 24 (with ECU 3.18 as receiver charges), and even at this price there was little guarantee about the speed of transactions. There were a host of reasons for these extreme cost levels, such as the absence of EU-wide clearing systems (hence the costs of correspondence banks at the retail level), costs due to the lack of a unified EU-wide payment method, lack of common technical standards, legal inconsistencies between the Member States and, not least, the lack of a common currency. There was nonetheless the perception that banks exercised market power, and earned high profits, in such fragmented markets. The banks have long dragged their feet, asking for self-regulation, which did not reduce costs significantly. Directive 97/5 on cross-border credit transfers set common rules for transparency and performance of

[30] See also *ECB Monthly Bulletin*, November 1999.

CASE STUDY 18.2 ***continued***

cross-border payments. This partial, multi-currency directive is a necessary but insufficient approach for the eurozone. In 2001 this was followed by Regulation 2560/2001 on cross-border payments, eliminating pay differences between domestic and cross-border transactions. Since 1999, the ECB has engaged itself because its task is to promote the smooth operation of payment systems. At retail level, correspondent banks were then still heavily used and interbank structures are inadequate. Now that the euro is a reality there is no reason to make any distinction between 'domestic' and 'rest of eurozone' payments. But that is not what one reads in the ECB's recent progress report *Towards a Single Euro Payment Area* (2004). As a consequence, the Commission proposed a far-reaching directive on payment services[31] with a deadline of 2010, replacing the 1997 and 2001 regulations.

The stages approach was agreed as follows.[32] Stage 1 began July 1990, that is, before the treaty negotiations had started officially. It included the abolition of exchange controls, to be made irrevocable by virtue of Article 56 EC once the second stage was reached (on 1 January 1994). Furthermore, initially there was a drive to include as many EU currencies in the EMS as possible: the pound, peseta and escudo all entered, and the lira moved into the narrow band. The currency crisis of 1992–93 (see Case Study 17.1) led to retrogression, with the pound and the lira opting out of the EMS, besides the great widening of the band.

A third element of stage 1 was the strengthening of economic policy coordination. Some weak forms of coordination existed before, based on a 1974 Council decision on what was called 'economic convergence'. The latter never referred to the strict standards for convergence imposed by the Maastricht Treaty. The actual policy impact of the pre-1990 coordination at EU level was at best minor. With stage 1 a more elaborate mechanism was put in place, called 'multilateral surveillance', based on a new Council decision in 1990. This was extended by the Maastricht Treaty with the national 'convergence' programmes, aiming to meet the entry conditions of monetary union over the medium-run.[33] This pursuit of nominal convergence is discussed in some detail later. How much stronger this mechanism really is, is unclear. As noted, the Council exercises prudence about individual Member States and the new coordination remains voluntary. However, what has given it 'teeth' is that the incentives behind the 'convergence' programmes do not depend on the Council but derive directly from the treaty's entry conditions for monetary union. The large majority of Member States actively cherished the prospect of monetary union membership and this meant that convergence programmes had a high political profile. The compromise formula in the treaty of combining dates with conditionality has proved to be very effective. In strict monetary terms, stage one meant little, however.

Stage 2 began on 1 January 1994 (Article 116 EC), and practically without conditions.[34] The substance of this stage has never been fully clear. The stage became necessary because of the doctrine of the indivisibility of (national) monetary policy: a transfer of monetary policy has to be complete, and until that moment national monetary policy cannot be 'partly' centralised. Many provisions for the stage are therefore procedural and will not be dealt with here. The main device is the establishment of the European Monetary Institute (EMI) which prepared the final transition to stage 3. Apart from the 'visibility' of having one 'European' central banker,[35] EMI had mainly low-key preparatory functions: it built up qualified staff for monetary analysis on

[31]COM (2005) 603 of 1 December 2005.

[32]The present book cannot hope to provide the fine details of Title VII (EMU) of the treaty. For detailed analysis see Gros & Thygesen (1998, chapter 12) and for legal aspects, Chuck & Phinnemore (1994, pp. 150–75, especially box 8). See also Bini-Smaghi & Gros (2000).

[33]One should add the medium-term credit facilities, linked to the EMS, but based on ECOFIN decisions with conditionality; they have existed since 1979. Such loans have been taken up by, for example, Italy and Greece.

[34]Other than the three elements of stage 1, just mentioned. The 'economist' school wanted greater conditionality.

[35]EMI's first president was Alexandre Lamfalussy, a Belgian. Dutch Wim Duisenberg succeeded him and later became the first ECB president, succeeded in 2003 by Jean-Claude Trichet from France (until 2011).

a European basis – without which the ECB could not function in stage 3 – and was deeply involved in the technical groundwork for the switch to common or similar banknotes as well as for the integration of national payments systems (see Case Studies 18.2 and 18.3).

Stage 2 is characterised by two other aspects: coordination and the realignment issue. The multilateral surveillance is extended by including the 'excessive deficits' procedure (Article 104 EC) and the 'broad guidelines' about overall economic policy of Member States (Article 99 EC). Of course, the EMI was also involved in coordination. The excessive deficits procedure during stage 2 is driven by the desire to be eligible for monetary union membership.

A final issue of stage 2 concerns realignments.[36] The idea of an ultimate realignment is not mentioned in the treaty, of course, but neither is it formally ruled out before establishing monetary union. However, with the very wide band of 2 × 15 per cent, the probability of speculative attacks was drastically reduced. In the end no ultimate realignment took place.

18.3.2 EMU's entry ticket and the outsiders

We list here the entry conditions for stage 3 and provide a rationale, based on Barro–Gordon-type incentive problems (see Chapter 17). A brief word follows on the (negative) side effects of this road to monetary union. Finally, calendar, membership and ERM-II are set out.

The entry ticket is earned once four (nominal) convergence criteria are met by an EU country, as summarised in Table 18.2. Why these entry criteria?[37] First, there is low inflation. If inflation preferences differ (as in Figure 17.6) between Member States, Germany will always have to compromise on a higher inflation average than it wants. So it will enter only if it can strongly condition the institutions of the currency union and allow only low-inflation countries to join. In section 18.4 the ECB will be discussed – it is modelled closely on the Bundesbank. By requiring low inflation at the time of entry, Germany would minimise its welfare loss to (close to) zero. If the 'high inflation' countries could manage their preferences ('flatten the *I* curves' in Figure 17.6) during stage 2, the EU would in fact engineer a true *regime change* – it would succeed in building 'a stability culture', shared by what used to be high(er)- and low-inflation countries.

Table 18.2 Convergence criteria as EMU entry ticket

Treaty (Art. 121)	Protocols (specification)
A high degree of price stability	No more than 1.5% inflation above the average of the three lowest-inflation Member States
Sustainability of the country's financial (i.e. fiscal, JP) position: applies Art. 104(6)	No larger government deficit than 3% of GDP: no higher (public) debt than 60% of GDP; on debt the treaty adds that one may qualify if the debt/GDP ratio is 'sufficiently diminishing and approaching [60%] at a satisfactory pace'
No devaluation in the 'normal' band of the EMS for two years	(No specifications, but see text)
Durability of convergence as reflected in long term	Points above the average interest rate no more than 200 basis levels in the three lowest-inflation countries in the EU (note: not those with lowest interest rates)

Second, there is budgetary convergence. Once again, the criteria can be explained by fear of (higher) inflation. This is clearest for the debt criterion. With high outstanding debt, a country has a strong incentive to create surprise inflation so as to lower the real debt burden. With the entry condition being a (relatively) low debt/GDP ratio, the incentive to push for inflation would be squeezed out of the system. The deficit percentage can be explained as a function of the debt ratio[38] given a growth forecast. The exact figures of 60 per cent and 3 per cent are therefore arbitrary, but the idea behind it makes sense; moreover, 60 per cent and 3 per cent are easy to monitor. Still, having a deficit of, say, 3.2 per cent in recessionary circumstances just when eager to

[36]Readers might be interested in yet another issue which had to be ignored in this book, namely the option of a parallel EC currency. There are many variants in the literature, but especially the 'hard-ECU' proposal by the British government might have played a role in the second stage, had it been adopted. See Gros & Thygesen (1998, pp. 416–18).

[37]The following is based on de Grauwe (2003, chapter 6).

[38]Thus, for a debt/GDP ratio of 60 per cent (= 0.6), the deficit would be 3 per cent of GDP (= 0.03) and the nominal growth rate 5 per cent (= 0.05), for debt to be stabilised as a percentage of GDP (because 0.03 = 0.05 × 0.6).

enter the eurozone, would prompt a candidate euro country to impose pro-cyclical measures and this is not desirable.

Third, the two-year no-devaluation rule was clearly meant to prevent a kind of competitive depreciation before entry. In fact, it turned out to have stifling effects, even immediately after the signing of the Maastricht Treaty. Italy could have opted for several (small) adjustments of the central rate in the ERM in 1992 and 1993 but this entry condition led it to 'freeze' too early. Later in the 1990s this condition hardly mattered, because the 'normal' band had been stretched to 30 per cent (2×15 per cent).

Fourth, the long-term interest convergence was apparently based on the prospect of huge arbitrage in the capital market, if bonds in different EMS currencies were to show interest rate disparities. There were fears that this arbitrage could disturb capital markets. However, since the road to the third stage was six or eight years, the capital gains and losses were incurred much earlier. Once a currency was firmly expected to enter (and this was easy to monitor, given the criteria), long-run interest rates would converge anyway. Given the long road to the euro, this criterion was thus redundant. One can argue that it does matter for the new Member States since their passage has to go through ERM-II.

One advantage of the entry conditions was clarity. Imagine if the criteria had been taken from optimum currency area theory, such as flexibility, divergence and speed of adjustment. These criteria are much harder to operationalise and politicisation would no doubt have caused problems. So for national governments the entry criteria were a great help, since the message of conditionality was straightforward in domestic politics. It must be said that this combination of clarity and the calendar worked miracles. Suddenly, it turned out to be possible to 'flatten' the indifference curves and accept temporary but considerable adjustment costs of the kind portrayed in Figure 17.8. Furthermore, the countries with the highest debt/GDP ratio (Belgium, Italy, later Greece) succeeded in stabilising the ratio and moving it down by several percentage points a year. Since interest payments on high debt were huge, the surplus on the primary budget (budget excluding interest payments) had to be pushed up to around 6 per cent of GDP just before entry. The price of regaining credibility was therefore high, yet no less than eleven countries resorted to both monetary and fiscal restrictiveness in order to get in. And the determination of the eleven helped the new Greek government to achieve the near impossible; by 2000, Greece had achieved compliance despite very high debt and deficits in the mid-1990s, and without ever having been in the ERM of the EMS. Greece also set out to change its economy into a more flexible and market-oriented one, with privatisation, more competitive exposure and a range of reforms.

The calendar was as follows. After some hiccups with ratification (the Danes said 'no' in June 1992, at first), the Commission was to report in late 1996 whether it could identify seven complying Member States. If yes, monetary union could be initiated by the European Council in 1997. But on a strict interpretation, 1996 data would only allow Luxembourg in. However, by early 1998, there would be a second step: this time the Council had to initiate a monetary union with two or more countries. On 2 May 1998, the European Council admitted eleven countries to the monetary union, which would start on 1 January 1999.[39] For three years the euro would be used between banks and for all new bond issues, but not yet as cash; of course, it could be used for electronic bank transfers by everybody. By 1 January 2002, conversion of existing currencies into euro coins and notes would begin (see Case Study 18.3) and legal tender of existing currencies would be ended on 30 June 2002. With the 'ins' forming the eurozone, any exchange rate arrangement with the 'outs' (the UK, Sweden, Denmark, and initially Greece; nowadays also the new Member States) would be factually different from the ERM. Beginning in 1999, the euro would always dominate the relationship. Formally, an ERM II was proposed on a voluntary basis, but only Greece and Denmark entered it (and Greece subsequently left it for the euro). So, *de facto*, the notion that the eurozone could, together with the 'outs', find ways to guarantee exchange rate stability so as to protect the single market has failed. Each one of the four 'outs' has gone its own way, for domestic political reasons.[40]

Despite the failure to ensure exchange rate stability for the single market (a problem much reduced by the dominance of the euro), the overall success of the Maastricht design to establish monetary union is undeniable. Not only was a major currency union founded, on

[39]Greece was to join the euro by 1 January 2001.

[40]Greece used ERM-II for what it is meant for – a stepping-stone to enter the eurozone. Denmark is in ERM-II (and is *de facto* a member of the eurozone) but has obtained a right to hold a referendum (in September 2000 a slight majority was against the euro). The UK has the right to opt out (as it does now) but also to opt in. Sweden has purposely avoided ever to enter ERM-I (of the EMS) so that it can legally claim that there is no obligation to enter. The Swedes voted 'no' in a referendum on the euro in 2004.

schedule, but in the process existing socio-political preferences were appreciably adapted. And this success was certainly not made easier by a major recession in 1992–93, two EMS crises, the aftermath of German unification (with high debt for Germany), and the Asian financial crisis and its contagion in late 1997. Almost in passing, the Union enlarged its membership in 1995 with Austria, Finland and Sweden and concluded ambitious Europe Agreements with ten central European countries.

CASE STUDY 18.3 Introducing the euro

The Madrid European Council of December 1995 chose 'Euro' as the name for the single currency of the monetary union. The true reason for the switch to the euro is to move away from the soft currency image of the ECU in the ERM-currency countries. After all, the euro should be as good as the Deutschmark, whereas the ECU steadily declined against the Deutschmark and the guilder because its basket comprised weaker currencies as well.

Introducing the euro was a complicated and costly affair. One might be inclined to think of the direct costs of printing new banknotes and coins, changing automated teller machines, and the invoicing and accounts of enterprises. Indeed, the massive operation took years to prepare and entailed considerable one-off costs. But some fascinating and critical other questions arose as well. Introducing the euro amounted to a 'sequencing' problem in that the decision to go for monetary union (in 1998) preceded the date for irrevocably fixing the conversion rates (1 January 1999), at which point in time further sequencing choices had to be made. One idea was to have a 'big bang': when fixing the rates, the euro would also be introduced as the exclusive currency in the monetary union, replacing national moneys (or the ECU, where relevant) in all its functions. Later, doubts emerged whether a short transition period would be possible. However, the longer the transition period the greater the uncertainty in financial markets whether active trading in 'deep' euro-denominated markets could be expected in the transition period. Not unlike the emergence of a telecoms network with strong positive network externalities beyond an attractive minimum number of connected subscribers (the 'critical mass'), the irreversibility of the process of introducing the euro would be best guaranteed by creating incentives in markets for a changeover based on such positive externalities. But the authorities must then take the lead in generating the 'critical mass' to begin with.

The Madrid European Council backed up these ideas. Stage 3 of EMU (see text of chapter) was divided into two substages: one of three years, following the irrevocable fixing of exchange rates, and one of at most six months to make the euro the sole legal tender. During stage 3A (1999–2001), notes and coins in euro did not yet circulate and the private sector, including financial markets and wholesale and retail payment systems (see Case Study 18.2 on European payment systems) were free to use the euro or not. Since this might have led to hesitations, two obligations contributed to an emerging 'critical mass': all payment obligations of banks under the ECB monetary policy (starting immediately) had to be in euro; all new tradable public debt had to be issued in euro by the Member States of the monetary union. In foreign exchange markets the use of the euro was encouraged by the Eurosystem. It was hoped that foreign trade invoicing, ECB funds (from the reserve requirements the ECB might establish) traded among banks, wholesale foreign exchange transactions (with huge volumes), and the market-based use of the TARGET system (linking the national payments settlement systems) together would provide the decisive boost to achieve a smooth 'passage to the euro' in a market-based fashion. By 2000 it seemed to have worked.

Far more difficult were the timing and logistics of the switch from national notes and coins to euronotes and coins. This turned out to be an enormous logistical operation without any parallel in history. It included, among other things, years of coinage at full capacity in all Member States, the organisation of massive daily shipments of notes and coins in January 2002 (so massive that several countries employed the army to discourage the Mafia), dual pricing of goods and services until mid-2002, incessant information campaigns and the euro-compatibility of payment terminals throughout the eurozone (at cost no higher

CASE STUDY 18.3 *continued*

than domestic payments). Introducing the euro also implied a large variety of complicated legal issues in world capital markets.

Stenkula (2004) has tested why differences in the pace of introduction (in 2002) between euro countries emerged. He finds that (1) the large pre-distribution of euros greatly accelerated the speed of the changeover, (2) that large countries tend to be slower (this is explained by considering money as a network good), (3) dual circulation should be short, no longer than logistical and technical problems require, (4) more bank branches help the speed of introduction, and (5) that national pride played no role whatsoever.

The euro introduction was a smooth and successful process, yet, a few years later, consumers in several EU countries (such as Italy and the Netherlands) did revolt. Although inflation had remained historically low, it turned out that, in a small number of goods and services such as bars, restaurants and a few food items, entrepreneurs had managed to raise prices sharply during the introductory period of the euro. In the Netherlands, this was compounded by a badly timed tax reform reducing discretionary spending, causing some people to firmly believe it was all due to the euro. This goes to show how crucial it is to monitor this aspect closely in order to pre-empt a discrediting of the euro, a possible lesson for the changeovers in the new Member States later on. Indeed, this is a real possibility since an increasing number of citizens in central Europe fear extra inflation (or cheating at the retail level) when the euro is introduced.[41]

Nevertheless, the strategy was economically costly. Not only did all potential entrants employ restrictive monetary and fiscal policies, they did this simultaneously so that a 'deflationary trap' emerged: the restrictiveness of policies in A caused a negative spillover to B, and vice versa. In this restrictive climate, budget cutting for Maastricht purposes was often 'undone' by the increase in spending because of 'stabilisers' (as unemployment shot up from an EU average of 8 per cent in 1991 to nearly 12 per cent in 1997). As a result, all the seven countries initially below or around the 60 per cent debt ratio had increased their ratio by 1997. Of the four countries with higher or very high debt ratios, Ireland, the Netherlands and Belgium lowered them (and so complied) but Italy did not. Taking into account the cyclical reasons and the development of the primary budgets, the Council felt that the debt criteria were met, nonetheless.

What about the new Member States in their passage to the euro? Note that they are obliged to enter the eurozone, eventually, but the entry conditions must be met. They have to pass two years in ERM-II.[42] In 2004, the inflation criterion (reference then 2.4 per cent) was met by four new Member States out of ten; the long-term interest rate criterion by eight; the deficit criterion by four, and the debt ratio criterion by eight, with the other two just over 70 per cent. These scores are not bad when compared with those of the eurozone countries back in the early 1990s. In particular, the inflation criterion had caused worries but there seems to be no clear pattern: fast growers Estonia and Lithuania have very low inflation whereas fast grower Slovakia has over 8 per cent; the Czech Republic had years of high budget deficits yet consistently low inflation.[43] It would appear that the new Member States can enter if they really want to, just like the current eurozone countries. However, they may, wisely, choose to be more flexible in their budgetary position for a few years more, in view of the many demands of reform and infrastructure; they can

[41]COM (2005) 545 of 4 November 2005, *Second Report on the Practical Preparations for the Future Enlargement of the Euro Area*.

[42]Late 2005, six new Member States were in ERM-II, namely Estonia, Lithuania and Slovenia since 27 June 2004 and Cyprus, Latvia and Malta since 2 May 2005. The first three are expected to enter the eurozone by 1 January 2007 if the entry conditions are fulfilled.

[43]The worries originate from the Balassa–Samuelson effect, which predicts a trend appreciation of real exchange rates determined by higher productivity growth in the tradables than in the non-tradables sector. This wage inflation in the tradable sector is not in itself a worry; quite the contrary, it is a sign of catch-up growth. But this higher, though good, inflation might be 'punished' by the strict inflation condition upon entry in euroland. The Balassa–Samuelson effect has often been estimated (e.g. Pelkmans *et al.*, 2000a; Halpern & Wyplosz, 2001) and might be 1 or 2 per cent, perhaps more when catch-up growth occurs. The data in the text do not seem to reflect this effect, which is puzzling.

afford deficits in the light of their low debt ratios. As far as Romania and Bulgaria are concerned, they also have low debt ratios and no deficits (in 2005); their first problem is inflation (falling rapidly though).

18.4 What kind of monetary union?

What kind of monetary union is the eurozone? The four key words to answer this question are: centralisation of monetary policy; centralisation of exchange rate policy, if any (with some discretion for ECOFIN); independence of the ECB; and, most important of all, an overriding objective of price stability.

The counterpart to the notion that Member States' monetary policy is 'indivisible' is, of course, that monetary policy of the ECB is also indivisible. On this account *centralisation of monetary policy* was based on a consensus. If 'subsidiarity' were (falsely) invoked to reduce such centralisation, the effective control of the Union's money stock, the equal treatment in terms of mandatory reserve requirement and the regional neutrality in open market operations would be endangered. Thus, subsidiarity suggests centralisation here. Therefore, even the decentralisation of the execution of monetary policy is severely limited: operating profits do not accrue to national central banks and, more generally, Article 12.1 of the Protocol on the Statute of the ESCB and of the ECB speaks of 'the necessary instruction to national central banks' following from the mandate to the Executive ECB Board to 'implement monetary policy'. Only to 'the extent deemed possible and appropriate . . . the ECB shall have recourse to national central banks to carry out operations . . . '.

The degree of centralisation is even greater since both decision making and implementation will be centralised. This makes economic sense. Nevertheless, national central banks were hesitant to transfer fully all foreign exchange reserves in non-Union currencies (and gold) to the ECB. An arbitrary sum of ECU 50 billion for the ECB has been fixed (Article 30.1 Statute), while the holding of IMF reserve positions and SDRs (special drawing rights under IMF rules) are not even included, although they could be added later (Article 30.5). An important reason for this limitation on reserve pooling is the current disparity among EU countries' reserve positions: their contributions would strongly diverge, and arbitrarily so. The limit need not be a problem since it is almost impossible to fix the optimum level of reserves for the ECB, as noted earlier.

Let us now study the *independence* of the ECB a little more closely. The independence of the ECB has functional and political reasons, all to do with the (better) pursuit of price stability. The political reason is obvious but, precisely therefore, requiring a fundamental political consensus among Member States. If governments – especially the finance ministers having to fund public expenditure – have a hold on the central bank, the credibility of the ECB with respect to its primary task would be compromised. One may extend the argument by imagining that other objectives of economic policy – notably, employment and growth – would somehow compete with low inflation, so that the ECB could be forced to accommodate spending policies going counter to the maintenance of price stability.

In this political sense, the ECB is truly independent. Germany has obtained a model close to that of the Bundesbank. Legally, this has been provided for by independence (from instructions) from Member States (Article 7 Statute),[44] the personal independence of members of the Executive Board and the Governing Council[45] and the constitutional nature of the ECB Statute, hence, attempts to alter it require ratification in all EU Member States.

But the functional back-up of this independence is likely to be at least as important. As with other market-oriented bodies fulfilling public service tasks (see Chapter 8), unbundling of tasks into separate agencies is likely to enhance efficiency. In the case of central banks, the power to create money is their core function, and this ought to be fully separated from the (public) power to spend.[46]

The most powerful provision for the ECB's independence, though, is the Bank's constitutional obligation to give primacy to price stability, over and above other economic policy objectives.

This leaves one danger: *exchange rate policy*. The danger is remote but not excluded. It may become relevant once the ECOFIN exercises its potential power over exchange rate policy. This Council can, with QMV, formulate general orientations for exchange rate policy

[44]Note that this applies to both the ECB and the ECSB, that is, also the national central banks.

[45]Via appointment rules: eight years, non-renewable for Board members and a minimum of five years the national central bank governors in the Governing Council (Arts 11.2 and 14.2 of the Statute).

[46]Watertight guarantees require even stricter rules, for example, a prohibition for the central bank to conduct open market operations in securities other than those with the highest credit rating, or other than any government securities.

'without prejudice to the primary objective . . . to maintain price stability' (Article 111(2) EC). If, say, interventions in euro/dollar or euro/yen are desired by the ECOFIN, there is no automatic imposition on the ECB, and even then sterilisation is still possible. The greater threat would arise if the ECOFIN (with unanimity) were to agree to a new peg to other major currencies. In such a new world exchange rate regime, crises could lead to capital flows so massive that the EU's price stability might be undermined. Both the unlikelihood of such a world regime and of such a decision of the ECOFIN would appear to make it most improbable that the independence is actually going to be put in jeopardy.[47] Thus far, there has been no sign of it when the euro was low *vis à vis* the US dollar or, for that matter, when the euro was high.

The strong emphasis on *price stability* forms the bedrock of the monetary constitution. The question arises whether there are solid economic arguments to support the primacy of price stability.

As noted in Chapter 17, inflation can be anticipated or not. With respect to the former, there are microeconomic costs. Since the social costs of producing money is practically zero, inflation should tend to zero. If inflation is positive, the private opportunity costs of holding money will depend on the alternative use of that money, for example, buying durable goods or holding bonds; hence the costs will become positive. The study of Emerson *et al.* (1990) estimates that inflation of 10 per cent could reduce significantly the transaction advantages of a single currency of Table 18.1 as the costs could be 0.1–0.3 per cent of GDP. At the macro level, it is known from extensive empirical work that higher inflation does not lower unemployment in the longer run. Gros & Thygesen (1998, pp. 483–5) also find a negative association between inflation and real growth in the EU, which is statistically highly significant.

The notion that unanticipated or surprise inflation may have temporary, real effects, has further drawbacks, because it raises the unpredictability and variability of inflation, which – as evidence shows – increases with the average level of inflation. An irregular but repeated recourse to surprise inflation must lead to 'stop–go' policies, which are bound to increase the macroeconomic costs of inflation in the longer run.

These constitutional features determine what kind of monetary union the EU has opted for. It is an amazingly powerful and functional construction, probably 'harder' than any other in the world. In the following, other characteristics of the eurozone are discussed which are perhaps not constitutional but still of interest for a good understanding of the nature and potential impact of the euro.

18.5 Monetary and fiscal policies in the eurozone

Macroeconomic policy making in the eurozone is a mixture of centralised monetary policy and decentralised fiscal policies under constraints. The reason why these constraints were imposed is discussed below.

18.5.1 Monetary policy

In order to manage the monetary policy of the newly created monetary union a new institution had to be set up: this was the European System of Central Banks (ESCB). We first describe this institution, then we consider the objectives, strategy and instruments of monetary policy. Finally, we briefly evaluate the ESCB's functioning to date.

18.5.1.1 The European (System of) Central Bank(s)

The European System of Central Banks was created by the Maastricht Treaty. It is made up of the European Central Bank and the national central banks (NCBs) of all the Member States of the EU. A smaller grouping, called the Eurosystem, consists of the ECB and the NCBs of the Member States participating in the monetary union (the eurozone). The ESCB has the same three decision-making bodies as the ECB. The first is the Executive Board which comprises the president and vice-president of the ECB and four other members, appointed by common accord of the governments of (all) the Member States. Its main tasks are to implement the monetary policy decisions taken by the Governing Council and to ensure the daily management of the ECB. The second decision-making body is the Governing Council which is made up of the Executive

[47] There have been two attempts to introduce exchange rate targets for the euro. One was when stage 3 was about to begin and the French (Strauss-Kahn) and German (Lafontaine) finance ministers pleaded for 'target zones'. In the autumn of 2000, when the euro fell sharply *vis-à-vis* the dollar (and the dollar-denominated oil price shot up), the ECB and others intervened because price stability was under pressure. However, no targets have been pursued.

Board and the Governors of the NCBs of the eurozone. Its chief responsibilities are (1) the definition and implementation of the monetary policy of the eurozone; (2) the conduct of foreign exchange operations, as well as the holding and management of foreign exchange reserves of the eurozone; and (3) promoting the smooth operation of payment systems. Prudential supervison of credit institutions and the stability of the financial system is not its responsibility (see also Chapter 9) but the Eurosystem is expected to contribute to the smooth conduct of policies pursued by the authorities who are in charge of them. The third body is the General Council which will exist as long as there are Member States of the EU that do not take part in the monetary union. Its members are the president and vice-president of the ECB as well as all the governors of the NCBs of the EU. It has no say in monetary policy making in the eurozone.

The E(S)CB is independent. In a democratic society, such independence brings with it other obligations, namely transparency and accountability. Winkler (2000) defines transparency as the degree of genuine understanding of the monetary policy process and policy decisions by the public. This requires some degree of disclosure by the ECB: disclosure of policy objectives, of economic information used for monetary policy decisions and of procedures followed to reach decisions, a prompt announcement of policy decisions, the reasons underlying them as well as indications of likely future policy actions, and finally, disclosure of how the ECB's decisions are implemented (de Haan *et al.*, 2005). The ECB has no formal obligation to transparency or accountability but it claims to be very open.

18.5.1.2 Objectives, strategies and instruments of monetary policy

Objectives. The EC treaty states that the 'primary objective of the ESCB shall be to maintain price stability'. But the treaty does not define what is meant by price stability, leaving this up to the ECB. On 13 October 1998, the Governing Council of the ECB defined price stability as a year-on-year increase in the Harmonised Index of Consumer Prices (HICP) for the euro area of below 2 per cent; in May 2003 it was specified as close to 2 per cent over the medium term. In this way, the ECB intended to 'provide a sufficient safety margin to guard against the risks of deflation', and to address 'the issue of the possible presence of a measurement bias in the HICP', as well as 'the implications of inflation differentials within the euro area.'

The EC treaty also assigns to the ESCB a secondary objective: 'without prejudice to the objective of price stability, the ESCB shall support the general economic policies in the Community with a view to contributing to the achievement of the objectives of the Community as laid down in Article 2'. However, the ECB also stated that 'maintaining price stability in itself contributes to the achievement of output and employment goals' (*ECB Monthly Bulletin*, January 1999, p. 40). In this way, the ECB reduced the two objectives to a single one.

Strategy. In order to achieve the ECB's objective(s), the Governing Council established a 'two-pillar' strategy. Originally the first pillar was the so-called monetary pillar where a prominent role was assigned to money, signalled by the announcement of a quantitative reference value for the growth of a broad monetary aggregate. A reference value for the rate of growth of the monetary aggregate, M3, was calculated on the basis of the quantity theory of money: the reference rate of growth of money stock equals the maximum allowed inflation rate plus the trend growth rate of output minus the rate of change in the velocity of circulation of money. The reason why a single value was announced for M3 rather than a range was that a reference range might be falsely interpreted as implying that interest rates would be changed automatically if monetary growth were to move outside the boundaries of the range. The second pillar was a broadly based assessment of the outlook for price developments and risks to price stability in the euro area which would encompass a wide range of economic and financial indicator variables. While developments in individual countries must be taken into account when performing the above analyses, the ECB makes its policy decision on the basis of the behaviour of the euro area aggregates.

In May 2003, the ECB reversed the order of the two pillars. First came the 'economic analysis' pillar and then the 'monetary analysis' pillar. On 28 October 2005, Otmar Issing, a member of the Executive Board of the ECB, explained that the ECB looked not only at the rate of growth of M3 but also at the reasons underlying that rate of growth. Only if it was felt that an increasing demand for money was feeding into higher spending on goods and services and were not just portfolio shifts, would the Central Bank consider that there was a risk to inflation. Finally, the conclusions regarding inflationary pressures resulting from each pillar were cross-checked against each other.

Instruments. We now describe how the ECB implements its monetary policy, or what is known as the operational framework. The guiding principles are that the EC treaty requires the ESCB to 'act in accordance with the principle of an open market economy with free competition', that implementation is decentralised through the NCBs though coordinated by the ECB, and that the ESCB is a monopoly supplier of monetary base to the commercial banking sector. The main instruments used by the ESCB are (1) standing facilities, (2) open market operations, and (3) minimum reserve requirements. There are two standing facilities: the marginal lending facility, which allows 'counterparties'[48] to borrow money overnight at a pre-specified interest rate from the ESCB against eligible assets; and the deposit facility which allows counterparties to make overnight deposits at the ESCB at a pre-specified interest rate. These two facilities serve to set an upper and lower bound to the overnight interbank interest rate. The minimum reserves requirement was a much used instrument in the toolkit of central banks but is used less and less because of the cost to commercial banks. The ECB requires credit institutions to deposit a certain fraction of their own liabilities with the NCBs. By raising the minimum reserves requirements ratio, central banks can create a liquidity shortage. Since the money deposited to satisfy this requirement can be profitably used otherwise by credit institutions, the requirement carries a cost, which is why it is less and less used as central banks have moved to more market-based instruments. Nevertheless, the Bundesbank insisted that it be maintained in the arsenal of instruments available to the ESCB in case it ever needed to create a liquidity shortage. For the moment it is used in order to smooth interest rates: banks must satisfy the requirement on average over the month. Finally, the most important instrument used by the ESCB is open market operations which consist in the buying and selling of securities by the ECB in order to inject or to withdraw liquidity from the interbank market and influence the interest rate in this manner. The main open market operation used by the ESCB is the main refinancing operation which occurs weekly by tender.

The ESCB uses the above instruments in order to control a very-short-term interest rate index known as the EONIA, the European Overnight Index Average. This is a measure of the interest rate prevailing in the euro interbank overnight market. The ECB uses various forms of open market operations to steer the EONIA rate within the bands set by the standing facilities rates.

The ESCB controls a single interest rate. As a consequence its policy will not be adapted or suitable for all the eurozone countries (the *one size fits all* problem) unless all countries happen to be in a similar business cycle phase or subject to the same shocks. But this is also true of the USA, for example. Also, the monetary transmission mechanism by which the interest rate controlled by the ECB affects the economy will differ from country to country since it depends on structural features of the economy, both real and financial. There is some evidence that, since monetary union, there has been some convergence in the monetary transmission mechanisms of the eurozone countries.

Evaluation. For a detailed evaluation of the first six years of existence of the monetary policy of the ESCB, the reader is referred to de Grauwe (2005) and de Haan *et al.* (2005). We briefly consider a few issues here.

The ECB is confronted with one basic problem in setting its monetary policy: it sets a single monetary policy (more concretely, a set of interest rates) which then applies to all the countries composing the euro area. De Grauwe (2005, p. 185) applied Taylor's rule[49] to the different countries of the euro area for the year 2003 and came up with a large variation of desired interest rates, from 1.22 per cent for Germany to 7.87 per cent for Ireland. Nevertheless, the ECB is obliged to set an interest rate corresponding to the average performance of the euro area, and it is from this perspective that its interest rate policy should be evaluated. Many economists feel that the ECB's monetary policy has been close to optimal given the above constraint.

How does one go about evaluation the ECB's performance with respect to transparency and accountability? One measure of *ex ante* transparency is the ability of markets to correctly forecast the interest rates that will be set by the ECB. From this point of view, the communication strategy of the ECB has been successful: by and large the ECB policy moves were in line with financial markets' expectations. Accountability is much more difficult to evaluate. While the ECB has made a number of moves to appear accountable (though not obliged to do so) through its publications and the speeches of its board members, and regular appearances of the ECB president in the EP, economists differ in their views regarding the extent to which it has actually accounted sufficiently for its actions.

[48] A counterparty is the opposite party in a financial transaction. In our context, the ECB draws up annually a list of counterparties with which it is willing to transact.

[49] The rule that Taylor established was the following: $i_t = \pi_t + r^* + 0.5(\pi_t - \pi^*) + 0.5(y_t)$, where i is the federal funds rate, r^* is the equilibrium real federal funds rate, π is the the actual inflation rate (GDP deflator), π^* is the target inflation rate, and y is the output gap (the deviation of actual output from its potential level). It verifies whether inflation is close to target and real output close to its long-run potential output.

The main criticism against the ECB has been with regard to its two-pillar strategy. A comprehensive inflation-targeting approach to monetary policy would subsume the monetary analysis pillar into the economic analysis pillar as one of the determinants of inflation, and not give it a separate role. An independent role for the monetary pillar properly interpreted has been strongly defended by Otmar Issing, a member of the Executive Board of the ECB (see above).

Has the ECB been successful in its main objective, namely, price stability? In order to evaluate its success we must distinguish between two issues: the ECB's definition of price stability and whether it has been able to stick to it. The ECB has been heavily criticised, first, for setting so low a ceiling to inflation, namely, 2 per cent, and, second, for defining price stability in an asymmetric way. Two reasons have been given for why the target should not be set too low. The first reason is macroeconomic in nature. Macroeconomic stabilisation may at times require negative real interest rates. Since nominal interest rates cannot fall below zero, a ceiling of 2 per cent to inflation places a lower bound of –2 per cent on real interest rates. The microeconomic reason is that inflation tends to 'oil' the economy: if there is downward nominal wage and price rigidity, relative wages and prices across sectors can be adjusted only by raising wages and prices in certain sectors.

The ECB has defined price stability as inflation between zero and 2 per cent. This could be taken to mean that the bank aims at an inflation target 1 per cent and allows for a one percentage point deviation on either side. But this does not seem to be the case, especially since the monetary policy review in May 2003 when the Governing Council stated that its objective was an inflation rate (as measured by the HICP) of close to 2 per cent.[50] Questions arise as to whether this results in an asymmetric monetary policy in the sense that the Governing Council is more sensitive to a rise in inflation above 2 per cent than to a fall in inflation to around 1 per cent. During the first six years of monetary union, the ECB has tolerated periods of inflation higher than 2 per cent. Its justification was that this was the result of temporary phenomena and did not reflect medium-run tendencies in inflation.

18.5.2 Fiscal policies in the monetary union

During the 1980s and early 1990s there was a huge increase in the ratio of government debt to GDP in the OECD countries. By 1995, the ratio had reached 133 per cent in Belgium and 123 per cent in Italy, the GDP weighted average for the EU as a whole being 70 per cent. The evolution of government debt was on an unsustainable path and there was a need for fiscal discipline of some sort.

There are various reasons why government budgets in modern democracies are often characterised by a deficit bias (see Calmfors, 2005, pp. 14–22). While these reasons may justify the need for fiscal rules at the national levels, they are not sufficient to require Community-level rules. In a monetary union, however, there are reasons to impose fiscal rules at a supranational level.

It is often held that the fiscal rules described above are excessively strict since capital markets have the capacity to differentiate between country borrowers by varying risk premiums. What the EMU constraints express is a conviction that capital markets do this either imperfectly (for instance, too late[51]) or in such a disruptive way (for example, by cutting credit lines totally) that the social costs of sudden austerity would be unacceptable. Without fiscal rules an irresistible pressure could be exerted on the ECB to lower interest rates. Behind this conviction lurks the possible lack of fiscal discipline in a single currency area. As noted in Chapter 17, fiscal policy is effective in stimulating output but at the costs of external deficits or depreciation; however, the latter discipline disappears in EMU. Indeed, during the preparations of the Amsterdam Treaty, repeated calls for tougher sanctions in the case of excessive deficits under a single currency were made.[52]

There are three aspects to the issue of fiscal policy in the monetary union of the EU: (1) regulatory constraints for national fiscal policy, (2) broader questions of macroeconomic policy coordination, of which fiscal policy (again, of the Member States) is a part, and (3) the option of a stabilisation function at the EU level.

The regulatory constraints ought to prevent the undermining of price stability, as pursued by the ECB, caused

[50]One of the reasons for redefining its inflation objective as inflation close to 2 per cent was the upward biases in the HICP which led to its overestimating inflation.

[51]Since a debt crisis will cause capital flight, it may force large devaluations the prospect of which intensifies the initial capital flight. Such a spiral would no longer apply once a single currency exists, so, for example, the Mexican peso crisis of December 1994 is not an instructive example. An appropriate case study might be the 1975 crisis for New York City.

[52]Gros (1995), for instance, proposes that the excessive deficit procedure in stage 3 be automatic, and not subject to Council decisions, and that non-compliance should lead to expulsion from EMU.

by destabilising fiscal policies of the Member States. The three constraints are:

1 no monetary financing of fiscal deficits;
2 a no-bail-out clause (that is, other Member States or the EU do not rescue a defaulting Member State);
3 excessive deficits (above 3 per cent, as a rule) are forbidden, subject to sanctions in stage 3 of EMU, and as an entry condition before stage 3.

The fear that a currency union, once the entry conditions are no longer relevant, could have an inflationary bias because of a lack of effective discipline of (national) fiscal policy, was tackled in the Stability and Growth Pact (SGP) which became effective with the start of the monetary union. The Pact consists of two elements, each of which was subject to a regulation.

The first regulation (1466/97), known as the preventive arm of the Pact, contains the obligation of a medium-term budget position 'close to balance or surplus', supported by annual 'stability programmes', showing the path to or maintenance of this position. The budget in question was later interpreted as being the cyclically adjusted budget (CAB). The other regulation (1467/97), called the corrective arm of the Pact, was a clarification of the excessive-deficit procedure in the treaty (Article 104 EC). The excessive-deficit procedure in essence states that deficits above a 'reference value' (the protocol fixed it at 3 per cent, not the treaty) are excessive. This can lead to sanctions, including non-interest-bearing deposits and, eventually, fines. Although 3 per cent is arbitrary, the idea is that recessions will cause fiscal stabilisers to work, resulting in deficits up to 3 per cent (only rarely would this not suffice). But, of course, this 'room' is available only if the budget is balanced before the recession hits. It is here that the Pact comes in. Its starting point is precisely that, in the medium-term, balanced budgets are necessary in order to create 'room' for the automatic fiscal stabilisers in recessionary periods, without endangering fiscal discipline. If truly exceptional,[53] a temporary excess of 3 per cent is allowed, otherwise sanctions follow. The deposit has a fixed component of 0.2 per cent of GDP and a flexible component which depends on the size of the excessive deficit. After two years, (part of) the deposit 'is urged always' to be converted into a fine.

When it came to the crunch, the fiscal rules turned out to be too restrictive, and the procedural rules for the Council to establish the existence of and eventually sanction an excessive deficit became unenforceable. Soon after the start of monetary union, the EU countries experienced a sharp downturn in economic activity. This led to an increase in public sector deficits; and since a number of countries had not achieved a government deficit in balance by then but were still suffering from deficits, several ran into trouble with the excessive-deficit constraint. Among the larger countries, Germany and France were the most difficult cases and did not respond to admonitions under the excessive-deficit procedure to improve their budget situations. Nevertheless, when the Commission recommended the initiation of the next step in the excessive-deficit procedure, the Council did not succeed in martialling a qualified majority to vote in the recommendation. This occurred in November 2003. The SGP had become a dead letter.[54]

These incidents prompted a reformed SGP which came into force in July 2005. Two new regulations (1055/2005 and 1056/2005) replaced the previous ones. The reform boils down to little more than fine-tuning and these details go beyond the scope of this book. On the whole, the new SGP is less strict (although, at the end of the day, the 3 per cent still stands, also because of the treaty protocol) in that an adjustment path of (only) 0.5 per cent a year is mentioned and that overshooting 3 per cent is already allowed in a recession (any negative growth), not only a deep recession.

With a little more attention to debt ratios rather than deficits (because it is unsustainable debt which could be a motive to exert pressure on the ECB) as well as to pension reform and the relation to overall economic 'governance' of the EU (see the softer coordination discussed in section 18.1.2.), the new SGP has some positive aspects, too. The crux of the matter, however, is whether such a relatively decentralised coordination, the 'policing' of which is run by exactly the ministers who are causing the problems, can actually work. The answer is: only imperfectly. For them the euro is a collective good and this severely limits their 'free-riding' in the Eurogroup of finance ministers. But some free-riding they are tempted to do and some colluding not to be too harsh to sinners is bound to occur. Commission officials and others have suggested that electoral budget cycles are too attractive for national ministers and the Pact is not strong enough to

[53]If the recession caused a decline in GDP by 2 per cent, a higher deficit is temporarily allowed. If growth is between 0.75 and –2 per cent, the Council decides whether more than 3 per cent is justified or not.

[54]The Council went further and adopted a new set of recommendations which had not been proposed by the Commission. This part of the Council's decision was annulled by the EC Court when the Commission appealed against the Council's decisions.

rein them in. One test to see if the new Pact has effect is whether, in the expected upturn of the EU economy in 2006 and 2007, the debt ratios in euroland start falling again.

Finally, there is a third way of looking at fiscal policy making in euroland. Since 1999 the EU has had a monetary union without any form of common fiscal stabilisation, and this is (nowadays) unique. Is it feasible in the long run? This brings us back to the substance and possible development of a kind of political union, where an EU-level fiscal function would result from some kind of central taxation, and perhaps some social expenditure functions as well. Such a scenario is very far off and is not pursued here. As noted, there are plausible arguments to defend the view that decentralisation might do. In the long run, a less rigid and restrictive solution for stabilisation problems might be wanted. During the Maastricht negotiations there was some attention paid to a Union-wide shock absorption mechanism. The Commission proposal was rejected, probably out of fear of a sizable expansion of the Union budget. However, as Italianer & Vanheukelen (1993) show, a degree of stabilisation as high as 19 per cent of the shock can be achieved with an estimated annual cost of only 0.2 per cent of EU GDP. The shock absorption mechanism they propose is a pure stabilisation scheme, that is, only the presence and the size of a shock determine eligibility. In other words, relative prosperity does not play a role. Its operation would depend on changes in unemployment rates relative to the EU average. Since the mechanism works as an insurance pool, the actual payments to Member States from the central pool are far smaller than the theoretical maximum payments one could imagine.[55]

18.6 External aspects of the euro

There are two external aspects of the euro which merit attention: whether euroland should care about the exchange rate of the euro, and the possible international role of the euro.[56]

Although there are provisions about the possible influence of the Council on exchange rate policy, and about the conclusion of exchange rate systems (Article 111 EC), the current position is one of 'benign neglect'. There is no policy or any target for that matter. However, if (say) the euro/dollar rate were to slide fast enough, it could lead to strong price increases of tradable goods, and hence increase overall inflation. This scenario unfolded in the summer and autumn of 2000, when, in addition, dollar-denominated oil prices shot up. Together, they had the tendency to push inflation in euroland over the 2 per cent ceiling. In the press, however, the discussion was centred on the 'weak' euro. The ECB strictly followed benign neglect because the fundamentals in the eurozone were good and there was no exchange rate target. Nevertheless, the euro became greatly undervalued and inflation was creeping up. In October and early November 2000, a few interventions were used to signal to the markets that the loss of confidence had no justification whatsoever. The euro stabilised but only began to climb again once the US boom was perceived to be over.

The international role of the euro is mainly dependent on the three determinants of a world currency role: a size effect, stability reputation and liquidity advantages. The size effect, if represented by GDP, might eventually lead to a world role. In 2004, euroland had a GNP of 16 per cent of world GNP, second after the USA with 21 per cent. Since the eurozone will grow in the years to come, the size effect will augment. If the UK comes in besides the new Member States, size might become important. The stability reputation of the euro is undisputed, with the hardest monetary constitution in the world. But this is internal to euroland. Its external value depends on the USA and Japan and their currencies. The liquidity properties of financial markets in the EU are rapidly improving as a result of recent financial market integration and modernisation (see Chapters 9 and 10). Further deepening might still take place. The question is, however, is the EU the cheapest place to do capital market business? Are markets as deep and as swift as in the USA?

Table 18.3 provides a bird's eye view of the international role of the euro in 2004. There are certainly signs of an interest in the euro for particular functions for particular players in selected cases. The main conclusion from Table 18.3 is that the euro has acquired the status of a 'regional international currency' but there

[55]The authors suggest that a payments ceiling and minimum thresholds for shocks would further limit the actual payments. Simulations for the 1980s bring this out. Note also that anti-cyclical devices have been proposed in more 'centralist' ways in the MacDougall report (MacDougall *et al.*, 1977). For a new variant, see Majocchi & Rey (1993).

[56]Other issues are ignored such as the proper (preferably, single) representation of euroland in the IMF, OECD, and bilaterally with the USA and Japan..

Table 18.3 Euro as international currency?

Euro functions	Specific roles	Importance of euro
Public role	Anchor, reserve, intervention (and privately) parallel	• 40 countries in 2004 . . . • but mainly –micro states in Europe –new Member States –candidate countries • Pegs with African franc zone
Euro role in world markets	Unit of account • invoicing • quotations	• Strongly in Europe; little outside Europe
	Means of exchange • payments • vehicle currency (intermediate between two little-traded currencies)	• Distant second to the US$ (share 96% out of 200%; two-sided trade; euro share 44% out of 200%; pound and yen ±20%)
	Store of value • financing	• (In stocks of euro-dominated debt) a rise to 31% in 2004, at the costs of the yen-share, and a little of the US share
	• investment	• Loans and deposits, picture complicated but euro-share considerable, for all links with Europe; fully outside Europe, euro shares small; note that UK financial business dominates the exchanges here

Source: ECB, 2005

are few, if any, signs of a rivalry with the dollar. There is also no intention to seek an international role (even if there is a minor gain in terms of seignorage, the gain on euro banknotes not returning to euroland). The inertia in invoicing in commodity markets is strong (why change a well-working set of world markets and its network infrastructure and tacit knowledge?) and the same is true for a vehicle role. The only speculation one might consider is the possibility of portfolio shifts out of the US dollar into the euro; given the instability of the dollar – its net debtor position and ever large deficits – this cannot be dismissed entirely.

18.7 Summary

Two contrasting concepts of economic union are, first, that of a fully fledged internal market (all that it takes for its establishment and proper functioning) and, second, that of the economic integration needed for monetary union to function properly. In the latter concept the E and the M of EMU are twins; in the former, exchange rate stability will do. In the Maastricht Treaty (and ever since), the E of EMU remains undefined. The implicit economic union in the treaty is far richer and more robust as a foundation for a single currency than with the first EMU attempt in the early 1970s (Case Study 18.1). A wide and very deep single market is in place (except perhaps for labour), and competition policy is well developed. With respect to cohesion, in its efficiency function there is no connection with monetary union; with respect to equity, there is a catch-up philosophy, in other words, no permanent redistribution. Finally, economic policy coordination is 'soft' in the 'open method of coordination' in the economic union (Lisbon) and stricter, with sanctions, for national fiscal policy, because it is tied to monetary union. The soft coordination is desirable

Summary *continued*

for a better functioning but the Lisbon incentive structure (given its very weak position in domestic politics) largely fails.

Currency unification prompts the question of why we need to have exchange rates. The main benefit is the ease, hence the low costs, of adjustment to a shock. The benefits of a single currency are microeconomic and, in principle, are not exhausted before all countries of the world are covered. Optimum currency area theory requires answers to four questions, all about the costs of giving up the exchange rate: the nature and sources of shocks, the alternative adjustments in the (for example, labour) market, what policies might facilitate adjustment, and what sacrifice is there in irrevocably fixing exchange rates in terms of short-run macroeconomic stabilisation. There are four benefits of irrevocably fixed exchange rates: avoidance of the costs of exchange rate volatility, of transactions, of exchange rate uncertainty, and the weakening of 'home bias'. Once a single currency is adopted, these benefits are enhanced by some extra gains (such as seignorage) and strategic gains for integration at large ('inner dynamics'). The latter are not measurable *ex ante* but have almost ceratinly been important *ex post* in the EU since the late 1990s.

Applied to the EU, both the probability and the empirical significance (for example for unemployment) of asymmetric shocks are low. Although cross-border labour mobility is low, so is intra-Member-State labour mobility. Moreover, the costs of intra-EU labour mobility are also perceived as high. The alternative of wage adjustment, helped by fiscal stabilisers is more problematic. Real wage rigidity in the EU is strong, and in an EMU, there must be decentralisation of fiscal stabilisers (since the EU budget is very small, and balanced). However, in the presence of real wage rigidity, exchange rates cannot be an effective policy instrument. And fiscally, decentralised stabilisation will do (and is forceful).

If monetary policy (hence, exchange rate policy) is seen as powerless in influencing real variables (for example, employment) beyond a short period, the EU may well be close to an optimum currency area. Current euroland might well have positive net benefits. No doubt, those costs decline further once adjustment mechanisms work better and the economy becomes more flexible. This is a task in the economic union.

The measurable benefits of a single currency in the EU are a little higher than 1 per cent of GDP. These benefits will not be fully obtained if EMU only irrevocably fixes the exchange rates but does not create a single currency. One important reason is found in the gains of integrating payment and settlement systems which would then not take place (see Case Study 18.2).

There are three stages to EU monetary integration in the 1990s. Stage 1 preceded the Maastricht Treaty and emphasised removal of capital controls and exchange rate stabilisation. Stage 2 (started 1 January 1994) brought the EMI and a stricter element of coordination: the 'excessive deficit' procedure. The real issue of stage 2 for the Member States was to obtain an entry ticket for EMU in 1999. The convergence criteria are perhaps arbitrary, especially the fiscal deficit and the debt ratio ones, although rational from a German point of view, given the risk of what it might lose from monetary union. The Maastricht strategy of strict entry conditions worked miracles: no less than eleven EU countries entered in 1999 and Greece in 2001, despite seemingly hopeless starting positions in the mid-1990s. Nevertheless, the strategy was economically costly as it was overly restrictive, with high additional unemployment. It is likely that no less than six new Member States will enter euroland before 2008.

The EU monetary union has a robust monetary constitution. It centralises monetary (and exchange rate, if any) policy, the ECB is independent and the price stability objective is overriding. The introduction of the euro is a fascinating experiment with major sequencing and logistical problems (see Case Study 18.3).

Monetary policy is not fundamentally different from 'national' monetary policy, although there is a 'one-size-fits-all' problem. And, of course, the ECB as an institution is more complex than a national central bank. Price stability is defined as inflation close to 2 per cent. The one-size-fits-all problem in years such as 2002 and 2003 turned out to be considerable, but such problems are by definition temporary and may concern different countries differently at different points in time. The ECB 'two-pillar' strategy (why not merge the broad economic and the monetary pressures for inflation?) is still the subject of much debate. Fiscal policy is decentralised but it is at the same time rather constrained (no bail-out; no

Summary ***continued***

excessive deficits). The Stability and Growth Pact has imposed a medium-run balanced budget so as to have 'room' for fiscal stabilisers in case of a recession. The SGP was not followed to its logical (sanctions) conclusion when it mattered most, so it has a credibility problem. The new SGP is not *a priori* more credible.

As to the external aspects of the euro, the exchange rate approach is a non-policy of 'benign neglect', and the international role of the euro increases slowly in importance. The euro is now (2005) a 'regional international currency' and the reader is unlikely to witness a challenge to the dollar in the near future.

CHAPTER 19

Assessing the EU Budget

Topics covered

If the Union is about 'rules, not money', as is noted in Chapter 2, the EU budget cannot be very important. The media and, at times, ministers of finance (or of the national budget), tend to make one believe differently, however. Even government leaders engage in what invariably are described as 'European budget battles'. Nevertheless, these political games have a heavy dose of 'make believe' and most of the noises in the media are for domestic political consumption. The facts are that the EU budget is trivial by any reasonable standard: it amounts to only 1 per cent of the Union's GDP and less than 3 per cent of the total of the national budgets. It is restricted in a number of ways which are explained later. Despite the facts, the EU budget has continued to fascinate many observers of the EU and, not least, academic economists and advisers. This fascination may be prompted by the political sensation of these 'battles', or, by the fear that budget battles may stifle the activism at EU level (as in the period 1980–84) or, rather, by grand new ideas of what might be done with an EU budget of very different design and functions from the one of today. For these reasons, there is a case for bringing clarity about the role and impact of the EU budget and, perhaps first of all, about what the EU budget is not and does not do. The perspective from which we assess the EU budget is 'subsidiarity'.

Section 19.1 briefly sketches the contrast between the overblown politics and very modest economics of the EU budget. The subsidiarity test is applied to the current budget and its public economic functions in section 19.2. Section 19.3 attempts to grasp the budget logic for four categories of expenditure: the CAP, cohesion, efficiency and several incipient EU public goods such as an EU zone of security or joint peacekeeping in other parts of the world. The revenue side is addressed in section 19.4. A long-run view of the budget brings out the strategic choices more clearly: they are juxtaposed in section 19.5.

19.1 Politics versus economics of the EU budget

The EU budget is tiny. A total of over €100 billion annually might appear to be an appreciable sum of money, but it still amounts to no more than between 2 and 3 per cent (on average) of the annual budget of the Member States. The structure of the EU budget is incomparable to that of national budgets. Two reasons make the two budgets incomparable. First, Member States have kept practically all the expenditures of the so-called spending ministries on their budget such as social and employment benefits, welfare payments, health benefits and health care, education, social housing, infrastructure, defence, police and justice. Only agriculture is split between the EU level and the national level. The unavoidable result is that, whatever policy expenditures the EU budget does include, their share of the total of EU spending *must* be much larger than a national budget would ever have. In other words, in and of itself a relatively high share of agriculture or of cohesion cannot be used as a good indicator of the economic impact. Second, the revenue side of the EU budget is not based on the taxation of EU citizens (directly and/or indirectly) and companies. Instead, a strange blend of what in European law is called 'own resources' of the EU level itself and Member States' contributions ensures enough revenue to cover EU spending.

The EU budget is subject to a host of technical and economic restrictions. Its administrative provisions are overly rigid, essentially because Member States are not willing to give too much discretion to the EU institutions other than the Council itself (and even then, in cumbersome procedures). It is an expression of the somewhat intergovernmental traditions which surround the European budget. Rather than relying on the routine 'Community method' (see Chapter 1), the Commission merely proposes the draft budget but is formally not allowed to play the same role as in the case of draft legislation. It is up to the EU budget authority which is jointly exercised by the Council and the European Parliament. Of course, the Commission remains quite active as a broker in the decision-making process but it can do no more when the going gets rough between the Council and the EP. In the constitutional treaty (not yet ratified) the Commission would obtain a formal role also after the submission of the draft budget. Budget ceilings are no longer set annually (a source of perennial friction) but are instead set for a period of six or seven years in the so-called *financial perspectives,* under veto. At the time of writing (2005), the ceiling is 1.24 per cent of GNI (that is, 1.27 per cent of GDP), but the actual budget expenditures since 2000 have hovered only just above 1 per cent of GDP. The new financial perspectives have been set for the period 2007–13 and the budget 'battle' in 2005 was precisely about these ceilings, the main categories of spending under that ceiling and, not least, about who pays into EU revenue both on a gross and a net basis. The *annual* budget debates within the seven-year period tend to be far more functional because the political boundaries are already carved in stone.

The economic restrictions include that the EU cannot run a deficit at any time and that borrowing is severely restricted. Since the EU does not avail of tax income or revenue from social charges either, the EU budget cannot have any macroeconomic function at all. Finally, there is also no link between the EU budget and the national budgets other than the annual contributions.

The conclusion is that the EU budget is of marginal economic importance. Its weight and role do not justify long-drawn-out budget battles between Member States which unduly focus on what net payments or receipts Member States can defend at home. The cardinal neglect in all these battles is the EU interest itself. This is the cost of the quasi-intergovernmentalism of the Union budget regime. The point is not so much that budget debates, whether in the national or EU context, should not be politicised; of course, they should since choices have to be made and communicated in a politically clear fashion. Rather, the point is that the incentive system of the EU budget regime is heavily distorted since the 'domestic' orientations of the Member States (which act as a brake on any tendency of the EU level ever to grow into a kind of Leviathan) are not counterbalanced by a strong defender of the common interest worth paying for via budget outlays.

Let us ignore the politics for a moment and assume a strictly economic perspective of the ideal role of the EU budget. Such a role would follow from answering five queries:

1 Does the pursuit of common objectives suggest the use of expenditure as an instrument?
2 Can markets or the internal market as such (sufficiently) achieve the common objectives?
3 If, and to the extent that, markets or the internal market cannot achieve the common objectives (sufficiently), can (EU) regulation not do it (subject to RIAs) or would regulation not be suitable?
4 If, therefore, the common objectives ought be pursued with money (not to speak of taxes), should this best be done at the Member States level but with credible coordination, or is it better to do it at the EU level in a common budget?
5 If it is to be done at EU level, how can representative democracy, transparency and accountability be organised that EU voters (far removed from the EU circuit in their daily lives) perceive the correspondence between what they want, what they pay for and what the EU accomplishes? How can the discretion at EU level, that the 'political distance' between voters and the EU circuit inevitably provides, be protected against undue influence of vested interests organised

at the EU level, be it to maintain EU expenditures or to insert new spending?

Such a functional test is difficult to follow rigorously at all times. Nevertheless, it is a useful starting point to formulate the EU budget and can serve as a test for any draft budget. The reality of EU budgets is far removed from living up to this test and the gap is worrying for efficiency and effectiveness. A dysfunctional political economy causes the following shortcomings. First, the subsidiarity test is not executed, or is executed only very superficially and selectively at best. Second, the path dependency (determined by vested interests which block alternative options) is very strong and greatly helped by unanimity. Two items in the budget add up to nearby 80 per cent of all expenditures (CAP and cohesion) and, although cohesion has gained as a share compared with the CAP, the CAP spending has never declined absolutely and the two together had already assumed a similar share 25 years ago. It is doubtful, to say the least, that actual CAP spending would pass the above test. Third, there is a dramatic lack of flexibility in the EU budget which renders a close correspondence with common objectives (which are subject to change, of course) almost impossible: shifts between categories of spending within an annual budget are cumbersome and slow, and next to impossible over the medium-run financial perspectives; the (*de facto*) ceiling of 1 per cent is the same as before 1988 but now applies to a Union with many more goals and tasks and with a clear cohesion aim for many relatively poor Member States. Fourth, the politics of the EU budget debate distort the functionality of what the EU does: citizens in net paying countries hear only about the 'sacrifices' and little if anything about the joint benefits; those in net receiving countries hear only about the political unwillingness of the net payers to live up to the 'solidarity' written in the treaty; worst of all, citizens are not made aware that the EU budget is a marginal issue in European integration, that the manifold benefits (economic and political, if not in security as well) have little or nothing to do with the EU budget and that net-payers are not net losers precisely because the core of European integration and its benefits are not expressed in or via the budget.

19.2 Subsidiarity and EU budget functions

The ingredients from a subsidiarity test as applied to the budget can be taken from Chapter 3. The test inspects the three public economic functions that the EU budget might possibly support, namely efficiency (or, the allocation function), equity and macroeconomic stabilisation. In principle, the test could be applied both to expenditures and to the revenue side. Sections 19.2 and 19.3 concentrate on the expenditures, section 19.4 on revenues.

In a setting of two-tier government, the central budget should be assigned with the *efficiency function* if (1) positive externalities across intra-EU borders are significant, and the solution of 'prisoners' dilemmas' for Member States are best solved by common funding; (2) negative intra-EU cross-border spillovers can better be prevented or minimised by common budgetary outlays (and not by prohibitions or EU regulation, for example); (3) scale or critical mass requires joint production or pooling of resources backed up by joint funding. Ideally, this is combined with a proportionality test (step 5). The latter should be specified in greater detail as follows. Even if positive externalities or scale are non-trivial, a shift to the EU level of funding (step 4) is not appropriate if the heterogeneity of preferences in a particular area of policy is strong. Ultimately, this is a political decision. In the case of negative externalities, the conflict must somehow be resolved. Dependent on the willingness to accept functional solutions, shifts to the EU level are an option. The problem is that negative externalities, if powerful enough, might be a manifestation of strongly held positions for which a functional solution is politically impossible. The choice is then one between making a mockery of the internal market and finding a common solution consistent with subsidiarity (given the imperative of a common market) but not with proportionality. The latter was the original issue for the CAP. In having to make two imperatives compatible, namely, the internal agricultural market and the interventionist protection of farmers' incomes via prices at the Member States level, the only way out was to conduct the heavy interventionism jointly. The upshot was a significant role in the EU budget for price support, behind the high tariff protection of the EU.

The proportionality issue is also affected by the capability of the centre of 'differentiating' policy instruments to diversity at the national or regional level. If that capability is low due to transaction costs or asymmetries of information about local preferences, the costs of centralisation can be perceived as (too?) high. This question might well play a role in the programming requirements of the Structural Funds which need not fit local needs.

Equity functions in multi-layer governments are basically a political function of sentiments of solidarity and, more often than not, of nationhood. All federations among the developed countries have quite powerful equity mechanisms at the federal level, although the redistributive effects differ considerably among them. The EU is not a nation or a country and does not aspire to become one. On this account alone, the EU cannot be expected to have strong equity functions. Moreover, equity functions are usually connected to both the revenue (that is, taxation) and expenditure sides. Yet, the Union has no instruments at the revenue side because there is no legal basis for EU taxes; even the constitutional treaty (not yet ratified) does not provide such a basis. This would mean not only that any equity function would have to be pursued solely with spending, but also that the political legitimacy of equity-based payments is not based on the dictum, 'no taxation without representation'. In other words, having tax power greatly strengthens the political debate about what is the 'right' form and degree of equity, and this is indispensable for legitimacy with voters/tax payers.

The EU budget cannot have *macroeconomic stability* functions in its current set-up. This was briefly referred to above as well as in section 3.6. An ingenious border case is the suggestion of a European unemployment fund, which could co-finance unemployment benefits in an EU country hit by idiosyncratic shocks, while the fund's income would be obtained from other countries not hit or in the upswing phase of the business cycle. Such an insurance-based fund could be integrated into the EU budget or remain a stand-alone fund. The Council has never shown any interest in ideas like this. In the eurozone the debate about the so-called policy mix is always about the central monetary policy combined with the overall 'fiscal stance' of the member countries of the zone, never about a possible combination of central monetary policy with the EU budget. The EU budget cannot play any role owing its miniscule size, its no-deficit rule, and the unusual characteristics of its revenue sources preempting any 'automatic stabiliser' role. Any suggestions of endowing the EU budget with at least some macroeconomic stabilisation functions all date from the 1970s (for example, the MacDougall report) and have since been ignored.

Without resorting to any figures, the subsidiarity test already severely limits the expected size and range of functions of the EU budget. No wonder a trivial budget remains. One could augment such a budget marginally by, for example, substituting specific national expenditures by EU-level ones, in case cross-border externalities or scale arguments are quite strong or when EU public goods are commonly produced and financed. In this way, the total of national and EU budget does not increase but the effectiveness of expenditures (everything else equal) will improve. Cases that come to mind include aspects of justice and home affairs (such as the 'common border guards' of the EU as a zone of security) or parts of fundamental research best done together. However, thus far such substitution has not taken place in any meaningful fashion. Its scope is likely to be modest, presumably. The upshot is that even with substitutive expenditures the EU budget will remain a marginal feature of European integration.

19.3 Today's EU budget under scrutiny

19.3.1 Basic facts

In this section, the 2005 EU budget is used to illustrate the policy choices the EU has made. Remembering the strong path dependency of the main categories of expenditures, the 2005 budget can be considered as broadly representative of the substance of the EU budget debates. The choices for the medium run, for which one might expect greater policy freedom to modify assignments to the EU level in ways suggested by subsidiarity, will be discussed in section 19.5. Here we focus on the expenditure side, in section 19.4 on the revenue side.

The EU budget technically works with two categories of spending: 'appropriations for commitments' (the disbursement of which may or may not (fully) occur in the same budget year) and 'appropriations for payments'. These and other technicalities will be ignored as we are interested solely in major choices and their rationale. The total of the EU budget (appropriations for commitments) for 2005 amounted to €116.5 billion, exactly 1 per cent of the Union's GNI (slightly higher for GDP). The overall spending ceiling is 1.24 per cent of GNI which means that there is a considerable margin left. Although in the history of the EU budget there have episodes of rapid growth of expenditures, the long-run trend is one of modest growth and considerable restraint in the share of GNI. Thus, the 1 per cent GNI share of 2005 is about the average for the period since 1992: over these thirteen years the GNI share hovered between 1.14 per cent (1993) and 0.91 per cent (2001). The 2005 budget is for a Union of 25 Member States and the average GNI per capita has of course declined with the entry of 10 new Member States in May 2004. Despite this artifact, the GNI share has barely gone up from 2003 (when it was 0.98 per cent). Keeping up spending discipline is a good sign but the restraint on extra spending when 10 relatively poor Member States come in is not easy to reconcile with the rhetoric of solidarity under cohesion, unless this is due to natural limits of their absorption capacity.

Figure 19.1 gives a bird's eye view of the history of EU spending. It shows clearly that agricultural and cohesion together have dominated EU spending for several decades, be it that the share of cohesion-type spending has

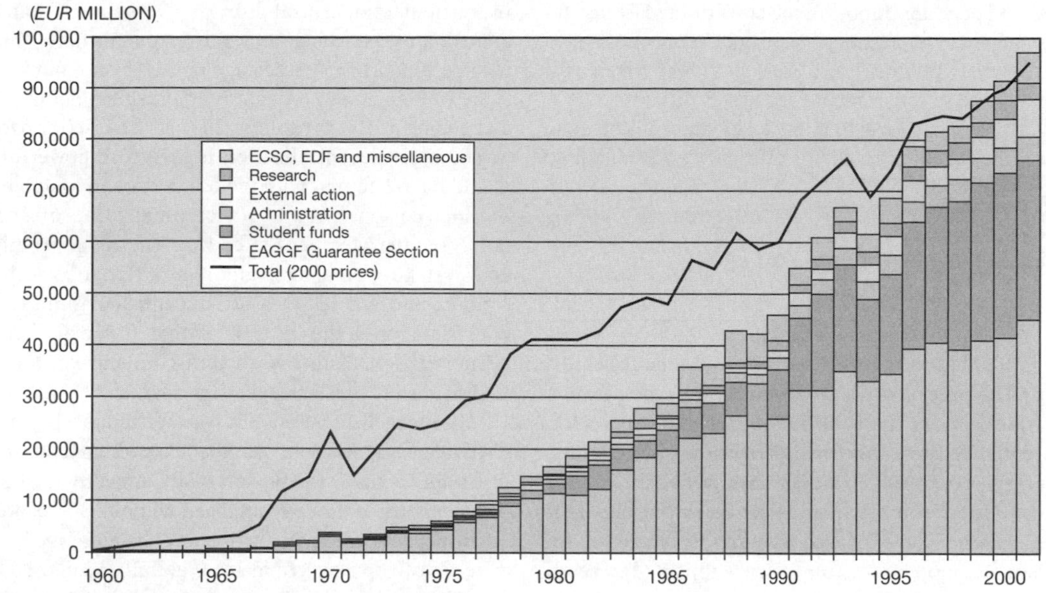

Figure 19.1 Expenditures history, 1960–2001
Source: European Commission, 2000b, Chart 1, p. 32

increased and that of agriculture decreased. Recently, one observes a modest reduction in their common share to just under 80 per cent.

Figure 19.2 provides a specification of the breakdown into main spending categories for the 2005 budget. It confirms once again the dominance of cohesion and agricultural spending: if one adds up agricultural spending (42.8 per cent, which includes rural expenditures, but see section 19.3.2) and structural operations (35.4 per cent, which includes the Cohesion Fund), one arrives at 78.2 per cent. The hard core of European integration receives only 7.8 per cent (internal policies), which can be interpreted as a confirmation of the motto 'rules, not money', or as evidence of being crowded out by the two dominant

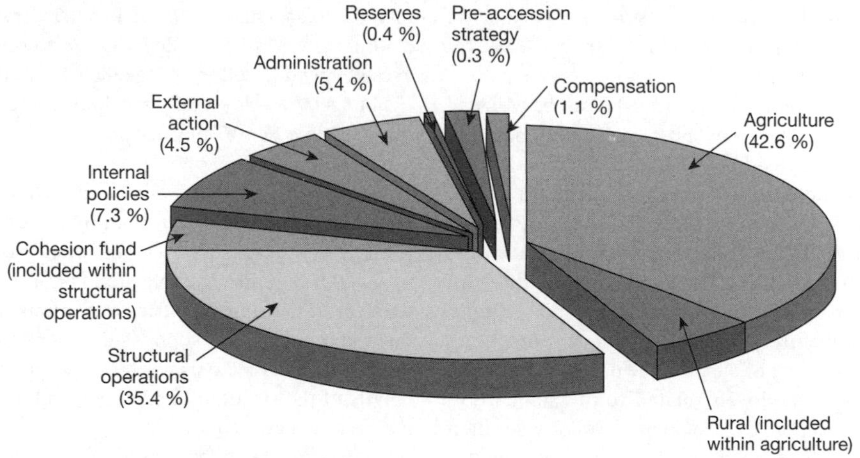

Figure 19.2 Figures by financial perspective heading, in commitment appropriations (aggregate, 2005)
Source: European Commission, 2006, p.9

forms of spending. Ignoring the costs of the EU institutions and some minor items, another 6.5 per cent is spent on external policies and pre-accession (Bulgaria, Romania and to some extent Croatia and Turkey).

With the basic facts in mind, let us study a little more closely the spending on equity, efficiency and (emerging) EU public goods.

19.3.2 What rationale for equity expenditures?

The EU budget contains two distinct (and large) equity items. The oldest one is money to support the incomes of farmers under the CAP. Of course, their income is also enhanced by high trade protection of temperate-zone agro-goods but this is ignored here as it is not a budget issue. From Chapter 11 we know that the three CAP reforms have caused a drastic change in the method of support – from price support, indirectly helping farmers' income, to direct income payments – but not much in the budget totals for farmers. Following a European Council agreement of 2003, the nominal growth of agro-spending up to 2013 (inclusive) is kept at 1 per cent a year, hence less than inflation (likely to remain around 2 per cent a year). In the medium-run budget agreement concluded in December 2005, it was formally accepted that, by 2008 or so, a new discussion about the EU budget would be foreseen in which the CAP spending ceilings could be challenged. Therefore, the 'iron' path dependency on agro-spending, which was already weakened since the late 1980s, will further diminish. It is possible that the WTO Doha Round might also tighten these constraints of subsidies.

Nevertheless, this peculiar and selective instance of 'equity', only for farmers, remains a special case for quite a while into the future.

The budget rationale of this spending can be assessed by asking two key questions. First, is CAP spending in accordance with subsidiarity? The answer is that the larger part (namely, direct income payments) is not. Even if one accepts that farmers are a special case, their income support ought to be roughly in line with the national or local standard of living. The standards of living differ markedly in the Union whereas central income payments are uniform (per relevant unit); not surprisingly, the level of support per unit (for example, of cattle or land) is closely related to the standard of living of the richer EU countries, otherwise their farmers would suffer from the shift to direct income payments. The upshot is that farmers in relatively poor areas of the Union are disproportionately remunerated, in particular in central Europe. Remember that the annual increase of central European farmers' direct income support is 5 percentage points (beginning with a share of 30 per cent of what EU15 farmers get in 2004 and ending at 100 per cent in 2013). The case for partial or complete decentralisation is therefore powerful. It would be in keeping with the unquestioned assignment of 'interpersonal equity' (a cardinal issue of social policy) to the Member State level. The EU level might keep a stake in rural expenditure as a form of structural support and would set a strict control regime (also, consistent with the WTO) so that national income support is not distortive or anti-competitive, but the CAP items in the EU budget would largely disappear.

The second key question is whether and to what extent CAP money is crowding out other expenditure that would justifiably support the pursuit of EU objectives. If path dependency is politically imposed without any regard to other spending with potentially more 'bang for the buck', there are two options left: increase overall spending so that crowding out is avoided, or accept crowding out as a result of strict ceilings on the budget's total. Since the greater prominence of cohesion, the CAP was forced into reforms because the budgetary consequences of the old CAP became unsustainable (quite apart from other drawbacks). Thus, the relative path dependency of CAP spending was broken, but (up to 2013) the real reduction has barely begun. Since the Lisbon process, aiming for a higher economic growth via the promotion of the 'knowledge economy' (see section 14.4) and greater 'competitiveness', a new contender for extra budget outlays has emerged: much more EU spending on research and technology, including ambitious environmental technology. The 'need to act in common' (step 2) in a number of instances in research and technology is well justified. Given the strict ceiling on overall EU expenditure, however, it proved exceedingly difficult to change the policy emphasis in the EU budget towards spending on knowledge-related items. Also on this score, the dominance of CAP spending cannot be justified.

The other equity item is of course cohesion. However, besides the equity motive – reflected in who is eligible – there is a critical efficiency issue of catch-up growth. The idea of cohesion is not to pay transfers for ever to lagging countries or regions, but to enable them to improve their supply side and capacity to attract productive factors so as to enjoy real convergence. The details of the structural and cohesion funding need not concern us here. Again, in terms of budget rationale, two questions can be posed. First, with respect to equity, the eligibility tends to be mixed up with net paying positions or *juste retour*. Thus, net paying but

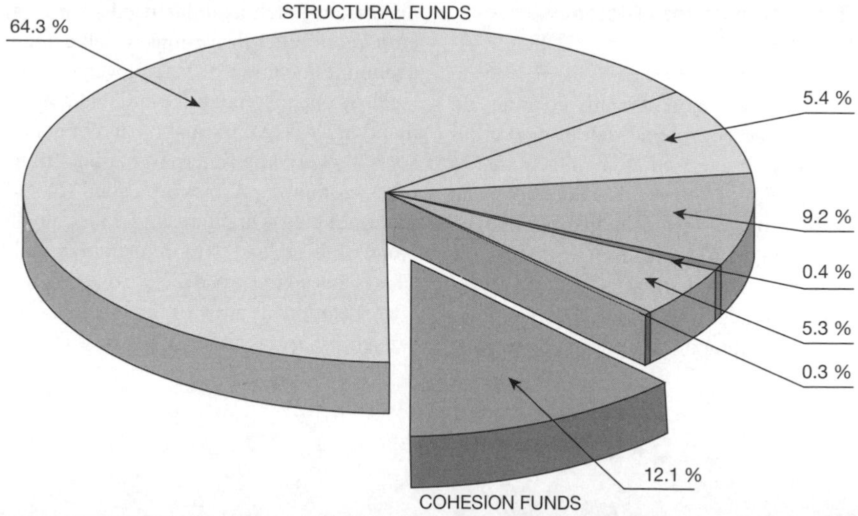

Heading 2: Structural operations	Budget 2005
STRUCTURAL FUNDS	**37, 291.56**
— Objective 1	27, 283.06
— Objective 2	3, 544.29
— Objective 3	3, 911.06
— Other structural measures (outside Objective 1 areas)	180.03
— Community initiatives	2, 258.57
— Innovative measures and technical assistance	114.56
COHESION FUND	**5, 131.93**
Total	**42, 423.50**

Figure 19.3 Structural and cohesion expenditure, 2005
Source: European Commission, 2006, p. 19

rich EU countries together obtain some 40 per cent of the transfers under Objective 1 (see Figure 19.3) for their lagging regions. This goes against the capacity-to-pay principle, universally accepted as a guiding principle for equity. But these countries insist not only under the pressure of these regions, obviously, but also because it reduces their net paying positions. Moreover, it leads to a curious and pointless pumping around of money from rich countries A, B, etc. to Brussels and subsequently back to their poor regions, under conditionality and considerable bureaucracy. The remedy is clear: decentralisation of this part of regional policy. This would purify the EU pursuit of equity in this policy field. An additional advantage would be that the domestic choices of relatively rich countries to allow great income per capita disparities are no longer addressed at the EU level. As one can observe from Figure 16.3, the richer EU countries differ significantly in this respect (with the UK as the extreme case of internal disparities) and there is no reason why countries that cherish a strategy of preventing such disparities at home would have to pay for other countries which allow much sharper disparities. In section 19.4 we shall add another remedy of a more general nature to address this equity issue. Second, the structural and cohesion flows are ultimately motivated by catch-up growth and the removal of obstacles to get out of local stagnation.

The Sapir report (Sapir *et al.*, 2003) has proposed to separate the transfers targeting real convergence from those addressing obstacles (in regions struggling disproportionately with restructuring) to move out of stagnation. A convergence fund would solely address the catching-up of poor countries and their lagging regions and a restructuring fund would focus on any regional restructuring of sufficient magnitude, with suitable means. It is worth considering merging the Objective 2 flows (going typically to stagnating regions that have lost their former production base) with those of the Social Fund and the Fisheries Fund into such a restructuring fund as the difficulties to be tackled are quite similar. This would also offer an opportunity to clarify the subsidiarity arguments for the Social Fund which, at the moment, are not very convincing (see Case Study 16.3).

19.3.3 What rationale for efficiency expenditure?

With only selective and very modest equity goals and no expenditure having a macroeconomic stabilisation influence, the EU can be characterised as mainly geared to efficiency in a wide sense. However, this does not mean that *therefore* it must be reflected in the EU budget. Economic integration in the EU is realised predominantly via the liberalisation of markets (that is, via free movements and free establishment over intra-EU borders), via competition policy preventing market power or removing distortions (such as unjustified state aids), via the pre-emption of other distortions which could undermine the economic meaning of free movement or establishment (such as open, competitive and unbiased public procurement) and via approximation and/or common regulation so as to overcome (internal) market failures. In specific cases, common policies are called for such as common trade policies which are imperative under subsidiarity. None of these lead to more than marginal EU spending. This is indeed the broad picture one gets from Figure 19.4.

A detailed scrutiny of these categories is beyond the present chapter as such a study requires much and

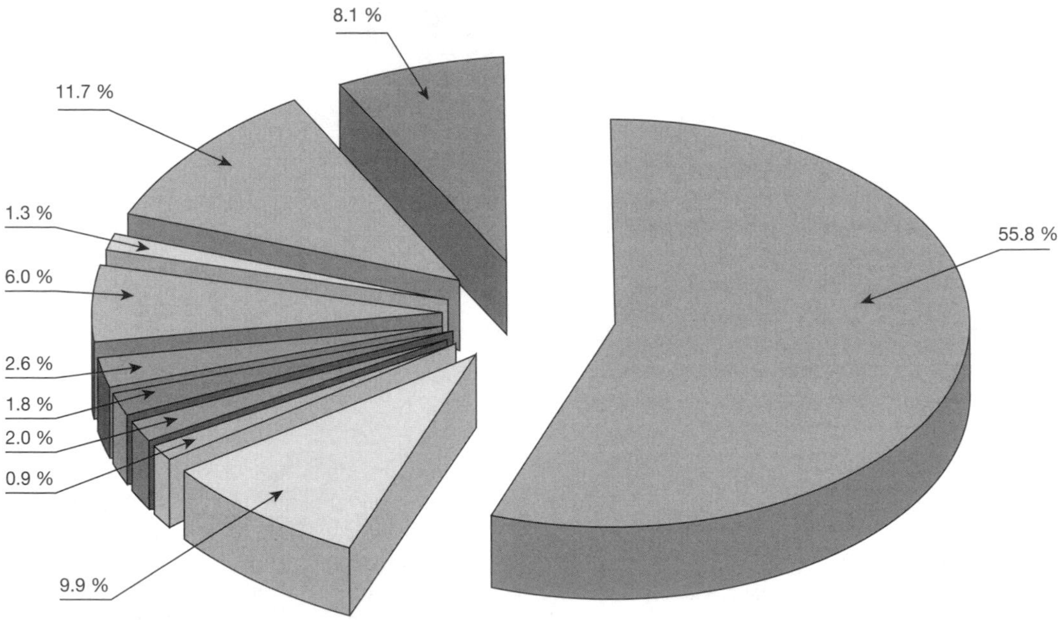

Heading 3: Internal policies	Budget 2005
Sixth framework programme for research and technological development	5, 047.0
Education and culture	896.6
Economical and financial affairs	83.3
Employment	178.2
Enterprise (excluding the sixth framework programme)	159.4
Environment	235.5
Justice and home affairs	540.2
Health and consumer protection	120.6
Energy and transport (excluding the sixth framework programme)	1, 056.1
Others	735.0
Total	**9, 052.0**

Figure 19.4 EU expenditure on internal policies, 2005
Source: European Commission, 2006, p. 20

well-structured information. Over half of this spending is not related to the proper functioning of the internal market in its widest sense: it refers to the Sixth Framework programme of research. Research is an activity which is subject to both scale and cross-border externalities, which suggests that in a number of instances a subsidiarity case can be made for common spending at the EU level. For further discussion we refer to Chapter 14. Indeed, in the light of the Lisbon objective and the EU's need to shift more forcefully to high value-added activities in services and manufacturing, it is not improbable that more EU spending (perhaps substituting for less effective or duplicative national expenditures) can be justified. This is also likely to be the case for technology, in particular for very risky, long-run development projects, for example in energy and environment. Where scale suggests a European size in any event, the choice is whether the EU or an effective intergovernmental agency is the right option. The latter can work well, as has been shown, in areas such as space and nuclear particles. In a few well-identified cases, an EU-based infrastructure is called for which embodies the technology. The infrastructure ought to be EU-based if it is essential for a better functioning of the internal market, as is the case for air traffic control. It is a political choice if the argument is a sufficient and guaranteed EU independence, as in the case of Galileo, or if the quality of interconnection between European universities is felt to require a common, high quality infrastructure (as in the case of the GEANT supernetwork). Galileo in fact has such strong cross-border externalities that it is hard to distinguish it from a common public good. GEANT is more like a collective good, the initial production of which needs EU initiative and funding.

19.3.4 Should the EU spend on public goods?

Public goods are crucial to the emergence and the very existence of countries. The classical examples of defence and a guaranteed access to justice in a uniform legal system are at the roots of most countries in the world. This is also likely to apply to foreign policy and diplomacy. Some public or collective goods (see above) consist of common infrastructures and may or may not be financed by user charges; the critical issue in such cases is the initial production of the public or collective good and there are instances that the EU is the right level and has credible instruments to fulfil that role.

The question briefly discussed here is whether the standard public good analogy from the economics of federalism can be applied to the Union. In section 3.4.1 this question was answered with a firm no. The reasons are a matter of politics and their underlying preferences.

ADDITIONAL READING

The EU conducts a so-called common foreign and security policy (CFSP) but this is predominantly a consensual, diplomatic process. After a cautious trial period since the early 1970s, the Maastricht Treaty created a special pillar for it (in Title V of the Maastricht Treaty, amended as Article 11-28, EU treaty nowadays; see also chapter II, Title V of the constitutional treaty [not yet ratified]). Its machinery has been deepened and widened, no doubt, but that is still a far cry from a truly common policy. It is an intergovernmental process, with great sensitivities in areas where no deep agreement prevails. Where common positions are formulated, the concrete consequences rarely go beyond mere diplomacy. The three tools, which can be considered as extensions of foreign policy, show this clearly. One is what is called in diplomacy 'technical cooperation' or, at times, 'economic cooperation'. These are typically project-based forms of support or common initiatives and may involve some spending. The budget outlays for 'external action' in Figure 19.2 consist mainly in such instances of cooperation with many countries in the world. Another tool is development cooperation which the EU channels via the European Development Fund, which is actually a fund of the Member States jointly, hence *not* on the EU budget.[1] In practice, the EU economic cooperation with developing countries often comprises development projects, too. In its various manifestations (bilateral of individual Member States, jointly in the European Development Fund, and economic or technical cooperation under CFSP) the EU is a leader in development aid, as an expression of its values. At

[1]Member States also pursue bilateral development policies on an individual basis, separate from this fund.

ADDITIONAL READING *continued*

the same time, the complex blend of three approaches testifies that Member States attach great value to their own foreign relations and diplomacy. The third tool is a range of more assertive action possibilities where the Union or a subset of its countries (but with EU blessing) exercises forms of power. This range includes peacekeeping operations under UN or OSCE mandate,[2] trade sanctions or boycotts or even possible support of UN interventions if the UN Security Council insists on it. A highly selective and prudent approach to initiate EU defence capabilities on a voluntary basis[3] began in the late 1990s.

All these details confirm that the Union is still very far away from the kind of common public goods that foreign policy and defence in federations typically would imply. This is so because Member States' populations are still deeply attached to their national autonomy in such areas, even though one recognises that more functional cooperation in CFSP is to be fostered and, in extreme instances, the Union can use its considerable muscle. The EU budget has, as yet, no common defence spending and its cooperative diplomacy is constrained to issues where intra-EU consensus (or the external extension of other policies such as trade, energy, environment) is well established. The words 'still very far away' are meant as an observation, not necessarily as a point on a trend towards a form of federalism with such public goods at the central level. What the preferences are in these sensitive areas, has been revealed much more systematically in the Convention, drafting the early version of the constitutional treaty, than one could ever acquire from polls or specific governments' declarations. Despite the wide spectrum of opinions and visions in the Convention, some desiring more progress on CFSP and defence than others, it was not possible to distil anywhere near a common desire to begin to centralise such policies. Subsidiarity strongly suggests centralisation for such public goods, as by definition it is far more effective to combine and streamline such efforts, *if and only if* the preferences are homogeneous enough to allow stepping up the ladder of the test. Such homogeneity is not there and it is impossible to say whether it might develop over time.

19.4 The Union's (own?) revenues

In 1970 the then EEC decided that the Community as such should be independent in its budgetary means. The system of 'own resources' was installed. However, the Member States have gradually shown less and less respect for this decision. The current set-up[4] of EU revenues is only a very pale reflection of what was intended initially. The idea was that the revenues of the Community would all be 'owned' by the Community, that is, not be regarded or treated as 'contributions' from the Member States. Nowadays, there are four sources of revenue: (1) the customs duties,[5] of which no less than 25 per cent is deducted for the costs of collecting them; (2) sugar levies, paid by sugar producers to pay for export subsidies; (3) a tiny percentage of every country's VAT basis;[6] (4) an equal percentage of every country's GNI. The first

[2]The Organisation for Security and Cooperation in Europe (OSCE) was founded after the fall of communism as a minimal common architecture on the Continent to promote human rights, certain common values, democracy (e.g. observers in elections) and to mediate in local conflicts. It includes all European countries and all countries of the former Soviet Union, also those in central Asia.

[3]It should be realised that several EU countries are not a NATO member as they have remained neutral. In any event, defence initiatives are highly circumscribed and not centralised, except when all EU countries agree about a defensive or UN-type action, and even then each country remains completely free to participate or not. The constitutional treaty (not yet ratified) renders this set-up slightly more effective, without essential changes.

[4]Based on Council Decision 2000/597. We shall not deal with the question whether the current set-up is in accordance with the treaty. The reader can ponder whether there is any lack of clarity in the first line of Art. 269 EC: 'Without prejudice to other revenue, the budget shall be financed wholly from own resources'.

[5]Including the agricultural ones. The distinction between agro-duties and customs duties ceased to exist when the levy system no longer incorporated 'variable levies'.

[6]Since VAT is regressive, the VAT basis is capped at 50 per cent to reduce negative effects for poor Member States.

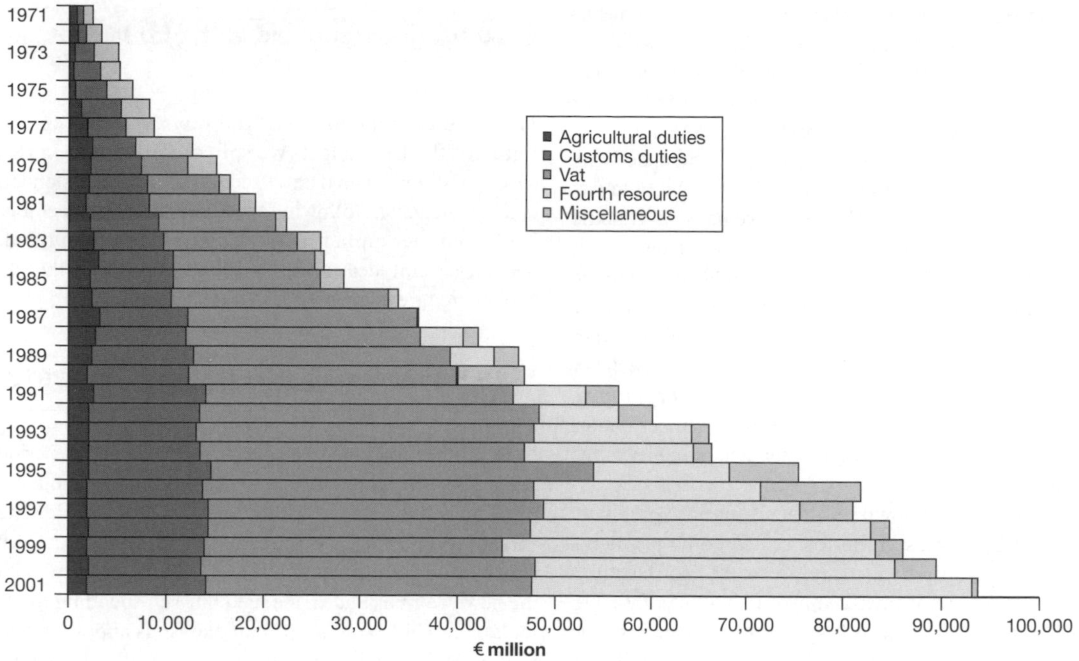

Figure 19.5 Evolution of EU revenues, 1971–2001
Source: European Commission, 2000b, Chart 5, p. 44

two revenue streams are called the 'traditional own resources' (adding up to only 11.6 per cent of EU revenue in 2005), the third one is called 'own resource' by the Commission[7] and yielded 14.4 per cent of EU revenue in 2005, and, finally the fourth and dominant one is just a resource (with 73 per cent of revenue).[8] Figure 19.5 shows the emergence of the fourth resource since around 1990.

The basis for any comparison with fiscal federalism is lacking: think of taxation (and, of course, representation, so that taxing citizens becomes legitimate and linked to what voters want), ability to pay, equity and common taxes on mobile factors. All of it seems to be irrelevant to the EU system. There is no legal basis for an EU tax of any kind. The budget powers of the European Parliament are considerable but not complete in a key area such as agriculture.[9] Equity or considerations of ability to pay are disregarded because poor Member States either pay proportionally (for the 73 per cent of the revenue) or suffer even from regressive 'own resources' (especially the VAT, some 14 per cent). In multi-tier government systems, it is not possible for the state/provincial level to tax mobile factors or footloose activities effectively; therefore, usually, a combination of federal taxation and tax coordination takes place. The EU could rebuild its own resources by introducing a common tax on mobile factors such as financial capital. Other possibilities include a carbon tax for emitters not in the EU carbon tradable permit scheme under the Kyoto protocol. Repeatedly, such proposals have been made but never have they been given any serious hearing by Council. The upshot is that (1) the own resources system prescribed by the treaty is on the way out because the 'traditional own resources' are shrinking as a result of trade liberalisation;

[7]Not least because the 1977 harmonisation of the VAT base was introduced for reasons of equal treatment between Member States, with the Community 'taking out' a similar percentage for every country.

[8]Technically, the UK rebate is also part of the revenue side. The UK paid (in 2005) some €5.1 billion less than it would if based on the regular calculation. The key reason for this decision (going back to 1984) is the large net outflows caused by the UK's being a net importer of CAP goods with few financial benefits from the CAP. The rebate was reduced in the European Council December 2005 decision on the medium-term financial perspectives up to 2013.

[9]The distinction between compulsory (mainly CAP obligations) and non-compulsory expenditure still exists. The rules do not give the EP a direct say over compulsory expenditure. Of course, the EP always has what is known as the nuclear option: it has the power to reject the EU budget as a whole. The leverage is often sufficient for Council to compromise.

(2) Member States have only tax coordination as a means to restore effective taxation of mobile factors or activities. Tax coordination is a cumbersome and slow approach, subject to unanimity and, moreover, highly uncertain (see Case Study 9.1 where the final result took 15 years).

The EU revenue system therefore lacks an underlying logic. The least one should expect is that the ability-to-pay principle would be applied on the revenue side by some kind of automatic rule. Rather than proportionality for all Member States (based on GNI), one could apply a range of multipliers moving from (say) 0.7 (times the average percentage of GNI) for the Member States below 75 per cent of the EU average GNI per capita, via 0.9 for Member States up to 90 per cent of the EU average GNI per capita, and increasing further, up to 1.3 for Member States enjoying a GNI per capita of 125 per cent or higher of the EU average.

This would boil down to 'general-purpose grants' to poor Member States in the form of forgoing payments to Brussels, would be a straightforward manifestation of equity, would not involve any bureaucracy linked to Funds and would leave full spending autonomy to the poor Member States. It would also reduce the heavy politicisation of seeking to fulfil solidarity solely on the expenditures side.

It would also make functional sense to introduce a simple EU tax piggybacking on national tax collection. The motive for such a tax is the 'fiscal equivalence' principle (Caesar, 2001): efficient and responsible budget decisions should assign political accountability to law makers deciding not only on spending (as is now the case in the EU) but also on the revenues for it. In this way, the political costs or legitimacy of the tax burden will be clarified and closer correspondence with voters' preferences should be ensured. The problem in the EU context is whether European voters will feel the same about the EP as about their national parliaments. There is a chicken-and-egg problem here. As long as taxation is not part and parcel of the EP's competences, the EP is bound to be far less interesting for voters and the media; on the other hand, this not being the case now (or, incidentally, in the constitutional treaty, not yet ratified), severely weakens the argument to confer tax power to the EP. An extra problem is, of course, that the EP does not face a true government but the Commission. The EP cannot send home the Council, and its power to sack the Commission (which it did in 1999) may prompt a crisis but not directly suggest a solution. All in all, introducing an EU tax is not really a functional decision but predominantly a political one and currently falls on deaf ears in the Union.

19.5 The future role of the EU budget

There are a number of insightful ways to reflect on the future of the EU budget. We split the reflection in two parts. First, the basic data of section 19.3.1 are extended to 2013 inclusive, following the agreement of December 2005, and the implicit policy choices are highlighted. Second, several ideas about the longer-run role of the EU budget are briefly reviewed.

19.5.1 Assessing the EU budget until 2013

In December 2005 the financial perspectives for the period 2007–13 were agreed. After the usual bickering about net positions, the (indeed rather special) UK rebate, the 'breaking open' of the (already in 2003) agreed CAP expenditure ceilings up to 2013, and the 'solidarity' with the new Member States, the medium-run spending totals look remarkably similar to what one finds about 2005 in Figure 19.2. Also, the average share (over the whole period) of GNI is 1.045 per cent (in 2005 exactly 1 per cent). Once again, the combination of path dependency and the political primacy of minimising net payment position (rather than focusing on the EU interest first of all) led to the impossibility of, for example, a growth-oriented budget. Nevertheless, if one takes a closer look at the year-on-year trends of three key categories (see Figure 19.6), one discerns weak but clear trends.

In 2004 euros, spending on agriculture declines a little (consistent with the 2003 agreement), that on economic cohesion increases but only marginally (still, by 2013, cohesion outlays will have outgrown agro-spending by €5 billion a year) and the competitiveness heading (which includes research and technology) grows by 50 per cent. Though attenuated, these new trends would seem to be in the broad EU interest. The other item that changes strongly (a doubling) is justice and security but from a tiny initial base. It is possible that the agro-spending is going to be further reduced after a new review in 2008.

19.5.2 Different futures of the EU budget

The purpose of this final subsection is to invite the reader to reflect on the EU budget in more fruitful ways than the marginal reshuffling in net-paying positions of Member States. The challenge is to develop a long-run logic of spending and revenue assignments to the EU,

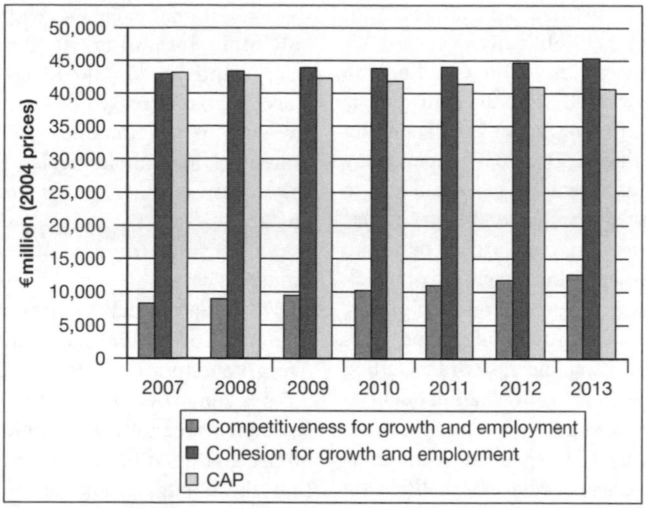

Figure 19.6 Main budget choices up to 2013

based on EU objectives over that same long run. We suggest three quite distinct ways of reflecting on the long-run budget. Of course, there is no claim that these three ways exhaust all options.

First, one way of thinking is the gradual *marginalisation* of the EU budget. The drivers of this process would be, first of all, the two main spending categories (CAP and cohesion) and, secondly, the continued lack of willingness even to consider a more functional (that is, subsidiarity based) approach to assigning the EU's spending when the case can be made. Over a period of, say, two decades or more, it is likely that the CAP spending share will have reduced a great deal more than the ± 37 per cent in 2013. Indeed, the December 2005 agreement suggests that in 2008 another review of CAP spending will take place. In particular, once the decentralisation of direct income payments is firmly accepted, the EU outlays for the CAP will drastically decline, also absolutely. As far as economic cohesion is concerned, the present outlook for economic convergence is solid. Two decades from 2005, Greece and Portugal should be close to the EU average and several new Member States might also have arrived at that level. The Baltic countries (started from a low GDP per capita but enjoying high catch-up growth) and Romania and Bulgaria (also starting from a low level and having appreciable rates of catch-up growth) might need a longer period but might nevertheless have become much more prosperous. The great unknown is Turkey, also starting from a low per-capita level and suffering from a 'dual economy' effect (see Case Study 20.2), but enjoying very healthy growth rates after 2001. At the moment there is no way of knowing whether Turkey will be admitted to the EU. The issue is whether, in the long run, the EU spending on cohesion will remain at present levels. The greater and faster economic convergence is, the greater the likelihood that, sooner or later, cohesion transfers will begin to shrink as well. With these two main spending categories reducing sharply, at some point in time the EU budget will become a trivial one. On the revenue side, the lack of progressivity in (own) resources will largely become irrelevant, too, because the total sums would shrink rather than increase. The motto 'rules, not money' would be consistently followed, except for relatively minor (yet presumably useful) expenditures on efficiency aspects and common initiatives (such as research). This would also assume that classic public goods such as foreign policy 'cooperation' and defence do not generate major spending at EU level.

A second way of thinking contrasts with the first one in that a *much more functional budget strategy* is gradually adopted. Such a process could develop once the CAP spending shrinks further and/or its direct income payments are partially or entirely decentralised. Partial decentralisation has the advantage that the EU control system of pre-empting distortions caused by national direct income payments can be tighter, with the leverage of (some) central disbursements. Once the CAP plays only a minor role in the EU budget, net paying positions of EU countries will be determined largely by the cohesion transfers and these are far less controversial. Moreover, many net paying countries might, at long last, be prepared to accept functional arguments for assigning the EU level with justified expenditures. Until today, many net payers object politically to such functional arguments because adding extra spending (no matter how well justified) would avoid the hard choices about path dependency of (especially) CAP spending and its effects on net positions. Once path dependency is broken, functionality might return. This would restore a focus on the EU interest rather than on budget battles with narrow national *juste retour* targets in mind. Functionality might open up many possibilities which need not be elaborated here. One could think of greater flexibility in the medium-run financial perspectives between spending categories, an increase of the ceiling for those financial perspectives (now 1.24 per cent of GNI) if the implied spending is well justified, the substitution of national by EU expenditures in areas where scale or intra-EU cross-border externalities are powerful (for example, research or specific aspects of intra-EU security under justice and home affairs), possibly the common production of limited EU public goods (perhaps some circumscribed aspects of defence or common defence procurement based on EU technology) and, on the revenue side, the introduction of a more 'progressive' resources system based on the ability to pay. Clearly, within the confines of spending limits, a better correspondence between EU objectives such as the Lisbon goal (in a new shape in 2025, one presumes) and spending categories can be accomplished as well.

The third way of thinking about the EU budget is to move beyond the sole focus on efficiency (and a modest cohesion approach) and *assign macroeconomic stabilisation elements* to it. The scope to do this is very small, however. Besides a European employment fund, based on insurance principles and small additional payments by the Member States,[10] the only other possibility would seem to be to amend the treaty and make the EU budget anti-cyclical. Nowadays, the treaty does not allow any deficits, and any surplus is immediately returned to the Member States on an annual basis. The problem with this suggestion is that, apart from overcoming the huge obstacle of treaty revision, the potential economic impact on the Union economy would be very small indeed. The MacDougall report (MacDougall *et al.*, 1977), in an era that Keynesian thinking was already in doubt, proposed a considerable increase in the overall economic size of the EU budget (first, up to 2.5 per cent of GDP, later to 5 per cent or possibly 10 per cent), precisely with a view to permit macroeconomic stabilisation properties. It is as well to realise that these suggestions have never been seriously considered. To begin with, they would revolutionise the Union as such a budget would almost certainly require an EU tax (and not a trivial one, as the introduction of a tax today would be) as well as major shifts of national expenditure to the EU level. In turn, this would only be feasible in a Union with very different political preferences. Moreover, in such a set-up it would probably be a necessary prerequisite that all Member States be in the eurozone and that any anti-cyclical policies be undertaken with due regard to the role of the ECB. The conclusion is then that in the longer run the Union, with a eurozone of 24 countries, will retain a small, acyclical budget and that fiscal coordination, under strict rules, will have to be pursued by the Member States directly. That this might be ineffective, and possibly inefficient too, is the price of a firm desire to retain national fiscal and budgetary autonomy.

19.6 Summary

The EU budget is small by any reasonable standard and of marginal economic importance. Comparisons with the structure of national budgets or their functions are misleading: what the so-called spending ministries do is virtually entirely spent via the national budget (and that makes up the bulk of national budgets) and revenues at the national level are tax based. The ceiling in the seven-year EU financial perspectives (the present one runs from 2007 to 2013) is 1.24 per cent of GNI – less than 0.03 per cent of the sum of the national budgets; the factual spending in 2005 was 1 per cent of GNI and is 1.04 per cent up to 2013 on average. Economic restrictions of the budget are severe: no deficits, annual surpluses are returned to the Member States and revenue is not tax based.

[10]Italianer & Vanheukelen (1993) suggest that one should think of contributions no higher than approximately 0.2 per cent of GDP annually.

Summary *continued*

The functional test whether the EU budget roles are justified is based on queries such as: Is money the proper tool for the objective pursued? Could markets not do it? Could regulation do it? If money is appropriate, should it be spent by Member States (in coordination) or at the EU level? If at the EU level, how best to achieve correspondence between what voters want and the spending? The reality for the EU budget is far removed from meeting the test. Among a series of shortcomings, the worst is the distorting nature of budget debates for the citizen: citizens in net paying countries hear only about the 'sacrifices' and little if anything about the joint benefits; those in net receiving countries hear only about the unwillingness of others to comply with solidarity. In general, no politician stresses the trivial nature of budget debates (the totals are small, the debate itself is about a fraction of it) and about the benefits lying elsewhere. The natural voice for the common EU interest (the Commission) has a limited role in the budget decision-making process.

A subsidiarity test for the budget yields that the EU budget does not and cannot have a macroeconomic stabilisation function and that the equity functions will be marginal at best. Even when the option of substituting national and EU spending is taken into account, a trivial budget is bound to remain. Today's EU budget can be scrutinised for the rationales of the spending outlays. The CAP spending could largely be decentralised; an additional advantage might be that 'crowding out' of well-justified expenditures can be overcome. The economic cohesion transfers do not live up to the ability-to-pay principle where relatively rich countries also receive such transfers. The efficiency rationale of EU action is powerful but this does not necessarily mean it has to be pursued with money. In 2005, less than 8 per cent was spent on efficiency-related items: is it crowded out or does it follow the motto 'rules, not money'? The EU might spend on public goods such as defence and foreign policy *if and only if* the preferences are homogeneous enough; that tough condition is not fulfilled today. The revenue system of the EU lacks an underlying logic. The 'own resources' idea is undermined, there is no taxation (which would help to link spending and revenue directly), the ability-to-pay principle for revenues (between poor and rich EU countries) does not apply, and mobile factors are not not taxed at the EU level. A progressive revenue basis would be a useful reform with many advantages.

The role of the budget in the medium run (to 2013) is little different from today, albeit that a weak trend of reducing the agro share is to continue. The long-run role of the EU budget can be stylised in three scenarios: the gradual marginalisation (due to the shrinkage of CAP and cohesion flows in, say, two decades from now); a more functional budget strategy (path dependencies broken, crowding out reduced and functionality might return); and the assumption of a macroeconomic stabilisation role (the probability of which approaches zero).

CHAPTER 20

EU Enlargement: Methods and Economic Analysis

Topics covered

20.1 The enlargement dynamics of the EU

20.2 The Union's enlargement strategy

20.3 The eastern enlargements

20.4 Beyond the EU27

20.5 Summary

The European Union has become a continental exercise in economic (and other) integration. This is the direct result of no less than six enlargements over a period of 35 years. Behind this quite stunning development when considering its beginning with the EEC6, there are profound changes in the power-political and security landscape in Europe and the demise of communism. However, there is undoubtedly also an attraction effect which plays a role. Such an enormous increase in size has not altered the Community beyond recognition, even if one might have expected this to be the case. Since about 1990, Europe has found itself in a process of pan-European economic integration. The process began in western Europe between a steadily enlarging EU and EFTA, accompanied by a series of ad hoc agreements with Mediterranean countries. After the collapse of Comecon,[1] the Warsaw Pact and finally the Soviet Union, preceded by the changes of regimes in central and east European countries, the process spread extremely rapidly. Although trade liberalisation initially assumed an important place in this process, for many countries the end goal quickly became membership of the EU. This end goal is a function of complex mixtures of economic, political (values, democracy), security (even without there being an EU army, EU membership is considered a major boost to their security) and cultural arguments.

In 2004, eight countries from central Europe and two Mediterranean islands (Cyprus – the Greek part – and Malta) entered. This EU25 has a string of deep FTAs and other agreements (for example, with Balkan countries) with European countries and an emerging 'neighbourhood' policy. Two so-called pre-accession countries (Romania and Bulgaria) will accede to the Union on the first day of 2007.

This chapter first explores the enlargement dynamics over three decades or more. It also asks the question whether full EU membership is always the only, and indeed the best, answer to the deepening interdependence on the continent. In section 20.2 we study the EU's enlargement strategy, its routine minimum requirements (a very demanding minimum, to be sure), and the nature and scope of accommodation to the special case of the eastern enlargements.

[1] Comecon, or officially the Council for Mutual Economic Assistance, was the trade organisation of the communist countries in Europe. It mainly fostered 'agreed' specialisation, barter exchange and residual (non-planned) imports. The negotiated prices were rarely based on world prices. The Soviet Union ensured energy security at subsidised prices. Comecon had no supranational power so the individual countries negotiated directly with the EC (to the extent that they were politically free to do so).

The eastern enlargements are analysed in section 20.3, both as to method and economic analysis. Finally, there is a need to look beyond the EU27, to the new neighbourhood policy and MED strategies or possible new EU membership. The latter also poses the question of the limits of domestic political legitimacy of a truly pan-European Union. Political legitimacy of 'enlargement for ever' is waning for fear of watering down effectiveness and of diversity beyond the perceived capacity of socio-cultural absorption.

20.1 The enlargement dynamics of the EU

Enlargement is a complicated process and it is certainly not only economic. This section first sets out the basic facts of 35 years of enlargement. Subsequently, we ask the question whether the EU has been able to combine deepening and widening (of scope) of its (economic) integration at the same time as it has been engaged in one enlargement after the other; in other words, were there no trade-offs? The enlargement dynamics cannot be grasped if one does not have at least some understanding of the political economy of the 'queuing up' for EU membership, that is, 'me-too' accession. Finally, a crucial query is why close (economic and political) relations with the Union in an interdependent Europe cannot take other forms than full EU membership.

20.1.1 Six enlargements, and more?

Barely four years after the Rome Treaty was signed, the UK applied informally for EEC membership. It eventually acceded in 1973. After the entry of the UK, Denmark and Ireland, four other enlargements have been completed[2] until 2004 and a sixth enlargement (with Bulgaria and Romania) will take place in 2007. From a group of six Member States beginning in 1958, with a population around 200 million, in 2007 the EU will count 27 countries with a total population of around 485 million. Table 20.1 provides a summary.

The enlargement dynamics may not have petered out yet, although the political limits might at long last get in the way (see section 20.4.1). In 2005, the EU had two candidate countries in pre-accession, that is, the countries negotiate the terms of accession while at the same time going through a most intense preparatory process of adopting the *acquis communautaire*, helped by the EU in terms of detailed advice, some co-financing and

Table 20.1 A summary of EU enlargements

Date	Key event	Comments
25 Mar. 1957	Rome (EEC) Treaty signed	The same six as the signatories of the ECSC treaty of Paris (1951)
1 Jan. 1958	EEC begins	
1 Jan. 1973	First enlargement	UK, Denmark, Ireland (UK, DK leave EFTA)
1 Jan. 1981	Second enlargement	Greece
1 Feb. 1985	Greenland withdraws from the EEC	Greenland was a territory administered by Denmark
1 Jan. 1986	Third enlargement	Spain and Portugal (Portugal leaves EFTA)
3 Oct. 1990	German unification	East Germany 'enters' the EU via Germany
1 Jan. 1995	Fourth enlargement	Sweden, Finland, and Austria (all three leave EFTA)
1 May 2004	Fifth enlargement (1st eastern enlargement)	Besides Malta and Cyprus, eight central European countries: Estonia, Latvia, Lithuania, Poland, Czech Republic, Slovakia, Hungary and Slovenia
1 Jan. 2007	Sixth enlargement (2nd eastern enlargement)	Romania and Bulgaria

[2]Not counting the entry of East Germany, via the unification of Germany in 1990.

early cohesion-type funding. These two candidate countries are Turkey (an associate since 1964) and Croatia. It is difficult to predict whether they will come in and when. Other western Balkan (that is, ex-Yugoslavia) countries are currently in a process of rebuilding their economies and attempting to forge bonds and reconciliation between former adversaries in the Balkan war of the first half of the 1990s. This might well lead to later applications for EU membership, beginning with Macedonia presumably. Still other countries such as Georgia and Ukraine have made firm political statements that they prepare for EU membership but, realistically, this is far off if only because of the very deep reforms needed and internal political obstacles to such developments. Finally, it is worth noting that two countries have explicitly voted (in referenda) that they want very close economic integration with the EU, but no EU membership: Norway and Switzerland. In the case of Norway, this is due to a blend of political autonomy and refusals to accept specific parts of the *acquis* (such as fisheries, agriculture and free movement of workers). In the Swiss case, it is perhaps an even more fundamental political objection in the light of the unique Swiss model of (direct) democracy, in addition to specific sensitivities in the *acquis*.

20.1.2 Deepening, widening and enlargement: no trade-offs?

The powerful, secular enlargement drive of the EU is nothing less than amazing. For a long time, the fear was expressed that repeated enlargements would endanger the *acquis*, or, even if the *acquis* were kept, processes of deepening the *acquis* and widening the scope of policy areas and freedoms (of movement) under the *acquis* would be hampered. The trade-offs were considered as follows: a genuine and credible deepening is so demanding (for example for the internal market, not to speak of the euro) that enlargement might stop or discredit it. A similar effect might occur where more policy fields were brought into the EU remit. Indeed, these fears were not without foundation. The UK held a referendum on withdrawal only two years after it entered the Community, in 1975, and a 'no' vote would almost certainly have changed profoundly the very open attitude to enlargement that has characterised the Union ever since. However, a firm yes followed. Inside the EU, the UK challenged several aspects of the *acquis* right from the start. Examples include the CAP itself, the 'old' very detailed approach to harmonisation and European standardisation, and the omission of pursuing a regional policy at the EU level as well. All this goes to show that entrants do affect the new *acquis* and may influence the methods in the existing *acquis*. To be sure, such influence may well be to the better for the Community. The UK's urge and influence to begin a 'new approach' to approximation has certainly been beneficial (of course, this was beginning to be recognised by other countries as well, Germany first of all). Its criticism of the CAP led to a politicisation of the 'net payment' position of the country around 1980 and the subsequent budget debate poisoned the atmosphere in the Council up to the Fontainebleau deal of mid-1984. A degree of paralysis marked this episode and one can have different views about the cost and benefits of this *juste retour* crusade. As to regional policy, the UK pushed strongly for a Regional Development Fund which came into being in 1975. It is ironical to observe that precisely the UK, in its new view of cohesion, advocates a return of regional policy to the Member States.[3] Similar changes in the emphases on policy, rules or liberalisation, or, for that matter, transfers (for example, Greece in the 1980s with its insistence of the Mediteranean programmes; Spain and Portugal insisting on far greater transfers which were adopted in 1988, and on a Cohesion Fund, which was established in 1993) can be found for other new Member States. When Finland, Sweden and Austria came in, a push for greater transparency led to laws on right of information and a change of conduct to some extent.

Another fear consisted in a widening gap between formal adoption of the *acquis* and the effective implementation of, in particular, internal market measures so important for business and the competitive stimulus they might exert. It is this fear, above all, which has prompted a far more strict EU 'management' of the period of preparation of candidate countries for their entry. Without proper implementation, the enlarged internal market would *de facto* still be fragmented. In other words, requiring thorough preparation is to pre-empt a trade-off between deepening and enlargement by conditioning even the pre-accession period. One additional reason to do this is to prevent an overburdening of the EU judicial system when massive recourse to courts and the EC Court (or its Court of First Instance) would probably clog the system, discredit its authority and cause disillusion among businesses and consumers.

[3] *An EU Framework for a Devolved Regional Policy* (HMSO, London, March 2003).

The EU has reasonably succeeded in combining deepening (which has been more or less permanent since the mid-1980s), widening (which has been happening since the 1970s) and the several enlargements. The avoidance of trade-offs is the result of an ever more ambitious and strategic approach to enlargement (see section 20.2).

20.1.3 The political economy of 'me-too' accession: EFTA

Market access to large economies, and even more when the economic distance to them is small, is crucial for many countries. For small economies this holds true *a fortiori*. When the EEC6 went ahead in 1956 after the Spaak report, most of the other OEEC countries at the time decided to improve market access in a free trade area among themselves, namely EFTA. Except for the UK, all participants in EFTA were small economies and, no matter how welcome free trade in EFTA was to them, what really mattered was access to the EEC6. At a later stage, the desire for access for reasons of scale production and viability of their export industries, became compounded by the fact that EFTA countries' multinationals did an increasing share of their business in the internal market of the EU. When the EU started deepening with ambition and with an expected positive impact for EU multinationals, further direct investment in EFTA countries was seen as yielding a sufficient return only if EFTA and the EU became or at least approximated to a single market. It is these aspects – the terms of market access and the (relative) competitive positioning that follows from it – that are the underlying drive of a chain of enlargements, even if political motives often played a role as well. Let us look a little more closely at the example of EFTA, which is instructive.

EFTA was a credible and successful free trade area in industrial goods.[4] To a large extent, this was due to its modesty. As an FTA it was not 'deep' in terms of regulatory approximation, it had no competition policy or any other common policy, let alone of course a common trade policy (as it was an FTA), and no further widening or deepening was pursued for a long time. Eventually, however, EFTA was going to be absorbed into the Union almost entirely. It is useful to understand why and how.

The history of EFTA and its gradual absorption into the Union is largely determined by a hegemony effect and a magnet effect. The preponderance of the Community was a direct result of the enormous importance for EFTA of EFTA exports to the EU. One may argue that – over time – this preponderance increased. In the course of the 1980s, this began to be translated into a long-run strategy to lead western Europe to ever 'deeper' trade liberalisation. In pursuing this strategy the EU acted as a leader. Hegemony in power politics has a negative connotation. In economic interdependence, however, there is a positive connotation. In a stream of literature inspired by Kindleberger (1973), the economic leader[5] is indispensable in accomplishing the international public good of a stable free trade system. Without hegemonic leadership, including the incentive of access to its big market, the public good may never be realised, as all partners would prefer to free ride. They do this given the tiny influence their own concessions may have on the continental free trade. Applied to Europe, the enlargement, widening and deepening of the EU may be interpreted as generating *hegemonic effects* in the sense that the Community began to assume credible leadership in pan-European trade and regulatory liberalisation. When the cold war was over – and for some countries, even earlier – this was combined with a *magnet effect*: the desire to join the EU or at least enjoy the economic benefits of association with it as much as possible.

The EU has always dominated the life and fate of EFTA. EFTA's functional success and stability stood in sharp contrast to its shrinking membership over time. However, not a hidden failure of EFTA, but dynamic magnet effects of the Community were the cause of the gradual shrinkage of EFTA to its current irrelevance. Already in 1961, in a sudden change of course, the UK applied for EU membership. The sole reason it took until 1973 before it entered the EU was a veto by President de Gaulle of France in 1963 and another one in 1967. That Ireland became an EC member had to do with the long-standing free trade with (and easy migration to and from) the UK[6] and with the expected benefits of the CAP (for Ireland). However, Ireland quickly exploited EU membership to initiate an aggressive campaign for foreign direct investment as a 'gateway' to Europe, an original move in those days. Denmark joined the EU together with the UK, first of all to safeguard its agricultural exports to Britain,

[4]For a short assessment, see section 18.2.1 in the second edition of this book, pp. 373–4.

[5]An economic leader may also use political incentives (or sweeteners, as they are called). See, for example, Hirsch & Doyle (1977), Keohane (1984), Snidal (1985) and Kindleberger (1986).

[6]A free trade agreement was concluded in 1965 but this crowned a decades-long tradition of easy mutual access.

although its interdependence with Germany is likely to have played a role as well.[7]

In 1986, Portugal left EFTA for the EU. Among the more prominent reasons for joining were the need for greater exposure to competition (without at the same time feeling 'ready' for too much world exposure), the opportunities to boost shielded exports in goods such as clothing (that is, trade diversion), the attraction of the EU Structural Funds and the positive impact on democracy and political stability (a hegemony effect). None of these perceived benefits could be had from EFTA. Curiously enough, the accession of Spain was not a prominent reason for Portugal as Spain and Portugal have liberalised their mutual access only because of the EU.

The deepening and widening due to EC-1992 was a major challenge for the remaining EFTA. EFTA's nature had hardly changed for over 25 years; its deepening and widening were trivial and never sudden. In 1984, the Luxembourg process was initiated between the EU and EFTA. It consisted of low-key bargaining on some fifteen areas with regulatory barriers, in anticipation of EC-1992. Without political impetus and without a clear overall goal, negotiations fizzled out precisely when EC-1992 became successful. The Oslo process, suggested by the EU and started in 1989, formed a radical break with EFTA traditions. It can be typified as a hegemonic deepening of EFTA. Once the EFTA countries recognised that the liberalisation and regulatory regimes generated by EC-1992 could only be accessed by engaging in an equivalent exercise, the sudden, far-reaching deepening and widening of EFTA was *de facto* determined by EC-1992, hardly by EFTA itself. EFTA countries merely decided where they would *not* mimic the EU. A second aspect was perhaps even harder to swallow for EFTA: the Oslo process departed from the existing bilateral FTAs concluded in 1973 between all EFTA countries separately with the EU. The new idea was to let all EFTA countries, and the EU as a whole, join a European Economic Area (EEA). This would in fact mean that the existing EFTA would go through a major reform, perhaps even lose its identity. Since the economic weight of the remaining EFTA was small compared with that of the EC12,[8] the economic impact of the EEA on the EU was minor[9] whereas the economic and regulatory impact of the EEA on EFTA was significant.

The EEA extended the internal market regime, as widened and deepened by EC-1992, to EFTA. This implied the adoption of a large stock of old – and new – approach regulation overcoming technical barriers, most of the services liberalisation (which was a radical change for EFTA), the fully fledged application of (EC) competition law and policy – another reform – and selected other regulation (for example, intellectual and industrial property, and so on). EFTA countries did not go all the way, however, so that, in technical GATT terms, the EEA is still an FTA. Trade policy and indirect taxation were excluded, as was agriculture. As a result, the customs frontiers remained in place. Other exceptions related to fish and the free movement of labour. This hegemonic deepening was accepted, above all, to prevent relocation of EFTA companies to the EC12 and, for EFTA, to remain an attractive investment area.

Of course, the EEA greatly narrowed the differences between the EU *acquis* and that of EFTA. This led to queries about the actual influence of EFTA countries on EU policy development, which – in the EEA – would be denied. These queries became even more insistent after the great obstacle to becoming an EU member – political neutrality for four EFTA countries – was made irrelevant by the collapse of the Warsaw Pact and later the Soviet Union. The motivation for having a vote inside the EU being much greater with the EEA, and the political unfeasibility having waned, Austria, Finland, Sweden, Switzerland and Norway applied for EU membership. But meanwhile the EU negotiated the Maastricht Treaty and became a politically deeper Union. This further deepening, added to the well-published grass-roots resistance in some EU countries against the Maastricht Treaty, prompted the Swiss population to reject the EEA (and thereby, implicitly, EU membership). Norway's referendum in November 1992 led to a rejection of EU membership. In 1995 the other three joined the EU.

The radical changes in Europe's political and economic landscape and the hegemonic deepening had almost terminated EFTA. Since 1995 Iceland, Norway and tiny Liechtenstein are in the EEA,[10] Switzerland is in EFTA (but in practice has negotiated many elements of the EEA bilaterally with the EU) and other EFTA countries have switched to the EU.

[7]A referendum in Norway in 1972 led to a refusal by the population to become an EU member.

[8]EFTA had 30 million consumers (albeit all high-income ones) and the EC12, after East Germany had come in in October 1990, over 340 million consumers.

[9]Also because the EU rules remained virtually unchanged.

[10]Apart from the EU itself, the EEA covers less than 5 million consumers this way.

20.1.4 The political economy of 'me-too' accession: less prosperous countries

For less prosperous countries in Europe, the above political economy – though clearly at play as well – is blended with powerful elements of what one might call 'anchorage'. This means that applications for EU membership can best be understood as the combination of three effects: (1) the *magnet* (market access and affluence); (2) *anchor effects* (lock-in of hard reforms, macroeconomic stability and credibility, and political anchorage of values and democracy (often after episodes of autocracy or worse) and, in some undefined but strongly perceived sense, security), and (3) *hegemony effects* (leadership in direction, rule setting, sanctions and ambition, both political and economic, but equally the expectation of special concessions, aid and transfers). A few reminders should suffice to grasp the drives behind these processes.

Spain, Portugal and Greece were all under authoritarian rule in the late 1960s and the first half of the 1970s. In the period 1973–75 each of them found ways to restore democracy and, in the wake of this U-turn, to modernise and open up its economy. The EU, both as a Community and individual countries, was clearly seen as an anchor to firmly pre-empt reversals of a political or economic policy nature. The Greek case is the most revealing. Greece was not considered ready for EU membership according to the official advice of the Commission to the Council, yet the Council overruled this economically and legally sound but 'narrow' opinion and voted in favour on the primacy of fundamental political arguments. For Spain and Portugal, political arguments were equally at play but the strategy chosen was to minimise expected adverse economic effects for (especially) France and Italy before it was felt that politics could prevail; hence, the extremely cumbersome treaties of Accession for Iberia full of exceptions and temporary derogations.

For central Europe, the magnet, anchor and hegemony effects were perhaps even more important. Emerging out of communism and on their way towards a market economy, both 'transitions' in the early 1990s desperately required first a minimum security architecture in Europe. The OSCE was not seen by the former Soviet Union satellites as a sufficiently credible response to these needs. Therefore, many countries sought to move simultaneously over various tracks to underpin their sense of security. At the basic level of political and human rights, they looked for credibility under the Council of Europe with its European Court of Human Rights. As to economic fundamentals, they turned to the OECD with the result that a set of basic economic principles of the market economy and a commitment of support (especially with the European Bank of Reconstruction and Development, the EBRD in London) was ensured. For further deepening, however, for the credible lock-in of a solid reform path, for attractive market outlets and for a much more profound sense of belonging to, indeed 'returning to Europe' (as President Havel of Czechoslovakia expressed it), these countries quickly designed consensual domestic strategies (irrespective of the coalition in power) to enter the EU. They made no secret of their perception of 'security' once they belonged to the EU, despite the fact that the Union has no common defence and a relatively soft common foreign policy. Apparently, the economic might of the Union and the fact that most EU countries are active members of NATO appeared convincing enough. Finally, practically all central European countries also turned to NATO for greater security, not least because of the direct involvement of the USA.

Once the post-cold-war security architecture in Europe began to be settled, the economic arguments became far more pronounced. Even if narrowed to economics, all three effects played a role and clearly still do for countries of central and eastern Europe eager to anchor more firmly their frail market economies ('in transition'), feel the magnet effect of a huge and prosperous market next door for exports and for a future nexus between exports and attracted FDI as well as be authoritatively directed towards well-functioning market institutions and rapid modernisation. Whereas in theory these countries could have opted for multilateral liberalisation instead of the route of economic regionalism in and with the EU, in practice the risks of such a multilateral route would have been extremely high. Not only have studies of transition shown time and again that succesful transition in Europe was directly related to proximity to the EU and with closer economic and regulatory interdependence (see, for example, Fischer, 1998; Wolf, 1999), the detailed work on pre-accession has revealed how wide and deep the great needs of institutional, regulatory and policy improvements were even in the relatively advanced EU candidate countries. One ought not to forget that the political stability of these newly restored democracies was shaky, not least because the initial misery with extreme restructuring without serious social safety nets, if not outright poverty, created fertile soil for populism or radicalism of dangerous sorts. Indeed, of all the transition countries that have moved out of communism, very few have a stable form of democracy, other than the ten EU candidates in the late 1990s. It is this very combination of profound political *and* economic transition which renders the transition process even more tenuous than it inevitably is by its nature[11] and which, far more than any narrow economic rationale, explains the absolute priority of the central European countries to commit to prepare for EU membership, almost irrespective of what it would take. At a later stage, when transition was ensured, the lure of EU membership acquired a more similar meaning to that held by other countries willing to become part of the internal market. Nevertheless, there is an additional attraction in that the EU disposes of what for relatively poor countries amount to sizable funds for economic cohesion. In addition, the macroeconomic stability which is an obligation since the Maastricht Treaty, yet a major problem for countries in transition when on their own, has undoubtedly served as a desired form of anchor too.

20.1.5 Alternatives to 'you-too' enlargement

The attractiveness of the EU was not foreseen by the founding fathers. Half a century later, the EU is confronted with a potential queue of further candidates which cannot *a priori* be regarded as ready to become part of an ambitious system, with very demanding political, legal, institutional and economic properties. This raises the issue of possible alternatives to (full) EU membership, instead of being forced into a 'you-too' arrangement with dire consequences for the internal market and the credibility of implementation, risking permanent frictions with the new Member State. In a weak form, the experience with Greece up to the early 1990s served as a wake-up call for the EU because the Union turned out to be ill-prepared for a situation of continuous disregard of EU rules and proper application. Neither microeconomically nor macroeconomically was Greece living up to what EU membership was all about. A letter in 1993 by Commission president Delors (which was leaked to the press), expressing the frustration of all the Member States and the Commission, has perhaps signalled the beginning of a reversal since the mid-1990s. Whereas, until the mid-1990s, Greece did not converge in income per capita, its U-turn has brought economic growth back to the country and it even managed to restore macroeconomic stability in a record time so that it could enter the eurozone (in 2001). It should be noted that, precisely in the case of Greece, the Commission had cautioned against immediate membership in 1980.

With the profound difficulties of 'transition' or dramatic disparities in prosperity between applicant countries and the Union, there is every reason to be prudent as the consequences of failure 'inside' the Union might well be more severe than in the case of Greece. Strictly speaking, the EU cannot expel a country, and therefore it has to anticipate what a proper arrangement should be.[12]

The arrangements thus far are essentially two. First, countries can become 'associates' and this can be formulated with or without a possibility of EU membership. In principle, EU membership is open to 'European' countries. However, associates inside Europe typically want to become a member sooner or later. Still, a much more gradual process of readying for membership is sensible for countries which do not yet possess credible and experienced market institutions or otherwise are too vulnerable (for example, due to entrenched protectionism). The critical question then is whether and to what extent the EU can and is prepared to use its leverage actively to support domestic reforms in the associated country and, no less, whether the associate is prepared to accept deep and often painful reforms on the way to a serious application of EU membership. The examples of Turkey and Greece – associates since the early 1960s – are surely not the ones to follow. But the Union has learned lessons. It has learned the hard way that benign forms of hegemony and anchorage are necessary, though not sufficient, conditions for the potential success of association as a stepping stone for pre-accession. The contrast between the old cases of Greece and Turkey and the highly intrusive way in which the association agreements with the central European countries were used creatively to engage in factual preparation of the *acquis communautiare* is almost black and white (see section 20.3.1). The new arrangements with Turkey since the customs union of 1996, but in particular since its acceptance as a candidate country, have hardly any resemblance to the old days of superficial diplomacy, without any ambition, legitimacy and clear roadmaps.

The associates outside Europe (for example, the MED countries) have also become more ambitious but the powerful incentives for possible EU membership are lacking, which also deprives the EU of a natural (and thus benign) hegemony to influence domestic reform processes.

The other arrangement is the EEA with the EFTA countries Norway, Liechtenstein and Iceland. The EEA is

[11]The Chinese model of gradual transition to a market economy, avoiding big losers and refusing democracy, need not suffer from these extreme difficulties but such choices were simply not desired by the peoples of central Europe. See Roland (2000) for a rigorous economic analysis of the advantages of the Chinese model of transition.

[12]There are weak sanctions in the case of violation of fundamental values, but not for matters such as the internal market.

very ambitious, the deepest FTA in the world by far. The reason for that is straightforward: the countries depend in an economic sense strongly on the EU, hence on the internal market, and hence wish to participate in it, yet do not accept all the obligations while their peoples do not accept the political consequences of full EU membership. The reason why the EEA works well is that, for the EU, it accommodates the wishes of these countries without deviating from the relevant *acquis*, while for the three 'EFTAns', it represents what they want and what they do not want. The problem of this model as an alternative for new applicants is that, more often than not, the applicants do not wish to go for a kind of EEA without full membership. For most of the economies of the internal market, the EEA is just as credible and powerful (including competition policy and a special EEA Court) but, somehow, this is feared to be not sufficient for anchorage or credible enough for lock-in or to gain the confidence of foreign investors. The new neighboorhood policy might eventually generate countries for which this dilemma might play a role. As far as Turkey is concerned, it is not prepared at the moment to negotiate any other arrangement than full membership, even when this may only occur around 2015 or so (which seems what the EU is aiming for). The current arrangement with Switzerland is a patchwork of separate agreements, more or less adding up to an EEA of sorts but without the clear set of obligations of a general kind, without a Court and without engagements for new EU *acquis*. Again, complicated as it is, the Swiss do not aim for entry.

20.2 The Union's enlargement strategy

20.2.1 Routine elements of every enlargement

Joining the EU is essentially done on the terms set by the Union. It is therefore a misnomer – yet, a misnomer which stubbornly remains popular – to speak of accession negotiations. The negotiations are predominantly an exchange about, followed by extremely detailed and intrusive screening of, the domestic institutions, competences, norms, regulations, jurisprudence, budgets, etc. of the candidate country, and only to a limited extent about temporary derogations from the *acquis* which can truly being negotiated. In the distant past (in the cases of Spain and Portugal for example), accession treaties could be cumbersome owing to an array of agricultural provisions full of temporary clauses. These types of technical derogations still persist but large derogations and for longer periods tend to be strongly resisted. The *acquis* should be accepted. Of course, sometimes the EU is demander. The free movement of workers has been victimised in the enlargement with Greece, Portugal, Spain and the central European countries. There can be sanctions when the overall treaty is agreed but the *acquis* is not adhered to sufficiently. The example that comes to mind is the tough *acquis* on veterinary and phyto-sanitary rules and institutions (with quality assessment, for example of slaughterhouses) which led the EU in 2004 to maintain highly specific exceptions to the free movement of the relevant goods (mainly plants, milk and meat) for some new Member States. Permanent derogations need an exceptionally strong justification and normally will be rejected.[13]

What is new since the early 1990s is that the Union formulates explicit accession strategies. The landmark decision is the Copenhagen European Council of December 1993. The so-called Copenhagen criteria have meanwhile become explicit conditions for eligibility. A crude summary of the routine elements of the EU enlargement strategy can be found in Table 20.2.

The details and depth of the scrutiny far ahead of the days of signing the accession treaty, let alone ratification, still more, actual entry, have become very demanding in the 1990s but – interestingly – only after the entry of Austria, Finland and Sweden was already decided. The annual reports on pre-accession, essentially the early adoption of the *acquis* and the fulfilment of the Copenhagen criteria, contain a wealth of information and assessments, especially if they are studied for a series of consecutive years.[14] The idea behind this scrutiny is to minimise the risk of an ultimate high-level political decision to refuse accession, which would inflict serious political and diplomatic damage, and an assurance for the EP, the Member States and, not least, business and the press that the enlargement process is credible in fulfilling

[13]Examples of detailed work on the technicalities of enlargement negotiations include Nicolaides & Raja Boean (1997), Mayhew (1998) and WRR (2001).

[14]Take, by way of example, the 2005 Comprehensive Monitoring report on Romania, SEC (2005) 1354 and COM (2005) 534 of 25 October 2005, and compare with the 2004 Regular report on Romania (COM (2004) 657 of 6 November 2004) and earlier years. For the first eastern enlargement, take, e.g., the Regular reports on Poland (SEC (2002) 1408 of 9 October 2002) and that of the Czech Republic (COM (2002) 1402 of October 2002), on the basis of which the final admission was agreed by the European Council.

Table 20.2 Routine elements of enlargement strategy

Origin	Principal condition(s)
Treaty (Art. 49 EU)	'Every European state' can apply for EU membership
Copenhagen (Dec. 1993)	• Stable institutions, guaranteeing democracy, rule of law, human rights, and respect for and protection of minorities
	• A functioning market economy
	• The capacity (of that economy) to withstand competitive pressures and market forces within the Union
	• The capacity to take on obligations of EU membership, including the objectives of political, economic and monetary union
Madrid (Dec. 1995)	Administrative capacity guaranteeing the effective implementation of the *acquis*

the Copenhagen criteria without late surprises. Another advantage is that the demanding reforms, and many of them at the same time, can be pursued in the candidate countries without giving opportunist political forces much of a chance. Indeed, the regular reports have been a cardinal factor in the eastern enlargements for the coherence and continuity of the pre-accession reforms. This is important for all 30 chapters of the accession negotiations but most of all for the 23 chapters belonging to the internal market in the wide sense. It is therefore very difficult for a candidate country to play games of 'window dressing'. This, in turn, raises the probability that the country, once a member, will be wedded to the *acquis* as part of its own market regime. There are forceful signals that international business utilised the regular reports for appraisals of direct investment opportunities and risks in candidate countries.

20.2.2 How special are the eastern enlargements?

There are several reasons why the two eastern enlargements are special and hence routine elements of enlargements are not entirely suitable. First, the countries all emerge from communism and autocratic or outright totalitarian rule. The transition processes that have followed are extremely complex transformations. Even after one and a half decades there are, dependent on the country, still legacies of the previous regimes (for example, a lack of initiative among the older population; extreme mistrust of governments, hence political instability from one cabinet to the next; corruption as a routine mode of survival; high structural unemployment in areas where state enterprises were dominant) or serious delays in arriving at the standards necessary to make the internal market function properly (for example, a well-functioning judicial system with enough speed of access to justice to help market players; reliable and agile public institutions), or political pressures on independent regulatory agencies or competition authorities. Second, it is a group of relatively poor countries. Never before was the average per-capita income at the time of entry so low. Whereas Ireland, Greece and Portugal hovered around 65 per cent of the EU average when coming in, and Spain close to 80 per cent, the ten central European countries (as a group) hovered around 52 per cent in 2004. Figure 16.2 shows that the dispersion among them is considerable, too; nonetheless, the majority lag far behind the average of the EU15. Third, they have *de facto* been operating as a group, even if the EU officially declared in Copenhagen in 1993 that each and every country's accession would be judged on its own merits. For a while, different models of accession queues, each country coming in alone, were discussed (such as the 'regatta' model), but nothing came of it.

These three reasons together render the two eastern enlargements somewhat special. It is entirely reasonable to argue that the routine strategy does not fit this kind of enlargement in some respects. In particular, this is the case when different levels of development entail distinct preference sets influencing the costs and the nature of benefits of regulation. At lower levels of development, the risk profiles of workers and companies, and even consumers, are different from the risk-evading attitudes of wealthy consumers and workers in highly developed countries. Also, priorities in environment and certain aspects of health need not necessarily be identical to those in affluent countries. This implies that EU risk regulation as a part of the *acquis* may, in part, be excessively costly for the new

Member States. This can be inevitable where the internal market would be distorted by differences in obligations of companies, generating artificial competitive advantages. One can query, however, whether EU occupational health and safety rules, with all their costly detail and precision, do not impose undue costs on often small and medium-sized companies in central Europe which are disproportionate given the level of development. Pushing indiscriminately the *acquis* without any regard to these queries can be characterised as 'raising rivals' costs', indeed, precisely those new, competitive rivals which accentuate competitive pressure and exploit the internal market.

Another instance where the Union ought not to go about as if the eastern enlargements were not special, is a set of extremely expensive directives on water, waste and (some) air pollution.[15] These directives require heavy investments and this in an area of environmental problems which is predominantly local rather than cross-border. It is one thing whether subsidiarity can regulate, say, drinking water requirements beyond a minimum set by the WHO, because it is conceivable that EU15 countries have homogeneous preferences here, and in any event there is no cross-border water trade that would turn these rules into a priority; it is, however, quite another when poor countries are forced to give priority to investments in this area only because it happens to be in the *acquis* (determined by rich countries who can afford it). Estimates vary over a range of no less than €80–110 billion and this is without considerable operation and maintenance costs.

A third instance of where indiscriminate imposition of the *acquis* is problematic is nuclear safety requirements. Strictly speaking, the EU (in fact, Euratom) did not have more than quite general safety requirements for the simple reason that Member States, until very recently, refused to give up their autonomy. In itself, this is quite remarkable since the potentially disastrous cross-border externalities can hardly be more forceful than in this area. During pre-accession and in fact earlier in political terms, the EU15 imposed the closure of a number of nuclear power plants in central Europe, with the argument that Chernobyl-type reactors could not be safe. Again, the costs of this decision for some of the countries (especially Lithuania) are very high, even though the upgrading of the plant had been blessed by the IAEA in Vienna as safe. Notably, too, the EU imposed a rule which did not exist in the *acquis*: Member States themselves do not live up to an EU requirements regime.

Fourth, the strategy was tightened considerably during the 1990s. The idea of pre-accession did not exist for Spain and Portugal and only in a very light form for the 1995 enlargement. But the most radical innovation was the emphasis on the 'administrative capacity' of the candidate countries, a clear sign that the legacies of transition were suspected to linger on to some degree, and probably rightly so. The great importance of the quality of market and economic policy institutions in the build-up to a well-functioning market economy, in particular when coming out of communism, is widely recognised and documented. The EBRD annual transition reports go at great length into indicators in order to attempt to measure empirically the relationship between such institutions and economic performance (including FDI attraction). All these four examples are linked with the predicament of central European countries and with legacies of their past. Only quite late in the pre-accession process has the EU begun to appreciate that a tough attitude about a timely adoption of the *acquis* – justifiable in itself – should be distinguished from an indiscriminate imposition of the *acquis* in every respect.

20.3 The eastern enlargements

In one decade, central Europe has moved from satellite status under the influence of the Soviet Union (including the Warsaw Pact and Comecon) to ten independent countries, transformed into democracies, and concluded the transition towards a functioning market economy, while accomplishing rapidly increasing economic integration with the EU. These ten countries have also opened up to the world economy and all of them have, in the same period, joined the WTO.

Clearly, such a dramatic transformation cannot be simplified for the purpose of economic analysis. This section first discusses the methods of association and pre-accession, just before EU membership, as well as the terms of accession itself. In section 20.3.2 a sketch of the economic impact is given, followed by a closer look at the microeconomics of catch-up growth of the new Member States.

[15]See WRR (2001) and COM (2001) 304 of 8 June 2001 on environmental financing in the candidate countries.

20.3.1 Accession and its elaborate method

After successive trade agreements and numerous adaptations and additions in a short episode, a total of ten association agreements were signed with the EU between 1991 and 1996.[16] Figure 20.1 illustrates the structure of the first six association agreements with the EU. The later ones are similar.

The political and economic aims, overarching the four pillars of the association, explain the radical character of the trade liberalisation. They also explain the dynamic nature of the cooperation. The hegemonic and anchor effects (expressed in the aims) were also important for the fragile democracies, suffering from huge economic shocks during the first three years of transition. To get around lengthy ratification procedures, interim trade agreements permitted the immediate start

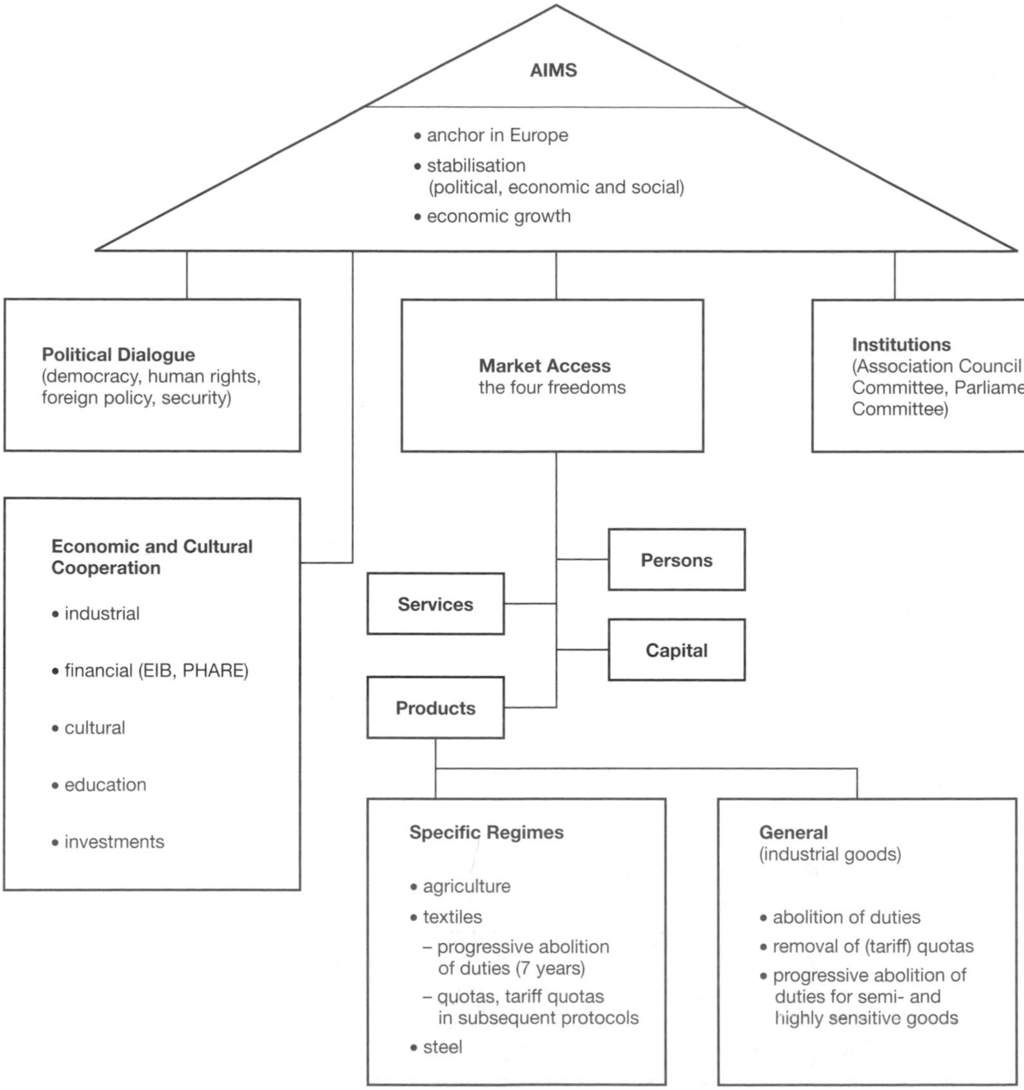

Figure 20.1 Association agreements with central European countries

[16]For a survey of the numerous changes in trade cooperation between the EU and central European countries as of 1988, see Pelkmans (1994b, especially table 5.4). The ten countries are Poland, Czech Republic, Slovakia, Hungary, Bulgaria, Romania, Slovenia and the three Baltic countries Estonia, Latvia and Lithuania.

of a rapid liberalisation process (in 1992 and following years, dependent on the country). Focusing on economic substance, the hard core of the association is the market access pillar, especially with respect to tariffs and quotas in goods markets. The association agreements also have the character of a framework for all kinds of deeper economic cooperation. They contain explicit references to the eventual accomplishment of the free movement of services, capital and, conditionally, even persons. Technical aid and infrastructural support is granted via the European Investment Bank and the PHARE programme.[17] Other programmes include industrial cooperation and the promotion of (EU) direct investment in central Europe. Even for goods markets proper, the potential dynamics of the cooperation can be read from the long-run commitment of the central European countries to align their economic regulation to that of the EU via an extensive programme of approximation.[18] This would eventually move the association close to the substance of the EEA.

Market access for goods was to be fully liberalised on both sides in a period of (maximum) ten years for central Europe and five years for the EU. However, no free market access for agriculture was envisaged.[19]

Also the central European countries have proved to be liberal. After shaking off communism, they established fairly liberal trade regimes, with relatively low tariffs and few quotas, though industrial tariffs were, on average, more than double the (low) EU tariffs. During 1993 and 1994, when the first recovery in central Europe proved to be very weak, the degree of restrictiveness of their tariffs increased somewhat. On the whole, however, EU producers had no serious access problems in trade policy. The initial problems for EU exports related more to weak or unstable demand, frequent changes in government, weak legal regimes with even weaker enforcement of market rules and property rights. Local producers or buyers also suffered from a fragile banking system. Exchange rate volatility and incomplete convertibility have caused problems as well. Thus, the main problems of trade with central Europe were a consequence of the transition of their economies.

One trade problem long remained unresolved: agriculture. As with EC/EFTA and the EEA, agricultural market access was selective and minimal. Because of the political expectations raised by the Union's recognition of its economic hegemonic and anchor roles, carefully measured concessions had to be made by the EU in agriculture. Compared with industry, and considering the vital importance of maintaining demand for central Europe's agricultural produce,[20] the partial retention of high agricultural EU barriers for associates was an inconsistent and protectionist policy response. The roots of this reticence are to be found in the EU's 'domestic' agricultural problem. Already under pressure in those early years, in the Uruguay Round to agree to tariffication and reduction of levies and to lower export subsidies while negotiating an internal CAP reform, further market opening was politically unfeasible. Moreover, central Europe's agricultural potential in the long run is large and East Germany (with many large farms) had already entered via German unification. As a result, the negotiations on concessions for the associates were difficult. Even restrictive quotas for specific products were perceived as extra concessions by EU farmers and as disappointing protectionism by the associates. The latter were also disillusioned because of the asymmetry in agricultural market access: easy for EU's agro-exports to them, difficult and at times trivially small for central Europe's export to the EU (except for wine, for example). The EU also continued to pay export subsidies on its exports to central Europe, thereby making it even more difficult for local agro-markets to compete.

The actual accession in 2004, and in 2007 for Romania and Bulgaria, is broadly based on the routine

[17]The PHARE programme began as an OECD-wide programme, coordinated by the EU (in 1989). The EU's own PHARE programme has grown to a huge technical aid policy supporting the association and its dynamic development, in addition to OECD-wide coordination of other aspects in the aid. The latter is embedded in multilateral efforts, joined by the World Bank and the new European Bank for Reconstruction and Development (in London). Later, the EU PHARE programme was woven into the pre-accession agreements (see Case Study 20.1).

[18]The very comprehensive nature of this approximation commitment and the complications for central Europe – in combining demanding economic reform for the transition, with demanding approximation of law for the association – can be read from the Commission's White Paper *Preparation [of these countries] for Integration into the Internal Market of the Union*, COM (95) 163 of 10 May 1995 and its detailed Annex specifying 899 directives and decisions in 23 chapters of the *acquis*. This White Paper's ambition cannot be justified on the basis of the one substantive approximation article in the Europe Agreements, merely containing a list of policy areas without any further detail. Rather, the White Paper is best understood as a guide for the introduction of the internal market *acquis*, one of the conditions for EU membership as defined in Copenhagen (December 1993) and later.

[19]For more detail, see section 18.4.1 of the 2nd edition.

[20]This demand was badly affected by the collapse of export demand from the ex-USSR as well as by the severe reduction in local purchasing power due to the transition.

elements of Table 20.2. The 'functioning market economy' criterion was in essence interpreted as the conclusion of transition. During the pre-accession this was scrutinised with many hard and soft indicators, and reforms were urged where indicators remained unsatisfactory. Once this criterion is fulfilled, however, and given the openness of their economies and the *acquis* obligations as well, the readiness to withstand competitive pressures should go hand in hand. The adjustment process would probably imply painful (relative) price and quality adjustment and inter-sectoral reallocation of resources – in a functioning market economy this can be a short-run problem, not a long-run issue. Participation in the economic union, especially in the internal market, has become ever more precise over time. It is *de facto* meant to include the full implementation of the 1995 White Paper (see fn 18), if not more of the *acquis*, *before* accession. It also implies sufficient 'administrative capacity' to enforce the *acquis* – an overly demanding condition to achieve during pre-accession. There are bound to be a number of temporary derogations (for environment and agriculture mainly), just as with previous enlargements. This is justified, if only because the investments and adjustment costs associated with the full *acquis* in certain policy areas would be so high as to reduce the rate of catch-up growth for many years.[21] The obligation to participate in the monetary union implies that it is ultimately subject to the entry conditions of the eurozone. In practice, acceding countries step into Stage 2 of EMU first, subsequently (but without a deadline) enter ERM-II and, after two years in ERM-II, become part of the eurozone (see also Chapter 18).

Finally, note that in adopting the *acquis* upon entry, some truly centralised aspects of the *acquis* only come into force at that date. Apart from certain obvious legal aspects (the EC Court's jurisdiction for them can only begin on the formal date of entry, for example), the main element is trade policy. Accession meant roughly a halving of industrial tariffs for the new Member States and a mixed picture of agricultural tariff adjustment.

From the EU side, one conspicuous element in the terms of accession has been the (maximum) seven years' derogation from the free movement of workers. Nothing new here, as Greece, Spain and Portugal were all confronted with the same period as well; in fact, this time it is marginally better because a few EU15 countries have not opted for restrictions (for example, the UK) and the derogation can be lifted in the interim. The sensitivity about migration is caused by the large wage gap, which is perceived as putting downward pressure on wages in the EU15 or crowding out of local workers in a few sectors such as building, restaurants and transport. Apparently, the insistence on host country control, already shrinking labour demand for legal immigrants so strongly, is still not enough.

CASE STUDY 20.1 Lock-in via pre-accession

For the ten central European countries, 'pre-accession agreements' provide a multi-annual framework for the domestic preparation for EU membership, and the EU's legal, advisory and financial roles in this process. The agreements go into extreme detail because the conditions for EU membership in this enlargement have been pushed up higher than ever before. Great technical assistance about almost every chapter in the *acquis*, very detailed legal advice in drafting laws, inspection of the actual implementation of hundreds of domestic laws reflecting the *acquis* (especially of the internal market and related approximation concerning health and safety, prudential supervision, environmental product standards, veterinary and plant health measures, application of customs rules, liberalisation of telecoms, sexual equality laws, and so on), assessment of the performance of the executive agencies and enforcement bodies for some forty areas of the internal market provisions, and conditional subsidies for infrastructure, environmental clean-up and proper institutions for regional and agricultural structural policy – these constitute the more important efforts under pre-accession. In effect, this might be considered as a massive exercise of lock-in of reforms, new policies and better administrative practices, that would in any case be required for successful transition to a market economy and for rapid development.

[21]For a detailed exposition of these and other enlargement issues, see Pelkmans *et al.* (2000a), WRR (2001) and the examples in section 20.2.2. See also the Kok report (Kok *et al.*, 2003).

CASE STUDY 20.1 *continued*

But the lock-in goes further still because the EU was sensitive to the risk that some of the candidate countries would only superficially change their economy and laws while in fact becoming new 'Mezzogiornos', dependent on EU transfers and without catch-up growth. So, not only do so-called regular reports (annually) provide 'scores' on how far the countries have gone in meeting the condition of a 'functioning market economy' (which is a sound idea), but the European Commission (DG Economic and Financial Affairs) and the candidate countries have concluded Joint Medium-term Economic Strategies as well. These synthesis documents integrate microeconomic aspects of transition (at least for the ten central European countries) and of pre-accession, with the budgetary and investment requirements of major domestic reforms (such as those affecting health, education, pensions) as well as of EU-led reforms (for example, environment, veterinary and sanitary inspections, energy sector), in a medium-term macroeconomic (growth) perspective. Crucial is the overall economic consistency of the many demanding policies with strict macroeconomic stability conditions, given the overriding aim of catch-up growth. Clearly, the annual rollover of the Joint Medium-term Economic Strategies, in a context of preparing for EU membership, creates yet another powerful lock-in which should greatly help governments to overcome resistance of vested interests or opportunistic political action against the painful parts of the policy package. All the same, from a political point of view, this unprecedented and deep lock-in is also meant to reassure EU Member States that this eastern enlargement will strengthen, not weaken the EU economy.

20.3.2 Economic impact of the eastern enlargement

There have been many *ex ante* studies of the economic impact of the eastern enlargement. A few general remarks are useful before going into some detail. First, unlike the impression one might get from the nature of the debate in political or social circles in the Union, eastern enlargement cannot exert a major economic impact on the EU economy. The most important reason is that the economic size of the ten central European economies in 2005 is about 6 per cent of the GDP of the EU15. Another reason is that the accession itself was preceded by a decade or more of mutual opening up in industrial goods markets and at least somewhat in agricultural ones as well as services. Therefore, the more interesting questions in terms of economic impact are likely to be posed for the acceding countries themselves where the impact is relatively much larger, both quantitatively and qualitatively. In this light it is crucial to structure the analytical approach to economic impact according to (1) the impact of what? (full membership, pre-accession only, or only the Europe Agreements), and (2) whether a comparatively static question is asked (membership as a one-off shock, usually free trade in goods and lower other 'trading costs' as a proxy for a deeper internal market) or a more dynamic question, namely whether EU membership exerts a stimulating influence on catch-up growth. The catch-up issue is addressed in section 20.3.3.

It is key to focus on: the impact of what? We discuss the initial east–west trade liberalisation first, subsequently the Europe Agreements and finally the potential economic impact of EU membership. Economic impact analysis of the strong liberalisation of trade between central Europe and the EU in the 1990s is made very difficult because of the simultaneity of diverse causes. One might be inclined to attribute all the trade flow changes between the two to the association agreements and the preceding liberalisation between the two. There are strong indications that this would be mistaken. With respect to the possible future trade impact, trade flows of some orders of magnitude have been widely quoted which are, almost certainly, misleading as well.

Let us begin with the fundamental reorientation of the trade of central Europe. The rather sudden transformation led economists to fall back on 'gravity models' to 'guesstimate' the long-run growth of trade between central Europe and the EU.[22] A gravity model is useful only when very aggregate trade flows are studied and if one is interested in a rough measure of the 'normal'

[22]See, for example, Hamilton & Winters (1992) and Baldwin (1994). See also Gros & Steinherr (1995).

potential of bilateral trade flows. The model explains the bilateral trade flow between any two trading partners in terms of their economic masses (hence 'gravity'), usually represented by GDP, and the economic distance between them. Applying it to European east–west trade, the idea is that, before 1989, the associates' potential trade with the EU had been artificially diverted to Comecon and suppressed by EU's barriers against 'state-trading' countries. The transition and liberalisation would lead to an explosive trade growth with the EU, and gravity models would give a clue about how far this process would go. However, Brenton & Gros (1995) have shown that these guesstimates are flawed, because they are based on pre-reform income levels (which were heavily distorted and much too high in dollar terms). By 1993, observed trade flows between the EU and central Europe were about as large as one would expect from gravity models with post-reform (1992) income levels. The authors also show that 1993 trade openness ratios (exports plus imports divided by GDP) of central European countries are similar to the ratios of EU countries of similar size. The conclusion is that the expected 'flood' of imports from central Europe will not materialise, and trade growth will be strong but quite gradual over a long period.

Brenton & Gros's conclusion would seem to permit a standard trade criterion and diversion analysis of the association agreements, later in the 1990s. However, this is hard to accomplish as the pre-FTA situation – heavily distorted as it was – cannot be based on the analysis of Figure 13.4. Several other determinants have played a role in the rapid increase of trade between central Europe and the EU in the first half of the 1990s. They are:

- drastic changes in relative prices in central Europe, for example a large rise in energy and minerals prices and a fall in low-quality industrial goods;
- a collapse in the east European (ex-USSR) demand for central European goods, whether agricultural or industrial, and the sharp reduction of intra-central Europe trade, even though it is no longer planned or monopolised;
- a sharp reduction in domestic demand, given a severe decline in incomes, at least initially;
- an initial strategy of strongly undervalued exchange rates, so as to facilitate the removal of exchange controls, and provide some protection to hard-hit import-competing producers while boosting exports to the EU; subsequently, real exchange rates have appreciated, usually via inflation.[23] Over half a decade the real swings have been considerable and have no doubt influenced trade flows.

The trade impact of the association has been important quantitatively, but what is attributable to the FTA is not clear. The ten associates already traded heavily with the EU15 in 1996: on their import side, the EU share hovered between 37 per cent (for Slovakia) and 68 per cent (for Slovenia); on their export side the EU share had gone up to anywhere between 33 per cent (Lithuania) and 66 per cent (Poland). Progress in transition did seem to matter. The more advanced candidate countries all have more than 60 per cent EU share in imports, and more than 53 per cent in their exports. These shares are close to those of the cohesion countries in the EU, and sometimes exceed the EU share of, for example, the UK. The attribution problem (that is, is it all due to the FTA in the Europe Agreement?) is caused by the sharp decline of domestic and east European demand, leaving the EU as the main source of survival for many companies.

Several authors have studied intra-industry trade (IIT) and quality aspects of EU–central Europe trade.[24] The main conclusions are that a deepening of IIT (horizontally) is not the reason for the rapid export expansion of central European exports to the EU (but relative prices are); that vertical IIT accounts for 80–90 per cent of total IIT (with central Europe specialising in the lower-quality segment within most sectors); and that, up to 1996 inclusive, there was no significant catching up in the quality of products exported by central Europe relative to the EU and only selectively relative to east Asian exporters.

However, there are good reasons not to extrapolate these conclusions to the post-1996 period. One such reason is the inflow of FDI, mainly but not only from the EU. Brenton and di Mauro (1999) find (using a gravity model) that FDI in the more advanced candidate countries is already greater (up to 1996 inclusive) than one would expect given their current level of income, market size and relative proximity. They also find that FDI inflows tend to give a boost not only to exports but also, to some degree, to imports. Another reason is that economic growth returned to central Europe, with medium-term annual growth after 2000 around 5 per cent for most countries. Given the stabilisation of market rules and institutions approaching those of EU quality, this should lead to entrepreneurial activity

[23] See, for example, Halpern & Wyplosz (1995).

[24] See Aturupane *et al.* (1999), Brenton (1999) and Ulff-Moller Nielsen (2000), among others.

emphasising greater quality. Central European countries are relatively well endowed with skilled labour, which, after a decade of transition, should be capable of generating high-quality products.

A special case is agriculture. The sharp decline in central European agriculture was a surprise to many EU observers.[25] As a result, the bilateral trade balance swung dramatically in the EU's favour. The free access for agro-exports of central Europe, is bound to act as a much-needed stimulus to continue structural reform, and raise productivity and quality in central Europe. Enlargement with all ten adds 50 per cent more agricultural land to that of the EU15, and nearly doubles the number of farm workers. Nevertheless, a careful study of the specialised literature (Pelkmans & Casey, 2003) shows that central European agriculture has suffered enormously from transition problems, severely damaging its competitiveness. It is only recently, stimulated by agro-food FDI, full membership and the prospect of EU direct income payments, that further restructuring away from very-low-productivity agriculture to high-value-added agriculture, combined with modern processing and marketing, is emerging (Swinnen, 2005).

Following the initial east–west trade liberalisation and the Europe Agreements, what could be the additional economic impact of EU membership? To appreciate the economic impact of EU membership, one can assume two complementary perspectives: on the one hand, the fundamental influence of growth prerequisites and appropriate economic institutions, and, on the other hand, economic simulation and empirical modelling. The first perspective is often taken for granted in developed countries, but has proved to be a critical issue in the transition from communism to functioning market economies in central Europe, while it also matters a lot in less prosperous countries trying to catch up. EU membership firmly seals a series of 'growth prerequisites' for the new Member States. These include political stability and democracy (stability fosters solid institutions and trust, over time), macroeconomic stability (which is good for growth, *ceteris paribus*) and credibility. The long road to EU membership also ensures appropriate economic institutions, which help markets to function well, which in turn helps sustain long-run growth and adjustment. Such institutions also legitimise the market economy in being fundamentally in the public interest and not in the short-run private interests of only some.

As far as the analytical approach is concerned, it would be wrong to model the economic impact of enlargement (in the goods markets) as the change from discriminated outsiders to preferred insiders. In terms of Figure 13.4 and Chapter 6, enlargement implies the shift from an industrial FTA to a CU, and from (incomplete) preferential agricultural trade to an agricultural CU. The latter is bound to have a significant sectoral impact, in simultaneously improving mutual market access and raising (often) external tariffs (on average) in agro-products.[26] Even without data and elasticities, one can say that the CU will act as a strong incentive to improve efficiency and enlarge production in central Europe's agriculture. Of course, price levels matter. Based on the Agenda 2000 CAP reform proposals (not the outcome), Frandsen *et al.* (2000) compute large output increases induced by a CU between the EU15 and central Europe: wheat up to 85 per cent, bovine meat by 56 per cent and dairy products by 22 per cent; output of some other CAP products falls modestly. The value of agro-exports from central Europe to the EU15 more than doubles, in part a (higher) price effect. The authors also fear that enlargement, in this respect, will be WTO-inconsistent.

The impact of the industrial CU is likely to be negligible for the EU and, at most, of some selective importance for central Europe, namely, where *ex ante* tariffs were high (for example, clothing and cars). A more speculative approach is that central Europe may see its trade with the EU increase by perhaps 20–40 per cent because other 'trade costs' are significantly lowered. In fact, in joining the CU, central Europe also joins the single market and this should facilitate intra-European trade beyond the level reached in the FTA.[27]

One might add a third general fact about enlargement: the adjustment costs of accession will be relatively low for the candidates, after the tremendous social costs of severe output decline due to transition and other costs of reallocation, induced by exposure to foreign competition and the reorientation of trade.

[25]It is caused by a number of transition problems such as conflicts about property rights (land), collapse of local demand and Comecon demand, the lack of agricultural banks (e.g. ensuring seasonal finance for fertilisers and seeds) and the EU's protectionism as well as its export subsidies.

[26]See Pelkmans & Casey (2003) for the complicated picture in *ex ante* tariffs, e.g. with fruits and vegetable tariffs and those for non-bovine meat often being higher than the CET of the EU15. Candidate countries did differ, however, which increases the problems of impact analysis.

[27]An example is in Baldwin *et al.* (1997). The basic idea behind the lowering of trade costs is found in Chapter 6, especially in section 6.6.

FDI may increase especially in parts of central Europe, at first regarded by investors as relatively risky or costly (such as Romania and Bulgaria). What was decisive for more FDI, even before their EU membership, is probably that the transition process was completed and legal certainty and 'administrative capacity' were enhanced. Also with respect to FDI, fears particularly about 'delocalisation' exist in the EU. Abraham & Konings (1999), however, show that such investment relocation is rarely the motive of FDI in central Europe, and even in such cases it may still generate additional exports of intermediate goods.

Finally, in the enlargement process there is great sensitivity about potential immigration into the EU, following EU membership. As noted in Chapter 10 (see also Figure 10.3) the determinants of migration flows are many, and large intra-EU migratory flows have never occurred, not even when income disparities were considerable. Two important points should be noted before extrapolating these conclusions to the eastern enlargements. First, the income disparities for some groups and some candidate countries are likely to be bigger than with any previous enlargement. This fuels the expectation that migration flows will be large, and especially in low-skilled categories, thereby negatively affecting wages and job opportunities of the low skilled in the EU15. Second, and significantly damping these expectations, it is little realised that national labour markets in the EU apply the host country principle (see Chapter 9), meaning that there is no wage competition between legal immigrants and locals. So, in most instances, workers will migrate only if their skills overcompensate the non-wage disadvantages of being a foreign worker, or, if this does not apply, they will find illegal employment or fill up labour shortages in sectors or in countries with tight labour markets. For EU countries with high unemployment, the truly sensitive issue is, therefore, illegal migration. Long transition periods to delay immigration do not prevent illegal migration. Only for Austria and (eastern) Germany do frontier workers present a potential problem, if the labour market is not tight.[28]

Furthermore there are significant distributive issues, if only because transfers (via the CAP and for cohesion purposes) are expected to play a major role after enlargement for decades to come. As to transfers, we refer the reader to Chapters 16 and 19.

20.3.3 Microeconomics of catch-up growth

Apart from security, values and a sense of political and cultural belonging, the new Member States joined the EU because they want prosperity. Therefore, the static economic impact analysis is secondary to the impact of EU membership on catch-up growth. The underlying microeconomics of catch-up growth propelled by market integration have been touched upon in several chapters, but notably in Chapter 16 on cohesion.[29] It is generally held that economic integration impacts positively on real convergence between countries, whereas the impact on regions can be both convergent and divergent (and this may also differ over time). Ben-David (1993) found a positive correlation between trade intensity and the speed of convergence. Since the former clearly rises with EU membership, it would support catch-up growth. Cuadrado-Roura (2001) showed that migration from low-income regions in the EU explains part of catch-up growth in the 1960s.

One prominent driver of catch-up growth of the new Member States is the trade–FDI nexus, which, under certain conditions, steadily improves dynamic comparative advantage. Such dynamic impetus would come on top of the static and pro-competitive effects of market integration analysed in Chapter 6. Dynamic comparative advantage assumes a continuous process of improving a country's capability to exploit higher value-added opportunities in the internal market. The country would move up the quality ladder, and this would require new or enhanced determinants in the production function, such as more and higher skills, more and better technology or a capacity to innovate, or a more systematic use of higher-quality services supporting output. Dynamic comparative advantage is strengthened by FDI. At an initial stage, when wages are low, reflecting low productivity (perhaps also because of a lack of equipment, infrastructure and services), FDI would accentuate this comparative advantage with footloose establishments and relatively little upskilling and spread effects into the wider economy. However, FDI inflows and rising exports will still propel (initial) extra growth but would eventually tend to lock in unpromising specialisation in a global context. However, EU membership will impose a quite sophisticated infrastructure for industrial and consumer standards, conformity assessment, quality control (ISO 9000), and so forth. Thus, at almost any level of the quality ladder, EU membership will assume

[28]For a detailed analysis for Austria, see Fidrmuc & Nowotny (2000). Economic studies of potential migration after enlargement include Bauer & Zimmerman (1999) and Boeri & Bruecker (2000).

[29]The reader is also referred to Chapters 6, 9 and 10.

a minimum infrastructure, appropriate skill levels and a premium on quality properties. If institutions work, this creates an attractive basis for FDI in (intermediate or final) goods with more value-added. At later stages this could lead to high-quality operations such as co-makerships with leading manufacturers (for example, around Skoda/Volkswagen in the Czech Republic in the mid-1990s and connected to the revival of Dacia/Renault in Romania is 2004/05).

Such a stepwise movement up ladders of higher value-added is powerfully stimulated by intra-EU trade and FDI, and hence they serve as channels of convergence. Early empirical work by Landesmann (2003) and Havlik (2005) reveals clear signals that these convergence channels between the new Member States and the EU15 work. Thus, between 1995 and 2001, intra-EU industrial exports of the new Member States was rising (in shares of industrial output) in labour-intensive industries in relatively low-wage countries such as Latvia, Romania and Bulgaria but falling in, for example, the Czech Republic, Hungary and Poland. With respect to technology-driven industries, all new Member States see their exports (in shares of industrial output) rise. The exceptions are Bulgaria and Romania, starting from a lower base. The upward jumps in these higher value-added sectors for Hungary, Slovakia, the Czech Republic and Poland are impressive. Focusing on skill decomposition, a similar pattern emerges but even more pronounced. The Bulgarian and Romanian share of industrial output in low-skill intensive sectors is far higher (above 60 per cent) than in other new Member States in the late 1990s, and in all other these sectors also shrink (in shares). When it comes to high-skill intensive sectors, all new Member States shift, with different speeds, towards higher shares. Other indicators point in a similar direction such as rising IIT shares and a rising demand in all new Member States for medium- and high-skilled labour, contrasting with falling demand for labour with only primary school education. The quality ladder is often measured with so-called export price gaps, that is, unit export price deviations from the average unit EU import prices. The new Member States are all in the process of rapidly closing this export price gap (which is, however, still negative).

Finally, central Europe has withstood the menace of a major collapse of FDI inflows during and after the 2001–03 recession in Europe, Japan and the USA. FDI inflows keep on increasing year after year and begin to swell also for countries such as Bulgaria, Slovakia and Romania, which were initially less successful in attracting them. Altogether, it is possible, therefore, to indicate powerful signals for a sustained catch-up growth of central Europe (at the micro level). To attribute this firmly to EU membership would be too much to ask from this kind of analysis, although the likelihood of a significant accession effect (even before actually coming in) is quite high.

20.4 Beyond the EU27

20.4.1 Further enlargement and its political legitimacy

The absorption capacity of the EU has been stretched to the limit. More 'me-too' accession is in principle welcome if applications come from 'European States' (Article 49 EU) which are 'democratic' (Article 6 EU). But six enlargements have clearly caused a fatigue, prompted an urge to consolidate first, not only in terms of the *acquis* and all that it takes, but also in terms of values, culture and political identity, and aroused fears in the social domain which engender blockages of further extension of the Union. In fairness, there is another reason as well, often hard to distinguish from the previously mentioned anxieties. Suppose, Switzerland or Norway were to apply for EU membership and not request to be treated in a special way or not insist on permanent derogations of substance. It is, of course, difficult to substantiate, but it would seem reasonable to expect that the enlargement fatigue would not apply to them. Their regulations and arrangements with the EU would not cause much of an *acquis* shock and their high level of development would not cause any strain, except for agriculture and (for Norway) fisheries. The Copenhagen criteria would not pose any problem whatsoever. The crux here is not so much a matter of west versus east or south, but rather that further enlargement (other than Switzerland or Norway, from whom no application is expected in any event) would inevitably involve solely relatively poor countries, often with fragile democracies and weak states or with a host of other problems. The only exception emerging from any list of candidates 'beyond the EU27' that is regarded as a reasonably promising case is Croatia. Croatia became an official candidate country in October 2005 when negotiations were opened.

The list of 'me-too' prospective candidate countries consist (in 2005) of the western Balkan countries (Albania, Bosnia and Herzegovina, the former Yugoslav republic of Macedonia, Serbia and Montenegro, and Kosovo). Turkey and Croatia are official candidate countries in negotiations about the adoption of the *acquis* and the terms of accession. Other countries have announced that they will eventually apply for EU membership after political consolidation and economic reforms have proceeded: they include in any case Moldova, Ukraine and Georgia. The present book is not the place for a political assessment of all these demands of a 'me-too' character. It is submitted, however, that, for a considerable period ahead, the EU will attempt to be as accommodating as possible but on the basis of alternative arrangements, not full EU membership. This should not be too difficult for a while because the Copenhagen criteria are demanding for these countries and their domestic resolve to satisfy these criteria will be crucial. With the western Balkan countries the EU has concluded Stability and Association Agreements (SAAs) or is in the process of doing so, which are reminiscent of the Europe Agreements for central Europe. The critical difference is the far stronger military and foreign policy element in them as a legacy of the bloody Yugoslav civil war of the first half of the 1990s and the ethnic tensions underlying it. The operational aspects such as roadmaps of reforms (and their sequencing) and a host of other specifics are dealt with in so-called European Partnerships which are expected to become part and parcel of the domestic political priorities and agenda, which in turn opens up quite considerable legal, institutional and financial EU assistance. The only country for which a prospect of 'candidacy' can be discerned in late 2005 is Macedonia. This would mean that, if it fulfils at the same time the political part of the Copenhagen criteria, accession negotiations might be started in 2006 or 2007. The predicament of the other former Yugoslav states is far less clear. Their competitiveness is frail and their fragmentation presents a problem. One possibly useful way to support their restoration of trade competitiveness is to consider a customs union as a group, together with the one Turkey already enjoys, with the EU. This could replace the bilateral FTAs under the SAAs and facilitate trade (without complicated rules of origin and their verification) significantly. Remembering the cold shower that Turkey received upon the establishment of the customs union, the fear in the western Balkans is that such an approach is too radical. Indeed, the difference is external protection against third countries but the competition from the competitive EU remains just as tough in the bilateral FTAs.[30]

CASE STUDY 20.2 Turkey: dual track to accession

The association with Turkey dates back to 1964. It was long an industrial FTA, with some exceptions, such as informal textiles and clothing quotas on the EU side and a range of derogations on the Turkish side. In April 1987, Turkey applied for EU membership. Its application was frozen, basically for human rights reasons. In many ways Turkey is part of Europe and its cooperative tradition (for example, Council of Europe, many private associations) as well as wider organisations with great importance for Europe (such as OECD, NATO). Using an article in the old association agreement (so that no ratification procedure had to be risked), a customs union was concluded and came into force in 1996. In 1997, Turkey was declared an eligible candidate for EU membership, but now under the same conditions as central Europe. Since 1999, Turkey has been engaged in similar pre-accession programmes to those set out in Case Study 20.1 and every November a detailed regular report is published about the adoption, implementation and administrative capacity of the *acquis*. Despite the fact that Turkey has never been a communist country, the multiple and profound economic interventionism reported in the regular reports made the Commission hesitant to accord the 'functioning market economy' status to Turkey. It did so only in 2004, following the post-2001-crisis reforms as supported by the IMF. Turkey was finally accepted as a negotiation partner in December 2004 and negotiations were initiated in October 2005. Turkey is clearly on a dual-track towards accession: one track concerning human rights, respect for minorities and some constitutional issues, where sensitivities are great and improvement is only recent; the other economic, where Turkey, with a more stable and more credible government, can pursue its economic reforms and inspire confidence in the EU about its growth potential. If Turkey were to pursue this dual track effectively, the economic

[30]The customs union idea has been floated, e.g. by Emerson (2005).

CASE STUDY 20.2 *continued*

analysis of enlargement would have to be rewritten. Researchers have long not assumed it is (politically) realistic that Turkey would soon enter. The economic size of Turkey is nearly that of central Europe as a whole. Despite its political and ethnic troubles, the economy has repeatedly shown its powerful growth potential under stability. The post-2001 growth rates hover between 4 and 9 per cent.

The customs union has had the effect of drastically lowering external protection to EU levels, both MFN and in regionalism with others. This has had a cold-shower effect (see section 6.2), which might boost efficiency. Turkey has also entered into an FTA with Israel and joined the new MED agreements. In agriculture, the CAP will eventually be introduced in order to allow free movement of agricultural products (Article 22/23). However, there has been little progress thus far. In practice, agro-liberalisation is likely to become a pre-accession activity on the 'economic' track. Agriculture is still poorly analysed but seems largely uncompetitive (except for fruits)

The customs union is also deep in other ways – it is much like a Europe Agreement (even though it is a customs union) with an almost exhaustive approximation programme for goods, provisions for intellectual property rights, and a wholesale adoption of EC-type competition rules as well as an independent competition authority (established in 1997). One should expect the initial screening of Turkish laws and institutions (the first stage of the negotiations) to take at least one and a half years. Subsequently, negotiations about the 30 chapters, frequently implying deep domestic reforms, will begin. Turkey is also a 'dual' economy, with low literacy rates in Anatolia and other peripheral regions. Cleary, this duality has to be overcome with major initiatives.

It can be argued, however, that the real test case of further enlargement is Turkey. Case Study 20.2 elaborates. Even if Turkey is capable of demonstrating consistency of reforms and steady economic growth – as it has been doing since the new government came to power in 2001 – the negotiations are still expected to take many years, possibly up to ten, because of the exceptional width and depth of institutional (indeed, partly constitutional) reforms and adaptation of customs and practices. Despite the kemalist separation of Islam and the state (a model taken over from the French *laïcité*), the country is widely regarded as Islamic and this causes hesitations. The size of the country is yet another source of inhibition, even if a Turkey of 85 million inhabitants, by the time it might come in, is still no more than perhaps 15 per cent of the EU population. It is well understood, however, that a prosperous and stable, democratic Turkey would be a tremendous benefit to the Union too.

20.4.2 The Union's orbit: neighbourhood and MED strategies

With the repeated enlargements, the Union has become a continental economic power, with – in terms of values at least – a strong explicit position. It is a beacon of democracy and a proven source of stability and prosperity for many adjacent countries at the edge of Europe, the Middle East or the southern Mediterranean. The EU has gradually come to understand the profound change in its international status. Both in terms of global responsibility as well as in its enlighted self-interest, the Union had to come up with a more strategic approach to its often flammatory or unstable orbit to the east, and south of the Mediterranean. In 2004 it unfolded a 'European neighbourhood policy' which attempts to offer adhanced market access (in FTAs, hence mutual) together with more political and reform commitments and assistance. In 1995, following a long history of programmes for the Mediterranean area, the so-called Barcelona process was set up for the North African and Middle East Mediterranean countries, mostly Arab except Israel (usually denoted as the MED countries). This Barcelona Euro-MED process attempted to strengthen and widen the chain of bilateral FTAs the EU had to conclude (so as to remain WTO compatible), substituting for the unilateral preferences formerly granted to the MED countries. Over time, some €9 billion of assistance was sunk into the Barcelona process, vigorous attempts have been made to move the MEDs into freer trade among themselves (only a four-country Agadir Agreement was harvested and its implementation is still to be started) and numerous reform debates have been held. The process is, broadly speaking, a failure. The visions of the Arab MEDs about where the process should be moving, contrasts with the reform-minded approach of the EU. The trade preferences and new FTAs are very problematic (dell'Aquila & Kuiper, 2003) and the underlying problems in many MEDs have hardly been tackled. New roadmaps agreed in 2005 are unlikely to help if visions differ and countries are not prepared to connect such processes with deep domestic reforms.

The new 'neighbourhood policy' is best regarded as an alternative to EU membership. It has this in common with the MED strategy. However, whereas the MED countries cannot be considered as 'European states', countries such as Moldova, Ukraine and Georgia are clearly European both geographically and culturally. One might also make the same argument for other potential participants of the neighbourhoud policy such as Azerbaijan and Armenia.[31] The European neighbourhood policy is to serve as a political, legal, trade (market access) and financial framework for systematic deepening with countries sharing values and a desire for stability and economic interdependence, based on WTO and OECD principles as much as possible. How this will work out in practice is unclear. The encouragement of domestic reforms can be really effective if (1) countries themselves are willing and (2) if there is a prospect of EU membership. Strictly speaking, such a prospect is not a necessary condition, but a superficial inspection of what enormous and consistent influence the Union has been able to wield in countries considered almost hopeless, when in transition, clarifies that the lack of prospect of membership – no doubt a key reason for the policy from the EU point of view – is exactly the critical weakness of the new policy. It is of course possible that countries such as Ukraine, now expressing a powerful desire to become EU member, will exploit faithfully all the options and opportunities of the neighbourhood policy and this way earn credibility, first with foreign direct investors, and gradually with the Union itself. However, this is not so probable given the large number of domestic obstacles and the long path to be travelled before such credibility can be accomplished. The time perspective of the policy is one of decades and it is far too early to cast judgements (see Emerson & Noutcheva, 2005; Milcher & Slay, 2005).

20.5 Summary

The six enlargements of the EU over 35 years are amazing. Yet another queue of likely 'me-too' applicant countries can be discerned. The sheer size effect (from 6 to 27 countries) is one element of the surprise, but what is just as unexpected is the apparently unproblematic combination of a permanent enlargement drive with ongoing deepening of the EU and widening of the scope of its rules and policies. The EU devised a tough enlargement strategy, precisely in order to pre-empt trade-offs between having ever more members, on the one hand, and deepening and widening, on the other hand. Enlargement has invariably been a 'me-too' phenomenon, but the motivations to apply are different in the case of most EFTA countries (predominantly the magnet effect; for Portugal, also anchoring and hegemony for the purpose of locking in democracy and reform) from those in central Europe, Turkey and the western Balkans (hegemony, anchor and magnet effects together). Indeed, for EFTA the radical deepening of the EU's internal market prompted new applications for EU membership as well as a far deeper FTA with the EU (in the EEA). The current queue comprises countries which clearly have decades of deep reform ahead of them. The question is whether alternative arrangements to EU membership can be designed, and can be acceptable, which still bring most of the gains of closer alignment with the Union.

The EU enlargement strategy is tough (the terms of accession are simple: accept the *acquis* of the club) and extremely demanding in terms of preparation, reporting, timely implementation of a huge and complex *acquis* and other aspects of compliance. Thus, there is little to 'negotiate' other than temporary derogations. The political and economic Copenhagen

[31]Note that Belarus is not taken into account given its current dictatorship and Russia has its own special relationship with the Union in a Partnership and Cooperation Agreement (signed in 1994, in force since 1997). Also, Moldova and Ukraine signed such agreements in 1994 but it should be realised that, recently, the changes in governments have radically altered the outlook *vis-à-vis* the EU, with a much greater sense of urgency to deepen the relationship with the Union.

Summary *continued*

criteria as well as proven 'administrative capacity' to implement and enforce the *acquis* at home are meticulously scrutinised before the Commission advises the Council to sign accession treaties, so that ratification can begin. The eastern enlargements are special but not because the Copenhagen criteria are compromised. They are special owing to their 'transition' out of autocratic regimes to democracy, and out of (badly) planned economies to functioning market economies, their relative poverty in a rich Union and the large number of countries entering together. In selected areas, therefore, there are sound economic reasons to adapt the enlargement strategy so as to reduce unjustified costs for the new Member States.

The eastern enlargements have been handled far more strategically and intrusively than ever before. The Europe (association) Agreements look, on the face of it, little more than industrial FTAs, with some flanking provisions. However, they were turned into a framework for a decade-long and intense preparation for EU membership. Later, this was reorganised into detailed pre-accession deals, emphasising minute plans for the domestic adoption of the *acquis*. The lock-in effects of this approach have no precedent anywhere in the world. Economic impact studies were, at first, very crude owing to data problems and the vagaries of 'transition'. The impact for the EU15 must be small for the simple reason that, economically, the new Member States together add up to some 6 per cent of the GDP of the EU15. The debate in the EU15 is mainly about the sensitive migration of workers despite the restrictive host country control principle which governs such migration. Rapprochement between central Europe and the EU generated a complete turnaround of trade structures and rapid growth of east–west European trade. Still, it is difficult to attribute this to the Europe Agreement, the pre-accession and EU membership. In the final analysis, what matters is the road to prosperity for these countries; in other words, will EU membership generate or at least stimulate a secular catch-up process? In terms of institutions and market rules, the prospects for catch-up are good and one powerful indicator is the continuous large FDI inflow into the region. Early empirical analysis of the microeconomics of catch-up growth confirms that these processes work in central Europe and that a gradual ascent of the (quality, skill and technology) ladder of dynamic comparative advantage is beginning to take place.

What about moving 'beyond the EU27'? One way of looking at this issue is to consider further enlargement in the light of the waning political legitimacy of it with EU citizens. Accepted candidates include Turkey and Croatia, soon probably Macedonia as well. A string of future applicants such as other western Balkan countries as well as Georgia, Moldova and Ukraine is not far-fetched, even if that might take another decade. Although the political debate is dominated by a possible Turkish membership, in fact, the 'limits' of the EU concern a much wider question. If Turkey were to get into the EU, it might have almost the same economic impact as the two eastern enlargements together. Another way to address the question has recently been formulated as the new 'neighbourhood policy' of the Union. This policy can be viewed as offering alternatives to EU membership, at least for a while and only for European countries, or as the upshot of the EU27 having become a truly continental power with an orbit which is economically dependent on economic intercourse with the Union. It includes a revival of the ten-year-old MED policy and a more structured approach to the countries around the Black Sea.

Bibliography

Abraham, F. (1992) *The Social Dimension of an Integrated EC–Nordic Economic Area,* International Economic Research Paper, no. 92, Leuven (October).

Abraham, F. (1999) *Regional Competition in the EU,* International Economics Discussion Paper, IERP no. 42, Leuven (March).

Abraham, F. & Konings, J. (1999) Does the opening of central and eastern Europe threaten employment in the West? *The World Economy,* Vol. 22, 4 (December).

Abraham, F. *et al.* (1991) *The Effect on Intra-Community Competition of Export Subsidies to Third Countries – the case of export credits, export insurance and official development aid,* Study for the EC Commission, Brussels.

Adler, M. (1970) Specialisation in the ECSC, *Journal of Common Market Studies,* Vol. 8.

AEA (2005) *AEA Yearbook 2005,* AEA, Brussels.

Aichinger, K. (2001) *Europe's position in quality competition, Enterprise Papers,* no. 4.

Aitken, N. (1973) The effect of the EEC and EFTA on European trade, a temporal cross-section analysis, *American Economic Review,* Vol. 63, 5 (December).

Albert, M. & Ball, R. (1983) *Towards European Economic Recovery in the 1980s,* European Parliament Working Party Document 1983/83, Luxembourg (July).

Alesina, A., Spolaore, E. & Wacziarg, R. (2000) Economic Integration and Political Disintegration, *American Economic Review,* American Economic Association, Vol. 90, 5, pp. 1276–96.

Allen, C., Gasiorek, M. & Smith, A. (1998) The competition effects of the single market in Europe, *Economic Policy,* no. 27 (October).

Alonso-Villar, O. (2005) The effects of transport costs revisited, *Journal of Economic Geography,* Vol. 5, pp. 589–604.

Anderson, J. & van Wincoop, E. (2004) Trade costs, *Journal of Economic Literature,* Vol. 62, 3 (September).

dell'Aquila, C. & Kuiper, M. (2003) *Which Road to Liberalisation? A First Assessment of the EuroMED Association Agreements,* ENAPRI Working Paper no. 2, Brussels (October). www.enapri.org.

Arndt, S. (1968) On discriminatory vs non-preferential tariff policies, *Economic Journal,* Vol. 78.

d'Aspremont, C. & Jacquemin, A. (1988) Cooperative and non-cooperative R&D in duopoly with spillovers, *American Economic Review,* Vol. 78, 5 (December) and 1990 Vol. 80, 3 (June).

Atkins, W.S. (1997) *Technical Barriers to Trade,* Single Market Review, subseries III.1, OOPEC, Luxembourg and Kogan Page, London.

Aturuphane, C., Djankov, S. & Hoekman, B. (1999) Horizontal and vertical intra-industry trade between eastern Europe and the EU, *Weltwirtschaftliches Archiv,* Vol. 135, 1.

Audretsch, D. (1993) Industrial policy and international competitiveness, in Nicolaides, P. (ed.) *Industrial Policy in the EC,* Nijhoff, Dordrecht.

Baden-Fuller, C. (1979) Art. 86 EEC: Economic analysis of the existence of a dominant position, *European Law Review,* Vol. 4, 4 (December).

Bakker, A.F.P. (1996) *International Financial Institutions,* Addison-Wesley-Longman, Harlow.

Balassa, B. (1961) *The Theory of Economic Integration,* Irwin, Homewood, Ill.

Balassa, B. (1975) Trade creation and trade diversion in the European Common Market: an appraisal of the evidence, in Balassa, B. (ed.) *European Economic Integration,* North-Holland, Amsterdam.

Balassa, B. (1976) Types of economic integration, in Machlup, F. (ed.) *Economic Integration Worldwide, Regional, Sectoral,* pp. 17–31, Macmillan, London.

Baldwin, R. (1989) The growth effects of 1992, *Economic Policy,* no. 9.

Baldwin, R. (1994) *Towards an Integrated Europe,* CEPR, London.

Baldwin, R. & Cave, M. (1999) *Understanding Regulation,* Oxford University Press, Oxford.

Baldwin, R. & Daintith, R. (eds) (1992) *Harmonisation and Hazard: Regulating Workplace Health and Safety in the EC,* Graham & Trotman, London.

Baldwin, R. & Krugman, P. (1987) Industrial policy and international competition in wide-bodied jet aircraft, in Baldwin, R. (ed.) (1988) *Trade Policy Issues and Empirical Analysis,* University of Chicago Press, Chicago.

Baldwin, R. & Seghezza, E. (1996) *Growth and European Integration: Towards an Empirical Assessment,* CEPR Discussion Paper no. 1393, London (May).

Baldwin, R. & Venables, A. (1995) Regional economic integration, in Grossman, G. & Rogoff, K. (eds), *Handbook of International Economics,* Vol. 3, North Holland, Amsterdam.

Baldwin, R. & Wyplosz, Ch. (2003) *The Economics of European Integration,* McGraw-Hill, London.

Baldwin, R., Francois, J. & Portes, R. (1997) The costs and benefits of enlargement: the impact on the EU and central Europe, *Economic Policy,* Vol. 24 (October).

Bangemann, M. (1992) *Establishing a Successful European Industrial Policy,* Kogan Page, London.

Bauer, T. & Zimmermann, K. (1999) *Assessment of Possible Migration Pressure and its Labour Market Impact following EU Enlargement to Central and Eastern Europe,* Study for the UK Department for Education and Employment, London.

Bayoumi, T. & Eichengreen, B. (1992) *Shocking Aspects of European Monetary Unification,* CEPR Discussion Paper no. 643, London.

Bayoumi, T. & Masson, T. (1995) Fiscal flows in the US and Canada: lessons for monetary union in Europe, *European Economic Review,* Vol. 39, 2 (February).

Begg, I. (2005) Slide on coordination channels. Lecture, Policy coordination in EU economic governance, Course, European macroeconomic policy, Economics Department, College of Europe, Bruges.

Bellis, J.F. (1990) The EEC anti-dumping system, in Jackson, J. & Vermulst, E. (eds) *Anti-dumping Law and Practice, A Comparative Study,* Harvester Wheatsheaf, London.

Ben-David, D. (1993) Equalizing Exchange: Trade Liberalization and Income Convergence, *The Quarterly Journal of Economics,* Vol. 108, 3, pp. 653–79, MIT Press, Mass.

Berglöf, E. (1997) Reforming corporate governance: redirecting the European agenda, *Economic Policy,* no. 24 (April).

Besley, T. & Seabright, P. (1999) The effects and policy implications of state aids to industry: an economic analysis, *Economic Policy,* no. 28 (April).

Best, E. & Bossaert, D. (eds) (2002) *From Luxembourg to Lisbon and Beyond,* Maastricht, European Institute of Public Administration. http://www.eipa.nl.

Bhagwati, J. (ed.) (1969) *International Trade,* Penguin Education, Harmondsworth.

Bianchi, P. & Labory, S. (eds) (2006) *International Handbook of Industrial Policy,* Edward Elgar, Cheltenham.

Bini-Smaghi, L. & Gros, D. (2000) *Open Issues in European Central Banking,* Macmillan, London.

Bini-Smaghi, L. & Tristani, O. (1995) The 1992–1993 EMS crisis, assessing the macro-economic costs, *Temi di discussioni,* no. 250, Banca d'Italia, Rome (February).

Bini-Smaghi, L. & Vori, S. (1993) Rating the EC as an optimal currency area, *Temi di discussioni,* no. 187, Banca d'Italia, Rome (January).

Bird, R. & Gendron P. (2000) CVAT, VIVAT and dual VAT: vertical sharing and interstate trade, *International Tax and Public Finance,* Vol. 5, 3, pp. 429–42.

Blanchard, O. (2005) *Macroeconomics,* 4th edn, Prentice Hall, Upper Saddle River, NJ.

Blind, K. (2004) *The Economics of Standards,* Edward Elgar, Cheltenham.

Bocconi (1997) *Advertising,* Single Market Review, subseries II. 7, Impact on Services, OOPEC, Luxembourg and Kogan Page, London.

Boeri, T. (2002) *Let social Europe(s) compete!* paper prepared for the Mondragone conference, Rome, July 26, 6.

Boeri, T. & Bruecker, H. (2000) The impact of eastern enlargement on employment and labour markets in the EU Member States, Part B, Berlin/Milan, Study for DG Employment and Social Affairs of the European Commission.

Boeri, T., Nicoletti, G. & Scarpetta, S. (2000) Deregulation and labour market performance, in Galli, G. & Pelkmans, J. (eds) *Regulatory Reform and Competitiveness in Europe,* Vol. I, Edward Elgar, Cheltenham.

Boldrin, M. & Canova, F. (2001) Inequality and convergence in Europe's regions: reconsidering European regional policies, *Economic Policy,* April, pp. 207–53.

Bossard, Idate & Devotech (1997) *Telecommunications – Liberalised Services,* Single Market Review, subseries II.6, OOPEC, Luxembourg and Kogan Page, London.

Braunerhjelm, P., Faini, R., Norman, V., Ruane, F. & Seabright, P. (2000) *Integration and the Regions of Europe,* CEPR, London.

Brenton, P. (1996) *The Impact of the Single Market on FDI in the EU,* report for the Single Market Review, CEPS, Brussels.

Brenton, P. (1999) *Trade and Investment in Europe: The Impact of the Next Enlargement,* CEPS, Brussels.

Brenton, P. (2003) *Rules of Origin in Free Trade Agreements,* Trade Note no. 4, The World Bank, Washington, DC, (May).

Brenton, P. & Gros, D. (1995) *Trade between the EU and Central Europe: An Economic and Policy Analysis,* CEPS Working Document, no. 93, Brussels.

Brenton, P. & Ikezuki, T. (2005) *The Value of Trade Preferences for Africa,* Trade Note no. 21, World Bank, Washington, DC, May.

Brenton, P. & di Mauro, F. (1999) The potential magnitude and impact of FDI inflows to CEECs, *Journal of Economic Integration,* Vol. 14, 1.

Brenton, P. & Nunez Ferrer, J. (1999) *EU Agriculture, the WTO and Enlargement,* CEPS Working Document no. 134, Brussels.

Bruelhart, M. & Tortensson, J. (1996) *Regional Integration, Scale Economies and Industry Location in the EU,* CEPR Discussion Paper no. 1435, London (July).

Buigues, P. & Sapir, A. (1993) Market services and European integration, issues and challenges, *European Economy/Social Europe,* no. 3, Reports and Studies.

CAA (1993) *Airline Competition in the Single European Market,* (CAP 623), Civil Aviation Authority, London.

CAA (1998) *The Single European Aviation Market: The First Five Years* (CAP 685), Civil Aviation Authority, London.

Caesar, R., 2001, An EU tax? – not a good idea, *Intereconomics,* Vol. 36, 5 (September/October).

Cairncross, A. (1973) *Control of Long-term International Capital Movements,* Brookings Institution, Washington, DC.

Cairncross, A. *et al.* (1974) *Economic Policy for the European Community: The Way Forward,* Macmillan, London.

Calmfors, L. (2005) What remains of the Stability Pact and what next? *SIEPS,* no. 8 (November) www.sieps.se.

Calmfors, L. *et al.* (2003) *Report on the European Economy 2003,* CESifo, Munich, chapter 3.

Cave, M. & Valletti, T. (2000) Regulation and competition in telecommunications, in Galli, G. & Pelkmans, J. (eds) *Regulatory Reform and Competitiveness in Europe,* Vol. II, Edward Elgar, Cheltenham.

Cecchini, P. *et al.* (1988) *The European Challenge 1992,* Wildwood House, Aldershot (also published in all other EC languages under different titles).

Cegos (1998) *Insurance,* Single Market Review, subseries II. 1, Impact on Services, OOPEC, Luxembourg and Kogan Page, London.

CEPII (1998) *Trade Patterns inside the Internal Market,* Single Market Review, subseries IV.2, OOPEC Luxembourg and Kogan Page, London.

CEPR (1993) *Making Sense of Subsidiarity: How much Centralization for Europe?* CEPR, London.

CEPR (2003) *Built to Last: A Political Architecture for Europe,* CEPR, London.

CEPS (1989) *Indirect Tax Harmonisation in the EC,* CEPS Working Party Report no. 1, Brussels (September) (Rapporteur: Stephen Smith).

CEPS (1992a) *The EC without Technical Barriers,* Working Party Report no. 5, CEPS, Brussels.

Cheh, J. (1974) US concessions in the Kennedy Round and short-run labour adjustment costs, *Journal of International Economics,* Vol. 4.

Christodoulakis, N. & Kalyvitis, S. (2000) The effects of the second Community support framework 1994-1999 on the Greek economy, *Journal of Policy Modelling,* Vol. 22, 5, pp. 611–24.

Chuck, C. & Phinnemore, D. (1994) *European Union and European Community: A Handbook and Commentary on the Post-Maastricht Treaties,* Harvester Wheatsheaf, New York/London.

Church, J. & Ware R. (2000) *Industrial Organisation: A Strategic Approach,* McGraw-Hill, New York.

Clinch, P. (2000) Environmental policy reform in the EU, in Galli, G. & Pelkmans, J. (eds) *Regulatory Reform and Competitiveness in Europe,* Vol. 1, Edward Elgar, Cheltenham.

Cnossen, S. (ed.) (1987) *Tax Coordination in the EC,* Kluwer, Deventer/London.

Constantopoulos, M. (1974) Labour protection in western Europe, *European Economic Review,* Vol. 5.

Cooper, C.A. & Massell, B.F. (1965) A new look at customs union theory, *Economic Journal,* Vol. 75 (December).

Copenhagen Economics (2005) *Economic Assessment of the Barriers to the Internal Market for Services,* January, DG Enterprise, Copenhagen and Brussels.

Corden, W. (1972) Economies of scale and customs union theory, *Journal of Political Economy,* Vol. 80, 3 (May/June).

Corden, W. (1975) The costs and consequences of protection: a survey of empirical work, in Kenen, P. (ed.) *International Trade and Finance,* Frontiers for Research, Cambridge University Press, New York.

Courchene, T. (1986) *Economic Management and the Division of Powers,* Study no. 67 for the Macdonald Commission, University of Toronto Press.

Crandall, R. & Winston, C. (2003) Does anti-trust policy improve consumer welfare? Assessing the evidence, *Journal of Economic Perspectives,* Vol. 17, 4 (Fall).

Cuadrado-Roura, J. (2001) Regional convergence in the EU: from hypothesis to the actual trends, *Annals of Regional Finances,* Vol. 35, pp. 333–56.

Curzon Price, V. (1974) *The Essentials of Economic Integration,* Macmillan, London.

Dang Nguyen, G. & Genton C. (2006) *Has the European ICT Sector a Chance to be Competitive?,* College of Europe BEEP Briefing no. 14. www.coleurop.be/eco/publications.htm.

Davies, D. (1998) The home market, trade and industrial structure, *American Economic Review,* Vol. 88/5, December.

Davis, E., *et al.* (1989) *'1992': Myths and Realities,* London Business School, London.

Dekker, P. *et al.* (2003) Social Europe (in Dutch), The Hague, CPB & SCP, *Europese verkenning* no. 1.

Delors, J. *et al.* (1989) *Report on the Economic and Monetary Union in the European Community,* Office for Official Publications of the EC, Luxembourg.

Dermine, J. (1996) *European Banking with a Single Currency,* INSEAD Working Papers 96/03/FIN, Fontainebleau.

Dermine, J. (1998) *Eurobanking: The Strategic Issues,* INSEAD Working Papers 98/74/FIN, Fontainebleau.

Dermine, J. (1999) *The Economics of Bank Mergers in the EU: A Review of the Public Policy Issues,* INSEAD Working Papers 99/35/FIN, Fontainebleau.

Devereux, M., Griffith, R. & Klemm, M. (2002) Corporate income tax: reforms and tax competition, *Economic Policy,* no. 35, pp. 451–95.

Dickinson, G. (1993) Insurance, *European Economy/Social Europe,* no. 3, Reports and Studies, Market Services and European Integration.

Diebold, W. (1980) *Industrial Policy as an International Issue,* McGraw-Hill, New York.

Diller, H. & Bukhari, I. (1994) Pricing conditions in the European Common Market, *European Management Journal,* Vol. 12, 2 (June).

Dixit, A. & Kyle, A. (1985) The use of protection and subsidies for entry promotion and deterrence, *American Economic Review,* Vol. 75, pp. 139 ff.

Dunning, J. (1979) Explaining changing patterns of international production: in defence of an eclectic theory, *Oxford Bulletin of Economics and Statistics,* Vol. 41.

Dunning, J. (1997) The European internal market programme and inbound direct investment, *Journal of Common Market Studies,* Vol. 35, 1.

Dunning, J. & Robson, P. (1987) Multinational corporate integration and regional economic integration, *Journal of Common Market Studies,* Vol. 26, 2 (December).

Eaton, J., Gutierrez, E. & Kortum, S. (1998) European technology policy, *Economic Policy,* no. 27 (October).

ECB (2004) *Towards a Single Euro Payment Area,* 3rd Progress Report, Frankfurt.

ECB (2005) *Review of the International Role of the Euro,* Frankfurt, January.

ECMT (2003) *Reforming Transport Taxes,* Paris, OECD/ECMT.

Ederveen, S., Gorter, J. de Mooij, R. & Nahuis, R. (2002) *Funds and Games: The Economics of European Cohesion Policy,* The Hague, CPB (April).

Ederveen, S., van der Horst, A. & Tang, P. (2005) *Is the European Economy a Patient, and the Union its Doctor?* CPB document no. 80, The Hague.

Egger, P. & Pfaffermayr, M. (2004) Foreign direct investment and European integration, *The World Economy,* Vol. 27, 1 (January).

Eichengreen, B. (1993) European monetary integration, *Journal of Economic Literature,* Vol. 31, 3 (September).

Eichengreen, B., Tobin, J. & Wyplosz, C. (1995) Two cases for sand in the wheels of international finance, *Economic Journal,* Vol. 105, 428 (January).

Eijffinger, S. & de Haan, J. (2000) *European Monetary and Fiscal Policy,* Oxford University Press, Oxford.

Emerson, M. (2005) An interim Plan for south-eastern Europe: customs union with the EU and a regional Schengen for the free movement of people, *CEPS Neighbourhood Watch,* no. 9 (October), pp. 9–11. www.ceps.be.

Emerson, M. *et al.* (1990) One market, one money, *European Economy,* no. 44 (October).

Emerson, M. & Noutcheva, G. (2005) *From Barcelona Process to Neighbourhood Policy: Assessments and Open Issues,* CEPS Working Document no. 220, (March). www.ceps.be.

Emerson, M., Vahl, T. & Woolcock, S. (2002) *Navigating by the Stars – Norway, the European Economic Area and the EU,* CEPS, Brussels.

Engel, Ch. & Rogers, J. (2004) European product market integration after the euro, *Economic Policy,* no. 19 (July).

ERE (1997) *Credit Institutions and Banking, Single Market Review,* subseries II.3, Impact on Services, OOPEC Luxembourg and Kogan Page, London.

ERG (2005) *Common Position on EC Recommendation on Cost Accounting and Accounting Separation.* ERG (05) 29, Brussels.

Esping-Andersen, G., Gallie, D., Hemerijck A. & Miles, J. (2001) *A New Welfare Architecture for Europe?* report to the Belgian presidency of the EU (September).

Ethier, W. (1986) The multinational firm, *Quarterly Journal of Economics,* Vol. 101 (November).

European Commission (1970) *The Industrial Policy of the Community* (Colonna–di Paliano memorandum), Brussels.

European Commission (1985) *Completing the Internal Market,* COM (85) 314 (14 June), Brussels.

European Commission (1988) The economics of 1992 (Cecchini report), *European Economy,* no. 35 (March).

European Commission (1990) *Industrial Policy in an Open and Competitive Environment* (Bangemann memorandum), Working Paper, 14 September.

European Commission (1991) *New Location Factors for Industries and Services,* study financed by EC and authored by NEI and Ernst & Young, Brussels.

European Commission (1993) White Paper on growth, competitiveness and employment, *Bulletin EC,* Supplement 93/6 (December).

European Commission (1994a) *An Industrial Competitiveness Policy for the EU* (second Bangemann memorandum) COM (94) 319 (September), Brussels.

European Commission (1994b) *Panorama of EU Industry,* OOPEC, Luxembourg.

European Commission (1994c) *On the EU Automobile Industry* (includes 'The automobile industry', a strategy document), COM (94) 49 (February), Brussels.

European Commission (2000) *2nd Cabotage Report,* COM (2000) 105 (28 February).

European Commission (2000b) *The Community Budget: The Facts in Figures,* OOPEC, Luxembourg. http://europa.eu.int/comm/budget/publications/other_en.htm

European Commission (2001) White Paper, *European transport policy for 2010: time to decide,* COM (2001) 370 final.

European Commission (2002) *Report from The Commission to The Council and The European Parliament on the state of the internal market for services presented under the first stage of the Internal Market Strategy for Services,* COM (2002) 441 final (5 June).

European Commission (2003) *The Competitiveness of Business-related Services and their Contribution to the Performance of European Enterprises,* COM (2003) 747 (4 December 2003).

European Commission (2004) *Third report on economic and social cohesion,* COM (2004) 107, OOPEC, Luxembourg (18 February). http://europa.eu.int/comm/regional_policy/sources/docoffic/official/reports/cohesion3/cohesion3_en.htm

European Commission (2005) *Opening the Door to Development: Developing Country Access to EU Markets 1999–2003,* DG Trade. http://europa.eu.int.

European Commission (2006) *General Budget of the European Union for the Financial Year 2006,* OOPEC, Luxembourg. http://europa.eu.int/comm/budget/publications/budget_in_fig_en.htm

European University Association (2005) *Strong Universities for a Strong Europe* (Glasgow Declaration), Brussels.

Evenett, S. & Vermulst, E. (2005) The politicisation of EC anti-dumping, *The World Economy,* Vol. 28, 5 (May).

Faini, R. (1999) Trade union and regional development, *European Economic Review,* Vol. 43, 2 (February).

Faini, R., Galli, G. & Giannini, C. (1992) Finance and development, the case of Southern Italy, in Giovanni, A. (ed.) *Finance and Development; Issues and Experience,* Cambridge University Press, Cambridge.

Fehr, H., Rosenberg, C. & Wiegard, W. (1994) Should the EU adopt the origin principle for VAT after 1997? *Finanz Archiv,* Vol. 51, 1.

Fidrmuc, J. & Fidrmuc, J. (2000) *Disintegration and trade,* unpublished paper, Centre for European Integration, Bonn (September).

Fidrmuc, J. & Nowotny, T. (2000) The effects of EU's eastern European enlargement on Austria, *Focus on Transition,* no. 1, Austrian National Bank, Vienna.

Fischer, S. (1998) From transition to market: evidence and growth prospects, in Zecchini, S. (ed.) *Lessons from the Economic Transition,* Dordrecht, Kluwer.

Fishwick, F. (1993) *Making Sense of Competition Policy,* Kogan Page, London.

Flam, H. (1992) Product markets and 1992: full integration, large gains, *Journal of Economic Perspectives,* Vol. 6, 4.

Flam, H. (1998) Discussion, *Economic Policy,* no. 27 (October).

Ford, R. & Suyker, H. (1990) Industrial subsidies in the OECD economics, *OECD Economic Studies,* no. 15 (Autumn).

Forte, F. (1977) Principles for the assignment of public economic functions in a setting of multi-layer government, in Commission of the European Communities, *Report of the Study Group on the Role of Public Finance in European Integration,* Vol. II (MacDougall report), Brussels.

Frandsen, S., Jensen, H. & Vanzetti, D. (2000) Expanding fortress Europe: agricultural trade and welfare implications of European enlargement for non-member regions, *The World Economy,* Vol. 23, 3 (March).

Friedman, M. (1953) The case for flexible exchange rates, in Friedman, M., *Essays in Positive Economics,* University of Chicago Press, Chicago.

de la Fuente, A. (2000) Convergence across countries and regions: theory and empirics, *EIB Papers,* Vol. 5, 2.

de la Fuente, A. (2002) *The Effects of Structural Funds Spending on the Spanish Regions: An Assessment of the 1994–99 Objective 1 CSF,* Barcelona, Universidad Autonomo, Instituto de Analisis Economico.

de la Fuente, A. & Vives, X. (1995) Infrastructure and education as instruments of regional policy: evidence from Spain, *Economic Policy,* Vol. 20 (April).

Gabel, L. (1991) *Competition Strategies for Product Standards,* McGraw-Hill, London.

Galal, A. & Hoekman, B. (eds) (1997) *Regional Partners in Global Markets: Limits and possibilities of the Euro–MED Agreements*, CEPR, London.

Galli, G., & Pelkmans, J. (2000) Introduction: aims, structure and overview, in Galli, G. & Pelkmans, J. (eds) *Regulatory Reform and Competitiveness in Europe,* Vol. I, Edward Elgar, Cheltenham.

Garber, P. & Taylor, M. (1995) Sand in the wheels of foreign exchange markets, a skeptical note, *Economic Journal,* Vol. 105, 428.

Gasiorek, M., Davidson, R., Davies, S., Lyons, B., Ulph, D., Vaughan, R. & Winters, L.A. (2004) The impact of a single currency in Europe on product markets: theory and evidence, in Dierx, A., Ilzkovitz, F. & Sekkat, K. (eds) *European Integration and the Functioning of Product Markets,* Edward Elgar, Cheltenham.

Gasiorek, M., Smith, A. & Venables, A. (1992) '1992': trade, factor prices and welfare in general equilibrium, in Winters, L.A., (ed) *Trade Flows and Trade Policy After '1992',* Cambridge University Press, Cambridge and CEPR, London.

Gasiorek, M., Smith A. & Venables, A. (2002) The accession of the UK to the EC: a welfare analysis, *Journal of Common Market Studies,* Vol. 40, 3, pp. 425–47.

Gatsios, K. & Seabright, P. (1989) Regulation in the European Community, *Oxford Review of Economic Policy,* Vol. 5, 2.

GATT (1994a) *The Results of the Uruguay Round of Multi-lateral Trade Negotiations, The Legal Texts,* GATT, Geneva.

GATT (1994b) *Trade Policy Review – Australia,* Vol. 1.

George, K. and Jacquemin, A. (1990) Competition policy in the European Community, in Comanor, W. S. *et al.* (eds) *Competition Policy in Europe and North America: Economic Issues and Institutions,* Harwood Academic, Chur and London.

Geroski, P. (1989a) European industrial policy and industrial policy in Europe, *Oxford Review of Economic Policy,* Vol. 5, 2.

Geroski, P. (1989b) The choice between diversity and scale, in Davis, E. *et al.* (eds) *1992 – Myths and Realities,* Centre for Business Strategy, London Business School.

Geroski, P. & Jacquemin, A. (1985) Industrial change, barriers to mobility and European industrial policy, *Economic Policy,* Vol. 1, 1.

Ghosh, A. (1995) International capital mobility amongst the major industrialized countries: too little or too much? *Economic Journal,* Vol. 105 (January).

Ghosh, A. & Wolf, H. (1994) *How Many Monies? A Genetic Approach to Finding Optimum Currency Areas,* NBER Working Paper 4805 (July).

Giannetti, M. *et al.* (2002) *Financial Market Integration, Corporate Financing and Economic Growth,* Economic Papers no. 179, European Commission, DG Economic and Financial Affairs, Brussels.

Giavazzi, F., Micossi, S. & Miller, M. (eds) (1989) *The European Monetary System,* Cambridge, University Press, Cambridge.

Giovannini, A. *et al.* (2002) *Cross-border Clearing and Settlement Arrangements in the EU,* Economic Papers no. 163, European Commission, DG Economic and Financial Affairs, Brussels.

Goldberg, P. & Verboven F. (2005) Market integration and convergence to the law of one price: evidence from the European car market, *Journal of International Economics,* Vol. 65, pp. 49–73.

de Grauwe, P. (1995) *Paradigms of Macroeconomic Policy for the Open Economy,* CES Discussion Paper no. 112, Leuven.

de Grauwe, P. (1996) The Economics of convergence: towards monetary union in Europe, *Weltwirtschaftliches Archiv,* Vol. 132, 1.

de Grauwe, P. (2000) *Economics of Monetary Union,* 4th edn, Oxford University Press, Oxford.

de Grauwe, P. (2003) *Economics of Monetary Union,* 5th edn, Oxford University Press, Oxford.

de Grauwe, P. (2005) *Economics of Monetary Union,* 6th edn, Oxford University Press, Oxford.

de Grauwe, P. & Skudelny, F. (2000) The impact of EMU on trade flows, *Weltwirtschaftliches Archiv,* Vol. 136, 3.

de Grauwe, P. & Vanhaverbeke, W. (1991) *Is Europe an Optimum Currency Area?* CEPR Discussion Paper no. 658, London.

Greenaway, D. (1989) Regional trading arrangements and intra-industry trade: evidence and policy issues, in Greenaway, D. *et al.* (eds) *Economic Aspects of Regional Trading Arrangements,* Harvester Wheatsheaf, Hemel Hempstead.

Greenaway, D. & Hine, R. (1991) Intra-industry specialisation, trade expansion and adjustment in the European Economic Space, *Journal of Common Market Studies,* Vol. 29.

Greenaway, D. & Milner, C. (1986) *The Economics of Intra-industry Trade,* Basil Blackwell, Oxford.

Greenaway, D. & Torstensson, J. (1997) Back to the future: taking stock on intra-industry trade, *Weltwirtschaftliches Archiv,* Vol 123, 2.

Grilli, E. (1993) *The EC and the Developing Countries,* Cambridge University Press, Cambridge.

Gros, D. (1995) *Towards a Credible Excessive Deficit Procedure,* CEPS Working Document no. 95, CEPS, Brussels.

Gros, D. (1996a) *Towards Economic Monetary Union,* CEPS Paper no. 65, CEPS, Brussels.

Gros, D. (1996b) *A Reconsideration of the Optimum Currency Area Approach,* CEPS Working Document no. 101, Brussels.

Gros, D. & Lannoo, K. (2000) *The Euro Capital market,* Wiley, Chichester.

Gros, D. & Micossi, S. (2005) *A Better Budget for the EU,* CEPS Policy Brief, no. 66 (February), Brussels. www.ceps.be.

Gros, D. & Steinherr, A. (1995) *Winds of Change: Economic Transition in Central and Eastern Europe,* Longman, London.

Gros, D. & Thygesen, N. (1988) *The EMS: Achievements, Current Issues and Directions for the Future,* CEPS Paper no. 35, Brussels.

Gros, D. & Thygesen, N. (1998) *European Monetary Union, from the EMS to EMU,* 2nd edn, Addison-Wesley-Longman, Harlow.

Grossman, G. (1990) Promoting new industrial activities, *OECD Economic Studies,* Vol. 14.

Grossman, G. & Horn, H. (1988) Infant-industry protection reconsidered: the case of informational barriers to entry, *Quarterly Journal of Economics,* Vol. 103.

Gual, J., (2003) *The Integration of EU Banking Markets,* IESE Business School, Barcelona.

Gual, J. & Neven, D. (1993) Banking, in *European Economy/Social Europe,* 1993/3, Reports and Studies, Market Services and European Integration.

Gyselen, L. (1994) Anti-competitive state measures under the EC treaty: towards a substantive legality standard, *European Law Review,* special issue on Competition Law Checklist – 1993, pp. CC 55–106.

de Haan, J., Eijffinger S. & Waller S. (2005) *The European Central Bank: Credibility, Transparency, and Centralization,* MIT Press, Cambridge, Mass.

Hönekopp, E. & Werner, H. (2000) Is the EU labour market threatened by a wave of immigration?, *Intereconomics,* Vol. 35, 1.

Hagedoorn, J. (1996) Trends and patterns in strategic technology partnering since the early seventies, *Review of Industrial Organisation,* Vol. 11, pp. 601–16

Hagedoorn, J. & Shakenraad, J. (1993) A comparison of private and subsidised R & D partnerships in the European IT industry, *Journal of Common Market Studies* , Vol. 31, 3 (September).

Hallet, M. (2000) *Regional Specialisation and Concentration in the EU,* Economic Papers, no. 141, European Commission, DG Economic and Financial Affairs, Brussels.

Halpern, L. & Wyplosz, C. (1995) *Equilibrium Real Exchange Rates in Transition,* CEPR Discussion Paper no. 1145, London.

Halpern, L. & Wyplosz, C. (2001) Economic transformation and real exchange rates in the 2000s: the Balassa–Samuelson connection, *Economic Survey of Europe* 2001, no.1, UN/ECE.

Hamilton, C. (1991) EC external protection and 1992: VERs applied to Pacific Asia, *Weltwirtschaftliches Archiv,* Vol. 127.

Hamilton, C. & Winter, L.A. (1992) Opening up international trade with eastern Europe, *Economic Policy,* no. 14 (April).

Harbord, D. & Yarrow, G. (1999) State aids, restructuring and privatisation, *European Economy,* Reports & Studies, no. 3.

Harris, R. (1984) Applied general equilibrium analysis of small open economies with scale economies and imperfect competition, *American Economic Review,* Vol. 74, 5.

Havlik, J. (2005) Structural change, productivity and employment in the new EU member states, Vienna, WIIW Research Paper no. 313.

Head, R. & Mayer, T. (2000) Non-Europe: the magnitude and causes of market fragmentation in the EU, *Weltwirtschaftliches Archiv,* Vol. 126, 2.

Hegarty, J. (1993) Beyond liberalisation to deregulation; creating a single European market in accountancy services, FEE, Brussels (unpublished).

Helpman, E. (1981) International trade in the presence of product differentiation, economies of scale and monopolistic competition: a Chamberlin–Heckscher–Ohlin approach, *Journal of International Economics,* Vol. 11, 3 (August).

Helpman, E. & Krugman, P. (1985) *Market Structure and Foreign Trade,* MIT Press, Cambridge, Mass.

High Level Expert Group (2005) *Frontier Research: The European Challenge,* Brussels. http://europa.eu.int/comm/research/future/basic_research/documents_en.htm

Hine, R. (1985) *The Political Economy of European Trade,* Wheatsheaf, Brighton.

Hine, R. (1994) International economic integration, in Greenaway, D. & Winters, L.A. (eds) *Surveys in International Trade,* Blackwell, Oxford.

Hirsch, F. & Doyle, M. (1977) Politicisation in the world economy: necessary conditions for an international economic order, in Hirsch, F. *et al.* (eds) *Alternatives to Monetary Disorder,* McGraw-Hill, New York.

Hishow, O. (2005) Lessons from Lisbon, or why leisure harms, *Intereconomics,* Vol. 40, 2 pp. 70–4.

Hocking, R., (1980) Trade in motorcars between the major European producers, *Economic Journal,* Vol. 90, 1 (September).

Hoekman, B. (1995) *The WTO, the EU and the Arab World: Trade Policy Priorities and Pitfalls,* CEPR Discussion Paper no. 1226, London (August).

Hoekman, B. & Kostecki, M. (1995) *The Political Economy of the World Trading System,* Oxford University Press, Oxford.

Hoeller, P. & Louppe, M.O. (1994) The EC's internal market: implementation and economic effects, *OECD Economic Studies,* no. 23 (Winter).

Holmes, P. (1997) *Study on the Economics and Industrial Aspects of Anti-dumping Policy,* Sussex European Institute Working Paper no. 22, Brighton (in cooperation with Jeremy Kempton).

Hönekopp, E. & Werner, H. (2000) Is the EU labour market threatened by a wave of immigration? *Intereconomics*, Vol. 35, 1.

House of Commons (2003) *European Social Fund,* Vol. 1, Work and Pensions Ctee, HC 680, HMSO, London.

Hufbauer, G. & Chilas, J. (1974) Specialization by industrial countries: extent and consequences, in Giersch, H. (ed.) *The International Division of Labour: Problems and Perspectives,* Mohr, Tübingen.

Hufbauer, G. & Schott, J. (1992) *North American Free Trade: Issues and Recommendations,* Institute for International Economics, Washington, DC.

Hughes, K. (ed.) (1993) *European Competitiveness,* Cambridge University Press, Cambridge.

IFO (1998) Currency Management Costs, Single Market Review, subseries III. 6, Office for Official Publications of the EC, Luxembourg and Kogan Page, London.

Ilzkovitz, F. & Meiklejohn, R. (eds) (2006) *European Merger Control, Do We Need An Efficiency Defence?* Edward Elgar, Cheltenham.

IMF (1984) *The Exchange Rate System: Lessons of the Past and Options for the Future,* IMF Occasional Papers no. 30, IMF, Washington, DC.

IMF (1994) *Exchange Rate Volatility and World Trade,* IMF Occasional Papers, no. 28, Washington, DC.

Inzerillo, U, Morelli, P. & Pittaluga, G. (2000) Deregulation and changes in the European Banking Industry, in Galli, G. & Pelkmans, J. (eds) *Regulatory Reform and Competitiveness in Europe,* Vol. 2, Edward Elgar, Cheltenham/Northampton (USA).

Italianer, A. (1990) *'1992': Hype or Hope, a Review,* Economic Papers, no. 77, DGII (February).

Italianer, A. (1994) Whither the gains from European economic integration? *Revue Economique,* Vol. 45, 3 (May).

Italianer, A. & Vanheukelen, M. (1993) Proposals for Community stabilisation mechanisms, some historical applications, *European Economy,* Reports and Studies no. 5, Economics of Community Public Finance.

Jackson (1990) *Restructuring the GATT System,* Pinter/Royal Institute of International Affairs, London.

Jacobs, B., Nahuis, R. & Tang, P. (2001) Sectoral productivity growth and R&D spill-overs in the Netherlands, *De Economist,* Vol. 149.

Jacquemin, A. & de Jong, H. (1977) *European Industrial Organization,* Macmillan, London.

Jacquemin, A. & Sapir, A. (1988) European integration or world integration? *Weltwirtschaftliches Archiv,* Vol. 124.

Johnson, H. (1958) The gains from freer trade in Europe, an estimate, *Manchester School,* Vol. 26.

de Jong, H. (1995) European capitalism: between freedom and social justice, *Review of Industrial Organisation,* Vol. 10, 4 (August).

Katsirea, I. (2003) Why the European broadcasting quota should be abolished, *European Law Review,* Vol. 28, pp. 190–209.

Kay, N. (1991) Industrial collaborative activity and the completion of the internal market, *Journal of Common Market Studies,* Vol. 29.

Kay, N. (1993) Mergers, acquisitions and the competition of the internal market, in Hughes, K. (ed.)

European Competitiveness, Cambridge University Press, Cambridge.

Keen, M. & Smith, S. (1996) The future of value added tax in the EU, *Economic Policy,* no. 23 (October).

Kenen, P. (1969) The theory of optimum currency areas: an eclectic view, in Mundell, R. & Swoboda, A. (eds) *Monetary Problems of the International Economy,* University of Chicago Press, Chicago.

Kenen, P. (1992) *EMU after Maastricht,* Group of Thirty, Washington, DC.

Keohane, R. (1984) *After Hegemony, Cooperation and Discord in the World Economy,* Princeton University Press, Princeton, NJ.

Kessides, I. & Willig, R. (1998) Restructuring regulation of the rail industry for the public interest, *Railways: Structure, Regulation and Competition Policy,* OECD, Paris, pp. 147–81.

Kiehl, M. & Werner, H. (1998) Die Arbeitsmarktsituation von EU Buergern and Angehoerigen von Drittstaaten in der EU (The labour market situation of EU citizens and residents from third countries in the EU), *IAB Werkstattbericht,* no. 7 (July).

Kindleberger, C. (1973) *The World in Depression, 1929–1939,* University of California Press, Berkeley.

Kindleberger, C. (1986) International public goods without international government, *American Economic Review,* Vol. 76, 1 (March).

Kleimeyer, S. & Sander, H. (2000) Regionalisation vs globalisation in European financial market integration: evidence from co-integration analysis, *Journal of Banking and Finance,* Vol. 24, pp. 1005–43.

Kok, W. (2003) *Enlarging the EU: Achievements and Challenges,* report to the European Commission, European University Institute, R. Schuman Centre, Florence/Brussels.

Kok, W. *et al.* (2003) *Jobs, Jobs, Jobs: Creating More Employment in Europe,* report of the Employment Task Force, Brussels (November).

Kok, W. *et al.* (2004) *Facing the Challenge: The Lisbon Strategy for Growth and Employment,* report from the High Level Group, Brussels (November).

Kol, J. (1988) *The Measurement of Intra-industry Trade,* Erasmus University Press, Rotterdam.

Koopman, G. (1993) Transport demand, modal choice and the completion of the internal market, *European Economy/Social Europe,* no. 3, Reports and Studies, Market Services and European Integration (Special box, pp. 251–7).

Koopman, G. & Muennich, F. (1999) *National and International Developments in Technology – Trends, Patterns and Implications for Policy,* HWWA Discussion Paper no. 76, Hamburg.

Kox H., Lejour A. & Montizaan R. (2004) *The Free Movement of Services within the EU,* CPB Document no. 69, CPB, The Hague (October).

Kreinin, M. (1972) Effects of the EEC on imports of manufactures, *Economic Journal,* Vol. 82 (September).

Kroes, N. (2005a) *European Competition Policy, delivering better markets and better choices,* speech for the European consumer and competition day, London.

Kroes, N. (2005b) *Preliminary Thoughts on Policy Review of Art. 82,* Fordham Corporate Law Institute, New York (September).

Krugman, P. (1979) Increasing returns, monopolistic competition, and international trade, *Journal of International Economics,* Vol. 9, 4.

Krugman, P. (1987) Is free trade passé? *Journal of Economic Perspectives,* Vol. 1, 1 (Fall).

Krugman, P. (1991) *Geography and Trade,* MIT Press, Cambridge, Mass.

Krugman, P. & Obstfeld, M. (1991) *International Economics,* Scott, Foreman, Glenview, Ill.

Krugman, P. & Obstfeld, M. (2003) *International Economics,* 6th edn, Scott, Foreman, Glenview, Ill.

Krugman, P. & Venables, A. (1990) Integration and the competitiveness of peripheral industry, in Bliss, C. & Braga de Macedo, J. (eds) *Unity with diversity in the European economy,* Cambridge University Press, Cambridge.

Krugman, P. & Venables, A. (1994) *Globalisation and the Inequality of Nations,* CEPR Discussion Paper no. 1015 (September).

Krugman, P. & Venables, A. (1995) Globalisation and the inequality of nations, *Quarterly Journal of Economics,* Vol. 100, 4.

Labory, S. & Malgarini, M. (2000) Regulation in Europe: justified burden or costly failure? in Galli, G. & Pelkmans, J. (eds) *Regulatory Reform and Competitiveness in Europe,* Vol. I, Edward Elgar, Cheltenham.

Laffont, J.J. & Tirole, J. (1993) *A Theory of Incentives in Procurement and Regulation,* MIT Press, Cambridge, Mass.

Landesmann, M. (2003) *Structural Features of Economic Integration in an Enlarged Europe: Patterns of Catching Up and Industrial Specialisation,* Economic Papers no. 181, European Commission, DG Economic and Financial Affairs, Brussels (January).

Langhammer, R. (1987) *Hat der europaeische Integrationsprozess die Integration der nationalen Märkte gefördert?* Kiel Discussion Papers no. 140 (June), Kiel Institute for World Economics.

Langhammer, R. & Sapir, A. (1987) *Economic Impact of Generalised Tariff Preferences,* Gower/Trade Policy Research Centre, Aldershot.

Lannoo, K. (1999) A European perspective on corporate governance, *Journal of Common Market Studies,* Vol. 37, 2 (June).

Lannoo, K. (2000) *Challenges to the Structure of Financial Supervision in the EU,* Report of a CEPS Working Party, CEPS, Brussels.

Lannoo, K. & Levin M. (2003) *Pan-European Asset Management: Achievements and Regulatory Impediments,* Report of the CEPS Task Force no. 44, CEPS, Brussels (April).

Larsen, A. *et al.* (1994) EC agricultural policy for the 21st Century, *European Economy,* no. 4, Reports & Studies.

Lasgni, A. (2000) Does country-targeted anti-dumping policy by the EC create trade diversion? *Journal of World Trade,* Vol. 34, 4, pp. 137–59.

Lawrence, R. (1991) Emerging regional arrangements: building blocks or stumbling blocks, in O'Brien, R. (ed.) *Amex Bank Review Price Essays,* Oxford University Press, Oxford.

Lawton, T.C. (1999) *European industrial policy and competitiveness: concepts and instruments,* Macmillan Business/St. Martin's Press, Basingstoke/New York.

Lejour, A., de Mooij R. & Nahuis, R. (2001) *EU Enlargement: Economic Implications for Countries and Industries,* CPB Document no. 11, CPB, The Hague.

Levin, M. (2003) *Competition, Fragmentation and Transparency: Assessing the ISD Review,* CEPS Task Force Report, no. 46 (April).

Llewellynn, D. (1999) *The Economic Rationale for Financial Regulation,* Occasional Paper Series no. 1, Financial Services Authority, London.

London Economics (2002) *Quantification of the Macro-economic Impact of Integration of EU Financial Markets* (November).

Machado Jorge, H. (1995) *Assured Performance: The Role of Conformity Assessment in Supporting the Internal Market,* CEPS Paper no. 60, CEPS, Brussels.

MacDougall, G. (1958) The benefits and costs of private investment from abroad: a theoretical approach, *Economic Record,* as reprinted in Bhagwati, J. (ed.) (1969) *International Trade,* Penguin Education, Harmondsworth.

MacDougall, G. *et al.* (1977) *Report of the Study Group on the Role of Public Finance in European Integration,* European Commission, Economic and Finance Series, 2 vols, General Report, Brussels.

Maijoor, S. (1995) An economic analysis of the market, the office functions and the auditing process of accountants (in Dutch, inaugural lecture), Maastricht University, Economics Department.

Majocchi, A. & Rey, M. (1993) A special financial support scheme in economic and monetary union, need and nature, in *European Economy,* Reports and Studies, no. 5, The Economics of Community Public Finance.

Majone, G. (2002) What price safety? The precautionary principle and its policy implications, *Journal of Common Market Studies,* Vol. 40.

Marjolin, R. *et al.* (1975) *Report of the Study Group 'Economic and Monetary Union 1980',* Brussels, (March).

Markusen, J. (1995), The boundaries of multinational enterprises and the theory of international trade, *Journal of Economic Perspectives,* Vol. 9, 2 (Spring).

Markusen, J. & Venables, A. (1996) *The Theory of Endowment, Intra-industry and Multinational Trade,* CEPR Discussion Paper no. 1341, February.

Martin, Ph. (1999) Are European regional policies delivering? *EIB Papers,* Vol. 4, 2.

Martin, S. (1993) *Industrial Economics, Economic Analysis and Public Policy,* 2nd edn, Prentice Hall, Englewood Cliffs, NJ.

Martinez, F. (2000) *Patents and the European Internal Market: Background and Recent Developments,* CEPS Working Document no. 155 (November), CEPS, Brussels.

di Mauro F. (2000) *The Effect of Economic Integration on FDI Flows: An Empirical Analysis and a Comparison with Trade,* CEPS Working Document no.135, CEPS, Brussels.

Mauro, P., Prasad, E. & Spilimbergo, A. (1999) *Perspectives on Regional Unemployment in Europe,* IMF Occasional Paper no. 177, Washington, DC.

Mayes, D. (1978) The effects of economic integration on trade, *Journal of Common Market Studies,* Vol. XVII, 1 (September).

Mayhew, A. (1998) *Recreating Europe,* Cambridge University Press, Cambridge.

Mayhew, A. (2000) *Enlargement of the EU: An Analysis of the Negotiations with the Central and Eastern European Candidate Countries,* Sussex European Institute Working Paper, Brighton (November).

McCahery J., Renneboog L., Ritter P. & Haller S. (2003) *The Economics of the Proposed European Takeover Directive,* research report, CEPS, Brussels (April).

McGowan, F. (1993) Air transport, *European Economy/Social Europe,* no. 3, Reports & Studies, Market Services and European Integration.

McGowan, F. (2000) Air transport regulation in the EU, in Galli, G. & Pelkmans, J. (eds) *Regulatory reform and Competitiveness in Europe,* Vol. II, Edward Elgar, Cheltenham.

McKinnon, R. (1963) Optimum currency areas, *American Economic Review,* Vol. 53, 4 (September).

McLure C. (2000) Implementing subnational value added taxes on internal trade: the compensating VAT (CVAT), *International Tax and Public Finance,* Vol. 7, 6, pp. 723–40.

McMorrow, K. (1996) The wage formation process and labour market flexibility in the Community, the US and Japan, *Economic Studies,* no. 118, European Commission, DG Economic and Financial Affairs, Brussel (October).

Meester, G. (1980) *Doeleinden, instrumenten en effecten van het landbouwbeleid in de EG,* LEI Agricultural-Economic Institute, The Hague.

Meicklejohn, R. (1999) The economics of state aid, *European Economy,* Reports and Studies, no. 3.

de Melo, J., Panagariya, A. & Rodrik, D. (1993) Regional integration, an analytical and empirical overview, in de Melo, J., Panagariya, A. (eds) *New Dimensions in Regional Integration,* Cambridge University Press, Cambridge.

Menil, G. (1999) Real capital market integration in the EU, *Economic Policy,* no. 28 (April).

Messerlin, P. (1989) The EC anti-dumping regulations, a first economic appraisal, *Weltwirtschaftliches Archiv,* Vol. 125, 3.

Messerlin, P. & Nogushi, Y. (1991) *The EC Anti-dumping and Anti-circumvention Regulations: A Costly yet Futile Exercise; The Case of Photocopiers,* Paris/Tokyo, September (mimeo).

Micco A., Stein, E. & Ordoñez, G. (2003) The currency union effect on trade: early evidence, *Economic Policy,* no. 37, pp. 317–56.

Midelfart-Knarvik, K.H., Overman, H., Redding, S. & Venables, A. (2000) *The Location of European Industry,* Economic Papers no. 142, European Commission, DG Economic and Financial Affairs, Brussels.

Milcher, S. & Slay, B. (2005) *The economics of the European neighbourhood policy: an initial assessment,* paper presented at a conference of CASE in Warsaw. www.case.com.pl.

Molle, W. (1994) *The Economics of European Integration: Theory, Practice, Policy,* 2nd edn, Dartmouth, Aldershot.

Molle, W. & van Mourik, A. (1988) International movements of labour under conditions of economic integration: the case of western Europe, *Journal of Common Market Studies,* Vol. 26, 3.

Monti, M. (1996) *The Single Market and Tomorrow's Europe,* OOPEC, Luxembourg and Kogan Page, London.

Morsink, R. & Molle, R. (1991) Direct investments and monetary integration, *European Economy* Special edition no. 1 on the Economics of EMU.

Mortensen, J. (2003) *Cross-border Portability of Pension Rights,* Report of a CEPS Task Force, no. 45 (April).

Motta, M. & Polo, M. (1997) Concentration and public policies in the broadcasting industry: the future of television, *Economic Policy,* no. 25 (October).

Mueller, J. (1981) Competitive performance and trade within the EEC, Generalizations from several case studies with specific reference to the West German economy, *Zeitschrift für die Gesamte Staatswissenschaften,* Vol. 137, 3, pp. 638–63.

Mundell, R. (1957) International trade and factor mobility, *American Economic Review,* Vol. 47, 2 (June).

Mundell, R. (1961) A theory of optimum currency areas, *American Economic Review,* Vol. 51, 4 (September).

Mundell, R. (1964) Tariff preferences and the terms of trade, *Manchester School,* Vol. 32 (January).

Mundell, R. (1968) *International Economics,* Macmillan, London.

Munk, K.J. (1994) The development of agricultural policies and trade relations in response to the transformation in central and eastern Europe, *European Economy,* Reports and Studies no. 5, The economics of the CAP, pp. 37–47.

Munk, K. & Thomson, K. (1994) The economic costs of agricultural policy, *European Economy/Social Europe,* no. 4, Reports and Studies, chapter B.

Murphy, A. (1990) *The EC and the International Trading System,* Vol. I (CEPS Paper no. 43) and Vol. II (CEPS Paper no. 48), Brussels.

Myrdal, G. (1956) *Economic Theory and Underdeveloped Regions,* Duckworth, London.

Narula, R. & Hagedoorn, J. (1999), Innovating through strategic alliances: moving towards international partnerships and contractual agreements, *Technovation,* Vol. 19, pp. 283–94.

NEA (1997) *Road Freight Transport, Single Market Review,* subseries II.5, OOPEC, Luxembourg and Kogan Page, London.

Neary, P. (2001) Of hype and hyperbolas: introducing the new economic geography, *Journal of Economic Literature,* Vol. 39, pp. 857–80.

Neary, P. (2002) *Foreign Direct Investment and the Single Market,* CEPR Paper no. 3419, London (June).

Neven, D. & Gougette, C. (1994) *Regional Convergence in the EC,* CEPR Discussion Paper no. 904 (February).

Neven, D., Nuttal, R. & Seabright, P. (1993) *Mergers in Daylight,* The Economics and Politics of European Merger Control, CEPR, London.

Neven, D. & Roeller, L. (1991) European integration and trade flows, *European Economic Review,* Vol. 35, pp. 1295–309.

Neven, D., Papandropoulos, P. & Seabright, P. (1998) *Trawling for Minnows: European Competition Policy and Agreements between Firms,* CEPR, London.

Nickell, S. & J. van Ours (2000) The Netherlands and the United Kingdom: a European unemployment miracle? *Economic Policy.* Vol. 15, no. 30. pp. 135–80.

Nicodème, G. & Sauner-Leroy, J.B. (2004) *Product market reforms and productivity: a review of the theoretical and empirical literature on the transmission channels,* Economic Papers no. 218, European Commission, DG Economic and Financial Affairs, Brussels (December).

Nicolaides, P. (ed.) (1993) *Industrial Policy in the EC,* Nijhoff, Dordrecht and EIPA, Maastricht.

Nicolaides, P. & Raja Boean, S. (1997) *A guide to the enlargement of the EU: determinants, process, timing, negotiations,* European Institute of Public Administration, Maastricht.

Nicolaides, P. & van Wijngaarden, R. (1993) Reform of anti-dumping regulations – the case of the EC, *Journal of World Trade,* Vol. 27, 3 (June).

Nicolas, F. & Repussard, J. (1995) *Common Standards for Enterprises,* OOPEC, Luxembourg.

Nicoletti, G. & Scarpetta S. (2003) Regulation, productivity and growth, *Economic Policy,* no 36 (April), pp. 9–72.

Oates W. (1999) An essay in fiscal federalism, *Journal of Economic literature,* Vol. 37, 3, pp. 1120–49.

OECD (1990) *OECD Economic Surveys — Spain,* OECD, Paris.

OECD (1992) *Technology and the Economy, the Key Relationships,* OECD, Paris.

OECD (1997) *The OECD Report on Regulatory Reform,* 2 vols, OECD, Paris.

OECD (2004) *A New World Map in Textiles and Clothing,* Policy Brief, October, OECD, Paris.

OECD (2005) *Agricultural Policies in OECD Countries: Monitoring and Evaluation 2005, Highlights,* OECD, Paris.

Ogus, A. (1994) *Regulation, Legal Form and Economic Theory,* Oxford University Press, Oxford.

Ohly, C. (1993) *What have we learned about the economic effects of European integration?* Economic Papers no.103, European Commission, DG II, Brussels.

Olechowski, A. & Sampson, G. (1980) Current trade restrictions in the EEC, the US and Japan, *Journal of World Trade Law,* Vol. 14, 3 (May/June).

Olsen, O. & Pelkmans, J. (1996) *Towards a Single Market in Utilities,* CEPS Working Party Report no. 14, CEPS, Brussels (July).

Ottaviano, M. & Thisse, J.F. (2005) New economic geography: what about the N? *Environment and Planning,* Vol. 37, pp. 1707–25.

Özden, Ç. & Reinhardt, E. (2003) *The Perversity of Preferences: The Generalized System of Preferences and Developing Country Trade Policies, 1976–2000,* Trade Working Paper no. 2955, World Bank, Washington, DC.

Padoa-Schioppa, T. (1984) *Money, Economic Policy and Europe,* OOPEC, Luxembourg.

Padoa-Schioppa, T. *et al.* (1987) *Efficiency, Stability and Equity: A strategy for the evolution of the economic system of the European Community,* Report of a study group appointed by the EC Commission, Brussels.

Panagariya, A. (2002) *Developing Countries at Doha: A Political Economy Analysis,* Vol. 25, 1 (September).

Pangestu, M. (2003) New regionalism: options for China and East Asia, in Krumm, K. & Kamas, H. (eds) *East Asia Integrates: A Trade Policy Agenda for Shared Growth,* World Bank, Washington, DC.

Pavitt, K. & Sharp, M. (1993) Technology policy in the 1990s: old trends and new realities, in Bekemans, L. & Tsoukalis, L. (eds) *Europe and Global Economic Interdependence,* College of Europe, Bruges.

Pearce D. & Howarth A. (2000) *Technical Report on Methodology: Cost Benefit Analysis and Policy Responses,* Report 481 505020, RIVM, Bilthoven (NL).

Peeperkorn, L. (1998) The economics of verticals, *Competition Policy Newsletter,* no. 2 (June), European Commission, DG Competition, Brussels.

Pelkmans, J. (1982a) The assignment of public functions in economic integration, *Journal of Common Market Studies,* Vol. 21.

Pelkmans, J. (1982b) Customs union and technical efficiency, *De Economist,* Vol. 130, 4.

Pelkmans, J. (1984) *Market Integration in the European Community,* Nijhoff, The Hague/New York.

Pelkmans, J. (ed.) (1985a) *Can the CAP be Reformed?* European Institute for Public Administration, Working Document 85/02, Maastricht.

Pelkmans, J. (1985b) The institutional economics of European integration, in Cappeletti, M., Weiler J. & Secombe, M. (eds) *Integration through Law – Europe and the American Federal Experience,* Vol. I, Book I, Walther de Gruyter, New York/Berlin.

Pelkmans, J. (1986) *Completing the Internal Market for Industrial Products,* OOPEC, Luxembourg.

Pelkmans, J. (1987) The new approach to technical harmonisation and standardisation, *Journal of Common Market Studies,* Vol. 25 (March).

Pelkmans, J. (1988) Liberalisation of product markets in the EC, in Giersch, H. (ed.) *Free Trade in the World Economy,* Mohr, Tübingen.

Pelkmans, J. (1990) Regulation and the single market, an economic perspective, in Siebert, H. (ed.) *The Completion of the Single Market,* Mohr, Tübingen.

Pelkmans, J. (1991) Towards economic union, in Ludlow, P. (ed.) *Setting EC Priorities, 1991–1992,* Brasseys, London.

Pelkmans, J. (1992a) EC 92 as a challenge to economic analysis, in Borner, S. & Grubel, H. (eds) *The EC after 1992,* Macmillan, London.

Pelkmans, J. (1992b) The EC internal market for air transport: issues after 1992, in Bannister, D. & Button, K. (eds) *Transport in a Free Market Economy,* Macmillan, London.

Pelkmans, J. (1994a) The significance of EC-1992, *The Annals* (of the American Academy of Political and Social Sciences), January, no. 531.

Pelkmans, J. (1994b) *Opening up the Euromarket for Textiles,* CEPS Paper no. 54, CEPS, Brussels.

Pelkmans, J. (1995) Condemned to conflicts, cooperation and consensus: the EU and the US in the Uruguay Round, in Breuss, F. (ed.) *The World Economy after the Uruguay Round,* Service Fachverlag, Vienna.

Pelkmans, J. (1998) A European Telecoms Regulator? in Vass, P. (ed.) *Network industries in Europe: Preparing for Competition,* Centre for the Study of Regulated Industries, London.

Pelkmans, J. (1999) *The GSM Standard: Explaining a Success Story,* CEPS Working Documents no. 132, CEPS, Brussels.

Pelkmans, J. (2001a) Making EU network industries competitive, *Oxford Review of Economic Policy,* autumn, Vol. 17, 3.

Pelkmans, J. (2001b) The GSM standard: explaining a success story, *Journal of European Public Policy,* special issue, Vol. 8, 3 (June).

Pelkmans, J. (2005a) Mutual recognition in goods and services: an economic perspective, in: F. Kostoris Padoa–Schioppa (ed.) , *The principle of mutual recognition in the European integration process,* Houndsmill, Palgrave Macmillan.

Pelkmans, J. (2005b) REACH: getting the chemistry right in Europe, in Hamilton, D. & Quinlan, J. (eds) *Deep Integration: How Transatlantic Markets are Leading Globalisation,* Johns Hopkins, SAIS, Center for Transatlantic Relations, Washington, DC and CEPS, Brussels.

Pelkmans, J. (2006) European industrial policy, in Bianchi, P. & Labory, S. (eds) *International Handbook of Industrial Policy,* Edward Elgar, Cheltenham.

Pelkmans, J. & Brenton, P. (1999) Bilateral trade agreements with the EU: driving forces and effects, in Memedovic, O., Kuyvenhoven, A. & Molle, W. (eds) *Multilateralism and regionalism in the post Uruguay Round era,* Kluwer Academic Publishers, Boston/Dordrecht.

Pelkmans, J. & Carzaniga, A. (1996) The trade policy review of the EU, *The World Economy,* Vol. 19, Special issue on Global Trade Policy.

Pelkmans, J. & Casey, J.P. (2003) EU enlargement: external economic implications, *Intereconomics,* Vol. 38, 4 (July/August).

Pelkmans, J. & Casey, J.P. (2004) *Can Europe deliver growth?* College of Europe BEEP Briefing no. 6 (January). www.coleurop.be/eco/publications.htm and www.ceps.be.

Pelkmans, J. & Fukasaku, K. (1995) Evolving trade links between Europe and Asia: towards 'Open Continentalism?' in Fukasaku, K. (ed.) *Regional Co-operation and Integration in Asia,* OECD, Paris.

Pelkmans, J. & Gremmen, H. (1983) The empirical measurement of static customs union effects, *Rivista Internazionale di Scienze Economiche e Commerciali,* Vol. 30, 7 (July).

Pelkmans, J. & Labory, S. (1998) *European Regulation and Cost-benefit Analysis, a Methodology for Non-specialists.* Paper for DG Enterprise, European Commission, CEPS, Brussels (unpublished, for internal distribution only).

Pelkmans, J. & Murphy, A. (1992) Strategies for the Uruguay Round, in Ludlow, P. (ed.) *Europe and North America in the 1990s,* CEPS Paper no. 52, Brussels.

Pelkmans, J. & Vanheukelen, M. (1988) The internal markets of North America, fragmentation and integration in the US and Canada, *Research on the 'Cost of Non-Europe', Basic Findings,* Vol. 16, OOPEC, Luxembourg.

Pelkmans, J. & White, P. (2000) *Sustainable mobility in Europe,* CEPS Working Party report no. 26, Brussels (September).

Pelkmans, J. & Winters, L.A. (1988) *Europe's Domestic Market,* Routledge, London.

Pelkmans, J. & Young, D. (1998) *Telecoms-98,* CEPS, Brussels.

Pelkmans, J., Gros, D. & Nunez Ferrer, J. (2000a) *Long-run Economic Aspects of the EUs Eastern Enlargement,* Working Document W109, WRR, The Hague.

Pelkmans, J., Labory, S. & Majone, G. (2000b), Better EU regulatory quality: assessing current initiatives and new proposals, in Galli, G. & Pelkmans, J. (eds) *Regulatory Reform and Competitiveness in Europe,* Vol. I, Edward Elgar, Cheltenham.

Pelkmans, J., Vos, E. & di Mauro, L. (2000c), Reforming product regulation in the EU: a painstaking, iterative two-level game, in Galli, G. & Pelkmans, J. (eds) *Regulatory Reform and Competitiveness in Europe,* Vol. I, Edward Elgar, Cheltenham.

Peltzman, S. (1976) Towards a more general theory of regulation, *Journal of Law and Economics,* Vol. 19 (August).

Peltzman, S. (1989) The economic theory of regulation after a decade of deregulation, *Brookings Papers on Economic Activity* (Microeconomics series), pp. 1–59.

Petersen, L. (1982) Capital movements and payments under the EEC treaty after Casati, *European Law Review,* Vol. 7, pp. 167 ff.

di Pietrantonio L. & Pelkmans J. (2004) The economics of EU railway reform, *Journal of Network Industries,* Vol. 5, 3/4 (December).

Pisani-Ferry, J. (2005) Speeding up European reform: a master plan for the Lisbon process, *CESinfo Forum,* Vol. 6, 2 (Summer).

van der Ploeg, R. (1991) Macro-economic policy coordination during the various phases of economic and monetary integration in Europe, in *European Economy,* Special edition no. 1 on the Economics of EMU.

Pomfret, R. (1986) *Mediterranean Policy of the EC, A Study of Discrimination in Trade,* Macmillian, London.

Pomfret, R. (1988) *Unequal Trade: the Economics of Discriminatory International Trade Policies,* Blackwell, Oxford.

Ponti, M. & Cappiello, M.A. (2000) Road transport, in Galli, G. & Pelkmans, J. (eds) *Regulatory Reform and Competitiveness in Europe,* Vol. 2, Edward Elgar, Cheltenham.

Pratten, C. (1988) A survey of the economies of scale, in *Research on the Costs of Non-Europe: Basic Findings,* Vol. II, OOPEC, Luxembourg/Brussels.

Prewo, W. (1974) Integration effects in the EEC: an attempt at quantification in a general equilibrium framework, *European Economic Review,* Vol. 3.

Puga, D. (2002) European regional policies in light of recent location theories, *Journal of Economic Geography,* Vol. 2, pp. 373–406.

Quehenberger, M. (2000) Ten years after: Eastern Germany's convergence at a halt? *EIB Papers,* Vol. 5, 2.

Radaelli C. (2003) Impact assessment in the EU: innovations, quality and good regulatory governance, paper prepared for the EU RIA conference, Brussels, 3 December.

Razin, A. & Sadka, F. (1995) *Resisting Migration: Wage Rigidity and Income Distribution,* CEPR Discussion Paper no. 1091, London (January).

Rees, R. & Kessner, E. (1999) Regulation and efficiency in European insurance markets, *Economic Policy,* no. 20 (October).

Renneboog, L. (1999) *Corporate Governance Systems: The role of Ownership, External Finance and Regulation,* CEPS Working Document no. 23, Brussels (September).

Resnick, S. & Truman, E. (1975) An empirical examination of bilateral trade in western Europe, in Balassa, B. (ed.) *European Economic Integration,* North-Holland, Amsterdam.

Riedel, J. (1977) Tariff concessions in the Kennedy Round and the structure of protection in West Germany, *Journal of International Economics,* Vol. 7, 2 (May).

Roberts, G. & Salop, S. (1996) Efficiencies in dynamic merger analysis, *World Competition,* Vol. 19, 4, June.

Rodríguez-Pose, A. & Fratesi, U. (2005) Between development and social policies: the impact of European Structural Funds in Objective 1 regions, *Regional Studies,* Vol. 38, 1, pp. 97–113.

Rødseth, A., (2000) *Open Economy Macroeconomics,* Cambridge University Press, Cambridge.

Roland, G. (2000) *Transition and Economics: Politics, Firms, Markets.* MIT Press, Cambridge, Mass.

Rose, A. (2000) One money, one market: the effect of common currencies on trade, *Economic Policy,* no. 30 (April).

Rose A. & Stanley T. (2004) A meta-analysis of the effect of common currencies on international trade, University of California at Berkeley, Haas School of Business. http://faculty.haas.berkeley.edu/arose

Rose, A.K. & van Wincoop, E. (2001) National Money as a Barrier to International Trade: The Real Case for Currency Union, *American Economic Review,* Vol. 91, 2, pp. 386–90, American Economic Association.

Rubalcaba-Bermejo, L. (1999) *Business Services in European Industry: Growth, Employment and Competitiveness,* OOPEC, Luxembourg.

Saint-Paul, G. (1994) *Searching for the virtues of the European model,* CEPR Discussion Paper no. 950, London (May).

Sala-i-Martin, X. & Sachs, J. (1992) Fiscal federalism and optimal currency areas, in Canzeroni, M. *et al.* (eds) *Establishing a Central Bank: Issues in Europe and Lessons from the US,* Cambridge University Press, Cambridge.

Sampson, G. & Snape, R. (1980) Effects of the EEC's variable import levies, *Journal of Political Economy,* Vol. 88, 5.

Sapir, A. (1992) Regional integration in Europe, *Economic Journal,* Vol. 102, pp. 1491–506.

Sapir, A. (1993) Sectoral dimension, *European Economy/Social Europe,* Reports and Studies, no. 3, Market Services and European Integration.

Sapir, A. (1995) *Europe's Single Market: The Long March to 1992,* CEPR Discussion Paper no. 1245, London (September).

Sapir, A. (2005) *Globalisation and the reform of European social models,* Discussion paper, Bruegel, Brussels, (September).

Sapir, A. *et al.* (2003) *An Agenda for a Growing Europe: Making the System Deliver,* Report of the Independent High Level Group, Brussels and Oxford University Press, Oxford (July).

Sapir, A. & Winter, C. (1994) Services trade, in Greenaway, D. & Winters, L.A. (eds) *Surveys in International Trade,* Blackwell, Oxford.

Scherer, F. & Ross, D. (1990) *Industrial Market Structure and Economic Performance,* 3rd edn, Houghton Mifflin, Boston.

Schenk, H. (1999) Are international acquisitions a matter of strategy rather than wealth creation? Management Report no. 42-1999, Erasmus University, School of Management, Rotterdam.

Schiff, M. & Winters, A. (2003) *Regional Integration and Development,* World Bank, Washington, DC.

Schultze, G. (1983) Industrial policy, a dissent, *Brookings Review,* Vol. 2, 1 (Fall).

Scitovsky, T. (1958) *Economic Theory and Western European Integration,* Allen & Unwin, London.

Segre, G. (2000) *European EMU and FDI: A Survey of the Theoretical and Empirical Literature,* CES, *Discussion Paper IERP* no. 152, Leuven (March).

Sekkat, K. (1998) *Exchange Rate Variability and EU Trade,* Economic Papers no. 127, European Commission, DG Economic and Financial Affairs, Brussels (February).

Servan-Schreiber, J. (1967) *Le défi américain,* Denoel, Paris. English translation *The American Challenge,* Atheneum, New York (1968).

Shaw, R., & Shaw, S. (1983) Excess capacity and rationalisation in the west European synthetic fibre industry, *Journal of Industrial Economics,* Vol. 32 (December).

Shibata, H. (1967) The theory of economic unions: a comparative analysis of customs union, free trade areas and tax unions, in Shoup, C. (ed.) *Fiscal Harmonisation in Common Markets,* Vol. I, Columbia University Press, New York.

Shonfield, A. (1973) *Europe: Journey to an Unknown Destination,* Penguin, Harmondsworth.

Siebert, H. (ed.) (1990) *The Completion of the Internal Market,* Mohr, Tübingen.

Sinn, H.W. & Ockel, W. (2003) Social union, convergence and migration, *Journal of Common Market Studies,* Vol. 41, 5, pp. 869–96.

Sleuwaegen, L., Pol, F. & Lashek, S. (1993) Road haulage, *European Economy/Social Europe,* no. 3, Reports & Studies, Market Services and European Integration.

Smith, A. & Venables, A. (1988) Completing the internal market in the EC, some industry simulations, *European Economic Review,* Vol. 32, pp. 1451–75.

Smith, A. & Venables, A. (1991) Counting the costs of VERs in the European car market, in Helpman, E. & Razin, A. (eds) *International Trade and Trade Policy,* MIT Press, Cambridge, Mass.

Smith, P.M. (1999) From industrial policy to enterprise policy, speech, conference of Philip Morris Institute, Brussels, 25 November.

Smith, S. (1993) Subsidiarity and the coordination of indirect taxes in the EC, *Oxford Review of Economic Policy,* Vol. 9, 1 (Spring).

Snidal, D. (1985) The limits of hegemonic stability, *International Organization,* Vol. 39, 4 (Autumn).

Soete, L. & ter Weel, B. (1999) *Innovation, knowledge creation and technology in Europe,* MERIT, Maastricht.

Somma, E. (1994) Intra-industry trade in the European computers industry, *Weltwirtschaftliches Archiv,* Vol. 130, 4.

Sorensen, P.B. (1998) Discussion, *Economic Policy,* no. 27 (October).

Spaak, P.H. *et al.* (1956) *Report of the Heads of Delegation of the Foreign Ministries* (Spaak report, in French), Brussels, mimeo.

Spulber, D. (1989) *Regulation and Markets,* MIT Press, Cambridge, Mass.

Steenbergen, J. (1980) The Common Commercial Policy, *Common Market Law Review,* Vol. 17, 2 (May).

Steinherr A. (2000) *Derivatives, The wild beast of finance,* A path to effective globalisation? 2nd edn, Wiley, Chichester.

Stenkula, M. (2004) The Euro-cash changeover process, *Kyklos,* Vol. 57, 2, pp. 265–85.

Stigler, G. (1971) The theory of economic regulation, *Bell Journal of Economics,* Vol. 2 (Spring).

Sun, J. & Pelkmans, J. (1995a) Regulatory competition in the internal market, *Journal of Common Market Studies,* Vol. 33, 1 (March).

Sun, J. & Pelkmans, J. (1995b) Why liberalisation needs centralisation: subsidiarity and EU telecoms, *The World Economy,* Vol. 18, 5 (September).

Sutton, J. (1991) *Sunk Costs and Market Structure: Price Competition, Advertising and the Evolution of Concentration,* MIT Press, Cambridge, Mass.

Swann, G.M.P. (2000) *The Economics of Standardization,* final reports for standards and technical regulations, Department of Trade and Industry/University of Manchester.

Swinnen, J. (2005) The dynamics of agri-food supply chains in transition countries, presentation at EBRD seminar, 26 April, London.

Tabellini, G. (2002) *The assignment of tasks in an evolving EU,* CEPS Policy Briefing, Brussels. www.ceps.be

Tharakan, P. & Waelbroeck, J. (1994) Anti-dumping and countervailing duties decisions in the EC and in the US, an experiment in comparative political economy, *European Economic Review,* Vol. 38.

The Economist (2004) Special report: Low cost airlines, 10 July, pp. 61–3.

Thomson, K. (1994) EC agriculture, past and present, *European Economy,* no. 4, Reports and Studies, Chapter A.

Thorbecke, E. & Pagoulatos, E. (1975) The effects of European economic integration on agriculture, in Balassa, B. (ed.) *European Economic Integration,* North-Holland, Amsterdam.

Tietmeyer, H. (1994) Europaische Waehrungsunion und Politische Union – das Modell mehrere Geschwindigkeiten, *Europa-Archiv,* Vol. 49, 16.

Tinbergen, J. (1954) *International Economic Integration,* North-Holland, Amsterdam.

Thisse, J.F. (2000) Agglomeration and regional imbalance: why? And is it bad? *EIB Papers,* Vol. 5, 2.

Tokarick, S. (2005) Who bears the cost of agricultural support in OECD countries? *The World Economy,* Vol. 28, 4 (April).

Tovias, A. (1977) *Tariff Preferences in Mediterranean Diplomacy,* Macmillan, London.

Tovias, A. (1982) Ex-post studies of the economic integration on trade: problems in measuring trade-flow and welfare effects, *Journal of European Integration,* Vol. 5, 2 (Winter).

Tovias, A. (1990) The impact of liberalising government procurement policies of individual EC countries on trade with non members, *Weltwirtschaftliches Archiv,* Vol. 126, 4, pp. 722–36.

Tovias, A. (1994) A survey of the theory of economic integration, in Michelmann, H. & Soldatos, P. (eds) *European Integration, Theories and Approaches,* University Press of America, Lanham, MD.

Truman, E. (1969) The European Economic Community: trade creation and trade diversion, *Yale Economic Essays* (Spring).

Truman, E. (1975) The effects of European economic integration on the production and trade of manufactured products, in Balassa, B. (ed.) *European Economic Integration,* North-Holland, Amsterdam.

Tsoukalis, L. (1977) *The Politics and Economics of European Monetary Integration,* Allen & Unwin, London.

Ulff-Moller Nielsen, J. (2000) Price–quality competition in the exports of the CEECs, *Intereconomics,* Vol. 35, 2 (March/April).

UNICE (2000) *Stimulating Creativity and Innovation in Europe,* UNICE Benchmarking Report 2000, Brussels.

Vahl, T. (2003) *Whither the Common European Economic Space?* CEPS, Brussels.

Vaulont, N. (1981) *The Customs Union of the European Community,* Commission of the EC, Brussels.

Veil, S. *et al.* (1997) *Report of the High Level Panel on the free movement of persons to the Commission,* Brussels (18 March).

Venables, A. (1990) Economic integration of oligopolistic markets, *European Economic Review,* Vol. 34, 4 (June).

Venables, A. (1995) Economic integration and the location of firms, *American Economic Review,* Vol. 85, 2 (May).

Venables, A. (1998) The assessment: trade and location, *Oxford Review of Economic Policy,* Vol. 14, 2 (Summer).

Verdoorn, P. & Schwartz, A. (1972) Two alternative estimates of the effects of EEC and EFTA on the pattern of trade, *European Economic Review,* Vol. 3, 3 (November).

Verwaal E. & Cnossen S. (2002) Europe's new border taxes, *Journal of Common Market Studies,* Vol. 40, 2, pp. 309–30.

Veugelers, R. & Vandenbussche, H. (1999) European anti-dumping policy and the profitability of national and international collusion, *European Economic Review,* Vol. 43, 1 (January).

Vickers, J. & Hay, D. (1987) The economics of market dominance, in Hay, D. & Vickers, J. (eds) *The Economics of Market Dominance,* Blackwell, Oxford.

Viner, J. (1950) *The Customs Union Issue,* Carnegie Endowment for International Peace, New York.

Viscusi W.K., Vernon J. & Harrington J. (2000) *Economics of Regulation and Competition,* 3rd edn, MIT Press, Cambridge, Mass.

Walkner C. & Raes J.P. (2005) *Integration and Consolidation in EU Banking – An Unfinished Business,* Economic Papers no. 226, European Commission DG Economic and Financial Affairs, Brussels (April).

Walsh, C. (1993) Fiscal federalism: an overview of issues and a discussion of their relevance to the EC, *European Economy,* no. 5, Reports and Studies, The Economics of Community Public Finance.

Walter, I. & Smith, R. (2000) *High Finance in the Eurozone,* Pearson, London.

Werner, P. *et al.* (1970) *Rapport intérimaire concernant la réalisation par étapes de l'Union Economique et Monétaire,* EEC Council and the European Commission, Brussels.

Weyerbrock, S. (1998) Reform of the EU's CAP: how to reach GATT-compatibility? *European Economic Review,* Vol. 42, 2 (February).

White, W. (1998) *The Coming Transformation of Continental European Banking?* BIS Working Papers no. 54, Basel (June).

Williamson, O. (1968) Economics as an anti-trust defence, the welfare trade-offs, *American Economic Review,* Vol. 58 (March) (correction in December 1969, Vol. 59).

Williamson, J. & Bottrill, A. (1973) The impact of customs unions on trade in manufactures, in Kraus, M. (ed.) *The Economics of Integration,* Allen & Unwin, London.

Winkler, B. (2000) *Which kind of transparency? On the need for clarity in monetary policy-making,* Working Paper no. 26, European Central Bank (August).

Winters, L.A. (1987) Britain in Europe: a survey of quantitative trade studies, *Journal of Common Market Studies,* Vol. 25.

Winters, L.A. (1990) The so-called 'non-economic' objectives of agricultural support, *OECD Economic Studies,* no. 13 (Winter).

Winters, L.A. (ed.) (1992) *Trade Flows and Trade Policy after 1992,* Cambridge University Press, Cambridge.

Winters, L.A. (1994) The EC and protection: the political economy, *European Economic Review,* Vol. 38, pp. 596–603.

Winters, L.A. & Venables, A. (eds) (1991) *European Integration: Trade and Industry,* Cambridge University Press, Cambridge.

Wolf, H. (1999) Transition strategies: choices and outcomes, *Princeton Studies in International Finance,* no. 85, June.

Wonnacott, P. & Wonnacott, R. (1981) Is unilateral tariff reduction preferable to a customs union? The curious case of the missing foreign tariffs, *American Economic Review,* Vol. 71, 4 (September).

World Bank (2000) *Trade Blocs: A World Bank Policy Research Report,* Oxford University Press, Oxford.

WRR (2001) *Towards a Pan-European Union,* WRR, The Hague. www.wrr.nl.

WRR (2003) *Capacity to Act in the Pan-European Union* (in Dutch), Report to the Government, WRR, The Hague. www.wrr.nl.

WTO (1995) *Trade Policy Review – European Community,* 2 vols, WTO, Geneva.

WTO (2000) *Trade Policy Review – the European Union,* 2 vols, WTO, Geneva.

WTO (2004) *Trade Policy Review – the European Communities,* 2 vols, WTO, Geneva [ref. WT/TPR/G/136].

Wyatt, D. & Dashwood, A. (1980) *The Substantive Law of the EEC,* Sweet & Maxwell, London.

Yannopoulos, G.N. (1990) Foreign direct investment and European integration: the evidence from the formative years of the European Community, *Journal of Common Market Studies,* Vol. 28, 4.

Index